Blackwell Handbook of Adolescence

Blackwell Handbooks of Developmental Psychology

This outstanding series of handbooks provides a cutting-edge overview of classic research, current research and future trends in developmental psychology.

- Each handbook draws together 25–30 newly commissioned chapters to provide a comprehensive overview of a sub-discipline of developmental psychology.
- The international team of contributors to each handbook has been specially chosen for its expertise and knowledge of each field.
- Each handbook is introduced and contextualized by leading figures in the field, lending coherence and authority to each volume.

The *Blackwell Handbooks of Developmental Psychology* will provide an invaluable overview for advanced students of developmental psychology and for researchers as an authoritative definition of their chosen field.

Published

Blackwell Handbook of Infant Development
Edited by Gavin Bremner and Alan Fogel

Blackwell Handbook of Childhood Social Development
Edited by Peter K. Smith and Craig H. Hart

Blackwell Handbook of Childhood Cognitive Development
Edited by Usha Goswami

Blackwell Handbook of Adolescence
Edited by Gerald R. Adams and Michael D. Berzonsky

The Science of Reading: A Handbook
Edited by Margaret J. Snowling and Charles Hulme

Blackwell Handbook of Early Childhood Development
Edited by Kathleen McCartney and Deborah A. Phillips

Forthcoming

Blackwell Handbook of Language Development
Edited by Erika Hoff and Marilyn Shatz

Blackwell Handbook of Adolescence

Edited by

Gerald R. Adams and Michael D. Berzonsky

© 2003, 2006 by Blackwell Publishing Ltd
except for editorial material and organization © 2003, 2006 by Gerald R. Adams and
Michael D. Berzonsky

BLACKWELL PUBLISHING
350 Main Street, Malden, MA 02148-5020, USA
9600 Garsington Road, Oxford OX4 2DQ, UK
550 Swanston Street, Carlton, Victoria 3053, Australia

The right of Gerald R. Adams and Michael D. Berzonsky to be identified as the Authors of
the Editorial Material in this Work has been asserted in accordance with the UK Copyright,
Designs, and Patents Act 1988.

First published 2003
First published in paperback 2006 by Blackwell Publishing Ltd

2   2007

Library of Congress Cataloging-in-Publication Data

Blackwell handbook of adolescence / edited by Gerald R. Adams and
    Michael D. Berzonsky.
            p. cm. – (Blackwell handbooks of developmental psychology ; 4)
        Includes bibliographical references and index.
        ISBN 978-0-631-21919-4 (hbk : alk. paper) — ISBN 978-1-4051-3302-9 (pbk : alk. paper)
    1. Adolescent psychology. I. Adams, Gerald R., 1946– II. Berzonsky,
    Michael D. III. Series.

    BF724 .B487 2003
    155.5–dc21

                                                            2002151837

A catalogue record for this title is available from the British Library.

Set in 10.5 on 12.5 pt Adobe Garamond
by SNP Best-set Typesetter Ltd, Hong Kong
Printed and bound in Singapore
by Utopia Press Pte Ltd

The publisher's policy is to use permanent paper from mills that operate a sustainable forestry
policy, and which has been manufactured from pulp processed using acid-free and elementary
chlorine-free practices. Furthermore, the publisher ensures that the text paper and cover board
used have met acceptable environmental accreditation standards.

For further information on
Blackwell Publishing, visit our website:
www.blackwellpublishing.com

Contents

Contributors

Gerald R. Adams is a Distinguished Professor of Teaching at the University of Guelph. He has been the editor for the *Journal of Adolescent Research* and associate editor for the *Journal of Primary Prevention* and the *Journal of Early Adolescence*. His research interests focus on the study of identity formation, parent–adolescent relationships, and social development during childhood, adolescence, and young adulthood.

Andrea Bastiani Archibald, Ph.D. is a Research Scientist at the Center for Children & Families, Teachers College, Columbia University. Her research focuses on the transition to puberty and adolescence for girls, and has examined the role of pubertal factors in adolescent adjustment and the development of psychopathology. Her work on the impact of puberty and family relations on girls' eating problems was recently published in the *Journal of Research on Adolescence* and the *International Journal of Eating Disorders*.

David E. Bard is a graduate student in the Quantitative Psychology program at the University of Oklahoma. He earned a BA in Psychology from Bethany College in Kansas in 1998, and an MA in Psychology from the University of Oklahoma in 2001. His research interests include behavior genetics, sports statistics, health psychology, and statistical test theory.

Bruce K. Bayley is a doctoral student in the Family and Human Development Department at Utah State University. He received his undergraduate degree in Sociology and a Master's degree in Family Ecology from the University of Utah. His current areas of interest include bidirectional relationships between crime/delinquency and the family; adolescent perceptions of crime and law enforcement; delinquency, crime analysis and mapping; and the use of Graphic Information System (GIS) technologies in social research.

Michael D. Berzonsky is Professor of Psychology at the State University of New York at Cortland. His current research interests focus on self-processes, identity formation, and social-cognitive development during adolescence and young adulthood.

Laurie Biebelhausen, MSSA, LSW is a doctoral candidate in Social Welfare at Case Western Reserve University. She is a Research Assistant at the Institute for the Study and Prevention of Violence at Kent State University and a clinical therapist at Applewood Centers, Inc. in Cleveland, Ohio.

Heather A. Bouchey is Assistant Professor of Psychology at the University of Vermont. She received her Ph.D. in Developmental Psychology from the University of Denver and was a NICHD postdoctoral fellow at the University of Michigan. Her research focuses on socio-cognitive development in adolescence, including both the social and self-processes underlying academic achievement and the formation and maintenance of romantic relationships. She is currently examining the role of romantic self-concept in adolescent development.

Jeanne Brooks-Gunn, Ph.D. is the Virginia & Leonard Marx Professor in Child Development and the Director of the Center for Children & Families, Teachers College, Columbia University. Dr. Brooks-Gunn has co-directed the Adolescent Study Program for the past 18 years and is a renowned expert on adolescent development. She has published 15 books and over 340 articles on child and adolescent development, as well as family processes and neighborhood contexts.

B. Bradford Brown is a Professor of Human Development in the Department of Educational Psychology and Research Scientist in the Wisconsin Center for Education Research at the University of Wisconsin-Madison, where he has been since receiving his Ph.D. from the University of Chicago in 1979. His research focuses on adolescent social development, especially teenage peer relationships and peer influence processes. He is the Editor of the *Journal of Research on Adolescence* and the co-editor of two books: *The Development of Romantic Relationships in Adolescence* (with Wyndol Furman and Candice Feiring, 1999), and *The World's Youth: Adolescence in 8 Regions of the Globe* (with Reed Larson and T. S. Saraswathi, 2002).

James P. Byrnes is Professor of Human Development in the Department of Human Development at the University of Maryland, College Park. He received his Ph.D. in Developmental Psychology from Temple University and held posts of Postdoctoral Fellow (City University of New York) and Visiting Assistant Professor (University of Michigan) prior to moving to the University of Maryland. His research has mainly addressed the following questions: (1) Why do adolescents sometimes fail to demonstrate deductive reasoning competence? (2) Why are certain topics in mathematics difficult for children and adolescents to understand? (3) Why are there gender and ethnic differences in mathematics achievement? (4) What does it mean to be a competent decision-maker, and does this competence develop during adolescence? His most recent publications include *Cognitive Development and Learning in Instructional Contexts* (2nd ed., 2001) and

Minds, Brains, and Learning: The Psychological and Educational Relevance of Neuro-scientific Research (2001). He is a Fellow of Division 15 of the American Psychological Association.

Deborah M. Capaldi is a Senior Scientist at the Oregon Social Learning Center in Eugene, Oregon. Originally from England, she received her Ph.D. from the University of Oregon. Her research centers on the causes and consequences of antisocial behavior across the lifespan, including aggression in young couples' relationships, health-risking sexual behaviors, and the intergenerational transmission of risk.

Mathew Christensen is a doctoral student in the Family and Human Development Department at Utah State University. He completed his undergraduate work in Sociology and Psychology at the University of Oregon and received a Master's degree in Family and Human Development from Utah State University. His research interests are the origins and sequelae of adolescents' adjustment to adoption, prevention of adolescent problems (e.g., risky sexual behavior and pregnancy), and creating bridges between scientific knowledge and normal human development within relationship contexts.

David A. Cole is a professor in clinical psychology and developmental psychopathology at Vanderbilt University. He earned his doctorate at the University of Houston, interned at the University of Minnesota Hospitals, and was a professor at the University of Notre Dame until 2001 when he accepted his current position at Vanderbilt. His research focuses on childhood depression, adolescent suicide, and methodology. He is particularly interested in the development and differentiation of cognitive features of depression during middle childhood. He teaches courses in developmental psychopathology, family therapy, research methodology, and statistics.

W. Andrew Collins is Morse-Alumni Distinguished Teaching Professor at the Institute of Child Development, University of Minnesota. A long-time contributor to research on adolescence, he has specialized in studies of parent–adolescent relationships and romantic relationships during adolescence, as well as the impact of mass media on children and adolescents. He was an associate editor of *Child Development* from 1989 to 1996. From 2000 to 2002, he served as president of the Society for Research on Adolescence, and he is currently secretary of the Society for Research in Child Development.

James E. Côté, Ph.D. is a Professor of Sociology and has authored or coauthored four books, including *Generation on Hold: Coming of Age in the Late Twentieth Century* (1996), *Arrested Adulthood: The Changing Nature of Identity and Maturity in the Late Modern World* (2000), and *Identity Formation, Agency, and Culture: A Social Psychological Synthesis* (2002), and two dozen journal articles. He teaches courses in the sociology of education, social psychology, the sociology of youth, socialization, and mass society, and his research interests include the social psychology of education and personal development; socialization, human development, and the life course; cross-cultural and historical studies of adolescence and adulthood; psychological and sociological approaches to identity; and the Mead–Freeman controversy in anthropology.

Diana D. Coyl is an Assistant Professor of Family Studies in the College of Education at University of New Mexico. She received her Master's degree and Ph.D. from the Department of Family and Human Development, Utah State University. Her research interests include normal adolescent development, adolescent problems (e.g., sexual behavior and pregnancy), school adjustment, identity development, peer relationships during adolescence and childhood, and attachment issues in infancy through young adulthood.

Lisa J. Crockett is Professor of Psychology at the University of Nebraska-Lincoln. Her research interests include adolescent problem behavior, the development of behavioral trajectories, gender issues, and the transition to adulthood. She is co-editor, with Ann C. Crouter, of *Pathways Through Adolescence: Individual Development in Relations to Social Contexts* (1995) and, with Rainer K. Silbereisen, of *Negotiating Adolescence in Times of Social Change* (2000). She is associate editor of the *Journal of Research on Adolescence* and serves on the editorial boards of the *Journal of Early Adolescence* and *the Journal of Adolescent Research*.

Richard Crosby is an Assistant Professor in the Department of Behavioral Sciences and Health Education in the Rollins School of Public Health at Emory University. He received his BA degree in school health education from the University of Kentucky in 1981 and his MA in health education from Central Michigan University in 1984. His Ph.D. (1998) is in health behavior and is from Indiana University. Dr. Crosby's research interests are focused adolescent populations. He is primarily involved in research and service that contributes to the reduction of the HIV/AIDS epidemic. Currently affiliated with the Emory Center for AIDS Research, Crosby has published numerous articles that report empirical findings relevant to the sexual risk behaviors of adolescents and adults.

Steven J. Danish, Ph.D. is Director of the Life Skills Center and Professor of Psychology, Preventive Medicine, and Community Health at Virginia Commonwealth University. He previously served as Chair of the Department of Psychology and has held academic positions at Penn State University and Southern Illinois University. He received his doctorate from Michigan State University. He is a fellow of the American Psychological Association (APA), the American Psychological Society (APS), and the Association for the Advancement of Applied Sport Psychology (AAASP) and is past president of the Society of Community Research and Action (a Division of the APA). He has written in the areas of counseling, community, and life-span developmental psychology; health and nutrition; substance abuse prevention; and sport psychology.

Nancy Darling is Associate Professor of Psychology at Bard College. Her research focuses on adolescent social relationships and their influence on the development of competence. Currently, she is studying parental monitoring and adolescents' decisions to share information with their parents, the association of social relations with adolescent academic performance and problem behavior, and the influence of adolescents' experiences with family and friends on the formation of new romantic relationships. She is particularly interested in how social development varies as a function of community and cultural context.

Lisa M. Diamond is Assistant Professor of Psychology and Gender Studies at the University of Utah. Her research focuses on adolescent and young adult social and sexual development, as well as the psychobiology of affectional bonding. Dr. Diamond also investigates the longitudinal course of same-sex sexuality, and has been conducting the first long-term, prospective study of sexual-identity transitions among sexual-minority women. She also studies how peer-attachment relationships help adolescents and adults regulate negative emotions and physiological stress, and whether romantic relationships are uniquely beneficial in this regard. Along these lines, she has been particularly interested in "passionate friendships" among young women: i.e., intense bonds that straddle the boundary between friendship and romantic love.

Ralph J. DiClemente is Charles Howard Candler Professor of Public Health and Chair, Department of Behavioral Sciences and Health Education at the Rollins School of Public Health, Emory University. He is also Professor in the School of Medicine, Department of Medicine, Division of Infectious Diseases and the Department of Pediatrics. Professor DiClemente was trained as a Health Psychologist at the University of California, San Francisco, where he received his Ph.D. in 1984 after completing his MS in Behavioral Sciences at the Harvard School of Public Health and his undergraduate degree at the City University of New York. Among his extensive publication record recent books include *Emerging Theories in Health Promotion Practice and Research* (co-edited with R. A. Crosby and M. Kegler; 2002) and *Handbook of Adolescent Health Risk Behavior* (co-edited with L. Ponton and L. K. Brown; forthcoming).

Thomas J. Dishion received his Ph.D. in Clinical Psychology from the University of Oregon. His interests include understanding the development of antisocial behavior and substance abuse in children and adolescents, as well as designing effective interventions and prevention programs. In particular, he and colleagues have examined the contribution of peer and family dynamics to escalations in adolescent substance use, delinquency, and violence. His intervention research focuses on the effectiveness of family-centered interventions, and the negative effects of aggregating high-risk youth into intervention groups. He is currently Science Coordinator of the Child and Family Center and Professor of Clinical Psychology, both at the University of Oregon. Prior to that, he was a research scientist at Oregon Social Learning Center. He has published over 90 scientific reports on these topics, a book for parents on family management, and two books for professionals working with troubled children and their families.

Jerome B. Dusek, Ph.D. is Professor of Psychology and Director of Graduate Studies at Syracuse University. His textbook, *Adolescent Development and Behavior* (3rd ed., 1996), has been a widely used text across North America. His research interests focus on the development of self-esteem in adolescents, coping and personality development, adolescent identity development, sex-role development, parental rearing influences on personality development, and adolescent romantic relationships.

Jacquelynne S. Eccles, Ph.D. is currently the McKeachie Collegiate Professor of Psychology, Women's Studies and Education at the University of Michigan. She has also been on the faculty at Smith College and the University of Colorado. Her administrative experiences include: Interim Chair of Psychology at UM, Chair of the Combined Program in Education and Psychology at UM, Chair of the MacArthur Foundation Network on Middle Childhood, Program Chair for Society for Research on Adolescence (SRA) and APA Division 35, president of APA Division 35, president-elect of SRA, council member for SRA and SPSSI, Chair of the National Academy of Science (NAS) Committee on Community-Based Programs for Youth, and Chair of the NSF SBE Directorate. Her awards include the Sarah Power Award for Outstanding Service from UM, APS's Cattell Fellows Award, and SPSSI's Kurt Lewin Award. Her research focuses on gender, ethnicity, and school and family influences on social development during the K-12 years and on the transition into adulthood.

Robert J. Fazio is a Ph.D. student in Counseling Psychology with a subspecialty in Performance Excellence at Virginia Commonwealth University. He earned his Master's degree in Athletic Counseling from Springfield College and his undergraduate degree from Pennsylvania State University. Rob has consulted with a variety of athletes and teams ranging from recreational athletes to athletes on the national level. He has served as the student representative on the executive board of the Association of the Advancement of Applied Sport Psychology (AAASP) and is currently the co-representative for Division 47 (exercise and sport psychology) of the American Psychological Association (APA).

Daniel J. Flannery, Ph.D. completed his doctoral training in psychology at Ohio State University. He is Professor of Justice Studies and Director of the Institute for the Study and Prevention of Violence at Kent State University. The Institute is an interdisciplinary research program focused on the study of causes and prevention of violence.

Wyndol Furman is Professor of Psychology and Director of Clinical Training at the University of Denver. He received his doctorate in clinical psychology from the University of Minnesota and publishes regularly on children's and adolescents' relationships with parents, friends, siblings, and romantic partners. He recently co-edited *The Development of Romantic Relationships in Adolescence* (1999) with B. Bradford Brown and Candice Feiring.

Julia A. Graber, Ph.D. is Associate Professor of Psychology at the University of Florida in Gainsville. She investigates girls' development during the transition from childhood to adolescence, with a particular emphasis on bio-psychosocial changes during adolescence. She recently co-edited *Transitions Through Adolescence* (1996), and has recently published articles in the *Journal of Youth and Adolescence* and the *Journal of Research on Adolescence*.

Isabela Granic received her Ph.D. in Human Development and Applied Psychology from the University of Toronto. Her theoretical and empirical work is in developmental psychopathology, with a focus on studying normative and antisocial adolescent development from a dynamic systems perspective. Her interests include identifying the processes that account for change and stability in adolescents' family and peer relationships, the heterogeneous family patterns underlying childhood aggression, and the mechanisms that account for change in interventions. She and her colleagues have developed new dynamic systems methods to study change processes in these domains. She is currently a Research Scientist in Toronto at the Hospital for Sick Children.

Thomas P. Gullotta is Chief Executive Officer of the Child and Family Agency and is a member of the psychology and education departments at Eastern Connecticut State University. He is the senior author of the fourth edition of *The Adolescent Experience* (2000) and is editor emeritus of the *Journal of Primary Prevention*. He is the senior book series editor for "Issues in Children's and Families' Lives." Tom holds editorial appointments on the *Journal of Early Adolescence, Adolescence,* the *Journal of Adolescent Research,* and the *Journal of Educational and Psychological Consultation*. He serves as vice-chairman for the Substance Abuse Task Force on the Board of the National Mental Health Association and co-chairs the Advisory Committee for the federal-funded Safe Schools Technical Assistance Center. He has published extensively on adolescents and primary prevention.

Stephen F. Hamilton is Professor of Human Development and Co-Director of the Family Life Development Center at Cornell University. His research in adolescent development and education investigates the interaction of school, community, and work during the transition from adolescence to adulthood. A major portion of his responsibility involves developing and supporting youth programs through Cooperative Extension. As a Fulbright Senior Research Fellow, Professor Hamilton spent a year studying Germany's apprenticeship system. The book that resulted from that study, *Apprenticeship for Adulthood: Preparing Youth for the Future* (1990), helped guide the School-to-Work Opportunities Act of 1994, as did the youth apprenticeship demonstration project that he and Mary Agnes Hamilton directed. He is currently engaged in a study of how adult mentors teach and advise youth at work. He was a member of the Committee on the Health and Safety Implications of Child Labor convened by the National Research Council and the Institute of Medicine.

C. Peter Herman is a Professor of Psychology at the University of Toronto, where he has taught since 1976, mainly in the areas of personality and research methodology. His research interests are in appetitive behavior and social influence, and he has published close to 100 papers on these and related topics. He is co-author of *Breaking the Diet Habit: The Natural Weight Alternative* (1983), as well as the third and fourth editions of *Psychology*. He is currently on the editorial board of *Psychological Assessment* and was formerly editor-in-chief of the *Journal of Personality*.

Tom Hollenstein received his MS in Psychology from the University of Oregon. He is a doctoral candidate in the Developmental Science program at the University of Toronto, under the supervision of Dr. Marc Lewis. His research interests include the application of dynamic systems methods to the study of developmental change.

David L. Hussey, Ph.D. is Assistant Professor of Justice Studies and a Faculty-Associate of the Institute for the Study and Prevention of Violence at Kent State University. He is also the Director of Research at Beech Brook in Cleveland, Ohio.

Farrah M. Jacquez is a graduate student in Clinical Psychology at Vanderbilt University. She attended college at Marshall University and has a Master's degree in Counseling Psychology from the University of Notre Dame. Her previous work has focused on risk factors for negative behavioral outcomes in adolescence (particularly adolescent suicide and high school dropout). Her current focus of interest is the relation between parental criticism and adolescent depression.

Christa Klute is a Ph.D. student in the Department of Educational Psychology at the University of Wisconsin-Madison. She received a BA in psychology with a certificate in criminal justice in 1993, and an MS in educational psychology in 2001 at the University of Wisconsin-Madison. In 2001, Ms. Klute received the U.W. Dean's Club Graduate Student Research Award for her work on the relationship between adolescent peer crowds and the styles of adolescent substance use.

Jane Kroger is currently Professor of Psychology, University of Tromsø, Norway. She holds a Ph.D. in Child Development from Florida State University, a BA in psychology and an M.Sc. in child development from the University of California, Davis, and a Diploma in Sociology from the University of Stockholm, Sweden. Her current research interests are identity development through adolescence and adulthood. Her most recent books include *Identity in Adolescence: The Balance Between Self and Other* (1996) and *Identity Development: Adolescence through Adulthood* (2000).

Spencer C. Leavitt is a doctoral candidate in the Department of Family and Human Development at Utah State University. He received a BA in Political Science from Brigham Young University and an M.Soc.Sc. in Human Resource Management from Utah State University. His current research interests include adolescent sexual behavior, marital relations and satisfaction, and the relationship between marital and family functioning and child well-being. He is interested in developing interventions that will improve child outcomes by building stable and beneficial marriage relationships.

Michael Lewis, Ph.D. is University Distinguished Professor of Pediatrics and Psychiatry, and Director of the Institute for the Study of Child Development at Robert Wood Johnson Medical School–University of Medicine and Dentistry of New Jersey. He is also Professor of Psychology at Rutgers University. His research has focused on normal and deviant emotional and intellectual development in the opening years of life. His work mapping the course of emotional development, presented in his 1983 book, *Children's Emotions and Moods*, has been heralded as the first attempt to delineate the normal course of emotional growth.

Julie Guay McIntyre, Ph.D. is Associate Professor of Psychology and Director at the Russell Sage College Honors Program. Her research interests focus on the study of stress and coping among adolescents and adults, parenting and the development of coping styles, the relation between stress, coping and health, coping and patient-controlled variables in analgesia (PCA), and the teaching of psychology.

Brent C. Miller is Vice-President for Research and a Professor in the Department of Family and Human Development at Utah State University. He is a fellow of the National Council on Family Relations, and received the Outstanding Graduate Mentor Award at Utah State University in 2000. He has written about research methods, marriage, and parent–child relations, but his recent work has focused on adolescent sexual behavior and pregnancy, especially as related to family relationships and contexts. Dr. Miller has been actively involved with the Effective Programs and Research Task Force of the National Campaign to Prevent Teen Pregnancy.

Jennifer S. Mills received her Ph.D. in Psychology from the University of Toronto and is an Assistant Professor of Psychology at York University. She also works with patients in the Eating Disorders Program of the Toronto General Hospital. Her research interests are in the broad area of eating and its disorders, with a particular emphasis on the factors that influence women to undertake or continue dieting and the psychological conse-quences of restrictive eating.

Kristin L. Moilanen is a graduate student of psychology at the University of Nebraska-Lincoln. She received her BA from Albion College and her MA from the University of Nebraska. Her main research interests include adolescent relationships and problem behavior.

Marilyn J. Montgomery, Ph.D. is Assistant Professor of Psychology and is the author *of Building Bridges to Parents: Tools and Techniques for Counselors* (1999). Her recent journal publications in the area of personal adjustment and the college experience include, "Flow theory as a model for enhancing student resilience," "Opportunity knocks only once? Challenging common beliefs about adulthood," "An investigation of the daily lived experience of women with eating disorders: Implications for counselors," and "The critical contact: A study of recruiter verbal behavior during campus interviews." She is the director of the International Youth Development Project at Florida International University; and is also mentor for the Psychology Research Initiative Mentoring (PRIME) program, which fosters the recruitment, retention, and success of minority students in Psychology.

Janet Polivy is currently a Professor in the Departments of Psychology and Psychiatry at the University of Toronto, where she has taught a variety of undergraduate and graduate courses and supervised numerous doctoral students. She is author of *Breaking the Diet Habit: The Natural Weight Alternative* (1983), as well as the third and fourth editions of *Psychology*, and more than a hundred journal articles and book chapters. Janet is also a consulting editor for the *Journal of Abnormal Psychology*, the *Journal of Consulting and Clinical Psychology*, the *International Journal of Eating Disorders*, the *Journal of Social and Clinical Psychology*, and *Eating Behavior*. She was elected to the Council of the College of Psychologists of Ontario from 1994 to 2000, where she served as Chair of the Regis-tration, Fitness to Practice, and Government Relations Committees, and served as Vice-President of Council. She is also active in other professional associations, and has served on several federal government panels.

Erik J. Porfeli is a doctoral candidate in the Department of Human Development and Family Studies at Pennsylvania State University. After receiving his undergraduate degree in Psychology at the University of Pittsburgh, he spent the next five years as a social worker and earning a degree in Rehabilitation Counseling from Kent State University. His research interests are focused on early career development and on advanced methods for studying career trajectories.

Marcela Raffaelli is an Associate Professor with a joint appointment in the Department of Psychology and the Institute for Ethnic Studies at the University of Nebraska-Lincoln. Her main research interest is in understanding and preventing sexual risk-taking among adolescents and young adults, with a particular focus on gender and cultural issues. She also has programs of research focusing on development among impoverished children and adolescents in the United States and Latin America. She is co-editor, with Reed Larson, of *Homeless and Working Youth around the World: Exploring Developmental Issues, New Directions in Child Development, 85* (1999). She is on the editorial board of the *Journal of Research on Adolescence* and is currently editor of the Society for Research on Adolescence *Newsletter*.

Geoffrey L. Ream is a Ph.D. candidate in Human Development at the Cornell University College of Human Ecology. He holds an MA in Human Development from Cornell University and a BA in Psychology from the University of Michigan. His research interests include social and personality development of adolescents, risk and resiliency factors, and the role of religion in the lives of sexual-minority youth.

Joseph Lee Rodgers is Robert Glenn Rapp Foundation Presidential Professor of Psychology at the University of Oklahoma. He holds a B.S. in Mathematics from the University of Oklahoma and a Ph.D. in Quantitative Psychology from the University of North Carolina. His research has focused on adolescent development, human fertility and reproduction, behavior genetics, mathematical modeling, and behavioral statistics. He has held visiting research and teaching appointments at the University of Hawaii, Ohio State University, the University of North Carolina, Duke University, Odense University in Denmark, and the Max Planck Demographic Institute in Rostock, Germany.

Robert W. Roeser is currently an Assistant Professor of Education at Stanford University. He received his Ph.D. in Education and Psychology from the University of Michigan in 1996. Dr. Roeser also holds a BA in Psychology from Cornell University and Master's degrees in Western Spirituality and Psychology (Holy Names College), Developmental Psychology, and Clinical Social Work (both University of Michigan). Consistent with his training, he approaches his work from an interdisciplinary perspective. His research focuses on the relation between children's and adolescents' academic, social–emotional, and behavioral functioning, as well as on how aspects of the classroom and school context relate to outcomes in these domains during and across the childhood and adolescent years.

Gianine D. Rosenblum, Ph.D. is Assistant Professor of Pediatrics at the Institute for the Study of Child Development at Robert Wood Johnson Medical School–University of Medicine and Dentistry of New Jersey. She received her doctorate in Clinical Psychology from Rutgers University. Dr. Rosenblum's research has focused on adolescent development, with particular emphasis on the development of body image and its relation to other psychological variables. Her other research and clinical interests include childhood obesity, the impact of illness on development, as well as the sequelae and prevention of childhood trauma, maltreatment and interpersonal violence.

Ritch C. Savin-Williams is Professor of Clinical and Developmental Psychology and former Director of Graduate Studies in the Department of Human Development at Cornell University. Professor Savin-Williams has written six books on adolescent development. His latest is *Mom, Dad, I'm Gay: How Families Negotiate Coming Out* (2001), which details the coming-out process of sexual-minority youths. It follows . . . *And Then I Became Gay: Young Men's Stories* (1998) and (co-edited with Kenneth M. Cohen) *The Lives of Lesbians, Gays, and Bisexuals: Children to Adults* (1996). He is also a licensed clinical psychologist with a private practice specializing in identity, relationship, and family issues among young adults, and has served as an expert witness on same-sex marriage, adoption, and Boy Scout court cases. He is currently writing about the experiences of growing up female with same-sex attractions, suicide attempts among gay youth, and other aspects of sexual-minority youth development.

Alesha D. Seroczynski is an Assistant Professor of Psychology at Bethel College in Mishawaka, Indiana. She did her undergraduate work at the University of Texas at Dallas. She obtained a Master's degree in Counseling Psychology and a Ph.D. in Developmental Psychology from the University of Notre Dame. Alesha's research interests have included genetic and environmental influences on aggression across the lifespan, the relationship between aggression and depression in childhood and adolescence, and the nature of relational versus physical aggression. She is currently beginning a new line of research on the Christian woman's identity in early adulthood.

Katherine Hames Shaver has a Master's degree in Human Development and Family Studies from Pennsylvania State University. She is currently working as a research associate studying social patterns relating to nursing in North Carolina.

Joann Wu Shortt is a research scientist at Oregon Social Learning Center, Eugene, Oregon. She received her Ph.D. from the University of Washington. Her research focuses on development that occurs within the context of family and peer relationships and her interests include familial risk and protective factors, emotional development (affective and physiological processes), developmental trajectories and outcomes for children growing up in the same family, and gender differences in adolescent development.

Judith G. Smetana is Professor of Psychology and Pediatrics at the University of Rochester. Her research focuses on children's and adolescents' social-cognitive development, including moral reasoning and development. Dr. Smetana has done extensive research on adolescent–parent relationships in different cultural contexts. Her works are published in journals such as *Child Development, Developmental Psychology,* and in *Annals of Child Development* (Vol. 10, 1995).

Tanya E. Taylor is a Ph.D. student in the Counseling Psychology program at Virginia Commonwealth University. She received her undergraduate and Master's degrees from the University of New Brunswick in Fredericton, New Brunswick, Canada. Research interests include adolescent life skill development, adolescent sport experience, and qualitative and quantitative methodologies.

Elliot Turiel is Chancellor's Professor of Education at the University of California, Berkeley. His research focuses on children's social-cognitive development, including moral reasoning and development. Dr. Turiel has examined social hierarchy and social conflicts within cultures. He is the author of numerous articles in journals such as *Developmental Psychology* and the *Journal of Moral Education,* and books including *The Development of Social Knowledge: Morality and Convention* (1983), *Annals of Child Development* (Vol. 10, 1995), *Development and Cultural Change: Reciprocal Processes* (1999), and *The Culture of Morality: Social Development, Context, and Conflict* (2002).

Fred W. Vondracek is Associate Dean for Undergraduate Studies and Outreach in Penn State University's College of Health and Human Development. He started his career as a tile-setter's apprentice in Germany, and then emigrated to the United States after obtaining his journeyman's license. He studied psychology at Concord College and at Pennsylvania State University, completing his Ph.D. in 1968. After completing a post-doctoral internship with the US Veterans Administration, he joined the faculty of Pennsylvania State University, where he has been since 1969. Since the 1980s, Dr. Vondracek's work has focused on the formulation of a developmental-contextual approach to career development.

Kelly L. Wester, MA is a doctoral candidate in the Counseling and Human Development program at Kent State University. She is also a Research Associate at the Institute for the Study and Prevention of Violence.

Heather Wheeler received her BA from the University of Guelph, and her MA from the University of Toronto, where she continues to pursue her Ph.D. The focus of her dissertation research is eating, dieting, and exercise as they relate to personality and identity.

Michael Windle is a Professor of Psychology and Director of the Center for the Advancement of Youth Health and the Comprehensive Youth Violence Center at the University of Alabama at Birmingham (UAB). He is a developmental psychopathologist with interests in risk and protective factors for child and adolescent alcohol and other substance use, mental health, and violence. Among his current funded projects, Dr. Windle received an NIH MERIT award for a longitudinal study, currently in Year 15, to investigate risk and protective factors for adolescent alcohol and other substance use and mental health. Dr. Windle also has other ongoing grants focused on child and adolescent nutrition, physical activity, violence, mental health, and sexual behavior. He has published over 150 journal articles and three books – *Children of Alcoholics: Critical Perspectives* (1990), *The Science of Prevention* (1997), and *Alcohol Use Among Adolescents* (1999).

Rebecca C. Windle completed her Master's degree in Social Work at the State University of New York, Buffalo in 1997. She has research interests in adolescent health issues, including sexual behavior and teen pregnancy, cigarette use, and suicide. She is currently a Research Associate at the University of Alabama at Birmingham and is actively involved in longitudinal research pertaining to risk and protective factors for adolescent health and the relevance of such findings for intervention applications.

Melanie J. Zimmer-Gembeck (Ph.D., Portland State University, Oregon) is Senior Lecturer (Assistant Professor) in the School of Applied Psychology at Griffith University-Gold Coast, Queensland, Australia. She completed a multidisciplinary NIMH post-doctoral fellowship in the Life Course Center and the Institute of Child Development, University of Minnesota. Her primary interests are the interface of peer relationships (friendships, romantic relationships, and peer status) and psychosocial development during adolescence and emerging adulthood. Her interests also include adolescent health and sexuality, and prevention science. She coauthored a Society for Research in Child Development monograph with E. A. Skinner and J. P. Connell that summarized results of a three-year prospective study of the influence of teacher warmth and structure on children's development of perceptions of control and motivation in the classroom.

Introduction by the Editors

Although more than two thousand years ago Greek philosophers like Aristotle (384–322 B.C.) and Plato (437–347 B.C.) wrote about the problems and characteristics of adolescents or postpubertal youth, the founding of adolescent psychology as an academic discipline is generally dated from 1904. In that year Granville Stanley Hall, who is credited with establishing the discipline, published a two-volume work entitled *Adolescence: Its Psychology and Its Relations to Physiology, Anthropology, Sociology, Sex, Crime, Religion, and Education.* As the discipline (which now includes more than psychology) prepares for its centennial celebration, we are pleased to edit the *Blackwell Handbook of Adolescence.* The discipline advanced dramatically in the twentieth century, and the chapters in the *Blackwell Handbook* provide an excellent overview of the status of adolescent development as we enter a new millennium.

Historically, scientific and lay conceptions of adolescents have diverged. The personal experiences everyone has had being an adolescent and dealing with adolescents have most likely contributed to this disconnect. Generally people find information derived from vivid firsthand experiences to be more compelling than scientific data (Tversky & Kahneman, 1973). In addition, misconceptions tend to result from the way adolescents are portrayed in the mass media. Accounts of adolescent behavior presented in movies, newspapers, and magazines tend to be sensational in that they focus on what is unusual and newsworthy rather than what is normative. For instance, media coverage of some tragic episodes of school violence in the late 1990s (e.g., shootings in Littleton, Colorado in 1999) contributed to widespread public concerns, fears, and political posturing about how increasingly dangerous and violent American schools were becoming. Scientific evidence, however, revealed that throughout the 1990s there had been a progressive decline in school violence in particular and adolescent violence in general (Brener et al., 1999; National School Safety Center, 2001).

Media explanations of adolescent behaviors and problems also tend to be simplified. For example, risky sexual behaviors, excessive drinking, violence, drug abuse, and so forth are often presented as being the direct result of isolated mechanical factors such as peer pressure, media influences, parental structure, economic conditions, and so on. Although factors like peer pressure for deviant behavior certainly play a role in adolescent behavior, research demonstrates that not all adolescents are equally susceptible to that pressure. Personal factors like need for approval, internalized standards, and self-control moderate the effect that peer pressure for deviancy will have on adolescents. Such complex elaborations require considerable time to present and process and they are rarely emphasized in media coverage. Media communication often leads to perceived normalization of relatively rare or infrequent events. In the course of a single day, people may hear repeated messages about a behavior or event through multiple forms of media. Repeated exposure can lead to perceived normalization. Likewise, copycat behaviors through imitation can magnify the salience of infrequent events and atypical behaviors, making them appear normal or common place.

Like adolescents, scientific disciplines also have a developmental history. Despite Stanley Hall's ill-fated attempt to explain adolescent behavior within the theoretical context of evolutionary recapitulation, he did initiate the scientific study of adolescence by identifying a number of the issues, processes, and developmental phenomena familiar to most contemporary students of adolescence. He and his students set the tone for subsequent adolescent research efforts with their observational and, especially, questionnaire studies on topics such as adolescent stress, religion and moral experiences, school processes, emotions, intellectual development, puberty, and physical growth (Hall, 1904). During the first half of the twentieth century, however, the study of adolescent development was overshadowed by the child psychology movement. Only one chapter (Dennis, 1946) in the first edition of Leonard Carmichael's *Manual of Child Psychology*, for example, was devoted to adolescence. Dennis' review suggested that most studies of adolescents, especially early in the century, were descriptive accounts focused, for instance, on the physiological and endocrinological changes associated with puberty and social and cultural differences in adolescent behavior. Again, only one chapter in the second edition of Carmichael's *Manual* emphasized adolescence (Horrocks, 1954), but some major advances in forthcoming research were foreshadowed. For instance, in addition to focusing on physical and sexual maturation, researchers were beginning to examine age-related changes in adolescent social, intellectual, emotional, and personality development. This emphasis was bolstered by ongoing longitudinal studies at, for instance, Berkeley and Harvard, that were starting to yield information about developmental changes during the second decade of life. An awareness of the ephemeral nature of many "adolescent" findings and the role that previous (cohort) and current (time of testing) social and cultural influences may play in developmental (or at least age-related) findings was also beginning to emerge (Horrocks, 1954). However, relatively few theory-driven investigations were being conducted, a tendency that was to persist for several more decades. Also, few graduate programs offered separate courses on adolescent development and fewer yet provided programs where students could specialize in research on adolescent processes.

By 1980 a rising tide of scientific activity could be detected. Locating it, however, required some effort. Grinder (1982), for instance, identified five active but "isolated" research domains devoted to adolescence: conventional academic studies; policy research that examined the impact that practices within social institutions had on adolescents' lives; research on how adolescents interact within different behavioral settings; research on preventive or remedial effects of action programs; and status reviews of demographic data relevant to various social priorities like health or educational needs. During the last quarter of the twentieth century adolescent research has flourished and come into its own. A number of peer-reviewed journals exclusively devoted to research on adolescents and youth were published (e.g., *Youth & Society, Journal of Youth and Adolescence, Journal of Adolescence, Journal of Early Adolescence, Journal of Research on Adolescence*, and the *Journal of Adolescent Research*); the Society for Research on Adolescence was formed; a diversity of textbooks was written by social scientists actively engaged in adolescent research; a *Handbook of Adolescent Psychology* edited by Joseph Adelson (1980) appeared; and book series such as *Advances in Adolescent Development* provided theoretical critiques and critical reviews of research on adolescent processes.

The chapters in the present *Handbook* provide a statement on the status of current research on adolescent processes and offer some projections about future directions and perspectives. This brief introduction cannot do justice to the richness and diversity reflected in the individual contributions. Therefore we will attempt to highlight what we think are some major issues and directions. The first part deals with biological bases of adolescence. A major theme, based on findings from behavioral genetics, is the pervasive influence that genetic variation has on adolescent development. The nature–nurture debate seems to have been resolved (see Turkheimer, 2000). As Rodgers and Bard note in the first chapter of this *Handbook*, the key question is not whether adolescent traits and processes are heritable, since virtually all are: from the social and behavioral domains of personality traits, mental-health indicators, and problem behaviors to the biological domains of puberty, physical growth, and sexual behaviors. Instead, more interesting questions have to do with attempting to specify the reciprocal interactive processes that account for adolescent development, and attempting to identify environmental factors that contribute to the considerable amount of reliable "nonshared" residual variance that is found after genetic and shared environmental effects have been accounted for (Turkheimer, 2000).

Recent advances in neuroscience may eventually provide another way to map some of the biological underpinnings of complex adolescent processes. Ramachandran and Blakeslee (1998), for example, review evidence suggesting that neural connections in different parts of the brain may be implicated in constructing self-images (e.g., a physical or embodied self) and performing self-processes (e.g., executive control and emotional expression). A unified sense of identity, they suggest, may result from neural processes that connect executive functioning represented in the frontal lobes with emotional, volitional, and other self-processes represented in other areas of the brain (Ramachandran & Blakeslee, 1998). Cognitive development also appears to be associated with neural changes and reorganizations in the frontal lobes of the brain (see Byrnes in this *Handbook*; Case, 1992). As Byrnes points out, however, changes in neural circuitry during adolescence may be the result, rather than the cause, of cognitive advances and increased acquisition of declarative and procedural knowledge.

The second section deals with adolescence within social contexts. In Adelson's (1980) *Handbook* developmental theoretical frameworks, especially Freudian psychodynamic and Piagetian cognitive-developmental perspectives, were dominant: three individual chapters focused on the former and the cognitive perspective was so pervasive that the editor considered it to be "probably the dominant approach in [contemporary] adolescent research" (Adelson, 1980, p. ix). Twenty years later, psychoanalytic interpretations are scant. Although cognitive factors are mentioned in numerous chapters in the current *Handbook*, Piagetian views in particular and cognitive accounts in general play a less focal role than they did in the early 1980s. The diminished interest in cognitive processes during adolescence is somewhat surprising given the central role that cognitive development plays in child development (Kuhn & Siegler, 1998) and the burgeoning discipline of social-cognition (Fiske & Taylor, 1991). As Byrnes notes in his chapter on cognitive development, although we know a lot about different aspects of adolescent reasoning, the field lacks a unified theoretical account that can be effectively applied to a wide range of problems and situations.

Although a pervasive interest in developmental change is apparent, organismic-stage models in particular and grand theoretical frameworks in general seem to have fallen from favor. One exception is the chapter by Granic, Dishion, and Hollenstein that considers family relationships during adolescence within a dynamic systems perspective on development. Dynamic systems approaches attempt to explain how novel qualities and irreducible complex forms emerge in the course of development (see Lewis, 2000). A key principle is that developmental changes in physical, chemical, social, and biological, as well as psychological, systems are self-regulated: the effect of conflict-induced changes and feedback is constrained by and dependent upon the existing state of a system's organizational structure. Development follows an iterative, self-organized course that results in states of increasing coherence, adaptiveness, and complexity. Although a dynamic-systems perspective has been used to examine various developmental processes (see e.g., Kunnen & Bosma, 2000; Lewis & Granic, 2000; van Geert, 1998), the majority of the chapters in the present *Handbook* suggest that, as yet, its impact in adolescent development has been limited. However, the developmental-contextual themes that are emphasized may lend themselves to potential evolution into a dynamic-systems perspective.

The chapters of this *Handbook* on social context and personal relationships highlight much of what is currently known about the social processes and interpersonal mechanisms that influence adolescent behavior, attitudes, and psychological states. Socialization processes and practices are examined within a variety of settings and contexts including: conversion and apostasy in religion; extracurricular school activities; the nature and functions of part-time work; transitions within educational settings; peer relationships and school performance; gender differences associated with stereotypes and occupational choice; teaching practices and the ecology of schools; ethnic or immigration cultural status; peer relationships and school success; friendships among peers and social interaction patterns; and contextual contributions to educational attainment. Social context and domains of interpersonal intimacy are also considered within the material on adolescent personal relationships. Developmental changes in the quality and depth of human relationships during adolescence are examined and vividly portrayed in chapters on adolescent dating and romantic experiences, personal friendships, premarital sex, desire and love, the nature of intimacy, diversity in sexual behaviors and orientations, and relationships with non-parent adults. These sections, in tandem with chapters on the developmental course of basic adolescent processes such as autonomy, identity, cognition, morality, emotions, and self-processes (self-esteem and self-conceptions), provide a comprehensive examination of normative development in its various forms and manifestations.

The research upon which many of these chapters is based has increasingly been transformed from single-variable or single-domain cross-sectional approaches to multivariate longitudinal designs. However, relatively few long-term investigations employing sequential designs and sequential-analytic strategies have yet been completed. A tendency among investigators using longitudinal designs to attempt to obtain data on the pre-adolescent and post-adolescent years appears to be occurring. Contextual and ecological information is increasingly being included within data sets. There also appears to be a growing concern with variables such as gender, ethnicity, culture, economic status, biology and puberty, and community settings that may moderate developmental changes and contribute to inter-individual diversity. In the not too distant future, one may find scholars writing data-based chapters placing adolescent development and behavior within the context of the entire life course, thereby providing a macro understanding of the adolescent experience within a life-span developmental frame. This possibility remains a potential and not yet a reality.

As Aristotle and Plato wrote of the problems of adolescence and G. Stanley Hall underscored the turmoil and stress of adolescence, a view of *Strum and Drang* was promulgated. Clearly, there are individual differences in the amount of stress and tension accompanying the adolescent transition (Berzonsky, 1982). Research indicates, however, that during adolescence states of all-consuming anxiety and conflict or severe problem behaviors are neither inevitable nor normative: most youth experience few problems or ones with transitory, relatively short-term effects (Montemayor, Adams & Gullotta, 1990). With maturity most adolescents become relatively productive young adults, who successfully launch careers, enter into the commitment of cohabitation or marriage, start a family, and enter into various sorts of community involvement. Unfortunately, a minority of youth does not escape the "window of vulnerability" that emerges around puberty (Adams, Bennion, Openshaw, & Bingham, 1990). A number of chapters in the *Handbook* examine the etiology, prevalence, and the psychological and social dynamics of common problems that occur during adolescence including sexually transmitted diseases, pregnancy, alcohol and substance use, conduct problems, crime and delinquency, depression, eating disorders, and running away. Again, one finds contextual perspectives being adopted. Not only are contemporary scholars suggesting strategies and ideas for treatment and rehabilitation, they are devoting increasing attention to identifying risk factors and developing prevention strategies and policies. It is possible that prevention science may become a central strand in the fabric of adolescent research. The long-term effectiveness of prevention and intervention programs, for the most part, has yet to be demonstrated. Rigorous program evaluations and longitudinal follow-ups are necessary to determine whether interventions have a significant long-term impact on adolescents and, if so, whether those effects are positive or negative (iatrogenic effects). At least some research demonstrates that at least some intervention programs, especially those in which high-risk adolescents associate with deviant peers, may actually produce elevated levels of problem behaviors like substance abuse, delinquency, and violence (Dishion, McCord, & Poulin, 1999; McCord, 1978). There is a need for a more collaborative climate between basic adolescent researchers and practitioners and service providers, with the latter playing an active role in framing questions and setting the research agenda.

Information about pathways into disordered or problem behaviors is provided, for example, in the chapters on crime, delinquency and youth gangs and adolescent eating disorders. The role that genetic, social, and personality factors play in an adolescent's susceptibility to problem behaviors and developmental pathology is examined. Most of this work has risk or protective components that are often considered in prevention or intervention sciences. As yet, interconnections or linkages between normative development themes and adolescent problem behaviors are not well articulated, leaving the two arenas of research relatively distinct. Perhaps more integrative approaches will emerge in the coming years.

Finally, it is important to recognize that while a few decades ago relatively few scholars were investigating adolescent processes, one now finds a multitude of scholars from a variety of disciplines and professions studying adolescent development and behavior. This diversity of scholars in the allied social sciences, medicine, biology, education, and prevention/intervention sciences has contributed multiple theoretical and conceptual perspectives, a variety of methodological and analytical strategies, and numerous creative insights to the study and understanding of the nature of adolescence. The chapters in this *Handbook* have been prepared by prominent scholars of adolescence and provide integrated theoretical and empirical accounts about the adolescent experience. It is our hope that the *Handbook* provides not only a substantive foundation for an improved understanding of adolescent development, behaviors, and problems, but that it also helps to enrich the study of adolescents and services provided to them.

References

Adams, G. R., Bennion, L. D., Openshaw, K. D., & Bingham, C. R. (1990). Windows of vulnerability: Identifying critical age, gender, and racial differences predictive of risk for violent deaths in childhood and adolescence. *Journal of Primary Prevention, 10*(3), 233–240.

Adelson, J. (Ed.) (1980). *Handbook of adolescent psychology.* New York: Wiley.

Brener, N. D., Simon, T. R., Krug, E. G., & Lowry, R. (1999). Recent trends in violence-related behaviors among high school students in the United States. *Journal of the American Medical Association, 282,* 440–446.

Berzonsky, M. D. (1982). Inter- and intra-individual differences in adolescent storm and stress: A life-span developmental view. *Journal of Early Adolescence, 2,* 211–217.

Case, R. (1992). The role of the frontal lobes in the regulation of cognitive development. *Brain and Cognition, 20,* 51–73.

Fiske, S. T., & Taylor, S. E. (1991). *Social cognition* (2nd ed.). New York: McGraw-Hill.

Dennis, W. (1946). The adolescent. In L. Carmichael (Ed.), *Manual of child psychology* (pp. 633–666). New York: Wiley.

Dishion, T. J., McCord, J., & Poulin, F. (1999). When interventions harm: Peer groups and problem behavior. *American Psychologist, 54,* 755–764.

Grinder, R. E. (1982). Isolationism in adolescent research. *Human Development, 25,* 223–232.

Hall. G. S. (1904). *Adolescence: Its psychology and its relations to physiology, anthropology, sociology, sex, crime, religion, and education* (2 vols.). New York: Appleton-Century-Crofts.

Horrocks, J. E. (1954). The adolescent. In L. Carmichael (Ed.), *Manual of child psychology* (2nd ed., pp. 697–734). New York: Wiley.

Kuhn, D., & Siegler, R. S. (Eds.) (1998). W. Damon (Series Ed.), *Handbook of child psychology: Vol. 2. Cognition, perception, and language* (5th ed.). New York: Wiley.

Kunnen, E. S., & Bosma, H. A. (2000). Development of meaning-making: A dynamic systems approach. *New Ideas in Psychology, 18*, 57–82.

Lewis, M. D. (2000). The promise of dynamic systems approaches for an integrated account of human development. *Child Development, 71*, 36–43.

Lewis, M. D., & Granic, I. (Eds.) (2000). *Emotion, development and self-organization: Dynamic systems approaches to emotional development.* New York: Cambridge University Press.

McCord, J. (1978). A thirty-year follow-up of treatment effects. *American Psychologist, 33*, 284–289.

Montemayor, R., Adams, G. R., & Gullotta, T. P. (1990). *From childhood to adolescence: A transitional period? Advances in Adolescent Development, Vol 2.* Newbury Park, CA: Sage.

National School Safety Center (2001, September 5). Report of school associated violent deaths. Retrieved October 10, 2001 from http://www.nssc1.org

Ramachandran, V. S., & Blakeslee, S. (1998). *Phantoms in the brain: Human nature and the architecture of the mind.* London: Fourth Estate.

Turkheimer, E. (2000). Three laws of behavior genetics and what they mean. *Current Directions in Psychological Science, 9*, 160–164.

Tversky, A., & Kahneman, D. (1973). Availability: A heuristic for judging frequency and probability. *Cognitive Psychology, 5*, 207–232.

van Geert, P. L. C. (1998). A dynamic systems model of basic developmental mechanisms: Piaget, Vygotsky, and beyond. *Psychological Review, 105*, 634–677.

PART I

Biological and Genetic Processes

CHAPTER ONE

Behavior Genetics and Adolescent Development: A Review of Recent Literature

Joseph Lee Rodgers and David E. Bard

Introduction

Behavior genetics is a quantitative method, and adolescent development is a psychological topic. Treating the cross between these two arenas appears, at the surface, to require collecting research in which the method has been applied to study the topic, and reviewing that research for coherence and common themes. But the challenge is rather more difficult than the surface level view might suggest. Below the surface is a great deal of shifting sand, which makes organizing the topic difficult. Because of this instability, it is critical that we carefully and explicitly define a foundational starting point. In the introduction to this article, we begin with some definitions, and then we describe the difficulties inherent in reviewing "behavior genetics and adolescent development." We conclude our introduction with a summary of the foundation on which we will base our review. In the next section, we carefully build that foundation. Following, we summarize the relevant research, and embed it within the organizational foundation.

Definitions: Why Is This Chapter Difficult to Frame?

The starting point for most behavior genetic modeling is the conceptual partitioning of sources of variance into genetic, shared environmental, and nonshared environmental (e.g., Rowe & Plomin, 1981). Some of the similarity between individuals in the same family may be caused by sharing the same genes. For example, monozygotic (MZ) twins share 100 percent of their genes, and should be approximately identical on traits or behaviors that are strongly under genetic control (e.g., height, eye color). Dizygotic (DZ) twins and full siblings on average share .50 of their genes, half siblings share .25, cousins share

.125, etc. Alternatively, some of the similarity between individuals in the same family has as its etiological source the shared environment; this theoretical source of influence causes related individuals to be similar because they share a common environment within the family. For example, parental discipline style may be a shared environmental influence that is in common to all children in a family and that results in similarities between the children in a measure of response to authority. Finally, the nonshared environment is a theoretical source of influence that causes individuals in the same family to be different from one another, that is, these influences are not shared in common among siblings. For example, a particularly outstanding teacher that a child had in first grade (but who was not the teacher of the other children in the family) could create nonshared environmental influences on reading motivation. Or, even within the family, parents may be more authoritative with their sons than with their daughters (which would result in parental discipline style being a nonshared rather than shared environmental influence).

It is well known to behavior geneticists – if not necessarily to the general population of researchers – that measures of variance related to genetic processes (heritabilities, or h^2) and shared environmental processes (sometimes called the common environment, or c^2) are *not* immutable (see Angoff, 1988). The basic biometrical model (e.g., Falconer, 1981) partitions the overall variance in the dependent variable into that attributable to genes, that attributable to the shared environment, and that attributable to the nonshared environment. (Most estimation procedures confound the latter source – nonshared environmental variance, often called e^2 – with measurement error, although there are statistical ways around this problem; see Rodgers, Rowe, & Li, 1994.)

Two critical features of this definition must be appreciated. First, h^2, c^2, and e^2 depend on both the amount of variance relevant to their conceptual domain, and they also depend on the amount of *overall* variance. The conceptual formulas are h^2 = genetic variance/total variance, c^2 = shared environmental variance/total variance, and e^2 = nonshared variance/total variance. (Total variance is often referred to as "phenotypic variance" in the behavior genetic literature.) These three coefficients necessarily add up to 100 percent, so that each one may be interpreted as the proportion of total variance attributable to genetic, shared environment, and nonshared environment sources, respectively. Thus, for example, if genetic variance remains fixed, but overall variance in the dependent variable (phenotypic variance) increases substantially, then h^2 goes down due to the denominator, without any shift in the genetic contribution itself. Second, h^2, c^2, and e^2 *must* be interpreted in a variance context; that is, the genetic and environmental contributions explain individual differences, and not general properties of traits or behaviors. For example, genes perfectly determine eye color. Yet, in a setting with few non-brown-eyed people, heritability would be very low (because there is little phenotypic variation). In other words, h^2 indicates how much *variance* in a trait or behavior is related to genetic sources. It does not indicate whether the existence of the trait or behavior has any genetic etiology. Similarly, c^2 and e^2 indicate how much *variance* in a trait or behavior is attributable to these two environmental sources, not whether the trait or behavior has underlying environment etiology. For example, a person's accent is obviously influenced by the environment. But a measure of accent would show very low c^2, for the simple reason that there is very little overall variance to explain. Even otherwise responsible behavior geneticists often misuse their language, and refer to "genetic or environmental influences on a trait," when what they really mean is "genetic or environmental influences on *variance in* or *individual differences* in a trait."

The explanation above refers to the basic *additive* genetic model. This model implies that a number of separate genetic sources each contribute separate and additive pieces of influences on the variance in a trait or behavior of interest. Of course, some genetic processes are nonlinear and nonadditive (e.g., basic principles of Mendelian inheritance are inherently non-additive). Quantitative modeling in behavior genetics supports fitting dominance models (e.g., Neale & Cardon, 1992), and the concept of emergenesis has been proposed to account for configural genetic contributions (Lykken et al., 1992). On the other hand, another type of nonlinear genetic process, epistasis, involves genetic interactions of alleles across genetic loci (as opposed to Mendelian dominance, which involves interactions of alleles within a genetic locus). Epistasis is difficult to model in behavioral genetic settings (e.g., Neale & Cardon, 1992). In this review, we will focus on efforts to fit additive genetic models to adolescent data, primarily because little attention has been given to nonlinear or non-additive models in the literature. Besides genetic nonadditivity, a second problem occurs when there are genetic-environmental interactions that are not accounted for within the model. Turkheimer (1998) showed that the effect of failing to account for genetic/environmental interactions is to bias estimates of h^2 and c^2. While there is little published literature, efforts to account for gene-environment interactions are ongoing (and several will be mentioned in reviewing the literature).

Both h^2 and c^2 (and, implicitly, e^2) can shift and change over time and over age, as the variances in both the numerators and the denominators shift and change. At adolescence in particular, phenotypic variance in many traits and behaviors can shift substantially. For a few years, height (and most other physiological measures) becomes more highly variable, as children reach puberty at a wide range of ages. In less obvious ways, there can be shifts in overall variance of intelligence, many personality traits, and especially in social and health behaviors. Smoking provides a good example. Among 8-year-olds, smoking behavior has virtually no heritability. Obviously, this is not because genetic influences do not contribute to smoking in general, but because there is little phenotypic variance in measures of smoking among 8-year-olds. By age 14, smoking heritabilities begin to be detectable in a measure like age-at-first cigarette (but not so much in measures of smoking addiction). By age 20, measures of smoking intensity, smoking duration, and smoking addiction all show heritable components. These points about genetic influences apply equally to both shared and nonshared environmental influences as well. It is in this context that we refer to the "shifting sand" on which we observe genetic and environmental influences.

There are several proper ways to treat these problems. The first is interpretational; authors must be clear about what h^2, c^2, and e^2 mean, and what they don't mean. Second, there are direct measures of these influences; for example, some behavior geneticists emphasize the importance of computing heritabilities, and also computing coefficients of genetic variation, which are not affected by the overall variance of the DV itself (see, e.g., Houle, 1992). Third, the shifts in h^2 and c^2 values can provide a great deal of information in and of themselves. For example, Kohler, Rodgers, and Christensen (1999) documented a substantial shift in h^2 of fertility, using secular twin data from Denmark. The dramatic upward shifts in h^2 values that they observed occurred simultaneously with the two fertility transitions in Denmark, which provided a framework within which to explain this rapid change in heritability.

The difficulties defined in this introductory section are all related to the method (and, importantly, to improper interpretation of the design and purpose of the method). The "shifting sand" problem of interpreting heritabilities is only a problem if it is allowed to be. We will attempt to carefully extract the proper information from the studies we review, and we invite the reader to bring healthy critical inspection into this investigation with us. As Maccoby (2000) noted, "knowing only the strength of genetic factors . . . is not a sufficient basis for estimating environmental ones" (p. 1). Turkheimer (1998) suggested that heritability studies lead only to the "banal tautology that all behavior is ultimately based in the genotype and brain" (p. 782). While we are more sanguine about the value of such studies than Turkheimer, we applaud the skeptical approach that this position implies.

Finally, we intend to respond to the "shifting sand" problem by firmly tying down our treatment with theoretical orientations from both social and biological domains that focus on the topic and not on the method. The study of adolescence in general, and especially adolescent development, focuses attention on the process of change. We have used three different social theories in our past work to frame the process of adolescent development. More properly, these are closer to motivating orientations than they are to formal theories, because we in no sense test or evaluate the structures. Rather, we let them guide our investigation and review. The three approaches are the Transition Behavior Perspective, the Life Course Perspective, and Problem Behavior Theory. In addition, the biological perspective that best informs the study of adolescent development is to consider hormonal influences that affect both physiological changes and behavioral changes.

Theoretical Framework

Adolescence embedded in a social and temporal ecology

The Transition Behavior Perspective is developed more completely in Ensminger (1987) and in Rodgers and Rowe (1993). This orienting framework views adolescence as a period of expanded behavioral opportunity. Adolescents begin to have choices within a behavioral ecology that were not available to them during childhood. How much to study, whether to smoke and drink, what parties to attend, what school clubs to join, and management of health behaviors are emerging issues within the decision-making framework of many adolescents. In addition, consumer behavior offers expanded opportunity in adolescence as well. Transition behaviors are defined as behaviors that adolescents use – either overtly or implicitly – to signal impending adulthood. These behaviors may have other purposes as well, but at least part of their status is to socially represent the transitional features of adolescence. Some of those behaviors are unhealthy, or at least socially proscribed. Examples include risky sexual behavior, reckless driving, smoking, drinking to excess, drug use, and cheating on homework. Some transition behaviors are healthy and socially normative. Examples include playing in the school band, checking out library books, playing on a tennis team, and joining a church group. The reason the Transition Behavior Perspective is valuable in the context of the current review is that is orients attention toward behaviors that many consider to be prototypical adolescent behavior.

Most of the attention to transition behaviors in the social science (and behavior genetic) literature is on behaviors that we have previously labeled mildly and severely deviant (see Rodgers, Billy, & Udry, 1984; Rodgers & Rowe, 1993). While the socially appropriate transition behaviors deserve much more attention than they have received, we will focus on those that have received substantial research attention. Those include smoking, drinking, drug use, and dating/sexual behavior.

A second theoretical perspective helps motivate some of the behavior genetic literature in this domain. Problem Behavior Theory (Jessor & Jessor, 1977) suggests that a number of both mildly and severely deviant behaviors may group together. The question of whether problem behaviors group together was expanded by Moffit (1993) into a theory of "adolescence-limited" versus "life-course-persistent" deviant behavior. Rodgers and Rowe (1990) found that sexual behavior had a somewhat unusual status in the context of Problem Behavior Theory; while it did covary with other mildly deviant behaviors (e.g., smoking, drinking, and driving illegally), it also contained substantial unique variance of its own that did not overlap with those other variables. The methodology of behavior genetics provides a powerful approach to investigating this perspective, and we will review several studies that consider the multivariate relationships between two or more problem behaviors.

A third theoretical approach that is useful is the Life Course Perspective, which suggests that norms are established by society to define age-appropriate behavioral transitions; "age differentiation is expressed in the sequence of roles and events, social transitions, and turning points that depict the life course" (Elder, 1975). Hogan and Astone (1986) suggested that transitions from adolescence into and through adulthood have ordered stages, and that society has normative expectations about age-appropriate life transitions; Rindfuss, Swicegood, and Rosenfeld (1987) investigated deviations from those normative ordered stages. Most of the examples of events of high salience in the Life Course Perspective are demographic transitions such as marriage, first child, or education. In combining the Transition Behavior and the Life Course Perspective, we bring a whole new domain of behaviors under this umbrella. In this combined perspective, the first cigarette, the first drink, and loss of virginity can also be considered to have "life course status," in that we organize our thinking and plans in relation to the timing of these events. Further, they are of particular salience in defining the "adolescent experience," an observation that brings Problem Behavior Theory into this integrative framework. Indeed, we suspect that many individuals (both adults and adolescents themselves) would define these mildly and severely deviant behaviors as closer to "adolescent prototype behaviors" than the more socially normative transition behaviors like joining clubs and playing in the band.

Nevertheless, we note the existence of certain cognitive and personality transitions that may also be motivated by Transition Behavior and Life Course perspectives. Certain subjects in school may be perceived in a Life Course perspective. One example would be bright students taking pre-calculus in 11th grade, or Advanced Placement English as seniors. Another would be the transition in junior- or mid-high to having a study hall (and associated expectations) as part of the school experience. A third would be expanding social autonomy, such as the choice to attend a school dance or to have lunch off-campus. A fourth would be the emergence of leadership in a high-school social/political structure.

Adolescence embedded in a hormonal ecology

The idea of adolescent "raging hormones" has been overplayed; for example, most adolescents are not nearly as sexually active in response to those hormones (even those who are nonvirgins are not nearly as sexually active) as many media portrayals might suggest (see, e.g., Rodgers, 1996). The proper phrase is probably closer to "changing hormones." Indeed, hormones drive many of the physiological changes during adolescence, which in turn have tremendous impacts on behavioral processes.

Buchanan, Eccles, and Becker (1992) developed an integrated framework in which to view the influence that hormonal changes during adolescence have on adolescent behaviors and traits. They noted that

> Historically, most of the changes in mood and behavior were presumed to be negative and to be the result of biological factors, particularly of hormones. . . . More recently, psychologists have questioned both the prevalence of such negative changes and their hypothesized biological roots. . . . Emphasis has shifted to contextual (i.e., family, school, peer group) and psychological (i.e., self-esteem, gender role orientation) factors. (p. 62)

Their review shows hormonal changes to potentially influence adolescent self-esteem, happiness, concentration, aggression and behavior problems, and social relationships. Udry et al. (1985) showed a link between androgenic hormones and male adolescent sexual behavior, and Udry and Talbert (1988) documented personality responses to hormonal changes. Susman et al. (1985) showed a link between adolescent hormone levels and socio-emotional behaviors.

Introductory summary

Behavior genetic modeling too often occurs in its own vacuum. This introduction was designed to create a larger context for the upcoming review of behavior genetic studies of adolescent behaviors and traits. Genes influence hormones. Hormones have both overlapping variance with and can change traits and behaviors. All occur at an organic level, within an individual who is embedded in a social environment of family, friends, school, church, and other social influences. Further, all of these complex interrelations are defined temporally, and may mean different things at different ages and stages. The Life Course and Transition Behavior Perspectives, along with Problem Behavior Theory, can help us appreciate this complex interplay. Recent work in the behavior genetic literature has shifted our orientation away from a strict causal flow from the genome to behavior, and has substituted various complex and fascinating feedback loops involved in the causal process (see, e.g., Brown, 1999; Gottlieb, 2000). We will return to this broader perspective in a concluding section, where we place in context the results of our review of genetic and environmental influences that emerge from the behavior genetic literature.

Methodology Used in This Review

To identify relevant empirical studies to be reviewed in this chapter, we partitioned our title into three component keywords: "behavior genetic," "adolescence," and "development." Our initial literature review identified primary journals in each area: *Behavior Genetics* for the first, *Adolescence* for the second, and *Developmental Psychology* for the third. We obtained copies of each article that involved behavior genetic analysis of a topic related to adolescent development from 1985 to 2000. In reviewing those articles, we identified a number of additional articles that were obtained as well. In addition, several recent chapters in *Annual Review of Psychology* provided both material and references to support this review (see Maccoby, 2000; Plomin & Rende, 1991; Rose, 1995; Steinberg & Morris, 2001).

By far the majority of our articles reviewed here come from *Behavior Genetics* and *Developmental Psychology*. Further, most are recent articles. Though we searched for relevant articles in each area back to 1985, most that were relevant had been published more recently than that, many in the latter half of the 1990s.

Behavior Genetic Research on Adolescence: The Social/Behavioral Ecology

The social/behavioral domains represented within the articles we have collected include adolescent transition behaviors (smoking, drinking, sexual behavior, and other risk-taking activities), social/mental health among adolescents (including depression and antisocial behavior), indicators of social relationships within the family (parents and siblings), and treatment of cognitive and personality development during adolescence.

Transition behaviors

Behavior genetic studies have shown that there is genetic variance underlying adolescent transition behaviors, and have also indicated some of the dynamics underlying the social/environmental correlates. While a general consideration of problem behaviors spreads out beyond the boundaries covered by transition behavior, they certainly overlap substantially with that domain, especially through alcohol and drug use.

Within the domain of problem behaviors, Gjone et al. (1996) used the Child Behavior Checklist (CBCL) to measure internalizing and externalizing problem behaviors among Norwegian same-sex twins born during the 1970s and 1980s. Their results showed significant heritabilities for both domains, with increasing h^2 and decreasing c^2 as the severity of the problem behavior increased for both internalizing and externalizing behaviors (although rescaling of those variables dampened this pattern). Van den Oord, Boomsma, and Verhulst (1994) also used the CBCL with a sample of international adopted children in the Netherlands. Like Gjone et al., they found significant heritability for externalizing behaviors; however, they did not match their result for internalizing behaviors. They also found larger variance for males than for females for aggressive behavior, which they speculated might have genetic origins. Eaves et al. (1993) studied conduct disorder items from the Rutter Parent Questionnaire using 8–16-year-old male twins from the Virginia Adolescent Behavioral Development study. Their model identified four underlying latent classes, which were themselves shown to be heritable. However, their model rejected a unidimensional interpretation of the latent processes underlying conduct disorder. Rodgers, Rowe, and Li (1994) studied measures obtained from the Behavioral Problem Index (BPI) using 5–11-year-old children from respondents in the National Longitudinal Survey of Youth (NLSY), nationally representative data from adolescents born between 1958 and 1965. For the six subscales of the BPI, they found strong heritabilities for the more trait-based subscales (Anxiety, Hyperactivity, and Dependent) and weaker heritabilities for the social subscales (Antisocial, Peer Conflict, and Headstrong). Further, the three social subscales showed significant shared environmental variance. The quality of the home environment (measured by the HOME) showed significant nonshared influences on siblings in the same household for all of the subscales except for Peer Conflict. Van der Valk et al. (1998) used an adoption design with 10–18-year-old Dutch children to investigate the longitudinal stability of problem behaviors. Their dependent measures came from the Child Behavior Checklist. They found stability in an externalizing factor, primarily genetic in origin, and more shared environmental influence at the early ages than at the later ones. Rowe, Almeida, and Jacobson (1999) studied adolescent aggression using the Add Health data. They found an $h^2 = .32$, with little shared environmental variance. The heritability increased from this value with increases in family warmth measured at the school level. Finally, van den Oord and Rowe (1997) investigated social maladjustment using the BPI measures in the NLSY. Their findings suggested that nonshared environmental influences had the most effect on children's problem behaviors. They also found support for a "liability model," suggesting "a stable underlying liability may be the 'third variable' that explains the relations between subsequent levels of problem behaviors" (pp. 319–320).

Several studies addressed specific transition behaviors. Koopmans et al. (1999) studied smoking initiation and quantity using a twin study of Dutch adolescents. They fit a bivariate model, and found that there were separate dimensions underlying smoking initiation and smoking quantity. They found substantial $h^2 = .39$ and even greater $c^2 = .54$ for smoking initiation, while h^2 and c^2 became negligible for smoking quantity. This finding – that there are separate (though potentially overlapping) liabilities for smoking onset and smoking persistence – was also obtained by Madden et al. (1999) and Heath et al. (1999) using adult samples.

Viken et al. (1999) used twins from a Finnish birth cohort born in 1975–9 to study self-reported alcohol consumption. Like the smoking results above, they found that shared environmental influences were important in drinking initiation, but that additive genetic effects became more important in explaining variance in drinking frequency among those who had already begun drinking. Buster and Rodgers (2000) used measures of light and heavy drinking from adolescents in the NLSY. They found significant h^2 for adolescent males in the NLSY for light drinking, with the shift to significant c^2 for heavy drinking. Adolescent females had a strong genetic basis (and non-significant c^2s) for both light and heavy drinking.

Carey (1992) and Meyer and Neale (1992) used a simulated dataset to investigate onset of drug use among teenagers. Carey simulated the dataset to represent three processes, diffusion/exposure, initial use, and persistence. Meyer and Neale fit models to show that, at least in this artificial dataset, the shared environment accounted for twin similarity in drug use onset and timing.

While multiple stage theories that include social influence processes have been developed to explain the spread of adolescent transition behaviors like smoking and drinking (e.g., Rowe & Rodgers, 1991; Rowe et al., 1996), the basic and simple distinction between onset and maintenance appears to be the most abiding and valuable one to emerge from this investigation (e.g., Mayhew, Flay, & Mott, 2000). The coherent result across these studies is that onset is driven socially, but after initiation has occurred, the variance in the amount is genetically based.

As discussed above, not all transition behaviors are necessarily problem behaviors. Participation in sports is a positive transition behavior (along with other extracurricular activities, church programs, hobbies, etc.). Boomsma et al. (1989) studied participation in sports using teenaged twins from Amsterdam and their parents. They found a genetic component to sports participation, and a strong shared environmental component for females (but not for males). Further, they developed a bivariate model between sports participation and heart rate, and found heart rate to have a stronger genetic basis and sports participation to have a stronger environmental basis. We encourage additional research falling into this domain, in which healthy adolescent transition behaviors are evaluated through behavior genetic and other methodologies.

Sexual behavior is a transition behavior that becomes socially normative with increasing age. Several behavior genetic studies have identified significant heritabilities for measures of age-at-first-intercourse (e.g., Dunne et al., 1997; Rodgers, Rowe, & Buster, 1999), which typically occurs during adolescence in the cultures studied. Miller et al. (1999) showed a relationship between dopamine receptors and age at first intercourse, providing information about a potential genetic mechanism to help explain this link.

Social/mental health

Rende et al. (1993) fit biometrical models to measures of depression in adolescents. They found a significant heritability in the overall depression distribution. However, the genetic component disappeared when models were fit to evaluate extreme depression. In other words, there did not seem to be any different or additional genetic component to extreme depression over and above its status as an extreme form of the overall variance in depression. Pike et al. (1996) used US sibling pairs who were within four years of one another in age, including twins, siblings, half-siblings, and unrelated siblings. Depression was measured in three ways, using the Child Depression Inventory, the BPI-Depression sub-scale, and the Behavior Events Inventory (BEI). They found that the "model attributes the variance of depressive symptoms to substantial genetic influence, negligible shared environmental influence, and moderate nonshared environmental influence" (p. 597). Further, they also found that mother's negativity was associated with adolescent depression through the nonshared environment, independent of genes and the shared environment. Results for father's negativity were similar. Jacobson and Rowe (1999) used the kinship structure in the National Longitudinal Survey of Adolescent Health (Add Health) to study the relation between social connectedness and adolescent depression. They found different models for males and females. Genetic influences were stronger for females than for males for both depression indicators, and also for the covariation between social connectedness and depression.

Other (overlapping) literature has investigated antisocial behavior in adolescents. The study by Pike et al. (1996) reviewed above that treated depression also investigated anti-social behavior using subscales from the BPI and the BEI. Antisocial behavior showed more shared environmental variance than did depression, but genetic and nonshared environmental influences also accounted for significant variance. As with depression, the non-shared environment accounted for covariation between mother's negativity and antisocial behavior, and genetic and shared environmental influences contributed variance as well. In a study by O'Connor et al. (1998) using Colorado Adoption Project (CAP) data from late childhood and early adolescence (ages 7–12), antisocial behavior was assessed using constructed measures for parental antisocial behavior and the Child Behavior Checklist (CBC) for children. They were interested in the causal directionality of parenting behavior and children's antisocial behavior. They found that the covariation between negative parenting and antisocial behavior was not evoked by the child; however, their results were consistent with a plausible parental effect on children's antisocial behavior.

Finally, a study by Topolski et al. (1997) used data from the Virginia Twin Study of Adolescent Behavioral Development to study separation anxiety disorder (SAD), over-anxious disorder, and manifest anxiety. Moderate heritabilities were found for each of the three, with meaningful shared environmental variance for SAD. There were no strong age or gender differences.

Social relationships with family members

There has been substantial research on adolescents from a behavior genetic perspective on family relationships. Both the Transition Behavior and Life Course perspectives provide motivation for changing relationships to emerge between adolescents and their family. Because adolescents have a new and broader behavioral repertoire, because they are beginning the transition into the independence and autonomy of adulthood, and because society notes several specific markers during adolescence as particularly salient (e.g., transition to high school, first car, leaving home, etc.), these social relationships may be subtle, volatile, and/or dynamic.

In an interesting methodological study, Plomin et al. (1994) showed that a number of measures of the family environment in fact contain substantial genetic variation: "On average, more than a quarter of the variance of these environmental measures can be accounted for by genetic differences among children" (p. 32). This study, a part of the Nonshared Environment in Adolescent Development (NEAD) project, recruited adolescents from both non-divorced and stepfamilies randomly chosen from the US population. This project grew out of a large effort showing the importance of nonshared environmental influences on individual differences in human (including adolescent) behavior. This particular study demonstrated the difficulty in cleanly separating measures into genetic and environmental categories.

Elkins, McGue, and Iacono (1997) took a developmental perspective in a study of parent–son relationships during adolescence. They used the Minnesota Twin Family Study and a Parental Environment Questionnaire that assessed various aspects of the parent–child relationship. They found different etiologies for twins around age 11 compared to those around age 17. Both ages showed heritability of adolescents' perceptions of the quality of parent–son relationships, with substantially higher h^2 for the older twins. These effects were stronger for the father–son relationship than for the mother–son relationship. Neiderhiser et al. (1998) used data from same-sex siblings in the NEAD project described above to study adolescent perceptions of parenting. Adolescent perceptions of parenting did mediate parent conflict measures and adolescent antisocial measures, and the association between parental and child maladjustment had a strong genetic component. Bussell et al. (1999) used the same data source to investigate the basis for the common finding that parent–child relationships are related to the quality of sibling relationships. Most of the covariance between quality of the mother–child relationship and the quality of the sibling relationship was attributable to the shared environment, although significant genetic and nonshared environmental components were identified as well. Neale (1999) challenged some of the assumptions from the Bussell et al. study, but supported the finding of the importance of the shared environment for both sibling and parent–child relationships (see also Neiderhiser et al., 1999, who replied to Neale's criticisms).

Personality

A number of researchers have fit biometrical models based on behavior genetic designs to measures of personality. McGue, Bacon, and Lykken (1993) used data from twins in Minnesota High Schools during the 1970s, measured in late adolescence and then around ten years later. They used the Multidimensional Personality Questionnaire, which has subscales of positive emotionality (similar to extraversion), negative emotionality (similar to neuroticism/aggression), and constraint (harm avoidance and traditionalism). They found reduction in genetic influence over the two age periods for negative emotionality, stability in overall personality structure that was primarily based on genetic processes, and change in personality structure that was primarily based on environmental factors. Billig et al. (1996) used data from 17-year-old male twins from the Minnesota Twin/Family Study with measures of personality (obtained from the Multidimensional Personality Questionnaire) and a second survey called Life Events Interview for Adolescents. In this second instrument, respondents indicated which of a wide variety of life events they had experienced, which were themselves divided into family events (e.g., the whole family moved into a new house), nonfamily events independent of the respondent's behavior (e.g., a close friend moved away), and nonfamily events not independent of the respondent's behavior (e.g., suspended from school). Biometrical modeling showed a genetic basis to nonindependent nonfamily life events and genetic covariance between nonindependent nonfamily life events and personality (especially with the personality factor, constraint). Finally, Macaskill et al. (1994) used the Eysenck Personality Scales with Australian twins aged 11 to 18. After partialling out age and gender, they found genetic influence for psychoticism and neuroticism.

Other treatment of more specific personality topics can also be found. Koopmans et al. (1995) studied sensation seeking using Dutch twins aged 12–24 and their parents. They used Zuckerman's Sensation Seeking Scale, which has several non-overlapping subscales. They found that "genes play a major role in the individual differences in sensation seeking" (p. 354), replicating results from Fulker, Eysenck, and Zuckerman. (1980). No shared environmental influences were significant. Eaves et al. (1997) used a 28-item social attitude survey to study conservatism. They found an important age difference, with twins younger than 20 having their conservatism related to shared environmental factors, while those older than 20 had conservatism variance that was primarily related to genetic influence.

Cognitive abilities

Using an Egyptian sample of twins aged 12–19, Abdel-Rahim, Nagoshi, and Vandenberg (1990) studied measures from a broad battery of cognitive measures. They found different results from those obtained from Western studies, with little difference between MZ and DZ twin scores and lower MZ correlations in general. They provide a cross-cultural interpretation of this result, although they hasten to note several methodological concerns, including low sample size and absence of height heritability. Nagoshi and Johnson (1993) used family data from the Hawaii Family Study of Cognition along with (age-corrected) measures of verbal ability, spatial ability, perceptual speed, and visual memory. They found a race difference (between those of Caucasian ancestry and those of Japanese ancestry), with similar c^2 for adolescents and adults. Petril and Thompson (1993) used twin data from the Western Reserve Twin Project cognitive measures from the WISC-R, the Colorado Test of Specific Cognitive Abilities, the Metropolitan Achievement Test, and the Cognitive Abilities Test. Univariate analysis showed both genetic and shared environmental variance underlying individual differences in cognition and achievement, and multivariate analysis showing covariance between them (especially genetic influence). Rodgers, Rowe, and May (1994) used PPVT, PIAT, and Digit Span measures from children and those transitioning into adolescents (aged 5–12) in the NLSY-Children dataset to study intelligence/achievement. They found moderate h^2 (median $h^2 = .50$) and smaller c^2 (median $c^2 = .16$) across five ability measures. Their particular focus, however, was on the nonshared environmental influences. They used specific measures of the nonshared environment, including differences among siblings in trips to the museum, owning books, parental reading, spanking, and HOME scores. They found a significant relationship of books to the PIAT Reading Recognition subscale, and a significant relationship of trips to the museum to the PIAT Math subscale.

Plomin et al. (1997) used a longitudinal sample of Colorado adoptive and biological children to study biometrical stability across ages 1–16. They found that over time, children became more like their parents in cognitive performance. Further, during adolescence, adoptive children became similar to their biological parents, suggesting that "genes that stably affect cognitive abilities in adulthood do not all come into play until adolescence" (p. 442). In a meta-analysis of literature from 1967–85, McCartney, Harris, and Bernieri (1990) found that the importance of shared environment as it contributed to differences in IQ decreased with age.

Behavior Genetic Research on Adolescence: The Biological/Hormonal Ecology

Very recently, the human genome has been mapped. This effort stimulated both knowledge of and interest in the way our human genetic structure influences human behavior. Critics have long decried efforts to link genetic structure to behavioral outcomes. More properly, we should simply understand that genetic influences will show up in virtually all domains. As Turkheimer (1998) notes, "Everything is biological; everything is genetic" (p. 789). He did not mean, of course, that everything is *only* genetic.

Knowledge of the human genome permits specification of mechanisms. Specific genetic loci have been identified as having influence (in a correlational rather than deterministic sense) on a number of adolescent behaviors that have been treated in this review, including risk-taking, smoking, and alcohol use. Behavior genetics offers a less direct indicator of genetic involvement than molecular genetic methods. On the other hand, the QTL (Quantitative Trait Loci) method simply correlates structure in the genome with measured traits of interest. A number of "false leads" have emerged using QTL studies, although the method will certainly be valuable in the long run. Activity in both molecular and behavioral genetic arenas has accelerated during the past decade, and in many ways the two approaches complement one another.

Physical growth

A number of behavior genetic studies have been made of adolescent development from a biological perspective. Most of these studies have treated measures of growth or other biological markers that would be expected to have strong genetic influences. In these cases, the important questions are often whether there are any environmental influences of note. Analysis of weight development and weight gain is a good case in point. While adult weight has a strong heritable component (h^2 equals around .80 in one review; see Grilo & Pogue-Geile, 1991), it seems reasonable that environmental influence might also affect weight, and many of those might reasonably emerge from the family.

Jacobson and Rowe (1998) studied adolescent Body Mass Index (BMI) among US Add Health respondents from a behavior genetic standpoint. They found substantial heritability, consistent with previous studies, and found evidence that the genes influencing BMI are similar for males and females. However, they found some differences in the genetic/environment apportionment for males/females and for blacks/whites. Further, they found an important source of shared environmental influence for white females. Beunen et al. (1998) studied subcutaneous fat distribution using Belgian twin pairs. They measured stature, weight, BMI, and five subcutaneous skinfold indicators. They found genetic and nonshared environmental variance to underlie individual differences in body fat, but no shared environmental influences. Their results suggested that all of the skinfolds were influenced by the same set of genes.

Another growth process is that related to puberty. Studies of pubertal development using behavior genetic methods have been conducted, although those will be reviewed below in our section on human reproduction.

Hormones

Harris, Vernon, and Boomsma (1998) studied testosterone in Dutch twin-parent data. Unlike the BMI findings, they found different genetic influences for males and females for plasma testosterone concentrations, with heritabilities of around $h^2 = .60$ for males and $h^2 = .40$ for females. Different genetic factors appeared to emerge in adulthood for males, while they were the same for females. Other research on hormones that is not directly tied to behavior genetic methods is nevertheless relevant to this treatment. Udry and his colleagues (Udry et al., 1985; Udry, Talbert, & Morris, 1986) showed links between androgens and adolescent sexual behavior among both males and females.

Sexual behavior and human reproduction occur at the boundary between social and biological processes (or, more properly, we should probably say that they substantially cross the boundary). The biological marker signaling reproductive potential is puberty. Doughty and Rodgers (2000) fit biometrical models to measures of age at menarche for US female adolescents from the NLSY. They found a significant and substantial heritability, with the rest of the variance attributable to the nonshared environment/measurement error. They also found that father absence was related to age at menarche, a finding originally developed by Belsky and his colleagues (e.g., Belsky, 2000) and given substantial attention in the evolutionary psychology literature. Rodgers and Buster (1994) found a seasonal component to menarche, with disproportionate numbers of NLSY females reporting first menstruation in the summer. Further, they estimated a large heritability of $h^2 = .62$ for seasonal menarche, and no shared environmental component.

Sexuality and human reproduction

We have reviewed several studies of age at first intercourse earlier in our section on transition behaviors. In addition, Rodgers and Doughty (2000) did a biometrical analysis of NLSY adolescent fertility expectations, fertility ideals, and fertility outcomes. They found a substantial heritability of $h^2 = .60$ for ideal fertility reported at ages 14–21 in 1979, although the estimate was much lower when it was reassessed two years later. Moderate heritabilities were found for late adolescents (ages 17–24 in 1982) for fertility expectations. Though few of the NLSY respondents had had children by 1982, enough had done so to estimate heritabilities for this cohort of 17–24-year-olds; they found a remarkably high $h^2 = .73$, with no shared environmental variance. Obviously, a number of adolescent sexual and reproductive behaviors have genetic components, a finding that might appear to some to be inconsistent with the tenets of Fisher's Fundamental Theorem of Natural Selection (Fisher, 1930). This inconsistency is only apparent and not real, however. Rodgers, Rowe, and Miller (2000) provide broad empirical treatment and Rodgers et al. (2001) discuss the role of genetic influences on human fitness and resolve the apparent inconsistency with Fisher's theorem, from both behavior genetic and molecular genetic standpoints.

Summary Statements and Conclusion

By themselves, behavioral genetic studies can appear somewhat sterile. At one extreme, such studies often report the "usual moderate heritability," the absence of any meaningful shared environment (or at least the interpretable shared environment), much non-shared environmental and measurement error, and little beyond (see Turkheimer, 2000, for a formalization of this set of findings). But at the other extreme, they can identify processes underlying human behavior, suggest interesting and intricate genetic/environmental interactions, show interpretable gender and race differences, complement studies from other domains (such as developmental psychology, molecular genetics, etc.), and strongly inform our models of human behavior. One of the strongest values of behavior genetic modeling is philosophical; this approach has helped to break researchers out of the extreme and unhealthy tendency toward social determinism. As Plomin and Rende (1991) have noted, behavior genetic models can be as powerful for studying the environment as for studying genetic influences; in that sense, it is a misnomer to call this set of models and methods behavior "genetics."

This review has identified a number of coherent patterns across studies, which will be summarized here. Genetic influences are ubiquitous in the adolescent development process. That statement is not surprising in regard to primarily biological domains like pubertal development, hormones, and physical development. But, interestingly, the heritabilities for many social and behavioral processes are generally of the same magnitude as those for the more biological domains. This result strongly supports the position taken in Rodgers, Rowe, and Li (1994) with regard to studies of genetic or environmental influences: "Each type of influence can [i.e., should] be controlled in the study of the other" (p. 374). In no sense would behavior genetic findings of genetic influence obviate the importance of developing social models of adolescent development. But if those social models do not control for or otherwise account for the automatic similarity among related kin caused by shared genes, then the validity of those findings is threatened at a very fundamental level.

This review has also identified a few shared environmental influences, and many non-shared environmental influences. Turkheimer and Waldron (2000) evaluated the status of nonshared environmental influences, and expressed pessimism that we will identify specific influences that have much importance. Further, Turkheimer (1999) and Molenaar, Boomsma, and Dolan (1997) have shown the effects of failing to account for genetic/environmental interactions, which can bias the many estimates of heritability and shared environmental variance in standard biometrical models. The search is still on for the specific causes of the large portion of variance that behavior geneticists call "the nonshared environment."

We have also specified a number of gender differences, and other demographic sub-groups show differences in genetic partitioning as well. In relation to sexual or repro-ductive behaviors, such differences are virtually axiomatic. In other domains, they can help identify useful treatment approaches (e.g., in relation to mental health), useful inter-ventions (e.g., in relation to problem behaviors), or useful components of behavioral models in basic research.

We conclude with some comments about the three theoretical perspectives we have used repeatedly in past research to inform and organize our thinking: Transition Behav-ior Theory, the Life Course Perspective, and Problem Behavior Theory. Both Transition Behavior Theory and the Life Course Perspective suggest that there are social markers to which adolescents attend in their developmental process. Examples include starting high school, the first cigarette, puberty, initiation of sexual behavior, and beginning to drive. It seems clear that there is genetic variance underlying virtually all of the individual dif-ferences in these various behaviors. Some behavior and molecular genetic research reviewed above has even been able to evaluate whether there are shared genetic influences common to these different domains. In fact, we consider that bivariate and multivariate models showing the genetic and environmental overlap provide some of the most excit-ing and valuable models to apply to future kinship data using behavior genetic designs. A number of such models have been developed previously, and have provided valuable and exciting findings. Others will follow.

Adolescence provides a fascinating "age-graded laboratory" for the study of develop-mental processes. Behavior genetic methods have been fruitfully applied within this laboratory. The findings from those studies, and the way those findings interact with those outside the boundaries of behavior genetics, have and will continue to provide stimulat-ing and valuable science.

Key Readings

Buster, M. A., & Rodgers, J. L. (2000). Genetic and environmental influences on alcohol use: DF analysis of NLSY kinship data. *Journal of Biosocial Science, 32,* 177–189.
This article applies biometrical modeling to adolescent and young adult use of alcohol. DF analysis is a simple regression-based approach to estimating genetic and environmental variance components.

Jacobson, K. C., & Rowe, D. C. (1999). Genetic and environmental influences on the relation-ships between family connectedness, school connectedness, and adolescent depressed mood: Sex differences. *Developmental Psychology, 35*(4), 926–939.
This article estimates biometrical models for adolescents relating family, school, and mental health.

McCartney, K., Harris, M. J., & Bernieri, F. (1990). Growing up and growing apart: A developmental meta-analysis of twin studies. *Psychological Bulletin, 107*, 226–237.
This article is a meta-analysis showing how behavior genetic findings relating genetic and environmental influences to various outcomes must be conditioned on the age of the respondent. It motivates the study of behavior genetic patterns in adolescents as potentially different than for other age groups.

Plomin, R., & Rende, R. (1991). Human behavioral genetics. In M. R. Rosenzweig & L. W. Porter (Eds.), *Annual Review of Psychology* (Vol. 42, pp. 161–190). Palo Alto, CA: Annual Reviews.
This review article accounts broadly for biometrical/behavior genetic findings across many different domains and ages.

Rodgers, J. L., Rowe, D. C., & Li, C. (1994). Beyond nature versus nurture: DF analysis of nonshared influences on problem behaviors. *Developmental Psychology, 30*(3), 374–384.
This article goes beyond the usual partitioning of influences in genetic and shared environmental influences – a model is defined to account explicitly for measured, nonshared environmental influences. The model is applied to the study of problem behaviors in older childhood and young adolescent respondents.

Turkheimer, E. (2000). Three laws of behavior genetics and what they mean. *Current Directions in Psychological Science, 9*, 160–164.
This article presents some of the methodological and empirical difficulties of doing research on behavior genetics. The caveats that emerge should inform all behavior genetic modeling efforts.

References

Abdel-Rahim, A. R., Nagoshi, C. T., & Vandenberg, S. G. (1990). Twin resemblances in cognitive abilities in an Egyptian sample. *Behavior Genetics, 20*(1), 33–43.
Angoff, W. H. (1988). The nature–nurture debate, aptitudes, and group differences. *American Psychologist, 43*, 713–720.
Belsky, J. (2000). Conditional and alternative reproductive strategies: Individual differences in susceptibility to rearing experiences. In J. L. Rodgers, D. C. Rowe, & W. B. Miller (Eds.), *Genetic influences on human fertility and sexuality* (pp. 127–168). Boston: Kluwer.
Beunen, G., Maes, H. H., Vlietinck, R., Malina, R. M., Thomis, M., Feys, E., Loos, R., & Derom, C. (1998). Univariate and multivariate genetic analysis of subcutaneous fatness and fat distribution in early adolescence. *Behavior Genetics, 28*(4), 279–288.
Billig, J. P., Hershberger, S. L., Iacono, W. G., & McGue, M. (1996). Life events and personality in late adolescence: Genetic and environmental relations. *Behavior Genetics, 26*(6), 543–554.
Boomsma, D. I., van den Bree, M. B. M., Orlebeke, J. F., & Molenaar, P. C. M. (1989). Resemblances of parents and twins in sports participation and heart rate. *Behavior Genetics, 19*(1), 123–141.
Brown, B. (1999). Optimizing expression of the common human genome for child development. *Current Directions in Psychological Research, 8*, 37–41.
Buchanan, C. M., Eccles, J. S., & Becker, J. B. (1992). Are adolescents the victims of raging hormones: Evidence for activational effects of hormones on moods and behavior at adolescence. *Psychological Bulletin, 111*, 62–107.
Bussell, D. A., Neiderhiser, J. M., Pike, A., Plomin, R., Simmens, S., Howe, G. W.,

Hetherington, E. M., Carroll, E., & Reiss, D. (1999). Adolescents' relationships to siblings and mothers: A multivariate genetic analysis. *Developmental Psychology, 35*(5), 1248–1259.

Buster, M. A., & Rodgers, J. L. (2000). Genetic and environmental influences on alcohol use: DF analysis of NLSY kinship data. *Journal of Biosocial Science, 32,* 177–189.

Carey, G. (1992). Simulated twin data on substance abuse. *Behavior Genetics, 22,* 193–196.

Doughty, D., & Rodgers, J. L. (2000). Behavior genetic modeling of menarche in U. S. females. In J. L. Rodgers, D. C. Rowe, & W. B. Miller (Eds.), *Genetic influences on human fertility and sexuality* (pp. 169–182). Boston: Kluwer.

Dunne, M. P., Martin, N. G., Statham, D. J., Slutske, W. S., Dinwiddie, S. H., Bucholz, K. K., Madden, P. A., & Heath, A. C. (1997). Genetic and environmental contributions to variance in age at first sexual intercourse. *Psychological Science, 8,* 1–6.

Eaves, L., Martin, N., Heath, A., Schieken, R., Meyer, J., Silberg, J., Neale, M., & Corey, L. (1997). Age changes in the causes of individual differences in conservatism. *Behavior Genetics, 27*(2), 121–124.

Eaves, L. J., Silberg, J. L., Hewitt, J. K., Rutter, M., Meyer, J. M., Neale, M. C., & Pickles, A. (1993). Analyzing twin resemblance in multisymptom data: Genetic application of a latent class model for symptoms of conduct disorder in juvenile boys. *Behavior Genetics, 23*(1), 5–19.

Elder, G. E. (1975). Age differentiation and the life course. *Annual Review of Sociology, 1,* 165–190.

Elkins, I. J., McGue, M., & Iacono, W. G. (1997). Genetic and environmental influences on parent–son relationships: Evidence for increasing genetic influence during adolescence. *Developmental Psychology, 33*(2), 351–362.

Ensminger, M. E. (1987). Adolescent sexual behavior as it relates to other transition behaviors in youth. In S. Hofferth & C. D. Hayes (Eds.), *Risking the future* (Vol. 2, pp. 36–55). Washington, DC: National Academy Press.

Falconer, D. S. (1981). *Introduction to quantitative genetics.* New York: Longman.

Fisher, R. A. (1930). *The genetical theory of natural selection.* Oxford: Clarendon.

Fulker, D. W., Eysenck, S. B. G., & Zuckerman, M. (1980). A genetic and environmental analysis of sensation seeking. *Journal of Research on Personality, 14,* 261–281.

Gjone, H., Stevenson, J., Sundet, J. M., & Eilertsen, D. E. (1996). Changes in heritability across increasing levels of behavior problems in young twins. *Behavior Genetics, 26*(4), 419–426.

Gottlieb, G. (2000). Environmental and behavioral influences on gene activity. *Current Directions in Psychological Research, 9,* 93–97.

Grilo, C. M., & Pogue-Geile, M. R. (1991). The nature of environmental influences on weight and obesity: A behavior genetic analysis. *Psychological Bulletin, 110,* 520–537.

Harris, J. A., Vernon, P. A., & Boomsma, D. I. (1998). The heritability of testosterone: A study of Dutch adolescent twins and their parents. *Behavior Genetics, 28*(3), 165–171.

Heath, A. C., Kirk, K. M., Meyer, J. M., & Martin, N. G. (1999). Genetic and social determinants of initiation and age at onset of smoking in Australian twins. *Behavior Genetics, 29,* 395–407.

Hogan, D. P., & Astone, N. M. (1986). The transition to adulthood. *Annual Review of Sociology, 12,* 109–130.

Houle, D. (1992). Comparing evolvability and variability of quantitative traits. *Genetics, 130,* 195–204.

Jacobson, K. C., & Rowe, D. C. (1998). Genetic and shared environmental influences on adolescent BMI: Interaction with race and sex. *Behavior Genetics, 28*(4), 265–278.

Jacobson, K. C., & Rowe, D. C. (1999). Genetic and environmental influences on the relationships between family connectedness, school connectedness, and adolescent depressed mood: Sex differences. *Developmental Psychology, 35*(4), 926–939.

Jessor, R., & Jessor, S. L. (1977). *Problem behavior and psychosocial development: A longitudinal study of youth*. New York: Academic Press.

Kohler, H.-P., Rodgers, J. L., & Christensen, K. (1999). Is fertility behavior in our genes? Findings from a Danish twin study. *Population and Development Review, 25*, 253–288.

Koopmans, J. R., Boomsma, D. I., Heath, A. C., & van Doornen, L. J. P. (1995). A multivariate genetic analysis of sensation seeking. *Behavior Genetics, 25*(4), 349–356.

Koopmans, J. R., Slutske, W. S., Heath, A. C., Neale, M. C., & Boomsma, D. I. (1999). The genetics of smoking initiation and quantity smoked in Dutch adolescent and young adult twins. *Behavior Genetics, 29*(6), 383–393.

Lykken, D. T., McGue, M., Tellegen, A., & Bouchard, T. J. (1992). Emergenesis: Genetic traits that may not run in families. *American Psychologist, 12*, 1565–1577.

Macaskill, G. T., Hopper, J. L., White, V., & Hill, D. J. (1994). Genetic and environmental variation in Eysenck Personality Questionnaire scales measured on Australian adolescent twins. *Behavior Genetics, 24*, 481–491.

Maccoby, E. E. (2000). Parenting and its effects on children: On reading and misreading behavior genetics. In S. T. Fiske, D. L. Schacter, & C. Zahn-Waxler (Eds.), *Annual Review of Psychology* (Vol. 51, pp. 1–27). Palo Alto, CA: Annual Reviews.

Madden, P. A. F., Heath, A. C., Pedersen, N. L., Kaprio, J., Koskenvuo, M. J., & Martin, N. G. (1999). The genetics of smoking persistence in men and woman: A multicultural study. *Behavior Genetics, 29*, 423–431.

Mayhew, K. P., Flay, B. R., & Mott, J. A. (2000). Stages in the development of adolescent smoking. *Drug and Alcohol Dependence, 59*(1), S61–S81.

McCartney, K., Harris, M. J., & Bernieri, F. (1990). Growing up and growing apart: A developmental meta-analysis of twin studies. *Psychological Bulletin, 107*, 226–237.

McGue, M., Bacon, S., & Lykken, D. T. (1993). Personality stability and change in early adulthood: A behavioral genetic analysis. *Developmental Psychology, 29*(1), 96–109.

Meyer, J. M., & Neale, M. C. (1992). The relationship between age at first drug use and teenage drug use liability. *Behavior Genetics, 22*(2), 197–213.

Miller, W. B., Pasta, D. J., MacMurray, J., Chiu, C., Wu, H., & Comings, D. E. (1999). Dopamine receptors are associated with age at first sexual intercourse. *Journal of Biosocial Science, 31*, 91–97.

Moffit, T. E. (1993). Adolescence-limited and life-course-persistent antisocial behavior: A developmental taxonomy. *Psychological Review, 100*, 674–701.

Molenaar, P. C. M., Boomsma, D. I., & Dolan, C. V. (1997). The detection of genotype-environment interaction in longitudinal genetic models. In M. LaBuda, E. Grigorenko, I. Ravich-Scherbo, & S. Scarr (Eds.), *On the way to individuality: Current methodological issues in behavior genetics* (pp. 53–70). Commack, NY: Nova Science.

Nagoshi, C. T., & Johnson, R. C. (1993). Familial transmission of cognitive abilities in offspring tested in adolescence and adulthood: A longitudinal study. *Behavior Genetics, 23*(3), 279–285.

Neale, M. C. (1999). Possible confounds and their resolution in multivariate genetic analyses: Comment on Bussell et al. (1999). *Developmental Psychology, 35*(5), 1260–1264.

Neale, M. C., & Cardon, L. R. (1992). *Methodology for genetic studies of twins and families*. London: Kluwer.

Neiderhiser, J. M., Bussell, D. A., Pike, A., Plomin, R., Simmens, S., Howe, G. W., Hetherington, E. M., & Reiss, D. (1999). The importance of shared environmental influences in explaining the overlap between mother's parenting and sibling relationships: Reply to Neale (1999). *Developmental Psychology, 35*(5), 1265–1267.

Neiderhiser, J. M., Pike, A., Hetherington, E. M., & Reiss, D. (1998). Adolescent perceptions as mediators of parenting: Genetic and environmental contributions. *Developmental Psychology, 34*(6), 1459–1469.

O'Connor, T. G., Deater-Deckard, K., Fulker, D., Rutter, M., & Plomin, R. (1998). Genotype-environment correlations in late childhood and early adolescence: Antisocial behavioral problems and coercive parenting. *Developmental Psychology, 34*(5), 970–981.

Petrill, S. A., & Thompson, L. A. (1993). The phenotypic and genetic relationships among measures of cognitive ability, temperament, and scholastic achievement. *Behavior Genetics, 23*(6), 511–518.

Pike, A., McGuire, S., Hetherington, E. M., Reiss, D., & Plomin, R. (1996). Family environment and adolescent depressive symptoms and antisocial behavior: A multivariate genetic analysis. *Developmental Psychology, 32*(4), 590–603.

Plomin, R., Fulker, D. W., Corley, R., & DeFries, J. C. (1997). Nature, nurture, and cognitive development from 1 to 16 years: A parent–offspring adoption study. *Psychological Science, 8*, 442–447.

Plomin, R., Reiss, D., Hetherington, E. M., & Howe, G. W. (1994). Nature and nurture: Genetic contributions to measure of the family environment. *Developmental Psychology, 30*(1), 32–43.

Plomin, R., & Rende, R. (1991). Human behavioral genetics. In M. R. Rosenzweig & L. W. Porter (Eds.), *Annual Review of Psychology* (Vol. 42, pp. 161–190). Palo Alto, CA: Annual Reviews.

Rende, R. D., Plomin, R., Reiss, D., & Hetherington, E. M. (1993). Genetic and environmental influences on depressive symptomatology in adolescence: Individual differences and extreme scores. *Journal of Child Psychology and Psychiatry, 34*, 1387–1398.

Rindfuss, R. R., Swicegood, C. G., & Rosenfeld, R. A. (1987). Disorder in the life course: How common and does it matter? *American Sociological Review, 52*, 785–801.

Rodgers, J. L. (1996). Sexual transitions in adolescence. In J. A. Graber, J. Brooks-Gunn, & A. C. Petersen (Eds.), *Transitions through adolescence: Interpersonal domains and context* (pp. 85–108). Mahwah, NJ: Erlbaum.

Rodgers, J. L., Billy, J. O. G., & Udry, J. R. (1984). A model of friendship similarity in mildly deviant behaviors. *Journal of Applied Social Psychology, 14*, 413–425.

Rodgers, J. L., & Buster, M. (1994). Seasonality of menarche among U.S. females: Correlates and linkages. In K. L. Campbell & J. W. Wood, *Human reproductive ecology: Interactions of environment, fertility, and behavior*. New York: New York Academy of Sciences.

Rodgers, J. L. & Doughty, D. (2000). Genetic and environmental influences on fertility expectations and outcomes using NLSY kinship data. In J. L. Rodgers, D. C. Rowe, & W. B. Miller (Eds.), *Genetic influences on human fertility and sexuality* (pp. 85–106). Boston: Kluwer.

Rodgers, J. L., Hughes, K., Kohler, H.-P., Christensen, K., Doughty, D., Rowe, D. C., & Miller, W. B. (2001). Genetic influence helps explain variation in human fertility outcomes: Evidence from recent behavioral and molecular genetic studies. *Current Directions in Psychological Science*, in press.

Rodgers, J. L., & Rowe, D. C. (1990). Adolescent sexual activity and mildly deviant behavior: Sibling and friendship effects. *Journal of Family Issues, 11*, 274–293.

Rodgers, J. L., & Rowe, D. C. (1993). Social contagion and adolescent sexual behavior: A developmental EMOSA model. *Psychological Review, 100*, 479–510.

Rodgers, J. L., Rowe, D. C., & Buster, M. (1999). Nature, nurture, and first sexual intercourse in the USA: Fitting behavioral genetic models to NLSY kinship data. *Journal of Biosocial Science, 31*, 29–41.

Rodgers, J. L., Rowe, D. C., & Li, C. (1994). Beyond nature versus nurture: DF analysis of nonshared influences on problem behaviors. *Developmental Psychology, 30*(3), 374–384.

Rodgers, J. L., Rowe, D. C., & May, K. (1994). DF analysis of NLSY IQ/achievement data: Nonshared environmental influences. *Intelligence, 19*, 157–177.

Rodgers, J. L., Rowe, D. C., & Miller, W. B. (2000). *Genetic influences on human fertility and sexuality: Theoretical and empirical contributions from the biological and behavioral sciences.* Boston: Kluwer.

Rose, R. J. (1995). Genes and human behavior. In J. T. Spence, J. M. Darley, & D. J. Foss (Eds.), *Annual Review of Psychology* (Vol. 46, pp. 625–654). Palo Alto, CA: Annual Reviews.

Rowe, D. C., Almeida, D. M., & Jacobson, K. C. (1999). School context and genetic influences on aggression in adolescence. *Psychological Science, 10,* 277–280.

Rowe, D. C., Chassin, L., Presson, L., & Sherman, S. J. (1996). Parental smoking and the epidemic spread of cigarette smoking. *Journal of Applied Social Psychology, 26*(5), 437–454.

Rowe, D. C., & Plomin, R. (1981). The importance of nonshared (E1) environmental influences in behavioral development. *Developmental Psychology, 17,* 517–531.

Rowe, D. C., & Rodgers, J. L. (1991). Adolescent smoking and drinking: Are they epidemics? *Journal of Studies on Alcohol, 52*(2), 110–117.

Steinberg, L., & Morris, A. S. (2001). Adolescent development. In S. T. Fiske, D. L. Schacter, & C. Zahn-Waxler (Eds.), *Annual Review of Psychology* (Vol. 52, pp. 83–110). Palo Alto, CA: Annual Reviews.

Susman, E. J., Nottelmann, E. D., Inoff-Germain, G. E., Dorn, L. D., Cutler, G. B., Loriaux, D. L., & Chrousos, G. P. (1985). The relationship of relative hormone levels and physical development and socio-emotional behavior in young adolescents. *Journal of Youth and Adolescence, 14,* 245–264.

Topolski, T. D., Hewitt, J. K., Eaves, L. J., Silberg, J. L., Meyer, J. M., Rutter, M., Pickles, A., & Simonoff, E. (1997). Genetic and environmental influences on child reports of manifest anxiety and overanxious disorders: A community-based twin study. *Behavior Genetics, 27,* 15–28.

Turkheimer, E. (1998). Heritability and biological explanation. *Psychological Review, 105,* 782–791.

Turkheimer, E. (2000). Three laws of behavior genetics and what they mean. *Current Directions in Psychological Science, 9,* 160–164.

Turkheimer, E., & Waldron, M. (2000). Nonshared environment: A theoretical, methodological, and quantitative review. *Psychological Bulletin, 126,* 78–108.

Udry, J. R., Billy, J. O. G., Morris, N. M., Groff, T. R., & Raj, M. H. (1985). Serum androgenic hormones motivate sexual behavior in adolescent boys. *Fertility and Sterility, 43,* 90–94.

Udry, J. R., & Talbert, L. M. (1988). Sex hormone effects on personality at puberty. *Journal of Personality and Social Psychology, 54,* 291–295.

Udry, J. R., Talbert, L. M., & Morris, N. M. (1986). Biosocial foundations for female adolescent activity. *Demography, 23,* 217–230.

van den Oord, E. J. C. G., Boomsma, D. I., & Verhulst, F. C. (1994). A study of problem behaviors in 10- to 15-year-old biologically related and unrelated international adoptees. *Behavior Genetics, 24*(3), 193–205.

van den Oord, E. J. C. G., & Rowe, D. C. (1997). Continuity and change in children's social maladjustment: A developmental behavior genetic study. *Developmental Psychology, 33*(2), 319–332.

van der Valk, J. C., Verhulst, F. C., Neale, M. C., & Boomsma, D. I. (1998). Longitudinal genetic analysis of problem behaviors in biologically related and unrelated adoptees. *Behavior Genetics, 28*(5), 365–380.

Viken, R. J., Kaprio, J., Koskenvuo, M., & Rose, R. J. (1999). Longitudinal analyses of the determinants of drinking and of drinking to intoxication in adolescent twins. *Behavior Genetics, 29,* 455–461.

CHAPTER TWO

Pubertal Processes and Physiological Growth in Adolescence

Andrea Bastiani Archibald, Julia A. Graber, and Jeanne Brooks-Gunn

Introduction

"What happens? What changes? How does it feel?" (3rd-grade girl)

"I'm nervous because I don't know what is going to happen." (5th-grade girl)

"I have to wear a bra now, and when I run in P.E. all the boys watch me. I'm getting underarm hair and hair in private parts and . . . I don't want this here." (5th-grade girl)

"Popular kids are trying to grow up real fast. They're into getting boobs and wearing make-up." (7th-grade girl)

Each of these statements exemplifies pre- and early adolescents' anxieties and questions about the transition to adolescence, and puberty, in particular. While becoming older brings with it new-found freedoms and independence, children and adolescents also recognize the mysteries of the transition to puberty, and many report feeling relatively unprepared for the profound physical, social, and emotional changes they are experiencing (Girl Scouts of the USA, 2000).

In their discussion of adolescence as one of the most fascinating and complex transitions in the life span, the Carnegie Council on Adolescent Development (1996) remarks that this is a time of accelerated growth and physical change second only to infancy. By the end of puberty, the majority of adolescents have experienced hormonal changes, attained secondary sexual characteristics, and grown in both height and weight (Grumbach, 1975; Reiter & Grumbach, 1982). These changes result in mature bodies judged both by physical/reproductive capabilities, as well as outward appearance. It is widely acknowledged that in traversing the phase of life between childhood and adulthood, adolescents face

The authors were supported by grants from the National Institute of Mental Health (MH56557) and the National Institute of Child Health and Human Development (HD32376). Correspondence should be addressed to Andrea B. Archibald, Ph.D., Center for Children & Families, Box 39, Teachers College, Columbia University, 525 W. 120th Street, New York, NY 10027.

numerous social and emotional challenges (e.g., Feldman & Elliott, 1990; Graber, Brooks-Gunn, & Petersen, 1996). However, puberty itself is a key developmental challenge of adolescence (Brooks-Gunn & Petersen, 1983; Brooks-Gunn & Reiter, 1990). As children's and adolescent's bodies develop, they not only have to adjust to their altered appearances and feelings around these changes, but they must also cope with other's responses to their maturing bodies.

The present chapter overviews pubertal growth and the physiological changes that occur during the preadolescent to adolescent years. First, the hormonal and physical changes of puberty are discussed. This section is followed by a discussion of the onset, rate, and progression of pubertal events for girls and boys. Finally, the special topic of pubertal timing is addressed. Of note is that in this chapter we look at puberty from biological, social, and emotional perspectives. Thus, in each section, particular mention will be made of research that has investigated corresponding social and emotional aspects of pubertal processes and physiological development during adolescence. In addition to differential experiences by gender, sections will highlight what is known in each area in terms of the diversity of the experience of adolescents (e.g., racial, ethnic, and/or socioeconomic status (SES) differences among adolescents).

Overview of Pubertal Development

Pubertal development or puberty is not a single process or stage. Instead, it is a continuum of development that began prenatally, and involves a series of interconnected hormonal and physical changes resulting in both adult reproductive capabilities, and adult appearance (Grumbach & Styne, 1998; Tanner, 1962). Marshall and Tanner (1974) have identified five general areas for the internal and external changes at puberty: (1) acceleration followed by deceleration of skeletal growth, or "growth spurt"; (2) increases in and/or redistribution of body fat and muscle tissue; (3) development of the circulatory and respiratory systems, and thus increased strength and endurance; (4) maturation of secondary sexual characteristics and reproductive organs; and (5) changes in hormonal/endocrine systems which regulate and coordinate the other pubertal events. This coordination by the endocrine system by necessity begins before the outwardly visible signs of puberty are evidenced, with organizational activity beginning before birth (Goy & McEwen, 1980). As would be expected from the extent of physical and physiological change, puberty is not an overnight event but rather takes five to six years for most adolescents (Petersen, 1987; Brooks-Gunn & Reiter, 1990). All of the aforementioned pubertal processes are influenced by an interaction of genetic, nutritional, and hormonal factors (Brooks-Gunn & Reiter, 1990).

Hormonal Changes at Puberty

Hormone levels begin to rise in middle childhood, and continue to increase more rapidly through early adolescence. Physical maturation and adult reproductive functioning are controlled by the endocrine system which operates first through the hypothalamus–pituitary–adrenal axis (HPA system) and then through the hypothalamus–pituitary–gonadal (HPG) axis (Grumbach & Styne, 1998). During the prenatal period, hormones called androgens organize the reproductive system (Brooks-Gunn & Reiter, 1990; Goy & McEwen, 1980). These hormones are then suppressed postnatally and through early childhood, until the reproductive system is reactivated and the hormones are no longer suppressed – signaling that pubertal development is to begin (Reiter & Grumbach, 1982).

Most children begin pubertal development during the middle childhood years, with the first increases in adrenal androgens beginning around age 8 for boys and age 6 for girls. About two years later, gonadal hormones begin to increase with increases in hormones for boys lagging increases observed in girls. The aforementioned initial rise in hormones occurring at an average age of 7 (boys and girls), is often called "adrenarche." This event precedes other hormonal changes of puberty as well as the onset of external signs of physical development (Cutler & Loriaux, 1980). Maturation of the reproductive system results in the production of gonadotropin-releasing hormone (GnRH) by the bursts of gonadotropins, luteinizing hormone (LH), and follicle-stimulating hormone (FSH). Thus, "gonadarche" follows adrenarche approximately two years later, with variable bursts of LH and FSH (Reiter & Grumbach, 1982). LH and FSH are secreted at low levels by the pituitary during childhood, and pulsatile releases of these hormones, particularly during the nighttime hours, are characteristic of stages of early puberty. Increases in LH and FSH are some of the earliest measurable hormonal indications of pubertal development, and have been found to rise progressively during puberty (Reiter & Grumbach, 1982). Episodic nocturnal bursts of low levels of LH are indicative of early pubertal stages for both boys and girls (Grumbach & Styne, 1998). During the latter stages of pubertal development, LH is released throughout the day in adult-like patterns (Grumbach & Styne, 1998). LH and FSH are especially important for producing sex hormones, androgens and estrogens, to stimulate the development of reproductive capabilities.

In girls, FSH stimulates production of ovaries to ripen eggs, and LH stimulates production of the hormones, progesterone and estrogen when levels get low (Katchadourian, 1977). FSH has a parallel rise to LH at puberty in boys. However, FSH rises slightly earlier than LH, and as such, is a sensitive indicator of early pubertal change in boys. As puberty progresses, FSH is correlated with maturation of sertoli cell function, leading to sperm production in boys. The adult-like pattern of tonic release is characteristic of hormonal regulation of reproduction in both boys and girls, such that the hypothalamus monitors levels of circulating sex steroids (e.g., estrogen and testosterone) and responds via alterations in release of the gonadotropins. For boys, spermatogenesis occurs when adult levels of androgens, and adult-like release of gonadotropins, is attained.

Psychological correlates of hormonal changes at puberty

Hormonal factors are believed to account, at least in part, for the increase in negative and variable emotions that are characteristic of adolescents (Brooks-Gunn, Graber, &

Paikoff, 1994; Buchanan, Eccles, & Becker, 1990; Archibald et al., submitted). Studies of adolescents suggest that higher levels of gonadotropins and other pubertal hormones are associated with negative affect and adjustment difficulties in adolescence (Archibald et al., submitted; Paikoff, Brooks-Gunn & Warren, 1991; Susman et al., 1985; Warren & Brooks-Gunn, 1989). For example, in 1985, Susman and her colleagues cross-sectionally investigated associations between hormone levels and adjustment difficulties in 9–14-year-old girls and boys. These researchers hypothesized that absolute hormone concentrations regardless of age may impact the psychological well-being of adolescents differentially, and over and above effects of pubertal timing. Adolescents had blood drawn that was assayed for the following pubertal hormones: luteinizing hormone, follicle-stimulating hormone, testosterone, estradiol, and adrenal androgens (DHEA, DHEAS). More hormone-affect associations were found for boys, than were found for girls. For girls, it was found that having high-for-age level of FSH, but not LH, was associated with reports of sad affect and psychopathology. However, it was not found that hormones impacted girls' adjustment over and above the influence of maturational timing (Susman et al., 1985). In a later study using the same sample, Susman and colleagues (1987) examined associations among hormone levels, emotional dispositions, and aggressive attributes. Interestingly, hormone levels were related to emotional dispositions and aggressive attributes for boys, but not for girls. Specifically, higher levels of androgens were related to acting-out problems in boys. Additionally, ratio of testosterone-estradiol was negatively related to boys' sad affect and acting-out behavior.

Brooks-Gunn and her colleagues (Brooks-Gunn & Warren, 1989; Paikoff et al., 1991; Warren & Brooks-Gunn, 1989) have also conducted work in this area with their longitudinal study of early adolescent girls in grades 5 through 8. In their investigations, they sought to test the hypothesis that "associations between negative emotional expression and hormonal changes will occur when the endocrine system is being 'turned on,' in the sense of moving from prepubertal to postpubertal levels" (Brooks-Gunn & Warren, 1989, p. 41). Measurements of serum FSH, LH, estradiol, DHEAS, and testosterone were made. Girls were then divided into four hormonal categories based on their levels of estradiol (because these levels show the most dramatic increases during puberty). Indeed, cross-sectional, nonlinear effects were found, and girls' negative affect did increase during the time of the onset or *initial* rapid rises in hormones (Brooks-Gunn & Warren, 1989; Warren & Brooks-Gunn, 1989). Hormones accounted for a small, but significant percentage of the variance in negative affect. In a longitudinal study with the same sample, these researchers produced similar findings (Paikoff et al., 1991).

Most recently, in a sample of preadolescent girls, Archibald and colleagues (submitted) found that increases in concentration of LH relative to FSH over a nine-month period in middle to late childhood were significantly associated with girls' reports of more intense anger over time. Importantly, this relationship remained significant after accounting for secondary sexual characteristic development; that is, after accounting for visible signs of pubertal development. These are the first longitudinal findings of effects of the earliest hormone changes on pre-adolescent girls' daily mood states.

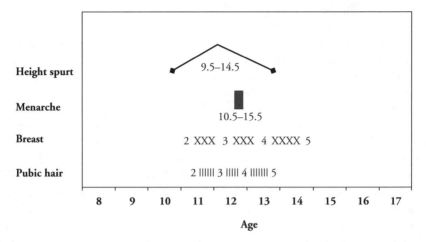

Figure 2.1   The developmental course of four pubertal processes for girls. Redrawn from Tanner, 1962, p. 36. Copyright ©1962 by Blackwell Scientific. Reprinted with permission.

The Onset, Rate, and Progression of Pubertal Events

Pubertal development is characterized not only by hormonal changes, but more often by the development of secondary sexual characteristics. These characteristics usually appear and develop in a set sequence, although variations in terms of which characteristic appears first or which develops more quickly are not uncommon. Moreover, differences in the onset or timing of pubertal events and the rate at which individuals progress through all pubertal events can differ among individuals (Brooks-Gunn, Petersen, & Eichorn, 1985; Eichorn, 1975). Similarly, systematic differences in timing, onset, and rate of pubertal development have been found between boys and girls, and for adolescents of different races (Grumbach & Styne, 1998; Herman-Giddens et al., 1997).

Physical changes of puberty

Figure 2.1 shows the basic sequencing of events in girls' pubertal development. Specific ages reported in the figure are based on Tanner's work from the 1950s with white, institutionalized youth in Great Britain; updated information on ages is provided whenever available.

For girls, breast budding is generally the first sexual characteristic to appear. This generally occurs between ages 8 and 13, with a mean age of 9.96 for white girls and a mean age of 8.87 for black girls (Herman-Giddens et al., 1997; Kaplowitz et al., 1999). Pubic hair development often begins shortly after breast budding. However, approximately 20 percent of girls experience pubic hair development prior to breast budding (Brooks-Gunn & Reiter, 1990). The continuous development of the breasts and pubic hair have been divided into five rough stages of growth for girls (Marshall & Tanner, 1969). The first stage indicates that no breast development has begun, the second is characterized by breast

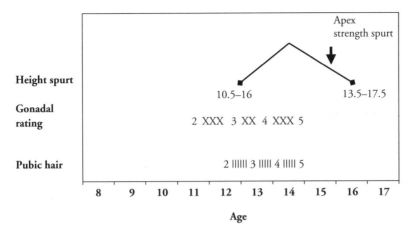

Figure 2.2 The developmental course of four pubertal processes for boys. Redrawn from Tanner, 1962, p. 30. Copyright ©1962 by Blackwell Scientific. Reprinted with permission.

budding, and subsequent stages indicate further growth until stage 5, being the mature stage of breast development. The latter stages involve the breasts becoming more enlarged, the separation between the contours of the two breasts becoming more distinct, and the areola having grown and receded into the general contour of the breast. The process of developing mature breasts from breast budding takes about 4.5 years, regardless of whether or not girls entered puberty earlier or later than average (Brooks-Gunn & Reiter, 1990).

Acceleration in height begins at approximately the same time as breast budding. Rapid growth in height peaks in mid-puberty for girls and then slows over time. Menarche follows the peak in height velocity, with a mean age of 12.88 for white girls, and 12.16 for black girls (Herman-Giddens et al., 1997). Taken together, while it appears that black girls begin puberty earlier than their white peers, this implies that black girls take longer to transition from early- to mid-adolescence.

Figure 2.2 shows the basic sequencing of physical events in boys' pubertal development. As with girls' development, ages reported in the figure are based on Tanner's work from the 1950s with white, institutionalized youth. Whereas ages for pubertal markers are thought to be lower now than those previously reported for girls, boys' puberty does not seem to have undergone the same trend for earlier onset. (Hypotheses explaining changes in girls' development will be discussed in the next section.)

As can be seen in figure 2.2, boys typically begin pubertal development 1–2 years later than girls. While not as outwardly visible as that for girls, the initial sign of sexual development in boys is the onset of testicular growth. This occurs at between about ages 11 and 11.5; however, some boys begin to develop in this area as early as age 9.5 (Brooks-Gunn & Reiter, 1990). Similar to the stages of breast development for girls, Tanner stages have been developed for boys' penile and pubic hair growth (Marshall & Tanner, 1969). In the first stage, the genitalia increase slightly in overall size but there is no change in overall appearance. In Stage 2, the scrotum has begun to enlarge and there is some reddening and change in the texture of the scrotal skin. The third stage involves the penis increasing predominantly in length, though slightly in breadth, also, along with further growth of the testes. This process continues through Stage 5 of mature (adult size and shape) genitalia. The bulk of testicular volume developed over these stages is attributable to sperm-producing tubules (Brooks-Gunn & Reiter, 1990; Grumbach & Styne, 1998). Virtually no boys have developed pubic hair by the onset of testicular growth. Pubic hair growth begins on average at about age 12. However, 41 percent of boys are in Tanner Stage 4 by the time pubic hair growth is first seen. Approximately three years pass between the initial signs of genital growth and the development of mature genitalia in boys. Again, given that variation among individuals is common, a lapse of five years is still within the normal range (Brooks-Gunn & Reiter, 1990).

Testicular growth is generally followed closely by initiation of height spurt at approximately 11.7 years. The age of peak height velocity is between 13 and 14 years for most adolescent boys. Spermarche, or the first ejaculation, most frequently occurs between 13 and 14 years of age and relatively early in pubic hair growth. In addition, to secondary sexual characteristics specifically, other physical changes of puberty for boys include voice change and the appearance of facial hair. These changes, along with the growth in height, are more noticeable to others than events like pubic hair growth (except, of course, in the locker room). On average, boys' voices first break around age 14 and have changed by age 15. Facial hair usually starts to grow during pubic hair Stage 3 with growth on the upper lip and cheeks; facial hair will not fill in until after pubic and genital development are completed. While these changes occur predominantly in early adolescence (from about 11 to 14 years), pubertal growth can continue into midadolescence (ages 15–18) as well. Thus, a potentially lengthy period of adjustment to physical aspects of pubertal development, as well as the corresponding social and emotional changes, is not uncommon (Brooks-Gunn & Reiter, 1990).

Body composition. Both girls and boys experience changes in their body composition – distribution of fat and muscle – during pubertal development (Grumbach & Styne, 1998; Marshall & Tanner, 1974). Increases and/or redistribution of body fat are another of the physiological changes of puberty and adolescence. Lean body mass (more muscular parts of the body), bone mass, and body fat are about equal in prepubertal boys and girls. However, postpubertal boys have 1.5 times the lean body mass and bone mass of postpubertal girls, and postpubertal girls have twice as much body fat as postpubertal boys (Grumbach & Styne, 1998). In fact, shortly after the growth spurt in height, there is a growth spurt in strength for boys. The differences in fat distribution for boys and girls are due in part to the fact that males have more and larger muscle cells than females; by the end of puberty, 54 percent of a typical boy's body weight is muscle. During puberty, hips and breasts enlarge for girls, though girls experience little change in waist circumference. This generally results in fat predominantly located in the lower body and a pear shape, or fat distributed in the upper and lower body and an hourglass shape.

Specific fat distribution patterns may be related to an individual girl's levels of reproductive hormones (Grumbach & Styne, 1998). By the time they finish puberty, girls have gained an average of 24 pounds (Warren, 1983). However, these pounds include lean body mass, bone mass, and fat. Interestingly, girls seem to experience increases in fat and weight around the same time they reach menarche (Frisch, 1983; Berkey et al., 2000). Researchers have suggested that a certain amount of body fat is necessary for the onset and maintenance of normal reproductive functioning in females. They have found adolescent girls to have a similar percentage of body fat when they get their periods, regardless of their ages and prepubertal sizes. The higher proportion of body fat in girls is believed to be necessary to provide metabolic support for pregnancy (Frisch, 1983).

Other physical changes. The physical changes already discussed are those that researchers have focused on more heavily as they are thought to have an impact on psychological adjustment of adolescents and/or reproductive functioning. However, the sources of common concerns of adolescents are also part of the physical changes of adolescence. That is, both boys and girls experience acne during puberty. In fact, acne may be one of the first visible signs of puberty in girls, preceding pubic hair growth or breast development (Grumbach & Styne, 1998). In addition, types of acne occurring during adolescence will vary in severity, with some youth having serious skin problems. Boys and girls also experience growth and changes in hair under the arms and over the body, usually during the later stages of puberty. These changes are accompanied by maturation of axillary and subcutaneous sweat glands. Although such changes are not associated with the end goal of puberty, that is, reproductive capability, they are undoubtedly salient to the adolescents themselves.

Variations in the onset of puberty

As indicated, there is a wide age range for the onset of puberty for boys and girls. Onset during the 4–5-year age ranges specified is within the normal range. Again, the sequence of pubertal events seems to be fairly standard within gender, although some variations occur. We have mentioned that girls' development appears to be earlier than reported in prior decades and that there are differences among girls by race and possibly by ethnicity. Note that racial and ethnicity differences have only been documented in the literature in the past decade. In contrast, the onset of pubertal development does not seem to have changed for boys over the last few decades (Kaplowitz et al., 1999). Furthermore, race and/or ethnicity differences in the onset of puberty have not been reported for boys to date. However, whereas a few large studies of girls' puberty have been launched in recent years, very few new studies of boys' puberty have been conducted recently (see Biro et al., 1995, as an exception). Given the limited data from racially diverse samples, the assumption of no racial or ethnicity effects on boys' puberty should be made with caution.

As we have indicated, the reports of differences among girls in timing of the onset of puberty have only emerged in the most recent investigations of girls' puberty. As such, this issue requires further explication. Certainly, it is feasible that racial and/or ethnic differences have always existed among girls but that prior studies did not include sufficient diversity to find this difference. The 1995 National Survey of Family Growth has data relevant to this issue as this survey was conducted with women ages 15–44 (National Center for Health Statistics, 1997). Examination of the ages of menarche in this sample of women indicates that there were no race or ethnic difference among the oldest group of women (ages 40–44); age of menarche was 12.7 for white, non-Hispanic women, 12.5 for Hispanic women, and 12.6 for non-Hispanic black women. In contrast, the youngest group (ages 15–19) in this study had younger ages of menarche as well as ethnic differences in menarche; age of menarche was 12.4 for white, non-Hispanic women, 12.1 for Hispanic women, and 12.0 for non-Hispanic black women. These data support the notion that puberty has been getting earlier for girls/women over recent decades, despite the fact that today extremely few women are under- or malnourished in Western countries. Furthermore, although inferences from this survey are not conclusive evidence, these data also suggest that the racial/ethnic difference has been developing over this time period.

Identifying a "race" or "ethnicity" difference does not, of course, establish why the difference has occurred. In particular, in the United States, race/ethnicity is frequently confounded with SES. Given that African American girls and women are disproportionately represented in the lower end of the income distribution and white girls and women are disproportionately represented in the upper end of income in the United States, it is difficult to determine the source of racial differences. To date, only a few studies have examined both SES and race/ethnicity; findings have not been consistent among these studies. Most recently, Obeidallah and her colleagues (Obeidallah et al., in press) investigated timing of menarche in a study of girls that were sampled by race/ethnicity and high, low, and middle SES in Chicago, Illinois. In this study, controlling for SES reduced differences in age at menarche between Latina and white girls. However, this study did not find a significant race difference in age at menarche between white and African American girls, with or without controlling for SES. In contrast, race differences were not accounted for by SES in a large, nationally representative sample of girls recruited as part of an investigation of cardiovascular risk (National Heart, Lung, & Blood Institute Growth and Health Study Research Group, 1992). This particular study reported race differences in the onset of pubertal development, consistent with that found by Herman-Giddens and her colleagues (1997). Race differences in onset of breast development, onset of pubic hair growth, and age at menarche based on Herman-Giddens and colleagues (1997) are shown in figure 2.3. In this case, though, indices of economic factors were not assessed with as much depth, as was done for the study by Obeidallah and her colleagues (in press). Certainly, additional research is needed to determine the role of race/ethnicity and SES as factors in the onset of puberty; moreover, other factors that may be associated with race/ethnicity or may be the potential underlying cause of race/ethnicity differences need to be identified.

The timing of the onset of puberty for both boys and girls has been linked to genetics, nutrition, behavior, and other environmental factors. Concern over the trend for earlier pubertal timing in girls has been given extensive press coverage recently in the news and popular media, as evidenced by the October 30, 2000 cover story of *Time* magazine, "Early puberty: Why are girls growing up faster?" Given this trend for girls as a group, in contrast with the absence of a similar trend for boys, many hypotheses have emerged to explain this phenomenon. Some of these include exposure to environmental toxins (including prenatal exposure), increasing rates of obesity or body fat mechanisms, and experience of psychosocial stress. We will briefly describe each. In the case of environmental toxins, it has been shown that some toxins, such as DDE (a breakdown produce

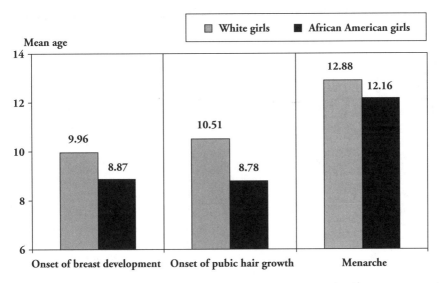

Figure 2.3 Age of attainment of pubertal characteristics for white and African American girls. Based on data reported in Herman-Giddens et al., 1997, in their clinic-based study of girls' pubertal development.

of the pesticide DDT) and PCBS, formerly used as flame retardants in electrical equipment, mimic estrogen; therefore, exposure to these toxins would stimulate pubertal development. Such exposure may occur prenatally or during childhood, as yet, data are limited in this area (e.g., Gladen, Ragan, & Rogan, 2000). If these toxins were prevalent, this hypothesis would explain why girls' puberty has become earlier. Furthermore, this hypothesis may also apply to race/ethnicity differences, given that substantial residential segregation exists in the United States and environmental toxins may be disproportionately distributed in neighborhoods with particular race or ethnic compositions. As indicated, the hypothesis is intriguing, but further investigation is required to draw conclusions.

Population-level changes in body fat may also be a factor in earlier maturation for girls. Recent studies have focused on the connections among the hormone leptin, regulation of body fat, and puberty in girls (e.g., Clayton & Trueman, 2000). Leptin is associated with weight gain and increases dramatically during periods of rapid weight gain as seen during puberty (Horlick et al., 2000). Leptin also appears to influence gonadotropin activity in the brain. As indicated, rates of obesity and overweight have been increasing over the past several decades for adults and children in the United States (Schreiber et al., 1996). Thus, more girls would be expected to mature at earlier ages due to elevated leptin levels. That is, childhood obesity would trigger increased leptin levels which would trigger pubertal development. However, studies to date have only shown correlations indicating that leptin levels increase with puberty. There is no evidence that leptin levels *cause* pubertal onset or changes. It may be more likely that changes in leptin levels are a product of pubertal onset and are a normative part of hormonal changes at puberty (Clayton & Trueman, 2000). In this case, obesity or overweight may trigger another mechanism that starts pubertal development and leptin levels increase as a result of this other causal chain. Again, weight and puberty associations have been found for girls but not boys, and racial differences exist for rates of obesity (although, again, SES differences are thought to be important factors in this difference).

Finally, it has also been suggested that the experience of psychosocial or environmental stress influences the timing of the onset of puberty. Several studies have now found that social stressors, in particular, stressful family situations, were predictive of earlier onset of puberty (e.g., Graber, Brooks-Gunn, & Warren, 1995; Moffitt et al., 1992; Surbey, 1990). Both father absence in the childhood years (Surbey, 1990), as well as lower warmth in family relations in two-parent (biological mother and father) families (Graber et al., 1995), resulted in earlier maturation for girls. Individually, each study is not conclusive. For example, Surbey's original study relied on retrospective accounts of both puberty and family factors (Surbey, 1990). Other studies did not control for the possibility that puberty may have already begun when the studies were initiated (Moffitt et al., 1992). In our own work, lower warmth in parent–child relationships resulted in earlier age at menarche after controlling for the effect of maternal age at menarche and level of breast development (Graber et al., 1995). In contrast, reports of number of stressful life events were not predictive of age at menarche; only family relations were significant. These findings taken together, along with other research on this topic, suggest that family dysfunction or stress influences onset of puberty. To date, the underlying mechanisms for these associations have not been defined. Notably, evidence is amassing that demonstrates that stress specifically influences estrogen systems in adult women and these effects are involved in a range of health outcomes (e.g., McEwen, 1994). Similar processes are likely to be the cause of associations of familial stressors and earlier maturational timing in girls.

Other hypotheses explaining timing differences in puberty are emerging. Further research is needed to examine potential race, ethnicity, and SES differences in the experience of different types of stress and how stress may be associated with puberty in girls in diverse samples. Investigations of mechanisms associated with weight gain and the influence and sources of environmental toxins also require more extensive study.

Psychological Correlates of Pubertal Events

As with hormonal changes during puberty, it has been suggested that the experience of the physical changes of puberty may be important psychologically to youth (Brooks-Gunn et al., 1985; Jones & Mussen, 1958). As indicated in the prior sections, the physical changes of puberty are dramatic, and moreover, are unpredictable in that the specifics of the final outcome are unknown (e.g., eventual size of one's breasts, height, etc.). In addition, other people respond to an adolescent's physical changes. When individuals look older they are often treated more like adults than children by adults (e.g., parents, teachers) and by other adolescents. Thus, the psychological impact, separate from hormonal changes of puberty, has also been of interest in the study of adolescent development.

Significance of secondary sex characteristics

Brooks-Gunn and colleagues have conducted research into the significance of breast and pubic hair development to adolescent girls (Brooks-Gunn, 1984; 1988). In their studies of early adolescent, 5th-and 6th-grade girls, when girls are asked about their reactions to breast and pubic hair growth, virtually all girls (82 percent) reported that breast growth was more important to them than pubic hair growth, because "other people can tell." In addition, this research shows that mothers more frequently talk to their daughters about breast than pubic hair development – although girls often report feeling uncomfortable during these discussions. These studies find that girls generally feel positively about the onset of breast development as exhibited in pride or excitement. However, as breast development advances girls are more likely to experience teasing by family members and boys about their breast development (Brooks-Gunn, 1988; Brooks-Gunn et al., 1994). In fact, anecdotal reports suggest that middle school girls experience a great deal of harassment by boys about breast development and their changing bodies (Orenstein, 1994). It is likely that positive feelings about development decline, and may do so more rapidly depending upon girls' comfort levels with peers and significant others, in school and other social contexts.

While girls' breast development can spur both emotional responses from the girls themselves, and social responses from others, boys' initial pubertal changes (i.e., testicular development) are a more private matter. Clearly, boys are likely to have emotional reactions about their growth and feelings of varying degrees of preparedness about their development. However, to the authors' knowledge, no studies have reported on boys' reactions to their maturing bodies. Like girls, boys also seem to experience harassment at school that is related to their bodies; however, the exact nature of these experiences is not well defined (AAUW, 1995). The severity and range of responses to these events has yet to be fully documented for boys or girls.

Similar to hormonal links to negative affect in adolescence, pubertal status has also been associated with adolescent mood. Given findings that rapid changes in hormones may be particularly salient to changes in mood or adjustment, our group conducted a small pilot study examining reports of depressive and anxious symptoms as girls changed from prepubertal, to beginning pubertal (initial breast development), to post-menarcheal. Significant increases in depressive and anxious symptoms were found in this study when girls changed from no pubertal development to beginning puberty (see figure 2.4). Again, analyses were based on a very small pilot study ($N = 10$) of girls, but findings are suggestive of the importance of examining the initial hormonal changes that occur during puberty in order to understand changes in emotion during the entry into adolescence.

Pubertal changes have also been linked to clinical depression in girls. In a study of early and mid-adolescent girls, Angold and colleagues (1998) found reaching Tanner Stage 3 of pubertal status was associated with increased levels of depression in girls. However, when Angold and colleagues (1999) later tested whether hormonal changes would also be associated with girls' depression, they found that girls' elevated estradiol and testosterone levels were predictive of their becoming clinically depressed, and that these effects eliminated effects due to secondary sexual characteristics. However, they found no effects

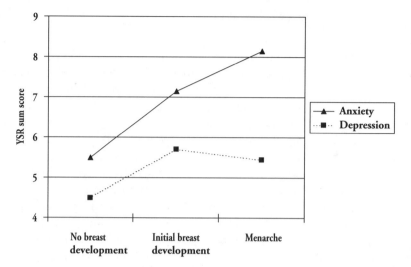

Figure 2.4   Univariate repeated measures of analysis of change in Anxiety and Depressive affect scores based on the Youth Self-Report were significant ($p < .05$). Analyses were of ten girls who were prepubertal at the first assessment, and were subsequently assessed when they had initial breast development, and again after menarche.

for FSH and LH. These studies illustrate the importance of investigating both hormones and secondary sexual characteristics when attempting to tease apart the effects of each on adolescents' adjustment.

Significance of menarche and spermarche

Interestingly, while menarche is frequently viewed as synonymous with the *start* of puberty, it actually occurs rather late in the maturational sequence – after pubic hair and breast development are well underway, after peak growth velocity, and during the rapid increase in weight and body fat (Gross, Dexter, & McCormick, 1982; Tanner, 1978). However, given that it is a salient and singular event, the psychological significance of menarche has been studied fairly extensively (Brooks-Gunn & Petersen, 1983; Brooks-Gunn & Ruble, 1982; Greif & Ulman, 1982; Koff, Reirdan, & Sheingold, 1982). Several studies have questioned girls about their reactions to menarche. In these studies, girls typically describe both positive and negative feelings (Petersen, 1983; Ruble & Brooks-Gunn, 1982). In studies conducted by Brooks-Gunn and Ruble (1982), girls were interviewed within two to three months of getting their periods for the first time. Twenty percent of girls reported only positive reactions, 20 percent reported only negative reactions, 20 percent reported ambivalent feelings, such as "felt same" or "felt funny," and the last 40 percent reported both positive and negative reactions (Ruble & Brooks-Gunn, 1982). Their studies also found that while the first months after menarche are characterized by secretiveness from others (except mothers), by about six months after menarche, girls begin sharing information and experiences with their friends (e.g., attitudes towards menarche, experience of menstrual-related pain and symptoms). Girls almost never discuss menarche with boys or their fathers and often report discomfort just thinking about discussions of puberty that might include Dad (Brooks-Gunn et al., 1994).

These patterns of information transmission are in contrast to what premenarcheal girls thought they would do when they got their periods. Premenarcheal girls expect to tell their girlfriends sooner as well as tell more people than they actually tell once they have gotten their periods. Similarly, discrepancies regarding menstrual symptoms and attitudes also exist prior to and post-menarche. Premenarcheal girls expect to experience more menstrual-related pain, water retention and negative affect then they actually report experiencing, when surveyed after menarche (Brooks-Gunn & Ruble, 1982).

It is believed by some that spermarche is as significant for boys as menarche is for girls. However, very little is known about the meaning of this, or any other pubertal changes to boys. In a small study, middle adolescent boys were interviewed about their reactions to their first ejaculation, their preparedness for the event and sources of information, and the extent to which they discussed this with friends (Gaddis & Brooks-Gunn, 1985). Responses to spermarche overall were more positive than girls' responses to menarche, though about two-thirds of the sample did report being "a little frightened." Although the vast majority of boys reported feeling "somewhat prepared," for the event, very few sources of information were mentioned. Finally, none of these boys, all of whom had ejaculated, had told their peers about their experience, although they all joked about it generally. Subsequent studies have found similar patterns of experience in men giving retrospective reports of their first ejaculation (Downs & Fuller, 1991), and in another small interview study, of older adolescents (Stein & Reiser, 1994). These studies also exemplify the importance of wording when asking about puberty. Other studies have asked men to report retrospectively on their first nocturnal emission as a means of assessing when they went through puberty (Graber, Petersen, & Brooks-Gunn, 1996); however, many boys have their first ejaculation during masturbation (Gaddis & Brooks-Gunn, 1985). Gaddis and Brooks-Gunn (1985) surmise that the secrecy around spermarche is likely due in part to the connection between ejaculation and masturbation.

Significance of changes in growth and body composition

Normal changes in height and weight at puberty are often experienced positively by boys, especially increases in muscle mass and height. Western cultures seem to favor boys who are larger and stronger. In contrast, girls more frequently experience normal height and weight changes negatively, particularly the increases in weight and/or fat. This is likely due to the fact that Western cultures, in which media images are dominated by white women, value the thin physique of a prepubertal body over the mature body for girls (Attie & Brooks-Gunn, 1989; Parker et al., 1995).

While teenage girls often adapt to their changing bodies by altering their body image (Steiner-Adair, 1986), they must also cope with their family's and peers' responses to their maturing bodies. Along the same lines, girls who engage in activities that value a pre-pubertal body, such as dancing, modeling, figure skating, or gymnastics, may also have an especially challenging time dealing with their increases in body fat. Not surprisingly, increases in body fat occurring with puberty have been associated with desires to be thinner, and other eating problems such as strict dieting, excessive exercising to lose weight, and/or bingeing and purging. For example, higher levels of body mass were associated with the development of eating problems in longitudinal studies of middle- and late-adolescent girls (Attie & Brooks-Gunn, 1989; Graber et al., 1994). Interestingly, these studies included a majority of normal-weight (not obese) girls. In a different investigation of precursors of eating problems in 5th- and 6th-grade boys and girls, Keel, Fulkerson, and Leon (1997) found that for 5th-grade girls, greater body mass as well as more advanced levels of pubertal development were predictive of eating prob-lems one year later.

Notably, there has been increased attention in the past several years to how girls' body image changes during adolescence and how weight changes of puberty are a factor in sub-sequent unhealthy behavioral patterns (e.g., dieting, depressive affect). Often, it is assumed that boys are more immune to societal or media pressures about their bodies. However, a few recent studies (Leit, Gray, & Pope, 2002) and journalistic reports (Hall, 1999; Trebay, 2000) suggest that media images of men are becoming as unrealistic and unattainable as media images of women. "Healthy" men in the media usually are "pumped-up," with large shoulder muscles and clearly defined abdominal muscles. Such physiques do not occur as a result of puberty but rather develop only when puberty is combined with extensive physical training. Some boys may be engaging in obsessive train-ing, similar to exercise activities of bulimics seeking to control their body shapes and weight via exercise. Other boys may engage in steroid use to obtain fast results. And, still others may simply experience dissatisfaction with their bodies during adolescence and young adulthood that may lead to depressive affect or other emotional problems. Ultimately, more research is needed to document the extent of these behaviors and to identify which boys may be at highest risk for health-compromising behaviors.

Normal height and weight changes may also be especially stressful for girls *and* boys who are overweight or obese in their prepubertal years. As there is a greater emphasis on looks and appearance for dating and peer acceptance in adolescence, normal weight changes for already overweight children may be particularly difficult for them.

Significance of other physical changes at puberty

As noted, little attention, from a research perspective, has been paid to changes such as voice change, acne, or changes in body hair and how these changes are experienced psy-chologically by young adolescents. In contrast, companies seeking to sell products to adolescents have clearly targeted acne and hair removal (for girls) as key problems of adolescence. For young adolescents, dermatology concerns are the second most common reason for a doctor visit (Ziv, Boulet, & Slap, 1999), which is even more indicative of adolescent concerns about acne when one considers the extent to which adolescents under-utilize medical services in general.

Significance of rate of development

There has been little work addressing whether and which periods of change (or stability) in pubertal development are most closely associated with negative and/or positive adjustment for adolescents. However, a short-term longitudinal study conducted by our group (Archibald et al., submitted) found interesting links between preadolescent girls' rates of breast and pubic hair development (combined) and their self-reported moods over a nine-month period. Specifically, girls who were experiencing initial pubertal changes exhibited decreases in positive mood and increases in sad mood, over time. Interestingly, girls who had begun puberty but had little change over time, reported the most intense and stable positive affect at each time of assessment. Additionally, girls who were in the mid-pubertal stages and continued to develop over time reported less intense sad mood at the second time point. Taken together, these findings suggest that beginning secondary sexual characteristic development at a fast pace may be experienced most negatively by girls over the short term, and that stability or slower rate of change in development (at least in the earliest stages of puberty) may be experienced most positively. Certainly all girls will demonstrate increases in pubertal development over time; however, it is possible that the rate of change may be most salient to mood. Finally, it appears that girls advancing in the later stages of puberty do not experience their development as negatively as they did during the initial pubertal changes, and may, in fact, see these changes as positive. These preliminary findings illuminate the need for researchers in adolescent development to consider not only the stages, but also the rate and possibly critical periods of, pubertal development. There has been a dearth of work that has investigated the *rate* of girls' pubertal changes in relation to their adjustment and virtually no studies of rate and boys' adjustment (Brooks-Gunn & Reiter, 1990; Graber, Petersen, & Brooks-Gunn, 1996).

Significance of pubertal timing

We discussed, in a previous section, factors that are associated with the timing of the onset of puberty as well as the range of ages in which normative development is seen for different aspects of puberty. Given the wide range of ages at which individuals may begin puberty or experience different stages of puberty, timing differences within a cohort of youth have been of interest in studies of psychosocial development in adolescence. In this case, timing refers to being earlier, on time, or later than most boys or girls in a particular cohort. Beginning with Jones and her colleagues (Jones & Bayley, 1950; Jones & Mussen, 1958), pubertal timing has been thought to have significance in the social world of adolescents and these social experiences may also impact psychological development (Brooks-Gunn, Petersen, & Eichorn, 1985; Petersen & Taylor, 1980). Timing may confer risk to adolescents in that those who are off-time or who go through puberty earlier or later than their peers may feel more self-conscious about their development or out of synch with others. It has also been suggested that being an early maturer, specifically, confers risk as these individuals face puberty before anyone else in their cohort and therefore do not have a social referent for the experience. Also, these individuals may have less developed social and cognitive skills when they begin puberty in comparison to peers who will have a few more years before reaching puberty. In this case, early maturing girls would be most at risk for difficulties as they begin puberty before any other group of children. In contrast, early maturing boys will actually be going through puberty at about the same time as the majority of girls. From a social comparison perspective, late-maturing boys may also be at risk as they mature later than any other group of adolescents. Research on the effects of pubertal timing has seen a resurgence in recent years, with studies testing whether effects exist, if so, for whom, and if so, why.

Existence of timing effects and for whom. Beginning with the existence of timing effects and for whom, evidence has begun to amass demonstrating that girls who mature earlier than their peers have poorer adjustment along several dimensions than other girls or boys (Blyth, Simmons, & Zakin, 1985; Caspi & Moffitt, 1991; Duncan et al., 1985; Graber et al., 1994; Petersen et al., 1991; Stattin & Magnusson, 1990). In a recent epidemiological study (Graber et al., 1997) that included both boys and girls in high school, links between pubertal timing and subclinical and clinical levels of psychopathology were examined. Early maturation for girls was associated with lifetime history of serious mental disorder including depression, conduct disorder, substance abuse, and suicide attempts. Early maturation in girls was also linked to elevated symptom levels of depressive affect and lower coping skills. Late-maturing girls also had elevated rates of lifetime history of depression in comparison to on-time maturers. These girls experienced elevated symptoms of self-consciousness and reported more conflict with parents than on-time girls.

Other studies have found comparable negative effects for early maturation with middle school-age girls as well (Hayward et al., 1997). In this case, early maturation was again linked to depressive disorder. Across studies, early maturation for girls has been linked with body image disturbance (Blyth, Simmons, & Zakin, 1984; Duncan et al., 1985), eating problems and dieting (Cauffman & Steinberg, 1996; Graber et al., 1994) as well as earlier initiation of sexual behaviors, including intercourse (Smolak, Levine, & Gralen, 1993; Cauffman & Steinberg, 1996). However, most of the studies in this area have only examined white, middle-class girls. Interestingly, Hayward and his colleagues (Hayward et al., 1999) subsequently examined depressive affect comparing same-aged pre- and post-menarcheal girls from three racial/ethnic backgrounds. White, post-menarcheal girls (early maturers) had higher depression scores than other girls; a timing effect was not found among African American or Hispanic/Latina girls. This finding is unique in that few studies have included sufficient numbers of non-white participants to test for timing effects. Even in this study, most participants were white. Additional work on whether timing effects are as prevalent for non-white groups of girls and boys is needed, especially if it is hypothesized that social context influences whether or not timing effects occur.

Recent studies of timing that have included boys also suggest that timing effects may exist for boys but that effects are not as serious as those documented for girls (Graber et al., 1997). Interestingly, early maturation for high school-age boys was also associated with psychopathology (as was early maturation for girls), but in connection to less severe problems such as elevated depressive symptoms and increased engagement in tobacco use in comparison to on-time maturing boys. Late-maturing boys in this study reported more problems with schoolwork, along with internalizing problems and greater self-consciousness in comparison to on-time maturers. Andersson and Magnusson (1990) also find that off-time pubertal development in boys is a risk for alcohol use and abuse in a study of older adolescent/young adult males. The existence and severity of pubertal timing effects on boys' development in adolescence have not been studied as often as effects for girls; virtually no information is available for diverse groups of boys.

Evidence for underlying mechanisms explaining timing effects. We have identified some of the hypothetical reasons that being off-time in puberty, or being early, may confer risk to young adolescents. As with the literature that has begun to establish whether or not timing effects occur, potential causes have also been identified. As indicated, one factor in being off-time is that fewer peers are having the same experiences as the individual. Because fewer pubertal timing effects have been documented for boys, less work has focused on why timing effects occur for boys. Therefore, most of the following discussion is based on studies of girls; information regarding boys' development is included when available.

Early-maturing girls may have an especially difficult time with pubertal weight changes. Girls who mature earlier than their peers gain weight at a time when most girls their age still have childlike appearances. So, early-maturing girls are not fitting the societal norm when other girls do. For this reason, early-maturing girls may have lower self-esteem, particularly as related to their body image, than girls who mature on-time or later than their peers (Graber, Petersen, & Brooks-Gunn, 1996). For late-maturing boys, the absence of physical development may be a problem. Some evidence suggests that body image is poor for late-maturing boys during the early adolescence period but it improves (as boys grow) by later adolescence (Graber et al., 1996).

Other hypotheses that have found support also focus on contextual factors that may interact with timing. For example, going through a school change at the same time as going through peak pubertal development has been identified as an experience that sets adolescents on the course for poorer adjustment across adolescence (Petersen, Sarigiani, & Kennedy, 1991). In this case, it is the fact that the adolescent is having concurrent life events that may overwhelm coping systems (Brooks-Gunn, 1991; Simmons & Blyth, 1987). Notably, early-maturing girls are more likely to make a school change during the peak pubertal period, and thus, these girls were more likely to have depressed affect than other girls and boys (Petersen et al., 1991).

Context may also determine whether or not being off-time is important. Again, drawing on studies of girls, Brooks-Gunn and her colleagues have found that pubertal timing did not influence the same behaviors when comparing adolescent girls who were ballet dancers and other girls (Gargiulo et al., 1987). That is, early-maturing girls often date at earlier ages than their peers and thus are more likely to experience sexual and relationship pressures at earlier ages (Cauffman & Steinberg, 1996; Smolak, Levine, & Gralen, 1993). In contrast, among adolescent ballet dancers, timing effects on dating were not found. Because training took so much time, the focus on a professional athletic/artistic endeavor seemed to be a protective factor for early-maturing girls.

Schools, themselves, are an important context for interpreting puberty and adolescent behaviors. Caspi and colleagues compared single-sex and coeducational school enrollment in New Zealand and reported that early maturing girls in single-sex schools did not seem to have greater behavior problems (Caspi et al., 1993). Rather, it was early-maturing girls who were in coeducational schools who had more difficulties. It has been suggested that coeducational schools simply tolerate a greater level of problem behavior on the assumption that it is more normative for boys. In contrast, it may be that interactions with boys are a stimulus to early-maturing girls, or a context for these girls, for problem behaviors. That is, early maturers are viewed by themselves and others as being old enough to try out certain behaviors (i.e., dating, drinking alcohol, etc.).

Along these lines, in one of the few longer-term, longitudinal studies of pubertal timing effects, Stattin and Magnusson (1990) found that it was early-maturing girls who associated with older peers (especially older boys) who were more likely to engage in problem behaviors at earlier ages than their peers. In their study of girls in Sweden, girls were followed from early adolescence into adulthood (age 30). By late adolescence, timing did not differentiate girls on these types of behaviors (e.g., sexual activities, drinking alcohol) as it was more normative for all girls to do these things. By age 30, women who had been early maturers had completed less education and thus had entered lower-level careers than other women. Notably, as adolescents, these girls had not differed from other girls on school achievement or other indicators of educational ability. Early engagement in non-school activities or focus on social experiences may have set early-maturing girls on pathways to earlier marriage and less connection with education over time; there were some indications that early maturers in this sample married at earlier ages than other women.

The hypotheses discussed thus far focus on experiences and context that shape experiences in the later periods of puberty. However, as with any transition, experiences or predispositions that are in place prior to the transition will shape how it is experienced by the adolescent (Graber & Brooks-Gunn, 1996). Caspi and Moffitt (1991) demonstrated that prior adjustment was important in determining whether early pubertal maturation resulted in difficulties for girls. In this study, early-maturing girls who did not have prior behavioral problems in middle childhood did not develop them during adolescence. Instead, the girls with the most behavioral problems as adolescents were early-maturing girls who had prior behavioral problems; Caspi and Moffitt (1991) refer to this as an accentuating effect of timing on behavioral problems. In our own work, we have found a similar interaction between pubertal timing and hormonal activity such that girls with high levels of adrenal activity who were also early maturers had elevated depressive symptoms (Graber, Brooks-Gunn, & Warren, in press). Again, early maturers who did not have high adrenal activity also did not have elevated symptoms. Overall, such findings indicate that multiple types of predispositions – temperament, behavior problems, biological factors – need to be taken into account in understanding why early maturation may or may not be problematic for girls.

Conclusions

As noted, aspects of the pubertal transition may have important influences on the mental health and behaviors of adolescents. Despite an increased interest in adolescent development as a whole, there is still a dearth of studies that have followed the same children through puberty and adolescence into adulthood. Thus, there are some studies of the experience of puberty and its short-term consequences but few studies that speak to long-term consequences (but see Stattin & Magnusson, 1990, as an exception). More research that studied adolescents is following these individuals into adulthood (e.g., Allen & Hauser, 1996), although not all of this took pubertal development into account.

To date, we are beginning to understand multiple aspects of pubertal development but it is interesting that there are still many facets that are unknown. Examinations of why onset may be earlier on average for girls are providing insights into processes that regulate the "activation" of the pubertal system. At the same time, such studies are highlighting the complexity of the interactions among the biological, social, and psychological in shaping any one individual's pubertal development and the repercussions of puberty on subsequent development.

References

Allen, J. P., & Hauser, S. T. (1996). Autonomy and relatedness in adolescent–family interactions as predictors of young adults' states of mind regarding attachment. *Development & Psychopathology, 8,* 793–809.

American Association of University Women (AAUW) (1995). *How schools shortchange girls.* New York: Marlowe.

Andersson, T., & Magnusson, D. (1990). Biological maturation in adolescence and the development of drinking habits and alcohol abuse among young males: A prospective longitudinal study. *Journal of Youth and Adolescence, 19,* 33–41.

Angold, A., Costello, E. J., Erkanli, A., & Worthman, C. M. (1999). Pubertal changes in hormone levels and depression in girls. *Psychological Medicine, 29,* 1043–1053.

Angold, A., Costello, E. J., & Worthman, C. M. (1998). Puberty and depression: The roles of age, pubertal status, and pubertal timing. *Psychological Medicine, 28,* 16–51.

Archibald, A. B., Graber, J. A., Brooks-Gunn, J., & Warren, M. P. (submitted). Moody girls: Is puberty to blame?

Attie, I., & Brooks-Gunn, J. (1989). Development of eating problems in adolescent girls: A longitudinal study. *Developmental Psychology, 25,* 70–79.

Berkey, C. S., Gardner, J. D., Frazier, A. L., & Colditz, G. A. (2000). Relation of childhood diet and body size to menarche and adolescent growth in girls. *American Journal of Epidemiology, 152,* 446–452.

Biro, F. M., Lucky, A. W., Huster, G. A., & Morrison, J. A. (1995). Pubertal staging in boys. *Journal of Pediatrics, 127,* 100–102.

Blyth, D. A., Simmons, R. G., & Zakin, D. F. (1985). Satisfaction with body-image for early adolescent females: The impact of pubertal timing within different school environments. *Journal of Youth and Adolescence, 14,* 207–225.

Brooks-Gunn, J. (1984). The psychological significance of different pubertal events to young girls. *Journal of Early Adolescence, 4,* 315–327.

Brooks-Gunn, J. (1988). Antecedents and consequences of variations in girls' maturational timing. *Journal of Adolescent Health Care, 9,* 365–373.

Brooks-Gunn, J. (1991). How stressful is the transition to adolescence for girls? In M. E. Colten & S. Gore (Eds.), *Adolescent stress: Causes and consequences* (pp. 131–149). Hawthorne, NY: Aldine de Gruyter.

Brooks-Gunn, J., Graber, J. A., & Paikoff, R. L. (1994). Studying links between hormones and adaptive and maladaptive behavior: Models and measures. *Journal of Research on Adolescence, 4*, 469–486.

Brooks-Gunn, J., Newman, D., Holderness, C., & Warren, M. P. (1994). The experience of breast development and girls: Stories about the purchase of a bra. *Journal of Youth and Adolescence, 3*, 271–294.

Brooks-Gunn, J., & Petersen, A. (Eds.) (1983). *Girls at puberty: Biological and psychosocial perspectives.* New York: Academic.

Brooks-Gunn, J., Petersen, A. C., & Eichorn, D. (1985). The study of maturational timing effects in adolescence. *Journal of Youth and Adolescence, 14*(3), 149–161.

Brooks-Gunn, J., & Reiter, E. O. (1990). The role of pubertal processes. In S. S. Feldman & G. R. Elliott (Eds.), *At the threshold: The developing adolescent* (pp. 16–53). Cambridge, MA: Harvard University Press.

Brooks-Gunn, J., & Ruble, D. (1982). The development of menstrual related beliefs and behaviors during early-adolescence. *Child Development, 53*, 1567–1577.

Brooks-Gunn, J., & Warren, M. P. (1989). Biological contributions to affective expression in young adolescent girls. *Child Development, 60*, 372–385.

Buchanan, C. M., Eccles, J. S., & Becker, J. B. (1992). Are adolescents the victims of raging hormones: Evidence for activational effects of hormones on moods and behavior at adolescence. *Psychological Bulletin, 111*, 62–107.

Carnegie Council on Adolescent Development (1996). *Great transitions: Preparing adolescents for a new century.* New York: Carnegie Corporation.

Caspi, A., Lynam, D., Moffit, T. E., & Silva, P. A. (1993). Unraveling girls' delinquency: Biological, dispositional and contextual contributions to adolescent misbehavior. *Developmental Psychology, 29*, 19–30.

Caspi, A., & Moffit, T. E. (1991). Individual differences are accentuated during periods of social change: The sample case of girls at puberty. *Journal of Personality and Social Psychology, 61*, 157–168.

Cauffman, E., & Steinberg, L. (1996). Interactive effects of menarcheal status and dating on dieting and disordered eating among adolescent girls. *Developmental Psychology, 32*, 631–635.

Clayton, P. E., & Trueman, J. A. (2000). Leptin and puberty. *Archives of Disease in Childhood, 83*, 1–4.

Cutler, G., & Loriaux, D. L. (1980). Adrenarche and its relationship to the onset of puberty. *Federation Proceedings, 39*, 2384–2390.

Downs, A. C., & Fuller, M. J. (1991). Recollections of spermarche: An exploratory investigation. *Current Psychology: Research & Reviews, 10*, 93–102.

Duncan, P. D., Ritter, P. L., Dornbusch, S. M., Gross, R. T., & Carlsmith, J. M. (1985). The effects of pubertal timing on body image, school behavior, and deviance. *Journal of Youth and Adolescence, 14*, 227–235.

Eichorn, D. H. (1975). Asynchronizations in adolescent development. In S. E. Dragastin & G. H. Elder, Jr. (Eds.), *Adolescence in the life cycle: Psychological change and social context* (pp. 81–96). Washington, DC: Hemisphere.

Feldman, S. S., & Elliot, G. R. (Eds.) (1990). *At the threshold: The developing adolescent.* Cambridge, MA: Harvard University.

Frisch, R. E. (1983). Fatness, puberty, and fertility: The effects of nutrition and physical training on menarche and ovulation. In J. Brooks-Gunn & A. C. Petersen, *Girls at puberty: Biological and psychosocial perspectives* (pp. 29–50). New York: Plenum.

Gaddis, A., & Brooks-Gunn, J. (1985). The male experience of pubertal change. *Journal of Youth and Adolescence, 14*, 61–69.

Gargiulo, J., Attie, I., Brooks-Gunn, J., & Warren, M. P. (1987). Girls' dating behavior as a function of social context and maturation. *Developmental Psychology, 23,* 730–737.

Girl Scouts of the USA (2000). *Teens before their time.* New York: Girl Scouts of the USA.

Gladen, B. C., Ragan, N. B., & Rogan, W. J. (2000). Pubertal growth and development and prenatal and lactational exposure to polychlorinated biphenyls and dichlorodiphenyl dichloroethene. *Journal of Pediatrics, 136,* 490–496.

Goy, R. W., & McEwen, B. S. (1980). *Sexual differentiation of the brain.* Cambridge, MA: MIT Press.

Graber, J. A., & Brooks-Gunn, J. (1996). Reproductive transitions: The experience of mothers and daughters. In C. D. Ryff & M. M. Seltzer (Eds.), *The parental experience in midlife* (pp. 255–299). Chicago: University of Chicago Press.

Graber, J. A., Brooks-Gunn, J., Paikoff, R. L., & Warren, M. P. (1994). Prediction of eating problems: An eight year study of adolescent girls. *Developmental Psychology, 30,* 823–834.

Graber, J. A., Brooks-Gunn, J., & Petersen, A. C. (1996). Pubertal processes: Methods, measures, and models. In J. A. Graber, J. Brooks-Gunn, & A. C. Petersen (Eds.), *Transitions through adolescence: Interpersonal domains and context* (pp. 23–53). Mahwah, NJ: Erlbaum.

Graber, J. A., Brooks-Gunn, J., & Warren, M. P. (1995). The antecedents of menarcheal age: Heredity, family environment, and stressful life events. *Child Development, 66,* 346–359.

Graber, J. A., Brooks-Gunn, J., & Warren, M. P. (in press). Pubertal effects on adjustment in girls: Moving from demonstrating effects to identifying pathways. *Journal of Youth & Adolescence.*

Graber, J. A., Lewinsohn, P. M., Seeley, J. R., & Brooks-Gunn, J. (1997). Is psychopathology associated with the timing of pubertal development? *Journal of the American Academy of Adolescent and Child Psychiatry, 36,* 1768–1776.

Graber, J. A., Petersen, A. C., & Brooks-Gunn, J. (Eds.) (1996). Pubertal processes: Methods, measures, and models. In *Transitions through adolescence: Interpersonal domains and context* (pp. 23–53). Mahwah, NJ: Erlbaum.

Greif, E. B., & Ulman, K. J. (1982). The psychological impact of menarche on early-adolescent females: A review of the literature. *Child Development, 53,* 1413–1430.

Gross, R. T., Dexter, K., & McCormick, S. (1982, January). Patterns of maturation: Their effects on behavior and development. Paper presented at the Symposium on Middle Childhood: Developmental Variation and Dysfunction Between Six and Fourteen Years. New Orleans.

Grumbach, M. M. (1975). Onset of puberty. In S. R. Berenberg (Ed.), *Puberty: Biologic and social components* (pp. 1–21). Leiden: HE Stenfert Kroese.

Grumbach, M. M., & Styne, D. M. (1998). Puberty: Ontogeny, neuroendocrinology, physiology, and disorders. In J. D. Wilson, D. W. Foster, & H. M. Kronenberg (Eds.), *Williams textbook of endocrinology* (pp. 1509–1625). Philadelphia: W. B. Saunders.

Hall, S. S. (1999, August 22). Bully in the mirror. *New York Times Magazine,* pp. 31–35, 58, 62–65.

Hayward, C., Gotlib, I. H., Schraedley, P. K., & Litt, I. F. (1999). Ethnic differences in the association between pubertal status and symptoms of depression in adolescent girls. *Journal of Adolescent Health, 25,* 143–149.

Hayward, C., Killen, J. D., Wilson, D. M., Hammer, L. D., Litt, I. F., Kraemer, H. C., Haydel, F., Varady, A., Taylor, C. B. (1997). Psychiatric risk associated with early puberty in adolescent girls. *Journal of the American Academy of Child & Adolescent Psychiatry, 36,* 255–262.

Herman-Giddens, M. E., Slora, E. J., Wasserman, R. C., Bourdony, C. J., Bhapkar, M. V., Koch, G. G., & Hasemeier, C. M. (1997). Secondary sexual characteristics and menses in young girls seen in office practice: A study from the pediatric research in office settings network. *Pediatrics, 99*(4), 505–511.

Horlick, M. B., Rosenbaum, M., Nicolson, M., Levine, L. S., Fedun, B., Wang, J., Pierson, R. N.,

Jr., & Leibel, R. L. (2000). Effect of puberty on the relationship between circulating leptin and body composition. *Journal of Clinical Endocrinology & Metabolism, 85,* 2509–2518.

Jones, M. C., & Bayley, N. (1950). Physical maturing among boys as related to behavior. *Journal of Educational Psychology, 41,* 129–148.

Jones, M. C., & Mussen, P. H. (1958). Self-conceptions, motivations, and interpersonal attitudes of early- and late-maturing girls. *Child Development, 29,* 491–501.

Kaplowitz, P. B., Oberfield, S. E., & the Drug and Therapeutics and Executive Committees of the Lawson Wilkins Pediatric Endocrine Society (1999). Reexamination of the age limit for defining when puberty is precocious in girls in the United States: Implications for evaluation and treatment. *Pediatrics, 104,* 936–941.

Katchadourian, H. (1977). *The biology of adolescence.* San Francisco: W. H. Freeman.

Keel, P. K., Fulkerson, J. A., & Leon, G. R. (1997). Disordered eating precursors in pre- and early adolescent girls and boys. *Journal of Youth and Adolescence, 26,* 203–216.

Koff, E., Rierdan, J., & Sheingold, K. (1982). Memories of menarche: Age, preparation, and prior knowledge as determinants of initial menstrual experience. *Journal of Youth and Adolescence, 11,* 1–9.

Leit, R. A., Gray, J. J., & Pope, H. G. (2002). The media's representation of the ideal male body: A cause for muscle dysmorphia? *International Journal of Eating Disorders, 31*(3), 334–338.

Marshall, W. A., & Tanner, J. M. (1969). Variations in the pattern of pubertal changes in girls. *Archives of Disease in Childhood, 44,* 291–303.

Marshall, W. A., & Tanner, J. M. (1974). Puberty. In J. D. Douvis & J. Drobeing (Eds.), *Scientific foundations of pediatrics* (pp. 124–151). London: Heinemann.

McEwen, B. S. (1994). How do sex and stress hormones affect nerve cells? *Annals New York Academy of Sciences, 743,* 1–18.

Moffitt, T. E., Caspi, A., Belsky, J., & Silva, P. A. (1992). Childhood experience and the onset of menarche: A test of a sociobiological model. *Child Development, 63,* 47–58.

National Center for Health Statistics (1997). *Fertility, family planning and women's health: New data from the 1995 National Survey of Family Growth.* DHHS Publication No. (PHS) 97–1995. Hyattsville, MD: US Department of Health and Human Services.

National Heart, Lung, and Blood Institute Growth and Health Study Research Group (1992). Obesity and cardiovascular disease risk factors in black and white girls: The NHLBI growth and health study. *American Journal of Public Health, 82,* 1613–1620.

Obeidallah, D. A., Brennan, R., Brooks-Gunn, J., Kindlon, D., & Earls, F. E. (in press). Socioeconomic status, race, and girls' pubertal maturation: Results from the Project on Human Development in Chicago Neighborhoods. *Journal of Research on Adolescence.*

Orenstein, P. (1994). *School girls: Young women, self-esteem, and the confidence gap.* New York: Doubleday.

Paikoff, R. L., Brooks-Gunn, J., & Warren, M. P. (1991). Effects of girls' hormonal status on depressive and aggressive symptoms over the course of one year. *Journal of Youth and Adolescence, 20,* 191–215.

Parker, S., Nichter, M., Nichter, M., Vuckovic, N., et al. (1995). Body image and weight concerns among African American and white adolescent females: Differences that make a difference. *Human Organization, 54,* 103–114.

Petersen, A. C. (1983). Menarche: Meaning of measures and measuring meaning. In S. Golub (Ed.), *Menarche* (pp. 35–61). Lexington, MA: Lexington Books, D. C. Heath.

Petersen, A. C. (1987). The nature of biological–psychosocial interactions: The sample case of early adolescence. In R. M. Lerner & T. T. Foch (Eds.), *Biological–psychosocial interactions in early adolescence: A life-span perspective* (pp. 35–61). Hillsdale, NJ: Erlbaum.

Petersen, A. C., Sarigiani, P. A., & Kennedy, R. E. (1991). Adolescent depression: Why more girls?

Journal of Youth and Adolescence, 20, 247–271.

Petersen, A. C., & Taylor, B. (1980). The biological approach to adolescence: Biological change and psychological adaptation. In J. Adelson (Ed.), *Handbook of adolescent psychology* (pp. 117–155). New York: Wiley.

Reiter, E. O., & Grumbach, M. M. (1982). Neuroendocrine control mechanisms and the onset of puberty. *Annual Review of Physiology, 44,* 595–613.

Ruble, D., & Brooks-Gunn, J. (1982). The experience of menarche. *Child Development, 53,* 1557–1566.

Schreiber, G. B. B., Robbins, M., Striegel-Moore, R., Obarzanek, E., Morrison, J. A., & Wright, D. J. (1996). Weight modification efforts reported by Black and White preadolescent girls: National Heart, Lung, and Blood Institutes Growth and Health Study. *Pediatrics, 98,* 63–70.

Simmons, R. G., & Blyth, D. A. (1987). *Moving into adolescence: The impact of pubertal change and school context.* New York: Aldine de Gruyter.

Smolak, L., Levine, M. P., & Gralen, S. (1993). The impact of puberty and dating on eating problems among middle school girls. *Journal of Youth & Adolescence, 22,* 355–368.

Stattin, H., & Magnusson, D. (1990). *Paths through life: Vol. 2. Pubertal maturation in female development.* Hillsdale, NJ: Erlbaum.

Stein, J. A., & Reiser, L. W. (1994). A study of white middle-class adolescent boys' responses to "semenarche" (the first ejaculation). *Journal of Youth and Adolescence, 23,* 373–384.

Steiner-Adair, C. (1986). The body politic: Normal adolescent development and the development of eating disorders. *Journal of the American Academy of Psychoanalysis, 14,* 95–114.

Surbey, M. K. (1990). Family composition, stress, and the timing of human menarche. In T. E. Ziegler & F. B. Bercovitch (Eds.), *Socioendocrinology of primate reproduction* (pp. 11–32). New York: Wiley.

Susman, E. J., Nottelmann, E. D., Inoff-Germain, G., Dorn, L. D., & Chrousos, G. P. (1987). Hormonal influences on aspects of psychological development during adolescence. *Journal of Adolescent Health Care, 8,* 492–504.

Susman, E. J., Nottelmann, E. D., Inoff-Germain, G. E., Dorn, L. D., Cutler, G. B., Loriaux, D. L., & Chrousos, G. P. (1985). The relation of relative hormone levels and physical development and social–emotional behavior in young adolescents. *Journal of Youth and Adolescence, 14*(3), 245–264.

Tanner, J. M. (1962). *Growth at adolescence.* New York: Lippincott.

Tanner, J. M. (1978). *Fetus into man: Physical growth from conception to maturity.* Cambridge: Harvard University Press.

Trebay, G. (2000, August 20). Scrawn to brawn: Men get muscles. *New York Times,* ST1, ST4.

Warren, M. P. (1983). Physical and biological aspects of puberty. In J. Brooks-Gunn & A. C. Petersen (Eds.), *Girls at puberty: Biological and psychosocial perspectives* (pp. 3–28). New York: Plenum.

Warren, M. P., & Brooks-Gunn, J. (1989). Mood and behavior at adolescence: Evidence for hormonal factors. *Journal of Clinical Endocrinology and Metabolism, 69,* 77–83.

Ziv, A., Boulet, J. R., & Slap, G. B. (1999). Utilization of physician offices by adolescents in the United States. *Pediatrics, 104,* 35–42.

Part II

The Social Context of Adolescence

CHAPTER THREE

Religious Development in Adolescence

Geoffrey L. Ream and Ritch C. Savin-Williams

Introduction

Gen-X Religion (Flory & Miller, 2000) is a collection of ethnographic studies of religious contexts created by young people, for young people. Syncretism of the values and culture of recent generations with timeless religious belief systems produces modes of religious expression that challenge traditional definitions based on established, mainstream religious organizations. Young members of these religious groups attend services dressed as they are, piercings and all (Jensen, 2000), and express their commitment by means of hip-hop and rap music (Walsh, 2000), multimedia presentations (Prieto, 2000), body modification (Jensen, Flory, & Miller, 2000), and anything else that can be infused with religious meaning. Rather than being the generation to whom nothing is sacred, this is the generation to whom nothing is profane. Sacred space is any place, any context, or any medium in which genuine people share a genuine commitment to personally held beliefs, identify with their coreligionists in a community, and are otherwise free to be who they are as individuals (Flory, 2000).

The focus of this chapter is the choices that young people make in their religious lives and the reasons behind these choices. Although family is the main influence on the belief systems of youth, the choices available to the youth as well as the quality of the youth's parental attachment are also significant factors. The focus of this chapter moves from the global to the specific, from a description of the American religious landscape and adolescents' roles within it to the developmental trajectories of individual youth.

Religious Choices Available: Church, Sect, Cult

Academics recently noted the fact that traditional definitions of religion as an institutionalization of society's ideas about the sacred and profane (e.g. Durkheim, 1915; Weber,

1922) are inadequate to describe modern religion, particularly that of young people. Recent theories of the sociology of religion emphasize the diversity of religious choices available, the inclusive nature of many religious groups, and the easy syncretism, almost as if the goal were marketability, between religion and various cultural expressions. Rational choice theorists of religion (Iannaccone, 1990; Stark & Bainbridge, 1985, 1987, 1996; Warner, 1993) speak of a religious marketplace, and America as a buyer's market. Religious organizations market religious goods, which are, specifically, a system of compensation for rewards and goals that are thwarted in the secular world. The supernatural is a necessary part of religion because, in the present state of modern medicine, it is impossible to talk about life after death without evoking the supernatural. Individuals merely shop for the organizations that afford them the relationship with the divine that makes the most sense to them.

Religious organizations exist on a continuum from churches to sects and cults (Stark & Bainbridge, 1985, 1987). The sect end of the continuum represents newer religious groups that place considerable demand on their members for time, energy, and behavioral regulation. Sects and cults also provide strong and comprehensive general compensators to their members for rewards unattained in earthly life, such as an unswerving belief in the afterlife and in the end times. They usually exist at odds with the values of mainstream society, and therefore attract members who already identify themselves as outsiders within the modern world. (Within sociology of religion, the difference between sects and cults is that sects tend to be splinter groups from churches, while cults spring up on their own. These are, admittedly, loaded words.)

If a sect exists long enough and attracts sufficient members, it is likely to gain power and influence in society, which the mainstream and privileged attempt to co-opt and control. Thus, the religious organization becomes a church. Churches, as opposed to sects or cults, are aligned with the values of mainstream society; exist with the blessing of the privileged; provide little to their members in terms of compensators; and demand little of their members in terms of time, energy, or adherence to strict dogma. ("Church" here is the term that sociologists of religion use to refer to any religious group that meets this theoretical definition, not necessarily a Christian one. The term is admittedly Christocentric.) When churches fail to meet the needs of members who are searching for stronger general compensators, cults and sects, which provide for those needs, gain market share (Stark & Bainbridge, 1985, 1987, 1996).

Academic theories of secularization (Berger, 1967), therefore, tend to only acknowledge one side of this process, the aging and decline of institutional churches. Research informed by secularization theory tends to only pay attention to old, mainline religious groups with membership in the millions and ignore the birth of cults and sects. Incidentally, secularization paradigms also exclude the contributions of young people in terms of Pentecostal urban missions, Islamic outreach to African Americans, and campus fellowships such as Hillel and InterVarsity. More comprehensive data indicate that newer, evangelical religious groups are growing as fast as older, staid religious groups are declining, and thus overall attendance at religious services in the United States has remained relatively constant for several decades (Gallup & Lindsay, 1999). Similar trends are visible in many Western nations (Kelley & De Graaf, 1997).

Thus far we have described the "supply-side" of young people's religion, that is, what choices are available to them. Most investigations of the religion of young people, however, focus on the "demand side," or the reasons youth make their particular choices. Although knowing what exists on the supply side is important to understanding the religious lives of youth, the availability of various religious choices is a moot point in predicting the choices that individual American youth will make. This is simply because contemporary America is so saturated with religious groups of all types that youth can find anything they want on the church–sect–cult spectrum. Particularly when youth attend college, parents can seldom influence the religious choices of their young adult offspring by limiting their options.

Religion and Adolescence

Adolescence, according to the classical developmental theorist G. Stanley Hall (1904), is *the* age of conversion. Hall defined conversion broadly as a culmination of the biological, psychological, cognitive, and social changes of adolescence, and of the shift of youths' energy from themselves to their relationships with other people. This is the task of identity formation assigned to adolescents by Erikson (1968), who proposed that the central task of adolescence is identity development, and the central route to identity consolidation is an emerging understanding of the self in a social context.

According to both Hall (1904) and Strommen (1979), adolescents are concerned with questions of who they are, not just in the context of other people but of life's greater meaning and their reason for being. Religion is the natural medium for exploring these questions, particularly in a religion-saturated environment such as the United States. Religion has been proposed as the natural remedy for the experience of meaninglessness and instability in the lives of many troubled youth (Garbarino, 1999). Far from making youth dull and compliant to the wishes of adults, religion contributes to the development of "vibrant" youth who are actively engaged in helping their communities (Youniss, McLellan, & Yates, 1999).

There are many reasons why youth would want to be involved in religion, as well as many reasons why religious organizations compete for market share among young people. According to Erikson (1964) in *Insight and Responsibility*:

As cultures, through graded training, enter into the fiber of young individuals, they also absorb into their lifeblood the regenerative power of youth. Adolescence is thus a vital regenerator in the process of social evolution; for youth selectively offers its loyalties and energies to the conservation of that which feels true to them and to the correction and destruction of that which has lost its regenerative significance. (p. 126)

Thus, a mutually beneficial relationship exists between young people and the religious organizations that seek to sustain themselves by recruiting them. In individual cases, these relationships are best conceptualized as social attachment relationships (Dudley & Muthersbaugh, 1996). Attachment to religious organizations is, understandably, closely related to the mental models of attachment figures that develop from attachments to parents (Kirkpatrick & Shaver, 1990).

Parental Attachment and Religious Socialization

One of the most consistent findings in the literature on religious socialization is that the quality of a youth's relationship with his or her parents determines the effectiveness of parental religious socialization (Dudley, 1999; Dudley & Laurent, 1988; Gamoran, 1992; Hernandez & Dudley, 1990; Hoge, Petrillo, & Smith, 1982; Nelsen, 1980). The religiosity of securely attached youth, or youth who rate their relationship with their parents positively, generally corresponds with the religiosity of their parents. The religiosity of insecurely attached youth tends to be different from that of their parents. Some youth disaffiliate with religion in order to make a decisive break from a religiously charged dysfunctional family system. Others convert, seeking religion-based attachments that were lacking in their family systems (Granqvist, 1998; Kirkpatrick, 1998; Kirkpatrick & Shaver, 1990; Streib, 1999).

Gender is an important factor in the effectiveness of parental religious socialization. Mothers, even in the new millennium, are the keepers of the home and of the faith: Women are more religious than men, girls are more religious than boys, and mothers have a greater impact on religious socialization than do fathers (Acock & Bengston, 1978; Nelsen, 1980). Although psychodynamic conventional wisdom predicts that youth will respond better to the socialization efforts of the parent of their own gender, research has not found this to be the case (Acock & Bengston, 1978; King, Elder, & Whitbeck, 1997; Nelsen, 1980).

Family socialization and parental attachment, as well as life-course factors and the availability of religious choices, help determine the path of religious development that any given youth will follow. A review of the literature generally uncovers four developmental paths. *Continuous religiousness* and *continuous religious non-involvement* are, in general, the patterns of securely attached youth who are satisfied with the answers provided by the belief system with which they were socialized, and who thus assume the religiousness or the non-religiousness of their parents. *Conversion* and *apostasy* are, in general, the paths of youth who are dissatisfied with the belief system they have inherited or with their parental or social attachments, and who want to take a substantially different path with respect to these issues (Greeley, 1978; Richardson, Stewart, & Simmonds, 1978; Streib, 1999).

Conversion

Youth primarily convert to new religious groups for three reasons: because the religious groups offer a new perspective on life that allows youth to cope more effectively with, or even escape from, whatever problems they are having; because the group provides them with new friends and a sense of belonging in a social network; and/or because of some prior religious socialization (or possibly a biological predisposition; see Wulff, 1997) to seek religious or spiritual solutions to problems (Kox, Meeus, & 't Hart, 1991; Richardson et al., 1978; Zinnbauer & Pargament, 1998).

Cults and extreme sects recruit young people as aggressively as other religious organizations. In a narrative study, youths who tended toward occult and fundamentalist religiousness reported deep emotional and spiritual needs that were not being met by their families and home churches (Streib, 1999). The frequent life transitions and changes of social context that adolescents and young adults experience make them good customers for the intensive social interaction and simplifying assumptions to life that cults and extreme sects provide (Hunter, 1998). It is important to understand that, although the perception of a group as a cult is in the eye of the beholder (some Christian groups label the Jehovah's Witnesses, the International Church of Christ, and the Church of Latter-Day Saints as cults), some cults are indeed psychologically and physically dangerous. This is important to concerned adults because a parent whose child is particularly vulnerable to cults is, according to attachment theory of religion, the same parent who is ill equipped to rescue their daughter or son. Thus, the task may require the intervention of non-parent concerned adults.

Apostasy

In the same manner that conversion provides an escape from a difficult family situation, apostasy provides a vehicle for youths who want to distance themselves from their families by disaffiliating with their religion (Greeley, 1978). Attachment theory, the most useful theory for predicting whether a youth will deviate from the religion of his or her parents, does not specify in which direction a particular youth will deviate. If a child is raised as a fairly secular Jew and becomes dissatisfied as an adolescent with the family system and its religion, the predictors of whether he or she will join a Hasidic congregation or disaffiliate with religion completely lie outside of the family system.

Research does not support the view that increased intellectual or cultural sophistication causes apostasy (Greeley, 1978). According to studies on church youth, other aspects of the religious organization, namely relationships with pastors and youth ministers, are significant factors (Dudley & Laurent, 1988). Apostate youth are likely to be those who are not only dissatisfied with their family system and its religion, but who also do not have access to relationships with significant non-parent adults in their religious organizations.

Other patterns of development resemble apostasy. One study revealed a pattern of accumulative heresy, in which individuals attend religious groups long enough to have their immediate needs met, but avoid investing time or energy in the groups or making a commitment (Streib, 1999). Another investigation identified a pattern of continuous nominal involvement, in which youths with otherwise satisfying family relationships adopted the halfhearted beliefs and sporadic "only when we have to" religiousness of their parents (Ream, 2001). Thus, for questions of religion and developmental outcomes for youth, why they are involved with religion is as important as whether they are involved.

Religion as a Developmental Asset for Youth

Regardless of what a youth decides about her or his own religious involvement, empirical findings do not support older conceptualizations of religion as a compensation for psychopathology (Freud, 1927) or as an indication of social and cultural incompetence (cited in Greeley, 1978). A review of the research literature on the positive effects of religious involvement finds that religious involvement and commitment increase the qualities in youth that society values, such as school achievement, attendance, and self-esteem. Religiousness mitigates against undesirable behavior, such as delinquency, juvenile court referrals, substance use, teen pregnancy, and sexual permissiveness (Thomas & Carver, 1990).

Many religious adolescents internalize their religions' messages about care and concern for other people. In a study of youths who identify as Catholic, stronger practice of the faith was associated with more highly developed thought around forgiveness (Enright, Santos, & Al-Mabuk, 1989). A summary of findings from the Monitoring the Future survey (Youniss et al., 1999) reveals that religious youth are almost three times as likely to engage in community service as non-religious youth. This would appear to be attributable to a bias in self-reporting, but the measures in the study were of service behavior, not intentions. Further, religious undergraduates at a Christian college participated in community service more than non-religious undergraduates, even though the two groups were not significantly different with regard to self-reported intentions to perform community service (Bernt, 1999). These studies describe religious youths as "vibrant," engaged in their communities, and caring about the welfare of themselves and others.

Religion is also an asset to the communities in which youth live. The Search Institute, a youth development think-tank, recently commissioned a study on faith-based programs for youth in inner cities. Pragmatically, in many cases, churches are the only organizations capable of initiating efforts to work with youth, especially now that much of the public-sector infrastructure, such as school-based programs, has fallen apart or moved out. Search Institute also found that religion answers questions of greater meaning, purpose, and direction for these youth (Trulear, 2000), an important service to provide when the only world many of these youth have known has been urban pathos (Kozol, 1995; Shannon, Kleniewski, & Cross, 1997).

Conclusions

The take-home message is that young people are not passive recipients of religious socialization. Rather, they select from a variety of religious choices available in an open market (Sherkat, 1991). Religious organizations, similar to other cultural institutions, sustain themselves by recruiting and retaining young people (Erikson, 1964). In turn, they offer needed religious goods, such as a sense of purpose and meaning to life, norms and standards for behavior, and a belief system that helps an individual to make sense of the senseless aspects of life, such as tragedy and death (Stark & Bainbridge, 1985, 1987).

Religion is a process of attachment, to others in the organization, to the organization itself, and to the divine. Depending on the needs of an individual young person, his or her religious attachment pattern will likely correspond with what went right in the family system and/or compensate for what went wrong (Granqvist, 1998). Those who seek a strong religion are merely those who have strong needs for that which they feel religion will provide (Streib, 1999). The influence of religion in the lives of youth is only rarely negative (Hunter, 1998), when youth find their way into an unhealthy situation, such as a doomsday cult. For the most part, religion acts as a developmental asset, both in the lives of individual youth (Youniss et al., 1999) and in their communities (Trulear, 2000).

The ministries most successful at recruiting and retaining youth are those that, if they are not run by youths themselves, make religion relevant and personal, give youth some measure of agency and voice in the organization, and stress religious experience over religious ideology (Flory, 2000). Similarly, the most successful ways of understanding religion in the lives of young people allow room for the diversity and individuality of religious expression in the current generation. Scanning the membership rolls of older, institutional religious organizations will tell a different story about modern American youth than asking Jewish adolescents about their youth group trip to Israel, attending a Christian rock concert, or participating in a revival meeting with Latino gang youth in East Los Angeles. Concerned adults who seek to better understand the religious lives of adolescents need to first understand that the relationships of young people with the divine are their own, and as individual as the young people themselves.

Key Readings

Flory, R. W., & Miller, D. E. (Eds.). (2000). *Gen-X religion.* New York: Routledge.
A collection of ethnographic studies of religious contexts on the West Coast of the United States that are created by young people, for young people. Flory describes a grounded theory of Gen-X religion based on the empirical works.

Kirkpatrick, L. A., & Shaver, P. R. (1990). Attachment theory and religion: Childhood attachments, religious beliefs, and conversion. *Journal for the Scientific Study of Religion, 29,* 315–334.
This article broke new ground for the study of religious commitment as an attachment process.

Stark, R., & Bainbridge, W. S. (1996). *Religion, deviance, and social control.* New York: Routledge.
A comprehensive theory of the sociology of religion, applying a rational-choice perspective to the various functions of religion in the lives of individuals.

Trulear, H. D. (2000). *Faith-based institutions and high-risk youth: First report to the field.* Philadelphia, PA: Public/Private Ventures.
Reports findings on a study of the role of inner-city religious organizations in ministering to high-risk youth, including inferences about the role of religion in the lives of youth. Available online, along with similar resources, at www.ppv.org

References

Acock, A. C., & Bengston, V. L. (1978). On the relative influence of mothers and fathers: A covariance analysis of political and religious socialization. *Journal of Marriage and the Family, 40*(3), 519–530.

Berger, P. L. (1967). *The sacred canopy: Elements of a sociological theory of religion.* Garden City, NY: Doubleday.

Bernt, F. M. (1999). Religious commitment, attributional style, and gender as predictors of under-graduate volunteer behavior and attitudes. *Journal of Psychology and Theology, 27*(3), 261–272.

Dudley, R. L. (1999). Youth religious commitment over time: A longitudinal study of retention. *Review of Religious Research, 41*(1), 110–121.

Dudley, R. L., & Laurent, C. R. (1988). Alienation from religion in church-related adolescents. *Sociological Analysis, 49*(4), 408–420.

Dudley, R. L., & Muthersbaugh, H. P. (1996). Social attachment to the Seventh-Day Adventist Church among young adults. *Review of Religious Research, 38*(1), 38–50.

Durkheim, E. (1915). *The elementary forms of the religious life* (trans. Joseph Ward Swain). London: George Allen & Unwin.

Enright, R. D., Santos, M. J., & Al-Mabuk, R. (1989). The adolescent as forgiver. *Journal of Adolescence, 12*(1), 95–110.

Erikson, E. H. (1964). *Insight and responsibility; lectures on the ethical implications of psychoanalytic insight.* New York: Norton.

Erikson, E. H. (1968). *Identity, youth, and crisis.* New York: Norton.

Flory, R. W. (2000). Toward a theory of Generation X religion. In R. W. Flory & D. E. Miller (Eds.), *GenX religion* (pp. 231–250). New York: Routledge.

Flory, R. W., & Miller, D. E. (Eds.). (2000). *Gen-X religion.* New York: Routledge.

Freud, S. (1927). *The future of an illusion* (trans. J. Sterachey, 1961). Garden City, NY: Anchor Books.

Gallup, G. J., & Lindsay, D. M. (1999). *Surveying the religious landscape: Trends in U.S. beliefs.* Harrisburg, PA: Morehouse.

Gamoran, A. (1992). Religious participation and family values among American Jewish youth. *Contemporary Jewry, 13*, 44–59.

Garbarino, J. (1999). *Lost boys: Why our sons turn violent and how we can save them.* New York: Free Press.

Granqvist, P. (1998). Religiousness and perceived childhood attachment: On the question of compensation or correspondence. *Journal for the Scientific Study of Religion, 37*(2), 350–367.

Greeley, A. M. (1978). Religious musical chairs. *Society, 15*(4), 53–59.

Hall, G. S. (1904). *Adolescence, its psychology, and its relations to physiology, anthropology, sociology, sex, crime, religion, and education* (Vol. 2). New York: D. Appleton & Co.

Hernandez, E. I., & Dudley, R. L. (1990). Persistence of religion through primary group ties among Hispanic Seventh-day Adventist young people. *Review of Religious Research, 32*(2), 157–172.

Hoge, D. R., Petrillo, G. H., & Smith, E. I. (1982). Transmission of religious and social values from parents to teenage children. *Journal of Marriage and the Family, 44*(3), 569–580.

Hunter, E. (1998). Adolescent attraction to cults. *Adolescence, 33*(131), 709–714.

Iannaccone, L. R. (1990). Religious practice: A human capital approach. *Journal for the Scientific Study of Religion, 29*(3), 297–314.

Jensen, L. (2000). When two worlds collide: Generation X culture and conservative evangelical-ism. In R. W. Flory & D. E. Miller (Eds.), *GenX religion* (pp. 139–162). New York: Routledge.

Jensen, L., Flory, R. W., & Miller, D. E. (2000). Marked for Jesus: Sacred tattooing among evan-gelical GenXers. In R. W. Flory & D. E. Miller (Eds.), *GenX Religion* (pp. 15–30). New York: Routledge.

Kelley, J., & De Graaf, N. D. (1997). National context, parental socialization, and religious belief: Results from 15 nations. *American Sociological Review, 62* (August), 639–659.

King, V., Elder, G. H. J., & Whitbeck, L. B. (1997). Religious involvement among rural youth: An ecological and life-course perspective. *Journal of Research on Adolescence, 7*(4), 431–456.

Kirkpatrick, L. A. (1998). God as a substitute attachment figure: A longitudinal study of adult attachment style and religious change in college students. *Personality and Social Psychology Bulletin, 24*(9), 1998.

Kirkpatrick, L. A., & Shaver, P. R. (1990). Attachment theory and religion: Childhood attachments, religious beliefs, and conversion. *Journal for the Scientific Study of Religion, 29,* 315–334.

Kox, W., Meeus, W., & 't Hart, H. (1991). Religious conversion of adolescents: Testing the Lofland and Stark model of religious conversion. *Sociological Analysis, 52*(3), 227–240.

Kozol, J. (1995). *Amazing grace: The lives of children and the conscience of a nation.* New York: HarperPerennial.

Nelsen, H. M. (1980). Religious transmission versus religious formation: Preadolescent–parent interaction. *Sociological Quarterly, 21*(2), 207–218.

Prieto, L. (2000). An urban mosaic in Shangri-La. In R. W. Flory & D. E. Miller (Eds.), *GenX religion* (pp. 57–73). New York: Routledge.

Ream, G. L. (2001). The development of intrinsic religious commitment and religious participation in young adulthood, and the religious development of gay, lesbian, and bisexual adolescents. MA thesis, Cornell University, Ithaca.

Richardson, J. T., Stewart, M. W., & Simmonds, R. B. (1978). Conversion to fundamentalism. *Society, 15*(4), 46–52.

Shannon, T. R., Kleniewski, N., & Cross, W. M. (1997). *Urban problems in sociological perspective.* Prospect Heights, IL: Waveland Press.

Sherkat, D. E. (1991). Religious socialization and the family: An examination of religious influence in the family over the life course. Ph.D. dissertation, Duke University, Durham, NC.

Stark, R., & Bainbridge, W. S. (1985). *The future of religion.* Berkeley, CA: University of California Press.

Stark, R., & Bainbridge, W. S. (1987). *A theory of religion.* New York: Peter Lang.

Stark, R., & Bainbridge, W. S. (1996). *Religion, deviance, and social control.* New York: Routledge.

Streib, H. (1999). Off-road religion? A narrative approach to fundamentalist and occult orientations of adolescents. *Journal of Adolescence, 22,* 255–267.

Strommen, M. P. (1979). *Five cries of youth.* San Francisco: Harper & Row.

Thomas, D. L., & Carver, C. (1990). Religion and adolescent social competence. In T. P. Gullotta, G. R. Adams, & R. Montemayor (Eds.), *Developing Social Competency in Adolescence* (Vol. 3, pp. 195–219). Newbury Park, CA: Sage.

Trulear, H. D. (2000). *Faith-based institutions and high-risk youth: First report to the field.* Philadelphia, PA: Public/Private Ventures.

Walsh, A. S. (2000). Slipping into darkness: Popular culture and the creation of a Latino evangelical youth culture. In R. W. Flory & D. E. Miller (Eds.), *GenX religion* (pp. 74–91). New York: Routledge.

Warner, R. S. (1993). Work in progress toward a new paradigm for the sociological study of religion in the United States. *American Journal of Sociology, 98*(5), 1044–1093.

Weber, M. (1922). *The sociology of religion* (trans. Ephraim Fischoff, 1963). Boston: Beacon Press.

Wulff, D. M. (1997). *Psychology of religion: Classic and contemporary views.* New York: Wiley.

Youniss, J., McLellan, J. A., & Yates, M. (1999). Religion, community service, and identity in American youth. *Journal of Adolescence, 22,* 243–253.

Zinnbauer, B. J., & Pargament, K. I. (1998). Spiritual conversion: A study of religious change among college students. *Journal for the Scientific Study of Religion, 37*(1), 161–180.

CHAPTER FOUR

The Family Ecology of Adolescence: A Dynamic Systems Perspective on Normative Development

Isabela Granic, Thomas J. Dishion, and Tom Hollenstein

Introduction

Several scholars have comprehensively reviewed the role of parents in normative adolescent development (e.g., Collins, 1990, 1995; Collins & Laursen, 1992; Hill, 1987; Hill & Holmbeck, 1986; Holmbeck, 1996; Holmbeck, Paikoff, & Brooks-Gunn, 1995; Laursen & Collins, 1994; Laursen, Coy, & Collins, 1998; Paikoff & Brooks-Gunn, 1991; Silverberg, Tennenbaum, & Jacob, 1992; Steinberg, 1990). Our goal in this chapter is to approach this growing literature through the lens of a dynamic systems framework, moving from a person-centered perspective to a focus on relationships, and the community and cultural context in which these relationships are embedded. In the first section, we introduce an ecological framework to serve as a heuristic for organizing the multiple systemic factors that impact on adolescent development. In the second section, we argue that although the ecological framework is critical for demarcating global influences, it falls short of specifying the mechanisms by which they transform family relationships and

This project was supported by a Postdoctoral Fellowship award to the first author, granted by the Social Sciences and Humanities Research Council of Canada, by grant DA 07031 from the National Institute on Drug Abuse at the National Institutes of Health to the second author, by grant MH 46690 from the National Institute of Mental Health to John Reid, Ph.D., and by grant MH 37940 from the National Institute of Mental Health to Deborah Capaldi, Ph.D.
Correspondence regarding this research may be addressed to Isabela Granic, Ph.D., Child and Family Center, 195 West 12th Avenue, Eugene, OR 97401-3408; phone (541) 346-4575, fax (541) 346-4858; email, igranic@darkwing.uoregon.edu

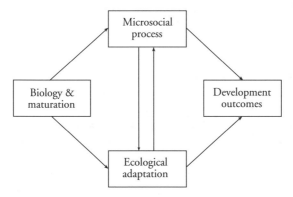

Figure 4.1 An ecological model.

adolescent outcomes. Thus, to identify these underlying mechanisms, we introduce a number of dynamic systems (DS) principles which are particularly relevant for understanding change and stability in developmental trajectories.

Next, we use these DS explanatory tools to understand the intra-individual and interpersonal processes that transform during adolescence. We follow this largely theoretical discussion with some preliminary results from an ongoing longitudinal project with parents and adolescents. Finally, we conclude the chapter by returning to broader ecological considerations, including the interrelations between the family and peer systems and the influence of community and culture on adolescent adjustment.

Ecological Framework

Our first step in discussing normative adolescence and the role of the family is to create an organizing framework for considering the domains of influence and time scales within which adolescent development unfolds. Our model builds on the insightful works of other developmental theorists (Bronfenbrenner, 1989; Hinde, 1989). Figure 4.1 summarizes the ecological framework, consistent with previous work on understanding problematic development in adolescence (Dishion, French, & Patterson, 1995b; Dishion, Poulin, & Medici Skaggs, 2000).

There are four domains that mutually interact to create many of the dynamics we see in adolescence. Biological change is considered the "prime mover" of development. Changes in hormone levels, physical growth, brain development, and concomitant refinements in emotion and cognition initiate transformations in both microsocial processes and social environments. In turn, reciprocal interactions between microsocial processes and ecological adaptations influence long-term developmental outcomes.

For example, parents are often concerned about the social niche in which their children participate. They manage their children's social relationships with an eye toward the future (Parke et al., 1988). They compete for opportunities to have their child on the "best soccer team," enroll them in private schools, and become involved in various organizations, church groups, and so on. These ecological adaptations, in turn, affect the types of microsocial interactions in which children participate.

Moreover, the kinds of ecologies available, and the nature of the constituent interactions, vary from culture to culture. For example, in non-Western cultural contexts, adolescents may spend more time within an extended family network of aunts, uncles, cousins, and grandparents than with their own nuclear family. In contrast, in Western cultures, adolescents often coregulate network connections between peer groups (unrelated to biological families) and some variation of a biological family. Each of these contexts constrain microsocial interactions and have implications for developmental outcomes.

Across many cultures, in terms of family life in particular, a great deal of research suggests that a parenting context characterized by high degrees of warmth and responsiveness on the one hand, and firm behavioral control and maturity demands on the other, is critical for promoting healthy development (e.g., Baumrind, 1991; Steinberg et al., 1995). Responsive parenting during adolescence includes encouragement of independence, negotiation through verbal "give-and-take," and warmth and support. Although proper monitoring is critical for minimizing problem behavior (Baumrind, 1991; Dishion & McMahon, 1998; Patterson, Reid, & Dishion, 1992), under "normal" circumstances, monitoring might better be conceptualized as a bidirectional, cooperative family process (Dishion & McMahon, 1998; Stattin & Kerr, 2000) in which the adolescent has learned what is expected of her and parents generally trust that these expectations will be met. Thus, the family relationship context shapes adolescents' patterns of adaptation and, in turn, these behavioral adaptations influence family relations.

Finally, in figure 4.1, we consider the joint influence of microsocial processes and ecological adaptations as jointly impacting on the long-term outcomes associated with adolescence. The gist of this model is that communities, and the family and peer systems embedded within these communities, self-organize around the changes in childhood and adolescence to assure that socialization does not go astray and that successful outcomes are guaranteed for nearly all members. In the classic cross-cultural study reported by Whiting and Whiting (1975), for example, cooperation with family members (e.g., involvement in family chores) was the key process that contributed to adolescents' prosocial development. In addition, a warm, supportive family context has been found to relate to a host of positive psychosocial outcomes including high self-esteem, self-confidence, and competence in areas of school achievement (e.g., Hill, 1987; Hill & Holmbeck, 1986; Holmbeck et al., 1995; Steinberg, 1990; Steinberg et al., 1995).

Although a large body of research has focused on identifying optimal family contexts, much less is known about the specific mechanisms by which these different levels of the ecological framework influence one another. Can we identify the processes responsible for initiating the various biological, emotional, and cognitive reorganizations occurring at the individual level? And by what process do these intrapersonal factors stabilize and become coordinated with broader ecological contexts, such that pathways of normative socialization proceed relatively undisturbed?

To address these process-level questions, and to better understand the mechanisms underlying both change and stability that characterize this developmental phase, we introduce a number of dynamic systems principles. The application of these principles within a broader ecological framework has provided us with an integrative model that can address intraindividual and interpersonal processes, as well as the diversity and equifinality of adolescent development. Before proceeding with our modeling efforts, we provide a brief overview of the relevant DS principles (more detailed explanations of DS principles can be found in reviews by Thelen & Smith, 1994; Fogel, 1993; Lewis, 2000).

Principles of Dynamic Systems

Overview

Some scholars have suggested that systems approaches to studying development have provided an interesting metaphor, but offer little more (Cox & Paley, 1997; Reis, Collins, & Bersheid, 2000; Vetere & Gale, 1987). Perhaps this has been the state of affairs for general systems theory or, more specifically, family systems theory, but we argue that the application of DS principles to understanding development provides the conceptual toolkit necessary for considering the complexity surrounding normative adolescent development.

In fields as diverse as physics (e.g., Haken, 1977), chemistry (e.g., Prigogine & Stengers, 1984), biology (e.g., Kauffman, 1993; Kelso, 1995), neuroscience (Freeman, 1995) and evolution (e.g., Goerner, 1995), DS principles have proven critical for providing explanations of change and stability. Several developmentalists have begun applying these principles to ontogenesis (e.g., Fogel, 1993; Fogel & Thelen, 1987; Keating, 1990a; Lewis, 1995; Lewis & Granic, 2000; Thelen & Smith, 1994; Thelen & Ulrich, 1991). Social psychologists (Vallacher & Nowak, 1994, 1997) and developmental psychopathologists (Cicchetti & Rogosch, 1997; Lewis & Granic, 1999; Pepler, Craig, & O'Connell, 1999) have also begun to explore their utility. For these theorists, DS principles of feedback, multistability, interdependent time scales and nonlinear change have been particularly useful in extending conventional models of psychological functioning. Strictly speaking, dynamic (or dynamical) systems theory is a technical, mathematical language. Following other developmentalists (e.g., Fogel, 1993; Fogel & Thelen, 1987; Keating, 1990a; Lewis, 1995, 1997; Pepler et al., 1999; Thelen & Smith, 1994; Thelen & Ulrich, 1991), our approach has been to import the DS language as a heuristic tool for explaining the processes that give rise to, and maintain, developmental relationships. Table 4.1 provides a summary of the relevant principles, definitions, and psychosocial illustrations of each principle.

Feedback processes

Dynamic systems self-organize through the interplay of two basic mechanisms: positive and negative feedback. Feedback processes have powerful implications for understanding stability and change in developing systems. *Positive feedback* is the means by which interactions among system elements amplify particular variations, leading to the emergence of novelty. Through *negative feedback*, elements remain linked, deviations are dampened, and stability is realized. Dynamic systems develop and become more complex through the interaction of both feedback processes; positive feedback catalyzes hierarchical reorganization in response to environmental changes and these new organizations are maintained through the self-stabilizing properties of negative feedback (e.g., Prigogine & Stengers, 1984).

Feedback on both real- and developmental-time scales may be the mechanism by which novel parent–adolescent interaction patterns emerge, develop, and stabilize. As discussed earlier, figure 4.1 illustrates the feedback relations between real-time patterns (microsocial processes) and developmental ones (ecological adaptations) that are expected to give rise to particular adolescent outcomes. In terms of feedback on the real-time scale, several socialization theorists have used this principle to describe dyadic processes, such as mother–infant vocalizations, deviancy training, coercion, and bullying relationships (e.g., Dishion et al., 1996; Maccoby & Martin, 1983; Patterson, 1982, 1995; Patterson & Bank, 1989; Pepler et al., 1999; Wilson & Gottman, 1995; see Granic, 2000, for a review). However, the explanatory power of feedback may best be realized when framed within the larger DS metatheoretical package. For instance, although feedback processes have been discussed by several theorists interested in the family, most have focused exclusively on the self-stabilizing mechanism of negative feedback (e.g., Bell's control model, Bell, 1968; Bell & Chapman, 1986; and systems theorists' cybernetic models, Minuchin, 1974; Robin & Foster, 1989).

Positive feedback, however, may be the mechanism by which new variations in the parent–adolescent relationship (e.g., new interpersonal goals, growing cognitive abilities) become amplified and result in new styles of relating (e.g., more egalitarian, cooperative relationships). We discuss these processes in detail later, but for now, consider the example of a parent relinquishing control and allowing her adolescent to take responsibility for a particular family decision. If the adolescent is perceived to have successfully negotiated this opportunity, the parent may be more likely in the future to ask the adolescent for help and, in turn, the adolescent may feel more competent to rise to the challenge. Thus, one critically timed event may become amplified through positive feedback processes resulting in a qualitative shift toward a more egalitarian parent–adolescent relationship. As shown in table 4.1, this is an example of positive feedback on a developmental scale.

Ex Positive

Multistability

Through feedback among lower-order (more basic) system elements, stable patterns of interactions emerge; they are referred to as *attractors* in DS terminology. Novel attractors emerge through positive feedback and they stabilize and are maintained by negative feedback. Attractors may be understood as absorbing states that "pull" the system from other potential states. Behavior moves toward these attractors in real time. Over developmental time, attractors represent recurrent patterns that stabilize and become increasingly predictable. As noted by Thelen and Smith (1994), all developmental acquisitions can be described as attractor patterns that emerge over weeks, months, or years.

As recurring stable forms, attractors can be depicted topographically as valleys on a dynamic landscape. The deeper the attractor, the more likely it is that behavior falls into it and remains there, and the more resistant it is to small changes in the environment. As the system develops, a unique *state space*, defined as a model of all possible states a system can attain, is configured by several attractors. Living systems are characterized by *multistability* (Kelso, 1995); that is, their state space (i.e., behavioral repertoire) includes several coexisting attractors.

Recurrent patterns of parent–adolescent can be conceptualized as dyadic attractors on a state space that represents the range of dyadic interactions that are possible. At any one time, a number of attractors on this state space may be available to a dyad; contextual constraints probabilistically determine the attractor toward which a dyad will move (Fogel, 1993; Fogel & Thelen, 1987). The concept of multistability suggests that all parent–adolescent dyads are characterized by a landscape of diverse attractors (e.g., playful, coercive, neutral) and that these attractors are related to one another. Thus, the emphasis moves from the more conventional, trait-focused approach of observing either negative or positive interactions exclusively to the recognition that a variety of interaction patterns characterize any one dyad. From this alternative perspective, not only can we ask what the attractors are in a particular parent–adolescent dyad's repertoire, but also, under what specific conditions does this system move from one type of attractor (e.g., cooperative) to another (e.g., conflictual). These ideas will become clearer when we look at potential candidates for dyadic attractors in the next section.

Interdependent time scales

The third DS premise we highlight is the interplay between different time scales. Self-organization at the moment-to-moment (real-time) scale constrains self-organization at the developmental scale which, in turn, constrains real-time behavior (van Gelder & Port, 1995). The notion of interdependent time scales suggests that developmental parent–child patterns arise from real-time interactions that recur and stabilize. As these patterns recur, they produce deeper attractors on a dyadic state space. Consequently, based on prior experience, the likelihood of a parent and child interacting in one of a limited number of ways is increasingly predetermined. Generally, this stability is maintained until the system undergoes a phase transition.

Phase transitions

The final, and most critical, principle of dynamic systems for our current purposes is their tendency to exhibit discontinuous or nonlinear change. Through the amplification properties of positive feedback, fluctuations in the organizational structure of a dynamic system can be observed. These fluctuations have the potential to resolve into abrupt changes, or *phase transitions*, and they occur at *points of bifurcation*, or junctures in the system's development.

At these thresholds, small variations have the potential to disproportionately affect the status of feedback among system elements, leading to the emergence of new forms. Novelty does not have to originate from outside the system; it can emerge spontaneously through feedback within the system. At bifurcation points, systems are extremely sensitive, adapting rapidly to both internal and environmental perturbations. Between these points, however, dynamic systems tend toward coherence and stability (Prigogine & Stengers, 1984). The family system may cross several bifurcation points along its developmental trajectory and early adolescence may be one of its most dramatic (Granic, 2000).

Modeling adolescence as an instantiation of a phase transition has particularly compelling implications. Phase transitions are characterized by a dramatic increase in variability and flux; adolescence is second only to infancy in terms of the massive reorganization that occurs in multiple domains. In the sections that follow, we specify the various intra- and interindividual processes that transform radically at this bifurcation point and speculate about the implications for the family system.

Applying DS Principles to Intraindividual and Interpersonal Processes

Like other systems theorists, we contend that the family system, itself comprising several dyadic systems (e.g., father–daughter, mother–son, father–mother), represents a fundamental unit of analysis. In order to understand these relationships, we may first need to examine the intraindividual (emotional and cognitive) systems that underlie them. Past research has uncovered several intraindividual processes (e.g., cognitive maturation, puberty), interindividual processes (e.g., emotional closeness, communication patterns) and a number of contextual factors (e.g., socioeconomic status, ethnicity) that seem essential for understanding the parent–adolescent relationship. But these insights have remained largely unintegrated; a coherent model that can explicate the connections among these various findings is needed.

Intraindividual processes

Cognitive development in early adolescence can be characterized as a discontinuous reorganization toward a higher level of complexity – a phase transition with profound implications for the parent–adolescent relationship. Although a detailed discussion of these cognitive changes is beyond the scope of this chapter (for reviews, see chapter 11 in this volume; Graber & Petersen, 1991; Keating, 1990b), several key points should be highlighted. Early adolescence marks the onset of formal operational thinking (e.g., Inhelder & Piaget, 1958). In contrast to earlier stages of development, the adolescent acquires the capacity to think abstractly – she or he is able to plan step-by-step activities toward a future goal, hold in mind and manipulate abstract concepts, and develop and test personal theories about the world around him or her.

One result of developing increasingly abstract thinking skills is that the adolescent becomes preoccupied with understanding the self in relation to others. She begins to reflect on the multifaceted components of her personality. She is able to see herself as charming and low-key with her father, angry and rebellious with her mother, vivacious and fun-loving with her friends, and sometimes sullen and depressed by herself. All these aspects of personality begin to be understood as parts of one integrated self – it is as if the adolescent recognizes for the first time the multistable nature of his or her state space (table 4.1). Parental figures also become de-idealized and multifaceted during this time (e.g., Steinberg, 1990). The adolescent discovers that her parents can often be wrong in their opinions, that their views can be inconsistent, and that they often endorse beliefs and values that are contrary to other parents' views.

These shifts in thinking styles must be intricately linked to emotional processes; a large body of evidence has accrued showing that emotion and cognition are inseparable across the lifespan (e.g., Lewis, 1995; Siegel, 1999; Sroufe, 1995). Neuroscientific evidence has emerged that suggests that the brain undergoes massive reorganizations during adolescence, particularly in the prefrontal cortex and limbic regions (for a review, see Spear, 2000). Spear's and others' work suggests that the adolescent's brain seems to function more "emotionally" during this transitional phase. The regulation and resolution of emotional experiences seem to be central tasks of adolescence and yet these processes have rarely been examined on a fine-grained level. This is surprising, given the central role that emotions have been given in human development in general and parent–child relationships in particular (for a review, see Granic, 2000; Maccoby & Martin, 1983; Schore, 1994). To begin speculating along these lines, we borrow a number of insights from the emotional development camp.

Emotional development theorists have suggested that emotions and cognitive appraisals are the basic psychological elements that interact to form global personality structures (e.g., Izard, 1977; Lewis, 1995; Tomkins, 1987, 1991; Magai & McFadden, 1995; Malatesta & Wilson, 1988). Emotions are elicited from cognitive evaluations of events *relative to an individual's personal goals* (Frijda, 1986; Lazarus, 1982, 1984). Conversely, and bidirectionally, emotions focus an individual's attention on certain aspects of a situation, prompting changes in action readiness (Frijda, 1986). Thus, anger is elicited when a goal is perceived to be intentionally blocked and appraisals of blame are elicited, sadness emerges when a blocked goal is appraised as insurmountable, shame is elicited when the goal of being admired is thwarted and appraisals of worthlessness are triggered, and so on. Over developmental time, recurrent emotion–cognition amalgams sensitize the individual to particular ways of processing information and engaging with the world (Izard, 1977; Lewis, 1995; Malatesta & Wilson, 1988).

Bidirectional influences between cognitive processes and emotion have been conceptualized as a feedback loop (e.g., Lewis, 1995, 1997; Teasdale, 1983; Teasdale & Barnard, 1993). Lewis's model (1995, 1997), based on DS principles, is particularly relevant. He posits that positive feedback between emotion and cognition is the basis for self-organizing personality development. Appraisals are conceptualized as emerging in coordination with emotions, each amplifying the other in real time (figure 4.2).

According to this view, from moment to moment, emotion focuses an individual's attention on particular goal-relevant elements in a situation. An appraisal forms, further generating emotion, which is in turn fed back into the system through repeated iterations. Stable personality structures, conceptualized as attractors, develop as recurring personal goals are blocked or partially blocked, and specific appraisals and emotions arise and persist over similarly frustrated occasions (Lewis, 1995, in press).

Table 4.1 Definitions and Examples of Dynamic Systems Principles

Dynamic system (DS) principles	Definition	Psychosocial examples
Feedback processes		
Positive feedback	Self-amplifying mechanism in which two or more processes influence each other, giving rise to novel patterns	(1) Real time: while talking with a peer, an aggressive adolescent introduces an antisocial topic (e.g., lying to parents), peer laughs, the aggressive youth joins in the laughter and brings up increasingly more antisocial topics (stealing, drugs), and the conversation culminates in an excited plan to rob a store (2) Developmental time: parent allows adolescent to have a party with no supervision, adolescent acts responsibly (makes sure no one drives drunk, cleans the house afterwards), parent is reassured of adolescent's competence, adolescent is given increasingly more freedom, adolescent responds with increasing responsibility, and a more egalitarian relationship arises
Negative feedback	Self-stabilizing mechanism in which two or more processes influence each other by minimizing or dampening variations	(1) Real time: Bell (1968) control model; parent and child have upper and lower limits of tolerance for the intensity, frequency, and acceptability of specific behaviors; when the upper limit of one member of the dyad is approached by the other, the former attempts to change or redirect the other's intolerable behavior; when the lower limit is reached, attempts to stimulate the other are initiated so as to maintain a state of equilibrium (2) Developmental time: a parent starts with a lax limit-setting strategy with no curfew, the adolescent comes home later than she promises, the parent responds by stricter limits with an early curfew, the adolescent begins to come home on time and to act more responsibly by calling when late, the parent responds by loosening the rules, the adolescent comes home on time generally, but when she is late, the parent again responds by setting a stricter curfew

Multistability	Characteristic of all living systems; property describing a system with several coexisting stable states	(1) Intraindividual: an adolescent girl may wake up one day feeling vivacious and fun-loving, by lunchtime, she may be in a lonely and sullen attractor and she may go to bed that night in an angry, rebellious attractor; each of these states are personality configurations that make up this girl's intraindividual state space
Attractor	An absorbing state that a system is drawn toward, predictably from a range of nearby states	(2) Interindividual: a parent and adolescent may be in a cooperative and loving dyadic attractor when cooking together, they may move to an angry and coercive attractor when discussing curfew, and a neutral dyadic state when watching television together; all of these interaction styles are part of this dyad's behavioral repertoire, or dyadic state space
State space	A model of all possible states a system can attain; the repertoire of available states for a given system	
Interdependent time scales	Real-time (moment-to-moment) interactions among system elements lay down developmental patterns which, in turn, constrain the nature of the real-time activities of system elements	On a real-time scale, a parent demands that her adolescent boy help with the dishes, the boy refuses, she insists, he threatens to run away, she withdraws her demands, he stays home; over many similarly repeated occasions, coercive dyadic habits stabilize in development, increasing the likelihood that the boy will refuse and the mother will acquiesce; this dyad will also be increasingly less likely to engage in cooperative exchanges
Phase transition	A nonlinear, discontinuous change in the organizational structure of a system; characterized by a temporary increase in variability in real- and developmental time	(1) Real time: family interactions in early adolescence may be characterized by many different mood states and rapid moment-to-moment transitions between one emotional state and another (2) Developmental time: early adolescence is marked by major reorganizations in multiple domains (biological, cognitive, social); this transition period is sandwiched between stable periods during which development proceeds relatively unperturbed

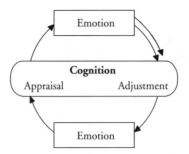

Figure 4.2   Positive feedback in cognition–emotion (adapted from Lewis, 1995).

Critical for our modeling purposes is the idea that feedback between emotion and cognition is always in relation to a goal. What sorts of goals might be relevant for the early adolescent? A number of theorists have suggested at least two macro-goals: identity formation (e.g., Erikson, 1968; Kroger, this volume) and autonomy from parents (Collins et al., 1997; chapter 9 in this volume). Subsumed under these broad developmental goals might be more immediate subgoals, including the need to be accepted and admired by the peer group, the need to participate in romantic relationships, and the desire to be recognized and respected by parents and other authority figures.

We propose that many of the adolescent's most important micro- and macro-goals are *interpersonal* in nature (e.g., to be trusted by parents, to be accepted by peers). The day-to-day pursuit of these goals fashions unique affective–cognitive structures which go on to constrain developmental patterns as personality consolidates. To clarify this argument further, we need to move to a discussion of interpersonal processes.

Interpersonal processes

Development does not proceed in a vacuum. Quite the contrary, development is fundamentally a relational process (e.g., Fogel, 1993; Fogel & Thelen, 1987; Granic, 2000; Laible & Thompson, 2000; Patterson & Reid, 1984; Schore, 1994). To understand adolescent development in the context of the family, we extend Lewis's individual personality model (1995, 1997) and argue that the separate affective–cognitive structures of the parent and the adolescent are the interacting subsystems that self-organize in dyadic interactions.

Through repeated feedback cycles, particular parent and adolescent affective–cognitive couplings may reciprocally select one another and become further coupled into a qualitatively more complex dyadic configuration (figure 4.3). Over time, the parent–child dyad develops a repertoire of various relational states, each accessible in certain contexts and not in others. A unique parent–adolescent state space may be one way to represent the range of possible interaction patterns toward which dyadic self-organization can evolve in real time (see table 4.1 for review). It can also inform us of the developmental history of that parent–adolescent system.

dyad = couple

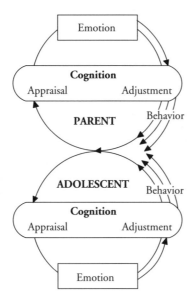

Figure 4.3   Parent–adolescent interacting feedback loops (adapted from Lewis, 1995).

Research on cognitive–emotional processes in parenting is one way to ground the notion of intercoupled parent and adolescent attractors and frame dyadic self-organization in terms of goal-relevant behaviors. Prior to adolescence, socialization in childhood often involves the clash of incompatible goals (Grusec, Rudy, & Martini, 1997) and invariably these processes are emotional (Dix, 1991): Parents want children to get enough sleep or to clean up their room, which may be incompatible with children's wishes to stay up late or watch television. The specific emotions involved in these conflict episodes may depend, in part, on the parent's short- and long-term goals (Kuczynski, 1984), the parent's appraisals of why the child is compliant or not, and the degree to which she controls these outcomes (e.g., Abramson, Seligman, & Teasdale, 1978; Dix, 1991; Hastings & Grusec, 1997, 1998; Weiner, 1979).

The direction of influence may be extended to the child or adolescent, as well. The extent to which a teen is angry at her mother for not letting her stay out late may depend on appraisals of why the parent is being so rigid and the degree to which the youth feels she has control over the situation. For each partner, the perception of the other's goal-facilitating or blocking behaviors may promote coupling between his or her emergent attractors.

There is some empirical support for this dyadic attractor model. Parpal and Maccoby (1985) have shown that children comply more with parental commands if the parent previously complied with the child's directives. This work suggests reciprocal coupling of cognitive–affective structures. In terms of adolescent issues, it may be that teenagers who perceive their parents as furthering their goals (e.g., letting them drive the car) feel positive emotions which feed back with appraisals of the parent as a cooperative and supportive partner. This affectionate–supportive attractor may be expressed behaviorally by complying with the parent's next demand (e.g., to bring the car back at a specific time).

The teen's responsible behavior, in turn, may trigger goal-facilitating appraisals and positive emotions in the parent. This parent–adolescent pattern may stabilize over development, providing the context in which mutual socialization goals may be realized.

Alternatively, Patterson, Reid, & Dishion (1992) have found a different interactional pattern characterizing clinically referred families. Their research shows that an aggressive child experiences an aversive intrusion from a family member at least once every minute (Patterson, 1982, 1995). In response, the child tends to be noncompliant and counterattacks by arguing and whining. After years of similarly repeated disciplinary attempts, a mother may develop an affective–cognitive structure, characterized by anger and appraisals of her child as obstinate and inherently "bad" (Granic, 2000). Simultaneously, the child may develop his own compatible cognitive–emotional configuration, constituted by anger and attributions of his mother as hostile and unfair (MacKinnon-Lewis et al., 1992). Through repeated interactions, their two attractors may become linked in a feedback loop such that the mother's attractor and the behavior with which it is expressed "pulls for" her son's angry attractor and the behaviors to which it is linked. Each member's behavior amplifies the other's anger and accompanying appraisals, coalescing into a hostile dyadic attractor.

Most importantly, based on the DS principle of multistability, both supportive/cooperative and coercive attractors may coexist as potential parent–adolescent states. At any one time, the likelihood of arriving at one attractor versus another depends on contextual constraints. The specific contextual factors that will "push" a dyad toward one versus another attractor depends entirely on the developmental history of that family system.

A DS Model of Conflict in Parent–Adolescent Relationships

Summary of past research

The majority of research on family relationships in adolescence has focused on the content and frequency of conflict. Before articulating our DS model of conflict in parent–adolescent relationships, we provide a brief review of these past findings. The history of the conflict literature represents an extreme pendulum swing with contemporary views having come to rest in the middle. At one end are the early psychoanalytic theorists (e.g., Blos, 1962, 1979; Freud, 1937, 1958), who argued that adolescence was a time of turbulence, during which conflict and antisocial behavior were not only normative, but necessary for healthy development to proceed. Among other reasons, the psychoanalytic approach was criticized for having been developed largely on the basis of clinical samples; subsequent research began to focus on more representative, non-clinical samples (Smetana, 1996).

This next body of work directly contradicted the stormy characterization of the adolescent–parent relationship (for recent reviews, see Baumrind, 1991; Collins, 1990, 1995; Holmbeck, 1996; Laursen & Collins, 1994; Laursen et al., 1998; Montemayor, 1986; Smetana, 1996; Steinberg, 1990). Evidence from a series of classic studies (e.g., Kandel & Lesser, 1972; Offer, 1969; Rutter et al., 1976), seemed to indicate that adolescence was largely conflict-free and painless. Only a very small proportion of adolescents in

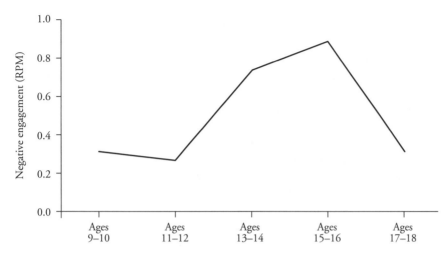

Figure 4.4   Observed rate-per-minute of negative engagement between mother and son across five waves of data collection.

the general population (5–20 percent) were found to experience significant conflict with their parents. Those adolescents who did show extreme levels of conflict in the family were already experiencing relationship difficulties during earlier stages of development (Collins, 1990; Hill, 1987; Montemayor, 1983; Rutter et al., 1976; Steinberg, 1990).

This optimistic view of adolescent–parent conflict also came under attack. A number of researchers (Smetana, 1996; Silverberg et al., 1992; Steinberg, 1987) argued that these studies relied too heavily on global assessments of family functioning that was summarized from questionnaires and interviews. No observations of actual family conflicts were made, nor were reports of daily hassles and arguments collected (Smetana, 1996).

Since the mid-1980s, these criticisms have been largely addressed and contemporary views of the parent–adolescent relationship now fall between the two extreme views (Baumrind, 1991; Smetana, 1996). Recent research has shown that most parents and adolescents maintain a close, affectionate bond during adolescence (e.g., Baumrind, 1991; Hill & Holmbeck, 1986). On the other hand, they share less time together (Csikszentmihalyi & Larson, 1984; Montemayor, 1982) and conflicts do seem to increase in early adolescence, gradually abating over the years (see Laursen et al., 1998, for a meta-analysis; Montemayor, 1983).

In our longitudinal project with the Oregon Youth Study (OYS) boys, we asked the boy and his parent(s) to discuss actual family problems every other year from age 10 through 18 (Forgatch, 1984; Forgatch, Fetrow, & Lathrop, 1985). We coded the 30 minutes of videotape with the Family Process Code (FPC; Dishion et al., 1983), and derived several clusters, including a negative engagement cluster, which primarily defined the family's level of conflict. The rate-per-minute of negative engagement is summarized in figure 4.4 and shows a marked increase in observed mother–son conflict beginning in early adolescence (13–14 years old) and declining after age 16.

An increase in parent–adolescent conflict seemed to be ubiquitous across the sample and did not appear indicative of any particular pathology. We suggest that this increase in family conflict around puberty (for boys) is developmentally functional in that it provides the context in which issues of autonomy are negotiated. Striving for autonomy is a key developmental task in adolescence (chapter 9 in this volume, 1990; Collins et al., 1997; Hill & Holmbeck, 1986), but it is important to note that autonomy need not, and most often does not, entail a divorce from parental ties. Most adolescents stay connected to the family and recent research has shown that close family relations, or secure attachments, facilitate independence during this transitional phase (Hill & Holmbeck, 1987; Larson et al., 1996). Adolescent maturity is thought to grow from "the balance between agency and communion, between separation and connectedness, and between conflict and harmony" (Baumrind, 1991, p. 120).

This more complex, dynamic view of parent–adolescent relationships seems to call for research that goes beyond examining the frequency and content of conflicts. Parents indeed argue more with their adolescent, but they also stay involved and loving. It is apparent from watching the videotapes gathered in our research that in middle childhood, parents dominated the problem-solving discussion at all levels, from problem definition, to problem solution. In contrast, during adolescence, parents responded to the expanding cognitive and emotion regulations skills of the adolescent by beginning to negotiate and integrate the adolescent's views and emotional reactions.

What are the specific mechanisms that trigger these types of changes in family interaction patterns? The DS concept of phase transitions is particularly appropriate for addressing this question.

Adolescence as a phase transition

Over the course of childhood, the parent and child develop characteristic ways of interacting with the other – individual personality configurations become more and more entrenched over occasions and, in parallel, dyadic attractors increasingly deepen and become stronger. The developmental result is a highly articulated parent–child state space that has been configured from similarly recurring family interactions, but the transition from childhood to adolescence represents an important perturbation to the family system.

Early adolescence can be viewed as a phase transition – a discontinuous shift – in the parent–child system. The characterization of the transition to adolescence as discontinuous is consistent with psychoanalytic (e.g., Blos, 1962, 1979; Freud, 1937, 1958), sociobiological (Steinberg, 1989, 1990), and cognitive-developmental models (Selman, 1981; Smetana, 1988; Youniss, 1980; for a review and an alternative perspective, see Laursen & Collins, 1994). According to DS principles, when the parent–child system reaches this bifurcation point, there is a temporary increase in the potential for new dyadic attractors to arise.

The specific types of novel interaction patterns that self-organize through this phase shift will depend partially on previously established structures – the history of that parent–adolescent relationship. But the relational system is also highly sensitive to fluctuations at this threshold of instability. The increase in degrees of freedom may mean that minor incidents (e.g., the parent allows her adolescent to make a small family decision, the youth begins to drive a car) can result in a cascade toward a major change in the parent–adolescent system.

Particularly during this early adolescent phase transition, conflict episodes may represent a rich microcosm through which novel parent–adolescent attractors emerge and stabilize. Whereas the power differential in childhood ensured that parental goals held most of the weight, this assumption becomes less clear as the adolescent grows older and vies for power and for legitimizing his or her own personal goals. Thus, there are far more opportunities for the parent to act as a goal-blocking agent for the adolescent.

A great deal of empirical and theoretical work supports the idea that early adolescence begins a period of shifting power dynamics, which may give rise to competing goals and result in a higher density of conflict episodes. Smetana (e.g., 1988, 1989, 1991) has shown that, as a result of domain-specific cognitive maturation, the issues adolescents previously perceived to be under parental jurisdiction become re-evaluated as personal decisions. Selman (1981) and Youniss (1980), arguing from a more global cognitive development perspective, have suggested that adolescents begin to re-evaluate the hierarchy of family roles and to work toward more egalitarian relationships. Parents, however, often do not share this goal and are reluctant to relinquish their position of authority. Pubertal development (Hill et al., 1985; Steinberg, 1987, 1988), increased time outside the home with peers (Hill, 1987), and observations of how other parents behave are also triggers that may give rise to beliefs and goals that are incompatible with those of parents.

Collins's (1990, 1992, 1995, 1997; Collins & Laursen, 1999) study of discrepant expectancies in parent–adolescent relationships is most relevant to this discussion. He has argued that the rapid nature of changes in multiple domains associated with the transition to adolescence initiates discrepancies in parents' and adolescents' expectations for one another. When interactional sequences are interrupted by behaviors that violate expectancies "conflict and emotional arousal occur" (Collins, 1992, p. 179). Collins's research has shown that discrepancies in expectations are greatest during early adolescence, compared with pre- and late adolescence (e.g., Collins, 1990, 1992, 1995; Collins & Laursen, 1999).

From a DS perspective, early adolescence constitutes a bifurcation point characterized by disequilibrium, which is in large part driven by changing and conflicting goals and the emotions they elicit. These changes provide numerous goal-blocking opportunities which, in turn, provoke conflict. In some cases, these conflict episodes may drive family members to reassess and "realign" their beliefs and goals to match the maturing needs of the adolescent (Collins, 1992). Particularly resonant with the DS approach, Collins refers to this transitional phase as a time for the "reestablishment of equilibrium" (p. 179). Upon passing through this phase transition, a new landscape of relational possibilities may stabilize for the family system.

A clear link exists between Collins's notion of expectations and our emphasis on goals. In some of Collins's work (e.g., 1992), he explicitly defines socialization goals as one type of expectancy. Although his notion of expectancies in family relationships has been central in our thinking, we prefer the concept of goals for the following reasons. First, as described earlier, the notion that cognitive–emotional processes function in the service of goals is a general principle that has been well-established in the emotional development literature. Second, expectancies can be considered "passive" or "active." One can expect the sun to rise every day, but that may not impact on behavior in any meaningful way. Active expectancies may be better conceptualized as goals – they direct behavior. Third, Collins's assertion that when expectancies are violated, conflict and emotional arousal are triggered seems too general to us. It is only when expectancies are higher or more positive than actual behavior that conflict has a chance to occur. For example, based on his own adolescence, a parent may expect his son to stay out past curfew and get caught drunk a few times during his teenage years, but his son may not be predisposed to act out in this way. In this case, a violation of expectancies may induce feelings of pride or perhaps even concern, but these emotions would not necessarily lead to conflict.

Thus, while maintaining the main gist of Collins's framework, we suggest that goals may provide a more specific term that helps us to model the cognitive–emotional organizations underlying parent–adolescent conflicts. Further, we propose that DS principles provide the mechanisms by which discrepant goals give rise to conflict. Specifically, at points of bifurcation, conflict episodes may trigger new emotion–cognition configurations for each dyad member which, through the amplification properties of positive feedback, may underpin the emergence of new parent–adolescent patterns.

As mentioned previously, a great deal of research has focused on the degree to which these parent–adolescent relationships are conflictual. With a DS approach, we can move this question forward considerably. For example, we can ask *process-level* questions regarding the temporal unfolding of these episodes: Under what conditions do some dyads "fall into" a hostile attractor versus other available attractors? How long do they remain there and how easily can they move out of the hostile attractor to a more amiable, cooperative one?

We can also inquire about the developmental course and *function* of these interaction patterns: By what processes does conflict trigger the reorganization of previously stable patterns of relating, and when do these new patterns become crystallized? Does a dyadic state space with many available attractors imply a more "adaptive" relationship, versus one that is more "rigid" and configured by only a few attractors? Finally, we can examine changes in the *organizational structure* of parent–adolescent interactions: What does a developmental transition look like in terms of parent–adolescent interactions, and how can we characterize the restabilization of family relationships? In other words, how do the family relationships of young adolescents reorganize in such a way as to accommodate more negativity and conflict while remaining warm and secure? We have recently become particularly interested in addressing this last set of questions.

Our aim was to extend past research on the content and frequency of conflict during this transitional phase by studying changes in the *organizational structure* of family interactions. According to our DS-inspired model (Granic, 2000), over the course of childhood, the parent and child develop characteristic ways of interacting with the other. The result is a highly predictable parent–child system which has been configured from many similarly repeated family interactions. For some families, these stable patterns may be characterized generally as supportive and warm. For other families, coercive (Patterson, 1982) patterns may have stabilized over time, and for still others, withdrawn and sad dyadic interaction styles may have emerged. Regardless of their content, however, at the onset of the phase transition – as underlying reorganizations in multiple domains are occurring – the family behavioral system undergoes a period of reorganization as well.

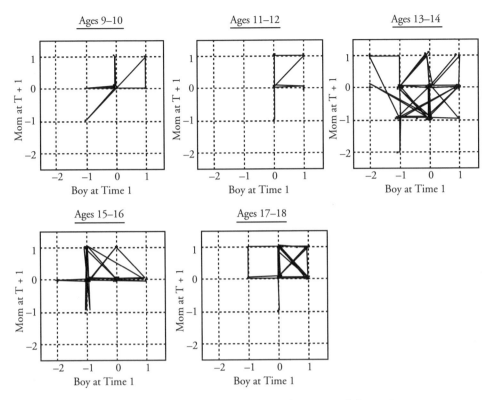

Figure 4.5 State space grids for one OYS family, across five waves of observation.

This period should be characterized by an increase in the variability of dyadic patterns: behavioral states should change frequently from one type to another (e.g., from playful to hostile interactions, from teasing to withdrawn behaviors). After the phase transition, the parent–adolescent system should return to a more stable, less flexible behavioral landscape.

As a preliminary step toward tracking these changes, we used a variation of Lewis and colleagues' (1999) state space grid method. Inspired by a DS framework, this method offers an intuitively appealing way to view the unfolding of complex, interactional behavior by displaying how behavior clusters in certain regions of a state space and changes over time. For this study, state space grids were particularly useful for depicting the relative stability and flexibility of dyads' behavioral repertoires.

The study, based on a subsample of OYS boys, involved 61 dyads who engaged in problem-solving discussions. Each conversational turn was coded with the FPC, which were subsequently collapsed into a 4-point scale (−2 = hostile, −1 = negative, 0 = neutral, and +1 = positive). Figure 4.5 shows the state space grids for one dyad's problem-solving sessions over five waves of data collection (every other year from ages 10 to 18). The x-axis of the grids represents the child's behavior at lag 0 and the y-axis represents the parent's behavior that followed (lag 1). The numbers on the axes represent the coding

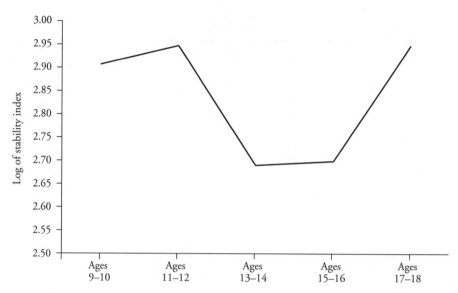

Figure 4.6   Logged "stability index" for the full sample across five waves of data collection.

categories. Each point on the grid represents two conversational turns (a dyadic state) and the line represents the behavioral trajectory across time. For our current purposes, it is particularly important to note the dispersion of behavior across the cells of the state space grid.

Figure 4.5 illustrates a sequence of grids for one dyad; a pattern characteristic for many of the families in the sample. The grids showed that dyadic behavior during early adolescence (ages 13–14 for boys) looked more flexible (less stable) than either the period before or after. In the first two waves, the dyad in figure 4.5 "visited" relatively few cells; they remained generally in the mutually neutral regions, with a few forays into the mutually positive region and one or two negative turns. In contrast, during the third wave, dyadic behavior became much more variable; almost every region of the state space was visited at least once. After this transitional phase, the grids for the next two waves indicated a restabilization or, in Collins's terms, a "reestablishment of equilibrium." Thus, inspection of the grids provided preliminary support for our hypothesis that early adolescence represents a phase transition marked by increased variability in dyadic behavior.

To begin quantifying the impressions gathered from the grids, we calculated a "stability index" for each dyad at each wave. We simply counted the number of conversational turns and divided by the number of cells visited: The higher the number, the more stable (i.e., the less variable) the behavioral pattern on the state space grid. Figure 4.6 illustrates the logged results for the sample as a whole. As expected, a quadratic pattern was revealed, indicating that dyadic behavior became considerably less stable (more variable) at ages 13–14.

Although we are only at the preliminary stages of our analyses, and we are still in the process of developing more sophisticated analytic strategies, we are encouraged by the results yielded by this new DS methodology. In future research, we plan on further examining the organizational structure, in conjunction with the content, of these patterns to examine more closely the process by which early adolescence ushers in a period of disequilibrium.

Mutual Constraints Among Hierarchical Levels and Relationship Systems

Constraints between intra- and interindividual processes

The systemic concept of hierarchical integration is critical for understanding adolescent development in the context of the family. We have considered how intraindividual attractors seem to couple to form particular dyadic attractors, but it is important to note that these dyadic patterns constrain the very individual structures by which they are constituted. This means that as the adolescent develops, his or her unique personality state space is partially configured by the dyadic attractors in which he or she participates.

Consider, for example, Steinberg's (1988) evidence that shows that emotional distance and conflict in the mother–daughter relationship accelerates pubertal maturation, while a close relationship postpones such development. From a DS perspective, this seems to be a compelling instance in which dyadic attractors (i.e., conflictual patterns) constrain the features of intraindividual biological processes (i.e., onset of puberty). Particular patterns of family relations have also been shown to influence adolescent ego development and to foster advanced levels of identity exploration (e.g., Brooks-Gunn, Graber, & Paikoff, 1994; Steinberg, 1990).

Similarly, peer relations may also influence intraindividual processes in profound ways. One example may be seen with antisocial adolescents and their peer systems. In distressed families, antisocial boys are likely to seek the company of peers, specifically antisocial peers, at earlier ages (see chapter 22 in this volume; Dishion et al., 1995b, 1996, 1997; Patterson et al., 1992). Compared with their normative counterparts, antisocial boys tend to have a series of short-term friendships with like-minded antisocial peers. How might these relationships influence adolescents' intraindividual development?

According to Piaget (1965), one of the main functions of peer interactions in adolescence is to induce conflict which, in turn, is thought to trigger intraindividual cognitive disequilibrium. This internal cognitive conflict leads to the eventual development of more sophisticated thinking skills. But because antisocial boys are likely to terminate their friendships immediately after conflicts arise, many of them may never reach this state of cognitive disequilibrium. In fact, programmatic studies of friendship interactions have established that antisocial boys spend a great deal of their time engaging in deviant talk organized through positive affective exchanges (Dishion et al., 1995a, 1996, 1997). We argue that, far from inducing conflict, these interactions serve to reinforce antisocial beliefs and attitudes among like-minded adolescents. As a result, the serial "hopping" from one antisocial friend to another may impinge upon, or retard, conceptual sophistication by failing to induce conflicts that members feel obliged to resolve amiably and productively.

Constraints between parental and peer relationships

Not only do hierarchically embedded system levels exert mutual influences over one another, but relationship contexts are also mutually embedded and reciprocally influential (Bronfenbrenner, 1989; Hinde, 1989). Particularly relevant during the adolescent phase transition are the bidirectional constraints between family and peer systems. For example, for attachment theorists, the adolescent is considered to have developed an internal working model (a representational template of the primary relationship) that forms the basis for the types of interactional/ relationship patterns that are developed with other partners (Allan & Land, 1999; Hartup & Laursen, 1999; Reis, Collins, & Bersheid, 2000). The securely attached child who learned to trust his environment and rely on support from the caregiver during times of stress is expected to develop relationships with peers that are similarly characterized by trust and support (e.g., Allan et al., 1998; Allan & Land, 1999; Zimmermann, Scheuerer-Englisch, & Grossmann, 1996).

Feedback processes over developmental time between the family and peer systems may not only reinforce old relational styles like the example given above, they also may catalyze major changes in one or both relational systems. For instance, early pubertal development is associated with increased parent–adolescent conflict, particularly for girls (Steinberg, 1988). Increased conflict in the home may prompt early maturing daughters to spend more time away from the home with peers. These girls are most likely to belong to a peer group that includes older boys (Magnusson, Stattin, & Allen, 1985). This increasing attention from males may prompt girls to dress more maturely and become sexually active at a younger age (Dishion et al., 2000). In turn, parent–adolescent conflict may become amplified as the parent becomes increasingly concerned about her daughter's well-being and the adolescent feels she is unable to express her individuality. Over these developmental feedback cycles, mother and daughter may become increasingly angry and resentful toward one another, each perceiving the other as impinging on critical interpersonal goals. Thus, through developmental feedback processes, relationships with family and peers reciprocally shape one another.

Ecological considerations

Although parenting practices are central to our understanding of adolescent development, it has become clear throughout our discussion that the adolescent's socialization context reaches beyond the home. In this final section, we broaden our discussion to consider the community and cultural contexts within which the adolescent's family and peer system is embedded. As many investigators have noted, most of what we currently understand about parent–adolescent relationships has come from research on white, middle-class, intact families (e.g., Collins, 1995; Hill, 1987; Holmbeck, 1996; Paikoff & Brooks-Gunn, 1991; Sessa & Steinberg, 1991; Spencer & Dornbusch, 1990; Steinberg, 1990; Steinberg et al., 1995). Fortunately, results from recently conceived ecologically-based research agendas have begun to paint a much more rich and complex picture of adolescent development (e.g., Deater-Deckard & Dodge, 1997; Dishion et al., 1995b; Dishion & Bullock, in press; Steinberg et al., 1995; McLoyd, 1990).

For example, Steinberg and colleagues (1995) launched a programmatic study of the adolescent's family in broader contexts. Instead of controlling for demographic variables, these researchers set out to systematically examine how parent–adolescent relationship patterns vary across different ethnic groups and socioeconomic levels. They were also interested in investigating the processes through which peer relationships moderate family influences. Not surprisingly, their results were complex. Authoritativeness was found to vary across different ecological niches (i.e., it was most prevalent in European American, middle-class, intact families), but the effects of authoritativeness varied to a much lesser extent. Across ethnic, SES, and family structure contexts, adolescents raised in authoritative homes were more self-reliant, less depressed and less likely to engage in delinquent activity.

In terms of scholastic achievement, however, African American and Asian American youth raised with authoritative parents performed no better than those who were not. To understand these results, Steinberg and colleagues turned to the peer group. The influence of peers versus parents on school performance was found to be relatively more powerful for minority than European American adolescents. A link between parenting practices and adolescent personality traits was discovered, and these traits, in turn, predicted membership in different types of cliques (antisocial or prosocial), however, *these associations were not evident for minority youth* (see also Cairns et al., 1988; Dishion & Bullock, in press). The authors suggested that minority youth are much more restricted in terms of their choices of peer groups and may often have difficulty joining an academically strong clique. For example, although African American parents encourage academic success (they score among the highest on measures of parental involvement in school), the influence of a less academically-minded peer group may offset these family influences.

Steinberg and associates also found some intriguing neighborhood effects. For instance, results revealed that a family's social integration within a neighborhood is related to scholastic achievement and the lack of antisocial behavior. However, these findings only hold when the neighborhood in which the family is well integrated is characterized by a high proportion of families exhibiting good parenting. Taken together, these findings suggest that the impact of authoritative parenting on adolescent development is far more complex than previously conceptualized.

Much of this work is based on global reports of parenting practices. In our own work, we have completed macro ratings of family management practices based on in-home videotaped interactions among successful and high-risk European American and African American families with adolescents. Figure 4.7 shows the results for the parenting construct we labeled "limit-setting." Our findings revealed that the covariation between limit-setting and the youths' status as successful or high risk (as defined by teachers) was exactly the opposite for each cultural group (Dishion & Bullock, in press). There was a statistically reliable interaction between risk status and ethnic group. As expected, high scores on the macro ratings of parent limit-setting characterized successful, and not high-risk, European American families. This was expected, given the measure was based on 20 years of research with primarily European American families (e.g., Patterson, Reid and Dishion, 1992). Paradoxically, however, low scores on observations of parental limit-setting were characteristic of successful African American families, not the high-risk families.

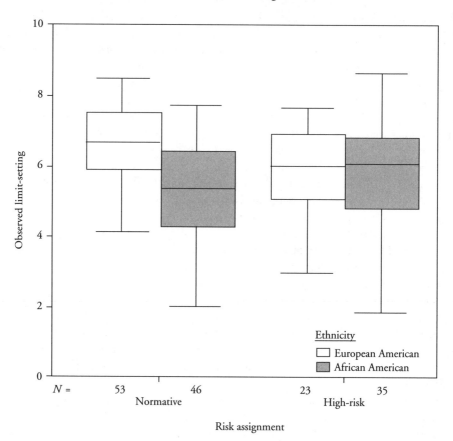

Figure 4.7 Limit-setting by ethnicity.

The principal explanation for this finding is that our measures of parenting were ethnically biased; that is, a firm, strict parenting style meant something different in the African American community than it did for the European American community. Our measures tapped the extent to which explicit discussion of family rules and punishment strategies was observed. But perhaps effective parenting among African American families evolves not so much from an explicit laying down of rules and regulations, but from a shared understanding between the adolescent and parent about the form and function of parenting in adolescence (Deater-Deckard & Dodge, 1997). Over many years, families construct a "verbal cocoon" that provides explanations for what are appropriate ways in which members respond to particular behaviors (Dishion & Bullock, in press). This family framework is not easily captured in a 30-minute observation session. Our challenge as researchers is to accurately tap the meaning of these subtle (and perhaps not so subtle) messages that contribute to the diversity of emergent family contexts.

Our proposal that socialization processes are embedded within the meaning attributed by the larger community is buttressed by the important acculturation research. This line of work suggests that families are strained when the youngsters in the family adopt cultural values that are radically different from those endorsed by the adult caregivers (Masten & Coatsworth, 1995); the shared understanding necessary for smooth socialization is disrupted. Interventions that develop bicultural training enhance parenting potential and reduce problem behavior in adolescence (Coatsworth et al., 1996; Szapocznik et al., 1996).

In the 1800s, the United States adopted a policy that sent Native American youth to boarding schools for "re-education." The resilient and powerful socialization practices of the Native American communities could only be disrupted by physically sending youth away from their family community into boarding schools where their way of life was challenged at every level, from introducing physical discipline, to forcing them to adopt a foreign language, dress and new set of beliefs (Duran & Duran, 1995). Thus, developmental processes at the intraindividual and interpersonal levels were targeted for change. In addition, multiple levels of the systemic hierarchy including parent–child, peer, teacher–student, community and cultural systems were disrupted. Remarkably, even under these extreme conditions, it took several generations of boarding schools to perturb traditional indigenous socialization practices. Today we witness, as Black Elk predicted, that the seventh generation is rejuvenating indigenous practices. This is a compelling example of how cultural identity underlies community self-organization, and how relatively resilient to countervailing forces individuals embedded in these rich contexts can be, not only during adolescence, but indeed across the life course, and across generations.

Summary and Conclusion

The current chapter represents our preliminary attempts at developing a coherent model of the family ecology during adolescence. We propose that such a model requires a shift both down the systemic hierarchy to considerations of intraindividual factors, and up to the community and cultural levels. We began by introducing a broad ecological framework that served as a heuristic for organizing the various interacting systems which contribute to the transformations in adolescence. Then, in order to be more specific about the underlying causal mechanisms that may be driving these changes, dynamic systems principles were introduced.

In terms of intra- and interpersonal processes, we argued the following:

1. Throughout childhood, specific combinations of emotions and appraisals arise and persist when interpersonal goals are unmet, or partially met;
2. As these similarly frustrating occasions recur, particularly in the family context, specific emotion–cognition attractors stabilize;
3. Early adolescence can be described as a phase transition characterized by increased variability in the system. At this time those early attractor patterns may break down and novel relationship patterns have the potential to emerge;
4. One potential mechanism by which these new family patterns emerge may be related to changing goals. During early adolescence, new interpersonal goals arise for the

teenager which are likely to be blocked, or partially blocked, by parents; thus, parent–adolescent conflict is likely;

5. Through repeated conflict scenarios during which similar issues are addressed (e.g., curfew, dating practices), positive feedback processes fashion new and unique emotion–cognition attractors;

6. A finite set of these attractors stabilize after the phase transition (in mid- to late-adolescence) and form the basis of subsequent personality patterns; and

7. These personality patterns then go on to constrain the types of future interpersonal relationships – family and peer relationships – that develop for the maturing adolescent.

We ended our discussion by returning to the ecological framework and addressing some critical community and cultural factors. Like others before us, we argued that adolescent socialization cannot be conceptualized without broadening our lens to include the peer, community, and cultural processes that reciprocally interact to shape developmental outcomes. In conclusion, we have been inspired by the potential for new insights that has emerged from amalgamating the ecological framework with DS concepts. It seems clear to us that a great deal of exciting future research can be undertaken at the crossroads of these two approaches.

Key Readings

Dishion, T. J., Poulin, F., & Medici Skaggs, N. (2000). The ecology of premature adolescent autonomy: Biological and social influences. In K. A. Kerns, J. Contreras, & A. M. Neal-Barrett (Eds.), *Explaining associations between family and peer relationships* (pp. 27–45). Westport, CT: Praeger.
This chapter explores the integration of evolutionary and social interaction theory in accounting for extreme levels of problem behavior in early to mid-adolescence. It was hypothesized that attentuated relationships with parents and other adults in early adolescence provides a context of vulnerability to peer influences. Peer relationships and interaction patterns are functional during puberty because of the secondary gain of promoting heterosexual relationships. These ideas were confirmed using structural equation modeling with a sample (n = 220), showing a combination of poor family management, school failure, and puberty predicting involvement with a deviant peer group, which in turn predicted early sexual intercourse.

Granic, I., & Hollenstein, T. (in press). Dynamic systems methods for models of developmental psychopathology. *Development and Psychopathology*.
This article provides a survey of novel designs and methodological techniques currently being used and refined by developmental dynamic systems researchers. The methodological review is aimed at introducing and encouraging developmentalists and developmental psychopathologists to expand their analytic repertoire with techniques that are more amenable to the study of change. One particularly promising method for the study of family interactions, state space grid analysis, is elaborated and its clinical utility is highlighted.

Lewis, M. D., & Granic, I. (Eds.) (2000). *Emotion, development and self-organization: Dynamic systems approaches to emotional development*. New York: Cambridge University Press.

This edited book was part of the Cambridge series on Social and Emotional Development. The volume includes contributions from leaders in the fields of emotion theory (e.g., Klaus Scherer, John Gottman), emotional development (e.g., Carroll Izard, Linda Camras, Marc D. Lewis, Ross Thompson, Allan Schore), and neuropsychology (e.g., Walter Freeman, Jaak Panksepp, Don Tucker). These scholars and others agreed to participate in this effort to identify and launch what is essentially a new area of specialization. Senior contributors who had not explicitly identified themselves with the dynamic systems approach reconceptualized their work from this perspective, and contributors who have been applying dynamic systems approaches for years summarized their program of research for the volume.

References

Abramson, L. Y., Seligman, M., & Teasdale, J. (1978). Learned helplessness in humans: Critique and reformulation. *Journal of Abnormal Psychology, 87*, 49–74.

Allan, J. P., & Land, D. (1999). Attachment in adolescence. In J. Cassidy & P. R. Shaver (Eds.), *Handbook of attachment theory, research, and clinical applications* (pp. 319–335). New York: Guilford.

Allan, J. P., Moore, C., Kuperminc, G., & Bell, K. (1998). Attachment and adolescent psychosocial functioning. *Child Development, 69*, 1406–1419.

Baumrind, D. (1991). Effective parenting during the early adolescent transition. In P. A. Cowan & M. Hetherington (Eds.), *Family transitions* (pp. 111–163). Hillsdale, NJ: Erlbaum.

Bell, R. Q. (1968). A reinterpretation of the direction of effects in studies of socialization. *Psychological Review, 75*, 81–95.

Bell, R. Q., & Chapman, M. (1986). Child effects in studies using experimental or brief longitudinal approaches to socialization. *Developmental Psychology, 22*, 595–603.

Blos, P. (1962). *On adolescence.* New York: Free Press.

Blos, P. (1979). *The adolescent passage.* Madison, CT: International Universities Press.

Bronfenbrenner, U. (1989). Ecological systems theory. In R. Vasta (Ed.), *Annals of child development, Vol. 6. Six theories of child development: Revised reformulations and current issues* (pp. 187–249). London: JAI Press.

Brooks-Gunn, J., Graber, J., & Paikoff, R. L. (1994). Studying links between hormones and negative affect: Models and measures. *Journal of Research on Adolescence, 4*, 469–486.

Cairns, R. B., Cairns, B. D., Neckerman, H. J., Gest, S. D., & Gariépy, J. L. (1988). Social networks and aggressive behavior: Peer support or peer rejection. *Developmental Psychology, 24*, 815–823.

Cicchetti, D., & Rogosch, F. (Eds.) (1997). Special issue: Self-organization. *Development and Psychopathology, 9*, 595–929.

Coatsworth, J. D., Szapocznik, J., Kurtines, W., & Santisteban, D. A. (1996). Culturally competent psychosocial interventions with antisocial problem behavior in Hispanic youth. In D. M. Stoff, J. Breiling, & J. Maser (Eds.), *Handbook of antisocial behavior* (pp. 395–404). New York: JohnWiley.

Collins, W. A. (1990). Parent–child relationships in the transition to adolescence: Continuity and change in interaction, affect, and cognition. In R. Montemayor, G. R. Adams, & T. P. Gullotta (Eds.), *From childhood to adolescence: A transitional period? Advances in Adolescent Development, Vol. 2* (pp. 85–106). London: Sage.

Collins, W. A. (1992). Parents' cognitions and developmental changes in relationships during adolescence. In I. E. Sigel & A. V. McGillicuddy-DeLisi (Eds.), *Parental belief systems: The psychological consequences for children* (2nd ed., pp. 175–197). Hillsdale, NJ: Erlbaum.

Collins, W. A. (1995). Relationships and development: Family adaptations to individual change. In S. Shulman (Ed.), *Close relationships and socioemotional development* (pp. 128–154). Norwood, NJ: Ablex.

Collins, W. A. (1997). Relationships and development during adolescence: Interpersonal adaptation to individual change. *Personal Relationships, 4*, 1–14.

Collins, W. A., & Laursen, B. (1992). Conflict and the transition to adolescence. In C. U. Shantz & W. W. Hartup (Eds.), *Conflict in child and adolescent development* (pp. 216–241). Cambridge: Cambridge University Press.

Collins, W. A., & Laursen, B. (1999). *Relationships as developmental contexts.* Mahwah, NJ: Erlbaum.

Collins, W. A., Laursen, B., Mortensen, N., Luebker, C., & Ferreira, M. (1997). Conflict processes and transitions in parent and peer relationships: Implications for autonomy and regulation. *Journal of Adolescent Research, 12*, 178–198.

Cox, M. J., & Paley, B. (1997). Families as systems. *Annual Review of Psychology, 48*, 243–267.

Csikszentmihalyi, M., & Larson, R. (1984). *Being adolescent.* New York: Basic Books.

Deater-Deckard, K., & Dodge, K. A. (1997). Externalizing behavior problems and discipline revisited: Nonlinear effects and variation by culture, context, and gender: Target Article. *Psychological Inquiry, 8*, 161–175.

Dishion, T. J., & Bullock, B. (in press). In J. G. Borkowski, S. Ramey, & M. Bristol-Power (Eds.), *Parenting and the child's world: Influences on intellectual, academic, and social-emotional development.* Mahwah, NJ: Erlbaum.

Dishion, T. J., Capaldi, D. M., Spracklen, K. M., & Li, F. (1995a). Peer ecology of male adolescent drug use. *Development and Psychopathology, 7*, 803–824.

Dishion, T. J., Eddy, J. M., Haas, E., Li, F., & Spracklen, K. (1997). Friendships and violent behavior during adolescence. *Social Development, 6*, 207–223.

Dishion, T. J., French, D. C., & Patterson, G. R. (1995b). The development and ecology of antisocial behavior. In D. Cicchetti & D. J. Cohen (Eds.), *Developmental psychopathology. Vol. 2: Risk, disorder, and adaptation* (pp. 421–471). New York: Wiley.

Dishion, T. J., Gardner, K., Patterson, G. R., Reid, J. B., & Thibodeaux, S. (1983). The Family Process Code: A multidimensional system for observing family interaction. Unpublished coding manual. Available from Oregon Social Learning Center, 160 East 4th Avenue, Eugene, OR 97401-2426.

Dishion, T. J., & McMahon, R. J. (1998). Parental monitoring and the prevention of child and adolescent problem behavior: A conceptual and empirical formulation. *Clinical Child and Family Psychology Review, 1*, 61–75.

Dishion, T. J., Poulin, F., & Medici Skaggs, N. (2000). The ecology of premature autonomy in adolescence: Biological and social influences. In K. A. Kerns, J. M. Contreras, & A. M. Neal-Barnett (Eds.), *Family and peers: Linking two social worlds* (pp. 27–45). Westport, CT: Praeger.

Dishion, T. J., Spracklen, K. M., Andrews, D. W., & Patterson, G. R. (1996). Deviancy training in male adolescent friendships. *Behavior Therapy, 27*, 373–390.

Dix, T. (1991). The affective organization of parenting: Adaptive and maladaptive processes. *Psychological Bulletin, 110*, 3–25.

Duran, E., & Duran, B. (1995). *Native American postcolonial psychology.* Albany, NY: State University of New York Press.

Erikson, E. H. (1968). *Identity, youth and crisis.* New York: Norton.

Fogel, A. (1993). *Developing through relationships: Origins of communication, self and culture.* Chicago: University of Chicago Press.

Fogel, A., & Thelen, E. (1987). The development of early expressive and communicative action: Re-interpreting the evidence from a dynamic systems perspective. *Developmental Psychology, 23*, 747–761.

Forgatch, M. S. (1984). A two-stage analysis of family problem-solving: Global and microsocial. Doctoral dissertation, University of Oregon. Eugene, OR.

Forgatch, M. S., Fetrow, B., & Lathrop, M. (1985). Solving problems in family interactions. Unpublished training manual. Available from Oregon Social Learning Center, 160 East 4th Avenue, Eugene, OR 97401-2426.

Freeman, W. (1995). *Societies of brain: A study in the neuroscience of love and hate.* Hillsdale, NJ: Erlbaum.

Freud, A. (1937). *The ego and mechanisms of defense.* London: Hogarth Press.

Freud, A. (1958). Adolescence. *Psychoanalytic Study of the Child, 13,* 255–278.

Frijda, N. H. (1986). *The emotions.* New York: Cambridge University Press.

Goerner, S. (1995). Chaos, evolution and deep ecology. In R. Robertson & A. Combs (Eds.), *Chaos theory in psychology and the life sciences* (pp. 17–38). Mahwah, NJ: Erlbaum.

Graber, J. A., & Petersen, A. C. (1991). Cognitive changes in adolescence: Biological perspectives. In K. R. Gibson & A. C. Petersen (Eds.), *Brain maturation and cognitive development: Comparative and cross-cultural perspectives* (pp. 253–279). New York: Aldine de Gruyter.

Granic, I. (2000). The self-organization of parent–child relations: Beyond bidirectional models. In M. D. Lewis & I. Granic (Eds.), *Emotion, development, and self-organization: Dynamic systems approaches to emotional development* (pp. 267–297). New York: Cambridge University Press.

Grusec, J. E., Rudy, D., & Martini, T. (1997). Parenting cognitions and child outcomes: An overview and implications for children's internalization of values. In J. E. Grusec & L. Kuczynski (Eds.), *Parenting and children's internalization of values: A handbook of contemporary theory* (pp. 259–282). New York: Wiley.

Haken, H. (1977). *Synergetics – An introduction: Nonequilibrium phase transitions and self-organization in physics, chemistry and biology.* Berlin: Springer-Verlag.

Hartup, W. W., & Laursen, B. (1999). Relationships as developmental contexts: Retrospective themes and contemporary issues. In W. A. Collins & B. Laursen (Eds.), *Relationships as developmental contexts: The Minnesota symposia on child psychology, Vol. 30* (pp. 13–35). Mahwah, NJ: Erlbaum.

Hastings, P., & Grusec, J. E. (1997). Conflict outcome as a function of parental accuracy in perceiving child cognitions and affect. *Social Development, 6,* 76–90.

Hastings, P., & Grusec, J. E. (1998). Parenting goals as organizers of responses to parent–child disagreement. *Developmental Psychology, 34,* 465–479.

Hill, J. P. (1987). Research on adolescents and their families: Past and prospect. In C. E. Irwin (Ed.), *Adolescent social behavior and health: New directions for child development* (No. 37, pp. 13–31). San Francisco: Jossey-Bass.

Hill, J. P., & Holmbeck, G. N. (1986). Attachment and autonomy during adolescence. In G. J. Whitehurst (Ed.), *Annals of child development* (Vol. 3, pp. 145–189). Greenwich, CT: JAI Press.

Hill, J. P., & Holmbeck, G. N. (1987). Familial adaptation to biological change during adolescence. In R. M. Lerner & T. T. Foch (Eds.), *Biological–psychosocial interactions in early adolescence: A lifespan perspective* (pp. 207–223). Hillsdale, NJ: Erlbaum.

Hill, J. P., Holmbeck, G. N., Marlow, L., Green, T. M., & Lynch, M. E. (1985). Pubertal status and parent–child relations in families of seventh-grade boys. *Journal of Early Adolescence, 5,* 31–44.

Hinde, R. A. (1989). Ethological and relationship approaches. In R. Vasta (Ed.), *Annals of child development: Vol. 6: Six theories of child development: Revised reformulations and current issues* (pp. 251–285). London: JAI Press.

Holmbeck, G. N. (1996). A model of family relational transformations during the transition to adolescence: Parent–adolescent conflict and adaptation. In J. A. Graber, J. Brooks-Gunn, &

A. C. Petersen (Eds.), *Transitions through adolescence: Interpersonal domains and contexts* (pp. 167–199). Mahwah, NJ: Erlbaum.

Holmbeck, G. N., Paikoff, R. L., & Brooks-Gunn, J. (1995). Parenting adolescents. In M. Bornstein (Ed.), *Handbook of parenting: Vol. 1. Children and parenting* (pp. 91–118). Mahwah, NJ: Erlbaum.

Inhelder, B., & Piaget, J. (1958). *The growth of logical thinking from childhood to adolescence: An essay on the construction of formal operational structures.* New York: Basic Books.

Izard, C. E. (1977). *Human emotions.* New York: Plenum.

Kandel, D. B., & Lesser, G. A. (1972). *Youth in two worlds.* San Francisco: Jossey-Bass.

Kauffman, S. A. (1993). *The origins of order: Self-organization and selection in evolution.* New York: Oxford University Press.

Keating, D. P. (1990a). Developmental processes in the socialization of cognitive structures. *Development and learning: Proceedings of a symposium in honour of Wolfgang Edelstein on his 60th birthday* (pp. 37–72). Berlin: Max Planck Institute.

Keating, D. P. (1990b). Adolescent thinking. In S. S. Feldman & G. R. Elliot (Eds.), *At the threshold: The developing adolescent* (pp. 54–89). Cambridge, MA: Harvard University Press.

Kelso, J. A. S. (1995). *Dynamic patterns: The self-organization of brain and behavior.* Cambridge, MA: Bradford/MIT Press.

Kuczynski, L. (1984). Socialization goals and mother-child interaction: Strategies for long-term and short-term compliance. *Developmental Psychology, 20,* 1061–1073.

Laible, D. J., & Thompson, R. A. (2000). Attachment and self-organization. In M. D. Lewis & I. Granic (Eds.), *Emotion, development, and self-organization: Dynamic systems approaches to emotional development* (pp. 298–323). New York: Cambridge University Press.

Larson, R. W., Richards, M. H., Moneta, G., Holmbeck, G., & Duckett, E. (1996). Changes in adolescents' daily interactions with their families from ages 10 to 18: disengagement and transformation. *Developmental Psychology, 32,* 744–754.

Laursen, B., & Collins, W. A. (1994). Interpersonal conflict during adolescence. *Psychological Bulletin, 115,* 197–209.

Laursen, B., Coy, K. C., & Collins, W. A. (1998). Reconsidering changes in parent–child conflict across adolescence: A meta-analysis. *Child Development, 69,* 817–832.

Lazarus, R. (1982). Thoughts on the relations between emotion and cognition. *American Psychologist, 37,* 1019–1024.

Lazarus, R. (1984). On the primacy of cognition. *American Psychologist, 39,* 124–129.

Lewis, M. D. (1995). Cognition–emotion feedback and the self-organization of developmental paths. *Human Development, 38,* 71–102.

Lewis, M. D. (1997). Personality self-organization: Cascading constraints on cognition-emotion interaction. In A. Fogel, M. C. D. P. Lyra, & J. Valsiner (Eds.), *Dynamics and indeterminism in developmental and social processes* (pp. 193–216). Mahwah, NJ: Erlbaum.

Lewis, M. D. (2000). The promise of dynamic systems approaches for an integrated account of human development. *Child Development, 71,* 36–43.

Lewis, M. D. (in press). Interacting time scales in personality (and cognitive) development: Intentions, emotions and emergent forms. In N. Granott & J. Parziale (Eds.), *Microdevelopment: Transition processes in development in learning.* Cambridge: Cambridge University Press.

Lewis, M. D., & Granic, I. (1999). Who put the self in self-organization? A clarification of terms and concepts for developmental psychopathology. *Development and Psychopathology, 11,* 365–374.

Lewis, M. D., & Granic, I. (Eds.) (2000). *Emotion, development and self-organization: Dynamic systems approaches to emotional development.* New York: Cambridge University Press.

Lewis, M. D., Lamey, A. V., & Douglas, L. (1999). A new dynamic systems method for the analysis of early socioemotional development. *Developmental Science, 2,* 457–475.

Maccoby, E. E., & Martin, J. A. (1983). Socialization in the context of the family: Parent–child interaction. In P. H. Mussen (Series Ed.) & E. M. Hetherington (Vol. Ed.), *Socialization, personality and social development* (Vol. IV, 4th ed., pp. 1–101). New York: Wiley.

MacKinnon-Lewis, C., Lamb, M. E., Arbuckle, B., Baradaran, L. P., & Volling, B. L. (1992). The relationship between biased maternal and filial attributions and the aggressiveness of their interactions. *Development and Psychopathology, 4,* 403–415.

Magai, C., & McFadden, S. H. (1995). *The role of emotions in social and personality development: History, theory, and research.* New York: Plenum.

Magnusson, D., Stattin, H., & Allen, D. L. (1985). Biological maturation and social development: A longitudinal study of some adjustment processes from mid-adolescence to adulthood. *Journal of Youth and Adolescence, 14*(4), 267–283.

Malatesta, C. Z., & Wilson, A. (1988). Emotion cognition interaction in personality development: A discrete emotions, functionalist analysis. *British Journal of Social Psychology, 27,* 91–112.

Masten, A. S., & Coatsworth, J. D. (1995). Competence, resilience, and psychopathology. In D. Cicchetti & D. J. Cohen (Eds.), *Developmental psychopathology: Vol. 2: Risk, disorder, and adaptation* (pp. 715–752). New York: Wiley.

McLoyd, V. C. (1990). The impact of economic hardship on Black families and children: Psychological distress, parenting, and socioemotional development. *Child Development, 61,* 311–346.

Minuchin, S. (1974). *Families & family therapy.* Cambridge, MA: Harvard University Press.

Montemayor, R. (1982). The relationship between parent–adolescent conflict and the amount of time adolescents spend alone and with parents and peers. *Child Development, 53,* 1512–1519.

Montemayor, R. (1983). Parents and adolescents in conflict: All families some of the time and some families most of the time. *Journal of Early Adolescence, 3,* 83–103.

Offer, D. (1969). *The psychological world of the teenager.* New York: Basic Books.

Paikoff, R. L., & Brooks-Gunn, J. (1991). Do parent–child relationships change during puberty? *Psychological Bulletin, 110,* 47–66.

Parke, R. D., MacDonald, K. B., Beitel, A., & Bhavnagri, N. (1988). The role of the family in the development of peer relationships. In R. Peters & R. J. McMahon (Eds.), *Social learning systems approaches to marriage and the family* (pp. 17–44). New York: Brunner/Mazel.

Parpal, M., & Maccoby, E. E. (1985). Maternal responsiveness and subsequent child compliance. *Child Development, 56,* 1326–1334.

Patterson, G. R. (1982). *Coercive family processes.* Eugene, OR: Castalia.

Patterson, G. R. (1995). Coercion as a basis for early age of onset for arrest. In J. McCord (Ed.), *Coercion and punishment in long-term perspectives* (pp. 81–105). New York: Cambridge University Press.

Patterson, G. R., & Bank, L. (1989). Some amplifying mechanisms for pathologic processes in families. In M. R. Gunnar & E. Thelen (Eds.), *Systems and development: The Minnesota symposia on child psychology, Vol. 22* (pp. 167–209). Hillsdale, NJ: Erlbaum.

Patterson, G. R., & Reid, J. B. (1984). Social interactional processes within the family: The study of moment-by-moment family transactions in which human development is embedded. *Journal of Applied Developmental Psychology, 5,* 237–262.

Patterson, G. R., Reid, J., & Dishion, T. J. (1992). *Antisocial boys.* Eugene, OR: Castalia.

Pepler, D., Craig, W., & O'Connell, P. (1999). Understanding bullying from a dynamic systems perspective. In A. Slater and D. Muir (Eds.), *The Blackwell reader in developmental psychology* (pp. 440–451). Malden, MA: Blackwell.

Piaget, J. (1965/1932). *The moral judgment of the child.* New York: Free Press.

Prigogine, I., & Stengers, I. (1984). *Order out of chaos.* New York: Bantam.

Reis, H. T., Collins, W. A., & Berscheid, E. (2000). The relationship context of human behavior and development. *Psychological Bulletin, 126*, 844–872.

Robin, A. L., & Foster, S. L. (1989). *Negotiating parent–adolescent conflict: A behavioral-family systems approach.* New York: Guilford.

Rutter, M., Graham, P., Chadwick, O. F. D., & Yule, W. (1976). Adolescent turmoil: Fact or fiction? *Journal of Child Psychology and Psychiatry, 17*, 35–56.

Schore, A. N. (1994). *Affect regulation and the origin of the self: The neurobiology of emotional development.* Mahwah, NJ: Erlbaum.

Selman, R. L. (1981). The development of interpersonal competence: The role of understanding in conduct. *Developmental Review, 1*, 401–422.

Sessa, F. M., & Steinberg, L. (1991). Family structure and the development of autonomy during adolescence. *Journal of Early Adolescence, 11*, 38–55.

Siegel, D. J. (1999). The developing mind: *Toward a neurobiology of interpersonal experience.* New York: Guilford.

Silverberg, S. B., Tennenbaum, D. L., & Jacob, T. (1992). Adolescence and family interaction. In V. B. van Hasselt & M. Hersen (Eds.), *Handbook of social development: A lifespan perspective* (pp. 347–370). New York: Plenum.

Smetana, J. (1988). Concepts of self and social convention: Adolescents' and parents' reasoning about hypothetical and actual family conflicts. In M. R. Gunnar & W. A. Collins (Eds.), *Development during the transition to adolescence. The Minnesota symposia on child psychology, Vol. 21* (pp. 79–122). Hillsdale, NJ: Erlbaum.

Smetana, J. (1989). Adolescents' and parents' reasoning about actual family conflict. *Child Development, 60*, 1052–1067.

Smetana, J. (1991). Doing what you say and saying what you do: Reasoning about adolescent–parent conflict in interviews and interactions. *Journal of Adolescent Research, 6*, 276–295.

Smetana, J. (1996). Adolescent–parent conflict: Implications for adaptive and maladaptive development. In D. Cicchetti & S. L. Toth (Eds.), *Adolescence: Opportunities and challenges. The Rochester symposia on developmental psychopathology, Vol. 7* (pp. 1–46). Rochester, NY: University of Rochester Press.

Spear, L. P. (2000). The adolescent brain and age-related behavioral manifestations. *Neuroscience and Biobehavioral Reviews, 24*, 417–463.

Spencer, M. B., & Dornbusch, S. M. (1990). Challenges in studying minority youth. In S. S. Feldman & G. L. Elliott (Eds.), *At the threshold: The developing adolescent* (pp. 123–146). Cambridge, MA: Harvard University Press.

Sroufe, L. A. (1995). *Emotional development: The organization of emotional life in the early years.* New York: Cambridge University Press.

Stattin, H., & Kerr, M. (2000). Parental monitoring: A reinterpretation. *Child Development, 71*, 1072–1085.

Steinberg, L. (1987). Recent research on the family at adolescence: The extent and nature of sex differences. *Journal of Youth and Adolescence, 3*, 191–197.

Steinberg, L. (1988). Reciprocal relation between parent–child distance and pubertal maturation. *Developmental Psychology, 24*, 122–128.

Steinberg, L. (1989). Pubertal maturation and parent–adolescent distance: An evolutionary perspective. In G. Adams, R. Montemayor, & T. Gullotta (Eds.), *Biology of adolescent behavior and development* (pp. 82–114). Newbury Park, CA: Sage.

Steinberg, L. (1990). Autonomy, conflict, and harmony in the family relationship. In S. Feldman & G. Elliot (Eds.), *At the threshold: The developing adolescent* (pp. 255–276). Cambridge, MA: Harvard University Press.

Steinberg, L., Darling, N. E., Fletcher, A. C., Brown, A. B., & Dornbusch, S. M. (1995). Authoritative parenting and adolescent adjustment: An ecological journey. In P. Moen, G. H. Elder Jr., & K. Luscher (Eds.), *Examining lives in context: Perspectives on the ecology of human development* (pp. 423–466). Washington, DC: American Psychological Association.

Szapocznik, J., Kurtines, W., Santisteban, D. A., Pantin, H., Scopetta, M., Mancilla, Y., Aisenberg, S., MacIntosh, S., Perez-Vidal, A., & Coatsworth, J. D. (1996). The evolution of a structural eco-systems theory for working with Hispanic families in culturally pluristic context. In J. Garcia & M. C. Zea (Eds.), *Psychological interventions and research with Latino populations.* New York: Allyn & Bacon.

Teasdale, J. D. (1983). Negative thinking in depression: Cause, effect or reciprocal relationship? *Advances in Behavior Research and Therapy, 5,* 3–25.

Teasdale, J. D., & Barnard, P. J. (1993). *Affect, cognition, and change: Re-modeling depressive thought.* Hillsdale, NJ: Erlbaum.

Thelen, E., & Smith, L. B. (1994). *A dynamic systems approach to the development of cognition and action.* Cambridge, MA: Bradford/MIT Press.

Thelen, E., & Ulrich, B. D. (1991). Hidden skills: A dynamic systems analysis of treadmill stepping during the first year. *Monographs of the Society for Research in Child Development, 56*(1) (Serial No. 223).

Tomkins, S. S. (1987). Script theory. In J. Aronoff, A. I. Rabin, & R. A. Zucker (Eds.), *The emergence of personality* (pp. 147–216). New York: Springer.

Tomkins, S. S. (1991). *Affect, imagery, consciousness. Vol. 3: Anger and fear.* New York: Springer.

Vallacher, R. R., & Nowak, A. (Eds.) (1994). *Dynamical systems in social psychology.* San Diego, CA: Academic.

Vallacher, R. R., & Nowak, A. (1997). The emergence of dynamical social psychology: Target article. *Psychological Inquiry, 8,* 73–99.

van Gelder, T., & Port, R. F. (1995). It's about time: An overview of the dynamical approach to cognition. In R. F. Port & T. van Gelder (Eds.), *Mind as motion: Explorations in the dynamics of cognition* (pp. 1–43). Cambridge, MA: MIT Press.

Vetere, A., & Gale, A. (1987). The family: A failure in psychological theory and research. In A. Vetere & A. Gale (Eds.), *Ecological studies of family life* (pp. 1–17). Chichester: Wiley.

Weiner, B. (1979). A theory of motivation for some classroom experiences. *Journal of Educational Psychology, 71,* 3–25.

Whiting, B. B., & Whiting, J. M. (1975). *Children of six cultures: A psychocultural analysis.* Cambridge, MA: Harvard University Press.

Wilson, B. J., & Gottman, J. M. (1995). Marital interaction and parenting. In M. H. Bornstein (Ed.), *Handbook of parenting, Vol. 4: Applied and practical parenting* (pp. 33–35). Mahwah, NJ: Erlbaum.

Youniss, J. (1980). *Parent and peers in social development.* Chicago: University of Chicago Press.

Zimmermann, P., Scheuerer-Englisch, H., & Grossmann, K. E. (1996, May). Social relationships in adolescence: Continuity and transformations. Paper presented at the biennial meeting of the European Association for Research on Adolescence, Liège, Belgium.

CHAPTER FIVE

Enhancing Adolescent Development through Sports and Leisure

Steven J. Danish, Tanya E. Taylor, and Robert J. Fazio

Youth development ought not to be viewed as a happenstance matter. While children can, and often do, make the best of difficult circumstances, they cannot be sustained and helped to grow by chance arrangements of makeshift events. Something far more intentional is required: a place, a league, a form of association, a gathering of people where value is placed on continuity, pre-dictability, history, tradition, and a chance to test out new behaviors. (Youth Development Committee of the Lilly Endowment, 1991)

Overview

The term "youth development" has become a popular one and has replaced "prevention" in many circles as the term of choice when discussing interventions with adolescents. Unfortunately, the meaning of "youth development" is so fraught with confusion that it is difficult to determine either the goals of an intervention designed to enhance youth development or the processes needed to achieve these goals. For this reason, one of our aims in this chapter is to clarify what we mean by enhancing youth development and how it differs from prevention.

A second aim we have is to delineate both the role of sport and leisure in the enhancement process and under what conditions these activities can make a difference. Researchers studying the role of extracurricular activities such as sport have assumed that all of these activities conform to the definition proposed by Mahoney and Stattin (2000). This is far from accurate. To understand the potential of an activity, it is necessary to know specifically how it is implemented. We will propose a model for implementing programs specifically designed to enhance development.

Defining Positive Youth Development

How we define youth development significantly affects the kinds of interventions developed. For some, especially individuals who are prevention-oriented, youth development refers to the elimination of problems. However, defining everything in terms of problem reduction is limiting. We do not assess people in terms of problems, or lack of problems, but in terms of their potential. Being problem-free is not the same as being competent or successful. Therefore, we must define and teach youth the skills, values, attitudes, and knowledge necessary to succeed with the same intensity as we work to teach the prevention of certain health-compromising behaviors and attitudes.

Numerous organizations have identified competencies related to positive youth development. For example, in a series of reports the Carnegie Council on Adolescent Development identified a number of desired adolescent development outcomes. In 1989, the Council identified five desired outcomes: (a) the ability to process information from multiple sources and communicate clearly; (b) to be en route to a lifetime of meaningful work by learning how to learn and therefore being able to adapt to different educational and working environments; (c) to be a good citizen by participating in community activities and feeling concern for, and connection to, the well-being of others; (d) to be a caring and ethical individual by acting on one's convictions about right and wrong; and (e) to be a healthy person. In 1995, the Council identified others associated with personal and social development. They include: (a) finding a valued place in a constructive group; (b) learning how to form close and lasting relationships; (c) feeling a sense of worth; (d) achieving a reliable basis for informed decision-making, especially on matters of large consequence; (e) being able to use available support systems; (f) having a positive future orientation; (g) learning respect (Carnegie Corporation of New York, 1989, 1995).

However, other researchers and groups identified other desirable outcomes. Pittman (1996) focused on the need to be motivated to be competent in academic, vocational, physical, emotional, civic, social, and cultural areas. Bloom (2000) delineated the needed competencies as the ability to work well, play well, love well, think well, and serve well. We believe that "be well" should be added to the list. Earlier Danish and his colleagues (Danish, D'Augelli, & Ginsberg, 1984) defined competence as the ability to do life planning, be self-reliant, and be able to seek help from others. Danish (2000) believed that such competencies would enable adolescents to better be able to develop confidence in the future, acquire a sense of personal control over themselves and their environment, and become better citizens.

What is interesting about these different sets of competencies is the overlap between the lists, even though they are labeled and defined slightly differently. Moreover, many of these sets of competencies are not of recent origin. The concept of developing competency in youth has existed for several decades. In fact, the foundation of this concept extends back to Erikson (1959) and White (1963).

The Paucity of Programs Directed at Positive Youth Development

So why have there been few intervention efforts directed at promoting youth development or enhancing competency? There are several reasons. First, although there are general statements about what constitutes positive youth development, many of the competencies that make up the concept are vague and difficult to measure. As a result of the vagueness, we have not defined the developmental benchmarks or the steps necessary to reach these benchmarks (Pittman, 1996). Second, because many research and intervention programs are federally supported, we often focus our research toward federal priorities. These priorities tend to emphasize research designed to reduce health-compromising or problem behaviors. Consequently, research and programming focusing on promoting development or teaching competencies is downplayed, and as a result, there are fewer resources available for those who have avoided involvement but are "at risk." In fact, it sometimes seems that even when more competent behavior can prevent or moderate involvement in negative behaviors, competency per se seems to have little value for itself.

A third reason is that we are a society that likes to focus on fixing problems first, especially in times of emergencies. Such an orientation, while especially attractive to funding sources, the media, and individuals, is antithetical to enhancing development, or for that matter, prevention. Consider the following fable as an illustration.

An individual is sitting on a riverbank enjoying a sunny day. All of a sudden she sees a body floating down the river. It is a child struggling to stay afloat. Immediately she jumps into the water, pulls the young boy out, and performs mouth-to-mouth resuscitation. Just as the child is beginning to breathe normally, there is more yelling from the river. She turns around to see another child floating down the river in a similar state. Again she jumps into the river, pulls the child out, and performs mouth-to-mouth resuscitation. As the child regains her breathing, the woman is again startled by the screaming behind her. A third child is floating down the river.

This situation is repeated several more times. Each time the woman rescues a child she becomes more tired and frustrated. She wonders why children are falling into the water, but is in a quandary. If she tries to go upstream to find out why the children are falling in and to try to prevent it from happening, she will be unable to help the children who are already in the river and floating downstream. However, if she does not go upstream, eventually she will be so tired and fatigued she will be unable to continue to pull children out. She feels helpless. What should she do? Should she direct her energies toward the children in present need or at the community of children at large? If she chooses the latter, how should she intervene? Should she try to put up a temporary barrier to prevent children from falling in, or teach the children how to swim and how to make effective decisions about what is appropriate risk-taking?

This fable highlights two important issues: (1) How prevalent are our concerns with fixing immediate problems? (2) If we decide to intervene at a community level, should we choose to change environments to accommodate a lack of competence, or focus our efforts on teaching competencies to the children and the community?

Until our priorities become focused on developing youth and the communities in which they live as opposed to simply trying to protect them from the temptations and realities of the real world, we will be fighting a losing battle. Not only is it nearly impossible to isolate them from what happens but in attempting to do so, the adolescent may be missing some critical developmental experiences.

A fourth reason so few youth development programs exist is that it is unclear how and where they should be taught. A great deal depends on what is going to be taught. Programs that focus on enhancing or promoting development can teach knowledge, skills and/or attitudes and values. Teaching facts or information is the easiest to do, but least likely to produce behavior change. At the other extreme, teaching attitudes and values are hardest to do, but most likely to result in the development of new attitudes and values. Skills are in the middle in terms of the ease with which the material can be taught, and the likelihood that behavior will be changed as a result of what is taught (Danish, 2000).

Character and value education have become popular topics in our society recently. As noted above, developing character is a difficult task and one which to date has resulted in more rhetoric than action. Several possible settings for imparting these attributes are the home, religious institutions, schools, or after-school programs. Home, and to a lesser extent, churches, synagogues, and mosques, are ideal settings to learn the values and character traits necessary to be a competent adolescent. It is critical that these attributes are taught in settings where youth are continuously exposed to individuals of social influence. For children, these individuals are most likely to be parents. Unfortunately, too many parents have abdicated this role because of time constraints, an absence of these qualities themselves, or other related reasons. As a result, this responsibility has been left to other adults such as teachers, coaches, and religious and community leaders. Some adults have assumed this role effectively; others have not. Even when these nonparental adults want to serve as role models, they may not have the time, skills, or a receptive adolescent. The receptivity of an adolescent diminishes with age as peers become the major source of influence (Danish, 2000).

Some organizations believe that schools have an important role in this kind of education for positive youth development. We disagree, especially given the demands on teachers' time and the decisions schools have made relative to extracurricular activities. Schools have increasingly become single-mindedly focused on teaching the three R's and the "background knowledge for functional literacy" (Hirsch, 1988, p. xi). Despite the best efforts of organizations such as the Character Education Partnership (CEP) and the Collaborative for Academic, Social and Emotional Learning (CASEL) to teach character and values, when the emphasis is on having students pass achievement-based tests to graduate and these same test scores determine whether schools remain accredited and/or funded and teachers keep their jobs, concerns with youth development, regardless of how the term is defined, are minimized (Danish, 2000). Furthermore, extracurricular activities such as intramural sports have been de-emphasized in schools and replaced by competition between schools. Thus, the school environment is often not a conducive place to teach character or values, although more skill-based programming such as life skills still may be taught in some schools if the administration provides the necessary opportunities.

Given that schools have decided that activities such as the sports and the arts are unimportant to teach in school, after-school settings have become the default environment for the teaching of such attributes as character life skills. Fortunately, the time after school may be ideal for the teaching of skills designed to promote adolescent development (Danish & Gullotta, 2000).

However, no one should underestimate the challenges of implementing after-school programming. The obvious setting for conducting these programs is in youth-serving agencies such as the Boys and Girls Clubs, 4-H Clubs, and YM/YWCAs. Unfortunately, there are concerns about the capacity of these youth-serving organizations to be the implementation site.

Informal reports about who is served by after-school programs in youth-serving organizations suggest that up to one-third of all children and youth are unserved, most of them disadvantaged, urban, or of color. Moreover, as youth age, the opportunities for maximal impact diminish.

Lack of participation among inner-city disadvantaged youth is related to fees, equipment and/or uniforms. Fees are variable by organization and affiliate. Lack of ability to pay requires organizations to raise funds from elsewhere to serve youth who cannot pay. If there are multiple children in a family, the problem is compounded. Families are reluctant to trade off one child for another, often with the result that none of the children attend the program. Lack of available or affordable transportation to and from programs and issues of safety can also compound the problem.

Another challenge is the lack of programming for girls. There is less funding for girls. This is true for all girls but especially for girls of color, particularly in cities. Boys and Girls Clubs do not serve as many girls as boys, and in some organizations serving girls, the percentage of girls of color is small.

The lack of opportunity for girls has become more critical because there is new concern about girls' involvement in negative behaviors, heretofore considered more likely to be the domain of boys and young men. One area where there is critical need for programs is for girls who have been the victims of physical and sexual abuse. Other youth who are especially underserved or unserved are immigrant youth and those with disabilities.

Although there is apparent willingness to serve more youth in after-school organizations, the mission and capacity of these organizations to expand is limited. At present there is no consensus about the need to serve every child or youth. What is required are more resources for such items as increased staffing, staff training, upgraded facilities, insurance, and technical assistance (Edmundson, 2000).

The role of volunteers presents additional challenges. Volunteers are viewed in a mixed way by youth organizations. They are necessary, but require recruitment, training and support, which in turn strains the capacity and resources of the organization and staff. For some organizations, especially those in big cities, they are essential to expand their service base; for others, the ability to professionalize current paid staff is much more important. Even when the number of volunteers is sufficient, their training is often inadequate.

What is evident is that if youth-serving organizations are to pick up the slack left when schools decided to de-emphasize programs to teach students how to live and decided to focus exclusively on what it is necessary to know, more financial support and related resources will be required.

The Potential of Sport as a Positive Youth Development Activity

The impact of sports on our society is pervasive. American culture places a tremendously high value on sport. It is a major source of entertainment for both young and old. Only family, school, and television involve children's time more than sport (Institute for Social Research, 1985). Ewing, Seefeldt, and Brown (1996) estimated that there are 48,374,000 children and adolescents in the 5–17 age range participating in sport in the United States. Twenty-two million or 45 percent of the youth are involved in community-based sport organizations such as Little League Baseball and Pop Warner Football. Almost 2.5 million or 5 percent are paying to participate in sport activities such as ice-skating and swimming; 14.5 million or 30 percent participate in recreational sports programs; 451,000 participate in intramural sports in middle, junior, and senior high school; and 12 percent of all adolescents play interscholastic sports. By far the largest number of youth participate in non-school-based sports programs. Therefore, if we expect to reach adolescents, we should consider trying to reach them where they are and want to be – involved in physical activity and sport (Danish, 2000; Hodge & Danish, 1999). In sum, sport is a cultural phenomenon that permeates all of society.

Participation in sport can be a significant factor in the development of an adolescent's identity, self-esteem, and competence (Danish, Petitpas, & Hale, 1990; Fejgin, 1994; Fox, 1992; Kleiber & Kirshnit, 1991; Zaharopoulos & Hodge, 1991). Kleiber and his colleagues (Kleiber & Kirshnit, 1991; Kleiber & Roberts, 1981) have observed that sport is a forum, a structured test, for learning the skills associated with character values such as responsibility, conformity, persistence, risk taking, courage, and self-control. Moreover, because sport is so important to youth, it is an environment where they spend time willingly. This is not always true for time spent at school, and it is well known that we learn best when we are in environments where we want to be.

Despite the claim of many educators and researchers that participation in sport facilitates positive adolescent development, there is nothing about sport itself that is magical. Being on the field or the court does not contribute to development (Hodge & Danish, 1999). It is the experience of sport that may facilitate adolescent development. Researchers who have studied the effects of participation in sport and leisure activities have found both positive and negative effects (Mahoney & Stattin, 2000, Strean & Garcia Bengoechea, 2001). Mahoney and Stattin (2000) found that the structure and context of the activity was important in determining whether participation led to positive or negative outcomes. Strean and Garcia Bengoechea (2001) found that it was the individual's experience of sport and physical activity that determined whether participation was viewed as positive or negative. Therefore, it may not be the mere participation in sport that enhances positive development. The individual's experience in sport may be the critical factor.

An individual's experience in sport may encompass a number of different factors and may be defined differently by different individuals. For the purposes of this chapter the term experience includes such things as the development of sport and life skills, transferability of these skills, positive coach–athlete relationships, and positive interaction with peers.

A number of life skills can be learned while participating in sports. Life skills may include goal setting, communicating effectively, problem solving, dealing with conflict, managing emotions, providing and receiving feedback, accepting interdependence, appreciating differences, and managing time and stress (Danish et al., in press, b). These skills can serve individuals both in their athletic and personal development. The ability to transfer these skills from sport to other domains is perhaps the most crucial step in facilitating the adolescent's development.

In addition to having the experience of learning skills, adolescents who participate in sport also have the opportunities to interact with coaches and peers. Research has shown that the type of leadership and relationship experienced with the coach is a major determinant in the youth sport experience (Smith & Smoll, 1996). Within the sporting domain the coach has the major responsibility of creating the ideal conditions to foster positive development. In creating a positive learning environment nothing is more important than the coach being aware of the impact she or he has on the adolescents involved.

The interactions between peers will also affect adolescent development because peers replace parents as the most important source of influence during this development stage. Because of the nature of sport, especially team sports, with its emphasis on teamwork and leadership, adolescents have the opportunity to interact and build relationships with a number of peers.

However, whether sport provides these opportunities really depends on the structure and the context of the sport experience. Mahoney and Stattin (2000) concluded that youth activities that prevent health-compromising behaviors (e.g., a decrease in antisocial behavior) have more structure compared to activities that may produce negative outcomes in youth. Other research has highlighted the importance of structure in the activities in which adolescents participate (Brown, 1988; Osgood et al., 1996). The research conducted by Mahoney and Stattin (2000) also delineated other critical factors including: emphasizing skill building that increases in complexity and challenge and requires attention; having regular participation schedules; being rule-guided; having adult supervision; and providing feedback. Research has also identified other critical components in addition to structure that should be included in the development of the activity. These include: connecting participants with competent peers and adults (Csikszentmihalyi, Rathunde, & Whalen, 1993; Fletcher, Elder, & Mekos, 1996); building on participants' existing skills and interests (Csikszentmihalyi, 1990; Jones & Offord, 1989; Mahoney, 2000); and creating opportunities where adolescents feel competent and accepted (Eder, 1985; Eder & Parker, 1987; Kinney, 1993).

As the adolescent increases his/her skill level, the skill level of the activity should increase. Sport is an example of an activity that can provide these aspects to enhance development. In the next section we will consider how sport can be designed to enhance positive youth development.

Designing Sport Programs to Enhance Adolescent Development

General considerations

In the previous section we stressed the importance of developing organized activities so that the benefits of participation accrue. The major benefit is the attainment of one's personal goals and the satisfaction derived from doing so (Danish et al., 1993). Successful and satisfying goal accomplishment is regarded as a powerful mediator of psychosocial development. One of the advantages of using sport examples to signify goal accomplishment is that the goals in sport are typically tangible, short-term and easily measured. This gives the adolescent a better opportunity to see the value in goal setting and to experience success in setting and achieving goals. Lifestyle goals such as developing good nutritional habits, avoiding tobacco and alcohol, or attaining academic and job skills are often less tangible and clear-cut. Additionally, because these lifestyle goals typically require a longer time period to achieve, youth tend to lose sight of their goal and fail to fully appreciate the worth of goal setting and the life-skill benefits of successful goal accomplishment.

Although we should not deny youth their dreams, and many of them have dreams of being a professional athlete, we must recognize that of the millions who play sports, a very small percentage eventually become elite athletes and/or have some kind of career in sport. It is imperative then that youth understand that sport provides an opportunity to further define their identity, discover other skills and interests and, most importantly, apply some of the valuable principles learned during sport participation to other areas of their lives. If the sport participant focuses totally on sport dreams and goals, the consequences may be negative. Too much involvement in sport during adolescence can lead to overtraining problems such as being prone to injury. Because youth are beginning participation earlier and earlier, burnout is possible as well, especially when parents and coaches require more and more practice. Too great an investment in sports may lead youth, especially boys, to avoid learning other skills or participating in other activities, and as a result, seek security instead of fully searching for their identity (Petitpas & Champagne, 1988). Finally, because of its inherently competitive nature, sport tends to reinforce an orientation toward ego goals rather than task goals. Researchers have concluded that the latter is most adaptive for psychosocial development (Roberts, 1993). If sport is to be a positive force for development, it must facilitate the attainment of both task and ego goals. This balance is often difficult to achieve because the focus in sport is predominantly on winning and social comparison criteria. This is especially true for boys in sport. Indeed, it has been suggested that sport is the social context in which boys use social comparison processes to determine their status with their peers and their self-esteem (Veroff, 1969).

On the other hand, when the outcome of sports is structured toward psychosocial development, it is more likely that the goals set forth by Baron De Coubertin, the founder of the Olympics, will be attained. In describing his aims for participants, he commented:

> Sport plants in the body seeds of physio-psychological qualities such as coolness, confidence, decision etc. These qualities may remain localised around the exercise which brought them into being; this often happens – it even happens most often. How many daredevil cyclists there are who once they leave their machines are hesitant at every crossroads of existence, how many swimmers who are brave in the water but frightened by the waves of human existence, how many fencers who cannot apply to life's battles the quick eye and nice timing which they show on the boards! The educator's task is to make the seed bear fruit throughout the organism, to transpose it from a particular circumstance to a whole array of circumstances, from a special category of activities to all the individual's actions. (1918)

It is one thing to know the goals of a sport program designed to promote adolescent development; it is an entirely different thing to know how to deliver such a program. Three factors critical in program delivery are the special challenges of developing and implementing after-school programs in underserved areas, issues of program leadership, and how the skills taught can be transferred from sport to other life domains.

Issues of leadership

Although sport may exist in a structured environment, it may vary in other aspects, such as what is the hoped-for outcome and the type and quality of adult supervision. The goals of sport participation for any adolescent are largely determined by the coach, adult supervisors of the sport, and the parents. Gould (2001) delineates three ways for coaches and other adults to view the outcome of sport: to win; to build better athletes; or to build better people through sport.

In a classic series of studies on coaching behavior, Smith and Smoll (1996) evaluated the effectiveness of different coaching styles for young athletes. They concluded that when coaches were trained to reward participants' performance early and often, to reward effort as much as outcome, and to have realistic age- and skill-level expectations, participants thrived. They enjoyed playing more, had a greater desire to play, believed their coach was more knowledgeable and a better teacher, and liked the team more. Such an orientation does not imply that winning and competition are unimportant. Competition is a key aspect that differentiates sport from many other activities. It is a "situation in which a comparison of an individual's performance is made with some standard of excellence, in the presence of others who are aware of the criteria (standard) . . . and can evaluate the comparison process" (Martens, 1975, p. 74). It is important to note that in the definition of competition, comparisons need not be made with others' performance. The standard on which competition can be based is one's actual or expected performance.

All in all, what makes sport enjoyable for adolescents is when the coach demonstrates physical, social, and life skills, increases their competence level, establishes a positive caring and trusting relationship with them, and facilitates positive interaction with other adolescents. Identifying what coaches "should" do to make a sport experience more positive and what they are trained in and feel comfortable doing is quite different. Gould, Damarjian, and Medbery (1999) studied why mental-skill information was not being taught to junior elite tennis players. Their conclusion was that the coaches did not feel comfortable teaching such information. Many probably did not possess the skills themselves. Instead their focus was on physical skill development and on emphasizing winning. In effect, the coaches were coaching the sport, not the adolescent.

Preparing coaches for this new role will not be easy. Their educational preparation, if they have had specific training and many have not, focuses much more on teaching the skills rather than the individual. If they are coaching in a competitive environment, they may be reinforced only for winning, if they are reinforced at all. The number of staff available for after-school, youth-serving programs is woefully inadequate, their pay is low, and they have little or no training. Therefore, many youth coaches, especially in after-school programs, are parents volunteering to coach. While parents in wealthier neighborhoods are eager to volunteer, in poorer neighborhoods recruiting and retaining volunteers is so difficult that many youth are either unserved or underserved, and the quality of programming is uneven (Edmundson & Dithmer, 1997; Reid & Tremblay, 1994).

To develop quality programming, coach education programs must be instituted for staff and volunteers. These programs must have some or all of the following characteristics:

1   modular: have multiple components built from these modules that can be taught both independently or together;
2   flexible: be applicable to a wide variety of sport and leisure activities so it can be customized to the audience. There should be a common core as well as different components appropriate for different activities such as sports or the arts;
3   cost- and time-effective: be sensitive to time constraints so that training can be viewed as a process of learning over time;
4   training and program material should be multimedia: be available in multiple formats (manuals, workbooks, handouts, videos, etc.) to maintain a high level of interest;
5   consistent: have a common viewpoint and philosophy among the critical program elements;
6   teachable: be capable of being taught and learned by different people at different times in different settings to facilitate community ownership of the program;
7   scale-able: be transportable, replicable, and sufficiently robust to facilitate community ownership and be applicable to settings with different levels of resources; and
8   evaluable: contain multiple levels of assessment and evaluation, many of which can be embedded in the delivery of the program (Danish, 2000).

Dealing with leadership issues will require a serious commitment of time and money. Three issues must be addressed. First, we must be willing to commit the time and resources to expand our pool of adult leaders. Given that the schools are no longer an ideal setting to assume the responsibility of providing the needed leadership, it would seem the need has increased. Second, we must delineate what factors are keeping us from engaging in this task. Third, we must decide what initial steps we are going to take to remedy the situation.

We have a second leadership issue with which to contend as well – parents. The recent news reports of parents fighting officials, coaches, other parents, and even adolescent participants are startling. Coaches and other staff may want to meet with parents prior to the season to explain the team or league philosophy so that parents have an expectation of what to expect and can remove their child if their expectations do not match those of the coach or league. Parents have to recognize that to be most effective they need to be a contributing part of the team, not a distraction.

However, not all parents are invested in their son's and daughter's activities. The place of parents in after-school programs conducted by youth-serving organizations is confusing. Sometimes programs serve as substitutes for parents. In some families, parents need some of the supports being provided for their children. Because parents are working, unavailable, or unreliable, many youth-service programs do not automatically have programs for the caring parent or relative. Nor do they expect their help in delivering the programs. Given the vast number of challenges in serving youth, involving parents, care-givers, and "gatekeepers," where possible and appropriate, is an important way to serve these youth and, at the same time, increase parenting and caregiving skills. Unfortunately, few programs have the resources to develop and sustain such programming.

Developing effective leaders is just one issue we face. How to deliver programs that teach life and sport skills together is another difficult issue.

Issues in program implementation

If the sports program is designed to help the adolescent learn both sport and life skills, what is learned in the athletic venue must be able to be transferred to non-sport settings. There are a number of strategies that can enhance the transfer. They include: (1) design-ing conditions to enhance transfer at the beginning of the activity; (2) creating similari-ties between the environment of the activity and the environment where the transfer is to occur; (3) providing opportunities to practice transfer during the activity; (4) provid-ing opportunities to reflect on the experiences; (5) involving peers who have successfully completed the activity; (6) involving significant others in the learning process; and (7) providing follow-up experiences to reinforce learning (Gass, 1985).

In the case of sport-based life-skills programs, the similarity between teaching sport skills and life skills provides an immediate advantage. Both sets of skills must be taught, not caught. Simply participating in sport itself is insufficient. There is nothing about a ball or a sport venue that teaches life skills or any aspect of positive development. Com-bining sport participation with lectures about the dangers of alcohol and drugs, manag-ing anger, and staying in school given by well-known athletes is also inadequate. First, being told what not to do is common fodder for youth and, although the messenger may be important to them, the message often has a limited impact. If messages are to be imparted, they need to focus on what has made the messenger successful, on and off the field – for example, their strength of character, steely determination, and deep desire to succeed regardless of the hardships and barriers placed in front of them. These are some of the life skills that can make adolescents succeed. When this side of an athlete is revealed, youth can truly appreciate their accomplishments and know what may be possible for them.

Second, and perhaps more important, it is necessary to remember that adolescents are active individuals. Their life experiences suggest they learn best by doing rather than by talking. If it is true that individuals remember only 10 percent of what they hear, the per-centage for adolescents may be lower. A Chinese proverb best describes the ideal teach-ing process – I listen – and forget, I see – and remember, I do – and understand.

In fact, teaching life skills is similar to teaching any new skill. The basic process for skill teaching is: name it, describe it, and give a rationale for its use; demonstrate the skill so correct and incorrect uses of the skill can be observed; and provide opportunities for extensive, supervised practice of the skill with continuous feedback. When integrating life skills and sport skills, special considerations exist. It is beneficial to provide a seamless transition between the two, yet if a goal of the program is to promote transference from one setting to another, some separation of the activities is necessary.

After trial and error, we have concluded that if the life-skill instruction were taught too separately from the sport instruction, the life skills would simply be ignored or easily forgotten. If the life-skill instruction were fully integrated into the sport instruction, it would be hard for the youth to understand how the life skills could be applied outside of sport. As a result of these experiences, we developed the following instructional design. We teach the general concept of the skill first. As part of the instruction we emphasize that successful athletes need to improve both their "below the neck" (physical skills) and "above the neck" (mental skills) abilities. Further, we explain and provide examples through activities for how both physical and mental skills can be practiced and improved in sport settings and how the mental skills can be practiced and improved in non-sport settings. Opportunities are then made available to apply and practice the skill in the sport venue. We also have the participants apply the skill to other areas of their lives and help them develop a plan to practice the skill in these other domains. Finally, we have the participants report successes and failures in applying the skill in both contexts, both during the session and at the next session.

Examples of Sport-based Life-Skills Programs

The SUPER Programs (Sports United to Promote Education and Recreation) (Danish et al., in press, a) are examples of integrated sport and life-skills programs. SUPER is a really series of sports-based life skills that are taught within sports clinics and form the basis of a program. Sessions involve three sets of activities: learning the physical skills related to a specific sport; learning life skills related to sports in general and how these skills are applicable outside of sport; and playing the sport. Skill modules are adapted to fit the specific sport and time. Each of the three activities lasts between 20 and 45 minutes.

One example of a SUPER Program has been done with basketball. An NCAA Division I men's and women's basketball team was trained to teach the program to middle school students. The program took place once per week for 12 weeks after school. The middle school students were placed in teams of approximately 10, with two college student-athletes serving as their coaches. During the 90-minute sessions, there were three stations: basketball fundamentals, basketball games, and life-skills teaching. Some of the life skills taught were how to dream, turning dreams into reachable goals, developing plans to reach the goals, overcoming goal roadblocks, developing social support, managing emotions, and learning positive self-talk. All of these skills have applicability beyond sport.

Student-athlete coaches were also taught how to use the Sport Observation System (SOS). The SOS involves focusing on how youth participate and not just on how well they perform. Understanding "how" provides information on the mental skills participants have in dealing with coaching/teaching and is likely to be indicative of how they will respond to other forms of instruction such as school and job training. The SOS is presented below.

The Sport Observation System

- How attentive are participants when given instructions or observing demonstration?
- What happens when they cannot perform an activity to their expectations?
- Do they initiate questions when they do not understand something, or do they wait for someone else to talk first?
- Do they initiate conversation with others, or do they wait for someone else to talk first?
- How do they respond when they have a good or a bad performance?
- How do they respond when others have a good or a bad performance?
- How do they respond when someone gives them praise or criticism?
- Do they give up when they don't do well, or do they persist?
- Do they compete or cooperate with teammates?

SUPER student-athlete leaders were asked to speak to the members of their team about what they observed. A "life-skills card" was given to each middle school participant at the end of the program. The report card provided feedback to the participants on the "how" and "how well" they had done.

Hodge, Heke, and McCarroll (2000) have used the SUPER model to develop the Rugby Advantage Program (RAP) in New Zealand and Danish and his colleagues (Danish, in press; Danish et al., 2000) have extended the model to golf with the development of the First Tee Life Skills Program.

Although the life-skill programs described above have been taught to individuals who live in their country's dominant culture, a life-skills program loosely based on the SUPER Program has been developed by and for an indigenous population in New Zealand. The Hokowhitu Program (Heke, 2001) is a sport-based drug and alcohol intervention program designed by New Zealand Maori for New Zealand Maori.

Concluding Comments

We have always known that sport is more than a physical activity. Plato said, "The moral value of exercises and sports far outweigh the physical value" (1920, p. 46). Pope John Paul II recently called sport "a total valorization of the body, a healthy spirit of competition, an education in the values of life, the joy of living" (Anon., 2000). When sport meets these objectives, it is an ideal vehicle to teach positive youth development. Unfortunately, too often these programs are not successful in reaching these objectives.

To be successful, we will face many challenges. We must develop skills in instructional design and program development and evaluation. However, we must do much more. We must reach more adolescents with these programs. Providing opportunities for more adolescents to experience programs that teach both sport and life skills will require recruiting and training new coaches and retraining old coaches to teach these programs. It will require expanding a community's capacity to offer such programs by reaching out to its largest and most untapped, yet valuable resource – youth. Peers are an excellent resource in teaching life-skills programs to younger peers (Danish, 2000).

Finally, we must encourage organizations that conduct sport and physical activity programs for youth, both school-based and after-school-based, to adopt these programs. Sport is a well-established institution worldwide with well-developed mores and traditions. Many individuals and organizations, including some adolescent researchers, believe that sport already teaches life skills and there may be resistance. Collaborating with national organizations, including professional sports organizations, to disseminate effective programs will be necessary if we wish to dramatically expand the number of adolescents we reach.

Sport can be an essential element in personal growth when programs are designed to enhance life's lessons. This is especially true when youth are taught to compete against themselves; more specifically, when competition is focused on maximizing one's own potential and achieving one's own goals. In other words, participation in sport is best when the focus is on knowing oneself as opposed to proving oneself.

Key Readings

Bloom, M. (2000). The uses of theory in primary prevention practice: Evolving thoughts on sports and after-school activities as influences of social competence. In S. J. Danish & T. P. Gullotta (Eds.), *Developing competent youth and strong communities through after-school programming.* Washington, DC: CWLA Press.
Dr. Bloom examines a number of different sport and after-school experiences and the potential benefits and drawbacks to each from the perspective of developing competence. He is a thought-provoking writer who comes at the topic both theoretically and with an intimate knowledge of the literature.

Csikszentmihalyi, M. (1990). *Flow: The psychology of optimal experience.* New York: Harper & Row.
This book helps us to understand what makes a task intrinsically motivating. The critical elements are: the need for balance between skill and challenge; complete absorption in the activity; the merging of action and awareness; total concentration in the activity; a sense of control; and a feeling of effortless movement. As one can see from these elements, it is not an everyday occurrence or a state someone tries to reach.

Danish, S. J., & Gullotta, T. P. (Eds.) (2000). *Developing competent youth and strong communities through after-school programming.* Washington, DC: CWLA Press.
A variety of after-school programs are described in sufficient detail that one could replicate them. Efforts are made to discuss some of the components across the programs that make them effective.

Smith, F. L., & Smoll, R. E. (1996). *Children and youth in sport: A biopsychological perspective.* Madison, WI: Brown & Benchmark.
Based on their classic research in 1979 about coaching youth, the authors examine children's psychosocial development through sport and how to enhance the experience for youth. They identify some best coaching practices that work!

References

Anon. (2000, May 22). Sport as seen by the Pope. *Sports Illustrated, 94,* 26.
Bloom, M. (2000). The uses of theory in primary prevention practice: Evolving thoughts on sports

and after-school activities as influences of social competence. In S. J. Danish & T. P. Gullotta (Eds.), *Developing competent youth and strong communities through after-school programming* (pp. 17–66). Washington, DC: CWLA Press.

Brown, B. B. (1988). The vital agenda for research on extracurricular influences: a reply to Holland and Andre. *Review of Educational Research, 58*, 107–111.

Carnegie Corporation of New York (1989). Turning points: Preparing American youth for the 21st century. Reports of the Carnegie Council on Adolescent Development. Waldorf, MD: Carnegie Corporation.

Carnegie Corporation of New York (1995). Great transitions: Preparing adolescents for a new century. Reports of the Carnegie Council on Adolescent Development. Waldorf, MD: Carnegie Corporation.

Csikszentmihalyi, M. (1990). *Flow: The psychology of optimal experience.* New York: Harper & Row.

Csikszentmihalyi, M., Rathunde, K., & Whalen, S. (1993). *Talented teenagers: The roots of success & failure.* Cambridge: Cambridge University Press.

Danish, S. J. (2000). Youth and community development: How after-school programming can make a difference. In S.J. Danish & T. P. Gullotta (Eds.), *Developing competent youth and strong communities through after-school programming* (pp. 275–302). Washington, DC: CWLA Press.

Danish, S. J. (in press). Teaching life skills through sport. In M. Gatz, M. A. Messner, & S. J. Ball-Rokeach (Eds.), *Paradoxes of youth sport* (pp. 49–60). Albany, NY: State University of New York Press.

Danish, S. J., Brunelle, J., Fazio, R., & Hogan, C. (2000). The First Tee National Youth Golf and Leadership Academy: First evaluation report. Unpublished.

Danish, S. J., D'Augelli, A., & Ginsberg, M. (1984). Life development intervention: Promotion of mental health through the development of competence. In S. Brown & R. Lent (Eds.), *Handbook of counseling psychology* (pp. 520–544). New York: Wiley.

Danish, S. J., Fazio, R., Nellen, V., & Owens, S. (in press, a). Teaching life skills through sport: Community-based programs to enhance adolescent development. In J. Van Raalte & B. Brewer (Eds.), *Exploring sport and exercise psychology* (2nd ed.). Washington, DC: American Psychological Association.

Danish, S. J., & Gullotta, T. P. (Eds.). (2000) *Developing competent youth and strong communities through after-school programming.* Washington, DC: CWLA Press.

Danish, S. J., Hodge, K., Heke, I., & Taylor, T. (in press, b). Promoting healthy development of youth through physical activity and sport. In T. P. Gullotta & M. Bloom (Eds.), *Encyclopedia of primary prevention.*

Danish, S. J., Petitpas, A. J., & Hale, B. D. (1990). Sport as a context for developing competence. In T. P. Gullotta, G. Adams, & R. Montemar (Eds.), *Developing social competency in adolescence* (Vol. 3, pp. 169–194). Newbury Park, CA: Sage.

Danish, S. J., Petitpas, A. J., & Hale, B. D. (1993). Life development intervention for athletes: Life skills through sports. *Counseling Psychologist, 21*(3), 352–385.

De Coubertin, P. (1918). What we can now ask of sport. Address to the Greek Liberal Club of Lauranne, France, February 24, 1918. (Trans. J. Dixon, in *The Olympic idea: Discoveries and essays.* Köln: Carl Diem Institut, 1966).

Eder, D. (1985). The cycles of popularity: Interpersonal relations among female adolescents. *Sociology of Education, 58*, 154–65.

Eder, D., & Parker, S. (1987). The cultural production and reproduction of gender: the effect of extracurricular activities on peer-group culture. *Sociology of Education, 60*, 200–214.

Edmundson, K. (2000). Issues in after-school youth development programming. In S. J. Danish & T. P. Gullotta (Eds.), *Developing competent youth and strong communities through after-school programming* (pp. 217–238). Washington, DC: CWLA Press.

Edmundson, K., & Dithmer, B. (1997). Developing opportunities for participation in structured activities for children and youth. Unpublished report for the Robert Wood Johnson Foundation.

Erikson, E. (1959). Identity and the life cycle: Selected papers. *Psychological Issues, 1*(1), 5–165.

Ewing, M., Seefeldt, V., & Brown, T. (1996). The role of organized sport in the education and health of American children and youth. Unpublished paper commissioned by the Carnegie Corporation, New York.

Fejgin, N. (1994). Participation in high school sports: A subversion of school mission or contribution to academic goals? *Sociology of Sport Journal, 11*, 211–230.

Fox, K. (1992). The complexities of self-esteem promotion in physical education and sport. In T. Williams, L. Almond, & A. Sparkes (Eds.), *Sport and physical activity: Moving towards excellence* (pp. 383–389). London: E & F. N. Spon.

Gass, M. (1985). Programming the transfer of learning in adventure education. *Journal of Experimental Education, 8*(3), 18–24.

Gould, D. (2001, February). Coaching the child not the sport. Presentation made to the VCU Conference on Learning Life Lessons through Sport: Focus on Youth Development. Richmond, VA.

Gould, D., Damarjian, N., & Medbery, R. (1999). An examination of mental skills training in junior tennis coaches. *Sport Psychologist, 13*, 127–143.

Heke, I. (2001). The Hokowhitu Program: Designing a sporting intervention to address alcohol and substance abuse in adolescent Maori. Manuscript, University of Otago, Dunedin, New Zealand.

Hirsch, E., Jr. (1988). *Cultural literacy.* New York: Vintage.

Hodge, K., & Danish, S. J. (1999). Promoting life skills for adolescent males through sport. In A. Horne & M. Kiselica (Eds.), *Handbook of counseling boys and adolescent males* (pp. 55–71). Thousand Oaks, CA: Sage.

Hodge, K., Heke, J. I., & McCarroll, N. (2000). The Rugby Advantage Program (RAP). Manuscript, University of Otago, Dunedin, New Zealand.

Institute for Social Research. (1985). Time, goods & well-being. Ann Arbor, MI: Michigan State University, unpublished.

Jones, M. B., & Offord, D. R. (1989). Reduction of antisocial behavior in poor children by nonschool skill-development. *Journal of Child Psychology and Psychiatry, 30*, 737–750.

Kinney, D. A. (1993). From nerds to normals: The recovery of identity among adolescents from middle school to high school. *Sociology of Education, 66*, 21–40.

Kleiber, D. A. & Kirshnit, C. E. (1991). Sport involvement and identity formation. In L. Diamant (Ed.), *Mind–body maturity: Psychological approaches to sports, exercise, and fitness* (pp. 193–11). New York: Hemisphere.

Kleiber, D. A., & Roberts, G. C. (1981). The effects of sport experience in the development of social character: An exploratory investigation. *Journal of Sport Psychology, 3*, 114–122.

Mahoney, J. L. (2000). School extracurricular activity participation as a moderator in the development of antisocial patterns. *Child Development, 71*, 502–516.

Mahoney, J. L., & Stattin, H. (2000). Leisure activities and adolescents' antisocial behavior: The role of structure and social context. *Journal of Adolescence, 23*, 113–127.

Martens, R. (1975). *Social psychology and physical activity.* New York: Harper & Row.

Osgood, D. W., Wilson, J. K., O'Malley, P. M., Bachman, J. G., & Johnston, L. D. (1996). Routine activities and individual deviant behavior. *American Sociological Review, 61*, 635–655.

Petitpas, A. L., & Champagne, D. E. (1988). Developmental programming for intercollegiate athletes. *Journal of College Student Development, 29*(5), 454–460.

Pittman, K. J. (1996). Programs that work. @ online. http://www.iyfnet.org/document.cfm/22/general/51

Plato (1920). Protagoras. In A. Cubberly (Ed.), *Readings in the history of education* (p. 46). New York: Houghton-Mifflin.

Reid, I., & Tremblay, M. (1994). Canadian youth: Does activity reduce risk? Report to the Inter-Provincial Sport and Recreation Council, University of New Brunswick, Fredericton, NB, Canada.

Roberts, G. (1993). Motivation in sport: Understanding and enhancing the motivation and achievement of children. In R. Singer, M. Murphey, & L. K. Tennant (Eds.), *Handbook of research on sport psychology* (pp. 405–420). New York: Macmillan.

Smith, F. L. & Smoll, R. E. (1996). *Children and youth in sport: A biopsychological perspective.* Madison, WI: Brown & Benchmark.

Strean, W. B., & Garcia Bengoechea, E. (2001, October). Fun in youth sport: Perspectives from coaches' conceptions and participants' experiences. Paper presented at the Association for the Advancement of Applied Sport Psychology, Orlando, FL.

Task Force on Education of Young Adolescents (1989). *Turning points: Preparing American youth for the 21st century.* New York: Carnegie Corporation.

Veroff, J. (1969). Social comparison and the development of achievement motivation. In C. P. Smith (Ed.), *Achievement-related motives in children* (pp. 46–101). New York: Russell Sage.

White, R. (1963). Ego and reality in psychoanalytic theory: A proposal regarding independent ego energies [Monograph 11]. *Psychological Issues, 3*(3), New York: International University.

Zaharopoulos, E., & Hodge, K. (1991). Self-concept and sports participation. *New Zealand Journal of Psychology, 20,* 12–16.

CHAPTER SIX

The World of Work and Careers

Fred W. Vondracek and Erik J. Porfeli

Introduction

Theorists in the field of human development generally agree that one of the main tasks during adolescence is to become prepared for eventually assuming a viable role in the world of adult work. According to some, adolescents become adults when they first undertake a "real job" (Inhelder & Piaget, 1958). Bandura (1995, p. 23) noted that

> the choices people make during formative periods shape the course of their lives. Such choices determine which of their potentialities they cultivate, the types of options that are foreclosed or remain realizable over their life course, and the life-style they follow. Among the choices that affect life paths, those that center on occupational choice and development are of special import.

Developmental theorists, however, are not the only ones placing work in a central position within the course of adolescence. Across a variety of cultures, studies of adolescents' hopes, aims, and aspirations for the future have demonstrated that adolescents themselves are most interested in their future education and occupation (cf. Nurmi, 1991). For example, a survey of students conducted in Germany indicated that they judged finding a place in the world of work to be their most pressing concern (Foerster & Friedrich, 1996). In the Netherlands, Bosma (1992) reported that in identity interviews, adolescents most frequently mentioned the area of school/(future) occupation as important. After all, having a "real job" and getting paid for one's work represents a big step toward independence, autonomy, and adulthood.

Work touches the lives of adolescents in many different domains. Educational track and attainment and academic achievement reflect and impact adolescents' work aspirations. Adolescents frequently choose peers from within the school setting and often from within their educational track. Hence, one's choice of friends shapes and is shaped by academic and vocational choices, abilities, and interests. In addition to the school context, it is well known that the adolescent's early or initial experiences of work often occur within the context of the family. Doing chores in the home and receiving tangible and intangible feedback may be the earliest work experiences available to children and adolescents. Adolescents also vicariously experience the world of work through their parents' recount of and reaction to their own work experience. In spite of the pervasiveness of work in the lives of children, relatively little is known about how adolescents can be encouraged to view work as an opportunity, rather than a burden, and as a means to create and structure their own lives. Relatively little is also known about how adolescents acquire the values that determine the types of rewards and satisfactions they will ultimately seek from work. Part of the reason for this relative lack of knowledge is that the study of adolescents' relationship to the world of work is not the domain of one discipline or field of study. Rather, it is distributed over many disciplines, ranging from psychology and sociology to education and economics. The diversity of research, albeit scarce, not only demonstrates the centrality of work within the human experience, but also points toward the need to understand work as more than just a psychological or sociological phenomenon.

In this chapter we will review much of what is currently known about adolescence and the world of work. We will pull together findings from a number of different fields and organize them according to what we call a developmental-contextual framework. To look at adolescence from anything but a developmental perspective would make little sense. Adolescent development is not the same, however, for all adolescents. Boys and girls experience adolescence quite differently. Moreover, adolescents grow up in different families, in different cultures, under different economic circumstances, and in different physical environments. Their schools are different, as are their peer groups both within the school and neighborhood context. Therefore, to talk about development without taking the context into account also makes little sense. While discussion of all of these contextual factors is well beyond the scope of the present chapter, it is worth noting that there is a large literature in life-course sociology that is based upon the observation that the various contexts that are enumerated above structure the pathways of vocational development in adolescence and throughout the life-course (e.g., Clausen, 1993; Kohn & Schooler, 1983), and that individual development takes place within the constraints and opportunities created by these socially constructed pathways.

Using a developmental-contextual perspective means paying simultaneous attention to both individual differences in development and differences in the various contexts of adolescent development. Because of our focus on work, we will be referring to the vocational or career development of adolescents throughout this chapter. Obviously, some adolescents' vocational development proceeds smoothly and leads to just the kind of career they envisioned as children. They love what they do, they are good at it, and they are rewarded for doing it. Other adolescents' vocational development may not have such a positive tone to it. They may struggle to find any job at all, they may dislike what they end up doing, and they may feel inadequately compensated. How is it that such dramatically different pathways can characterize the vocational development of adolescents? What are the factors that lead to a satisfying and successful career, or to frustration and failure in the world of work? To search for answers to these questions, we will examine how adolescents explore the world of work, how they develop work-related interests and values, and finally, how they decide what line of work or what career to pursue.

Exploring the World of Work

In Western societies, children and adolescents are encouraged to explore the world of work in preparation for eventually entering the labor force and becoming productive citizens. Much of this exploration occurs informally, and includes avocational activities such as hobbies and leisure pursuits. Most adolescents also acquire knowledge regarding occupations through the subjects they study in school. Prominent career theorists have emphasized that the roles of leisurite and student, which have the highest salience during adolescence, offer many opportunities for adolescents to prepare for the world of work (Super, 1980). Holland (1997) stressed that leisure activities are chosen on the basis of the same personality factors and interests that guide the eventual selection of an occupation. Indeed, adolescents do not draw significant distinctions between leisure, school, and work activities (Vondracek & Skorikov, 1997). Each aspect of life offers opportunities for exploration and learning, provided the adolescent is receptive. The contexts of leisure and school are discussed elsewhere in this volume. Consequently, we now turn our attention to the role of part-time work in adolescents' career development.

The Experience of Part-Time Work

Work experience plays an important role in the way adolescents define themselves. Experiencing the reality of paid work may prompt adolescents to seriously consider, often for the first time, who they would like to be (or not to be), or who they could be in the world of work. Nevertheless, there is controversy about whether work experience during adolescence is a good, bad, or indifferent factor in their career development. Should adolescents work at all? Some parents consider it reasonable to let their adolescents concentrate on their education (which could be viewed, however, as a particular kind of work). Others feel that paid work promotes a greater respect for work and underscores the value of labor as a means to obtain things one needs and wants.

Parents are not the only ones who may disagree about whether work promotes healthy adolescent development. Researchers have reached somewhat conflicting findings in their studies of adolescent work over the past two decades. One widely quoted study (Greenberger & Steinberg, 1986) focused on the negative aspects of adolescent work, concluding that adolescents who work part-time during their high school years are more likely to use tobacco and marijuana than those adolescents who do not work. Moreover, the study concluded that part-time work, especially when it involved more than 15–20 hours per week, interfered with schoolwork and resulted in cynical attitudes toward paid work. Other studies found that students who worked were more likely to be involved in various forms of misconduct (Steinberg & Dornbusch, 1991), and consumed more alcohol (Mortimer et al., 1996). In almost all instances where negative consequences were found to be associated with adolescent work, the adolescents worked excessively long hours, thereby reducing their opportunities to have typical adolescent social relationships (Greenberger, 1988) and increasing the risks associated with unhealthy lifestyles and overexertion (Bachman & Schulenberg, 1993). Interestingly, Mortimer et al. (1996) found that high school seniors who worked moderate hours had better grades than those who worked more than 20 hours, but they also had better grades than those who did not participate in paid work.

Positive consequences of adolescent part-time work have often been reported along-side some of the negative consequences summarized earlier. For example, Greenberger and Steinberg (1986) concluded that, in spite of a preponderance of negative consequences, working adolescents reported that they were more punctual, dependable, and responsible than their nonworking peers. These findings are consistent with reports that adolescents' work experiences increase their employability at the conclusion of school (Kablaoui & Pautler, 1991; Stern & Nakata, 1989). Another study examined the impact of part-time work on adolescents' valuing of various aspects of work, finding that working adolescents decreased the value they placed on peripheral aspects of work (e.g., status, power, prestige) and increased the value they placed on central aspects of work such as creativity, achievement, and self-development (Skorikov & Vondracek, 1997). The former are usually associated with extrinsic values and motivation, i.e., rewards derived from work but external to the work itself, while the latter represent intrinsic values and motivation (i.e., rewards derived from the work itself) (Mortimer & Lorence, 1995). Finally, there is evidence to suggest that part-time work may enhance adolescents' relationships with their parents because parents appreciate the increased autonomy and independence that is usually associated with work (Phillips & Sandstrom, 1990; Shanahan et al., 1996).

Clearly, the question of whether part-time work is either good or bad for adolescents is too simplistic (cf. Hamilton & Lavine-Powers, 1990). As Finch, Mortimer, and Ryu (1997, p. 327) observe, "the consequences of the transition to part-time work depend on the quality of the work experience, its meaning, and the context in which it occurs." Whether young people directly enter the labor market out of high school or proceed to college is one of the key factors determining the utility of part-time work during the high school years. Those who plan to go on to college are more likely to view their work experience as "something to do" and as a source of extra income. They are less likely to view their part-time jobs as preludes to working in their future occupations and they are unlikely to expect occupational advancement as a result of such jobs. Students who plan to leave school after high school graduation (or before) are much more likely to expect (and eventually experience) continuity in their part-time job and their eventual full-time work. It is reasonable, therefore, to hold a differentiated view regarding the meaning of part-time work among working adolescents.

A differentiated view of adolescent work is clearly present in the various theoretical and conceptual models that attempt to account for the role of work in the lives of adolescents. Erikson (1959, 1968) has been most explicit in his view that the experience of work shapes the developmental course of individuals, as they advance from childhood to adolescence and adulthood. Work and the antecedents of work in childhood and early adolescence are viewed as requiring (and promoting) ever-changing adaptive capacities that are necessary for advancement from one stage of development to the next. As children and adolescents begin to understand the difference between work and play, they become capable of being workers and they realize that they must find a place for themselves, an identity, in the world of occupations. Thus, adolescent work is clearly conceptualized as a means toward developmental advancement including, most importantly, the achievement of a self-chosen identity.

A quite different theoretical perspective on adolescent part-time work maintains that it can be a positive or a negative influence, depending on the social and historical context within which it occurs (Vondracek, Lerner, & Schulenberg, 1986). Accordingly, adolescent work may undermine the ability of parents to monitor and control their children (Greenberger & Steinberg, 1986), or it may bring parents and children closer together, as was often the case during the Great Depression, when the work performed by adolescents was an important contributor to the cohesion and even survival of many families (Elder, 1974). Moreover, adolescents' part-time work may have a different meaning (e.g., Greenberger & Steinberg, 1986) and different consequences (Shanahan et al., 1994), depending on whether they live in urban or rural settings. Obviously, adolescent work has many dimensions, and this complexity has contributed to the mixed view of adolescent work as an experience that can lead to functional and dysfunctional outcomes.

Because neither theory nor empirical evidence offers a clear answer, we would like to repeat some observations made quite a few years ago:

> Adolescents are most likely to benefit from part-time work if they are physically and mentally capable of handling the demands of the job, if the job is likely to enhance their commitment to work, if the work does not interfere with school or with important peer relationships, and if the adolescent is sufficiently emotionally mature, conscientious, and reliable to have a good chance of experiencing work as something positive, something that leads to desired rewards. (Vondracek & Schulenberg, 1984, p. 348)

What adolescents consider to be the desirable rewards of work varies widely and is usually considered in discussions of work values (Super, 1973) or work-aspect preferences (Pryor, 1982). Next, we will review how adolescents acquire work values and how these values may differ across adolescents depending on a number of factors, including their family context and social and cultural background.

The Development of Work Values

The most prominent theoretical framework for examining how children and adolescents acquire work values has been called the "occupational linkage hypothesis" (Kohn & Schooler, 1983; Mortimer & Kumka, 1982; Ryu & Mortimer, 1996). The basic idea behind this hypothesis or model is that parental work and occupational values and behaviors are transmitted in a variety of ways to their offspring during childhood and adolescence. For example, parents' encouragement and support influence adolescent occupational aspirations and attainments in directions that reflect parents' work values (Hauser, Tsai, & Sewell, 1983). Recent research has suggested that the process of transmitting values from parents to their children involves complex relationships which may be different for mother–daughter and father–son dyads. In fact, Ryu and Mortimer

(1996) concluded that the occupational linkage hypothesis is far more applicable to the development of work values in boys than in girls, and that adolescents generally tend to be more influenced by their same-sex parent than by their opposite-sex parent.

The fact that girls and boys hold different work values has been demonstrated in numerous studies (e.g., Eccles & Hoffman, 1984; Tittle, 1988; Wijting, Arnold, & Conrad, 1978). Findings have generally centered on the observation that boys prefer extrinsic and instrumental values such as job security, risk-taking and high financial rewards, while girls tend to prefer expressive and socially oriented values such as friendship and altruism (Erez, Borochov, & Mannheim, 1989). Other studies have called into question the persistence of these traditional sex differences in view of the changing climate toward gender equality in the workplace. For example, Vodanovich and Kramer (1989) found that male and female college students were quite similar in how they ranked traditionally masculine and traditionally feminine work values. Thus, it is quite possible that shifting cultural values are leading to an androgynous work-values pattern in which men and women value both extrinsic and intrinsic outcomes (Beutell & Brenner, 1986). Further support for the changing patterns of work values is offered by a recent study that examined a large sample of both Caucasian and African American adolescents. Although both extrinsic and intrinsic work values were highly valued in this sample, intrinsic values were rated highest, and between midadolescence and early adulthood extrinsic values declined in importance. Most important in the socialization of young people toward work were parental aspirations and race (Cotton, Bynum, & Madhere, 1997).

The view that the cultural context is important in the acquisition of work values stresses enculturation as the most important means for the transmission of work values to children and adolescents. Enculturation works through the adolescent's social group affiliation and the social group's socioeconomic and cultural (e.g., national, religious) characteristics (Krau, 1987). Even in this broad model, however, the family and the school are viewed as the primary socializing agents influencing the work-values socialization of adolescents. For example, in Krau's Israeli sample, students in the Catholic monastic schools reflected "Christian work morale," while students in the Arab schools had work values that reflected the problems of national identity and rights (Krau, 1987, p. 117). These findings clearly illustrate a central thesis of this chapter, namely, that outcomes are produced through the dynamic interaction of the developing individual within his or her multiple and hierarchically structured contexts (Vondracek, Lerner, & Schulenberg, 1986). Viewed from this perspective, simple answers are rarely correct. The transformation of adolescents into productive workers is a complex process that is expressed through a multitude of possible pathways, chosen by the individual in relation to the affordances offered by his or her context. Precisely how adolescents make their career choices will be the subject of the next section.

Career Decision-Making

Thus far we have seen that adolescents can acquire experience and knowledge about the world of work through part-time work. In addition, as a result of socialization experiences in the family, school, community, and cultural contexts, they gradually formulate values regarding work, and they quite naturally become curious about which occupations might allow them to implement their work values. Thus, adolescents become interested in the issue of what occupation will cause people to look up to them, what occupation will facilitate their making a lot of money, or what occupation will optimize their chances for personal growth. A logical corollary to this process is a growing awareness of the variety of preparatory pathways that one must travel to eventually arrive at the occupational destiny that is desired. The process of translating hard-earned knowledge of the world of work and of one's own preferences and values into occupational reality requires that good decisions be made regarding the occupational paths one follows.

In fact, however, many adolescents short-circuit the process of learning about themselves and the world of work and making rational decisions based on what they learn. Unfortunately, this is true for most adolescents who drop out of school and for most of those who finish high school and enter the labor force without additional schooling or training (particularly in the United States). This circumstance has led to a clear distinction between the transition from school to *work* versus the transition from school to *career,* reflecting what some have called a great divide between those who work after high school (and get *jobs*) and those who go on to college (and start *careers*) (Hamilton & Lavine-Powers, 1990).

Decisions about careers are not what they used to be. In the middle of the twentieth century, it was not uncommon for individuals to choose to work for a company or organization and then to spend their entire career with that employer. Those days are gone, for the most part, as rapid changes in the global economy and the inexorable rise of technology are causing mergers, restructuring, and bankruptcies at an alarming rate. Whole branches of industry or commerce become obsolete and new ones are invented, seemingly overnight. Consequently, making decisions about careers must be viewed as work in progress, not just during adolescence, but throughout the course of adult life as well. Perhaps surprisingly, this notion, although brought into renewed focus by rapid economic changes, has been around for quite a long time. Phillips and Pazienza (1988, p. 3) observed that

> by 1929, Kitson was already warning against the misconceptions underlying the attempt to "find out what I'm cut out for," and he made a strong case for the adaptability of individuals in terms of their suitability for a number of occupations and their capacity for developing new interests and abilities as a function of their life experiences.

In short, adolescents are unlikely to simply "choose a career" or occupation. Instead, with their first tentative decision of what they want to be, they initiate a lengthy process of decision-making that may not run its course until old age.

Given the ubiquity of decision-making throughout the course of one's career, it is appropriate to examine what is involved in the process, what it takes to make good decisions and, more importantly, what it takes to make decisions that lead to good outcomes. A number of authors have proposed models that describe a process of moving through a number of stages before a decision can be reached. For example, Tiedeman and O'Hara (1963) described an elaborate stage model that later formed the basis of Harren's (1979) sequential stage model of the career decision-making process, which included the stages of awareness, planning, commitment, and implementation. Another elaborate model of career decision-making, relying on social learning theory, describes the learning of various component skills as the prerequisite for good career decision-making (Krumboltz, Mitchell, & Jones, 1976).

A different approach to career decision-making was taken by Gati (1986; Gati, Fassa, & Houminer, 1995). Basically, he asserted that while individuals may be able to learn about themselves in relation to work, they could not realistically be expected to learn enough about the ever-changing world of work. Moreover, even if individuals were perfectly knowledgeable about themselves and the world of work, they would still not necessarily be good decision makers. To overcome these difficulties, Gati (1986, 1990) adapted in his Sequential Elimination Model (SEM) core features of Tversky's (1972) theory of choice, which has as its central focus a procedure called "elimination-by-aspects." The SEM, when applied to career decision-making, requires the identification and ranking (according to their relative importance) of various occupational aspects, including objective features such as abilities or physical constraints, and more subjective features such as work values. When a desirable aspect is identified, all alternatives that do not incorporate it are eliminated from further consideration. This process continues until only a few (or one) alternatives remain. Gati and his colleagues (1995) have shown how the SEM is readily usable in counseling designed to help adolescents or young adults to rationally proceed toward making sound decisions. Their nine-step SEM procedure starts with defining and structuring the decision problem, e.g., choosing an occupation or choosing a field of study, which leads to identifying those aspects of the decision problem that are relevant to the individual, and progresses to ranking the importance of the aspects that have been identified. Preferences are progressively narrowed and the procedure culminates by determining the steps necessary to actualize the most preferred alternative(s).

Even if the initial career choices are made rationally, there is no assurance that the decisions made are the best decisions possible, or that they will not require revision some time in the future. In fact, revising one's career decisions in light of new insights and preferences and in light of new learning about the world of work and labor market and macro-economic conditions would be considered adaptive and functional. Ultimately, the choices associated with one's career should contribute to the development of a vocational identity that is well articulated and well integrated into one's overall identity. In other words, who one is occupationally ought to be well connected to who one is as a person, as a human being. The processes of vocational or occupational identity development will be the focus of the next section.

Vocational Identity Development

"I'm a lifeguard" or "I'm a cashier at Burger King" are statements that reflect the adolescents' emerging sense of who they are in the world of work. In other words, they are beginning to have a vocational identity. Erikson (1959) is generally credited with erecting the foundation for present-day thinking about identity development. Most pertinent to the present discussion, he wrote that: "In general, it is primarily the inability to settle on an occupational identity which disturbs young people" (Erikson, 1959). He went on to observe that he had used the construct of ego identity "to denote certain comprehensive gains which the individual, at the end of adolescence, must have derived from all of his preadult experience in order to be ready for the task of adulthood" (p. 101). In Western society, being a productive worker is certainly one of the cardinal tasks of adulthood, and it is during adolescence and early adulthood that the processes of vocational development culminate in the development of a vocational identity, an identity which may be revised repeatedly, however, if personal and /or contextual circumstances demand it.

In spite of Erikson's relative emphasis on vocational (occupational) identity development, most identity researchers (e.g., Kroger, 2000) have tended to ignore the possibility that individuals may experience highly differentiated and domain-specific identity development, although the work on ethnic identity is an exception (e.g., Phinney, 1990; Phinney & Rosenthal, 1992). Archer and Waterman (1983) identified domains other than Erikson's (1968) original three (vocation, ideology, and family), including vocational plans, values, and sex-role orientation. Bosma (1992) has contributed to the discussion through investigating different areas of exploration and commitment among Dutch adolescents, and by suggesting that there are significant intraindividual, as well as interindividual differences in identity formation among adolescents. Archer (1989) has suggested that for different people, different identity domains are salient. Accordingly, vocational identity development should be most salient during adolescence, when individuals are attempting to define and establish their place in the world of work (see also Super, 1980). One supporting piece of evidence comes from a study of junior/senior high school students, which clearly demonstrated that vocational identity development tended to be more advanced in the vocational domain than in a number of other domains, including those of religion, lifestyle, and politics (Skorikov & Vondracek, 1998).

Individual differences in how people go about exploring themselves and their contexts in order to resolve the crisis of identity have been the focus of several researchers and theorists (Berzonsky, 1990; Grotevant, 1987). Berzonsky (1990), for example, has proposed that there is a "normative-oriented" style of identity development that tends to lead to foreclosure, an "information-oriented" style that may lead to moratorium or identity achievement, and an "avoidant-oriented" style that is associated with diffusion. Moreover, these different styles of identity development may also be associated with "dispositional differences in the way in which individuals appraise and attempt to manage stressors" (Berzonsky, 1992, p. 206). Because adolescents may experience vocational development, especially career decision-making, as stressful, different styles of identity formation may be associated with differences in vocational decision status. In other words, those with an information-oriented identity style may be decided (identity achieved) or actively exploring alternatives (moratorium); those with a normative-oriented style may have decided to stick with family tradition (foreclosure); and those with an avoidant-oriented style may be undecided and not working on reaching a decision through exploration (diffusion). Consistent with this differentiated view, it has been shown that the identity statuses are quite clearly associated with differences in career-decision status and various types of career indecision (Vondracek et al., 1995).

Regardless of specific theoretical orientation, there is general agreement that our occupation plays a central role in how we think about ourselves and in how others perceive and evaluate us. After all, knowing a person's occupation is a "shorthand" for a person's education and income, social standing, and lifestyle. "So, what do you do for a living?" What other question could possibly convey so much about who a person is?

Sex Differences in Career Development

In their important book on the career psychology of women, Betz and Fitzgerald (1987) identified three significant problems in women's labor-force participation: (1) a significant difference in the wages paid to men and women, with women earning only about 60 percent of the wages earned by men in similar positions; (2) a pronounced and chronic underutilization of talent and ability in women; and (3) a pronounced role-choice overload, caused by the fact that most career women are expected to not only pursue their career but be mothers and homemakers at the same time. Although progress has been made in addressing these issues, the social, economic, and cultural contexts that contributed to the creation of these problems still exist today. More importantly, these same circumstances contribute to the maintenance of an environment in which girls are still much more likely than boys to pursue careers as secretaries and nurses rather than aim toward becoming executives or physicians (Gustafson & Magnusson, 1991).

Several factors have been identified as important contributors to the persistent differences in the occupational experience of men and women. Perhaps most important among these is sex-role stereotyping. Sex-role stereotyping manifests itself in the pervasive, socially condoned assignment of different roles to both sexes across the lifespan. These differential roles are normative in society and represent approved, sex-based behavioral patterns for males and for females. Sex-role stereotypes are acquired by children quite early in their development when they are encouraged to play with different, "sex-appropriate" toys (Maccoby & Jacklin, 1974), when teachers reinforce different behaviors in boys and in girls (Guttentag & Bray, 1976), and when parents communicate that they have different (often lower) aspirations for girls than for boys (Marini, 1978). Along with the learning of sex-role stereotypic behavior, children acquire occupational stereotypes, which define the appropriateness of various occupations for males and females (Looft, 1971).

Because these occupational stereotypes are formed early and are relatively stable, they tend to profoundly influence the range of occupations considered by male and female adolescents (Gottfredson, 1981). Females tend to prefer stereotypically female occupations, while males prefer stereotypically male occupations. Some of the negative consequences of this segregation are due to the fact that female-stereotyped occupations tend to be lower-paying, lower-status occupations than the male-stereotyped occupations. Moreover, this segregation often results in women having far more limited opportunities for advancement than is typical for men (Baron & Bielby, 1985; Betz, 1994). There have been some changes in the past two decades, with a slowly increasing number of adolescent girls choosing non-traditional (i.e., male-dominated) careers (Nauta, Epperson, & Kahn, 1998). At the same time, adolescent boys are as likely as ever to stick with traditionally male occupational choices. This is most likely the case because female-dominated occupations tend to be lower-paying (O'Brien et al., 2000), but also because there is far less support for boys wishing to pursue nontraditional careers than there is for girls who wish to do so.

Although sex-role stereotyping and the stereotyping of occupations account for much of the observed difference in the vocational development and occupational preferences of male and female adolescents, they do not account for all of it. There is evidence to suggest that, even today, young women are much more likely to feel that pursuing a family, as opposed to pursuing a career, has top priority in their lives. One study reported that between the ages of 17 and 22, women changed their career plans to select more traditional and less prestigious careers, possibly to accommodate their plans for family and children (O'Brien et al., 2000). Clearly, many women's lives are shaped, to a large extent, by the biological destiny of childbearing and of nurturing children, priorities that are most often detrimental to the career trajectories typical in male-dominated, and thus more prestigious, occupations. It has also been established that some aspects of work valued by females tend to be different from those valued by males (Beutell & Brenner, 1986; Pryor, 1983). Females are more likely to link personal achievement with helping others (Super & Hendrix, 1968), they tend to consider good relationships with their coworkers as very important, and they value working in pleasant surroundings. In contrast, males rate creativity, money, and physical activity to be most important (Vondracek et al., 1990).

Beliefs of personal efficacy have also been shown to play an important role in vocational development (Betz, 1994; Betz & Hackett, 1981). For example, when adolescents perceive their efficacy in a particular occupational or educational area to be high, they invest more time and effort in exploring and pursuing a future in that area. Conversely, when they perceive their efficacy to be low in a particular area, they are unlikely to make it part of their possible futures (Betz, 1994; Betz & Hackett, 1981; Lent, Brown, & Larkin, 1986). Male and female high school students have been shown to have different patterns of occupational self-efficacy, with boys having higher self-efficacy perceptions in traditionally male occupations and in science, while girls have higher self-efficacy perceptions in traditionally female occupations.

Many of the sex differences found in the vocational development of adolescents and in the career development of young adults are based on a complicated mix of social, cultural, and biological factors. They tend to be associated with negative consequences for women, and progress toward their elimination or reduction has been slow. Consequently, Hackett (1995) has argued for instituting programs to enhance the career self-efficacy of women and minorities, who are underrepresented in technical and scientific fields. The successful application of such interventions would help to reduce the negative consequences of sex differences in the vocational development of girls and young women, and it would also be a boon to an economy that is experiencing a shortage of skilled and well-prepared workers in the sciences and in technology.

Non-College-Bound Youth

Although about 50 percent of all graduating seniors report a baccalaureate degree as their educational aspiration, approximately 75 percent of all adolescents in the United States do not attain this goal (cf. Stern & National Center for Research in Vocational Education, 1995). Approximately half of all adolescents, called the "forgotten half" in a noted Grant Foundation report, have finished their formal education when they leave high school, often without a diploma (Youth and America's Future, 1988, p. 1). Consequently, the majority of adolescents enter the labor market in the United States with the intention of simply finding a job; developing a career is something many of them will not have thought about or considered seriously for a variety of reasons. Having only a high school education and some part-time work experience when they set out in search of a job places these adolescents at an immediate disadvantage in the new, technology-driven global economy that places a premium on credentials and strong educational preparation, especially in mathematics and in the sciences and engineering. As a consequence, many non-college-bound youth can expect several years of career instability characterized by periods of unemployment and a series of dead-end, minimum-wage jobs. The reasons for this pattern are complex and, like other aspects of career development, involve individual and contextual issues.

None of the above should be interpreted to mean that the work performed by non-college-bound youth is unimportant. Moreover, a minority of non-college-bound youth become successful entrepreneurs or become highly valued by their employers because of special talents or personal attributes. Most of them, however, work in fast-food restaurants, service stations, convenience stores, and small businesses, performing repetitive and at times monotonous tasks. It is likely that neither the adolescents themselves, nor their parents, started out with such low aspirations. The question remains, however, how so many high school students, who often enter adolescence with lofty goals and high aspirations, find themselves in such a relatively undesirable position when they enter the labor force.

Data from the National Longitudinal Survey of Young Americans (cf. Youth and America's Future, 1988) demonstrate that 1980 high school graduates in the bottom quarter were only one-fifth as likely as those in top half of their class to be in college five years after graduation. Those in the top half "were 70 times more likely to be enrolled in college and majoring in engineering, math or physical science programs than those in the bottom quarter" (p. 31). Those in the bottom fifth were 8.8 times more likely to have left high school without a diploma. It should not be surprising that economically disadvantaged students with academic difficulties end up in vocational and nonacademic tracks that are frequently associated with significant employment difficulties upon entrance into the labor force.

These difficulties are demonstrated by data that show that during 1993, the unemployment rate for 18–19-year-olds was 19 percent, while for 20–24-year-olds the rate stood at 11 percent. At the same time, the national average for 25–54-year-olds was only 5.4 percent. In addition to these large differences in unemployment rates, data from the National Longitudinal Survey of Young Americans demonstrated that young adults between the ages of 18 and 27, who did not enroll in post-secondary education even though they graduated from high school, had moved through approximately six different jobs and experienced five bouts of unemployment (cf. Stern & National Center for Research in Vocational Education, 1995). Apart from this obvious instability in the occupational domain, non-college-bound youth are likely to experience collateral instability and disadvantage in the interpersonal and economic areas of functioning. For example, while federal aid for college students amounted to approximately $15,200 per college graduate annually, those who did not attend college received only about $1,460 (Worthington & Juntunen, 1997).

These data suggest that those who are fortunate enough to have the family and socio-economic background and personal attributes to make college attendance and graduation likely, continue to be favored in virtually all aspects of life, including their chances for a successful and rewarding career. These conclusions are supported by Pimentel (1996), who found that parental education, family income, and school performance predicted educational aspirations of high school students and that a higher grade-point average, parental education (for boys), and family income (for girls) predicted higher educational attainment six months after graduation. Moreover, the advantages of the college-bound continue to accumulate, as do the disadvantages of the non-college-bound. This is under-scored by Stern and the National Center for Research in Vocational Education (1995), who documented significant financial rewards of having a baccalaureate degree as well as completion of something as modest as a two-year degree. How to involve increasing numbers of non-college-bound youth in this all-important additional training has occu-pied policy makers, practitioners, and academics for decades. One notable effort by Blustein and colleagues (1997) involved the development of theoretical models that incor-porate individual and contextual factors that affect the school-to-work transition of "work-bound" adolescents. A specific aim of this work and similar efforts has been to gain improved understanding of the complex circumstances that contribute to the quality and ultimate outcome of the transition to work. Another has been to develop, imple-ment, and evaluate programs that provide additional educational and vocational resources to ease the school-to-work transition for non-college-bound youth.

Strategies and programs used in countries other than the United States to facilitate the transition from school to work and to ensure a highly trained, competitive workforce, have received considerable attention as possible means for improving the work careers of non-college-bound youth in the United States. Most notable among these has been the apprenticeship model that has been credited, to a large extent, with the economic vitality of Germany. MIT economist Lester Thurow has been quoted as saying that "the German secret weapon is the education of the high school graduate who doesn't go on to university [training]. . . . After you get through a German apprenticeship training program, you're simply the best educated person in the world at your level" (see Smith, 1995, p. 127). Others have joined in citing the potential of the apprenticeship model for addressing the problems of non-college-bound youth, but they have cautioned that the German model cannot be imported without significant adaptation because of its deep institutional roots (Hamilton, 1990).

Nevertheless, there are lessons to be learned from the German experience. In the years following World War II, an essential aspect of the apprenticeship system was collaboration among all of the key players: Labor unions worked hand-in-hand with business and indus-try in supporting a national educational policy that fostered and supported the develop-ment of skilled labor. Training positions for relatively young adolescents (14–16 years of age) were created in almost every company and local schools offered relevant education that allowed apprentices to spend four-fifths of their time in the work setting. A comprehensive examination (in both practical skill and school learning) concluded the apprenticeship training, placed the successful apprentice in a well-paying position (usually) and opened the possibility of qualifying (after five years) to take the Master's examination. Those who successfully absolved the Master's examination were allowed to open their own businesses if they so desired. Reasons for the sensational postwar success of the model included the very limited enrollment in universities and technical colleges, cultural factors that precluded otherwise qualified adolescents from lower socioeconomic backgrounds to seriously consider a university or college education, and the extremely low pay apprentices received from their employers. Those conditions have been reversed, for the most part, creating much less favorable conditions for the modern-day system of apprenticeships in Germany. Although many good features of the system have persisted, it clearly is no longer the virtually guaranteed route to occupational success for youth that it once was.

Opponents of the school-to-work movement and specifically the apprenticeship model argue that technological advancement may or may not require additional skills and training and that the employment difficulties of work-bound youth go far beyond a lack of training or vocational socialization (Kantor, 1994). For example, African American students were more likely to be enrolled in vocational (i.e., work-bound) programs and Asian and white students were more likely to be placed in academic (i.e., college-bound) tracks (Oakes & Guiton, 1994). This racial difference can be seen after graduation as well. The high school graduating class of 1995 experienced differential unemployment rates by race six months after graduation where the white student rate was 14.2 percent and the African American and Latino rates were 29.1 percent and 40.5 percent, respectively (cf. Worthington & Juntunen, 1997). Worthington and Juntunen (1997) warn that the school-to-work option may not gain credibility if the associated programs are reserved for or dominated by minorities and students deemed problematic by the school or the community. Although the aforementioned programs may improve the skills of the youngest segment of the non-college-educated workforce, until employers begin to acknowledge and accept the additional training as valuable and needed, the employment landscape for non-college-bound youth will remain relatively unchanged.

Conclusions

The period of adolescence makes incredibly complex demands on the developing individual. In addition to coping with rapid biological and cognitive changes, adolescents must make well-balanced commitments of time and effort to determine how to deal with family and peer relationships, school, leisure, and work. Effort expended in one area may reduce the amount of effort available for another. Choices made about school may increase or constrict the number of choices available in the world of work. Abilities and skills nurtured or neglected in childhood and adolescence could be the difference between a life of satisfaction and success and one of misery and failure. Although adolescents must ultimately be responsible for their own successes and failures, it is incumbent upon policy makers and upon the adolescents' communities and schools to provide them with the opportunities necessary for success. Most important of all, their parents must constantly strive to find the delicate balance between giving guidance and direction and inhibiting their freedom to be self-directing; between providing the necessary emotional support and being harsh or unresponsive; between fostering aspirations that are too high and aspirations that are too low.

If all goes well, as adolescents approach adulthood, they are well prepared for the challenge of becoming productive workers and embarking on a successful career. This challenge takes on additional meaning with the insight that the realization of virtually all life aspirations may very well be closely related to the development of one's vocational career (Krau, 1997). Krau observes that as individuals seek meaning in their lives, they most likely find it to be closely linked to their work. Vocational careers are thus seen as the main instrument to achieving self-realization throughout the course of life. Conventional wisdom also affirms that individuals who love their work tend to be happier, healthier, and more productive than are people who only see work as a necessary chore. The pervasive, lifelong impact of career development and career-related choices during adolescence represent powerful arguments for promoting further study and better understanding of the underlying processes.

Key Readings

Blustein, D. L., Phillips, S. D., Jobin-Davis, K., Finkelberg, S. L., & Roarke, A. E. (1997). A theory-building investigation of the school-to-work transition. *Counseling Psychologist, 25*(3), 364–402.
This article is one of the few that addresses the developmental and contextual issues associated with the transition to work for non-college-bound youth.

Mortimer, J. T., & Finch, M. D. (Eds.). (1996). *Adolescent work and family: An intergenerational developmental analysis*. Thousand Oaks, CA: Sage.
This text is a fine representation of the sociological approach to the study of career development. The contributing authors use data from the Youth Development Study to address a variety of work- and career-related questions.

Vondracek, F. W., Lerner, R. M., & Schulenberg, J. E. (1986). *Career development: A lifespan developmental approach*. Hillsdale, NJ: Erlbaum.
This text is an adaptation of the developmental-contextual framework to the area of career development and was intended to demonstrate the centrality of the career development process in human development.

Vondracek, F. W. (2001). The developmental perspective in vocational psychology. *Journal of Vocational Behavior, 59*, 252–261.
This article, addressing career development from a developmental perspective, appears as one of several in a special issue on future directions in vocational psychology.

References

Archer, S. L. (1989). Gender differences in identity development: Issues of process, domain and timing. *Journal of Adolescence, 12*(2), 117–138.

Archer, S. L., & Waterman, A. S. (1983). Identity in early adolescence: A developmental perspective. *Journal of Early Adolescence, 3*(3), 203–214.

Bachman, J. G., & Schulenberg, J. (1993). How part-time work intensity relates to drug use, problem behavior, time use, and satisfaction among high school seniors: Are these consequences or merely correlates? *Developmental Psychology, 29*(2), 220–235.

Bandura, A. (1995). Exercise of personal and collective efficacy in changing societies. In A. Bandura (Ed.), *Self-efficacy in changing societies* (pp. 1–45). New York: Cambridge University Press.

Baron, J. N., & Bielby, W. T. (1985). Organizational barriers to gender equality: Sex segregation of jobs and opportunities. In A. S. Rossi (Ed.), *Gender and the life course* (pp. 233–251). New York: Aldine.

Berzonsky, M. D. (1990). Self-construction over the life-span: A process perspective on identity formation. In G. J. Neimeyer & R. A. Neimeyer (Eds.), *Advances in personal construct psychology: A research annual, Vol. 1. Advances in personal construct psychology* (pp. 155–186). Greenwich, CT: Jai Press.

Berzonsky, M. D. (1992). A process perspective on identity and stress management. In G. R. Adams & T. P. Gullotta (Eds.), *Adolescent identity formation. Advances in adolescent development: Vol. 4* (pp. 193–215). Newbury Park, CA: Sage.

Betz, N. E. (1994). Career counseling for women in the sciences and engineering. In W. B. Walsh & S. H. Osipow (Eds.), *Career counseling for women. Contemporary topics in vocational psychology* (pp. 237–261). Hillsdale, NJ: Erlbaum.

Betz, N. E., & Fitzgerald, L. F. (1987). *The career psychology of women.* San Diego, CA: Academic.

Betz, N. E., & Hackett, G. (1981). The relationship of career-related self-efficacy expectations to perceived career options in college women and men. *Journal of Counseling Psychology, 28*(5), 399–410.

Beutell, N. J., & Brenner, O. C. (1986). Sex differences in work values. *Journal of Vocational Behavior, 28,* 29–41.

Blustein, D. L., Phillips, S. D., Jobin-Davis, K., Finkelberg, S. L., & Roarke, A. E. (1997). A theory-building investigation of the school-to-work transition. *Counseling Psychologist, 25*(3), 364–402.

Bosma, H. A. (1992). Identity in adolescence: Managing commitments. In G. R. Adams & T. P. Gullotta (Eds.), *Adolescent identity formation. Advances in adolescent development, Vol. 4* (pp. 91–121). Newbury Park, CA: Sage.

Clausen, J. (1993). *American lives.* New York: Free Press.

Cotton, L., Bynum, D. R., & Madhere, S. (1997). Socialization forces and the stability of work values from late adolescence to early adulthood. *Psychological Reports, 80,* 115–124.

Eccles, J. E., & Hoffman, L. W. (1984). Sex roles, socialization, and occupational behavior. In H. W. Stevenson & A. E. Siegel (Eds.), *Child development research and social policy.* Chicago: University of Chicago Press.

Elder, G. H. (1974). *Children of the Great Depression.* Chicago: University of Chicago Press.

Erez, M., Borochov, O., & Mannheim, B. (1989). Work values of youth: Effects of sex or sex role typing? *Journal of Vocational Behavior, 34*(3), 350–366.

Erikson, E. H. (1959). *Identity and the life-cycle.* New York: International Universities Press.

Erikson, E. H. (1968). *Identity: Youth and crisis.* New York: Norton.

Finch, M. D., Mortimer, J. L., & Ryu, S. (1997). Transition into part-time work: Health risks and opportunities. In J. Schulenberg, J. Maggs, & K. Hurrelmann (Eds.), *Health risks and developmental transitions during adolescence* (pp. 321–344). Cambridge: Cambridge University Press.

Foerster, P., & Friedrich, W. (1996). Jugendliche in den neuen Bundesländern: Ergebnisse einer empirischen Studie zum Wandel der Meinungen, Einstellungen und Werte von Jugendlichen in Sachsen 1990 bis 1994 [Youth in the new federal states: Results of an empirical study regarding changing values of youth in Saxony, 1990–1994]. Aus Politik und Zeitgeschichte, Beilage zur Wochenzeitung *Das Parlement, B19/96,* 19–29.

Gati, I. (1986). Making career decisions – A sequential elimination approach. *Journal of Counseling Psychology, 33*(4), 408–417.

Gati, I. (1990). Interpreting and applying career decision-making models: Comment on Carson and Mowsesian. *Journal of Counseling Psychology, 37*(4), 508–514.

Gati, I., Fassa, N., & Houminer, D. (1995). Applying decision theory to career counseling practice: The sequential elimination approach. *Career Development Quarterly, 43,* 211–220.

Gottfredson, L. S. (1981). Circumscription and compromise: A developmental theory of occupational aspirations. *Journal of Counseling Psychology, 28*(6), 545–579.

Greenberger, E. (1988). Working in teenage America. In J. T. Mortimer & K. M. Borman (Eds.), *Work experience and psychological development through the life span. AAAS Selected Symposia Series, No. 107* (pp. 21–50). Boulder, CO: Westview Press.

Greenberger, E., & Steinberg, L. (1986). *When teenagers work: The psychological and social costs of adolescent employment.* New York: Basic Books.

Grotevant, H. D. (1987). Toward a process model of identity formation. *Journal of Adolescent Research, 2*(3), 203–222.

Gustafson, S. B., & Magnusson, D. (1991). *Female life careers: A pattern approach.* Hillsdale, NJ: Erlbaum.

Guttentag, M., & Bray, H. (1976). *Undoing sex stereotypes: Research and resources for educators.* New York: McGraw-Hill.

Hackett, G. (1995). Self-efficacy in career choice and development. In A. Bandura (Ed.), *Self-efficacy in changing societies* (pp. 232–258). New York: Cambridge University Press.

Hamilton, S. F. (1990). *Apprenticeship for adulthood: Preparing youth for the future.* New York: Free Press.

Hamilton, S. F., & Lavine-Powers, J. (1990). Failed expectations: Working-class girls' transition from school to work. *Youth and Society, 22*(2), 241–262.

Harren, V. A. (1979). Research with the assessment of career decision making. *Character Potential: A Record of Research, 9*(2), 63–69.

Hauser, R. M., Tsai, S. L., & Sewell, W. H. (1983). A model of stratification with response error in social and psychological variables. *Sociology of Education, 56*(1), 20–46.

Holland, J. L. (1997). Making vocational choices: A theory of vocational personalities and work environments (3rd ed.). Odessa, FL: Psychological Assessment Resources.

Inhelder, B., & Piaget, J. (1958). *The growth of logical thinking from childhood to adolescence: An essay on the construction of formal operational structures.* New York: Basic Books.

Kablaoui, B. N., & Pautler, A. J. (1991). The effects of part-time work experience on high school students. *Journal of Career Development, 17*(3), 195–211.

Kantor, H. (1994). Managing the transition from school to work: The false promise of youth apprenticeship. *Teachers College Record, 95*(4), 442–461.

Kohn, M. L., & Schooler, C. (1983). *Work and personality: An inquiry into the impact of social stratification.* Norwood, NJ: Ablex.

Krau, E. (1987). The crystallization of work values in adolescence: A socio-cultural approach. *Journal of Vocational Behavior, 30,* 103–123.

Krau, E. (1997). *The realization of life aspirations through vocational careers.* Westport, CT: Praeger.

Kroger, J. (2000). Ego identity status research in the new millennium. *International Journal of Behavioral Development, 24*(2), 145–148.

Krumboltz, J. D., Mitchell, A. M., & Jones, G. B. (1976). A social learning theory of career selection. *Counseling Psychologist, 6*(1), 71–81.

Lent, R. W., Brown, S. D., & Larkin, K. C. (1986). Self-efficacy in the prediction of academic performance and perceived career options. *Journal of Counseling Psychology, 33*(3), 265–269.

Looft, W. R. (1971). Sex differences in the expression of vocational aspirations by elementary school children. *Developmental Psychology, 5*(2), 366.

Maccoby, E. E., & Jacklin, C. N. (1974). *The psychology of sex differences.* Stanford, CA: Stanford University Press.

Marini, M. M. (1978). Sex differences in the determination of adolescent aspirations: A review of research. *Sex Roles, 4*(5), 723–753.

Mortimer, J. T., Finch, M. D., Ryu, S., Shanahan, M. J., & Call, K. T. (1996). The effects of work intensity on adolescent mental health, achievement, and behavioral adjustment: New evidence from a prospective study. *Child Development, 67,* 1243–1261.

Mortimer, J. T., & Kumka, D. S. (1982). A further examination of the "occupational linkage hypothesis." *Sociological Quarterly, 23,* 3–16.

Mortimer, J. T., & Lorence, J. (1995). The social psychology of work. In K. S. Cook, G. A. Fine, & J. S. House (Eds.), *Sociological perspectives on social psychology* (pp. 497–523). Boston: Allyn & Bacon.

Nauta, M. M., Epperson, D. L., & Kahn, J. H. (1998). A multiple-groups analysis of predictors of higher level career aspirations among women in mathematics, science, and engineering majors. *Journal of Counseling Psychology, 45*(4), 483–496.

Nurmi, J.-E. (1991). How do adolescents see their future? A review of the development of future orientation and planning. *Developmental Review, 11*(1), 1–59.

Oakes, J., & Guiton, G. (1994). Matchmaking: The dynamics of high school tracking decisions. *American Educational Research Journal, 32,* 3–34.

O'Brien, K. M., Friedman, S. M., Tipton, L. C., & Linn, S. G. (2000). Attachment, separation, and women's vocational development: A longitudinal analysis. *Journal of Counseling Psychology, 47*(3), 301–315.

Phillips, S., & Sandstrom, K. L. (1990). Parental attitudes toward youth work. *Youth & Society, 22*(2), 160–183.

Phillips, S. D., & Pazienza, N. J. (1988). History and theory of the assessment of career development and decision making. In W. B. Walsh & S. H. Osipow (Eds.), *Career decision making* (pp. 1–31). Hillsdale, NJ: Erlbaum.

Phinney, J. S. (1990). Ethnic identity in adolescents and adults: Review of research. *Psychological Bulletin, 108*(3), 499–514.

Phinney, J. S., & Rosenthal, D. A. (1992). Ethnic identity in adolescence: Process, context, and outcome. In G. R. Adams & T. P. Gullotta (Eds.), *Adolescent identity formation. Advances in Adolescent Development, Vol. 4* (pp. 145–172). Newbury Park, CA: Sage.

Pimentel, E. E. (1996). Effects of adolescent achievement and family goals on the early adult transition. In J. T. Mortimer & M. D. Finch (Eds.), *Adolescents, work, and family: An intergenerational developmental analysis. Understanding Families, Vol. 6* (pp. 191–220). Thousand Oaks, CA: Sage.

Pryor, R. (1982). Values, preferences, needs, work ethics, and orientations to work: Toward a conceptual and empirical integration. *Journal of Vocational Behavior, 20,* 40–52.

Pryor, R. G. (1983). Sex differences in the levels of generality of values/preferences related to work. *Journal of Vocational Behavior, 23*(2), 233–241.

Ryu, S., & Mortimer, J. T. (1996). The "occupational linkage hypothesis" applied to occupational value formation in adolescence. In J. T. Mortimer & M. D. Finch (Eds.), *Adolescents, work, and family: An intergenerational developmental analysis. Understanding Families, Vol. 6* (pp. 167–190). Thousand Oaks, CA: Sage.

Shanahan, M. J., Elder, G. H., Burchnial, M., & Conger, R. D. (1996). Adolescent paid labor and relationships with parents: Early work–family linkages. *Child Development, 67,* 2183–2200.

Skorikov, V., & Vondracek, F. W. (1998). Vocational identity development: Its relationship to other identity domains and to overall identity development. *Journal of Career Assessment, 6*(1), 13–35.

Skorikov, V. B., & Vondracek, F. W. (1997). Longitudinal relationships between part-time work and career development in adolescents. *Career Development Quarterly, 45,* 221–235.

Smith, H. (1995). *Rethinking America.* New York: Random House.

Steinberg, L., & Dornbusch, S. M. (1991). Negative correlates of part-time employment during adolescence: Replication and elaboration. *Developmental Psychology, 27*(2), 304–313.

Stern, D., & Nakata, Y. F. (1989). Characteristics of high school students' paid jobs, and employment experience after graduation. In D. Stern & D. Eichorn (Eds.), *Adolescence and work: Influences of social structure, labor markets, and culture* (pp. 189–233). Hillsdale, NJ: Erlbaum.

Stern, D., & National Center for Research in Vocational Education (US) (1995). *School to work: Research on transition programs in the United States.* Washington, DC: Falmer Press for the National Center for Research in Vocational Education.

Super, D. E. (1973). The work values inventory. In D. G. Zytowski (Ed.), *Contemporary approaches to interest measurement* (pp. 189–205). Minneapolis: University of Minnesota Press.

Super, D. E. (1980). A life-span, life-space, approach to career development. *Journal of Vocational Behavior, 16,* 282–298.

Super, D. E., & Hendrix, V. L. (1968). Factor dimensions and reliability of the Work Values Inventory. *Vocational Guidance Quarterly, 17,* 269–274.

Tiedeman, D. V., & O'Hara, R. P. (1963). *Career development: Choice and adjustment.* Princeton, NJ: College Entrance Examination Board.

Tittle, C. K. (1988). Validity, gender research, and studies of the effects of career development interventions. *Applied Psychology: An International Review, 37*(2), 121–131.

Tversky, A. (1972). Choice by elimination. *Journal of Mathematical Psychology, 9*(4), 341–367.

Vodanovich, S. J., & Kramer, T. J. (1989). An examination of the work values of parents and their children. *Career Development Quarterly, 37,* 365–374.

Vondracek, F. W., Lerner, R. M., & Schulenberg, J. E. (1986*). Career development: A life-span developmental approach.* Hillsdale, NJ: Erlbaum.

Vondracek, F. W., & Schulenberg, J. E. (1984). Adolescence and careers. In R. M. Lerner & N. L. Galambos (Ed.), *Experiencing adolescents: A sourcebook for parents, teachers, and teens* (pp. 7–359). New York: Garland.

Vondracek, F. W., Schulenberg, J., Skorikov, V., Gillespie, L. K., & Wahlheim, C. (1995). The relationship of identity status to career indecision during adolescence. *Journal of Adolescence, 18*(1), 17–29.

Vondracek, F. W., Shimizu, K., Schulenberg, J., Hostetler, M., & Sakayanagi, T. (1990). A comparison between American and Japanese students' work values. *Journal of Vocational Behavior, 36*(3), 274–286.

Vondracek, F. W., & Skorikov, V. B. (1997). Leisure, school, and work activity preferences and their role in vocational identity development. *Career Development Quarterly, 45*(4), 322–340.

Wijting, J. P., Arnold, C. R., & Conrad, K. A. (1978). Generational differences in work values between parents and children and between boys and girls across grade levels 6, 9, 10, and 12. *Journal of Vocational Behavior, 12*(2), 245–260.

Worthington, R. L., & Juntunen, C. L. (1997). The vocational development of non-college-bound youth: Counseling psychology and the school-to-work transition movement. *Counseling Psychologist, 25*(3), 323–363.

Youth and America's Future (Organization) (1988). *The forgotten half – non-college youth in America: An interim report on the school-to-work transition.* Washington, DC: [The Commission].

CHAPTER SEVEN

Schools as Developmental Contexts

Jacquelynne S. Eccles and Robert W. Roeser

Introduction

Despite the increasing recognition that schools play a critical role in cognitive and social development, our understanding of the impact of schools on development is still quite rudimentary. Only recently have researchers interested in schools looked beyond the intellectual domain to examine how experiences in classrooms and schools influence adolescents' feelings, identity-related beliefs, and behavioral choices. For the most part, developmental researchers focus on the family and the peer group rather than schools; in contrast, educational researchers focus on the impact of schools on intellectual rather than social–emotional outcomes. Although there are important exceptions to this characterization, the need for increased interdisciplinary collaboration among researchers interested in "school effects" on adolescent development has been noted by several scholars (Eccles et al., 1998; Speece & Keogh, 1996). Instead, researchers in education, psychology, psychiatry, and sociology have typically worked independent of one another and have used a variety of approaches to study how schools influence development. Such diversity has made it difficult to compare findings and build an integrated body of knowledge about school effects. In this chapter, we briefly review the five major streams of these research efforts.

School-Level Resources and Structure

Early studies of schools focused primarily on objective characteristics of schools such as school size, teacher–student ratios, number of books in the library, and per-pupil expenditures (Barker & Gump, 1964). School size emerged as one of the most important of these structural characteristics: Both students and their teachers scored better on a wide variety of indicators of successful development if they were in small schools rather than large schools. There has been a renewed interest in both school size and school-level resources. A recent example of the work on school size can be found in the 2000 book *Children of the Land*, by Glen Elder and Rand Conger. These investigators found that school size is associated with a wide range of social and academic outcomes for adolescents attending high schools in Iowa during the 1990s. On all indicators, the adolescents attending smaller schools, on average, did better than the adolescents attending larger schools after critical family and individual level predictors were controlled. Elder and Conger argued that these effects likely reflect two processes: the greater opportunities for students at small schools to play significant roles in the fabric of their high school culture and the greater likelihood of teachers being able to monitor and support all of the students in the school. Recent work using national samples suggests that there may be a curvilinear relation between school size and adolescent development – being in a very small secondary school can have negative consequences for those adolescents who do not fit well with the social groups and teachers in the school, being in a secondary school larger than 1000 has negative consequences for many adolescents (Lee & Smith, 2001).

The continuing ethnic group differences in academic achievement and performance on standardized tests have forced a reconsideration of the role of other school-level resources on adolescents' development. Thirty-seven percent of African American youth and 32 percent of Hispanic youth, compared to 5 percent of European American and 22 percent of Asian youth are enrolled in the 47 largest city school districts in this country; in addition, African American and Hispanic youth attend some of the poorest school districts in this country. Twenty-eight percent of the youth enrolled in city schools live in poverty and 55 percent are eligible for free or reduced-cost lunch, suggesting that class may be as important (or more important) as race in the differences that emerge. Teachers in these schools report feeling less safe than teachers in other school districts, dropout rates are highest, and achievement levels at all grades are the lowest (Council of the Great City Schools, 1992). Finally, schools that serve these populations are less likely than schools serving more advantaged populations to offer either high-quality remedial services or advanced courses and courses that facilitate the acquisition of higher-order thinking skills and active learning strategies. Even adolescents who are extremely motivated are likely to find it difficult to perform well under these educational circumstances.

Schools as Social Organizations

Schools are formal organizations and have their own characteristics (values, norms, activities, and everyday routines) that can impact on adolescents' intellectual, social–emotional, and behavioral development. A second group of researchers has focused on these characteristics and their impact on adolescent development. Rather than examining the relation of demographic and economic inputs with achievement outputs, these researchers examine the mediating organizational and social processes enacted by teachers, principals, and school staff. In this chapter, we review the evidence for school climate, shared values and goals, and curricular tracking.

School climate and shared values/goals

Some of the researchers interested in school climate study schools that have the reputation of being particularly good or unusually bad. Others do intensive studies of school-level interventions designed to change the "school climate" (e.g., Bandura, 1994; Bryk et al., 1993; Cauce, Comer, & Schwartz, 1987; Comer, 1980; Goodenow, 1993; Lee & Smith, 2001; MacIver, Reuman, & Main, 1995; Rosenbaum et al., 1988; Rutter, 1983). Using these strategies, researchers have demonstrated the advantages of the following types of school climate-related processes: organizational features of the school such as strong leadership, opportunities for all students to participate in school activities, and strong and clear norms and rules related to order and discipline; social/cultural features such a sense of community among teachers, students, and staff, and both positive teacher expectations and a high sense of shared teacher efficacy; and instructional features such as a press for achievement and an emphasis on clear curricular goals. For example, in their analysis of higher achievement in Catholic schools, Bryk et al. (1993) discuss how the culture within Catholic schools is fundamentally different from the culture within most public schools in ways that positively affect the motivation of students, parents, and teachers. This culture values academics, has high expectations that all children can learn, and affirms the belief that the business of school is learning.

Similarly, Maehr, Midgley and their colleagues have argued that a school-level emphasis on different achievement goals creates a school psychological environment that affects students' academic beliefs, affect, and behavior (e.g., Maehr & Midgley, 1996; Roeser, Midgley, & Urdan, 1996). For example, schools' use of public honor rolls and assemblies for the highest achieving students, class rankings on report cards, differential curricular offerings for students of various ability levels, and so on are all practices that emphasize relative ability, competition, and social comparison in the school and create a school-level ability rather than mastery/task focus. In contrast, through the recognition of academic effort and improvement, rewards for different competencies that extend to all students, and through practices that emphasize learning and task mastery (block scheduling, interdisciplinary curricular teams, cooperative learning), schools can promote a school-level focus on discovery, effort and improvement, and academic mastery. In turn, this focus on mastery goals supports the school attachment and academic achievement of students of all ability levels (see Eccles et al., 1998 for a review).

The academic goal focus of a school also has important implications for students' mental health. In a series of studies, Roeser and Eccles found that the belief that their school is ability-focused leads to declines in students' educational values, achievement, and self-esteem, and increases in their anger, depressive symptoms, and school truancy as they move from seventh to eighth grade (Roeser & Eccles, 1998; Roeser, Eccles, & Sameroff, 1998). Effects of school-wide academic climate and goals on delinquency were found by Fiqueira-McDonough (1986). Apparently, schools that emphasize ability alienate a significant number of students who cannot perform at the highest levels, leading to anxiety, anger, disenchantment, and self-selection out of the school environment (Eccles & Midgley, 1989; Finn, 1989). In contrast, schools that emphasize effort, improvement, task mastery, and the expectation that all students can learn appear to include more adolescents in the learning process, promote adaptive attributions (e.g., achievement is based on effort and is therefore malleable), reduce depression, and decrease the frustration and anxiety that can be generated in achievement settings.

Finally, school-level academic goal emphases are strongly correlated with adolescents' perceptions of the school social climate. Adolescents who perceive a task-orientation in their school also report that their teachers are friendly, caring, and respectful. These factors, in turn, predict an increased sense of belonging in school among adolescents. In contrast, perceptions of a school ability-orientation are negatively correlated with adolescents' perceptions of caring teachers (Goodenow, 1993; Roeser et al., 1996). From the adolescents' perspective, a de-emphasis on comparison and competition and an emphasis on effort and improvement are intertwined with their view of caring teachers.

Curricular tracking

Another school-level feature that is strongly related to adolescent development is curricular tracking (Oakes, Gamoran, & Page, 1992). The process of providing different educational experiences for students of different ability levels is a widespread yet very controversial practice in American schools. At the secondary school level this practice usually involves between-class grouping of students bound for different post-secondary school trajectories (college prep, general, vocational). Differentiated curricular tracking affects development in two ways: First, tracking determines the quality and kinds of opportunities to learn each student receives (Rosenbaum, 1980; Oakes, Gamoran, & Page, 1992), and second, it determines exposure to different peers and thus, to a certain degree, the nature of social relationships that youth form in school (Fuligni, Eccles, & Barber, 1995).

The common justification for curricular tracking derives from a person–environment fit perspective. Students should be more motivated to learn if the material they are asked to master is appropriate for their current competence level and interests. There is some evidence consistent with this perspective for adolescents placed in the college tracks (Fuligni, Eccles, & Barber, 1995; Gamoran & Mare, 1989; Pallas et al., 1994; Slavin, 1990). In contrast, the results for adolescents placed in low-ability and non-college tracks do not support this hypothesis. By and large, when long-term effects are found for this group of students, they are negative primarily because these adolescents are typically provided with inferior educational experience and support (Pallas et al., 1994; Rosenbaum, 1980; Rosenbaum, Kulieke, & Rubinowitz, 1988). Low track placement is related to poor attitudes towards school, feelings of incompetence, and problem behaviors both within school (nonattendance, crime, misconduct) and in the broader community (drug use, arrests) as well as to educational attainments (Oakes, Gamoran, & Page, 1992). But whether or not academic tracks promote such outcomes or reflect preexisting differences remains a matter of considerable debate. It is also important to note that these negative effects result from the stereotypically biased implementation of ability-grouping programs. A different result might emerge for the low-competence students if the teachers implemented the program more in keeping with the goals inherent in the person–

environment fit perspective – that is, by providing *high*-quality instruction and motivational practices tailored to the current competence level of the students.

Another important and controversial aspect of curriculum differentiation involves how students get placed in different classes and how difficult it is for students to move between class levels as their academic needs and competencies change once initial placements have been made. This issue is especially important in adolescence, when course placement is linked directly to the kinds of educational options that are available to the student after high school. Minority youth, particularly African American and Hispanic boys, are more likely to be assigned to low-ability classes and non-college-bound curricular tracks than other groups; furthermore, many of these youth are incorrectly assigned to these classes (Oakes, Gamoran, & Page, 1992; Rosenbaum, Kulieke, & Rubinowitz, 1988).

The consequences of such misassignment are great. Dornbusch (1994) described the impact of tracking on a large, ethically diverse sample of high school students in northern California. Analyzing the data course by course, Dornbusch found that 85 percent of his sample stayed in the same track during high school – there was little mobility. Furthermore, Dornbusch found that many average students, particularly average students of color, were incorrectly assigned to lower-track courses. This mistake had long-term consequences for these students, in effect putting them on the wrong path toward meeting the requirements for getting into California's higher educational system. Of particular concern was the fact that these youth and their parents, who were more likely to be of color and poor, were never informed of the potential consequences of course decisions made by school personnel during the child's early high school career. Thus, curricular differentiation and school–home communication practices exerted a profound influence over the life paths of these average students who, though able, were placed in lower-ability classrooms in high school.

Classroom-Level Practices Linked to Academic Outcomes

A third group of researchers focus on the classroom-level practices that enhance academic outcomes. These researchers have demonstrated the importance of two general characteristics: a strong emphasis on high-quality instruction and high expectations that all students can master the curriculum (see, for example, Ames, 1992; Bransford, Brown, & Cocking, 1999; Darling-Hammond, 1997; Jackson & Davis, 2000; MacIver, Reuman, & Main, 1995; Pintrich & Schunk, 1996; Wehlage et al., 1989). A full review is beyond the scope of one chapter, but there is growing consensus that the following teaching strategies and techniques are important:

- Active construction of knowledge in which students are asked to construct or produce knowledge rather than just reproducing or repeating facts and views expressed by teachers and textbooks.
- Disciplined inquiry in which students are encouraged to engage in deep cognitive work "that requires them to rely on a field of knowledge, search for understanding,

and communicate in 'elaborated forms' their ideas and findings" (Jackson & Davis, 2000: 69). This characteristic also includes active instruction in the metacognitive skills needed to monitor one's own learning and progress.

- Relevance of material being studied to the student and his or her community and culture. The work that students are doing in school should be valued and recognized as important beyond the school and classroom.
- Regular feedback on progress so that students understand what they know and what they still need to learn and master. The feedback needs to focus on progress and on new learning needs, rather than one's current performance level compared with others in the class or learning group.
- Abundant opportunities to rethink one's work and understanding.
- Differentiated instruction that recognizes individual differences in levels of current knowledge, interests, and learning styles and provides multiple ways of learning new material and demonstrating that learning.
- Cooperative and highly interactive learning activities that allow students to work with and tutor each other and allow instructors to work with them in designing learning activities that provide the kinds of experiences listed above.

Classroom-Level Influences on Motivation and Social Development

Another group of researchers focus on classroom-level influences on students' achievement motivation and more general social development (see Ames, 1992; Connell & Wellborn, 1991; Deci & Ryan, 1985; Eccles, Wigfield, & Schiefele, 1998; Maehr & Midgley, 1996; Newmann, Wehlage, & Lamborn, 1992; Pintrich & Schunk, 1996; Roeser & Eccles, 1998; Skinner & Belmont, 1993; Stipek, 1996). These investigators often focus on two sets of influences: teachers' beliefs and teacher practices. Not surprisingly, many of the practices shown to influence academic outcomes also influence student motivation. For example, the following practices all support high student motivation to learn:

- Teaching and grading practices that stress improvement rather than social comparison based on current competence levels.
- Practices that reflect high teacher expectations for all students' performance.
- Practices that make sure all students participate fully in the learning activities of the classroom.
- Practices that involve hands-on activities (like laboratory exercises and field-based data collection efforts).
- Practices that support student autonomy and decision making.
- Practices that are compatible with the students' culture and home values.
- Practices that help students understand the importance and larger meaning of what they are being taught.
- Practices that create a positive and supportive teacher–student relationship.
- Practices that create a positive and supportive peer climate for all students.

We summarize briefly a few of these conclusions.

Teacher expectations

There is a long history of research on teacher expectancy effects. A great deal of this work has focused on differential treatment related to gender, race/ethnic group, and/or social class. Most of this work has documented the small but fairly consistent undermining effects of low teacher expectations on girls (for math and science), on minority children (for all subject areas), and on children from lower social-class family backgrounds (again for all subject areas) (see Brophy, 1988; Eccles & Wigfield, 1985; Ferguson, 1998; Jussim, Eccles, & Madon, 1996; Valencia, 1991).

Recently, Claude Steele (e.g., Steele & Aronson (1995)) has linked this form of differential treatment, particularly for African American students, to school disengagement and disidentification (the separation of one's self-esteem from all forms of school-related feedback). Steele argues that African American students become aware of the fact that teachers and other adults have negative stereotypes of African Americans' academic abilities. This awareness increases their anxieties, which, in turn, lead them to disidentify with the school context to protect their self-esteem.

Integrated approaches to studying classroom-level influences on development

Goal theory. Recently, there has been a shift to a more global, integrated view of the impact of learning contexts on motivation. Goal theorists, for example, have proposed two major achievement goal systems: mastery-oriented goals and performance-oriented goals. Students with mastery-oriented goals focus on learning the material and on their own improvement over time. Students with performance-oriented goals focus on doing better than other students in their class. Goal theorists further argue that a mastery orientation sustains school engagement and achievement better than a performance orientation (see Ames, 1992; Dweck, 1999; Nicholls, 1984; Maehr & Midgley, 1996). Finally, these theorists suggest that the publicness of feedback, particularly social comparative feedback and a classroom focus on competition between students, undermines mastery motivation and increases performance motivation. Evidence supporting both sets of hypotheses has come from the work of Covington (1992) and MacIver (1988). More recently, the work of Midgley, Maehr, and their colleagues has shown that school reform efforts to reduce such classroom practices as social comparative grading systems, and ego-focused, competitive motivational strategies have positive consequences for adolescents' academic motivation, persistence on difficult learning tasks, and socioemotional development (e.g., Maehr & Midgley, 1996).

Girl-friendly classrooms. Research on group differences in achievement is another example of an attempt to identify a broad set of classroom characteristics that might influence development. The work on gender differences in interest in math, physical science, and engineering is one example of this approach. Courses in these subject areas are often taught in a manner that females find either boring, irrelevant to their interests, or threatening (Eccles, 1989; Hoffmann & Haeussler, 1995). Females respond more positively to math and science instruction when it is taught in a cooperative or individualized manner rather than a competitive manner, when it is taught from an applied/person-centered perspective rather than a theoretical/abstract perspective, when it is taught using a hands-on approach rather than a "book-learning" approach, when the teacher avoids sexism in its many subtle forms, and when the examples used to teach general concepts reflect both stereotypically female and male interests (e.g., using the heart as an illustration of the principles associated with pumps). The reason often given for these effects is the fit of the teaching style and format with females' values, goals, motivational orientation, and learning styles (see Eccles, 1989). This conclusion is a good example of person–environment fit perspectives on the impact of contexts on human development. Lack of cultural and developmental fit are two other powerful examples of this perspective. We will discuss this issue further later on in this chapter.

Psychological influences on motivation. Many of these same researchers have also looked at the psychological influences on student school motivation and learning (e.g., see Ames, 1992; Bandura, 1994; Dweck, 1999; Eccles, Wigfield, & Schiefele, 1998; Ford, 1982; Fuligni, 1997; Graham, 1994; Gutman & Midgley, 2000; Jencks & Phillips, 1998; Pintrich & DeGroot, 1990; Roeser, Midgley, & Urdan, 1996; Stipek, 1996; Wang & Gordon, 1994). Most recently, these researchers have focused on three sets of beliefs: expectancy- or efficacy-related beliefs, task value-related beliefs, and personal goals. They have documented the powerful influence of students' beliefs regarding their ability to master challenging academic work on both their engagement in learning tasks and their actual academic achievement. Similarly, they have shown that students do better on school-related tasks that they both enjoy and think are important. Finally, they have documented the influence of both short- and long-term goals on adolescents' engagement and performance in school. Most of the work on short-term goals has focused on the immediate goals students have as they are performing school-related tasks. For example, is the students' primary goal in doing a particular assignment to demonstrate that they are smarter or better than the other students in the class, or to learn as much as they can from the assignment? In other words, are the students more concerned about demonstrating their ability (or avoiding demonstrating a lack of ability – often labeled an ability-goal focus) or about mastering the material (often labeled a task-mastery focus)? These types of studies demonstrate that students with a task-mastery focus learn more from the task, and are more likely to persist following difficulty or failure, than students with an ability focus. Most of the work on long-term goals has focused on educational and occupational aspirations. These studies show that students do better on tasks and courses that they believe will be instrumental in helping them to achieve these aspirations. As noted above, classroom practices are directly related to the development of these self-perceptions and values.

The nature of academic work

Another important classroom experience is the academic work itself. Two aspects of academic tasks are important: the content of the curriculum and the design of instruction.

The nature of academic content has an important impact on students' attention, interest and cognitive effort. Long ago, Dewey (1902/1990) proposed that academic work that is meaningful to the historical and developmental reality of children's experience will promote sustained attention, high investment of cognitive and affective resources in learning, and strong identification with educational goals and aims. In general, research supports this hypothesis. Content that provides meaningful exploration is critical given that boredom in school, low interest, and perceived irrelevance of the curriculum are associated with poor attention, diminished achievement, disengagement, and finally, alienation from school (e.g., Finn, 1989; Jackson & Davis, 2000; Larson & Richards, 1989). Curricula that represent the "voices," images, and historical experiences of traditionally underrepresented groups is particularly important. The disconnection of traditional curricula from the experiences of these groups can explain the alienation of some group members from the educational process, sometimes eventuating in school dropout (Fine, 1991; Sheets & Hollins, 1999). For example, in reflections on the failure of urban schools in Watts, California to meet the needs of African American males who eventually dropped out, Glasgow (1980, pp. 58, 62) wrote: "what really made these men angry was the explicit and implicit put-down of those things that were the core of their lives. . . . The message of cultural inferiority was conveyed in myriad ways, from outright speech corrections to the omission of everyday Black referents and the absence of Black history in the curriculum."

From a developmental perspective, there is evidence that the nature of academic work does not change over time in ways that are concurrent with the increasing cognitive sophistication, diverse life experiences, and identity needs of adolescents as they move from the elementary into the secondary school years (Carnegie Council on Adolescent Development, 1989). As one indication of this, middle school students report the highest rates of boredom when doing schoolwork, especially passive work (e.g., listening to lectures) and in particular classes such as social studies, math, and science (Larson & Richards, 1989). Similarly, the *content* of the curriculum taught in schools does not broaden to incorporate either important health or social issues that become increasingly salient as adolescents move through puberty and deal with the identity explorations associated with adolescence (Carnegie Council on Adolescent Development, 1989).

Experiences of racial/ethnic discrimination

Researchers interested in the relatively poor academic performance of adolescents from some ethnic/racial groups have suggested another classroom-based experience as critical for adolescent development: experiences of racial/ethnic discrimination (Feagin, 1992; Fordham & Ogbu, 1986; Rosenbaum, Kulieke, & Rubinowitz, 1988; Ruggiero & Taylor, 1995; Taylor et al., 1994; Wong, Eccles, & Sameroff, under review). Two types of discrimination have been discussed: (1) anticipation of future discrimination in the labor market which might be seen as undermining the long term benefits of education (Fordham & Ogbu, 1986), and (2) the impact of daily experiences of discrimination on one's mental health and academic motivation (Wong, Eccles, & Sameroff, under review).

Both types of discrimination are likely to influence adolescent development but research on these issues is in its infancy. Wong, Eccles, and Sameroff (under review) found that anticipated future discrimination leads to increases in African American youth's motivation to do well in school, which in turn leads to increases in academic performance. In this sample, anticipated future discrimination appeared to motivate the youth to do their very best so that they would be maximally equipped to deal with future discrimination. In contrast, daily experiences of racial discrimination from their peers and teachers led to declines in school engagement and in confidence in one's academic competence and grades, along with increases in depression and anger.

Person–Environment Fit

A fifth group of researchers focuses on person–environment fit. Researchers in this tradition argue that development and learning are maximized when there is a good fit between the needs/characteristics of the learner and the characteristics of the learning environment. Specific research projects have taken many different foci. Some researchers focus on the relation between current ability levels and instructional practices – arguing that there needs to be a good fit between current ability level and both the nature and the difficulty level of instructional practices in order to provide adequate challenge coupled with high probability for success (see Eccles, Wigfield, & Schiefele, 1998; Jackson & Davis, 2000).

Other researchers focus on the issue of cultural fit (e.g., Arkunkumar, Midgley, & Urdan, 1999; Bowers & Flinders, 1990; Deyhle & LeCompte, 1999; Fuligni, 1997; Gay, 1999; Reynolds, 1999; Rosenbaum, Kulieke, & Rubinowitz, 1988; Suarrez-Orozco & Suarrez-Orozco, 1995; Valencia, 1991). These researchers have shown that school achievement is lower than expected when the practices at school do not fit very well with the cultural practices in the students' homes and communities. Poor fit can result from a wide variety of practices, including the language of instruction, the values of the teachers, the design of parent involvement, the authority relations between teachers and students, the content of the instructional materials, and the nature of psychological services provided.

Still other researchers within this tradition focus on the fit between the opportunities afforded in school and the *developing* child's changing needs and competencies. These researchers have extended the person–environment fit perspective to a developmentally sensitive, dynamic view of context × person interactions. For example, several motivational researchers have suggested that a good fit of the school context to the developmental needs and competencies of students is needed for optimal socioemotional as well as for cognitive development. Eccles and her colleagues (1993) have labeled this type perspective *stage–environment fit* to capture the idea that there is a link between the developmental appropriateness of the characteristics of any specific social context and the nature of the developmental outcomes obtained in that context. Eccles and her colleagues have used this approach to study the negative changes in motivation and behavior in school settings often associated with the transition to junior high school.

The middle grades school transition

There is substantial evidence of declines in academic motivation, attachment to school and academic achievement across the early adolescence years (approximately ages 11–14; e.g., Anderman & Maehr, 1994; Eccles & Midgley, 1989; Eccles et al., 1993; Maehr & Midgley, 1996; Rosenbaum, 1980; Roeser, Eccles, & Freedman-Doan, 1999; Simmons & Blyth, 1987; Wigfield et al., 1991). In many cases, the declines in motivation and achievement coincide with the transition into either middle school or junior high school. Eccles and Midgley (1989) proposed that these negative developmental changes result from the fact that traditional junior high schools do not provide developmentally appropriate educational environments for early adolescents. For example, Eccles, Midgley, and their colleagues have argued that junior high school classrooms are more likely than elementary school classrooms to manifest the following age-inappropriate characteristics: high teacher control with little support for student autonomy and decision-making, unsupportive teacher–student relationships, grading practices likely to create an ability- or performance-focused motivational orientation among students rather than a performance- or mastery-focused motivational orientation, whole-class instruction likely to focus attention on social comparison, and lowered teacher sense of personal efficacy to teach all students. Empirical studies have supported these suggestions and have shown how these characteristics undermine early adolescents' school-related motivation and self-perceptions (Anderman, Maehr, & Midgley, 1999; Finger & Silverman, 1966; Midgley, Anderman, & Hicks, 1995; Midgley & Feldlaufer, 1987; Midgley, Feldlaufer, & Eccles, 1988, 1989a, 1989b; Oakes, Gamoran, & Page, 1992; Roderick, 1993; Simmons & Blyth, 1987).

Similarly, Simmons and Blyth (1987) pointed out that most junior high schools are substantially larger than elementary schools and instruction is more likely to be organized departmentally. As a result, junior high school teachers typically instruct several different groups of students, making it very difficult for students to form a close relationship with any school-affiliated adult precisely at the point in development when they need guidance and support from nonfamilial adults. Such changes in student–teacher relationships are also likely to undermine the sense of community and trust between students and teachers, leading to a lowered sense of efficacy among the teachers, an increased reliance on authoritarian control practices by the teachers, and an increased sense of alienation among the students. Finally, such changes are likely to decrease the probability that any particular student's difficulties will be noticed early enough to get the student necessary help, thus increasing the likelihood that students on the edge will be allowed to slip onto negative motivational and performance trajectories, leading to a decline in grades and, frequently, subsequent school dropout (Lord, Eccles, & McCarthy, 1994; Roderick, 1993; Simmons & Blyth, 1987).

Changes such as these are likely to have a negative effect on many students' motivational orientation toward school at any grade level. But Eccles and Midgley (1989) argued that these types of school environmental changes are particularly harmful at early adolescence, given what is known about psychological development during this stage of life. Evidence from a variety of sources suggests that early adolescent development is characterized by increases in desire for autonomy, peer orientation, self-focus and self-consciousness, salience of identity issues, concern over heterosexual relationships, and capacity for abstract cognitive activity (see Brown, 1990; Eccles and Midgley, 1989; Keating, 1990; Simmons & Blyth, 1987; Wigfield, Eccles, & Pintrich, 1996). Simmons and Blyth (1987) argued that early adolescents need safe, intellectually challenging environments to adapt to these shifts. In light of these needs, the environmental changes often associated with transition to junior high school seem especially harmful in that they emphasize competition, social comparison, and ability self-assessment at a time of heightened self-focus; they decrease decision-making and choice at a time when the desire for control is growing; they emphasize lower-level cognitive strategies at a time when the ability to use higher-level strategies is increasing; and they disrupt social networks at a time when adolescents are especially concerned with peer relationships and may be in special need of close adult relationships outside of the home. The nature of these environmental changes, coupled with the normal course of individual development, is likely to result in a developmental mismatch so that the "fit" between the early adolescent and the classroom environment is particularly poor, increasing the risk of negative motivational outcomes, especially for adolescents who are having difficulty succeeding in school academically.

Middle school reform efforts.   Based on the pattern of results discussed in this section, the Carnegie Foundation, along with other agencies, has funded several major middle school reform efforts since 1985. Jackson and Davis (2000) recently summarized many of these efforts. They concluded that the following middle school characteristics support both learning and positive youth development:

- A curriculum grounded in rigorous academic standards and current knowledge about how students learn best.
- A curriculum that is relevant to the concerns of adolescents.
- Instructional methods designed to prepare all students to achieve at the highest standards.
- Staff who are trained experts at teaching young adolescents.
- Ongoing professional development opportunities for the staff.
- Organizational structures that support a climate of intellectual development.
- Organizational structures that support a caring community climate with shared educational goals.
- Democratic governance that involves both the adults and the adolescents.
- Extensive involvement of parents and the community.
- High levels of safety and practices that support good health.

In another building-level middle school reform effort, Maehr and Midgley (1996) demonstrated the power of practices designed to reduce focus on performance goals and increase focus on task/mastery goals. These practices include grading based on progress rather than normative performance, other reward structures based on progress and mastery of challenging materials rather than competitive performance, grouping of students by interest or choice rather than ability level, use of tests to diagnose what still needs to be learned rather than to compare students to each other, provision of ample opportunities for student choice and decision making as well as self-scheduling and self-regulation, and cooperative learning structures rather than competitive learning structures.

The high school transition

Although there is less work on the transition to high school, the existing work suggests quite similar problems (Coleman & Hoffer, 1987; Jencks & Brown, 1975; Lee, Bryk, & Smith, 1993; Lee & Smith, 2001; Wehlage, 1989; Wehlage et al., 1989). For example, high schools are typically even larger and more bureaucratic than junior high schools and middle schools. Lee and Smith (2001) provide numerous examples of how the sense of community among teachers and students is undermined by the size and bureaucratic structure of most high schools. There is little opportunity for students and teachers to get to know each other. Consequently, there is distrust between them and little attachment to a common set of goals and values. There is also little opportunity for the students to form mentor-like relationships with a nonfamilial adult and little effort is made to make instruction relevant to the students. Such environments are likely to further undermine the motivation and involvement of many students, especially those not doing particularly well academically, those not enrolled in the favored classes, and those who are alienated from the values of the adults in the high school.

Most large public high schools also organize instruction around curricular tracks that sort students into different groups. As a result, there is even greater diversity in the educational experiences of high school students than of middle grades students; unfortunately, this diversity is often associated more with the students' social class and ethnic group than with differences in the students' talents and interests (Lee & Bryk, 1989). As a result, curricular tracking has served to reinforce social stratification rather than foster optimal education for all students, particularly in large schools (Dornbusch, 1994; Lee & Bryk, 1989). Lee and Bryk (1989) documented that average school achievement levels do not benefit from this curricular tracking. Quite the contrary – evidence comparing Catholic high schools with public high schools suggests that average school achievement levels are increased when all students are required to take the same challenging curriculum. This conclusion is true even after one has controlled for student selectivity factors.

Summary and Conclusions

We have now completed our discussion of school influences on adolescent development. We have outlined many ways in which schools affect the development of adolescents and tried to make it clear that schools operate at several levels to influence development. We also stressed the need to take both a developmental and a person–environment fit perspective on schools. To understand how schools influence development, one needs to understand change at both the individual and the institutional level. Stage–environment fit theory provides an excellent example of the linking of these two developmental trajectories. Imagine two trajectories: one at the school level and one at the individual level.

Schools change in many ways over the grade levels. The nature of these changes can be developmentally appropriate or inappropriate in terms of the extent to which they foster continued development toward the transition into adulthood and maturity. Youth move through this changing context as they move from grade to grade and from school to school. Similarly, youth develop and change as they get older. They also have assumptions about their increasing maturity and the privileges it ought to afford them. We believe optimal development occurs when these two trajectories of change are in synchrony with each other – that is, when the changes in the context mesh well with, and perhaps even slightly precede, the patterns of change occurring at the individual level. Furthermore, we summarized evidence that the risk of negative developmental outcomes is increased when these two trajectories are out of synchrony – particularly when the context changes in a developmental regressive pattern. School reform efforts have shown that schools can be made more developmentally appropriate for adolescents; when they are, adolescents remain engaged in their own schooling and connected to schools as valued social institutions.

We also tried to make it clear that the fit between what goes on in school and the needs, beliefs, and cultural values of individual adolescents is key to optimal development. Adolescents are unlikely to thrive in schools that fail to teach material that is relevant to the students and their cultural groups. School reform efforts to improve cultural fit can be quite successful in improving the achievement levels of the students. Adolescents are also unlikely to thrive in schools that allow racial, ethnic, gender-based, and sexual-orientation-based discrimination to occur. Repeated exposure to such insults to one's personhood will undermine both the adolescents' development and their attachment to the school's agenda itself.

Key Readings

Bryk, A. S., Lee, V. E., & Holland, P. B. (1993). *Catholic schools and the common good.* Cambridge, MA: Harvard University Press.
This is a classic book that summarizes the evidence for high achievement in Catholic schools and provides a thorough discussion of the reasons for their success.

Covington, M. V. (1992). *Making the grade: A self-worth perspective on motivation and school reform.* New York: Cambridge University Press.
This book provides an excellent summary of Martin Covington's work on self-worth as well as concrete suggestions for how to implement his principles in school reform.

Darling-Hammond, L. (1997). *The right to learn: A blueprint for creating schools that work.* San Francisco: Jossey-Bass.
The book provides an outstanding discussion of the needs for school reform in American schools.

Deci, E. L., & Ryan, R. M. (1985). *Intrinsic motivation and self-determination in human behavior.* New York: Plenum.
This book outlines Deci and Ryan's classic self-determination theory.

Dewey, J. (1902/1990). *The child and the curriculum.* Chicago: University of Chicago Press.
A classic book on the best way to think about curriculum.

Eccles, J. S., Midgley, C., Wigfield, A., Buchanan, C. M., Reuman, D., Flanagan, C., & MacIver, D. (1993). Development during adolescence: The impact of stage-environment fit on adolescents' experiences in schools and families. *American Psychologist, 48,* 90–101.
The article summarizes stage environment-fit theory and discusses reasons why junior high schools are doing such an inadequate job educating early adolescents.

Eccles, J. S., Wigfield, A., & Schiefele, U. (1998). Motivation. In N. Eisenberg (Ed.), *Handbook of Child Psychology* (Vol. 3, 5th ed., pp. 1017–1095). New York: Wiley.
This chapter provides a broad overview of achievement motivation and summarizes what we know about the impact of schools, families, and peers on school motivation and performance.

Elder, G. H. Jr., & Conger, R. D. (2000). *Children of the land.* Chicago: Chicago University Press.
The book provides a summary of the findings from the longitudinal study of adolescent development in farming communities conducted by Elder, Conger, and their colleagues.

Fine, M. (1991). *Framing dropouts: Notes on the politics of an urban public high school.* Albany: State University of New York Press.
This book summarizes the results of a longitudinal qualitative study of the causes of school dropout.

Jackson, A. W., & Davis, G. A. (2000). *Turning points 2000: Educating adolescents in the 21st century.* New York: Teachers College Press.
The book provides a summary of the results from all middle school reform efforts across the USA since the 1980s.

Lee, V. E., & Smith, J. (2001). *Restructuring high schools for equity and excellence: What works.* New York: Teachers College Press.
The book provides a summary of the findings from the National Educational Longitudinal Study related to reforming American high schools.

Maehr, M. L., & Midgley, C. (1996*). Transforming school cultures to enhance student motivation and learning.* Boulder, CO: Westview Press.
The book summarizes the middle school reform study conducted by Carol Midgley and Martin Maehr. Their reform implemented Goal Theory to increase mastery motivation among students and teachers in grades 6–9.

Pintrich, P. R., & Schunk, D. H. (1996). *Motivation in education: Theory, research, and application.* Englewood Cliffs, NJ: Prentice Hall.
The book provides a broad summary of work in motivation and education.

Sheets, R. H., & Hollins, E. R. (Eds.) (1999). *Racial and ethnic identity in school practices: Aspects of human development.* Mahwah, NJ: Erlbaum.
The volume contains several excellent chapters on the issues of race, ethnicity, and school experiences.

Simmons, R. G., & Blyth, D. A. (1987). *Moving into adolescence: The impact of pubertal change and school context.* Hawthorn, NY: Aldine de Gruyter.
This book is the classic summary of the longitudinal work of Roberta Simmons on adolescent development. It compares the development of adolescents attending K-8, 9–12-grade configuration schools with adolescents attending K-6, 7–9, 10–12-grade configuration schools.

Suarrez-Orozco, M., & Suarrez-Orozco, C. (1995). *Transformations: Immigration, family life, and achievement motivation among Latino adolescents.* Stanford, CA: Stanford University Press.
The book summarizes the qualitative research the authors have done on Latino youth and school achievement.

References

Ames, C. (1992). Classrooms: Goals, structures, and student motivation. *Journal of Educational Psychology, 84,* 261–271.

Anderman, E. M., & Maehr, M. L. (1994). Motivation and schooling in the middle grades. *Review of Educational Research, 64,* 287–309.

Anderman, E. M., Maehr, M. L., & Midgley, C. (1999). Declining motivation after the transition to middle school: Schools can make a difference. *Journal of Research and Development in Education, 32,* 131–147.

Arunkumar, R., Midgley, C., & Urdan, T. (1999). Perceiving high or low home-school dissonance: Longitudinal effects on adolescent emotional and academic well-being. *Journal of Research on Adolescence, 9,* 441–466.

Bandura, A. (1994). *Self-efficacy: The exercise of control.* New York: W. H. Freeman.

Barker, R., & Gump, P. (1964). *Big school, small school: High school size and student behavior.* Stanford, CA: Stanford University Press.

Bowers, C. A., & Flinders, D. (1990). *Responsive teaching: An ecological approach to classroom patterns of language, culture, and thought.* New York: Teachers College Press.

Bransford, J. D., Brown, A. L., & Cocking, R. R. (Eds.) (1999). *How people learn: Brain, mind, experience, and school.* Washington, DC: National Academy Press.

Brophy, J. (1988). Research linking teacher behavior to student achievement: Potential implications for instruction of Chapter 1 students. *Educational Psychologist, 23,* 235–286.

Brown, B. B. (1990). Peer groups and peer culture. In S. S. Feldman & G. R. Elliott (Eds.), *At the threshold: The developing adolescent* (pp. 171–196). Cambridge, MA: Harvard University Press.

Bryk, A. S., Lee, V. E., & Holland, P. B. (1993). *Catholic schools and the common good.* Cambridge, MA: Harvard University Press.

Carnegie Council on Adolescent Development (1989). *Turning points: Preparing American youth for the 21st century.* New York: Carnegie Corporation.

Cauce, A. M., Comer, J. P., & Schwartz, D. (1987). Long-term effects of a systems-oriented school prevention program. *American Journal of Orthopsychiatric Association, 57,* 127–131.

Coleman, J. S., & Hoffer, T. (1987). *Public and private high schools: The impact of communities.* New York: Basic Books.

Comer, J. (1980). *School power.* New York: Free Press.

Connell, J. P., & Wellborn, J. G. (1991). Competence, autonomy, and relatedness: A motivational analysis of self-system processes. In R. Gunnar & L. A. Sroufe (Eds.), *Minnesota symposia on child psychology* (Vol. 23, pp. 43–77). Hillsdale, NJ: Erlbaum.

Council of the Great City Schools (1992). *National urban education goals: Baseline indicators, 1990–91.* Washington, DC: Council of the Great City Schools.

Covington, M. V. (1992). *Making the grade: A self-worth perspective on motivation and school reform.* New York: Cambridge University Press.

Darling-Hammond, L. (1997). *The right to learn: A blueprint for creating schools that work.* San Francisco: Jossey-Bass.

Deci, E. L., & Ryan, R. M. (1985). *Intrinsic motivation and self-determination in human behavior.* New York: Plenum.

Dewey, J. (1902/1990). *The child and the curriculum.* Chicago: University of Chicago Press.

Deyhle, D., & LeCompte, M. (1999). Cultural differences in child development: Navaho adolescents in middle schools. In R. H. Sheets & E. R. Hollins (Eds.), *Racial and ethnic identity in school practices: Aspects of human development* (pp. 123–140). Mahwah, NJ: Erlbaum.

Dornbusch, S. M. (1994). Off the track. Presidential address at the biennial meeting of the Society for Research on Adolescence, San Diego, CA.

Dweck, C. S. (1999). *Self-theories: Their role in motivation, personality and development.* Philadelphia: Psychology Press.

Eccles, J. S. (1989). Bringing young women to math and science. In M. Crawford & M. Gentry (Eds.), *Gender and thought: Psychological perspectives* (pp. 36–57). New York: Springer.

Eccles, J. S., & Midgley, C. (1989). Stage/environment fit: Developmentally appropriate classrooms for early adolescents. In R. Ames & C. Ames (Eds.), *Research on motivation in education* (Vol. 3, pp. 139–181). New York: Academic.

Eccles, J. S., Midgley, C., Wigfield, A., Buchanan, C. M., Reuman, D., Flanagan, C., & MacIver, D. (1993). Development during adolescence: The impact of stage–environment fit on adolescents' experiences in schools and families. *American Psychologist, 48,* 90–101.

Eccles, J., & Wigfield, A. (1985). Teacher expectations and student motivation. In J. B. Dusek (Ed.), *Teacher expectations* (pp. 185–217). Hillsdale, NJ: Erlbaum.

Eccles, J. S., Wigfield, A., & Schiefele, U. (1998). Motivation. In N. Eisenberg (Ed.), *Handbook of child psychology* (Vol. 3, 5th ed., pp. 1017–1095). New York: Wiley.

Elder, G. H. Jr., & Conger, R. D. (2000). *Children of the land.* Chicago: Chicago University Press.

Feagin, J. R. (1992). The continuing significance of racism: Discrimination against Black students in White colleges. *Journal of Black Studies, 22,* 546–578.

Ferguson, R. F. (1998). Teachers' perceptions and expectations and the Black–White test score gap. In C. Jencks & M Phillips (Eds.), *The Black–White test score gap* (pp. 273–317). Washington, DC: Brookings Institute Press.

Fine, M. (1991). *Framing dropouts: Notes on the politics of an urban public high school.* Albany: State University of New York Press.

Finger, J. A., & Silverman, M. (1966). Changes in academic performance in the junior high school. *Personnel and Guidance Journal, 45,* 157–164.

Finn, J. D. (1989). Withdrawing from school. *Review of Educational Research, 59,* 117–142.

Fiqueira-McDonough, J. (1986). School context, gender, and delinquency. *Journal of Youth and Adolescence, 15,* 79–98.

Ford, M. E. (1982). Social cognition and social competence in adolescence. *Developmental Psychology, 18,* 323–340.

Fordham, S., & Ogbu, J. U. (1986). Black students' school success: Coping with "the burden of 'acting white.'" *Urban Review, 18,* 176–206.

Fuligni, A. J. (1997). The academic achievement of adolescents from immigrant families: The role of family background, attitudes, and beliefs. *Child Development, 68,* 351–363.

Fuligni, A. J., Eccles, J. S., Barber, B. L. (1995). The long-term effects of seventh-grade ability grouping in mathematics. *Journal of Early Adolescence, 15*(1), 58–89.

Gamoran, A., & Mare, R. D. (1989). Secondary school tracking and educational inequality: Compensation, reinforcement, or neutrality? *American Journal of Sociology, 94,* 1146–1183.

Gay, G. (1999). Ethnic identity development and multicultural education. In. R. H. Sheets & E. R. Hollins (Eds.), *Racial and ethnic identity in school practices: Aspects of human development* (pp. 195–212). Mahwah, NJ: Erlbaum.

Glasgow, D. G. (1980). *The Black underclass: poverty, unemployment, and entrapment of ghetto youth* (1st ed.). San Francisco: Jossey-Bass.

Goodenow, C. (1993). Classroom belonging among early adolescent students: Relationships to motivation and achievement. *Journal of Early Adolescence, 13*(1), 21–43.

Graham, S. (1994). Motivation in African Americans. *Review of Educational Research, 64*, 55–117.

Gutman, L. M., & Midgley, C. (2000). The role of protective factors in supporting the academic achievement of poor African American students during the middle school transition. *Journal of Youth and Adolescence, 29*, 223–248.

Hoffmann, L., & Haeussler (1995, April). Modification of interests by instruction. Paper presented at Annual AERA Meeting in San Francisco, CA.

Jackson, A. W., & Davis, G. A. (2000). *Turning points 2000: Educating adolescents in the 21st century.* New York: Teachers College Press.

Jencks, C. L., & Brown, M. (1975). The effects of high schools on their students. *Harvard Educational Review, 45*, 273–324.

Jencks, C., & Phillips, M, (Eds.) (1998). *The Black–White test score gap.* Washington DC: Brookings Institute Press.

Jussim, L., Eccles, J. S., & Madon, S. (1996). Social perception, social stereotypes, and teacher expectations: Accuracy and the quest for the powerful self-fulfilling prophecy. In L. Berkowitz (Ed.), *Advances in experimental social psychology* (pp. 281–388). New York: Academic.

Keating, D. P. (1990). Adolescent thinking. In S. S. Feldman & G. R. Elliott (Eds.), *At the threshold: The developing adolescent* (pp. 54–89). Cambridge, MA: Harvard University Press.

Larson, R., & Richards, M. (Eds.) (1989). The changing life space of early adolescence. *Journal of Youth and Adolescence, 18* (special issue), 501–626.

Lee, V. E., & Bryk, A. S. (1989). A multilevel model of the social distribution of high school achievement. *Sociology of Education, 62*, 172–192.

Lee, V. E., Bryk, A. S., & Smith, J. B. (1993). The organization of effective secondary schools. In L. Darling-Hammond (Ed.), *Review of Research in Education* (Vol. 19, pp. 171–267). Washington, DC: American Educational Research Association.

Lee, V. E., & Smith, J. (2001). *Restructuring high schools for equity and excellence: What works.* New York: Teachers College Press.

Lord, S., Eccles, J. S., & McCarthy, K. (1994). Risk and protective factors in the transition to junior high school. *Journal of Early Adolescence, 14*, 162–199.

MacIver, D. (1988). Classroom environments and the stratification of students' ability perceptions. *Journal of Educational Psychology, 80*, 1–40.

MacIver, D. J., Reuman, D. A., & Main, S. R. (1995). Social structuring of school: Studying what is, illuminating what could be. In M. R. Rosenzweig & L. W. Porter (Eds.), *Annual review of psychology* (Vol. 46, pp. 375–400).

Maehr, M. L., & Midgley, C. (1996). *Transforming school cultures to enhance student motivation and learning.* Boulder, CO: Westview Press.

Midgley, C., Anderman, E., & Hicks, L. (1995). Differences between elementary and middle school teachers and students: A goal theory approach. *Journal of Early Adolescence, 15*, 90–113.

Midgley, C., & Feldlaufer, H. (1987). Students' and teachers' decision-making fit before and after the transition to junior high school. *Journal of Early Adolescence, 7*, 225–241.

Midgley, C., Feldlaufer, H., & Eccles, J. S. (1988). The transition to junior high school: Beliefs of pre- and post-transition teachers. *Journal of Youth and Adolescence, 17*, 543–562.

Midgley, C. M., Feldlaufer, H., & Eccles, J. S. (1989a). Changes in teacher efficacy and student self- and task-related beliefs during the transition to junior high school. *Journal of Educational Psychology, 81*, 247–258.

Midgley, C., Feldlaufer, H., & Eccles, J. S. (1989b). Student/teacher relations and attitudes toward mathematics before and after the transition to junior high school. *Child Development, 60*, 981–992.

Newmann, F. M., Wehlage, G. G., & Lamborn, S. D. (1992). The significance and sources of student engagement. In F. M. Newmann (Ed.), *Student engagement and achievement in American secondary schools* (pp. 11–39). New York: Teachers College Press.

Nicholls, J. G. (1984). Achievement motivation: Conceptions of ability, subjective experience, task choice, and performance. *Psychological Review, 91*, 328–346.

Oakes, J., Gamoran, A., & Page, R. N. (1992). Curriculum differentiation: Opportunities, outcomes, and meanings. In P. Jackson (Ed.), *Handbook of Research on Curriculum* (pp. 570–608). New York: Macmillan.

Pallas, A. M., Entwisle, D. R., Alexander, K. L., & Stluka, M. F. (1994). Ability-group effects: Instructional, social, or institutional? *Sociology of Education, 67*, 27–46.

Pintrich, P., & De Groot, E. V. (1990). Motivational and self-regulated learning components of classroom academic performance. *Journal of Educational Psychology, 82*, 33–40.

Pintrich, P. R., & Schunk, D. H. (1996). *Motivation in education: Theory, research, and application.* Englewood Cliffs, NJ: Prentice Hall.

Reynolds, A. L. (1999). Working with children and adolescents in the schools: Multicultural counseling implications. In R. H. Sheets & E. R. Hollins (Eds.), *Racial and ethnic identity in school practices: Aspects of human development* (pp. 213–230). Mahwah, NJ: Erlbaum.

Roderick, M. (1993). *The path to dropping out: Evidence for intervention.* Westport, CT: Auburn House.

Roeser, R. W., & Eccles, J. S. (1998). Adolescents' perceptions of middle school: Relation to longitudinal changes in academic and psychological adjustment. *Journal of Research on Adolescence, 88*, 123–158.

Roeser, R. W., Eccles, J. S., & Freedman-Doan, C. (1999). Academic functioning and mental health in adolescence: Patterns, progressions, and routes from childhood. *Journal of Adolescent Research, 14*, 135–174.

Roeser, R. W., Eccles, J. S., & Sameroff, J. (1998). Academic and emotional functioning in early adolescence. Longitudinal relations, patterns, and prediction by experience in middle school. *Development and Psychopathology, 10*, 321–352.

Roeser, R. W., Midgley, C. M., & Urdan, T. C. (1996). Perceptions of the school psychological environment and early adolescents' psychological and behavioral functioning in school: The mediating role of goals and belonging. *Journal of Educational Psychology, 88*, 408–422.

Rosenbaum, J. E. (1980). Social implications of educational grouping. *Review of Research in Education, 7*, 361–401.

Rosenbaum, J. E., Kulieke, M. J., & Rubinowitz, L. S. (1988). White suburban schools' responses to low-income Black children: Sources of successes and problems. *Urban Review, 20*, 28–41.

Ruggiero, K. M., & Taylor, D. M. (1995). Coping with discrimination: How disadvantaged group members perceive the discrimination that confronts them. *Journal of Personality and Social Psychology, 68*, 826–838.

Rutter, M. (1983). School effects on pupil progress: Research findings and policy implications. *Child Development, 54*, 1–29.

Sheets, R. H., & Hollins, E. R. (Eds.) (1999). *Racial and ethnic identity in school practices: Aspects of human development.* Mahwah, NJ: Erlbaum.

Simmons, R. G., & Blyth, D. A. (1987). *Moving into adolescence: The impact of pubertal change and school context.* Hawthorn, NY: Aldine de Gruyter.

Skinner, E. A., & Belmont, M. J. (1993). Motivation in the classroom: Reciprocal effects of teacher behavior and student engagement across the school year. *Journal of Educational Psychology, 85*, 571–581.

Slavin, R. E. (1990). Achievement effects of ability grouping in secondary schools: A best-evidence synthesis. *Review of Educational Research, 60*, 471–499.

Speece, D. L., & Keogh, B. K. (1996). *Research on classroom ecologies: Implications for inclusion of children with learning disabilities.* Mahwah, NJ: Erlbaum.

Steele, C. M., & Aronson, J. (1995). Stereotype threat and the intellectual test performance of African-Americans. *Journal of Personality and Social Psychology, 69,* 797–811.

Stipek, D. J. (1996). Motivation and instruction. In R. C. Calfee & D. C. Berliner (Eds.), *Handbook of educational psychology.* New York: Macmillan.

Suarrez-Orozco, M., & Suarrez-Orozco, C. (1995). *Transformations: Immigration, family life, and achievement motivation among Latino adolescents.* Stanford, CA: Stanford University Press.

Taylor, R. D., Casten, R., Flickinger, S., Roberts, D., & Fulmore, C. D. (1994). Explaining the school performance of African-American adolescents. *Journal of Research on Adolescence, 4,* 21–44.

Valencia, R. R. (Ed.) (1991). *Chicano school failure and success: Research and policy agendas for the 1990s.* London: Falmer.

Wang, M. C., & Gordon, E. W. (Eds.) (1994). *Educational resilience in inner-city America.* Hillsdale, NJ: Erlbaum.

Wehlage, G. (1989). Dropping out: Can schools be expected to prevent it? In L. Weis, E. Farrar, & H. Petrie (Eds.), *Dropouts from school.* Albany, NY: State University of New York Press.

Wehlage, G., Rutter, R., Smith, G., Lesko, N., & Fernandez, R. (1989). *Reducing the risk: Schools as communities of support.* Philadelphia: Falmer.

Wigfield, A., Eccles, J., MacIver, D., Reuman, D., & Midgley, C. (1991). Transitions at early adolescence: Changes in children's domain-specific self-perceptions and general self-esteem across the transition to junior high school. *Developmental Psychology, 27,* 552–565.

Wigfield, A., Eccles, J. S., & Pintrich, P. R. (1996). Development between the ages of eleven and twenty-five. In D. C. Berliner & R. C. Calfee (Eds.), *The handbook of educational psychology* (pp. 148–185). New York: Macmillan.

Wong, C. A., Eccles, J. S., & Sameroff, A. (under review). The influence of ethnic discrimination and ethnic identification on African-American adolescents' school and socio-emotional adjustment. *Journal of Personality.*

CHAPTER EIGHT

College as a Transition To Adulthood

Marilyn J. Montgomery and James E. Côté

The Promise of Higher Education

Entering college is, for many young people, a major step in the journey into adulthood. The college experience itself represents an intensive preparatory socialization process, where many stakeholders have related but distinct goals: the business community wants eager employees with human capital skills; civil society needs an informed and committed citizenry; parents hope college will enhance their offspring's happiness and self-sufficiency; and college students themselves aspire to improve their professional and personal prospects. In addition, professors and administrators attempt to nurture particular abilities and values that they hope will become an enduring part of students' intellectual life.

At the same time, public support for higher education is widespread; impressive amounts of wealth have been expended on undergraduate programs. In addition to the billions of dollars spent each year by governments worldwide on higher education, some colleges have individual endowments in excess of one billion dollars. This tremendous support appears to be based on the faith placed in post-secondary institutions and the higher social status of college graduates (Pascarella & Terenzini, 1991). As college has become a part of the transition to adulthood for an increasing number of young people, it is both appropriate and timely to reexamine and reevaluate the impact of this experience on those who participate in it.[1]

Does higher education fulfill its promises?

Do colleges and universities indeed substantiate the hopes of students and expectations of society? Our answer to this question is, "Basically, yes." However, as in all things academic, it would be more accurate to say, "It depends." It depends, in part, on how one looks at the question (e.g., one's theoretical perspective and interests), and concomitantly, one's choice of outcome variables. For example, from one perspective, the important question to ask is whether college lives up to its promise to render graduates who are broadly educated, informed citizens and developmentally enhanced human beings. From another perspective, the important question is whether college lives up to its promise to provide a context that opens doors to better standards of living and a higher quality of life than is available to those with lower levels of academic attainment. As it turns out, both are important questions and both perspectives are well represented in the literature.

Extensive efforts to understand the college experience have been underway since the 1950s. During the 1950s and 1960s, studies proliferated gauging the impact of the university experience on student development, primarily in terms of various forms of psychological adjustment and change (see Barton, 1959; Feldman & Newcomb, 1969; Heath, 1968; Jacob, 1957; Katz et al., 1968; and Sanford, 1967; for reviews). Studies undertaken in the 1970s and 1980s became more focused on how higher education affects students' social outcomes, and theoretical models of student change were developed (e.g., Astin, 1977; Tinto, 1975, 1987). In a review of these decades of studies, Pascarella and Terenzini (1991) list about 20 formal theories or models of student change that were advanced.[2] These theories, they suggest, can be categorized into two "general families" of theories, namely, those rooted in a developmental perspective and those rooted in a sociodemographic or contextual perspective.

A developmental perspective generally looks at individual growth along certain dimensions of psychological or cognitive development. When used to evaluate the impact of college on students, a developmental perspective suggests that we ask how attending college (as a social institutional experience) affects developmental markers of change (e.g., stage of moral reasoning or growth in autonomy). A contextual perspective, in contrast, suggests that we ask how demographic features such as socioeconomic status, gender, or ethnicity, and situational variables such as type of learning environment, impact both developmental (e.g., advances in formal thought) and non-developmental (e.g., college completion or employment rates) markers of change.

Both types of questions are important and both help us answer the question of whether (and for whom) college fulfills its promise. Both developmental and contextual perspectives independently have much to contribute to our understanding of college as a transition to adulthood. However, there is also a growing recognition of the utility of combining levels of analysis and integrating variables from both perspectives into a "developmental contextualist" perspective. This perspective looks for ways in which people differ in their "goodness of fit" with a given context (Lerner, 1995; Lerner & Kauffman, 1985). This differential response between person and context can be summarized as follows:

> Just as a [person] brings his or her characteristics of individuality to a particular social setting, there are demands placed on the [person] by virtue of the social and physical components of the setting. These demands may take the form of (a) attitudes, values, or stereotypes that are held by others in the context regarding the person's attributes . . . ; (b) the attributes (usually behavioral) of others in the context with whom the [person] must coordinate, or fit, his or her attributes . . . for adaptive interactions to exist; or (c) the physical characteristics of a setting . . . that require the [person] to possess certain attributes . . . for the most efficient interaction within the setting to occur. (Lerner, 1995, p. 22)

Lerner (1995) also argues that those "whose characteristics match most of the settings within which they exist receive supportive or positive feedback from the contexts and show evidence of the most adaptive behavioral development" (p. 23).

Applying this combined perspective to higher educational settings should help us better understand how people "fit" into various contexts (see Côté and Levine's [1997, 2000] "integrated paradigm of student development" for one effort). Accordingly, the basic framework of this chapter is to employ a developmental contextual perspective in order to address the question of how well various higher educational settings fulfill their promises to students and to society. Thus, we focus on two basic issues. First, what facilitates the successful transition to, and through, college – and for whom? Second, what is the long-term practical impact of college on later quality of life, and who benefits most? These two issues are particularly appropriate and timely, given the evidence (discussed below) strongly suggesting that completing a college education has a significant practical impact on long-term markers of enhanced quality of life, but that many young people experience the college context as a difficult aspect of the transition to adulthood.

Before turning to the primary question of whether college fulfills its promises, however, it is important to further delimit the scope of the chapter by examining in more detail the issue of who participates in the college experience. College, we said, has become a part of the transition from adolescence to adulthood for an increasingly greater number of young people. However, as we discuss in the next section, it is not the only way or even the predominant way to make the transition to adulthood.

Who goes to and through college?

One index of the significance of college in the transition to adulthood is the proportion of the adolescent/young adult population that actually participates in college and eventually attains a degree. There is no doubt that college attendance increased dramatically over the twentieth century, going from an elite experience to a common experience (Spitzberg & Thorndike, 1992). However, although a cursory glance at statistics suggests that the majority of young people now attend college, closer examination reveals that this is not the case. The confusion seems to arise with the periodic press releases stating that about two-thirds of American college students now begin their studies directly out of high school (up from 45 percent in 1960; US Census Bureau, 1999, p. 192). While these entry statistics appear valid (similar rates can be found in other countries, like Canada), the way in which they are reported obscures several things. First, the denominator for this statistic is first-year college students, not final-year high school students. In other words, out of the total population of freshmen in 1999, 67 percent came directly from high school. (It is difficult to reliably track people the other way, from high school forward.) Second, the misleading figures regarding those going directly from high school (or its equivalent) to college include freshmen of varying ages (mainly 17–24), not a cohort of equal age (e.g., 18). Not everyone finishes high school at the same age. Just as in college, some high-school students "stop out" or go at a slower pace because of work and family demands, but eventually about 90 percent of Americans will now obtain a high-school diploma or its equivalent *by age 24*. (Of the entire US population over age 25, 82.8

percent were high school graduates in 1998; up from 41.1 percent in 1960; US Census Bureau, 1999, p. 169.)

Even in the United States, which has the highest college attendance rate in the world, only about 40 percent of 18- and 19-year-olds are actually in college either part-time or full-time (about 37 percent of males and 45 percent of females; National Commission on Excellence in Education, 1998). According to the Census Bureau (1999) about 10 percent of 18- to 21-year-olds were still in high school in 1997, 13 percent were high school dropouts, and 45 percent were in college. The remaining one-third of this age group included high school graduates who were working, traveling, or unemployed. Similarly, using data from the National Longitudinal Survey of Youth, Velum and Weiss (1993) report that among those aged 14–18 as of January 1, 1978, and followed through January 1990 (when they were 26–30), 12.7 percent had not completed high school, 45.4 percent did complete at least high school, 20.7 percent had completed "some college," and only 21.2 percent were actual college graduates. They also report that a disproportionate number of blacks and Hispanics had not completed high school (19.7 percent and 22.6 percent, respectively), and were less likely than whites to be college graduates (11.7 percent and 8.4 percent). When viewed longitudinally, then, college clearly is *not* the most common route to adulthood. Instead, it is but one of several routes.

This fact is also borne out with international comparisons of the percentage of the 25–34-year-old population with a BA degree. In 1996, 26.5 percent of Americans in this age group had a BA degree or higher; in Japan, 23 percent; in Canada, 20.1 percent; in the UK, 15 percent; and in France and Germany, 13 percent (National Commission on Excellence in Education, 1999).

Although open to a variety of interpretations, the main trends in these findings illustrate several points that counter conventional wisdom concerning the relative proportion of young people who experience college as a transition to adulthood. Fewer than 50 percent of young Americans attempt a college degree, and at best three-quarters of these eventually obtain degrees (cf. Gilbert, 1991). Thus, although college attendance has become an important part of the transition to adulthood for an increasingly greater number of young people, it is not the predominant way of entering the labor force and adulthood. Moreover, a substantial portion of those who experience college as part of their transition to adulthood encounter difficulties in doing so; about one-quarter who begin the process do not complete it. Consequently, our discussion of the impact of college on the transition to adulthood represents the experience of fewer than half of those moving through this age period.

Fulfilling the Promise: A Developmental Perspective

A developmental perspective, we said, generally attempts to determine how attending college impacts developmental markers of change. From such a perspective, the important question to ask is whether college lives up to its promise to turn out graduates who are broadly educated, mature citizens and enriched human beings.

Does college enhance human development? As we noted, our answer to this question is, "Basically, yes." However, in answering this question, one must specify what constitutes developmental enhancement,[3] and acknowledge the methodological problems in sorting out gains that can be attributed to college-related development versus other causes. In evaluating the studies, a central question is whether or not the changes observed among college attendees can be attributed wholly, or even in part, to the actual experiences provided by colleges. People are continually changing and developing, especially between ages of 18 and 22 – the age period when college is most commonly attended. Thus, maturation effects are difficult to distinguish from the effects attributable to college experiences. In addition, people have different abilities when they begin college. Those with greater abilities may change because of those abilities, and not necessarily because of their experiences in college. Similarly, certain types of people may respond only to certain types of higher-educational environments. Further, it is possible that some of the effects of higher education are multiplicative over the course of the lifespan but not necessarily detected with short-term studies (Tuijnman, 1989). Thus, we currently can only roughly estimate the direct developmental effects of the college experience. Ideally, future research will more thoroughly explore whether or not the changes observed among college students take place among those that do not attend college, using, for example, matched samples of college and non-college young adults with longitudinal samples (see Pascarella, 1999). However, such research undertakings are expensive and difficult endeavors, and therefore rare.

Nevertheless, several decades of literature on college effects have explored the ways in which college might fulfill its promise of stimulating forms of human development. For example, researchers using psychosocial developmental models such as vectors of student development (Chickering, 1969), ego strength (Adams, Ryan, & Keating, 2000), and identity status (Berzonsky & Kuk, 2000; Marcia, 1966; Waterman, 1993); cognitive-structural theories of epistemological development (Perry, 1970) and ethical development (Kohlberg, 1969); and topological models (e.g., the person–environment interaction theories of Astin, 1968; Holland, 1966), have looked for ways in which college enhances student psychosocial, cognitive, and moral development as well as student personal adjustment. (See also chapters 9 and 11 in this volume for reviews of identity and moral development.)

After examining the many studies conducted during the 1970s and 1980s, Pascarella and Terenzini (1991) concluded in their book, *How College Affects Students*, that

> students not only make statistically significant gains in factual knowledge and in a range of general cognitive and intellectual skills; they also change on a broad array of value, attitudinal, psychosocial, and moral dimensions. . . . changes in intellectual skills [tend] to be larger in magnitude than changes in other areas, but . . . the change that occurs during the college years does not appear to be concentrated in a few isolated areas. Rather, the research portrays the college student as changing in an integrated way, with change in any one area appearing to be part of a mutually reinforcing network or pattern of change in other areas. (p. 557)

While the breadth and scope of these changes are encouraging in terms of the hopes and aspirations that many people have regarding the positive benefits of higher education, the direct effects of college experiences are difficult to sort out due to the aforementioned methodological problems. The few studies that have done so make more modest claims about the impact of college. From their review of this literature, Pascarella and Terenzini concluded that the evidence more consistently supports intellectual as opposed to psychosocial change, with the strongest evidence pointing to verbal and quantitative skills, critical thinking, and the use of principled reasoning in judging moral issues. However, the magnitude of net effects, when clear (i.e., for verbal and quantitative skills and critical thinking), was not great (about one-quarter to one-third of a standard deviation).

In some of the psychosocial areas of greatest interest to developmental psychologists, the evidence Pascarella and Terenzini (1991) reviewed is mixed. It is strongest for variables like political liberalism, various forms of self-concept, personal adjustment, and psychological well-being, with effect sizes similar to the "intellectual" variables. However, they found little demonstrable effect of college attendance for variables like identity and ego development, interpersonal relationships, maturity, and general personality development, though research on these topics was scant. This may be because some deep-seated personal characteristics are resistant to change during this period (Côté & Allahar, 1996; Côté & Levine, 2000), or simply that these factors are not systematically targeted at most colleges (whereas the intellectual variables *are*), so expectations of substantive changes may be unrealistic.

Empirical studies conducted since the 1990s reconfirmed that the college experience does indeed enhance cognitive development (Whitt et al., 1999), critical thinking (Battistoni, 1995), civic responsibility (Ehrlich, 2000), human capital skills (Côté & Levine, 1997), and academic and intellectual orientation (Terenzini et al., 1995; Wilder et al., 1996). However, as mentioned above, while recent research informed by a developmental perspective illustrates the ways that college promotes positive development, its focus tends to be on how college affects short-term outcome variables (e.g., Cramer, 1998; Adams, Ryan, & Keating, 2000). Few studies address the longitudinal maintenance of these effects (for exceptions, see Côté, 2000; Josselson, 1987). Research programs examining links between college experience and markers of developmental change, markers of contextual effects on income and social status, and markers of quality of life (e.g., health and well-being) are few.

Although the developmental literature is informative, much work remains to be done in order to better understand how college is important in producing mature citizens and developmentally enhanced human beings. The broad strokes we have provided must suffice, as we move on to the practical issues of the impact of college on the long-term material quality of life, and the college and student characteristics associated with successful completion of college. To explore these issues, we next turn to the literature examining the impact of college on students' social context.

Fulfilling the Promise: A Contextual Perspective

A contextual or sociodemographic perspective, we said, generally attempts to determine how social context variables impact both developmental and non-developmental markers of change. From such a perspective, an important question is whether college fulfills its promise of enhancing students' short- and long-term material quality of life, and for whom.

Does college enhance students' material quality of life? As with the developmental perspective, our answer to this question is also "Basically, yes." The literatures suggest many ways in which college does fulfill its promise of enhancing the quality of students' lives in the long term. Research using college impact models such as Astin's (1977) Input–Environment–Output (I–E–0) model and Tinto's (1987) theory of student departure provide support for the view that college enhances markers of short-term gains (e.g., career choice and grade attainment) as well as long-term gains in quality of life indices (e.g., income and social status). In this section, we summarize the college-impact literature to illustrate the effects that college can have on occupational attainment and earnings.

Long-term impact

The research examining the difference between attending and not attending college clearly shows that the sheer fact of having completed any college degree is of greater significance than the type of college attended or specific experiences within a given college. Since most of this research compares college attenders with nonattenders, the results are essentially estimates of the effects of college extended over a period of time. Some of these effects are directly attributable to having a college degree, but other effects are indirect in the sense that a college degree opens up opportunities that lead to a variety of experiences unavailable to those who do not graduate from college. In other words, the initial investment in one's higher education yields both direct and indirect dividends, and those dividends can subsequently multiply (see Côté, 1997). Of course, the same methodological caveats that apply to the developmental literature apply to these findings, particularly the questions of selection and maturation: those who go to college tend to be of higher aptitude and enter at higher levels of psychosocial and cognitive development, and so they might have matured or grown in certain ways even without attending college. This caveat does not apply, however, with respect to the "credential value" of a college degree, because the degree itself is essential in gaining access to certain jobs and professional programs.

Employment outcomes

As noted, occupational effects are both direct and indirect: having the degree both opens doors and provides advantages throughout one's career. College graduates, on average, have higher earnings, more stable employment, more career mobility, and higher career attainment (e.g., Human Resources Development Canada, 2000; Organization for Economic and Cooperative Development, 2000). The baccalaureate degree can both open doors and help one climb ladders. In fact, the BA has been called "the single most important educational rung on the socioeconomic attainment ladder" (Pascarella & Terenzini, 1991, p. 575). The "socioeconomic positioning effect" produces subsequent benefits by giving graduates various "material and nonmaterial resources and opportunities" (p. 577) with which to further their occupational position and personal development, and the jobs they have access to are more conducive to subsequent forms of psychosocial and cognitive development as well as career mobility (see Côté's 1997 identity capital model). In one analysis, a Bachelor's degree was estimated to grant an advantage over a high school diploma in the magnitude of one standard deviation on occupational status scales, between 20 percent and 40 percent higher earnings than high school graduates, and an average 10 percent annual private rate of return on personal money and time invested in one's education (Pascarella & Terenzini, 1991). Rates of private return for Canadian graduates has been estimated at about 22 percent for women and 14 percent for men (Human Resources Development Canada, 2000).

That is the good news. The bad news is related to the fact that the modern college is embedded in the system of "credentialism" in terms of its relationship to the workplace (Fallows, 1985). In contrast to the past, now virtually all people in non-menial jobs need to be "credentialed" in some way before entering the workforce, rather than acquiring skills and knowledge as a part of on-the-job learning and apprenticeships. This situation has produced a situation referred to as the "credentialism paradox" by Allahar and Côté (1998) because many of the skills and much of the knowledge acquired during college are often not directly applicable in subsequent jobs, yet without the credential the person does not have access to those jobs.

Extensive research has been conducted on this problem in Canada, originally referring to it as underemployment (Côté & Allahar, 1996; Allahar & Côté, 1998), and more recently as overqualification (e.g., Kelly, Howatson-Leo, & Clark, 1997). Because of the large supply of credentialed workers in countries like Canada and the United States, positions requiring higher skills are now filled by MAs and Ph.D.s. This "downward mobility" has resulted in a cascading displacement effect, resulting in reduced demand for lower levels of educational attainment (such as the BA), especially for those with skills not directly tied to current economic needs (Pryor & Schaffer, 1999). Students from many disciplines, especially the Arts and Social Sciences, now face the prospect of their degrees offering fewer occupational opportunities (at least in the short run) than in the past, when undergraduate degrees virtually guaranteed high occupational attainment (Luffman, 2001). For example, throughout the 1980s and 1990s, up to one-half of Canadian university graduates found themselves in jobs not requiring a university degree two years after graduation (Frenette, 2000), a figure which declined to about one-third after five postgraduation years (Nobert, McDowell, & Goulet, 1992). In 1994, 37 percent of those aged 20–29 with Bachelor's degrees felt they were overqualified for their jobs (compared with 22 percent for all Canadian workers with college or university degrees; Kelly, Howatson-Leo, & Clark, 1997).

Back to the good news: while a minority of college graduates may be overqualified or underemployed in terms of what they actually do on the job – especially initially, and especially humanities and social sciences graduates – the lifetime earning advantage, even for underemployed college graduates, is substantially higher than for high school graduates (in the magnitude of between $500,000 and $1 million lifetime benefit per individual; Allahar & Côté, 1998). In short, completing a college education is on average a wise investment, although this investment works out better for some than for others. Moreover, the knowledge, skills, and personality development acquired during the college years may have "sleeper" or indirect effects in that long-term occupational and lifestyle outcomes are enhanced in ways that are difficult to calculate. In a recent study of the long-term employment rates and salaries of Canadian graduates, Giles and Drewes (2001) conclude that in comparison with applied-program graduates, those

> graduating from programs in the humanities and social sciences had considerably more difficulty with the school-to-work transition. . . . But once that transition was made, the generic nature of the skills they acquired appeared to stand them in good stead – because of these skills they have a greater longevity and . . . [aptitude for] continued lifelong learning in the face of labor market changes. (p. 33)

Differential employment outcomes for students exist, and are most evident with respect to race and gender, with nonwhites and women obtaining greater relative benefits from an undergraduate education (Pascarella & Terenzini, 1991). In part, this is due to the fact that college has a compensation effect with respect to helping people make up for lower socioeconomic starting points. On the other hand, students from high socioeconomic backgrounds appear to enjoy a greater net impact when they attend higher-quality colleges. As Pascarella and Terenzini (1991) note: "students from advantaged social backgrounds are not only more likely to attend elite undergraduate colleges than their counterparts from less advantaged social origins; they may also be more likely to convert the status conferred by such an institution into greater economic success" (p. 632).

While both genders benefit from attending college, and getting a college degree appears to have an even greater impact on the postgraduate earning power of young women, gender differences continue to exist in the potential academic benefit students glean from college. Unfounded beliefs about sex differences in cognitive abilities are often conveyed by parents and teachers to prospective college students (Eccles, Jacobs, & Harold, 1990; Jussim & Eccles, l992), and these strongly influence their course of study (see also chapter 7 in this volume). In particular, girls or women have historically been thought to lack the potential to excel in either math or science courses or in occupations that require this training, and have been counseled instead into fields that require verbal ability, such as library science and elementary education. Unfortunately, these career areas typically have a lower lifetime earning trajectory than do (historically male-dominated) scientific or technical fields. However, there are some signs that the segregation by major that has characterized college for decades has begun to loosen, at least in service delivery careers. For example, in 1990, women earned 40 percent of all degrees conferred by law schools in the United States, up from 9 percent in 1970. Similarly, women earned 30 percent of all medical degrees in 1990, up from 5 percent in l970 (Bianchi, 1995).

Between-college effects

"Which college should I choose?" Many young people who ask this question pore over recruitment materials and attend college fairs, searching for the answer; high school counselors vigorously encourage them to make the best choice. In addition, many colleges heavily recruit students and imply that choice of college can have life-changing impact. Is all this effort merited? Are some colleges better than others in stimulating short-term change and making a long-term difference among their students? The answer to this question is a very reserved "Yes." Some studies have found differences in terms of between-college effects, but these are nowhere near as strong as people might expect, especially people with strong loyalties to their alma maters.

There are several possible reasons for the weak between-college differences. One reason may be that there is more variability within many institutions than across them, even among private four-year colleges. Another reason may be that colleges have more in common than their different recruitment materials suggest: curriculum, instructional practices, and educational goals are very similar among ostensibly different colleges.

Several observations hold across the between-college studies. First, the differences attributable to college quality, often assessed in terms of student selectivity and academic prestige, is remarkably small given the variations in resources available to various colleges. Second, even when it comes to more "objective" factors like career success and ultimate earnings, the differential quality of colleges tend to be of minor importance after taking into consideration the characteristics of the students who attend the college. Colleges that are prestigious draw upon a pool of students with greater initial aptitude and occupational aspirations; hence, these institutions merely have to maintain those initial levels. Moreover, attending elite institutions only modestly enhances occupational attainment, and "the magnitude of the effect that can actually be attributed to college quality and not other influences is quite small, a good deal smaller than is commonly believed" (Pascarella & Terenzini, 1991, pp. 596–597). Student input factors are greater predictors of outcome.

Finally, other between-college differences that have been examined are of interest here. For example, attending a predominantly black college has modest positive effects on both the cognitive development and educational attainment of black students (Flowers & Pascarella, 1999), and black women benefit even more in terms of their academic and social self-image (Pascarella & Terenzini, 1991). Similarly, women who attend all-women colleges have greater educational attainment, are more likely to go into male-dominated careers, and achieve greater prominence in a field (Pascarella & Terenzini, 1991). Nevertheless, the larger conclusion remains that the impact of attending (versus not attending) any college is more pronounced than differential impacts attributable to attending different kinds of college.

The College Experience: Adjusting to and Finishing School

Given the evidence strongly suggesting that completing a college education – any college education – is a wise investment, and that developmental changes taking place during the college years may also have long-term implications for enhanced occupational and lifestyle outcomes, it is helpful to have some understanding of (1) what the college experience is like for those who use this route to adulthood, (2) some of the challenges of making it through college, and (3) some of the factors that serve as potential mediators or moderators to the completion of college.

The transition to college

For those who choose college as a route to adulthood, the first serious hurdle is the transition from high school and home environment to college life. What kinds of psychological adjustment and development are involved in this transition to college?

The literature suggests that students generally face many demands as they negotiate the passage from high school and home environment to college life. Many students experience the initial adjustment to college as stressful and as negative in various ways (Pancer et al., 2000; Wintre & Yaffe, 2000). Moreover, record numbers of first-year students now report that they frequently feel overwhelmed by academic demands: 29.6 percent in 1999 versus 16 percent in 1985 (Sax et al., 1999). Both resident and home-based students exhibit increased psychological disturbance and absentmindedness after beginning school, but those who are homesick experience greater disturbance and cognitive failure (Fisher & Hood, 1987). Perhaps to avoid homesickness, most students do not go far from home when they enter college as freshmen; 80 percent attend college in their home state (US Department of Education, 1997). When asked about the reason for selecting the college that they did, 22 percent said they wanted to live near home (*Chronicle of Higher Education*, 1997). These statistics indicate that many students choose colleges from which they are able to come and go from home with relative ease.

Family support seems to be a key to facilitating new students' emotional adjustment to college. Most students request and receive at least some emotional and instrumental support from their parents (Valery, O'Connor, & Jennings, 1997). Those students who enjoy close relationships with their family, and who have parents who are supportive and demanding, as well as autonomy-granting, do better on many indices of student adjustment (Strage & Brandt, 1999; Strage, 1998; Hickman, Bartholomae, & McKenry, 2000). This seems to be true for both students who leave home and for students who continue to live at home and commute to class.

College also offers new opportunities for young adults to renegotiate relationships with the family and to experience desired autonomy. In fact, 17 percent of students in a recent survey said their choice of college was based on their desire to move away from home (*Chronicle of Higher Education*, 1997). However, psychologically healthy autonomy is not detachment; rather, it is a psychological status in which parents and children accept each other's individuality (see chapter 9 in this volume for a discussion of the development of autonomy in adolescence and young adulthood). A related area of interest in developmental studies is the quality of the attachment relationship between college students and their parents. Secure attachment to parents is consistently related to students' academic, interpersonal, and emotional well-being (e.g., Berman & Sperling, 1991; Bloom, 1987; Rice & Whaley, 1994). Further, students' attachment to their parents appears to be quite stable despite the growth in autonomy they experience through the college years (Rice et al., 1995; Sun et al., 2000).

When young adults go away to college, they not only experience diminished dependence on parents and others who have served important support functions. They must also establish new guidelines and limits for their own behavior related to time and money management and involvement in relationships with peers, with limited direct input from parents. Home leaving seems to improve parent–child relationships; students who attend college away from home begin to have more positive thoughts and feelings about their parents and actually express more affection toward them (Sullivan & Sullivan, 1980).

However, as noted previously, many students continue to live at home while they attend college. For these students, parental input on matters of peer involvement and time management continues, solicited or not. These students see the quality of their relationships with their parents as more conflictual than do students who have left home (Sullivan & Sullivan, 1980). For home-based students, the challenge of gaining autonomy is more difficult in some ways, but they have more ready access to the soothing and support functions of their family when they need them.

Regardless of resident status, students who perceive themselves as adaptable to change and in control of their environments, who use good problem-solving skills to meet their new challenges, and who enjoy both closeness and autonomy in their family relationships adjust especially well during the first year of college (Brooks & DuBois, 1995; Holmbeck & Wandrei, 1993).

The quality of the college experience

Students who persist through the initial transition to college life are faced with making a social and academic adjustment to the environment in which they find themselves. What facilitates a good college experience? Who gets the most out of college?

Colleges differ in the extent to which they foster students' social and academic adjustment and integration, and these two broad factors are related to student persistence and educational attainment. For example, Strage's (1999) survey of students found strong relationships between five indices of academic and social integration (academic confidence, social confidence, perception of oneself as a leader among one's peers, a positive rapport with one's teachers, and an internal locus of control) and actual successful student outcomes (as indexed by Grade Point Average (GPA) and persistence/task-involvement). These strong relationships between academic and social adjustment and student success held across ethnic groups, and for both first and later-generation college students.

Fostering student academic adjustment. Certainly, as college catalogues boast, the resources and opportunities for involvement that colleges provide to students are important (Côté and Levine, 1997). There are a number of such factors that positively impact students' academic adjustment, such as living on campus, the "academic experience" (engagement in academic work), exposure to effective teaching and stimulating subject matter presented in a logical sequence (Braxton, Bray, & Berger, 2000), interaction with faculty in informal non-classroom settings focusing on intellectual matters, and involvement in extracurricular involvement in subject-focused groups (Adams, Ryan, & Keating, 2000).

Students also benefit when they perceive their college to be concerned about the individual student, and when there is an emphasis on supportive services (advising, orientation, and individualized courses that develop academic survival skills (Pascarella & Terenzini, 1991)). This type of normative, nurturing environment has a small but significant impact on learning, cognitive development (especially critical thinking and adult reasoning skills), the career chosen, and the type of career entered (Côté & Levine, 1997).

Fostering student social adjustment. Environments that foster students' perception of being socially integrated also have an important impact on their experience of college. Students benefit when a college fosters a strong peer culture in which students participate frequently in college-sponsored activities and develop close campus friendships (Pascarella & Terenzini, 1991).

Perhaps one of the most significant factors impacting the quality of the college experience is being a member of a racial or ethnic minority. Although women made inroads into the predominantly male academy in the 1920s and 1930s, the 1950s government assistance for armed service personnel following World War II provided the first college inroads for ethnic minority students – in fact, racial and ethnic diversity on campuses is a trend that is only a few decades old (Spitzberg & Thorndike, 1992). Some argue that it is no surprise, then, that minority students are at increased risk for feeling that their college has a "chilly climate" for students like themselves, and this can impact their success (Cabrera et al., 1999). Unfortunately, despite many institutions' commitment to diversity-positive institutional change, as many as 20 percent of minority students still report that they have experienced bias incidents of verbal or physical aggression while on campus (Grieger & Toliver, 2001). Although minority students tend to experience college less positively than majority students, maintaining or building a strong ethnic identity through associating with similar others seems to facilitate a positive experience (Hatter & Ottens, 1998). Joining ethnic organizations provides support for students' ethnic identity, and has no negative impact on larger campus adjustment or involvement (Saylor & Aries, 1999). However, minority students' general sense of overall integration into the college environment is also very important. For example, several studies have found that when in predominantly white settings, the quality of African American students' relationships with peers, faculty, and administrators is almost as important to their academic achievement as individual academic effort (e.g., Schwitze et al., 1999; Watson & Kuh, 1996).

Whereas the college environment is experienced as liberating by some, it can also be a particularly difficult and overwhelming experience for students with physical disabilities (Wright & Stimmel, 1983). During college, students usually develop intimate relationships and make major decisions such as choosing an occupation. Coping with a physical disability is difficult at any age, but physically disabled students can become overwhelmed with their limitations in this future-oriented setting. College environments vary in the extent to which they provide support services and address the practical constraints these students face (Borland & James, 1999).

Student effort and involvement. Student characteristics and effort are even stronger factors influencing the quality of the college experience than college characteristics, by merit of the fact that certain kinds of students engage in behaviors that tend to maximize the impact of colleges. Based on their analysis of the literature, Pascarella and Terenzini (1991) conclude that

> one of the most inescapable and unequivocal conclusions we can make is that the impact of college is largely determined by the individual's quality of effort and level of involvement in both academic and nonacademic activities. . . . Such a conclusion suggests that the impact of college is not simply the result of what a college does for or to a student. Rather the impact is a result of the extent to which an individual student exploits the people, programs, facilities, opportunities, and experiences that the college makes available. . . . From this perspective it is the individual student who perhaps most determines the extent to which college makes a difference. (pp. 610–611)

Students' motivations for being in college make a difference. Those who are motivated to achieve personal and intellectual development experience more positive outcomes (Côté & Levine, 2000) than the estimated 38 percent who go to college because their parents want them to (*Chronicle of Higher Education*, 1997). Still, instructional approaches can interact with student personality characteristics. Students with higher needs for independent achievement and those with an internal locus of control do better with the complementary teaching approach that requires self-direction and independent learning. Conversely, students with more dependent and conforming personalities, along with those with an external locus of control, learn better in structured environments where teachers monitor them closely (cf. Côté & Levine, 1997).

In sum, the evidence thus suggests that young people find that there are both positive and negative aspects to the college experience. The greatest impact on the quality of college experiences is an interaction between the student' s total level of engagement in the college and the resources the college provides, especially when those resources are coordinated to maximize targeted outcomes.

Just how difficult is college?

There is evidence that completing college has become an increasingly difficult challenge. Unfortunately, many students encounter so much difficulty with the high school-to-college transition that they drop out in the first year. The data on retention and completion rates provide some evidence for the difficulty of college as a transition to adulthood (ACT, 2001).

With respect to retention rates, about one-quarter of those who were freshmen in 1995 failed to register in 1996 for a second year in the same college (figures for 2000 show a slight increase [about 1 percent] in the return rate; ACT, 2001). However, these figures vary by type of school: highly selective schools (where students have Scholastic Aptitude Test (SAT) scores above 1200) have freshman dropout rates of less than 10 percent and five-year graduation rates of 70 percent, while "open" schools (where students have SAT scores lower than 950) have freshman dropout rates approaching 50 percent. Dropout rates also tend to be higher for blacks, Hispanics, and Native Americans, perhaps due in part to the aforementioned "chilly climate" that some minorities perceive on predominately white college campuses (Ponterotto, 1990). Thus, although about half of high school graduates go directly on to higher education, a substantial portion are at risk: "some of them aren't prepared – whether academically, financially or socially – to succeed. Unless they're offered and take advantage of course-placement recommendations and participate in developmental courses and other support services, they can quickly find themselves in over their heads" (ACT, 2001).

These retention-rate statistics do not tell the whole story, however. The "school-leaver" statistics include transfers to other institutions, "stopouts" who take time off to work, travel, or start a family, and "true dropouts." The "moratorium" from college can be a period during which personal reintegration takes place (Riviere, 1999). Subsequently, about two-thirds of those who stop out eventually complete their degrees (National Commission on Excellence in Education, 1999), and only about 20–30 percent of those who begin college become "true dropouts."

Still, in reference to completion rates, statistics available from a variety of sources show that even in selective colleges, more than half of students are not finishing their studies in the expected four-year period. According to American College Testing Program (ACT, 2000) statistics, only about 43 percent of those in four-year public institutions who began in 1991 had completed their "four-year" degrees five years later in 1996 (see also Levine & Cureton, 1998). This represents a continual decrease since 1983, when about 52 percent completed their degrees within five years. Figures for 2000 show a continuing downward trend, with only 41.9 percent of those in public institutions, and 55.5 of those in private institutions, finishing their four-year degrees within five years. Overall, the median time spent from completing high school to earning a BA in 1993 was 6.29 years, with 74.3 percent completing it in six years or less, 64.7 percent completing it in five years or less, and 42.5 percent doing so in four years or less (US Census Bureau, 1999, p. 203). Clearly, many students face personal, social, academic, and financial challenges that prevent them from obtaining a four-year degree from their initial college of choice in a straight-forward fashion,[4] and these challenges seem to be increasing.

Factors related to leaving school. The data on retention and completion rates provide evidence for the general difficulty of completing college; we can also identify some specific factors that are related to dropping out. Conventional wisdom predicts that academic preparation and aptitude (as indicated by GPA, SATs, etc.) would be related to persistence and/or attrition in college, and there is evidence that this is the case (Daugherty & Lane, 1999; Frehill, 2000). There is also strong evidence for other factors that are related to students' success or failure in making it through. In one study, students' financial and social support variables (full-time employment, lack of financial support, difficult living arrangements, and lack of encouragement to attend college) were more predictive of attrition than were students' psychological coping resources (Ryland, Riordan, & Brack, 1994). This suggests that dropping out may have more to do with the support systems in students' lives than with other stressors.

Other studies involving dropouts suggest that students' lack of social and academic integration is a very important factor. For example, in one large longitudinal study of commuters, students' perception of the quality of their faculty–student and staff–student interaction was the most important factor distinguishing dropout students from successful ones – even more important than GPA, remedial status, or perceptions of academic climate (Johnson, 1997). Other students who leave prematurely experience a growing sense of "mutual maladaptation" (Riviere, 1999) that is characterized by a global sense of malaise. For example, a study that surveyed college seniors who dropped out before graduating found that their premature exit was predicted by several factors: dissatisfaction with academic guidance, dissatisfaction with access to school-related information, dissatisfaction with the quality of education, and feelings of institutional alienation (Mohr, Eiche, & Sedlacek, 1998).

Another way that college attrition has been studied is by examining currently enrolled students' level of commitment to stay in school. Due to the higher dropout rates of minority students, several studies have focused on how diversity issues might be related to students' commitment to remain in school. In a survey of both minority and non-minority students at a large, prestigious university with a diverse student population, researchers found that for all students, commitment to remain in college was positively related to identification with the university, and the commitment to remain in school was negatively related to experience of "disrespect" (Zea et al., 1997). When students (regardless of race) perceived the environment as unwelcoming because of their race, ethnicity, or religion, their desire to continue attending college diminished. Minority students were more likely than majority students to report experiencing disrespect.[5]

Searching for other factors related to dropout among minority students, Hurtado and Carter (1997) used Tinto's (1975) theoretical model of students' departure from college to analyze longitudinal data from the National Survey of Hispanic Students. As also noted above, students' perceptions of a hostile racial climate had a negative effect on their sense of belonging at college. However, when students discussed course content with others outside of class and were members of campus-based religious and social-community organizations, they experienced a much stronger sense of belonging.

Interventions for student success. In an effort to capitalize on what we know about factors related to dropout vs. commitment to remain in school, programs for at-risk students have been developed at many campuses. These interventions, such as Upward Bound, Project Advancement Via Individual Determination, Graduation Really Achieves Dreams, and the Young Scholars Program appear to mediate the difficulties of college and increase graduation rates (Newman & Newman, 1999). A review of the body of evaluation research on these programs suggests that they succeed in improving college attendance rates by (1) creating meaningful bonds between students and teachers, (2) giving students opportunities to work while at school, (3) allowing students high-status roles in the school, (4) providing academic support, and (5) helping students see an attainable future (Fashola & Slavin, 1998).

Taken together, the studies on student dropout and dropout prevention indicate that while not all students persist until graduation, a successful passage through college is fostered in several ways. To succeed, students need conducive life circumstances (such as student loans or part-time work opportunities), an academic environment that is a good fit with their goals and needs, and a subjective sense of positive integration into both academic and social aspects of campus life. Fortunately, many of these factors are amenable to change when they are lacking.

Discussion and Conclusions

As we noted at the beginning of the chapter, college has become a part of the transition from adolescence to adulthood for an increasing number of young people. As a consequence, impressive amounts of wealth have been expended, based on the belief that college will significantly enhance the quality of life for each successive generation of adolescents moving into adulthood. Thus, we focused this chapter on two basic questions. First, what is the long-term practical impact of college on later quality of life? Second, what facilitates students' successful transition to, and through, college?

Using a developmental-contextual framework to answer these questions, we now come to several broad conclusions. The first conclusion is that going to college itself – any college – is more important than going to any particular college. Thus, it is imperative that those who want to be stimulated in terms of occupational and personal development should attend college and *finish* it.

The second conclusion is that "what goes in" is highly related to "what comes out." In other words, input factors like student aptitude level and motivation to learn have a great bearing on output factors like the magnitude of skills acquired and the degree of personal change. This does not mean that the environment experienced in between is unimportant, but that high-aptitude students will generally have higher outcomes because they start at higher levels, and have greater inherent potential for change. However, this also means that students with less aptitude (or "underachievers") need extra attention to help them compensate for past deficits and maximize beneficial college effects. In a sense, their change *could be* greater because they have further to go on indices of positive growth.

This point brings us to the third conclusion; that college can be a mixed experience for students, providing them with opportunities for academic and psychosocial growth but also with many challenges and stresses. Those students who are able to find peers, teachers, and administrators with whom they can develop personal and academic relationships experience a sense of "social integration"; those who do not experience a sense of "mutual maladaptation." Social integration may be the most crucial ingredient for students to feel positive enough about college to endure the stressors, achieve academic success, and enjoy the many opportunities for growth and development.

Our fourth conclusion is that student *effort and involvement* in the academic environment while in college makes a big difference in the gains that are made (throughput versus input). Even in the most nurturant and benign environment in the highest-quality school, what students get out of their experience is a function of what they put into it. This also goes for schools that do not necessarily make an effort to provide the nurturant and benign settings: good students can still get much out of their experience. Students who meet their learning environments "halfway" are more likely to find nurturance and to benefit from their experiences (Côté & Levine, 1997).

Taken together, the overall lesson we can learn from several decades of research is that motivated students with the appropriate aptitude and a supportive social environment can gain a great deal from attending college if they put sufficient effort into it. The benefits may not accrue immediately, either occupationally or personally, but the chances are that they will in the long term.

Notes

1. Throughout this chapter, we use the term "college" to represent the undergradute experience, as per the American convention, instead of the more accurate but cumbersome phrase "college and university." Additionally, we refer primarily to the "college-aged" undergraduates who begin in their late teens, as opposed to older returning students. We also refer mostly to American and Canadian studies and statistics, because making extensive international comparisons would require more space than is available here.

2.   Given the space restraints in this chapter and because of the extensiveness and conclusiveness of their review of the literature – some 3,000 studies – we rely on a number of their conclusions that hold a decade after their book was published, and we update those where significant new information is available.

3.   The US National Education Goals 1990 set a goal for the year 2000 which read, "The proportion of college graduates who demonstrate an advanced ability to think critically, communicate effectively, and solve problems will increase substantially" (Greenwood, 1993). Individual institutions often develop statements listing more specific criteria, such as "thinking actively, taking responsibility, learning independently, working and learning cooperatively, communicating effectively, appreciating diversity, applying specific knowledge and skills, using technology and solving problems . . . critical thinking, self-appraisal, and self-esteem" (Highline Community College, 1994).

4.   Another indicator of the increasingly lengthy "four-year" degree is that the median age (in Canada) for completing a BA was 24 in 1995 (Taillon & Paju, 1999).

5.   In colleges where white students are a minority, they experience problems similar to those that minority students experience in predominantly white settings. In one such college, the demographic category of student most likely to drop out of college is the white male (Florida International University Office of Institutional Research, 2001).

Key Readings

Astin, Alexander W. (1993). *What matters in college? Four critical years revisited.* San Francisco: Jossey-Bass.

The book presents an extensive study of how students change and develop in college and reveals how colleges can enhance that development. Based on surveys of more than 20,000 students, 25,000 faculty members, and 200 institutions, this book examines how academic programs, faculty, student peer groups, and other variables affect students' college experiences. Examines environmental characteristics of institutions in relation to students' personality and self-concept, behavior patterns, values and beliefs, academic and cognitive development, career development, and satisfaction with the college environment.

Côté, J. E., & Levine, C. (1997). Student motivations, learning environments, and human capital acquisition: Toward an integrated paradigm of student development. *Journal of College Student Development, 38,* 229–243.

This article presents the integrated paradigm of student development, which identifies the importance of a goodness of fit between student motivations and educational environments for optimal skill and grade attainment outcomes. Reports findings of an empirical study that point to the importance of students being motivated to engage in reciprocal relationships with their learning environments in order to enhance their human capital skills.

Levine, A., & Cureton, J. S. (1998). *When hope and fear collide: A portrait of today's college student.* San Francisco: Jossey-Bass.

The book examines the cohort passing through colleges during the 1990s, finding that while these students feared a great many things both on a global level and on a local level, they were less pessimistic than the previous cohort. The focus is on how students come to grips with the challenges of politics, academics, and personal relationships on campus and draws implications for their futures. This book offers advice on how students can chart a course through college.

Pascarella, E. T., & Terenzini, P. T. (1991). *How college affects students: Findings and insights from 20 years of research.* San Francisco: Jossey-Bass.
This volume is the landmark review of 20 years of research and some 3,000 studies that examine the ways in which students have been found to benefit from, and change as a result of, attending college.

Sax, L. J., Astin, A. W., Korn, W. S., & Mahoney, K. (1999). *The American Freshman: National norms for fall 1999.* Los Angeles: Higher Education Research Institute, UCLA.
This is one of many annual reports of the largest ongoing study of higher education in the United States. Beginning in 1966, several hundred thousand students at hundreds of institutions have been assessed each year on a variety of measures relevant to their attitudes, values, behaviors, and aspirations. Summary reports can be accessed at http://www.gseis.ucla.edu/heri/news.htm

Key Websites

American College Testing Program (ACT)
http://www.act.org/
ACT, Inc. is an independent, not-for-profit organization that provides assessment, research, information, and program-management services in educational planning, career planning, and workforce development. The site is designed to help students make better decisions regarding their postsecondary education and to provide relevant information to colleges. Program areas include: recruiting students, advising and placing students, enhancing teaching and learning, retaining students, and promoting institutional effectiveness.

National Commission on Excellence in Education
http://nces.ed.gov/
The Commission is the primary federal entity responsible for collecting and analyzing educational statistics for the United States and other nations. Up-to-date statistics on all aspects of all educational levels.

Organization for Economic and Cooperative Development (OECD)
http://www1.oecd.org/media/publish/
This is an excellent source for international educational statistics and focused studies on issues of international interest (e.g., http://www1.oecd.org/media/publish/pb00-10a.htm).

References

ACT Program (2000). *Fewer college freshmen drop out, but degree rate also falls.* Iowa City, Iowa: www.act.orgnews/releases
ACT Program (2001). More first-year college students return for second year: Fewer students graduate in five years. Iowa City: www.act.orgnews/releases
Adams, G. R., Ryan, B. A., & Keating, L. (2000). Family relationships, academic environments, and psychosocial development during the university experience: A longitudinal study. *Journal of Adolescent Research, 15,* 99–122.
Allahar, A., & Côté, J. E. (1998). *Richer and poorer: The structure of social inequality in Canada.* Toronto: Lorimer.

Astin, A. W. (1968). *The college environment.* Washington, DC: American Council on Education.

Astin, A. W. (1977). *Four critical years.* San Francisco: Jossey-Bass.

Barton, A. H. (1959). *Studying the effects of college education.* New Haven: Edward W. Hazen Foundation.

Battistoni, R. (1995). Service learning, diversity and the liberal arts curriculum. *Liberal Education, 81*, 30–35.

Berman, W. H., & Sperling, M. B. (1991). Parental attachment and emotional distress in the transition to college. *Journal of Youth and Adolescence, 20*, 427–440.

Berzonsky, M., & Kuk, L. S. (2000). Identity status, identity processing style, and the transition to university. *Journal of Adolescent Research, 15*, 81–80.

Bianchi, S. M. (1995). The changing economic roles of women and men. In R. Farley (Ed.), *State of the union: America in the 1990s* (pp. 134–157). New York: Russell Sage.

Bloom, M. V. (1987). Leaving home: A family transition. In J. Bloom-Feshbach & S. Bloom-Feshbach (Eds.), *The psychology of separation and loss: Perspectives on development, life transitions, and clinical practice* (pp. 232–266). San Francisco: Jossey-Bass.

Borland, J., & James, S. (1999). The learning experience of students with disabilities in higher education: A case study of a UK university. *Disability and Society, 14*, 85–101.

Braxton, J. M., Bray, N. J., & Berger, J. B. (2000). Faculty teaching skills and their influence on the college student departure process. *Journal of College Student Development, 41*, 215–227.

Brooks, J. H., & DuBois, D. L. (1995). Individual and environmental predictors of adjustment during the first year of college. *Journal of College Student Development, 36*, 347–360.

Cabrera, A., Nora, A., Terenzini, P. T., Pascarella, E., & Hagedorn, L. S. (1999). Campus racial climate and the adjustment of students to college: A comparison between White students and African-American students. *Journal of Higher Education, 70*, 134–160.

Chickering, A. W. (1969). *Education and identity.* San Francisco: Jossey-Bass.

Chronicle of Higher Education (1997, August 29). *Almanac: Facts about the U.S., each of the 50 states, and D.C., 44,* Washington, DC: *Chronicle of Higher Education.*

Côté, J. E. (1997). An empirical test of the identity capital model. *Journal of Adolescence, 20*, 577–597.

Côté, J. E. (2000). Late modernity, individualization, and identity capital: Some longitudinal findings with a middle-class sample. Paper presented at the Nordic Youth Research Information Symposium, Helsinki, Finland.

Côté, J. E., & Allahar, A. L. (1996). *Generation on hold: Coming of age in the late twentieth century.* New York: New York University Press.

Côté, J. E., & Levine, C. (1997). Student motivations, learning environments, and human capital acquisition: Toward an integrated paradigm of student development. *Journal of College Student Development, 38*, 229–243.

Côté, J. E., & Levine, C. (2000). Attitude versus aptitude: Is intelligence or motivation more important for positive higher educational outcomes? *Journal of Adolescent Research, 15*, 58–80.

Cramer, P. (1998). Freshman to senior year: A follow-up study of identity, narcissism, and defense mechanisms. *Journal of Research in Personality, 32*, 156–172.

Daugherty, T. K., & Lane, E. J. (1999). A longitudinal study of academic and social predictors of college attrition. *Social Behavior and Personality, 27*, 355–362.

Eccles, J. S., Jacobs, J. E., & Harold, R. D. (1990). Gender role stereotypes, expectancy effects, and parents' socialization of gender differences. *Journal of Social Issues, 46*, 183–201.

Ehrlich, T. (2000). *Civic responsibility and higher education.* Phoenix, AZ: Oryx Press.

Fallows, J. (1985, December). The case against credentialism: Bad for business. *Atlantic Monthly,* 49–67.

Fashola, O. S., & Slavin, R. E. (1998). Effective dropout prevention and college attendance programs for students placed at risk. *Journal of Education for Students Placed at Risk, 3,* 159–183.

Feldman, K. A., & Newcomb, T. M. (1969). *The impact of college on students.* San Francisco: Jossey-Bass.

Fisher, S., & Hood, B. (1987). The stress of the transition to university: A longitudinal study of psychological disturbance, absent-mindedness and vulnerability to homesickness. *British Journal of Psychology, 78,* 425–441.

Florida International University Office of Institutional Research (2001). *FIU 2000–2001 Factbook.* Miami, FL: www.fiu.edu.oir/fb0001.html

Flowers, L., & Pascarella, E. T. (1999). Cognitive effects of college racial composition on African American students after 3 years of college. *Journal of College Student Development, 40,* 669–677.

Frehill, L. M. (2000). Race, class, and gender in college completion: The 1980 high school senior cohort. *Race, Gender & Class in Education, 7,* 81–107.

Frenette, M. (2000). Overqualified? Recent graduates and the needs of their employers. *Education Quarterly Review (Statistics Canada), 7*(1), 6–20.

Gilbert, S. (1991). *Attrition in Canadian universities.* Guelph, Ont.: Commission of Inquiry on Canadian University Education.

Giles, P., & Drewes, T. (2001, Autumn). Liberal arts degrees and the labour market. *Perspectives on Labour and Income,* 27–33.

Greenwood, A. (1993). *National assessment of college student learning: Getting started.* NCES Publication No. 93116. Washington, DC: US Government Printing Office.

Grieger, I., & Toliver, S. (2001). Multiculturalism on predominantly white campuses: Multiple roles and functions for the counselor. In J. G. Ponterotto, J. M. Casas, L. A. Suzuki, & C. M. Alexander (Eds.), *Handbook of multicultural counseling* (2nd ed., pp. 825–848). Thousand Oaks, CA: Sage.

Hatter, D. Y., & Ottens, A. J. (1998). Afrocentric world view and Black students' adjustment to a predominantly White university: Does worldview matter? *College Student Journal, 32,* 472–480.

Heath, D. H. (1968). *Growing up in college: Liberal education and maturity.* San Francisco: Jossey-Bass.

Hickman, G. P., Bartholomae, S., & McHenry, P. C. (2000). Influence of parenting style on the adjustment and academic achievement of traditional college freshmen. *Journal of College Student Development, 41,* 41–54.

Highline Community College (1994). *Highline Community College outcomes: Student abilities across the curriculum and within departments.* ERIC Document Reproduction Service No. JC950064. Des Moines, WA: Highline Community College.

Holland, J. L. (1966). *The psychology of vocational choice: A theory of personality types and model environments.* Waltham, MA: Blaisdell.

Holmbeck, G. N., & Wandrei, M. L. (1993). Individual and relational predictors of adjustment in first-year college students. *Journal of Counseling Psychology, 40,* 73–78.

Human Resources Development Canada (2000). Profile of Canadian youth in the labour market. Ottawa, Human Resources Development Canada: http:/www.hrdc-drhc.gc.ca/arb

Hurtado, S., & Carter, D. F. (1997). Effects of college transition and perceptions of the campus racial climate on Latino college students' sense of belonging. *Sociology of Education, 70,* 324–345.

Jacob, P. E. (1957). *Changing values in college: An exploratory study of the impact of college teaching.* New York: Harper & Row.

Johnson, J. L. (1997). Commuter college students: What factors determine who will persist and who will drop out? *College Student Journal, 31*, 323–332.

Josselson, R. (1987). *Finding herself: Pathways to identity development in women.* San Francisco: Jossey-Bass.

Jussim, L., & Eccles, J. S. (1992). Teacher expectations: Construction and reflection of student achievement. *Journal of Personality and Social Psychology, 63*, 947–961.

Katz, J. & Associates (1968). *No time for youth: Growth and constraint in college students.* San Francisco: Jossey-Bass.

Kelly, K., Howatson-Leo, L., & Clark, W. (1997). "I feel overqualified for my job . . ." *Canadian Social Trends, Winter,* 11–16, Ottawa: Statistics Canada.

Kohlberg, L. (1969). Stage and sequence: The cognitive-developmental approach to socialization. In D. A. Goslin (Ed.), *Handbook of socialization theory and research* (pp. 347–480). Chicago: Rand McNally.

Lerner, R. M. (1995). *America's youth in crisis: Challenges and options for programs and policies.* Thousand Oaks, CA: Sage.

Lerner, R. M., & Kauffman, M. B. (1985). The concept of development in contextualism. *Developmental Review, 5*, 309–333.

Levine, A., & Cureton, J. S. (1998). *When hope and fear collide: A portrait of today's college student.* San Francisco: Jossey-Bass.

Luffman, J. (2001). School-to-work transition: A focus on arts and culture graduates, *Education Quarterly Review, 7*, 24–30.

Marcia, J. E. (1966). Development and validation of ego identity status. *Journal of Personality and Social Psychology, 3*, 551–558.

Mohr, J. J., Eiche, K., & Sedlacek, W. E. (1998). So close, yet so far: Predictors of attrition in college seniors. *Journal of College Student Development, 39*, 343–354.

National Commission on Excellence in Education (1998). *Projections of Education Statistics to 2008.* http://nces.ed.gov/pubs98

National Commission on Excellence in Education (1999). *Overview of the condition of education.* http://nces.ed.gov/pubs99/conditions99

Newman, R., & Newman, B. M. (1999). What does it take to have a positive impact on minority students' college retention? *Adolescence, 34*, 483–492.

Nobert, L., McDowell, R., & Goulet, D. (1992). *Profile of post-secondary education in Canada 1991 edition.* Ottawa: Department of the Secretary of State of Canada.

Organization for Economic Cooperation and Development (2000). *From initial education to working life: Making transitions work.* Paris: OECD.

Pancer, S. M., Hunsberger, B., Pratt, M. W., & Alisat, S. (2000). Cognitive complexity of expectations and adjustment to university in the first year. *Journal of Adolescent Research, 15*, 38–57.

Pascarella, E. T. (1999). The development of critical thinking: Does college make a difference? *Journal of College Student Development, 40*, 562–569.

Pascarella, E. T., & Terenzini, P. T. (1991). *How college affects students: Findings and insights from 20 years of research.* San Francisco: Jossey-Bass.

Perry, W. G. (1970). *Forms of intellectual and ethical development in the college years.* New York: Holt, Rinehart & Winston.

Ponterotto, J. G. (1990). Racial/ethnic minority and women students in higher education: A status report. *New Directions for Student Services, 52*, 45–59.

Pryor, F. L., & Schaffer, D. L. (1999). *Who's not working and why: Employment, cognitive skills, wages, and the changing U.S. labor market.* New York: Cambridge University Press.

Rice, K. G., Fitzgerald, D. P., Whaley, T. J., & Gibbs, C. L. (1995). Cross-sectional and longitudinal examination of attachment, separation-individuation, and college student adjustment. *Journal of Counseling and Development, 73*, 463–474.

Rice, K. G., & Whaley, T. J. (1994). A short-term longitudinal study of within-semester stability and change in attachment and college student adjustment. *Journal of College Student Development, 35*, 324–330.

Riviere, B. (1999). The psychosocial process of college dropout: The CEGEP experience. *Canadian Journal of Counselling, 33*, 277–292.

Ryland, E. B., Riordan, R. J., & Brack, G. (1994). Selected characteristics of high-risk students and their enrollment persistence. *Journal of College Student Development, 35*, 54–58.

Sanford, N. (1967). *The American college: A psychological and social interpretation of higher learning*. New York: Wiley.

Sax, L. J., Astin, A. W., Korn, W. S., & Mahoney, K. (1999). *The American Freshman: National norms for fall 1999*. Los Angeles: Higher Education Research Institute, UCLA.

Saylor, E. S., & Aries, E. (1999). Ethnic identity and change in social context. *Journal of Social Psychology, 139*, 549–566.

Schwitzer, A. M., Griffin, O. T., Ancis, J. R., & Thomas, C. R. (1999). Social adjustment experiences of African American college students. *Journal of Counseling and Development, 77*, 189–197.

Spitzberg, I. J., & Thorndike, V. V. (1992). *Creating community on college campuses*. Albany, NY: State University of New York Press.

Strage, A. A. (1998). Family context variables and the development of self-regulation in college students. *Adolescence, 33*, 17–31.

Strage, A. A. (1999). Social and academic integration and college success: Similarities and differences as a function of ethnicity and family educational background. *College Student Journal, 33*, 198–205.

Strage, A. A., & Brandt, T. S. (1999). Authoritative parenting and college students' academic adjustment and success. *Journal of Educational Psychology, 91*, 146–156.

Sullivan, K., & Sullivan, A. (1980). Adolescent–parent separation. *Developmental Psychology, 16*, 93–104.

Sun, S. W., Bell, N. J., Feng, D., & Avery, A. W. (2000). A longitudinal analysis of parental bonds and relational competencies during the college years. *International Journal of Adolescence and Youth, 8*, 149–181.

Taillon, J., & Paju, M. (1999). *The class of '95: Report on the 1997 national survey of 1995 graduates*. Ottawa, Human Resources Development Canada: http:/www.hrdc-drhc.gc.ca/arb

Terenzini, P. T., Springer, L., Pascarella, E. T., & Amaury, N. (1995). Academic and out-of-class influences on students' intellectual orientations. *Review of Higher Education, 19*, 23–44.

Tinto, V. (1975). Dropout from higher education: A theoretical synthesis of recent research. *Review of Educational Research, 45*, 89–125.

Tinto, V. (1987). *Leaving college: Rethinking the causes and cures of student attrition*. Chicago: University of Chicago Press.

Tuijnman, A. (1989). *Recurrent education, earnings, and well-being: A fifty-year longitudinal study of a cohort of Swedish men*. Stockholm: Stockholm Studies in Educational Psychology.

US Census Bureau (1999). *Statistical abstracts of the United States*. Washington, DC: US Census Bureau.

US Department of Education (1997). *The condition of education: 1997*. Washington, DC: US Government Printing Office.

Valery, J. H., O'Connor, P., & Jennings, S. (1997). The nature and amount of support college-age adolescents request and receive from their parents. *Adolescence, 32*, 323–337.

Velum, J. R., & Weiss, A. B. (1993). Education and the work histories of young adults. *Monthly Labor Review*, April, 11–20.

Waterman, A. S. (1993). Developmental perspectives on identity formation: From adolescence to adulthood. In J. E. Marcia, A. S. Waterman, D. R. Matteson, S. L. Archer, & J. L Orlofsky (Eds.), *Ego identity: A handbook for psychosocial research* (pp. 42–68). New York: Springer.

Watson, L., & Kuh, G. D. (1996). The influence of dominant racial environments on student involvement, perceptions, and educational gains: A look at historically black and predominantly white liberal arts institutions. *Journal of College Student Development, 37*, 415–424.

Whitt, E., Edison, M., Pascarella, E. T., Nora, A., & Terenzini, P. T. (1999). Interactions with peers and objective and self-reported cognitive outcomes across 3 years of college. *Journal of College Student Development, 40*, 61–78.

Wilder, D. H., McKeegan, H. F., Midkiff, R. M., Skelton, R. C., & Dunkerly, R. E. (1996). Higher education impact on student objectives: Longitudinal change in Clark–Trow educational philosophies. *Research in Higher Education, 37*, 279–298.

Wintre, M. G., & Yaffe, Y. (2000). First-year students' adjustment to university life as a function of relationships with parents. *Journal of Adolescent Research, 15*, 9–37.

Wright, L. S., & Stimmel, T. (1983). Perceptions of parents and self among college students reporting learning disabilities. *Exceptional Child, 31*, 203–208.

Zea, M. C., Reisen, C. A., Beil, C., & Caplan, R. D. (1997). Predicting intention to remain in college among ethnic minority and nonminority students. *Journal of Social Psychology, 137*, 149–160.

PART III

Developmental Patterns and Processes

CHAPTER NINE

Autonomy Development during Adolescence

Melanie J. Zimmer-Gembeck and W. Andrew Collins

Introduction

Throughout life autonomy advances and declines as individuals develop new competencies, previously acquired skills decline, and changing conditions require altered behavior (Baltes & Silverberg, 1994). During adolescence the development of autonomy typically accelerates because of rapid physical and cognitive changes, expanding social relationships, and additional rights and responsibilities. Self-reliance and personal decision-making increase, the self and identity are gradually consolidated, and affect, behavior, and cognition are increasingly self-regulated. Failures in these tasks can mark a variety of widely recognized problem behaviors and other difficulties (Adams, Montemayor, & Gullotta, 1996; Allen et al., 1994a, 1994b; Baltes & Silverberg, 1994; Blos, 1979; Chen & Dornbusch, 1998; Douvan & Adelson, 1966; Erikson, 1969; A. Freud, 1958; Ryan, Deci, & Grolnick, 1995; Silverberg & Gondoli, 1996).

In this chapter, we address the question of how autonomy emerges from this mix of maturational, social, and psychological changes. The chapter is divided into four parts. In the first part, we describe the concept of autonomy, its definition, relation to other aspects of psychosocial development, and functional significance for behavior and adjustment. We next review key theoretical perspectives on, and processes in, the development of autonomy during adolescence. Third, we consider the role of context in the development of autonomy, focusing particularly on the role and impact of close relationship part-

Preparation of this manuscript was in part supported by a National Institute of Mental Health training grant (PI, Jeylan Mortimer) to the Life Course Center, Department of Sociology, University of Minnesota (Melanie J. Zimmer-Gembeck) and by the Rodney T. Wallace Professorship for the Advancement of Teaching and Learning, College of Education and Human Development, University of Minnesota (W. Andrew Collins).

ners. Finally, we examine common variations in autonomy and autonomy development for females and males and for adolescents from differing cultures.

The Nature and Function of Autonomy

Defining autonomy

The term "autonomy" is used widely to refer to a set of psychosocial issues that are of particular importance during adolescence. Yet the particular meaning of the term is often difficult to specify. Moreover, explaining how individuals become autonomous – and why some either do not or do so only partially – varies, depending upon one's initial assumptions about the meaning and significance of autonomy.

Developmental and social theorists have proposed a variety of definitions, as table 9.1 shows. Some view autonomy as a quality of the individual (e.g., actions that are initiated and regulated by the core self; Ryan et al., 1995), whereas others define autonomy as partially or fully dependent upon an adolescent's relationship with others or a response to others (e.g., as disengagement from parental ties and control; A. Freud, 1958). Likewise, some definitions emphasize *freedom from* the constraints of childhood dependence on others, whereas others focus on the *freedom to* make choices, pursue goals, and regulate one's own behavior, cognition, and emotion (Collins, Gleason, & Sesma, 1997; Hill & Holmbeck, 1986). In general, current perspectives incorporate several features of these earlier definitions by proposing that socially responsible and optimal autonomous functioning follows from the continuing maintenance of connections to social partners, while becoming increasingly self-regulating, self-motivating, and independent (e.g., Collins et al., 1997; Grotevant & Cooper, 1986; Hill & Holmbeck, 1986). Definitions generally are complicated, however, by two characteristics of common ways of thinking about autonomy: the fact that autonomy refers to multiple dimensions of thought, action, and emotions; and the overlap between autonomy and other terms that describe increasingly mature individual functioning.

Multiple dimensions. The construct of autonomy has been conceptualized as having behavioral, cognitive, and affective dimensions (Steinberg, 1990; Sessa & Steinberg, 1991; Steinberg & Silverberg, 1986). The behavioral dimension of autonomy has been defined as active, independent functioning including self-governance, self-regulation of behavior, and acting on personal decisions (Feldman & Quatman, 1988; Feldman & Rosenthal, 1991; Sessa & Steinberg, 1991). Cognitive autonomy most often has been defined as a "sense of self-reliance, a belief that one has control over his or her own life, and subjective feelings of being able to make decisions without excessive social validation" (Sessa & Steinberg, 1991, p. 42; also see Brown et al., 1993; Greenberger et al., 1975). The third dimension, emotional autonomy, has been defined as a sense of individuation from parents and relinquishing dependence on them (also see chapter 10 in this volume). Emotional autonomy implies changing conceptions of, and relations with, parents, including developing more mature conceptions of parents as people (Steinberg & Silverberg, 1986). Research in which all three constructs have been measured reveals some overlap in the dimensions of autonomy, suggesting that they do not develop independently (see Collins & Repinski, 1994; Youniss & Smollar, 1985).

These three components of autonomy, though conceptually distinct, all appear to increase during adolescence. Adolescents gradually seek and receive greater independence from parental control with age. Adolescents also increasingly report feeling more autonomous (Greenberger, 1984; Greenberger & Sorenson, 1974), more individuated, less likely to idealize parents, and less likely to express childish dependency on them (Steinberg & Silverberg, 1986). Much more information is needed, however, about the nature of the interrelations among behavioral, cognitive, and emotional autonomy and whether all three are equally significant components of adolescent psychosocial development (Collins et al., 2000).

Autonomy and other aspects of psychological maturity. The multidimensional nature of autonomy results in further conceptual challenges. These challenges are complicated by the shared variation between autonomy and other psychosocial concepts such as identity, competence, control, and self-regulation (Baltes & Silverberg, 1994; Baumeister et al., 1998; Skinner, 1996). For example, Baltes and Silverberg (1994) proposed that healthy autonomy might encompass psychosocial functioning in many domains, including competence in academic, work, and social domains; emotion regulation and impulse control; leadership; and positive self-esteem and identity. Recent findings indeed show considerable overlap between measures of both emotional and behavioral autonomy, current and earlier measures of social competence, and both early childhood and middle childhood measures of sociability, initiative, and self-assertion (Collins et al., 2000). A key question for the future is whether autonomy can be defined and measured independent of other aspects of psychosocial maturity, or – to put it another way – exactly what the concept of autonomy adds to our understanding of psychosocial maturity (Steinberg, 2000).

Functions of autonomy

Achieving autonomy is one of the key normative psychosocial developmental issues of adolescence, and all perspectives on the development of autonomy emphasize the problematic outcomes that may follow from a lack of appropriate support for autonomy. For example, Blos (1979) contended that failure to individuate from parents could result in one of two extreme outcomes: the avoidance of regression marked by "flight into adultomorphic roles" (p. 103), or continuation of the regressed state. Blos believed that both extremes almost certainly would result in emotional illness. Similarly, the ability to act independent of others and an interest in connecting with others are thought to be associated with physical and psychological well-being, but an unusual level of independence not tempered by a positive orientation to others can be psychologically, physically, and socially damaging (Bakan, 1966; Helgeson, 1994).

Table 9.1 A Selection of Definitions of Autonomy and Related Constructs

Authors	Year	Construct	Definition
A. Freud	1958	Detachment	Increasing disengagement from parental ties and controls.
Bakan	1966	Agency	Urges of self-affirmation and individualization; involves self-affirmation, self-assertion, and self-expansion.
Bakan	1966	Unmitigated agency	Agency not balanced by cooperation, caring, and the formation of connections with others.
Greenberger & Sorenson	1974	Self-reliance	An aspect of psychosocial maturity marked by an absence of excessive dependency on others, a sense of control over one's life, and initiative.
Berndt	1979	Autonomy	Resistance to parental and peer pressure.
Blos	1979	Individuation	A process of emotional disengagement from parents.
Grotevant & Cooper	1986	Self-assertion	Having an awareness of one's own point of view and being responsible for communicating it clearly.
Grotevant & Cooper	1986	Separateness	The ability to express differences between the self and others.
Hill & Holmbeck	1986	Autonomy	Freedom to carry out actions on the adolescent's own behalf while maintaining appropriate connections to significant others.
Steinberg & Silverberg	1986	Emotional autonomy	Individuation from parents, nondependency on parents, deidealization of parents, and increasing perceptions of parents as people.
Bandura	1989	Agency	The capacity to exercise control over one's thought processes, motivation, and action.
Ryan & Lynch	1989	Autonomy, self-determination	Self-governance and self-regulation; the opposite is heteronomy defined as being controlled by external forces or compulsions, the relative absence of volition.
Crittenden	1990	Autonomy	Capacities for taking responsibility for one's own behavior, making decisions regarding one's own life, and maintaining supportive relationships.
Lamborn & Steinberg	1993	Emotional autonomy	The development of mature, realistic, and balanced perceptions of parents that accompanies the acceptance of primary responsibility for personal decision-making, values, and emotional stability.

Table 9.1 *Continued.*

Authors	Year	Construct	Definition
Turner et al.	1993	Autonomy	Self-governance, self-regulation, and independence, but not freedom from appropriate limits set by parents.
Baltes & Silverberg	1994	Autonomy	The attainment of greater self-reliance; growing capacity to be self-regulating with respect to the learning process and behavior; self-initiative; self-direction and independence vs. obedience to rules and authority.
Skinner & Wellborn	1994	Autonomy	Need for self-determined (i.e., choiceful) interactions with the environment.
Helgeson	1994	Communion	Focus on or orientation toward others.
Helgeson	1994	Unmitigated communion	Communion not mitigated by agency; an extreme focus on others precluding attending to oneself
Ryan, Deci, & Grolnick	1995	Autonomy	Operating agentically and authentically from one's core sense of self; to be self-initiating and self-regulating; not independence and detachment; a need of all humans throughout the lifespan.
Collins, Gleason, & Sesma	1997	Behavioral autonomy	Active, overt manifestations of independent functioning, includes regulation of one's own behavior and decision making.
Collins, Gleason, & Sesma	1997	Emotional autonomy	Individuation from parents and relinquishing of dependence on them.
Collins, Gleason, & Sesma	1997	Cognitive autonomy	A sense of self-reliance, a belief that one has control over one's own life, and subjective feelings of being able to make decisions without excessive social validation.
Herman et al.	1997	Psychological autonomy	An independent sense of identity, even while preserving connection to parents.
Deci & Ryan	2000	Autonomy	The organismic desire to self-organize experience and behavior and to have activity; be concordant with one's integrated sense of self; acting from one's integrated sense of self, and endorsing one's actions.
Skinner & Edge	2000	Autonomy	Need to express one's authentic self and to experience that self as the source of action.

Much evidence shows that autonomy support provided by others and adolescents' ability to function relatively autonomously have positive influences on other aspects of adolescent functioning. As autonomy increases during middle and late adolescence, parents and peers have less influence on adolescents' opinions and decisions, despite generally increasing "peer pressure" during these periods (Brown, Clasen, & Eicher, 1986). Even in early adolescence, those adolescents whose parents increasingly involve them in decision making are less likely to be exceedingly oriented to peer opinions and peer acceptance than those adolescents whose parents allow less involvement in decision making (Fuligni & Eccles, 1993). In short, a balance between independent, self-confident action and positive relationships with others appears to be optimal for psychological adjustment and development (Helgeson, 1994; Sessa & Steinberg, 1991).

Theoretical Views of Autonomy Development

Theoretical perspectives on the development or function of autonomy not only imply differing definitions, but also offer different explanations of the origins and development of autonomy (Baltes, Reese, & Nesselroade, 1970). These varying explanations underscore the diverse influences and processes that contribute to the development of autonomy. In this section, we briefly describe three general perspectives on autonomy: organismic-maturational views primarily based in psychoanalytic perspectives; perspectives emphasizing self and motivation; and perspectives emphasizing social influences and relationships.

Organismic–maturational views

The earliest influential perspective on autonomy and its development, the psychoanalytic theory of Anna Freud (1958), described the development of autonomy as an outgrowth of drives of the organism that promoted detachment and disengagement from parental ties and controls. In psychoanalytic views this loosening of ties with parents is essential to becoming an autonomous individual capable of being responsible for what he or she thinks, does, believes, feels, decides, and becomes. A contemporary extension of this view (Blos, 1979) asserted that autonomy relies not on detachment from parents, but individuation from them. Individuation is a process of emotional disengagement from the caregivers that first occurs in early childhood (around age 2) and then reoccurs in adolescence.

One common conviction among these theoretical perspectives is that detachment and individuation from caregivers is prompted by development of the organism. Drives, primarily sexual, are assumed to arise during puberty and are manifested as either behavioral or cognitive rebelliousness and defiance toward parents or other caregivers. As a result, relations between parents and their adolescents are marked by a "normal conflictual condition" which stimulates dissolution of ties to parents and reduction of parental controls (Blos, 1979, p. 77). Only through detachment and individuation can young people move outside the family to find healthy extrafamilial adult love and hate objects. In this complex way "the constancy of self-esteem and of mood become increasingly independent from external sources or, at best, dependent on external sources of one's own choosing" (Blos, 1979, p. 143).

The close relation between detachment from parents and some aspects of autonomy was evident in a well-known series of papers by Steinberg and his colleagues and Ryan and Lynch. Influenced by the theory of Blos (1979), Steinberg and Silverberg (1986) operationalized emotional autonomy as adolescents' changing perceptions of parents. This measure was labeled the Emotional Autonomy Scale (EAS). The scale consisted of two affective scales (non-dependency and individuation) and two cognitive scales (perceiving parents as people and deidealization). All four scales were designed to measure childlike dependencies on parents and individuation. In the first study using the EAS (Steinberg & Silverberg, 1986), adolescents' (11–14-year-olds) scores on the EAS were inversely related to resistance to peer pressure and self-reliance. The authors argued that early adolescents are in a transitional period during which initial feelings of emotional autonomy can leave young people vulnerable to peer pressure. At later ages, however, increasing emotional autonomy should be positively related to self-reliance and resistance to peer pressure.

Challenging this interpretation, Ryan and Lynch (1989) contended that the EAS measured detachment from parents rather than emotional autonomy. They further posited that detachment can result in both positive and negative experiences. Positive experiences of detachment from parents might include self-reliance and self-regulation, whereas negative experiences might include separation and loss of valuable supportive connections. These negative experiences potentially lead to additional adverse outcomes, such as lack of a consolidated identity, a reduced base of support, lower self-esteem, and problem behaviors.

The disagreement about the appropriate interpretation of the EAS illustrates the difficulty of measuring autonomy independent of a variety of other indicators of competence, including degree of distancing from parents. In more recent work, Steinberg and colleagues (Lamborn & Steinberg, 1993) sought to better understand the conditions within which emotional autonomy measured by the EAS is linked to negative or positive adolescent functioning. They found that a combination of emotional autonomy and supportive relationships differentiated various subgroups of adolescents. Consistent with Steinberg and Silverberg's (1986) prediction, 14- to 18-year olds with relatively higher scores on the EAS and higher amounts of support from parents also scored higher on psychosocial development and academic competence than their peers. By contrast, consistent with Ryan and Lynch's (1989) prediction, those adolescents with high EAS scores and low support from parents showed problematic adjustment profiles. Similarly, Fuhrman and Holmbeck (1995) examined the association between emotional autonomy, maternal warmth, parental control, parent–adolescent conflict, family cohesion, and adolescent adjustment (behavioral problems, competence, and academic achievement) among adolescents ages 10 to 18. Their results also indicated that in a context of positive parent–adolescent relationships, low emotional autonomy (i.e., little detachment from parents) is associated with more positive adolescent adjustment. In a context of negative parent–adolescent relationships, however, high emotional autonomy (i.e., higher levels of detachment from parents) is associated with relatively more positive adolescent adjustment. These findings are indications that autonomy is neither inimical to relationships nor separate from them in an adolescent's psychological life. Future research that considers emotional and cognitive aspects of autonomy (as well as behavioral autonomy) in conjunction with qualities of relationships with parents and peers will be most promising for understanding the growth of competencies and other developmental outcomes in adolescence and adulthood.

In addition to highlighting the importance of parent–adolescent relationships to the development of emotional and cognitive autonomy, the most recent studies (Lamborn & Steinberg, 1993; Fuhrman & Holmbeck, 1995) provide evidence that the EAS needs additional psychometric work to unconfound autonomy and the quality of the adolescent–parent relationship. Schmitz and Baer's (2001) recent examination of the psychometric properties of the EAS questions whether this measure is sufficiently sound for future research. The factor structure of the scale differed from that proposed in the original study (Steinberg & Silverberg, 1986) and the structure of the scale differed depending on the age and race/ethnicity of adolescents. Hence, our conceptualizations of autonomy have been advancing while our measurement may require additional work. These authors propose that some of the seemingly contradictory results of research based upon the EAS (Fuhrman & Holmbeck, 1995; Lamborn & Steinberg, 1993; Ryan & Lynch, 1989; Steinberg & Silverberg, 1986) may be a result of the inadequacies of the scale rather than differences in the meaning of the measure as either detachment (an indication of problems) or emotional autonomy (a normative aspect of development). They further note that these findings may indicate "the need for more work at the conceptualization level in the research process" (Schmitz & Baer, 2001; p. 217). Although conceptualization has advanced, revised or new measures are important next steps for further progress in research on adolescent autonomy development.

Views emphasizing self and motivation

In comparison to organismic–maturational perspectives on adolescent autonomy, views emphasizing aspects of the self and motivation attribute autonomy development to internal processes, as well, but describe different processes of interaction between the individual and the environment in the emergence of autonomy. Among the views we place in this category are the self-determination theory of Ryan, Deci, and colleagues (Deci & Ryan, 1985; Ryan, Kuhl, & Deci, 1997; Ryan & Lynch, 1989), Bandura's theory of self-efficacy (Bandura, 1989, 1997), a motivational theory of psychological needs described by Connell, Skinner and others (Connell, 1990; Connell & Wellborn, 1991; Ryan, et al., 1995; Skinner & Edge, 2000; Skinner & Wellborn, 1994), and a theory of the three roots of the self (Baumeister, 1998).

A common theme in these theories is that autonomy requires a sense of agency. Ryan et al. (1995) refer to autonomy as "the extent that one is operating agentically, from one's core sense of self . . . To be autonomous thus means to be *self*-initiating and *self*-regulating" (p. 621, italics in original). In this sense, agency combines features of both cognitive autonomy and behavioral autonomy. Skinner, Connell, and colleagues (Skinner,

1996; Patrick, Skinner, & Connell, 1993) have shown that actions and perceptions that fulfill needs for autonomy are separate from those that fulfill needs for competence. Within this perspective, needs for autonomy are met when one perceives oneself as the *origin* of one's own actions (the agent; a perceived internal locus of causality), while the need for competence is met when one feels *effective* at causing desirable and preventing undesirable outcomes (internal locus of control). An internal perceived locus of causality (autonomy) is evidenced as a perceived freedom to choose one's own course of action, while control is the expectation of a contingency between one's actions and outcomes. An innate need for autonomy energizes and motivates all individuals to seek their own course of behavior, while a need for relatedness to others simultaneously promotes behaviors that maintain connections with others. Autonomy is evident in intrinsic motivation to engage in certain behaviors and joy in choosing to engage in certain behaviors rather than others.

Bandura's (1989) social–cognitive perspective on agency evolved from social learning theory and self-efficacy theory. These earlier theories were focused on perceived competence and the influences of the environment on individuals' goal-directed actions. In Bandura's view, agency implies that actions, beliefs, emotions, and motivations arise from a continuous pattern of interaction between individuals and environment. Thus, autonomy is not an innate need of individuals, and the environment does not simply endow individuals with the ability to be autonomous and self-regulating. Rather, individuals construct the ability to regulate one's own cognitions, emotions, and behavior from a history of transactions with the environment. Individuals must engage in self-regulatory practices to develop autonomous functioning.

In addition, the theoretical perspective and research of Baumeister and colleagues (Baumeister, 1998; Baumeister et al., 1998) provide direction on the interface of self-regulation and autonomy. In his review of theory and research on the self within a symbolic interactionist framework (e.g., Mead, 1934), Baumeister (1998) describes three roots of selfhood including the (a) reflexive consciousness; (b) interpersonal aspect of selfhood; and (c) agent, executive function, controller, or origin of the self. The first root of selfhood, the reflexive consciousness, encompasses self-awareness. The second root, the interpersonal aspect of the self, recognizes that selves exist and develop within relationships with others and that we learn and create models of the self through interactions with others. The third root, the executive function, is responsible for self-regulation and autonomous functioning of the self (Baumeister et al., 1998). Consisting of experiences of being an active agent and decision-maker and of independently regulating cognition, emotion, behavior, and motivation by making choices, taking action, and taking responsibility, the executive function also regulates behavior and emotion by monitoring and modifying initial reactions. In this view, autonomy is but one of the roots of the self. Increasingly, failures of self-regulation, which depend upon this executive function of the self, have been implicated in a range of problem behaviors during adolescence and adulthood, including aggression and drug abuse (Baumeister, 1996; Baumeister et al., 1998; Baumeister, Heatherton, & Tice, 1994).

All of these theoretical perspectives assert that particular forms of relations with others support the development of a sense of agency. Although these perspectives do not view detachment from others, individuation, defiance of parents, and conflict with parents as a necessary or even central event in autonomy development, they do highlight the importance of social interactions in the development of autonomy. For example, Deci and Ryan (2000) describe the opposite of autonomy as the experience of being controlled, coerced, compelled, or manipulated into actions that do not freely emerge from the core self ("heteronomy"). Baumeister (1998) proposed that the three roots of the self are interrelated. One must be aware of the self to monitor and regulate the self. Yet awareness of the self is most likely dependent on interactions with others and is often extracted from one's understanding of others' perceptions. In addition, interpersonal relationships serve to initiate and guide self-regulatory actions and capacities. Hence, connections with others and autonomous regulation of action are interrelated and mutually influential. Successful autonomous functioning includes having an adequate awareness of the self, understanding and internalizing social information, and having the means to regulate and modify the self.

Autonomous actions thus are distinct from those that are deliberate responses to the influence of others in that they involve individuals' perceptions of choice and willingness. Because autonomy is defined apart from the social context, autonomous actions can occur while dependent on or attached to another. In fact, attachment and emotional bonds that include interactions that support autonomy (that is, that are not overly coercive and controlling), rather than detachment from close relationships, can promote individuation and autonomous functioning (Ryan & Lynch, 1989).

Views emphasizing social relationships and influences

During the 1980s and 1990s, many other developmental scientists challenged classic psychoanalytic theories of the development of autonomy, proposing that autonomy does not necessitate severing of ties with parental figures (e.g., Allen et al., 1994a, 1994b; Collins, 1990; Collins & Repinski, 1994; Grotevant & Cooper, 1986; Hill & Holmbeck, 1986; Gilligan, 1982; Ryan & Lynch, 1989; Steinberg, 1990; Youniss & Smollar, 1985). Instead, as also proposed by self and motivation theorists, these developmental perspectives proposed that autonomy and connections to others coexist and influence each other bidirectionally. Socially responsible autonomous functioning and self-regulation depend upon continuing, but transformed, attachments and connections to others (especially caregivers) (Grolnick, Deci, & Ryan, 1997). For example, adolescents with supportive, warm, and involved parents and who also provide appropriate structure and demand mature behavior may be more likely to feel capable of making independent decisions while seeking appropriate input from others, exploring their environments, expressing themselves, and engaging in behaviors that reflect their true selves (Steinberg, 1990). In addition, autonomous functioning may be more likely when exchanges between adolescents and adults honor and respect the adolescents' capabilities and permit and support autonomous behaviors and decision making while also maintaining positive emotional connections. The nature and function of adult–child relationships are adjusted as the young person gains capacity for independent functioning and desires more responsibility and autonomy (Collins et al., 1997a, 1997b).

Scholars in this tradition further specified the process of autonomy development in the context of parent–child relationships. Kobak and Cole (1994) portray the development of autonomy as a transaction between the individual and the interpersonal environment. They describe a process by which early attachment to parents facilitates or impedes children's development of "meta-monitoring," defined as the ability to monitor one's own models of self and others, reflect on these models, and revise them, if necessary. The growing capacity for meta-monitoring allows the adolescent to become more autonomous and to regulate his or her behaviors. Instead of detaching from parents, young people revise their models of their relationships with their parents as they move into adolescence in ways that maintain connections, but reflect the increasing autonomy of the adolescent and transformations in relationships with their parents (see also Collins, 1990, 1995). Allen and colleagues (Allen et al., 1994a, 1994b; Allen & Land, 1999) posit a similar process in which autonomy and relatedness balance each other in well-adjusted adolescents. For example, using an observational coding scheme, these researchers reported that interactions between parents and their 14-year-old adolescents that were lower in autonomous-relatedness (defined as allowing disagreement, statements of positions, validation of others' positions, and attention to others' statement) were linked to increases in depressed affect among adolescents at age 16 (Allen et al., 1994a, 1994b).

Additional evidence for the importance of child–parent relationships to the development of autonomy comes from work by Kremen and Block (1998). In this study, the influence of parenting qualities in preschool on adolescents' ego-control and ego-resilience was examined. Ego-control was conceptualized as a system of attentional, cognitive, affective, and action processes that manage an individual's impulses and desires by organizing and motivating behavior. Controlling for preschool ego-control, parenting behaviors in preschool, including support and encouragement of autonomy, and warmth or lack of hostility, were linked to relatively greater regulation of impulses and behavior in adolescence.

Significant social relationships (most often with parents) that are thought to foster socially adaptive autonomy are those that allow disagreement and the expression of alternative views, while not being intrusive, overinvolved, or manipulative (e.g., Steinberg, 1990; Lamborn & Steinberg, 1993). Terminology for describing these relationships varies, as is apparent from the list of terms that have been used to describe the behaviors of individuals and institutions that influence the development of autonomy among children and adolescents (see table 9.2). Behaviors that constrain or limit the development of autonomy typically are described as exerting psychological control, a phenomenon increasingly studied in the field today (e.g., Barber, 1996).

In sum, the theoretical perspectives summarized here do not necessarily conflict with one another. Each emphasizes a different aspect of the complex process of autonomy development, and all three contribute to a comprehensive account of how autonomy emerges during adolescence. In the next section, we briefly review findings showing the interrelation of these factors in autonomy development during adolescence.

Processes in Adolescent Autonomy

The key questions for those seeking to understand adolescents and their development are how changes in the individual, influences from others, and environmental opportunities,

Table 9.2 Behaviors and Styles of Parents and Other Social Partners That May Affect Adolescents' Development of Autonomy

Authors	Year	Construct	Definition
Grotevant & Cooper	1986	Mutuality	The demonstration of sensitivity to and respect for beliefs, feelings, and ideas of others.
Grotevant & Cooper	1986	Permeability	The responsiveness or openness of an individual to the ideas of others; the giving of permission and encouragement to the other to develop a point of view.
Grotevant & Cooper	1986	Parent–child disagreement	Allows the adolescent to form and argue for his or her own ideas and opinions.
Feldman & Rosenthal	1991	Demanding	Involvement in decision-making, conformity, organization, and achievement orientation.
Brown et al.	1993	Joint decision making	Efforts to engage a young person in joint decision making.
Allen et al.	1994a	Exhibiting autonomy-relatedness	Speech patterns that express and allow discussion of reasons for disagreement, provide evidence of confidence in one's position, validate others' positions, and attend to others' speeches.
Allen et al.	1994a	Inhibiting autonomy	Speech patterns that make it more difficult for individuals to discuss reasons for positions including over-personalizing disagreement, pressuring others to agree, and recanting positions to foreclose discussion.
Skinner & Wellborn	1994	Coercion	Contexts that constrain, manipulate, or control the young person; can include verbal and physical threats, punishment, love withdrawal, guilt induction, competition and comparison, or rewards and bribes.
Ryan, Deci, & Grolnick	1995	Autonomy support	The encouraging of self-initiation, providing choice, allowing independent problem-solving, minimizing control and power assertion; taking children's perspectives, offering choices, using minimal controls.
Barber	1996	Psychological control	Control attempts that intrude into the psychological and emotional development of the child; measured as invalidating feelings, constraining verbal expression, personal attack, and love withdrawal.

Table 9.2 *Continued.*

Authors	Year	Construct	Definition
Ryan & Solky	1996	Autonomy support	Contact and encouragement of the self in the context of interpersonal interactions; the readiness of a person to assume another's perspective or internal frame of reference and to facilitate self-initiated expression and action; acknowledgement of the other's perceptions, acceptance of the other's feelings, and an absence of attempts to control the other's experience and behavior.
Barber & Olsen	1997	Psychological autonomy granting	The extent to which socialization processes facilitate and do not intrude on the child's development of an independent sense of identity, efficacy, and worth; an aspect of socialization in which children are permitted to experience, value, and express their own thoughts and emotions, leading to the development of a stable sense of self and identity.
Collins et al.	1997	Parent–child conflict	Conflict stimulates realignment toward more age-appropriate expectations especially in the area of behavioral autonomy.
Eccles et al.	1997	Autonomy support	The provision of opportunities for autonomous behavior and decision making.
Herman et al.	1997	Psychological autonomy granting	The extent to which parents employ noncoercive, democratic discipline and encourage the individuality of the adolescent.
Gray & Steinberg	1999	Psychological autonomy granting	The extent to which parents employ noncoercive, democratic discipline and encourage young people to express individuality in the family.
Skinner & Edge	2000	Autonomy support	Provided when social partners or institutions respect and defer to young people allowing them freedom of expression and action, and encouraging them to attend to, accept, and value their inner states, preferences, and desires. The opposite of autonomy support is coercion or controlling social conditions.

demands, and constraints combine in the growth of autonomous functioning. This question is not only a matter of intellectual curiosity. Knowing the essential ingredients of adaptive behavioral, cognitive, and emotional autonomy development may provide a basis for intervening with adolescents who face difficulties in such areas as self-determination, initiative, planning, goal setting, socially appropriate inhibition of impulse, motivation, problem-solving, coping with challenges, and problem behaviors (Allen et al., 1997; Larson, 2000; Skinner & Edge, 2000).

Autonomy in social contexts

Recently, Collins and colleagues (Collins et al., 1997b) described how the nature and quality of social contexts promote or limit adolescents' internalization of the desires of others. This process of internalization results in more or less socially responsible autonomy and self-regulated action. They describe the common view of adolescence as a "period of tension between two developmental tasks: increasing conformity to societal expectations, while attaining autonomy from the influences of others" (p. 78), and provide evidence that this perspective has been biased toward intra-individual processes, rather than relational processes. They proposed that internalization and autonomy or self-regulation result from a transactional process of acknowledging and modifying one's own needs and desires, while maintaining connections to others, beginning to own socially approved behaviors, and recognizing and resisting unnecessary or negative influences. In short, the challenge to adolescents is to transform socially sanctioned values into personal values, while also discarding negative or unnecessary opinions and evaluations. Similarly, Kremen and Block (1998) proposed that internalization of social standards is the likely mechanism that would account for associations between warm, structured, and autonomy-supportive parental behaviors in preschool and adaptive levels of adolescent self-regulation.

This description of attaining autonomy implies several component achievements. One achievement is the development of a sense of self as unique and somewhat distinctive from others. Harter (1999) describes how the development of the self during adolescence is influenced by and emerges from interactions with others. During early adolescence, young people are sensitive to feedback from others about who they are as persons. Later, during middle adolescence, young people increasingly become preoccupied with opinions and expectations of important others. During this time, they have difficulties consolidating all of the information they receive about the self. By late adolescence, young people begin to consolidate their conceptions of self and internalize some values that may have originally been socialized by significant others. An implication of Harter's view is that some preoccupation with the evaluations and opinions of others during adolescence is normative, but continued preoccupation may indicate difficulties with autonomy.

A second attainment is distinguishing between actions based on one's individually held principles, rather than on others' behaviors and expectations. Ryan and Connell (1989; see also Deci & Ryan, 2000) have proposed a categorization of actions as more or less autonomous, depending on whether behaviors were dependent on others' evaluation and influence. Actions coerced or evoked by others were defined as least autonomous, whereas actions arising from the core self were most autonomous. Children's reasons for completing school assignments were placed on a continuum according to whether the action was completely regulated by others (not autonomous) or regulated and valued by the self (autonomous). The proposed reasons, ranging from least to most autonomous, were labeled external (representing compliance to others), introjected (adopted from others), identified (behaviors matched to others with whom one feels similarity or an affinity), and internalized (or integrated) regulation. External regulation was evident in actions such as engaging in schoolwork to avoid parental anger. Introjected regulation was evident in behaviors that were still externally motivated, but had become more internalized. For example, actions might be performed because of the expectation that feelings of shame or guilt would follow if schoolwork was not completed. Identified regulation occurs when actions are still externally motivated, but have become a part of one's identity. Internalized (integrated or intrinsic) regulation was evident when actions were motivated by a real desire by the self to engage in behaviors for fun or because one believed in, wanted, or enjoyed the behavior. Across ages, children shift from external to more internal regulation of actions that are desired by the social world.

Empirical methods to examine the degree of internalization of social standards are still in their infancy. Yet there is some evidence that developmental advantages seem to accompany a relatively more internalized form of self-regulation. Conversely, feelings of being externally coerced and compelled are accompanied by developmental disadvantages (Harter, 1999; Higgins, 1991; Ryan, et al., 1995, 1997). In a study of children of elementary school age, Ryan and Connell (1989) found that more internalized reasons for behaviors in the achievement domain were associated with mastery motivation, internal control, positive coping, effort and enjoyment in schoolwork, empathy, and positive relatedness to mother and teacher. Although research similar to that of Ryan and colleagues (Ryan & Connell, 1989; Deci & Ryan, 2000) has not been completed with adolescents, it is likely that the self-regulation of behavior and cognition based on internalized social standards has even greater developmental advantages during adolescence and beyond. Harter (1999) states that adolescents who do not move to the stage of internal standards, but continue to rely on external social standards and feedback, will be "at risk, because they have not developed an internalized, relatively stable sense of self that will form the basis for subsequent identity development" (p. 188).

Social interactions and autonomy

Many developmental theorists and researchers have considered whether particular behaviors of parents, peers, and teachers, and what particular styles of interacting with young people, facilitate the development of autonomous functioning. Terminology and conceptualizations vary when describing these influential features. Variations among parents' rearing behaviors provide an example. Table 9.2 lists a variety of parental behaviors relevant to autonomy, including authoritative, authoritarian and permissive parenting styles; intrusive or overinvolved parenting; autonomy support; coercion; psychological control; psychological autonomy granting; behavioral control; enabling, constraining, and autonomy promoting; and demands for mature behavior (e.g., see Baumrind, 1991a, 1991b; Best, Hauser, & Allen, 1997; Connell & Wellborn, 1991; Gray & Steinberg, 1999; Grotevant & Cooper, 1986; Herman et al., 1997; Patrick et al., 1993; Ryan & Solky, 1996). These descriptive terms encompass specific parenting behaviors such as directive statements (Eccles et al., 1997), manipulation tactics (e.g., psychological control; Barber, 1996; Barber & Olsen, 1997), and engaging the child in joint decision making (Brown et al., 1993) , as well as global parenting styles in which warmth or involvement, monitoring, and discipline behaviors are combined (e.g., authoritative, authoritarian, or permissive parenting styles; Baumrind, 1991a, 1991b).

Researchers recently have turned to illuminating the conjoint influence of a number of parenting behaviors (e.g., composites of multiple dimensions or interaction effects) such as warmth, connection, involvement, monitoring, and autonomy support (e.g., joint decision making, lack of psychological control, emotional autonomy, autonomy grant-ing, or support for autonomy) on adolescent behaviors and outcomes (Allen et al., 1994a, 1994b; Barber, 1996; Barber & Olsen, 1997; Brown et al., 1993; Eccles et al., 1997; Gray & Steinberg, 1999). For example, Gray and Steinberg (1999) examined independent and joint effects of three aspects of parenting on adjustment in a cross-sectional study of a diverse sample of 8,700 adolescents (ages 14 to 18). Aspects of parenting examined were acceptance-involvement, strictness-supervision (behavioral control), and psychological autonomy-granting. Adolescent adjustment outcomes included behavior problems (anti-social behavior, deviance, drug use, peer conformity), psychosocial development (work orientation, self-reliance, self-esteem), internal distress (psychological symptoms, somatic symptoms), and academic competence (academic self-competence and grade-point average). In general, both individual and joint effects of aspects of parenting were related to most of the adolescent outcomes. Of primary interest here were the strong positive curvilinear associations of parental acceptance-involvement and psychological autonomy granting with psychosocial development. Although there were gains in psychosocial devel-opment as parental acceptance-involvement and psychological autonomy granting increased from low to high, there were even greater gains as parental acceptance-involvement increased from low to moderate and as psychological autonomy granting increased from moderate to high. Behavioral control had a weaker relation with psycho-social development, but there was also a curvilinear association between behavioral control and psychosocial development. Specifically, both a moderate level of behavioral control was associated with relatively more positive adolescent psychosocial functioning. Overall, research examining joint effects of all three parenting dimensions on psycho-social development revealed that parental autonomy granting yields the highest levels of adolescent psychosocial development when parental acceptance-involvement and behav-ioral control are also high.

In addition to parents, teachers and peers can influence adolescent functioning by behaving in ways that are either autonomy-granting or coercive (Allen et al., 1997; Barber & Olsen, 1997; Eccles et al., 1997; Larson, 2000; Skinner & Edge, 2000). However, few researchers have focused on the direct effects of these extrafamilial characteristics on self-reliance, emotional autonomy, behavioral autonomy, and initiative or intrinsic motiva-tion. Instead, most focus on behaviors that have been associated with autonomy or decision making, such as grade-point average, problem behaviors, self-concept, and depression. In a cross-sectional study of 1,387 7th-grade students, Eccles and colleagues (1997) operationalized autonomy support from parents, siblings, teachers, and peers. For example, autonomy support by teachers was operationalized as students' ratings of teachers as being willing to listen to student suggestions, encouraging choice, and involving students in decision making. Eccles et al. found that connection (warmth and involvement), behavioral regulation, and autonomy support by parents, within sibling relationships, in school contexts, and in peer contexts all made significant positive contributions to some aspect of adolescent development. For example, higher levels of behavioral regulation by parents, peers, and schools were all associated with relatively lower levels of adolescent problem behaviors. In a similar cross-sectional study with 925 5th- and 8th-grade students, Barber and Olsen (1997) found that levels of connection, regulation and psychological control or autonomy support by family and peers were most strongly associated with outcomes of depression and antisocial behavior; relatively lower connection, lower regulation, and higher psychological control were associated with increased depression and antisocial behavior. Connection, regulation, and autonomy support by teachers were most strongly predictive of achievement. In addition, aspects of peer relationships were significantly more predictive of the functioning of young people with poor family relationships and were not as strongly associated with adolescent functioning among those with more positive relationships with family.

Communities and organizations are additional contexts that may promote or undermine the development of socially responsible autonomous behavior, emotion, and cognition. Larson (2000) and Allen and colleagues (Allen et al., 1994c, 1997) discuss the ways that youth organizations and intervention and prevention programs might increase autonomous and socially adaptive functioning by developing adolescents' initiative within a context of support from peers and adults. Their suggestions include encouraging engagement in the environment, personal projects, and goals. Strategies included encouraging participation in volunteer work or in structured activities apart from schoolwork such as hobbies, artwork, or sports, and access to a greater variety of adult role models who are excited about their interests and careers. However, few organizations and programs thus far have both explicitly stated autonomy and initiative development as a goal. Among those that have done so, few have evaluated the effectiveness of their efforts. Moreover, the few existing evaluation studies provide weak evidence of effectiveness at best, because participation in the target youth development programs lacked random assignment and were cross-sectional (Larson, 2000). Researchers evaluating Teen Outreach, a program designed to reduce teen pregnancy and school dropout by increasing participation in volunteer activities and providing structured discussions of future life options, report that youth programs are most beneficial when adolescents can select the work they will do within limits, adults assist adolescents to make choices that result in their feelings of competence and relatedness to others, and they provide an environment within which young people feel safe to discuss their views, are listened to, and respected (Allen et al., 1994c, 1997). Larson (2000) summarizes three features of youth organizations that are most likely to facilitate agency and initiative in youth. These include (1) program administration that is youth-based so that the motivation, direction, and goals come from the youth;

(2) adults providing structure in the form of specifying rules and constraints, while emphasizing the importance of the youth-based aspects of the organization; and (3) structuring organizations around a period of activity followed by the completion of a project or goal.

Additional work has shown that an adolescent's autonomous functioning may change depending on the context. Harter and colleagues (Harter, 1999; Harter, Waters, & Whitesell, 1997; Harter et al., 1998) have reported that adolescents' level of voice (saying what one is thinking, expressing opinions) varies depending on the support for voice provided within the context (e.g., by parents, teachers, male classmates or female classmates). In addition, level of voice is systematically higher in some contexts than others. For example, voice is highest with close friends and lowest with classmates of the opposite gender, parents, and teachers (Harter et al., 1997, 1998).

Transformations in family relationships and conflict. Other researchers have investigated the transformations within families as adolescents become more capable of self-regulation and desire more autonomy. One view of this process comes from Maccoby (1984). She observed that autonomy appears to follow a three-phase developmental sequence, beginning with parental regulation of children, to gradually increasing co-regulation between children and parents, to eventual self-regulation. Middle childhood and early adolescence were depicted as the period during which co-regulatory processes are especially important to the eventual achievement of responsible autonomy.

In a similar, but more elaborated model, Collins (1990, 1995) has proposed autonomy results from successive transformations of dyadic interactions in response to violated expectancies. He reasoned that the rapid physical, cognitive, and behavioral changes of adolescence and slower, but notable changes of mid-life for parents result in frequent violations of expectancies about the behavior of each member of the pair. Repeated violations stimulate each member of the pair to alter expectancies, eventually reaching a level appropriate to the interactions of parent and more adult-like offspring. Therefore, violations of expectancies and the family challenges or conflict that may result are likely adaptive and can stimulate important changes in family relationships and individual development (Collins et al., 1997a; Holmbeck & Hill, 1991; Steinberg, 1990). In a short-term longitudinal study, Holmbeck and O'Donnell (1991) found that adolescents (ages 10 to 18) and their mothers who had discrepant judgments concerning the locus of decision making and the granting of behavioral autonomy at time 1 reported increased conflict and decreased cohesiveness from time 1 to time 2. These findings suggest that family interactions are perturbed when mother–adolescent pairs have discrepant perceptions and expectancies regarding adolescent autonomy. However, these perturbations are likely time-limited and result in realignment of expectancies, adaptation to the developmental changes of family members, and decreased conflict affect. Collins and Luebker (1994) reported that the expectancies of parents and adolescents gradually converge between early and late adolescence, providing support for a key premise of Collins's (1995) model. In addition, emotional strains are most prominent during early adolescence (Steinberg, 1981, 1990; Laursen, Coy, & Collins, 1998), but adolescents' emotional experiences when interacting with family become increasingly positive starting in early to late high school (Larson et al., 1996).

Culture, Gender, and Autonomy Development

We have described how support provided in different contexts is important to the development of autonomy within those specific contexts. In this section, we examine two additional sources of variation in autonomy development: culture, and, within cultures, gender.

Cultural variations in autonomy and autonomy development

Autonomy, individuality, and personal freedom are strong cultural values in the United States and in most Western industrialized societies. Within this tradition, parents generally socialize their children to make their own decisions, parents will expect young adolescents to begin to demonstrate autonomy and take on additional responsibility, adolescents will have increasing desires for individual rights and responsibility, and older adolescents will move out of the home of origin and attempt to make it on their own. However, these expectations and desires vary among cultures within and outside of the United States. For example, within the United States, some cultures place higher value on collective support and allegiance to the group and thus value individual autonomy less highly than European Americans do (Cooper, 1994; Feldman & Rosenthal, 1990, 1991). These differences in values and norms may affect the development of autonomy during adolescence and appear as cultural differences in patterns of interactions between adolescents and others (particularly parents). Nevertheless, even though these generalizations often hold when describing groups of individuals classified in predefined cultural categories such as "European American" or "Chinese American," there is most likely significant variation among individuals within each group as well.

To date, our understanding of the interface of culture and adolescent autonomy has been limited to the documentation and explanation of differences between cultures. Fuligni (1998) compared Mexican, Chinese, Filipino, and European adolescents residing in the United States with respect to acceptability of disagreements with mothers and fathers, endorsement of parent authority, expectations for behavioral autonomy (e.g., no longer tell your parents where you are going, go out on dates), conflict, and cohesion. In contrast to European adolescents, American adolescents of Mexican and Filipino heritage expressed more respect for parental authority, and Chinese American adolescents expected to be granted behavioral autonomy later in life. Fuligni (1998) found, however, that differences in timetable expectations of behavioral autonomy were accounted for by whether parents and/or adolescents were foreign-born or not; he found no differences among racial/ethnic groups in conflict or cohesion with mothers or fathers.

Using the same measure of behavioral autonomy, Feldman and Rosenthal (1990) also reported that Chinese American and Chinese Australian adolescents had later autonomy expectations than their European American and Anglo/Celtic Australian counterparts did. This finding applied to both first-generation and second-generation Chinese adolescents. Yet, Chinese Australian adolescents were somewhat more similar to Anglo/Celtic Australian adolescents than Chinese American adolescents were to their US counterparts.

This cross-cultural pattern likely was due to the greater opportunity to maintain cultural norms and values in the United States, because of a greater concentration of Chinese in the region (San Francisco) in which the research was conducted. These findings suggest that racial and ethnic differences in autonomy striving and autonomy granting by parents may decline or disappear as immigrants adapt to a new culture. Whether acculturation occurs gradually or more quickly may depend on initial differences between cultures and the ability to maintain support for traditional cultural norms and values in the new country.

Besides attitudes regarding timetables for autonomy development, cultural variations also occur in values and conceptions of the self as independent and autonomous. In these studies, self-concept often is differentiated as individualistic, independent, autonomous, or agentic versus collectivistic or relational (Feldman & Rosenthal, 1991; Kashima et al., 1995; Markus & Kityama, 1991). In a recent study of adults (Kashima et al., 1995), conceptions of the self were placed on three dimensions – independent (assertive and agentic self), relational ("self as a relational being", p. 928), and collectivist (self as a member of a group with group needs taking priority over individual needs). Adults in Korea, Japan, Australia, the United States, and Hawaii differed on independent and collectivist conceptions of the self, but differed most markedly in independence. Individuals in Korea, Japan, and Hawaii reported being less agentic and assertive than individuals in the United States and Australia. Feldman and Rosenthal (1991) conceptualized values of individualism–collectivism as a single dimension and reported that Australian and US adolescents manifested more individualistic values than adolescents in Hong Kong. In all three cultures, however, higher levels of individualistic values were associated with earlier expectations for behavioral autonomy.

The study of autonomy as manifested in diverse cultures is in its infancy. What we know now, however, is that the frequently heard generalization that autonomy is irrelevant to development in non-industrialized cultures is misleading. Rather, the particular form of autonomy, and the process of autonomy development that is most adaptive, may vary both between and within cultures. Cultural variations thus may be more a matter of when and how autonomy is evinced, rather than whether or not autonomy is relevant to human action and emotion.

Gender and autonomy

Girls generally have later expectations for *behavioral* autonomy than boys, regardless of race/ethnicity (Fuligni, 1998). Yet, gender differences in expectations for behavioral autonomy appear to be less pronounced today than in the past, and gender differences may be greater in some cultures than in others (Feldman & Rosenthal, 1990). Less is known about why gender differences occur and whether gender differences occur in other dimensions of autonomy (i.e., cognitive autonomy or emotional autonomy).

Gender differences in behavioral autonomy may be related to the distinction between agency and communion. Agency has been defined as self-assertive and independent behaviors, which reflect an individual orientation toward the self. Communion has been defined as interpersonal concern, caring, and cooperation, and reflects an orientation toward others (Helgeson, 1994; Saragovi et al., 1997). Both agency and communion relate to aspects of behavioral, cognitive, and emotional autonomy. At the same time, agency is considered more characteristic of US males than females, whereas communion is considered more typical of females than males. Research findings show that females are more likely to report personality characteristics of communion and relatedness to others, while males are more likely to have agentic and assertive personality characteristics (Helgeson, 1994). Not surprisingly, agency and communion commonly are operationalized as masculine and feminine traits, respectively, in such commonly used measures as the Bem Sex-Role Inventory (Bem, 1974) and the Personal Attributes Questionnaire (Spence, Helmreich, & Stapp, 1974).

Some observers believe gender differences in autonomy expectations partly reflect these gender differences in agency and communion. Gilligan and colleagues (Brown & Gilligan, 1992; Gilligan, 1982; Gilligan, Lyons, & Hanmer, 1989) and others (see Chodorow, 1989; Miller, 1986; Pipher, 1995) have criticized theories that highlight autonomy and independence without recognizing the important role that relationships and connections play in female development. Gilligan (1982) and Pipher (1995) further link gender differences in autonomy to what they call a "loss of voice" that young women experience as they enter adolescence. Loss of voice has been defined as the suppression of opinions, emotions, thoughts or behaviors of the authentic self. These concepts also overlap somewhat with conceptualizations of behavioral, emotional, and cognitive autonomy. Research findings raise doubts, however, that females and males manifest these phenomena differently during adolescence. Harter and colleagues (Harter, 1999) have recently demonstrated that recognition of false-self behavior escalates during adolescence for both genders. Average levels of voice for females and for males were similar among middle school and high school students (Harter et al., 1997, 1998). Most important to the study of autonomy is Harter and colleagues' (Harter 1999) evidence that adolescents feel more or less authentic when interacting with different social partners such as fathers, mothers, close friends, teachers, and romantic partners, and that these variations were more pronounced in some subgroups than in other subgroups. For example, one group of females (a minority of all females) characterized by a feminine gender orientation with few masculine characteristics reported lower levels of voice than males did when interacting with teachers, male classmates, and female classmates (i.e., in public contexts). By contrast, level of voice did not differ between males and females when in more private contexts with parents and friends. Apparently, females who report high connection and caring, but low independence and individualism (a feminine gender orientation), are most likely to manifest lower levels of voice in public domains.

Among both males and females, extremes of either agency or communality may be inimical to healthy adjustment. Bakan (1966) proposed that higher levels of agency and communion are associated with greater physical and psychological well-being, but that agency not tempered by communion, called unmitigated agency, can be psychologically, physically, and socially damaging. Helgeson (1994) summarized evidence supporting the detrimental correlates of unmitigated agency and unmitigated communion. Unmitigated agency and unmitigated communion are both quantitatively and qualitatively different from agency and communion. For example, as Helgeson (1994) and Saragovi and colleagues (1997) describe, someone who has markers of unmitigated agency, such as being arrogant, is qualitatively different from someone who is high in agency in the form of self-assertiveness or self-confidence. An individual who is high in unmitigated communion is subservient to another by tolerating insults, accepting verbal abuse, and repeatedly apologizing. This person is qualitatively different from someone who is highly interpersonally sensitive.

Helgeson (1994) found that unmitigated agency and unmitigated communion did exist among adults and were associated with differing physical and mental health functioning of males and females. Agency was correlated with improved psychological well-being, and communion was associated with more positive social relationships and social support. Yet, agency was also associated with Type A behavior, poor health care, and behavioral problems, while communion was associated with greater psychological distress. Unmitigated agency was associated with greater hostility, and unmitigated communion was related to psychological distress. It should be noted that some researchers (e.g., Saragovi et al., 1997) question whether the qualitative differences are always distinguishable from the simple combination of quantitative levels of agency and communion.

Although information on agency and communion among adults provides insight into the possible life-course pathways of autonomy development among males and females, information is still limited on gender similarities or differences in autonomy development during adolescence. Yet, the results of recent prospective research (Kremen & Block, 1998) has begun to suggest that parenting behaviors may have different effects on the development of adolescent behavioral autonomy and self-regulation among females as compared to males. In this study a relatively higher level of autocratic parenting behavior in preschool (ages 3 to 5), including more hostile interactions and fewer autonomy supportive behaviors, was associated with patterns of ego-control in later adolescence and young adulthood (ages 18 and 23) that differed by gender. Specifically, autocratic parenting behaviors when children were in preschool was associated with overcontrol of behavior among adolescent females and undercontrol of behavior among adolescent males. In other words, autocratic parenting behaviors were associated with the development of more rigid, compliant, and complacent behavior among females and impulsive, aggressive, dominating, and restless behavior among males. In addition, females with autocratic parents tended to place relatively more focus on the other, while males tended to be more likely to take advantage of others. In contrast, when parents were more responsive, supportive, and encouraging of choice and independence when their children were in preschool, females were relatively more undercontrolled in late adolescence and males were relatively more overcontrolled. This study provides initial evidence that the some parenting behaviors (i.e., autocratic behaviors) socialize females and males differently, but the same parenting style (i.e., a combination of supportive, responsive, contingent, and autonomy supportive parenting behaviors) is associated with adaptive development for both males and females.

Much more information is needed regarding the parenting behaviors, peer relationships, and community contexts that are most beneficial for the development of adaptive autonomous functioning among females as compared to males. In addition, no longitudinal research provides a basis for focusing on intra-individual change in autonomy or level of voice among males, as compared to females. Nevertheless, the evidence that orientations to agency and communion are correlated with gender, and the same parenting behaviors may result in gender differences in behavioral, cognitive, and emotional autonomy, imply that the question of how autonomy development proceeds in both females and males is an important one.

Conclusions

Autonomy in adolescence and across the lifespan is a multidimensional construct that has been conceptualized in a variety of ways over the last decades. Theories also differ by either proposing that autonomy in adolescence arises in predictable ways among all adolescents or that the development of socially adaptive autonomous behavior, cognition, and emotion is an outgrowth of the active human organism interacting within all levels of the environment from the microsystem (e.g., within families and with friends) to the macrosystem (e.g., social policies; see Bronfenbrenner, 1977). Most recent theoretical perspectives tend to propose the latter and link the development of autonomy to the development of the self and changing conceptions of relationships with others. Research findings show the relevance of all of these observations to adolescent autonomy development and challenge researchers to, first, provide clear conceptualizations of autonomy, and, second, further investigate the links among socially adaptive autonomous behavior, the self, and relationships and other contexts of development.

In future research on autonomy, several themes require particular attention. One is the impact of relationships with significant others. In what ways do important relationships support or undermine an individual's efforts to become autonomous? Another significant future theme is whether relationships and other aspects of the environment operate differently for females and males, and for adolescents from cultures that have varying levels of support for cooperation and competition in educational pursuits, work roles, athletics, and other arenas. We also need to better understand the conditions under which autonomous behavior contributes to future adaptation and healthy individual development, and the conditions under which one develops the capacity for choice and socially adaptive behavior, and the circumstances within which one can be either overly self-reliant or too dependent on others for guidance and support. Finally, conceptualizations of the multidimensional construct of autonomy during adolescence have been advancing, but valid and reliable measurement of clearly defined dimensions requires our attention before the majority of these questions can be pursued.

Key Readings

Baltes, M. M., & Silverberg, S. B. (1994). The dynamics between dependency and autonomy: Illustrations across the life span. In D. L. Featherman, R. M. Lerner, & M. Perlmutter (Eds.), *Life-span development and behavior* (Vol. 12, pp. 41–90). Hillsdale, NJ: Erlbaum.
This is one of the few chapters available that examines the interface of autonomy and dependency throughout the life span. The demands and opportunities for both autonomy and dependency are

proposed as dynamic, influenced by physical, social/cultural and psychological factors, and linked to developmental tasks of different life phases.

Blos, P. (1979). *The adolescent passage: Developmental issues.* New York: International Universities Press.
This is a classic book describing the challenges of autonomy development during adolescence, as well as other adolescent developmental issues.

Grusec, J. E., & Kuczynski, L. (Eds.). (1997). *Parenting and children's internalization of values: A handbook of contemporary theory.* New York: Wiley.
Chapters in this edited volume, especially those by Collins and colleagues, and Grolnick and colleagues, describe the development of autonomy and self-determination in childhood and adolescence. The emphasis is on the behaviors of parents that socialize and permit self-regulated action, and support autonomy and self-determination. In addition, it is suggested that children's internalization of values may mediate associations between parents' behavior, parent–child interactions, and adolescents' ability to select and carry out their own socially responsible actions.

Connell, J. P., & Wellborn, J. G. (1991). Competence, autonomy, and relatedness: A motivational analysis of self-system processes. In M. R. Gunnar & L. A. Sroufe (Eds.), *The Minnesota symposia on child development: Vol. 23: Self processes and development* (pp. 43–77). Hillsdale, NJ: Erlbaum.
Based on a motivational perspective, this chapter describes a theoretical model of the study of the self and development. The focus is on three fundamental individual needs (i.e., competence, autonomy, and relatedness) that motivate behavior throughout life, and the characteristics of social contexts (i.e., structure/chaos, autonomy support/coercion, and involvement/neglect) that may or may not meet these needs. In combination, individual needs and social contextual characteristics promote or undermine engagement or disaffection from the environment in the form of changes in behavior, emotion, and orientation.

Deci, E. L., & Ryan, R. M. (1985). *Intrinsic motivation and self-determination in human behavior.* New York: Plenum.
This book thoroughly describes a developmental theory of motivation, proposing that intrinsic motivation in humans is based in the innate, organismic needs for competence and self-determination. It is argued that competence and self-determination energize a wide variety of behaviors and psychological processes for which the primary rewards are the experiences of effectance and autonomy.

Gray, M. R., & Steinberg, L. (1999). Unpacking authoritative parenting: Reassessing a multidimensional construct. *Journal of Marriage and the Family, 61,* 574–587.
This is one of a number of recent studies that have examined multiple dimensions that, in combination, form a parenting style. Three parent behavioral dimensions were assessed in this large study of almost 9,000 young people, including acceptance-involvement, strictness-supervision, and psychological autonomy-granting. Associations between parental dimensions, and adolescent problems and psychosocial development/competence were examined.

Hill, J. P., & Holmbeck, G. N. (1986). Attachment and autonomy during adolescence. *Annals of child development, 3,* 145–189.
Although not yet 20 years old, this is a classic and often cited summary of the centrality of both attachment and autonomy among adolescents living in Western industrialized cultures. Topics

discussed include sociohistorical issues; definitions, and classic and contemporary theoretical perspectives; and a review of selected empirical research.

Silverberg, S. B., & Gondoli, D. M. (1996). Autonomy in adolescence: A contextualized perspective. In G. R. Adams, R. Montemayor, & T. P. Gullotta (Eds.), *Psychosocial development during adolescence: Progress in developmental contextualism* (pp. 12–61). Thousand Oaks, CA: Sage.
Silverberg and Gondoli provide an extension of Hill and Holmbeck's classic article. These authors begin by addressing definitional issues and major theories. They also review selected empirical work including the autonomy versus detachment debate (see Steinberg & Silverberg, 1986 and Ryan & Lynch, 1989); research using the Emotional Autonomy Scale (Steinberg & Silverberg, 1986); describe studies of autonomy within context, including the influence of parenting behaviors and styles on adolescent autonomy development; and propose future directions for researchers.

Steinberg, L. (1990). Autonomy, conflict, and harmony in the family relationship. In S. S. Feldman & G. R. Elliott (Eds.), *At the threshold: The developing adolescent* (pp. 255–276). Cambridge, MA: Harvard University Press.
A chapter that focuses on family relationships and autonomy development with a special focus on early adolescents. Topics reviewed include psychoanalytic, neoanalytic, and more recent theories of autonomy development during adolescence, whether detachment from the family is desirable, the functions of conflict between parents and their adolescents, and the impact of the authoritative parenting style on adolescent emotional and behavioral autonomy.

References

Adams, G. R., Montemayor, G. R., & Gullotta, T. P. (Eds.). (1996). *Psychosocial development during adolescence: Progress in developmental contextualism.* Thousand Oaks, CA: Sage.

Allen, J. P., Hauser, S. T., Bell, K. L., & O'Connor, T. G. (1994a). Longitudinal assessment of autonomy and relatedness in adolescent-family interactions as predictors of adolescent ego development and self-esteem. *Child Development, 65,* 179–194.

Allen, J. P., Hauser, S. T., Eickholt, C., Bell, K. L., & O'Connor, T. G. (1994b). Autonomy and relatedness in family interactions as predictors of expressions of negative adolescent affect. *Journal of Research on Adolescence, 4,* 535–552.

Allen, J. P., Kuperminc, G. P., Philliber, S., & Herre, K. (1994c). Programmatic prevention of adolescent problem behaviors: The role of autonomy, relatedness, and volunteer service in the Teen Outreach Program. *American Journal of Community Psychology, 22,* 617–638.

Allen, J. P., & Land, D. (1999). Attachment in adolescence. In J. Cassidy & P. R. Shaver (Eds.), *Handbook of attachment: Theory, research, and clinical applications* (pp. 319–335). New York: Guilford.

Allen, J. P., Philliber, S., Herring, S., & Kuperminc, G. P. (1997). Preventing teen pregnancy and academic failure: Experimental evaluation of a developmentally based approach. *Child Development, 64,* 729–742.

Bakan, D. (1966). *The duality of human existence.* Chicago: Rand McNally.

Baltes, M. M., & Silverberg, S. B. (1994). The dynamics between dependency and autonomy: Illustrations across the life span. In D. L. Featherman, R. M. Lerner, & M. Perlmutter (Eds.), *Life-span development and behavior* (Vol. 12, pp. 41–90). Hillsdale, NJ: Erlbaum.

Baltes, P. B., Reese, H. W., & Nesselroade, J. R. (1988). *Life-span developmental psychology: Introduction to research methods.* Hillsdale, NJ: Erlbaum.

Bandura, A. (1989). Human agency in social cognitive theory. *American Psychologist, 44,* 1175–1184.

Bandura, A. (1997). Self-efficacy: The exercise of control. New York: W. H. Freeman.

Barber, B. K. (1996). Parental psychological control: Revisiting a neglected construct. *Child Development, 67,* 3296–3319.

Barber, B. K., & Olsen, J. A. (1997). Socialization in context: Connection, regulation, and autonomy in the family, school, and neighborhood, and with peers. *Journal of Adolescent Research, 12,* 287–315.

Baumeister, R. F. (1996). Self-regulation failure: An overview. *Psychological Inquiry, 7,* 1–15.

Baumeister, R. F. (1998). The self. In D. T. Gilbert, S. T. Fiske, & G. Lindzey (Eds.), *Handbook of social psychology* (4th ed.). New York: McGraw-Hill.

Baumeister, R. F., Heatherton, T. F., & Tice, D. M. (1994). *Losing control: How and why people fail at self-regulation.* San Diego, CA: Academic.

Baumeister, R. F., Leith, K. P., Muraven, M., & Bratslavsky, E. (1998). Self-regulation as a key to success in life. In D. Pushkar, W. M. Bukowski, A. E. Schwartzman, D. M., Stack, & D. R. White (Eds.), *Improving competence across the lifespan: Building interventions based on theory and research* (pp.). New York: Plenum.

Baumrind, D. (1991a). Parenting styles and adolescent development. In J. Brooks-Gunn, R. Lerner, & A. C. Peterson (Eds.), *The encyclopedia of adolescence* (pp. 746–758). New York: Garland.

Baumrind, D. (1991b). The influence of parenting style on adolescent competence and substance use. *Journal of Early Adolescence, 11,* 56–95.

Bem, S. L. (1974). The measurement of psychological androgyny. *Journal of Consulting and Clinical Psychology, 42,* 155–162.

Berndt, T. J. (1979). Developmental changes in conformity to peers and parents. *Developmental Psychology, 15,* 608–616.

Best, K. M., Hauser, S. T., & Allen, J. P. (1997). Predicting young adult competencies: Adolescent era parent and individual influences. *Journal of Adolescent Research, 12,* 90–112.

Blos, P. (1979). *The adolescent passage: Developmental issues.* New York: International Universities Press.

Bronfenbrenner, U. (1977). Toward an experimental ecology of human development. *American Psychologist, 32,* 513–531.

Brown, B. B., Clasen, D. R, & Eicher, S. A. (1986). Perceptions of peer pressure, peer conformity dispositions, and self-reported behavior among adolescents. *Developmental Psychology, 22,* 521–530.

Brown, B. B., Mounts, N., Lamborn, S. D., & Steinberg, L. (1993). Parenting practices and peer group affiliation in adolescence. *Child Development, 64,* 467–482.

Brown, L., & Gilligan, C. (1992). *Meeting at the crossroads: Women's psychology and girls' development.* Cambridge, MA: Harvard University Press.

Chen, Z., & Dornbusch, S. M. (1998). Relating aspects of adolescent emotional autonomy to academic achievement and deviant behavior. *Journal of Adolescent Research, 13,* 293–319.

Chodorow, N. (1989). *Feminism and psychoanalytic theory.* New Haven, CT: Yale University Press.

Collins, W. A. (1990). Parent–child relationships in the transition to adolescence: Continuity and change in interaction, affect, and cognition. In R. Montemayor, G. R. Adams, & T. P. Gullotta (Eds.), *Advances in adolescent development: Vol. 2: From childhood to adolescent: A transitional period?* (pp. 85–106). Thousand Oaks, CA: Sage.

Collins, W. A. (1995). Relationships and development: Family adaptation to individual change. In S. Shulman (Ed.), *Close relationships and socioemotional development: Vol. 7: Human development* (pp. 128–154). Norwood, NJ: Ablex.

Collins, W. A., Gleason, T., & Sesma, Jr., A. (1997b). Internalization, autonomy, and relationships: Development during adolescence. In J. E. Grusec & L. Kuczynski (Eds.), *Parenting and children's internalization of values: A handbook of contemporary theory* (pp. 78–99). New York: Wiley.

Collins, W. A., Hyson, D. M., Zimmer-Gembeck, M. J., Siebenbruner, J., & Foo, G. (2000, July). Middle-childhood correlates of adolescent autonomy: Longitudinal perspectives. Poster presented at the biennial meeting of the International Society for the Study of Behavioral Development, Beijing, China.

Collins, W. A., Laursen, B., Mortensen, N., Luebker, C., & Ferreira, M. (1997a). Conflict processes and transitions in parent and peer relationships: Implications for autonomy and regulation. *Journal of Adolescent Research, 12,* 178–198.

Collins, W. A., & Luebker, C. (1994). Parent and adolescent expectancies: Individual and relational significance. In J. G. Smetana (Ed.), *Beliefs about parenting: Origins and developmental implications: Vol. 66: New directions for child development* (pp. 65–80). San Francisco: Jossey-Bass.

Collins, W. A., & Repinski, D. J. (1994). Relationships during adolescence: Continuity and change in interpersonal perspective. In R. Montemayor, G. R. Adams, & T. P. Gullotta (Eds.), *Personal relationships during adolescence* (pp. 7–36). Thousand Oaks, CA: Sage.

Connell, J. P. (1990). Context, self, and action: A motivational analysis of self-system processes across the life span. In D. Cicchetti & M. Beeghly (Eds.), *The self in transition: Infancy to childhood* (pp. 610–97). Chicago: University of Chicago Press.

Connell, J. P., & Wellborn, J. G. (1991). Competence, autonomy, and relatedness: A motivational analysis of self-system processes. In M. R. Gunnar & L. A. Sroufe (Eds.), *The Minnesota symposia on child development: Vol. 23: Self processes and development* (pp. 43–77). Hillsdale, NJ: Erlbaum.

Cooper, C. R. (1994). Cultural perspectives on continuity and change in adolescents' relationships. In R. Montemayor, G. R. Adams, & T. P. Gullotta (Eds.), *Personal relationships during adolescence* (pp. 78–100). Thousand Oaks, CA: Sage.

Crittenden, P. M. (1990). Toward a concept of autonomy in adolescents with disability. *Children's Health Care, 19,* 162–168.

Deci, E. L., & Ryan, R. M. (1985). *Intrinsic motivation and self-determination in human behavior.* New York: Plenum.

Deci, E. L., & Ryan, R. M. (2000). The "what" and "why" of goal pursuits: Human needs and the self-determination of behavior. *Psychological Inquiry, 11,* 227–268.

Douvan, E., & Adelson, J. (1966). *The adolescent experience.* New York: Wiley.

Eccles, J. S., Early, D., Frasier, K., Belansky, E., & McCarthy, K. (1997). The relation of connection, regulation, and support for autonomy to adolescents' functioning. *Journal of Adolescent Research, 12,* 263–286.

Erikson, E. E. (1969). *Identity: Youth and crisis.* New York: Norton.

Feldman, S., & Quatman, T. (1988). Factors influencing age expectations for adolescent autonomy: A study of early adolescents and parents. *Journal of Early Adolescence, 8,* 325–343.

Feldman, S., & Rosenthal, D. (1991). Age expectations of behavioral autonomy in Hong Kong, Australian, and American youth: The influences of family variables and adolescents' values. *International Journal of Psychology, 26,* 1–23.

Feldman, S. S., & Rosenthal, D. A. (1990). The acculturation of autonomy expectations in Chinese high schoolers residing in two Western nations. *International Journal of Psychology, 25,* 259–281.

Freud, A. (1958). Adolescence. *Psychoanalytic study of the child, 13,* 255–278.

Fuhrman, T., & Holmbeck, G. N. (1995). A contextual-moderator analysis of emotional autonomy and adjustment in adolescence. *Child Development, 66,* 793–811.

Fuligni, A. J. (1998). Authority, autonomy, and parent–adolescent conflict and cohesion: A study of adolescents from Mexican, Chinese, Filipino, and European backgrounds. *Developmental Psychology, 34,* 782–797.

Fuligni, A. J., & Eccles, J. S. (1993). Perceived parent–child relationships and early adolescents' orientation toward peers. *Developmental Psychology, 29,* 622–632.

Gilligan, C. (1982). *In a different voice: Psychological theory and women's development.* Cambridge, MA: Harvard University Press.

Gilligan, C., Lyons, N., & Hanmer, T. J. (1989). *Making connections.* Cambridge, MA; Harvard University Press.

Gray, M. R., & Steinberg, L. (1999). Unpacking authoritative parenting: Reassessing a multidimensional construct. *Journal of Marriage and the Family, 61,* 574–587.

Greenberger, E. (1984). Defining psychosocial maturity in adolescence. *Advances in Child Behavioral Analysis & Therapy, 3,* 1–37.

Greenberger, E., Josselson, R., Knerr, C., & Knerr, B. (1975). The measurement and structure of psychosocial maturity. *Journal of Youth and Adolescence, 4,* 127–143.

Greenberger, E., & Sorenson, A. (1974). Toward a concept of psychosocial maturity. *Journal of Youth and Adolescence, 3,* 329–358.

Grolnick, W. S., Deci, E. L., & Ryan, R. M. (1997). Internalization within the family: The self-determination theory perspective. In J. E. Grusec & L. Kuczynski (Eds.), *Parenting and children's internalization of values: A handbook of contemporary theory* (pp. 135–161). New York: Wiley.

Grotevant, H. D., & Cooper, C. R. (1986). Individuation in family relationships: A perspective on individual differences in the development of identity and role-taking skill in adolescence. *Human Development, 29,* 82–100.

Harter, S. (1999). *The construction of the self: A developmental perspective.* New York: Guilford.

Harter, S., Waters, P., & Whitesell, N. R. (1997). False self-behavior and lack of voice among adolescent males and females. *Educational Psychologist, 32,* 153–173.

Harter, S., Waters, P. L., Whitesell, N. R., & Kastelic, D. (1998). Level of voice among female and male high school students: Relational context, support, and gender orientation. *Developmental Psychology, 34,* 892–901.

Helgeson, V. S. (1994). Relation of agency and communion to well-being: Evidence and potential explanations. *Psychological Bulletin, 116,* 412–428.

Herman, M. R., Dornbusch, S. M., Herron, M. C., Herting, J. R. (1997). The influence of family regulation, connection, and psychological autonomy on six measures of adolescent functioning. *Journal of Adolescent Research, 12,* 34–67.

Higgins, E. T. (1991). Development of self-regulatory and self-evaluative processes: Costs, benefits, and tradeoffs. In M. R. Gunnar & L. A. Sroufe (Eds.), *Self processes and development: The Minnesota Symposia on Child Development* (Vol. 23, pp. 125–166). Hillsdale, NJ: Erlbaum.

Hill, J. P., & Holmbeck, G. N. (1986). Attachment and autonomy during adolescence. *Annals of Child Development, 3,* 145–189.

Holmbeck, G. N., & Hill, J. P. (1991). Conflictive engagement, positive affect, and menarche in families with seventh-grade girls. *Child Development, 62,* 1030–1048.

Holmbeck, G. N., & O'Donnell, K. (1991). Discrepancies between perceptions of decision making and behavioral autonomy. In R. L. Paikoff (Ed.), *Shared views in the family during adolescence. Vol. 51: New directions in child development* (pp. 51–69). San Francisco: Jossey-Bass.

Kashima, Y., Yamaguchi, S., Kim, U., Choi, S., Gelfand, M. J., & Yuki, M. (1995). Culture, gender, and self: A perspective from individualism–collectivism research. *Journal of Personality and Social Psychology, 69*, 925–937.

Kobak, R., & Cole, H. (1994). Attachment and meta-monitoring: Implications for adolescent autonomy and psychopathology. In D. Cicchetti & S. L. Toth (Eds.), *Rochester Symposium on Developmental Psychopathology: Vol. 5: Disorders and dysfunctions of the self* (pp. 267–297). Rochester, NY: University of Rochester Press.

Kremen, A. M., & Block, J. (1998). The roots of ego-control in young adulthood: Links with parenting in early childhood. *Journal of Personality and Social Psychology, 75*, 1062–1075.

Lamborn, S. D., & Steinberg, L. (1993). Emotional autonomy redux: Revisiting Ryan and Lynch. *Child Development, 64*, 483–499.

Larson, R. W. (2000). Toward a psychology of positive youth development. *American Psychologist, 55*, 170–183.

Larson, R. W., Richards, M. H., Moneta, G., Holmbeck, G., & Duckett, E. (1996). Changes in adolescents' daily interactions with their families from ages 10 to 18: Disengagement and transformation. *Developmental Psychology, 32*, 744–754.

Laursen, B., Coy, K. C., & Collins, W. A. (1998). Reconsidering changes in parent–child conflict across adolescence: A meta-analysis. *Child Development, 69*, 817–832.

Maccoby, E. E. (1984). Socialization and developmental change. *Child Development, 55*, 317–328.

Markus, H. R., & Kityama, S. (1991). Culture and the self: Implications for cognition, emotion, and motivation. *Psychological Review, 98*, 224–253.

Mead, G. H. (1934). *Mind, self, and society.* Chicago: University of Chicago Press.

Miller, J. B. (1986). *Toward a new psychology of women.* Boston: Beacon Press.

Patrick, B. C., Skinner, E. A., & Connell, J. P. (1993). What motivates children's behavior and emotion? Joint effects of perceived control and autonomy in the academic domain. *Journal of Personality and Social Psychology, 65*, 781–791.

Pipher, M. B. (1995). *Reviving Ophelia: Saving the selves of adolescent girls.* New York: Ballantine Books.

Reese, H. W., & Overton, W. F. (1970). Models of development and theories of development. In L. R. Goulet & P. B. Baltes (Eds.), *Life-span developmental psychology: Research and theory.* New York: Academic.

Ryan, R. M., & Connell, J. P. (1989). Perceived locus of causality and internalization: Examining reasons for acting in two domains. *Journal of Personality and Social Psychology, 57*, 749–761.

Ryan, R. M., Deci, E. L., & Grolnick, W. S. (1995). Autonomy, relatedness, and the self: Their relation to development and psychopathology. In D. Cicchetti & D. J. Cohen (Eds.). *Developmental psychopathology: Volume 1: Theory and methods* (pp. 618–655). New York: Wiley.

Ryan, R. M., Kuhl, J., & Deci, E. L. (1997). Nature and autonomy: An organizational view of social and neurobiological aspects of self-regulation in behavior and development. *Development and Psychopathology, 9*, 701–728.

Ryan, R. M., & Lynch, J. H. (1989). Emotional Autonomy versus detachment: Revisiting the vicissitudes of adolescence and young adulthood. *Child Development, 60*, 340–356.

Ryan, R. M., & Solky, J. A. (1996). What is supportive about social support? On the psychological needs for autonomy and relatedness. In G.R. Pierce, B.R. Sarason, & I.G. Sarason (Eds.), *Handbook of social support and the family* (pp. 249–267). New York: Plenum.

Saragovi, C., Koestner, R., Dio, L. D., & Aubé, J. (1997). Agency, communion, and well-being: Extending Helgeson's (1994) model. *Journal of Personality and Social Psychology, 73*, 593–609.

Schmitz, M. F., & Baer, J. C. (2001). The vicissitudes of measurement: A confirmatory factor analysis of the Emotional Autonomy Scale. *Child Development, 72*, 207–219.

Sessa, F. M., & Steinberg, L. (1991). Family structure and the development of autonomy during adolescence. *Journal of Early Adolescence, 11*, 38–55.

Silverberg, S. B., & Gondoli, D. M. (1996). Autonomy in adolescence: A contextualized perspective. In G. R. Adams, R. Montemayor, & T. P. Gullotta (Eds.), *Psychosocial development during adolescence: Progress in developmental contextualism* (pp. 12–61). Thousand Oaks, CA: Sage.

Skinner, E. A. (1996). A guide to constructs of control. *Journal of Personality and Social Psychology, 71*, 549–570.

Skinner, E. A., & Edge, K. (2000). Self-determination, coping, and development. Unpublished manuscript, Portland State University.

Skinner, E. A., & Wellborn, J. G. (1994). Coping during childhood and adolescence: A motivational perspective. In D. L. Featherman, R. M. Lerner, & M. Perlmutter (Eds.), *Life-span development and behavior* (Vol. 12, pp. 91–133). Hillsdale, NJ: Erlbaum.

Spence, J. T., Helmreich, R., & Stapp, J. (1975). The Personal Attributes Questionnaire: A measure of sex role stereotypes and masculinity–femininity. *JSAS Catalog of Selected Documents in Psychology, 4*, 43–44.

Steinberg, L. (1981). Transformations in family relations at puberty. *Developmental Psychology, 17*, 833–840.

Steinberg, L. (1990). Autonomy, conflict, and harmony in the family relationship. In S. S. Feldman & G. R. Elliott (Eds.), *At the threshold: The developing adolescent* (pp. 255–276), Cambridge, MA: Harvard University Press.

Steinberg, L. (2000). Discussant's remarks. In J. Smetana (chair), Autonomy during adolescence: Developmental processes in diverse context. Symposium presented at the biennial conference of the Society for Research on Adolescence, Chicago, IL.

Steinberg, L., & Silverberg, S. (1986). The vicissitudes of autonomy in early adolescence. *Child Development, 57*, 841–851.

Turner, R. A., Irwin, C. E, Tschann, J. M., & Millstein, S. G. (1993). Autonomy, relatedness, and the initiation of health risk behaviors in early adolescence. *Health Psychology, 12*, 200–208.

Youniss, J., & Smollar, J. (1985). *Adolescent relations with mothers, fathers, and friends.* Chicago: University of Chicago Press.

CHAPTER TEN

Identity Development during Adolescence

Jane Kroger

Introduction

Billy, the adolescent hero in Cormac McCarthy's novel, *The Crossing* (1994), pauses in his search for the path that will lead him to his stolen horses and, symbolically, point the way into his own adult life. He listens to the words of an older opera singer as she conveys something of the road ahead. That journey one must make alone, she informs him. It is difficult even for two brothers to travel together on such a journey, for each person will have a different understanding of the same road. And some may not even wish to see what lies before them in plain sight. Everyone's journey upon the road will lead some- where, whether to their original purposes or not.

The road lying in front of Billy holds many fearful, painful, as well as pleasurable rites of passage and symbolizes the journey that each youth must make into the unknown terrain of adult life. Billy is equipped with a goal (to retrieve stolen horses and avenge his parents' deaths), with his own mental and physical skills sharpened for survival in pursuit of this goal, and with the companionship of his younger brother and a girl. It is the vision of a desired future, retrieving horses, which enables Billy to set out on a road. And it is *this* particular desired future that causes him to select the particular road that he chooses, from among many possibilities. Community response, sometimes sage, sometimes shattering, provides Billy with a sense of where his boundaries are and who and what he will become.

Correspondence regarding this article should be sent to Jane Kroger, Psychology Department, Uni- versity of Tromsø, N-9037 Tromsø, Norway. I would like to extend my grateful appreciation to Dr. Stephen J. Haslett, Director, Statistics Research and Consulting Centre, Massey University, Palmerston North, New Zealand, and Dr. Monica Martinussen, Psychology Department, Univer- sity of Tromsø, Tromsø, Norway, for their helpful comments regarding methodological issues dis- cussed in this chapter.

It is this very unique combination of Billy's individual interests, needs, wishes, defenses (psychological elements), physical features such as his gender, strengths, limitations (biological elements), coupled with social response (social elements), that combine to form what Erik Erikson (1968) would refer to as Billy's sense of "ego identity." Key concepts used by Erikson to define identity and explain its developmental process are highlighted below, and empirical efforts to refine further Erikson's ideas will provide the frame for this chapter. Erikson's attempts to define and understand ego identity seek ultimately to explain how youths, like Billy, come to find meaningful directions in the search for a way into adult life.

What is Identity?

Erikson adopted a psychosocial approach to understanding identity by describing the interplay between the individual biology, psychology, and social recognition and response within an historical context. He gave equal emphasis to these elements, also stressing the importance of historical context for their definition. Later theorists, however, have differentially emphasized these particular elements both in defining identity and in researching its parameters. Historical, structural stage, sociocultural, and narrative models have all offered alternatives to a psychosocial definition of identity. These approaches, respectively, emphasize the overarching role of historical epoch in giving rise to identity questions, developmentally different ways in which individuals construct meaning and identity, social and cultural forces that create and shape identity, and the narrative of one's own life story as the creation and foundation of identity. All of these approaches hold their own strengths and limitations, and a more complete review can be found in Kroger (2000).

Erikson's Theory of Identity: Key Concepts

Erikson has detailed many important concepts in describing the nature of ego identity and its developmental course over the years of adolescence. Some key Eriksonian contributions include the concept of *ego identity*, the *Identity vs. Role Confusion* task of adolescence, the *identity-formation process*, *identity crisis*, and the phenomenon of a *psychosocial moratorium*.

By *ego identity*, Erikson (1968) refers both to a conscious sense of individual uniqueness as well as an unconscious striving for continuity of experience; an optimal identity is experienced as a psychosocial sense of well-being. "[Ego identity's] most obvious concomitants are a feeling of being at home in one's body, a sense of 'knowing where one is going', and an inner assuredness of anticipated recognition from those who count" (Erikson, 1968, p. 165).

Identity vs. Role Confusion marks the fifth in Erikson's eight-stage lifespan sequence of developmental tasks, which comes to the fore during adolescence. During this time, adolescents will seek to find some resolution between these two poles. Optimally, adolescents undergo the *identity-formation process.* This process involves the ego's ability to synthesize and integrate important earlier identifications into a new form, uniquely one's own. Erikson also stresses the important role played by the community in both recognizing and being recognized by the maturing adolescent. Erikson viewed a *psychosocial moratorium* to be an important developmental process in which young adults freely experiment with various possible adult roles in order to find one that seems to provide a unique fit (Erikson, 1968, p. 156). Perhaps one of Erikson's most widely used and related concepts has been that of the *identity crisis.* By crisis, he does not mean an impending catastrophe, but rather a critical turning point in the life history of an individual, in which development can only move forward by taking a new directional course.

Empirical Operationalizations of Identity

Over the years since Erikson first presented these concepts, there have been many attempts to operationalize and empirically examine each of them. Attempts to study Erikson's fifth psychosocial task of Identity vs. Role Confusion have been undertaken in different ways. One line of research has examined the place that "Identity vs. Role Confusion" holds in the eight-stage lifespan scheme (e.g. Constantinople, 1967, 1969; Rosenthal, Gurney, & Moore, 1981). A second line of work has focused on Erikson's fifth psychosocial stage alone and has conceptualized it in bipolar terms – as something one "has" to a greater or lesser degree (e.g., Simmons, 1970). A third, very general approach has attempted to study one or more dimensions of ego identity outlined by Erikson (e.g., Blasi & Milton, 1991).

Within this third tradition, a very popular approach has emerged in the attempt to understand the relationship between exploration and commitment variables to the formation of ego identity. The identity-status model developed by Marcia (1966, 1967) identifies four different styles (or statuses) by which late adolescents approach identity-defining roles and values. Various personality features, subjective experiences, and styles of interpersonal interaction have been associated with the four positions. Given the popularity of this model, it will be described in some detail below, and empirical findings and questions emerging from its use will be the focus for the remainder of this chapter.

Erikson had indicated that issues of vocational decision-making, adopting various ideological values, as well as a sense of sexual identity form the foundation of one's ego identity. Thus, Marcia and others have examined how an individual selects meaningful personal directions regarding these issues through the processes of exploration and commitment. Marcia reasoned that if an identity had been formed, an individual could be expected to have commitments in certain areas that Erikson had detailed. After his first 20 interviews, however, Marcia found that commitments were arrived at in different ways and the manner of being non-committed took different forms. The identity statuses thus emerged from the interview data itself (Marcia, personal communication, 2000).

The identity statuses were originally conceptualized by Marcia as topographical features of some underlying identity structures. The more areas or domains in which identity had been achieved, the greater the probability of a certain kind of identity structure being present. *Identity-achieved* individuals have undertaken explorations of meaningful life directions prior to their commitments, while *foreclosed* individuals have formed commitments without significant prior explorations. Many of the values and roles adopted by the foreclosed individual are based on parental values, with which an adolescent has strongly identified. Individuals in the *moratorium* identity status are very much in the process of searching for meaningful adult roles and values but have not yet formed firm commitments, while those in the *diffusion* status appear uninterested in finding personally expressive adult roles and values. These youths may lack commitment for a variety of reasons, ranging from merely a happy-go-lucky approach to life to severe psychopathology.

The original identity status interview lasted about 30–45 minutes and covered themes of vocation, religious and political values (ideology), and, later, sexual-expression and sex-role values (Marcia et al., 1993). Each identity domain was assigned an identity-status assessment, and an overall identity rating was given according to the clinical judgment of the rater. Independent reliability checks generally revealed 75–80 percent agreement percentages between two independent raters. Since the original identification and validation work on the identity statuses, further measures of identity status have also been developed.

Among the most popular of these instruments has been the Extended Objective Measure of Ego Identity Status-II (EOM-EIS-II; Adams, Bennion, & Huh, 1989; Adams, 1999), which has undergone several revisions. This paper-and-pencil measure comprises 64 items that assess the degree of identity achievement, moratorium, foreclosure, and diffusion for an individual within each of eight identity-defining areas. Occupational, political, religious, and philosophy of life values comprise a general ideological domain, and friendship, dating, sex-role, and recreational values comprise a general interpersonal domain. Items use a Likert-type scale format to assess the presence or absence of exploration and commitment an individual has experienced with regard to each statement.

While the Identity Status Interview (Marcia et al., 1993) and the EOM-EIS-II (Adams, Bennion, & Huh, 1989; Adams, 1999) have remained the most popular ways to assess ego-identity status, other alternatives have appeared. The Groningen Identity Development Scale (GIDS; Bosma, 1985, 1992) combines interview and questionnaire material to assess ego-identity status in the areas of school, occupation, leisure-time activities, parents, philosophy of life, friendship, and personal characteristics. The Dellas and Jernigan (1990) Identity Status Inventory assesses identity status (identity achievement, moratorium, foreclosure); diffuse-luck, having no commitment with dependence on luck or fate; and diffused-diffuse (having superficial search with no commitment) in the areas of occupation, religion, and politics. Mallory (1989) has developed a Q-sort personality profile for each of the four ego-identity statuses, based on Block's (1961/1978) California Q-set.

Additional measures have examined exploration and commitment components of identity in somewhat different ways than solely through Marcia's identity statuses. Balistreri, Busch-Rossnagel, and Geisinger (1995) have developed a self-report Ego Identity Process Inventory that focuses more fully on the processes of commitment and exploration in a number of identity-defining domains. This instrument provides continuous scale measures of exploration and commitment for each individual, though it is possible to derive an identity status assessment from it. Meeus et al. (1999) have focused on exploration and commitment variables to study identity transitions and pathways over time.

Criticisms of the Identity-Status Approach

Since 1988, several critical commentaries of the identity-status approach have appeared (Blasi & Glodis, 1995; Côté & Levine, 1988; van Hoof, 1999). One focus of criticism has been whether or not Marcia's identity-status approach captures Erikson's theoretical conception of identity. Blasi and Glodis (1995, p. 410) have criticized the identity-status construct for failing to address phenomenological dimensions of identity: "[Measures assessing ego identity status] neglect to address the experience of one's fundamental nature and unity, which, in Erikson's descriptions as well as in common understanding, constitutes the subjective side of the phenomenon." From a somewhat different perspective, Côté and Levine (1988) point to a theoretical hiatus between Marcia's formulations of identity and Erikson's theory. Côté and Levine note that while the identity-status paradigm has focused on at least one essential element expressed in Erikson's writings on identity (the formation of commitments during the identity formation process), the identity-status construct has largely ignored not only the role of developmental contexts but also the interaction between person and environment. A third critique has come from van Hoof (1999), who argues that Marcia's identity statuses ignore what she believes to be the core of identity – spatial–temporal continuity. She also points to construct underrepresentation of Erikson's theory in the identity-status approach and questions what construct actually underlies the ego-identity statuses.

At no time has Marcia claimed that his attempt to operationalize identity via the identity statuses captures all dimensions that Erikson included in his concept of ego identity. Any attempt to operationalize all of Erikson's identity dimensions in a single construct would be simply unwieldy, if not impossible. However, exploration and commitment variables used by Marcia to define the identity statuses were taken directly from part of Erikson's construct of identity. Similarly, the identity-defining roles and values of vocation, ideology, and sexuality, deemed by Erikson to be so critical for adolescents in the identity-formation process, are those same values which are examined in commonly used measures of ego-identity status. Clearly, Marcia's identity-status approach has been based on some of Erikson's key ideas regarding ego identity.

Berzonsky and Adams (1999) have addressed the question of whether or not the identity-status construct is a valid measure of Eriksonian identity. They point out that in the need to be precise and specific, operationally defining a construct involves a trade-off, often in the loss of theoretical richness and scope. Multiple measurements are also necessary to establish construct validity. The identity statuses are an operational attempt to define and expand some, but not all, of Erikson's rich, clinically based observations included in his identity construct. Certainly, it is important and necessary to operationalize and research other dimensions of Erikson's identity construct. The identity-status construct has given rise to an estimated 500 studies of various personality variables, family antecedents, and developmental consequences associated with the various identity statuses (Waterman, 1999). As van Hoof (1999) has pointed out, however, a number of these studies have failed to hypothesize relationships that are directly grounded in Eriksonian theory. Future identity status research should take heed of this criticism as well as focus on additional identity dimensions that Erikson has described.

A second issue under recent discussion has been the construct validation of the identity statuses themselves. Van Hoof (1999) has adopted the rather conservative position that each of the four identity statuses must respond statistically differently to variables used to help establish their construct validity. She points out that most commonly only one or two identity statuses differ significantly from remaining identity statuses on measures of constructs used for validation. She concludes, therefore, that construct validity of the four different identity positions has not been established. Waterman (1999) has addressed this issue by noting the lack of any typological or complex stage system in psychology that would likely satisfy this stringent criterion for construct validation. Validation of a construct, Waterman and others have argued, should require that a distinctive pattern of responses be demonstrated. Thus, construct validation of the identity statuses should require not that each identity status be related significantly differently to every other identity status on dependent variables used to help establish construct validation. Rather, only a distinctive and hypothesized pattern of response should be associated with the four identity-status positions.

One would not, furthermore, expect individuals in each identity status to score significantly differently from those in every other identity status on some variables used to help establish construct validity. (Although some data do discriminate among the four identity positions; see Berzonsky & Adams, 1999.) Thus, for example, moratoriums would be theoretically expected to score higher than the other identity statuses on a measure of anxiety because of the uncertainty and indecision likely to be associated with the identity-formation process. However, they may not score *significantly* higher than every other identity status, and no theoretical expectations would be held for the interrelationships among remaining identity statuses. According to more commonly used criteria for the establishment of construct validity in psychology, considerable evidence has accrued for expected patterns of responses for each of the four ego identity statuses. However, a useful direction for future research would be a meta-analysis of variables commonly researched in relation to the identity statuses. This procedure would provide a mean estimate of effect size and make it possible to study variation among studies in actual effect sizes, ultimately enabling one to determine whether or not the mean effect could be generalized across settings (Hunter & Schmidt, 1990).

Characteristics of the Adolescents in Various Identity-Status Groupings

Numerous studies have been undertaken to examine a broad range of personality features, interpersonal behaviors, family antecedents, and developmental patterns of movement for each of the identity statuses. Within many Western contexts, these characteristics have been found for both men and women in more recent decades. Early stages of identity status research through the 1970s focused primarily on core personality features of each identity status within the United States and Canada, with developmental patterns studied over only two data-collection points during adolescence. However, the past two decades have seen a wide range of personality features examined in many countries around the world. Developmental patterns have been examined over more points in time, and the study of identity-status patterns of change and stability has been extended into the years of early and middle adulthood. Recent criticism of the developmental nature of the identity statuses will be addressed in a subsequent section. The following section details personality variables, patterns of family interaction, and behavioral consequences associated with each of the four identity statuses.

Identity achieved

Identity-achieved individuals have shown such personality features as the high levels of achievement motivation and self-esteem (along with moratoriums; e.g., Orlofsky, 1978) and low neuroticism and high conscientiousness and extrovertedness (e.g., Clancy & Dollinger, 1993). Conversely, the identity-achieved have also shown the lowest use of defense mechanisms (e.g., Cramer, 1997), and low levels of shyness (e.g., Hamer & Bruch, 1994) relative to those of other identity statuses. They also have shown the highest levels of internal locus of control (e.g., Abraham, 1983).

In terms of cognitive processes, identity-achieved individuals have demonstrated the ability to function well under conditions of stress (e.g., Marcia, 1966) and to use more planned, rational, and logical decision-making strategies than other identity statuses (e.g., Blustein & Phillips, 1990; Boyes & Chandler, 1992). This group has also demonstrated the highest level of moral reasoning regarding issues of both justice and care (e.g., Rowe & Marcia, 1980; Skoe & Marcia, 1991). They have also demonstrated the highest levels of ego development in Loevinger's (1976) ego development scheme (e.g., Berzonsky & Adams, 1999).

Interpersonally, identity-achieved individuals have demonstrated the highest levels of intimacy relative to other identity positions (e.g., Kacerguis & Adams, 1980; Orlofsky, Marcia, & Lesser, 1973). They are able to develop mutual interpersonal relationships with both close friends and a partner, and they are genuinely interested in others. Identity-achieved individuals have shown the greatest willingness to reveal themselves to others (e.g., Adams, Abraham, & Markstrom, 1987), and have also shown the most secure patterns of attachment to their families (e.g., Kroger, 1985). Identity-achieved and moratorium adolescents have been least likely to report maternal socialization behaviors that control or regulate but rather encourage free and independent behavior (e.g., Adams & Jones, 1983). Families of both identity-achieved and moratorium adolescents have emphasized both individuality and connectedness in family relationships (e.g. Campbell, Adams, & Dobson, 1984).

Moratorium

Anxiety has been a key personality variable associated with those in the moratorium identity status (e.g. Marcia, 1967). Moratoriums are in the process of searching for identity-defining commitments, and this appears to be a very anxiety-provoking process. Anxiety regarding death has been found to be significantly higher among moratoriums compared with each of the other three identity statuses (e.g., Sterling & Van Horn, 1989). Moratoriums have been shown to use denial, projection, and identification to help keep general anxieties at bay (e.g., Cramer, 1995). In research by Berzonsky and Kuk (2000), the more self-exploration that students had engaged in (those in both identity-achieved and moratorium identity statuses), the more prepared they were to undertake tasks in a self-directed manner without needing to look to others for reassurance and emotional support. Moratorium individuals have also shown a greater disposition to adaptive regression than those in other identity statuses (e.g., Bilsker & Marcia, 1991).

Cognitively, students in a moratorium process have also been found to be skeptical about ever knowing anything with certainty (e.g., Boyes & Chandler, 1992). Moratoriums and achievements are significantly more experientially oriented compared with foreclosures and diffusions (e.g., Stephen, Fraser, & Marcia, 1992). They, like the identity achieved, have also demonstrated an analytic/philosophical cognitive style (e.g., Shain & Farber, 1989). In a study of adolescent females, both moratorium and achievement women were able to integrate and analyze information from a variety of perspectives, in contrast to other identity groups (e.g., Read, Adams, & Dobson, 1984). Berzonsky (1990) has found moratorium and achieved individuals to use an information-oriented style to construct a sense of identity. In general, moratorium adolescents have demonstrated the ability to reflect on diverse information in an analytical manner.

Interpersonally, those in the moratorium status have been found most frequently to be preintimate in their style of intimacy – that is, they are most likely to have established close friendship relationships which are characterized by respecting the integrity of others, being open and nondefensive, but have not yet committed themselves to a partner. In relation to their families, moratorium adolescents have appeared ambivalent; for men, conflictual independence from parents has predicted degree of identity exploration (e.g., Lucas, 1997). Parents of moratorium adolescents have emphasized independence in their child-rearing patterns (e.g., Campbell et al., 1984).

Foreclosure

Foreclosed individuals have consistently shown personality characteristics such as high levels of conformity, authoritarianism, and levels of aspiration change, coupled with low anxiety, and use of defensive narcissism (e.g., Cramer, 1995; Marcia, 1966, 1967). The foreclosed identity status has been associated with racial and homophobic prejudice (e.g., Fulton, 1997). Foreclosed individuals rely on dependent strategies for their decision making (e.g., Blustein & Phillips, 1990) and are not generally open to new experiences (e.g., Clancy & Dollinger, 1993). They use an external locus of control (e.g., Clancy & Dollinger, 1993) and are especially oriented toward the more distant future, compared with other identity statuses (e.g., Rappaport, Enrich, & Wilson, 1985).

Cognitively, foreclosed adolescents have been least able to integrate ideas and to think analytically; they, along with diffusions, have also been most likely to make errors in judgment because of reduced attention (e.g., Read, Adams, & Dobson, 1984). In addition, the foreclosed, along with the diffuse, are most likely to share the view that absolute certainty is attainable (e.g., Boyes & Chandler, 1992). Foreclosure adolescents have been found to use a normative orientation in constructing a sense of identity – they conform to the expectations of significant others and are concerned about preserving their existing identity structure (e.g., Berzonsky, 1990, 1992). Foreclosed and diffuse individuals are also most likely to be preconventional or conventional in their level of moral reasoning (e.g., Rowe & Marcia, 1980) and the foreclosed are more oriented toward others' needs only in their ability to care (e.g., Skoe & Marcia, 1991).

Interpersonally, foreclosures are most likely to be stereotyped in their styles of intimacy (more concerned with superficial features of a relationship) (e.g., Orlofsky, Marcia, & Lesser, 1973). Additionally, mutually identified best friends shared distinct similarities in ego-identity status; foreclosed adolescents were most likely to have best friends who were also foreclosed (e.g., Akers, Jones, & Coyl, 1998). In terms of family patterns of interaction, foreclosed adolescents have reported their families as very close and child-centered; in a study of adolescent females, when the mother is too close, involved, and protective of her daughter, the daughter mirrors parental values rather than exploring other possibilities (e.g., Perosa, Perosa, & Tam, 1996). Less reported conflict in families has also been associated with the foreclosed identity status (e.g., Willemsen & Waterman, 1991). Foreclosed adolescents have evidenced patterns of severe anxious attachment in the face of family separation threat more frequently than any other identity status (Kroger, 1985). Observational research has found parents who discourage the expression of individual opinions among family members have adolescents demonstrating low levels of identity exploration (e.g., Grotevant & Cooper, 1985). Youths who remain foreclosed during late adolescence have shown more anxious or detached attachment profiles relative to other identity statuses (e.g., Kroger, 1995).

Diffusion

Diffuse individuals have shown low levels of autonomy, self-esteem, and identity (e.g., Cramer, 1997; Marcia, 1966). Having no firm identity-defining commitments nor interest in making them, diffusions seem content to "go where the wind blows" or wherever circumstances push them; they have demonstrated the lowest sense of personal integrative continuity over time (e.g., Berzonsky, Rice, & Neimeyer, 1991). Diffusions are also most likely to have difficulties in adapting to a university environment (e.g., Berzonsky and Kuk, 2000) and are most likely to be shy (e.g., Hamer & Bruch, 1994). Adams et al. (1984) found diffusions to be most influenced by peer pressures toward conformity, compared with other identity statuses. Diffusions were also the most self-focused of all identity statuses on a task that required them to estimate being the focus of others' attention (Adams, Abraham, & Markstrom, 1987); grandiose self-expression as well as disagreeableness have been associated with the identity diffusion status (e.g., Blustein & Palladino, 1992; Clancy & Dollinger, 1993). Diffusions have also shown high levels of neuroticism (along with the moratoriums) and lowest levels of conscientiousness (e.g., Clancy & Dollinger, 1993). Taken together, these findings suggest impaired psychosocial development for the late adolescent diffuse individual.

Cognitively, the adolescent diffuse either rely on intuitive or dependent styles of decision-making or show an absence of systematic approaches to solving problems (e.g., Blustein & Phillips, 1990). A diffuse/avoidant orientation to identity construction has been associated with the diffusion identity status (e.g., Berzonsky, 1990). This social-cognitive style is marked by procrastination and defensive avoidance of issues, as well as reliance on an external locus of control. Diffusions have demonstrated preconventional, conventional, or generally low levels of moral reasoning (e.g., Podd, 1972; Skoe & Marcia, 1991). Conformist or preconformist levels of ego development have also characterized the identity diffuse and foreclosed (Ginsburg & Orlofsky, 1981). Diffusions have also scored highest of all the identity statuses on a measure of hopelessness (Selles, Markstrom-Adams, & Adams, 1994).

In terms of interpersonal relationships, diffusions have reported distant or rejecting caretakers or low level of attachment to parents (e.g., for males, Campbell, Adams, & Dobson, 1984; for females, Josselson, 1987). In addition, communication patterns have often been inconsistent. Memories of diffusions regarding their families has carried themes of a wistful quality, wishing for strong adults to care and set guidelines (e.g., Josselson, 1987). In terms of social relationships, diffusions have been most likely to use bribes and deception to exert influence on others compared with the other identity statuses (e.g. Read, Adams, & Dobson, 1984). Diffusions are most likely to be isolated or stereotyped in their styles of intimacy with others (e.g., Orlofsky, Marcia, & Lesser, 1973). In other words, they either have established no close relationships, or tend to have relationships focused on very superficial issues.

Developmental patterns and processes

Cross-sectional, longitudinal, and retrospective studies of identity status movements over time have all pointed to increasing numbers of adolescents in more mature (moratorium and achievement) identity statuses and decreasing numbers in less mature (foreclosure and diffusion) statuses over time. This pattern has appeared for identity status ratings assigned both in global terms as well as in most individual identity domains (e.g., Archer, 1982; Cramer, 1998; Fitch & Adams, 1983; Foster & LaForce, 1999; Josselson, 1987; Kroger, 1988, 1995; Kroger & Haslett, 1987, 1991; Marcia, 1976; Meilman, 1979; Waterman, Geary, & Waterman, 1974; Waterman & Goldman, 1976; Waterman & Waterman, 1971). It is noteworthy, however, that across all of the above studies, approximately one-half of late adolescents have retained a foreclosed or diffuse identity status, in both global or domain ratings, by the time of leaving tertiary study. This pattern suggests considerable scope for change through the years of adult life. Developmental research has benefited the most from longitudinal studies designed to enable the observation of intraindividual pathways of identity development. Because of the generally short duration of the moratorium status, it is also important for longitudinal researchers to collect data at reasonably frequent intervals to enable a fuller understanding of all steps taken in various developmental trajectories of adolescence.

Some additional issues regarding identity status change have also been explored. Some researchers are currently focusing on issues involved in the moratorium process and the examination of factors most likely to precipitate developmental change. Personality factors (including readiness for change, the experience of conflict, and openness to new experience), in combination with various environmental factors (for example, the importance of a "bridging other") all may be important to understand movement into the moratorium process. Bosma and Kunnen (2001) provide a good review of recent researches into issues of identity-status transitions. The study of identity-status trajectories involving three or four data collection points has also been an important recent addition to the study of identity status development through the years of adolescence and adulthood. Works by Adams, Montemayor, and Brown (1992), Goossens (1992), Josselson (1996), and Mallory (1983) have all pointed to diversity of pathways as lives unfold during late adolescence and beyond. The meaning of identity status movements after the identity formation process of adolescence raises some complex issues, however, and a discussion is beyond the scope of the present chapter.

Criticism Regarding the Developmental Nature of the Identity Statuses

Since 1988, several critiques have appeared regarding the developmental nature of the identity-status positions. One line of criticism has been directed at whether or not the identity statuses are sensitive enough to measure the identity formation process. Van Hoof (1999, p. 540) has argued that because a high percentage of adolescents remain stable in foreclosure or diffusion positions at the end of late adolescence (noted in the previous section), the identity statuses are "not sensitive enough" to measure the identity formation process. Other models of related developmental schemes have also noted the large percentages of individuals who do not move to more complex forms of identity resolutions by adult life. For example, a review of studies of Kegan's (1994) meaning-making construct point to the fact that approximately "one-half to two-thirds of the adult population appear not to have fully reached the fourth order of conscientiousness" [Eriksonian equivalent of attaining a sense of personal identity, Kegan, 1982] (Kegan, 1994, p. 191). It appears likely that a number of adolescents do retain less mature identity positions at the end of adolescence; among those who do change, however, movement is primarily in the predicted, progressive direction. Waterman (1999), too, has observed that because stability of identity status is common during adolescence, one cannot conclude that the identity statuses do not measure the identity-formation process for those who do change.

Another line of criticism has been directed at whether or not there is a continuum of identity-status movement and a theoretical rationale for it (Côté & Levine, 1988; Meeus et al., 1999; van Hoof, 1999). There is a clear, theoretical rationale for the prediction of movement from a foreclosed identity position to a moratorium to identity achievement. Erikson (1968, p. 159) has described a sequence in the movement of ego growth: "If we consider introjection, identification, and identity formation to be the steps by which the ego grows in ever more mature interplay with the available models, the following psychosocial schedule suggests itself." To Erikson, "tentative crystallizations of identity" occur during childhood, based upon identifying with the characteristics, roles, and values of important others. Identity attainment, at the end of adolescence, then, is "superordinated to any single identification with individuals of the past: it includes all significant identifications, but it also alters them in order to make a unique and reasonably coherent whole of them" (Erikson, 1968, p. 161).

Marcia's (1966) foreclosed identity status is defined by identity commitments without exploration – an identity derived from identifications with significant others. The moratorium status reflects the identity formation process of individual exploration of identity-defining alternatives, while the identity-achieved status reflects an identity resolution based on a unique synthesis of previous identifications, following a time of exploration, to a position which is uniquely one's own. These three identity positions identified by Marcia correspond directly to Erikson's stages of ego growth in the identity-formation process. Marcia's diffusion-identity status, reflecting a position of little or no identity exploration and a lack of identity-defining commitments corresponds directly to Erikson's notion of identity diffusion. In nonpathological circumstances, Marcia's diffusion status is developmentally most likely to precede identity foreclosure, before one has begun to consider issues of identity definition.

As Meeus and van Hoof both note, among those individuals who do change identity status during adolescence, the most common pattern of movement is a progressive one, at least from the less mature (foreclosure and diffusion) to more mature (moratorium and achieved) identity positions. This movement is in accordance with theoretical prediction. At present, longitudinal studies of identity status change over late adolescence often have two- to three-year intervals between assessments. The longitudinal assessment of ego-identity status change at more frequent intervals over time is needed, however, before complete details of the continuum of movement for those who do move can be fully evaluated.

Van Hoof (1999) has argued that the frequent patterns of stability or decrease in the moratorium identity status in longitudinal and cross-sectional studies of identity status change argue against the notion of a developmental continuum. However, it is difficult to interpret what overall change or stability in the moratorium status actually means. One is expected to be in the moratorium status in late adolescence for a relatively brief period of time (Waterman, 1999). Time estimates for the area of vocational identity, for example, show the probability of movement from a moratorium position over a one-year timespan during late adolescence/young adulthood to be 50–100 percent for various subgroups of the larger sample (Kroger & Haslett, 1987). At the same time, there is commonly a relatively long interval between identity-status assessments in both longitudinal and cross-sectional research. Thus, it is possible that considerable movement into and out of the moratorium status may have taken place unobserved. Such change may either fail to have been recorded by researchers at their infrequent data-collection points or appear as no change in cross-sectional studies, as comparable numbers of different individuals move into and out of this identity status.

Additionally, the times at which identity status assessments have been made in longitudinal studies of adolescent identity development are generally at entry and exit points of university attendance (e.g., Cramer, 1998; Kroger, 1988, 1995; Waterman & Goldman, 1976). University entry and exit times are unlikely to capture the moratorium identity-status position for those late adolescents who will undergo change. One might expect to find late adolescents in a moratorium position after they have had time for exposure to the diversity of new ideas and people in the university environment, as well as at the point of having to make identity-defining decisions such as choosing a college major or otherwise considering important adult life options, some time prior to university completion. Waterman and Waterman (1971) and Fitch and Adams (1983) have undertaken longitudinal studies over a 9–12-month interval following university entrance, when such processes are likely taking place. Both of these researches show considerable increases in the numbers of students moving into the moratorium position after 9–12 months at university. Longitudinal data collection at intermediate time intervals over the time of tertiary study is necessary to assess individual trajectories of movement across any identity-status continuum.

Kroger and Haslett (1987, 1991) and Meeus et al. (1999) have pointed to the advantages of the use of loglinear models and Markov chains for the analysis of identity-status movements over time as an alternative to chi-square analyses. Van Hoof (1999), however, has been highly critical of the use of Markov chains used to estimate the probabilities of being in a particular identity status at a particular age, while at the same time advocating the use of dynamic systems models. Markov chains belong in the general class of dynamic models (Kiiveri & Speed, 1982; Berzuini et al., 1997). Markov chains are, simply, dynamic models for categorical variables (Kroger & Haslett, 1987; Liu & Chen, 1998). Use of simulation techniques (e.g. Markov Chain Monte Carlo and Bootstrap: Gilks, Richardson, & Spiegelhalter, 1991) will in some circumstances add to the discussion of movement patterns for the various identity statuses at the cost of additional model complexity. However, Markov chains per se have both a sound and well-documented history. They have further potential in the study of processes with time-varying states or statuses, and this includes the study of identity-status movements over time.

Identity and Broader Social Contexts

Though Adams and Fitch (1983) first pointed to the important role of one context (differing academic environments) beyond the family in adolescent identity development, it has only been very recently that researchers have been increasingly focusing attention on social context and its role in adolescent identity development. Clear patterns of difference in identity-status pathways of movement have been found in various adult lifestyle contexts under study, even when key demographic variables such as education level, marital status, parental status, and/or age group have been held constant (Josselson, 1996; Kroger & Haslett, 1987, 1991). To date, however, it has been difficult to determine the direction of effects and the question remains open as to whether individuals with certain kinds of identity structures are attracted to particular kinds of settings, whether particular settings steer the process of identity development, or a combination of both factors. At this point, from the above research on contexts it seems that social circumstances may set broad limits to likely behaviors, though individual personality characteristics do play a key role in influencing the course of identity development over time.

Contexts, in broader terms, and their role in identity development have been a recent focus for several recent articles, including those by Adams and Marshall (1996), Côté (1996), and Yoder (2000). Adams and Marshall have stressed that identity develops out of both individual and social processes. They point out how processes of differentiation and integration underlie the relationship between individual and context, and how identity both shapes and is shaped by the surrounding milieu. An interesting issue that could be explored in future research would be developmentally different ways in which individuals become differentiated from and integrated with their contexts over time. Côté has stressed that the best way to understand the relationship between identity development in context is to delineate the levels or dimensions of identity being explored in relation to a given context. He has also stressed the need to understand particular individual factors such as ethnicity and gender and the particular meaning such issues take on within particular contexts. A further perspective has been stressed by Yoder, in which she details various external "barriers" to development and how they may limit individual developmental options. Barriers may appear and disappear over time, and Yoder stresses various characteristics of barriers (e.g., sociocultural bias) which may be identified over a continuum. Her formulations present an interesting new way of examining the impact of changing historical circumstances on the identity-formation process of adolescence.

Identity and Gender

Several years ago, I undertook an extensive review of identity status research regarding possible gender differences on three questions: (1) Are there gender differences in the identity-status distributions of adolescents and adults to deal with identity-defining roles and values? (2) Are there gender differences in the identity domains most important to self-definition? (3) Are there gender differences in the developmental process of identity formation? (Kroger, 1997). I examined all published studies appearing between 1966 and 1995 in the Social Science Citation Index that made use of one of the more common measures of identity status or style for both genders. After eliminating sample duplications, some 56 studies were examined.

Surprisingly few gender differences appeared in response to the above three questions. With regard to the question of possible gender differences in identity structure (global identity status ratings), some 35 studies reporting some 42 testings provided meaningful data. Only six distributions showed clearly statistically significant gender differences in identity status or style; there was no consistent pattern of gender differences across these studies. Some gender differences did appear in the identity-status distributions for the various identity content areas (or domains). However, no consistent patterns across studies could be observed with one exception. For the few studies that included both genders and the content area of family/career priorities and/or sexual values, women generally pre-dominated over men in moratorium and achievement-identity statuses. No gender dif-ferences appeared in the developmental pathways taken; both men and women showed increasing frequencies of moratorium and achievement ratings and decreasing foreclosure and diffusion ratings over time. By 1995, few studies had explored the issue of possible gender differences in relation to social context, with no trends apparent. In sum, there has been little evidence of gender differences regarding questions of identity structure, domain salience, or developmental process. It is important to note, however, that my review did not include an examination of possible gender × identity status interactions for dependent behavioral, psychological, or social variables. Recent work by Cramer (2000) suggests some gender × identity status differences in personality processes supporting identity development as well as in self-descriptions.

A promising line of future identity research is also likely to be exploring the poten-tially mediating impact of gender-role orientation (masculine, feminine, androgynous) on the identity-formation process of late adolescence. Preliminary evidence from five researches to date suggests that gender-role orientation, rather than gender per se, is an important predictor of difference in resolutions to questions of identity, moral reasoning, and intimacy (Bartle-Haring & Strimple, 1996; Cruise, as cited in Marcia, 1993; Dyk & Adams, 1990; Skoe, 1993; Sochting, Skoe, & Marcia, 1994). Future identity research must recognize considerable intrasex variation, particularly regarding gender-role adher-ence, and examine the impact of this potential mediator on dependent variables under study.

Identity and Ethnicity

For most Caucasian-American adolescents, awareness of their cultural ancestry is impor-tant, but not of vital concern to their sense of ego identity. However, for members of many ethnic minority groups living within majority cultures, questions regarding ethnic identity have prompted vital identity explorations. Indeed, Phinney and Alipura (1990) have shown that self-esteem for many ethnic minority group members has been directly related to the extent to which individuals had thought about and resolved identity issues concerning their ethnicity. Smith et al. (1999) have found self-esteem to be strongly related to one's ethnic identity. In the words of one of my own research participants from an ethnic minority group, "I think feeling comfortable with my ethnic identity is a prerequisite to discovering my personal identity" (Kroger, 2000, p. 126).

Jean Phinney has been a researcher active in the development of measures of ethnic identity. She has developed an interview means of assessing ethnic identity, with identity statuses reflecting the degrees of crisis and commitment to questions of ethnicity (Phinney, 1989). With this measure, Phinney found stages of ethnic identity development apparent across Asian American, black, and Hispanic high school students; interestingly, whites could not be reliably coded on this measure. Ethnically identity-achieved minority-group adolescents had the highest scores on independent measures of ego identity and psychological adjustment. Phinney and her colleagues (1999) have also developed the Multigroup Ethnic Identity Measure (MEIM). This measure has been used across a variety of ethnic groups and provides a global composite index of ethnic identity. Ethnic identity has been strongly related to measures of coping ability, mastery, self-esteem, and optimism and negatively related to loneliness and depression.

Studies over the past decade have examined a diversity of issues related to ethnic identity development in varied cultural settings. The relationship between Marcia's identity statuses (or exploration and commitment processes) and selected personality variables have been explored in various cultural settings (e.g., Alberts & Meyer, 1998; Nurmi, Poole, & Kalakoski, 1996). The relationship between ethnic community context and ethnic identity has been examined among aboriginal Sami adolescents living in coastal and inland communities in northern Norway (Kvernmo & Heyerdahl, 1996). Ethnic identity has been one predictor of fidelity among African American but not European American adolescents in a one-year longitudinal study (Markstrom & Hunter, 1999). Reviews of research that attempt to integrate the great diversity of important ethnic identity issues are badly needed. In addition, studies focusing on the impact of intercultural exposures to adolescent identity formation are a further area in need of investigation.

Summary and Conclusions

This chapter began by examining five general approaches to the study of identity development during adolescence that dominate the field today. Erik Erikson (1963, 1968) first used the term "ego identity," and has provided central, identity-related concepts which researchers continue to explore today in empirical and narrative investigations. Among researchers, Marcia's (1966, 1967) identity-status paradigm has provided a popular model for expanding and empirically investigating Erikson's notions regarding identity. This chapter has focused primarily on this paradigm, overviewing key personality factors associated with the identity statuses, as well as developmental patterns of movement over time. The chapter has also focused, in conclusion, on general issues related to identity development in context, as well as on questions regarding the relationship of gender and ethnicity to adolescent identity development. Individual sections have presented some possibilities for future research directions that might fruitfully be explored, and responses to recent major criticisms of the identity-status approach have been presented.

Key Readings

Erikson, E. H. (1968). *Identity: Youth and crisis.* New York: W. W. Norton.
This volume was written by Erikson to elaborate his notions of ego identity and to describe how identity issues are worked into each psychosocial stage of development, from infancy through old

age. The book overviews the origins of the construct and elaborates concepts related to identity in adolescence via Erikson's clinical experiences as well as through his work in other cultural contexts.

Kroger, J. (2000). *Identity development: Adolescence through adulthood.* Newbury Park, CA: Sage. Beginning with a general review of contemporary approaches to identity, this volume explores identity contents and processes from early adolescence through the years of later adulthood. Chapters on selected identity issues of adolescence and adulthood focus on such topics as adolescent immigrants and adoptees, as well as adults who have lost a significant other or who experience threats to physical integrity.

Marcia, J. E., Waterman, A. S., Matteson, D. R., Archer, S. L., & Orlofsky, J. L. (Eds.). (1993). *Ego identity: A handbook for psychosocial research.* New York: Springer. This volume contains a review of identity research through the early 1990s and has chapters focusing particularly on issues related to identity and gender, as well as identity processes. The manual also contains adolescent and adult forms of the Identity Status Interview.

Bosma, H. A., & Kunnen, E. S. (2001). Determinants and mechanisms in ego-identity development: A review and synthesis. *Developmental Review, 21*, 39–66. This article provides an overview of research both into mechanisms of change of change in identity transitions and factors associated with various identity transitions. It also provides suggestions for researchers wishing to explore issues associated with identity transitions.

References

Abraham, K. G. (1983). The relation between identity status and locus of control among rural high school students. *Journal of Early Adolescence, 3*, 257–264.

Adams, G. R. (1999). The objective measure of ego identity status: A manual on theory and test construction. Manuscript, University of Guelph, Ont., Canada.

Adams, G. R., Abraham, K. G., & Markstrom, C. A. (1987). The relations among identity development, self-consciousness, and self-focusing during middle and later adolescence. *Developmental Psychology, 23*, 292–297.

Adams, G. R., Bennion, L., & Huh, K. (1989). Objective measure of ego identity status: A reference manual. Manuscript.

Adams, G. R., & Fitch, S. A. (1983). Psychosocial environments of university departments: Effects on college students' identity status and ego stage development. *Journal of Personality and Social Psychology, 44*, 1266–1275.

Adams, G. R., & Jones, R. M. (1983). Female adolescents' identity development: Age comparisons and perceived child-rearing experience. *Developmental Psychology, 19*, 249–256.

Adams, G. R., & Marshall, S. K. (1996). A developmental social psychology of identity: Understanding the person in context. *Journal of Adolescence, 19*, 429–442.

Adams, G. R., Montemayor, R., & Brown, B. B. (1992). Adolescent ego-identity development: an analysis of patterns of development and the contributions of the family to identity formation during middle and late adolescence. Manuscript.

Adams, G. R., Ryan, J. H., Hoffman, J. J., Dobson, W. R., & Nielsen, E. C. (1984). Ego identity status, conformity behavior, and personality in late adolescence. *Journal of Personality and Social Psychology, 47*, 1091–1104.

Akers, J. F., Jones, R. M., & Coyl, D. D. (1998). Adolescent friendship pairs: Similarities in identity status development, behaviors, attitudes, and intentions. *Journal of Adolescent Research, 13*, 178–201.

Alberts, C., & Meyer, J. C. (1998). The relationship between Marcia's ego identity statuses and selected personality variables in an African context. *International Journal for the Advancement of Counselling, 20*, 277–288.

Archer, S. L. (1982). The lower age boundaries of identity development. *Child Development, 53*, 1551–1556.

Balistreri, E., Busch-Rossnagel, N. A., & Geisinger, K. F. (1995). Development and preliminary validation of the Ego Identity Process Questionnaire. *Journal of Adolescence, 18*, 179–192.

Bartle-Haring, S., & Strimple, R. E. (1996). Association of identity and intimacy: An exploration of gender and sex-role orientation. *Psychological Reports, 79*, 1255–1264.

Berzonsky, M. D. (1990). Self-construction over the life-span: A process perspective on identity formation. In G. J. Neimeyer & R. A. Neimeyer (Eds.), *Advances in personal construct psychology* (Vol. 1, pp. 155–186). Greenwich, CT: JAI Press.

Berzonsky, M. D. (1992). Identity style inventory, 3rd revision. Manuscript, State University of New York, Cortland.

Berzonsky, M. D., & Adams, G. R. (1999). Reevaluating the identity status paradigm: Still useful after 35 years. *Developmental Review, 19*, 557–590.

Berzonsky, M. D., & Kuk, L. S. (2000). Identity status, identity processing style, and the transition to university. *Journal of Adolescent Research, 15*, 81–98.

Berzonsky, M. D., Rice, K. G., & Neimeyer, G. J. (1991). Identity status and self-construct systems: Process X structure interactions. *Journal of Adolescence, 13*, 251–263.

Berzuini, C., Best, N. G., Gilks, W. R., & Larizza, C. (1997). Dynamic conditional independence models and Markov chain Monte Carlo methods. *Journal of the American Statistical Association, 92*, 1403–1412.

Bilsker, D., & Marcia, J. E. (1991). Adaptive regression and ego identity. *Journal of Adolescence, 14*, 75–84.

Blasi, A., & Glodis, K. (1995). The development of identity. A critical analysis from the perspective of the self as subject. *Developmental Review, 15*, 404–433.

Blasi, A., & Milton, K. (1991). The development of the sense of self in adolescence. *Journal of Personality, 59*, 217–242.

Block, J. (1961/1978). *The Q-sort method in personality assessment and psychiatric research*. Palo Alto, CA: Consulting Psychologists Press.

Blustein, D. L., & Palladino, D. E. (1992). Self and identity in late adolescence: A theoretical and empirical integration. *Journal of Adolescent Research, 6*, 437–453.

Blustein, D. L., & Phillips, S. D. (1990). Relation between ego identity statuses and decision-making styles. *Journal of Counseling Psychology, 37*, 160–168.

Bosma, H. A. (1985). *Identity development in adolescence: Coping with commitments*. Groningen: University of Groningen Press.

Bosma, H. A. (1992). Identity in adolescence: Managing commitments. In G. R. Adams, T. P. Gullotta, & R. Montemayor (Eds.), *Adolescent identity formation: Advances in adolescent development: Vol. 4* (pp. 91–121). Newbury Park, CA: Sage.

Bosma, H. A., & Kunnen, E. S. (2001). Determinants and mechanisms in ego-identity development: A review and synthesis. *Developmental Review, 21*, 39–66.

Boyes, M. C., & Chandler, M. (1992). Cognitive development, epistemic doubt, and identity formation in adolescence. *Journal of Youth and Adolescence, 21*, 277–304.

Campbell, E., Adams, G. R., & Dobson, W. R. (1984). Familial correlates of identity formation in late adolescence: A study of the predictive utility of connectedness and individuality in family relations. *Journal of Youth and Adolescence, 13,* 509–525.

Clancy, S. M., & Dollinger, S. J. (1993). Identity, self, and personality: I. Identity status and the five-factor model of personality. *Journal of Research on Adolescence, 3,* 227–245.

Constantinople, A. (1967). Perceived instrumentality of the college as a measure of attitudes toward college. *Journal of Personality and Social Psychology, 5,* 196–201.

Constantinople, A. (1969). An Eriksonian measure of personality development in college students. *Developmental Psychology, 1,* 357–372.

Côté, J. E. (1996). Identity: A multidimensional analysis. In G. R. Adams, R. Montemayor, & T. P. Gullotta (Eds.), *Psychosocial development during adolescence: Advances in adolescent development: Vol. 8* (pp. 130–180). Newbury Park, CA: Sage.

Côté, J. E., & Levine, C. (1988). A critical examination of the ego identity status paradigm. *Developmental Review, 8,* 147–184.

Cramer, P. (1995). Identity, narcissism, and defense mechanisms in late adolescence. *Journal of Research in Personality, 29,* 341–361.

Cramer, P. (1997). Identity, personality, and defense mechanisms: An observer-based study. *Journal of Research in Personality, 31,* 58–77.

Cramer, P. (1998). Freshman to senior year: A follow-up study of identity, narcissism, and defense mechanisms. *Journal of Research in Personality, 32,* 156–172.

Cramer, P. (2000). Development of identity: Gender makes a difference. *Journal of Research in Personality, 34,* 42–72.

Dellas, M., & Jernigan, L. P. (1990). Affective personality characteristics associated with undergraduate ego identity formation. *Journal of Adolescent Research, 5,* 306–324.

Dyk, P. H., & Adams, G. R. (1990). Identity and intimacy: An initial investigation of three theoretical models using cross-lag panel correlations. *Journal of Youth and Adolescence, 19,* 91–110.

Erikson, E. H. (1963). *Childhood and society* (2nd ed.). New York: W. W. Norton.

Erikson, E. H. (1964). *Insight and responsibility.* New York: W. W. Norton.

Erikson, E. H. (1968). *Identity: Youth and crisis.* New York: W. W. Norton.

Fitch, S. A., & Adams, G. R. (1983). Ego identity and intimacy status: replication and extension. *Developmental Psychology, 19,* 839–845.

Foster, J. D., & LaForce, B. (1999). A longitudinal study of moral, religious, and identity development in a Christian liberal arts college. *Journal of Psychology and Religion, 27,* 52–68.

Fulton, A. S. (1997). Identity status, religious orientation, and prejudice. *Journal of Youth and Adolescence, 26,* 1–11.

Gilks, W. R., Richardson, S., & Spiegelhalter, D. J. (1991). *Markov chain Monte Carlo in practice.* London: Chapman & Hall.

Ginsburg, S. D., & Orlofsky, J. L. (1981). Ego identity status, ego development, and locus of control in college women. *Journal of Youth and Adolescence, 10,* 297–307.

Goossens, L. (1992, September). Longitudinal trajectories of identity status development in university students. Paper presented at the Fifth European Conference on Developmental Psychology, Seville, Spain.

Grotevant, H. D., & Cooper, C. R. (1985). Patterns of interaction in family relationships and the development of identity exploration in adolescence. *Child Development, 56,* 415–428.

Hamer, R. J., & Bruch, M. A. (1994). The role of shyness and private self-consciousness in identity development. *Journal of Research in Personality, 28,* 436–452.

Hunter, J. E., & Schmidt, F. L. (1990). *Methods of meta-analysis: Correcting error and bias in research findings.* Newbury Park, CA: Sage.

Josselson, R. (1987). *Finding herself: Pathways to identity development in women.* San Francisco: Jossey-Bass.

Josselson, R. (1996). *Revising herself: The story of women's identity from college to midlife.* New York: Oxford University Press.

Kacerguis, M. A., & Adams, G. R. (1980). Erikson stage resolution: the relationship between identity and intimacy. *Journal of Youth and Adolescence, 9,* 117–126.

Kegan, R. (1982). *The evolving self: Problem and process in human development.* Cambridge, MA: Harvard University Press.

Kegan, R. (1994). *In over our heads: The mental demands of modern life.* Cambridge, MA: Harvard University Press.

Kiiveri, H., & Speed, T. P. (1982). Structural analysis of multivariate data: A review. *Sociological Methodology, 13,* 209–289.

Kroger, J. (1985). Separation-individuation and ego identity status in New Zealand university students. *Journal of Youth and Adolescence, 14,* 133–147.

Kroger, J. (1988). A longitudinal study of ego identity status interview domains. *Journal of Adolescence, 11,* 49–64.

Kroger, J. (1995). The differentiation of "firm" and "developmental" foreclosure identity statuses: A longitudinal study. *Journal of Research on Adolescence, 10,* 317–337.

Kroger, J. (1997). Gender and identity: The intersection of structure, content, and context. *Sex Roles, 36,* 747–770.

Kroger, J. (2000). *Identity development: Adolescence through adulthood.* Newbury Park, CA: Sage.

Kroger, J., & Haslett, S. J. (1987). An analysis of ego identity status changes from adolescence through middle adulthood. *Social and Behavioral Sciences Documents, 17* (Ms. 2792).

Kroger, J., & Haslett, S. J. (1991). A comparison of ego identity status transition pathways and change rates across five identity domains. *International Journal of Aging and Human Development, 32,* 303–330.

Kvernmo, S., & Heyerdahl, S. (1996). Ethnic identity in aboriginal Sami adolescents: the impact of the family and the ethnic community context. *Journal of Adolescence, 19,* 453–463.

Liu, J. S., & Chen, R. (1998). Sequential Monte Carlo methods for dynamic systems. *Journal of the American Statistical Association, 93,* 1032–1044.

Loevinger, J. (1976). *Ego development.* San Francisco: Jossey-Bass.

Lucas, M. (1997). Identity development, career development, and psychosocial separation from parents: Similarities and differences between men and women. *Journal of Counseling Psychology, 44,* 123–132.

Mallory, M. E. (1983). Longitudinal analysis of ego identity status. Doctoral dissertation, University of California, Davis.

Mallory, M. E. (1989). Q-sort definition of ego identity status. *Journal of Youth and Adolescence, 18,* 399–412.

Marcia, J. E. (1966). Development and validation of ego identity status. *Journal of Personality and Social Psychology, 3,* 551–558.

Marcia, J. E. (1967). Ego identity status: relationship to change in self-esteem, "general maladjustment," and authoritarianism. *Journal of Personality, 35,* 118–133.

Marcia, J. E. (1976). Identity six years after: A follow-up study. *Journal of Youth and Adolescence, 5,* 145–150.

Marcia, J. E. (1993). The relational roots of identity. In J. Kroger (Ed.), *Discussions on ego identity* (pp. 101–120). Hillsdale, NJ: Erlbaum.

Marcia, J. E., Waterman, A. S., Matteson, D. R., Archer, S. L., & Orlofsky, J. L. (Eds.). (1993). *Ego identity: A handbook for psychosocial research.* New York: Springer.

Markstrom, C. A., & Hunter, C. L. (1999). The roles of ethnic and ideological identity in predicting fidelity in African American and European American adolescents. *Child Study Journal, 29*, 23–38.

McCarthy, C. (1994). *The crossing*. London: Picador.

Meeus, W., Iedema, J., Helsen, M., & Vollenbergh, W. (1999). Patterns of adolescent identity development: Review of literature and longitudinal analysis. *Developmental Review, 19*, 419–461.

Meilman, P. W. (1979). Cross-sectional age changes in ego identity status during adolescence. *Developmental Psychology, 15*, 230–231.

Nurmi, J. E., Poole, M. E., & Kalakoski, V. (1996). Age differences in adolescent identity exploration and commitment in urban and rural environments. *Journal of Adolescence, 19*, 443–452.

Orlofsky, J. L. (1978). Identity formation, achievement, and fear of success in college men and women. *Journal of Youth and Adolescence, 7*, 49–62.

Orlofsky, J. L., Marcia, J. E., & Lesser, I. M. (1973). Ego identity status and the intimacy versus isolation crisis of young adulthood. *Journal of Personality and Social Psychology, 27*, 211–219.

Perosa, L. M., Perosa, S. L., & Tam, H. P. (1996). The contribution of family structure and differentiation to identity development in females. *Journal of Youth and Adolescence, 25*, 817–837.

Phinney, J. S. (1989). Stages of ethnic identity development in minority group adolescents. *Journal of Early Adolescence, 9*, 34–49.

Phinney, J. S., & Alipura, L. L. (1990). Ethnic identity in college students from four ethnic groups. *Journal of Adolescence, 13*, 171–183.

Podd, M. H. (1972). Ego identity status and morality: The relationship between two developmental constructs. *Developmental Psychology, 6*, 497–450.

Rappaport, H., Enrich, K. I., & Wilson, A. (1985). Relation between ego identity and temporal perspective. *Journal of Personality and Social Psychology, 48*, 1609–1620.

Read, D., Adams, G. R., & Dobson, W. R. (1984). Ego identity status, personality, and social influence style. *Journal of Personality and Social Psychology, 46*, 169–177.

Roberts, R. E., Phinney, J. S., Masse, L. C., Chen, Y. R., Roberts, C. R., & Romero, A. (1999). The structure of ethnic identity of young adolescents from diverse ethnocultural groups. *Journal of Early Adolescence, 19*, 301–322.

Rosenthal, D. A., Gurney, R. M., & Moore, S. M. (1981). From trust to intimacy: A new inventory for examining Erikson's stages of psychosocial development. *Journal of Youth and Adolescence, 10*, 526–537.

Rowe, I., & Marcia, J. E. (1980). Ego identity status, formal operations, and moral development. *Journal of Youth and Adolescence, 9*, 87–99.

Selles, T., Markstrom-Adams, C., & Adams, G. R. (1994, February). Identity formation and risk for suicide among older adolescents. Paper presented at the Biennial Meetings of the Society for Research on Adolescence, San Diego, CA.

Shain, L., & Farber, B. A. (1989). Female identity development and self-reflection in late adolescence. *Adolescence, 24*, 381–392.

Simmons, D. D. (1970). Development of an objective measure of identity achievement status. *Journal of Projective Techniques and Personality Assessment, 34*, 241–244.

Skoe, E. E. (1993). Sex role orientation and its relationship to the development of identity and moral thought. *Scandinavian Journal of Psychology, 36*, 235–245.

Skoe, E. E., & Marcia, J. E. (1991). A care-based measure of morality and its relation to ego identity. *Merrill-Palmer Quarterly, 37*, 289–304.

Sochting, I., Skoe, E. E., & Marcia, J. E. (1994). Care-oriented moral reasoning and prosocial behavior: A question of gender or sex role orientation? *Sex Roles, 31*, 131–147.

Smith, E. P., Walker, K., Fields, L., Brookins, C. C., & Seay, R. C. (1999). Ethnic identity and its relationship to self-esteem, perceived efficacy and prosocial attitudes in early adolescence. *Journal of Adolescence, 22,* 867–880.

Stephen, J., Fraser, E., & Marcia, J. E. (1992). Moratorium-achievement (Mama) cycles in life-span identity development: Value orientations and reasoning system correlates. *Journal of Adolescence, 15,* 283–300.

Sterling, C. M., & Van Horn, K. R. (1989). Identity and death anxiety. *Adolescence, 24,* 321–326.

Van Hoof, A. (1999). The identity status approach: In need of fundamental revision and qualitative change. *Developmental Review, 19,* 497–556.

Waterman, A. S. (1999). Identity, the identity statuses, and identity status development: A contemporary statement. *Developmental Review, 19,* 591–621.

Waterman, A. S., & Goldman, J. A. (1976). A longitudinal study of ego identity status development at a liberal arts college. *Journal of Youth and Adolescence, 5,* 361–369.

Waterman, A. S., Geary, P. S., & Waterman, C. K. (1974). Longitudinal study of changes in ego identity status from the freshman to the senior year at college. *Developmental Psychology, 10,* 387–392.

Waterman, A. S., & Waterman, C. K. (1971). A longitudinal study of changes in ego identity status during the freshman year at college. *Developmental Psychology, 5,* 167–173.

Willemsen E. W., & Waterman, K. K. (1991). Ego identity status and family environment: A correlational study. *Psychological Reports, 69,* 1203–1212.

Yoder, A. E. (2000). Barriers to ego identity status formation: A contextual qualification of Marcia's identity status paradigm. *Journal of Adolescence, 23,* 95–106.

CHAPTER ELEVEN

Cognitive Development during Adolescence

James P. Byrnes

Introduction

As children negotiate their way through the adolescent period, they confront many challenges and opportunities. If all goes well, these challenges and opportunities lead to improvements in their social, emotional, and intellectual competencies. If children lack access to important resources, however, little progress occurs. The goal of the present chapter is to chart the development of intellectual skills during the adolescent period. To this end, available research will be summarized within answers to the following five questions: (1) What is cognition? (2) How does it develop? (3) Why does it develop? (4) What factors moderate the expression of competence in adolescents? (5) What implications can be drawn from the research on cognitive development in adolescence?

What Is Cognition?

Theories are often said to "carve nature at its joints." In the case of psychological theories, the entity being carved is the human mind (Kosslyn & Koenig, 1994). The term *cognition* is used to refer to those aspects of the mind related to the acquisition, modification, and manipulation of knowledge in particular contexts (Bjorklund, 1999). Knowledge comes in many forms (e.g., math knowledge, self-knowledge), so the field of cognitive development has broad applicability. In fact, it is hard to think of a situation in which knowledge would not be involved. Nevertheless, when we say that researchers study cognitive development, we usually mean that they study such things as learning, memory, language, and reasoning.

More specifically, cognitivists make several important distinctions or "carvings" in their theorizing. The first is the distinction between behaviors (e.g., walking to a library) and mental entities that cause these behaviors (e.g., the desire to read a certain book and the belief it can be found in the library). Other important distinctions pertain to the different kinds of mental entities that have been proposed to explain various kinds of behaviors. At the highest level of analysis, three kinds of mental entities have been proposed: (a) knowledge, (b) cognitive processes and capacities, and (c) metacognitive orientations.

Knowledge refers to three kinds of information structures that are stored in long-term memory: declarative knowledge, procedural knowledge, and conceptual knowledge (Byrnes, 1999). *Declarative knowledge* or "knowing that" is a compilation of all of the facts an adolescent might know (e.g., knowing that two plus two equals four; knowing that Harrisburg is the capital of Pennsylvania). *Procedural knowledge* or "knowing how to" is a compilation of all of the goal-directed skills an adolescent might know (e.g., knowing how to add numbers; knowing how to drive a car). The third kind of knowledge, *conceptual knowledge*, is a form of representation that reflects an adolescent's understanding of his or her declarative and procedural knowledge (Byrnes, 1999). Conceptual knowledge might be called "knowing why" (e.g., knowing why one should use the least-common-denominator method to add fractions). One way to study cognitive development in adolescence, then, is to consider (a) the kinds of knowledge possessed by adolescents at different ages (e.g., do older adolescents have more conceptual knowledge in math than younger adolescents?) and (b) age changes in the interconnections among the different kinds of knowledge (e.g., are math strategies – a form of procedural knowledge – more likely to be linked to conceptual understandings of numbers with age?).

A second way to study cognitive development is to study age changes in the application of *cognitive processes* to an existing knowledge base. The most commonly studied cognitive processes are various forms of *reasoning* (e.g., inductive, deductive, analogical, decision making, and problem-solving). Other important processes include *encoding* (forming a mental representation of a situation), *learning* (i.e., getting information into long-term memory), and *retrieval* (getting information out of long-term memory). Unlike studies of knowledge in which a researcher considers whether a certain kind of knowledge exists in two or more age groups, studies of cognitive processes tend to focus on *how well* children in two or more age groups perform a mental operation. That is, researchers usually assume that children in two age groups are capable of performing the operation at some level, but they consider whether one group carries it out more effectively than the other. In the case of deduction, for example, researchers might ask: Are older adolescents more likely than younger adolescents to know which conclusions logically follow from a set of premises and which do not follow? As we shall see in subsequent sections, age changes in cognitive processes vary considerably according to the knowledge or content involved in a problem. Certain kinds of content produce large age differences in performance, while other kinds produce no age differences.

Other factors that affect performance are the biological *constraints* imposed on *cognitive capacity*. When adolescents attempt to think through a problem they face, there may be a number of things to consider. Coordinating all of this information is a little like trying to build a large and complicated object (e.g., a swing set for one's children) in a room that is too small to fit all of the pieces. When performance improves in some cognitive area during adolescence (e.g., deduction), this change may be due to the acquisition of increased working memory capacity. Hence, just as a complex piece of software runs better after one upgrades a computer to have more RAM, an adolescent may reason better after he or she acquires increased working memory capacity. But it is not just the mental "space" that determines performance in a situation. Sometimes an adolescent may need to keep information in mind before it fades. One way to overcome the time constraints imposed by fading short-term memories is to use a memory strategy (e.g., verbal rehearsal). Another way is to perform cognitive or behavioral operations very quickly. If biological changes during adolescence increase overall capacity or speed of processing, older adolescents may perform better on some cognitive task than younger adolescents for such reasons alone.

The third way to study cognitive development is to consider age changes in adolescents' ability to reflect on and evaluate their knowledge, cognitive processes, and behaviors (i.e., their *metacognitive orientations*). In other words, can adolescents articulate what they know? Can they formalize an intuitive notion? Do they "know when they don't know?" Do they tend to be absolutists or relativists? It is one thing to have knowledge and quite another to be more or less certain about this knowledge. Similarly, it is one thing to make a deductive inference and quite another to consciously reflect on the validity of this inference (Moshman, 1998).

How Does Cognition Develop during Adolescence?

Having defined cognition in terms of knowledge, cognitive processes, constraints, and metacognitive orientations, we can now consider age changes in these aspects of mind. Before proceeding, however, it is important to clarify how the term *development* is used in this chapter. The present author shares the view that cognition can be said to develop when (a) either a qualitative or quantitative change occurs in some aspect of cognition over time and (b) this change enhances an individual's ability to attain healthy or adaptive outcomes (e.g., better grades in school; stronger, more beneficial friendships; physical or emotional health). Note that such changes can either be local (i.e., confined to a particular domain) or global (i.e., domain-general or stage-like).

A second introductory point is that the vast majority of contemporary cognitive developmentalists strongly support the idea of domain-specificity (Wellman & Gelman, 1998). What children learn is obviously a function of what they are exposed to. If children grapple with certain topics more often than others in school and elsewhere, it stands to reason that their knowledge of the high-exposure topics will be more extensive, interconnected, and abstract than their knowledge of lesser-exposure topics (even a domain-general theorist such as Piaget would agree with such an assertion – see Piaget, 1983). This analysis suggests that older adolescents and adults would only tend to know more than younger adolescents for topics that are repeatedly expanded upon with age.

Knowledge

Various sources in the literature suggest that children's declarative, procedural, and conceptual knowledge all increase with age (Byrnes, 2001a). The clearest evidence of such changes can be found in the National Assessments of Educational Progress (NAEPs) that are conducted by the US Department of Education every few years. Each NAEP measures the declarative, procedural, and conceptual knowledge of 4th-, 8th-, and 12th-graders (*N*'s > 17,000) in one of seven domains: reading, writing, math, science, history, geography, and civics. In math, for example, NAEP results show that children in the 4th grade tend to know arithmetic facts and can sometimes solve simple word problems. By 12th grade, however, many children can also perform algebraic manipulations, create tables, and reason about geometric shapes (Reese et al., 1997). Similar results are found on the history NAEP. Some of the knowledge required on the latter include important dates and people (declarative knowledge), map-reading skills (procedural knowledge), and understanding of the significance of certain events (conceptual knowledge). Once again, these forms of knowledge are more evident in 12th-graders than in 4th- or 8th-graders (Beatty et al., 1996).

Although the trends on the other NAEPs are similar, in no case can it be said that a majority of 12th-graders demonstrate a deep conceptual understanding of a given skill or subject matter (Byrnes, 2001a). One reason for the low level of conceptual knowledge in 12th-graders is the abstract, multidimensional, and counterintuitive nature of many of the topics in question. Even in the best of circumstances, concepts such as *scarcity, civil rights, diffusion, limit,* and *conservation of energy* are difficult to grasp and illustrate. Moreover, the scientific definitions of such concepts run counter to students' preexisting ideas. The difficulty of concepts combined with an adolescent's preexisting naive conceptions mean that adolescents will routinely demonstrate hard-to-remediate misconceptions.

In general, then, one can summarize the results on knowledge as follows:

- In most school-related subject areas, there are modest, monotonic increases in declarative and procedural knowledge between the 4th grade and college years; smaller increases are found for conceptual knowledge.
- Misconceptions abound in most school subjects and are evident even in 12th-graders and college students.
- The most appropriate answer to the question, Does knowledge increase during adolescence?, is the following: It depends on the domain (e.g., math vs. interpersonal relationships) and type of knowledge (e.g., declarative vs. conceptual).
- Although there is little evidence of a domain-general shift in understandings that occurs at a particular age, there is evidence of within-domain levels of understanding through which children progress in adolescence. Hence, constructivism is alive and well despite empirical problems with the stage concept (Byrnes, 2001a).

Cognitive processes

As suggested earlier, there are a number of different kinds of cognitive processes that can be applied to an existing knowledge base. Because a comprehensive review of the literatures on all of these cognitive processes is beyond the scope of this chapter, the focus instead shall be on a sampling of recent findings in several areas that predominate in the literature on adolescent thinking. These areas are grouped as follows: (a) deductive reasoning and inductive reasoning; (b) other kinds of reasoning; (c) decision making; and (d) memory processes and constraints.

Deductive and inductive reasoning. People engage in deductive reasoning whenever they combine premises and derive a logically sound conclusion from these premises (Ward & Overton, 1990). For example, given the premises

(A1) *Either the butler or the maid killed the duke*
(B1) *The butler could not have killed the duke,*
one can conclude (C1) *The maid must have killed the duke.* Similarly, given the premises
(A2) *If today is Tuesday, then I have class*
(B2) *Today is Tuesday,* one can conclude (C2) *I have class.*

As can be seen, the premises describe rules for some states of affairs in the world that are known before the conclusion is known or derived. Although it might be said that deductive reasoning is an esoteric enterprise that is only used in introductory logic classes, in reality, deductive reasoning is likely to be applied in a variety of contexts as adolescents try to make sense of what is going on and what they are allowed to do in these contexts. Moreover, deductive reasoning is likely to be used by the police in solving crimes, authors and students as they write argumentative essays, lawyers as they try their cases, scientists as they test hypotheses, and high school students as they set up algebra and geometry proofs. It is thought to be a functionally important kind of reasoning that helps one avoid both minor errors (e.g., going to class on the wrong day) and serious errors (e.g., convicting the wrong person) if carried out correctly. In other words, the conclusions set up beliefs (e.g., the butler did it) that in turn determine behavior (e.g., spending no time investigating other suspects).

The best ways to avoid making deductive reasoning errors include (a) making sure that the premises are, in fact, true and (b) drawing only those inferences that logically follow from the premises. To illustrate the former, consider what would happen in the butler example above if there were three possible suspects but the reasoner thought that there were only two. In such a case, premise (A1) above (that either the butler or the maid murdered the duke) is not true. As a result, conclusion (C1) above (that the maid did it) would not follow from premises (A1) and (B1) (if the butler did not do it, either of the other two suspects could have – not just the maid). The best example of the second source of error are the reasoning fallacies common within conditional syllogisms. Given the premise (A2) *If it is Tuesday, then I have class* and (B2) *It is not Tuesday,* one cannot conclude that (C2) *I do not have class* (because I might have class on other days too). Those who accept C2 commit the so-called denial of antecedent fallacy. Similarly, one cannot infer that it is definitely Tuesday from premise (A2) and the fact that I have class. Those who do so commit the so-called affirmation of consequent fallacy.

Hence, there is an important difference between conclusions that logically follow from premises and conclusions that do not. Part of a person's deductive reasoning competence involves understanding this difference. But how should a person's competence be judged when he or she draws conclusions that are not warranted by the rules of logic, behaves on the basis of these conclusions, and ends up being regularly successful anyway? For example, what if a reasoner knows that he or she cannot conclude that the maid definitely committed the murder (because other suspects exist), but has strong suspicions that the maid did it? Should he or she not gather evidence on the maid? If a detective regularly followed these hunches and attained an excellent conviction rate, would it not be appropriate to say that he or she was a good reasoner?

As this example shows, there are other kinds of inferences besides the deductive kind that can help an individual be successful in the world. When the former involve extrapolation from a small number of cases to a general principle (e.g., my babysitter drives a Volvo so all babysitters probably do) or inferences that could be true (but may not be), we say that a person has made an inductive inference. Although it may be fallacious to draw inductive inferences (i.e., because single cases may not be representative and stereotypes derive from inductions), people who do so can be rather successful if they somehow manage to match up their guesses with objective probabilities in the world. In fact, researchers who study language acquisition suggest that children would never learn language as fast as they do if they did not make inductions (e.g., My pet is called a *dog*. Your pet looks like mine, so it is probably called *dog* too). Again, though, there is a difference between making an inductive inference and knowing that it could easily be wrong. The questions of interest here, then, are the following: (a) Do adolescents recognize the fallibility of their inductive inferences? (b) Do they think that these inferences are as certain as valid deductive inferences? and (c) How often do inductive inferences lead them on a course of success-enhancing behaviors?

The foregoing descriptions of deductive and inductive reasoning were provided to give a sense of what these processes entail. Understanding the nature and functional value of these inferences is the first step in knowing how to chart their development in empirical studies. But it is also important for researchers to make two important methodological decisions related to the response required of participants and the content of the tasks. As suggested earlier, participants could be (a) asked to say which conclusions follow from either premises or cases (e.g., give them premises A2 and B2 above and ask them to draw a conclusion); (b) asked to discriminate between conclusions that follow and those that do not; or (c) asked to indicate outcomes that would count against an hypothesis (e.g., the case of an underage drinker for the hypothesis "If a person is drinking beer, that person is at least 21 years old"). In addition, they could be asked to explain their answers or say how confident they are in each conclusion. As for the content of the tasks, they can be presented with premises (or cases) about real, familiar entities (e.g., animal species, driving laws), fantasy content that was invented for the experiment (e.g., the properties of alien creatures or fairy-tale characters), or abstract content about letters, shapes, or nonsense syllables. It turns out that each of these decisions affects the magnitude of age trends when children, adolescents, and adults are compared. As such, it has been difficult to establish both the age of onset of deductive and inductive competencies and the developmental course of these skills over the adolescent period. The effects of response mode and content have been further complicated by disagreements among researchers over the standards set to attribute competence. Some researchers attribute competence if a child makes at least some of the valid inferences for at least one kind of content (e.g., fantasy). Others only do so if a respondent consistently makes valid inferences, consistently avoids fallacious inferences, and does so over multiple contents (at a rate above chance). In part, these methodological decisions reflect the extent to which researchers align themselves with the current *Zeitgeist* favoring very early competence or align themselves with Piaget's theory (which suggests that higher levels of inductive and deductive skill emerge with the onset of formal operations in adolescence).

Notwithstanding all of these complications, there are identifiable developmental changes in deductive reasoning skills that occur between childhood and early adulthood. Competence is first manifested around age 5 or 6 in the ability to draw some types of conclusions from "if-then" (conditional) premises, especially when these premises refer to fantasy or make-believe content (e.g., Dias & Harris, 1988). Several years later, children begin to show insight into the difference between conclusions that follow from conditional premises and conclusions that do not follow (e.g., Byrnes & Overton, 1986; Janveau-Brennan & Markovits, 1999), especially when the premises refer to familiar content about taxonomic or causal relations. Next, there are monotonic increases through-out adolescence in the ability to draw appropriate conclusions, explain one's reasoning, and test hypotheses even when premises refer to unfamiliar, abstract, or contrary-to-fact propositions (Klaczynski, 1993; Moshman & Franks, 1986; Ward & Overton, 1990). But again, performance is maximized on familiar content about legal or causal relations (Klaczynski & Narasimham, 1998). When the experimental content runs contrary to what is true (e.g., All elephants are small animals. This is an elephant. Is it small?) or has no meaningful referent (e.g., If there is a D on one side of a card, there is a 7 on the other), less than half of older adolescents or adults do well. Performance on the latter tasks can, however, be improved in older participants if the abstract problems are presented after meaningful ones, or if the logic of the task is explained to participants (e.g., Klaczynski, 1993; Ward, Byrnes, & Overton, 1990). Even so, such measures generally have only a weak effect. These findings imply that most of the development after age 10 in deductive reasoning competence is in the ability to suspend one's own beliefs and think objectively about the structure of an argument (Moshman, 1998). Little evidence exists for an abstract, domain-general ability that is spontaneously applied to any content.

As for inductive reasoning competence, few studies exist and fewer still examine induc-tion in adolescents. In a large study conducted in Hungary (Csapo, 1997), over 2,400 students in the 3rd, 5th, 7th, 9th, and 11th grades were given six different kinds of induc-tion problems including number analogies, verbal analogies, number series (e.g., 1, 7, 13, ?), and letter series (e.g., a, c, e, ?). Results showed the following percentages correct for each of the grade levels: 33 percent (3rd), 45 percent (5th), 60 percent (7th), 70 percent (9th), and 75 percent (11th). Thus, performance generally improved with age, especially between the first three grade levels. However, these findings do not necessarily imply that a domain-general inductive reasoning competence emerges over time because (a) the correlations among the six kinds of items ranged between .48 and .67 and (b) age differences were larger on some kinds of items than others. A similar kind of domain-specificity in age trends was found in a study of inductive reasoning in 5th- and 7th-graders (Baker-Sennett & Ceci, 1996). As was alluded to earlier, these findings are probably attributable to knowledge increases between childhood and late adolescence as well as increased familiarity with such induction tasks. Older adolescents also show the ability to know when two analogies are formally similar (Nippold, 1994). This kind of second-order reasoning is similar to the conscious assessment required in deduction tasks that have contrary-to-fact content (as described above).

In two other studies, researchers tried to assess deductive and inductive approaches in the same subjects. Galotti, Komatsu, and Voelz (1997) presented 2nd–6th-graders with deductive or inductive problems and asked them to draw an inference, rate their confidence, and explain their answers. Results for confidence ratings and explanations showed increased sensitivity to the two kinds of problems with age. For example, by the 4th grade, confidence ratings for deductive problems were higher than those for inductive problems (as they should be since deductive conclusions must be true). In a study of 5th- and 8th-graders, Foltz, Overton, & Ricco (1995) presented children with a task in which a picture was covered by small, rectangular pieces of paper. The idea was to turn over as few pieces as possible to figure out which of several alternatives was underneath (the alternatives were similar in appearance). The deductive (and most efficient) strategy in this case was to turn over pieces that would rule out alternatives. The inductive strategy was to turn over pieces that were consistent with a favorite choice but also consistent with others. Results showed that children shifted toward the deductive strategy with age and that the deductive strategy was employed more often by children who performed well on a widely used deduction task (the Wason selection task).

Overall, one can conclude the following from the research on deductive and inductive reasoning:

- Although preadolescent children show the ability to make certain kinds of deductive and inductive inferences, children gain increased insight into the distinction between, and value of, these two kinds of inference throughout adolescence. Moreover, older adolescents show greater facility in suspending their own beliefs to evaluate the reasoning of someone else (but their performance is far from perfect) and can sometimes reason about arguments at an objective level (Moshman, 1998).
- Performance is greatly enhanced when adolescents are asked to apply these skills to an existing knowledge base. The latter finding is consistent with recent claims that reasoning skills have been designed by evolution to be knowledge-dependent (see Hirschfeld & Gelman, 1994).

Other kinds of reasoning. There are, of course, other kinds of reasoning besides deductive and inductive reasoning. For example, students engage in mathematical reasoning when they are given elements of a math problem and asked to solve it (as on the Scholastic Achievement Test), spatial reasoning when they manipulate spatial information (e.g., mentally rotating an object; using a map to figure out the most efficient route to a location), scientific reasoning when they set up hypotheses and test them appropriately, and so on. As all of these examples show, reasoning involves the goal-directed manipulation, combination, or elaboration of items of information. That is, when people reason, they "go beyond the information given" to figure out (a) what is true or could be true about the world or (b) how to proceed or attain desired outcomes in a particular situation.

For comparative reasons, it is of interest to determine whether age trends in other forms of reasoning parallel those found for deductive and inductive reasoning. Unfortunately, it is difficult to draw firm conclusions in the case of mathematical or spatial reasoning because researchers who study these forms of reasoning have generally not given the same task to children, adolescents, and adults. In addition, most studies in areas such as mathematical or spatial reasoning have focused on the competencies of preschoolers and elementary students (Byrnes, 2001a; Deloache et al., 1998). The few studies that exist in the area of math, however, do suggest that there are developmental changes in the ability to reason about the same mathematical content (e.g., Geary et al., 1997; Halford, 1978; Lester 1975; Sweller and Cooper, 1985).

In the area of spatial reasoning, researchers have also found age changes between childhood and adolescence. However, in most cases, the largest improvements occur for the speed with which children perform spatial operations. Accuracy is high at all ages (Kail, 1988; Levine, Preddy, & Thorndike, 1987; Merriman, Keating, & List, 1985; Waber, Carlson, & Mann, 1982).

The literature on scientific reasoning in adolescence is somewhat larger than that on mathematical or spatial reasoning, but again, it is hard to find direct comparisons of children, adolescents, and adults on the same task. Nevertheless, the following can be inferred from the literature as a whole: Through careful selection of content (e.g., crumbs left by a mouse who stole food), it is possible to show early insight into the use of evidence to make inferences (Sodian, Zaitchik, & Carey, 1991). In addition, training in the use of the isolation of variables technique has been effective in children aged 10 and over (e.g., Chen & Klahr, 1999). But the ability to consciously construct one's own hypotheses across a wide range of contents, test these hypotheses in controlled experiments, and draw appropriate inferences from the data is increasingly manifested throughout adolescence and early adulthood (Byrnes, 2001a; Klaczynski & Narasimham, 1998; Kuhn et al., 1995).

Decision making. The construct of decision making refers to a set of processes that come into play when an individual is trying to figure out how to attain a particular goal (Byrnes, 1998). After setting the goal, the person generates a set of options by either conducting a memory search or consulting external sources (e.g., mentors, peers, etc.). Next, the person has to evaluate the options in some way, choose the best one, and implement it. Finally, the person experiences the consequences of this decision.

Reviews of the literature show that researchers have not been interested in determining whether children, adolescents, and adults engage in goal-setting, option generation, option evaluation, and so on (because it is self-evident that they do at some level). Rather, they have been more interested in determining whether these aspects of decision making are carried out more effectively with age. So, they might ask, Are adolescents more likely to set multiple, adaptive goals with age? Are they more likely to generate a set of options that are highly likely to satisfy these goals? Are they likely to use strategies to help themselves discover the best way to proceed? Are older adolescents and adults more likely to anticipate the consequences of their decisions than younger adolescents and children? Is there evidence that children are more likely to learn from their decision-making successes and failures with age?

Because the literature on the development of decision making is still relatively sparse, it is not yet possible to provide definitive answers to these important questions (Byrnes,

1998; Klaczynski, Byrnes, & Jacobs, 2001). Nevertheless, there is evidence that older adolescents and adults are more likely than younger adolescents or children to (a) understand the difference between options likely to satisfy multiple goals and options likely to satisfy only a single goal (Byrnes & McClenny, 1994; Byrnes, Miller, & Reynolds, 1999); (b) anticipate a wider range of consequences of their actions (Lewis, 1981; Halpern-Felsher & Cauffman, 2001); and (c) learn from their decision-making successes and failures with age (Byrnes & McClenny, 1994; Byrnes, Miller, & Reynolds, 1999). There is also some suggestion that adolescents are more likely to make good decisions when they have metacognitive insight into the factors that affect the quality of decision making (Miller & Byrnes, 2001; Ormond et al., 1991). However, most of these studies involved laboratory tasks, hypothetical scenarios, or self-report. In real-world contexts, factors may come into play that seriously affect the quality of decisions. For example, adolescents may think they will find an outcome positive and learn later that it was not. Thus, lack of self-knowledge could lead to serious errors. Also, high states of emotional arousal or intoxication could lead to sharp reductions in the ability to generate, evaluate, and implement success-producing options. Hence, adolescents and adults who look good in the lab may nevertheless make many poor decisions in the real world if they lack appropriate self-regulatory strategies for dealing with such possibilities (e.g., self-calming techniques; coping with peer pressure to drink; etc.). Additional studies are clearly needed in this area to examine such issues and to replicate the work that has already been done.

Memory skills and processing constraints. Over the years, memory researchers have introduced a number of theoretical distinctions in order to accommodate a diverse set of findings from healthy and brain-injured individuals (Squire & Knowlton, 1995). For example, there is the distinction between the capacity to temporarily entertain information in consciousness (i.e., working memory) and information that is permanently stored in patterns of neural connections (i.e., long-term memory). Within working memory and long-term memory, other important distinctions have been made (e.g., verbal working memory versus spatial working memory). In addition, researchers have found it necessary to distinguish between subconscious improvements in skills over time (implicit memory) and information that one can talk about after it is retrieved from long-term memory (explicit memory). Other features of the human memory system include the constraints that limit the amount of information that can be simultaneously entertained in working memory before it fades, and strategies that can be used to overcome these constraints and store new information in long-term memory (e.g., rehearsal). Conceivably, researchers who study cognitive development could chart age changes in any one of these aspects of memory (e.g., working memory, implicit memory, strategies, etc.). As was the case for certain kinds of reasoning, however, most studies of memory have tended to focus on the changes that occur between birth and age 10. This preadolescent emphasis has been exaggerated in recent years as large numbers of researchers endeavored to determine the competencies of young children to serve as witnesses in criminal cases (Bjorklund, 1999).

Nevertheless, a handful of studies of memory development in adolescence have been conducted since the early 1990s. Paniak et al. (1998), for example, created age norms for 9–15-year-olds ($N > 700$) on the Logical Memory and Visual Reproduction scales of the

Wechsler Memory Scale-Revised (WMS-R). On the Logical Memory scale, individuals are asked to remember as much as they can about two paragraphs that are read to them. On the Visual Reproduction subtest, participants are presented with geometric designs for 10 seconds and then asked to find each design among four alternatives. Results showed that immediate recall scores on the Logical Memory scale improved monitonically with age (i.e., 43 percent in 9-year-olds to 63 percent for 16-year-olds) and that a delay produced about a 5 percent decrement at each age level. For the Visual Reproduction scale, performance increased monitonically from 73 percent in 9-year-olds to 89 percent in 15-year-olds. Another finding was that a delay manipulation produced twice as much loss in the 9–11-year-olds as in the 12–15-year-olds.

Zald and Iacono (1998) charted the development of spatial working memory in 500 14- and 20-year-olds. Spatial working memory was assessed by asking participants to remember the location of a symbol on a computer screen after a brief delay that included a verbal interference task (to limit covert rehearsal). The error rates after 8-second and 14-second delays were 83 percent and 93 percent, respectively, for the 14-year-olds, and 72 percent and 80 percent, respectively, for the 20-year-olds (the 20-year-olds did better). In a control condition with immediate recall and no interference, the error rates were only 24 percent at each age level. Thus, the delays and interference produced sharp drops in performance, especially in the younger subjects. The differences between age groups were significant in all conditions except for the control condition. Thus, spatial working memory does appear to improve during the adolescent period. Expressed as an effect size, the age difference in the most difficult condition was $d = .47$ (one-half of a standard deviation). Swanson (1999) obtained similar results for both verbal and spatial working memory in a normative sample of 778 people. Monotonic increases in memory were found between the ages of 6 and 35, which effect sizes in the .40s.

Wood et al. (1999) asked students in four grade levels to learn 60 facts either using their own approach or an approach called elaborative interrogation (providing answers to "why" questions about each fact). After a study period, students were asked to recall as many facts as they could. Results for students in the elaborative interrogation condition were as follows: Whereas 5th- and 6th-graders recalled 38 percent of the facts, 9th–10th-graders, college freshmen, and college seniors recalled 43 percent, 58 percent, and 60 percent, respectively. The corresponding figures for students in a self-study condition were 28 percent, 34 percent, 52 percent, and 59 percent, respectively. Wood et al. interpreted these results as suggesting that the elaborative interrogation approach was most effective for the younger students, presumably because older students were likely to use an elaborative technique on their own. The difference between the college seniors and 5th–6th-graders produced a substantial effect size in each condition (d's = 1.69, 2.32 for each condition).

Cycowicz et al. (2000) conducted a study to see whether performance on implicit memory tests would improve with age as much as has been found on explicit memory tests (such as those used by Paniak et al., 1998, Zald & Iacono, 1998, and Wood et al., 1999, above). Implicit memory was assessed using a picture fragment test. Here, portions of a picture would be added until an individual could identify it. After the identification part of the test, participants were then asked to recall the pictures and recognize them. To give a sense of the overall level of performance, Cycowicz et al. divided group means by the level of performance usually found in adult samples. Results showed that 5–7-year-olds recalled 31 percent as many pictures as adults, and recognized 33 percent as much. The corresponding figures for 9–11-year-olds were 68 percent (recall) and 54 percent (recognition); for 14–16-year-olds, the figures were 90 percent (recall) and 87 percent (recognition). Thus, by around age 15, the performance of adolescents closely approximates the performance of adults. The authors concluded that "implicit memory, like explicit memory, develops with age" (p. 19).

Lehman et al. (1998) assessed age changes in the ability to intentionally forget items of information. Here, cues indicated which items to remember and which to forget. Eighth- and 9th-graders showed significantly better memory for the to-be-remembered items and significantly poorer memory of the to-be-forgotten items than 3rd-graders. The authors explained this age difference by suggesting that younger children were less skilled in the process of encoding than older children.

In contrast to the previous four studies that found sizable age changes in memory performance between childhood and adolescence, several other studies have found much smaller changes or no change at all. For example, in a study of speed of retrieval, List, Keating, and Merriman (1985) found that there was a 44 percent reduction in the speed with which children could identify and judge letters between the 4th and 8th grades (884 msec to 587 msec). Between the 8th grade and college levels, retrieval speed was reduced by another 15 percent (587 msec to 507 msec), but the latter change was not significant. Thus, whereas students at all three levels were fairly quick in their responding, performance improved nevertheless between the ages of 9 and 13. In a study of false recognition, Seamon et al. (2000) found that few subjects in the 1st grade, 5th grade, and college levels made errors in identifying pictures they had seen before in a study trial. No significant age differences emerged.

Thus, age differences in memory do not always emerge in comparisons of children, adolescents, and adults. The variables that seem to affect the size of the age difference include: (a) whether students have to learn information during the experiment or retrieve something known already, and (b) the length of the delay between stimulus presentation and being asked to retrieve information.

Metacognitive orientations

The final aspect of cognition to be examined refers to the ability to reflect upon and evaluate one's own knowledge or someone else's knowledge (Moshman, 1998). To illustrate this ability, note that there is a difference between remembering a textbook description of an historical event (e.g., the Boston Massacre) and evaluating the quality of the evidence on which this description is based (e.g., How do we know for sure who fired the first shot?). Moreover, there should be a correspondence between the number of possible explanations that exist and one's level of certainty (Byrnes & Beilin, 1991). For example, if two suspects could have committed a crime, a detective should be more uncertain about the guilt of one individual than if only one person could have done it. Relatedly, one should be more certain about the occurrence of an historical event when large quantities of credible evidence exist than when very little or dubious evidence exists.

Finally, competent scientists are conscious of the difference between their theories and the evidence that would be needed to prove these theories (Kuhn, 1992). In addition, scientists know that experiments tend to raise more questions than they answer. At what point do adolescents come to agree with the old adage, "The more you know, the more know you don't know?"

Researchers from several distinct perspectives have focused on adolescents' ability to reflect upon the source of their knowledge and what they and others believe to be the case (Moshman, 1998). Some have asked adolescents to consider perspectives on controversial issues (e.g., the death penalty, evolution, suspected carcinogens), while others used questions that tapped into epistemological beliefs (e.g., "You either learn difficult material fast or not at all"). Results from all of these studies suggest that children start out as objectivists who usually assume that all knowledge is certain and can be learned quickly through observation. In early adolescence, there is a shift toward a relativism that is based on the idea that everyone's truth or perspective is as good as anyone else's. In late adolescence and early adulthood, there is growing insight into the idea that whereas there are often multiple perspectives, there are evidence-based or reasoning-based techniques for evaluating the accuracy or validity of each claim. In other words, all perspectives may not be equally "good" (Chandler, Boyes, & Ball, 1990; Kuhn, 1992; Kitchener et al., 1989; Schommer, 1998; Schommer et al., 1997).

Why Does Cognition Develop during Adolescence?

We have seen that in each area of cognition described in this chapter (i.e., knowledge, reasoning, decision making, memory, and metacognitive orientations), older adolescents and adults demonstrate more intellectual competence than younger adolescents. The latter, in turn, demonstrate more competence than children. The literature also suggests, however, that researchers have sometimes underestimated the reasoning skills of preadolescent children (i.e., they have more competence skill than was originally assumed) and sometimes overestimated the skills of older adolescents and adults (i.e., they have less competence than was originally assumed). What developmental mechanisms are responsible for this overall pattern of results? At present, no definitive answers can be given to this question, but several possibilities can be proposed and briefly evaluated.

The first is the Piagetian notion of equilibration. Although it is certainly reasonable to assume (a) there is a tension between assimilative and accommodative forces on knowledge growth and (b) there is an important role for experience in knowledge growth, the construct of equilibration remains difficult to test. Recent attempts to model equilibration in connectionist simulations, however, could provide a means by which specific claims about this elusive process could be evaluated empirically (Mareschal & Shultz, 1996).

The second possibility is a neurally-based process of some sort. Ideally, this process should be able to explain (a) increases in the ability to coordinate multiple dimensions of a problem; (b) changes in working memory, encoding, and retrieval; (c) increases in speed of processing that occur in multiple domains; and (d) the increase in metacognitive and reflection skills described in multiple sections of this chapter (Halford, Wilson, & Phillips, 1998; Kail, 1996; Moshman, 1998; Waltz et al., 1999). It has been suggested that the maturation of the frontal lobes could be responsible for many of the age trends reported in this chapter (Case, 1992). This claim seems plausible given that neurons in the frontal lobes continue to mature through adolescence (Byrnes, 2001b; Johnson, 1997), and neuroscientific studies have implicated the frontal lobes in both multi-dimensional thinking, self-awareness, metamemory, and working memory (Byrnes, 2001b; Halford et al., 1998; Waltz et al., 1999). Moreover, the frontal lobes are recipro-cally connected with multiple cortical and subcortical structures in the brain, which could provide a mechanism by which a domain-general increase in speed of processing could occur. However, neural changes could be a *consequence* of other developmental changes instead of being a cause of them. For example, it is known that the brain changes when people have experiences and gain knowledge (Byrnes, 2001b). Synaptic connections realign and myelin sheaths form over well-established, lengthier assemblies. In addition, people who have a great deal of knowledge (e.g., experts) remember more than people with less knowledge and demonstrate faster speeds of processing. Thus, one could explain several of the findings by appealing to knowledge alone. In addition, improvements in working memory and metacognitive orientations continue well past adolescence (and well past the time the frontal lobes finally mature). Thus, while the neural account is intrigu-ing, it remains to be sufficiently worked out and verified.

The third possibility is education. Clearly, the main source of knowledge changes during the adolescent period is high school and college coursework (Byrnes, 2001a). In addition, researchers who study deductive reasoning, decision making, argumentative reasoning, critical thinking, and metacognition orientations have all found or argued that education appears to be a key variable in explaining improvements in reasoning (Byrnes, Miller, & Reynolds, 1999; Kuhn, 1992; Kitchener et al., 1989; Pascarella, 1999; Schommer, 1998; Scribner, 1997).

Of course, it could also be the case that all three of these explanations are correct. For example, education and experience could beget knowledge and brain changes that corre-spond to this knowledge. These changes, in turn, could eventually lead to interconnec-tions and other changes that produce the capacity for multidimensional thinking, fast responding, and so on. Finally, connectionist models of knowledge change (and the cor-responding neural assemblies) can be used to explain the monotonic, conservative changes that occur.

What Factors Moderate the Expression of Cognitive Skills in Adolescents?

We have noted several times in this chapter that cognitive skills improve during the ado-lescent period, but the performance of older adolescents and adults is far from perfect. What factors limit the extent to which reasoning, memory, and metacognitive skills are expressed? A number of such factors have been identified over the years, but for the sake of brevity, only a few will be mentioned here. The first factor that greatly affects the level of performance is the content of any given task. As noted several times, through careful selection of content that is highly familiar and appropriately structured, researchers can elevate performance to very high levels and eliminate (or even reverse) age differences between children and adolescents, or adolescents and adults. The second factor is the motivational incentive of the task (Klaczynski et al., 2001). Adolescents and adults perform much better on reasoning and scientific thinking tasks when they are highly motivated to use their skills (as when their personal beliefs are under attack). The third factor is the processing demands of the task. The more dimensions that have to be co-ordinated and held in working memory, the greater likelihood that adolescents and adults will resort to focusing on a few salient issues. This general rule of thumb implies that researchers can elevate performance on complex tasks by providing lots of contextual supports or scaffolds (e.g., external memory aids, training, etc.; see Fischer, 1980). Finally, research on decision making has highlighted the important role of emotions in perfor-mance. Emotions not only drive the decision-making process (i.e., options are chosen to maximize the experience of positive emotions and minimize the experience of negative ones), but they can sharply interfere with performance when they are too intense (Byrnes, 1998). Part of being a good decision-maker is being able to use self-regulatory (e.g., self-calming) strategies to manage the effects of emotions.

To the extent that gender and ethnicity covary with knowledge (and education), moti-vation, processing capacity, and emotions, one would expect within-grade performance differences to emerge on tasks that tap into reasoning, memory, and metacognitive ori-entations. Thus, just as researchers can manipulate the size of age differences through careful selection of content and task demands, they can also manipulate the size of gender and ethnic differences in the same way (Byrnes, Miller, & Schaefer, 1999). However, it would be wrong to assume any "natural" connection between gender, ethnicity, and reasoning performance because gender and ethnicity are merely proxy variables for other, more determinative factors (e.g., education and experience; see Byrnes, 2001a, for a review of gender and ethnic differences in cognition).

Implications

Spurred on by early debates regarding the nature and extent of formal operational reasoning in children, adolescents, and adults (Byrnes, 1988; Keating, 1990), researchers have come to refine what it currently understood about cognition in adolescence. Notwithstanding the numerous attempts to demonstrate competence in young children since the 1980s, the present review suggests that cognitive skills do develop in several important ways during the adolescent period. Older adolescents and adults not only have more knowledge than younger adolescents and children, they demonstrate greater facility in making use of this knowledge to remember, reason, make decisions, and solve problems. In addition, older adolescents and adults seem to be more metacognitive, re-flective, and constructivist in their understanding of the mind than younger adolescents and children. And yet, the former's absolute level of performance generally hovers near the mediocre range when they are asked to learn or reason about required school topics (e.g., math, science, history) or controversial issues (e.g., the death penalty; global warming).

What are the implications of these findings for theories, research, and public policy? Theoretically, it would be important for researchers to take a synthetic perspective in which the best elements of Piagetian theory, information-processing theory, decision theory, motivation theories, and neuroscience are woven into a comprehensive account of adolescent thinking. No one theory in these separate domains can handle the full range of findings described in this chapter. The development of such a theory would be important for several reasons. First, it would provide the basis for new, innovative studies that go beyond a piecemeal accounting of small changes in individual skills. Second, it would provide a more coherent and useful basis for understanding the best ways to teach adolescents. The present review merely indicates that adolescents have trouble when they engage in the kind of higher-order thinking required in high school and college. It provides little insight into how to overcome their difficulties.

As for the policy and legal implications of the present results, the findings are still too tentative to say anything definitive. One important reason for the impasse is that researchers still disagree about the meaning of responses on reasoning and decision-making tasks (Klaczynski et al., 2001). If a response could either mean that a person is rational or irrational, such a response could not be used by lawyers or judges to attribute competence. Even if researchers came to agree on the best answer to give on a test, one has to also consider the powerful effect of moderating variables on performance (e.g., content, emotions, and so on). An adolescent may look competent when asked to reason about certain topics but incompetent when asked to reason about others. In addition, the adolescent may be able to say the right things in an assessment, but then fail to demonstrate this ability in real-world contexts due to motivational or emotional factors. Thus, there is a clear need for advancement in both the theoretical and assessment realms.

Key Readings

Moshman, D. (1998). Cognitive development beyond childhood. In W. Damon (Series Ed.), D. Kuhn & R. S. Siegler (Vol. Eds.), *Handbook of child psychology: Vol. 2. Cognition, language, and perception* (pp. 947–978). New York: Wiley.
This chapter provides an excellent summary of contemporary research in adolescent cognitive development and provides a different way of categorizing studies than that utilized in the present chapter. It highlights a key difference between child and adolescent thought: the ability to reflect upon one's own thinking.

Overton, W. F. (1990). *Reasoning, necessity, and logic: Developmental perspectives.* Mahwah, NJ: Erlbaum.
This book is an excellent review of the literature on a key of area of research in adolescent cognitive development: deductive reasoning. The chapters collectively establish the fact that children take quite some time to gain full mastery of deductive competencies.

References

Baker-Sennett, J., & Ceci, S. J. (1996). Clue-efficiency and insight: Unveiling the mystery of inductive leaps. *Journal of Creative Behavior, 30*, 153–172.

Beatty, A. S., Reese, C. M., Perksy, H. R., & Carr, P. (1996). *The NAEP 1994 U.S. History Report Card for the nation and the states.* Washington, DC: US Department of Education.

Bjorklund, D. F. (1999). *Children's thinking: Developmental function and individual differences.* Belmont, CA: Wadsworth.

Byrnes, J. P. (1988). Formal operations: A systematic reformulation. *Developmental Review, 8*, 66–87.

Byrnes, J. P. (1998). *The nature and development of decision-making: A self-regulation perspective.* Mahwah, NJ: Erlbaum.

Byrnes, J. P. (1999). The nature and development of representation: Forging a synthesis of competing approaches. In I. Sigel (Ed.), *Development of Representation* (pp. 273–294). Mahwah, NJ: Erlbaum.

Byrnes. J. P. (2001a). *Cognitive development and learning in instructional contexts* (2nd ed.). Needham Heights, MA: Allyn & Bacon.

Byrnes, J. P. (2001b). *Minds, brains, and education: Understanding the psychological and educational relevance of neuroscientific research.* New York: Guilford.

Byrnes, J. P., & Beilin, H. (1991). The cognitive basis of uncertainty. *Human Development, 34*, 189–203.

Byrnes, J. P., & McClenny, B. (1994). Decision-making in young adolescents and adults. *Journal of Experimental Child Psychology, 58*, 359–388.

Byrnes, J. P., Miller, D. C., & Reynolds, M. (1999). Learning to make good decisions: A self-regulation perspective. *Child Development, 70*, 1121–1140.

Byrnes, J. P., Miller, D. C., & Schaefer, W. D. (1999). Sex-differences in risk-taking: A meta-analysis. *Psychological Bulletin, 125*, 367–383.

Byrnes, J. P., & Overton, W. F. (1986). Reasoning about certainty and uncertainty in concrete, causal, and propositional contexts. *Developmental Psychology, 22*, 793–799.

Case, R. (1992). The role of the frontal lobes in the regulation of cognitive development. *Brain & Cognition, 20*, 51–73.

Chandler, M. J., Boyes, M., & Ball, L. (1990). Relativism and stations of epistemic doubt. *Journal of Experimental Child Psychology, 50*, 370–395.

Chen, Z., & Klahr, D. (1999). All other things being equal: Acquisition and transfer of the Control of Variables Strategy. *Child Development, 70*, 1098–1120.

Csapo, B. (1997). The development of inductive reasoning: Cross-sectional assessments in an educational context. *International Journal of Behavioral Development, 20*, 609–626.

Cycowicz, M., Friedman, D., Snodgrass, J. G., & Rothstein, M. (2000). A developmental trajectory in implicit memory is revealed by picture fragment completion. *Memory, 8*, 19–35.

Deloache, J. S., Miller, K. F., & Pierroutsakos, S. L. (1998). Reasoning and problem solving. In W. Damon (Series Ed.), D. Kuhn & R. S. Siegler (Vol. Eds.), *Handbook of child psychology: Vol. 2: Cognition, language, and perception* (pp. 801–850). New York: Wiley.

Dias, M. G., & Harris, P. L. (1988). The effect of make-believe play on deductive reasoning. *British Journal of Developmental Psychology, 6*, 207–221.

Fischer, K. W. (1980). A theory of cognitive development: The control and construction of hierarchies of skills. *Psychological Review, 87*, 477–531.

Foltz, C., Overton, W. F., & Ricco, R. B. (1995). Proof construction: Adolescent development from inductive to deductive problem-solving strategies. *Journal of Experimental Child Psychology, 59*, 179–195.

Galotti, K. M., Komatsu, L. K., & Voelz, S. (1997). Children's differential performance on deductive and inductive syllogisms. *Developmental Psychology, 33*, 70–78.

Geary, D. C., Hamson, C. O., Chen, G.-P., Liu, F., Hoard, M. K., & Salthouse, T. A. (1997). Computational and reasoning abilities in arithmetic: Cross-generational change in China and the United States. *Psychonomic Bulletin & Review, 4*, 425–430.

Halford, G. S. (1978). An approach to the definition of cognitive developmental stages in school mathematics. *British Journal of Educational Psychology, 48*, 298–314.

Halford, G. S., Wilson, W. H., & Phillips, S. (1998). Processing capacity defined by relational complexity: Implications for comparative, developmental, and cognitive psychology. *Behavioral & Brain Sciences, 21*, 803–864.

Halpern-Felsher, B. L., & Cauffman, E. (2001). Costs and benefits of a decision: Decision-making competence in adolescents and adults. *Journal of Applied Developmental Psychology, 22*, 257–274.

Hirschfeld, L. A., & Gelman, S. A. (1994). *Mapping the mind: Domain specificity in cognition and culture.* Cambridge: Cambridge University Press.

Janveau-Brennan, G., & Markovits, H. (1999). The development of reasoning with causal conditionals. *Developmental Psychology, 35*, 904–911.

Johnson, M.H. (1997). *Developmental cognitive neuroscience: An introduction.* Cambridge, MA.: Blackwell Publishers.

Kail, R. (1988). Developmental functions for speeds of cognitive processes. *Journal of Experimental Child Psychology, 45*, 339–364.

Kail, R. (1996). Nature and consequences of developmental change in speed of processing. *Swiss Journal of Psychology, 55*, 133–138.

Keating, D. P. (1990). Adolescent thinking. In S. S. Feldman & G. R. Elliott (Eds.), *At the threshold: The developing adolescent* (pp. 54–89). Cambridge, MA: Harvard University Press.

Kitchener, K. S., King, P. M., Wood, P. K., & Davidson, M. L. (1989). Sequentiality and consistency in the development of Reflective Judgment: A six-year longitudinal study. *Journal of Applied Developmental Psychology, 10*, 73–95.

Klaczynski, P. A. (1993). Reasoning schema effects on adolescent rule acquisition and transfer. *Journal of Educational Psychology, 85*, 679–692.

Klaczynski, P. A., Byrnes, J. E., & Jacobs, J. E. (2001). Introduction to the special issue on the development of decision-making. *Journal of Applied Developmental Psychology, 22*, 225–236.

Klaczynski, P. A., & Narasimham, G. (1998). Representations as mediators of adolescent deductive reasoning. *Developmental Psychology, 34*, 865–881.

Kosslyn, S. M., & Koenig, O. (1994). *Wet mind: The new cognitive neuroscience.* New York: Free Press.

Kuhn, D. (1992). Piaget's child as scientist. In H. Beilin & P. B. Pufall (Eds.), *Piaget's theory: Prospects and possibilities. The Jean Piaget symposium series* (pp. 185–208). Hillsdale, NJ: Erlbaum.

Kuhn, D., Garcia-Mila, M., Zohar, A., & Andersen, C. (1995). Strategies of knowledge acquisition. *Monographs of the Society for Research in Child Development, 60*, v-128.

Lehman, E. B., Morath, R., Franklin, K., & Elbaz, V. (1998). Knowing what to remember and forget: A developmental study of cue memory in intentional forgetting. *Memory & Cognition, 26*, 860–868.

Lester, F. K. (1975). Developmental aspects of children's ability to understand mathematical proof. *Journal for Research in Mathematics Education, 6*, 14–25.

Levine, G., Preddy, D., & Thorndike, R. L. (1987). Speed of information processing and level of cognitive ability. *Personality and Individual Differences, 8*, 599–607.

Lewis, C. (1981). How do adolescents approach decisions: Changes over grades seven to twelve and policy implications. *Child Development, 52*, 538–544.

List, J. A., Keating, D. P., & Merriman, W. E. (1985). Differences in memory retrieval: A construct validity investigation. *Child Development, 56*, 138–151.

Mareschal, D., & Shultz, T. R. (1996). Generative connectionist networks and constructivist cognitive development. *Cognitive Development, 11*, 571–603.

Merriman, W. E., Keating, D. P., & List, J. A. (1985). Mental rotation of facial profiles: Age-, sex-, and ability-related differences. *Developmental Psychology, 21*, 888–900.

Miller, D. C., & Byrnes, J. P. (2001). Adolescents' decision-making in social situations: A self-regulation perspective. *Journal of Applied Developmental Psychology, 22*, 237–256.

Moshman, D. (1998). Cognitive development beyond childhood. In W. Damon (Series Ed.), D. Kuhn & R. S. Siegler (Vol. Eds.), *Handbook of child psychology: Vol. 2. Cognition, language, and perception* (pp. 947–978). New York: Wiley.

Moshman, D., & Franks, B. A. (1986). Development of the concept of inferential validity. *Child Development, 57*, 153–165.

Nippold, M. A. (1994). Third-order verbal analogical reasoning: A developmental study of children and adolescents. *Contemporary Educational Psychology, 19*, 101–107.

Ormond, C., Luszcz, M. A., Mann, L., & Beswick, G. (1991). A metacognitive analysis of decision-making in adolescence. *Journal of Adolescence, 14*, 275–291.

Paniak, C., Murphy, D., Miller, H., & Lee, M. (1998). Wechsler memory scale-revised logical memory and visual reproduction norms for 9- and 15-year-olds. *Developmental Neuropsychology, 14*, 555–562.

Pascarella, E. T. (1999). The development of critical thinking: Does college make a difference? *Journal of College Student Development, 40*, 562–569.

Piaget, J. (1983). Piaget's theory. In P. H. Mussen (Series Ed.), W. Kessen (Volume Ed.), *Handbook of child psychology: Vol. 1: History, theory, and methods* (pp. 103–128). New York: Wiley.

Reese, C. M., Miller, K. E., Mazzeo, J., & Dossey, J. A. (1997). *The NAEP 1996 Mathematics Report Card for the Nation and the States*. Washington, DC: US Department of Education.

Schommer, M. (1998). The influence of age and education on epistemological beliefs. *British Journal of Educational Psychology, 68*, 551–562.

Schommer, M., Calvert, C., Gariglietti, G., & Bajaj, A. (1997). The development of epistemological beliefs among secondary students: A longitudinal study. *Journal of Educational Psychology, 89*, 37–40.

Scribner, S. (1997). Modes of thinking and ways of speaking: Culture and logic reconsidered. In E. Tobach, R. J. Falmagne, M. Parlee, L. M. W. Martin, & A. S. Kapelman (Eds.), *Mind and social practice: Selected writings of Sylvia Scribner* (pp. 125–144). New York: Cambridge University Press.

Seamon, J. G., Luo, C. R., Schlegel, S. E., Greene, S. E., & Goldenberg, A. B. (2000). False memory for categorized pictures and words: The category associates procedure for studying memory errors in children and adults. *Journal of Memory and Language, 42*, 120–146.

Sodian, B., Zaitchik, D., & Carey, S. (1991). Young children's differentiation of hypothetical beliefs from evidence. *Child Development, 62*, 753–766.

Squire, L. R., & Knowlton, B. J. (1995). Memory, hippocampus, and brain systems. In M. S. Gazzaniga (Ed.), *The cognitive neurosciences* (pp. 825–837). Cambridge MA: MIT Press.

Swanson, H. L. (1999). What develops in working memory? A life span perspective. *Developmental Psychology, 35*, 986–1000.

Sweller, J., & Cooper, G. A. (1985). The use of worked examples as a substitute for problem-solving in learning algebra. *Cognition and Instruction, 2,* 59–89.

Waber, D. P., Carlson, D., & Mann, M. (1982). Developmental and differential aspects of mental rotation in early adolescence. *Child Development, 53,* 1614–1621.

Waltz, J. A., Knowlton, B. J., Holyoak, K. J., Boone, K. B., Mishkin, F. S., de Menezes Santos, M., Thomas, C. R., & Miller, B. L. (1999). A system for relational reasoning in human pre-frontal cortex. *Psychological Science, 10,* 119–125.

Ward, S. L., Byrnes, J. P., & Overton, W. F. (1990). Organization of knowledge and conditional reasoning. *Journal of Educational Psychology, 82,* 832–837.

Ward, S. L. & Overton, W. F. (1990). Semantic familiarity, relevance, and the development of deductive reasoning. *Developmental Psychology, 26,* 488–493.

Wellman, H. M., & Gelman, S. A. (1998). Knowledge acquisition in foundational domains. In W. Damon (Series Ed.), D. Kuhn & R. S. Siegler (Vol. Eds.), *Handbook of child psychology: Vol. 2. Cognition, language, and perception* (pp. 524–573). New York: Wiley.

Wood, E., Willoughby, T., McDermott, C., Motz, M., Kaspar, V., & Ducharme, M. J. (1999). Developmental differences in study behavior. *Journal of Educational Psychology, 91,* 527–536.

Zald, D. H., & Iacono, W. G. (1998). The development of spatial working memory abilities. *Developmental Neuropsychology, 14,* 563–578.

CHAPTER TWELVE

Moral Development during Adolescence

Judith G. Smetana and Elliot Turiel

Introduction

During the 1920s, many social commentators in the United States were convinced that the nation was in serious moral decline. In large measure, the decline was blamed on American youth (including adolescents and young adults), because they abandoned traditional values, no longer respected authority, and gave in to their own interests and embraced individualistic concerns (Fass, 1977). At the same time, other social commentators believed that changes in the attitudes and behaviors of youth reflected a moral advance in that they were willing to defy authority and traditional norms in the service of fairness, equality, and self-determination. Such contrasting views of adolescence are common throughout the twentieth century and appear in many research findings. During the 1960s, for instance, American youth (adolescents as well as post-adolescents) were derided by some for their selfishness, lack of values, and radical individualism, whereas others praised their moral commitments to alleviating racism and poverty and their efforts to bring an end to a war.

In turn, during the late 1980s and the 1990s, a number of commentators have maintained that society is experiencing moral crisis and breakdown that has led to a rising tide of juvenile delinquency, adolescent drug and alcohol use, and teenage pregnancy and childbearing (Bennett, 1992; Whitehead, 1993; Wynne, 1986). In a similar vein, several sociologists have maintained that American society is in a state of moral confusion and decline, which has resulted from a lack of commitment to personal responsibility and an increased focus on personal goals and individual rights (Bellah et al., 1985; Etzioni, 1993; Putnam, 2000). American adolescents, we are told, are at the forefront of radical individualism, and this state of affairs needs to be remedied by renewing our commitments to community and society. Others, however, have argued that social commitments have not declined (Ladd, 1999) and that the nation's youth cannot be characterized as individualistic or detached from responsibility (Youniss, McLellan, & Yates, 1997; Youniss & Yates, 1997).

Research on social and moral development has yielded findings that appear to show that adolescents have similar conflicting orientations to morality. On the one side it seems that adolescents become highly relativistic and that they embrace a nihilistic approach to morality. Specifically, some findings suggest that adolescents maintain the view that moral values are arbitrary, that any position taken by individuals or groups is as valid as any other, and that people should be free to believe and do as they wish (Kohlberg, 1984; Kohlberg & Kramer, 1969; Perry, 1968). Yet, several analyses of moral development propose that understandings of society's moral underpinnings are first formed during adolescence (Colby & Kohlberg, 1987), and that principled moral judgments emerge in late adolescence (Kohlberg & Gilligan, 1971). Others have proposed that prosocial commitments emerge in adolescence (Eisenberg, 1990) and that an orientation toward care in interpersonal relationships also develops during adolescence (Gilligan, 1982).

A good deal of the research on morality in the adolescent years has been conducted in the context of efforts to examine transformations in moral judgments from childhood to adulthood. Kohlberg and his colleagues, who extended Piaget's (1932/1965) research on moral judgments in childhood to later ages, proposed that prior to adolescence, children are premoral. Eisenberg and her colleagues have examined an aspect of moral reasoning – prosocial judgments – that they believed was omitted in the previous research focusing on reasoning about rules and prohibitions. Gilligan and her colleagues also have focused on aspects of morality they believed were ignored in previous work – caring (as opposed to justice) in interpersonal relationships.

In this chapter, we review each of these approaches and research findings. It is necessary, however, to consider social commentators' claims that adolescents are individualistic and lack moral commitments, as well as the research findings that they are relativistic and nihilistic in their judgments. It is also necessary to explain these seemingly contradictory views of adolescents. Adolescents may simply maintain both orientations and live with (or are unaware of) the contradictions. Instead, our view is that an alternative theoretical approach to social and moral development is needed to reconcile the conflicting perspectives on adolescent morality. In reviewing empirical research we attempt to show that morality has been characterized too globally (e.g., in Kohlberg's formulation), thereby failing to account for other aspects of social judgments in development. In addition, such global characterizations have, in our view, inadequately characterized the development of moral judgments in childhood. Of course, this has implications for explanations of moral changes in adolescence. We propose that children develop moral judgments of welfare, justice, and rights, and in turn, that adolescents are not premoral in their moral judgments.

Moreover, the findings suggest that there is considerable diversity in adolescents' social and moral judgments and that adolescents' reasoning varies according to situational contexts. After discussing propositions on stages of moral and prosocial judgments and on caring, we provide an integrative framework for understanding this research evidence that considers adolescent moral development in the context of other developing social concepts. In contrast to the global stage view, we propose that adolescents' social judgments are heterogeneous and may focus on prescriptive judgments of justice, welfare and rights, judgments regarding society and social conventions, and judgments regarding personal goals and assertions of personal jurisdiction. Rather than viewing these as inconsistent or contradictory, we assert that these types of judgments are reflective of adolescents' social worlds and may be applied – separately or together – in situations of choice and conflict. Thus, to understand adolescent morality, researchers need to consider both developmental changes and situational variations in adolescents' social and moral judgments. A large number of studies have examined moral development during adolescence or have included adolescents as participants, along with younger children or older adults. Therefore, we cannot hope to provide an exhaustive review of the literature on adolescent moral development. Rather, we discuss research on a variety of topics that illustrates this position.

Are Adolescents Principled Moral Reasoners?

The dominant paradigm for research on adolescent moral development for several decades, reaching its peak in the 1970s and early 1980s, was Kohlberg's theory of moral judgment development (Colby & Kohlberg, 1987; Kohlberg, 1984). As is now well known, from responses to hypothetical dilemmas that opposed conflicting concerns with law, life, interpersonal obligations, trust, and authority, Kohlberg proposed that moral judgments develop through a series of six universal, sequential, and hierarchical stages of progressively more differentiated and integrated concepts of justice. His theory focused on the underlying structure of individuals' moral judgments rather than on the content, or particular decisions that children and adolescents made.

According to Kohlberg, moral judgments in middle and late childhood are structured by concerns with obedience, punishment avoidance, and instrumental needs (labeled "preconventional" reasoning and divided into two stages). Increased perspective-taking abilities were seen as liberating children from this external focus on obedience to authority and authority sanctions and leading to the development of broader interpersonal and societal perspectives on morality. At this next level, labeled "conventional" morality and consisting of two stages, moral judgments were seen as structured by an understanding of role obligations, interpersonal needs, and respect for societal rules and authority. Kohlberg described a further developmental level of "post-conventional" or principled moral judgments, structured by concerns with mutual respect, contractual arrangements among individuals and their rights and duties, and differentiated concepts of justice and rights.

The proposition that more advanced structures of thought emerge during the teenage years has rested partly on the claim that changes in adolescent moral structures are connected to the emergence of competencies in other domains, including the development of formal operational thought and the development of more advanced perspective-taking abilities. For instance, formal operational logic has been described as a "necessary but not sufficient" prerequisite for the development of principled moral reasoning. As formal operational logic (or, as recognized more recently, early formal operations) develops in early adolescence, early theorizing assumed that transitions to adolescence were marked by the emergence of principled moral judgments (Kohlberg & Gilligan, 1971).

Although Kohlberg's model focuses primarily on reasoning about prohibitions, Eisenberg has proposed a similar sequence in the development of prosocial moral reasoning, based on her extensive program of research (reviewed in Eisenberg, 1990, 1998). In this research, children and adolescents were presented with hypothetical dilemmas and asked to make judgments about whether it would be right to help or share with others, sometimes at a cost to the self, in situations where the influence of rules, laws, authorities, punishment, or formal obligations are minimized.

Eisenberg has described changes in prosocial moral reasoning in terms of a five-level sequence, with most of the changes seen as occurring prior to adolescence. More specifically, young children are hedonistic when reasoning about prosocial moral dilemmas, but during the elementary school years, there is an increase in reasoning, reflecting concern with others' approval. During the late elementary school years, reasoning about stereotypic conceptions of good and bad behavior, along with concerns with the approval or disapproval of others, increase in frequency. Preadolescence is characterized by increases in a self-reflective and empathic orientation that includes sympathetic concern for others and greater perspective-taking (Eisenberg, 1998). In the transition to adolescence, adolescents reason more in terms of internalized norms and values and positive affect related to living up to one's values (or guilt for not living up to values), as well as increased concern for others' rights, justice, and welfare. Although this sequence is viewed as reflecting developmentally more advanced modes of prosocial moral reasoning, these levels are not seen to reflect hierarchical and integrated structures, as Kohlberg has proposed. Therefore, individuals may use a variety of different levels in their reasoning, and reasoning can vary by situations and circumstances.

Longitudinal changes in moral and prosocial reasoning

Despite these claims, much of the research evidence from these perspectives has not provided compelling evidence that the majority of American adolescents develop principled moral reasoning or more internalized prosocial moral judgments. In Kohlberg's longitudinal research (Colby & Kohlberg, 1987), early adolescents were primarily found to be preconventional in their moral reasoning, and by middle adolescence, they remained preconventional or continued to demonstrate preconventional thinking as they transitioned to higher developmental stages. By late adolescence, nearly half of Kohlberg's participants remained at Stage 3, and for many adolescents, this stage of moral thought continued into adulthood. Principled moral reasoning, defined by Kohlberg as entailing understandings of rights and justice that are not contingent on societal conventions or rules, rarely emerged during adolescence, and conventional moral judgments, which best characterized the moral maturity levels of most adolescents in Kohlberg's and other studies, emerged at both the beginning or end of adolescence (Colby & Kohlberg, 1987). As Lapsley (1990) has concluded, these findings do not directly undermine Kohlberg's model of moral judgment development, but they do not clearly demonstrate that adolescence is a unique developmental period for the emergence of principled moral thought.

Likewise, longitudinal assessments following children from preschool ages through late adolescence (ages 19–20) have revealed a great deal of variation in the developmental pattern of prosocial moral judgments, although some general trends have been observed (Eisenberg, 1990, 1998). Consistent with Eisenberg's model, both interpersonally-oriented prosocial moral reasoning and stereotypic reasoning appear to peak in middle adolescence and then decrease in use in late adolescence and young adulthood. Also in line with predictions, both self-reflective and internalized reasoning have been found to increase in late adolescence. More surprisingly, however, the research also demonstrates increased use of lower level prosocial moral reasoning in late adolescence. For instance, several studies have demonstrated that hedonistic reasoning, which generally has been found to decline until early adolescence, increases from middle adolescence to late adolescence, particularly in situations where the cost of helping is high (Eisenberg, 1990, 1998). Thus, these findings suggest that presumably developmentally less mature hedonistic prosocial moral reasoning reemerges in late adolescence.

A similar set of findings were obtained from research on longitudinal changes, as measured by Kohlberg's methods. As first reported by Kohlberg and Kramer (1969), and reiterated later in relation to other longitudinal studies (Colby & Kohlberg, 1987), Kohlberg and his colleagues have found that a small but notable percentage of their middle-class samples dropped or regressed in their moral thinking between late high school and the first two years of college (e.g., between approximately 17 and 20 years of age). The adolescents who regressed generally had been the most advanced, typically scoring as having a mixture of conventional (Stage 4) and principled (Stage 5) reasoning. All of the change entailed a regression to Stage 2 instrumental relativism. These findings are inconsistent with the theory, in which stages are seen to represent progressively more equilibrated structures that are transformed with development. The findings could be interpreted to mean that the small proportion of adolescents who actually attain principled moral thought lose it quickly by the end of adolescence, to be replaced by the types of value relativism, situation ethics, and egoism so soundly censured by Bellah et al. (1985) and Etzioni (1993).

Gender differences in adolescent morality

Gilligan (1982) has criticized Kohlberg's theory of moral judgment as being biased against females and as underestimating the developmental maturity of girls' moral reasoning. She claimed that girls' moral reasoning, which is typically scored as Stage 3 interpersonal morality (in comparison to boys, whose reasoning is typically scored as Stage 4 law and order morality), actually represents a different, rather than less mature moral orientation. More specifically, Gilligan claimed that boys' morality is oriented toward rules, rights, and the self as an autonomous agent, whereas girls' morality is structured by care, entailing responsibility to others, the need to avoid harm, and the self as embedded in relationships. Gilligan asserted that the morality of care has been overlooked in theories of moral development because the prominent theorists were males and, in the case of Kohlberg, the theory was originally developed entirely on a sample of boys.

However, extensive reviews, as well as a meta-analysis of 80 studies that included males and females on Kohlberg's stages, have revealed few sex differences in moral stages, particularly when educational and occupational levels were controlled (Walker, 1984, 1991). Sex differences, though rare, favored females in childhood and early adolescence and favored males in late adolescence and young adulthood, although these differences were not significant in the meta-analysis (Walker, 1984). Moreover, along with Kohlberg's longitudinal studies, Walker found that neither males nor females developed to the stages of principled moral thought.

Gilligan's claim (1982) that girls' moral reasoning is oriented toward care rather than justice has received a great deal of research attention and scrutiny. Research on several primarily adolescent samples (that also included some young adults; Gilligan & Attanucci, 1988) has demonstrated that adolescent males and females use both justice and care orientations, although females focus on care somewhat more than do males. Moreover, the results of numerous studies testing Gilligan's claims have demonstrated that regardless of age, the patterns vary according to the situational contexts in which justice and care are assessed.

Walker (1991) has argued convincingly that sex differences in moral reasoning can be attributed primarily to differences in dilemma content, although in his longitudinal study of moral discussions in families, Walker (1991) found few sex differences in adolescents' reasoning about either hypothetical or actual moral dilemmas. Sex differences did emerge – but only in adults' reasoning about self-generated moral dilemmas, and these differences were entirely due to differences in dilemma content. Adult females' self-generated conflicts focused more on personal moral issues (involving specific individuals or groups with whom the participant had an ongoing and significant relationship), and these dilemmas were more likely to generate a care orientation. In contrast, adult males focused more on impersonal content (involving institutions or people whom the participant did not know well), which, in turn, more often elicited a justice orientation.

Further evidence for the situational or contextual basis for adolescents' moral orientations was found in a study specifically designed to examine the balance between justice and welfare in children and adolescents' moral reasoning (Smetana, Killen, & Turiel, 1991). This study found that both adolescent boys and girls gave greater priority to maintaining interpersonal obligations or justice concerns depending on the features of the situations. For instance, adolescents (as well as children) were more likely to favor maintaining interpersonal obligations when the interpersonal relationships were depicted as close (a friend rather than acquaintance) or when unfairness was minimized. However, when fairness was made more salient, adolescents gave less priority to maintaining interpersonal relationships. Therefore, the research indicated that there were considerable inconsistencies both within and across individuals in their reasoning that were not simply due to gender. Rather, the situational features of the dilemmas accounted for the variations.

Consistency in moral reasoning across contexts. Although a basic tenet of the theoretical paradigm used by Kohlberg (1984) is that stages are "structured wholes" and that individuals should demonstrate consistency across tasks and contexts in their developmental level of moral reasoning, the research evidence casts doubt on this assumption with regard to the particular stage sequence proposed by Kohlberg. Numerous findings indicate that adolescents reason at lower levels on alternative dilemmas to Kohlberg's standardized moral judgment dilemmas than on his standardized dilemmas. For instance, Gilligan and colleagues (1971) found that adolescents typically reasoned at Stage 2 when responding to sexual dilemmas, although the same individuals reasoned at Stage 4 when assessed on Kohlberg's standardized moral judgment interview. Similar results were reported by Krebs et al. (1991) using a variety of dilemmas focusing on drunk driving, business and free trade, and choices to engage in prosocial acts. In each of these cases, disparities between alternative and standardized dilemmas were frequently greater than a stage and typically entailed lower scores on the alternative dilemma than on Kohlberg's interview. Indeed, a high proportion of adolescents' moral reasoning on these dilemmas was scored as Stage 2 instrumental relativism.

Morality as a Distinct Domain of Social Knowledge

The sets of findings we have considered are, in significant ways, inconsistent with the theoretical frameworks from which they stem. In particular, there are greater variations by contexts and more judgments that appear contrary with the type of moral judgments expected. The findings also show greater contextual variations than would be expected from a global view like Kohlberg's. And, there are greater variations in justice and care judgments on the part of both males and females than expected from a gender-based view like the one Gilligan has proposed. The findings also show that adolescents make more relativistic and self-oriented judgments than would be expected if the shift from childhood to adolescence were one from premoral or preconventional judgments to an understanding of moral rules and authority.

These findings, however, are consistent with an alternative view of the development of moral judgments that places them alongside other domains of social and personal judgments that begin to form in early childhood. The contextual variations evident in the research with adolescents are, in this view, due to the application and coordination of different domains in situational contexts. The social world of adolescents is complex and entails different types of interactions, including those pertaining to justice, welfare, and rights (morality), to social organization, hierarchical structures, society, and social conventions, and to individuals' psychological reality and their attempts to gain a psychological understanding of self and others. These different types of social interactions and judgments have been described in what has come to be known as a domain-specificity perspective on moral and social development.

Kohlberg (Colby & Kohlberg, 1987; Kohlberg, 1984) has proposed that the process of development involves the gradual differentiation of principles of justice or rights from nonmoral (e.g., conventional, pragmatic, and prudential) concerns. In contrast to this assertion, an extensive body of research has demonstrated that an understanding of justice, welfare, and rights develops early in ontogenesis (see Smetana, 1995b, Tisak, 1995; Turiel,

1983, 1998 for reviews of research supporting these claims) and is differentiated through-out development from other social concepts, including concepts of social convention and personal issues.

In this view, morality regulates the social interactions and social relationships of individuals within societies and is defined as individuals' prescriptive moral understanding of how people ought to behave toward each other. Prescriptive moral judgments are based on concepts of welfare (harm), justice, and rights. Children and adolescents across a broad age range have been found to evaluate moral issues as prescriptive, obligatory, generalizable, and independent of authority sanctions or punishment. Thus, moral transgressions are seen as wrong because of their features, like their consequences for others' rights and welfare.

However, not all social concepts are moral. Moral concepts differ both analytically and empirically from individuals' understanding of social organization, social systems, and social conventions. Social conventions have been defined as the arbitrary, agreed-on, and shared regularities that coordinate the interactions of individuals within social systems and that thereby promote the smooth and efficient functioning of social groups. Social conventional acts themselves are arbitrary in that alternative actions could serve the same function; thus they are relative to the social context. In different social systems, conventional regularities may differ and yet serve the same symbolic function of providing individuals with a set of expectations regarding appropriate behavior. Although moral prescriptions are an aspect of social organization, they are not defined by social organization, but rather are determined by factors inherent to social interactions (Gewirth, 1978; Turiel, 1983, 1998). This distinction between morality and convention is consistent with philosophical analyses of morality (cf. Dworkin, 1978; Gewirth, 1978; Rawls, 1971).

Morality also has been distinguished conceptually from individuals' psychological knowledge, or their attempts to understand the self and others as psychological systems. Personal issues are one aspect of psychological knowledge that bears in important ways on the scope and nature of morality. Although concepts of rights and rights claims are an integral aspect of morality, it has been proposed that rights are grounded in individuals' attempts to establish and maintain a sense of personal agency (Dworkin, 1978; Gewirth, 1978; Nucci, 1996; Nucci & Turiel, 2000). In turn, personal agency may be exercised when asserting control and making claims about personal issues. Personal issues pertain only to the actor and therefore are considered to be outside the realm of conventional regulation and moral concern (Nucci, 1996; Smetana, 1995b; Turiel, 1983, 1998); indeed, the right to make autonomous decisions is an aspect of the self that forms the boundary between the self and the social world. Issues of personal choice are part of the private aspects of one's life and entail issues of preference and choice. They are seen as psychologically necessary in maintaining a sense of agency and uniqueness.

Morality, social conventions, and psychological knowledge develop from children's and adolescents' differentiated social experiences and social interactions (for evidence in support of this claim, see Smetana, 1995b; Tisak, 1995; Turiel, 1998). A number of observational studies of children's naturally occurring interactions have described the types of differentiated social interactions that are thought to lead to the development of moral, conventional, and personal knowledge (Smetana, 1995b). Social domain theory proposes that morality, social convention, and personal issues are separate, self-regulating developmental and conceptual systems. Much of the research from the domain perspective has focused on how children, adolescents, and adults differentiate and coordinate different types of social concepts in their judgments and justifications. In the studies of domain differentiation, children and adolescents typically are presented with stimuli viewed as prototypical of the domains and are asked to judge the stimuli on a set of theoretical criteria hypothesized to differentiate the domains (e.g., universalizability, unalterability, and independence from rules and authority in the case of morality, and contextual relativity, alterability, and contingency on rules and authority in the case of conventions). This research has provided strong support for the claim that from early childhood on, children differentiate among different types of social events, acts, and transgressions. To a lesser extent, research has examined the developmental trajectory of concepts within each domain.

The research indicates that moral concerns in middle childhood with strict equality and equal treatment between persons (Davidson, Turiel, & Black, 1983; Nucci, 2001) are transformed in preadolescence into a concern with equity, or an understanding that fair treatment may entail unequal treatment when considering individual differences in needs and statuses (Damon, 1977, 1980; Nucci, 2001). Early adolescents continue to consolidate their moral understanding of equity and equality (Nucci, 2001), and combined with the prescriptive and universalizable element of morality, are more readily able to extend their moral concepts of fairness and welfare to abstract others and beyond their own group. During middle adolescence, concepts of fairness become more broadly comprehensive and universally applicable. Thus, moral reasoning during adolescence becomes both more generalizable across situations and more able to take situational variations into account.

In contrast, the development of conventional knowledge entails a progressive understanding of conventions as functional to societal regulation and social order and an increasing understanding of society as a hierarchically structured social system (Turiel, 1983). However, conventional understanding develops through a series of successive oscillations between affirmations and negations of the importance of conventions in structuring social life (Turiel, 1983). During early and late adolescence, conventions are negated as "nothing but" the arbitrary dictates of authority (in early adolescence) or the expectations of society (in late adolescence). These findings suggest that what has been described as regression in late adolescents' moral concepts can be understood, instead, in terms of coordinations between adolescents' developing concepts of morality, social convention, and personal jurisdiction (Nucci & Turiel, 2000).

Coordinations in Moral and Social Concepts

The hypothetical situations in the interview developed by Kohlberg posed participants with different moral considerations such as stealing and the value of life. They also involve situations where moral considerations (for instance, stealing) are pitted against a conventional concern (such as obeying a parent). Rather than reflecting downward shifts in adolescents' moral thinking and an apparent increase in moral relativism, Kohberg's obser-vations of late adolescents' moral thinking may instead be related to the multifaceted (mixed moral and conventional) nature of the dilemmas that adolescents were asked to consider. Instead of indicating regression to Stage 2 instrumental relativism, Kohlberg and Kramer's (1969) findings appear to reflect adolescents' systematic attempts to coor-dinate their developing moral conceptions of justice and rights with their understanding of society, conventions, and social systems (Nucci, 2001; Turiel, 1974, 1977). Conflicts and confusions occur as adolescents attempt to differentiate and integrate their under-standing of morality as autonomous and universally applicable with their developing understandings of conventions as arbitrary, relativistic, and serving societal functions (Turiel, 1974). In particular, what Kolhberg and Kramer (1969) characterized as regres-sion in adolescents' moral thinking instead appears to entail adolescents' inability to coordinate (and researchers' inability to differentiate) between adolescents' developing understanding of morality as increasingly universal and broadly applicable, with their developing understanding of social conventions. Social conventions take a turn toward negation during late adolescence and are seen as "nothing but" societal standards that are codified through habitual use (Nucci, 2001). In contrast, the affirmations of convention that characterize adolescents' understanding of social conventions at both earlier and later developmental phases, along with adolescents' more universally applicable conceptions of morality, appear to have been treated by researchers as illustrations of principled moral reasoning.

Analyses of structural changes in moral concepts may be important to an under-standing of adolescents' moral development. However, this example (and the findings of distinct social domains, more generally) suggests that a thorough account of adolescent development must entail analyses of how adolescents coordinate moral and nonmoral (e.g., conventional, personal, or practical or pragmatic) issues in their thinking. Indeed, the distinctive features of adolescent social development may pertain to how adolescents weigh and coordinate competing moral and nonmoral concerns in different types of social situations – and the novel types of social situations that adolescents encounter as they venture beyond the family into the world of peer groups. The different attributions that have been made about the nature of adolescent morality (as principled or autonomous versus relativistic or egoistic) may be related to a general failure in much research to sep-arate different types of social concepts in adolescents' thinking and to consider how ado-lescents apply their moral, conventional, and personal knowledge in social situations. Some examples of this are provided later in the chapter.

Adolescents' social world is complex. Although this is obvious, a less obvious obser-vation is that in straightforwardly moral situations, adolescents may generally think and act morally. That is, the overwhelming majority of adolescents routinely refrain from hitting, hurting, killing, stealing, maiming, acting dishonestly, or harassing others, although countless opportunities exist on a daily basis to do so. Although these situations may not require extensive moral reflection, adolescents' ability to desist from these acts may reflect more than merely moral "habits" (e.g., Damon, 1988), but rather, evaluations that morality ought to be upheld. Furthermore, many of the issues that are contested during adolescence may not be moral issues at all, as research on parental authority and adolescent–parent conflict illustrates. This research indicates that morality may be upheld in some situations and that conflicts may occur at the intersection between other domains. This research also indicates that adolescents' judgments about what they consider to be areas of personal jurisdiction loom large. The research on parental authority strongly suggests that the coordination of the personal with morality and social convention is central in the social lives of adolescents.

Adolescent Judgments of Legitimate Adult Authority

A number of studies have examined adolescents' judgments of the legitimacy of different adult authorities to make rules about hypothetical moral, social conventional, and personal issues (see Smetana, 1995a for a review). The findings from this research are highly consistent. They indicate that across the second decade of life, adolescents of varying ethnicities and cultural backgrounds overwhelmingly view moral issues as legitimately regulated by adults – and that they are obligated to obey parental moral rules, once established. However, adolescents' judgments of adults as legitimate moral authorities are contextually bounded. For instance, research has indicated that adolescents are nearly unanimous in viewing parents as having the moral authority to regulate moral acts in the home, but not in school. In contrast, teachers and principals are seen as having the legitimate authority to regulate adolescents' moral behavior in school, but not at home.

The conclusion that adolescents generally view adults as having the legitimate authority to regulate (contextually appropriate) moral issues is supported by research indicating that moral issues are also infrequent sources of conflict in adolescent–parent relationships (reviewed in Smetana, 1995a, 2002). Across numerous studies, adolescents and parents in different cultures rarely reason about actual conflicts in moral terms. Moral conflicts pertained primarily to adolescents' interpersonal relationships with siblings or friends; these issues became conflicts with parents only when parents were drawn in as third parties to settle the disputes. Thus, these findings, as well as the research on adolescents' conceptions of legitimate adult authority, suggest that moral issues are not contentious in parent–adolescent relationships because adults' (contextually appropriate) moral authority is rarely challenged (although we would expect it to be challenged when parents take unjust positions).

However, the research also illustrates that adolescents challenge adults' authority on other fronts. A number of studies have revealed that adolescents of varying ethnicities (including Chinese American, Mexican American, and Filipino American adolescents described by Fuligni, 1998 and African American adolescents described by Smetana, 2000) uniformly judge that parents do not have the legitimate authority to regulate personal issues and preferences, while the majority of parents disagree with these judgments. Parents generally believe themselves to have legitimate authority over acts that adolescents view as within their personal domain.

Moreover, these findings are echoed in the research on adolescent–parent conflict, which indicates that adolescents and parents have different views of disputes. Parents justify their perspectives on conflicts by appealing to social conventions or to pragmatic concerns, whereas adolescents primarily appeal to exercising or maintaining personal jurisdiction (see Smetana, 1995a, 2002; Smetana & Gaines, 1999). An extensive and growing body of research has demonstrated that although the boundaries and content of the personal domain may be canalized by culture, adolescents in Western and non-Western cultures alike assert a personal domain (see reviews by Killen, McGlothlin, & Lee-Kim, 2002; Nucci, 1996; Smetana, 2002). One interpretation of these findings is that adolescents' appeals to personal jurisdiction reflect the individualistic orientation of American culture, with its focus on personal goals, individual rights, and personal agency (Bellah et al., 1985).

But the research findings are inconsistent with this account, because appeals to personal jurisdiction have been found among adolescents in varying cultural and ethnic contexts, including ones that are described as prototypically collectivist. This has included Chinese adolescents in Hong Kong and mainland China (Yau & Smetana, 1996, 2001), as well as American adolescents from Chinese American, Mexican American, and Filipino backgrounds (Fuligni, 1998). Thus, these findings do not appear to reflect a selfish or hedonistic focus on personal goals and individual rights, as the social commentators described at the outset of the chapter have asserted. Rather, this research is consistent with several other lines of investigation that have demonstrated that appeals to personal jurisdiction reflect an aspect of children's developing social knowledge and serve an important psychological function. For instance, as reviewed elsewhere (Killen, McGlothlin, & Lee-Kim, 2002; Nucci, 2001; Smetana, 2002), a growing number of studies have indicated that from early ages on, children assert claims to an arena of personal discretion and personal freedom, and these claims are not restricted to North American samples. Similar findings have been obtained in diverse cultures, although judgments of personal choice and personal entitlements have been found to vary as a function of several variables, including where in the social hierarchy one stands (see Nucci, 2001; Smetana, 2002; Turiel, 2002 for more discussion of these issues). Furthermore, mothers in diverse cultural and ethnic contexts (see Smetana, 2002 for a review) have been found to endorse an arena of personal control as important for their children's development.

Thus, the research on adolescent–parent conflict indicates that rather than reflecting egoistic or selfish moral orientations, adolescents' appeals to personal jurisdiction serve to increase adolescents' agency, or enlarge their sphere of personal action, and thus reflect adolescents' developing autonomy or distinctiveness from others (see Nucci & Turiel, 2000, Smetana, 1995a, 2002 for elaboration). Adolescents' appeals to personal jurisdiction in the context of adolescent–parent conflict provide a mechanism for renegotiating and enlarging the boundaries of adolescents' authority over the self. It is important to recognize that parents and adolescents do not simply have different conceptions of the personal realm. Many of the activities that adolescents judge as personal are also considered personal by parents – but as applicable to individuals older than their offspring. Indeed, the research demonstrates that activities parent think they should control for their young adolescents are left to personal choice on the part of their older adolescents (Smetana, 2002).

In the research on parental authority, clear distinctions were made among moral, conventional, and personal issues and justifications. But not all situations can be evaluated as solely moral or nonmoral. Many situations may be ambiguous from a moral point of view. For instance, research from the domain perspective suggests that in the research where Kohlberg's stage model was applied to adolescents' reasoning about sexuality or other issues such as fair trade and business practices, the issues investigated in the alternative dilemmas may have been morally ambiguous or may not have been construed as moral issues at all.

Before assuming that reasoning about an issue can be analyzed for moral judgments, it is first necessary to ascertain the types of social knowledge that are applied, and whether individuals view the action as morally relevant. (Our concern here is whether adolescents view an issue as within or outside the moral realm – using theoretically derived criteria to define morality rather than adolescents' naïve moral theories – and not whether they view a particular act or behavior as moral or immoral or right or wrong.) Research on adolescents' evaluations of risk-taking behaviors provides a useful illustration of this issue.

Adolescent Moral Reasoning in Situations of Risk

Adolescence has been described as a time of increased risk-taking (Baumrind, 1987), and risk-taking behaviors such as alcohol and substance use have enormous consequences to society. Most of the available research has focused on the parenting and personality factors that predict increased risk, but a growing number of studies have examined whether adolescents' conceptions of these issues are informed by moral concerns.

In several studies (Berkowitz, Guerra, & Nucci, 1991; Killen, Leviton, & Cahill, 1991; Nucci, Guerra, & Lee, 1991), adolescents of various ages have been asked to classify behaviors related to alcohol and substance use (such as use of alcohol, caffeine, nicotine, marijuana, cocaine, and crack) as moral or nonmoral (and pertaining to conventions, personal choice, or prudential concerns) and to rate their harmfulness to self and others. In general, the studies indicate that the "harder" the drug, the more likely it is to be classified as moral, based on adolescents' justifications and their judgments that the acts are right or wrong regardless of existing laws. The more harmful adolescents rated the drug to be, the more likely they were to use moral justifications. Although the classification of particular drugs varies somewhat from study to study, use of crack and cocaine was generally viewed as a moral transgression. In contrast, in different studies, smoking cigarettes, occasional drinking, use of nicotine, and caffeine were overwhelmingly seen as matters of personal choice or as prudentially acceptable ("all right, but foolish because it harms you"; Nucci, Guerra, & Lee, 1991). The majority of adolescents judging drug use as acceptable also endorsed individuals' right to harm themselves, but not when the acts were described as having negative consequences for others (Killen, Leviton, & Cahill, 1991).

Furthermore, adolescents' views of drugs were related to their level of drug use. High drug users were more likely than low drug users to view drug use as a personal rather than a prudential issue and to view drug use as less harmful and less wrong (Nucci, Guerra, & Lee, 1991). Moreover, Berkowitz, Guerra, and Nucci (1991) found that adolescents who viewed substance use as a moral issue were more likely to rate the behavior as harmful to self and others, which in turn was related to less frequent use of that substance. Judgments of harmfulness predicted whether adolescents categorize substance use (alcohol, cigarettes, and marijuana) as moral or not, and domain categorization, in turn, significantly predicted substance use (Berkowitz et al., 1998). Lower levels of moral reasoning predicted substance use only when the issue was categorized as moral.

Thus, adolescents' categorization of alcohol and substance use as moral issues (using theoretical and definitional criteria to define morality) was related to their beliefs about whether these behaviors are harmful to self and others. These findings are consistent with recent research, which has demonstrated that individuals' informational assumptions, or the facts, beliefs, or theories they hold about the social world, are clearly separable from individuals' moral evaluations (Wainryb, 1991) and that altering informational assumptions can change moral evaluations by changing the meaning of the acts.

Separating the moral, conventional, and personal components of acts also helps understanding of how features of situations affect judgments, including whether issues are moral or nonmoral. Moral decisions become problematic primarily in situations where the moral status of the situation is ambiguous or contested or where moral concerns come into conflict with other types of considerations. In some situational contexts, moral concerns may predominate, and adolescent moral thinking may be autonomous. For instance, Helwig (1995b) has proposed that there may be a general developmental pattern where increasingly more abstract and complex moral concepts are applied first in straightforward moral situations, and then in complex or multifaceted situations, entailing conflicts between moral and conventional concerns. As described in the following section, this pattern has been obtained in several different programs of research, including research on adolescents' conceptions of civil liberties and research on exclusion and inclusion in social groups.

Coordinations in Adolescent Reasoning

Educating adolescents for citizenship and participation in democracy has been identified as an important goal of character and moral education programs for adolescents (Berkowitz & Fekula, 1999). Therefore, there has been a call for more research linking adolescents' ideas about society and fair government to adolescents' developing moral concepts (Torney-Purta, 1990). However, recent research has indicated the importance of separating moral concerns with justice or rights from conventional concepts. Employing such an approach, recent research on adolescents' conceptions of civil liberties has provided a way of clarifying inconsistencies found in previous research, as well as contributing to an understanding of developmental processes in adolescent morality.

Previous survey research on Americans' attitudes toward civil liberties (discussed extensively in Turiel, Killen, & Helwig, 1987) indicates that although individuals support freedoms and rights when questions about these issues are posed abstractly, the same individuals express substantially less support when civil liberties are described in various concrete contexts. Such findings have been viewed as indicating adolescents' lack of principled moral thinking. In contrast, Helwig (1995a) has proposed that these findings reflect conflicts between various moral concepts and principles applied in complex situations.

To test this proposition, Helwig (1995a) asked adolescents (7th- and 11th-graders and college students) to reason and make judgments about two examples of civil liberties (freedom of speech and freedom of religion) presented in different types of situations. He found that when civil liberties were decontextualized and presented abstractly or when they were presented in contextualized situations where there were no other competing moral concerns, early adolescents displayed sophisticated conceptions of civil liberties; they nearly unanimously endorsed civil liberties and judged them using moral criteria.

However, concepts of civil liberties were not fully applied when early adolescents judged situations where freedom and rights were described as in conflict with laws and equality. In these multifaceted situations, freedom of speech and religion were less likely to be affirmed and more likely to be subordinated to other concerns. In general, older adolescents gave priority to civil liberties across a broader range of situations than did younger adolescents. Late adolescents were better able to integrate their evaluations of legal systems and acts and evaluate both legal restrictions on rights and acts violating restrictive laws from the perspective of abstract rights. Furthermore, when judging multifaceted situations that depicted conflicts between concerns pertaining to rights versus equality (e.g., between competing moral concerns), older adolescents were better able to coordinate their notions of equality with differences in individuals, as would be predicted from Nucci's (2001) account of developmental changes in moral concepts. Thus, these findings indicate that judgments that appear to entail exceptions to general principles may be explained in terms of conflicts in multifaceted situations. In this study, failures to endorse civil liberties in early adolescence were due to adolescents' difficulties in coordinating different principles and concerns in their social judgments, and these abilities increased from early to late adolescence.

A similar developmental pattern has been observed in recent research on children's and adolescents' (7–13-year-olds') judgments of inclusion and exclusion from social groups (Killen & Stangor, 2001). This research examined evaluations of acts that entailed peer-group exclusion based on stereotypes regarding gender or race. The researchers first identified a set of peer-group activities that are gender- (e.g., doing ballet or playing baseball) or racially-stereotyped (e.g., doing math or playing basketball). Then, study participants were asked to evaluate and justify different types of peer exclusion (e.g., boys excluding girls or white children excluding a black child). Consistent with Helwig's (1995a) findings, the research revealed that when the acts were presented in straightforward contexts with no other competing concerns, children across ages applied moral concepts and evaluated the acts as wrong, regardless of whether or not the acts conformed to stereotypes.

The situations also were presented in multifaceted situations. Participants made judgments either about two children who were equally qualified or unequally qualified in that a child who fit the stereotype was better at the activity. In these conditions, children made clear distinctions. When children were described as equally qualified, most children picked the child who did not fit the stereotype, based on moral concerns with equal treatment. Overall, when choices pertained to unequal qualifications, children and adolescents selected the child who was better qualified, based on (conventional) concerns with group processes. However, early adolescents were more likely than preadolescents to attempt to coordinate moral concerns of fairness with – conventional concerns with group processes (with greater emphasis given to group processes among early adolescents). In other words, although there were variations in social judgments about inclusion and exclusion from social groups, adolescents became increasingly able to weigh and coordinate both moral and conventional concerns in complex situations where they conflicted.

Another interesting finding emerged from this research. In both straightforward and multifaceted contexts, girls were more consistently concerned with fairness and equal access than were boys. These findings are in contrast to Gilligan's (1982) hypothesis that concerns with fairness characterize the moral orientation of boys rather than girls. Killen and Stangor (2001) hypothesized that these findings may be due to girls' greater experiences with, and hence sensitivity to, the moral aspects of exclusion.

An extension of this research provides indirect support for this notion. Horn (in press) examined how adolescents' identification with either high- versus low-status peer groups (cheerleaders, jocks, or preppies versus dirties, druggies, and gothics) influenced their judgments of peer-group inclusion and exclusion. Adolescents who belonged to high-status groups judged exclusion from peer groups as less wrong than did adolescents who either did not belong to a group or who belonged to low-status groups. Thus, moral concepts of fairness or equal treatment were influenced both by the moral parameters of the situation as well as adolescents' position in the social hierarchy.

These findings are consistent with findings obtained in an extensive body of cross-cultural research on judgments of rights and personal choices among the Druze in Israel, who live in a hierarchical society (described in Turiel, 1998, 2002). This research indicated that children's, adolescents', and adults' evaluations of the fairness of different social arrangements depends on where in the social hierarchy one stands. Those in subordinate roles (e.g., females), who experienced greater restrictions in their choices and freedoms as a function of their social position, evaluated certain social practices as more unfair than did those in more dominant positions, who may be accorded greater entitlements and choices (Wainryb & Turiel, 1994). Along with Horn (in press), these findings demonstrate the complexity and heterogeneity of moral and social judgments that is not captured by schemes that describe morality as developing in a series of hierarchical stages. The studies just reviewed indicate the importance of considering moral judgments as intertwined but separable from other types of social concepts.

Moral commitment and community service

A final question is whether the development of principled moral judgments and concepts of society should be facilitated among adolescents. It has been speculated that providing adolescents with opportunities to engage in community service and to reflect on and discuss their experiences may facilitate greater moral commitment (Hart et al., 1995). Service programs are becoming increasingly common in high schools and are seen as having a positive impact on the community, as well as on participating youth. Indeed, in contrast to the highly publicized recent claims that American youth are demonstrating less commitment to personal responsibility, and increased self-interest and individualism (Bellah et al., 1985; Etzioni, 1993), national survey data indicate that nearly two-thirds of high school seniors have participated at least occasionally in community service over the previous year and that rates of participation in community service have not changed since the mid-1970s (Youniss & Yates, 1997).

Yates and Youniss (1996; Youniss & Yates, 1997) have hypothesized that the opportunity to engage in critical reflection and discussion of the issues and conflicts that arise while engaging in community service facilitates political and moral understanding. To test this hypothesis, they examined the effects of reflective discussion of participation in community service in a sample of socioeconomically mixed, primarily African American middle adolescents in Washington, DC. Adolescents participated in community service (serving food to the homeless in a soup kitchen) over the course of a year. Youniss and Yates (1997) have asserted that adolescents' experiences led to increased compassion, greater interdependence, and broader conceptions of justice. Comparisons of students' essays describing their experiences, collected over a three-month period, revealed increases in "transcendent" reasoning, reflecting greater understanding of justice and responsibility and more theorizing about society or political processes (Yates & Youniss, 1996). This research suggests that involvement in service learning, combined with critical reflection on those experiences, can positively affect adolescents' understanding of justice (morality), society and societal functioning (social conventions), and developing psychological knowledge and self-esteem, and that these effects may continue into adulthood (Youniss, McLellan, & Yates, 1997).

Summary and Conclusions

The research reviewed in this chapter suggests that there is considerable contextual variability and heterogeneity in adolescents' moral and social thinking. Adolescents are not consistently principled moral thinkers, as some have claimed, nor are they morally confused and selfish individualists, as others have asserted. Adolescents make autonomous moral judgments in some situations and focus on personal goals in others.

We have proposed that adolescent moral development must be understood within the broader context of adolescents' developing social knowledge. In thinking about the social world or deciding on the right course of action, adolescents bring to bear their moral knowledge, which can be in conflict with or subordinated to other types of social concerns. Moral concerns may be uncontested in some social situations, while conflicts in social judgments may occur at the boundaries between other domains, as the research on adolescent–parent relationships demonstrated. Other social situations may be morally ambiguous and depend on one's informational assumptions, for instance about whether an act causes harm, as illustrated by the research on adolescents' conceptions of alcohol and substance abuse. Many social situations are multifaceted and require individuals to weigh and coordinate moral and nonmoral (e.g., personal, prudential, conventional, or pragmatic) concerns.

Thus, we have proposed that an adequate account of the variability in adolescents' moral thinking and decision making must include a consideration of adolescents' social and moral judgments in interaction with the contextual features of situations. This interaction may lead adolescents to endorse moral concerns in some situations and to subordinate or coordinate them in others. The development of adolescents' moral thinking entails their ability to apply more abstract and complex moral concepts in complex or multifaceted situations involving conflicts between moral and other social or nonsocial concerns.

Key Readings

Colby, A., & Kohlberg, K. (Eds.) (1987). *The measurement of moral judgment* (2 Vols.). New York: Cambridge University Press.
These volumes provide a comprehensive description of Kohlberg's theory of the development of moral judgments. They also include a detailed description of interviews used in assessing moral judgments, interviews and procedures for scoring in accord with Kohlberg's scheme of six stages, and evidence for the reliability and validity of the methods. Several chapters describe the results of longitudinal, cross-cultural studies, including Kohlberg's original, 20-year longitudinal study of moral development in US males.

Eisenberg, N. (1990). Prosocial development during early and mid-adolescence. In R. Montemayor, G. R. Adams, & T. P. Gullotta (Eds.), *From childhood to adolescence: A transitional period?* (pp. 240–268). Newbury Park, CA: Sage.
This chapter provides an overview of theoretical issues in studying prosocial development during adolescence and reviews relevant empirical research examining age-related changes in prosocial development across adolescence.

Helwig, C. C. (1995). Adolescents' and young adults' conceptions of civil liberties: Freedom of speech and religion. *Child Development, 66*, 152–166.
This article examines age-related changes in adolescents' conceptions of civil liberties. Previous research had conceptualized children's and adolescents' understanding of rights primarily in terms of qualitative shifts in the development of moral judgments. This study provides a perspective that considers how adolescents coordinate abstract conceptions of rights with their application in concrete situations.

Smetana, J. G. (1995). Context, conflict, and constraint in adolescent–parent authority relationships. In M. Killen & D. Hart (Eds.), *Morality in everyday life: Developmental perspectives* (pp. 225–255). Cambridge: Cambridge University Press.
This chapter challenges earlier theoretical accounts that view adolescent autonomy as a stage of thinking that develops from an earlier stage entailing parental constraint. Instead, theory and research are reviewed here in support of the view that different forms of adult authority coexist during childhood and adolescence, and that adolescents actively renegotiate the boundaries of adult authority.

Turiel, E. (2002). *The culture of morality: Social development, context, and conflict.* Cambridge: Cambridge University Press.
This book examines how explanations of social and moral development inform our understandings of morality and culture, and challenge commonly held views that dichotomize cultures as individualistic or collectivist. A position is presented that emphasizes the heterogeneity of moral and social judgments, as well as conflicts among people in different positions in the social hierarchy.

It is shown that people of lesser power, such as women and minorities, often oppose and try to change cultural arrangements.

Youniss, J., & Yates, M. (1997). *Community service and social responsibility in youth.* Chicago: University of Chicago Press.
This book reviews previous research on community service during adolescence and describes the results of the authors' research on the impact of community service on adolescents' moral development. Youniss and Yates provide a theoretical framework for understanding how engagement and reflection in community service may facilitate adolescents' moral conceptions.

References

Baumrind, D. (1987). A developmental perspective on adolescent risk taking in contemporary America. In C. E. Irwin, Jr. (Ed.), *New directions for Child Development: Adolescent social behavior and health* (pp. 93–125). San Francisco: Jossey-Bass.

Bellah, R. N., Madsen, R., Sullivan, W. M., Swidler, A., & Tipton, S. M. (1985). *Habits of the heart: Individualism and commitment in American life.* New York: Harper & Row.

Bennett, W. J. (1992). *The de-valuing of America: The fight for our culture and our children.* New York: Free Press.

Berkowitz, M. W., Guerra, N., & Nucci, L. (1991). Sociomoral development and drug and alcohol abuse. In J. L. Gewirtz & W. M. Kurtines (Eds.), *Handbook of moral behavior and development, Vol. 3: Applications* (pp. 35–53). Hillsdale, NJ: Erlbaum.

Berkowitz, M. W., & Fekula, M. J. (1999). Civics and moral education. In M. Ben-Peretz, S. Brown, & R. Moon (Eds.), *Routledge International Companion to Education* (pp. 897–909). London: Routledge.

Berkowitz, M. W., Giese, J. K., Begun, A., & Zweben, A. (1998, June). Sociomoral predictors of adolescent substance use: A structural equation analysis. Paper presented at the Jean Piaget Society, Chicago.

Colby, A., & Kohlberg, K. (Eds.) (1987). *The measurement of moral judgment* (2 Vols.). New York: Cambridge University Press.

Damon, W. (1977). *The social world of the child.* San Francisco: Jossey-Bass.

Damon, W. (1980). Patterns of change in children's social reasoning: A two-year longitudinal study. *Child Development, 51,* 1010–1017.

Damon, W. (1988). *The moral child: Nurturing children's natural moral growth.* New York: Free Press.

Davidson, P., Turiel, E., & Black, A. (1983). The effect of stimulus familiarity of criteria and justifications in children's social reasoning. *British Journal of Developmental Psychology, 1,* 49–65.

Dworkin, R. (1978). *Taking rights seriously.* Cambridge: Harvard University Press.

Eisenberg, N. (1990). Prosocial development during early and mid-adolescence. In R. Montemayor, G. R. Adams, & T. P. Gullotta (Eds.), *From childhood to adolescence: A transitional period?* (pp. 240–268). Newbury Park, CA: Sage.

Eisenberg, N. (1998). Prosocial development. In N. Eisenberg (Ed.), William Damon (Series Ed.), *Handbook of child psychology, 5th ed., Vol. 3: Social, emotional, and personality development* (pp. 701–778). New York: Wiley.

Etzioni, A. (1993). *The spirit of community: The reinvention of American society.* New York: Touchstone.

Fass, P. (1977). *The damned and the beautiful: American youth in the 1920's.* New York: Oxford University Press.

Fuligni, A. J. (1998). Authority, autonomy, and parent–adolescent conflict and cohesion: A study of adolescents from Mexican, Chinese, Filipino, and European backgrounds. *Developmental Psychology, 34,* 782–792.

Gewirth, A. (1978). *Reason and morality.* Chicago: University of Chicago Press.

Gilligan, C. (1982). *In a different voice.* Cambridge: Harvard University Press.

Gilligan, C., & Attanucci, J. (1988). Two moral orientations: Gender differences and similarities. *Merrill-Palmer Quarterly, 34,* 223–237.

Gilligan, C., Kohlberg, L., Lerner, J., & Belenky, M. (1971). Moral reasoning about sexual dilemmas. *Technical Report of the President's Commission on Obscenity and Pornography* (Vol. 1, pp. 141–174). Washington, DC: US Government Printing Office.

Hart, D., Yates, M., Fegley, S., & Wilson, G. (1995). Moral commitment in adolescence. In M. Killen & D. Hart (Eds.), *Morality in everyday life* (pp. 317–341). Cambridge: Cambridge University Press.

Helwig, C. C. (1995a). Adolescents' and young adults' conceptions of civil liberties: Freedom of speech and religion. *Child Development, 66,* 152–166.

Helwig, C. C. (1995b). Social context in social cognition: Psychological harm and civil liberties. In M. Killen & D. Hart (Eds.), *Morality in everyday life: Developmental perspectives* (pp. 166–200). Cambridge: Cambridge University Press.

Horn, S. S. (in press). Adolescents' reasoning about exclusion from social groups. *Developmental Psychology.*

Killen, M., Leviton, M., & Cahill, J. (1991). Social reasoning regarding drug use in adolescence. *Journal of Adolescent Research, 6,* 336–356.

Killen, M., McGlothlin, H., & Lee-Kim, J. (2002). Between individuals and culture: Individuals' evaluations of exclusion from social groups. In H. Keller, Y. Poortinga, & A. Schoelmerich (Eds.), *Between biology and culture: Perspectives on ontogenetic development* (pp.159–190). Cambridge: Cambridge University Press.

Killen, M., & Stangor, C. (2001). Children's social reasoning about inclusion and exclusion in gender and race peer group contexts. *Child Development, 72,* 174–186.

Kohlberg, L. (1984). *Essays on moral development: Vol. 2: The psychology of moral development.* San Francisco: Harper & Row.

Kohlberg, L., & Gilligan, C. (1971). The adolescent as philosopher: The discovery of self in a post-conventional world. *Daedalus, 110,* 1051–1086.

Kohlberg, L., & Kramer, R. (1969). Continuities and discontinuities in childhood and adult moral development. *Human Development, 12,* 93–120.

Krebs, D. L., Vermeulen, S. C. A., Carpendale, J. I., & Denton, K. (1991). Structural and situational influences on moral judgment: The interaction between stage and dilemma. In W. M. Kurtines & Jacob L. Gewirtz (Eds.), *Handbook of moral behavior and development: Vol. 2: Research* (pp. 139–169). Hillsdale, NJ: Erlbaum.

Ladd, E. C. (1999). *The Ladd report.* New York: Free Press.

Lapsley, D. K. (1990). Continuity and discontinuity in adolescent social cognitive development. In R. Montemayor, G. R. Adams, & T. P. Gullotta (Eds.), *From childhood to adolescence: A transitional period?* (pp. 183–204). Newbury Park, CA: Sage.

Nucci, L. P. (1996). Morality and personal freedom. In E. S. Reed, E. Turiel, & T. Brown (Eds.), *Values and knowledge* (pp. 41–60). Mahwah, NJ: Erlbaum.

Nucci, L. (2001). *Education in the moral domain.* Cambridge: Cambridge University Press.

Nucci, L. P., Guerra, N., & Lee, J. (1991). Adolescent judgments of the personal, prudential, and normative aspects of drug usage. *Developmental Psychology, 27,* 841–848.

Nucci, L. P., & Turiel, E. (2000). The moral and the personal: Sources of social conflict. In L. P. Nucci, G. Saxe, & E. Turiel (Eds.), *Culture, thought, and development* (pp. 115–137). Mahwah, NJ: Erlbaum.

Perry, W. (1968). *Forms of intellectual and ethical development in the college years.* New York: Holt, Rinehart, & Winston.

Piaget, J. (1932/1965). *The moral judgment of the child.* New York: Free Press.

Putnam, R. D. (2000). *Bowling alone: The collapse and revival of American community.* New York: Simon & Schuster.

Rawls, J. (1971). *A theory of justice.* Cambridge, MA: Cambridge University Press.

Smetana, J. G. (1995a). Context, conflict, and constraint in adolescent–parent authority relationships. In M. Killen & D. Hart (Eds.), *Morality in everyday life: Developmental perspectives* (pp. 225–255). Cambridge: Cambridge University Press.

Smetana, J. G. (1995b). Morality in context: Abstractions, ambiguities, and applications. In R. Vasta (Ed.), *Annals of child development* (Vol. 10, pp. 83–130). London: Jessica Kingsley.

Smetana, J. G. (2000). Middle class African American adolescents' and parents' conceptions of parental authority and parenting practices: A longitudinal investigation. *Child Development, 71,* 1672–1686.

Smetana, J. G. (2002). Culture, autonomy, and personal jurisdiction in adolescent–parent relationships. In H. W. Reese & R. Kail (Eds.), *Advances in child development and behavior, Vol. 29* (pp. 51–87). New York: Academic.

Smetana, J. G., & Gaines, C. (1999). Adolescent–parent conflict in middle class African American families. *Child Development, 70,* 1447–1463.

Smetana, J. G., Killen, M., & Turiel, E. (1991). Children's reasoning about interpersonal and moral conflicts. *Child Development, 62,* 629–644.

Tisak, M. (1995). Domains of social reasoning and beyond. In R. Vasta (Ed.), *Annals of child development* (Vol. 11, pp. 95–130). London: Jessica Kingsley.

Torney-Purta, J. (1990). Youth in relation to social institutions. In S. S. Feldman & G. R. Elliot (Eds.), *At the threshold: The developing adolescent* (pp. 457–477). Cambridge, MA: Harvard University Press.

Turiel, E. (1974) Conflict and transition in adolescent moral development. *Child Development, 45,* 14–29.

Turiel, E. (1977). Conflict and transition in adolescent moral development. II. The resolution of disequilibrium through structural reorganization. *Child Development, 48,* 634–637.

Turiel, E. (1983). *The development of social knowledge: Morality and convention.* Cambridge: Cambridge University Press.

Turiel, E. (1998). Moral development. In N. Eisenberg (Ed.), William Damon (Series Ed.), *Handbook of child psychology, 5th Ed., Vol. 3: Social, emotional, and personality development* (pp. 863–932). New York: Wiley.

Turiel, E. (2002). *The culture of morality: Social development, context, and conflict.* Cambridge: Cambridge University Press.

Turiel, E., Killen, M., & Helwig, C. (1987). Morality: Its structure, functions, and vagaries. In J. Kagan & S. Lamb (Eds.), *The emergence of morality in young children* (pp. 155–243). Chicago: University of Chicago Press.

Wainryb, C. (1991). Understanding differences in moral judgments: The role of informational assumptions. *Child Development, 62,* 840–851.

Wainryb, C., & Turiel, E. (1994). Dominance, subordination, and concepts of personal entitlements in cultural contexts. *Child Development, 66,* 390–401.

Walker, L. J. (1984). Sex differences in the development of moral reasoning: A critical review. *Child Development, 55,* 677–691.

Walker, L. J. (1991). Sex differences in moral reasoning. In J. L. Gewirtz & W. M. Kurtines (Eds.), *Handbook of moral behavior and development* (Vol. 2, pp. 333–364). Hillsdale, NJ: Erlbaum.

Whitehead, B. D. (1993, April). Dan Quayle was right. *Atlantic Monthly*, 47–84.

Wynne, E. A. (1986). The great tradition in education: Transmitting moral values. *Educational Leadership, 43*, 4–9.

Yates, M., & Youniss, J. (1996). Community service and political–moral identity in adolescents. *Journal of Research on Adolescence, 6*, 271–284.

Yau, J., & Smetana, J. G. (1996). Adolescent–parent conflict among Chinese adolescents in Hong Kong. *Child Development, 67*, 1262–1275.

Yau, J., & Smetana, J. G. (2001). Adolescent–parent conflict in Hong Kong and Mainland China: A comparison of youth in two cultural contexts. Manuscript, Indiana Wesleyan University.

Youniss, J., & Yates, M. (1997). *Community service and social responsibility in youth.* Chicago: University of Chicago Press.

Youniss, J., McLellan, J. A., & Yates, M. (1997). What we know about engendering civic identity. *American Behavioral Scientist, 40*, 620–631.

CHAPTER THIRTEEN

Emotional Development in Adolescence

Gianine D. Rosenblum and Michael Lewis

Introduction

While it is a truism to say that adolescence is a period of great change, there is more than one way to characterize the changes of adolescence. In one view, the developmental events of adolescence represent a "step up" to adulthood. Hormone levels, cognitive ability, and social experiences all shift during adolescence from their childhood to adult forms. Once so transformed, these factors stabilize for much of adulthood. In this view, adolescence represents a portal to adulthood, and adjustment in this period represents adaptation to the child-to-adult shift that takes place. Many cultural and religious rituals (e.g., the bar/bat mitzvah in Jewish tradition) reflect this view, in that they treat a particular moment in adolescence as the point when an individual makes the transition from child to adult, with adult levels of responsibility and duty. An alternative view conceptualizes the period of adolescence as possessing unique characteristics, apart from the need for adjustment to adult levels of various factors. Adolescence is seen as a temporary, transitional period, with inherent characteristics not expected to persist into adulthood.

The theory and research reviewed in this chapter indicate that with regard to emotion, both views may be correct. During adolescence, young people experience adult-like body chemistry, cognition, and physique for the first time. The changes in cognitive and bodily status first occur in adolescence, then persist into adulthood. However, the novelty of these phenomena and the adolescent's inexperience with them when they first occur makes the adolescent experience different from that of adults. Adolescent emotional experience is in part a function of the incorporation of new cognitive and physiological events and their influence on the adolescents' perceptions of their development.

In addition to events that represent the acquisition of adult status, there are happenings unique to adolescence which do not persist into the adult years, including social environments and expectations that are particular to the developmental period. Some theorists hold that the confluence of cognitive, physiological, social/environmental, and emotional events of adolescence provide for internal and external worlds which are unique in development. This distinct adolescent experience is viewed as necessary for maturation and allows for the development of the complex cognitive, emotional, and self-structures essential for adult functioning.

In this chapter, we first review the foundations of emotional life developed prior to adolescence. This includes the emotions felt, as well as the skills for understanding and controlling emotion acquired in childhood. Cognitive development, hormonal changes, and life events are viewed as three of the most highly salient influences on adolescent emotional growth. We review research which describes how these factors impact on emotional functioning as children enter and proceed through adolescence. The chapter then turns to research on adolescent emotional experience. Reports on adolescents' day-to-day emotional lives, their experience of negative emotions, their emotional competencies, as well as the relation of emotion to identity in adolescence are reviewed. Finally, a summary of the tasks of emotional development in adolescence is presented.

Emotional Life Prior to Adolescence

In order to clarify the issues related to the development of emotion, researchers have differentiated between various aspects of emotional phenomena including emotional states, emotional experiences, and emotional expressions (Lewis & Michalson, 1983).

Emotional states

Emotional states are inferred constructs involving the specific physiological changes, and consequent changes in behavior, which occur in response to a particular stimulus.

Emotional experience

Emotional experience is an individual's interpretation and evaluation of their emotional state and their behavior. Emotional experience requires a concept of self, because by experiencing an emotion we mean being able to make reference to the self as having that state.

Emotional expressions

Emotional expressions are the potentially observable changes in face, voice, body, and activity level which occur in response to emotional states and experiences. While emotional expressions are typically used as indices of emotional states and experiences, emotional expressions are capable of being masked, dissembled, and controlled, beginning early in childhood (Saarni, 1999). Thus, emotional expression may not match well with emotional experience or internal emotional state.

Much research has explored the emergence and development of emotions in infancy and early childhood. These earlier developments create the background for children's emotional lives as they enter adolescence. During the first year of life, infants develop and express what have come to be known as the six primary emotions: interest, joy, disgust, sadness, anger, and fear. The more complex emotions such as embarrassment, pride, and shame do not emerge until later. For them to emerge, the child needs to develop consciousness or self-awareness. Self-awareness emerges in the second year of life (Lewis & Brooks-Gunn, 1979) and allows for a new class of emotions called the "self-conscious" emotions, which include evaluative and non-evaluative components (Lewis, 1992). The self-conscious emotions of embarrassment, envy, and empathy arise when the self is the object of attention, and are not evaluative in nature. The self-conscious evaluative emotions, shame, pride, and guilt, require self-awareness as well as the ability to compare one's self and or one's behavior to an internal or external standard, rule, or goal (Lewis, 1999). Succeeding relative to a standard, and thinking we are responsible for the success, gives rise to feelings of pride. Failing and thinking we are generally no good gives rise to feelings of shame. Focusing on the specific actions that gave rise to the failure triggers guilt or regret (Lewis, 1992). Thus, by the third year of life, most children exist within a fairly elaborate and complex emotional landscape. Their emotional lives include diverse and differentiated emotional states, experiences, and expressions.

In the years from early childhood to adolescence, few new emotions emerge. Rather, once young children possess the capacity for primary and self-conscious emotions, they set about using their increasing cognitive skills to elaborate them. Cognitive development allows for more complex and nuanced representations of events, and the ability to compare current events with ever-increasing memory stores of prior events. Increasingly complex emotions are the consequence of increasingly personal and psychological interpretations of internal and external events, and conscious or unconscious judgments about their significance (Thompson, 1989). Across childhood, children develop an enhanced understanding of their own emotional lives and acquire a series of emotional skills and abilities related to interpersonal relationships and intrapersonal emotional functioning. Many of these skills are firmly in place prior to adolescence.

Emotional Competencies in Early Childhood

By preschool age, children in Western cultures have learned the Western cultural idea that the emotion provoked by a situation is determined by cognitive factors, including the beliefs and desires of the individual in the situation (Harris, Olthof, & Terwogt, 1981). Saarni connects the emergence of the increasingly complex emotional life of children to the development of "emotional competencies," or "self-efficacy in the presence of emotion-eliciting social transactions" (Saarni, 1993, p. 442). Emotional competence encompasses the development of regulation/coping skills, expressive behavior skills, and relationship-building skills. Children must progressively build skills in these areas to achieve successful development outcomes. By the end of middle childhood, normally adjusted children have achieved many major milestones in the development of emotional competence.

The emergence of conscious self-awareness in the second year allows for tremendous developments in children's emotional and social lives. Children are now able to think of the other as well as the self, and comprehend the relation of self to other and other to self. This is a basic prerequisite of empathic responding, another ability developed in a basic form during childhood. The self-conscious emotions strongly influence behavior and skill development as children seek out behaviors and contexts associated with pride and avoid behaviors and contexts associated with shame, guilt, and regret (Lewis, 1992, 2000).

Theory of mind and the understanding of emotions

Theory of mind research has sought to discover what young children know about beliefs, desires, feelings, intentions, and the like. In the years between ages 2 and 6, children come to understand a great deal about mental states. For example, they know that others will act in accordance to the beliefs they hold, even if they are in contradiction to actual facts (Wimmer & Perner, 1983). And at the end of the preschool period, children have some understanding of what it means to "know" something (Montgomery, 1992). Children's developing comprehension of mental states includes increasing understanding about emotions and the emotional lives of others. Several researchers have examined children's understanding of others' emotional expressions. Early on, children look to the facial expressions of others to glean information about their emotional states and experiences (Gross & Ballif, 1991). Over time, children incorporate information from situations into their inferences about emotions. When the situation and the expressed emotion appear to be in conflict children tend to look to the stronger cues (i.e., the situation, or the person's expression) to determine what emotion the other person is likely to be feeling (Wiggers & Van Lieshout, 1985).

In later childhood, an increasingly complex understanding of the workings of the mind allows for a more complex and sophisticated prediction of others' emotional responses based on both obvious (e.g., facial) and more subtle (inferred) cues. Gnepp and Gould (1985) found that among kindergartners, 5th-graders, and college students, only the college students consistently relied upon personal information about the other person to predict what their emotions might be. Thus, it is during adolescence that the ability to incorporate new and subtle information into emotional understanding is developed.

Control over emotional expression and dissemblance

Children also come to understand that outward emotional expressions may not correspond with internal emotional experience. By ages 3 or 4 children have some appreciation of the fact that it is not always accepted to express how you feel and that their culture has rules for the appropriate display of certain emotions (Cole, 1986). Two years later, children can understand the difference between felt and expressed emotion, and understand that emotion is private and may not always be shown. Children's understanding of the social rules for verbal and facial emotional expression increases during the early school years, but has been shown to level off after fifth grade. Thus, by early adolescence the capacity to exert control over emotional expression, at least in some situations, is present (Saarni, 1984). It is not until adolescence, however, that young people can articulate the psychic conflict inherent in feeling one thing while expressing another (Harris & Gross, 1988).

Influences on Adolescent Emotional Life

Events unique to, or first lived in adolescence, have significant implications for emotions during this period. Influential events include the development of formal operational thought, the hormonal and other physiological changes of puberty, changing identity structures, heightened peer orientation, multiple salient life events, and a shift in social demands and expectations triggered by emergence into adolescence.

Cognitive development

In the conceptualization of emotion used here, cognitive evaluation and processing of events is critical to emotional production. As cognitive skills develop, the potential for emotional reactivity also develops (Lewis, 1999). Adolescence heralds significant cognitive developments which impact greatly on emotional life as changes in children's ability to reason about the world also brings new abilities to reason about emotions. In early adolescence, sometime around age 11, formal operations replace concrete operations as information-processing abilities increase in complexity and sophistication (Piaget & Inhelder, 1969). During this cognitive transformation children develop the ability to understand abstractions and symbolic logic. They are no longer restricted to the use of concrete representations of perceived data, but can now conceive of and reason with less tangible generalities not bounded by time and space (Fischer & Ayoub, 1994). Adolescents begin to know their world through imagined and deduced events and see essential similarities underlying superficial differences. Different actions can be seen to reflect the same fundamental concepts. Cause and effect relations are more readily recognized as complex event sequences and multiple determinants can be held in mind (Piaget, 1970; Piaget & Inhelder, 1958). These changes in memory and information processing allow for the generation of hypotheses about relations between events and a generally greater historical perspective (Kaplan, 1991).

Cognitive developments also influence the way adolescents understand what it means to know something. Very young children are highly context-dependent. Their representations of fact do not correspond to an understanding of one, immutable "real" world. They are the ultimate relativists who appear to accept that there may be different realities for different contexts or different people. By school age, cognitive development allows for an understanding of the idea that there is a single "real" world, and that all incoming information must be compared against that standard. Forguson and Gopnick (1988) describe school-age children as "hyperrealists" (p. 239). At this age, children lose their relativistic cognitive flexibility to such a degree that they may be intolerant of other options and rigidly apply their known rules in circumstances where several alternatives may be equally "realistic." Chandler (1987, 1988) posits that adolescence marks the reemergence of an awareness of relativism. Prior to adolescence, concrete operational children (Piaget, 1970) are aware that different individuals may have different points of view and, thus, may hold different opinions about the same facts or events. However, they maintain a perception that there is one absolute truth. If two individuals hold differing opinions it is assumed to be because one of them has been deprived of information. Thus, despite the recognition of differing opinions, preadolescent, i.e., concrete operational children, can presumably take comfort in the belief that there is out there somewhere a knowable reality and absolute truth.

The initial apprehension of abstract thought brings with it a host of novel experiences with emotional implications. Emotions may now be triggered by abstract ideas, anticipated future events, and recalled past events. Emotional responses to interpersonal relationships intensify as adolescents begin to understand people as "personalities" rather than simply agents of action. The underlying characteristics which tie together individuals' seemingly disparate behaviors are now grasped. Adolescents can analyze their own and others' personalities, experience emotional responses to, and join in relationships based on common personality properties (Fischer & Ayoub, 1994). Enhanced cognitive capabilities allow for recognition of the complex, multiple, and multiply determined emotions of self and others. Adolescents are more able to introspect and examine their own emotional lives. Also, there is now recognition of the fact that the same event may reasonably trigger differing emotional responses in different people.

In addition, the development of formal operational thought permits young people to simultaneously hold cognitive representations of their own and others' ideas. Adolescents' newly attained capacities for higher-order abstraction leads them to think about their own and others' thoughts and examine their efforts to make sense out of ambiguous data. This cognitive development allows for the nascent realization that the process of coming to know something is inherently subjective, and that differences in understanding or interpretations will not necessarily be resolvable by an appeal to the "facts." Chandler (1987) cites the emotional implications of awakening to the ambiguity and subjective nature of meaning. In adolescents' attempts to cope with the loss of knowability, they may adopt a stance of rigid dogmatism or vacillate between this and an abandonment of efforts to know anything at all. The loss of the ability to trust what is known results in a tendency to choose actions based on emotion, or to act with apparent emotional indifference. Furthermore, the emotional reaction to the awareness of subjectivity is described by numerous scholars (see Chandler, 1987, 1994). Descriptions of this experience of "Cartesian anxiety" are replete with references to negative emotions. This includes the "dread of madness and chaos where nothing is fixed" (Bernstein, 1983), and feelings of loneliness, isolation, homelessness, and loss. The adolescent must develop a strategy for coping with the relativity of knowledge and managing the anxiety and generally negative affect triggered by this awareness.

Thus, completing a successful transition from childhood to adulthood involves not just the cognitive acquisition of formal operations, but an emotional adjustment to this new way of perceiving the world. During the adolescent period, skills and competencies must be developed for understanding and managing the emotions generated by new points of view, for integrating new cognitive skills adaptively, and for coping with ambiguity.

Hormonal events

Adolescence is a time of significant biological change, and research indicates several possible relations between hormonal changes and emotional states. The instability of emotion in early adolescence may be related to inconsistency and variability of hormonal levels in this period of development (Buchanan, Eccles, & Becker, 1992). Adolescents may be particularly sensitive to small alterations in hormone levels due to their lack of prior exposure to these chemicals. Adaptation to new hormone levels over time may help explain why moods become less extreme as children progress through adolescence into adulthood (Deiner, Sandvik, & Larsen, 1985). In a review of the literature, Buchanan et al. (1992) point out that the hormonal changes of puberty begin early, and most effects on mood variability have been found in young adolescents. Research which finds no hormone-mood association may assess children too late in adolescence to detect effects, after hormone levels have stabilized or after adaptation to new, elevated levels.

In addition to effects on mood variability, hormones have been shown to have effects on the experience of positive and negative affect, with puberty related to increased negative affect (e.g., Brooks-Gunn, Graber, & Paikoff, 1994). However, most research indicates that hormonal effects are small and exist in complex interactions with other factors (see Buchanan et al., 1992). Pubertal timing provides a good example. While the onset of puberty in girls brings with it a host of dramatic hormonal changes, several studies have indicated that the timing of puberty relative to peers is a more important predictor of psychosocial functioning than measures of pubertal level per se (Alsaker, 1992).

The emotional changes brought on by hormonal fluctuations represent an experience largely unique to the adolescent period (although menopause may be somewhat comparable). Hormonal increases and instability, particularly in early adolescence, may contribute to changeable and more negatively toned emotional experiences. Emotional stabilization over time may reflect regulation of hormone levels as well as physiological adaptation to new levels. Even so, adolescent emotional responses are also clearly linked to the timing and social environment in which the hormonal changes take place. In fact, the contextual variables may contribute as much or more to the emotional experience of adolescents than actual hormone fluctuations.

Life experiences

Some researchers have posited that early adolescence is not only a period of cognitive and physiological transformation, but a period in which multiple life changes occur simultaneously, resulting in a "pile-up" of life events with which adolescents must struggle to cope (Simmons et al., 1987). Each of these life events might independently influence the emotional development and emotional tone of adolescence, but collectively these stressors contribute to greater upheaval. This pile-up comprises the changes brought on by puberty, as well social and environmental events. Some of these events are normative and predictable, while others are randomly occurring.

The hormonal changes discussed above may influence subjective or private experience of emotions, as hormone fluctuations shape emotional proclivities. The overt changes to physical appearance brought on by puberty are likely to have private effects on an adolescent's body image, for example (Brooks-Gunn, 1984). Physical development also affects the adolescent's social environment as changing appearance triggers changing expectations and behaviors in others (Blyth, Simmons, & Zakin, 1985).

Many American children experience a sudden change in school setting coincident with entry into early adolescence (Simmons et al., 1987). The school transition brings the stress of a novel environment and new social hierarchies. At this age, students frequently transition from a smaller to larger school with more complex schedules and less personal attention. Early adolescents may have to separate from friends and leave other supportive relationships. All of these elements constitute significant potential stressors. Higher risk for emotional and behavioral difficulties exists for adolescents who go through the predictable, normative events of pubertal onset and school transitions, and simultaneously experience other changes like family disruption, relocation to a new community, or the initiation of dating (Simmons & Blyth, 1987).

Even the socially normative expectations of adolescent romantic involvement can precipitate additional emotional stress. Adolescents report emotional distress related to feeling pressure to "be in love" (Simon, Eder, & Evans, 1992), concern over choosing the right romantic partner, and suffering the loss of a break-up (Larson, Clore, & Wood, 1999b). Furthermore, social pressure to engage in sexual activity, unwanted sexual attention or harassment, as well as unwanted or regretted sexual experiences are other important potential contributors to adolescents' overall emotional experience. Coping skills developed in childhood may be considerably strained by the multiple new stresses encountered at adolescence. Adolescents must expand their emotional competencies in order to succeed in soothing themselves when in distress and to modulate their emotional expression in accord with their new social environments.

Let us turn now to examining what is known about adolescent emotional experience and expression, and the ways in which the development of new emotional skills and abilities impacts upon the adolescent emotional landscape.

Adolescent Emotional Experience

For generations, Western culture has viewed adolescence as a period of emotional upheaval and turmoil (Arnett, 1999). Historically, development from childhood into adolescence has been thought to include an increase in the intensity of emotions, the experience and expression of emotional lability or "mood swings" (Hall, 1904), and an increase in negatively valenced emotions (Freud, 1969). Currently, popular depictions of adolescents and youth use words like "alienated," "desperate," and "overwhelmed" to describe youths' inner lives (Underwood, 1999). The public typically perceives adolescence to be a troubled time, and believes that adolescents are more likely than younger children to have problems with family conflicts, anxiety, insecurity, and depression (Buchanan et al., 1990; Holmbeck & Hill, 1988).

Recent research has emphasized collection of empirical data on the emotional lives of children as they make the transition from childhood into early adolescence and beyond. While some data contradict the conceptualization of adolescence as a period of turmoil, there are many indications that the emotional landscape of adolescent life differs from the periods that precede and follow it.

Adolescents' day-to-day emotional lives

Several studies have now been conducted by Larson and colleagues using the "experience sampling method" (ESM) (e.g., Larson & Lampman-Petraitis, 1989; Larson et al., 1990). This method provides adolescents with electronic pagers, and "beeps" them at random times during two-hour intervals throughout their waking hours. When beeped, the participants record their immediate situation and corresponding emotions. This allows for descriptions of the adolescents' emotions, including emotional intensity, variability, and events that trigger emotions.

The ESM research indicates that adolescent emotional experience does differ in intensity, frequency, and persistence from that of older and younger individuals. Compared to their parents, adolescents experience greater extremes of emotion, with a bigger range between higher and lower moods (Larson, Csikzentmihalyi, & Graef, 1980); this was particularly true for negative emotions. Adolescents also reported experiencing negative moods more frequently than adults. Though adolescents reported experiencing extreme positive moods more frequently than adults, on average, adults' mood states were more positive than adolescents'. Adults reported feeling more in control, more active, and more alert than adolescents. In addition to being more negative, adolescents' mood states were less persistent and quicker to dissipate than those of adults. The frequency of very "high highs," and very "low lows," and the fleeting quality of their emotional states, lends some credibility to adults' stereotypic perceptions of adolescents as moody and changeable.

Adolescents' emotional experiences also differed from those of younger children (Larson & Lampman-Petraitis, 1989). Larson and Lampman-Petraitis (1989) found that average daily mood declines as children progress from 5th to 9th grade. Across grades both boys and girls reported a 50 percent decrease in the experience of feeling "very happy." In girls, highly positive emotion declined, and was replaced by an increase in lesser positive and mildly negative moods. For boys, there was an increase only in mildly negative moods. Overall, children's emotional experience during early adolescence appears to include less happiness than during childhood (Arnett, 1999).

There also are differences in the events adolescents perceive to be triggers for emotion. Larson and Asmussen (1991) found that fifth and sixth graders were likely to attribute emotions to the activity they were immediately engaged in, while adolescents were more reactive and sensitive to past and future events. Adolescents were also more sensitive to smaller events throughout their day than were younger children. These developments are likely related to enhancements in cognitive functioning as adolescents are able to attend to more subtle cues, hold and examine complex events in the memory, and anticipate the implications of future events.

There also appears to be a relationship between heightened adolescent emotionality and adolescents' emergence into the romantic sphere. When asked to report the reasons for their emotions, adolescents frequently gave romantic relationships (heterosexual, real, or imagined) as the cause. Having a boy/girlfriend was associated with wide mood swings (Larson et al., 1999b). The ephemeral nature of adolescent romantic attachments (Feiring, 1996) likely adds to the vacillation between emotional highs and lows. The mood-romance relation is so marked that Larson and colleagues argue for these relationships, in particular, romantic disappointments and frustrations, to be identified as the major source of stress and emotional pain for adolescents (Larson et al., 1999b).

Negative affect, depression, and shame

It is also notable that in the realm of negative affect, important gender differences exist. While rates of depressed mood increase overall with the onset of adolescence, this elevation is significantly greater for girls than boys (Nolen-Hoeksema & Girgus, 1994). Prior to early adolescence, depressed mood and clinical depression do occur, but at lower rates and similar frequencies in both genders (Brooks-Gunn & Petersen, 1991). Sex differences develop in the early adolescent years, approximately across ages 11 to 12 (Ohannessian et al., 1999). By age 13, girls show reliably greater frequencies of depressive symptoms than boys (Nolen-Hoeksema & Girgus, 1994). Drops in self-esteem at adolescence, low perceived competence in academic, peer-social, and behavioral domains, low levels of perceived support from peers and parents, as well as poor body image have been linked to depressed mood in adolescence (Harter & Whitesell, 1996; Nolen-Hoeksema & Girgus, 1994).

In addition, as in adults, poor mood and depressive symptoms in adolescents are associated with a cognitive style which includes negative automatic thoughts, hopelessness, helplessness, and a tendency toward rumination over problems and worries (Garber, Weiss, & Shanley, 1993; Nolen-Hoeksema & Girgus, 1994). In general, girls are more likely than boys to manifest the factors associated with depressed mood. Prior to the appearance of gender differences in depression and anxiety, girls exhibit lower levels of perceived competence than boys. Girls exhibit poorer mood and more feelings of hopelessness in the presence of fewer risk factors than boys (Harter & Whitesell, 1996), perhaps indicating a greater underlying vulnerability. In addition, pubertal maturation tends to occur earlier in girls, in synchrony with school transitions, leading to an increased risk for the "pile-up" phenomenon discussed earlier.

In one study of normal adolescents (Stapley & Haviland, 1989), negative, self-directed emotions were found to be more salient (i.e., were experienced with greater frequency, intensity, and duration) for girls than boys. This developmental phenomenon is likely related to the gender difference in clinical depression seen in adolescents and adults (Nolen-Hoeksema, 1987). Adolescent boys also report salient negative emotions, though they do not conform to the classical representation of depression. Girls report increased salience of shame, guilt, sadness, shyness, and self-directed hostility, particularly in interpersonal contexts. In contrast, boys report an increase in feelings of contempt and report that their experience of negative emotion is related more to activities and achievement than interpersonal life. Boys also are more likely to deny having feelings at all. Thus, estimates of gender differences in adolescent depression may be related to our definition of depression, which more closely follows the emotional experience of girls and women than that of boys and men (Hamilton & Jensvold, 1992).

Shame is another important facet of the adolescent emotional world (Reimer, 1996). Numerous factors contribute to early adolescents' vulnerability to shame, including the public nature of bodily changes brought on by puberty and the conflict between individuation and the need to maintain the approval and love of significant others. Psychosexual development prompts the emergence or intensification of sexual feelings, desires, and experiences (e.g., sexual desire and fantasy, nocturnal emissions, cross-gender identification, homosexual orientation). These new experiences may trigger feelings of shame, particularly if they are perceived to be socially unacceptable or as a potential threat to important attachments.

Adolescent girls may be at particular risk for experiencing shame. At all ages, girls tend to be more shame-prone than boys (Tangney, 1990). This may be related to early childhood gender-role socialization which tends to provide girls with more global feedback and boys with more specific feedback (Lewis, 1992), but there are many factors in adolescence which may exacerbate feelings of shame in girls. Social pressure to conform to sex roles intensifies further when girls reach adolescence. This creates heightened expectations for girls to be solicitous to the needs of others and vigilant for other's responses to them. This in turn increases the risk for girls to experience shame (Reimer, 1996).

Bodily change also is more likely to elicit shame in girls than boys. As a normal consequence of puberty, girls experience an increase in body mass that is at odds with the dominant culture's standard for feminine beauty. The loss of the prepubescent body and the increasing disparity between their real and ideal bodies causes adolescent girls dissatisfaction, distress, and shame (Blyth et al., 1985; Reimer, 1996; Rosenblum & Lewis, 1999). Western society's glorification of idealized female beauty creates an environment in which girls' bodily shame may easily generalize into global feelings of shame (Rodin, 1992). Furthermore, objectification theory (Fredrickson & Roberts, 1997) holds that Western girls are socialized to be constantly cognizant of whether their bodies and physical appearances are pleasing to others. A chronic state of anxiety may be generated by the concerns about maintaining a satisfactory appearance. Additionally, entry into sexual maturity simultaneously heightens girls' concerns about sexual attractiveness, and their awareness that they may become the targets of sexual violence. As girls mature, further anxiety may be generated by fears about, or the experience of, sexual victimization and harassment.

Emotion and identity

Adolescence is also a time of identity development. Haviland et al. (1994) theorize that emotion serves as "glue" connecting separate events via shared emotional processes or emotional valence. Certain emotions may become "content elaborated" by virtue of being associated with numerous types of events. Certain events or themes may become "emotionally elaborated" as they are associated with many different emotions. Emotional association thereby provides a source of organization and meaning for disparate experiences (Haviland-Jones & Kahlbaugh, 2000). As systems which provide meaning, emotions are inextricably bound to identity; when emotional experience changes, identity also changes. As a child enters adolescence, the organizational structure of childhood identity is lost. A new identity, with the resilience to carry the individual through to adulthood, must then be constructed (Chandler, 1994). Haviland views the process of identity reconstruction as inextricably linked to the development of new emotion-event linkages and emotional processes in general (Haviland et al., 1994).

Adolescence is replete with novel experiences which for the first time are available to serve as emotional triggers. Adolescence also brings changes in whether and what types of emotions are triggered by events. For example, age-related changes in emotional associations are linked to adolescents' shift away from family, and increased focus on peers. When asked about what sorts of experiences trigger emotional reactions, younger children are most likely to associate emotional experience to family happenings. In contrast, adolescents are more likely to link their emotions to peer, especially opposite-sex peer, events (Csikszentmihalyi & Larson, 1984). In addition to age effects, adolescence also brings sex differences in the types of situations that are emotionally charged. For girls, interpersonal experiences take on the highest emotional salience. During adolescence, girls' affiliative experiences become connected to multiple emotions in complex ways. In contrast, while both boys and girls maintain a significant emotional connection to activities and achievement in adolescence, boys do not undergo an increase in the emotional charge of relationship events (Haviland-Jones, Gebelt, & Stapley, 1997).

Novel affect-experience connections appear in adolescence and are the basis for a substantive change in the associative network of events and emotions. Construction of this new network is a prominent feature of adolescent emotional and identity development. Identity structures that are developing in adolescence may include new elements or feature a change in prominence of the roles of friend, best friend, and romantic partner, and more elaboration of roles outside of home and school (Haviland et al., 1994). These new aspects of identity exist in part because new and compelling emotional experiences gave them heightened salience.

Emotion Skills and Abilities Developed or Enhanced in Adolescence

The emotional experiences (i.e., the moment-to-moment, or day-to-day feelings) of adolescence are likely to be confined to the developmental period. In contrast, emotional skills and abilities developed during adolescence are expected to persist into adulthood, and serve as the building blocks for adult emotional functioning. This includes the ability to experience and reflect on mixed and conflicting emotions, more sophisticated skill in emotional dissemblance, and the capacity for a mature experience of empathy.

Mixed emotions

The term "mixed emotions" is part of everyday adult parlance. Adult life frequently is described as filled with "bittersweet" moments and "ambivalent" feelings about people and events. Young children do not share this experience. Only with the cognitive skills of early adolescence are children capable of acknowledging the simultaneous coexistence of two conflicting emotions. Harter and Buddin (1987) describe a five-stage developmental sequence, at the end of which (level 4; approximately age 12) children express understanding of simultaneous conflicting emotions. The youngest children initially deny the possibility of mixed emotions. Slightly older children describe experiencing two different emotions by vacillating between them, depending on the target of their focus (e.g., focusing on an object: the chewed toy versus the new puppy; or focusing on a point in time: during the party versus after the party). Only at level 4 were children able to articulate having two simultaneous, opposite valence feelings elicited by the same target in the same moment. This development allows for a more sophisticated emotional experience, particularly in the interpersonal realm.

Emotional dissemblance

Early in life children learn that felt emotions need not necessarily be expressed. Over time, children learn to dissemble their external expressions from their internal feeling states. The skill of separating emotional experience from emotional expression evolves and increases in sophistication from simply reducing the amount of emotion expressed, to the more challenging substitution of a preferred expression for a less desired one (Ekman & Friesen, 1975). Children develop dissemblance due to a number of motivations, including the desire to avoid negative outcomes, protect their own self-esteem, to defend relationships, and behave in accordance with social norms and rules. As children progress toward adolescence, choices to control emotional expression become increasingly linked to the management of interpersonal relationships (Saarni, 1999). In the increasingly complex emotional world of the adolescent, the skills of dissemblance become at once more important and more challenging. The relatively new experience of mixed emotions may leave adolescents confused about what they are feeling and what can be shown, and to whom.

By adolescence, knowledge about the existence of display rules has been in place for many years and skills for control of expression have had time to develop. During adolescence children must adopt the display rules governing more mature interpersonal interactions and adult discourse. The ability to control expression and strategically display a desired "look" exists on a developmental continuum, however. Even at age 15 adolescents' skills are still modest. Similar to younger children, tenth graders reported that in some situations they would control their words but not their facial expressions (Gnepp & Hess, 1986). In an earlier study (Harris et al., 1981), adolescents reported doubts that they could control their facial displays of emotions. The more intense emotional states and experiences of adolescence may be felt so keenly that self-efficacy for emotional display control is particularly low.

Overall, adolescents' abilities to discern and conform to the norms governing the use of adult emotional signaling behavior, and their awareness of the more subtle and complex rules governing mature interaction, are limited. Their first attempts to use adult emotion communication strategies can be unsubtle and incomplete, reflecting their immaturity and lack of finesse (Haviland-Jones et al., 1997). It is one of the tasks of adolescence to practice and develop these skills. Over time, healthy adolescents with access to appropriate adult role models become more adept and skillful at mature roles.

Adolescents also may possess idiosyncratic display rules particular to their social subculture. The need to maintain a calm, stoic exterior, to disguise internal emotional turmoil, and to ward off castigation by peers is felt keenly by youths (Von Salisch, 1991). Thus, adolescents may be particularly motivated to learn emotional dissemblance skills for use with peers. In addition to managing social situations, the strategy of adopting a strong front may serve to reduce the level of internal emotional distress, as one "acts as if" one were calm and in control while confronting a stressor. Saarni (1999) points out that this "strong front" behavior might elicit positive social feedback, which would in turn reinforce maintaining emotional control in a difficult situation.

Empathy

The cognitive growth of adolescence makes another key emotional development possible by allowing for an enhanced capacity to be aware of the emotion experienced by others, that is, the experience of empathy. Empathy is the product of the coordinated operation of both emotional and cognitive processes (Hoffman, 1984). Cognitively, awareness of the self–other distinction is fundamental to the experience of empathy. A child must know herself, have a sense of the other, and understand that it is possible for these selves to communicate through the process of empathy (Lewis, 1997). Comprehension of another's feelings is necessary for empathy to occur. Emotional arousal in response to another's situation must trigger cognitive processes, such as perspective taking, in order to maintain the self–other boundary and determine what actions will be generated. The child must be capable of an affective response which is concordant to what the other person is perceived to feel.

Younger children may respond with emotion to witnessing another's experience; however, it is likely that they are experiencing a reaction to the event they have witnessed, rather than responding to the other person's emotions. Over time, other-awareness increases. Between ages 7 and 13, children's focus shifts such that they attend to the emotional experience of the person rather than the event (Strayer, 1993). Children who are more other-person focused have a greater ability to accurately match their affect with that of the other. The ability to be other-focused corresponds with the development of cognitive role-taking skills which increase as children mature into adolescence. In turn, role-taking skills have been shown to be predictive of empathy (Roberts & Strayer, 1996).

The cognitive developments of adolescence also allow emotional responses to become uncoupled from acute, immediate events. Newly developed abstract reasoning permits adolescents to extrapolate from the more limited emotional experiences of an individual to the emotions of a group of people, other organisms, or the "feelings" of the earth itself. Adolescents for the first time can be mobilized toward social action due to the experience of sharing the pain of others on a larger scale. As abstract thinking advances, adolescents are more able to anticipate and be responsive to shifts in the emotional states, experiences, and expressions of others. Their ability to detect dissemblance in others may also increase, as they take into consideration the contexts and multiple determinants of emotional displays.

The ability to become empathically aware of others' emotions does not necessarily translate into socially appropriate or supportive emotional responding, however. It is clear that by adolescence, children have in place the basic skills necessary for empathic responding. They are self-aware and have the ability to infer the emotional experiences of others. However, additional emotion-regulation skills are influential in the experience and expression of empathy. Empathic responding is largely concentrated on apprehending the suffering, sorrow, and other negative emotions experienced by others, whereas empathy for positive emotions may be an experience linked to rarer and more intimate interpersonal bonds (Royzman & Kumar, 2000). In order to engage in empathic response, the empathizer must be able to tolerate the affect generated by an empathic connection (Eisenberg et al., 1994). In the presence of the negative affect of another, individuals who are poorly regulated in this regard may experience high levels of negative arousal and personal distress. This self-focused distress may prompt them to avoid empathic responding altogether, flee the situation, or otherwise prematurely terminate an empathic connection (Eisenberg, 2000).

There is evidence that levels of sympathy and empathy are stable over time from early adolescence to adulthood (Davis & Franzoi, 1991). If emotional regulation and dysregulation are associated with empathic responding, then skills for coping with negative affect will impact upon children's capacity to empathize with others throughout their lives (Eisenberg et al., 1991). Research with disordered youths supports the notion that emotional dysregulation and the inability to self-soothe interferes with empathy. Cohen and Strayer (1996) found that adolescents with Conduct Disorder experienced more personal distress than non-Conduct Disordered adolescents when confronted with scenarios designed to evoke empathic responding. These youths were also less able to accurately match the affect state of the other person, perhaps because their own level of distress prevented them from attending to cues indicating the other person's affect state. The Conduct Disordered adolescents were not un-emotional or indifferent, rather, their emotional experience was more self-focused and aversive. This undermined their ability to keep the experience of others in the foreground.

Emotional Competence in Adolescence and Beyond

Some of the emotional experiences and challenges of adolescence are presented by the unique circumstances of the developmental period; this is the temporary, transitional element of adolescence. These challenges may provoke skill-building efforts and facilitate the development of a more sophisticated cognitive-emotional framework that will persist into adulthood. It is significant, however, that a number of aspects of adolescent life are linked to distress and negative emotional experience. Though the new cognitive skills and abilities at work in adolescence allow for the anticipation of future positive events and deeper interpersonal relationships, frequently they appear to produce painful emotions (e.g., Larson & Asmussen, 1991). Those adolescents who are not able to cope success-fully with the increased emotional burdens of adolescent life may experience negative con-sequences, including proneness to depression and feelings of shame, anxiety, pathological anger, and emotional volatility. Such emotional dysfunctions may in turn trigger other difficulties like drug use, or the loss of important supportive relationships. These emotional problems and related difficulties may then persist in to adulthood.

It is clear that healthy children have many emotional skills in place by the end of middle childhood (Saarni, 1999). However, in order to make a successful passage through adolescence the average young person must develop and utilize a broad range of addi-tional competencies. Adolescents must develop the ability to:

- regulate intense emotions
- modulate rapidly vacillating emotions
- self-soothe independently
- achieve awareness of and successfully attend to their own emotions without becom-ing overwhelmed by them (Mayer & Salovey, 1997; Saarni, 1999)
- understand the consequence to self and others of genuine emotional expression versus dissemblance (Saarni, 1999)
- use symbolic thought to reframe (i.e., transform the meaningfulness of) a negative event to one that is less aversive (Saarni, 1999)
- separate momentary emotional experience from identity, and recognize that the self can remain intact and continuous despite emotional fluctuation (Chandler, 1994; Larson et al., 1999b)
- distinguish feelings from facts to avoid reasoning based on emotion, as in: "I feel it, therefore it must be true" (Saarni, 1999)
- negotiate and maintain interpersonal relationships in the presence of strong emotion
- manage the emotional arousal of empathic and sympathetic experiences
- use cognitive skills to gather information about the nature and sources of emotion.

Though this list is only a partial representation of the emotional competency tasks in adolescence, research indicates that healthy youths ought to possess the basic cognitive-emotional building blocks necessary to accomplish these tasks. It is these accomplish-ments, rather than the transitory emotional states and experiences, that adolescents will carry into adulthood. Additional research is needed to explore how and when adolescents develop these skills and whether their acquisition is predictive of healthy emotional development into adulthood.

Recently, there has been a greater emphasis on the beneficial factors related to development of positivity, happiness, and general emotional well-being in adults (Seligman & Csikszentmihalyi, 2000). Overall emotional tone tends to be stable from adolescence into adulthood and emotionality has been tied in significant ways to numerous measures of morbidity and mortality (e.g., Salovey et al., 2000). Therefore, in addition to supporting basic healthy emotional development, we might do well to educate adolescents about, and nurture the development of, these beneficial factors prior to and during adolescence. This might include emphasizing the development of close kin and deep friendship ties, fostering skills to increase the likelihood of selecting an appropriate life-mate, promoting the ability to engage in cooperation and reciprocal interaction, and reducing materialism, as well as nurturing optimism, positivity, and humor (Valiant, 2000).

Key Readings

Arnett, J. J. (1999). Adolescent storm and stress reconsidered. *American Psychologist, 54*(5), 317–326.
This article provides a thorough and up-to-date review of the literature on adolescent emotional experience. It critiques conceptualizations of adolescence that do not take into account recent empirical evidence on adolescent development.

Buchanan, C. M., Eccles, J. S., & Becker, J. B. (1992). Are adolescents the victims of raging hormones: Evidence for activational effects of hormones on moods and behavior at adolescence. *Psychological Bulletin, 111*(1), 62–107.
An extensive review of the research on the relation between the hormonal changes of puberty and adolescent mood states.

Chandler, M. (1987). The Othello effect: Essay on the emergence and eclipse of skeptical doubt. *Human Development, 30*(3), 137–159.
This article offers a theoretical approach to adolescent development which highlights the emotional and behavioral implications of the emergence of epistemic doubt. It casts typical adolescent behaviors as by-products of attempts to establish intellectual authority.

Lewis, M. (1992). *Shame: The exposed self.* New York: Free Press.
This is a seminal text on the development of the powerful emotion of shame. It provides a framework for understanding the role of shame and self-conscious self-awareness in shaping human emotion and behavior.

Lewis, M., & Michalson, L. (1983). *Children's emotions and moods: Developmental theory and measurement.* New York: Plenum.
This book is a classic work in the understanding of emotional development in children. It provides the fundamental building blocks for conceptualizing emotional development in any developmental period.

Saarni, C. (1999). *The development of emotional competence.* New York: Guilford.
This volume exhaustively reviews the literature on emotional development in children. The author synthesized her own research with that of others, including cross-cultural research, to develop a comprehensive picture of children's development of specific skills in emotional competence.

References

Alsaker, F. D. (1992). Pubertal timing, overweight, and psychological adjustment. *Journal of Early Adolescence, 12*(4), 396–419.

Arnett, J. J. (1999). Adolescent storm and stress reconsidered. *American Psychologist, 54*(5), 317–326.

Bernstein, R. (1983). *Beyond objectivism and realism.* Philadelphia: University of Philadelphia Press.

Blyth, D. A., Simmons, R. G., & Zakin, D. F. (1985). Satisfaction with body image for early adolescent females: The impact of pubertal timing within different school environments. *Journal of Youth and Adolescence, 14,* 207–225.

Brooks-Gunn, J. (1984). The psychological significance of different pubertal events to young girls. *Journal of Early Adolescence, 4,* 315–327.

Brooks-Gunn, J., Graber, J. A., & Paikoff, R. L. (1994). Studying links between hormones and negative affect: Models and measures. *Journal of Research on Adolescence, 4,* 469–486.

Brooks-Gunn, J., & Petersen, A. C. (1991). Studying the emergence of depression and depressive symptoms during adolescence. *Journal of Youth and Adolescence, 20,* 115–119.

Buchanan, C. M., Eccles, J. S., & Becker, J. B. (1992). Are adolescents the victims of raging hormones: Evidence for activational effects of hormones on moods and behavior at adolescence. *Psychological Bulletin, 111*(1), 62–107.

Buchanan, C. M., Eccles, J. S., Flanagan, C., & Midgley, C. (1990). Parents' and teachers' beliefs about adolescents: Effects of sex and experience. *Journal of Youth and Adolescence, 19,* 363–394.

Chandler, M. (1987). The Othello effect: Essay on the emergence and eclipse of skeptical doubt. *Human Development, 30*(3), 137–159.

Chandler, M. (1988). Doubt and developing theories of mind. In J. W. Astington, P. L. Harris, & D. R. Olson (Eds.), *Developing theories of mind* (pp. 387–413). Cambridge: Cambridge University Press.

Chandler, M. (1994). Adolescent suicide and the loss of personal continuity. In D. Cicchetti & S. L. Toth (Eds.), *Rochester symposium on developmental psychopathology: Disorders and dysfunctions of the self* (Vol. 5, pp. 371–390). Rochester, NY: University of Rochester Press.

Cohen, D., & Strayer, J. (1996). Empathy in conduct-disordered and comparison youth. *Developmental Psychology, 32,* 988–998.

Cole, P. M. (1986). Children's spontaneous control of facial expression. *Child Development, 57,* 1309–1321.

Csikszentmihalyi, M., & Larson, R. (1984). *Being adolescent: Conflict and growth in the teenage years.* New York: Basic Books.

Davis, M. H., & Franzoi, S. (1991). Stability and change in adolescent self-consciousness and empathy. *Journal of Research in Personality, 25,* 70–87.

Deiner, E., Sandvik, E., & Larsen, R. J. (1985). Age and sex effects for emotional intensity. *Developmental Psychology, 21,* 542–546.

Eisenberg, N. (2000). Empathy and sympathy. In M. Lewis & Haviland-Jones (Eds.), *Handbook of emotions* (pp. 677–693). New York: Guilford.

Eisenberg, N., Fabes, R., Murphy, B., Smith, P., O'Boyle, C., & Suh, K. (1994). The relations of emotionality and regulation to dispositional and situational empathy-related responding. *Journal of Personality and Social Psychology, 66,* 776–797.

Eisenberg, N., Fabes, R. A., Schaller, M., Carlo, G., & Miller, P. A. (1991). The relations of parental characteristics and practices to children's vicarious emotional responding. *Child Development, 62,* 1393–1408.

Ekman, P., & Friesen, W. V. (1975). *Unmasking the face.* Englewood Cliffs, NJ: Prentice Hall.

Feiring, C. (1996). Concepts of romance in 15-year-old adolescents. *Journal of Research on Adolescence, 6,* 181–200.

Fischer, K., W., & Ayoub, C. (1994). Affective splitting and dissociation in normal and maltreated children: Pathways for self in relationships. In D. Cicchetti & S. L. Toth (Eds.), *Rochester symposium on developmental psychopathology: Disorders and dysfunctions of the self* (Vol. 5, pp. 149–222). Rochester, NY: University of Rochester Press.

Forguson, L., & Gopnik, A. (1988). The ontogeny of common sense. In J. W. Astington, P. L. Harris, & D. R. Olson (Eds.), *Developing theories of mind* (pp. 226–243). Cambridge: Cambridge University Press.

Fredrickson, B. L, & Roberts, T.-A. (1997). Objectification Theory: Toward understanding women's lived experiences and mental health risks. *Psychology of Women Quarterly, 21,* 173–206.

Freud, A. (1969). Adolescence as a developmental disturbance. In G. Caplan & S. Lebovici (Eds.), *Adolescence: Psychosocial Perspectives* (pp. 5–10). New York: Basic Books.

Garber, J., Weiss, B., & Shanley, N. (1993). Cognitions, Depressive Symptoms, and Development in Adolescents. *Journal of Abnormal Psychology, 102,* 47–57.

Gnepp, J., & Gould, M. (1985). The development of personalized inferences: Understanding other people's emotional reactions in light of their prior experiences. *Child Development, 56,* 1455–1464.

Gnepp, J., & Hess, D. L. (1986). Children's understanding of verbal and facial display rules. *Developmental Psychology, 22,* 103–108.

Gross, A. L., & Ballif, B. (1991). Children's understanding of emotions from facial expressions and situations: A review. *Developmental Review, 11,* 368–398.

Hall, G. S. (1904). *Adolescence: Its psychology and relation to physiology, anthropology, sociology, sex, crime, religion, and education* (2 vols.). Englewood Cliffs, NJ: Prentice Hall.

Hamilton, J. A., & Jensvold, M. (1992). Personality, psychopathology, and depressions in women. In L. S. Brown & M. Ballou (Eds.), *Personality and psychopathology* (pp. 116–143). New York: Guilford.

Harris, P. L., & Gross, D. (1988). Children's understanding of real and apparent emotion. In J. W. Astington, P. L. Harris, & D. R. Olson (Eds.), *Developing theories of mind* (pp. 295–314). Cambridge: Cambridge University Press.

Harris, P. L., Olthof, T., & Terwogt, M. M. (1981). Children's knowledge of emotion. *Journal of Child Psychology and Psychiatry and Allied Disciplines, 22,* 247–261.

Harter, S., & Buddin, B. J. (1987). Children's understanding of the simultaneity of two emotions: A five-stage developmental acquisition sequence. *Developmental Psychology, 23,* 388–399.

Harter, S., & Whitesell, N. R (1996). Multiple pathways to self-reported depression and psychological adjustment among adolescents. *Development and Psychopathology, 8,* 761–777.

Haviland, J. M., Davidson, R. B., Ruetsch, C., & Gebelt, J. L. (1994). The place of emotion in identity. *Journal of Research on Adolescence, 4,* 503–518.

Haviland-Jones, J., Gebelt, J. L., & Stapley, J. C. (1997). The questions of development in emotion. In P. Salovey & D. J. Sluyter (Eds.), *Emotional development and emotional intelligence* (pp. 233–256). New York: Basic Books.

Haviland-Jones, J., & Kahlbaugh, P. (2000). Emotion and identity. In M. Lewis & J. Haviland-Jones (Eds.), *Handbook of Emotions* (pp. 293–305). New York: Guilford.

Hoffman, M. L. (1984). Interaction of affect and cognition in empathy. In C. E. Izard, J. Kagan, & R. B. Zajonc (Eds.), *Emotions, cognitions and behavior* (pp. 103–131). New York: Cambridge University Press.

Holmbeck, G. N., & Hill, J. P. (1988). Storm and stress beliefs about adolescence: Prevalence, self-reported antecedents, and effects of an undergraduate course. *Journal of Youth and Adolescence, 17,* 285–306.

Kaplan, E. H. (1991). Adolescents age fifteen to eighteen: A psychoanalytic developmental view. In S. I. Greenspan & G. H. Pollock (Eds.), *The course of life: Adolescence* (Vol. IV, pp. 201–233). Madison, WI: International Universities Press.

Larson, R., & Asmussen, L. (1991). Anger, worry, and hurt in early adolescence: An enlarging world of negative emotions. In M. E. Colten & S. Gore (Eds.), *Adolescent stress: Causes and consequences* (pp. 21–41). New York: Aldine de Gruyter.

Larson, R., Csikzentmihalyi, M., & Graef, R. (1980). Mood variability and the psychosocial adjustment of adolescents. *Journal of Youth and Adolescents, 9,* 469–490.

Larson, R., & Lampman-Petraitis, C. (1989). Daily emotional states as reported by children and adolescents. *Child Development, 60,* 1250–1260.

Larson, R. W., Clore, G. L., & Wood, G. A. (1999b). The emotions of romantic relationships : Do they wreak havoc on adolescents? In W. B. Furman, B. B. Brown, & C. Feiring (Eds.), *The Development of Romantic Relationships in Adolescence* (pp. 19–49). New York: Cambridge University Press.

Larson, R. W., Raffaelli, M., Richards, M. H., & Ham, M. (1990). Ecology of depression in late childhood and early adolescence: A profile of daily states and activities. *Journal of Abnormal Psychology, 99,* 92–102.

Lewis, M. (1992). *Shame: The exposed self.* New York: Free Press.

Lewis, M. (1997). *Altering fate: Why the past does not predict the future.* New York: Guilford.

Lewis, M. (1999). The role of self in cognition and emotion. In T. Dalgleish & M. J. Power (Eds.), *Handbook of cognition and emotion* (pp. 125–142). Chichester: Wiley.

Lewis, M. (2000). Self-conscious emotions: Embarrassment, shame, pride and guilt. In M. Lewis & J. Haviland-Jones (Eds.), *Handbook of Emotions* (Vol. 2, pp. 265–280). New York: Guilford.

Lewis, M., & Brooks-Gunn, J. (1979). *Social cognition and the acquisition of the self.* New York: Plenum.

Lewis, M., & Michalson, L. (1983). *Children's emotions and moods: Developmental theory and measurement.* New York: Plenum.

Mayer, J. D., & Salovey, P. (1997). What is emotional intelligence? In P. Salovey & D. Sluyter (Eds.), *Emotional development and emotional intelligence: Educational implications* (pp. 3–34). New York: Basic Books.

Montgomery, D. E. (1992). Young children's theory of knowing: The development of a folk epistemology. *Developmental Review, 12,* 410–430.

Nolen-Hoeksema, S. (1987). Sex differences in unipolar depression: Evidence and theory. *Psychological Bulletin, 101,* 259–282.

Nolen-Hoeksema, S., & Girgus, J. S. (1994). The emergence of gender differences in depression in adolescence. *Psychological Bulletin, 115,* 424–443.

Ohannessian, C. M., Lerner, R. M., Lerner, J. V., & Von Eye, A. (1999). Does self-competence predict gender differences in adolescent depression and anxiety? *Journal of Adolescence, 22,* 397–411.

Piaget, J. (1970). *Science of education and the psychology of the child* (Trans. D. Coltman). New York: Orion.

Piaget, J., & Inhelder, B. (1958). *The growth of logical thinking from childhood to adolescence.* New York: Basic Books.

Piaget, J., & Inhelder, B. (1969). *The psychology of the child.* New York: Basic Books.

Reimer, M. (1996). "Sinking into the ground": The development and consequences of shame in adolescence. *Developmental Review, 16,* 321–363.

Roberts, W., & Strayer, J. (1996). Empathy, emotional expressiveness and prosocial behavior. *Child Development, 67,* 449–470.

Rodin, J. (1992). *Body traps.* New York: William Morrow.

Rosenblum, G. D., & Lewis, M. (1999). The relations among body image, physical attractiveness, and body mass in adolescence. *Child Development, 70,* 50–64.

Royzman, E. B., & Kumar, R. (2000). On the relative preponderance of empathic sorrow and its relation to common-sense morality (Ideas in progress). Manuscript.

Saarni, C. (1984). An observational study of children's attempts to monitor their expressive behavior. *Child Development, 55,* 1504–1513.

Saarni, C. (1993). Socialization of emotion. In M. Lewis & J. Haviland (Eds.), *Handbook of emotions* (pp. 435–446). New York: Guilford.

Saarni, C. (1999). *The development of emotional competence.* New York: Guilford.

Salovey, P., Rothman, A. J., Detweiler, J. B., & Steward, W. T. (2000). Emotional states and physical health. *American Psychologist, 55,* 110–121.

Seligman, M. E. P., & Csikszentmihalyi, M. (2000). Positive psychology. *American Psychologist, 55,* 5–14.

Simmons, R. G., & Blyth, D. A. (1987). *Moving into adolescence: The impact of pubertal change and school context.* Hawthorne, NY: Aldine de Gruyter.

Simmons, R. G., Burgeson, R., Carlton-Ford, S., & Blyth, D. A. (1987). The impact of cumulative change in early adolescence. *Child Development, 58,* 1120–1234.

Simon, R. W., Eder, D., & Evans, C. (1992). The development of feeling norms underlying romantic love among adolescent females. *Social Psychology Quarterly, 55,* 26–46.

Stapley, J. C., & Haviland, J. M. (1989). Beyond depression: Gender differences in normal adolescents' emotional experiences. *Sex Roles, 20,* 295–308.

Strayer, J. (1993). Children's concordant emotions and cognitions in response to observed emotions. *Child Development, 64,* 188–201.

Tangney, J. P. (1990). Assessing individual differences in proneness to shame and guilt: The development of self-conscious affect and attribution inventory. *Journal of Personality and Social Psychology, 59,* 102–111.

Thompson, R. A. (1989). Causal attributions and children's emotional understanding. In C. Saarni & P. L. Harris (Eds.), *Children's understanding of emotion* (pp. 117–150). New York: Cambridge University Press.

Underwood, A. (1999). How well do you know your kid? *Newsweek International,* May 10.

Valiant, G. E. (2000). Adaptive mental mechanisms: Their roles in positive psychology. *American Psychologist, 55,* 89–98.

Von Salisch, M. (1991). *Kinderfreundschaften.* Göttingen: Hogrefe.

Wiggers, M., & Van Lieshout, C. (1985). Development of recognition of emotion: Children's reliance on situational and facial expressive cues. *Developmental Psychology, 21,* 338–349.

Wimmer, H., & Perner, J. (1983). Beliefs about beliefs: Representation and constraining function of wrong beliefs in young children's understanding of deception. *Cognition, 13,* 103–128.

CHAPTER FOURTEEN

Self-Concept and Self-Esteem Development

Jerome B. Dusek and Julie Guay McIntyre

Introduction

As DuBois and Hirsch (2000) have noted, investigations of the "self," whether called self-concept, self-esteem, identity, self-regard, or some other term, abound. The study of the self in its many facets has arguably been more plentiful than research in any other area of psychology in general and developmental psychology in particular. Questions concerning the self have been addressed by psychologists from a variety of subdisciplines. Hence, cognitive psychologists, those investigating attachment concerns, investigators of clinical and personality development, and social psychologists all contribute to our growing understanding of concerns surrounding the self (Harter, 1999).

The richness of these endeavors has gone far in delineating the important contributors to development of self-views, the significance of holding healthy self-views, and the advancement of theory concerning self-views. In addition, these efforts have stimulated reconsideration and reconceptualization that has allowed refinements in theory and application while at the same time opening new avenues of pursuit.

Issues of definition

The widespread interest in the self has sparked a number of controversies. One entails matters of definition. In general usage, many employ the terms self-concept and self-esteem interchangeably, which also is the case in much of the published literature. Others investigating the self, however, prefer to define self-concept as the dimensions or categories along which we view the self (e.g., student, athlete, friend), a qualitative measure, and self-esteem as our evaluation or assessment of our self (e.g., on a Likert scale) on each dimension, a quantitative measure. While all adolescents have a student self-concept they vary in their assessment of their judgment of how good a student they are and how important this dimension is to their overall self-esteem. The distinction between the terms self-concept and self-esteem, then, is more than a matter of semantics because it guides research efforts, for example, in the realm of global vs. domain-specific aspects of the self discussed below.

In order to simplify matters for the reader, we choose to not debate the distinction between the terms self-esteem and self-concept here. Although the vast majority of the research cited below concerns self-esteem, we shall, as is common in the literature, use the terms self-concept and self-esteem in a manner consistent with usage by the researchers whom we cite.

Global vs. domain-specific selves

An important issue for researchers interested in delineating relations between the self and other aspects of development centers on how many selves we have. Initial research measured what today is referred to as global self-esteem (e.g., Coopersmith, 1967; Rosenberg, 1979), an aggregate self-perspective drawn from the various domains of the self. Although this approach offers simplicity, it does not allow an assessment of the adolescent's sense of competence in specific domains (e.g., academic, athletic, social). Moreover, the notion of a global self-esteem presumes (a) that the adolescent indeed somehow summarizes the self across various domains and that (b) each domain is equally important both for each adolescent and for adolescents in the aggregate, each a highly tenuous assumption (e.g., Harter, 1999; Marsh & Hattie, 1996).

Current approaches, then, take the perspective that the concept of the self involves a variety of specific domains and that adolescents may feel more or less positively about their domain-specific selves. Hence, researchers measure the adolescent's self-esteem in a variety of domains, with some of these being more salient during different times in the adolescent's life or at different times during daily interactions (Dusek, 1996). As a result, it has become possible to examine differential influences on specific domains of the self. This is not to say that researchers have entirely abandoned the concept of a general self; indeed, some of the most commonly used scales include a "general" self-esteem measure. Nonetheless, the emphasis tends to be focused on domain-specific assessments.

To further complicate matters, Rosenberg (1986) has distinguished between barometric and baseline self-esteem. The former refers to evaluations of the self at a particular moment in time, and is presumed to fluctuate with immediate experiences. The latter is a more long-term view of the self based on one's developmental history in a particular domain of the self. Hence, receiving a very good or very poor grade on a test, for example, might substantially alter one's barometric self-esteem but likely would not alter one's baseline self-esteem. Changes in baseline self-esteem occur, of course, but they are more slow and gradual; continued increases or decreases in school performance, for example, could result in an increased or decreased baseline academic self-esteem, respectively. It is the relative consistency of the baseline self-esteem that plays the important role of tempering the momentary fluctuations in barometric self-esteem; several days or less after receiving an unexpected test grade one's academic self-esteem will return to its prior state.

In the research cited below, the instruments employed generally assess baseline self-esteem, unless otherwise noted. In a number of instances domain-specific measures were employed.

Measuring self-concept and self-esteem

Measurement of self-concept or self-esteem emphasizes two related concerns: how the measurement is made (self-report, informed observer) and the reliability and validity of the measure used (Dusek, 2000). The vast majority of studies employ self-report measures. Participants are asked to make a self-judgment by choosing between two bipolar choices, writing a self-description, or using a Likert scale to indicate their self-evaluation. These various self-report measures generally have sound reliability and validity. Studies utilizing other measures of the self (e.g., informed observer) vary in their reliability and validity, and are rarely seen. To date, little by the way of research comparing differing measures of self as related to research findings has been done. Research using multi-trait–multimethod approaches (Campbell & Fiske, 1959) could be very useful in helping to disentangle disparate findings and pointing the way to more profitable research, as Marsh, Craven, and Debus (1998) have indicated.

Reliability of measures of the self generally has involved test–retest or internal consistency data. Validity of the various measures of self come in the form of construct validity; measures of self are related to academic achievement, personality (e.g., depression), adjustment, other measures of self, and other constructs. Generally, the measures employed in the research reported below fare well both with regard to reliability and validity.

A historical concern of developmental psychologists, namely, the equivalence of a measuring instrument across an age span, has generally been ignored. Two widely used and notable exceptions are the scales developed by Harter (1985, 1988) and Marsh (Marsh & Hattie, 1996). These investigators have developed scales applicable to different age groups and have shown that the scales developed for different age groups measure equivalent constructs.

In the literature we review below we report findings noting the type of measure used. While one cannot argue for a single, one-size-fits-all measure, it is important to note that these concerns can be the root of disparate findings and confusing conclusions (Dusek, 2000). In this chapter, then, we report findings and make some note, where appropriate, that differences in findings between studies might be related to differences in the measures employed.

Scope of this chapter

Several limitations have been placed on the material included below. First, we do not review research dealing with identity development; it is detailed in chapter 9 of this volume. We limit our review to research in the domains of self-concept and self-esteem. While there are many interesting facets to the study of these aspects of the self, due to space limitations a number cannot be addressed. We have chosen to focus this chapter on moderating influences on the self. To this end we review information on biological factors related to self-development, the role of the school in self-development, and parental influences. Unfortunately, we could not include other areas in which exciting research is being done, for example, the role of peers in the formation and maintenance of self-esteem (e.g., Berndt, 1996; Keefe & Berndt, 1996). Finally, while of necessity we must limit our discussion of methodological concerns, such as some of those noted above, we raise them within the context of these other foci. Following our review we discuss some directions for promising future research.

Some Moderating Influences on Self-Concept/ Self-Esteem Development

There are many factors that impact on the adolescent's developing sense of self. Adolescence begins with the biological changes leading up to and through the growth-spurt years. This maturation has wide-ranging impacts, including its influence on the sense of self. We discuss those influences first. Next, we examine research on the relation of schooling to the self. Adolescents spend much of the day for nine months of the year in the school environment, and it has a substantial impact on self-esteem. Parents have a long-standing relationship with the adolescent and that developmental history continues through the adolescent years. Then we discuss parental influences on the self.

Maturational influences on self-esteem

Pubertal timing. Since the 1950s, a number of studies have examined the impact of early, late, or on-time physical development on self-esteem/self-image. Two general theories have been posited to address the differential effects that timing of physical development relative to one's peers has on overall adjustment. The deviance hypothesis (e.g., Petersen & Crockett, 1985; Petersen & Taylor, 1980) states that being pubertally off time, whether early or late, causes difficulties for adaptation because it places the adolescent in a socially deviant category. Being different is particularly troublesome for adolescents who have yet to achieve their identity and, therefore, seek to fit in by being as much like their peers as possible until they have established their own sense of self. Alternatively, the developmental stage termination hypothesis (e.g., Peskin & Livson, 1972; Peskin, 1973) states that early maturation interrupts the acquisition and consolidation of adaptive skills that characterize middle childhood. Early maturers are more at risk for developmental difficulties because they are more likely to be involved in roles and activities that they do not yet have the skills/ability to handle.

It should be noted that a wide range of methods have been employed to categorize adolescents into one of these three groups: bone ossification, hormone levels, age at peak height velocity, age at menarche, and self-ratings and ratings by nurses/medical personnel on specific indices of pubertal growth (such as pubic hair growth and pattern and breast development in females, and facial hair in males). More recently, adolescents' self-reports of global pubertal development, based on a six-point rating scale indicating how much physical change they have noticed, and perception of pubertal development in relation to classmates, have been used outside of medical settings (e.g., Alsaker, 1992). Therefore, in some studies, maturational timing was based on how participants compared to others in the sample on some objective criterion or measure. For example, in the Berkeley and Oakland Growth Studies, those in the upper and lower 20 percent of the sample on skeletal age were classified as early and late maturers, respectively. Interestingly, these researchers not only studied those at the extremes of the pubertal timing spectrum, but also excluded "on-time" maturers. In other studies (e.g., Brooks-Gunn and Warren, 1985), individuals were classified by comparing some criterion, in Brooks-Gunn and Warren's case age at menarche, to national norms. Finally, in other cases subjective self-assessments have been used to classify subjects into pubertal timing groups (e.g., Alsaker, 1992). Regardless of the method used for classifying participants into pubertal timing groups, the terms "early," "late," and "on-time" are relative. Therefore, a person classified as a late maturer in one sample may have been classified as "on-time" in another, depending on the classification measure and the comparison group. On the one hand, the lack of a standard measure of pubertal timing can be seen as a significant difficulty in identifying reliable findings. On the other hand, the adolescent's self-rating of being early, on-time, or late in physical growth likely is more important than objective assessments to any psychological consequences of pubertal timing on development.

Females. Because simply asking females their age of menarche is an easy means of measuring pubertal timing and because body image historically has been the focus of research with females, the impact of pubertal timing on self-esteem has been studied more in adolescent girls than in their male counterparts. Cumulatively, research has shown that being "early" has the most detrimental effects on females' self-esteem, as well as on other correlates of self-esteem such as body image and appearance. There are two main reasons for this finding: (1) girls in general are already about two years ahead of their male counterparts in terms of physical development (referring to peak growth); if they are early maturers, they may be as much as five to six years ahead of normal maturing boys and as much as two to three years ahead of their same-sex peers. Drawing upon the deviance hypothesis, being this out of sync with peers may lead to feelings of isolation and confusion at a time when social comparison is so important. (2) Consistent with the developmental stage termination hypothesis, early maturing girls are at risk for delinquency, depression, drug and alcohol use, premature sexual activity, and school-related problems (Silbereisen et al., 1989), perhaps, in part, because they associate with older adolescents. These girls often may be forced to cope with issues and activities (e.g., dating) that most of their peers have yet to encounter. Furthermore, because they look so much older than they are, adults as well as peers may have inappropriate expectations for psychological maturity that can be stressful for the early maturing adolescent.

Whether it is best for females to be "late" or "on-time" seems to be somewhat more inconclusive than the pervasive disadvantages of being "early." Perhaps the contradictory results are due, at least in part, to the particular social context that is salient for the adolescent female and the specific measure(s) used to tap feelings about the self (e.g., body image, global self-esteem, physical appearance). Consider the following example that highlights the importance of context. Tobin-Richards, Boxer, and Petersen (1983) found that being on-time was associated with more positive feelings about attractiveness and body image among girls. Brooks-Gunn and Warren (1985), on the other hand, found that among ballet dancers, it was the late maturers who had the most positive body image. These findings are explained in terms of a "goodness of fit" between the requirements of the environmental setting and the physical and/or behavioral characteristics of the person. It would be interesting to determine if late-maturing girls who are dancers, gymnasts, or figure skaters, groups who are likely to be advantaged in terms of body image, feel less positive about themselves when this role is a less salient part of the self. For example, if these measures were taken "off season" or in a context that places greater emphasis on physical maturity (e.g., a school dance), results may be different.

One consistent finding is that girls who report less satisfaction with their body shape and weight tend to have lower self-esteem than do those who have a more positive body image (Martin et al., 1988). More recent research has examined whether specific aspects (i.e., weight, body shape) and general aspects (i.e., overall feelings about appearance) of body image make distinct, independent contributions to the prediction of self-esteem among adolescent females. In their study of Scottish females, Williams and Currie (2000) found that early maturation and lower ratings of body image were associated with lower reported levels of self-esteem among 11-year-olds. They also found a mediational effect of body image – the negative effects of off-time maturation on self-esteem were due to heightened experiences of body-image concerns. Among 13-year-olds, body-size concerns, poorer perceived appearance, and late maturation all were predictive of lower self-esteem. However, there was no mediational role for body image in the association between late pubertal timing and lower self-esteem. The authors explain that among older adolescent females the negative effects of late pubertal timing might be attributable more to social factors (e.g., lower popularity with boys) than to individual psychological factors (e.g., body image).

Males. Overall, it seems that being an early maturer is best for male's sense of self-esteem. Consistent with the deviation hypothesis, early maturing males are more in sync (or at least, less out of sync) with the physical development of their female peers, who, on average, are two years more physically mature. Furthermore, being an early maturer also means being taller and more muscular, both advantageous, or at least considered attractive, in a society that values athletic prowess if one is interested in excelling in athletics. According to the stage termination hypothesis, however, being an early maturer should be a disadvantage. Although some research has documented negative outcomes, e.g., increased anxiety, lower intellectual curiosity, and increased submissiveness, for early maturing males during the initial stages of the growth spurt (see Peskin, 1967, 1973), these negative effects on correlates of self-esteem do not seem to be long-lived. Perhaps the temporary setbacks of being an early maturing male are outweighed by the advantages of early maturity.

Pioneering research by Mussen and Jones (1957) concluded that peers rated early maturers as more self-assured compared to late maturers. Using projective techniques that are scored by analyzing the central theme in one's story, they also found that the early maturers made more positive self-attributions to the central figures. For the most part, the self-esteem advantage for early-maturing males has been replicated. In his study of Norwegian adolescents, Alsaker (1992) also found positive effects of early maturation and negative effects of late maturation on self-esteem for males. However, he also noted that 8th-grade boys who perceived themselves as early had more negative global self-evaluations than those who were on-time. This may be another example of the context effect; perhaps in other cultures a more mature physical stature does not bring with it the same meaning as it does in the United States, where most of this research has been conducted.

Methodological issues. As noted above, researchers have used a variety of methods (some objective, others subjective) to determine maturational status and to measure self-esteem (most utilize global measures). These differing methods of identifying early and late maturers may contribute to conflicting findings. Furthermore, the use of global measures of self-esteem may limit the identification of important relationships and/or mask important discrepancies in findings involving various aspects of the self. In addition, males have been studied much less frequently than females. Perhaps this underrepresentation of research with males helps explain why the findings seem more clear-cut for males than for females.

Most research conducted on maturational influences on self-esteem has been in the United States, often with white, middle-class samples. Generalizability should not be taken for granted, as issues of weight and maturational timing likely have different meaning in different cultures and subcultures. For example, African American adolescents are less likely than Latino or white adolescents to judge themselves as overweight. Furthermore, African American and white women have different perspectives on body size, with greater weight connoting power for African Americans (see Pritchard, King, & Czajka-Narins, 1997). More comparative studies need to be conducted to better understand the meaning of relative timing of physical maturation and how it impacts self-esteem across diverse contexts and among various ethnic groups.

School transitions and self-esteem

In addition to the many physiological and psychosocial changes of adolescence, multiple transitions at school also occur. In early adolescence some students move from elementary school to junior high and then to high school (grades K-6/7–9/10–12 or the 6/3/3 pattern). Others experience fewer transitions by staying in the same school until 8th grade, then moving onto high school (grades K-8/9–12 or the 8/4 pattern). Much research conducted in the 1970s and through the 1980s by Simmons, Blyth, and colleagues examined the differential effects of these grade-level organizational patterns on self-esteem and achievement (as well as other variables beyond the scope of this chapter) among adolescents. Perhaps the most intriguing finding they reported was that the transition in seventh grade (the 6/3/3 pattern) was accompanied by a decrease in self-esteem (Simmons et al., 1979; Blyth, Simmons, & Carlton-Ford, 1983) for girls. They further reported that a recovery to initial levels of self-esteem failed to occur for a sizable proportion of the girls who made the junior high transition (Simmons & Blyth, 1987).

Wigfield and Eccles (1994) also found an initial decline in self-esteem following the transition to junior high school but, unlike the findings of Simmons and Blyth (1987), this was true for both males and females. Still, boys reported higher self-esteem than did girls at all four waves of the study. Among their students, self-esteem increased during seventh grade; therefore, the disruption in self-esteem did not appear to be as long-lasting as it was for many of the females in Simmons and Blyth's sample. Other researchers have reported that self-esteem increased during seventh grade (see Nottleman, 1987) and throughout the high school years (see O'Malley & Bachman, 1983; Dusek & Flaherty, 1981), perhaps because adolescents were becoming more comfortable with the physical changes of the growth spurt and because the identity crisis was being resolved.

A number of hypotheses have been posited to explain the "vulnerability" in self-esteem when adolescents move to a new school in seventh grade. According to the overload hypothesis, too many changes are experienced at the same time and, therefore, the adolescent is bombarded with stressors without adequate coping strategies (Simmons et al., 1987). Changes in school routines, attending a larger school, and meeting a large number of new students, all require adjustments that have not been experienced by most adolescents in the recent past.

Another contributor to the drop in self-esteem during the transition to seventh grade may result from the fact that adolescents are becoming more cognitively sophisticated, engaging in social comparison and consequently developing a more realistic view of their capabilities than they may previously have had. Marsh (1989) has even suggested that a drop in self-esteem should not be equated as "bad" and should not be blamed on the educational system. It may be that adolescents are simply more capable than younger children of incorporating feedback about themselves; therefore, they are painfully aware that they are not always the best at everything as they may have thought or may have been told.

Finally, according to the mismatch hypothesis (Eccles & Midgely, 1989), when adolescents move from elementary to junior high they enter into a school system with more rules and restrictions at precisely the time when they are striving for independence. New teacher expectations for performance, more stringent grading criteria, less personal attention from teachers, and a disruption in social networks occur at a time when, in many ways, adolescents most need the support provided by teachers and friends in earlier grades.

At first glance, none of the above hypotheses explain why males in Simmons and Blyth's (1987) sample did not experience similar decreases in self-esteem similar to those of their female counterparts during this 7th-grade transition. After all, they, too, were experiencing many physiological changes while adjusting to the multiple new stressors of a new school environment. And they also had the advanced social comparison skills of their female counterparts, which might have put them at risk for a decrease in self-esteem and the mismatch between person and environment experienced by the females in the study. Perhaps the explanation of the gender difference lies in the general earlier maturity of adolescent females. Consistent with research findings on gender differences in body image cited above, the girls in Simmons and Blyth's research rated themselves as less good-looking than their male counterparts and indicated that they were less satisfied with their looks, weight and body build. In addition, in the 7th grade they began to care more than boys about their looks and about body build. As discussed in the previous section, adolescent girls often rate themselves lower in physical attractiveness than do boys (see Harter, 1990; Pliner, Chaiken, & Flett, 1990). Furthermore, their perception of physical attractiveness is tied more closely to self-esteem than is true for males (Allgood-Merten, Lewinsohn, & Hops, 1990). These discrepancies, which may account for the gender differences, may also have existed in the Wigfield and Eccles (1994) sample, but their effects may not have been identified because Wigfield and Eccles employed only a global measure of self-esteem.

The school transition research reviewed above was conducted primarily with white students, thereby limiting the generalizability of the findings. Although the original data set of Simmons et al. (1987) included African Americans, their most widely cited and best known research examined only the subsample of white students. What is less well known is that the African American girls from the overall sample reported increases in self-esteem over these same transitions. Furthermore, many studies have reported that African American girls have a much more positive body image than their white counterparts, which suggests that the mediating effect of physical changes on the relation between school transitions and self-esteem may differ as a function of ethnicity.

More recent research on the impact of the school transition on self-views has begun to focus on ethnically diverse samples from various socioeconomic backgrounds, as well as on the moderators that underlie the relation between school transition and self-views (see Fenzel, 2000). Seidman et al. (1994) examined the impact of school transitions in early adolescence among poor black, white, and Latino urban youth. They found that self-esteem declined across the school transition regardless of whether the transition was made before (in 5th or 6th grades) or during seventh grade. Interestingly, there were no significant gender or race/ethnicity effects.

Seidman et al. (1996) sampled an ethnically diverse population of poor black, European American, Latino, and Asian American urban youth. They, too, examined the impact of the school transition on self-esteem, but their focus was on the transition to senior high, less frequently a focus of research than the earlier transition to middle school or junior high. No significant change in self-esteem was found across the high school transition (contrary to findings of Simmons & Blyth, 1987 and Seidman et al., 1994). It may be that because this was the second transition for these adolescents, so they had better coping skills to bring to bear on the stressors associated with the transition. Consistent with Seidman et al. (1994), there were also no significant gender or race/ethnicity interaction effects. The authors note that this may be due to the homogeneous socioeconomic status of the sample, which may, in essence, override the effects of race and ethnicity. Perhaps differences would have been detected in both of these studies if specific domains of self-esteem were tapped in addition to global self-worth.

More research needs to be conducted to understand ethnic group differences in the effects of the school transition on self-views. It may be that the mediating role of physical development differs for black and white female adolescents because black females develop approximately a year earlier than their white counterparts (Herman-Giddens et al., 1997). The earlier physical maturity of black females may allow them to adapt to changing physical characteristics, such as body shape and size, prior to experiencing the stresses of changing schools. White females, in contrast, may have to adapt to both changes (along with others) simultaneously, which may be more difficult. Further research clarifying the nature of these ethnic group differences is needed in order to develop appropriate intervention and/or prevention programs for those at risk during this developmentally "vulnerable" time.

Methodological concerns in the study of achievement and self-esteem. Prior to reviewing the literature on the relation between self-esteem and school performance, it is necessary to point out some of the problems that pervade this area of research. This is particularly important because from a common-sense view and at first glance, it may seem rather obvious that positive or high self-esteem should facilitate academic achievement (good grades) and vise versa – good grades should enhance self-esteem. Students readily note that they like some courses because they do well in them, and dislike others because they do not do well; in each case this is a self-judgment, a form of self-esteem. However, both the strength of these relations (correlations) between self-esteem and school performance, as well as the direction of causation in the relationship, continue to be debated.

There are many reasons for the discrepant findings in the strength of the relation between measures of self-esteem and school performance. First, various levels of self-esteem, from global self-esteem, to overall academic self-concept, to self-perceptions in particular academic disciplines, such as math, English or science, have been employed. Generally, correlations are stronger when linking self-esteem and achievement within a particular domain. For example, Marsh (1993) found that math achievement was substantially correlated with math self-concept (median r = 0.33), very slightly less correlated with general academic self-concept (median r = 0.26), and even less strongly correlated with English self-concept (median r = 0.10). Clearly, the strength of the relation depends on the specificity and congruity of the self-esteem measure vis-à-vis the subject matter.

Second, measures of academic achievement have varied across studies. Some studies have included objective measures, such as standardized test scores; others have included subjective measures, such as teacher ratings or teacher-assigned grades, and/or self-perceptions of academic competence. Because teacher-assigned grades and self-perceptions are more subject to measurement error and other biases, they are a less desirable measure of achievement for the study of relations between school achievement and self-esteem.

Third, as Byrne (1996) noted, the formats of the instruments, both self-esteem and achievement, employed have varied in terms of scaling format, number of scale points, number of items, and specificity of item content. In addition, the construct validity of the self-concept and achievement measures has varied dramatically across studies (Byrne, 1996). Some have been widely used and have proven psychometric properties, while others may only have been employed in a particular study with little evidence of psychometric soundness (Byrne, 1984; Hattie, 1992; Wylie, 1974, 1979). A smaller number of scale points for grades, self-esteem scores, or both, can attenuate the magnitude of the relations found. Validity concerns also are critical to interpreting findings.

Finally, as Hattie (1992) has pointed out, samples have varied widely in terms of gender, age, grade level, academic ability, socioeconomic status, and ethnicity. Without the type of systematic research we note below, it is very difficult to make general statements with a high degree of confidence.

Relations between self-esteem and academic achievement. The majority of studies have found positive correlations between self-esteem and academic achievement, although often the correlations were not very large (West, Fish, & Stevens, 1980; Hansford & Hattie, 1982; Hattie, 1992; Wylie, 1979). Even when strong correlations have been reported, determining the direction of causality has proven difficult. As DuBois and Tevendale (1999) note, "long-term prospective studies are needed in which self-esteem and criterion aspects of adjustment are assessed on multiple occasions over extended portions of development and examined with respect to their ongoing interrelationships with one another across time" (p. 112). Although several longitudinal studies have been conducted to clarify issues of causation and direction of effect, the results have been far from crystal clear. In fact, it seems the more research that is done, the more murky the waters. Some have found a causal predominance of grades over self-esteem, others have found a causal predominance of self-esteem over grades, others have been unable to establish causal dominance (Calsyn & Kenny, 1977; Shavelson & Bolus, 1982; Byrne, 1986; Maruyama, Rubin, & Kingsberry, 1981; Pottebaum, Keith, & Ehly, 1986; Newman 1984; Marsh, 1987). Even when using the same data set, researchers have come to different conclusions (see Newman, 1984; Marsh, 1987) regarding causal predominance in the relation between self-esteem and school achievement. Still others (e.g., Skaalvik & Hagtvet, 1990) have reported different directions of causality for different age groups.

In many ways, this lack of consistency is not surprising, given the list of methodological problems mentioned above as well as variations in the time frames studied. As Skaalvik and Hagtvet (1990) reminded us, if the time lag between measures is too short, little change may occur. On the other hand, if the time lag is too long, developmental trends may be masked. It is probably safe to assume that the relation between self-esteem and achievement is reciprocal, with the direction of effect changing at different developmental levels and as different variables, prior to adolescents' becoming more salient.

In an attempt to unravel the confusing findings, more recent researchers have employed both zero-order correlations and structural equation-modeling techniques (Hoge, Smit, & Crist, 1995). These researchers concluded that "the real influences are weaker than correlational studies led us to believe" but that grades have "a bit more influence on self-concept than the opposite" (p. 312). In other words, the reciprocal relationship may be present, but the influence of grades on self-esteem is a bit stronger.

Researchers are also beginning to examine racial differences in the relation between self-esteem and academic outcomes. For example, in a comparison of African American and European American students, Osborne (1995) found a weakening correlation between self-esteem and academic outcomes from 8th to 10th grades for African American students. The most striking finding (and the only statistically significant one) was that this decreasing correlation over time was strongest for African American males. Using Steele's (1992) disidentification hypothesis, Osborne suggested that these males may detach their self-esteem from academic outcomes as a means of protecting their overall self-esteem. The African Americans in this sample scored lower on measures of academic achievement but reported higher global self-esteem. It would be interesting to determine whether those who disidentify the most score highest on ethnic identity, a measure not included in this study. Furthermore, more research examining the direction and strength of effect needs to be conducted with other ethnically diverse populations, as most studies have been conducted in the United States with white/European Americans.

The role of parents and family

Interest in the role of parents and family on self-views has a long and rich history. Modern researchers have focused on the impact of parents and family from several different approaches. One method that has been used is to examine parental rearing practices and their effect on self-esteem. Hence, researchers have examined parental warmth, general home atmosphere, and predominant rearing style as related to the development of self-views. A second approach in this regard has been to relate adolescents' self-views to family characteristics, such as living in a mother-custody home, being in a family undergoing divorce, and family socioeconomic standing.

Parental rearing practices. Initial research on the influence of parental rearing practices on self-development focused on single dimensions of rearing. For example, in one of the earliest studies of its kind, Coopersmith (1967) reported that 5th- and 6th-grade boys with high self-esteem perceived their parents as highly warm, supportive, and accepting. They described their home atmosphere as one of tolerance and understanding, with clear rules, fair punishment, mutual respect between parents and adolescents, and little hostility. In contrast, low-self-esteem boys were reared by parents who were either too permissive, and perhaps even neglectful, or who were harsh disciplinarians.

These same general findings have been reported for 7th- through 9th-grade males and females (Litovsky & Dusek, 1985, 1988) and for adolescents of differing ethnic backgrounds, including African American, Asian, and Hispanic adolescents (Felson & Zielinski, 1989; Harter, 1990; Leiderman, Meldman, & Ritter, 1989). Regardless of the adolescent's ethnic background or gender, parents who employ positive rearing practices raise adolescents who value themselves and are able to learn their competencies because the home atmosphere is supportive and conducive to personal growth, and who get along better with peers (Dekovic & Meeus, 1997). In contrast, parental intrusiveness and use of guilt to control the adolescent's behavior is associated with poorer self-esteem (Litovsky & Dusek, 1985).

More recent approaches to examining the influence of parental rearing practices on self-views has focused less on individual dimensions of rearing and more on global measures of parental rearing styles. Generally, these styles involve classifying parents into different groups based on adolescents' perceptions of parenting on a combination of rearing dimensions. Drawing on Baumrind's (1978) earlier work, Maccoby and Martin (1983) identified four general parental rearing styles. The authoritative style is characterized by a high degree of responsiveness (warmth, supportiveness, nurturing, acceptance) as well as a high degree of demandingness of age-appropriate behavior. The authoritarian style involves relatively low levels of responsiveness and high levels of demandingness. The indulgent style involves high levels of responsiveness but low levels of demandingness. The final parenting style, indifferent, involves relatively low levels of both responsiveness and demandingness.

The research evidence overwhelmingly supports the view that the authoritative rearing style is associated with the most positive outcomes. Adolescents who perceive their parents as using authoritative rearing practices do better in school (Dornbusch et al., 1987; Steinberg et al., 1992), have better skills in coping with stress (Dusek & Danko, 1994; McIntyre & Dusek, 1995), are better psychologically adjusted as assessed by a variety of instruments, and have better self-esteem (Lamborn et al., 1991). Research shows these benefits for African American, Hispanic, and white adolescents (Steinberg et al., 1994). In contrast, adolescents who perceive their parents as using predominantly one of the other rearing styles rated themselves higher on less desirable outcomes, such as delinquency (Indulgent, Indifferent), extreme dependency on parents (Authoritarian), somatic distress (Authoritarian), and irresponsible, socially immature behavior (Indulgent). Finally, some evidence (Steinberg et al., 1994) indicates that continued exposure to authoritative parenting is associated with continued good psychological adjustment, but that continued exposure to alternative rearing styles is associated with increases in undesirable outcomes, such as declining school performance and increased somatic distress.

Theorists have posited a variety of explanations for the apparent superiority of authoritative parenting. One important component of the authoritative rearing style is the use of inductive discipline, which involves explaining to the adolescent why what was done was unacceptable and providing alternative means of behaving. Inductive discipline uses a punishment situation as a teaching/learning opportunity, and promotes a give and take in a warm, affectionate atmosphere fostering identification with the parents (Steinberg et al., 1992). In turn, the adolescent learns that mistakes are tolerable and feels more self-assurance in trying new things and exploring competencies, both of which are important to self-esteem. The power-assertive (e.g., the use of physical punishment, withdrawal of privileges, or the threat of these) and love-withdrawal (e.g., ignoring the child, the use of guilt, or other means of implicitly threatening abandonment) discipline techniques foster extreme dependency – a precursor of a number of psychological disorders – do not teach alternative means of behaving, and indeed may teach inappropriate means of social interaction.

By placing limits that are appropriate to the adolescent's competencies, and by allowing rules to be flexible as the situation dictates (e.g., staying out late on a school night for some special event), authoritative parents promote the learning of limits and competencies. The limits imposed teach that there are rules to be followed, in contrast to the indulgent parenting style, for example, in which rule enforcement is lax. The latter, of course, is related to increasing delinquent behavior and the poor self-esteem associated with it (Wells, 1989).

The warmth and acceptance exhibited by authoritatively oriented parents is associated with a sense in the adolescent of being valuable, which in turn is related to a more positive self-esteem. Although one must be concerned about attributing causal predominance to parental rearing practices, the small amount of longitudinal research that exists (e.g., Steinberg et al., 1994) is consistent with the perspective that rearing practices foster the sound psychological development with which they are associated.

Cautions about rearing styles. A number of cautions must be noted. First, the study of rearing styles, or even more simply the study of how rearing dimensions relate to outcomes, relies largely on offspring report of perceptions of parental rearing practices (as well as many of the measures to which they are related). As Schaefer (1965a, 1965b) initially pointed out, it is these perceptions which affect offspring and hence may be most effective in understanding the link between parenting practices and offspring outcomes. Indeed, differences in perceptions of rearing practices may account in part for differences in self-esteem of adolescent siblings. In turn, however, alternative measures of rearing styles and practices could result in different findings. Relying on sibling reports, laboratory observations of adolescent–parent interactions, or parental reports of rearing ractices no doubt would help clarify the complexity involved in the relation between child-rearing and self-esteem.

Second, it is important to note that no parent uses solely a single rearing style. What adolescents report is a predominant style. No doubt, some of the confusions that exist about the relation between child-rearing and self-esteem is the result of parental use of differing styles, or of parental changes in styles of rearing, such as may occur under times of extreme distress (e.g., divorce, death of a loved one, mid-life crisis). Little research has been conducted on these concerns.

Third, despite the increase in single-parent families and the percentage of adolescents who will spend some time in a single-parent family, the majority of adolescents live in two-parent homes. While some research (e.g., Litovsky & Dusek, 1988) suggests perceived maternal warmth and nurturing may be more important than perceived paternal warmth to sound self-esteem, research on the differential influences of maternal and paternal rearing styles on self-esteem is virtually nonexistent. Until such information is more available, the role of rearing on self-development remains incomplete.

Finally, in interpreting the findings of research on parental rearing practices it is important to note that a number of methodological concerns temper the conclusions one may draw. Research in these areas is not experimental – children cannot be assigned randomly to parents, parents cannot be assigned randomly to rearing styles, and families cannot be assigned randomly to socioeconomic circumstances, for example – but rather is correlational. As a result, concerns of direction of causality constantly are present. In addition, researchers have assumed implicitly that parenting styles are consistent over time and have remained so from early in the child's life. Of course, circumstances can cause changes in the parent's predominant rearing mode, and we know little of the impact of such changes.

Family circumstances. Adolescents not only have parents who rear them, but also grow up in a family structure: one vs. two parents, step-parent family, families undergoing divorce, and families from differing economic circumstances and ethnic backgrounds. Because these influences on adolescent development are central to other chapters we mention them only briefly here.

Rosenberg (1985) reported that adolescents living only with their mothers had lower self-esteem than adolescents living with both parents. This was especially true for those who were younger adolescents or who had mothers who were younger relative to the age of the adolescent. Rosenberg suggested that older adolescents have better coping skills for living in a single-parent family and that these skills allow them to maintain a better self-esteem. In addition, he suggested that older mothers may be better able to cope with divorce and its associated stressors and therefore not experience as great a decline in parenting skills as younger mothers. Maintenance of sound parenting skills is associated with better self-esteem in offspring.

Relations between social class and self-esteem have been the subject of numerous investigations. One can find evidence supporting the notion that adolescents from poorer backgrounds have lowered self-esteem (e.g., Demo & Savin-Williams, 1983; Bachman & O'Malley, 1986), but it appears that it is not socioeconomic status per se that is at the root of this finding. Rather, it appears that related conditions, such as links between economics and school performance and one's friends' social standing and self-esteem (Filsinger & Anderson, 1982), mediate the relation between socioeconomic status and the adolescent's self-esteem.

Summary and Conclusions

We reviewed the literature on three important influences on the adolescent's development of self-esteem: the physical changes undergone during the growth-spurt years, the impact of school transitions and school achievement, and parental rearing practices and family circumstances. We identified a number of important relations between these influences and the adolescent's self-views. Importantly, it is clear from the extant literature that although generalizations are reasonable and possible, individual difference characteristics are critical mediators that cannot be ignored. Physical growth impacts on the adolescent's self-perceptions, but the result depends on pubertal timing and ethnic group membership. School and school achievement help shape self-views, but they do so differently for those coming from the K-8 and the K-6 school systems. Dimensions of rearing and general parenting styles clearly play an important role in the adolescent's perception of the self, but these influences, too, are mediated by other family circumstances.

The role of other influences on self-esteem are being identified. For example, recent research on self-esteem development among adolescents in different social settings (urban vs. kibbutz; Orr & Dinur, 1995) points to the need to examine macro influences in the development of self-views. In this regard, some researchers (e.g., Hirsch et al., 2000) have begun to identify at a more micro level the components of these wider settings that are responsible for their influence on the self.

Other researchers (e.g., Kaplan & Lin, 2000; Scheier et al., 2000) are furthering our understanding of the role of self-esteem in aspects of deviant development (e.g., violence, school difficulties, alcohol use). Of special interest is research linking negative self-views to the later development of deviant behavior. By expanding the perspective of self-esteem to include both positive and negative self-views it will be possible to enhance our understanding of the role of the self even further.

Key Readings

Bracken, B. A. (Ed.). (1996). *Handbook of self-concept.* New York: Wiley.
This book makes a major contribution to the field by providing historical background on the constructs of self-esteem and self-concept as well as reviewing the literature in a variety of areas (e.g., family self-concept, physical self-concept, academic self-concept, age, race and gender issues). The author concludes by discussing his multidimensional model and its clinical applications.

DuBois, D. L., & Tevendale, H. D. (1999). Self-esteem in childhood and adolescence: Vaccine or epiphenomenon? *Applied and Preventative Psychology, 8,* 103–117.
This article provides an up-to-date review of the self-esteem debate: that self-esteem is highly influential on individual adjustment vs. the view that self-esteem effects do not exist at all. Of particular note is coverage of counterintuitive research linking high levels of self-esteem with maladaptive outcomes.

Dusek, J. B. (2000). Commentary on the special issue: The maturing of self-esteem research with early adolescents. *Journal of Early Adolescence, 20,* 231–240.
This article summarizes the findings of eight studies of self-esteem during the early adolescent years and points to some ways in which future researchers may further our understanding of self.

Harter, S. (1999). *The construction of the self: A developmental perspective.* New York: Guilford.
This book examines the question of how cognitive, social, and emotional processes work together in constructing a sense of self. An overarching theme is the diversity of pathways to self-worth and its correlates. Cognitive and social intervention strategies are reviewed as well as helpful suggestions for effective program evaluation.

References

Allgood-Merten, B., Lewinsohn, P. M., & Hops, H. (1990). Sex differences and adolescent depression. *Journal of Abnormal Psychology, 99,* 55–63.

Alsaker, F. D. (1992). Pubertal timing, overweight, and psychological adjustment. *Journal of Early Adolescence, 12*(4), 396–419.

Bachman, J. G., & O'Malley, P. (1986). Self-concepts, self-esteem, and educational experiences: The frog pond revisited (again). *Journal of Personality and Social Psychology, 50,* 35–46.

Baumrind, D. (1978). Parental disciplinary patterns and social competence in children. *Youth and Society, 9,* 239–276.

Berndt, T. J. (1996). Friendship in adolescence. In N. Vanzetti & S. Duck (Eds.), *A lifetime of relationships* (pp. 181–212). Pacific Grove, CA: Brooks Cole.

Blyth, D. A., Simmons, R. G., & Carlton-Ford, S. (1983). The adjustment of early adolescents to school transitions. *Journal of Early Adolescence, 3,* 105–120.

Bronfenbrenner, U. (1989). Ecological systems theory. In R. Vasta (Ed.), *Annals of child development: Vol. 6: Theories of child development: Revised formulations and current issues* (pp. 187–249). Greenwich, CT: JAI Press.

Brooks-Gunn, J., & Warren, M. P. (1985). The effects of delayed menarche in different contexts: Dance and nondance students. *Journal of Youth and Adolescence, 14,* 285–300.

Byrne, B. M. (1984). The general/academic self-concept nomological network: A review of construct validation research. *Review of Educational Research, 54,* 427–456.

Byrne, B. M. (1986). Self-concept/academic achievement relations: An investigation of dimensionality, stability, and causality. *Canadian Journal of Behavioural Science, 18,* 173–186.

Byrne, B. M. (1996). Academic self-concept: Its structure, measurement, and relation to academic achievement. In B. Bracken (Ed.), *Handbook of self-concept* (pp. 287–316). New York: Wiley.

Calsyn, R. J., & Kenny, D. A. (1977). Self-concept of ability and perceived evaluation of others: Cause or effect of academic achievement? *Journal of Educational Psychology, 69,* 136–145.

Campbell, D. T., & Fiske, D. W. (1959). Convergent and discriminant validation by the multitrait–multimethod matrix. *Psychological Bulletin, 56,* 81–105.

Coopersmith, S. (1967). *The antecedents of self-esteem.* San Francisco: Freeman.

Dekovic, M., & Meeus, W. (1997). Peer relations in adolescence: Effects of parenting and adolescents' self-concept. *Journal of Adolescence, 20,* 163–176.

Demo, D., & Savin-Williams, R. (1983). Early adolescent self-esteem as a function of social class: Rosenberg and Pearlin revisited. *American Journal of Sociology, 88,* 763–774.

Dornbusch, S. M., Ritter, P. L., Leiderman, P. H., Roberts, D. F., & Fraleigh, M. J. (1987). The relation of parenting style to adolescent school performance. *Child Development, 58,* 1244–1257.

DuBois, D. L., & Hirsch, B. J. (2000). Self-esteem in early adolescence: From stock character to marquee attraction. *Journal of Early Adolescence, 20,* 5–11.

DuBois, D. L., & Tevendale, H. D. (1999). Self-esteem in childhood and adolescence: Vaccine or epiphenomenon? *Applied and Preventative Psychology, 8,* 103–117.

Dusek, J. B. (1996). *Adolescent development and behavior* (3rd ed.). Upper Saddle River, NJ: Prentice Hall.

Dusek, J. B. (2000). Commentary on the special issue: The maturing of self-esteem research with early adolescents. *Journal of Early Adolescence, 20,* 231–240.

Dusek, J. B., & Danko, M. (1994). Adolescent coping styles and perceptions of parental childrearing. *Journal of Adolescent Research, 9,* 412–426.

Dusek, J. B., & Flaherty, J. (1981). The development of the self-concept during the adolescent years. *Monographs of the Society for Research in Child Development, 46*(4), Whole # 191.

Eccles, J. S., & Midgley, C. (1989). Stage/environment fit: Developmentally appropriate classrooms for early adolescents. In R. Ames & C. Ames (Eds.), *Research on motivation in education* (Vol. 3, pp. 139–181). New York: Academic Press.

Felson, R., & Zielinski, M. (1989). Children's self-esteem and parental support. *Journal of Marriage and the Family, 51,* 727–735.

Fenzel, M. (2000). Prospective study of changes in global self-worth and strain during the transition to middle school. *Journal of Early Adolescence, 20,* 93–116.

Filsinger, E., & Anderson, C. (1982). Social class and self-esteem in late adolescence: Dissonant context or self-efficacy? *Developmental Psychology, 18,* 380–384.

Hansford, B. D., & Hattie, J. A. (1982). The relationship between self and achievement/performance measures. *Review of Educational Research, 52,* 123–142.

Harter, S. (1985). Manual for the self-perception profile for children. Unpublished ms., University of Denver, CO.

Harter, S. (1988). The self-perception profile for adolescents. Unpublished ms., University of Denver, CO.

Harter, S. (1990). Identity and self development. In S. Feldman & G. Elliott (Eds.), *At the threshold: The developing adolescent* (pp. 352–387). Cambridge, MA: Harvard University Press.

Harter, S. (1999). *The construction of the self: A developmental perspective.* New York: Guilford.

Hattie, J. (1992). *Self-concept.* Hillsdale, NJ: Erlbaum.

Herman-Giddens, M. E., Slora, E. J., Wasserman, R. C., Bourdony, C. J., Bhapkar, M. V., Koch, T. G., & Hasemeier, C. D. (1997). Secondary sexual characteristics and menses in young girls seen in office practice: A study from the Pediatric Research in Office Settings Network. *Pediatrics, 99,* 505–512.

Hirsch, B. J., Roffman, J. G., Deutsch, N. L., Flynn, C. A., Loder, T. L., & Pagano, M. E. (2000). Inner-city youth development organizations: Strengthening programs for adolescent girls. *Journal of Early Adolescence, 20,* 210–230.

Hoge, D. R., Smit, E. K., & Crist, J. T. (1995). Reciprocal effects of self-concept and academic achievement in sixth and seventh grade. *Journal of Youth and Adolescence, 24*(3), 295–314.

Kaplan, H. B., & Lin, C. (2000). Deviant identity as a moderator of the relation between negative self-feelings and deviant behavior. *Journal of Early Adolescence, 20,* 150–177.

Keefe, K., & Berndt, T. J. (1996). Relations of friendship quality to self-esteem in early adolescence. *Journal of Early Adolescence, 16,* 1101–1129.

Lamborn, S. D., Mounts, N. S., Steinberg, L., & Dornbusch, S. M. (1991). Patterns of competence and adjustment among adolescents from authoritative, authoritarian, indulgent, and neglectful families. *Child Development, 62,* 1049–1065.

Leiderman, P. H., Meldman, M. A., & Ritter, P. L. (1989). Parent and peer influences on adolescent self-esteem in a multiethnic high school population. Paper presented at the biennial meetings of the Society for Research in Child Development, Kansas City, MO, March.

Litovsky, V. G., & Dusek, J. B. (1985). Perceptions of child-rearing and self-concept development during the early adolescent years. *Journal of Youth and Adolescence, 14,* 373–387.

Litovsky, V. G., & Dusek, J. B. (1988). Maternal employment and adolescent adjustment and perceptions of child-rearing. *International Journal of Family Psychiatry, 9,* 153–167.

Maccoby, E. E., & Martin, J. (1983). Socialization in the context of the family: Parent–child interaction. In E. M. Hetherington (Ed.), *Handbook of child psychology: Socialization, personality, and social development* (Vol. 4, pp. 1–102). New York: Wiley.

Marsh, H. W. (1987). The big-fish-little-pond effect on academic self-concept. *Journal of Educational Psychology, 79,* 280–295.

Marsh, H. W. (1989). Age and sex effects in multiple dimensions of self-concept: Preadolescence to early adulthood. *Journal of Educational Psychology, 81,* 417–430.

Marsh, H. W. (1993). Academic self-concept: Theory, measurement, and research. In J. Suls (Ed.), *Psychological perspectives on the self* (Vol. 4, pp. 59–98). Hillsdale, NJ: Erlbaum.

Marsh, H. W., Craven, R., & Debus, R. (1998). Structure, stability, and development of young children's self-concept: A multicohort–multioccasion study. *Child Development, 69,* 1030–1053.

Marsh, H. W., & Hattie, J. (1996). Theoretical perspectives on the structure of the self-concept. In B. A. Bracken (Ed.), *Handbook of self-concept* (pp. 38–90). New York: Wiley.

Martin, S., Housley, K., McCoy, H., & Greenhouse, P. (1988). Self-esteem of adolescent girls as related to weight. *Perceptual and Motor Skills, 67,* 879–884.

Maruyama, G., Rubin, R. A., & Kingsberry, G. G. (1981). Self-esteem and educational achievement: Independent constructs with a common cause? *Journal of Personality and Social Psychology, 40,* 962–975.

McIntyre, J. G., & Dusek, J. B. (1995). Perceived parental rearing practices and styles of coping. *Journal of Youth and Adolescence, 24,* 499–509.

Mussen, P. H., & Jones, M. C. (1957). Self-concepts, motivations, and interpersonal attitudes of late and early maturing boys. *Child Development, 28,* 243–256.

Newman, R. S. (1984). Children's achievement and self-evaluations in mathematics: A longitudinal study. *Journal of Educational Psychology, 76,* 857–873.

Nottelmann, E. D. (1987). Competence and self-esteem during the transition from childhood to adolescence. *Developmental Psychology, 23,* 441–450.

O'Malley, P. M., & Bachman, J. G. (1983). Self-esteem changes and stability between ages 13 and 23. *Developmental Psychology, 19,* 257–268.

Orr, E., & Dinur, B. (1995). Social setting effects on gender differences in self-esteem: Kibbutz and urban adolescents. *Journal of Youth and Adolescence, 24,* 3–27.

Osborne, J. W. (1995). Academics, self-esteem, and race: A look at the underlying assumptions of the disidentification hypothesis. *Personality and Social Psychology Bulletin, 21*(5), 449–455.

Peskin, H. (1967). Pubertal onset and ego functioning. *Journal of Abnormal Psychology, 72,* 1–15.

Peskin, H. (1973). Influence of the developmental schedule of puberty on learning and ego development. *Journal of Youth and Adolescence, 2,* 273–290.

Peskin, H., & Livson, M. (1972). Pre- and postpubertal personality and adult psychological functioning. *Seminars in Psychiatry, 4,* 343–353.

Petersen, A. C., & Crockett, L. (1985). Pubertal timing and grade effects on adjustment. *Journal of Youth and Adolescence, 14,* 191–206.

Petersen, A. C., & Taylor, B. (1980). The biological approach to adolescence: Biological change and psychological adaptation. In J. Adelson (Ed.), *Handbook of adolescent psychology* (pp. 117–155). New York: Wiley.

Pliner, P., Chaiken, S., & Flett, G. L. (1990). Gender differences in concern with body weight and physical appearance over the life span. *Personality and Social Psychology Bulletin, 16,* 263–273.

Pottebaum, S. M., Keith, T. Z., & Ehly, S. W. (1986). Is there a causal relation between self-concept and academic achievement? *Journal of Educational Research, 79,* 140–144.

Pritchard, M. E., King, S. L., & Czajka-Narins, D. M. (1997). Adolescent body mass indices and self-perception. *Adolescence, 32*(128), 863–880.

Roberts, A., Seidman, E., Pedersen, S., Chesir-Teran, D., Allen, L., Aber, J. L., Duran, V., & Hsueh, J. (2000). Perceived family and peer transactions and self-esteem among urban early adolescents. *Journal of Early Adolescence, 20,* 68–92.

Rosenberg, M. (1979). *Conceiving the self.* New York: Basic Books.

Rosenberg, M. (1985). *Society and the adolescent self-image.* Princeton, NJ: Princeton University Press.

Rosenberg, M. (1986). Self-concept from middle childhood through adolescence. In J. Suls & A. G. Greenwald (Eds.), *Psychological perspectives of the self* (Vol. 3, pp. 107–136). Hillsdale, NJ: Erlbaum.

Schaefer, E. S. (1965a). Children's reports of parental behavior: An inventory. *Child Development, 36,* 413–424.

Schaefer, E. S. (1965b). A configurational analysis of children's reports of parental behavior. *Journal of Consulting Psychology, 29,* 552–557.

Scheier, L. M., Botvin, G. J., Griffin, K. W., & Diaz, T. (2000). Dynamic growth models of self-esteem and adolescent alcohol use. *Journal of Early Adolescence, 20,* 178–209.

Seidman, E., Aber, J. L., Allen, L., & French, S. E. (1996). The impact of the transition to high school on the self-system and perceived social context of poor urban youth. *American Journal of Community Psychology, 24,* 489–515.

Seidman, E., Allen, L., Aber, J. L., Mitchell, C., & Feinman, J. (1984). The impact of school transitions in early adolescence on the self-system and perceived social context of poor urban youth. *Child Development, 65,* 507–522.

Seidman, E. Shavelson, R. J., & Bolus, R. (1982). Self-concept: The interplay of theory and methods. *Journal of Educational Psychology, 74,* 3–17.

Silbereisen, R. K., Petersen, A. C., Albrecht, H. T., & Kracke, B. (1989). Maturational timing and the development of problem behavior. Longitudinal studies in adolescence. *Journal of Early Adolescence, 9,* 247–268.

Simmons, R. G., & Blyth, D. A. (1987). *Moving into adolescence: The impact of pubertal change and school context.* New York: Aldine de Gruyter.

Simmons, R. G., Blyth, D. A., Van Cleave, E. F., & Bush, D. M. (1979). Entry into early adolescence: The impact of school structure, puberty, and early dating on self-esteem. *American Sociological Review, 44*(6), 948–967.

Simmons, R. G., Burgeson, R., Carlton-Ford, S., & Blyth, D. A. (1987). The impact of cumulative change in early adolescence. *Child Development, 58,* 1220–1234.

Skaalvik, E. M., & Hagtvet, K. A. (1990). Academic achievement and self-concept: An analysis of causal predominance in a developmental perspective. *Journal of Personality and Social Psychology, 58,* 292–307.

Steele, C. (1992). Race and the schooling of Black Americans. *Atlantic Monthly, 269*(4), 68–78.

Steinberg, L. D., Lamborn, S. D., Darling, N., Mounts, N. S., & Dornbusch, S. M. (1994). Over-time changes in adjustment and competence among adolescents from authoritative, authoritarian, indulgent, and neglectful families. *Child Development, 65,* 754–770.

Steinberg, L. D., Lamborn, S. D., Dornbusch, S. M., & Darling, N. (1992). Impact of parenting practices on adolescent achievement: Authoritative parenting, school involvement, and encouragement to succeed. *Child Development, 63,* 1266–1281.

Tobin-Richards, M. H., Boxer, A. M., & Petersen, A. C. (1983). Early adolescents' perceptions of their physical development. In J. Brooks-Gunn & A. C. Petersen (Eds.), *Girls at puberty: Biological and psychological perspectives* (pp. 127–154). New York: Plenum.

Wells, L. E. (1989). Self-enhancement through delinquency: A conditional test of self-derogation theory. *Journal of Research in Crime and Delinquency, 26,* 226–252.

West, C. K., Fish, J. A., & Stevens, R. J. (1980). General self-concept, self-concept of academic ability and school achievement: Implications for "causes" of self-concept. *Australian Journal of Education, 24,* 194–213.

Wigfield, A., & Eccles, J. S. (1994). Children's competence beliefs, achievement values, and general self-esteem: Change across elementary and middle school. *Journal of Early Adolescence, 14,* 107–138.

Williams J. M., & Currie, C. (2000). Self-esteem and physical development in early adolescence: Pubertal timing and body image. *Journal of Early Adolescence, 20*(2), 129–149.

Wylie, R. C. (1974). *The self-concept: A review of methodological considerations and measuring instruments.* Lincoln: University of Nebraska Press.

Wylie, R. C. (1979). *The self-concept: Vol. 2: Theory and research on selected topics.* Lincoln: University of Nebraska Press.

PART IV

Personal Relationships

CHAPTER FIFTEEN

Dating and Romantic Experiences in Adolescence

Heather A. Bouchey and Wyndol Furman

Introduction

If we were to enter a typical grade school playground in the United States, we would likely witness a curious process, wherein boys and girls sporadically tease each other with threats of "Cootie" infestation, kissing games, or other similar taunts. If we flash forward a few years, we are likely to see the same students interacting more regularly with members of the other sex. Although adolescents may have previously proclaimed that members of the other sex were "icky" or stupid, they have now become much more interested in these peers. If we look even further into the future, many of these individuals will be involved in an intense romantic relationship during adolescence or young adulthood. Some will have recognized that they are lesbian, gay, or bisexual, and turned their romantic interests to same-sex peers. Clearly, substantial changes have occurred in these peer interactions. What was once a short-lived interchange on the playground has become an intimate relationship that is central to an adolescent's or young adult's life.

In this chapter, we discuss the emergence and nature of adolescents' dating and romantic experiences. Existing research has primarily focused on heterosexual relationships, but we include literature on the experiences of lesbian, gay, and bisexual youth whenever possible (see also chapter 19 in this volume). We highlight common changes that occur in romantic experiences and relationships from early through late adolescence. We also describe individual differences in these experiences and discuss contextual influences on romantic relationships. The topic of adolescent romance is a relatively new one in the scientific literature; accordingly, we not only review the existing research, but also describe major gaps in our current knowledge and identify important directions for research and

This work was supported by Grant 50106 from the National Institutes of Health to Wyndol Furman, Ph.D. Please do not cite or quote without permission of the authors.

theory. We begin with an examination of the significance of romantic activity in adolescence.

The Significance of Romantic Experiences in Adolescence

Romantic relationships are a central aspect of most adolescents' social worlds. Well over one-half of 12- to 18-year-olds in the United States report having experienced a romantic relationship in the last 18 months (Carver, Joyner, & Udry, 1999). By the 10th grade (ages 15–16), adolescents interact more frequently with romantic partners than they do with parents, siblings, or friends (Laursen & Williams, 1997). Moreover, other-sex peers occupy much of adolescents' thoughts even when they are not interacting with them. High school students spend between five and eight hours per week thinking about actual or potential romantic partners (Richards et al., 1998).

Romantic partners are also a major source of support for many adolescents. By the tenth grade, they are tied for second with mothers in the hierarchy of support figures (Furman & Buhrmester, 1992). In college (age 19), romantic relationships are the most supportive relationship for males, and are among the most supportive relationships for females.

The other sex is a frequent source of strong emotions as well – in fact, a more frequent source than same-sex peers, parents, or school issues (Wilson-Shockley, 1995). The majority of these emotions are positive, but a substantial proportion are negative, indicating that other-sex relationships can be sources of stress as well.

Romantic involvements are thought to influence both intimacy and identity development – two crucial psychosocial processes that occur during adolescence (Dyk & Adams, 1987, 1990; Erikson, 1968; Fitch & Adams, 1983; Furman & Shaffer, in press). Various theorists have even suggested that experiences in adolescent romantic relationships may influence the nature of subsequent close relationships, including marriages (Erikson, 1968; Furman & Flanagan, 1997; Sullivan, 1953). In addition to encouraging a sense of relatedness to others, romantic experiences may help adolescents successfully establish autonomy as they explore extrafamilial relationships and come to rely less on parents (Dowdy & Kliewer, 1998; Furman & Shaffer, in press; Gray & Steinberg, 1999).

Whereas dating may confer several benefits to adolescents, it also entails risks. The elevated prevalence of teen pregnancy and sexually transmitted disease in the United States is clearly linked to romantic involvement. In fact, the strongest risk factor for sexual intercourse in 7th–12th grades is participation in a romantic relationship during the previous 18 months (Blum, Beuhring, & Rinehart, 2000). Romantic partners are the perpetrators of between one-half to two-thirds of sexual victimization incidents in late adolescence (Flanagan & Furman, 2000). More than 25 percent of adolescents are victims of dating violence or aggression (see Wolfe & Feiring, 2000), and dating violence precedes serious marital violence in 25 percent to 50 percent of cases (Gayford, 1975; Roscoe & Benaske, 1985). In terms of mental health, adolescent romantic breakups are one of the strongest predictors of depression, multiple-victim killings, and suicide attempts and completions (Brendt et al., 1993; Fessenden, 2000; Joyner & Udry, 2000; Monroe et al., 1999). Thus, romantic involvement has both benefits and risks. The specific effects of romantic experiences, however, vary from individual to individual, a topic we shall return to in a subsequent section.

Developmental Changes in Romantic Experiences

In this section, we describe the nature of adolescent heterosexual romantic experiences and the developmental changes that commonly occur from early adolescence to late adolescence and adulthood. We must emphasize at the outset that there is no single normative pattern of development in the romantic domain. Individuals vary with respect to when they develop romantic interests, when they begin to date, and how extensively they date. The sequence of experiences is also not fixed. For example, early romantic ventures tend to be short-lived, but a minority of them may develop into long-term relationships. Despite this variability in adolescent romantic involvement, there is some commonality in the nature and sequence of these experiences; a description of the developmental changes that often occur can be useful heuristically.

Changes in interest and activity with the other sex

One of the most noticeable developmental changes occurring in early adolescence is increased activity with the other sex. During the elementary school years, both boys and girls interact primarily with peers of the same sex, often actively avoiding interaction with other-sex playmates (Maccoby, 1988, 1990; Thorne, 1986). However, in early adolescence boys and girls begin to think about and engage more in activities with the other sex.

Dunphy (1963) first described this pattern of changes in his five-stage developmental model of adolescent peer-group interaction. In the first stage, unisexual cliques emerge. These cliques consist of four to six close friends with similar backgrounds who serve as the primary nonfamily social unit throughout early adolescence. In the second stage of Dunphy's (1963) model, male cliques and female cliques begin socializing together in a group context. A larger heterosexual peer group begins to emerge during the third stage, when clique leaders begin to date each other. In the fourth stage, the peer crowd is fully developed, and several heterosexual cliques closely associate with one another. Finally, males and females begin to develop couple relationships; the crowd begins to disintegrate, leaving loosely associated groups of couples.

Recent investigations have identified developmental changes that are congruent with Dunphy's model. For example, early adolescents spend much of their time thinking about members of the other sex, but it is not until later that they actually begin to spend a significant amount of time with them (Blyth, Hill, & Thiel, 1982; Richards et al., 1998). Typically, adolescents first interact with the other sex in a mixed group context, and then begin dating in a group context before finally forming dyadic romantic relationships (Connolly, Goldberg, & Pepler, under review). Those who are liked by many of their peers date more frequently (Franzoi, Davis, & Vásquez-Suson, 1994). Moreover, having a large number of close other-sex friends predicts having a larger other-sex network subsequently, which in turn predicts developing a romantic relationship with someone (Connolly, Furman, & Konarski, 2001). Finally, the percentage of adolescents who report having a boyfriend or girlfriend increases from early to late adolescence (Carver et al., 1999; Furman & Buhrmester, 1992). A recent national survey reports that 36 percent of adolescents at age 13 and 73 percent at age 18 report involvement with a romantic partner in the last 18 months (Carver et al., 1999). These relationships also become more intense and central over time, as interdependence and closeness between romantic partners increase with age (Laursen & Williams, 1997; Zimmer-Gembeck, 1999).

To date, the majority of theoretical and empirical work has focused on heterosexual youths' experiences. Few sexual-minority youth enter into romantic liaisons with same-sex peers during adolescence, because of the limited opportunities to do so (Sears, 1991). Many, however, have sexual experiences with same-sex peers (Herdt & Boxer, 1993; Savin-Williams, 1990, 1998). Moreover, many gay and lesbian youth report that they had dated and had sexual experiences with other-sex peers during adolescence (Savin-Williams, 1996). Experiences with the other sex may help clarify gay, lesbian, and bisexual youths' sexual orientation, and can provide a cover for their sexual identity (Diamond, Savin-Williams, & Dubé, 1999).

Changes in features of romantic relationships across adolescence

By early adolescence, individuals begin to differentiate between relationships with other-sex friendships and heterosexual romantic relationships, attributing features such as passion and commitment solely to the latter (Connolly et al., 1999). At the same time, adolescents' conceptualizations of dating and romance are not the same as adults' conceptions. Early notions of romance are quite idealized and commensurate with stereotyped media images of heterosexual love (Connolly, et al., 1999; Montgomery & Sorell, 1998). For instance, many adolescents report being in love even though they have rarely spoken to or are not in an actual relationship with the object of their desire (Montgomery & Sorell, 1998). Further, older adolescents report both falling in love at a later age and having dated less in the past than younger ones do, suggesting that concepts of romantic relationships change with development (Montgomery & Sorell, 1998; Shulman & Scharf, 2000).

Adolescents initially view these new relationships as opportunities for recreation, sexual experimentation, or status attainment. Dating relationships are not expected to meet many of the functions that are obtained in subsequent adult romantic relationships, such as the provision of support or caregiving (Connolly & Goldberg, 1999; Feiring, 1996; Roscoe, Diana, & Brooks, 1987). In fact, simply having a boyfriend or girlfriend during early and middle adolescence may be more important than the nature of the romantic interactions themselves. Of course, having the right boyfriend or girlfriend matters as well. A popular or attractive dating partner can be an avenue for garnering prestige and respect from one's peers (Brown, 1999; Furman & Wehner, 1997); an undesirable one can lead to ridicule or ostracism.

With time, adolescents acquire experience interacting with the other sex and begin to turn to their romantic partners to fulfill socio-emotional needs. Furman and Wehner (1994) proposed that romantic partners become important figures in the functioning of four behavioral systems – affiliation, sexual/reproduction, attachment, and caregiving. According to this model, the affiliative and sexual/reproduction systems are the first to become salient in romantic relationships (Furman & Wehner, 1994, 1997). In their initial romantic relationships, adolescents are likely to "hang out" with dating partners and engage in many leisure activities with them. They provide stimulation and frequently trigger positive emotions (Wilson-Shockley, 1995). In addition, adolescent romantic relationships present ideal opportunities for individuals to explore their sexual feelings, seek sexual gratification, and ascertain the kind of sexual activity with which they feel comfortable. Furman and Wehner (1994, 1997) posited that the attachment and caregiving systems become more important in romantic relationships during late adolescence and early adulthood. At this time, the press to find a new primary attachment figure increases as relationships with parents have transformed and many individuals have left home. The emergence of the attachment and caregiving systems takes time, however, and thus, these systems may be fully activated only in relatively long-term romantic relationships (Furman & Wehner, 1994, 1997).

Although the evidence is limited, existing data are consistent with this framework. For instance, both middle and late adolescents mention affiliative features more often than attachment and caregiving features in their descriptions of the advantages of romantic relationships (Feiring, 1996, 1999; Shulman & Scharf, 2000). Moreover, the emphasis on romantic partners' affiliative features tends to decrease or remain the same from middle to late adolescence, whereas the emphasis on attachment features tends to increase. Adolescents first turn to their peers for a safe haven, and subsequently rely on them as a secure base (Hazan & Zeifman, 1994). However, only long-term romantic partners are likely to serve as secure bases (Fraley & Davis, 1997; Hazan & Zeifman, 1994). Even in young adulthood, a substantial number of individuals still view parents as their primary secure base (Trinke & Bartholomew, 1997; Fraley & Davis, 1997).

Individual Differences in Romantic Relationships

Up to this point, we have emphasized the normative patterns of adolescent romantic development. What is at least as striking, however, is the diversity of romantic experiences adolescents have. Some begin dating early, whereas others wait until later in adolescence or even adulthood. Some date extensively, whereas others focus on alternative activities, such as schoolwork or sports, during adolescence. Not only does the timing and extent of adolescents' romantic experiences vary, but the nature of their experiences differs widely as well. For instance, some adolescents become involved with warm and supportive dating partners, whereas others report conflict-ridden, volatile relationships.

Investigators have begun to examine such individual differences in romantic activity, but a systematic framework for describing potential differences in romantic experiences has not yet emerged in the literature. Although it is beyond the scope of this chapter to fully propose such a framework, we believe that at least four dimensions are required to capture individual variation in experiences. These dimensions are (a) the timing of dating; (b) the intensity or quantity of experiences; (c) the quality of the relationships that develop; and (d) individuals' representations of these relationships. The empirical literature concerning each is described subsequently.

Much of the work on individual differences in the timing of dating experiences has focused on early participation in romantic relationships. Bullies are more likely to begin dating early, and their relationships are more likely to be characterized by a lack of support and physical and social aggression (Connolly et al., 2000). Those adolescents who are involved with a romantic partner at a young age have higher rates of alcohol and drug use as well as lower levels of academic achievement (Aro & Taipale, 1987; Grinder, 1966). However, the causal direction of the links between early involvement and these problems is not clear, as early relationships may engender some risk or adolescents at risk may be seeking out romantic relationships earlier (Aro & Taipale, 1987; Pawlby, Mills, & Quinton, 1997).

To date, little research has examined the developmental antecedents and sequelae for those adolescents who date at a later age than their peers do. In one study of 12th-grade students (ages 16–19), those with minimal dating experience were found to report greater symptomatology than those who had dated some (Furman, 2000). Coupled with the results on early dating, this suggests that being off the normative timetable is associated with psychological difficulties.

Once one takes into account early daters and nondaters, the correlates of the frequency or intensity of dating do not appear to be strong or are mixed in nature. For example, when minimal daters were excluded from the study just described, psychological symptomatology and self-esteem were unrelated to quantitative indices, such as the total number of people dated, the number dated in the last year, and whether one was currently dating (Furman, 2000). Similarly, middle adolescents who were currently dating and those who had not dated in the last six months did not differ in the frequency of behavioral problems (Kuttler, La Greca, & Prinstein, 1999). Those who had broken up with a partner in the last six months, however, reported more externalizing symptoms, underscoring the importance of distinguishing between the potential impact of romantic involvement and romantic breakups.

The quality of adolescents' relationships may also play an important role in their impact. For example, negative interactions and controlling behavior by one's partner are associated with greater symptomatology and lower self-esteem (Furman, 2000). Importantly, the degree of adolescents' dating involvement and their romantic relationship quality appear relatively unrelated. For example, whether one has a romantic relationship in one year is not very predictive of the quality of ones that develop, nor conversely, is the quality of the relationship in prior years predictive of whether one has a romantic relationship in subsequent years (Connolly et al., 2001).

Just as individuals have working models or representations of their relationships with parents, they also develop representations or views of their romantic relationships. We have proposed that the same framework used by attachment researchers to assess representations of relationships with parents can capture individual differences in romantic views (Furman & Simon, 1999; Furman & Wehner, 1994). That is, representations of romantic relationships, as well as those of parent–child relationships, can be classified into three categories – secure, anxious-avoidant (dismissing), and anxious-ambivalent (preoccupied). Most of the work to date has examined the links among views of different relationships (see next section), but some work has examined relations between romantic representations and adjustment. Specifically, preoccupied or anxious-ambivalent romantic styles and working models have been linked to greater symptomatology and poor self-esteem (Cooper, Shaver, & Collins, 1998; Furman, 2000). Secure styles are associated with greater self-esteem.

In a related vein, Downey and her co-workers have studied rejection sensitivity – the disposition to "anxiously or angrily expect, readily perceive, and react intensely to rejection" (Downey, Bonica, & Rincón, 1999, p. 149). Girls who are high in rejection sensitivity worry about whether their partner will cheat or betray them, are upset when their partner does things without them, and want to know exactly what their partner is doing (Purdie & Downey, 2000). They are more likely to get in physical fights or ignore their partner to make him feel badly.

Although relatively little empirical work has been conducted, it is apparent that marked variations exist in adolescents' romantic experiences. Moreover, such individual differences are linked to psychosocial adjustment.

Sociocontextual Factors and Romantic Experiences

Romantic relationships occur within a social context. Accordingly, adolescents' romantic experiences and views are likely linked to their close relationships with others, such as parents and friends. In addition, adolescents' experiences with particular romantic partners may influence their views and subsequent relationships. Finally, broad cultural messages, practices, and mores in society at large may also have an impact on adolescents' romantic views. We discuss each of these factors in the following sections.

Parent–child relationships

The premise that parent–child relationships influence romantic relationships is certainly not new. For instance, Freud (1940/1964) posited that the mother–infant relationship served as a template for all later love relationships. Social scientists have documented connections between adults' recollections and representations of their relationships with parents and romantic partners (see Furman & Flanagan, 1997), but as yet empirical data on such links in adolescence are sparse. Theorists have, however, hypothesized that parents may influence adolescent romantic relationships through a variety of mechanisms.

One process by which parents are thought to have an effect on adolescents' romantic views and experiences is via socialization practices. For example, a history of attentive and responsive caregiving from parents is expected to enhance adolescents' self-esteem and sense of self-worth, thereby affording them confidence in the novel domain of romantic experiences and relationships (Collins & Sroufe, 1999). Likewise, an authoritative parenting style is thought to help adolescents participate in and make sense of the romantic domain (Gray & Steinberg, 1999). Children whose parents effectively monitor their activities are hypothesized to feel supported and to develop the social competence necessary to negotiate romantic relationships. Further, parents' socialization practices may affect their adolescents' choices regarding whom to date.

Parents may also influence the construction of views regarding close relationships (Furman & Simon, 1999; Simon et al., 2000). According to Bowlby (1973), models of both self and other formed in the context of the initial caregiver–child relationship are carried forward to subsequent relationships in life. Thus, if a child experiences sensitive and consistent caregiving early on, he/she is likely to form secure representations of close relationships, and will in turn approach new relationships with the expectation of achieving intimacy and closeness. On the other hand, an individual who has experienced rejection or inconsistent/intrusive caregiving may develop insecure representations of close relationships. Empirical evidence indicates that views of relationships with parents and romantic partners are related, but the findings are somewhat inconsistent (Furman, 1999; Furman et al., in press). The links may become stronger in late adolescence and adulthood as attachment and caregiving features of romantic relationships become more salient than they were earlier in adolescence (Furman & Wehner, 1997).

Finally, parents' own marriage or romantic relationship may influence adolescents' romantic experiences in several different ways (Gray & Steinberg, 1999). Parents may model patterns of communication, conflict resolution, and support-seeking in their marital and romantic relationships – patterns that adolescents may subsequently imitate with their own romantic partners. As the parental marital relationship is likely a quite salient model of close egalitarian relationships for adolescents, they may rely on perceptions of their parents' marriage to interpret and make sense of novel romantic experiences. Further, parents' marriage may have an indirect effect on adolescent romantic relationships through its effect on the parent–adolescent relationship (see Fincham, 1998). Similarly, the marriage may affect the adolescent's adjustment, which in turn may affect his/her romantic experiences.

Studies of the cross-generational transmission of aggression have found links between parents' marriages and adolescents' aggression toward their romantic partner (Capaldi & Clark, 1998; Capaldi et al., 2001; Simons, Lin, & Gordon, 1998). The mechanisms responsible for the transmission, however, do not seem to be marital conflict per se, but unskilled or punitive parenting. These parenting practices seem to lead to antisocial behavior, which is in turn linked to dating violence.

Relationships with friends

Attachment theorists emphasized the role that parent–child relationships may play in the emergence of romantic relationships (e.g. Bowlby, 1973, Shaver & Hazan, 1988), but did not discuss the role that peer relationships may play. Furman (1999) proposed that peer relationships might influence the development of romantic relationships through at least three different mechanisms.

First, as was discussed in a prior section, the peer group provides a *context* for establishing heterosexual relationships. Peers introduce individuals to members of the other sex, as well as contribute to the interchanges between them. Adolescents' friends and acquaintances can serve as matchmakers, messenger services, and interpreters of romantic experience (Brown, 1999), thus somewhat protecting individual adolescents from overt rejection or unfavorable romantic experiences. Interacting in a group context may also be easier for young adolescents than more intense dyadic exchanges with members of the other sex.

Secondly, who one's peers and friends are may affect the nature of one's romantic relationships. Adolescents' peers are likely to affect their choices of potential partners, and their behavior toward these partners. For example, European American girls are influenced by their existing friends' sexual activity (Billy & Udry, 1985). Similarly, associating with deviant peers predicts hostile talk about women, which in turn predicts aggression toward romantic partners (Capaldi et al., 2001).

Finally, interactions in and representations of friendships might influence concomitant processes in romantic relationships. Friendships share a number of overt features with romantic relationships. Both entail affiliative characteristics, such as mutual co-construction of the relationship, companionship, and intimacy (Furman, 1999; Furman & Wehner, 1994). Both friendships and romantic relationships are egalitarian in nature, with the participants possessing relatively equal footing with one another. Thus, the social skills acquired in friendships would be expected to carry over to romantic relationships. Consistent with this idea, ratings of social support and negative interactions in friendships and romantic relationships are usually found to be correlated (Connolly & Johnson, 1996; Furman, 1999; Furman et al., in press). Similarly, romantic self-concepts are related to close-friend and peer self-concepts (Connolly & Konarski, 1994).

Given similarities in the features and qualities of close friendships and romantic relationships, adolescents' cognitive representations of these relationships are likely to be linked. Both high school and college students' self-reported relational styles with close friends are related to corresponding styles with romantic partners (Furman et al., in press; Furman & Wehner, 1994, 1997). Furthermore, adolescents' internal working models regarding friendships and romantic relationships are tied to one another (Furman, 1999; Furman et al., in press). In fact, the links between representations of friendships and romantic relationships are more consistent than those between parent–child relationships and romantic relationships.

Recently, investigators have explored the role of other-sex friendships in romantic relationship development. Friendships with members of the other sex are a common occurrence in adolescence, especially during high school (Kuttler et al., 1999). The existing literature suggests that such relationships influence adolescents' romantic experiences. Adolescents with more other-sex friends at age 13 were more likely to describe their romantic relationships in terms of self-disclosure and support at age 15 than those with fewer other-sex friends (Feiring, 1999). In contrast, adolescents with a smaller number of other-sex friends tended to focus on social status in their subsequent romantic relationship descriptions. Further, those adolescents with more other-sex friends at age 13 had longer romantic relationships at age 18. Interactions with other-sex peers are also associated with social and romantic competence, as well as high self-esteem (Bukowski, Sippola, & Hoza, 1999; Darling et al., 1999).

Peer relations for sexual minority youth are usually quite different. Few have the opportunity to be part of a group of adolescents with the same sexual orientation, and instead they may be teased or ostracized by heterosexual peers. Passionate same-sex friendships – intense yet avowedly non-sexual relationships – may fulfill some of the needs that heterosexual youth meet through romantic relationships (Diamond, Savin-Williams, and Dubé, 1999). Such relationships may also assist in the clarification and ascertainment of sexual identity.

Experiences with specific romantic partners

Although adolescents' patterns of interaction with both parents and friends may influence their views of close relationships with others, experiences in particular romantic relationships are also likely to impact subsequent ones. After all, many aspects of romantic relationships are specific to that domain. For instance, sexual behavior, infidelity, and breakups are all common occurrences in the romantic domain but uncommon in other relationships. To the extent that these events or other experiences are common across romantic relationships, adolescents may draw upon them to manage present situations with romantic partners. In addition to the acquisition of specific relational skills learned with romantic partners, adolescents' views of these relationships may also be influenced by their prior romantic experiences (Furman & Wehner, 1994). Those individuals who have experienced a positive initial romantic relationship may expect future partners to behave in similar ways. Those with less positive experiences may approach future relationships with some trepidation or may repeat past patterns of interaction.

Although it appears plausible that previous romantic experiences may influence adolescents' subsequent ones, it is unlikely that they would be completely the same. After all, one's partner is different and she or he would influence the course of the relationship as well. Moreover, adolescents are just learning about romantic relationships. Given adolescents' psychosocial need to establish a sense of identity and experiment with different possible selves (Erikson, 1968; Markus & Nurius, 1986), one might expect them to behave in different ways across romantic relationships.

Unfortunately, little is known empirically about the degree of consistency across relationships. In one study (Connolly et al., 2000), perceptions of support and negative interactions in romantic relationships were found to be highly stable across a year, even though the vast majority of the relationships were different at both times.

Cultural influences on romantic experiences

The previous discussion of socio-contextual influences on adolescent romantic experiences and views focused on relationships with significant others such as parents, friends, and dating partners. However, each of these relationships occurs against the backdrop of broader societal and cultural messages concerning the romantic realm. Societal or cultural influences on romantic relationships include numerous factors such as media portrayals of romance and norms about dating, sexuality, gender roles, and marriage. Many Western societies extol the value of dating, yet in more traditional societies dating and even pre-marital contact with the other sex are discouraged or actively prohibited (Hatfield & Rapson, 1996; Mulatti, 1995; Vaidyanathan & Naidoo, 1990).

Across cultures, considerable variability exists with respect to how romantic partnerships are formed. Autonomy and independence in the selection of romantic partners – a hallmark of dating in Western culture – is certainly not a universal cultural practice. In fact, free choice in the selection of one's romantic partners is a relatively rare occurrence worldwide (Stephens, 1963). The vast majority of adolescents do not get to independently select their potential mates. Rather, approval from parents or elders, as well as arranged marriages, is still quite common in many areas of the world (Buruma, 1994; Rosenblatt & Anderson, 1981; Sprecher & Chandak, 1992).

Cultural differences in the selection of romantic partners would likely have an impact on the development of romantic relationships and concomitant cognitive representations of such relationships. For instance, because mixed-sex group dating and exploration with a number of dating partners are not universal cultural practices, interactions within the peer network and the affiliative behavioral system may not be central aspects of romantic development for all youth. As previously discussed, contemporary Western scholars posit that these factors are crucial in the establishment of romantic relationships during adolescence, but it is not clear what role they play in non-Western societies. In cultures where mates are selected by community or family members, culturally prescribed roles and parents' modeling of marital behavior may have a stronger impact on romantic relationships than one's interactions with agemates (Simon et al., 2000).

Concluding Remarks

In this chapter, we have reviewed the significance, characteristics, and development of adolescent romantic experiences and relationships. We discussed normative shifts in mixed-sex interactions and features of romantic relationships across adolescence, as well as individual differences in the timing, quantity, and quality of romantic experiences and representations. Finally, we described a number of socio-contextual influences that are hypothesized to influence the emergence and nature of romantic relationships. This review highlights the considerable progress made within the past ten years in the field of adolescent romantic research. Despite this progress, however, much work remains to be done. As such, this area represents a rich avenue for further theoretical and empirical exploration.

We have emphasized the diversity of romantic experiences in adolescence. If anything, however, the diversity is even greater than we have stated. Most of the research to date has focused on the romantic experiences of middle-class, heterosexual youth in North America. We still know relatively little about the dating and romantic relationships of gay, lesbian, or bisexual youth, although progress is being made (see chapter 19 in this volume; Diamond, Savin-Williams, & Dubé, 1999; Savin-Williams, 1996). Further, except for demographic work on the timing of sexual intercourse and teen pregnancy rates, very few studies address the nature of romantic relationships in ethnic minority youth. Longitudinal studies of normative romantic development in African-American, Latino, Asian American, and Native American youth are necessary to broaden our current knowledge base. It is also likely that geographic norms concerning dating and romantic involvement may influence the nature of romantic experiences. For instance, the nature and timing of adolescent romantic experiences may differ for individuals growing up in a small, close-knit rural community and those in a suburban or urban inner-city environment. We also know relatively little about the romantic relationships of particular subgroups of adolescents, such as those expecting a child (Moore & Florsheim, 2001) or those with health problems (Seiffge-Krenke, 1997).

With few exceptions (e.g. Shulman et al., 1997), investigators have not examined gender differences in the nature and experience of adolescent romantic relationships. Given the extensive theoretical history positing that girls are more strongly socialized to value relationships and connection with others (e.g., Gilligan, 1986; Maccoby, 1998), the absence of work on the role of gender in the adolescent romantic domain is puzzling.

Most of the work to date has also focused on individuals and their romantic experiences, not the relationships per se. The vast majority of research has relied on the self-reported perceptions of one romantic partner, but an understanding of romantic relationships entails assessing the behavior and perceptions of the two persons involved. A few investigators have gathered data from both individuals in a dyad or coded patterns of interaction (e.g. Welsh et al., 1999), but additional work on the dyadic components of romantic relationships would be quite beneficial.

Finally, investigators have only begun to examine the links between childhood experiences and adolescent romantic relationships (e.g. Collins et al., 1997), and almost nothing is known about whether adolescent experiences are predictive of subsequent relationships (see Furman & Flanagan, 1997). Similarly, the evidence is beginning to indicate that adolescent romantic experiences are linked to psychosocial functioning, but systematic research that examines such relations, as well as the mechanisms by which such associations occur, remains relatively sparse. For instance, how do adolescent romantic experiences influence subsequent self-concept and identity development? Can interaction with romantic partners have either a deleterious or beneficial effect on adolescents' achievement and motivation beliefs? Are the effects of romantic experiences above and beyond the influence of other important persons in the adolescents' life? Do romantic experiences offer something unique to the socialization process? Although answers to these questions remain largely unanswered, we hope that this review will stimulate future theoretical debate and empirical work in the fascinating domain of adolescent romantic experiences.

Key Readings

Furman, W., Brown, B. B., & Feiring, C. (Eds.) (1999). *The development of romantic relationships in adolescence.* Cambridge: Cambridge University Press.
This edited volume compiles a variety of theoretical frameworks concerning the nature, function, and experience of adolescent romantic relationships. Topics covered include important mechanisms and processes underlying romantic relationship development, individual differences in romantic relationships, and their social context.

Furman, W., & Wehner, E. (1994). Romantic views: Toward a theory of adolescent romantic relationships. In R. Montemayor, G. R. Adams, & G. P. Gullotta (Eds.), *Relationships during* adolescence: *Advances in adolescent development, Vol. 6,* (pp. 168–175). Thousand Oaks, CA: Sage.

This chapter introduces a theoretical framework for conceptualizing the nature and function of romantic relationships during adolescence. Integrating romantic attachment and neo-Sullivanian theory, the authors contend that the behavioral systems approach best captures the complex phenomenon of romantic relationship development.

Shulman, S., & Collins, W. A. (Eds.) (1997). *Romantic relationships in adolescence: Developmental perspectives.* San Francisco: Jossey-Bass.

This edited issue of the *New Directions in Child Development* series integrates empirical findings and theoretical frameworks from an international perspective. The issues explored range from connections among family, peer, and romantic relationships to gender and physical health status as modifiers of romantic experiences.

References

Aro, H., & Taipale, V. (1987). The impact of timing of puberty on psychosomatic symptoms among fourteen- to sixteen-year-old Finnish girls. *Child Development, 58,* 261–268.

Billy, J. O., & Udry, J. R. (1985). Patterns of adolescent friendship and effects on sexual behavior. *Social Psychological Quarterly, 48,* 27–41.

Blum, R. W., Beuhring, T., & Rinehart, P. M. (2000). *Protecting teens: Beyond race, income, and family structure.* Center for Adolescent Health, University of Minnesota: Minneapolis, MN.

Blyth, D. A., Hill, J. P., & Thiel, K. S. (1982). Early adolescents' significant others: Grade and gender differences in perceived relationships with familial and nonfamilial adults and young people. *Journal of Youth and Adolescence, 11,* 425–449.

Bowlby, J. (1973). *Attachment and loss: Vol. 2: Separation.* New York: Basic Books.

Brendt, D. A., Perper, J. A., Moritz, G., Baugher, M., Roth, C., Balach, L. et al. (1993). Stressful life events, psychopathology, and adolescent suicide: A case control study. *Suicide and Life-Threatening Behavior, 23,* 179–187.

Brown, B. B. (1999). "You're going out with who?!": Peer group influences on adolescent romantic relationships. In W. Furman, B. B. Brown, & C. Feiring (Eds.), *The development of romantic relationships in adolescence* (pp. 291–329). Cambridge: Cambridge University Press.

Bukowski, W. M., Sippola, L. K., & Hoza, B. (1999). Same and other: Interdependency between participation in same- and other-sex friendships. *Journal of Youth and Adolescence, 28,* 439–459.

Buruma, I. (1994). *A Japanese mirror: Heroes and villains of Japanese culture.* New York: Viking Penguin.

Capaldi, D. M., & Clark, S. (1998). Prospective family predictors of aggression toward female partners for at-risk young men. *Developmental Psychology, 34,* 1175–1188.

Capaldi, D. M., Dishion, T. J., Stoolmiller, M., & Yoerger, K. (2001). Aggression toward female partners by at-risk young men: The contribution of male adolescent friendships. *Developmental Psychology, 37,* 61–73.

Carver, K., Joyner, K., & Udry, J. R. (1999). National estimates of adolescent romantic relationships. Unpublished manuscript. Carolina Population Center.

Collins, W. A., Hennighausen, K. C., Schmit, D. T., & Sroufe, L. A. (1997). Developmental precursors of romantic relationships: A longitudinal analysis. *New Directions for Child Development, 78,* 69–84.

Collins, W. A., & Sroufe, L. A. (1999). Capacity for intimate relationships: A developmental construction. In W. Furman, B. B. Brown, & C. Feiring (Eds.), *Contemporary perspectives on adolescent romantic relationships* (pp. 125–147). Cambridge: Cambridge University Press.

Connolly, J., Craig, W., Goldberg, A., & Pepler, D. (1999). Conceptions of cross-sex friendships and romantic relationships in early adolescence. *Journal of Youth and Adolescence, 28*, 481–494.

Connolly, J., Furman, W., & Konarski, R. (2001). The role of peers in the emergence of romantic relationships in adolescence. *Child Development, 71*, 1395–1408.

Connolly, J., & Goldberg, A. (1999). Romantic relationships in adolescence: The role of friends and peers in their emergence and development. In W. Furman, B. B. Brown, & C. Feiring, (Eds.), *The development of romantic relationships in adolescence* (pp. 266–290). Cambridge: Cambridge University Press.

Connolly, J., Goldberg, & Pepler, D. (under review) *Romantic development in the peer group in early adolescence.*

Connolly, J. A., & Johnson, A. M. (1996). Adolescents' romantic relationships and the structure and quality of their close interpersonal ties. *Personal Relationships, 3*, 185–195.

Connolly, J. A., & Konarski, R. (1994). Peer self-concept in adolescence. Analysis of factor structure and associations with peer experience. *Journal of Research in Adolescence, 43*, 385–403.

Connolly, J., Pepler, D., Craig, W., & Taradash, A. (2000). Dating experiences of bullies in early adolescence. *Child Maltreatment, 5*, 299–310.

Cooper, M. L., Shaver, P. R., & Collins, N. J. (1998). Attachment styles, emotion regulation, and adjustment in adolescence. *Journal of Personality and Social Psychology, 74*, 1380–1397.

Darling, N., Dowdy, B. B., Van Horn, M. L., & Caldwell, L. L. (1999). Mixed-sex settings and the perception of competence. *Journal of Youth and Adolescence, 28*, 461–480.

Diamond, L. M., Savin-Williams, R. C., & Dubé, E. M. (1999). Sex, dating, passionate friendships, and romance: Intimate peer relations among lesbian, gay, and bisexual adolescents. In W. Furman, B. B. Brown, & C. Feiring (Eds.), *The development of romantic relationships in adolescence* (pp. 175–210). Cambridge: Cambridge University Press.

Dowdy, B. B., & Kliewer, W. (1998). Dating, parent–adolescent conflict, and behavioral autonomy. *Journal of Youth and Adolescence, 27*, 473–492.

Downey, G., Bonica, C., & Rincón, C. (1999). Rejection sensitivity and adolescent romantic relationships. In W. Furman, B. B. Brown, & C. Feiring (Eds.), *The development of romantic relationships in adolescence* (pp. 148–174). Cambridge: Cambridge University Press.

Dunphy, D. C. (1963). The social structure of urban adolescent peer groups. *Sociometry, 26*, 230–246.

Dyk, P. A. H., & Adams, G. R. (1987). The association between identity development and intimacy during adolescence: A theoretical treatise. *Journal of Adolescent Research, 2*, 223–235.

Dyk, P. H., & Adams, G. R. (1990). Identity and intimacy: An initial investigation of three theoretical models using cross-lag panel correlations. *Journal of Youth and Adolescence, 19*, 91–110.

Erikson, E. H. (1968). *Identity, youth, and crisis.* New York: Norton.

Feiring, C. (1996). Concepts of romance in 15-year-old adolescents. *Journal of Research on Adolescence, 6*, 181–200.

Feiring, C. (1999). Other-sex friendship networks and the development of romantic relationships in adolescence. *Journal of Youth and Adolescence, 28*, 495–512.

Fessenden, F. (2000, April 9). They threaten, seethe, and unhinge, then kill in quantity. *New York Times*, p. 1.

Fincham, F. D. (1998). Child development and marital relations. *Child Development, 69*, 543–574.

Fitch, S. A., & Adams, G. R. (1983). Ego identity and intimacy status: Replication and extension. *Developmental Psychology, 19*, 839–845.

Flanagan, A. S., & Furman, W. C. (2000). Sexual victimization and perceptions of close relationships in adolescence. *Child Maltreatment, 5*, 350–359.

Fraley, R. C., & Davis, K. E. (1997). Attachment formation and transfer in young adolescents' close friendships and romantic relationships. *Personal Relationships, 4*, 131–144.

Franzoi, S. L., Davis, M. H., & Vásquez-Suson, K. A. (1994). Two social worlds: Social correlates and stability of adolescent status groups. *Journal of Personality and Social Psychology, 67*, 462–473.

Freud, S. (1940/1964). An outline of psycho-analysis. In J. Strachey (Ed. and Trans.), *The standard edition of the complete psychological works of Sigmund Freud, Vol. 23* (pp. 139–207). London: Hogarth.

Furman, W. (1999). Friends and lovers: The role of peer relationships in adolescent heterosexual romantic relationships. In W. A. Collins & B. Laursen (Eds.), *Relationships as developmental contexts: Minnesota Symposia on Child Development: Vol. 30* (pp. 133–154). Hillsdale, NJ: Erlbaum.

Furman, W. (April, 2000). Quantity and quality of romantic experiences: What matters? Poster presented at the meetings of the Society for Research in Child Development, Albuquerque, NM.

Furman, W., & Buhrmester, D. (1992). Age and sex differences in perceptions of networks of personal relationships. *Child Development, 63*, 103–115.

Furman, W., & Flanagan, A. (1997). The influence of earlier relationships on marriage: An attachment perspective. In W. K. Halford & H. J. Markman (Eds.), *Clinical handbook of marriage and couples interventions* (pp. 179–202). New York: Wiley.

Furman, W., & Shaffer, L. (in press). The role of romantic relationships in adolescent development. In P. Florsheim (Ed.), *Adolescent romantic relations and sexual behavior: Theory, research, and practical implications*. Mahwah, NJ: Erlbaum.

Furman, W., & Simon, V. A. (1999). Cognitive representations of adolescent romantic relationships. In W. Furman, B. B. Brown, & C. Feiring (Eds.), *The development of romantic relationships in adolescence* (pp. 75–97). Cambridge: Cambridge University Press.

Furman, W., Simon, V. A., Shaffer, L., & Bouchey, H. A. (in press). Adolescents' working models and styles for relationships with parents, friends, and romantic partners. *Child Development*.

Furman, W., & Wehner, E. A. (1994). Romantic views: Toward a theory of adolescent romantic relationships. In R. Montemayor, G. R. Adams, & G. P. Gullotta (Eds.), *Relationships during adolescence: Advances in adolescent development: Volume 6* (pp. 168–175). Thousand Oaks, CA: Sage.

Furman, W., & Wehner, E. A. (1997). Adolescent romantic relationships: A developmental perspective. In S. Shulman & W. A. Collins (Eds.), *Romantic relationships in adolescence: Developmental perspectives: New directions for child development* (pp. 21–36). San Francisco: Jossey-Bass.

Gayford, J. J. (1975). Wife battering: A preliminary survey of 100 cases. *British Medical Journal, 1*, 194–197.

Gilligan, C. (1986). *In a different voice: Psychological theory and women's development*. Cambridge, MA: Harvard University Press.

Gray, M. R., & Steinberg, L. (1999). Adolescent romance and the parent–child relationship: A contextual perspective. In W. Furman, B. B. Brown, & C. Feiring, (Eds.), *The development of romantic relationships in adolescence* (pp. 235–265). Cambridge: Cambridge University Press.

Grinder, R. E. (1966). Relations of social dating attractions to academic orientation and peer relations. *Journal of Educational Psychology, 57*, 27–34.

Hatfield, E., & Rapson, R. L. (1996). *Love and sex: Cross-cultural perspectives*. Boston, MA: Allyn & Bacon.

Hazan, C., & Zeifman (1994). Sex and the psychological tether. In K. Bartholomew & D. Perlman (Eds.), *Advances in personal relationships: Vol. 1: Attachment processes in adulthood* (pp. 151–180). London: Jessica Kingsley.

Herdt, G., & Boxer, A. M. (1993). *Children of Horizons: How gay and lesbian teens are leading a new way out of the closet.* Boston, MA: Beacon.

Joyner, K., & Udry, J. R. (2000). You don't bring me anything but down: Adolescent romance and depression. *Journal of Health and Social Behavior, 41,* 369–391.

Kuttler, A. F., La Greca, A. M., & Prinstein, M. J. (1999). Friendship qualities and social–emotional functioning of adolescents with close, cross-sex friendships. *Journal of Research on Adolescence, 9,* 339–366.

Laursen, B., & Williams, V. A. (1997). Perceptions of interdependence and closeness in family and peer relationships among adolescents with and without romantic partners. In S. Shulman & W. A. Collins (Eds.), *Romantic relationships in adolescence: Developmental perspectives* (pp. 3–20). San Francisco: Jossey-Bass.

Maccoby, E. E. (1988). Gender as a social category. *Developmental Psychology, 24,* 755–765.

Maccoby, E. E. (1990). Gender and relationships: A developmental account. *American Psychologist, 45,* 513–520.

Maccoby, E. E. (1998). *The two sexes: Growing up apart, coming together.* Cambridge, MA: Harvard University Press.

Markus, H., & Nurius, P. (1986). Possible selves. *American Psychologist, 41,* 954–969.

Monroe, S. M., Rohde, P., Seeley, J. R., & Lewinsohn, P. M. (1999). Life events and depression in adolescence: Relationship loss as a prospective risk factor for first onset of major depressive disorder. *Journal of Abnormal Psychology, 108,* 606–614.

Montgomery, M. J., & Sorell, G. T. (1998). Love and dating experience in early and middle adolescence: Grade and gender comparisons. *Journal of Adolescence, 21,* 677–689.

Moore, J., & Florsheim, J. (2001). Interpersonal processes and psychopathology among expectant and nonexpectant adolescent couples. *Journal of Consulting and Clinical Psychology, 69,* 101–113.

Mulatti, L. (1995). Families in India: Beliefs and realities. *Journal of Comparative Family Studies, 26,* 11–25.

Pawlby, S. J., Mills, A., & Quinton, D. (1997). Vulnerable adolescent girls: Opposite-sex relationships. *Journal of Child Psychology and Psychiatry, 38,* 909–920.

Purdie, V., & Downey, G. (2000). Rejection sensitivity and adolescent girls' vulnerability to relationship-centered difficulties. *Child Maltreatment, 5,* 338–349.

Richards, M. H., Crowe, P. A., Larson, R., & Swarr, A. (1998). Developmental patterns and gender differences in the experience of peer companionship during adolescence. *Child Development, 69,* 154–163.

Roscoe, B., & Benaske, N. (1985). Courtship violence experienced by abused wives: Similarities in patterns of abuse. *Family Relations, 43,* 419–424.

Roscoe, B., Diana, M. S., & Brooks, R. H. (1987). Early, middle, and late adolescents' views on dating and factors influencing partner selection. *Adolescence, 22,* 59–68.

Rosenblatt, P. C., & Anderson, R. M. (1981). Human sexuality in cross-cultural perspective. In M. Cook (Ed.), *The bases of human sexual attraction* (pp. 215–250). London: Academic Press.

Savin-Williams, R. C. (1990). *Gay and lesbian youth: Expressions of identity.* New York: Hemisphere.

Savin-Williams, R. C. (1996). Dating and romantic relationships among gay, lesbian, and bisexual youths. In R. C. Savin-Williams & K. M. Cohen (Eds.), *The lives of lesbians, gays, and bisexuals: Children to adults* (pp. 166–180). Fort Worth, TX: Harcourt Brace.

Savin-Williams, R. C. (1998). *. . . and then I became gay: Young men's stories.* New York: Routledge.

Sears, J. T. (1991). *Growing up gay in the South: Race, gender, and journeys of the spirit.* New York: Harrington Park Press.

Seiffge-Krenke, I. (1997). The capacity to balance intimacy and conflict: Differences in romantic relationships between healthy and diabetic adolescents. In S. Shulman & W. Andrew Collins (Eds.), *Romantic relationships in adolescence: Developmental perspectives: New directions for child development* (pp. 37–52). San Francisco: Jossey-Bass.

Shaver, P., & Hazan, C. (1988). A biased overview of the study of love. *Journal of Social and Personal Relationships, 5,* 473–501.

Shulman, S., Levy-Shiff, R., Kedem, P., & Alon, E. (1997). Intimate relationships among adolescent romantic partners and same-sex friends: Individual and systemic perspectives. *New Directions for Child Development, 78,* 37–51.

Shulman, S., & Scharf, M. (2000). Adolescent romantic behaviors and perceptions: Age- and gender-related differences, and links with family and peer relationships. *Journal of Research in Adolescence, 10,* 91–118.

Simon, V. A., Bouchey, H. A., & Furman, W. (2000). The social construction of adolescents' representations of romantic relationships. In S. Larose & G. M. Tarabulsy (Eds.), *Attachment and development: Vol. 2: Adolescence* (pp. 301–326). Quebec: Les Presses de l'Université du Quebec.

Simons, R. L., Lin, K., & Gordon, L. C. (1998). Socialization in the family of origin and male dating violence: A prospective study. *Journal of Marriage and the Family, 60,* 467–478.

Sprecher, S., & Chandak, R. (1992). Attitudes about arranged marriages and dating among men and women from India. *Free Inquiry in Creative Sociology, 20,* 1–11.

Stephens, W. N. (1963). *The family in cross-cultural perspective.* New York: Holt, Rinehart, and Winston.

Sullivan, H. S. (1953). *The interpersonal theory of psychiatry.* New York: Horton.

Thorne, B. (1986). Girls and boys together, but mostly apart. In W. W. Hartup & Z. Rubin (Eds.), *Relationship and development* (pp. 167–184). Hillsdale, NJ: Erlbaum.

Trinke, S. J., & Bartholomew, K. (1997). Hierarchies of attachment relationships in young adulthood. *Journal of Social and Personal Relationships, 14,* 603–626.

Vaidyanathan, P., & Naidoo, J. (1990). Asian Indians in western countries: Cultural identity and the arranged marriage. In N. Bleichrodt & P. Drenth (Eds.), *Contemporary issues in cross-cultural psychology* (pp. 37–49). Amsterdam: Swets & Zeitlinger.

Welsh, D. P., Galliher, R. V., Kawaguchi, M. C., & Rostosky, S. S. (1999). Discrepancies in adolescent romantic couples' and observers' perceptions of couple interaction and their relationship to depressive symptoms. *Journal of Youth and Adolescence, 28,* 645–666.

Wilson-Shockley, S. (1995). Gender differences in adolescent depression: The contribution of negative affect. Master's thesis, University of Illinois at Urbana-Champaign.

Wolfe, D. A., & Feiring, C. (2000). Dating violence through the lens of adolescent romantic relationships. *Child Maltreatment, 5,* 360–363.

Zimmer-Gembeck, M. J. (1999). Stability, change and individual differences in involvement with friends and romantic partners among adolescent females. *Journal of Youth and Adolescence, 28,* 419–438.

CHAPTER SIXTEEN

Friendships, Cliques, and Crowds

B. Bradford Brown and Christa Klute

Introduction

In the United States and Canada, adolescence is commonly viewed as a time to step away from the family and step more decisively into the world of peers. Young people are expected to spend more time with friends (and less with family), to build a social life around peer relationships, and to look to peers for emotional and instrumental support. Although the importance of age-mates is often overstated, peer relationships do become a major preoccupation for most adolescents. On average, they spend approximately one-third of their waking hours with friends (Hartup & Stevens, 1997). Yet, the salience of peers should not be taken for granted. There is considerable individual and cultural variability in both the quality and features of peer relationships during this stage of life (Hartup & Laursen, 1999; Larson et al., 2002).

This chapter will focus on two components of the adolescent peer system, namely, dyadic friendships and affiliations with groups of peers. Our primary concern is sketching normative patterns within these components and their consequences for adolescent adjustment. We confine our analysis to North American youth because a majority of research is concentrated on this population. As a comparison point, we will occasionally refer to youth in other nations. We will be more attentive to variability among North American adolescents with regard to ethnic or socioeconomic background.

Because of space limitations our review is not intended to be comprehensive. Rather, we articulate major themes in the research literature and major issues that are yet to be resolved. To put the study of friendships and peer groups in proper perspective, we begin with an overview of the organization of the peer social system and its transformations during adolescence. We then examine, in turn, research on friendships, small-group relationships (cliques), and the broader group system (crowds). This division among types – or more accurately, levels – of relationships is artificial because adolescents negotiate peer relationships concurrently across the levels of interaction. However, most studies have been confined to one level, and this simplification facilitates an understanding of the dynamics of peer relationships.

Background: Structure and Personal History

Adolescent peer relationships comprise a dynamic social system, an evolving set of relationships organized into different levels of interaction. An individual's success in negotiating this dynamic system is influenced by one's history of peer relationships and the social skills that one brings to relationships in adolescence. It is also influenced by features of both proximal and distal social contexts. Proximal social contexts are those that relate directly to peer interaction. They include the neighborhood or school, in which a substantial portion of peer interaction takes place, and the family, which is often charged with responsibility for oversight of peer interaction. Many investigators have examined connection between peer relationships and these proximal contexts, in what Bronfenbrenner (1999) would refer to as a *mesosystems* analysis. Less common are analyses that include more distal contexts (e.g., the juvenile justice system or work settings) in which peer interaction is less frequent and oversight less direct. A broader, *macrosystems* analysis – examining how cultural norms shape the quality and content of peer interaction – is rarer still, although becoming more significant as young people engage in peer interaction within the context of a multicultural society.

The structure of peer relationships

As individuals move into adolescence, the peer social system becomes more elaborate. New relationships and new levels of interaction emerge (for a more comprehensive discussion, see Brown, 1999). Throughout childhood individuals grow accustomed to *dyadic* peer relationships, with friends as well as siblings and cousins. These constitute the most immediate and concrete level of peer interaction, which is expanded to include new forms of relationships in adolescence – most notably, romantic and sexual relationships (see Part IV of this volume). Children also amass considerable experience negotiating interactions with small groups of peers. Some of these are formal relationships (organized and supervised by adults) that result from participation on sports teams, religious or community groups, youth organizations, or other structured activities. Others involve informal collectives (organized by youth with only indirect supervision from adults) that comprise a circle of friends or a neighborhood playgroup. A small group with circumscribed membership that shares a friendship orientation is often referred to as a *clique*. Whether formal or informal, peer associations at this level share the characteristic that they are *interaction-based*, identified by the fact that group members do things together.

Typically, adolescents participate in a variety of groups at this level, which vary in their duration and the stability of group membership. Overlap in membership among a person's small groups also varies. The friendship group of one teenager may be a subset of the members of one formal group such as a sports team, whereas another teen's circle of friends may be drawn from two or three formal groups, and yet another person's clique may feature no peers who are part of formal groups in which the person participates.

Based on sociological work on the advantages of diverse networks (Granovetter, 1983), one would expect that this variability in the composition of an adolescent's small groups would affect their function as a support network and reveal something about the adolescent's personality or social skills, but little attention has been paid to these issues.

Complementing dyads and cliques, which are defined by interaction patterns, a third level of peer-group association emerges at adolescence that is based more on the individual's reputation among peers. Adolescents in many schools and communities are associated with larger collectives called *crowds* or *sets*. These groups cluster together individuals who have established the same basic image or identity among peers. Crowd labels reflect a particularly prominent feature of group members, such as residential location (northsiders, project people), ethnic or socioeconomic background (Mexicans, richies), peer status (nobodies, snobs), or individual abilities and interests (jocks, skaters, brains, gangbangers). Most crowds feature a set of stereotypic norms that, collectively, define a distinctive lifestyle (Larkin, 1979; Stone & Brown, 1999). As with cliques, adolescents may be associated with more than one crowd, but this constitutes a dilution of their image among peers. Some adolescents are not clearly or consistently associated by peers with *any* crowd. Moreover, there are social contexts in which crowds are not easily discernible.

Unlike dyads and cliques, crowds are cognitive abstractions. Membership is determined by reputation rather than interaction. Nevertheless, affiliation with a particular crowd does tend to facilitate relationships with certain peers and constrain relationships with others. These constraints are well documented in American films (e.g., "The Breakfast Club," "Can't Buy Me Love," "American Pie") and novels about teenagers – such as *That Was Then, This Is Now* (S. E. Hinton, 1971). They are also the subject of some social scientific research that is examined in a later section of this chapter.

Personal history

Of course, young people do not move into this elaborated peer system at adolescence totally naive to its demands and expectations. They arrive with a history of relationships – with peers and others – and social skills (Sameroff, 1975). In most cases, prior to adolescence young people have initiated, nurtured, and abandoned friendships; established a certain level of popularity and social status within the social world of their elementary classroom or neighborhood; and fashioned a set of social skills to be used in pursuing peer interactions (for reviews of these topics, see Bukowski, Hoza, & Boivin, 1993; Parker & Asher, 1987; Rubin, Bukowski, & Parker, 1998). They have been guided by parents and other adults in developing these relationships and relationship skills (Parke & O'Neil, 1999). Older siblings and the mass media (especially, television shows, movies, and popular songs) have given them opportunities to witness and study adolescent peer relationships. Their behavior in various social settings has laid the foundation for a reputation that will channel them toward certain peer crowds. Moreover, many of the peer relationships that they engage in during early adolescence are continuations of childhood affiliations, especially in the realm of close friendships and formal group interactions (such as sports teams).

All of these become a repository of experiences that adolescents can draw upon as they negotiate the novel features of peer interactions in this new stage of life. They also form a trajectory that can vault young people toward a certain type or array of peer relationships and away from others. Unfortunately, investigators rarely have access to reliable information on experiences with peers prior to adolescence, so that we still have limited understanding of how these preadolescent experiences affect the course of peer relationships during adolescence. There is, however, a growing body of evidence that young people with limited success in peer relationships during childhood continue to struggle with relationships throughout adolescence. Hodges et al. (1999) show how youngsters without friends become more attractive targets for bullying, and being the victim of bullying, in turn, diminishes the chances of securing friendships. As these individuals enter adolescence their status as a victim becomes reified through their association with a rejected crowd. Such a label encourages a broader array of peers to join in the harassment, and would-be friends shy away for fear that they, too, will become the victims of peer derision (Merten, 1996). It is difficult for an adolescent to break out of this pattern of loneliness and peer rejection.

Summary

The experiences that adolescents have in interpersonal relationships prior to adolescence form the basis of their entry into the expanded world of peer interaction during adolescence. Most adolescents are called upon to engage in new types of relationships and new levels of interaction with peers. This would be bewildering if there was not some preparation during childhood, or if relationship experiences in childhood are inadequate. Unfortunately, investigators rarely take experiences prior to adolescence into account when studying adolescents' peer relationships.

Friendships in Adolescence

Of the many types and levels of peer associations in which adolescents are involved, investigators have concentrated most of their attention on friendship. Not only are friendships the easiest peer relationship to study; they are also generally regarded as the most important. It is difficult, however, to differentiate the literature on friendship *dyads* from studies of friendship *cliques*, because many investigators ask adolescents to report on "your closest friends" without clarifying whether they want respondents to generalize across several dyadic relationships or describe characteristics of the friendship group. Unless studies refer explicitly to group behavior or group dynamics, we will assume that they are intended to describe individual friendships, thus including their findings in this section.

The vast majority of adolescents report having at least one close friend, although the specific people nominated as closest friends can change considerably even over brief periods of time (six months or less). Erwin (1993) points out that friendships grow more stable during adolescence, largely because of advances in cognitive development and relationship management skills (especially the negotiation of conflict). As in childhood, adolescent friendships depend upon propinquity, but because teenagers have more mobility than younger children, they are less likely to confine close friendship choices to peers in the same immediate neighborhood or school classroom. Still, the importance of proximity should not be underestimated. Dubois and Hirsch (1990) found that urban African American boys were more likely than European American boys to maintain separate friendship networks in school and the neighborhood, largely because the African American youth were less likely to have neighborhood associates attending their school.

General truths about friendship

A succession of studies over a period of 30 years has confirmed several general truths about adolescent friendship. First, equality and reciprocity are considered normative mandates in friendship. Second, the individuals most likely to be selected as friends are peers who are similar to the self. Third, adolescents are especially likely to select same-gender peers as close friends; in multiethnic environments there is also a strong preference for same-race peers. Fourth, girls display more intimacy in their friendship than boys (at least in the frequency, if not the depth of intimate exchanges).

Despite extensive evidence in support of these general truths, they are not unequivocal. We can illustrate this with reference to the inclination to select similar peers as friends. Clark (1989) argues that similarity between friends is less pronounced among black adolescents than white youth because black teens may have less opportunity to select friends with similar characteristics. If they attend predominantly white schools and/or live in predominantly white neighborhoods, black adolescents may have to choose between selecting a same-race friend who is not particularly similar in interests or values, or choosing someone with similar interests and attitudes who is from a different racial background. There is also some evidence suggesting that African American youth are more tolerant of differences than European American youth, making similarity a less significant basis for close friendship.

A second limitation to the general truth of similarity concerns the consistency of similarities across friends. In asking about close friends in general, rather than assessing each close friend in turn, investigators have ignored the possibility that adolescents construct a network of friendships that feature disparate similarities. For example, adolescents may have one close friend who shares their musical tastes, another who is pursuing similar extracurricular activities, a third who espouses the same religious beliefs, and so on. Each friend is similar to the self, but in distinctive ways.

Of the many issues that investigators have examined in relation to adolescent friendships, we will highlight two that have been closely pursued and/or hotly debated in recent years: the degree to which friends influence adolescents' behavior (especially their misbehavior), and the significance of having high quality friendships.

Patterns of influence in friendships

One of the strongest correlates of an adolescent's behavior is the behavior of close friends. This has been observed with regard to both prosocial and antisocial activities. In the past, such correlations were commonly taken as evidence of the influence friends have over the individual. Yet, 25 years ago some investigators recognized that several factors could account for similarity among friends. Cohen (1977) pointed to three specific processes: *selection*, or the tendency of adolescents to become friends with peers who share their attitudes and activities; *deselection*, or the inclination to abandon a friendship if a peer changed attitudes or activities in a way that weakened similarity; or *influence* (also referred to as socialization), persuasion from the friend to alter opinions or behavior to be more similar to the friend. In reanalyses of data that Coleman (1961) collected for his classic portrait of the "adolescent society," Cohen found little evidence of a deselection process, but both selection and influence clearly contributed to the level of similarity between friends.

Denise Kandel (1978) conducted a now classic longitudinal study on a sample of New York teenagers, concluding that both selection and influence were factors in the similarity of drug-use attitudes and behaviors of friends. At the outset of the study, friendship pairs manifested more similarity in drug use than randomly generated pairs (based on comparison of self-reported behavior of each member of the pair). Nine months later, pairs who remained friends increased in similarity to a significantly greater extent than pairs whose friendship dissolved or randomly assigned pairs. Kandel also demonstrated that *perceived* similarity (based on adolescents' reports of their own and their friends' behavior) was higher than *actual* similarity (based on independent reports of each friend), and that similarity was stronger in reciprocated friendship dyads (in which both members nominated each other as a close friend) than non-reciprocated dyads. These findings cast doubts on results from a host of other studies that had assessed friend influence by asking adolescents to report their own and their closest friends' behavior at a single measurement point. Kandel's research became the standard by which to judge more recent studies of friend influence.

One intriguing finding of more recent investigations is that friends seem to have more influence over the initiation of a behavior than the cessation of the behavior. For example, drawing upon Latane's (1981) social impact theory, Ennett and Bauman (1994) examined the composition of friendship groups and changes in smoking behavior of adolescents over a one-year period. They found that nonsmokers who belonged to groups containing smokers were more likely to initiate cigarette use than nonsmokers in groups without any smokers. Interestingly, however, the number of group members who stopped smoking over the one-year period of the study did not predict whether or not an adolescent would also stop smoking.

Two intriguing and controversial findings about the initiation of heterosexual intercourse emerged from Bearman and Brückner's (1999) analyses of data from the National Longitudinal Study of Adolescent Health. The investigators identified the risk for "sexual debut" of all female participants who reported being virgins at the outset of the study, based on self-reports of characteristics that have been associated with the initiation of sexual activity in previous studies. The investigators found, first, that the individual's own risk status was *not* as influential in sexual debut (over a one-year period) as the risk status of members of their friendship group. Second, they reported that the risk status of the friendship group, collectively, was more influential than that of the respondent's best friend. In other words, membership in a low-risk peer group could protect adolescent girls at high risk for sexual debut from actually initiating sexual activity – and do so more effectively than one close relationship with a low-risk peer.

Thus, friends do, indeed, influence adolescents, particularly in the initiation of risky or problem behavior. It is easy to overestimate that influence, however, by simply looking at the degree of similarity between friends and ignoring the effects of friendship selection processes. Moreover, a comprehensive assessment of the degree of friend influence must be mindful of the structure of adolescent peer relationships, paying attention to the multiple, nested levels of peer relationships that adolescents negotiate, rather than assuming that all influence emerges from dyadic relationships with close friends.

Documenting the degree and locus of friends' influence is an important step toward building more effective intervention programs for youth (Bearman & Brückner, 1999). However, researchers also need to be attentive to the *mechanisms* of influence, how peers promote changes in adolescents' attitudes and behavior. Our understanding of these mechanisms remains remarkably weak. Most intervention programs that deal with peer influence are organized around the assumption that peers exert direct pressure on adolescents to engage in undesirable behavior. The programs offer peer-resistance training and practice in refusal strategies. Investigators have developed self-report measures of adolescents' perceptions of peer pressure (Clasen & Brown, 1985; Santor, Messervey, & Kusumakar, 2000), which have been used to document significant variation in the strength and direction of peer pressure in various domains; age trajectories and gender differences also vary across domains. Generally, speaking, however, adolescents claim that they encounter relatively little direct pressure from peers to engage in prosocial or anti-social behavior (Clasen & Brown, 1985).

This does not imply that peer influence is minimal. Adolescents may be unreliable reporters of peer pressure (little information exists on the validity of self-report measures). Moreover, Brown and Theobald (1999) argued that, in addition to peer pressure, there are three other major modes by which friends can exert influence. One is through normative regulation. Through interaction with peers, adolescents recognize that there are commonly accepted attitudes or behavior patterns that are expected within the friendship group. Although there is no overt pressure for an adolescent to conform to norms, the expectation is quite clear. Eder (1993) reported on conversations among early adolescent girls that set boundaries for interactions with boys. Macleod (1987) provides a similar illustration in a study of older, lower-class boys. In both instances, strident assertions were mixed with gentle teasing or mockery of specific group members in order to articulate and reinforce group norms. A particularly fascinating illustration of normative regulation comes from Dishion, Poulin, and Burraston's (2001) careful analysis of conversations among friendship pairs. They found that conversational cues such as laughter and attentiveness, or follow-up comments that signaled approval of the adolescent's stories about misbehavior served to strengthen the adolescent's acceptance of deviant activity.

Another mode of peer influence is through _modeling_. A classic illustration is found in Dunphy's (1963) depiction of how the leaders of early adolescent male and female cliques make a public display of their romantic relationship in order to illustrate to fellow group members how to conduct such a liaison. Modeling is not confined to close friends or admired peers, however. Eckert (1989) describes how members of one peer crowd in a Midwestern high school carefully observed the dress and grooming strategies, activity preferences, and behavior patterns of the other major crowd, then scrupulously adopted the antithesis of their rival crowd's characteristics as the norms of their own group.

Finally, peers can influence adolescents through _structuring opportunities_. In an update of Dunphy's (1963) classic work, Connolly, Furman, and Konarski (2000) examined how certain friendship groups encourage romantic relationships among members simply by exposing group members to the other sex. In this particular study, members of mixed-sex peer groups in middle school were more likely to move into dating relationships than adolescents whose friends were all the same gender as they were.

Even from this cursory review it is apparent that peer-influence processes are more complex than researchers and practitioners often recognize. They are not focused exclusively (or primarily) around overt pressure tactics, nor are they located strictly within dyadic relationships. A systematic examination of influence processes across several levels of peer interaction is needed in order to account for the changes over time in the degree of similarity that investigators have noticed between an adolescent and close friends.

Quality of friendships

A second area of significant progress in the study of friendship over the past several years concerns the quality of these relationships. Individuals enter adolescence with varying degrees of social skills, which ought to affect their capacity to form meaningful, lasting friendships. Criteria by which the quality of friendships are judged vary among studies, but the advent of reliable measures such as the Network of Relationships Inventory (Furman & Buhrmester, 1985) has made it easier to engage in comparative research about this topic.

Investigators have been especially concerned with three questions in this area: Which adolescents are most likely to display high quality friendships? Is the quality of adolescent friendships associated with features of relationships prior to adolescence? Do adolescents with high-quality friendships display better behavioral and emotional adjustment? With regard to the first question, Brendgen et al. (2001) reported that adolescent girls attribute higher quality to their friendships than boys do; the sex difference was confirmed in observations of friendship pairs. Smith and Schneider (2000) discovered that both male and female adolescents tended to attribute more quality to their relationships with girls than with boys. In this particular study, ethnic differences were nominal, but ethnic or cultural differences are more difficult to ascertain because most measures of friendship quality are derived from a European American perspective, thus potentially biased against other cultural groups.

Not surprisingly, investigators also have found significant associations between the quality of preadolescent relationships and friendship quality in adolescence. For example,

Markiewicz, Doyle, and Bregden (2001) found that adolescents who perceived a strong relational bond between their parents tended to report stronger attachment to parents, and this in turn was associated with higher self-perceived quality of their friendship relationships. Shulman and Scharf (2000) also found a correlation between the strength of bonds to parents and emotional involvement with friends and romantic partners. The implication is that, in negotiating friendships (and romantic relationships) during adolescence, individuals build upon the experiences they have had in family relationships. This is precisely what would be expected from attachment and social learning theories.

A more controversial set of findings emerges from studies of the relation between friendship quality and adjustment. Ordinarily, one would predict that adolescents with high-quality friendships would be better adjusted, and those manifesting behavior problems would also display difficulties with interpersonal relationships. As expected, adolescents with high-quality friendships do display higher emotional adjustment, but results related to behavioral outcomes are more complicated. Several investigators have found that teenagers who have high-quality relationships with deviant peers tend to display higher, not lower levels of behavioral problems such as drug use or delinquency (Dishion, Andrews, & Crosby, 1995; Hussong, 2000). Moreover, deviant adolescents are just as likely as nondeviant youth to display positive features in their friendships, but deviant youth are likely to manifest a higher number of negative features (Giordano, Cernkovich, & Pugh, 1986; Hussong, 2000). In other words, high-quality friendships may actually *promote* problem behavior if an adolescent is associating with deviant peers.

One important caveat to add is that high quality in friendship is not necessarily synonymous with the absence of any problematic features. Laursen (1993), for example, found that conflict is not uncommon in adolescent friendships. It tends to be handled differently, however, from conflict in other close relationships. Teenagers recognize that conflict is more of a threat to voluntary relationships such as friendships or romantic attachments, so there is more of an effort to resolve it.

Summary

In this section we have highlighted only a few themes within the extensive literature on adolescent friendships. Rather consistently, they display the complexity that investigators are beginning to discover in this type of adolescent peer relationship. The "general truths" about adolescent friendships are beginning to be qualified as investigators place the study of friendship in a more multicultural perspective. In moving beyond these general truths, investigators have focused more attention on the character and dynamics of this interpersonal relationship. Friend influence extends beyond simple notions about peer pressure; friendship quality can be a blessing as well as a problem, depending upon the behavior patterns of the person who is befriended. To build on insights derived from recent research, investigators will need to pay more attention to the friendship *dyad* rather than the perceptions of just one member. The most informative studies include both members of a friendship and follow the partners closely over time.

Adolescent Cliques

Particularly in adolescence, individual friendships do not exist in a social vacuum. They are nested within a network of peer relationships and are responsive to the norms and dynamics of that network. As we have already described, this network includes a variety of formal and informal groups of peers. In this chapter we will focus attention on just one type of group, the friendship clique, because it is likely to be the most significant part of the network for most adolescents. Certainly, it has received comparatively more attention from researchers. In comparison to studies of friendship, however, research on adolescent cliques is quite limited. Investigators have examined the structure as well as the dynamics of cliques. Research on clique dynamics has included more qualitative work and has concentrated on preadolescent and early adolescent age groups.

Cliques vary in size from three to ten members, with most having about five members (Ennett, Bauman, & Koch, 1994). They are more challenging to study than friendships because they are more difficult to identify. There are three major ways of defining and assessing cliques: social network analyses that employ nominations of friends from all participants in a social context to identify the major clusters of individuals that comprise each friendship group; information from selected informants about who interacts with whom (e.g., the social-cognitive mapping procedure of Cairns & Cairns, 1994); or systematic, direct observations of adolescents in their natural context, using ethnographic methods. We will draw upon studies using all three of these methods.

Clique structure

Although cliques seem synonymous with adolescence, not all people in this life stage actually belong to a clique. Most investigations of cliques have used a school as the social context for analyses, drawing data from the entire school population (or an entire grade level). Using social network analysis programs, several researchers have identified three different positions that adolescents can occupy within a clique structure: member (someone whose affiliations lie almost exclusively within one friendship group), isolate (someone with virtually no ties to a recognized clique), and liaison, who has ties to members of two disparate cliques and serves as a link between the two groups (Ennett & Bauman, 1996; Shrum & Cheek, 1987). The term, isolate, is a slight misnomer because many youth in this category actually have one or two friendships, but they do not have a sufficient number of ties to members of any one group to be considered part of that group.

The division of adolescents into distinctive cliques is most pronounced in early adolescence; with advancing age the number of isolates and, especially, liaisons increases (Shrum & Cheek, 1987). Thus, the group system is transformed from a set of disparate cliques to a more loose-knit collection of groups tied together by liaisons. Group membership is also fluid; it is rare for the membership of a clique to remain unchanged over the course of a school year. In one longitudinal study of high school youth, less than 10 percent of respondents reported that their clique had not experienced any changes over a three-year period (Engles et al., 1997). Rather than dissolving, most cliques seem to replace old members with new ones. Allowing for no more than 50 percent turnover in group membership, Ennett and Bauman (1996) reported that between 55 percent and 80 percent of the cliques they observed remain discernible over a one-year period (the percentage varied among schools participating in the study).

Like friendships, cliques display a predilection for similarity among members. This is most pronounced with regard to age and gender, but in multiethnic settings cliques tend to be ethnically homogeneous as well. The more tight-knit the clique, the less likely it is to have members of multiple ethnic groups (Zisman & Wilson, 1992). In fact, in a study of several multiethnic schools, Urberg et al. (2000) found that African American students were less integrated into the friendship-group network than European American students. According to Cairns and Cairns (1994), groups also display marked homogeneity in aggressiveness or delinquent behavior. This predilection for similarity delimits the pool of prospective new members. Cairns and Cairns (1994) found a high turnover in the membership of socially aggressive groups, but new members were likely to display roughly the same level of aggressiveness as old members.

Qualitative researchers frequently comment on the status hierarchy that is evident in adolescent cliques, especially among groups of girls (Adler & Adler, 1995; Eder, 1985). As would be expected, group leaders have the most authority in determining group membership. Other members can bring forward candidates for membership, but unless they are accepted by group leaders they will not be integrated into the clique.

Most studies of the structural features of cliques have been conducted in small to medium-sized schools in predominantly European American, suburban or rural communities. In part this is a matter of expedience because it is more difficult to gather data from a sufficient percentage of respondents in larger schools, and the number of cases would tax the limits of the social network programs. Nevertheless, it would be helpful to know how cliques are structured – and how that structure evolves – in a school with a large and highly mobile population. Much also could be learned from closer study of youth who change statuses – from clique member to liaison or from isolate to clique member – over a short period of time. What prompts this change? How does it affect their susceptibility to peer influence or sense of well-being?

Clique dynamics

The studies of clique structure provide a useful backdrop to the more intriguing analyses of interaction between groups and among group members. These portray cliques as instruments of socialization and social control, sometimes providing social support and other times engaging in ostracism and ridicule. Since Dunphy's (1963) classic portrayal of how friendship groups prepare adolescents for the heterosocial world of adult society, there has been a succession of rich ethnographic analyses documenting adolescents' daily experiences in cliques. These provide clues to the evolution of the clique system from the circumscribed groups of early adolescence to the looser network of relationships observable in middle to late adolescence. We will highlight results from three such studies, covering different portions of the adolescent period, in order to illustrate this evolution.

Over a seven-year period, Adler and Adler (1995) engaged in participant observations of the clique activities of (mostly middle-class, European American) youngsters in fourth through sixth grades at several public and private elementary schools. They noted the same pattern of extensive turnover in membership that quantitative researchers reported. They also found, however, that there was a highly structured process whereby new members were recruited into the clique. Membership shifts were carefully overseen by the highest status group members – clique leaders, whose position in the clique was far more stable than that of other members. The cliques also were arranged in a status hierarchy, with higher-status cliques manifesting tighter control over membership, but more appeal to outsiders. To enforce group norms, clique leaders ridiculed lower-status members of the group. They also tended to belittle outsiders and cajole group members to follow suit in this activity. Those who complained about their treatment to outsiders or adult authorities suffered even greater ridicule. Those who stuck up for a friend who was the object of ridicule were likely to get the same treatment themselves. These dynamics were much more apparent in high-status groups than lower-status groups.

In the face of these dynamics, it is little wonder that many adult women look back with dread on their early adolescence (Pipher, 1994). However, this organizational dynamic is very effective in redirecting young people's priorities from childhood to adolescent social norms. It sends a blunt message as to who is in charge of the peer social system (peers, rather than adults) and provides unequivocal information about how to proceed within that system. It also heightens the need for close and supportive friendships that can help young people negotiate the difficult dynamics of cliques without emotional upheaval.

The move into early adolescence and middle school seems to prompt some tempering of the rigid control of group members. In Eder's (1985) examination of a sample of Midwestern middle school girls, many elements of the preadolescent group system were still evident: a group-status hierarchy, envy of higher-status groups, normative regulation within the group, belittling of outsiders, and so on. Yet, the girls' behavior was not depicted in such stark terms. Ridicule and belittlement of group members gave way to teasing and, occasionally, cajoling. There seemed to be a shift in emphasis from social control to socialization, as much of the group's conversation centered upon building effective relationships with boys.

Macleod's (1987) study of late adolescent boys from lower socioeconomic strata affirmed the broader agenda of cliques in this older age group. He focused on two groups: the Hallway Hangers, a set of white youth performing marginally in school and engaged in delinquent activities; and the Brothers, a primarily black group working hard to do well in school. Conversations between the author and group members emphasized much more of a balance between social support and social control than was evident in the other two studies. Teasing was still common to keep group members in line with group norms, but most ridicule was reserve for outsiders; members readily rose to each other's defense. Moreover, members routinely disappeared from the group to accommodate the needs of a part-time job or romantic relationship. The group was a comfortable home base from which one could venture out and safely return without fear of exclusion.

Crowds

Crowds are a social cognitive construct: they require young people to construct a set of labels that venture beyond the concrete and thoroughly observable features of peers, reach consensus on the meaning of these labels, then apply the labels to peers who may not conveniently interact with each other to affirm their similarity. In view of these social cognitive demands, it is not surprising that individuals are not able to articulate a crowd system in their school or community much before middle adolescence. Brown, Mory, and Kinney (1994) linked peer crowds to the process of adolescent identity development, whereas Eckert (1989) suggested they are instrumental in reaffirming socioeconomic divisions within society, and Fordham and Ogbu (1986) implied that crowds assist in maintaining allegiance to ethnic group norms. These are not mutually exclusive objectives, suggesting that crowds serve multiple purposes within the peer social system.

Barbara and Phillip Newman emphasize the importance of "group identity" in early adolescence, either as a stepping stone toward a more individuated, autonomous sense of identity (Newman & Newman, 1976), or as an enduring complement to the North American emphasis on individuality (Newman & Newman, 2001). Crowds seem to embody this sense of group identity, giving young people a vocabulary for describing the distinctive categories of identity that are visible among peers, or the basic alternative lifestyles available in a given social system (Eckert, 1989; Larkin, 1979). In many reports, however, there is a disturbing lack of consensus about the features of a given crowd. In Eckert's (1989) study of youth in a suburban Michigan school, both the jocks and the burnouts vigorously defended their crowd against the derisive depictions that out-group members often had for their group. Stone and Brown (1999) make sense of this with reference to social identity theory (Tajfel, 1984), explaining that as individuals develop an attachment to their own group there is an inclination to exaggerate the strengths of their own group and limitations of outgroups. This is, of course, reminiscent of the inclination of early adolescent cliques to ridicule outsiders (Adler & Adler, 1995).

Crowds are very much a product of the social context, however. As a result, the specific crowds that teenagers recognize may vary substantially from one community to the next (Thurlow, 2001). In predominantly European American contexts, crowd labels reflect individual abilities and interests or social standing: brains, skaters, populars, nerds, and so on (see, e.g., Larkin, 1979). In multiethnic contexts, crowd labels can reflect ethnic divisions instead of or in addition to more person-specific characteristics (e.g., Matute-Bianchi, 1986). This is not a foregone conclusion, however. Peshkin (1991) described a multiethnic community in which ethnic divisions were largely ignored in young people's social interaction patterns. Not surprisingly, ethnic labels were not apparent in the major crowds that adolescents mentioned, except in undercurrents among a small portion of the community.

Although peer crowds are abstractions, they do have more concrete consequences for individuals. Urberg et al. (2000) found evidence to support Brown et al.'s (1994) contention that peer-crowd affiliations channel adolescents toward friendships with certain peers and not others. Adolescents reported that a disproportionate share of their close friends came from their own crowd. Just as friends influence adolescents by structuring opportunities to engage in certain behaviors, peer-crowd affiliations can structure opportunities for certain social relationships.

It seems, however, that the capacity of crowd affiliation to facilitate certain relationships and constrain others may fade across adolescence. In a longitudinal ethnographic study of youth in one Midwestern, predominantly European American community, David Kinney charted a substantial transformation in the peer-crowd system (see Brown et al., 1994). The basic division between populars and everyone else in middle school gave way to a more elaborated system of crowds with fairly impermeable boundaries in the early high school years. By the later portion of high school, however, distinctions between crowds began to blur; students enumerated several hybrid crowds composed of members of two groups that formerly were quite distinct. The older students also described how individuals associated much more freely across crowd lines than they had earlier in adolescence. This ethnographic evidence corresponds to quantitative studies suggesting that the importance of crowd affiliation diminishes toward the end of adolescence (Brown, Eicher, & Petrie, 1986). Again, there is a discernible parallel between studies of peer crowds and friendship groups, which appear to grow more loose-knit across adolescence (Zisman & Wilson, 1992).

Much of the literature on peer crowds, however, assumes that adolescents fit squarely in one and only one group. Like systems of classifying individuals into sociometric status categories, categorization schemes for classifying individuals into peer crowds often ignore the variability that exists in adolescents' associations with various groups. Some adolescents develop a consistent image among peers as a member of one specific crowd, whereas others may be viewed as straddling two groups; or some peers may associate an individual with one crowd while other peers place the person in a different crowd. One option to categorical assignment is to calculate a series of scores representing the proportion of peer nominations that an adolescent receives to each major crowd (as an example, see Brown et al., 1993). Another methodological issue is whether self-reported crowd affiliation is as reliable a measure as peer ratings. Some reports suggest that the two measurement schemes are sufficiently correlated that they produce little substantive difference in data analyses (Urberg et al., 2000), whereas other reports indicate that, at least in early adolescence, there are substantial biases in self-reports (Brown, Clasen, & Neiss, 1987). More work is needed to resolve these methodological questions.

Conclusion

One of the major challenges for North American youth as they move into adolescence is to negotiate a much more complex and elaborate system of peer relationships. Likewise, a challenge for researchers is to make sense of this system and the relationships that adolescents contract within it. In particular, researchers must face four particular realities of the adolescent peer system.

First, this system comprises multiple relationships operating on multiple levels simultaneously. Dyadic friendships exist within the constraints of a friendship network and under the shadow of the peer-crowd affiliations of the pair of friends. The impact of a friendship clique is undoubtedly conditioned by members' dyadic relationships within and beyond the clique itself. As difficult as it is to take these various types and levels of relationship into consideration, researchers must strive to be more attentive to them.

Qualitative research is helpful in this regard, although adolescents have a penchant for significant interactions with peers outside of adults' eyesight. Research designs will need to incorporate measures of various levels of peer interaction as moderators of the relationships that are the targets of a given inquiry.

Second, peer relationships are dynamic entities. Although friendships grow more stable during adolescence, it is not uncommon for young people to reorder their friendships or even abandon certain relationships in favor of new ones over the course of a year. In some cases, this means that even short-term longitudinal studies are essentially comparing apples and oranges. On the other hand, some friendships endure for long periods during adolescence, and it is unlikely that friendships of long duration operate the same way or provide the same benefits as less established relationships. Changes in clique composition, which are especially common in the early phases of adolescence, pose a similar challenge for longitudinal research. Studies need to be more attentive to these dynamic features of peer relationships by including assessments of the duration of relationships or consistency of peer-group composition over time.

Third, studies that make the relationship the unit of analysis are particularly useful in elucidating features of peer relationships and peer interaction. Because peer influence is a mutual phenomenon (an adolescent influences friends at the same time as being influenced by them), it doesn't make much sense to measure how much an adolescent moves toward a friend's attitudes and behavior over time without also considering how much the friend's attitudes and behavior have changed in the direction of the target adolescent.

A final issue that we have largely ignored in this chapter – in part because of space constraints and in part because of a dearth of research – is that the adolescent peer system is strongly influenced by cultural context. An increasing proportion of research studies involve individuals beyond the European American middle class. The ethnic diversity of North American societies and the increasing exposure of young people to foreign cultures demand that researchers be more attentive to cultural influences on and cultural variability in the course of friendships and peer-group relations during adolescence. In many societies it is still the case that adolescents' interactions with peers are highly circumscribed or constrained to blood relatives (Larson et al., 2002).

Still, there has been remarkable progress since the mid-1980s in our appreciation of the complexities of adolescents' relationships with peers. This constitutes an exciting base on which researchers can build in the future.

Key Readings

Bukowski, W. M., Hoza, B., & Boivin, M. (1993). Popularity, friendship, and emotional adjustment during early adolescence. In B. Laursen (Ed.), *Close friendships in adolescence. New directions for child development, No. 60* (pp. 23–37). San Francisco: Jossey-Bass.
The authors distinguish between adolescents' reputation among peers in general and their relationships with individual peers.

Cairns, R., & Cairns. B. (1994). *Lifelines and risks: Pathways of youth in our time.* New York: Cambridge University Press.

The book is a comprehensive report of long-term longitudinal study of how social group relationships affect and are affected by deviant behavior patterns of youth.

Furman, W., Brown, B. B., & Feiring, C. (Eds.) (1999). *The development of romantic relationships in adolescence.* London: Cambridge University Press.
This edited volume presents current research and theory on all major facets of romantic relationships in adolescence.

Hartup, W. W. (1999). Peer experience and its developmental significance. In M. Bennett (Ed.), *Developmental psychology: Achievements and prospects* (pp. 106–125). Philadelphia, PA: Psychology Press.
This chapter is an insightful theoretical analysis of the unique role played by peer relations in psychological and social development of children and youth.

Parker, J., & Asher, S. (1987). Peer acceptance and later personal adjustment. Are low accepted children at risk? *Psychological Bulletin, 102,* 357–389.
This article is a classic analysis of sociometric studies of youth, focusing on the effects of peer acceptance and rejection on long-term adjustment of youth.

Rubin, K. H., Bukowski, W. M., & Parker, J. G. (1998). Peer interactions, relationships, and groups. In W. Damon (Ed.), *Handbook of child psychology* (pp. 619–700). New York: Wiley.
This chapter is a comprehensive overview of research on peer relations in childhood and adolescence, including most major facets of adolescents' peer relations.

References

Adler, P. A., & Adler, P. (1995). Dynamics of inclusion and exclusion in preadolescent cliques. *Social Psychology Quarterly, 58,* 145–162.

Bearman, P., & Brückner, H. (1999). *Peer effects on adolescent sexual debut and pregnancy: An analysis of a national survey of adolescent girls.* Washington, DC: National Campaign to Prevent Teen Pregnancy.

Bronfenbrenner, U. (1999). Environments in developmental perspective: Theoretical and operational models. In S. L. Friedman & T. D. Wachs (Eds.), *Assessment of the environment across the life span* (pp. 3–28). Washington, DC: American Psychological Association.

Brendgen, M., Markiewicz, D., Doyle, A. B., & Bukowski, W. M. (2001). The relationship between friendship quality, ranked friendship preference, and adolescents' behavior with their friends. *Merrill Palmer Quarterly, 47,* 395–415.

Brown, B. B. (1999). Measuring the peer environment of American adolescents. In S. L. Friedman & T. D. Wachs (Eds.), *Assessment of the environment across the life span* (pp. 59–90). Washington, DC: American Psychological Association.

Brown, B. B., Clasen, D. R., & Neiss, J. (1987, April). Smoke in the looking glass: Adolescents' perceptions of their peer group status. Paper presented at the biennial meetings of the Society for Research in Child Development, Baltimore.

Brown, B. B., Eicher, S. A., & Petrie, S. D. (1986). The importance of peer group ("crowd") affiliation in adolescence. *Journal of Adolescence, 9,* 73–96.

Brown, B. B., Lamborn, S. L., Mounts, N. S., & Steinberg, L. (1993). Parenting practices and peer group affiliation in adolescence. *Child Development, 64,* 467–482.

Brown, B. B., Mory, M., & Kinney, D. A. (1994). Casting adolescent crowds in relational perspective: Caricature, channel, and context. In R. Montemayor, G. R. Adams, & T. P. Gullotta (Eds.), *Advances in adolescent development: Vol. 6: Personal relationships during adolescence* (pp. 123–167). Newbury Park, CA: Sage.

Brown, B. B., & Theobald, W. E. (1999). *How peers matter: A research synthesis on peer influences on adolescent pregnancy.* Washington, DC: National Campaign to Prevent Teen Pregnancy.

Bukowski, W. M., Hoza, B., & Boivin, M. (1993). Popularity, friendship, and emotional adjustment during early adolescence. In B. Laursen (Ed.), *Close friendships in adolescence. New directions for child development, No. 60* (pp. 23–37). San Francisco: Jossey-Bass.

Cairns, R., & Cairns, B. (1994). *Lifelines and risks: Pathways of youth in our time.* New York: Cambridge University Press.

Clark, M. L. (1989). Friendships and peer relations of Black adolescents. In L. Reginald (Ed.), *Black adolescents* (pp. 175–204). Berkeley, CA: Cobb & Henry.

Clasen, D., & Brown, B. B. (1985). The multidimensionality of peer pressure in adolescence. *Journal of Youth and Adolescence, 14,* 451–468.

Cohen, J. (1977). Sources of peer group homogeneity. *Sociology of Education, 50,* 227–241.

Coleman, J. (1961). *The adolescent society.* Glencoe, IL: Free Press.

Connolly, J., Furman, W., & Konarski, R. (2000). The role of peers in the emergence of heterosexual romantic relationships in adolescence. *Child Development, 71,* 1395–1408.

Dishion, T., Andrews, D., & Crosby, L. (1995). Antisocial boys and their friends in early adolescence: Relationship characteristics, quality, and interactional process. *Child Development, 66,* 139–151.

Dishion, T., Poulin, F., & Burraston, B. (2001). Peer group dynamics associated with iatrogenic effects in group interventions with high-risk young adolescents. In D. W. Nangle & C. A. Erdley (Eds.), *The role of friendship in psychological adjustment. New directions for child and adolescent development, No. 91* (pp. 79–92). San Francisco: Jossey-Bass.

Dubois, D., & Hirsch, B. (1990). School and neighborhood friendship patterns of blacks and whites in early adolescents. *Child Development, 61,* 524–536.

Dunphy D. (1963). The social structure of urban adolescent peer groups. *Sociometry, 26,* 230–246.

Eckert, P. (1989). *Jocks and burnouts: Social categories and identity in the high school.* New York: Teachers College Press.

Eder, D. (1985). The cycle of popularity: Interpersonal relations among female adolescence. *Sociology of Education, 58,* 154–165.

Eder, Donna (1993). "Go get ya a French!": Romantic and sexual teasing among adolescent girls. In Deborah Tannen (Ed.), *Gender and conversational interaction* (pp. 17–31). New York: Oxford University Press.

Engles, R. C. M. E., Knibbe, R. A., Drop, M. J., & de Haan, Y. T. (1997). Homogeneity of cigarette smoking within peer groups: Influence or selection. *Health Education & Behavior, 24*(6), 801–811.

Ennett, S. T., & Bauman, K. E. (1994). The contribution of influence and selection to adolescent peer group homogeneity: The case of adolescent cigarette smoking. *Journal of Personality and Social Psychology, 67*(4), 653–663.

Ennett, S. T., & Bauman, K. E. (1996). Adolescent social networks: School, demographic, and longitudinal considerations. *Journal of Adolescent Research, 11,* 194–215.

Ennett, S. T., Bauman, K. E., & Koch, G. G. (1994). Variability in cigarette smoking within and between adolescent friendship cliques. *Addictive Behaviors, 19,* 295–305.

Erwin, P. (1993). *Friendship and peer relations in children.* New York: Wiley.

Fordham, S. & Ogbu, J. (1986). Black students' school success: Coping with the "burden of acting White." *Urban Review, 18,* 176–206.

Furman, W., & Buhrmester, D. (1985). Children's perceptions of the personal relationships in their social networks. *Developmental Psychology, 21,* 1016–1024.

Giordano, P. C., Cernkovich, S. A., & Pugh, M. D. (1986). Friendships and delinquency. *American Journal of Sociology, 91,* 1170–1202.

Granovetter, M. S. (1983). The strength of weak ties: A network theory revisited. *Sociological Theory, 1,* 201–233.

Hartup, W. W., & Laursen, B. (1999). Relationships as developmental contexts: Retrospective themes and contemporary issues. In W. A. Collins & B. Laursen (Eds.), *Relationships as developmental contexts. The Minnesota symposia on child psychology, Vol. 30* (pp. 13–35). Mahwah, NJ: Erlbaum.

Hartup, W. W., & Stevens, N. (1997). Friendships and adaptation in the life course. *Psychological Bulletin, 121,* 335–370.

Hinton, S. E. (1971). *That was then, this is now.* New York: Viking.

Hodges, E., Boivin, M., Vitaro, F., & Bukowski, W. (1999). The power of friendship: Protection against an escalating cycle of peer victimization. *Developmental Psychology, 35,* 94–101.

Hussong, A. M. (2000). Distinguishing mean and structural sex differences in adolescent friendship quality. *Journal of Social and Personal Relationships, 17,* 223–243.

Kandel, D. (1978). Homophily, selection, and socialization in adolescent friendships. *American Journal of Sociology, 84,* 427–436.

Larkin, R. W. (1979). *Suburban youth in cultural crisis.* New York: Oxford University Press.

Larson, R., Wilson, S., Brown, B. B., Furstenburg, F. F., & Verma, S. (2002). Changes in adolescents' interpersonal experiences: Are they being prepared for adult relationships in the 21st century? *Journal of Research on Adolescence, 13,* 31–68.

Latane, B. (1981). The psychology of social impact. *American Psychologist, 36,* 343–356.

Laursen, B. (1993). The perceived impact of conflict on adolescent relationships. *Merrill-Palmer Quarterly, 39,* 535–550.

Macleod, J. (1987). *Ain't no makin' it.* Boulder, CO: Westview Press.

Markiewicz, D., Doyle, A. B., & Bregden M. (2001). The quality of adolescents' friendships: Associations with mothers' interpersonal relationships, attachment to parents and friends, and prosocial behaviors. *Journal of Adolescence, 24,* 429–445.

Matute-Bianchi, E. (1986). Ethnic identities and patterns of school success and failure among Mexican-descent and Japanese-American students in a California high school: An ethnographic analysis. *American Journal of Education, 95,* 233–255.

Merten, D. E. (1996). Visibility and vulnerability: Responses to rejection by nonaggressive junior high school boys. *Journal of Early Adolescence, 16,* 5–26.

Newman, B. M., & Newman, P. R. (2001). Group identity and alienation: giving the we its due. *Journal of Youth and Adolescence, 30,* 515–538.

Newman, P. R., & Newman, B. M. (1976). Early adolescence and its conflict: Group identity versus alienation. *Adolescence, 11,* 261–274.

Parke, R. D, & O'Neil, R. (1999). Social relationships across contexts: Family-peer linkages. In W. A. Collins and B. Laursen (Eds.), *Relationships as developmental contexts* (pp. 211–239). Mahwah, NJ: Erlbaum.

Parker, J., & Asher, S. (1987). Peer acceptance and later personal adjustment. Are low accepted children at risk? *Psychological Bulletin, 102,* 357–389.

Peshkin, A. (1991). *The color of strangers, the color of friends.* Chicago: University of Chicago Press.

Pipher, M. (1994). *Reviving Ophelia: Saving the selves of adolescent girls.* New York: Ballantine.

Rubin, K. H., Bukowski, W. M., & Parker, J. G. (1998). Peer interactions, relationships, and groups. In W. Damon (Ed.), *Handbook of child psychology* (pp. 619–700). New York: Wiley.

Sameroff, A. J. (1975). Transactional models in early social relations. *Human Development, 18*(2), 65–79.

Santor, D., Messervey, D., & Kusumakar, V. (2000). Measuring peer pressure, popularity, and conformity in adolescent boys and girls: Predicting school performance, sexual attitudes, and substance abuse. *Journal of Youth and Adolescence, 29*, 163–182.

Shrum, W., & Cheek, N. H. (1987). Social structure during the school years: Onset of the degrouping process. *American Sociological Review, 52*, 218–223.

Shulman, S., & Scharf, M. (2000). Adolescent romantic behaviors and perceptions: Age- and gender-related differences, and links with family and peer relationships. *Journal of Research on Adolescence, 10*, 99–118.

Smith, A. & Schneider, B. H. (2000). The inter-ethnic friendships of adolescent students: A Canadian study. *International Journal of Intercultural Relations, 24*(2), 247–258.

Stone, M. R., & Brown, B. B. (1999). Descriptions of self and crowds in secondary school: Identity claims and projections. In Jeffrey McClellan (Ed.), *The role of peer groups in adolescent social identity: Stability and change* (pp. 7–20). San Francisco: Jossey-Bass.

Tajfel, H. (1984). Intergroup relations, social myths and social justice in social psychology. In H. Tajfel (Ed.), *The social dimension: European developments in social psychology* (Vol. 1, pp. 695–715). Cambridge: Cambridge University Press.

Thurlow, C. (2001). The usual suspects? A comparative investigation of crowds and social-type labelling among young British teenagers. *Journal of Youth Studies, 4*, 319–334.

Urberg, K. A., Degirmencioglu, S., Tolson, J. M., & Halliday-Scher, K. (2000). Adolescent social crowds: Measurement and relationship to friendships. *Journal of Adolescent Research, 15*, 427–445.

Zisman, P., & Wilson, V. (1992). Table hopping in the cafeteria: An exploration of "racial" integration in early adolescent social groups. *Anthropology and Education Quarterly, 23*, 199–220.

CHAPTER SEVENTEEN

Relationships Outside the Family: Unrelated Adults

Nancy Darling, Stephen F. Hamilton, and Katherine Hames Shaver

Introduction

Adults outside the family touch the lives of adolescents in important ways, yet we know relatively little about this complex and understudied area of adolescent development. This chapter is organized around two key questions: Who are the unrelated adults in adolescents' lives? and Why should they matter? Research relevant to the first question may be distinguished as contextual, role-focused, or person-focused. Contextual approaches examine the settings and conditions under which adolescents engage in sustained contact with unrelated adults, comparing the contemporary United States with other countries and other eras. Role-focused approaches compare adolescents' relations with parents and other adult relatives with their relations with adults in other roles. Here the distinction between social role and functional role is important. Social role refers to an adult's place in the social system; e.g., teacher or parents' friend. Functional role is what the adult does for the adolescent; e.g., teach, advise, encourage. Person-focused approaches share a method of asking adolescents to identify the people who are important to them (or adults to identify those who were important when they were adolescents). These three approaches clearly overlap and are sometimes mixed in practice.

In the second major section of the chapter we adopt the perspective of ecological systems theory (Bronfenbrenner, 1992) to analyze the potential effect of relations with adults outside the family on adolescent development. This section is primarily theoretical, drawing on the limited empirical literature to substantiate these effects when possible. We focus on the functional role of mentor. Two themes that emerge are the interaction between parents and mentors – Do mentors substitute for or complement parents? – and the relative importance of instrumental versus emotional content in the relationship between mentors and adolescents.

Unrelated Adults: The Neglected Other

Adolescence is a transitional period between embeddedness within the family and the relative independence of adulthood. Among its defining qualities are an expanding range of social relations, greater ability to actively shape the social environment, and the development of a self-concept that includes awareness of both the current self and potential adult selves (Collins et al., 1997; Eccles et al., 1996; Eccles, Lord, & Buchanan, 1996). Adolescents' relations with parents undergo a transformation during adolescence (Collins et al., 1997) and relations with peers take on new qualities of reciprocity and intimacy during the same period (Laursen, 1998). Most research and theorizing about adolescents' social relations have been directed toward parents and same-sex peers, with little research focusing on relations with either cross-gender peers (Brown, Feiring, & Furman, 1999) or unrelated adults (Scales & Gibbons, 1996).

Why has the study of unrelated adults in adolescents' lives been so neglected? Four trends in the field of developmental psychology may have contributed. First, developmental research has tended to proceed from infancy to adulthood and from mother–infant interactions to increasingly distal relationships (Brown et al., 1999). Thus the area may have been neglected because of both the relative distance of unrelated adults from the social core of the family and the age of the developing person. There appears to be much more research on the role of nonfamilial adults in the lives of younger children (e.g., daycare providers, elementary school teachers) than in the lives of adolescents (see, for example, Pianta, 1992). A second tendency in developmental research may have contributed as well. Just as physical development tends to proceed from head to foot and from the center of the body outward, developmental research on social relationships in the United States has generally proceeded from studying what people think and feel (their head and heart) to what they do (their feet and hands). Because relationships with adults outside of the family tend to be less emotionally salient to adolescents than relationships with parents, peers, or siblings (Darling, Hamilton, & Niego, 1994; Darling et al., in press; Furman & Buhrmester, 1992; Galbo, 1986, 1989; Hamilton & Darling, 1996), their potential significance has been overlooked by investigators. Third, research on unrelated adults may have suffered from our stereotypes of adolescents themselves (Buchanan & Holmbeck, 1998). If adolescence is a period when individuals revel in peer relationships and rebellion from adult norms, why study relationships with unrelated adults? Adolescents have to interact with their parents. Isn't it likely that their major interactions with unrelated adults will be in attempts to avoid their constraints? Finally, research on unrelated adults may have suffered from a lack of theories that would provide clear hypotheses about the processes through which unrelated adults may influence adolescents (for a related discussion, see Brown et al., 1999). Because the focus of research on social development is on the emotional interaction of dyadic participants, and relations with unrelated adults tend to be relatively low in emotional content, theory has provided little guidance in this area. Much of the research on continuity between children's relationships with parents and with unrelated adults has been carried out based upon the attachment (e.g., Pianta, 1992) or social learning (Baumrind, 1971) perspectives. Although some research on continuity in the characteristics of adolescents' relationships with parents and adults has come from these same perspectives (see, e.g., Cotterell, 1992; Fletcher et al., 1995; Rhodes, Haight, & Briggs, 1999), the ties between theory and empirical analyses have been much looser. This lack of theoretical sharpness has also led to somewhat disappointing results in empirical studies of the phenomenon.

Who Are the Unrelated Adults in Adolescents' Lives?

Adolescents come in contact with unrelated adults through institutional involvement with schools, churches, and organized activities, through the social networks of their parents and peers, and through the settings they frequent, such as neighborhoods, malls, or the homes of their friends. Researchers examining the social-network characteristics of adolescents have taken one of three approaches to understanding the makeup of social networks: contextual, role-focused, or person-focused.

Contextual approaches

Adolescents today are probably more isolated from contact with unrelated adults than at any time in the past. Discontinuity in the transition to adulthood, and especially the extension of schooling, have resulted in adolescents spending much of their time in social contexts with a high concentration of peers and few opportunities to form close, trusting contacts with adults outside the family (Eccles et al., 1996). Historically, the workplace has been a major context in which youths have encountered unrelated adults. Although the majority of high school-aged students in the United States work, most jobs held by youths now involve them with other teenaged employees and supervisors not much older than themselves, rather than with unrelated adults (Greenberger & Steinberg, 1986). In addition, heavy involvement in part-time work may limit adolescents' opportunities to become involved in other activities that might put them in more meaningful contact with adults (for example, violin teachers, gymnastics coaches, or older members of a chess club) (Greenberger & Steinberg, 1986; Hamilton, 1990). The increasing number of families in which all adults work have left more adolescents unsupervised after school (Belle, 1999). In addition to making them less likely to spend time with their own parents, this is also likely to decrease their contact with the parents of their friends and to make it less likely that they will meet unrelated adults through the social networks of their parents. Extracurricular activities are another context in which adolescents have traditionally become involved with nonfamilial adults. Although the majority of adolescents are involved, the concentration of such activities within school settings and the increasingly stringent age segregation of community-based organizations have limited the number of adults engaged with adolescents in these settings (Kleiber, 1999).

This segregation of youth from adults stands in marked contrast to the more continuous transitions to adulthood that adolescents experienced prior to this century (Kett, 1977). Schooling was often abbreviated, sporadically attended, and much less age-segregated than is typical of classrooms today (Modell & Goodman, 1990). When most people earned their livelihood from farming and small shops, children and adolescents worked alongside parents and adult employees. Many young adolescents left home to work in shops, crafts, the new factories (e.g., textile mills) or as domestic help (Kett, 1977; Modell & Goodman, 1990). Coresidence with parents into early adulthood and the prevalence of sharing residence with nonfamily adults are also likely to have contributed to the integration of adults into the lives of youths. This kind of age integration is still observed in traditional societies, including Amish and Mennonite youth in the United States and Canada (Hostetler & Huntington, 1992). Girls in traditional societies are especially likely to spend considerable time in the company of their mother and other adult women. Although boys also spend time with their fathers and other adult men learning the skills they will need to succeed as adults, they tend to socialize with peers more than with men (Schlegel, 1995).

Cross-national comparisons call attention to differences in social arrangements that are taken for granted in any one country. Customary practices and the structure of social institutions, especially educational systems and social services, create varying opportunities for young people to interact with adults (Matsuda, 1989). A powerful illustration is the institution of apprenticeship found in Germany, Switzerland, Austria, Denmark, and some Eastern European countries. Apprentices, who may include half or more of the older adolescent population, spend a large amount of their time at work in the company of adults (Hamilton, 1987; Hamilton & Hamilton, 1999; Silverberg et al., 1998). This places them in direct and sustained contact with adults far more regularly than their age-mates who attend school full time. In Germany, other social arrangements also reduce the segregation of adolescents that is characteristic of US communities. For example, most of the activities that are sponsored by schools in the United States as extracurricular activities are sponsored by community clubs in Germany, in which members are drawn from the entire age spectrum. Instead of a middle school soccer team, adolescents play on a community team, with neighborhood adults playing on age-group teams in the same club. Similarly, in Japan, almost half of adolescents attend one or more "juku" – after-school lessons focusing on academic tutoring or the acquisition of cultural knowledge, such as martial arts, calligraphy, or music (Matsuda, 1989). Because these classes are very small, they afford more individualized contact between students and adults.

Adolescents' exposure to unrelated adults in a variety of settings may have important implications for development both because it increases the likelihood that adolescents will form strong bonds with individual adults and because it gives them access to information and other resources through "weak ties" (Granovetter, 1983). In addition, unrelated adults, especially those who are part of youths' social networks, contribute to the informal social control parents have over their adolescents (Sampson, 1992). Although historical and cultural comparisons of the contexts in which adolescents spend their time are suggestive of potential differences in adolescents' contacts and relations with unrelated adults, no study of which we are aware systematically documents typical patterns of adolescents' contact with unrelated adults in contemporary society. Given the potential for such variation to contribute to differences in the structural and relational qualities of adolescents' social networks (Cochran & Brassard, 1979), this represents a major gap in our knowledge of adolescent development.

Role-focused approaches

It is likely that there is great variability in the social roles of adults with whom different adolescents have contact. Despite this variability, in industrial societies, most adolescents have frequent contact with adults in particular social roles, such as teachers. Researchers taking a role-focused approach to understanding adolescents' social networks examine differences in the functional roles (Hamilton & Darling, 1989) enacted by individuals who differ in social roles. For example, to what extent are relationships with teachers characterized by emotional support or conflict compared with relationships with peers or parents? Such research differs from person-focused approaches (discussed in the next section), in which individuals are asked to name significant others in their lives, because the social roles to be rated are chosen by the researcher and the adolescent may or may not have a meaningful relationship with a person filling that role. Such research is informative in that it describes typical relationships, rather than optimally functioning ones. This is especially important because it increases comparability across social roles. For example, because virtually all adolescents in the United States name their parents among the most important influences on their lives, but many fewer name unrelated adults (Blyth & Foster-Clark, 1987; Darling et al., in press), comparisons of the functional roles of parents and unrelated adults compare the functioning of an *average* parent with the functioning of a *particularly important* unrelated adult. (Note that some researchers muddy this distinction by asking adolescents to select the single most important teacher they have had, rather than a particular or current teacher (see, for example, Lempers & Clark-Lempers, 1992), while other researchers have asked adolescents to describe "teachers" in general, rather than a specific teacher (e.g., Wentzel, 1997).) Analysis of the functionality of social networks based on social roles alleviates this problem.

Virtually all research taking a role-focused approach to understanding unrelated adults has compared the functional roles of teachers with those of parents, peers, and people occupying other social roles. Consistent evidence suggests that relations with teachers are less affectively charged than relationships with other adults (Galbo, 1989; Lempers & Clark-Lempers, 1992). For example, Lempers and Clark-Lempers (1992) compared early, middle, and late adolescents' perceptions of their relations with individuals in five social roles (mothers, fathers, peers, teachers, and siblings) across eight functional roles and asked about relationship satisfaction. Functional roles included admiration, affection, reliable alliance, companionship, conflict, intimacy, instrumental aid, and nurturance. In 48 of 54 comparisons (functional role by gender by age), teachers were ranked lower in the fulfillment of each functional role than parents, peers, or siblings. The only exception to this pattern was the provision of instrumental aid. Younger adolescents rated teachers as second in instrumental aid only to parents, middle adolescent boys rated them as providing more aid than siblings, and middle adolescent girls and older adolescents rated them as providing equally low instrumental aid as opposite sex parents and siblings. These authors concur with Galbo (1984) that "adolescents do not perceive teachers as important to them" (Lempers & Clark-Lempers, 1992). Thus although virtually all adolescents in developed nations spend significant amounts of time in the company of teachers, there is little evidence that their relationships with the average teacher are as emotionally significant as their relationships with the average parent or sibling, and certainly not as salient as their relationship with a close friend. In addition, Lempers and Clark-Lempers found that the higher adolescents rated their parents on each function, the lower they rated teachers. Reflecting on the fact that middle school and high school teachers typically meet multiple classes of 20–30 students daily, one should not be surprised by the scarcity of close personal relationships between teachers and students.

Person-focused approaches

Most researchers comparing the functionality of adolescents' social networks across social roles have used a person-centered approach, where adolescents list the most significant people in their lives and report on those relationships. The procedure used to elicit names of associates varies somewhat across researchers. Some researchers simply ask adolescents to name a limited number of individuals who they believe have been most significant in their lives (e.g., Darling et al., in press; Lanz et al., 1999; Tatar, 1998a). Other researchers go through a more complex process of first eliciting a range of associates in different social roles (for example, parents, unrelated adults, relatives, peers), and then either asking adolescents to choose the most significant individual or individuals in each category (e.g., Munsch & Blyth, 1993) or selecting the single associate named in the category who is "most functional" (i.e., associated with the most descriptors) (e.g., Blyth & Foster-Clark, 1987; Darling et al., in press). Still other researchers ask adolescents to choose the most important associate in each social role category and then name them, without the prior elicitation procedure (e.g., Greenberger, Chen, & Beam, 1998; Tatar, 1998a). Blyth, Hill, and Thiel (1982) provide an excellent discussion of the advantages and disadvantages of different elicitation procedures.

In open-ended listings of significant or influential others, peers are named more frequently than any other single category of associates (see, e.g., Blyth, Hill, & Thiel, 1982; Darling et al., in press; Hendry et al., 1992; Lanz et al., 1999; Tatar, 1998a). Not surprisingly, parents are named most frequently as significant adults, although there does appear to be some cultural variability in adolescents' perceptions that their parents are significant. For example, in one cross-cultural study (Darling et al., in press), virtually every college student from the United States named at least one mother and one father figure. (Several adolescents named stepparents as well as biological parents and included biological parents with whom they had very little contact because they felt their absence had been significant.) Using an identical procedure, fewer than 70 percent of male college students in Japan named their mothers as one of the ten most significant people in their life prior to college, and only 72 percent named their fathers. This is especially surprising given the very low rate of divorce in Japan. Because the number of others who can be named as significant is typically fixed, such variability in the naming of parents has important implications for the other associates who can be named. In the Darling et al. study, Japanese adolescents named more than twice as many peers, on average, as adolescents in the United States.

Although unrelated adults comprise only a small proportion of the social network members of adolescents elicited using person-centered approaches (one widely cited statistic is approximately 10 percent from a study by Blyth, Hill, and Thiel, 1982), most adolescents name at least one unrelated adult among their significant others. For example, in one retrospective study, 82 percent of college juniors named an unrelated adult as one of the ten most important people in their lives prior to entering college (Hamilton & Darling, 1996). When allowed to name unrelated adult associates separately from peer associates, 69 percent of 7th–8th-graders named an unrelated adult as currently important to them (Darling, 1990) and Blyth, Hill, and Thiel (1982) reported that adolescent boys named an average of 1.89 and girls an average of 2.31 significant non-kin adults. When confronted with a stressful life event, 56 percent of 7th- and 8th-graders said that they asked an unrelated adult for help with their problem (Munsch & Blyth, 1993). Thus, although unrelated adults are less commonly nominated as significant network members than parents or unrelated peers, they are perceived as among the most important members of their social networks by large numbers of adolescents.

Consistent with the implications of contextual approaches to understanding social networks, there appear to be both contextual and individual differences in the makeup of social networks elicited through these techniques. Garbarino and his colleagues found that urban children included more unrelated adults in their networks than their suburban or rural peers. However, when asked to name the individuals to whom they could turn for help with a problem, the urban sample named fewer adults than their nonurban peers (Garbarino et al., 1978). Variability has been found both across neighborhoods within the same city (Furstenberg, 1990) and across schools in the same community (Coleman & Hoffer, 1987), and appears to be one way in which communities contribute to variation in the development of adolescent problem behavior (Sampson, 1992). Children from families in which parents are divorced are also more likely to name unrelated adults as part of their social network than are their peers from intact families (Stinson, 1991). There are mixed findings about gender differences in the number of significant adults named, with some studies reporting more adults named by boys than by girls (Hamilton & Darling, 1989), and others reporting more adults named by girls (Blyth, Hill, & Thiel, 1982; Greenberger et al., 1998). Some of this variability may result from differences in procedures in eliciting names of significant others or, as suggested by Greenberger et al., differences in the age of participants. It may be more likely, however, that such differences reflect contextual differences peculiar to the samples. For example, in a cross-cultural comparison of network characteristics (Darling et al., in press), college students in both the United States and Japan were more likely to name same-sex than opposite-sex unrelated adults (results comparable to virtually all other studies in this area). However, this tendency was stronger for boys than for girls and in Japan than in the United States. These differences are likely to reflect both the lack of female teachers in Japan and stronger gender norms (the same pattern held for peers as well).

Another interesting cultural difference between the United States and Japan was in the extent to which variability in the functioning of social relationships could be attributed to between-person differences or within-person differences in the functioning of different associates. In Japan, relatively more of the variability in mentoring was attributable to differences between people, while in the United States, relatively more of the variability was attributable to differences between the associates an individual person named. This suggests that mentoring may be more role-constrained in the United States than in

Japan. Such differences in the prescriptiveness of social roles may be another source of contextual variability in the relational characteristics of social networks. For example, in Japan, the responsibility for learning is placed primarily on the student, while in the United States, a much greater emphasis is placed on the teachers as the driving force in student learning (Haase, 1998). One might hypothesize that individual differences in students' abilities to take advantage of learning situations might be more important determinants of role relationships in Japan than in the United States.

One line of research that has combined the contextual and person-centered approaches to understanding significant others is exemplified by comparisons of the individuals whom adolescents and adults thought had had a significant impact on their lives prior to adulthood (Lanz et al., 1999; Tatar, 1998a). Both studies found that peers were more likely to be nominated as significant nonfamily members by adolescents than by adults. Although one way of interpreting such differences is that adults had had more opportunities to form significant relationships with adults during their own adolescence than adolescents do today, an alternative explanation is that such differences reflect variations in how adolescents and adults define "significant" and understand how others have influenced them. Describing this variation, Tatar writes: "retrospective recall *(by adults)* enables an emphasis on the 'instrumental' aspects of relationships for future purposes, rather than on the 'affective' aspects which may be more salient among individuals who are currently adolescents" (1998a, p. 699). In other words, developmental differences in the life tasks of individuals cause them to understand the importance of others in their lives in different ways. Tatar reported that adults examining their lives retrospectively focused on individuals who changed their trajectory (for example, by changing a career focus or sparking a new interest), while adolescents tend to focus on individuals who are currently offering emotional support and companionship. Research on adolescents suggests that unrelated adults are named as significant or important because they are challenging, but supportive – especially of the adolescents' interests and abilities (Clark-Lempers, Lempers, & Ho, 1991; Hendry et al., 1992; Tatar, 1998a, 1998b; Werner, 1993). In the research reviewed by Galbo (1986, 1994), adults were valued for their honesty, understanding, openness, encouragement, and support. Interestingly, although nonparental adults were described by adolescents as equally uninvolved with problem behavior as parents, they were also somewhat less condemning of the adolescents' own problem behavior (Greenberger et al., 1998). This is consistent with the idea that unrelated adults may occupy something of a "middle ground" between parents and peers. Unrelated adults represent adult norms, but are less explicitly charged with socialization, are less likely to be in a position to sanction misbehavior, and may thus allow adolescents more latitude to discuss their own beliefs and noncompliance.

Like research from the role-centered perspective, adolescents' descriptions of their relationships with significant adults place relatively more emphasis on the instrumental, rather than emotional, components of the relationships. For example, Tatar (1998a) reports that both adults and adolescents describe the most important characteristics of teachers as challenger, teacher, believer, enabler. Others report similar results (Darling et al., in press; Hendry et al., 1992). In an analysis of the correlates of mentoring with other aspects of relationships, Darling et al. (in press) found that in both Japan and the United States, mentoring was less strongly associated with affective qualities of relationships (i.e., support, being "fun") for unrelated adults than for either parents or peers. This suggests that adolescents may be able to value and take advantage of the instrumental components of relationships with unrelated adults separately from the affective components.

Summary

Adolescents may come in contact with a greater variety of unrelated adults in some historical and cultural contexts than in others and the qualities of their relationships with unrelated adults may also vary as a function of cultural norms as well as individual differences. Although the unrelated adults with whom adolescents have the most prolonged contact (teachers) appear not to be emotionally salient, it is clear that the majority of adolescents form significant relationships with at least one unrelated adult and that many of the unrelated adults they name as significant are teachers. Thus, in a given classroom, the teacher may be important to only a very small number of adolescents. This does not imply that over the course of their schooling most of the adolescents in that classroom have not encountered one teacher whom they thought was significant and with whom they formed a strong bond. Concluding that teachers are unimportant to adolescents on the basis of ratings of comparisons of current teachers to current friends or to parents may be unwarranted, just as we would not judge the significance of peers to adolescents by asking adolescents to rate their relationship with the person who happened to be assigned to the seat next to them. The literature is clear, however, that unrelated adults are important to adolescents for different reasons than are either parents or peers. The focus of these relationships is more instrumental than emotional. (For a review and discussion of the implications of this difference, see Darling et al., 1994.) These findings suggest that our understanding of these relationships must be based in a firmer conception of how they function rather than a comparison with other relationships, which are demonstrably different.

Why Should Adults Matter?

Prior discussions of the role of unrelated adults in the lives of adolescence research has typically framed such relationships in terms of adolescents' relationships with the most significant adults in their lives: their parents (Darling et al., 1994). This is most obvious in discussions of unrelated adults as mentors. The word "mentor" derives from Homer's *Odyssey*. When Ulysses left Ithaca to fight in the Trojan wars, he asked his friend, Mentor, to serve as tutor and substitute father for his newborn son, Telemachus. From this perspective, unrelated adults should influence adolescent development to the extent that they provide similar functions to parents or compensate for inept or absent parenting (Freedman, 1993; Grossman & Tierney, 1998; Rhodes, 1994; Rhodes, Contreras, & Mangelsdorf, 1994; Rhodes, Ebert, & Fischer, 1992).

The presumed ability of an unrelated adult to perform a quasi-parental role accounts for much of the current popularity of programs matching single-parent children and adolescents with mentors. As Freedman points out (1993), another source of political support for mentoring is the inaccurate belief that it is cheap. Big Brothers/Big Sisters is the oldest, largest, and best developed mentoring program. Public/Private Ventures took advantage of the waiting list of young people maintained by most Big Brothers/Big Sisters programs, which results from the relative shortage of adult volunteers, to conduct an experiment designed to document the impact of having a mentor. Program operators in participating cities agreed to divide their applicants randomly into treatment and control groups. They then proceeded to match those in the treatment group while retaining the control-group applicants in the waiting list for 18 months, the length of time applicants ordinarily spend waiting (Grossman & Tierney, 1998).

This design yielded unusually robust findings for a program evaluation. Compared to mostly 10–14-year-old boys and girls whose assignment to a mentor was delayed for 18 months as a result of the random selection process, those with a Big Brother or Big Sister were less likely to begin using drugs and alcohol; were less likely to hit others; showed more positive attitudes toward school; had better grades and attendance; and reported better relations with peers and family members.

In the following sections, we take the perspective of ecological systems theory (Bronfenbrenner, 1992) to examine the potential contributions of unrelated adults to adolescent development. Ecological systems theory is a model of human development characterized by (a) an emphasis on an active person who influences and interprets, as well as is influenced by, the environment; (b) a focus on understanding the processes underlying development; and (c) the investigation of interrelationships among multiple contexts in which the developing person interacts. One of the basic premises of ecological systems theory is that adaptive development requires "participation in progressively more complex reciprocal activity, on a regular basis over extended periods of time with one or more other persons with whom the child develops a strong, mutual, irrational attachment, and who are committed to that child's development, preferably for life" (Bronfenbrenner, 1979, p. 5). This concept of the nature of developmentally instigative processes is reflected in Bronfenbrenner's definition of a mentor:

> A mentor is an older, more experienced person who seeks to further the development of character and competence in a younger person by guiding the latter in acquiring mastery of progressively more complex skills and tasks in which the mentor is already proficient. The guidance is accomplished through demonstration, instruction, challenge, and encouragement on a more or less regular basis over an extended period of time. In the course of this process, the mentor and the young person develop a special bond of mutual commitment. In addition, the young person's relationship to the mentor takes on an emotional character of respect, loyalty, and identification. (Bronfenbrenner, personal communication)

Bronfenbrenner's definition has four critical components: intentionality on the part of the mentor, a focus on activities and skills acquisition, interaction over a long period of time, and mutual commitment and emotional bonding. We discuss each in turn.

Intentionality on the part of the mentor

In his description of life-course development, Erikson states that generativity is the central issue of human development that has "made man the teaching and instituting as well as the learning animal" (Erikson, 1950, p. 266), emphasizing the psychological need of healthy adults to nurture and teach the younger generation. Defining generativity as a key developmental task for adults implies that mentoring, like parenting, is a natural and fulfilling function. However, little research has focused on adults' motivations for becoming involved in ongoing relationships with unrelated youth or on the effect of these motivations on the relationships themselves (although see McAdams & de St. Aubin, 1998, for a review of the literature on the course and correlates of generativity). Intentionality on the part of adults involved with adolescents may be an important factor in understanding adult–adolescent relationships because it influences (a) the likelihood that the relationship will form and be maintained; (b) the content of the relationships; and (c) the interpretation of the relationship by the developing person.

Within institutional settings, most individuals are drawn to professions where they work with youth because of their desire to teach, help, and form relationships with their students or clients (Ames & Ames, 1984; Sylvia & Hutchison, 1985). Similar motivations appear to underlie volunteering. Concern for others differentiates between those who volunteer and those who do not, as well as tenure within volunteer organizations (Clary et al., 1998). Thus, within institutional settings, it appears that most adults with whom adolescents come in contact are motivated to form relationships with them. Individual differences within institutional settings, however, suggest that the prevalence of mentoring (and presumably functional aspects of relationships as well) varies systematically depending upon both the personality of individuals involved and the institutional support and reward structure (Aryee, Chay, & Chew, 1996; Bigelow, 1999). Analyses also suggest that some historical periods are more characterized by a focus on intentionally fostering development among the younger generation than others (Moran, 1998).

Intentionality on the part of the mentor may also influence the content of the relationship. Bronfenbrenner's emphasis on intentionality is consistent with both Vygotskian (Wertsch, 1979, 1981) and social learning theory (Bandura, 1989) in suggesting that development occurs when the developing person internalizes aspects of an ongoing interaction with a more skilled other. Vygotsky explicitly assumes that adults involved in interactions with younger persons will adopt behaviors facilitating growth by the child because of both cultural demands and biological imperatives. The simplification of language used by adults when communicating to children is an example of such an adjustment. In addition, individual differences in the skill of adults at scaffolding tasks to facilitate development suggest both that most adults understand the importance of adjusting their behavior to enable youth to learn in their interactions with them and that individual adults differ in their skill at adjusting their behavior to appropriate levels (Wertsch, 1979, 1981). Research suggests that differences in teachers' goals and motivations are embedded in a value system that is shared by both students and teachers (Ames & Ames, 1984). For example, Ames discusses three types of motivational systems: ability-evaluative, task mastery, and moral responsibility (Ames & Ames, 1984). Teacher goal orientation helps to determine strategy choice and behavior in the classroom, which, in turn, helps to shape students' motivations, goals, values, and behaviors. It would be expected that differences in motivations would also change both the frequency and patterning of the classroom reward structure.

The role of the protégé or student has often been overlooked in the discussion of intentionality. At least one experimental study suggests that college students' *perceptions* of the motivations of adults for their involvement changes their perception of the mentor, their experiences with them, and their approach to the shared activity when the mentor was uninvolved (Wild, Enzle, & Hawkins, 1992). Students who believed their instructors were volunteers, rather than paid, enjoyed the activity more, perceived the instructors to be more creative and enthusiastic, enjoyed their lessons more and were more interested in continuing, and were more experimental and playful in their approach to the activity when on their own. In addition, studies of graduate students suggest that most mentor–protégé relationships develop as a result of student initiation or recruiting of mentors. Mentors are most likely to develop relationships with protégés whom they perceive to have similar interests to themselves and to be motivated (Pawlak, 1999). These results are consistent with Werner's (1990; 1995) interpretation of the prevalence of significant, nonparental adults in the lives of resilient children as resulting from these children's ability to seek out and develop such relationships for themselves. Thus, a mentor's intentional fostering of development may occur partly in response to characteristics of the protégé, including initiation of the relationship.

A focus on activities and skill acquisition

While adolescents' relations with family members are characterized by strong affect, their relations with adults who are not family members appear to be less affectively charged and to place relatively more emphasis on shared activities and instrumental functions (Blyth, Hill, & Thiel, 1982; Darling et al., 1994; Galbo, 1984; Lempers & Clark-Lempers, 1992). This focus on joint-activity participation may be important both because it provides a context for the development of the adolescent–adult relationship and because it changes the meaning of the interactions that occur within the relationship. Two important developmental tasks of adolescence may make this activity focus particularly salient: vocational selection and identity development. Both younger (Galbo, 1989) and older youth (Bigelow, 1999; Pawlak, 1999; Schmidt, 1998) seek out mentoring from adults whom they see as having shared interests that they hope to develop themselves. Adolescence is characterized by the development of a self-concept that includes an awareness of both the current self and potential adult selves. Contact with a broad range of unrelated adults with whom the adolescent shares some interests may facilitate exploration of several different vocational avenues. The weak and instrumental nature of the ties adolescents have to many adults in their environment may, in fact, be advantageous in the exploratory phase of career development. Resources accessed through individuals who are not part of a central social network tend to expand access to novel resources unavailable through close relationships (Granovetter, 1983). In addition, the lack of a strong emotional relationship between adolescent and adult may allow the adolescent to explore areas that are different from aspects of the self expressed in other contexts, and to drop areas that they have decided not to pursue, without fear of terminating an important source of emotional support or appearing inconsistent. The independence of emotional and instrumental functions characteristic of adolescents' relationships with unrelated adults (Darling et al., in press) may also facilitate adolescents maintaining access to instrumental resources in the absence of a strong emotional bond and without reliance on good interpersonal skills.

A second implication of the activity focus of adolescents' relations with unrelated adults is in how feedback from the significant other is internalized into the self. Two types of distinctions have been used to explain social role variability in the association between the person's perception of their relations with significant others and their self-concept: variability in the person's perception of the information source and variability in the aspect of the self which the person perceives the source to reflect upon. Unrelated adults may differ from parents and close friends both because of the value we place on their opinion and because of their credibility (Rosenberg, 1973). Although the level of emotional bonding typical of relationships with unrelated adults may decrease the salience of their opinions on global self-worth, their credibility as sources of information may be particularly high, in part because of this same emotional distance. Credibility refers to the extent to which we place faith in the truth or validity of the person's evaluation, and may increase as a function of perceived objectivity. As a result, a mother's assurance that "You tried hard" may not be very comforting to a 16-year-old athlete, while a coach's harsh criticism may not impinge on their emotional bond because the 16-year-old understands the coach's objectivity and commitment to improving performance.

It is important to note that adults need not be significant in order to influence activity selection. For example, a study suggested that unrelated adults are an important reason for dropping out of activities that adolescents were interested in (Hultsman, 1993). Although this study did not explore the reasons underlying the adolescents' decisions to quit, it seems likely that not liking the activity leader was prominent among reasons for dropout. This would be consistent with findings that adolescents' perceptions that their teachers cared about them significantly increased their interest and motivation in academic subjects (Wentzel, 1997).

Although Darling, Hamilton, and Niego (1994) have argued that understanding the instrumental focus of relationships with nonparental adults is critical in understanding the developmental impact of these relationships, other writers have disagreed. For example, Sullivan (1996) has argued that the emotional support provided by mentors may be particularly important in helping at-risk urban girls develop a stronger sense of self. Other research has suggested that emotional support predicts both stress and depression among young Latina mothers (Rhodes et al., 1994) and optimism about the career process among African American pregnant and parenting adolescents (Klaw & Rhodes, 1995). This finding stands in sharp contrast to the instrumental focus found in research on mentoring of gifted and talented youth (Pleiss & Feldhusen, 1995). It is unclear whether emotional support is particularly important in facilitating positive development in more vulnerable populations of at-risk youth or whether these differences result from the different emphases of the researchers.

Interaction over a long period of time

Adolescents' relationships with mentors assigned through voluntary or paid programs are frequently ended early because of volunteer frustration and burnout, relationship difficulties, and logistical difficulties in maintaining contact (Freedman, 1993; Grossman & Rhodes, in press; Hamilton, Hamilton, & Wood, 1991). It is thus particularly important to understand the consequences of early termination for development. Long-term mentoring relationships have been associated with positive outcomes such as lower involvement in drug and alcohol use, improved school performance, lower levels of emotional distress and better relations with parents and peers (for reviews, see Grossman & Rhodes, in press; Rhodes, Haight, & Briggs, 1999). Early termination of mentoring relationships has been associated with negative outcomes, including declines in global self-worth and scholastic competence (Grossman & Rhodes, in press). In addition, it is possible that adolescents who are sensitive to feelings of rejection as a result of previous relationship problems may be particularly vulnerable to perceived rejection in mentoring relationships (Downey & Feldman, 1996). Thus it appears that the benefits of mentoring relationships may take time to appear, and that unsuccessful matches may, in fact, be harmful (Grossman & Rhodes, in press).

Adolescents are more likely than preadolescents to terminate relationships with assigned mentors early (Grossman & Rhodes, in press). Although Grossman and Rhodes did not investigate the reasons underlying these differences, other, qualitative investigations suggest that mentor goals may be important determinants of such differences (Hamilton & Hamilton, 1993). As youth become more focused on peer relationships, they may become less interested in establishing relationships with adults based on friendship, and more interested in establishing relationships based on skill development. Mentors whose primary goal is the establishment of a strong emotional relationship with youth may become frustrated as their meetings are cancelled because of conflicts with parties, extracurricular activities, and other peer-centered youth activities. Those mentors whose goals are more instrumentally focused may be less likely to see these frustrations in terms of rejection and may be more flexible in dealing with obstacles. Although, as discussed previously, many of the interactions adolescents have with unrelated adults may be short-term and instrumental, it appears that length of time is an important component in establishing the benefits of mentoring in relationships where there is a clear expectation that a strong emotional bond should be formed.

Mutual commitment and emotional bonding

No study of which we are aware has examined the importance or nature of behavioral and emotional commitment in adolescents' relationships with unrelated adults. Several different theoretical orientations suggest that commitment on the part of the mentor should be important, however. For example, to the extent that relationships with unrelated adults compensate for problematic earlier relationships, attachment theory suggests that commitment by the mentor may help to realign the attachment system, moving it toward greater stability (Belsky & Cassidy, 1994). Such realignment would take time to develop and might be strengthened, rather than weakened, by sustained commitment in the face of threats. If relationships with unrelated adults develop on a similar timetable as adolescents' relations with other significant figures, it may be that the caregiving and attachment systems may become engaged only as the relationships develop over time (Hazan & Shaver, 1994). Investigations of mentors' motivations for developing ongoing relationships with protégés suggests both that they are attracted to motivated (i.e., committed) youth (Bigelow, 1999) and see the development of the protégé as enhancing their own prestige. Thus commitment by the protégé may enhance their relationship with their mentor.

Although research on adolescents' interpersonal relationships has focused on emotional functioning, the specific functions described by Bronfenbrenner – respect, loyalty, and identification – are infrequently touched upon. All are relevant, however, to understanding unrelated adults as potential role models. As defined by Kemper, a role model is one

> who demonstrates for the individual how something is done in the technical sense. . . . [The role model] is concerned with the "how" question. The essential quality of the role model is that he possesses skills and displays techniques which the actor lacks (or thinks he lacks) and from whom, by observation and comparison with his own performance, the actor can learn. (Kemper, 1968, p. 33)

A role model provides learners with observational opportunities that include imitation of new behaviors, inhibition of unsuccessful behaviors through observation of negative consequences, and the disinhibition of formerly constrained behaviors and increasing use of successful behaviors through observation of positive consequences (Bandura, 1989).

Pleiss and Feldhusen (1995) suggest that adolescents' interactions with adults who are important in their lives can be placed along a continuum from mentors, to role models, to heroes. Mentors are involved in ongoing interactions with their adolescent protégés, while heroes may be one-way attachments in which the adult has no knowledge of their importance to the developing person. Although the developmental importance of relationships such as this that are emotionally salient to youth but involve no interaction is unclear, research suggests that youth who have role models – even if they have no contact with them – may hold higher career aspirations than their peers.

As nothing more than a model of desired behavior, an unrelated adult role model need not have an emotional tie with a youth. Merton (1968), who is credited with coining the term "role model," pointed out that it implies identification with only a narrow aspect of a person – one role – rather than with the whole person. However, a mentor is by definition someone with whom a young person has direct contact, and the modeling function of a mentor is usually presumed to extend beyond a single role, encompassing, for example, values and ways of treating others in addition to specific skills and an occupational identity. The term "ego ideal" might be more appropriate in this context than role model. Positive emotional relationships with mentors appear to enhance the duration of mentor–protégé relationships (Grossman & Rhodes, in press), and are likely to increase both the credibility and value placed on feedback. This may be especially important when feedback is difficult or demands a change in behavior on the part of the adolescent.

It is important to note that although much of Bronfenbrenner's description of an ideal mentor–protégé relationship focuses on the active role of the mentor, mutual commitment and emotional bonding cannot occur without the protégé's participation; it must be reciprocal. Although an adult may have many of the qualities that would make him or her an excellent ego ideal, only the adolescent can make the decision that the adult is worthy of emulation and loyalty (Hendry et al., 1992). For theoretical reasons (e.g.

Bandura, 1989), one might expect differences in adolescents' perceptions of mentor quality or the influence of mentors based on perceived similarity. For example, one might hypothesize that same-gender or same-ethnic mentor–protégé relationships might be more influential than matches that crossed those lines. Although some effects consistent with those hypotheses have been noted, no major trends have emerged (Rhodes, in press).

Bronfenbrenner's definition of a mentor is idealized. It incorporates all the elements one might hope to embody as a mentor or to see in a mentor for one's own child. However, the term is widely applied to people and to relationships that do not have all four elements. The term has become prominent in corporate settings, as women have entered the executive ranks in growing numbers and found that the absence of female mentors has been another barrier to overcome (Zey, 1988). A workplace mentor for an adult or for a youth may be quite influential by teaching work-related competencies in the absence of a mutual emotional commitment. Haase (1998) described spending more than a year as an apprentice potter in Japan under a mentor who was emotionally abusive, causing him to leave eventually, but only after he had acquired substantial knowledge and skill despite the rather hostile relationship.

Future directions

By definition, mentors are the unrelated adults who are most influential on adolescent development. We would recommend, therefore, that one avenue of future research be directed toward the functional role or roles associated with mentors (i.e., what mentors do) rather than toward unrelated adults in social roles presumed to be influential (e.g., teacher). We have cited research on the extent to which adolescents identify unrelated adults as important to them, on who those adults are, and to some extent on what they do. Bronfenbrenner's definition of a mentor poses useful questions for future research about whether and under what conditions both instrumental and emotional functions are critical to mentoring. The research cited above suggests that emotional support from mentors may be critical for adolescents who lack such support from parents and other family members, but that instrumental functions may be more critical for adolescents with stronger families or other sources of emotional support. This indicates the importance of looking for the impact of mentors in the context of other relationships, especially with parents. Are mentors substitute parents, performing functions that would otherwise be absent, or do they complement parents, addressing specific needs while parents fulfill others? Surely both functions may be found. It seems likely that young people with both parents and other adults who act as mentors will benefit the most. Examining both the interactions between mentors and parents and the balance between instrumental and emotional functions performed by mentors promises both theoretical payoff and empirically-based guidance for programs that attempt to introduce mentors into adolescents' lives.

A second major thrust of future research on the roles played by unrelated adults in the lives of adolescents should be to recognize and explore what seems most unique and characteristic of these relationships: their instrumental and sometimes transient nature

(Darling et al., 1994). More research should focus on the nature of adolescents' ties with adults who may not be emotionally significant, but who may help shape their activities, goals, skills, and talents. Social network approaches, particularly those emphasizing structural network characteristics, may be particularly important in understanding individual differences in access to resources through unrelated adults and the consequences such differences may have for adolescent development and the successful transition to adulthood. One of the challenges that may come from tying non-network based approaches to specific adolescent outcomes is that different adolescents may be influenced by specific adults in somewhat unique and idiosyncratic ways. For example, although many children who have shown resilience in the face of developmental challenges have had unrelated adults play important roles in their lives (Werner & Smith, 1992), the specific roles played are quite varied, and different individuals have been affected in different ways. A combination of qualitative approaches and more exploratory "science in the discovery mode" (Bronfenbrenner & Morris, 1998) may be necessary before we come to understand adolescents' relationships with unrelated adults on their own terms, rather than trying to force them into the mold of relationships that are significant because of their powerful emotional force.

Key Readings

Blyth, D. A., Hill, J. P., & Thiel, K. S. (1982). Early adolescents' significant others: Grade and gender differences in perceived relationships with familial and nonfamilial adults and young people. *Journal of Youth & Adolescence, 11*(6), 425–450.
This article is a classic and frequently cited study overviewing social role variation in functional roles.

Clark-Lempers, D. S., Lempers, J. D., & Ho, C. (1991). Early, middle, and late adolescents' perceptions of their relationships with significant others. *Journal of Adolescent Research, 6*(3), 296–315.
The article is a more recent study of adolescents' relationships with a broad range of significant others.

Darling, N., Hamilton, S. F., & Niego, S. (1994). Adolescents' relations with adults outside the family. In R. Montemayor & G. R. Adams (Eds.), *Personal relationships during adolescence. Advances in adolescent development, Vol. 6* (pp. 216–235). Thousand Oaks, CA: Sage.
The chapter reviews the literature on unrelated adults, specifically distinguishing between their instrumental and emotional significance.

Rhodes, J. E. (1994). Older and wiser: Mentoring relationships in childhood and adolescence. *Journal of Primary Prevention, 14*(3), 187–196.
An article which gives an overview of the mentoring process.

Rhodes, J. E., Haight, W. L., & Briggs, E. C. (1999). The influence of mentoring on the peer relationships of foster youth in relative and nonrelative care. *Journal of Research on Adolescence, 9*(2), 185–201.
This article is a quasi-experimental study of the significance of nonparental adults.

References

Ames, C., & Ames, R. (1984). Systems of student and teacher motivation: Toward a qualitative definition. *Journal of Educational Psychology, 76*(4), 535–556.

Aryee, S., Chay, Y. W., & Chew, J. (1996). The motivation to mentor among managerial employees: An interactionist approach. *Group & Organization Management, 21*(3), 261–277.

Bandura, A. (1989). Human agency in social cognitive theory. *American Psychologist, 44*, 1175–1184.

Baumrind, D. (1971). Current patterns of parental authority. *Developmental Psychology, 4*(1, Pt. 2), 1–103.

Belle, D. (1999). *The after-school lives of children: Alone and with others while parents work.* Mahwah, NJ: Erlbaum.

Belsky, J., & Cassidy, J. (1994). Attachment: Theory and Evidence. In M. Rutter & D. Hays (Eds.), *Development through life* (pp. 373–402). London: Blackwell.

Bigelow, J. R., Jr. (1999). Mentor–protégé relationship formation in graduate psychology programs: A comprehensive literature review and proposal. Doctoral dissertation, George Fox University, Newberg, OR.

Blyth, D. A., & Foster-Clark, F. S. (1987). Gender differences in perceived intimacy with different members of adolescents' social networks. *Sex Roles, 17*(11–12), 689–718.

Blyth, D. A., Hill, J. P., & Thiel, K. S. (1982). Early adolescents' significant others: Grade and gender differences in perceived relationships with familial and nonfamilial adults and young people. *Journal of Youth & Adolescence, 11*(6), 425–450.

Bronfenbrenner, U. (1979). *The ecology of human development: Experiments by nature and design.* Cambridge, MA: Harvard University Press.

Bronfenbrenner, U. (1992). Ecological systems theory. In R. Vasta (Ed.), *Six theories of child development: Revised formulations and current issues* (pp. 187–249). London: Jessica Kingsley.

Bronfenbrenner, U., & Morris, P. (1998). The ecology of developmental processes. In R. M. Lerner (Ed.), *Handbook of child psychology. Theoretical models of human development* (5th ed., Vol. 1, pp. 993–1028). New York: Wiley.

Brown, B. B., Feiring, C., & Furman, W. (1999). Missing the Love Boat: Why researchers have shied away from adolescent romance. In W. Furman, B. B. Brown, & C. Feiring (Eds.), *The development of romantic relationships in adolescence. Cambridge studies in social and emotional development* (pp. 1–16). New York: Cambridge University Press.

Buchanan, C. M., & Holmbeck, G. N. (1998). Measuring beliefs about adolescent personality and behavior. *Journal of Youth & Adolescence, 27*(5), 607–627.

Clark-Lempers, D. S., Lempers, J. D., & Ho, C. (1991). Early, middle, and late adolescents' perceptions of their relationships with significant others. *Journal of Adolescent Research, 6*(3), 296–315.

Clary, E. G., Snyder, M., Ridge, R. D., Copeland, J., Stukas, A. A., Haugen, J., & Miene, P. (1998). Understanding and assessing the motivations of volunteers: A functional approach. *Journal of Personality & Social Psychology, 74*(6), 1516–1530.

Cochran, M. M., & Brassard, J. A. (1979). Child development and personal social networks. *Child Development, 50*(3), 601–616.

Coleman, J. C., & Hoffer, T. (1987). *Public and private high schools: The impact of communities.* New York: Basic Books.

Collins, W. A., Laursen, B., Mortensen, N., Luebker, C., & Ferreira, M. (1997). Conflict processes and transitions in parent and peer relationships: Implications for autonomy and regulation. *Journal of Adolescent Research, 12*(2), 178–198.

Cotterell, J. L. (1992). The relation of attachments and support to adolescent well-being and school adjustment. *Journal of Adolescent Research, 7*(1), 28–42.

Darling, N. (1990). *Control beliefs during early adolescence: A comparison of the niche formation and socialization models of development.* Ithaca, NY: Cornell University Press.

Darling, N., Hamilton, S. F., & Niego, S. (1994). Adolescents' relations with adults outside the family. In R. Montemayor & G. R. Adams (Eds.), *Personal relationships during adolescence. Advances in adolescent development, Vol. 6* (pp. 216–235). Thousand Oaks, CA: Sage.

Darling, N., Hamilton, S. F., Toyakawa, T., & Matsuda, S. (in press). Naturally-occurring mentoring in Japan and the United States: Social roles and correlates. *American Journal of Community Psychology.*

Downey, G., & Feldman, S. (1996). The implications of rejection sensitivity for intimate relationships. *Journal of Personality & Social Psychology, 70,* 1327–1343.

Eccles, J. S., Flanagan, C., Lord, S., Midgley, C., et al. (1996). Schools, families, and early adolescents: What are we doing wrong and what can we do instead? *Journal of Developmental & Behavioral Pediatrics, 17*(4), 267–276.

Eccles, J. S., Lord, S., & Buchanan, C. M. (1996). School transitions in early adolescence: What are we doing to our young people? In J. A. Graber & J. Brooks-Gunn (Eds.), *Transitions through adolescence: Interpersonal domains and context* (pp. 251–284). Mahwah, NJ: Erlbaum.

Erikson, E. H. (1950). *Childhood and society.* New York: W. W. Norton.

Fletcher, A., Darling, N., Steinberg, L., & Dornbusch, S. M. (1995). The company they keep: Relation of adolescents' adjustment and behavior to their friends' perceptions of authoritative parenting in the social network. *Developmental Psychology, 31,* 300–310.

Freedman, M. (1993). *The kindness of strangers: Adult mentors, urban youth, and the new voluntarism.* San Francisco: Jossey-Bass.

Furman, W., & Buhrmester, D. (1992). Age and sex differences in perceptions of networks of personal relationships. *Child Development, 63*(1), 103–115.

Furstenberg, F. F. (1990). How families manage risk and opportunity in dangerous neighborhoods. Paper presented at the 84th annual meeting of the American Sociological Association, Washington, DC.

Galbo, J. J. (1984). Adolescents' perceptions of significant adults: A review of the literature. *Adolescence, 19*(76), 951–970.

Galbo, J. J. (1986). Adolescents' perceptions of significant adults: Implications for the family, the school and youth serving agencies. *Children & Youth Services Review, 8*(1), 37–51.

Galbo, J. J. (1989). The teacher as significant adult: A review of the literature. *Adolescence, 24*(95), 549–556.

Galbo, J. J. (1994). Teachers of adolescents as significant adults and the social construction of knowledge. *High School Journal, 78*(1), 40–44.

Garbarino, J., Burston, N., Raber, S., Russell, R., & Crouter, A. (1978). The social maps of children approaching adolescence: Studying the ecology of youth development. *Journal of Youth & Adolescence, 7*(4), 417–428.

Granovetter, M. (1983). The strength of weak ties: A network theory revisited. *Sociological Theory, 1,* 201–233.

Greenberger, E., Chen, C., & Beam, M. R. (1998). The role of "very important" nonparental adults in adolescent development. *Journal of Youth & Adolescence, 27*(3), 321–343.

Greenberger, E., & Steinberg, L. (1986). *When teenagers work: The psychological and social costs of adolescent employment.* New York: Basic Books.

Grossman, J. B., & Rhodes, J. E. (in press). The test of time: Predictors and effects of duration in youth mentoring relationships. *American Journal of Community Psychology.*

Grossman, J. B., & Tierney, J. P. (1998). Does mentoring work? An impact study of the Big Brothers/Big Sisters program. *Evaluation Review, 22*(3), 403–426.

Haase, B. (1998). Learning to be an apprentice. In J. Singleton (Ed.), *Learning in likely places: Varieties of apprenticeship in Japan* (pp. 107–121). New York: Cambridge University Press.

Hamilton, M. A., & Hamilton, S. F. (1993). *Toward a youth apprenticeship system: A progress report from the Youth Apprenticeship Demonstration Project in Broome County, New York*. Ithaca, NY: Cornell University Press.

Hamilton, S. F. (1987). Apprenticeship as a transition to adulthood in West Germany. *American Journal of Education, 95*(2), 314–345.

Hamilton, S. F. (1990). *Apprenticeship for adulthood: Preparing youth for the future*. New York: Free Press.

Hamilton, S. F., & Darling, N. (1989). Mentors in adolescents' lives. In K. Hurrelmann & U. Engel (Eds.), *The social world of adolescents: International perspectives. Prevention and intervention in childhood and adolescence, Vol. 5* (pp. 121–139). Berlin: Walter de Gruyter.

Hamilton, S. F., & Darling, N. (1996). Mentors in adolescents' lives. In K. Hurrelmann & S. F. Hamilton (Eds.), *Social problems and social contexts in adolescence: Perspectives across boundaries* (pp. 199–215). New York: Aldine de Gruyter.

Hamilton, S. F., & Hamilton, M. A. (1999). Creating new pathways to adulthood by adapting German apprenticeship in the United States. In W. R. Heinz (Ed.), *From education to work: Cross-national perspectives* (pp. 194–213). New York: Cambridge University Press.

Hamilton, S. F., Hamilton, M. A., & Wood, B. J. (1991). *Creating apprenticeship opportunities for youth*. Ithaca NY: Cornell Youth and Work Program.

Hazan, C., & Shaver, P. R. (1994). Attachment as an organizational framework for research on close relationships. *Psychological Inquiry, 5*(1), 1–22.

Hendry, L. B., Roberts, W., Glendinning, A., & Coleman, J. C. (1992). Adolescents' perceptions of significant individuals in their lives. *Journal of Adolescence, 15*(3), 255–270.

Hostetler, J. A., & Huntington, G. E. (1992). *Amish children: Education in the family, school, and community* (2nd ed.). Forth Worth, TX: Harcourt Brace Jovanovich.

Hultsman, W. Z. (1993). The influence of others as a barrier to recreation participation among early adolescents. *Journal of Leisure Research, 25*(2), 150–164.

Kemper, T. (1968). Reference groups, socialization and achievement. *American Sociological Review, 33*, 31–45.

Kett, J. (1977). *Rites of passage: Adolescence in America, 1790 to the present*. New York: Basic Books.

Klaw, E. L., & Rhodes, J. E. (1995). Mentor relationships and the career development of pregnant and parenting African American teenagers. *Psychology of Women Quarterly, 19*(4), 551–562.

Kleiber, D. A. (1999). *Leisure experiences and human development: A dialectical interpretation*. New York: Basic Books.

Lanz, M., Iafrate, R., Marta, E., & Rosnati, R. (1999). Significant others: Italian adolescents' rankings compared with their parents'. *Psychological Reports, 84*(2), 459–466.

Laursen, B. (1998). Closeness and conflict in adolescent peer relationships: Interdependence with friends and romantic partners. In W. M. Bukowski & A. F. Newcomb (Eds.), *The company they keep: Friendship in childhood and adolescence. Cambridge studies in social and emotional development* (pp. 186–210). New York: Cambridge University Press.

Lempers, J. D., & Clark-Lempers, D. S. (1992). Young, middle, and late adolescents' comparisons of the functional importance of five significant relationships. *Journal of Youth & Adolescence, 21*(1), 53–96.

Matsuda, S. (1989). Significant partners in childhood and adolescence. In K. Hurrelman & U.

Engel (Eds.), *The social world of adolescents: International perspectives* (pp. 199–212). New York: Walter de Gruyter.

McAdams, D. P., & de St. Aubin, E. (Eds.). (1998). *Generativity and adult development: How and why we care for the next generation.* Washington, DC: American Psychological Association.

Merton, R. K. (1968). *Social theory and social structure.* New York: Free Press.

Modell, J., & Goodman, M. (1990). Historical perspectives. In S. S. Feldman & G. R. Elliott (Eds.), *At the threshold* (pp. 93–122). Cambridge, MA: Harvard University Press.

Moran, G. F. (1998). Cares for the rising generation: Generativity in American history, 1607–1900. In D. P. McAdams & E. de St. Aubin (Eds.), *Generativity and adult development: How and why we care for the next generation* (pp. 311–333). Washington, DC: American Psychological Association.

Munsch, J., & Blyth, D. A. (1993). An analysis of the functional nature of adolescents' supportive relationships. *Journal of Early Adolescence, 13*(2), 132–153.

Pawlak, S. A. (1999). The academic mentoring process: A survey of important aspects. Doctoral dissertation, University of Memphis, TN.

Pianta, R. C. (Ed.). (1992). *Beyond the parent: The role of other adults in children's lives* (Vol. 57). San Francisco: Jossey-Bass.

Pleiss, M. K., & Feldhusen, J. F. (1995). Mentors, role models, and heroes in the lives of gifted children. *Educational Psychologist, 30*(3), 159–169.

Rhodes, J. E. (1994). Older and wiser: Mentoring relationships in childhood and adolescence. *Journal of Primary Prevention, 14*(3), 187–196.

Rhodes, J. E. (in press). *Stand by me: The risks and rewards of mentoring today's youth.* Cambridge, MA: Harvard University Press.

Rhodes, J. E., Contreras, J. M., & Mangelsdorf, S. C. (1994). Natural mentor relationships among Latina adolescent mothers: Psychological adjustment, moderating processes, and the role of early parental acceptance. *American Journal of Community Psychology, 22*(2), 211–227.

Rhodes, J. E., Ebert, L., & Fischer, K. (1992). Natural mentors: An overlooked resource in the social networks of young, African American mothers. *American Journal of Community Psychology, 20*(4), 445–461.

Rhodes, J. E., Haight, W. L., & Briggs, E. C. (1999). The influence of mentoring on the peer relationships of foster youth in relative and nonrelative care. *Journal of Research on Adolescence, 9*(2), 185–201.

Rosenberg, M. (1973). Which Significant Others? *American Behavioral Scientist, 16,* 829–860.

Sampson, R. J. (1992). Family management and child development: Insights from social disorganization theory. In J. McCord (Ed.), *Facts, frameworks, and forecasts. Advances in criminological theory, Vol. 3* (pp. 63–93). New Brunswick, NJ: Transaction.

Scales, P. C., & Gibbons, J. L. (1996). Extended family members and unrelated adults in the lives of young adolescents: A research agenda. *Journal of Early Adolescence, 16*(4), 365–389.

Schlegel, A. (1995). A cross-cultural approach to adolescence. *Ethos, 23*(1), 15–32.

Schmidt, L. C. (1998). A motivational approach to the prediction of mentoring relationship satisfaction and future intention to mentor. Doctoral dissertation, University of Pittsburgh, PA.

Silverberg, S. B., Vazsonyi, A. T., Schlegel, A. E., & Schmidt, S. (1998). Adolescent apprentices in Germany: Adult attachment, job expectations, and delinquency attitudes. *Journal of Adolescent Research, 13*(3), 254–271.

Stinson, K. M. (1991). *Adolescents, family, and friends: Social support after parents' divorce or remarriage.* New York: Praeger.

Sullivan, A. M. (1996). From mentor to muse: Recasting the role of women in relationship with urban adolescent girls. In B. J. R. Leadbeater & N. Way (Eds.), *Urban girls: Resisting stereotypes, creating identities* (pp. 226–249). New York: New York University Press.

Sylvia, R. D., & Hutchison, T. (1985). What makes Ms. Johnson teach? A study of teacher motivation. *Human Relations, 38*(9), 841–856.

Tatar, M. (1998a). Significant individuals in adolescence: Adolescent and adult perspectives. *Journal of Adolescence, 21*(6), 691–702.

Tatar, M. (1998b). Teachers as significant others: Gender differences in secondary school pupils' perceptions. *British Journal of Educational Psychology, 68*(2), 217–227.

Wentzel, K. R. (1997). Student motivation in middle school: The role of perceived pedagogical caring. *Journal of Educational Psychology, 89*(3), 411–419.

Werner, E. E. (1990). Protective factors and individual resilience. In S. J. Meisels & J. P. Shonkoff (Eds.), *Handbook of early childhood intervention* (pp. 97–116). New York: Cambridge University Press.

Werner, E. E. (1993). Risk, resilience, and recovery: Perspectives from the Kauai Longitudinal Study. *Development & Psychopathology, 5*(4), 503–515.

Werner, E. E. (1995). Resilience in development. *Current Directions in Psychological Science, 4*(3), 81–85.

Werner, E. E., & Smith, R. S. (1992). *Overcoming the odds: High risk children from birth to adulthood*. Ithaca, NY: Cornell University Press.

Wertsch, J. V. (1979, 1981). The concept of activity in Soviet psychology: An introduction. In J. V. Wertsch (Ed.), *The concept of activity in Soviet psychology* (pp. 3–36). Armonk, NY: M. E. Sharpe.

Wild, T. C., Enzle, M. E., & Hawkins, W. L. (1992). Effects of perceived extrinsic versus intrinsic teacher motivation on student reactions to skill acquisition. *Personality & Social Psychology Bulletin, 18*(2), 245–251.

Zey, M. G. (1988). A mentor for all reasons. *Personnel Journal, 67*(1), 46–51.

CHAPTER EIGHTEEN

Adolescent Sexuality: Behavior and Meaning

Lisa J. Crockett, Marcela Raffaelli, and Kristin L. Moilanen

Introduction

The emerging sexuality that accompanies adolescence poses fundamental challenges for young people. These include adjusting to the altered appearance and functioning of a sexually maturing body, learning to deal with sexual desires, confronting sexual attitudes and values, experimenting with sexual behaviors, and integrating these feelings, attitudes, and experiences into a developing sense of self. The challenge is accentuated by the un-familiar excitement of sexual arousal, the attention connected to being sexually attractive, and the new level of physical intimacy and psychological vulnerability created by sexual encounters.

Adolescents' responses to these challenges are profoundly influenced by the social and cultural context in which they live. In the United States, in contrast to many other Western nations, adolescent sexuality has typically been viewed as inappropriate and troublesome rather than as normal and healthy. In part, this reflects cultural mores about nonmarital sexual activity; in part it reflects well-justified concerns about potential negative consequences of sexual activity (see chapters 20 and 27 in this volume). Cultural proscriptions against nonmarital sex are counterbalanced by permissive attitudes reflected in the media and in the values of many adults. These competing perspectives co-mingle, creating a situation where adolescents are exposed to sexual material in settings of daily life but given inadequate preparation to behave responsibly in sexual situations. Feelings of sexual desire and love collide with social prescriptions to show restraint, setting the stage for psychological conflict and behavioral inconsistency.

Despite a recognition of the subjective aspects of adolescent sexuality, the scientific literature has focused primarily on objective indicators such as having sex at certain ages, the behaviors adolescents practice, and the health-related outcomes of teen sexual activity (Moore & Rosenthal, 1993). While this approach helps define the scope of the "problem," it fails to address the intrapsychic and interpersonal processes that influence whether intercourse occurs and whether protection is used. Understanding these subjective dimensions is key to developing effective interventions to reduce risky sexual behavior; it is also critical for grasping the meaning young people ascribe to their experiences, and the ways in which sexuality is integrated into their identities and intimate relationships (e.g., Brooks-Gunn & Paikoff, 1997).

To provide an integrated picture of adolescent sexuality, we address three related issues: (1) recent trends in sexual behaviors among US adolescents; (2) individual and social factors influencing adolescent sexual behavior; and (3) how adolescents make sense of their sexual feelings and experiences. We highlight variations related to gender and ethnicity, but our scope is limited to heterosexual behavior (for a discussion of gay and lesbian youth, see chapter 19 in this volume). Wherever possible, we rely on recent national surveys for information on the attitudes and experiences of contemporary youth.

Sexual Behaviors

Both sexual ideation and activity increase over the adolescent period (e.g., Halpern et al., 1993). Teenagers engage in a spectrum of sexual behaviors ranging from fantasy and self-stimulation to various forms of intercourse.

Non-coital sexual behaviors

Fantasy. Erotic fantasy is the most common sexual behavior in adolescence. In a non-representative sample of 13–18-year-olds, 72 percent acknowledged having sexual fantasies (Coles & Stokes, 1985). Erotic fantasies serve several important functions for adolescents: along with creating pleasant sexual arousal and expressing sexual needs, they provide insight into sexual desires and preferences and are an opportunity to "rehearse" sexual encounters (Katchadourian, 1990).

Masturbation. Similar to fantasy, masturbation allows teenagers to explore their sexuality in a safe and private way, and is generally regarded as a normative activity (Katchadourian, 1990). In one survey, 46 percent of boys and 24 percent of girls reported masturbating (Coles & Stokes, 1985); among college students, 67 percent of males and 34 percent of females reported masturbating at age 15 (Leitenberg, Detzer, & Srebnik, 1993). However, masturbation remains a taboo topic in the United States. This taboo is apparent in a content analysis of sex-related items published in *Seventeen* magazine: masturbation was not mentioned at all in 1974 and appeared in less than 5 percent of items in 1984 and 1994 (Carpenter, 1998).

"Making out." Most US adolescents engage in physically intimate behavior, even if they do not have intercourse. In a sample of ethnic minority 14–17-year-olds who had not yet had intercourse, 86 percent had kissed, 47 percent had rubbed their body against

another, and 16 percent had engaged in genital touching (K. Miller et al., 1997). In a multiethnic sample of 12–15-year-olds, Smith and Udry (1985) found that white adolescents followed a typical progression from necking, to petting above the waist, to genital touching, to intercourse. A similar sequence emerged in a primarily white, Mormon sample (B. Miller et al., 1998). In contrast, black adolescents showed no predictable sequence of sexual behaviors, and many reported intercourse prior to heavy petting (Smith & Udry, 1985). Thus, the timing and sequencing of sexual behaviors appear to differ for blacks and whites.

Sexual intercourse

The majority of US adolescents experience intercourse by age 18. In recent national surveys, 50 percent of 9th–12th-graders reported they had had sex (Blum et al., 2000; CDC, 2000). The likelihood of intercourse increases with age, so that by 12th grade, approximately two-thirds of students have had sex (CDC, 2000). This is likely an underestimate, as school-based surveys exclude high school dropouts and youth enrolled in alternative schools, who are more likely to be sexually active.

The prevalence of adolescent intercourse differs by race and ethnicity. Among participants in the National Survey of Adolescent Health (Add Health), less than half of white (46 percent) and Hispanic (47 percent) high school students reported sexual intercourse, compared to two-thirds (67 percent) of blacks (Blum et al., 2000). Similarly, in 1995, 88 percent of black males aged 17–19 reported engaging in sex, compared to 64 percent of non-black males (Ku et al., 1998). Among females aged 15–19 in 1995, 60 percent of non-Hispanic blacks, 56 percent of Hispanics, and 51 percent of non-Hispanic whites reported intercourse (Singh & Darroch, 1999). Boys tend to initiate intercourse earlier than girls: in 1999, 45 percent of 9th-grade boys but 33 percent of 9th-grade girls reported intercourse (CDC, 2000).

Historical trends. Decreases in the age of pubertal onset over the twentieth century, combined with an increase in the age of marriage in recent decades, has resulted in a span of over ten years between sexual maturity and marriage (Brooks-Gunn & Paikoff, 1997). This extended interval makes premarital sex likely. Historical data on premarital intercourse indicate that adolescent sexual activity increased during the twentieth century, especially for white females. By 1979, about half of white high school seniors of each gender reported having sex (Chilman, 1986). Although rates of sexual activity among teenagers appear to have leveled off, recent data show a continued trend towards earlier ages at first intercourse among adolescents who do initiate sexual activity. In 1995, 19 percent of teenage girls engaged in sex before age 15, almost double the proportion in 1988 (Child Trends, 2000).

Partners. Two-thirds of girls and half of boys aged 14–18 report having fewer than two sexual partners in their lifetime (CDC, 1992; cited in Santelli et al., 1998). However, 13 percent of high school girls and 19 percent of high school boys report having four or more lifetime partners (CDC, 2000). Among sexually active adolescents, older youth are more likely to have multiple partners: 21 percent of 12th-graders compared to 12 percent of 9th-graders reported four or more partners (CDC, 2000). Thus, although most adolescents engage in serial monogamy, because their relationships are often short-lived, they may have several partners over time (see Moore & Rosenthal, 1993 for a discussion).

Sexual coercion. Not all sexual intercourse is voluntary, particularly for girls. Among 17–23-year-old female participants in the National Survey of Children, 7 percent had been "forced to have sex against [their] will or raped" at least once (Miller, Monson, & Norton, 1995). Similarly, the 1995 National Survey of Family Growth indicated that among 15–19-year-old girls who have had sex, 7 percent said their first intercourse was nonvoluntary and another 24 percent said it had been voluntary but unwanted. Rates of sexual coercion were especially high among girls who initiated sex before age 13: one-fifth said their first intercourse was non-voluntary and another half said it was voluntary but unwanted (SIECUS, 1997).

In sum, research since the 1980s has yielded a wealth of data about certain aspects of adolescent sexual behavior, particularly intercourse. About two-thirds of US teens experience first sexual intercourse by 12th grade; thus, initiating intercourse is a normative experience for teenagers. Next, we turn to an examination of biological, psychological, and sociocultural factors that influence adolescent sexual behavior.

Biological Influences

Puberty

Puberty encompasses dramatic changes in hormone levels, body shape, and physical size (see chapter 2 in this volume). Research has linked both stage of pubertal development and timing of puberty to adolescent sexual behavior. Among 7th- and 8th-grade boys, pubertal development over a six-month period was associated with concurrent changes in sexual ideation and precoital behavior, and pubertal stage predicted the transition to intercourse (Halpern et al., 1993). Among girls, pubertal stage predicted level of sexual experience the following year (Whitbeck, Conger, & Kao, 1993). For both genders, earlier pubertal onset relative to peers was associated with greater sexual experience (Flannery, Rowe, & Gulley, 1993; B. Miller et al., 1998). Among girls, early menarche was associated with a younger age at first intercourse (Magnusson, 1988; B. Miller et al., 1997); among boys, advanced pubertal maturation relative to peers was associated with earlier first intercourse (Capaldi, Crosby, & Stoolmiller, 1996).

Pubertal hormones may underlie the relation between pubertal development and sexual behavior. Testosterone administration increases sexual interest and behavior in women (Sherwin, Gelfand, & Brender, 1985) and in men with low testosterone levels (Kwan et al., 1983). Similarly, cross-sectional studies by Udry and colleagues demonstrated an association between androgen levels and both sexual motivation and behavior in early adolescence (Udry et al., 1985; Udry, Talbert, & Morris, 1986). However, longitudinal studies have not supported this linkage: increases in testosterone over early adolescence failed to predict changes in sexual behavior for either gender (Udry & Campbell, 1994). Among boys, initial testosterone levels were associated with concurrent and subsequent sexual behavior, but changes in testosterone did not predict changes in sexual ideation or behavior (Halpern et al., 1993). Among postmenarcheal girls, pubertal development significantly predicted non-coital behavior and intercourse, but testosterone levels did not (Udry & Campbell, 1994). Thus, rather than exerting a direct influence on sexual behavior, hormones may operate indirectly by stimulating physical maturation and sexual attractiveness.

Genetic factors

Age of puberty is partly inherited, providing a potential genetic basis for individual differences in the timing of first intercourse. Evidence of heritability is found in high intercorrelations in age at menarche between mothers and daughters and between sisters (Garn, 1980). Genetic effects are also implicated by the recent finding that dopamine receptor genes are associated with age of first intercourse (W. Miller et al., 1999). However, mother's age at menarche does not necessarily predict early initiation of intercourse by her children (Mott et al., 1996), so other mechanisms are likely involved.

Biosocial models

Recent models of adolescent sexual behavior incorporate both biological and social influences (e.g., Irwin et al., 1997). For example, Smith, Udry, and Morris (1985) found that pubertal indices and best friend's sexual behavior each predicted the sexual behavior of boys and girls; among girls, the impact of friend's sexual behavior was particularly pronounced at advanced stages of pubertal development. B. Miller et al. (1998) found direct effects of pubertal development for both genders, along with an indirect effect of parent–child communication about sex on girls' level of sexual experience two years later. These studies underscore the need to consider social as well as biological influences.

Sociocultural Influences

Human societies differ greatly in the cultural rules regulating sexual behavior and the vigor with which they are enforced. In some cultures premarital sex is encouraged because pregnancy allows a determination of the fertility of potential marriage partners; in other cultures premarital sex is strongly discouraged, especially for girls, because virginity is highly prized (Paige & Paige, 1985; Whiting, Burbank, & Ratner, 1986). The United States is an interesting case because of its ambivalent treatment of adolescent sexuality. Despite increased societal permissiveness since the 1950s (Chilman, 1986) and the fact that the majority of adolescents have sex, many adults are reluctant to accept adolescent intercourse. Whereas only a fourth of US adults in the early 1990s disapproved of premarital sex in general, two-thirds said that sex between adolescents was wrong (Smith, 1994). Because of these negative attitudes, adolescents, who are encouraged to prepare for adulthood in many arenas (e.g., by studying or getting a job), are given little guidance and training for sexual experimentation. The "abstinence-only" movement in sexuality education is a prime example of this neglect.

In regard to sexuality education, the contrast between the United States and other Western countries is striking. For example, the Swedish State Commission on Sex Education suggests that students should gain knowledge that "will equip them to experience sexual life as a source of happiness and joy in fellowship with other[s]" (Brown, 1983, p. 880, cited in Fine, 1988). In contrast, US sex education curricula have typically focused on the dangers of sex and on girls' need for protection from predatory males (Fine, 1988); more recently, federal mandates for "abstinence-only education" have further narrowed opportunities for federally funded programs to discuss the full range of sexual experiences and feelings. However, the former Surgeon General's call to action to promote sexual health and responsible sexual behavior suggests a renewed interest in open dialogue about sexuality (Satcher, 2001).

Cultural values and attitudes regarding sexuality are distilled through experiences in everyday social contexts. Interactions within families, peer groups, and other daily contexts can influence whether and when an adolescent will initiate sexual intercourse.

Family influences

Family processes. Parent–child relationships, parental control, and parent–child communication have all been implicated in adolescent sexual behavior. Better parent–child relationships are associated with postponing intercourse, less frequent intercourse and fewer sexual partners (for a review, see Miller, Benson, & Galbraith, 2001). Although most studies are cross-sectional, similar relations have been found longitudinally (Feldman & Brown, 1993; K. Miller et al., 1998.) Effects of mother–child relationship quality have emerged for both sons and daughters (Jaccard, Dittus, & Gordon, 1996; Weinstein & Thornton, 1989), and the quality of the father–child relationship is influential for boys (Feldman & Brown, 1993). Effects of parent–child closeness have been found among blacks and whites and in multiethnic samples (Dittus & Jaccard, 2000).

Several mechanisms may underlie the associations between family relationships and adolescent sexual activity. Poor parent–child relationships may enhance susceptibility to peer influences or increase the propensity to associate with deviant friends (Whitbeck, Conger, & Kao, 1993). Mechanisms may differ for girls and boys: Whitbeck and colleagues found that, for girls, the relation between low parental warmth and sexual behavior was mediated by depressed mood, whereas for boys it operated through alcohol use (Whitbeck et al., 1992). In a study of boys, those from families characterized by low support, high indulgence, and paternal rejection had lower self-restraint and more sexual partners (Feldman & Brown, 1993). Such mediating variables may explain why parent–child relationship quality does not always have significant effects on adolescents' sexual behavior when examined within multivariate models (Crockett et al., 1996; Small & Luster, 1994).

Parental control is also related to adolescent sexual activity. Typically, better monitoring is associated with postponing intercourse (Jacobson & Crockett, 2000) or less frequent intercourse (Benda & DiBlasio, 1994), although not all studies find this pattern (e.g., East 1996). Presumably, parental monitoring and supervision reduce adolescent intercourse by restricting opportunities for sexual activity; however, some studies indicate that sexual activity is more likely when parental control is excessive (Miller et al., 1986) or intrusive (Upchurch et al., 1999).

Direct communication is another way in which parents may influence their children's sexual behavior. However, family communication about sex is infrequent (Raffaelli, Bogenschneider, & Flood, 1998), and parents and teens often disagree about the frequency and content of these conversations (Jaccard, Dittus, & Gordon, 1998). Research on parent–adolescent communication and adolescent sexual activity has yielded complex and often contradictory findings. The impact of parent–child communication appears to depend on openness of the communication, a clear focus on sexual topics, the quality of the parent–child relationship, and the parent's values regarding adolescent sexual activity (see Miller, Benson, & Galbraith, 2001).

Parents' attitudes about adolescent sex predict their children's sexual attitudes and behavior (Thornton & Camburn, 1989; Treboux & Busch-Rossnagel, 1990). Moreover, adolescents' perceptions of parental disapproval of sex are associated with postponing intercourse (Jaccard, Dittus, & Gordon, 1996; Sieving, NcNeely, & Blum, 2000). These effects are enhanced when the parent-child relationship is close, indicating that values are more easily transmitted within supportive parent–child relationships (Dittus & Jaccard, 2000; Weinstein & Thornton, 1989).

Family composition and socioeconomic status. Consistent associations have been found between family structure (especially living in a single-parent family) and earlier first intercourse (B. Miller et al., 1997). This effect persists after controlling for demographic variables such as race, social class, and age. It has been attributed to modeling (Miller & Bingham, 1989), permissive parental attitudes (Thornton & Camburn, 1987), and reduced parental control (Newcomer & Udry, 1987). Single parents who date may be salient role models. In a study of recently divorced mothers and their adolescent children, maternal dating had a direct positive relation to sons' level of sexual experience; for daughters, the effect was mediated by girls' permissive sexual attitudes (Whitbeck, Simons, & Kao, 1994).

The sexual behavior of family members is also associated with adolescent sexual activity. Teenagers whose mothers initiated sex and childbearing at younger ages are more likely to have sex (Kowaleski-Jones & Mott, 1998) and to experience early sexual debut (Ku, Sonenstein, & Pleck, 1993a). Moreover, the presence of older sexually active siblings, especially teenage sisters who are pregnant or parenting, is related to younger siblings' sexual experience, earlier first intercourse, and pregnancy risk (East, Felice, & Morgan, 1993; Widmer, 1997). These associations could reflect modeling effects but may also be genetically mediated through early timing of puberty (Newcomer & Udry, 1984).

Finally, consistent associations have been found between family socioeconomic status and adolescent sexual activity. Lower family income (Upchurch et al., 1999) and lower parental educational attainment (Brewster, 1994; Sieving, McNeely, & Blum, 2000) are associated with a greater likelihood of teenage intercourse. These associations may reflect differences in perceived life opportunities and available social roles.

Peer influences

Peers are presumed to exert a major social influence on adolescent sexual behavior. Peer effects may operate at several levels. Same-sex peers are a major source of information about sex (Davis & Harris, 1982), and peers provide settings (e.g., cars, parties) where sex can occur (Rowe & Linver, 1995). Same-sex friends may influence the perceived acceptability of sexual behavior, and sexually experienced friends may serve as role models. Finally, romantic partners provide opportunities for sexual experimentation and may also exert pressure for sex (Wyatt & Riederle, 1994).

Friends. Associations between close friends' sexual behavior are well documented (East, Felice & Morgan, 1993; Rodgers & Rowe, 1990; Whitbeck et al., 1993). Although these patterns could indicate a peer socialization effect, selection may also play a role, if adolescents choose friends who are like themselves in attitudes and behavior (Bauman & Ennett, 1996; Billy, Rodgers, & Udry, 1984). In a longitudinal study, best friends' sexual experience was strongly associated with the initiation of intercourse for white females, but for white males the association appeared to reflect boys' selection of friends with levels of sexual experience similar to their own. No evidence of peer influence was found for blacks of either gender (Billy & Udry, 1985).

Associating with deviant peers has been linked to earlier initiation of intercourse (Rowe et al., 1989a; Whitbeck et al., 1999). Conversely, spending time with conventional peers in extracurricular activities is negatively associated with adolescent intercourse (Miller & Sneesby, 1988).

Jaccard, Blanton, and Dodge (2000) attempted to isolate peer socialization effects by controlling for potential confounds related to inaccurate reporting of friends' behavior, selection of friends, and common experiences (e.g., similar rate of pubertal development). Once statistical controls were applied, peer effects were small and occurred only between friends with similar sexual experience. Thus, effects of peer behavior may be limited; beliefs about friends' sexual behavior appear more influential than friends' actual behavior (Cvetkovich & Grote, 1980).

Romantic partners. Most teenagers become involved in romantic relationships (see chapter 15 in this volume). The proportion of Add Health respondents reporting a "serious romantic relationship" in the past 18 months increased from one-third of 13-year-olds to over half of 15-year-olds, to 70 percent of 17-year-olds (Raffaelli, unpublished analysis). Romantic or dating relationships often provide the context for adolescent sexual behavior. Early and steady dating predict sexual behavior for both genders (Miller et al., 1986; B. Miller et al., 1997; Thornton, 1990). Among adolescents in the Add Health study, being in a romantic relationship increased the likelihood of sexual activity (Dittus

& Jaccard, 2000). Finally, three-quarters of female National Survey of Family Growth (NSFG) participants aged 25 and under who had their first voluntary sexual intercourse before age 18 said they were "going steady" (73.9 percent) with or engaged to (1.9 percent) their first sexual partner'[1] (Manning, Longmore, & Giordano, 2000).

Neighborhood influences

Neighborhoods can be a source of models for and information about sexual behavior. Living in poor neighborhoods is associated with greater frequency of intercourse among males (Ku, Sonenstein, & Pleck, 1993b) and with higher rates of adolescent pregnancy (Hogan & Kitagawa, 1985). Community variables, such the percentage of women working full time, are negatively associated with rates of premarital intercourse for both black and white women (Billy, Brewster, & Grady, 1994) and help account for racial disparities in timing of first intercourse (Brewster, 1994). The proportion of middle-class neighbors is negatively associated with adolescent childbearing, whereas the prevalence of female-headed families is a positive predictor. These neighborhood "effects" may reflect the role models available to youth and the potential for collective monitoring by adults (Brooks-Gunn et al., 1993).

Media

Adolescents are frequently exposed to sexual material on television, in movies, and in magazines. Most sexual behavior on television takes places between unmarried adults and ignores the potential negative consequences of sexual intercourse; music videos often combine sex and violence (Huston, Wartella, & Donnerstein, 1998). However, the effect of media exposure on adolescents' sexual attitudes and behavior has not been sufficiently studied. Experimental studies show that exposure to sexual content can lead to more permissive attitudes about premarital sex, but a link between exposure and adolescent intercourse has not been established (Huston, Wartella, & Donnerstein, 1998).

Psychological and Behavioral Influences

Attitudes and values

Adolescents' attitudes about sex are shaped by family values and cultural proscriptions as well as personal experience. In 1967, Reiss argued that most adolescents subscribed to the notion that sexual intimacy was permissible in the context of affection (Reiss, 1967). Most 18–25-year-olds continue to approve of premarital sex under some conditions; less than 20 percent say premarital sex is always wrong (Smith, 1994). Nonetheless, there is considerable variability in adolescents' opinions about the appropriateness of premarital sex, especially casual sex. More permissive attitudes about sex predict adolescents' level of coital and precoital experience and their initiation of intercourse (Treboux & Busch-Rossnagel, 1990; Whitbeck et al., 1999). Young men hold more permissive sexual attitudes than young women (Feldman, Turner & Araujo, 1999).

Religion is often linked to adolescent sexual behavior (see Rostosky et al., in press, for a review). Youth who have no religious affiliation are most likely to initiate sex as teenagers (Forste & Heaton, 1988), and those who belong to churches that promote abstinence are least likely to have sex (e.g., Miller & Olson, 1988). Greater religiosity, as indexed by frequency of church attendance and perceived importance of religion, is associated with postponing intercourse (Cvetkovich & Grote, 1980; Jessor et al., 1983; Thornton & Camburn, 1989; Whitbeck et al., 1999). In a national sample, greater frequency of attending religious services decreased the odds of initiating intercourse among white males and white, Latina, and black women (Day, 1992).

Academic achievement and educational investment

Adolescents with higher educational aspirations and better academic performance tend to postpone first intercourse (Jessor et al., 1983; Miller & Sneesby, 1988) and have sex less often (Ohannessian & Crockett, 1993). Time spent in academic activities is also negatively related to early intercourse, especially for girls (Crockett et al., 1996; Whitbeck et al., 1999).

Psychosocial adjustment

Psychological well-being. Although low self-esteem has been proposed as a predictor of early intercourse, evidence of this relationship is weak. In longitudinal studies, the association is weak or nonsignificant (Crockett et al., 1996; Jessor et al., 1983; Whitbeck et al., 1999). A more robust effect has been found for depression: depressed affect is positively associated with girls' sexual experience (Whitbeck et al., 1992, 1993, 1999).

Problem behaviors. Consistent linkages have been found between early sexual activity and other forms of misconduct, including delinquent activities (Costa et al., 1995; Ketterlinus et al., 1992), substance use (Halpern-Felsher, Millstein, & Ellen, 1996), and such behaviors as cheating on tests (Rodgers & Rowe, 1990). Some scholars have suggested that the association among problem behaviors reflects a common deviance trait (Rowe et al., 1989b) or a personality disposition towards unconventionality (Costa et al., 1995). It could also represent an emerging lifestyle or pattern of adaptation. Bingham and Crockett (1996) found that adolescents who experienced early, middle, and late sexual debut exhibited distinct developmental trajectories, with those who initiated sex early showing a longitudinal pattern of poorer adjustment in multiple domains, including academic achievement, family relationships, and misconduct.

Risk tolerance and self-restraint

Adolescent sexual activity may also be linked to a general propensity to engage in potentially risky activities. Risk-proneness and involvement in problem behaviors predicted nonvirginity in both genders (Kowaleski-Jones & Mott, 1998). Among boys, self-restraint at ages 10–11 was inversely associated with number of sexual partners and level of misconduct four years later (Feldman & Brown, 1993). Finally, in a clinic sample, girls terminating a pregnancy were found to be more impulsive than those seeking contraceptive advice (Rawlings, Boldero, & Wiseman, 1995).

Making Sense of Sexuality

Adolescents must sort out what they believe about sexuality, just as they must grapple with other aspects of their personal identity. However, relatively little research exists on adolescents' constructions of sexuality. Their view of sex and the meaning it holds are likely based on internalized cultural images of sex and romance as well as on their own experiences of love and desire. These subjective elements, along with situational factors that affect decision making, play an important role in sexual choices and behavior. In the following paragraphs we review the meager literature on these issues.

Cultural templates

Long before adolescents actually engage in sexual intercourse, they have developed a complex set of ideas about sexuality and sexual encounters. Some theorists describe these mental representations as "scripts" that provide guidelines for heterosexual interactions (Gagnon, 1973, 1990). In fact, college students agree on how men and women should behave on a first date (Rose & Frieze, 1993), and adolescents agree about what behavior is appropriate at different ages. For example, Australian girls and boys tend to agree that kissing should occur at ages 12–14 and fondling, intercourse, and oral sex at ages 15–17 (Rosenthal & Smith, 1997). US college students endorse a similar sexual timetable (Feldman, Turner, & Araujo, 1999). Given the historical double standard, scripts for female sexuality have changed more in recent decades than scripts for male sexuality (Thompson, 1995). An examination of sexual discourse in *Seventeen* magazine from the 1970s to the 1990s revealed that young women went from being portrayed as sexual objects to being acknowledged as sexual agents (Carpenter, 1998). Nevertheless, later issues presented contradictory messages about sexuality, emphasizing victimization as well as choice, and morality as well as desire.

Despite a gender convergence in sexual behaviors, a double standard remained in the late 1980s such that girls were judged more harshly than boys for engaging in some types of sexual activities (Moore & Rosenthal, 1993). In qualitative interviews, girls were more likely than boys to express ambivalence about their sexuality and to be concerned about how they would be viewed if they were sexually active (Hillier, Harrison, & Warr, 1997).

This concern is well founded, as girls who have multiple sexual partners still risk being labeled "sluts" (Orenstein, 1994, cited in Graber, Brooks-Gunn, & Galen, 1998).

Constructions of love, desire, and sexual identity

Love. Although adults often discount adolescent relationships as "puppy love," the feelings associated with "crushes" and romantic relationships can be intense (see chapter 15 in this volume). Romantic feelings emerge at an early age. In one study, 7th- and 8th-graders spent 4–6 hours a week thinking about individuals of the other sex (Richards et al., 1998). Among 7th–12th-graders, being with someone of the other sex was associated with more positive moods and more frequent feelings of being "in love" compared to other social contexts (Richards et al., 1998). Romantic feelings have been linked to pubertal development. Feelings of being "in love" were associated with self-rated changes in body shape among 5th–9th-grade girls and with pubic hair growth among 5th- and 6th-grade boys (Richards & Larson, 1993). Importantly, feelings of love can affect sexual decision-making. As one girl stated, "When you're there with him and you love him so much, it's hard to say no" (Public Policy Productions, 1995).

Desire. Little is known about adolescents' experience of sexual desire. Of necessity, studies of adolescents' sexual feelings have been conducted with convenience samples, limiting their generalizability. Nonetheless, they provide important information about how adolescents make sense of their emerging sexuality. In general, males more often emphasize physical aspects of sex (e.g., satisfaction, release) whereas females emphasize emotional aspects such as love and intimacy (Moore & Rosenthal, 1993). However, recent research with adolescent girls reveals myriad perspectives about the connection between sex and love. Thompson (1995, p. 14) identified "girls who strove desperately to fuse sex and love . . . girls who preferred playing the field to pursuing steady love . . . girls who chose . . . to value work over love; girls who declined the right to separate sex and reproduction."

Similarly, in an analysis of discourses on sex, relationships, and reproduction (Lamanna, 1999), a third of young women (35 percent) emphasized sex avoidance and another third (35 percent) situated sex and reproduction in the context of a relationship characterized by love, caring, and domesticity. The remaining women characterized their sexual activity as lacking intentionality – something that "just happens" (16 percent) or as an act of self-development (14 percent).

Life circumstances may influence these diverse perspectives. Tolman and Szalacha (1999) analyzed the "narratives of desire" among 15–19-year-old girls attending a suburban (primarily white) school or an urban (largely minority) school. Almost half the narratives focused on vulnerability, 29 percent on pleasure, and 24 percent on a mix of themes. Urban girls told more narratives about vulnerability than pleasure, whereas suburban girls generated equal numbers of narratives on these two themes, unless they had experienced sexual violation. Only suburban girls who had not experienced violation talked about desire in a way that suggested a healthy "embodied sexuality" (Hillier, Harrison, & Bowditch, 1999): "Both sexual desire and sexual pleasure are known to them as profoundly physical experiences – as feelings they perceive in their own bodies"

(Tolman & Szalacha, 1999, p. 29). In contrast, urban girls and suburban girls who had been violated talked about their sexual experiences in a disconnected way.

Sexual identity. Ultimately, adolescents must develop a concept of themselves as sexual beings and integrate their sexual self into their overall identity. This process begins when young people first recognize their feelings of sexual arousal and may continue through-out life (Graber, Brooks-Gunn, & Galen, 1998). Key dimensions of the sexual self-concept may include sexual self-esteem, sexual self-efficacy/mastery, and beliefs about sexual self-image. Buzwell and Rosenthal (1996) identified five sexual styles among Australian adolescents: sexually naive, sexually unassured, sexually competent, sexually adventurous, and sexually driven. The clusters differed in gender, age composition, and sexual history (e.g., the sexually naive group contained more girls, virgins, and younger students). Notably, the five clusters also differed in their patterns of sexual risk-taking, suggesting the utility of this classification scheme in understanding how sexual self-concept might affect adolescents' behavior.

Situations of sexual possibility

Although sexual identity and sexual motives influence adolescents' decisions about whether to have sex, situational variables also play a role. Boys and girls in the United States have opportunities to be together in private, affording them what Roberta Paikoff (1995) has called "situations of sexual possibility." Opportunities for privacy increase with age. In one study, the amount of time adolescents spent alone with a person of the other sex increased from under three hours a week in 9th grade to over eight hours in 12th grade (Richards et al., 1998). When sexual opportunities occur, attitudes about sex and feelings about the partner influence whether intercourse occurs; furthermore, attitudes toward contraception and the ability to plan ahead influence whether sex is unprotected. However, other variables also enter into the equation. For many adolescents sex is sporadic and thus hard to predict. Moreover, some adolescents have ambivalent feelings about preparing for sex, even when they think it might occur. For example, girls may be concerned that they will appear "loose" if they carry condoms (Hillier, Harrison, & Warr, 1997). Thus, for various reasons adolescents may be unprepared for a sexual encounter.

We must also consider the effects of intense desire on the behavior of adolescents who have not let learned to control their emotions. Although adolescents demonstrate sound decision-making skills in laboratory settings, real-life decision making occurs under nonoptimal conditions, such as time pressure (Keating, 1990). Hamburg (1986) has suggested that sexual decision-making reflects "hot cognitions" as opposed to "cold cognitions," and may be less reasoned and logical. The use of alcohol or other drugs also affects judgment in sexual situations.

Additionally, some adolescents engage in sex for reasons other than desire. Parents of poor, urban, African American adolescents speculate that their teenagers have sex in exchange for protection from gangs and because they routinely witness sexual activity among older peers in their buildings (Brooks-Gunn & Paikoff, 1997). Sprecher and McKinney (1987) suggest that sex can represent an act of exchange, interdependence, maintenance, self-disclosure, intimacy, or love. Curiosity and pressure from peers and partners also plays a role in early sexual encounters (Wyatt & Riederle, 1994). What happens in situations of sexual possibility depends on the myriad functions sex can serve and the salience of these functions to the young people involved.

Finally, it is critical to recognize that there are two people involved in a sexual encounter. Thus, two people's desires, attitudes, and intentions need to be taken into account in predicting sexual behavior. Moreover, the partners likely differ in power, making one partner's wishes more influential (Fine, 1988; Hillier, Harrison, & Warr, 1997). Partners who are aware of the power differential perceive that they have more or less control in the situation; adolescents who perceive little control may not assert their wishes. In a study of Australian adolescents, two-thirds reported that they talked about condoms the last time they had sex, yet almost one-fifth of these youth did not use a condom (Hillier, Harrison, & Warr, 1997). Thus, sexual communication between partners does not guarantee better decision-making.

Conclusions and Directions for Future Research

Research on adolescent sexuality has tended to be behavior-focused, spurred by concerns about adolescent pregnancy and health risks. Such a focus affords only a partial understanding of adolescent sexuality, neglecting the subjective and interpersonal dimensions that provide the psychological context for sex. Thus, we know much about adolescents' sexual behavior, especially intercourse, but little about their reasons for having sex or the meaning they ascribe to their behavior.

Studies of adolescent sexual behavior have moved beyond identifying individual predictors of sexual activity to testing multivariate models that incorporate biological, psychological, and social factors (e.g., Crockett et al., 1996; Udry & Billy, 1987). However, most studies still focus on intercourse, rather than other forms of sexual expression that precede or co-occur with intercourse. Moreover, many studies of intercourse do not distinguish between vaginal, oral, and anal sex. Finally, most studies conceptualize intercourse dichotomously, as having occurred or not occurred. Fortunately, more sophisticated approaches are beginning to appear in the literature. Kim Miller and colleagues (1997) identified two subgroups of virgins in their white heterosexual sample: "delayers" had never engaged in intercourse and did not think they would in the next year, whereas "anticipators" reported a high likelihood of sexual initiation in the next year. Significant differences in non-coital experiences (kissing and genital touching) emerged between "anticipators" and "delayers" who would normally be pooled into a "not sexually active" group. Similarly, Luster and Small (1994) classified their sample of adolescents into high-risk youth (more than one lifetime sex partner and infrequent or no contraceptive use); low-risk youth (one partner and always used contraception); and abstainers. Significant differences emerged among the groups.[2] The differentiated approach exemplified in these typologies should lead to a more nuanced understanding of adolescent sexual behavior in future years.

Studies of sexual behavior and the determinants of sexual activity have revealed important differences related to gender, race/ethnicity, and socioeconomic status, but these variables have not been fully examined in studies of subjective aspects of sexuality. Attention has focused mainly on girls; thus, little is known about boys' experiences of sexuality. The picture that emerges from the scant literature is largely negative; boys come across as manipulators who will do anything to "get sex" and avoid emotional entanglements. The reality is more complicated, but only a handful of studies on boys' subjective experiences of sexuality have been conducted (e.g., Fine, 1987). Regarding ethnicity, the work of Tolman and her colleagues (e.g., Tolman & Szalacha, 1999) reveals important differences in how girls from suburban (mostly white) and urban (mostly minority) schools conceptualize their feelings of desire. However, additional research is needed to disentangle differences due to ethnicity from those due to location (urban vs. suburban), and to uncover the processes that produce these differences.

Although sexual activity typically involves two people who may have differing levels of arousal, distinct emotions and desires, and different levels of power, relatively little attention has been paid to adolescents' sexual partners, and most research has obtained data from only one member of the couple. Past research has shown the importance of relationship characteristics in influencing contraceptive use at first intercourse (Manning, Longmore, & Giordano, 2000); for example, female NSFG respondents younger than 18 whose partners were six or more years older were less likely to report contraceptive use at last intercourse than young women whose partners were within two years of their age; they were also more likely to become pregnant and bear a child (Darroch, Landry, & Oslak, 1999). Future research should examine the role of partners more fully.

There is an ongoing need for longitudinal research that tracks changes in attitudes, behaviors, and subjective experience over time. This is especially critical for building a picture of how sexual self-concept develops and how sexuality becomes integrated into the young person's identity and construction of relationships. Unfortunately, considerable challenges remain to conducting such studies, given the moral climate that persists in the United States. Until we accept adolescent sexuality, we will be unable to protect young people from potential negative consequences and foster their healthy sexual development.

Notes

1. 21.3 percent were "just friends" or "went out once in a while," and 2.9 percent had just met their sex partner.
2. For example, the high-risk group reported higher levels of abuse, and lower levels of parental monitoring and support, than the other two groups.

Key Readings

Brooks-Gunn, J., & Paikoff, R. (1997). Sexuality and developmental transitions during adolescence. In J. Schulenberg, J. L. Maggs, K. Hurrelmann, & L. Chassin (Eds.), *Health risks and developmental transitions during adolescence* (pp. 190–219). Cambridge: Cambridge University Press.

This chapter provides a basic overview of adolescent sexuality from a developmental perspective and includes an extensive reference list.

Fine, M. (1988). Sexuality, schooling, and adolescent females: the missing discourse of desire. *Harvard Educational Review, 58*(1), 29–53.
This article is a critique of traditional sex education that has emphasized danger rather than desire.

Miller, B. C., Benson, B., & Galbraith, K. A. (2001). Family relationships and adolescent pregnancy risk: A research synthesis. *Developmental Review, 21*, 1–38.
The article is a comprehensive review of research on how family factors affect adolescents' risk for pregnancy.

Moore, S., & Rosenthal, D. (1993). *Sexuality in adolescence.* New York: Routledge.
This volume is an in-depth review of current research on adolescent sexual development with an international focus.

Santelli, J. S., Lindberg, L. D., Abma, J., McNeely, C. S., & Resnick, M. (2000). Adolescent sexual behavior: Estimates and trends from four nationally representative surveys. *Family Planning Perspectives, 32*, 156–165, 194.
This article is a detailed description of adolescent sexual behavior drawing from multiple national surveys conducted at different timepoints.

References

Bauman, K. E., & Ennett, S. T. (1996). On the importance of peer influence for adolescent drug use: Commonly neglected considerations. *Addiction, 91*, 185–198.

Benda, B. B., & DiBlasio, F. A. (1994). An integration of theory: Adolescent sexual contacts. *Journal of Youth and Adolescence, 23*(3), 403–420.

Billy, J. O. G., Brewster, K. L., & Grady, W. R. (1994). Contextual effects on the sexual behavior of adolescent women. *Journal of Marriage and the Family, 56*, 387–404.

Billy, J. O. G., Rodgers, J. L., & Udry, J. R. (1984). Adolescent sexual behavior and friendship choice. *Social Forces, 662*, 653–678.

Billy, J. O. G., & Udry, J. R. (1985). The influence of male and female best friends on adolescents' sexual behavior. *Adolescence, 20*, 21–32.

Bingham, C. R., & Crockett, L. J. (1996). Longitudinal adjustment patterns of boys and girls experiencing early, middle, and late sexual intercourse. *Developmental Psychology, 32*, 647–658.

Blum, R. W., Beuhring, T., Shew, M. L., Bearinger, L. H., Sieving, R. E., & Resnick, M. D. (2000). The effects of race/ethnicity, income, and family structure on adolescent risk behaviors. *American Journal of Public Health, 90*, 1879–1884.

Brewster, K. L. (1994). Race differences in sexual activity among adolescent women: The role of neighborhood characteristics. *American Sociological Review, 59*, 408–424.

Brooks-Gunn, J., Duncan, G. J., Klebanov, P. K., & Sealand, N. (1993). Do neighborhoods influence child and adolescent development? *American Journal of Sociology, 99*(2), 353–395.

Brooks-Gunn, J., & Paikoff, R. (1997). Sexuality and developmental transitions during adolescence. In J. Schulenberg, J. L. Maggs, K. Hurrelmann, & L. Chassin (Eds.), *Health risks and developmental transitions during adolescence*, pp. 190–219. Cambridge: Cambridge University Press.

Brown, P. (1983). The Swedish approach to sex education and adolescent pregnancy: Some impressions. *Family Planning Perspectives, 15*(2), 92–95.

Buzwell, S., & Rosenthal, D. (1996). Constructing the sexual self: Adolescents' sexual self-perceptions and sexual risk-taking. *Journal of Research on Adolescence, 6*, 489–513.

Capaldi, D. M., Crosby, L., & Stoolmiller, M. (1996). Predicting the timing of first sexual intercourse for at-risk adolescent males. *Child Development, 67*, 344–359.

Carpenter, L. M. (1998). From girls into women: scripts for sexuality and romance in *Seventeen* magazine, 1974–1994. *Journal of Sex Research, 35*(2), 158–168.

Centers for Disease Control and Prevention [CDC] (2000). Youth risk behavior surveillance – United States, 1999. *MMWR, 49*(No. SS-5).

Chilman, C. S. (1986). Some psychosocial aspects of adolescent sexual and contraceptive behaviors in a changing American society. In J. B. Lancaster & B. A. Hamburg (Eds.), *School-age pregnancy and parenthood: biosocial dimensions* (pp. 191–217). Hawthorne, NY: Aldine de Gruyter.

Coles, R., & Stokes, G. (1985). *Sex and the American teenager*. New York: Harper & Row.

Costa, F. M., Jessor, R., Donovan, J. E., & Fortenberry, J. D. (1995). Early initiation of sexual intercourse: The influence of psychosocial unconventionality. *Journal of Research on Adolescence, 5*, 93–121.

Crockett, L. J., Bingham, C. R., Chopak, J. S., & Vicary, J. R. (1996). Timing of first sexual intercourse: The role of social control, social learning, and problem behavior. *Journal of Youth and Adolescence, 25*, 89–111.

Cvetkovich, G., & Grote, B. (1980). Psychological development and the social problem of teenage pregnancy. In C. Chilman (Ed.), *Adolescent pregnancy and childbearing: Findings from research* (pp. 15–41). Washington, DC: US Department of Health and Human Services.

Darroch, J. E., Landry, D. J., & Oslak, S. (1999). Age differences between sexual partners in the United States. *Family Planning Perspectives, 31*, 160–167.

Davis, S. M., & Harris, M. B. (1982). Sexual knowledge, sexual interests, and sources of sexual information of rural and urban adolescents from three cultures. *Adolescence, 17*, 471–492.

Day, R. D. (1992). The transition to first intercourse among racially and culturally diverse youth. *Journal of Marriage and the Family, 54*, 749–762.

Dittus. P. J., & Jaccard, J. (2000). The relationship of adolescent perceptions of maternal disapproval of sex and of the mother-adolescent relationship to sexual outcomes. Manuscript, Department of Psychology, State University of New York at Albany, NY.

East, P. L. (1996). The younger sisters of childbearing adolescents: Their attitudes, expectations, and behaviors. *Child Development, 67*, 267–282.

East, P. L., Felice, M. E., & Morgan, M. C. (1993). Sisters' and girlfriends' sexual and childbearing behavior: effects on early adolescent girls' sexual outcomes. *Journal of Marriage and the Family, 55*, 953–963.

Feldman, S. S., & Brown, N. (1993). Family influences on adolescent male sexuality: The mediational role of self-restraint. *Social Development, 2*, 16–35.

Feldman, S. S., Turner, R., & Araujo, K. (1999). Interpersonal context as an influence on sexual timetables of youth: gender and ethnic effects. *Journal of Research on Adolescence, 9*(1), 25–52.

Fine, G. A. (1987). *With the boys: Little league baseball and adolescent culture*. Chicago: University of Chicago Press.

Fine, M. (1988). Sexuality, schooling, and adolescent females: the missing discourse of desire. *Harvard Educational Review, 58*(1), 29–53.

Flannery, D. J., Rowe, D. C., & Gulley, B. L. (1993). Impacts of pubertal status, timing, and age on adolescent sexual experience and delinquency. *Journal of Adolescent Research, 8*, 21–40.

Forste, R. T., & Heaton, T. B. (1988). Initiation of sexual activity among female adolescents. *Youth and Society, 19*(3), 250–268.

Gagnon, J. H. (1973). Scripts and the coordination of sexual conduct. *Nebraska Symposium on Motivation, 21*, 27–59.

Gagnon, J. H. (1990). The explicit and implicit use of the scripting perspective in sex research. *Annual Review of Sex Research, 1*, 1–43.

Garn, S. M. (1980). Continuities and change in maturational timing. In O. G. Brim & J. Kagan (Eds.), *Constancy and change in human development* (pp. 113–162). Cambridge, MA: Harvard University Press.

Graber, J. A., Brooks-Gunn, J., & Galen, B. R. (1998). Betwixt and between: Sexuality in the context of adolescent transitions. In R. Jessor (Ed.), *New perspectives of adolescent risk behavior* (pp. 270–316). Cambridge: Cambridge University Press.

Halpern, C. T., Udry, J. R., Campbell, B., & Suchindran, C. (1993). Testosterone and pubertal development as predictors of sexual activity: A panel analysis of adolescent males. *Psychosomatic Medicine, 55*, 436–447.

Halpern-Felsher, B., Millstein, S. G., & Ellen, M. (1996). Relationship of alcohol use and risky sexual behavior: A review and analysis. *Journal of Adolescent Health, 19*, 331–336.

Hamburg, B. (1986). Subsets of adolescent mothers: Developmental, biomedical, and psychosocial issues. In J. B. Lancaster & B. A. Hamburg (Eds.), *School-age pregnancy and parenthood: Biosocial dimensions* (pp. 115–145). Hawthorne, NY: Aldine de Gruyter.

Hillier, L., Harrison, L., & Bowditch, K. (1999). "Neverending love" and "blowing your load": The meanings of sex to rural youth. *Sexualities, 2*(1), 69–88.

Hillier, L., Harrison, L., & Warr, D. (1997). "When you carry a condom all the boys think you want it": Negotiating competing discourses about safe sex. *Journal of Adolescence, 21*, 15–29.

Hogan, D. P., & Kitagawa, E. M. (1985). The impact of social status, family structure, and neighborhood on the fertility of black adolescents. *American Journal of Sociology, 90*(4), 825–855.

Huston, A. C., Wartella, E., & Donnerstein, E. (1998*). Measuring effects of sexual content in the media: A report to the Kaiser Family Foundation.* Washington, DC: Kaiser Family Foundation.

Irwin, C. E., Jr., Igra, V., Eyre, S., & Millstein, S. (1997). Risk-taking behavior in adolescents: the paradigm. In M. S. Jacobson, J. M. Rees, N. H. Golden, & C. E. Irwin (Eds.), *Adolescent nutritional disorders: prevention and treatment* (pp. 1–35). New York: New York Academy of Sciences.

Jaccard, J., Blanton, H., & Dodge, T. (2000). Peer influence on risk behavior. Manuscript, Department of Psychology, State University of New York at Albany, NY.

Jaccard, J., Dittus, P. J., & Gordon, V. V. (1996). Maternal correlates of adolescent sexual and contraceptive behavior. *Family Planning Perspectives, 28*(4), 159–185.

Jaccard, J., Dittus, P. J., & Gordon, V. V. (1998). Parent–adolescent congruency in reports of adolescent sexual behavior and in communication about sexual behavior. *Child Development, 69*, 247–261.

Jacobson, K. C., & Crockett, L. J. (2000). Parental monitoring and adolescent adjustment: An ecological perspective. *Journal of Research on Adolescence, 10*, 65–97.

Jessor, R., Costa, F., Jessor, S. L., & Donovan, J. E. (1983). Time of first intercourse: A prospective study. *Journal of Personality and Social Psychology, 44*(3), 608–626.

Katchadourian, H. (1990). Sexuality. In S. S. Feldman & G. R. Elliott (Eds.), *At the threshold: The developing adolescent* (pp. 330–351). Cambridge, MA: Harvard University Press.

Keating, D. (1990). Adolescent thinking. In S. S. Feldman & G. R. Elliott (Eds.), *At the threshold: The developing adolescent* (pp. 54–89). Cambridge, MA: Harvard University Press.

Ketterlinus, R. D., Lamb, M. E., Nitz, K., & Elster, A. B. (1992). Adolescent nonsexual and sex-related problem behaviors. *Journal of Adolescent Research, 7*, 431–456.

Kowaleski-Jones, L., & Mott, F. L. (1998). Sex, contraception and childbearing among high-risk youth: Do different factors influence males and females? *Family Planning Perspectives, 30,* 163–169.

Ku, L., Sonenstein, F. L., Lindberg, L. D., Bradner, C. H., Boggess, S., & Pleck, J. H. (1998). Understanding changes in sexual activity among young metropolitan men: 1979–1995. *Family Planning Perspectives, 30*(6), 256–262.

Ku, L., Sonenstein, F. L., & Pleck, J. H. (1993a). Factors influencing first intercourse for teenage men. *Public Health Reports, 108*(6), 680–694.

Ku, L., Sonenstein, F. L., & Pleck, J. H. (1993b). Neighborhood, family and work: influences on the premarital behaviors of adolescent males. *Social Forces, 72,* 479–503.

Kwan, M., Greenleaf, W. J., Mann, L., Crapo, L., and Davidson, J. M. (1983). The nature of androgen action of male sexuality: A combined laboratory and self-report study in hypogonadal men. *Journal of Clinical Endocrinology and Metabolism, 57,* 557–562.

Lamanna, M. A. (1999). Lining the postmodern dream: Adolescent women's discourse on relationships, sexuality, and reproduction. *Journal of Family Issues, 20*(2), 181–217.

Leitenberg, H., Detzer, M. J., & Srebnik, D. (1993). Gender differences in masturbation and the relation of masturbation experience in preadolescence and/or early adolescence to sexual behavior and sexual adjustment in young adulthood. *Archives of Sexual Behavior, 22*(2), 87–98.

Luster, T., & Small, S. A. (1994). Factors associated with sexual risk-taking behaviors among adolescents. *Journal of Marriage and the Family, 56,* 622–632.

Magnusson, D. (1988). *Individual development from an interactional perspective: A longitudinal study.* Hillsdale, NJ: Erlbaum.

Manlove, J., & Terry, E. (2000). *Trends in sexual activity and contraceptive use among teens* (Research Brief No. 2000–03). Washington, DC: Child Trends.

Manning, W. D., Longmore, M. A., & Giordano, P. C. (2000). The relationship context of contraceptive use at first intercourse. *Family Planning Perspectives, 32*(3), 104–110.

Miller, B. C., Benson, B., & Galbraith, K. A. (2001). Family relationships and adolescent pregnancy risk: A research synthesis. *Developmental Review, 21,* 1–38.

Miller, B. C., & Bingham, C. R. (1989). Family configuration in relation to the sexual behavior of female adolescents. *Journal of Marriage and the Family, 51,* 499–506.

Miller, B. C., McCoy, J. K., Olson, T. D., & Wallace, C. M. (1986). Parental discipline and control attempts in relation to adolescent sexual attitudes and behavior. *Journal of Marriage and the Family, 48,* 503–512.

Miller, B. C., Monson, B. H., & Norton, M. C. (1995). The effects of forced sexual intercourse on white female adolescents. *Child Abuse and Neglect, 19,* 1289–1301.

Miller, B. C., Norton, M. C., Curtis, T., Hill, E. J., Schvaneveldt, P., & Young, M. H. (1997). The timing of sexual intercourse among adolescents: Family, peer, and other antecedents. *Youth & Society, 29*(1), 54–83.

Miller, B. C., Norton, M. C., Fan, X., & Chistopherson, C. R. (1998). Pubertal development, parental communication, and sexual values in relation to adolescent sexual behaviors. *Journal of Early Adolescence, 18,* 27–52.

Miller, B. C., & Olson, T. D. (1988). Sexual attitudes and behavior of high school students in relation to background and contextual factors. *Journal of Sex Research, 24,* 194–200.

Miller, B. C., & Sneesby, K. (1988). Educational correlates of adolescents' sexual attitudes and behavior. *Journal of Youth and Adolescence, 17,* 521–530.

Miller, K. E., Sabo, D. F., Farrell, M. P., Barnes, G. M., & Melnick, M. J. (1998). Athletic participation and sexual behavior in adolescents: the different worlds of boys and girls. *Journal of Health and Social Behavior, 39,* 108–123.

Miller, K. S., Clark, L. F., Wendell, D. A., Levin, M. L., Gray-Ray, P., Velez, C. N., & Webber,

M. P. (1997). Adolescent heterosexual experience: A new typology. *Journal of Adolescent Health, 20,* 179–186.

Miller, W. B., Pasta, D. J., MacMurray, J., Chiu, C., Wu, H., & Comings, D. E. (1999). Dopamine receptor genes are associated with age at first sexual intercourse. *Journal of Biosocial Sciences, 31,* 43–54.

Moore, S., & Rosenthal, D. (1993). *Sexuality in adolescence.* New York: Routledge.

Mott, F. L., Fondell, M. M., Hu, P. N., Kowaleski-Jones, L., & Menaghan, E. G. (1996). The determinants of first sex by age 14 in a high-risk adolescent population. *Family Planning Perspectives, 28*(1), 13–18.

Newcomer, S. F., & Udry, J. R. (1984). Mothers' influence on the sexual behavior of their teenage children. *Journal of Marriage and the Family, 46,* 477–485.

Newcomer, S. F., & Udry, J. R. (1987). Parental marital status effects on adolescent sexual behavior. *Journal of Marriage and the Family, 49,* 235–240.

Ohannessian, C., & Crockett, L. (1993). A longitudinal investigation of the relationship between educational investment and adolescent sexual activity. *Journal of Adolescent Research, 8,* 167–182.

Orenstein (1994). *School girls: Young women, self-esteem, and the confidence gap.* New York: Doubleday. (Cited in Graber et al., 1998.)

Paige, K. E., & Paige, J. M. (1985). *Politics and reproductive rituals.* Berkeley: University of California Press.

Paikoff, R. L. (1995). Early heterosexual debut: Situations of sexual possibility during the transition to adolescence. *American Journal of Orthopsychiatry, 65*(3), 389–401.

Public Policy Productions (1995). *Teens, sex and the schools* (video).

Raffaelli, M., Bogenschneider, K., & Flood, M. F. (1998). Parent-teen communication about sexual topics. *Journal of Family Issues, 19*(3), 316–334.

Rawlings, D., Boldero, J., & Wiseman, F. (1995). The interaction of age with Impulsiveness and Venturesomeness in the prediction of adolescent sexual behavior. *Individual Differences, 19*(1), 117–120.

Reiss, I. (1967). *The social context of premarital sexual permissiveness.* New York: Holt.

Richards, M. H., Crowe, P. A., Larson, R., & Swarr, A. (1998). Developmental patterns and gender differences in the experience of peer companionship during adolescence. *Child Development, 69,* 154–163.

Richards, M. H., & Larson, R. (1993). Pubertal development and the daily subjective states of young adolescents. *Journal of Research on Adolescence, 3,* 145–169.

Rodgers, J. L., & Rowe, D. C. (1990). Adolescent sexual activity and mildly deviant behavior. *Journal of Family Issues, 11*(3), 274–293.

Rose, S., & Frieze, I. H. (1993). Young singles' contemporary dating scripts. *Sex Roles, 28,* 499–509.

Rosenthal, D. A., & Smith, M. A. (1997). Adolescent sexual timetables. *Journal of Youth and Adolescence, 26*(5), 619–636.

Rostosky, S. S., Wilcox, B. L., Comer Wright, M. L., & Randall, B. A. (in press). The impact of religiosity on adolescent sexual behavior: A review of the evidence. *Journal of Adolescent Research.*

Rowe, D., & Linver, M. (1995). Smoking and addictive behaviors: Epidemiological, individual, and family factors. In J. Turner & L. Cardon (Eds.), *Behavior genetic approaches in behavioral medicine: Perspectives on individual differences* (pp. 67–84). New York: Plenum.

Rowe, D. C., Rodgers, J. L., Meseck-Bushey, S., & St. John, C. (1989a). An "epidemic" model of sexual intercourse prevalences for black and white adolescents. *Social Biology, 36,* 127–145.

Rowe, D. C., Rodgers, J. L, Meseck-Bushey, S., & St. John, C. (1989b). Sexual behavior and nonsexual deviance: A sibling study of their relationship. *Developmental Psychology, 25*, 61–69.

Santelli, J. S., Brener, N. D., Lowry, R., Bhatt, A., & Zabin, L. S. (1998). Multiple sexual partners among U.S. adolescents. *Family Planning Perspectives, 30*, 271–275.

Satcher, D. (2001). The Surgeon General's call to action to promote sexual health and responsible sexual behavior. Retrieved from http://www.surgeongeneral.gov/library/ sexualhealth/call.htm.

Sherwin, B. B., Gelfand, M. M., & Brender, W. (1985). Androgen enhances sexual motivation in females: A prospective cross-over study of sex steroid administration in the surgical menopause. *Psychosomatic Medicine, 7*, 339–351.

SIECUS. (1997). Male involvement in teen pregnancy. *SHOP Talk (School Health Opportunities and Progress) Bulletin, 2*(8).

Sieving, R., McNeely, C., & Blum, R. (2000). Maternal expectations, mother–child connectedness, and adolescent sexual debut. *Archives of Pediatrics and Adolescent Medicine, 154*, 809–816.

Singh, S., & Darroch, J. E. (1999). Trends in sexual activity among adolescent American women: 1982–1995. *Family Planning Perspectives, 31*(5), 212–219.

Small, S. A., & Luster, T. (1994). Adolescent sexual activity: An ecological, risk-factor approach. *Journal of Marriage and the Family, 56*, 181–192.

Smith, E. A., & Udry, J. R. (1985). Coital and non-coital sexual behaviors of white and black adolescents. *American Journal of Public Health, 75*(10), 1200–1203.

Smith, E. A., Udry, J. R., & Morris, N. M. (1985). Pubertal development and friends: A biosocial explanation of adolescent sexual behavior. *Journal of Health and Social Behavior, 26*, 183–192.

Smith, T. W. (1994). Attitudes toward sexual permissiveness: Trends, correlates, and behavioral connections. In A. S. Rossi (Ed.), *Sexuality across the life course* (pp. 63–97). Chicago: University of Chicago Press.

Sprecher, S., & McKinney, K. (1987). Barriers in the initiation of intimate heterosexual relationships and strategies for intervention. Special issue: Intimate relationships: Some social work perspectives on love. *Journal of Social Work and Human Sexuality, 5*, 97–110.

Thompson, S. (1995). *Going all the way: Teenage girls' tales of sex, romance, and pregnancy.* New York: Hill & Wang.

Thornton, A. (1990). The courtship process and adolescent sexuality. *Journal of Family Issues, 11*(3), 239–273.

Thornton, A. D., & Camburn, D. (1987). The influence of the family on premarital sexual attitudes and behavior. *Demography, 24*, 323–340.

Thornton, A. D., & Camburn, D. (1989). Religious participation and adolescent sexual behavior and attitudes. *Journal of Marriage and Family, 51*, 641–653.

Tolman, D. L., & Szalacha, L. A. (1999). Dimensions of desire. *Psychology of Women Quarterly, 23*, 7–39.

Treboux, D., & Busch-Rossnagel, N. A. (1990). Social network influences on adolescent sexual attitudes and behaviors. *Journal of Adolescent Research, 5*, 175–189.

Udry, J. R., & Billy, J. O. G. (1987). Initiation of coitus in early adolescence. *American Sociological Review, 52*, 841–855.

Udry, J. R., Billy, J. O. G., Morris, N. M., Groff, T., & Raj, M. (1985). Serum androgenic hormones motivate sexual behavior in adolescent boys. *Fertility and Sterility, 43*, 90–94.

Udry, J. R., & Campbell, B. C. (1994). Getting started on sexual behavior. In A. S. Rossi (Ed.), *Sexuality across the life course* (pp. 187–207). Chicago: University of Chicago Press.

Udry, J. R., Talbert, L. M., & Morris, N. M. (1986). Biosocial foundations for adolescent female sexuality. *Demography, 23,* 217–230.

Upchurch, D. M., Aneshensel, C. S., Sucoff, C. A., & Levy-Storms, L. (1999). Neighborhood and family contexts of adolescent sexual activity. *Journal of Marriage and the Family, 61,* 920–933.

Weinstein, M., & Thornton, A. (1989). Mother–child relations and adolescent sexual attitudes and behaviors. *Demography, 26*(4), 563–577.

Whitbeck, L., Conger, R., & Kao, M. (1993). The influence of parental support, depressed affect, and peers on the sexual behaviors of adolescent girls. *Journal of Family Issues, 14*(2), 261–278.

Whitbeck, L. B., Conger, R. D., Simons, R. L., & Kao, M. (1993). Minor deviant behaviors and adolescent sexual activity. *Youth & Society, 25*(1), 24–37.

Whitbeck, L., Hoyt, D., Miller, M., & Kao, M. (1992). Parental support, depressed affect, and sexual experiences among adolescents. *Youth and Society, 24*(2), 166–177.

Whitbeck, L. B., Simons, R. L., & Kao, M. Y. (1994). The effects of divorced mothers' dating behaviors and sexual attitudes on the sexual attitudes and behaviors of their adolescent children. *Journal of Marriage and the Family, 56,* 615–621.

Whitbeck, L. B., Yoder, K. A., Hoyt, D. R., & Conger, R. D. (1999). Early adolescent sexual activity: a developmental study. *Journal of Marriage and the Family, 61,* 934–946.

Whiting, J. W., Burbank, V. K., & Ratner, M. S. (1986). The duration of maidenhood across cultures. In J. B. Lancaster & B. A. Hamburg (Eds.), *School-age pregnancy and parenthood: Biosocial dimensions* (pp. 273–302). Hawthorne, NY: Aldine de Gruyter.

Widmer, E. D. (1997). Influence of older siblings on initiation of sexual intercourse. *Journal of Marriage and the Family, 59,* 928–938.

Wyatt, G. E., & Riederle, M. H. (1994). Reconceptualizing issues that affect women's sexual decision-making and sexual functioning. *Psychology of Women Quarterly, 18,* 611–625.

CHAPTER NINETEEN

The Intimate Relationships of Sexual-Minority Youths

Lisa M. Diamond and Ritch C. Savin-Williams

Introduction

No previous handbook on adolescence contains a chapter that focuses primarily on sexual-minority youths. Although social and behavioral scientists began systematically studying adolescent same-sex sexuality in the early 1980s, most early studies were theoretically impoverished and methodologically flawed. This is no longer the case. The amount and quality of research on youths with same-sex attractions and relationships has dramatically increased, and we can now assert with some confidence how their experiences resemble *and* differ from those of heterosexual adolescents. We also know that adolescent same-sex experiences – from fantasies and attractions to full-blown romantic relationships – are more common than many have historically assumed. Thus, no substantive review of adolescent social and sexual development can afford to ignore adolescent same-sex sexuality.

Yet addressing this topic is more difficult than one might assume. Although discussions of adolescent same-sex sexuality are often framed as discussions of lesbian/gay/bisexual youth, this is not entirely accurate. Not all adolescents with same-sex attractions and experiences identify as lesbian, gay, or bisexual, and not all lesbian/gay/bisexual adults recall having experienced same-sex attractions during adolescence. What, then, is the proper topic of this chapter – self-identified lesbian/gay/bisexual youths, regardless of how their same-sex sexuality manifests itself, or adolescent same-sex intimacy, regardless of whether it culminates in a lesbian/gay/bisexual identification?

Both deserve attention. All aspects of same-sex sexuality violate current culturally defined sexual norms, and this alone has intrapsychic and interpersonal consequences even for youths who never identify as lesbian, gay, or bisexual. Thus, our concern in this chapter is with *sexual-minority youths*, defined as all youths who experience same-sex attractions. Although we cannot accurately predict these youths' *future* sexual desires and identities, their *current* desires clearly mark them as worthy of our theoretical and empirical attention.

The Importance of Intimate Relationships

The majority of extant research on sexual-minority youths has focused on their sexual behavior, identity development, stigmatization/victimization, and suicidality. One might conclude from this research that sexual-minority youths spend all of their time having sex, analyzing their sexual identity, fending off verbal and physical assaults, and contemplating suicide. This is obviously a distorted perception. Although each of these are important issues deserving of attention, researchers have generally overlooked the more mundane features of adolescent life, such as routine friendship formation and dissolution, relations with parents, and romances.

This is a notable shortcoming for efforts to understand sexual-minority youths' social development. Of the multiple transitions that take place during the adolescent and young adult years, those involving interpersonal relationships are some of the most salient and important. Adolescents of all sexual orientations undergo notable increases in their desires and capacities for emotional intimacy with peers, and these changes can profoundly reshape their close relationships and the sense of self they derive from these relationships. These transformations might be particularly meaningful for sexual-minority youths, given that same-sex sexuality is a fundamentally interpersonal as well as intrapsychic phenomenon. Same-sex attractions are, after all, desires for particular types of interactions with particular partners, and their highly charged social meaning derives directly from this fact.

Yet little attention has been devoted to sexual-minority youths' interpersonal worlds. Rather, it is often assumed that their close relationships are simply "mirror images" of heterosexual youths' close relationships, involving crushes and dates with the *same* sex instead of the other sex, and best friendships with the *other* sex instead of the same sex. The reality is far more complicated. Not only do most sexual-minority youths pursue intimate sexual and emotional relationships with *both* female and male peers over the course of adolescence (Savin-Williams, 1996a), but others develop unique same-sex and/or other-sex relationships that breach the conventional boundaries between friendship and romantic love (Diamond, 2000a).

Clearly, these youths' interpersonal experiences are far from mirror images of heterosexuals' experiences. This chapter reviews what is known regarding their unique patterns of relationship participation and the social-developmental implications of these patterns. The emphasis will be on youths' peer relationships – specifically, close friendships and romantic/sexual ties. Parental relationships, although obviously important, are beyond the scope of this chapter, and we direct interested readers elsewhere for substantive discussions of this topic (Floyd et al., 1999; Savin-Williams, 1998c, 2001).

Sexual Orientation and Same-Sex Intimacy

We begin by reviewing what is currently known about sexual orientation and its adolescent manifestations. *Sexual orientation* is typically defined as a consistent, enduring pattern of sexual desire for individuals of the same sex, the other sex, or both sexes. This is not to be confused with *sexual identity*, which is a culturally organized conception of the self according to a sexual label, usually *lesbian/gay*, *bisexual*, or *heterosexual*. Extensive research, speculation, and debate have been devoted to the nature and causes of sexual orientation. Are individuals born with a fixed predisposition to experience same-sex attractions, or are these attractions shaped by environmental experiences? If the former, when do such predispositions manifest themselves, and what else do they influence (i.e., affectional feelings, sex-typed behavior, etc.)? If the latter, what types of environmental experiences are involved, and do they shape and reshape sexual desires throughout the life course, or only during childhood?

Although these questions alone could occupy this entire chapter, we emphasize instead three points on which scientists increasingly agree, and which have important implications for understanding adolescent same-sex sexuality. First, sexual orientation is partly determined by genes in some people (reviewed in Bailey & Pillard, 1995). This conclusion is supported by chromosome research (Hamer & Copeland, 1994) and twin studies (Bailey & Pillard, 1991; Bailey et al., 1993), and provides a biological explanation for the fact that many sexual minorities experience their same-sex sexuality as a stable, unchanging trait that first manifests itself in early childhood (Savin-Williams, 1996c). Although investigators have found varying levels of familial concordance for same-sex orientation in line with genetic relatedness, it bears noting that no research has found perfect concordance of sexual orientation in identical twins, demonstrating that non-genetic factors are also involved.

This leads to the second point: Sexual orientation has multiple causes, and different combinations of causes may be operative for different individuals (Garnets & Kimmel, 1993; Richardson, 1987). For some, genetic factors outweigh environmental influences; for others, psychosocial and interpersonal factors are most important. Accordingly, same-sex sexuality develops at different rates and in different contexts across different individuals. Some sexual minorities recall having experienced same-sex attractions at an early age, in the context of spontaneous fantasies; others do not experience same-sex attractions until adulthood, in the context of specific long-standing relationships (Blumstein & Schwartz, 1990; Kitzinger & Wilkinson, 1995; Savin-Williams, 1996c).

We therefore arrive at our third point: Sexual orientation and same-sex intimacy are distinct phenomena. One need not possess a same-sex orientation to desire or enjoy same-sex intimacy, and one need not possess a heterosexual orientation to desire or enjoy other-sex intimacy. Rather, individuals typically experience a diverse array of attractions and behaviors during their adolescent years, some of which reflect curiosity and experimentation, some of which reflect social pressure, and some of which reflect an underlying sexual orientation (Bancroft, 1990; Cass, 1990; Laumann et al., 1994).

This complexity makes it difficult to specify a distinct set of behaviors and affects that reliably distinguishes lesbian/gay/bisexual adolescents from confused, experimenting, sexually adventurous, or curious adolescents. Perhaps the only way to be certain whether an adolescent's same-sex attractions will persist into adulthood is to observe whether they actually *do*. In the meantime, we should take our cues from how youths describe their experiences and interpret their desires and relationships, resisting the temptation to second-guess their reports on the basis of preconceptions about "typical" lesbian/gay/bisexual development.

Multiple Pathways of Sexual-Minority Development

The very notion of "typical" lesbian/gay/bisexual development is increasingly suspect. For example, although it was once thought that all sexual minorities experienced the emergence of their same-sex attractions prior to adolescence, we now know that this is not always the case. Rather, sexual minorities show remarkably diverse social and sexual developmental trajectories (Diamond, 1998, 2000b, in press; Diamond & Savin-Williams, 2000; Golden, 1987; Savin-Williams, 1998a, in press; Savin-Williams & Diamond, 2000), reporting various ages and contexts for first awareness of same-sex attractions, first sexual questioning, and first self-identification. They also have remarkably divergent patterns of sexual and romantic relationships (Diamond, Savin-Williams, & Dubé, 1999; Savin-Williams, 1996a), divergent patterns of friendship with sexual-minority and heterosexual age-mates and adults (Diamond & Dubé, 2001), and divergent degrees of openness about their sexuality to friends and family members (Cohen & Savin-Williams, 1996; Savin-Williams, 1998b).

Thus, a singular "sexual-minority developmental trajectory" does not exist. Rather, there are multiple pathways of development in different domains, and each of these pathways is sensitive to a youth's personal characteristics and local environments. Factors such as gender, ethnicity, and social class have obvious influences, but so do a youth's overall personality, confidence, sex drive, resilience, and attractiveness. Andersen and Cyranowski (1994) noted that individual differences in such domains might play a particularly formative role at the beginning of an individual's "sexual/intimate career."

Environmental factors are also critically important. It has long been noted that large urban centers tend to be more tolerant of same-sex sexuality than small, rural communities, and therefore youths from these two types of communities will likely face distinctly different normative pressures as they struggle to acknowledge, interpret, and accept their same-sex attractions. They will also have notably different degrees of access to support resources. Large urban centers are much more likely to have vibrant lesbian/gay/bisexual communities that sponsor youth groups and youth-focused recreational activities. Youths from rural areas might have little idea that such resources even exist. These differences directly influence how youths experience and interpret their same-sex sexuality, given that access to supportive lesbian/gay/bisexual resources likely speeds and eases the process of sexual-minority identity development.

Gender differences

Over twenty years of research has conclusively demonstrated that nearly all features of sexual-minority development and experience are differentiated by gender. Even the seemingly universal experience of homophobia impacts women differently than men. Male sexual minorities typically face considerably more outright stigmatization and violence than do females (D'Augelli, 1989), and research suggests that our culture is more often threatened and appalled by male than female same-sex sexuality (D'Augelli & Rose, 1990; Herek, 1988). Such differences have important implications for the types of intimate experiences that sexual-minority youths will have the opportunity to pursue, as well as the physical, interpersonal, and intrapsychic repercussions of these experiences.

Some of the largest gender differences concern the ways in which same-sex sexuality first unfolds. For example, whereas many gay men recall childhoods characterized by gender atypicality, feelings of "differentness," and early same-sex attractions (Bailey & Zucker, 1995; Herdt & Boxer, 1993; Isay, 1989; Savin-Williams, 1990), these experiences are less frequently recalled by sexual-minority women (Bailey, 1996; Diamond, 1998; Savin-Williams, 1998a, in press). Women also show greater variability in the age at which they first become aware of same-sex attractions, the age at which they consciously question their sexuality, and the age at which they first have same-sex sexual contact (reviewed in Savin-Williams & Diamond, 2000).

For example, male sexual-minority youths typically pursue sexual contact during their early teen years (Herdt & Boxer, 1993; Savin-Williams, 1998a), shortly after pubertal onset. In contrast, although some sexual-minority women experiment sexually with other girls during early adolescence, the majority do not have same-sex sexual contact until late adolescence or young adulthood, often a number of years *after* identifying as lesbian or bisexual (Diamond, 1998; Kitzinger & Wilkinson, 1995; Savin-Williams, in press; Savin-Williams & Diamond, 2000). Much of this variability is attributable to women's diverse social environments. Specifically, some young women have more opportunities to experiment with same-sex contact as a result of having more permissive environments, more freedom from parental supervision, and greater availability of willing same-sex partners.

Although these environmental factors also influence sexual-minority men's formative sexual experiences, they generally exert greater pressure on young women. Notably, this is consistent with research on heterosexual youths demonstrating that whereas the timing of male sexual initiation is directly dependent on pubertal increases in androgen levels, independent of social factors, the timing of female sexual initiation is predominantly dependent on social and interpersonal factors, independent of androgen levels (Udry & Billy, 1987; Udry, Talbert, & Morris, 1986). In other words, both sexual-minority *and* heterosexual male youths tend to seek sexual activity *when* and *with whom* they want, environment notwithstanding. For sexual-minority and heterosexual female youths, situational and environmental factors play a greater role in structuring sexual experiences.

Interpersonal factors – especially participation in emotionally intimate relationships – are particularly important in this regard. Women are more likely than men to report experiencing emotional same-sex attractions before experiencing physical same-sex desires, and physical desires often develop in the context of an existing emotional bond (Blumstein

& Schwartz, 1990; Rose, Zand, & Cimi, 1993; Vance & Green, 1984). For example, young women's first same-sex attractions are frequently directed toward close friends or female mentors, whereas young men's first same-sex attractions are often directed toward strangers or fantasy images of men (Savin-Williams & Diamond, 2000). Furthermore, women are more likely than men to report that they become attracted to – or fall in love with – "the person and not the gender" (Blumstein & Schwartz, 1990; Golden, 1987; Savin-Williams, 1998a, in press).

There is considerable debate about the source of these gender differences. Some attribute them to the fact that women have been historically socialized to restrict their sexual feelings and behaviors to intimate emotional relationships, whereas males have not (Gagnon & Simon, 1973). Others attribute them to essential differences between female and male sexuality, hypothesizing that women's weaker libidos inevitably grant social and interpersonal factors a greater role in structuring sexual responses (see Baumeister, 2000). Importantly, these provocative, ongoing debates should not overshadow the extent of diversity *within* each gender. Some male youths show "female-typed" patterns of same-sex desire and experience, and some female youths show "male-typed" patterns (Savin-Williams & Diamond, 2000). Research has begun to probe for the potential determinants of these diverse patterns.

Ethnicity

Ethnicity is another important source of variability in a sexual-minority youth's experiences. As noted earlier, environmental factors related to a youth's ethnic communities and identifications often play a critical role in shaping a youth's processes of acknowledging, interpreting, and acting on same-sex attractions (Dubé & Savin-Williams, 1999). In general, ethnic-minority communities tend to stigmatize same-sex sexuality more stringently than mainstream Anglo society (Chan, 1992; Collins, 1990; Hidalgo, 1984; Icard, 1986), reflected in the fact that some languages have no positive or neutral terms for "lesbian," "gay," or "bisexual" (Espin, 1997). Consequently, ethnic-minority youths with same-sex attractions often grow up with little sense that others share their experiences (Savin-Williams, 1996b).

Importantly, the nature, parameters, and underlying reasons for the stigmatization of same-sex sexuality vary considerably across ethnic groups, and these differences have correspondingly distinct implications for sexual-minority youths' experiences. For example, Latino, African American, Asian-Pacific Islander, and South Asian communities typically place considerable emphasis on family ties, and same-sex sexuality is often construed as a violation and betrayal of familial cohesion and loyalty (Chan, 1992; Hidalgo, 1984; Jayakar, 1994; Tremble, Schneider, & Appathurai, 1989; Vasquez, 1979; Wooden, Kawasaki, & Mayeda, 1983). Many South Asian families continue to arrange their children's marriages (Jayakar, 1994; Pasupathi, in press), and the social ties created by these marriages may have important implications for the family's integration into other social networks. Adolescents whose same-sex sexuality leads them to withdraw from this tradition may be viewed by their parents as making a selfish choice that impacts negatively on the family's entire social system. In these cases, adolescents may feel impossibly torn between familial loyalty and their deepest, inescapable desires. As a result, many delay disclosing their sexuality to parents until they have completed college or have established their independence (Dubé & Savin-Williams, 1999).

In ethnic groups that have sharply demarcated gender roles, same-sex sexuality carries the additional stigma of gender-role deviation (Carrier, 1989; Parker, 1989). For example, many Latino communities expect adolescent males to display the exaggerated masculine characteristics of "machismo" (courage, aggressiveness, power, and invulnerability) in order to gain status as mature, appropriately-behaving Latino men. Adolescent females must display suitable "etiqueta" (patience, nurturance, passivity, and subservience) to gain status as mature, appropriately-behaving Latino women. Because these cultures typically construe same-sex sexuality as gender nonconformity, adolescents who pursue same-sex sexuality are viewed by their communities as having fundamentally failed as men or women.

Within African American communities, same-sex sexuality is often associated with long-standing cultural stereotypes of African Americans as hypersexual and morally bankrupt (Clarke, 1983; Collins, 1990; Greene, 1986; Icard, 1986). Thus, sexual-minority youths often feel pressured to hide their same-sex sexuality, perhaps by engaging in opposite-sex romantic and sexual relationships, in order to present an image of normalcy to larger Anglo society and contradict these racist stereotypes (Clarke, 1983; De Monteflores, 1986; Gomez & Smith, 1990; Mays & Cochran, 1988). These pressures may fall particularly hard on youths, as these youths may themselves feel that their same-sex desires are signs of sickness or moral failings.

For all of these reasons, ethnic-minority youths may interpret and express their same-sex sexuality in markedly different ways than Anglo youths. Some might pursue exclusively sexual same-sex behavior with strangers to avoid thinking of themselves as gay, and maintain their most important romantic ties to other-sex partners (Carballo-Dieguez & Dolezal, 1994; Vasquez, 1979). Others might postpone same-sex behavior until they are certain they are gay (Dubé & Savin-Williams, 1999). Still others might identify as lesbian or gay and regularly pursue same-sex behavior, but resist larger participation in gay culture and choose to emphasize the cultural component of their identity in order to maintain their strong cultural ties (Icard, 1986; Mays & Cochran, 1988).

Sexual-Minority Youths' Romantic Relationships

How do sexual-minority youths' diverse intrapsychic experiences influence their romantic and sexual relationships? As noted earlier, this topic has been woefully understudied, but existing data suggest that one of the most important characteristics of sexual-minority youths' intimate relationships is how often they violate traditional expectations of adolescents' platonic and romantic ties. Because same-sex sexuality is highly stigmatized, youths who seek same-sex intimate relationships face a range of choices and constraints that heterosexual youths need never consider. They must often explicitly question *who* they want to be intimate with, in what types of ways, and what risks they are willing to take to obtain this intimacy. Do they want same-sex partners, other-sex partners, or both? What type of intimacy do they seek and expect from female versus male partners? In answer to these questions, sexual-minority youths frequently craft unique constellations of same-sex *and* other-sex intimate relationships that challenge common assumptions about what types of relationships are normal and healthy during adolescence.

Finding potential partners

Many of the unique features of sexual-minority youths' relationships are attributable to the simple fact that same-sex romances are exceedingly difficult to find and maintain during adolescence. However, although the majority of sexual-minority youths *desire* same-sex romantic relationships (Savin-Williams, 1990), a host of cultural, structural, interpersonal, and intrapsychic factors have typically blocked their access to such relationships. Thus, perhaps the most notable feature of adolescent same-sex romance is how elusive it can be. The first obstacle involves identifying potential partners. Whereas heterosexual youths can assume that just about any attractive peer is fair game, sexual-minority youths must restrict their pool of potential partners to other "known" sexual minorities (although some attempt to initiate relationships with heterosexual peers, taking notable risks of stigmatization and rejection).

Most sexual-minority youths find age-appropriate sexual-minority peers through lesbian/gay/bisexual community centers, most of which sponsor youth-support groups or recreational activities where adolescents can meet and socialize with other sexual-minority peers. These activities are invaluable for providing youths with a safe space in which to work through issues of self-identification and coming out, giving them opportunities to experience a taste of "normal" adolescence. These sexual-minority peer groups allow youths the chance to flirt, gossip, argue, play matchmaker, fall in love, and have their hearts broken – just like heterosexual youths. Although lesbian/gay/bisexual youth resources have proliferated dramatically over the past ten years, they are nonetheless out of reach for large numbers of sexual-minority youth, such as those living in small towns, rural areas, or who do not have access to transportation. Others may be hesitant to attend lesbian/gay/bisexual youth events because they realize that their presence at such events is tantamount to coming out as lesbian, gay, or bisexual, a step they might not be ready to take.

Even youths who navigate these multiple hurdles and find themselves with a sexual-minority peer group may nonetheless encounter considerable difficulty forming romantic relationships. First, their circle of sexual-minority friends is likely to be fairly small, and might not contain a single individual that the youth even finds physically or romantically attractive (or who finds the *youth* attractive). Second, a youth might be reluctant to jeopardize the few sexual-minority friendships he or she has by risking a romantic relationship with these friends. Third, even if he or she finds an attractive, available, and willing partner, this person might not want the same *type* of relationship the youth wants. As with heterosexual adolescents, some sexual-minority youths are only interested in casual sexual relationships, whereas others are only interested in serious romantic ties.

Diverse types of intimate relationships

Clearly, youths who succeed in forming and maintaining same-sex romantic ties may nonetheless have to settle for partners and relationships they consider less than ideal. Others adapt to these hurdles by seeking a diverse variety of sexual and affectionate same-sex bonds, many of which violate traditional conventional definitions of friendship and romance (Diamond, 2000a). It has been difficult to systematically chart and interpret such diverse relationship patterns because research on adolescent relationships has traditionally relied on vague, theoretically impoverished distinctions between different types of intimate relationships (Diamond, Savin-Williams, & Dubé, 1999). Rough lines are drawn between platonic and romantic relationships, and perhaps between casual and serious romances, but rarely do researchers probe the full range of affectional and sexual ties that adolescents from diverse backgrounds might consider *casual, serious, platonic,* or *romantic.* Yet important differences exist among these types of relationships that can shape youths' social and sexual development.

For example, one relationship pattern that is more common among male than female youths involves the pursuit of *exclusively* sexual same-sex liaisons (Diamond, Savin-Williams, & Dubé, 1999). Such a liaison often occurs in secret, and both youths may deny (to themselves as well as each other) that it has any relevance for their sexual orientation. Rather, they can safely characterize their behavior as simple sexual release. Such exclusively sexual relationships are rarely observed among young women (Savin-Williams, in press). Not only do women appear less interested in such relationships than men, but there is less of an adolescent subculture supporting such behavior among female youths (Gagnon & Simon, 1973).

Rather, young women who cannot safely or easily pursue same-sex romances may opt for an exclusively emotional bond with a same-sex peer (Diamond, Savin-Williams, & Dubé, 1999; Diamond, 2000a). These *passionate friendships*, which appear more common in women than men and in early rather than late adolescence, typically contain the affective and behavioral features of romantic relationships – such as emotional passion, possessiveness, exclusivity, and frequent physical affection – in the absence of explicit sexual desire or activity. Thus, they might provide youths with all of the benefits of a same-sex romantic relationship (most notably, social support and emotional intimacy), while avoiding many of the risks and complications. Notably, a similar degree of fluidity and ambiguity between friendships and romantic relationships is also observed among adult sexual-minority women (Nardi & Sherrod, 1994; Rose, Zand, & Cimi, 1993).

Thus, many sexual-minority youths' most extensive experience with same-sex intimacy occurs in relationships that look nothing like typical dating or romantic relationships. These diverse relationship types might be conceptualized as solutions to the problems all youths – but especially sexual-minority youths – face in balancing their needs and desires for sexual and affectional intimacy with the risks posed by particular types of intimate relationships, as well as the constraints they face in finding the partners and relationships they want.

Such same-sex relationships also give youths an opportunity to probe the nature of their sexual and affectional desires. Contrary to conventional wisdom, many youths have considerable difficulty discerning whether the feelings and fantasies they experience for same-sex partners (whether real or imagined) are "real" sexual desires. They may be particularly confused as to the association between their sexual and affectional feelings, and which type of feeling is better "evidence" of their sexual orientation. For example, one gay male adolescent interviewed by Savin-Williams (1998a) described sex with his former girlfriend as "satisfying physically, but not emotionally," whereas another claimed that despite his emotional attachment to a former girlfriend, "physically I didn't want her" (p. 110). Different youths might have notably divergent interpretations of such experiences, as might their parents, friends, and partners.

These conflicting interpretations highlight the fact that although adolescents are besieged with information on sexual behavior, pregnancy, sexually transmitted diseases, and even date rape, they typically receive no information (from health educators, parents, friends, or the culture at large) about exactly what the distinction between romantic love and platonic love feels like, or when an affectionate caress becomes an erotic overture. Thus, the diverse types of intimate same-sex relationships crafted by sexual-minority youths give them a chance to test whether their interest in same-sex peers is motivated by same-sex sexual desire, general sexual release, or romantic infatuation.

The importance of friends

Although it is typically assumed that romantic relationships "trump" close friendships as sources of intimacy, unconditional support, intense passion, and erotic titillation, this is not always the case among sexual minorities. In a sample of gay and lesbian adults, Nardi and Sherwood (1994) found that many granted a preeminent role to close friends as sources of support and emotional security, often considering these friends to be "chosen family." They attributed this pattern to the fact that many of these individuals did not expect or receive substantial support from family members as a result of their sexual orientation. Nardi and Sherwood also documented somewhat fluid boundaries between friendship and romantic involvement among these adults. For example, some gay men had periodic, casual sexual contact with their close friends, whereas some lesbians reported being in love with their close friends (currently or formerly).

Similar ambiguities have been detected among sexual-minority youths. For example, a recent study comparing sexual-minority and heterosexual youths' friendships and romantic relationships (Diamond & Dubé, 2001) found that sexual-minority male youths frequently ranked friends as more important sources of emotional support and security than serious romantic partners, in contrast with heterosexual adolescents and, interestingly, sexual-minority females. This might reflect sexual-minority males' expectations that supportive, intimate ties with same-sex romantic partners will be difficult to find or their internalization of cultural stereotypes portraying gay and lesbian relationships (and particularly gay men's relationships) as less stable, satisfying, and healthy than heterosexual romantic relationships (Kurdek & Schmitt, 1985–6; Testa, Kinder, & Ironson, 1987).

Another notable feature of male sexual-minority youths' close friendships is that they are disproportionally formed with *women*. Whereas heterosexuals and sexual-minority females typically have predominantly same-sex friendship networks and same-sex best friends, sexual-minority male youths show the opposite pattern (Diamond & Dubé, 2001). One possible explanation for this finding is that sexual-minority males might seek to avoid suspicion of their sexual orientation by avoiding close same-sex friendships. Expressions of intimacy and affection between men are often directly associated with same-sex sexual interest (Marsiglio, 1993; Nardi, 1992), whereas women are granted far more latitude in expressing emotional and physical affection for same-sex friends (Derlega et al., 1989; Stoneman, Brody, & MacKinnon, 1986). Thus, while a sexual-minority female adolescent may trust that her close same-sex friendships will not incur suspicion of her sexual orientation, young gay and bisexual men may "play it safe" by developing their closest ties with other-sex friends (Savin-Williams, 1996a).

Another factor to consider is the potentially disruptive effects of sexual attractions on close friendships. All youths in the aforementioned study reported having been sexually attracted to at least one close friend who was a potential romantic partner (Diamond & Dubé, 2001), but sexual-minority males reported these attractions more often than all other groups. Furthermore, sexual attractions to *male* friends were described by *all* groups as more disruptive than attractions to female friends, perhaps because males appear to have more difficulty keeping a friendship platonic when the friend in question is a potential romantic partner. Thus, sexual-minority males have the unique distinction of being *most* likely to develop the *most* disruptive attractions. Seeking intimate friendships with female friends might allow them to avoid these complications. Alternatively, some male sexual-minority youths may be unsuccessful in hiding their attractions, and find their male friends withdrawing from them over time.

Finally, sexual-minority males might receive or anticipate greater support and acceptance of their same-sex sexuality from female than male peers. Not only are female friends typically perceived and experienced as more sympathetic and helpful than male friends (Buhrke & Fuqua, 1987; George et al., 1998), but women are less likely than men to harass sexual minorities (D'Augelli & Rose, 1990; Herek, 1988). Thus, sexual-minority male youths may intentionally cultivate female friendships in order to maximize opportunities for social support. These provide just a few examples of how same-sex sexuality can have multiple interpersonal repercussions.

Other-Sex Romantic Relationships

One of the most common misconceptions about sexual-minority youths is that they neither pursue nor desire *other-sex* sexual and romantic relationships. This is false; most youths have either dated, "fooled around" with, had sex with, or been seriously romantically involved with other-sex peers (reviewed in Diamond, Savin-Williams, & Dubé, 1999). Even when these relationships are acknowledged, they typically receive little attention or are given much importance. Seemingly, once an adolescent's same-sex attractions are known, we take the liberty of unilaterally disregarding his/her other-sex relationships as intrinsically false, unpleasant, and irrelevant.

This is simply not the case. Detailed interviews conducted with sexual-minority youths reveal that their other-sex relationships are often critically important and deeply satisfying, often on both sexual and emotional levels (Diamond, 1998; Savin-Williams, 1998a; Savin-Williams & Diamond, 2000). Thus, contrary to conventional wisdom, the simple presence of same-sex attractions does not automatically render all other-sex interactions uniformly distasteful. Perhaps researchers have extrapolated too closely from the experiences of typical heterosexuals, whose other-sex desires are often accompanied by notable distaste for the very idea of same-sex sexual activity.

Of course, some sexual-minority youths *do* recall their other-sex sexual and romantic experiences as unsatisfying, boring, or downright unpleasant. The key point is that this is far from universal. Some youths report that the emotional closeness they felt with a high-school girlfriend or boyfriend overshadowed or even masked their lack of sexual desire for the partner. Others report that they experienced pleasurable sexual release in the relationship, despite the fact that they would have preferred same-sex partners if given the choice (Savin-Williams, 1998a; Savin-Williams & Diamond, 2000). Perhaps most importantly, it is often overlooked that a large proportion of sexual-minority youths and adults experience attractions for *both* sexes, although to varying degrees. We commonly speak of lesbian/gay individuals as if their same-sex attractions were as uniformly exclusive as we presume the other-sex attractions of heterosexuals to be. Yet, Laumann and colleagues' (1994) large-scale study of sexuality reveals that the majority of individuals who experience same-sex attractions also experience other-sex attractions, even if only slightly. This should not be surprising, given how aggressively most children are socialized toward heterosexual desire.

Thus, even a youth who rarely fantasizes about or becomes attracted to other-sex peers might nonetheless authentically enjoy his/her other-sex relationships. Given this fact, it is clearly important to consider sexual-minority youths' other-sex relationships when analyzing their social and sexual development. Similarly, one might argue that future research should pay closer attention to the *same-sex* relationships of heterosexual adolescents. Although the majority of heterosexual adolescents will likely never pursue an explicitly sexual or romantic relationship with a same-sex peer, some might nonetheless find themselves in same-sex relationships that become infused with ambiguous erotic elements at one time or another, or that spill over into secretive, experimental sexual contact. These experiences have garnered far too little attention by researchers studying adolescent development. If we want to understand the role of intimate relationships and social and sexual development of sexual-minority and heterosexual youths, *both* same-sex and other-sex intimate relationships must be studied in *both* groups.

What Counts As a Lesbian/Gay/Bisexual Relationship?

What should we make of youths who participate in same-sex intimate relationships, yet decline to identify as lesbian, gay, or bisexual? The standard explanation is that these youths are not yet ready to accept their same-sex sexuality or to disclose it to others. It is typically assumed that the adoption of a proud gay, lesbian, or bisexual identity is the only possible positive resolution of the sexual questioning process. However, this may not be the case. The scant research that has been conducted on youths who acknowledge same-sex attractions, but decline to identify as lesbian, gay, or bisexual, suggests that although they may face difficult pressures from friends, family members, and romantic partners to identify, they often feel as comfortable and happy with their sexuality as do openly identified lesbian/gay/bisexual youths, and feel that their unlabeled status leaves them open to all relationship possibilities (Diamond, in press).

Passionate friendships are of particular interest in this regard. These relationships have historically been interpreted as subverted lesbian/gay romances, but this is a vast over-generalization (Diamond, 2000a; Faderman, 1981). The underlying assumption is that the heightened emotional intensity of such relationships necessarily signals sexual interest, and that an adolescent's desire for emotional union with another person is yoked to a corresponding desire for sexual union. From this perspective, a same-sex passionate friendship is just as much a "lesbian/gay relationship" as a full-blown romantic and sexual affair between two adolescents of the same sex.

Yet, is this really the case? If passionate friendships are considered to be lesbian/gay relationships, how do we explain the fact that anthropologists and historians have docu-mented such friendships among otherwise heterosexual individuals in a variety of differ-ent cultures and historical periods, dating as far back as ancient Greece (Crowly, 1987; Faderman, 1981; Hansen, 1992; Rotundo, 1989; Smith-Rosenberg, 1975; Williams, 1992)? Were all of these people lesbian/gay/bisexual? Probably not. Rather, we must acknowledge that adolescents' and adults' capacities for same-sex affectional bonding are far more extensive than is typically assumed (for potential explanations for this phenomenon, see Diamond, 2001). Instead of amalgamating passionate friendships with more conventional same-sex romantic relationships, the distinctive features and social-developmental implications of each type of relationship should be noted for *both* sexual-minority and heterosexual youths.

Conclusion: Appreciating the Diversity of Youths and their Relationships

Perhaps the single most defining characteristic of sexual-minority youths' intimate rela-tionships is that they *have* no single defining characteristic: the types of casual, intimate, platonic, and romantic relationships these youths pursue with same-sex *and* other-sex peers are as diverse as the youths themselves. We would therefore caution both researchers and youth advocates to jettison preconceptions about what sorts of relationships are most typical of, most important to, and most developmentally significant for sexual-minority versus heterosexual youths. If we hope to understand how same-sex sexuality shapes ado-lescent social and sexual development, researchers and service providers must treat *all* of a youth's relationships as developmentally significant, not just those that fit neatly into familiar cultural categories. This requires greater awareness of the specific features linking *and* distinguishing between a youth's platonic friendships and romantic relationships. It also requires greater attention to relationships that breach the conventional boundary between "friend" and "lover," from close friendships involving periodic sexual contact to passionate attachments *lacking* such contact.

In considering the relevance of such relationship experiences for both sexual-identity development and general social/sexual development, it is critical to remember that relationship experiences are *always* embedded within highly specific sociocultural and interpersonal contexts, and these contexts must be carefully analyzed if we wish to accurately discern how and why particular sexual-minority youths experience a different range of developmental milestones, at different ages, with different implications. Thus, whereas early research on sexual-minority youths emphasized *commonalities* in their developmental experiences (especially commonalities that were attributable to their shared experience of stigmatization), researchers now face the more difficult task of charting the multiple, interacting factors producing *diversity* in their developmental pathways. In this review we have emphasized the contributions of gender and ethnicity to these diverse pathways, but future research will undoubtedly reveal a range of additional critical factors, such as personality, attachment style, sexual attitudes and expectations, self-efficacy, self-control, social skills, and even physical attractiveness.

Future research is also likely to reveal the importance of interactions between these personal characteristics and various environmental/situational contexts such as family relationships, community ties, socioeconomic status, access to educational and work opportunities, and access to information about sexuality. Notably, the aforementioned personal characteristics and environmental/situational contexts have long been topics of study with regard to *heterosexual* youths' social and sexual development (see for example Feldman et al., 1995; Goodson, Evans, & Edmundson, 1997; Udry, 1988), but have not been substantively investigated in the context of same-sex sexuality. This is likely to change as more and better data on sexual-minority adolescents increasingly becomes available (for example, see nationally representative data on youths with same-sex attractions reported by French et al., 1996; Garofalo et al., 1998, 1999; Russell & Joyner, in press; Russell, Seif, & Truong, 2001).

These data also highlight one of the first and most important points made in this chapter: that the full population of sexual-minority youths includes far more than simply lesbian/gay/bisexual-*identified* adolescents. Many adolescents experience same-sex attractions and sexual contact *without* identifying as lesbian/gay/bisexual, just as many openly identified lesbian/gay/bisexual adults report *never* having had same-sex attractions or sexual contact during the adolescent years. If we are to successfully describe and explain the extent to which same-sex sexuality exerts a distinctive press on adolescent social and sexual development, we must resist prematurely classifying youths into restrictive sexual typologies and instead describe and investigate the full range of their same-sex and other-sex desires, affections, and behaviors over time.

This is critical for any thoroughgoing understanding of the uniqueness of sexual-minority youths' intimate relationships. As we have noted, sexual-minority youths are just as strongly motivated to form intimate romantic ties as are heterosexual youths, but they face notable obstacles in doing so. The pervasive stigmatization of same-sex sexuality and the sheer difficulty of identifying potential romantic partners makes it difficult for many sexual-minority youths to pursue the prototypical adolescent experiences of flirting, dating, and falling in love. Yet these handicaps clearly do not prevent them from meeting the powerful needs for physical affection, emotional security, and simple companionship that underlie *all* adolescents' close relationships. Rather than forgoing intimate romantic ties altogether, sexual-minority youths often develop unique constellations of relationships that allow them to safely meet different types of needs within different types of social ties. Researchers, clinicians, and parents who seek to understand the unique experiences of sexual-minority youths must acknowledge the importance of these special ties. Although they challenge many conventional assumptions regarding the nature of intimate affection and the parameters of same-sex sexuality, they broaden our understanding of youths' capacities to craft rewarding, supportive ties to ease their pathway to adulthood.

Key Readings

Boxer, A., & Cohler, B. (1989). The life course of gay and lesbian youth: An immodest proposal for the study of lives. *Journal of Homosexuality, 17,* 315–355.
The publication of this article was a turning point in the study of lesbian, gay, and bisexual youth. The authors argued that instead of relentlessly searching for continuities between the childhood and adolescent/adult experiences of sexual minorities, researchers should seek to explain disconti-nuities in their developmental experiences. This article challenges many conventional assumptions about lesbian/gay/bisexual development (many of which persist to this day) and articulates a powerful vision for future research on this population.

Diamond, L. M. (2000). Passionate friendships among adolescent sexual-minority women. *Journal of Research on Adolescence, 10,* 191–209.
For years, young women involved in passionate, intense, same-sex friendships have been suspected of being lesbian, reflecting the assumption that same-sex emotional and physical intimacy are two sides of the same coin. This article challenges this view by documenting that although many sexual-minority women recall passionate, adolescent friendships with same-sex peers, many of these friendships contained no sexual undercurrent. The article suggests that researchers conceptualize "passionate friendships" as a unique type of adolescent relationship and attend to its potential developmental import for both sexual-minority and heterosexual adolescents.

Diamond, L. M. (2000). Sexual identity, attractions, and behavior among young sexual-minority women over a two-year period. *Developmental Psychology, 36,* 241–250.
Sexual-minority women typically recall more change and discontinuity in their sexual identity tra-jectories than men, but it has been difficult to interpret these experiences given that they are always recalled "after the fact." This article presents two-year follow-up data from the very first *prospec-tive* study of adolescent and young adult sexual-minority women. The findings demonstrate that although most women's sexual attractions are fairly stable, the prevalence of nonexclusivity in these attractions engenders considerable fluidity in their sexual-identity labels, sometimes many years after they first "come out."

Savin-Williams, R. C. (1998). *"...And then I became gay": Young men's stories.* New York: Routledge.
This book chronicles the childhood and adolescent experiences of a diverse sample of adolescent and young adult gay and bisexual men, using qualitative interviews to probe for the transitions and turning points in their sexual-identity development and the personal meaning of their diverse experiences. The results provide powerful evidence that there is no "prototypical" trajectory of lesbian/gay/bisexual development. Rather, each youth's pattern of childhood and adolescent experiences is shaped by multiple interacting factors.

Savin-Williams, R. C., & Cohen, K. M. (Eds.). (1996). *The lives of lesbians, gays, and bisexuals: Children to adults.* Fort Worth, TX: Harcourt Brace.

This is currently the only comprehensive "textbook" on lesbian/gay/bisexual development. It covers the entire sexual-minority lifespan, from early childhood to old age, and includes chapters on topics ranging from biological theories of sexual orientation to "coming out" to gender and ethnic-minority differences, all of which are written by renowned experts in the study of sexuality and sexual orientation.

Weinberg, M. S., Williams, C. J., & Pryor, D. W. (1994). *Dual attraction: Understanding bisexuality.* New York: Oxford University Press.

Many discussions of same-sex sexuality fail to acknowledge the existence of bisexual individuals, yet we now know that more sexual minorities experience *nonexclusive* than exclusive same-sex attractions. Although this book focuses on adults rather than adolescents, it is the largest and most systematic study of bisexuality to date, and provides critical information on gender differences, developmental issues, and special challenges facing bisexuals.

References

Andersen, B. L., & Cyranowski, J. M. (1994). Women's sexual self-schema. *Journal of Personality and Social Psychology, 67,* 1079–1100.

Bailey, J. M. (1996). Gender identity. In R. C. Savin-Williams & K. M. Cohen (Eds.), *The lives of lesbians, gays, and bisexuals: Children to adults* (pp. 71–93). Fort Worth, TX: Harcourt Brace.

Bailey, J. M., & Pillard, R. C. (1991). A genetic study of male sexual orientation. *Archives of General Psychiatry, 48,* 1089–1096.

Bailey, J. M., & Pillard, R. C. (1995). Genetics of human sexual orientation. *Annual Review of Sex Research, 6,* 126–150.

Bailey, J. M., Pillard, R. C., Neale, M. C., & Agyei, Y. (1993). Heritable factors influence sexual orientation in women. *Archives of General Psychiatry, 50,* 217–223.

Bailey, J. M., & Zucker, K. J. (1995). Childhood sex-typed behavior and sexual orientation: A conceptual analysis and quantitative review. *Developmental Psychology, 31,* 43–55.

Bancroft, J. (1990). Commentary: Biological contributions to sexual orientation. In D. P. McWhirter, S. A. Sanders, & J. M. Reinisch (Eds.), *Homosexuality/heterosexuality: Concepts of sexual orientation* (pp. 101–111). New York: Oxford University Press.

Baumeister, R. F. (2000). Gender differences in erotic plasticity: The female sex drive as socially flexible and responsive. *Psychological Bulletin, 126,* 247–374.

Blumstein, P., & Schwartz, P. (1990). Intimate relationships and the creation of sexuality. In D. P. McWhirter, S. A. Sanders, & J. M. Reinisch (Eds.), *Homosexuality/heterosexuality: Concepts of sexual orientation* (pp. 307–320). New York: Oxford University Press.

Buhrke, R. A., & Fuqua, D. R. (1987). Sex differences in same- and cross-sex supportive relationships. *Sex Roles, 17,* 339–352.

Carballo-Dieguez, A., & Dolezal, C. (1994). Contrasting types of Puerto Rican men who have sex with men (MSM). *Journal of Psychology and Human Sexuality, 6,* 41–67.

Carrier, J. M. (1989). Gay liberation and coming out in Mexico. *Journal of Homosexuality, 17,* 225–252.

Cass, V. (1990). The implications of homosexual identity formation for the Kinsey model and scale of sexual preference. In D. P. McWhirter, S. A. Sanders, & J. M. Reinisch (Eds.), *Homosexuality/heterosexuality: Concepts of sexual orientation* (pp. 239–266). New York: Oxford University Press.

Chan, C. S. (1992). Cultural considerations in counseling Asian American lesbians and gay men. In S. H. Dworkin & F. J. Gutierrez (Eds.), *Counseling gay men and lesbians: Journey to the end of the rainbow* (pp. 115–124). Alexandria, VA: American Association for Counseling and Development.

Clarke, C. (1983). The failure to transform: Homophobia in the Black community. In B. Smith (Ed.), *Home girls: A Black feminist anthology* (pp. 197–208). New York: Kitchen Table Press.

Cohen, K. M., & Savin-Williams, R. C. (1996). Developmental perspectives on coming out to self and others. In R. C. Savin-Williams & K. M. Cohen (Eds.), *The lives of lesbians, gays, and bisexuals: Children to adults* (pp. 113–151). Fort Worth, TX: Harcourt Brace.

Collins, P. H. (1990). Homophobia and Black lesbians. In P. H. Collins (Ed.), *Black feminist thought: Knowledge, consciousness, and the politics of empowerment* (pp. 192–196). New York: Routledge.

Crowly, J. W. (1987). Howells, Stoddard, and male homosocial attachment in Victorian America. In H. Brod (Ed.), *The making of masculinities* (pp. 301–324). Boston: Allen & Unwin.

D'Augelli, A. R. (1989). Lesbians' and gay men's experiences of discrimination and harassment in a university community. *American Journal of Community Psychology, 17*, 317–321.

D'Augelli, A. R., & Rose, M. L. (1990). Homophobia in a university community: Attitudes and experiences of heterosexual freshmen. *Journal of College Student Development, 31*, 484–491.

De Monteflores, C. (1986). Notes on the management of difference. In T. Stein & C. Cohen (Eds.), *Contemporary perspectives on psychotherapy with lesbians and gay men* (pp. 73–101). New York: Plenum.

Derlega, V. J., Lewis, R. J., Harrison, S., Winstead, B., & Constanza, R. (1989). Gender differences in the initiation and attribution of tactile intimacy. *Journal of Nonverbal Behavior, 13*, 83–96.

Diamond, L., Savin-Williams, R. C., & Dubé, E. M. (1999). Sex, dating, passionate friendships, and romance: Intimate peer relations among lesbian, gay, and bisexual adolescents. In W. Furman, B. Brown, & C. Feiring (Eds.), *The development of relationships during adolescence* (pp. 175–210). New York: Cambridge University Press.

Diamond, L. M. (1998). Development of sexual orientation among adolescent and young adult women. *Developmental Psychology, 34*, 1085–1095.

Diamond, L. M. (2000a). Passionate friendships among adolescent sexual-minority women. *Journal of Research on Adolescence, 10*, 191–209.

Diamond, L. M. (2000b). Sexual identity, attractions, and behavior among young sexual-minority women over a two-year period. *Developmental Psychology, 36*, 241–250.

Diamond, L. M. (2001). What does sexual orientation orient? Links and distinctions between the processes underlying romantic love and sexual desire. Manuscript under review.

Diamond, L. M. (in press). Was it a phase? Explaining changes in women's same-sex sexuality over a 5-year period. *Journal of Personality and Social Psychology*.

Diamond, L. M., & Dubé, E. M. (2001). Friendship and attachment among heterosexual and sexual-minority youths: Does the gender of your friend matter? Manuscript under review.

Diamond, L. M., & Savin-Williams, R. C. (2000). Explaining diversity in the development of same-sex sexuality among young women. *Journal of Social Issues, 56*, 297–313.

Dubé, E. M., & Savin-Williams, R. C. (1999). Sexual identity development among ethnic sexual-minority male youths. *Developmental Psychology, 35*, 1389–1398.

Espin, O. M. (1997). Crossing borders and boundaries: The life narratives of immigrant lesbians. In B. Greene (Ed.), *Ethnic and cultural diversity among lesbians and gay men* (pp. 191–215). Thousand Oaks, CA: Sage.

Faderman, L. (1981). *Surpassing the love of men*. New York: William Morrow.

Feldman, S. S., Rosenthal, D. R., Brown, N. L., & Canning, R. D. (1995). Predicting sexual experience in adolescent boys from peer rejection and acceptance during childhood. *Journal of Research on Adolescence, 5,* 387–411.

Floyd, F. J., Stein, T. S., Harter, K. S. M., Allison, A., & Nye, C. L. (1999). Gay, lesbian, and bisexual youths: Separation–individuation, parental attitudes, identity consolidation, and well-being. *Journal of Youth and Adolescence, 28,* 719–739.

French, S. A., Story, M., Remafedi, G., Resnick, M. D., & Blum, R. W. (1996). Sexual orientation and prevalence of body dissatisfaction and eating disordered behaviors: a population-based study of adolescents. *International Journal of Eating Disorders, 19,* 119–126.

Gagnon, J. H., & Simon, W. (1973). *Sexual conduct: The social sources of human sexuality.* Chicago: Aldine.

Garnets, L. D., & Kimmel, D. C. (1993). Lesbian and gay male dimensions in the psychological study of human diversity. In L. D. Garnets & D. C. Kimmel (Eds.), *Psychological perspectives on lesbian and gay male experiences* (pp. 1–51). New York: Columbia University Press.

Garofalo, R., Wolf, R. C., Kessel, S., Palfrey, S. J., & DuRant, R. H. (1998). The association between health risk behaviors and sexual orientation among a school-based sample of adolescents. *Pediatrics, 101*(5), 895–902.

Garofalo, R., Wolf, R. C., Wissow, L. S., Woods, E. R., & Goodman, E. (1999). Sexual orientation and risk of suicide attempts among a representative sample of youth. *Archives of Pediatrics and Adolescent Medicine, 153,* 487–493.

George, D., Carroll, P., Kersnick, R., & Calderon, K. (1998). Gender-related patterns of helping among friends. *Psychology of Women Quarterly, 22,* 685–704.

Golden, C. (1987). Diversity and variability in women's sexual identities. In Boston Lesbian Psychologies Collective (Ed.), *Lesbian psychologies: Explorations and challenges* (pp. 19–34). Urbana: University of Illinois Press.

Gomez, J., & Smith, B. (1990). Taking the home out of homophobia: Black lesbian health. In E. C. White (Ed.), *The Black women's health book: Speaking for ourselves* (pp. 198–213). Seattle, WA: Seal.

Goodson, P., Evans, A., & Edmundson, E. (1997). Female adolescents and onset of sexual intercourse: A theory-based review of research from 1984 to 1994. *Journal of Adolescent Health, 21,* 147–156.

Greene, B. (1986). When the therapist is white and the patient is Black: Considerations for psychotherapy in the feminist heterosexual and lesbian communities. *Women and Therapy, 5,* 41–66.

Hamer, D., & Copeland, P. (1994). *The science of desire: The search for the gay gene and the biology of behavior.* New York: Simon & Schuster.

Hansen, K. V. (1992). "Our eyes behold each other": Masculinity and intimate friendship in antebellum New England. In P. Nardi (Ed.), *Men's friendships* (pp. 35–58). Newbury Park, CA: Sage.

Herdt, G., & Boxer, A. M. (1993). *Children of Horizons: How gay and lesbian teens are leading a new way out of the closet.* Boston: Beacon Press.

Herek, G. M. (1988). Heterosexuals' attitudes toward lesbians and gay men: Correlates and gender differences. *Journal of Sex Research, 25,* 451–477.

Hidalgo, H. (1984). The Puerto Rican lesbian in the United States. In T. Darty & S. Potter (Eds.), *Women identified women* (pp. 105–150). Palo Alto, CA: Mayfield.

Icard, L. (1986). Black gay men and conflicting social identities: Sexual orientation versus racial identity. *Journal of Social Work and Human Sexuality, 4,* 83–93.

Isay, R. A. (1989). *Being homosexual: Gay men and their development.* New York: Farrar, Straus & Giroux.

Jayakar, K. (1994). Women of the Indian subcontinent. In L. Comas-Diaz & B. Greene (Eds.),

Women of color: Integrating ethnic and gender identities in psychotherapy (pp. 161–181). New York: Guilford.

Kitzinger, C., & Wilkinson, S. (1995). Transitions from heterosexuality to lesbianism: The discursive production of lesbian identities. *Developmental Psychology, 31,* 95–104.

Kurdek, L. A., & Schmitt, J. P. (1985–6). Relationship quality of gay men in closed or open relationships. *Journal of Homosexuality, 12,* 85–99.

Laumann, E. O., Gagnon, J. H., Michael, R. T., & Michaels, F. (1994). *The social organization of sexuality: Sexual practices in the United States.* Chicago: University of Chicago Press.

Marsiglio, W. (1993). Attitudes toward homosexual activity and gays as friends: A national survey of heterosexual 15- to 19-year-old males. *Journal of Sex Research, 30,* 12–17.

Mays, V. M., & Cochran, S. D. (1988). The black women's relationships project: A national survey of black lesbians. In M. Shernoff & W. A. Scott (Eds.), *The sourcebook on lesbian/gay health care* (pp. 54–62). Washington, DC: National Lesbian and Gay Health Foundation.

Nardi, P. M. (1992). That's what friends are for: Friends as family in the gay and lesbian community. In K. Plummer (Ed.), *Modern homosexualities: Fragments of lesbian and gay experience* (pp. 108–120). London: Routledge.

Nardi, P. M., & Sherrod, D. (1994). Friendship in the lives of gay men and lesbians. *Journal of Social and Personal Relationships, 11,* 185–199.

Parker, R. (1989). Youth, identity, and homosexuality: The changing shape of sexual life in contemporary Brazil. *Journal of Homosexuality, 17,* 269–289.

Pasupathi, M. (in press). Women and arranged marriages: What has love got to do with it? In M. Yalom & L. L. Carstensen (Eds.), *Rethinking the couple: Some feminist answers.* Berkeley, CA: University of California Press.

Richardson, D. (1987). Recent challenges to traditional assumptions about homosexuality: Some implications for Rose, S., Zand, D., & Cimi, M. A. (1993). Lesbian courtship scripts. In E. D. Rothblum & K. A. Brehony (Eds.), *Boston marriages* (pp. 70–85). Amherst: University of Massachusetts Press.

Rotundo, E. A. (1989). Romantic friendships: Male intimacy and middle-class youth in the northern United States, 1800–1900. *Journal of Social History, 23,* 1–25.

Russell, S., & Joyner, K. (in press). Adolescent sexual orientation and suicide risk: Evidence from a national study. *American Journal of Public Health.*

Russell, S. T., Seif, H., & Truong, N. L. (2001). School outcomes of sexual minority youth in the United States: Evidence from a national study. *Journal of Adolescence, 24,* 111–127.

Savin-Williams, R. C. (1990). *Gay and lesbian youth: Expressions of identity.* Washington, DC: Hemisphere.

Savin-Williams, R. C. (1996a). Dating and romantic relationships among gay, lesbian, and bisexual youths. In R. C. Savin-Williams & K. M. Cohen (Eds.), *The lives of lesbians, gays, and bisexuals: Children to adults* (pp. 166–180). Fort Worth, TX: Harcourt Brace.

Savin-Williams, R. C. (1996b). Ethnic- and sexual-minority youth. In R. C. Savin-Williams & K. M. Cohen (Eds.), *The lives of lesbians, gays, and bisexuals: Children to adults* (pp. 152–165). Fort Worth, TX: Harcourt Brace.

Savin-Williams, R. C. (1996c). Memories of childhood and early adolescent sexual feelings among gay and bisexual boys: A narrative approach. In R. C. Savin-Williams & K. M. Cohen (Eds.), *The lives of lesbians, gays, and bisexuals: Children to adults* (pp. 94–109). Fort Worth, TX: Harcourt Brace.

Savin-Williams, R. C. (1998a). *". . . And then I became gay": Young men's stories.* New York: Routledge.

Savin-Williams, R. C. (1998b). The disclosure to families of same-sex attractions by lesbian, gay, and bisexual youths. *Journal of Research on Adolescence, 8,* 49–68.

Savin-Williams, R. C. (1998c). Lesbian, gay and bisexual youths' relationships with their parents. In C. Patterson & A. R. D'Augelli (Eds.), *Lesbian, gay, and bisexual identities in families: Psychological perspectives* (pp. 75–98). New York: Oxford University Press.

Savin-Williams, R. C. (2001). *Mom, Dad. I'm gay.* Washington, DC: APA Press.

Savin-Williams, R. C. (in press). *". . . And then I kissed her": Young women's stories.* New York: Routledge.

Savin-Williams, R. C., & Diamond, L. M. (2000). Sexual identity trajectories among sexual-minority youths: Gender comparisons. *Archives of Sexual Behavior, 29,* 419–440.

Smith-Rosenberg, C. (1975). The female world of love and ritual: Relations between women in nineteenth century America. *Signs, 1,* 1–29.

Stoneman, Z., Brody, G. H., & MacKinnon, C. E. (1986). Same-sex and cross-sex siblings: Activity choices, roles, behaviors, and gender stereotypes. *Sex Roles, 9/10,* 495–511.

Testa, R. J., Kinder, B. N., & Ironson, G. (1987). Heterosexual bias in the perception of loving relationships of gay males and lesbians. *Journal of Sex Research, 23,* 163–172.

Tremble, B., Schneider, M., & Appathurai, C. (1989). Growing up gay or lesbian in a multicultural context. *Journal of Homosexuality, 17*(1–4), 253–267.

Udry, J. R. (1988). Biological predispositions and social control in adolescent sexual behavior. *American Sociological Review, 53,* 709–722.

Udry, J. R., & Billy, J. O. G. (1987). Initiation of coitus in early adolescence. *American Sociological Review, 52,* 841–855.

Udry, J. R., Talbert, L. M., & Morris, N. M. (1986). Biosocial foundations for adolescent female sexuality. *Demography, 23,* 217–230.

Vance, B. K., & Green, V. (1984). Lesbian identities: An examination of sexual behavior and sex role acquisition as related to age of initial same-sex encounter. *Psychology of Women Quarterly, 8,* 293–307.

Vasquez, E. (1979). Homosexuality in the context of the Mexican American culture. In D. Kukel (Ed.), *Sexual issues in social work: Emerging concerns in education and practice* (pp. 131–147). Honolulu: University of Hawaii, School of Social Work.

Williams, W. L. (1992). The relationship between male–male friendship and male–female marriage. In P. Nardi (Ed.), *Men's friendships* (pp. 187–200). Newbury Park, CA: Sage.

Wooden, W. S., Kawasaki, H., & Mayeda, R. (1983). Lifestyles and identity maintenance among gay Japanese-American males. *Alternative Lifestyles, 5,* 236–243.

PART V

Problem Behaviors

CHAPTER TWENTY

Adolescent Pregnancy and Childbearing

Brent C. Miller, Bruce K. Bayley, Mathew Christensen, Spencer C. Leavitt, and Diana D. Coyl

Introduction and Overview

World perspective on adolescent fertility behavior

Becoming pregnant and giving birth during the second decade of life is common in many countries, but it is exceedingly rare and discouraged in others. Over half of young women experience a birth before age 18 in sub-Saharan Africa and Bangladesh, whereas in Japan and Korea only 1 percent do so (Alan Guttmacher Institute, 1998). Setting aside countries in which adolescent parenthood is normatively accepted, this chapter addresses adolescent pregnancy and childbearing in societies where these events are considered to be premature, and where adolescent parenthood is increasingly recognized as a compelling problem with far reaching implications. The negative consequences of teen pregnancy are more thoroughly discussed later, but to summarize briefly at this point, early parenthood tends to disrupt the long period of education and training needed in developed societies for adult self-sufficiency. Infants and children born to adolescent mothers are more likely to experience cognitive, social, and economic disadvantages. Adolescent parenthood also imposes significant financial burdens on extended families and on society through various forms of public assistance.

Using the United States as the primary case study, this chapter provides a historical background, presents adolescent pregnancy rates and trends, summarizes the antecedents and consequences of adolescent parenthood, analyzes adolescent pregnancy-resolution decision making and outcomes, and concludes by describing prevention/intervention programs and policy initiatives.

Historical background in the United States

Girls and young women in the United States traditionally were viewed as <u>intrinsically innocent</u>, sexual activity before marriage was strictly forbidden, and pregnancy outside of wedlock was a public declaration of both religious and social deviance (Nathanson, 1991). Early in the twentieth century, societal perceptions of women began to change. As more young women became sexually active prior to marriage, the assumption of intrinsic innocence was replaced with one of <u>intrinsic sexuality</u> (Nathanson, 1991). The decreasing age of puberty coupled with the increasing age of marriage meant that adolescents were physically capable of reproduction long before they were prepared to become parents. Social control and shotgun marriages waned as societal attitudes became more permissive. Today, adolescent pregnancy carries less stigma, and policy changes in the United States allow teenagers to have sex, use contraception, have an abortion, and to bear and raise children outside of marriage.

Adolescent pregnancy was not seen to be a problem of national significance in the United States until the 1970s, which is somewhat ironic because US teen birthrates had been much higher in previous decades (Vinovskis, 1988). Even though birthrates of adolescents aged 15–19 steadily declined from more than 80 per thousand in the 1950s to less than 60 per thousand in 1983, attention became focused on the increase in premarital intercourse and teenage births out of wedlock. Because early nonmarital childbearing is linked with welfare dependency, a growing national debate centered around government spending for social programs. During the late 1970s and early 1980s new perceptions about the social and financial costs of adolescent pregnancy gave rise to national concern (AGI, 1994; Vinovskis, 1988).

There are several reasons why little attention was paid to adolescent pregnancy in the United States prior to the 1970s. In nineteenth-century America teen pregnancy was less likely because menarche occurred later (about 14 or 15 years of age) and teens were also much less likely to have sex before marriage (AGI, 1994; Vinovskis, 1988). In the event of unintended pregnancy it also was more common to get married (shotgun weddings) than it is today (Bachu, 1999). The gradual recognition of adolescence, as distinct from childhood and adulthood, also led to growing concern about adolescent issues, including adolescent pregnancy.

Key concepts

The terms teen *pregnancy, childbirth,* and *parenthood* are sometimes used interchangeably (and imprecisely), but these concepts need to be differentiated. Childbirth is the most common outcome of teen pregnancy in the United States (about 55 percent), but teen pregnancies also end in miscarriages (about 14 percent) and induced abortions (about 30 percent). To clarify these concepts, the sum and components of teen pregnancy can be stated as an equation:

TEEN PREGNANCY = MISCARRIAGES + ABORTIONS + LIVE BIRTHS

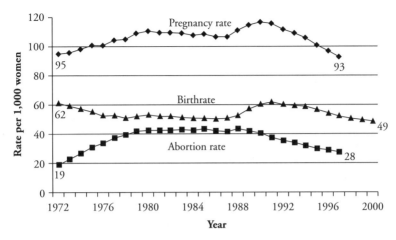

Figure 20.1   Pregnancy, birth, and abortion rates among females aged 15–19 in the United States, 1972–2000. Taken from data in Henshaw, 2001 and Moore et al., 2001.

Stillbirths are sometimes added to miscarriages to constitute fetal loss. Teen parenthood occurs if teen pregnancy results in birth, and if teen parents assume the responsibilities of providing and caring for their children.

About 80 percent of teen pregnancies and 60 percent of all pregnancies in the United States are unintended at conception (AGI, 1999; Henshaw, 1998). Relatedly, about 80 percent of teen births in the United States are nonmarital, compared to 34 percent of births to women of all ages. Marital status is strongly related to pregnancy intentions and pregnancy outcomes; in 1995 about three-quarters of pregnancies among married women resulted in live births, compared to less than half of pregnancies among unmarried women (Ventura et al., 1999).

Teen pregnancy rates and trends

After a 20-year rise in teen pregnancy, there have been significant decreases in teen pregnancy, birth, and abortion rates since 1991 (see figure 20.1). Overall, teen pregnancy rates have declined 19 percent since 1991, reaching their lowest level since 1973 (AGI, 1999). Similarly, the 2000 teen birthrate of 48.7 births per 1,000 15–19-year-old females is a new historic low. These declines have occurred in all race/ethnic groups (Moore et al., 1999). Because teen birthrates have declined along with teen pregnancy and abortion rates, changes in abortion do not explain decreases in teen births (Moore et al., 1999).

Despite recent reductions, rates of teen pregnancy and birth remain higher in the United States than all other Western industrialized countries, and are on a par with the highest rates for all developed countries (Singh & Darroch, 2000). Roughly 10 percent of females aged 15–19 become pregnant each year in the United States. The proportion that becomes pregnant is more than twice as high for older adolescent females (15.3

percent for ages 18–19) compared with middle adolescents (6.2 percent for ages 15–17) (AGI, 1999). The cumulative proportion of adolescent females who become pregnant increases during each year of age, so that before age 20, more than 40 percent of teenage females in the United States become pregnant (AGI, 1986). Although adolescent pregnancy and birthrates have declined in recent decades, nonmarital teen childbearing rose dramatically from the 1970s to the 1990s, so that a large majority (80 percent) of teen births now occur outside of marriage.

Research suggests two main reasons for recent declines in teen pregnancy rates: fewer adolescents are engaging in sexual intercourse and more sexually active teens are using contraceptives. Data from the National Survey of Adolescent Males (Sonenstein et al., 1998) show that the percentage of 15–19-year-old males who ever had intercourse was lower in 1995 (55 percent) than in 1988 (60 percent). Other analyses of national data (AGI, 1999; Hogan, Sun, & Cornwell, 2000; Kaufmann et al., 1998) report smaller decreases in the number of women aged 15–19 who ever had sexual intercourse between 1988 and 1995. The use of condoms, especially at first intercourse, increased dramatically in the 1980s and 1990s, and sexually active teens also are using more effective contraceptive methods such as contraceptive implants and injectables (Piccinino & Mosher, 1998). Declines in teen sexual intercourse, and increases in contraceptive use among the sexually active, have continued through the end of the 1990s. Analyses have shown that both declines in teen sexual intercourse and better contraceptive use have contributed to the reduction in teen pregnancy (Sawhill & Flanigan, 2000; Hogan et al., 2000).

Summary

In the United States, adolescent pregnancy and childbearing are considered premature and can have long-term negative implications for families and society. Societal perceptions of adolescent pregnancy have been influenced by changing views of adolescence, changes in the timing of female pubertal development, and shifts in government spending for social programs. During the late 1970s and 1980s, public attention focused on the social and financial costs associated with nonmarital adolescent childbearing, leading to a recognition of adolescent pregnancy as a significant social problem. Eighty percent of teen pregnancies are unintended at conception, and 80 percent of teen births are nonmarital. Despite recent decreases in the United States among all race/ethnic groups in teen pregnancy, birth, and abortion rates, the country has the highest rates of teen pregnancy and birth in the industrialized West. Recent declines in adolescent pregnancy and childbearing have been attributed both to decreases in teen sexual intercourse, and to increases in contraceptive use among sexually active teens.

Antecedents of Teen Pregnancy

The proximal determinants of teen pregnancy are sexual intercourse and contraceptive use. Therefore, research about teen pregnancy often has used sexual intercourse (e.g., age of onset, intercourse frequency, number of partners) or contraceptive use (e.g., use at first or most recent intercourse, consistency of use) as proxy outcome measures for teen pregnancy risk. The antecedents of teen pregnancy risk are presented next, from individual, to family, to broader contextual influences.

Individual influences

Most research about adolescent pregnancy has focused on environmental/contextual factors, but some researchers have explored genetic and biological contributions to adolescent sexual behavior and pregnancy. Three primary areas of investigation have emerged: (1) a focus on genetics and heredity; (2) hormone levels in relation to sexual motivation and behaviors; and (3) the role of early pubertal development.

Researchers have reported correlations between mother's, daughter's, and sister's ages of menarche (Garn, 1980; Mott et al., 1996; Newcomer & Udry, 1984), and noted that mothers' young age at first intercourse predicts sons' and daughters' having intercourse before age 14 (Mott et al., 1996). Behavior-genetic models of age at first intercourse, predicted by genetic, shared environmental, and nonshared environmental influences, indicates that genetic influences account for some of the variance in both early and late onset of first sexual intercourse (Rodgers, Rowe, & Buster, 1999). Among white opposite-sex pairs, heritabilities were found to predict age of first intercourse. A relationship between dopamine receptor genes and age at first intercourse has also been reported (Miller et al., 1999).

Research by Udry and colleagues (Udry, Talbert, & Morris, 1986; Udry, 1988) showed that free testosterone hormone levels are related to teen sexual motivation and behavior. There is little evidence, however, that changes in boys' testosterone levels directly affected their sexual behavior over three years; pubertal development was a much stronger predictor of sexual ideation and behavior than changes in testosterone levels (Halpern et al., 1993).

Several investigators have noted a relationship between early pubertal development, age of first intercourse, and subsequent adolescent sexual behavior and pregnancy (Flannery, Rowe, & Gulley, 1993; Zabin et al., 1986). Halpern et al. (1993) reported that early pubertal development was a significant predictor of adolescent males' transition to intercourse, and the risk ratio was about twice as great for earlier vs. later maturing boys. Miller et al. (1998) also reported that early development relative to peers was related to a higher level of sexual behavior two years later. Both theory and research findings suggest that early pubertal development is associated with early experiences in intimate relationships, including sexual involvement with larger numbers of sexual partners, and an increased likelihood of teen pregnancy (AGI, 1994).

Family influences

Family influences on adolescent pregnancy risk include the hereditary or biological transmission of potentially important individual characteristics already described, the contextual and structural features of families (e.g., parents' education, marital status, sibling composition), and family processes or practices of parenting (e.g., parental support, control, or supervision of teenagers). A few studies have analyzed the dependent variable of adolescents' reports of ever having been pregnant or causing a pregnancy, but most research has related family variables to the key proximal determinants – sexual intercourse and contraceptive behavior.

Parent–child relationships. Many researchers have investigated the relation between adolescents' pregnancy risk and family variables such as parental warmth, support, parent–child closeness and child attachment to parents (see Table 1 in the 20-year research review by Miller, Benson, and Galbraith, 2001). There is marked consistency in this body of about two dozen studies, with all but a few indicating that parent–child closeness is associated with reduced adolescent pregnancy risk through teens remaining sexually abstinent, postponing intercourse, having fewer sexual partners, or using contraception more consistently. For example, investigators reported that closeness to mother was related to daughters' and sons' postponement of sexual intercourse (Jaccard, Dittus, & Gordon, 1996; Weinstein & Thornton, 1989), and to more consistent contraceptive use by sexually active teens of both sexes (Jaccard, Dittus, & Gordon, 1996).

Most of the evidence shows that parents' supervision and monitoring of children (Miller, Benson, & Galbraith, 2001, Table 2) also is related to adolescents' sexual behaviors in ways that would lower their risk of pregnancy (not having intercourse, later sexual debut, or having fewer sexual partners). A possible explanation for the few contrary findings is that parental control is multidimensional, and it is associated with negative teen outcomes if it is excessive or coercive (Barber, 1996; Gray & Steinberg, 1999). Dorius and Barber (1998) and Upchurch et al. (1999) reported that intrusive maternal control was related to early age of first sexual intercourse, and Rodgers (1999) reported that parents' psychological control was related to high-risk behavior among sexually active daughters. In general, however, parental supervision and behavior monitoring directly reduces teen pregnancy risk, and does so indirectly through lower alcohol and drug use and less association with high-risk peers.

Associations between parent–child communication and adolescent pregnancy risk have been investigated in more than 30 studies (see Miller, Benson, & Galbraith, 2001, Table 3). Results are discrepant; there is no simple, direct effect. Several important issues complicate our understanding of the association between parent–child communication and adolescent pregnancy risk (Jaccard, Dittus, & Litardo, 1999). One is temporal order; does parent–child communication affect teen behavior or vice versa? Parent–teen communication content, frequency, and quality also vary greatly, and associations between parent/teen communication and adolescent sexual behavior are moderated by parents' values. Recent investigations (Jaccard, Dittus, & Litardo, 1996; Luster & Small, 1997; Miller et al., 1998, 1999) have demonstrated that parents' sexual values, in combination with parent–child communication, have an important effect on adolescents' intercourse experience.

A number of recent studies have identified mediating mechanisms, depicted in figure 20.2, that could help explain how parent–child relationships (especially closeness & supervision) influence adolescents' pregnancy risk. For example, parent–child closeness is

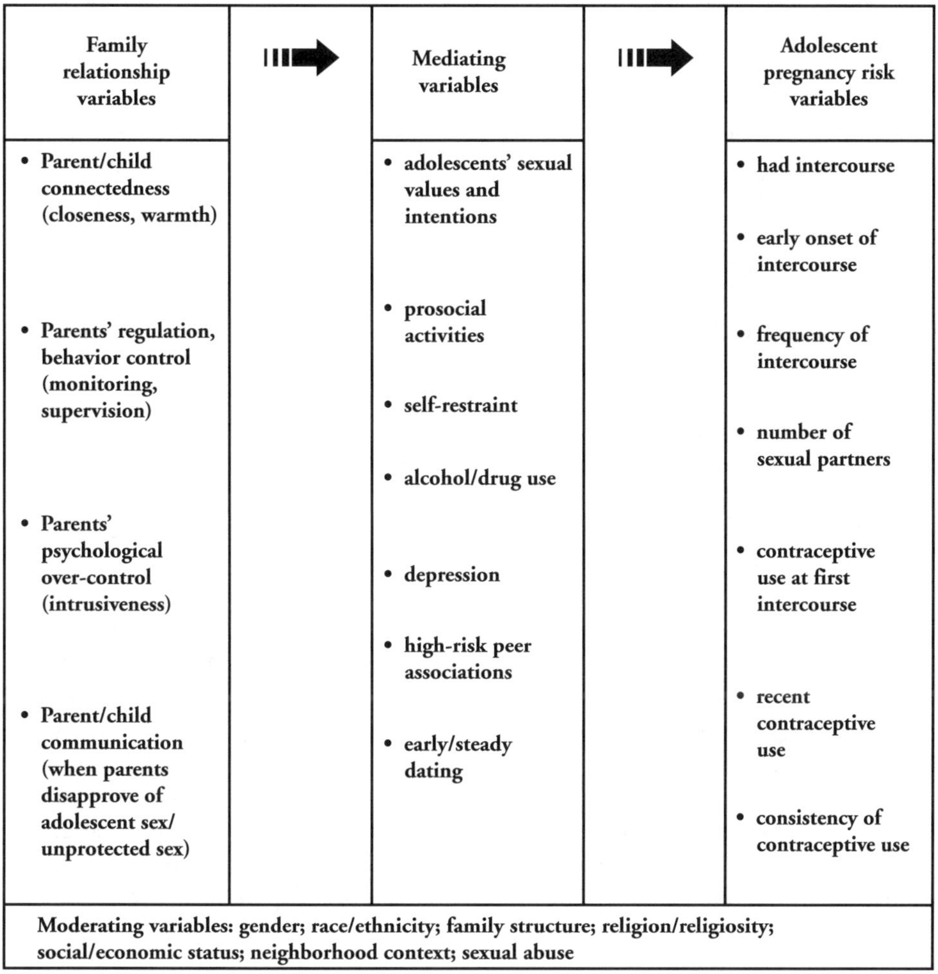

Family relationship variables		Mediating variables		Adolescent pregnancy risk variables
• Parent/child connectedness (closeness, warmth)	**III➡**	• adolescents' sexual values and intentions	**III➡**	• had intercourse • early onset of intercourse
• Parents' regulation, behavior control (monitoring, supervision)		• prosocial activities • self-restraint • alcohol/drug use		• frequency of intercourse • number of sexual partners
• Parents' psychological over-control (intrusiveness)		• depression • high-risk peer associations		• contraceptive use at first intercourse • recent contraceptive use
• Parent/child communication (when parents disapprove of adolescent sex/ unprotected sex)		• early/steady dating		• consistency of contraceptive use
Moderating variables: gender; race/ethnicity; family structure; religion/religiosity; social/economic status; neighborhood context; sexual abuse				

Figure 20.2   A mediated conceptual model of family relationships and adolescent pregnancy risk.

related to: teens' attitudes about having sex, feelings of depression, impulse control, academic and prosocial activities, use of substances, and association with sexually active peers, all of which are related to adolescent sexual behavior and pregnancy. Several investigators (Benda & DiBlasio, 1991; Feldman & Brown, 1993; Whitbeck et al., 1992) have suggested that a lack of closeness in the parent–teen relationship increases the negative influence of peers. In one longitudinal study (Scaramella et al., 1998) the effects of parental warmth and involvement in 7th grade were shown to affect teen pregnancy status in 12th grade through intervening mechanisms such as deviant peer affiliations, substance use, delinquency, and academic competence. As depicted in figure 20.2, parent–child involvement also can reduce teen sexual behavior indirectly by instilling values, providing youth with opportunities to develop prosocial skills, and to acquire a sense of competence and worth (Ramirez-Valles, Zimmerman, & Newcomb, 1998).

Combined effects of parent–teen relationship dimensions. Relatively few investigations have been designed to simultaneously test how multiple dimensions of parent–child relationships influence adolescent pregnancy risk. "Family assets" (Luster & Small, 1997) to prevent teen pregnancy can be viewed as including not only parental disapproval of teen sex (or unprotected teen sex), but also having a supportive parent/teen relationship (connectedness) and appropriately monitoring (regulation) teen activities. Some investigators (Jaccard, Dittus, & Gordon, 1996) have argued persuasively that parents' attitudes and values about teen sex and pregnancy strongly influence teens' pregnancy risk. Parents' values for their teens to avoid pregnancy (either through sexual abstinence or through contraceptive use) are most effectively transmitted when parents have a close relationship (connectedness) with their children (Jaccard, Dittus, & Gordon, 1998; Weinstein & Thornton, 1989).

Contextual family influences. Family structure provides a salient context because children grow up usually having primary relationships with one or two biological parents, and with or without older and younger siblings. With respect to parents' marital status, research consistently shows that living with a single parent is related to adolescents having sexual intercourse at younger ages (see Lammers et al., 2000; Miller, Benson, & Galbraith, 2001). Several investigators have shown that single or divorced parents have more permissive sexual attitudes (Thornton & Camburn, 1987), provide less parental supervision, and model dating activity themselves (Whitbeck, Simons, & Kao, 1994). These factors help explain why adolescents in some single-parent families are at increased risk of pregnancy. Having older siblings also is related to higher risk of pregnancy if older siblings have had sexual intercourse, and if the older sisters have experienced an adolescent pregnancy or birth (East, 1996a, 1996b, 1998; East & Kiernan, 2001). In many recent studies, investigators found that traumatic experiences, especially those involving sexual abuse, are related to higher adolescent pregnancy risk, through earlier onset of voluntary sexual intercourse, and through less consistent use of contraception (see Browning & Laumann, 1997; Miller, Benson, & Galbraith, 2001, Table 9).

Peer influences

Researchers first thought that the striking similarities among teenage friends were due simply to peer pressures that required conformity, but studies have shown that adolescents also are drawn to peers with similar attitudes, beliefs, and desires (Aloise-Young, Graham, & Hansen, 1994; Ennett & Bauman, 1994). Peers still are blamed by parents and the larger society for exerting negative peer pressures, but in a recent review Brown and Theobald (1999) concluded that this negative stereotyping of peer pressures is oversimplified. Adolescent peers often support one another in efforts to make thoughtful and safe decisions about risky vs. responsible sexual behavior (Bearman & Brückner, 1999). So, friends are affected by peer influence and pressure, but not as much, or as negatively, as has been presumed. Selection of a desired group of friends, and conforming to their normative behaviors in order to be befriended, are significant reasons why teenage friends share so many similar behaviors, risky or not.

Adolescents experience four kinds of peer influences which may or may not encourage risky behavior. Peer pressure, the most recognized form of peer influence, appears to be more influential among acquaintances rather than close friends. In one sample (Lightfoot, 1997), 85 percent of teens reported that they would be more likely to engage in new and risky behavior among acquaintances rather than close friends. Bearman and Brückner (1999) also reported that the larger group of general friends was much more likely to influence early sexual activity and pregnancy than were best friends. Traditionally, boys faced more peer pressure to engage in sex, while girls received more encouragement to wait until marriage (De Gaston, Weed, & Jensen, 1996; Brown, 1982).

Peer modeling, a second kind of influence on sexuality and pregnancy, has been difficult to study because sexuality and pregnancy are inherently private expressions. Eder (1993a) described the playful learning process among small groups of adolescent females as they took turns teasing and flirting with desired boys in school. As previously noted, investigators also have linked the increased risk of early sexual intercourse and pregnancy to younger teens living with older sexually active or pregnant sisters (Cox, Emans, & Bithoney, 1993; East, 1996). Television represents another potential source of modeling teen sexuality and how adolescents might learn to behave in intimate situations (Children Now and the Kaiser Family Foundation, 1996).

A third kind of peer influence, setting norms, refers to the regular behaviors and expectations adolescents must exhibit in order to feel accepted among their friends. Teens' perceptions of their peers' sexual activity has been strongly associated with adolescents' subsequent sexual intercourse (Furstenberg et al., 1987; Kinsman et al., 1998; Miller et al., 1997). Friends' positive attitudes toward sexual intercourse have been associated with adolescents' positive attitudes about sexual intercourse and their actual sexual behavior (Treboux & Busch-Rossnagel, 1995). Conversely, having friends with high educational expectations and good grades predicts lower teen pregnancy (Bearman & Brückner, 1999; Kasen, Cohen, & Brook, 1998).

Fourth, the term structuring opportunities refers to the creation of opportunities to engage in sexual intercourse. Teenage boys who have not had intercourse often cite the lack of opportunity as a major reason (Brown & Theobald, 1999). In peer groups where dating at young ages and early entry into romantic relationships are normative, teens are more likely to engage in early sexual activity (Dorius, Heaton, & Steffen, 1993; Miller et al., 1997).

Some peer groups appear to have a particularly powerful influence on teen sexual intercourse because popularity and peer status increase as a result of sexual activity in these groups. Among "jocks" and other highly popular groups, more sexual activity was reported at younger ages than among teens who were labeled "smarts" or "average" (Kinsman et al., 1998; Dolcini, 1997). In some groups there might be increased opportunities for sexual activity because popular kids are more often invited to social events, and they attract romantic partners more easily than "average" teens (Kinney, 1993). Not all evidence supports the hypothesis of increased risk among the most popular youth, however, Bearman and Brückner (1999) found that girls in the "leading crowd" were less than half as likely as other females to get pregnant during adolescence.

Another aspect of peer influence that has been studied is how adolescents balance influences they receive from peers and parents. There is some evidence of an oppositional relation between peers and parents, with peers being viewed as a negative influence and parents as positive (Hirschi, 1969). When bonds to parents are strong the negative effects of peers are low (Warr, 1993; Benda & DiBlasio, 1991). Sophisticated longitudinal research suggests that inadequate parenting may actually prompt association with deviant peers, as depicted in figure 20.2 (Dishion et al., 1995; Farrell & White, 1998; Scaramella et al., 1998).

Neighborhood

The role of community characteristics in adolescent pregnancy begins with a social framework that encourages or inhibits a variety of adolescent behaviors (Brewster, Billy, & Grady, 1993). This framework is not limited to availability of reproductive services, such as family planning clinics or abortion facilities, but also includes social, economic, and educational conditions that provide or deny adolescents with opportunities to achieve desired adult statuses.

Among the strongest of these conditions are a community's socioeconomic characteristics. Defined by housing values, income and poverty levels, and educational attainment levels, community socioeconomic status (SES) has been shown to effect males and females alike (Billy, Brewster, & Grady, 1994; Ku, Sonenstein, & Pleck, 1993). High neighborhood unemployment is a consistent predictor of the probability of teen fatherhood (especially among black males) and also has an adverse effect on females. In communities that offer few employment opportunities, female adolescents appear to be less motivated to delay the transition to sexual activity. In contrast, increased economic resources and positive female role models lessen these negative effects (Brewster, 1994b; Upchurch et al., 1999).

Community characteristics also shape and reinforce prevailing normative boundaries of acceptable behavior by directly prohibiting certain acts, and indirectly through various social, religious, economic, and political institutions. For example, in most analyses, adolescent religiosity has a positive, preventive effect on adolescent pregnancy (Billy, Brewster, & Grady, 1994; Thornton & Camburn, 1987). Social disorganization elevates the risk of adolescent pregnancy by increasing rates of teen sexual activity (Lauritsen, 1994; Billy, Brewster, & Grady, 1994). Societal influences also can take the shape of positive neighborhood monitoring. Adolescent pregnancy rates appear to be lower in communities where nonparental adults take an active role in the welfare of neighborhood teenagers (Small & Luster, 1994).

Race/ethnicity and socioeconomic status

Teenage pregnancy and birthrates vary greatly among race/ethnic groups in the United States (Ventura et al., 1999). African American teens had the highest birthrate in the mid-1990s, nearly double the national average for all races (112 vs. 60 per 1,000 females aged 15–19), whereas Asian/Pacific Islander teens had less than half the average birthrate (26 vs. 60 per 1,000). Birthrates among teens aged 15–19 decreased for all race/ethnic groups during the 1990s, but during this time the Latino teen birthrate surpassed the rate for African Americans. Birthrate differences between race/ethnic groups are projected to continue through 2050 (Day, 1996). In the late 1990s, African American and Latino pregnancy rates were about twice as high as those of non-Latino, white 15–19-year-olds (AGI, 1999).

There are no widely accepted explanations for race/ethnic differences in pregnancy and birthrates, but low SES of some race/ethnic groups has been associated with teen pregnancy and childbearing. Brewster (1994a) found that African American teens living in poverty in urban neighborhoods were more likely than whites to initiate sexual activity at young ages, and were less likely to use birth control. However, East (1998) reported that culture-specific age norms explained early sexual activity and nonmarital teen childbearing better than SES or family context; Furstenberg et al. (1987) also found more support for a cultural explanation of adolescent sexual intercourse than for SES. Some cultures may support a relatively more tolerant attitude toward teen childbearing, providing less of a deterrent to early unprotected sexual activity. East (1998) reported that Latino teens desired early and rapid transitions into the experiences of intercourse, marriage, and childbirth, in contrast to Asian teens, who desired later and more gradual transitions. Sanchez (1997) explained that the Latino normative cultural context prohibits premarital sex for female teens, but males are granted more sexual freedom. Pregnancy among Latino teenagers might result from denial: if teens are not having sex, there is no need for contraception. Even though southeast Asian families have relatively low incomes, they report high aspirations for teens' future education and employment, whereas Latino teens report low expectations for future education and employment. The relative emphasis on children's future educational and career success might partially explain the differing birthrates in these groups (Allen & Mitchell, 1998). Among groups with historically low educational attainment and career expectations, teen parenthood provides an immediate sense of purpose (Burton, 1990; Geronimus, 1992).

Poverty influences adolescent pregnancy, and adolescent parenthood usually, but not always, results in lower SES (Maynard, 1996). African American and Latino females disproportionately live in poor neighborhoods with school systems that contribute to low educational and career expectations. While these different cultural contexts may not cause poverty or adolescent pregnancy, they are associated (Furstenberg & Brooks-Gunn, 1986; Upchurch & McCarthy, 1990). Recent analyses suggest that about two-thirds of the racial difference in the risk of premarital childbearing can be explained by racial differences in neighborhood quality (South & Baumer, 2000).

Teenage childbearing may be more directly related to lower future expectations among some race/ethnic groups than it is to a specific contextual factor like poverty, dropping out of high school, or neighborhood job opportunities. Dropping out of high school precedes many teenage pregnancies rather than follows it (Fergusson & Woodward, 2000), and most teens who become pregnant eventually graduate from high school (Furstenberg & Brooks-Gunn, 1986; Olsen & Farkas, 1989; Upchurch & McCarthy, 1990). A cultural context of poverty, poor schools, and low-paying jobs appears to foster the perception of limited future possibilities. Teen childbearing may represent little threat to future opportunities for teens in poor families and neighborhoods. Rather, childbearing for poor teens may contribute to increased status and self-worth that is associated with parenthood, and having a baby may be seen as a way to ease immediate stressful circumstances by becoming eligible for welfare benefits.

Summary

Researchers who study teen pregnancy often substitute sexual intercourse and contraceptive use variables as proxies for teen pregnancy risk. These behaviors are affected by individual, family, and broader contextual influences. Individual contributions to teen pregnancy risk include genetic and hereditary influences, hormone levels associated with sexual motivation and behaviors, and early pubertal development. Family influences on adolescent pregnancy risk include parenting practices, parent/adolescent relationship qualities, family structure, and other contextual features of family life. Warm, supportive relationships between parents and adolescents and parental supervision and monitoring of adolescents serve as protective factors. In contrast, pregnancy risk is greater in families where parents provide less supervision and monitoring. Contextual family factors, including single or divorced parenthood and especially child sexual abuse, increase pregnancy risk. Peers can either encourage or discourage risky sexual behavior. Peer pressure, peer modeling, peer cultural norms, and structural opportunities have been identified as potential sources of peer influence. Community characteristics, such as low community socioeconomic status and poorer employment opportunities for adults and adolescents, increase the risk of pregnancy. Communities also shape and reinforce normative boundaries that influence adolescent pregnancy risk through social, religious, and other institutions and positive neighborhood monitoring. There are large differences in teen pregnancy and childbearing among race/ethnic groups in the United States, but there is no widely accepted explanation for these group differences. Some researchers suggest that culture-specific age norms help explain early sexual activity and nonmarital teen childbearing, and poverty, poor schools, and low-paying jobs foster the perception of limited future possibilities. Among poor teens, childbearing may actually contribute to increased status and self-worth.

Teen Pregnancy Decision-making and Resolution

The decision points that result in teen pregnancy and parenthood are shown in figure 20.3. As depicted there, having sexual intercourse without contraception and contraceptive failure lead to pregnancy. In the event of an unintended pregnancy, a woman – and often her partner and significant others – face essentially three options: to terminate the pregnancy, to place the child for adoption, or to parent the child (see the lower half of figure 20.3). The major factors that influence adolescents' pregnancy resolution decisions are: personal attitudes and socialization about abortion, parenting, and adoption (Custer, 1993; Donnelly & Voydanoff, 1991; Fox et al., 1987); the influence or pressure of significant others such as parents and partners (Dworkin, Harding, & Schreiber, 1993; Namerow, Kalmuss, & Cushman, 1993; Ortiz & Nuttall, 1987); and access to and

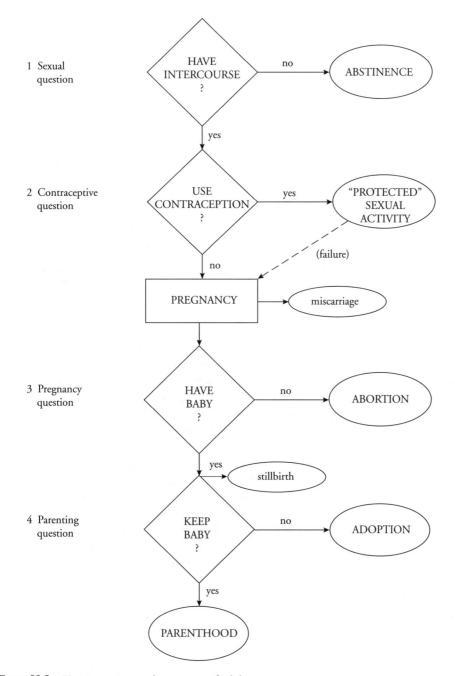

Figure 20.3 Turning points and outcomes of adolescent pregnancy.

utilization of pregnancy and adoption counseling, abortion, and prenatal services (Bachrach, 1986; Eisen & Zellman, 1983).

The decision to have an abortion or give birth

Abortion might be chosen by some adolescents because they wish to keep secret the fact that they are sexually active or that they became pregnant. A lack of economic resources is often cited, as well as concerns about how children would disrupt or interfere with the parents' school, work, or other life plans. Relationship difficulties or instability may also be reasons to have an abortion, and many adolescents feel unprepared to assume parental responsibilities at this stage in their lives (Donovan, 1995).

Several sociodemographic characteristics are associated with the decision to have an abortion. The relationship between income level and abortion rates is widely documented: As level of income increases, so does the likelihood of having an abortion (Donovan, 1995; AGI, 1994). In one study, about 70 percent of adolescents from higher-income families had abortions, compared with less than one-third of adolescents from poor/low-income families (Donovan, 1995).

Ortiz and Nuttall (1987) reported that mothers have the most influence among Puerto Rican teens who decided to carry their pregnancies to term, whereas sisters were most influential for those who decided to have an abortion. Fathers were the least influential, regardless of whether daughters chose to terminate their pregnancies or give birth. Related findings from a sample of African American adolescents also indicated that mothers were the most influential in their daughter's pregnancy experiences and outcomes, even more so than daughters' male partners or girlfriends (Murry, 1995).

In a study of post-decision satisfaction (six months after delivery or abortion), Eisen and Zellman (1983) found that satisfaction about having an abortion was predicted by positive pre-procedure abortion opinion, more liberal attitudes toward abortion for others, consistent contraceptive use following the abortion, and their mothers' higher educational attainment. Among adolescents who decided to give birth, positive attitudes toward single motherhood and lack of school attendance in the six months after delivery were associated with decision satisfaction. Murry (1995) reported that being older, having higher education, income, and access to health care clinics were related to African American teens' decisions to have an abortion. African Americans who reported a specific religious affiliation were more likely to have an abortion, in contrast with Stevans, Register, and Sessions' (1992) report that religious affiliation had no effect on how adolescents resolved their pregnancies. Among Latino adolescent females, being younger at the time of conception, and having never used or inconsistently used contraception, were factors that contributed to the decision to have an abortion. Informing adolescents' mothers of the pregnancy, and having well-educated mothers, were two family factors associated with choosing to have an abortion. Consistent with other findings (Stevans, Register, & Sessions, 1992), regular church attendance among Latino females was inversely related to the decision to terminate a pregnancy.

Caution is warranted in interpreting the findings of these studies about the correlates of abortion decision-making by adolescents because abortions are seriously under reported in major national surveys. In most surveys, the number of abortions must be more than doubled to compensate for underreporting, and underreporting abortions appears to be greater for non-white women (Jones & Forest, 1992).

The decision to parent or relinquish for adoption

Race, education and income level, future career and educational aspirations, and the influence of significant others (i.e., the mothers and birth fathers) historically were associated with unwed mothers choosing adoption (Bachrach, 1986; Bachrach, Stolley, & London, 1992; Chandra et al., 1999; Kalmuss, Namerow, & Cushman, 1991; Miller & Coyl, 2000; Namerow, Kalmuss, & Cushman, 1993; Warren & Johnson, 1989). White women have been much more likely to relinquish infants for adoption than black and Latino women, but most of the decline in adoption relinquishment in recent decades is due to white women becoming more like women of other races. Recent decreases in adoption relinquishment among unmarried white women have virtually eliminated what were previously large racial differences (Bachrach, Stolley, & London, 1992; Chandra et al., 1999).

Findings about the relationship between mother's age and the decision to relinquish a baby for adoption are inconsistent. Bachrach (1986) and Donnelly and Voydanoff (1991) reported that younger adolescents were more likely to relinquish than women who were 17–18 years or older, but Bachrach, Stolley, and London (1992) and Warren and Johnson (1989) reported that older adolescents were more likely to relinquish their infants than were younger mothers. Bachrach, Stolley, and London (1992) observed no relationship between relinquishment and mother's age using bivariate analysis, but more complex multivariate analysis revealed a significant positive relationship. "[The likelihood of relinquishment increased] 13% with each additional year of age" (1992, p. 31).

Miller (1995) summarized previous research showing that female adolescents with high educational and vocational goals were more likely to postpone sexual activity, to use birth control to prevent unwanted pregnancies, and to place infants for adoption, than were adolescents with lesser educational goals. Kalmuss, Namerow, and Cushman (1991) reported that unmarried young women in maternity residences who intended to place for adoption were more advantaged socioeconomically and more likely to anticipate attending college than those who did not consider placing. Low, Moely, and Willis (1989) and Donnelly and Voydanoff (1991) found that pregnant teens were more likely to place infants for adoption if they had chosen careers that require longer preparation time.

Young women who have personal experiences with adoption (e.g., knowing someone who was adopted or being adopted themselves) and those who live in maternity residences, are more likely than other young women to chose adoption (Namerow, Kalmuss, & Cushman, 1993). The role of significant others also predicts adoption decision making; young women whose mothers and boyfriends prefer adoption rather than parenting are more likely to relinquish infants for adoption, whereas young women who choose to parent are more likely to report that their mothers and boyfriends preferred parenting. Pregnant young women who believe that the future outcomes they desire are more likely to occur if they placed for adoption are more likely to place, and those who believe that parenting will provide the best outcomes are more likely to parent.

Adoption-related attitudes are different among pregnant young women who intend to place for adoption and those who intend to parent (Kalmuss, Namerow, & Kushman, 1991). Those who intend to place have the most favorable attitudes about adoption, whereas those who never consider adoption are the least positive. The proportion of young women who consider adoption is inflated when respondents are selected from maternity residences, but these findings are consistent with other research and theory which suggests that those who make an adoption plan tend to be disproportionally white, from advantaged backgrounds, to have intentions toward college and careers, and to have more positive attitudes about adoption than pregnant young women who choose to parent.

Father's age and roles

The male partners of teenage mothers went relatively unnoticed until the 1990s. It was generally assumed that these fathers were also teenagers, but recent studies have indicated that many of the partners of teen mothers are adult men (Darroch & Landry, 1999; Landry & Forrest, 1995; Males & Chew, 1996). In fact, only one-quarter of the men involved in the pregnancies of females under age 18 are less than age 19 themselves. Of the older male partners, nearly 40 percent are age 20 or older (AGI, 1999).

In the United States, males average about three years older than their female sex partners (Males & Chew, 1996), so it is not surprising that teenage girls also tend to have older partners. However, teenage girls who are involved with adult men are more likely to become pregnant than their peers whose partners are closer to their own age. Darroch and Landry (1999) found that 36 percent of sexually active teenage girls had a partner at least three years older, whereas 56 percent of births to girls aged 15–17 involved fathers at least three years older. Males and Chew (1996) reported that more than two-thirds of babies born to school-aged mothers were fathered by adult men. Landry and Forrest (1995) reported similar results, that about two thirds of teenage mothers had partners who were at least 20 years old. Lindberg and Sonenstein (1997) reported less dramatic findings, namely, that 27 percent of babies born to 15–17-year-old girls were fathered by men at least five years older. Discrepancies across these studies can be explained by noting that Darroch and Landry (1999), Landry and Forrest (1995), and Males and Chew (1996) examined the adult or nonadult status of fathers, whereas Lindberg and Sonenstein (1997) focused on specific age differences.

Lower contraceptive use might be one reason why teenage girls who are sexually involved with adult men are more likely to become pregnant. Darroch and Landry (1999) found that girls involved with adult men were less likely to use contraception than girls involved with teenaged boys, and that *unintended* pregnancy is lower among girls with adult partners. Whereas 82 percent of pregnancies were unintended among teenagers with peer-aged partners, only 70 percent were unintended among those with adult partners (Darroch & Landry, 1999), suggesting that contraceptive use may be less consistent among female teens with adult men.

Adult men who father children with teenage girls are different than adult men with same-age female partners in several respects. They are less likely to have finished high school or continue their education, they also are more likely to be unemployed (9.9 percent compared to 6.7 percent), and they are less likely to work in professional or managerial positions (24.4 percent compared to 32.1 percent). Lindberg and Sonenstein (1997) suggested that adult men might be more desirable to teenage girls than same-age partners because of perceived employment and marriageability advantages, but the above statistics show that the perceived superiority of older partners is unfounded.

One of the greatest concerns about teenage pregnancy is the number of single-parent households created by early childbearing. About 20 percent of teen mothers with peer-aged partners are married at the birth of their child, compared to 23 percent of those with adult partners. However, according to Lindberg and Sonenstein (1997), partners are much more likely to live together when the father is an adult (35 percent before the birth and 48 percent after) than when he is a minor (22 percent before and 28 percent after). These statistics suggest that older fathers may be more involved initially with teen mothers and their babies, but the long-term stability of these relationships is unknown. It is clear that the majority of fathers of children born to teenage mothers are not involved with the mother following conception. Further research is needed to understand the degree to which the fathers of these children are responsible for their support, both financially and emotionally.

Summary of pregnancy antecedents and decision making

A complete summary of risk factors for adolescent childbearing must consider at least two major stages: (a) becoming pregnant; and (b) resolving a pregnancy through unmarried parenthood (Miller, 1995). More specific turning points for adolescent pregnancy and parenthood include having early sexual intercourse, not using contraception, carrying an unintended pregnancy to term, and not relinquishing the child for adoption.

As shown in the first column of table 20.1, many individual, familial, and broader contextual variables are related to the timing of sexual intercourse in adolescence. Variables that make early sexual intercourse more likely (indicated by a "+" sign in table 20.1) are: early pubertal development; high testosterone levels; being African American; permissive sexual attitude; use of alcohol, tobacco, and other drugs; psychosocial deviance; poverty status; living with a single parent; and sibling and peer sexual activity. Conversely, sexual intercourse tends to be delayed or less likely (indicated with a "–" sign) among young teens with: good school grades and high educational aspirations; high religiosity; better-educated parents; close parent–child relationships; high parental supervision; and those who live in more advantaged neighborhoods.

Among sexually active teens, nonuse (or inconsistent use) of contraception is the major risk factor in unplanned pregnancy. As shown in the second column of table 20.1, sexually active adolescents are less likely to use contraception at all, or to use it consistently when they are young, if they are African American, ambivalent about pregnancy, use alcohol or drugs, live with a single parent or in poverty, and if they have been sexually abused. Contraceptive use is more likely (or more consistent) among adolescents who do well in school and have future educational plans, have favorable contraceptive attitudes, have more educated parents with whom they have a close relationship, have siblings and

Table 20.1　Correlates of Behaviors Linked to Adolescent Nonmarital Childbearing

Risk protective correlates	Pregnancy risk			Resolution of pregnancy		
	Sexual intercourse	*Use contraception*	*Choose abortion*	*Choose adoption*	*Parenthood Married*	*Unmarried*
Individual factors						
Young age	−	−	+	+	−	+
Early puberty	+					
Testosterone	+					
Race (black & Latino)	+	−		−	−	+
Edu plans, grades	−	+	+	+	+	−
Religiosity	−		−		+	−
Self-esteem			+			
Pregnancy ambivalence	−	−	−			+
Substance use	+	−				
Psychosocial deviance	+	−				
Proximate social factors						
Parents' education	−	+	+	+		−
Family income			+	+		−
Poverty status	+	−	−	−	−	+
Physical/sexual abuse	+	−				
Single parent	+	−	−	−	−	+
Family support	−	+				
Parental supervision	−	+				
Sib/friend behavior	+	+				+
Parent/peer acceptance	+	+	+	+		+
Poor rel w/ partner			+		−	+
Broader contextual factors						
Neighborhood SES	−	+				−
AFDC benefit level				−	−	+
Employment opp.		+				−
Family planning ser.		+				−
School sex ed.		+				−

* This table is an abbreviated summary of major research findings; see Kirby (2001), Miller, Benson, & Galbraith (2001), and Moore et al. (1995) for complete presentation. Plus sign means more likely, minus sign means less likely, blank means unknown or inconsistent results.

friends who support contraceptive use, live in more advantaged neighborhoods, and have received comprehensive sex education at school.

Regarding adolescent pregnancy resolution, many of the correlates of abortion and adoption are similar (as shown in columns 3 and 4 of table 20.1). Pregnant adolescents who are young are more likely to have an abortion rather than give birth, or to choose adoption rather than parenthood. African American adolescents are less likely than whites to choose adoption or to marry. Doing well in school, having high educational aspirations and more highly educated parents are related to resolving a pregnancy through abortion rather than through giving birth, and are more characteristic of adolescents who choose adoption rather than parenthood. Conversely, living in poverty and living with a single parent are inversely related to abortion and adoption decisions. Decisions about abortion and adoption are strongly influenced by significant others, especially by mothers. Abortion is less likely among those who are highly religious, but it is more likely when there is a poor relationship with the sexual partner.

Childbearing teens are less likely to marry if they are young, and some research suggests (column 5 in table 20.1) that marriage also is less likely among adolescent parents who are African American, live with a single parent or in poverty, have a poor relationship with their partner, and who live in an area with relatively higher AFDC (Aid to Families with Dependent Children) benefit levels. Conversely, marriage is more likely among adolescent parents who are religious and doing well in school. Single-parent family structure, especially the number of parents' marital disruptions, is positively related to having a nonmarital birth. The younger the age of first sexual intercourse, the greater the likelihood of beginning a family through nonmarital childbearing, rather than through marriage (Miller & Heaton, 1991).

Summary

In the event of an unintended pregnancy, three options arise: to terminate the pregnancy, to continue the pregnancy and place the child for adoption, or to parent the child. Individual, family, and broader contextual factors influence adolescents' pregnancy resolution decisions. The decision to have an abortion is positively associated with family income and education levels, and mother's and male partner's influence. Race, family socioeconomic status, and adolescents' future career and educational aspirations are among the most salient variables associated with choosing adoption. In the past, white females were much more likely to relinquish their infants for adoption to unrelated persons compared with black and Latino females, but recent decreases in adoption relinquishment among unmarried white females have nearly eliminated what were previously large racial differences. In the 1990s it was found that a substantial number of the male partners of teenage mothers were adult men. Pregnancy risk is higher in age-discrepant couples because girls involved with adult men are less likely to use contraception than girls involved with teenaged boys. Although older men may appear to have employment and marriageability advantages over male teens, these positive characteristics have not been found in studies of adult men who father children with adolescent females.

Consequences of Teen Parenthood

Consequences for adolescent mothers

Women who become parents as teenagers spend twice as much time between the ages of 14 and 30 as single parents when compared to those who postpone childbirth until their early twenties (Hotz, McElroy, & Sanders, 1997). In 1996, only 19 percent of adolescent mothers married the father of their first child before or directly after the birth of the child (Maynard, 1996). Of the teenage mothers who do marry, the likelihood of these unions ending in divorce is greater than those of their later-bearing counterparts (Bennett, Bloom, & Miller, 1995; Coley & Chase-Lansdale, 1998; Hotz, McElroy, & Sanders, 1997).

As single mothers, adolescent females are also more likely than their peers to drop out of high school (see table 20.2). Educational underachievement and high school dropout were significantly related to teenage pregnancy in a prospective New Zealand birth cohort analysis (Fergusson & Woodward, 2000). In an analysis of US teens who gave birth, only three out of ten earned a high school diploma by age 30, compared to over 85 percent of mothers who delayed childbirth (Hotz, McElroy, & Sanders, 1997). These figures, however, are disputed. Upchurch and McCarthy (1990) found that while teenage mothers are less likely to return to school after they have dropped out, there is no difference between them and their later-childbearing counterparts when making the decision to leave high school prior to completion.

Related to their lower education, adolescent mothers also have poorer employment opportunities and a lower earning potential (Hotz, McElroy, & Sanders, 1997). The difference in earnings between an adolescent mother and a mother who gave birth in her early twenties is, however, not as large as might be expected. In one study (Maynard, 1996), it was reported that over the course of early adulthood (ages 19 to 30), adolescent mothers earned an average of $1,522 per year more than their later-bearing counterparts ($6,323 vs. $4,801 in 1996). However, on average, adolescent mothers tended to put in more hours at work, approximately 34 percent more over the same period (see table 20.2).

Annual income for adolescent mothers varies depending on the contributions, or lack thereof, of the child's father. Typically, earned wages of adolescent mothers account for only one-third of their total income. The remaining two-thirds is usually made up of spousal income or child support, and public assistance. Adolescent mothers receive significantly higher levels of public assistance and, by age 30, have received about four times the amount of benefits received by later-bearing women (Hotz, McElroy, & Sanders, 1997).

Consequences for adolescent fathers

Adolescent males involved in teen births, like their female partners, also tend to complete less schooling by age 27 as compared to those who waited to father children until age 21 (11.3 vs. 13 years of school). Missing the final semester can mean the difference between becoming a high school graduate or dropout. Adolescent fathers are also significantly overrepresented in the blue-collar labor force, and are underrepresented in white-collar occupations (Buchanan & Robbins, 1990). Over a span of 18 years following the birth of a first child to an adolescent mother, fathers earn, on average, 25 percent less per year than their later father counterparts. More than half of this 25 percent deficit can be

Table 20.2 Summary of Teen Parenthood Consequences in the United States

Adolescent	(Compared to later-bearing mothers)
	1. Less likely to marry the father of their first child
	2. More likely to become divorced
	3. Twice as much time spent as a single parent prior to age 30
	4. More likely to drop out of school
	5. Less likely to earn a high school diploma by age 30
	6. Work more hours at a lower rate of pay
Adolescent	(Compared to later-bearing fathers)
	1. Less likely to earn a high school diploma
	2. More likely to work in a blue-collar occupation
	3. More likely to experience lower income levels
	4. More likely to engage in delinquent and criminal behaviors
Children of adolescent parents	(Compared to children of older parents)
	1. More likely to be born premature and of low birth weight
	2. More likely to experience serious or life-threatening medical conditions at birth
	3. Less likely to receive quality medical care and nutrition
	4. Less likely to receive necessary emotional support and cognitive stimulation
	5. More likely to drop out of school
	6. More likely to become involved in delinquent and criminal behaviors
	7. More likely to bear children out of wedlock
Society	
	1. Increased financial burden to taxpayers and extended families
	2. Additional strain on the resources of governmental programs and systems

directly attributed to adolescent parenting and other closely related factors (Brien & Willis, 1997).

Even if an adolescent male delays fatherhood until his early twenties, research has shown little or no benefit to the child or mother unless the couple marries or the father pays child support on a regular basis. On average, nonresident fathers earn a wage sufficient to offset as much as 40–50 percent of welfare support to the adolescent mother and their child. However, only 15 percent of never-married teen mothers have been awarded court-ordered child support, and most of those received less than half of the amount awarded.

As shown in table 20.2, adolescent fathers also appear to engage in more delinquent behaviors than older fathers. In the Rochester Youth Development Study (Thornberry, Smith, & Howard, 1997), early involvement in delinquent activities and illegal drug use were highly correlated with teenage fatherhood; 47 percent of high-rate delinquents and 70 percent of drug users were teen fathers (Stouthamer-Loeber & Wei, 1998). In the Pittsburgh Youth Study, a significant relationship also was found between delinquent activities and teenage fatherhood (Thornberry et al., 2000).

Consequences for children

Children of adolescent mothers are more likely to be born premature and are one and a half times more likely to be low-birth weight babies (less than $5\frac{1}{2}$ lb) when compared to children born to mothers in their early twenties (see table 20.2) (Moore, Morrison, & Greene, 1997; National Center for Health Statistics, 1994; Wolfe & Perozek, 1997). Medical problems at birth due to low birth weight are reflected by increased risks of infant death, blindness, deafness, chronic respiratory conditions, mental retardation, mental illness, and cerebral palsy. As low-birth weight infants grow older, they also become more prone to conditions such as dyslexia and hyperactivity.

Adolescent childbearing also has an effect on the type and quality of care and nutrition young children receive (see table 20.2). Typically, 60 percent of older mothers report their children's health as "excellent," compared to only 38 percent of adolescent mothers (Wolfe & Perozek, 1997). Based on these figures, the children of adolescent mothers might be expected to spend more time in the care of a physician, but the opposite is true; children of adolescent mothers see a physician about half as often (2.3 vs. 4.8 times a year) as children born to older parents (Wolfe & Perozek, 1997). Factors such as motivation, peer support or influence, and community context are responsible for at least one-third of this difference (Wolfe & Perozek, 1997). In spite of the less frequent doctor visits, adolescent mothers spend 20 percent more in medical care than their later-bearing counterparts. Of the $3,700 in medical services spent annually per child by adolescent mothers, about one-half is paid for through public assistance (Wolfe & Perozek, 1997).

Table 20.2 shows that children of adolescent mothers also are more likely to grow up in homes in which parents provide less emotional support and cognitive stimulation. Parental affection, books, games, and educational toys are less available, on average, especially in homes were the mother is working increased hours or the child's father is absent. Children born to teenage mothers ($\leq$17) score lower in cognitive tests of mathematics, reading recognition, and reading comprehension than children born to parents in their early twenties (Moore, Morrison, & Greene, 1997), even after controlling for differences in the mothers' socioeconomic backgrounds. When children of teenage mothers enter school, they are 70 percent less likely to be rated at the top of their class (Moore, Morrison, & Greene, 1997). As school performance lags, perhaps in part due to the low levels of cognitive stimulation at young ages and inferior nutritional and emotional support, children of adolescent mothers are also more likely to drop out of high school than peers with older mothers (Haveman, Wolfe, & Peterson, 1997). Approximately 57 percent of this difference can be attributed to the effects of adolescent childbearing and closely related factors (Maynard, 1996).

As they grow older, children of teenage mothers are at greater risk for running away from home (Moore, Morrison, & Greene, 1997) and sons born to teen mothers are 2.7 times more likely to spend part of their lives in prison (Grogger, 1997). Children of teenage mothers are also more likely to become parents themselves before the age of 19, and are more likely to bear children out of wedlock when compared to children born to women who delayed birth.

Consequences to society

Maynard (1997) estimated that adolescent childbearing cost American taxpayers about $7 billion annually in the mid-1990s. This was broken down across six categories: (1) increased incarceration expenses, $1 billion; (2) increased welfare and food stamp benefits, $2.2 billion; (3) increased medical expenses, $1.5 billion; (4) loss of tax revenue, $1.3 billion; and (4) increased foster care, $0.9 billion. The study also predicted a total savings to taxpayers, when combining these costs with other disadvantages faced by adolescent mothers, of between $13 billion and $19 billion savings per year *if* public policy could effectively delay adolescent childbearing and address the other disadvantages previously discussed. Beyond the direct monetary loss to society, adolescent childbearing also strains the time, resources, and effectiveness of governmental programs and systems. Controlling for a moderate range of background factors, researchers estimate the combined financial cost of adolescent childbearing at approximately $21 billion per year (Maynard, 1997).

Opposing views

Traditionally, teenage childbearing has been viewed as a serious social and economic problem with young, single, less educated mothers remaining financially dependent on social support systems. Recent research, however, portrays a different and less negative view of teenage parenthood. Some contemporary social scientists believe the average effect of a teenage birth is negligible, and that the natural variance among individuals negates a "one size fits all" conclusion (Hoffman, 1998). They argue that teenage mothers are not chosen from the population at random, and many young parents have prior associations with the same negative conditions that are reported as outcomes of teen parenthood (poverty, low education, etc.).

For example, Geronimus and Korenman (1992) compared sisters who had first births at different ages, and found that teenage births were not the cause of the mothers' problems, but that the problems were mostly likely a contributing factor for the births. Because of this, they believe the negative effects of teen motherhood have been overstated. They agreed that teenage mothers were less likely to be married or have a high school diploma, but the economic deficits, when compared to their later-bearing counterparts, were minimal.

Geronimus and Korenman are not alone in their belief that the negative effects of teenage births have been exaggerated. According to Hotz, McElroy, and Sanders (1997), who compared teenage mothers who gave birth to girls of a similar age who miscarried, those who had a teen birth were actually better off financially by their mid- to late twenties than those in the comparison (miscarried) group. Any differences in educational attainment or receipt of welfare benefits between the two groups were found to be negligible. Fergusson and Woodward (2000) also found that the links between teenage pregnancy and post-secondary educational attainment were largely noncausal.

Negative effects on the children of teen mothers also have been questioned. Using data from the National Longitudinal Survey of Youth–Child Supplement and the

National Survey of Children, Moore, Morrison, and Greene (1997) found that children of teenage mothers are no more at risk for depression, behavior problems, health problems, psychological well-being, or cognitive development than their later-born counterparts.

Summary

Although earlier research may have overstated the negative effects of teenage parenthood, which could be considered adaptive in some cultural contexts, substantial negative effects remain. Consequences for adolescent mothers included increased time spent single parenting, lower educational attainment, fewer employment opportunities, and lower earning potential compared with nonparenting peers. Significant health risks to both the mother and her child have also been identified. Adolescent males who father children also tend to complete less schooling, have more limited career opportunities, and poorer earning potential than male peers who wait to father children in their twenties. Research indicates that nonresident teen fathers tend to provide limited or no child support.

Negative consequences for children born to teen mothers may begin during the pregnancy and continue throughout their lives. Adolescent mothers are less likely to receive recommended prenatal care and their babies are at greater risk for being born prematurely and of low birth weight. In infancy, these children are at increased risk of infant death, and other physical and mental health problems. Despite these health risks, they are less likely to be seen by a physician. During childhood they are more likely to grow up in homes in which parents provide less emotional support and cognitive stimulation. These limitations have been related to lower scores on cognitive tests of math and reading ability, even after controlling for differences in mother's socioeconomic background. Poorer performance in school has been associated with increase risk of school dropout. During adolescence, children of teen mothers are at greater risk for running away from home, becoming single parents themselves before age 19. Males born to single adolescent women are more likely to spend part of their lives in prison compared with peers who experience more stable family patterns and home environments.

It is estimated that American taxpayers contribute $6.9 billion each year to subsidize the costs of adolescent childbearing. Other related costs to society include the strain on time, resources, and effectiveness of governmental programs and systems. It has been suggested that between $13 and $19 billion could be saved each year if public policy could effectively delay adolescent childbearing.

Conclusions and Implications

Contexts, antecedents, and consequences

Around the world, pregnancy and childbirth in the second decade of life are least common in highly developed countries, yet their occurrence tends to be considered much more of a problem in these countries. Since the mid-1970s there has been a clear trend of decreasing teenage pregnancy and birth in developed countries (Singh & Darroch, 2000). Teenage pregnancy and birthrates in the United States have been among the highest in the industrialized world, and it was not until the 1990s that pregnancies, births, and abortions all decreased in the United States.

Very divergent rates of pregnancy and birth exist across cultural contexts and race/ethnic groups in the United States, mirroring different rates in native countries throughout the world, and suggesting that lingering cultural influences play a role in US teenage pregnancy and childbirth. It is not clearly understood how race/ethnic groups and their cultural contexts influence adolescents' future aspirations, and desires for early pregnancy and childbirth. Research has established that disadvantaged circumstances and community contexts in which poverty and unemployment are high and average educational levels are low, place teens at increased risk for early pregnancy and childbirth. Some groups have been less thoroughly studied with regard to teen pregnancy and childbirth; for example, our understanding of the antecedents, consequences, and prevention of teen pregnancy is less conclusive for Native Americans and Asian Americans in particular.

Major antecedents of teen pregnancy include individual, family, and neighborhood factors, as well as broader contextual factors such as race/ethnicity and societal norms. Investigations of genetic and biological contributions to teen pregnancy have focused on the role of heredity, hormone levels in relation to sexual motivation and behaviors, and early pubertal development. Family influences that are clearly important for teen pregnancy risks are parent–child closeness and parental monitoring or supervision. Single-parent family structure, having older sexually active or parenting siblings, and abusive childhood experiences all elevate the risk of becoming pregnant or causing a pregnancy. Neighborhood characteristics appear to increase the risk of teen pregnancy through limited employment and educational opportunities, which may decrease adolescents' motivation to delay sexual intercourse and use contraception. Community norms and laws also influence adolescents' sexual behavior by directly prohibiting certain acts and by providing guidelines through social, religious, and political institutions. Adolescents' values and future expectations – influenced by race/ethnicity, cultural contexts, and SES – permeate their decisions regarding sexual behavior, pregnancy, and parenthood.

Major consequences of teen parenthood for females include the increased likelihood of single parenting, poverty, and health problems, as well as reduced educational and employment opportunities. For males, teen parenthood has negative effects on their education and employment. Children of adolescent mothers are more likely to grow up poor, to receive less education, and to have more behavior and health problems than children of older parents. The cost of adolescent childbearing to society includes increased welfare and food stamp benefits, medical expenses, loss of tax revenue, and increased foster care. Beyond the direct monetary loss to society, adolescent childbearing also strains the time, resources, and effectiveness of extended families and governmental programs and systems.

Prevention and intervention efforts

In recent decades countless programs to reduce teen pregnancy have been developed and implemented. Kirby (2001) reviewed five types of teen pregnancy-reduction programs in the United States: (1) curriculum-based small- or large-group education programs; (2) sex- and HIV-education programs for parents and their families; (3) clinic- or school-based programs that provide information and access to condoms and contraceptives; (4) community-wide pregnancy and HIV-prevention programs with multiple components; and (5) youth-development programs that affect, but do not focus on sexuality. Evaluations of such programs are often inhibited by methodological problems or constraints in program design and implementation, and few replication studies have been done.

Kirby's (2001) review indicated that sex- and HIV-education programs do not significantly increase adolescent sexual activity, a concern that has made adolescent sex-education programs controversial. Some programs did increase condom or contraceptive use while others did not. Evaluations of some school-based and community sex- and HIV-education programs that used random assignment, large sample sizes, and long-term follow-up showed statistically significant and programmatically important reductions in the frequency of sex, as well as increases in condom and contraceptive use, delays in sexual initiation, and decreases in unprotected sex (Coyle et al., 1999; Jemmott, Jemmott, & Fong, 1998; St. Lawrence, 1994).

Clinic programs and schools with health centers that provide one-on-one discussions with youth about their behavior, and information about abstinence, and that make condoms and/or other types of contraception available do not appear to impact adolescent sexual activity or decrease pregnancy or birthrates, but do consistently increase the use of condoms and contraception (Kirby, 2001). Programs designed to provide reproductive health services and to increase access to contraceptives may prevent thousands of adolescent pregnancies each year.

Community-wide pregnancy-prevention initiatives focusing on pregnancy prevention or condom use do not increase adolescent sexual activity in those communities. The most effective programs are those that are most intensive; however, when programs end, the use of condoms and pregnancy rates return to preprogram levels (Kirby, 2001).

Some youth-development programs significantly reduce teen pregnancy by addressing important nonsexual antecedents of teen pregnancy. The following components appear to be effective in these programs: the provision of employment opportunities for youth; instructional strategies designed to enhance adolescents' attachment to school; provisions for increasing academic success; and opportunities for community service. In addition, increased contact with caring adult leaders, monitored and supervised activities, and youth-volunteer opportunities appeared to serve as protective factors against sexual activity.

Kirby (2001) concluded that the teen pregnancy-prevention programs with strongest evidence of their effectiveness are sex-education programs that address both pregnancy and STD/HIV as well as youth-development programs, particularly those that have a service-learning component. His recommendations for middle and high school programs include: (1) instructional techniques that encourage youth involvement in and attachment to school; (2) sex-education programs that address both pregnancy and STD/HIV; (3) service-learning programs that incorporate community service and ongoing small group discussions; (4) school-based or school-linked clinics that focus upon reproductive health and give clear messages about abstinence and use of contraception; and (5) school condom-availability programs. Theoretically based programs that address the numerous antecedents and risk factors that affect teen pregnancy and provide information about sexual behavior and its consequences, as well as information about abstinence and access to contraception, are likely to be most effective in reducing teen pregnancy.

Conclusions

Adolescents are more likely to become pregnant if they begin having sex at an early age, partly because they are exposed to risk for a longer period of time, but also because those who begin early are more likely to be pressured or coerced, less likely to use contraception effectively, and to have sex more often with more partners. Adolescents who are most personally and socially disadvantaged are at greatest risk of becoming unmarried parents. That is, teens who do poorly in school, who have low future expectations, and who come from disadvantaged families and communities are more likely to initiate sex at a young age, are less likely to use contraception effectively, and, once pregnant, are more likely to bear a child, and particularly to give birth outside of marriage.

The influence of broader social contexts and opportunity structures on unwed teen childbearing must be considered in designing social policies and implementing interventions. To understand the contexts in which adolescents make decisions, one must take race/ethnicity into account, as well as the role of coercive sexual intercourse and, even when consensual, the dynamics of having older male partners. Social policies and interventions must be directed at multiple aspects of this complex problem because adolescents (and those who influence their decision making) respond differently to alternatives and constraints. That is, some adolescents can be influenced to abstain from or postpone onset of sexual intercourse, others will be sexually active but can be influenced to use contraception more effectively; and once pregnant, marriage, adoption, and abortion are options for some but not others.

Key Readings

The most current data and reports about adolescent pregnancy and childbearing are accessible through selected Internet sites. See http://www.teenpregnancy.org

Kirby, D. (2001). *Emerging Answers: Research Findings on Programs to Reduce Teen Pregnancy.* Washington, DC: National Campaign to Prevent Teen Pregnancy.
This comprehensive report details the evaluation designs and research findings of all major teen pregnancy-prevention/intervention programs. Programs with strongest evidence of their effectiveness are sex-education programs that address both pregnancy and STD/HIV and youth-development programs, particularly those that have a service-learning component. Ten program components are identified that are important in designing teen pregnancy-prevention/intervention programs.

Maynard, R. A. (Ed.) (1996). *Kids having kids: A Robin Hood Foundation special report on the costs of adolescent childbearing.* New York: Robin Hood Foundation.

This report summarizes studies about the consequences of teenage childbearing compared with later childbirth. Adolescent parents tend to have lower educational levels and reduced income when compared to their later-bearing counterparts. Infants born to adolescent parents are more likely to be born premature, resulting in low birth-weight problems, and children of adolescents are more likely to experience poor parenting, have trouble in school, drop out of school, run away from home, and incur more violations of the law when compared to children of older parents.

Miller, B. C., Benson, B., & Galbraith, K. A. (2001). Family relationships and adolescent pregnancy risk: A research synthesis. *Developmental Review, 21*(1), 1–38.

This article synthesizes 20 years of research on parental and family influences on whether teenagers become pregnant or cause a pregnancy. Parent–child and family interactions are emphasized, including parent–child connectedness, parental supervision, parent–child communications, and parental attitudes about teen sex. Parents influence the risk of pregnancy for their teens, especially through close, warm parent–child relationships, and parental supervision. Parent values are also important, as are parents' marital status and the behavior of older siblings.

Scaramella, L. V., Conger, R. D., Simons, R. L., & Whitbeck, L. B. (1998). Predicting risk for pregnancy by late adolescence: A social contextual perspective. *Developmental Psychology, 34*, 1233–1245.

An intensive longitudinal study of 368 adolescents from the 7th to 12th grades, with their parents and siblings. High parental warmth and involvement in 7th grade were found to be negatively related to deviant peer associations, educational connectedness, and adolescent risk-taking behavior, which were significant predictors of pregnancy status by the 12th grade. Academic competence was found to have a direct inverse relationship to adolescent pregnancy.

References

Alan Guttmacher Institute (AGI) (1986). Analysis of S. K. Henshaw, Teenage Pregnancy Statistics, New York: AGI, May, 1996; and J. D. Forest, Proportion of U.S. Women Ever Pregnant Before Age 20, New York, AGI, 1986, unpublished.

Alan Guttmacher Institute (AGI) (1998). *Sex and America's teenagers.* NewYork: AGI.

Alan Guttmacher Institute (AGI) (1998). *Into a New World.* New York: AGI.

Alan Guttmacher Institute (AGI) (1999). *Analyses of data from the 1988 and 1995 National survey of family growth.* New York: AGI.

Allen, L., & Mitchell, C. (1998). Racial and ethnic differences in patterns of problematic and adaptive development: An epidemiological review. In V. C. McLoyd, L. Steinberg, et al. (Eds.), *Studying minority adolescents: Conceptual, methodological, and theoretical issues* (pp. 29–54). Mahwah, NJ: Erlbaum.

Aloise-Young, P. A., Graham, J. W., & Hansen, W. B. (1994). Peer influence on smoking initiation during early adolescence: A comparison of group members and group outsiders. *Journal of Applied Psychology, 79*, 281–287.

Bachrach, C. A. (1986). Adoption plans, adopted children, and adoptive mothers. *Journal of Marriage and the Family, 48*, 243–254.

Bachrach, C. A., Stolley, K. S., & London, K. A. (1992). Relinquishment of premarital births: Evidence from national survey data. *Family Planning Perspective, 24*, 27–48.

Bachu, A. (1999). *Trends in premarital childbearing: 1930 to 1994.* Current Population Reports, Series P-23, No. 197.

Barber, B. K. (1996). Parental psychological control: Revisiting a neglected construct. *Child Development, 67*, 3296–3319.

Bearman, P., & Brückner, H. (1999). *Power in numbers: Peer effects on adolescent girls' sexual debut and pregnancy.* Washington, DC: National Campaign to Prevent Teen Pregnancy.

Benda, B. B., & DiBlasio, F. A. (1991). Comparison of four theories of adolescent sexual exploration. *Deviant Behavior, 12*(3), 235–257.

Bennett, N. G., Bloom, D. E., & Miller, C. K. (1995). The influence of nonmarital childbearing on the formation of first marriages. *Demography, 32*, 47–62.

Billy, J. O., Brewster, K. L., & Grady, W. R. (1994). Contextual effects on the sexual behavior of adolescent women. *Journal of Marriage and the Family, 56*(5), 387–404.

Brewster, K. L. (1994a). Neighborhood context and the transition to sexual activity among young black women. *Demography, 31*, 603–614.

Brewster, K. L. (1994b). Race differences in sexual activity among adolescent women: The role of neighborhood characteristics. *American Sociological Review, 59*(6), 408–424.

Brewster, K. L., Billy, J. O., & Grady, W. R. (1993). Social context and adolescent behavior: The impact of community on the transition to sexual activity. *Social Forces, 71*(3), 713–740.

Brien, M. J., & Willis, R. J. (1997). Costs and consequences for the fathers. In R. A. Maynard (Ed.), *Kids having kids: Economic costs and social consequences of teen pregnancy* (pp. 95–143). Washington, DC: Urban Institute Press.

Brown, B. B. (1982). The extent and effects of peer pressure among high school students: A retrospective analysis. *Journal of Youth and Adolescence, 11*, 121–133.

Brown, B. B., & Theobald, W. (1999). How peers matter: A research synthesis of peer influences on adolescent pregnancy. In *Peer potential: Making the most of how teens influence each other* (n.p.). Washington, DC: National Campaign to Prevent Teen Pregnancy.

Browning, C., & Laumann, E. (1997). Sexual contact between children and adults: A life course perspective. *American Sociological Review, 62*, 540–560.

Buchanan, M., & Robbins C. (1990). Early adult psychological consequences for males of adolescent pregnancy and its resolution. *Journal of Youth and Adolescence, 19*, 413–424.

Burton, L. M. (1990). Teenage pregnancy as an alternative life-course strategy in multigenerational black families. *Human Nature, 1*, 123–143.

Chandra, A., Abma, J., Maza, P., & Bachrach, C. (1999). *Adoption, adoption seeking, and relinquishment for adoption in the United States.* Advance data from vital and health statistics, No. 306. Hyattsville, MD: National Center for Health Statistics.

Children Now and the Kaiser Family Foundation (1996). *Sex, kids, and the family hour: A three-part study of sexual content on television.* A special report from Children Now and the Kaiser Family Foundation, Oakland, CA: Kaiser Foundation.

Coley, R. L., & Chase-Lansdale, P. L. (1998). Adolescent pregnancy and parenthood: Recent evidence and future directions. *American Psychologist, 53*(2), 152–166.

Cox, J., Emans, S. J., & Bithoney, W. (1993). Sisters of teen mothers: Increased risk for adolescent pregnancy. *Adolescent and Pediatric Gynecology, 6*, 138–142.

Coyle, K. K., Basen-Enquist, K. M., Kirby, D. B., Parcel, G. S., Banspach, S. W., Harrist, R. B., Baumler, E. R., & Weil, M. L. (1999). Short-term impact safer choices: A multi-component school-based HIV, other STD, and pregnancy prevention program. *Journal of School Health, 69*(5), 181–188.

Custer, M. (1993). Adoption as an option for unmarried pregnant teens. *Adolescence, 28*, 891–902.

Darroch, J. E., & Landry, D. J. (1999). Age differences between sexual partners in the United States. *Family Planning Perspectives, 31*, 160.

Day, J. C. (1996). Population projections of the United States by age, sex, race, and Hispanic origin: 1995 to 2050. *Current Population Reports, 25*, 1130.

De Gaston, J. F., Weed, S., & Jensen, L. (1996). Understanding gender differences in adolescent sexuality. *Adolescence, 31*, 217–231.

Dishion, T. J., Capaldi, D., Spracklen, K. M., & Li, F. (1995). Peer ecology of male adolescent drug use. *Development and Psychopathology, 7*, 803–824.

Dolcini, M. M. (1997, August). Young adolescent crowds and risk behavior: A longitudinal analysis. Paper presented at the annual meeting of the American Psychological Association, Chicago.

Donnelly, B. W., & Voydanoff, P. (1991). Factors associated with releasing for adoption among adolescent mothers. *Family Relations, 40*, 404–410.

Donovan, P. (1995). *Politics of blame – family planning and the poor.* New York: Alan Guttmacher Institute.

Dorius, G., & Barber, B. (1998). Parental support and control and the onset of sexual intercourse. Unpublished manuscript, Department of Sociology, Brigham Young University, Provo, UT.

Dorius, G., Heaton, T. B., & Steffen, P. (1993). Adolescent life events and their association with the onset of sexual intercourse. *Youth and Society, 25*, 3–23.

Dworkin, R. J., Harding, J. T., & Schreiber, N. B. (1993). Parenting or placing: Decision making by pregnant teens. *Youth & Society, 25*, 75–92.

East, P. L. (1996a). Do adolescent pregnancy and childbearing affect younger siblings? *Family Planning Perspectives, 28*(4), 148–153.

East, P. L. (1996b). The younger sisters of childbearing adolescents: Their attitudes, expectations, and behaviors. *Child Development, 67*, 267–282.

East, P. L. (1998). Racial and ethnic differences in girls' sexual, marital, and birth expectations. *Journal of Marriage and the Family, 60*, 150–162.

East, P. L., & Kiernan, E. A. (2001). Risks among youths who have multiple sisters who were adolescent parents. *Family Planning Perspectives, 33*(2), 75–80.

Eder, D. (1993). "Go get ya a French!": Romantic and sexual teasing among adolescent girls. In D. Tannen (Ed.), *Gender and conversational interaction* (pp. 17–31). New York: Oxford University Press.

Eisen, M., & Zellman, G. L. (1983). Factors predicting pregnancy resolution decision satisfaction of unmarried adolescents. *Journal of Genetic Psychology, 145*, 231–239.

Ennett, S. T., & Bauman, K. E. (1994). The contribution of influence and selection to adolescent peer group homogeneity: The case of adolescent cigarette smoking. *Journal of Personality and Social Psychology, 67*, 653–663.

Farrell, A. D., & White, K. S. (1998). Peer influences and drug use among urban adolescents: Family structure and parent–adolescent relationships as protective factors. *Journal of Consulting and Clinical Psychology, 66*, 248–258.

Feldman, S., & Brown, N. (1993). Family influences on adolescent male sexuality: the mediational role of self-restraint. *Social Development, 2*(1), 15–35.

Fergusson, D. M., & Woodward, L. J. (2000). Teenage pregnancy and female educational under-achievement: A prospective study of a New Zealand birth cohort. *Journal of Marriage and the Family, 62*(1), 147–161.

Flannery, D. J., Rowe, D. C., & Gulley, B. L. (1993). Impact of pubertal status, timing, and age on adolescent sexual experience and delinquency. *Journal of Adolescent Research, 8*(1), 21–40.

Fox, R. A., Baisch, M. J., Goldberg, B. D., & Hochmuth, M. C. (1987). Parenting attitudes of pregnant adolescents. *Psychological Reports, 61*, 403–406.

Furstenberg, F. F., & Brooks-Gunn, J. (1986). Teenage childbearing: causes, consequences and remedies. In Linda N. Aiken & David M. Mechanic (Eds.), *Applications of social science to clinical medicine and health policy* (pp. 316–317). New Brunswick, NJ: Rutgers University Press.

Furstenberg, F. F., Morgan, P. S., Moore, K. A., and Peterson, J. L. (1987). Race differences in the timing of adolescent intercourse. *American Sociological Review, 52*, 511–518.

Garn, S. M. (1980). Continuities and change in maturational timing. In O. G. Brim & J. Kagan (Eds.), *Constancy and change in human development* (pp. 113–162). Cambridge, MA: Harvard University Press.

Geronimus, A. T. (1992). The weathering hypothesis and the health of African American women and infants: Evidence and speculations. *Ethnicity and Disease, 2*, 207–221.

Geronimus, A. T., & Korenman, S. (1992). The socioeconomic consequences of teenage childbearing reconsidered. *Quarterly Journal of Economics, 107*, 1187–1214.

Gray, M. R., & Steinberg, L. (1999). Unpacking authoritative parenting: Reassessing a multi-dimensional construct. *Journal of Marriage and the Family, 61*, 574–587.

Grogger, J. (1997). Incarceration-related costs of early childbearing. In R. A. Maynard (Ed.), *Kids having kids: Economic costs and social consequences of teen pregnancy* (pp. 231–256). Washington, DC: Urban Institute Press.

Halpern, C, T., Udry, J. R., Campbell, B., & Suchindran, C. (1993). Testosterone and pubertal development as predictors of sexual activity: A panel analysis of adolescent males. *Psychosomatic Medicine, 55*, 436–447.

Haveman, R., Wolfe, B., & Peterson, E. (1997). Children of early childbearers as young adults. In R. Maynard (Ed.), *Kids having kids: Economic costs and social consequences of teen pregnancy* (pp. 257–284). Washington, DC: Urban Institute Press.

Henshaw, S. K. (1998). Unintended pregnancy in the United States, *Family Planning Perspectives, 30*(1), 24–29.

Henshaw, S. K. (2001). *U.S. Teenage pregnancy statistics with comparative statistics for women aged 20–24.* New York: Alan Guttmacher Institute.

Hirschi, T. (1969). *Causes of delinquency.* Berkeley: University of California Press.

Hoffman, S. D. (1998). Teenage childbearing is not so bad after all . . . Or is it? A review of the new literature. *Family Planning Perspectives, 30*, 236–243.

Hogan, D. P., Sun, R., & Cornwell, G. T. (2000). Sexual and fertility behaviors of American females aged 15–19 years: 1985, 1990, and 1995. *American Journal of Public Health, 90*(9), 1421–1425.

Hotz, V. J., McElroy, S. W., & Sanders, S. G. (1997). The impacts of teenage childbearing on the mothers and the consequences of those impacts for government. In R. Maynard (Ed.), *Kids having kids: Economic costs and social consequences of teen pregnancy.* Washington, DC: Urban Institute Press, 1997.

Jaccard, J., Dittus, P. J., & Gordon, V. V. (1996). Maternal correlates of adolescent sexual and contraceptive behavior. *Family Planning Perspectives, 28*, 159–165, 185.

Jaccard, J., Dittus, P. J., & Gordon, V. V. (1998). Parent–adolescent congruency in reports of adolescent sexual behavior and in communication about sexual behavior. *Child Development, 69*(1), 247–261.

Jaccard, J., Dittus, P. J., & Litardo, H. A. (1999). Parent–adolescent communication about sex and birth control: Implications for parent-based interventions to reduce unintended adolescent pregnancy. In L. J. Severy, W. B. Miller, & L. Sever (Eds.), *Advances in population: Psychological perspectives, Vol. III* (n.p.). London: Jessica Kingsley.

Jemmott, J. B., Jemmott, L. S., & Fong, G. T. (1998). Abstinence and safer sex: A randomized trial of HIV sexual risk-reduction interventions for young African-American adolescents. *Journal of the American Medical Association, 279* (19), 1529–1536.

Jones, E. F., & Forest, J. D. (1992). Under reporting of abortion in surveys of U.S. women: 1976 to 1988. *Demography, 29,* 113–126.

Kalmuss, D., Namerow, P. B., & Cushman, L. F. (1991). Adoption versus parenting among young pregnant women. *Family Planning Perspectives, 23,* 17–23.

Kasen, S., Cohen, P., & Brook, J. S. (1998). Adolescent school experiences and dropout, adolescent pregnancy, and young adult deviant behavior. *Journal of Adolescent Research, 13*(1), 49–72.

Kaufmann, R. B., Spitz, A. M., Strauss, L. T., Morris, L., Santelli, J. S., Koonin, L. M., & Marks, J. S. (1998). The decline in U.S. teen pregnancy rates, 1990–1995. *Pediatrics, 102,* 1141–1147.

Kinney, D. A. (1993). From nerds to normals: The recovery of identity among adolescents from middle school to high school. *Sociology of Education, 66,* 21–40.

Kinsman, S. B., Romer, D., Furstenberg, F. F., & Schwarz, D. F. (1998). Early sexual initiation: The role of peer norms. *Pediatrics, 102,* 1185–1192.

Kirby, D. (2001). *Emerging Answers: Research Findings on Programs to Reduce Teen Pregnancy* (Summary). Washington, DC: National Campaign to Prevent Teen Pregnancy.

Ku, L., Sonenstein, F. L., & Pleck, J. H. (1993). Neighborhood, family, and work: Influences on the premarital behaviors of adolescent males. *Social Forces, 72*(2), 479–503.

Lammers, C., Ireland, M., Resnick, M., & Blum, R. (2000). Influences on adolescents' decision to postpone onset of sexual intercourse: A survival analysis of virginity among youths aged 13 to 18 years. *Journal of Adolescent Health, 26*(1), 42–48.

Landry D. J., & Forrest, J. D. (1995). How old are U.S. fathers? *Family Planning Perspectives, 27,* 159–161, 165.

Lauritsen, J. L. (1994). Explaining race and gender differences in adolescent sexual behavior. *Social Forces, 72*(3), 859–884.

Lightfoot, C. (1997). *The culture of adolescent risk-taking.* New York: Guilford.

Lindberg, L. D., & Sonenstein, F. L. (1997). Age differences between minors who give birth and their adult partners. *Family Planning Perspectives, 29,* 61–66.

Low, J. M., Moely, B. E., & Willis, A. S. (1989). The effects of perceived parental preferences and vocational goals on adoption decisions: Unmarried pregnant adolescents. *Youth and Society, 20,* 342–354.

Luster, T., & Small, S. A. (1997). Sexual abuse history and number of sex partners among female adolescents. *Family Planning Perspectives, 29*(5), 204–211.

Males, M., & Chew, K. S. Y. (1996). The ages of fathers in California adolescent births, 1993. *American Journal of Public Health, 86,* 565–568.

Maynard, R. A. (1996). *Kids having kids: A Robin Hood Foundation special report on the costs of adolescent childbearing.* New York: Robin Hood Foundation.

Maynard, R. A. (1997). The costs of adolescent childbearing. In R. A. Maynard (Ed.), *Kids having kids: Economic costs and social consequences of teen pregnancy* (pp. 285–337). Washington, DC: Urban Institute Press.

Miller, B. C. (1995). Risk factors for adolescent nonmarital childbearing. In *Report to Congress on out-of-wedlock childbearing* (pp. 217–227). Department of Health and Human Services. Washington, DC: US Government Printing Office (DHHS Pub. No. [PHS] 95–1257).

Miller, B. C., Benson, B., & Galbraith, K. A. (2001). Family relationships and adolescent pregnancy risk: A research synthesis. *Developmental Review, 21*(1), 1–38.

Miller, B. C., & Coyl, D. D. (2000). Adolescent pregnancy and childbearing in relation to infant adoption in the United States. *Adoption Quarterly, 4*(1), 3–25.

Miller, B. C., & Heaton, T. B. (1991). Age at first sexual intercourse and the timing of marriage and childbirth. *Journal of Marriage and the Family, 53,* 719.

Miller, B. C., Norton, M. C., Curtis, T., Hill, E. J., Schvaneveldt, P., & Young, M. H. (1997). The timing of sexual intercourse among adolescents: Family, peer, and other antecedents. *Youth and Society, 29,* 54–83.

Miller, B. C., Norton, M. C., Fan, I., & Christopherson, C. R. (1998). Pubertal development, parental communication, and sexual values in relation to adolescent sexual behavior. *Journal of Early Adolescence, 18,* 27–52.

Miller, W. B., Pasta, D. J., MacMurray, J., Chiu, C., Wu, H., & Comings, D. E. (1999). Dopamine receptors are associated with age of first sexual intercourse. *Journal of Biosocial Science, 31,* 43–54.

Moore, K. A., Manlove, J., Terry-Humen, E., Williams, S., Papillo, A. R., & Scarpa, J. (2001). *Facts at a glance.* Washington, DC: Child Trends.

Moore, K. A., Miller, B. C., Glei, D., & Morrison, D. R. (1995). *Adolescent sex, contraception, and childbearing. A review of recent research.* Washington, DC: Child Trends.

Moore, K. A., Morrison, D. R., & Greene, A. D. (1997). Effects on the children born to adolescent mothers. In R. A. Maynard (Ed.), *Kids having kids: Economic costs and social consequences of teen pregnancy* (pp. 145–180). Washington, DC: Urban Institute Press.

Moore, K. A., Papillo, A. R., Williams, S., Jager, J., & Jones, F. (1999). *Teen birthrates for 1998: Facts at a glance.* Washington, DC: Child Trends.

Mott, F. L., Fondell, M. M., Hu, P. N., Kowaleski-Jones, L., & Menaghan, E. G. (1996). The determinants of first sex by age 14 in a high-risk adolescent population. *Family Planning Perspectives, 28*(1), 13–18.

Murry, V. M. (1995). An ecological analysis of pregnancy resolution decisions among African American and Hispanic adolescent females. *Youth and Society, 26,* 325–350.

Namerow, P. B., Kalmuss, D. S., & Cushman, L. F. (1993). The determinants of young women's pregnancy-resolution choices. *Journal of Research on Adolescence, 3,* 193–215.

Nathanson, C. A. (1991). *Dangerous passage: The social control of sexuality in women's adolescence.* Philadelphia, PA: Temple University Press.

National Campaign to Prevent Teen Pregnancy (NCPTA) (1999). *What about the teens? Research on what teens say about pregnancy: A focus group report.* Washington, DC: NCPTA.

National Center for Health Statistics (1994). Advance report on final natality statistics, 1992. *Monthly Vital Statistics Report, 43*(5) (Suppl.).

Newcomer, S. F., & Udry, J. R. (1984). Parental marital status effects on adolescent sexual behavior. *Journal of Marriage and the Family, 49,* 235–240.

Olsen, R. J., & Farkas, G. (1989). Endogenous covariates in duration models and the effect of adolescent childbearing on schooling. *Journal of Human Resources, 19,* 32–41.

Ortiz, C. G., & Nuttall, E. V. (1987). Adolescent pregnancy: Effects of family support, education, and religion on the decision to carry or terminate among Puerto Rican teenagers. *Adolescence, 22,* 897–917.

Piccinino, L. J., & Mosher, W. D. (1998). Trends in contraceptive use in the United States: 1982–1995. *Family Planning Perspectives, 30,* 4–10.

Ramirez-Valles, J., Zimmerman, M. A., & Newcomb, M. D. (1998). Sexual risk behavior among youth: Modeling the influence of prosocial activities and socioeconomic factors. *Journal of Health and Social Behavior, 39,* 237–253.

Rodgers, J. L., Rowe, D. C., & Buster, M. (1999). Social contagion, adolescent sexual behavior, and pregnancy: A nonlinear dynamic EMOSA model. *Developmental Psychology, 34*(5), 1096–1113.

Rodgers, K. B. (1999). Parenting processes related to sexual risk-taking behaviors of adolescent males and females. *Journal of Marriage and the Family, 61,* 99–109.

Sanchez, M. (1997). Families of Mexican origin. In M. K. DeGenova (Ed.), *Families in* cultural context: Strengths and challenges in diversity (pp. 61–84). Mountain View, CA: Mayfield.

Sawhill, I., & Flanigan, C. (2000). *What's behind the good news: Why the rates of teen childbirth have declined.* Washington, DC: National Campaign to Prevent Teen Pregnancy.

Scaramella, L. V., Conger, R. D., Simons, R. L., & Whitbeck, L. B. (1998). Predicting risk for pregnancy by late adolescence: A social contextual perspective. *Developmental Psychology, 34,* 1233–1245.

Singh, S., & Darroch, J. E. (2000). Adolescent pregnancy and childbearing: levels and trends in developed countries. *Family Planning Perspectives, 32,* 14–23.

Small, S. A., & Luster, T. (1994). Adolescent sexual activity: An ecological, risk-factor approach. *Journal of Marriage and the Family, 56*(2), 181–192.

Sonenstein, F., Ku, L., Lindberg, L., Turner, C., & Pleck, J. (1998). Changes in sexual behavior and condom use among teenaged males: 1988 to 1995. *American Journal of Public Health, 88,* 956–959.

South, S. J., & Baumer, E. P. (2000). Deciphering community and race effects on adolescent pre-marital childbearing. *Social Forces, 78*(4), 1379–1407.

Stevans, L. K., Register, C. A., & Sessions, D. N. (1992). The abortion decision: A qualitative choice approach. *Social Indicators Research, 27,* 327–344.

St. Lawrence, J. S. (1994). *Becoming a responsible teen: An HIV risk reduction intervention for African-American adolescents.* Jackson, MS: Jackson State University.

Stouthamer-Loeber, M., & Wei, E. H. (1998). The precursors of young fatherhood and its direct effect on delinquency of teenage males. *Journal of Adolescent Health, 22,* 56–65.

Thornberry, T. P., Smith, C. A., & Howard, G. J. (1997). Risk factors for teenage fatherhood. *Journal of Marriage and the Family, 59*(8), 505–522.

Thornberry, T. P., Wei, E. H., Stouthamer-Loeber, M., & Van Dyke, J. (2000). Teenage father-hood and delinquent behavior. *Juvenile Justice Bulletin,* January, Washington, DC: Office of Juvenile Justice and Delinquency Prevention.

Thornton, A., & Camburn, D. (1987). The influence of the family on premarital sexual attitudes and behavior. *Demography, 24*(3), 323–340.

Treboux, D., & Busch-Rossnagel, N. A. (1995). Age differences in parent and peer influences on female's sexual behavior. *Journal of Research on Adolescence, 5,* 469–487.

Udry, J. R. (1988). Biological predispositions and social control in adolescent sexual behavior. *American Sociological Review, 53,* 709–722.

Udry, J. R., Talbert, L. B., & Morris, N. M. (1986). Biosocial foundations for adolescent female sexuality. *Demography, 23*(2), 217–230.

Upchurch, D., & McCarthy, J. (1990). The timing of first birth and high school completion. *American Sociological Review, 55,* 218–227.

Upchurch, D. M., Aneshensel, C. S., Sucoff, C. A., & Levy-Storms, L. (1999). Neighborhood and family contexts of adolescent sexual activity. *Journal of Marriage and the Family, 61,* 920–933.

Ventura, S. J., Martin, J. A., Curtin, S. C., & Mathews, T. J. (1999a). *Births: Final Data for 1997.* National Vital Statistics System, Hyattsville, MD: National Center for Health Statistics.

Ventura, S. J., Mosher, W. D., Curtin, S. C., Abma, J. C., & Henshaw, S. (1999b). *Highlights of trends in pregnancies and pregnancy rates by outcome: Estimates for the United States, 1976–1996.* National Vital Statistics System, Hyattsville, MD: National Center for Health Statistics.

Vinovskis, M. A. (1988). *An "epidemic" of adolescent pregnancy?: Some historical and policy considerations.* New York: Oxford University Press.

Warr, M. (1993). Parents, peers, and delinquency. *Social Forces, 72,* 247–264.

Warren, K. C., & Johnson, R. W. (1989). Family environment, affect, ambivalence and decisions about unplanned adolescent pregnancy. *Adolescence, 24,* 505–522.

Weinstein, M., & Thornton, A. (1989). Mother–child relations and adolescent sexual attitudes and behaviors. *Demography, 26*(4), 563–577.

Whitbeck, L., Hoyt, D., Miller, M., & Kao, M. (1992). Parental support, depressed affect, and sexual experiences among adolescents. *Youth and Society, 24*(2), 166–177.

Whitbeck, L. B., Simons, R. M., & Kao, M. (1994). The effects of divorced mothers' dating behaviors and sexual attitudes on the sexual attitudes and behaviors of their adolescent children. *Journal of Marriage and the Family, 56*(3), 615–621.

Wolfe, B., & Perozek, M. (1997). Teen children's health and health care use. In R. A. Maynard (Ed.), *Kids having kids: Economic costs and social consequences of teen pregnancy* (pp. 181–203). Washington, DC: Urban Institute Press.

Zabin, L. S., Smith, E. A., Hirsch, M. B., & Hardy, J. B. (1986). Ages of physical maturation and first intercourse in black teenage males and females. *Demography, 23*(4), 595–605.

CHAPTER TWENTY-ONE

Alcohol and Other Substance Use and Abuse

Michael Windle and Rebecca C. Windle

Introduction

Substance use is pervasive among youth in many cultures and countries around the world. Although some level of substance use (e.g., alcohol use) may be condoned under certain circumstances (e.g., religious holidays), for the most part, moral and legal prohibitions against teen substance use exist in most countries. An important justification for these prohibitions is that substance use, especially at heavier levels and across long periods of time, is strongly associated with morbidity and mortality. For example, the short-term complications associated with cigarette smoking among teens include increased respiratory tract symptoms and infections, changes in pulmonary functioning, worsening of asthma, and declines in physical fitness (e.g., Pérez-Stable & Fuentes-Afflick, 1998); longer-term consequences include the development of life-threatening illnesses, such as cancer and cardiovascular disease (e.g., Britton, 1998). As a second example, substance abuse, especially in combination with depressive symptoms, represents a particularly serious risk factor for suicide attempts and completions (e.g., Windle & Windle, 1997). Yet a third example of great public concern is the relationship between the use of substances (often alcohol), driving, and fatal automobile crashes. Recent US statistics indicated that 33 percent of high school seniors reported either driving while drinking or riding with someone who had been drinking during the last two weeks, and 20 percent reported these behaviors after heavy drinking (i.e., five or more drinks in a row) (O'Malley & Johnston, 1999).

In addition to these concerns with adolescent substance use for morbidity and mortality, there are also concerns with the impact of adolescent substance use for human development (e.g., Baumrind & Moselle, 1985; Windle & Davies, 1999). For example, Baumrind and Moselle (1985) suggested that substance use may impair the adaptive capacities of adolescents to confront age-appropriate, normative developmental life tasks, such as developing a personal identity, forming constructive peer relationships, and renegotiating balances between autonomy and relatedness in the family. The failure to adequately address and resolve these age-appropriate life tasks may delay the development of optimal personal, cognitive, and social skills that may impact negatively subsequent transitions in adolescence and young adulthood.

In recent years, two foci of substance use research with adolescents have been to study the developmental processes that underlie the initiation and escalation of substance-use behavior, and to develop preventive interventions that interrupt these processes, thereby preventing or delaying teens' use of substances. In this chapter, we focus primarily on the first of these, though we provide some information about, and key references to, the extensive literature pertinent to adolescent substance interventions. We begin the next section with a description of epidemiological findings on adolescent substance use, and then provide a conceptual orientation to guide the investigation of adolescent substance use. Then, a brief description of a survey study that the authors are conducting is presented. Next, a sampling of empirical studies focusing on adolescent substance use is described, with specific reference to adolescent alcohol typologies, followed by information on the predictors of distinct phases of substance use (e.g., initiation, escalation, termination). This section is followed by a succinct description of substance-use prevention programs. Finally, we conclude with a summary section. It is important to observe that the adolescent substance-use literature is large and that "due justice" could not be done in this chapter to cover the extensive literatures on smoking, alcohol, and other substance use; we have attempted to provide a broad yet cohesive overview, and to identify some key research findings.

Trends in the Epidemiology of Adolescent Substance Use

The prevalence data presented in this section are based primarily on recent findings from the US Monitoring the Future Studies (MFS; Johnston, O'Malley, & Bachman, 1999, 2000). The MFS have collected substance-use data (e.g., lifetime, past year, and current use; binge drinking) annually on nationally representative samples of US high school seniors since 1975. In 1991, the MFS data collection was expanded to include 8th- and 10th-grade students. Trend data from the MFS on cigarette smoking, heavy alcohol consumption, and marijuana use for US teens is described below. (Due to their lower prevalence, trend data for other illicit drug use, e.g., heroin, cocaine, and amphetamines, are not covered in this section but are available in other publications such as Johnston, O'Malley, & Bachman, 1999, 2000.)

Rates of lifetime cigarette smoking among adolescents remained fairly stable across the 1990s. In 1991, the lifetime prevalence of smoking among 8th-, 10th-, and 12th-graders was 44.0 percent, 55.1 percent, and 63.1 percent, respectively; in 1999, these rates were 44.1 percent, 57.6 percent, and 64.6 percent (Johnston, O'Malley, & Bachman, 2000). Although the lifetime prevalence of cigarette smoking has fluctuated little since the 1990s, the percentage of adolescents who reported smoking during the past year, the past month, smoking more frequently (e.g., daily smoking), and heavier smoking (e.g., more than half a pack per day) has gradually increased, and these upward trends have been seen in both younger and older adolescents. In 1999, nearly one in four high school seniors (23.1 percent) reported daily smoking (Johnston, O'Malley, & Bachman, 2000).

Alcohol use is a statistically normative behavior among older adolescents, with 80 percent of seniors reporting lifetime consumption of alcohol, approximately 75 percent reporting consumption in the past year, and 51 percent reporting consumption in the past month (Johnston, O'Malley, & Bachman, 2000). As with cigarette smoking, the lifetime prevalence of alcohol use among US teens has remained fairly stable in recent years. However, the number of adolescents who reported heavier, more problematic alcohol use (e.g., being drunk, binge drinking) has been increasing gradually. While any level of alcohol use among teens is of concern, binge drinking, or heavy episodic drinking, is of particular concern. (Binge drinking is typically defined as the consumption of five or more drinks in a row within the past two weeks.) In 1999, one-third of high school seniors reported being drunk during the past month, and one in four 10th-graders reported binge-drinking behaviors (Johnston, O'Malley, & Bachman, 2000).

Although marijuana is an illicit substance in the United States, the trends in use across the decade of the 1990s was toward increasing numbers of 8th-, 10th-, and 12th-graders using marijuana and increasing frequency of use (Johnston, O'Malley, & Bachman, 2000). For example, in 1991, 10.2 percent of 8th-graders reported lifetime use of marijuana; in 1999, this figure had more than doubled to 22.0 percent. And, from 1991 to 1999, the percentage of 8th-graders who reported the use of marijuana in the past month tripled, from 3.2 percent to 9.7 percent (Johnston, O'Malley, & Bachman, 2000). Such trends as increasing levels of licit and illicit substance use, more frequent and heavier levels of use, and increasing use among younger adolescents is not unique to teens in the United States, but rather has been reported in Canada, Australia, and Western European countries (Bauman & Phongsavan, 1999; Fombonne, 1998).

Among adolescents, licit and illicit substance use varies by a number of important demographic variables, including gender, age, and race/ethnicity. In general, boys relative to girls are more likely to use substances, to use them more frequently and at higher levels of consumption, and to experience more substance-related problems (e.g., Barnes & Welte, 1986). However, gender differences in substance-use behaviors become more pronounced among older adolescents, as there are fewer gender differences in substance use among younger teens (Johnston et al., 1999). For instance, binge drinking among 8th-grade males and females occurs at a rate of 14.4 percent and 12.7 percent, respectively; in contrast, among high school seniors, 40 percent of males report binge drinking while 24 percent of females report this heavier level of alcohol use. A notable exception to the finding of gender differences among older teens is the use of cigarettes. That is, the prevalence of current cigarette use, daily use, and heavy use is highly similar for older male and female adolescents in the United States. However, Bauman and Phongsavan (1999) reported that a higher percentage of adolescent girls in Australia, Canada, the UK, and other Western European countries reported current smoking, relative to their male counterparts, but that many more adolescent males smoked in Asian countries compared to females. Clearly, cultural norms are a contributing factor to levels of smoking behavior among teens.

An additional demographic variable that consistently predicts patterns of substance use among teens is age (e.g., Barnes & Welte, 1986). Older adolescents relative to younger adolescents are more likely to use substances, to use them more frequently, and to consume them at heavier levels (Johnston, O'Malley, & Bachman, 1999). However, it is important to recognize that the age of substance-use initiation is decreasing for many substances. For example, the average age of first-time use of alcohol among US teens was 15.9 years in 1994, relative to 17.4 years in 1987; similarly, the average age of first-time use of marijuana was 16.3 years in 1994, relative to 17.8 years in 1987 (Office of National Drug Control Policy, 1997). In a longitudinal study investigating the developmental patterns of cigarette, alcohol, and marijuana use among teens, Duncan et al. (1995) found that the greatest increases in use across all three substances occurred between ages 13 and 14. These statistics are particularly troubling given that an earlier age of substance-use debut portends poorer long-term outcomes such as substance-related problems and substance disorders (Windle, 1999).

In relation to substance-use differences among racial and ethnic groups, African American teens report the lowest prevalence of licit and illicit substance use, and this is true for both younger and older adolescents. In contrast, a higher percentage of Hispanic 8th-graders report using substances relative to white 8th-graders. However, by 12th grade, these prevalence rates have reversed, with whites reporting the highest prevalence of substance use followed by Hispanics (Johnston, O'Malley, & Bachman, 2000). An exception to this general finding is that Hispanic students of all ages are the most likely to report some form of cocaine use relative to whites. Johnston, O'Malley, & Bachman (1999) have suggested that the cross-temporal shift from lower to higher rates of substance use among whites, and higher to lower rates among Hispanics, may be explained by a higher dropout rate among Hispanic students; thus, the representation of older Hispanic substance users in a national school-based survey is diminished as these youth disproportionately drop out of school.

While the percentage of adolescents using substances varies considerably across these three ethnic groups, the *patterns* or *trends* of substance use have generally moved in parallel (Johnston, O'Malley, & Bachman, 1999). For example, across a 20-year period (1977–97), whites had the highest percentage of 12th-graders reporting marijuana use in the past year, with an intermediate percentage of Hispanics reporting use, and with the lowest percentage of adolescents reporting use being African American teens. However, in terms of patterns or trends of marijuana use, these three ethnic groups have been highly similar, with all three groups showing decreases in use throughout the 1980s and an upturn in use beginning in the early 1990s. These findings suggest that broader factors (such as cultural norms, media messages, pricing, ease of availability) may influence national substance-use trends among different ethnic/racial groups in a similar manner.

A Conceptual Approach to the Investigation of Adolescent Substance Use

A number of conceptual models have been proposed to account for substance use and abuse among teens, including biogenetic and disposition models, socialization models, multivariate models, such as Problem Behavior Theory (PBT; Jessor & Jessor, 1977), and dynamic contextual models, such as a lifespan developmental psychopathology perspective (see Windle, 1999 for a review). The conceptual approach we have used to guide our research on the predictors, moderators, and mediating processes of adolescent internalizing and externalizing behaviors (including substance use) is a lifespan developmental psychopathology approach (Cicchetti & Rogosch, 1999; Windle & Davies, 1999). This developmental-conceptual approach focuses on risk and protective factors and processes that enhance or ameliorate adolescents' risk for adverse substance-use outcomes. It provides a multifaceted model specification that includes: (1) both distal and proximal etiologic factors that influence outcomes; (2) moderator variables that attenuate or exacerbate the relationship between dependent and independent variables; (3) mediator variables that help to explain the intervening risk and protective processes and mechanisms leading from antecedent variables to the outcomes of interest; (4) a recognition that such developmental processes occur as a function of ongoing, dynamic, bidirectional person–environment interactions that transpire within and are influenced by larger social contexts; (5) an appreciation that development occurs as a function of multiple experiences and events occurring across time, and that these experiences and events have a cumulative effect on later adaptation and functioning; and (6) a realization that there may be multiple developmental pathways leading to the same outcome (i.e., equifinality), or, conversely, that a single component or factor (e.g., family history of alcoholism) that is common across individuals will not inevitably result in a common outcome (e.g., alcohol disorder) but rather may result in varied outcomes among individuals (i.e., multifinality) (Cicchetti & Rogosch, 1999; Windle & Davies, 1999). In essence, a developmental process model attempts to map the ways in which constellations of factors coalesce into meaningful patterns (or organized behavioral regularities) across time to predict given outcomes.

Brief Description of the Middle Adolescent Vulnerability Study (MAVS)

In the following pages, we present empirical data related to patterns of initiation, escalation, and desistance of substance use within a community sample of adolescents. Findings from our longitudinal research project, entitled the Middle Adolescent Vulnerability Study (MAVS), are presented; for purposes of brevity, we have provided a brief description of the study participants and design below.

The MAVS is a prospective longitudinal study investigating the developmental trajectories of internalizing (e.g., depression) and externalizing (e.g., substance use and abuse, delinquency) problems among middle-aged adolescents. More specifically, we wanted to study the causal priority and time-ordered relations of vulnerability factors (e.g., temperament, family social support, peer relationships) to cross-temporal patterns of psychosocial dysfunction (e.g., development of alcohol use and alcohol-related problems). The design of the study involved four waves of data collection spaced six months apart with survey assessments in high school settings. The assessment protocol involved paper-and-pencil self-report forms, with data collection occurring in groups of 40–50 students during school hours. The first wave of data collection occurred with 10th-and 11th-grade students in the fall semester, with the second wave of collection occurring six months later in the spring, and two additional waves of collection in the fall and spring of the following school year, when students were in 11th and 12th grades. This short-term, intensive data collection design was chosen in order to optimize the identification of behavioral and emotional patterns of functioning during a period in the lifespan when adolescents are likely to initiate and increase their problem behaviors.

The MAVS subjects were 1218 predominantly white adolescents (97 percent) from three suburban high schools with approximately equal percentages of males and females (48 percent and 52 percent, respectively). The participation rate was 76 percent and participation required active informed consent from both the adolescent participant and their primary caregiver. In general, the students came from middle-income households (median family income was $40,000), and their mean age at the first assessment was 15.54 (±.66) years. Retention rates across the four waves of measurement were uniformly high (from 88 percent to 94 percent for contiguous waves of measurement), and 83.4 percent of the teens participated in all four waves of data collection.

Empirical Studies on Adolescent Substance Use

Substance-use behaviors among adolescents are highly variable. Teens differ with regard to the age at which they initiate substance use, the quantity and frequency of use, the number of substances used, the expression of substance-related problems, and the rate at which they develop and progress to different levels of substance use (e.g., Duncan et al., 1995). Some adolescents engage in initial experimentation that is quickly abandoned; other teens' use is characterized by infrequent and/or low-to-moderate levels of use across time; and some youth engage in more frequent and heavy use that may subsequently evolve into abusive levels with associated substance-related problems (e.g., missing school due to substance use, driving while under the influence of substances, engaging in physical aggression while using substances) and/or dependency symptoms.

In addition to the high variability of substance-use behaviors among teens, the developmental processes leading to different behaviors are also heterogeneous, and are characterized by different predictors and mediating mechanisms and by differing levels of risk (Clayton, 1992; Windle & Davies, 1999). For example, the socialization processes of role modeling, imitation, and social reinforcement, along with parent-to-child transmission of attitudes and beliefs about the positive effects of substance use, may be strong contributors to the initiation of tobacco or alcohol use for children. In contrast, adolescents characterized by a difficult temperament, low parental monitoring, and involvement with drug-using peer networks are at increased risk for the escalation of substance use, perhaps to abusive levels. Furthermore, the processes leading to specific substance-use behaviors (e.g., initiation, escalation, termination) may differ based on racial/ethnic and gender group differences.

An important implication of these observations is the need for greater specificity of substance-use interventions with teens at varying levels of risk (Windle & Windle, 1999). For example, universal, school-based prevention programs that teach youth the requisite skills to help them resist social pressures (e.g., from siblings, peers, the media) to use drugs may be relatively effective in preventing or delaying substance use among teens who come from lower-risk contexts. However, adolescents who, for example, are high on sensation seeking, come from neighborhoods with high levels of substance use and abuse, and experience low levels of parental involvement – and thus are at greater risk – may require more intensive interventions that are tailored to meet their particular needs in order to increase program efficacy (e.g., Harrington & Donohew, 1997; Thompson et al., 1997).

To further illustrate the variability in adolescent drinking practices, in the next section we describe an adolescent alcohol drinking typology that distinguishes alcohol-use behaviors among teens, and the differential correlates of these behaviors. Following this section, we describe empirical findings relevant to different substance-use behaviors among adolescents (e.g., initiation, escalation, desistance) and on the predictors and mediating processes of various substance-use outcomes. Finally, we will include a discussion of racial/ethnic group differences and, where available, gender differences.

An alcohol drinking typology: An illustration of the variability of alcohol use among teens

While there is a recognition that alcohol-use behaviors among adolescents are heterogeneous, recent studies have advanced the literature by focusing on the identification and validation of distinct alcohol-use profiles, or typologies, that incorporate multidimensional components of drinking behavior (e.g., quantity and frequency of drinking; heavy episodic, or binge, drinking; adverse alcohol-related consequences) (e.g., Colder & Chassin, 1999; Schulenberg et al., 1996; Windle, 1994, 1996). In attempting to identify constellations of drinking behaviors that characterize the alcohol consumption patterns of subgroups of adolescents, these studies have utilized a pattern-centered approach (e.g., Magnusson & Bergman, 1990). A major advantage of the pattern-centered approach is the identification of distinct subgroups based on specified parameters (e.g., different drinking behaviors) that, in turn, facilitates the study of distinct etiologic pathways and outcomes, and suggests alternative preventions and interventions for different alcohol-use subgroups (Windle, 1996).

Using data from the MAVS, Windle (1996) investigated the validity of an adolescent drinking typology by deriving five drinking groups based on variation in the quantity and frequency of alcohol consumption, heavy-drinking episodes, and alcohol-related adverse consequences. These groups represented a range of drinking behaviors, and included abstainers, light drinkers, moderate drinkers, heavy drinkers, and problem drinkers. The heavy and problem drinking groups consumed similarly high levels of alcohol, but unlike the heavy drinking group, the problem group also reported alcohol-related problems (e.g., missed school because of drinking, passed out from drinking). An important focus of the study was to compare heavy and problem drinkers on a number of important psychosocial variables (e.g., childhood externalizing problems, drinking disinhibitions, family social support), because differences between these groups may point to a need for more intensive and perhaps extensive interventions with problem-drinking youth to prevent long-term adverse outcomes (e.g., alcohol and other substance-related disorders).

The results indicated that boys were more highly represented among the heavy and problem drinking groups and girls somewhat more highly represented in the light and moderate drinking categories. Abstainers and light drinkers did not differ on most variables. Moderate drinkers differed significantly from light drinkers on several variables, with moderate drinkers reporting more disinhibitory behaviors while drinking (e.g., less likely to use a condom during sexual intercourse, more aggressive) and a higher percentage of friends who drink. Likewise, heavy drinkers differed significantly from moderate drinkers on a few variables (e.g., percentage of friends who use drugs). Importantly, problem drinkers were distinguished from heavy drinkers on a number of variables, with problem drinkers reporting higher levels of childhood externalizing behaviors (e.g., physical fighting, impaired peer relations, attentional deficits), more disinhibited drinking, the use of alcohol to cope with stressors, lower levels of perceived family support, higher levels of illicit drug use, and a higher percentage of friends who used illicit drugs. These findings applied to both boys and girls. In an earlier study using the same sample and alcohol typology, Windle (1994) found that problem drinkers relative to heavy drinkers had significantly higher levels of depressive symptoms (for boys only), higher levels of delinquent activity, and a greater probability of a family history of alcoholism.

Based on these findings, we suggested that adolescents who engaged in high levels of alcohol consumption *and* experienced alcohol-related problems had drinking trajectories that differed substantially from heavy drinking-only adolescents. The problem drinkers were more likely to come from alcoholic families, to manifest high levels of childhood behavior problems and current (adolescent) delinquent activities, to have lower family support and greater affiliation with drug-using peers, to use illicit substances in addition to alcohol, to use alcohol as a coping mechanism, and to experience more depressive symptoms. Thus, we argued that teens in the problem-drinking subgroup were characterized by a developmental trajectory in which problem behaviors emerged in childhood, continued through adolescence, and have a significant probability of carrying over into adulthood. Hence, the intervention needs of problem drinkers were substantially more extensive than those of light and moderate drinkers, and probably more extensive than those of heavy drinkers.

Predictors of substance-use behaviors

While demographic variables such as gender, age, and racial/ethnic group status are predictors of substance-use behaviors among teens, other factors in a number of domains (ranging from genetically to societally based) have been identified as concurrent and prospective predictors of adolescent substance use. These factors include individual factors (e.g., dispositional characteristics such as poor impulse control and sensation-seeking, early and persistent behavior problems, alcohol expectancies), peer influences (e.g., friends' substance use, peer norms favorable to substance use), family influences (e.g., family substance use and attitudes, parenting practices), and community-level factors (e.g., lack of enforcement of underage drinking laws) (for reviews, see Hawkins, Catalano, & Miller, 1992; Petraitis, Flay, & Miller, 1992; Windle, 1999). Below we focus on predictors of specific features, or aspects, of substance-use behaviors among adolescents, including the *initiation or onset* of substance use; *escalation in the frequency and/or quantity* of substance use and the occurrence of substance-related problems; and, although less-well researched, *decreases in or desistance from* substance use.

Initiation of substance use. The substances that adolescents are most likely to first experiment with are cigarettes and alcohol (e.g., Kandel, Yamaguchi, & Chen, 1992). A substantial body of research has focused on the predictors of the initiation or debut of substance use among adolescents, with findings suggesting that socialization processes play an important role in teens' initial use of alcohol or cigarettes (e.g., Duncan et al., 1995; Ellickson & Hays, 1991). Socialization models emphasize the role of socializing agents (such as parents, friends, and the media) as important influences on the adoption of substance use by adolescents. These models posit that the mechanisms by which, for example, parents and peers influence teens' substance use onset include both direct and indirect effects (Flay et al., 1994). An example of a direct socialization effect would be a significant other's modeling of a particular behavior (such as smoking or alcohol use) and the adolescent's imitation of that behavior. An example of an indirect socialization effect would be the transferral of normative standards, expectations, and beliefs about substance use to a child, with such cognitive factors, in turn, affecting substance-use intentions and behaviors. This socialization process model was supported by Flay et al. (1994) in their study of smoking onset. The influence of parents' and friends' cigarette use on the target adolescent's smoking onset was mediated through cognitive factors such as perceived friends' and parents' approval of smoking and the teen's smoking intentions. Additionally, friends', but not parents', smoking behavior directly contributed to smoking initiation among teens.

Duncan et al. (1995) investigated the developmental trends in adolescent substance use (i.e., cigarette, alcohol, and marijuana use) across time, and predictors of those trends. They found that adolescents who used higher levels of one substance tended to also use higher levels of the other substances; in addition, more rapid increases in the use of one substance was often accompanied by similar rapid increases in the use of other substances. Social factors predicted both initial substance use and cross-temporal developmental trends. For example, a higher level of family cohesion predicted lower levels of initial substance use but did not predict growth trajectories; in contrast, peer encouragement to use substances predicted higher levels of initial substance use and increases in the rate of substance use across time.

Catalano et al. (1992) compared the predictors of substance-use initiation (i.e., cigarettes, chewing tobacco, alcohol, marijuana) among a sample of African American, white, and Asian American 5th-grade boys and girls. Predictor variables were measured in the fall and substance-use initiation was measured in the spring of the following year. A composite score of the number of substances initiated by the spring assessment (i.e., tobacco, alcohol, and/or marijuana) was derived and used as the outcome variable in regression analyses. Among these 5th-grade students, whites had the highest rates of cigarette and alcohol-use initiation, followed by African Americans, and finally Asian Americans. Findings on predictors indicated that the groups differed on the *protective* factors that predicted a *lesser* variety of substances initiated by the follow-up assessment. For whites, significant predictors of a lesser variety of substance-use initiation included being female, proactive family management practices (e.g., parents know where child is when away from home, parents make family rules clear), parents not revoking privileges, absence of sibling drug use and delinquency, and parents' disapproval of the child's alcohol use. For Asian Americans, significant predictors were being female, absence of sibling drug use and delinquency, the child living with both parents, and parents' disapproval of the child's alcohol use. Finally, among African American adolescents, a strong attachment to parents and parents deciding which friends the child sees predicted a lesser variety in the substances initiated.

In general, the above findings indicate that social factors represent important risk and protective influences on adolescents' substance-use initiation. Positive interactional processes occurring within the family context (e.g., family cohesion, proactive family management practices, emotional attachment to parents, parents' disapproval of substance use) represent important protective factors that discourage or delay initiation of substance use among teens. Conversely, parents' and peers' modeling of substance-use behaviors and their positive attitudes regarding substance use predict substance initiation among youth. In discussing the influence of parents and peers on teens' substance-use initiation, it is important to recognize that most youth experience these debut events during the developmental period of early adolescence. This is a time in development when teens are still emotionally reliant on their parents, and have not yet confronted and negotiated the normative events of middle adolescence, such as identity formation, striving for autonomy, greater emotional bonding with peers, and forming romantic relationships. Thus, early adolescence – relative to midadolescence and beyond – is a period in the lifespan when parents still have greater influence than peers on their teen's behaviors, including substance-use behaviors.

In discussing social influences on substance use among teens, research consistently shows that white teens relative to African American teens initiate substance use earlier and use substances more frequently and at higher levels (e.g., Barnes & Welte, 1986; Ellickson & Morton, 1999; Johnston, O'Malley, & Bachman, 2000). Differential socialization processes may account for some of the variation in substance-use behaviors between these groups, and, more specifically, recent studies have identified differences in parental socialization practices among white and African American families. In a descriptive study comparing anti-tobacco socialization practices among white and African American parents of 12–18 year-old teens, Clark et al. (1999) found that African American parents differed significantly from white parents on a number of parenting practices that discouraged their adolescent's use of tobacco products. For example, significantly more African American parents set ground rules regarding children's tobacco use and relayed those rules to their children. Additionally, white parents were more likely to say that punishing children for trying tobacco was unlikely to keep them from trying it again. Finally, white parents were more likely to say that schools are more effective than parents in teaching children about the dangers of tobacco. These findings suggest that, in this sample, African American parents were more likely than white parents to believe that anti-tobacco socialization practices occurring within the home could be effective in preventing or delaying teens' use of tobacco products. While these findings are suggestive, research investigating racial and ethnic group differences in parental and family socialization practices related to adolescent substance use is in its nascent stages and provides a fertile domain for future research efforts.

Escalation of substance use. While social factors have been an important focus of research into the contributors of substance-use initiation, a broader range of factors (e.g., biogenetic, cognitive, psychological, social, academic, community, cultural) are believed to be influential determinants of escalating substance-use patterns (e.g., increases in quantity and frequency of use, binge drinking, substance-related problems, substance-use disorders). This is not to imply that socialization processes are not important contributors to escalating patterns of substance use; rather, it is to suggest that the developmental processes leading to increases in substance use and/or abusive levels of use are varied, multiple, and complex. For example, Colder and Chassin (1999) found that moderate alcohol use was related to socialization processes that supported the use of alcohol, whereas problem alcohol use was associated with high levels of family disruption and poor psychological functioning. Similarly, behavior-genetic findings have indicated that the drinking behaviors of parents, siblings, and friends influence alcohol initiation, but that differences in the frequency and quantity of alcohol use and of alcohol disorders are more strongly impacted by genetic than socialization factors (e.g., Rose, 1998).

In conjunction with the recognition that complex developmental processes underlie escalating patterns of substance use, researchers have begun to utilize integrated multivariate, conceptually driven models to test direct and indirect developmental pathways leading to increases in substance use among adolescents (e.g., Chassin et al., 1993; Cooper et al., 1995; Windle, 2000). These studies are important because they help us to model, and thus better understand, complex, interactional processes among multilevel variables (e.g., biological, psychological, social) that lead to substance-use and abuse outcomes among adolescents. In turn, empiricially validated, multivariate models of substance use and escalation provide researchers with important targets for effective secondary and tertiary interventions with substance-using adolescents.

Using structural equation modeling with the MAVS sample, Windle (2000) simultaneously tested three conceptual models (i.e., socialization, negative affect regulation, and biogenetic-dispositional models) of substance use and substance-related problems. Several findings are relevant to this discussion. First, developmental pathways were identified that supported socialization models of substance use. For instance, sibling substance use predicted the target adolescent's use of alcohol to cope with stressors; in turn, drinking to cope predicted both alcohol use and alcohol-related problems. From a socialization perspective, this finding suggests that adolescents may have observed their siblings using alcohol to cope with their own stressful life events; in turn, such observations may have contributed to the target adolescent's use of alcohol as a coping mechanism. An additional socialization pathway indicated that sibling substance use predicted the target adolescent's affiliation with substance-using peers which, in turn, predicted the adolescent's use of alcohol and illicit substances, and alcohol-related problems. One interpretation of this finding is that affiliation with an older sibling and his/her network of drug-using friends could increase the likelihood (e.g., via increased accessibility to substances and role-modeling processes) that the adolescent would use licit and illicit drugs and experience alcohol-related problems. These developmental pathways suggest a complex social-izing context in which the density of substance-using significant others creates an atmos-phere that encourages the adolescent's own use of alcohol and illicit substances and problem drinking behaviors. Integration into a context in which older siblings and peers are using substances at higher levels may be especially influential for middle-aged adolescents who tend to move away from parental influences and toward greater peer affiliation.

Second, the data supported the notion that adolescents in this study used alcohol to help regulate negative affect. That is, Windle (2000) found that stressful life events pre-dicted adolescents' use of alcohol for coping purposes (e.g., "I drink to forget my prob-lems"); in turn, coping motives for drinking predicted higher levels of alcohol-related problems. These findings, and others from the MAVS (Windle & Windle, 1996), suggest that adolescents who report higher levels of stressful life events may be consuming greater amounts of alcohol to help regulate the negative affect associated with their life stressors. In turn, they are also experiencing more alcohol-related problems which most probably contribute to their stressors and negative affect.

Third, the biogenetically based temperamental attributes of activity level and an approach orientation predicted associations with a denser network of substance-using peers; in turn, having substance-using peers predicted alcohol and illicit drug use and problems associated with alcohol use. Perhaps a higher activity level and a more gregari-ous, approach-oriented style are dispositional characteristics that contribute to adoles-cents' entrance into peer networks in which substance use is commonly practiced. In turn, integration into these networks encourages greater alcohol and illicit substance use, and a higher number of alcohol-related problems (e.g., missing school because of drinking, getting into trouble with the law while drinking).

In a study by Cooper et al. (1995), two developmental pathways contributed to alcohol use and alcohol problems among a sample of adolescents. The first pathway indicated that adolescents who were higher on the dispositional trait of sensation seeking and who expected alcohol to enhance their socioemotional functioning (e.g., "drinking alcohol makes me feel more friendly") reported drinking more frequently to enhance positive emotions and experiences. In turn, drinking to enhance positive emotions predicted high levels of alcohol use which, in turn, predicted more alcohol-related problems. A second pathway showed that teens who experienced higher levels of negative emotions, expected alcohol to alleviate their negative affect (e.g., "drinking alcohol helps me forget worries"), and engaged in avoidance coping (e.g., failed to confront a problem by denying its exis-tence) reported higher levels of drinking alcohol to cope; in turn, drinking to cope predicted both greater alcohol consumption and more alcohol-related problems. These pathways suggest that cognitive-based alcohol-related expectancies, dispositional charac-teristics, and coping styles motivate adolescents to use alcohol for enhancement and coping purposes. In turn, the use of alcohol for these reasons leads to higher levels of alcohol consumption and more alcohol-related problems.

Findings by Cooper et al. (1995), Windle (2000), and others (e.g., Chassin et al., 1993) provide models of complex mediational processes that lead to escalations in alcohol and illicit drug use among middle adolescents. These processes include dispositional (e.g., temperament), intrapersonal (e.g., drinking to cope with negative affect, alcohol expectancies), and social (e.g., sibling and peer substance use) influences that interact across time to produce escalating patterns of use and abuse. However, not directly represented (or capable of being disentangled) in these models are genetic variables and gene-environment processes (e.g., G-E interactions and correlations) that are important to our understanding of the development of abusive levels of substance use. As we indicated earlier in this chapter, research findings have pointed to correlates and developmental pathways of problem drinking that differentiate problem drinkers from other drinkers (e.g., moderate and heavy drinkers). Characteristics of teens who are on a developmental trajectory toward problematic levels of alcohol use include an earlier onset of substance use (e.g., before the age of 12 or 13), a family history of alcoholism, higher levels of externalizing childhood behaviors, and comorbid psychopathology (e.g., depression). Most of these critical risk factors have a potent genetic loading; however, it certainly appears that serious levels of alcohol use and alcohol disorders are phenotypes best viewed within a multifactorial gene-environment model. Which specific genes and gene-environment processes are most important in understanding the etiology and time-course of substance-use behaviors are among the most prominent issues confronting the substance-use field today.

Decreases in and desistance from substance use. In general, for both males and females, alcohol and marijuana use is initiated and escalates during the early and middle teen years, peaks in the late adolescent to early adult years, and declines thereafter; in contrast, cigarette use is initiated and increases during adolescence but continues to increase into adulthood (Bates & Labouvie, 1997; Raveis & Kandel, 1987). Relative to studies on substance-use initiation and escalation, there are fewer studies on decreasing or desisting patterns of use. Two related circumstances account for why researchers have focused on initiation and escalation rather than on desistance. First, in addition to increases in the initiation of use across adolescence, substance use manifests considerable cross-temporal continuity once teens have begun to use. Furthermore, for adolescents with more established patterns of use (e.g., problem drinking, daily smoking), the continuity and stability of use is substantial (Patton et al., 1998; Windle, 1996). Given the increases in and continuity of substance-use behaviors across time, it has been important to investigate underlying mechanisms that support and facilitate these patterns of use. Second, because of increasing use and continuity of use among teens, substance-use interventions with adolescents have understandably focused more on preventing or delaying such behaviors rather than on treating established problems and disorders once they occur; hence, research has been aimed at identifying influential risk and protective factors for initiation and escalation in order to develop more effective prevention programs. Nevertheless, understanding the developmental processes that are associated with reductions and desistance in substance-use behaviors is important, given that the majority of adolescent substance users will eventually decrease or end their use as they enter young and middle adulthood.

An informative study by Schulenberg et al. (1996) investigated those variables assessed in 12th grade that significantly predicted increases and decreases in frequent binge drinking across the transition into young adulthood (i.e., from approximately 18–24 years of age). Variables measured in the 12th grade that predicted *increases* in binge drinking included being male; lower levels of social conservatism; family role efficacy, self-efficacy, and identity focus; and higher levels of drinking to get drunk and a greater number of evenings out. Conversely, predictors of *decreases* in binge drinking included being female, higher levels of self-efficacy and work role readiness, and lower drinking to get drunk.

Other studies have looked at the predictors of decreases in or cessation from cigarette, alcohol, and marijuana use during the third decade of life, that is, young adulthood (e.g., Breslau & Peterson, 1996; Kandel & Raveis, 1989; Labouvie, 1996; Miller-Tutzauer, Leonard, & Windle, 1991; Rose et al., 1996). For example, variables that prospectively predict smoking cessation in young adults include a later age of smoking onset (i.e., after 13 years of age), higher levels of education, lower levels of previous smoking, having fewer smoking friends, valuing health, and being employed (Breslau & Peterson, 1996; Rose et al., 1996). The adoption of important social roles, such as marrying and becoming a parent, are important contributors to decreases in alcohol and other drug use (Labouvie, 1996; Miller-Tutzauer, Leonard, & Windle, 1991). Finally, significant predictors in the cessation of marijuana use include a lower frequency of past use, marrying, being a parent (for women), and a lower household income for men and a higher household income for women (Kandel & Raveis, 1989).

A prominent conceptual argument for decreases or desistance in deviant behaviors is the idea that most young people (although certainly not all) tend to "mature-out" of these types of behaviors as they assume adult roles and responsibilities in society at large. For example, Pulkkinen (1988) suggested that older adolescents and young adults engaging in delinquent acts terminate or lessen these behaviors as they move away from social contexts that foster them (e.g., exiting delinquent peer groups; moving to a different neighborhood), and as they assume adult roles that require higher levels of maturity (e.g., holding down a steady job, marrying, becoming a parent). Likewise, Labouvie (1996) postulated the importance of a self-correction process in which individuals decrease their substance use in order to maximize the attainment of adult goals that are incongruent with the heavier use of substances.

Substance-Use Prevention Efforts

Three types of preventive interventions are universal, selective, and indicated programs (Institute of Medicine, 1994). Universal programs include all persons in a particular population (e.g., all students in a school) without regard for level of substance-use risk. Selective programs target subgroups of individuals (e.g., children of alcoholics) who have a greater risk of developing a particular condition or problem (e.g., alcohol disorders). Indicated prevention programs are those that target individuals manifesting specific attributes or behaviors (e.g., drinking and driving) which place them at high risk for adverse outcomes (e.g., automobile fatalities).

The majority of substance-use prevention programs with youth in the United States have involved universal, school-based interventions aimed at delaying or preventing the onset of substance-use behaviors among children and young teens who have not yet initiated or become heavily involved in the consumption of licit and illicit drugs. In general, these programs are broadly administered to all youth in school settings using a curriculum-based format. As pointed out earlier in this chapter, research findings have indicated that social-influence factors are strong contributors to the initiation of substance-use behaviors. It is thus not surprising that the most popular form of substance-use prevention programs with youth have been developed based on social influence models (e.g., Botvin et al., 1990; Dielman et al., 1989; Ellickson & Bell, 1990). A critical goal of these programs has been to teach children and young teens the requisite skills to resist social influences that encourage drug use (Norman & Turner, 1993).

Evaluations of the short- and long-term efficacy of universal programs in preventing or reducing substance use among adolescents have been mixed (e.g., Botvin et al., 1995; Ellickson, Bell, & McGuigan, 1993; Shope et al., 1992). For example, several evaluation studies have suggested that universal programs are more effective in preventing substance-use behaviors among baseline non-users, but are less effective among baseline users who have initiated use at an earlier age and therefore may be at increased risk for future substance-related problems (Ellickson & Bell, 1990; Perry et al., 1996). This limitation of universal programs is related, in part, to their lack of attention to varying levels of substance-use risk among teens. In addition, universal prevention programs seem to be more effective in reducing the use of cigarettes and marijuana and less effective in reducing alcohol use (Botvin et al., 1990; Ellickson & Bell, 1990). In the United States, societal attitudes and media messages which condone, and indeed support, alcohol use are pervasive, and therefore prevention efforts that discourage teens' use of alcohol may be less effective than efforts to prevent their use of cigarettes and marijuana.

In recent years, there has been a movement within the scientific community to design and develop prevention programs that address some of the limitations of universal programs. For example, the Personal Growth Class (PGC; Thompson, Horn, & Hertig, 1997) and Jump Start (Harrington & Donohew, 1997) are two targeted prevention programs designed to meet the specific profiles and needs of two subgroups of at-risk adolescents. The PGC was designed to meet the emotional, academic, and substance-use prevention needs of adolescents at high risk for school dropout. Jump Start targeted African American teens who were economically disadvantaged and who were high on sensation seeking, a disposition associated with higher levels of substance use. Jump Start's program goals were to reduce substance-use behaviors and encourage completion of high school and pursuit of career goals. Program activities were designed specifically to appeal to adolescents high on sensation seeking (e.g., high-sensation value messages that were novel, complex, unconventional, and fast-paced). Evaluation studies indicated that both these programs experienced some success in attaining program goals with these high-risk groups of teens (Harrington & Donohew, 1997; Thompson et al., 1997).

In addition to recognizing the need for programs designed for adolescents at varying levels of risk, researchers have suggested that adolescent substance-use prevention programs should be comprehensive (i.e., target multiple domains of children's functioning such as intrapersonal, family, school, media, community) (Pentz et al., 1989), begin before the onset of substance-use behaviors (given the earlier onset of such behaviors among a number of adolescents, this suggests program implementation should begin with young children) (Williams et al., 1999), be of longer duration (Ellickson & Bell, 1990), and be designed to maximize adolescents' program exposure (Botvin et al., 1995). Multicomponent, comprehensive community prevention programs have been the response to some of these concerns. Two multicomponent community programs are the Midwestern Prevention Project (MPP; Pentz et al., 1989; Johnson et al., 1990) and Project Northland (Perry et al., 1996; Williams et al., 1999). A primary goal of these programs has been to reduce adolescents' substance-use behaviors by promoting anti-substance-use messages, practices, and norms at multiple contextual levels, including the family, school, and community. In both short- and long-term evaluation studies, findings indicated that the MPP was effective in *reducing the rate of growth* of substance use among program participants relative to control subjects (Johnson et al., 1990; Pentz et al., 1989). Results from Project Northland showed that intervention efforts were successful in reducing cigarette, alcohol, and marijuana use among baseline nonusers but not among baseline users (Perry et al., 1996).

We conclude this brief discussion of substance-use prevention programs with an acknowledgment that such programs must recognize that adolescents differ on important variables that contribute to substance use based on racial/ethnic group membership (e.g., Ellickson & Morton, 1999). For example, peers may be more influential in the use of substances among white and Hispanic teens, whereas dispositions (e.g., risk-taking) may be more important for African Americans. Differences in socialization practices occurring within the family may also impact on differential substance-use behaviors among white and African American youth (e.g., Clark et al., 1999). Thus, the development of preventive intervention protocols needs to reflect these differences in order to increase the probability of meeting program goals, such as preventing substance-use initiation and reducing escalation.

Summary

In the aggregate, prevalence data on adolescent substance use indicate a reasonably high degree of stability since the 1990s. Although these relatively high rates of use serve as a threat to adolescent morbidity and mortality, several recent trends are of particular concern. These trends include an increase in the percentage of adolescents using substances at more serious or severe levels, such as daily smoking, alcohol binge drinking, and the persistent use of highly potent forms of marijuana. A second trend of major concern is the earlier age of onset for the use of many substances, as many more children are engaging in substance use even prior to adolescence. This is of concern because early-onset substance use is a potent predictor of both health and social difficulties during adolescence as well as adulthood. Substance use and abuse during childhood and adolescence may undermine the development of important cognitive and social skills essential to optimal growth and to the preparation for the life tasks of adolescence and young adulthood.

As researchers and practitioners have further pursued the study of adolescent substance use it has become increasingly clear that there is enormous variation in the substance-use practices of adolescents. Adolescents initiate the use of substances at different times and display quite distinct patterns of intraindividual change in substance use across time.

Furthermore, the predictors of different aspects or features of substance use (e.g., initiation, escalation, desistance) may vary, as well as the predictors for different racial/ethnic and gender groups. An important next phase in the study of adolescent substance use will be to use methodological approaches (e.g., pattern-centered) and short-term prospective research designs that will facilitate our understanding of the causes and consequences of adolescent substance use. This knowledge may serve as a useful guide for targeted interventions that are based on an appreciation of the heterogeneity of influences associated with adolescent substance use and abuse.

Key Readings

Dryfoos, J. G. (1990). *Adolescents at risk: Prevalence and prevention.* New York: Oxford University Press.
This book provides a review of the prevalence of a wide range of adolescent high-risk behaviors (e.g., delinquency, substance abuse, pregnancy, and school failure and dropout) and an evaluation of prevention programs designed to eliminate or mitigate these high-risk behaviors.

Bukstein, O. G. (1995). *Adolescent substance abuse: Assessment, prevention, and treatment.* New York: Wiley.
This book provides an in-depth review of the causes, treatment, and prevention of adolescent substance abuse and provides strong coverage to issues related to comorbidity (i.e., co-occurring substance abuse and mental disorders) and to treatment modalities in treatment settings.

Schinke, S. P., Botvin, G. J., & Orlandi, M. A. (1991). *Substance abuse in children and adolescents: Evaluation and intervention.* Newbury Park, CA: Sage.
This book provides a comprehensive description and evaluation of several approaches to substance-abuse prevention among children and adolescents, including educational, psychosocial, mass-media, and comprehensive community-based.

Windle, M. (1999). *Alcohol use among adolescents.* Thousand Oaks, CA: Sage.
This book integrates research from multiple fields of study (e.g., epidemiology, pediatrics, developmental psychology) to examine risk and protective factors for alcohol use and abuse among adolescents, as well as to report findings from prominent prevention and treatment studies.

References

Barnes, G. M., & Welte, J. W. (1986). Adolescent alcohol abuse: Subgroup differences and relationships to other problem behaviors. *Journal of Adolescent Research, 1,* 79–94.
Bates, M. E., & Labouvie, E. W. (1997). Adolescent risk factors and the prediction of persistent alcohol and drug use into adulthood. *Alcoholism: Clinical and Experimental Research, 21,* 944–950.
Bauman, A., & Phongsavan, P. (1999). Epidemiology of substance use in adolescence: Prevalence, trends and policy implications. *Drug and Alcohol Dependence, 55,* 187–207.
Baumrind, D., & Moselle, K. A. (1985). A developmental perspective on adolescent drug abuse. *Alcohol and Substance Abuse in Adolescence, 2,* 41–67.
Botvin, G. J., Baker, E., Dusenbury, L., Botvin, E. M., & Diaz, T. (1995). Long-term follow-up

results of a randomized drug abuse prevention trial in a white middle-class population. *Journal of the American Medical Association, 273*, 1106–1112.

Botvin, G. J., Baker, E., Dusenbury, L., Tortu, S., & Botvin, E. M. (1990). Preventing adolescent drug abuse through a multimodal cognitive–behavioral approach: Results of a 3-year study. *Journal of Consulting and Clinical Psychology, 58*, 437–446.

Breslau, N., & Peterson, E. L. (1996). Smoking cessation in young adults: Age at initiation of cigarette smoking and other suspected influences. *American Journal of Public Health, 86*, 214–220.

Britton, G. A. (1998). A review of women and tobacco: Have we come such a long way. *Journal of Obstetric, Gynecologic, and Neonatal Nursing, 27*, 241–249.

Catalano, R. F., Morrison, D. M., Wells, E. A., Gillmore, M. R., Iritani, B., & Hawkins, J. D. (1992). Ethnic differences in family factors related to early drug initiation. *Journal of Studies on Alcohol, 53*, 208–217.

Chassin, L., Pillow, D. R., Curran, P. J., Molina, B. S. G., & Barrera, Jr., M. (1993). Relation of parental alcoholism to early adolescent substance use: A test of three mediating mechanisms. *Journal of Abnormal Psychology, 102*, 3–19.

Cicchetti, D., & Rogosch, F. A. (1999). Psychopathology as risk for adolescent substance use disorders: A developmental psychopathology perspective. *Journal of Clinical Child Psychology, 28*, 355–365.

Clark, P. I., Scarisbrick-Hauser, A., Gautam, S. P., & Wirk, S. J. (1999). Anti-tobacco socialization in homes of African American and white parents, and smoking and nonsmoking parents. *Journal of Adolescent Health, 24*, 329–339.

Clayton, R. R. (1992). Transitions in drug use: Risk and protective factors. In M. Glantz & R. Pickens (Eds.), *Vulnerability to drug abuse* (pp. 15–51). Washington, DC: American Psychological Association.

Colder, C. R., & Chassin, L. (1999). The psychosocial characteristics of alcohol users versus problem users: Data from a study of adolescents at risk. *Development and Psychopathology, 11*, 321–348.

Cooper, M. L., Frone, M. R., Russell, M., & Mudar, P. (1995). Drinking to regulate positive and negative emotions: A motivational model of alcohol use. *Journal of Personality and Social Psychology, 69*, 990–1005.

Dielman, T. E., Shope, J. T., Leech, S. L., & Butchart, A. T. (1989). Differential effectiveness of an elementary school-based alcohol misuse prevention program. *Journal of School Health, 59*, 255–263.

Duncan, T. E., Tildesley, E., Duncan, S. C., & Hops, H. (1995). The consistency of family and peer influences on the development of substance use in adolescence. *Addiction, 90*, 1647–1660.

Ellickson, P. L., & Bell, R. M. (1990). Drug prevention in junior high: A multi-site longitudinal test. *Science, 247*, 1299–1304.

Ellickson, P. L., Bell, R. M., & McGuigan, K. (1993). Preventing adolescent drug use: Long-term results of a junior high program. *American Journal of Public Health, 83*, 856–861.

Ellickson, P. L., & Hays, R. D. (1991). Antecedents of drinking among young adolescents with different alcohol use histories. *Journal of Studies on Alcohol, 52*, 398–408.

Ellickson, P. L., & Morton, S. C. (1999). Identifying adolescents at risk for hard drug use: Racial/ethnic variations. *Journal of Adolescent Health, 25*, 382–395.

Flay, B. R., Hu, F. B., Siddiqui, O., Day, L. E., Hedeker, D., Petraitis, J., Richardson, J., & Sussman, S. (1994). Differential influence of parental smoking and friends' smoking on adolescent initiation and escalation of smoking. *Journal of Health and Social Behavior, 35*, 248–265.

Fombonne, E. (1998). Increased rates of psychosocial disorders in youth. *European Archives of Psychiatry and Clinical Neuroscience, 248*, 14–21.

Harrington, N. G., & Donohew, L. (1997). Jump Start: A targeted substance abuse prevention program. *Health Education & Behavior, 24*, 568–586.

Hawkins, J. D., Catalano, R. F., & Miller, J. Y. (1992). Risk and protective factors for alcohol and other drug problems in adolescence and early adulthood: Implications for substance abuse prevention. *Psychological Bulletin, 112*, 64–105.

Institute of Medicine (1994). *Reducing risks for mental disorders: Frontiers for preventive intervention research.* Washington, DC: National Academy Press.

Jessor, R., & Jessor, S. L. (1977). *Problem behavior and psychosocial development: A longitudinal study of youth.* New York: Academic.

Johnson, C. A., Pentz, M. A., Weber, M. D., Dwyer, J. H., Baer, N., MacKinnon, D. P., Hansen, W. B., & Flay, B. R. (1990). Relative effectiveness of comprehensive community programming for drug abuse prevention with high-risk and low-risk adolescents. *Journal of Consulting and Clinical Psychology, 58*, 447–456.

Johnston, L. D., O'Malley, P. M., & Bachman, J. G. (1999). *National survey results on drug use from The Monitoring the Future Study, 1975–1998: Vol. I: Secondary school students.* National Institute on Drug Abuse, NIH Publication No. 99–4660. Washington, DC: US Government Printing Press.

Johnston, L. D., O'Malley, P. M., & Bachman, J. G. (2000). *The Monitoring the Future national results on adolescent drug use: Overview of key findings, 1999.* National Institute on Drug Abuse, NIH Publication No. 00–4690. Washington, DC: US Government Printing Press.

Kandel, D. B., & Raveis, V. H. (1989). Cessation of illicit drug use in young adulthood. *Archives of General Psychiatry, 46*, 109–116.

Kandel, D. B., Yamaguchi, K., & Chen, K. (1992). Stages of progression in drug involvement from adolescence to adulthood: Further evidence for the gateway theory. *Journal of Studies on Alcohol, 53*, 447–457.

Labouvie, E. (1996). Maturing out of substance use: Selection and self-correction. *Journal of Drug Issues, 26*, 457–476.

Magnusson, D., & Bergman, L. R. (1990). A pattern approach to the study of pathways from childhood to adulthood. In L. Robins & M. Rutter (Eds.), *Straight and devious pathways from childhood to adulthood* (pp. 101–115). New York: Cambridge University Press.

Miller-Tutzauer, C., Leonard, K. E., & Windle, M. (1991). Marriage and alcohol use: A longitudinal study of "maturing out." *Journal of Studies on Alcohol, 52*, 434–440.

Norman, E., & Turner, S. (1993). Adolescent substance abuse prevention programs: Theories, models, and research in the encouraging 80's. *Journal of Primary Prevention, 14*, 3–20.

Office of National Drug Control Policy: The national Drug Control Strategy–1997. Available at: http://www.ncjrs.org/htm/chapter/htm/

O'Malley, P. M., & Johnston, L. D. (1999). Drinking and driving among American high school seniors: 1984–1997. *American Journal of Public Health, 89*, 678–684.

Patton, G. C., Carlin, J. B., Coffey, C., Wolfe, R., Hibbert, M., & Bowes, G. (1998). The course of early smoking: A population-based cohort study over three years. *Addiction, 93*, 1251–1260.

Pentz, M. A., Dwyer, J. H., MacKinnon, D. P., Flay, B. R., Hansen, W. B., Wang, E. Y., & Johnson, C. A. (1989). A multicommunity trial for primary prevention of adolescent abuse. *Journal of the American Medical Association, 261*, 3259–3266.

Perry, C. L., Williams, C. L., Veblen-Mortenson, S., Toomey, T. L., Komro, K. A., Anstine, P. S., McGovern, P. G., Finnegan, J. R., Forster, J. L., Wagenaar, A. C., & Wolfson, M. (1996).

Project Northland: Outcomes of a communitywide alcohol use prevention program during early adolescence. *American Journal of Public Health, 86,* 956–965.

Petraitis, J., Flay, B. R., & Miller, T. Q. (1995). Reviewing theories of adolescent substance use: Organizing pieces in the puzzle. *Psychological Bulletin, 117,* 67–86.

Pulkkinen, L. (1988). Delinquent development: Theoretical and empirical considerations. In M. Rutter (Ed.), *Studies of psychosocial risk: The power of longitudinal data* (pp. 184–199). New York: Cambridge University Press.

Raveis, V. H., & Kandel, D. B. (1987). Changes in drug behavior from the middle to the late twenties: Initiation, persistence, and cessation of use. *American Journal of Public Health, 77,* 607–611.

Reed, M. D., & Rountree, P. W. (1997). Peer pressure and adolescent substance use. *Journal of Quantitative Criminology, 13,* 143–180.

Rose, J. S., Chassin, L., Presson, C. C., & Sherman, S. J. (1996). Prospective predictors of quit attempts and smoking cessation in young adults. *Health Psychology, 15,* 261–268.

Rose, R. J. (1998). A developmental behavior-genetic perspective on alcoholism risk. *Alcohol Health & Research World, 22,* 131–143.

Schulenberg, J., Wadsworth, K. N., O'Malley, P. M., Bachman, J. G., & Johnston, L. D. (1996). Adolescent risk factors for binge drinking during the transition to young adulthood: Variable- and pattern-centered approaches to change. *Developmental Psychology, 32,* 659–674.

Shope, J. T., Dielman, T. E., Butchart, A. T., Campanelli, P. C., & Kloska, D. D. (1992). An elementary school-based alcohol misuse prevention program: A follow-up evaluation. *Journal of Studies on Alcohol, 53,* 106–121.

Thompson, E. A., Horn, M., Herting, J. R., & Eggert, L. L. (1997). Enhancing outcomes in an indicated drug prevention program for high-risk youth. *Journal of Drug Education, 27,* 19–41.

Williams, C. L., Perry, C. L., Farbakhsh, K., & Veblen-Mortenson, S. (1999). Project Northland: Comprehensive alcohol use prevention for young adolescents, their parents, schools, peers, and communities. *Journal of Studies on Alcohol – Supplement, 13,* 112–124.

Windle, M. (1994). Coexisting problems and alcoholic family risk among adolescents. *Annals of the New York Academy of Sciences, 708,* 157–164.

Windle, M. (1996). An alcohol involvement typology for adolescents: Convergent validity and longitudinal stability. *Journal of Studies on Alcohol, 57,* 627–637.

Windle, M. (1999). *Alcohol use among adolescents.* Thousand Oaks, CA: Sage.

Windle, M. (2000). Parental, sibling, and peer influences on adolescent substance use and alcohol problems. *Applied Developmental Science, 4,* 98–110.

Windle, M., & Davies, P. (1999). Developmental theory and research. In K. E. Leonard & H. T. Blane (Eds.), *Psychological theories of drinking and alcoholism* (2nd ed., pp. 164–202). New York: Guilford.

Windle, M., & Windle, R. C. (1996). Coping strategies, drinking motives, and stressful life events among adolescents: Associations with emotional and behavioral problems, and academic functioning. *Journal of Abnormal Psychology, 105,* 551–560.

Windle, M., & Windle, R. C. (1999). Adolescent tobacco, alcohol, and drug use: Current findings. *Adolescent Medicine: State of the Art Reviews, 10,* 153–163.

Windle, R. C., & Windle, M. (1997). An investigation of adolescents' substance use behaviors, depressed affect, and suicidal behaviors. *Journal of Child Psychology and Psychiatry, 38,* 921–929.

CHAPTER TWENTY-TWO

Understanding Conduct Problems in Adolescence from a Lifespan Perspective

Deborah M. Capaldi and Joann Wu Shortt

Introduction

Conduct problems have probably been the topic of more academic and popular press writings than any other issue at adolescence. They have long been recognized as problematic and a source of distress to parents. In 1817, Jane Austen wrote: "the Musgraves had had the ill fortune of a very troublesome, hopeless son, and the good fortune to lose him before he reached his twentieth year . . . he was stupid and unmanageable . . . (and was) scarcely at all regretted" (Austen, 1997, pp. 55–56). Jane Austen's terminology of "troublesome" and "unmanageable" are hallmark descriptors of conduct problems used by many parents today in discussing their adolescents' behaviors. Parents spend many wakeful hours and much intense discussion anguishing about how best to respond to or manage the behaviors. In fact, having a child with conduct problems can be a great strain on a marital relationship (Jouriles, Bourg, & Farris, 1991). However, most parents would prefer a somewhat less radical solution to their problems than sudden death!

The authors would like to thank Jane Wilson, Rhody Hinks, and the data collection staff for commitment to high-quality data and to Sally Schwader for editorial assistance with manuscript preparation.

Support for the Oregon Youth Study was provided by Grant R37 MH 37940 from the Prevention, Early Intervention, and Epidemiology Branch, National Institute of Mental Health (NIMH), US PHS. Additional support was provided by Grant R01 MH 50259 from the Prevention, Early Intervention, and Epidemiology Branch, NIMH, US PHS; Grant P30 MH 46690 Prevention, Early Intervention, and Epidemiology Branch, NIMH, and Office of Research on Minority and Health (ORMH) US PHS; Grant R01 MH 37911 from the Behavioral Sciences Research Branch, NIMH, US PHS.

Some researchers feel, with reasonable justification, that there is an overemphasis on pathology in the field of psychology (Seligman & Csikszentmihalyi, 2000). However, even apart from assisting parents, there are several reasons why conduct problems should be a major focus of attention, with the aims of understanding the etiology of such behaviors and of informing and conducting preventive interventions and also treatment programs. First, a large proportion of youth show some engagement in illegal activities during adolescence. The frequency and prevalence of these behaviors rise dramatically in early adolescence, peak at around 15–16 years of age, and then decline almost as dramatically through early adulthood to relatively low levels by about 30 years of age (Blumstein et al., 1986). Such behaviors, especially property and person crimes, are costly both in financial terms and in distress to the victims. Second, teachers struggle to manage classrooms disrupted by the behavior of one or more students who display conduct problems (Walker, 1995). Behavior-management problems mar the educational experience for other students and usually result in poor academic skills on the part of the conduct-problem child. Finally, conduct problems cast long shadows into adulthood. Some individuals who display conduct problems in adolescence go on to criminal careers in adulthood (Blumstein et al., 1986). However, many who desist from criminal activities in young adulthood, or who mainly engaged in less criminal forms of conduct-problem behavior in adolescence, may experience other negative consequences as adults. Disabling injuries (or death) from car accidents (Junger, 1994); drug overdoses (Robins & Price, 1991); violence (Farrington, 1991); failure to finish high school (Elliott & Voss, 1974); lack of job skills and unemployment (Farrington et al., 1988); low income (Farrington et al., 1988); becoming a teenage parent with consequences including struggling to raise and support children or abandoning one's children by not keeping in contact (Capaldi & Stoolmiller, 1999; Fagot et al., 1998), and having a poor relationship with the child's other biological parent resulting in ongoing stress and conflict (Buchanan, Maccoby, & Dornbusch, 1991); incurable sexually transmitted diseases (Capaldi et al., 2002); substance addictions (i.e., tobacco, alcohol, or other drugs; Robins & Price, 1991); poor relationships with parents (Capaldi & Stoolmiller, 1999); and physical and psychological aggression toward intimate partners (Capaldi & Clark, 1998; Magdol et al., 1997) are just some of the adult correlates of adolescent conduct problems. Furthermore, most of these associations have been found for girls as well as for boys (Pajer, 1998).

Toward understanding conduct-problem behaviors in adolescence, this chapter will highlight relevant research, especially from the Oregon Youth Study (OYS), on the role of family processes and peer influences in the development of conduct disorders using a lifespan, individual–environment interaction model. Next, recent findings from the OYS regarding some key developmental problems associated with conduct problems in adolescence; namely, accelerated pathways to adulthood, co-occurrence with depressive symptoms, aggression toward a romantic partner (often termed "dating violence"), and health-risking sexual behavior are reviewed. Other associated problems at adolescence such as substance use and membership of gangs are addressed in separate chapters in this volume. We will conclude with a discussion of gender and cultural issues, followed by a brief description of prevention and treatment approaches.

Clinical Definitions and Prevalence of Conduct Disorder

Clinicians use the term "conduct disorder" to describe a persistent pattern of conduct problems that violate fundamental social rules and/or the basic rights of others (Eddy, 1996). Conduct disorders include six different diagnoses in the American Psychiatric Association (1994) *Diagnostic and Statistical Manual of Mental Disorders* (*DSM-IV*); namely, Conduct Problems (involving isolated acts rather than a pattern of behavior), Adjustment Disorder with or without emotional disturbance (both defined as in response to recent stressors); Disruptive Behavior Disorder (falling below criteria for the two more serious diagnoses – following); Oppositional Defiant Disorder (defined as a pattern of negativistic, hostile, and defiant behavior lasting at least six months); and Conduct Disorder (defined as a repetitive and persistent pattern of behavior in which the basic rights of others or major age-appropriate societal norms or rules are violated). Conduct-disordered behaviors include aggression toward people and animals, destruction of property, deceitfulness, theft, early onset of staying out at night, and truancy.

Regarding prevalence, it is estimated that in elementary school 2 percent of girls and 7 percent of boys meet a diagnosis for conduct disorder (Offord, Boyle, & Racine, 1991), with less severe disorders such as oppositional defiant disorder being more common at this age. The prevalence of conduct disorder for males is found consistently to be higher than that for females, partially due to the gender difference in physical harm to others. Estimates of prevalence rise through early to midadolescence to about 4–15 percent of boys and girls (Offord, Boyle, & Racine, 1991), with some decrease in gender difference in prevalence. Much research, until relatively recently, has focused on boys, yet conduct disorder is the second most common psychiatric diagnosis in girls, particularly in adolescence.

Some degree of conduct-problem symptoms or behaviors is, in fact, ubiquitous in childhood and adolescence. For self-reported delinquent acts, Elliott and Voss (1974) found that 95 percent of a large adolescent sample reported some participation in delinquent behavior, 62 percent admitted serious delinquent acts, 26 percent were known to the police, and 6 percent were adjudicated delinquents. Somewhat over one-half of the OYS sample had an arrest record in the juvenile period (prior to 18 years of age), and 20 percent had five or more arrests in the same period.

The Etiology of Conduct Problems

A great many risk factors in childhood from the domains of family contextual factors (e.g., poverty), parental factors (e.g., substance use), parenting behaviors (e.g., harsh discipline), child behavior (e.g., hyperactivity), and peer factors (e.g., peer rejection) are associated with conduct problems in adolescence. The important questions to address are how or by what processes these risk factors are associated with conduct problems, which factors play a causal role in the emergence of conduct problems, and how we can intervene on these factors to prevent or treat conduct problems.

An integrative theoretical framework that helps to clarify the role of the different domains of risk factors in the emergence of conduct problems is the lifespan developmental approach. This theory emphasizes the interaction between the individual's prior dispositions and learning and the environments in which s/he is placed or selects (Baltes, 1983; Dishion, French, & Patterson, 1995). At the heart of the lifespan or ecological approaches are individual interactions with the social environment.

Individual–Environment Interactions

Scarr and McCartney (1983) described individual–environment interaction effects that shape the environment and the individual's behaviors. The first type is *passive*, whereby the individual has no choice in the selection of environment and only limited ability to affect the environment. This pertains particularly to environments provided by caregivers in early childhood, but also to institutional environments, including schools and detention centers. The second effect is described as *evocative* (i.e., through responses elicited from others). Thus, explosive temper tantrums by a child may predict harsh parental discipline (Ge et al., 1996), and aggression toward peers may lead to peer rejection (Coie & Dodge, 1988). Such rejection by prosocial peers deprives the aggressive child of positive developmental influences in the peer group. Individuals may also *react* to environmental events (e.g., an aggressive response to an insult). The final type of environmental effect described by Scarr and McCartney is the *active* type, or through selection of environments by the individual. Individuals may select environments that suit their dispositions and goals. Thus, adolescents usually select their peer groups, and continued involvement with delinquent peers is considered to be a major contributor to continuance of conduct problems (Dishion, Andrews, & Crosby, 1995).

We suggest, however, that selection of environments is related to individual characteristics in an additional way, namely, that individual characteristics may expand or contract the range of environmental options (e.g., a boy who did not graduate from high school has limited employment and higher education options). *Restriction of environmental options* is an unintended but powerful consequence of conduct-problem behaviors. Remaining in or entering higher-risk and antisocial environments is more likely when these prior failures in development have occurred (Capaldi & Stoolmiller, 1999). Movement into environments that provide support for conduct problems and fewer interpersonal sanctions contributes to maintaining the stability of conduct problems or increasing engagement in such behavior. Family contextual factors, such as low income, also cause considerable limitations that restrict environmental options for children and adolescents (e.g., by living in a high-risk neighborhood). In the model presented below regarding the Oregon Youth Study, these individual–environment interactions are considered to be ongoing processes in the development of conduct problems.

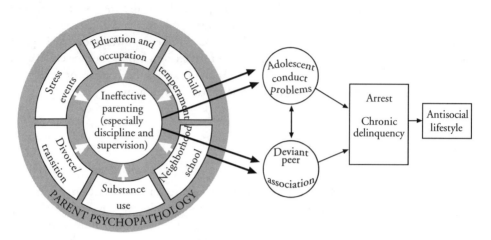

Figure 22.1   The mediational family model.

The Oregon Youth Study (OYS)

The OYS is a longitudinal study of males who were considered at risk for delinquency, and involves a community sample recruited from schools with a higher than usual incidence of delinquency in the neighborhood for a medium-sized metropolitan area. The sample was followed from childhood through young adulthood. All 4th-grade boys were invited to participate, and the recruitment rate was 74 percent. The sampling design was such that the boys would have an elevated risk for delinquency, but the majority did not have conduct problems in 4th grade. The sample is 90 percent European American. In the first year, the parents were 75 percent lower- and working-class. Yearly assessments were collected through young adulthood, including data from multiple sources (e.g., the boy, both parents, teachers, school and official records, peers, romantic partners), observational data of family, peer, and romantic partner interactions, as well as interview and questionnaire data. Participation rates in late adolescence and young adulthood averaged about 98 percent, or a sample size of around 200 (Capaldi et al., 1997). Constructs, such as conduct problems, were assessed by multiple indicators (e.g., parent, teacher, and self-reports, and arrest records).

Mediational Developmental Model

Shown in figure 22.1 is a developmental model for conduct problems in childhood and adolescence that combines family context, parental characteristics and behaviors, parenting practices, child temperament and behavior, and peer factors in a dynamic, mediational model. Parent psychopathology is viewed as an underlying risk context for the family and is related to other contextual risk factors (e.g., unemployment) and ineffective parenting. Parent psychopathology, as conceptualized in this model, includes, in particular, parental antisocial behavior, depression, and substance use. Each of the contextual variables identified in the general model in figure 22.1 has been shown to covary significantly with conduct problems in boys. These variables include parental antisocial behavior (Capaldi & Patterson, 1991), parental depression (Radke-Yarrow, 1998), divorce and parental transitions (Capaldi & Patterson, 1991), stress and depression (Forgatch, Patterson, & Skinner, 1988), neighborhood (Wilson, 1987), employment (Farrington et al., 1986), and occupation and education as indicators for socioeconomic status (Elliott, Huizinga, & Ageton, 1985). A major mechanism by which contextual risk factors are posited to be associated with the development of conduct problems is mediational, through either family or delinquent-peer group interactions.

Family Process and Conduct Problems

Stable or trait-like contextual factors (i.e., low socioeconomic status and antisocial personality) are thought to identify parents who are at risk because they acquired few parenting skills and/or learned inappropriate parenting behaviors such as aggressive or coercive techniques and harsh, abusive discipline. Less stable or state characteristics, including stress and depression, are posited to disrupt or diminish parenting by taking the parents' time and attention from their child or by producing depressed or irritable mood states. Negative social exchanges between the parent and child increase during times of family stress, indicating that prevention of these negative social exchanges may prevent increases in conduct problems for the child (Patterson, 1982). Evidence for the relation between the state characteristics (e.g., stress) and parenting practices is often difficult to establish because these state characteristics are related to the more stable parental characteristics (e.g., parental antisocial behavior predicts family stress). A further factor that may relate to an association between parental antisocial behavior and adolescent conduct problems is that parents showing higher levels of antisocial behavior may provide a more delinquent environment, where behaviors such as substance use and acts of rule-breaking behavior may be considered more acceptable than they would be by prosocial parents.

Temperamental Risk for Conduct Problems

Child temperament, primarily defined as emotional dispositions (Rothbart, Posner, & Hershey, 1995) and posited to be related to genetic influences and possibly to pre- and perinatal environmental stressors and insults, is hypothesized to have both a mediated and a direct effect on risk for the development of conduct problems (see figure 22.1). Direct effects are due to the fact that children who experience more negative and hostile affect are likely to be more aggressive, and children who act impulsively are more likely to engage in rule-breaking behaviors. The indirect effect through parenting practices is posited as being due to the fact that children who express negative affect may evoke more harsh responses from their parents (Ge et al., 1996). One physiological mechanism that could be genetically related and be associated with difficult temperament is hypoarousal. Hypoarousal appears to be indicative of qualities of fearlessness and stimulation seeking akin to characteristics of a disinhibited temperament seen during infancy (Raine, 1997).

Research on the association between parental criminality and children's criminality indicates an interactive effect, such that having a father with a criminal record is a risk factor for sons' criminality when there is also poor parenting (McCord, 1999). Similar effects have been found for the association of criminality in adopted children whose biological parents had a history of criminality – the child was at much higher risk if the adoptive parents were also criminals (Bohman, 1996). Overall, findings regarding genetic vulnerability and parenting indicate the importance of both nature and nurture for positive child development and of examining the nature of the joint contributions of both genetic and environmental effects (Collins et al., 2000).

Early versus Late Onset of Conduct Problems

It has been estimated that about 6 percent of juveniles account for 50 percent of juvenile arrests (Wolfgang, Figlio, & Sellin, 1972). This has led to research efforts to identify characteristics of this severe and chronic group of offenders. Age of onset of conduct problems is posited by several researchers to be a defining developmental characteristic relating to the severity and course of the behaviors. Patterson and colleagues (e.g., Patterson et al., 1998) argue that early starters, with onset of conduct problems in childhood and an arrest before 14 years of age, are likely to be severe and chronic offenders and continue into adulthood. Late starters, with adolescent onset, are posited to be much more likely to desist from offending in adulthood. Similarly, Moffitt (1993) has characterized the early onset group as life-course persistent, and the late onset group as adolescent limited. The extent to which age of onset of conduct problems can predict accurately persistence and desistance of antisocial behavior in adulthood has yet to be tested thoroughly.

Currently, there is some controversy regarding both the occurrence of the increase in aggression during early childhood for the early onset group and the existence of adolescent onset of conduct problems (or late starters). Tremblay et al. (1999) found that 17-month-old toddlers show relatively high levels of physically aggressive acts and that these levels tend to *decrease* with age, thus, overt aggressive acts seem to decrease with development in early childhood. However, in a synthesis of longitudinal research, Lipsey and Derzon (1998) found evidence for the early onset group, in that the strongest predictors of serious and violent delinquency at 15–25 years of age were the presence of general offending and substance use prior to age 11. A further aspect of the controversy is that studies of developmental trajectories of self-reported delinquency do not converge on an adolescent onset group (Wiesner & Capaldi, 2001).

Delinquent-Peer Association

Models of peer influence in the development of conduct problems have received much less attention than parenting models. We concur with the position of Collins et al. (2000) that it is critical to consider the role of peers as well as of parenting in the socialization of children. Delinquent-peer association has been identified repeatedly as strongly associated with conduct problems and delinquent behavior at adolescence (e.g., Dishion, French, & Patterson, 1995). Several mechanisms are related to risk for delinquent-peer association in adolescence. First, the density of delinquent peers in the neighborhood and school is related to living in high-risk neighborhoods; thus, the latter contextual factor is posited to show a direct association with delinquent-peer association (see figure 22.1). Second, poor parenting may be associated with delinquent–peer association, either because it drives the child or adolescent to seek the company of peers (e.g., due to harsh or rejecting behavior by the parent) or because the parent is not adequately supervising the child. The development of conduct problems also relates to delinquent–peer association in two major ways. First, aggressive children tend to be rejected by prosocial peers (Coie & Dodge, 1988). This unintended consequence of their aggressive behavior limits their choices regarding peers who are willing to spend time with them and tends to push them toward associations with antisocial peers (Dishion et al., 1991). Second, conduct-problem children may actively select peers who like to engage in the same behaviors as they do themselves (Scarr & McCartney, 1983).

Conduct problems and association with friends who also engage in conduct problems (i.e., delinquent-peer association) are very closely related constructs, especially in middle to late adolescence (Dishion, French, & Patterson, 1995). Stoolmiller (1994) found that growth in delinquent-peer association and conduct problems at adolescence were highly related. Elliott et al. (1985) found that self-reported involvement in a delinquent-peer group accounted for involvement in subsequent levels of self-reported delinquency in middle and late adolescence, even after accounting for previous levels of delinquency.

Similar to boys, girls with a childhood history of externalizing behavior problems become familiar with delinquent peers during early adolescence (Caspi et al., 1993). Because of the gender differences in conduct problems, boys will tend to have more delinquent male peers in their peer groups with girls commonly associating with a mixed-sex peer group (Giordano & Cernkovich, 1997). Association with delinquent peers appears to be more common among girls who have an early onset of pubertal maturation (Stattin & Magnusson, 1990), however, early pubertal maturation appears to be related to the development of adolescent behavior and emotional problems only when it occurs in the context of additional risk factors (Caspi & Moffitt, 1991).

Peer delinquency training

Dishion and colleagues (e.g., Dishion, Andrews, & Crosby, 1995) examined the processes by which conduct problems can form the basis for adolescent friendships. Their observations of discussions between adolescent males and their friends indicated that rein-forcement of rule-breaking talk occurred for some of the dyads. They conceptualized this process as delinquency training. The delinquency training occurred within these friend-ships via a process by which rule-breaking talk organized the positive affective exchanges within the friendship. In other words, in some friendship dyads, laughter was more likely during discussions of breaking rules. In contrast, prosocial boys tended to laugh mostly in normative discussions. Antisocial dyads also showed higher overall frequencies of anti-social talk. This process of delinquency training in adolescence predicted escalations in serious delinquent behavior (Dishion et al., 1996). Interviews with delinquent adolescent girls indicate that they are also involved in friendship networks that encourage their delin-quent behavior (Giordano & Cernkovich, 1997). What appeared to be particularly salient was the perception of peer approval for law violations. These findings suggest that ado-lescence is a critical period for the influence of peers, with respect to establishing norms, values, and behaviors that account for subsequent individual differences in adjustment.

Accelerated Pathways to Adulthood

The ecology of conduct problems at adolescence is such that they are associated with more rapid entry into adult roles. This may seem counterintuitive, because successful adjustment and associated mental maturity are commonly thought of as attributes of developmental progress. Newcomb (1987) has described the process whereby risk or problem behaviors are associated with more rapid movement into adult roles as "pseudo-maturity," indicating that the taking on of such roles does not necessarily indicate the capacity to succeed in them. Similarly, Burton, Obeidallah, and Allison (1996) have described the accelerated life courses of inner-city African American adolescents. We posit that high school dropout is a large factor in such acceleration, because adolescents are then likely to enter employment earlier and leave the family-of-origin home prior to 18 years of age (Capaldi & Stoolmiller, 1999). Dropping out of high school is strongly asso-ciated with conduct problems (Elliott & Voss, 1974). A second factor posited to be asso-ciated with an accelerated pathway to adulthood is early age at initiation of sexual intercourse. Early initiation of intercourse is strongly predicted by childhood and ado-lescent conduct problems (Capaldi, Crosby, & Stoolmiller, 1996). Furthermore, a back-ground of risk and conduct problems predicts earlier entry into a romantic relationship (Capaldi & Crosby, 1997). It may be that the higher levels of delinquent-peer group involvement and risk taking for the young men who are higher in conduct problems are also related to early partnering.

Adolescent Pregnancy and Parenthood

Conduct problems are also predictive of adolescent parenthood for both boys (Capaldi & Stoolmiller, 1999) and girls (Scaramella et al., 1998). Related to their conduct problems is the increased risk for inadequate parenting by teen mothers (Serbin et al., 1998) and for the development of behavior problems in their children (Lahey et al., 1988). However, although early entry into motherhood may be associated with difficulties in parenting and relationship difficulties, these family commitments are thought to help girls pull themselves out of delinquent-peer groups and discontinue engaging in delinquent activities outside the home (Giordano & Cernkovich, 1997). Thereby, teenage delinquent mothers may have more favorable long-term outcomes compared to teenage fathers, if the fathers are not living with their children.

The strong association of early parenthood and conduct problems is emphasized by findings for the OYS sample. The boys who became fathers during adolescence showed over twice as many arrests in the juvenile period and were similarly about twice as likely to have dropped out of school, to use tobacco daily, and to show patterned marijuana use. They were also over four times as likely to show patterned use of other drugs (Fagot et al., 1998). As predicted by the developmental-failure model associated with conduct problems (Capaldi, 1991, 1992; Patterson & Capaldi, 1991), these adolescent fathers with higher levels of conduct problems and low personal capital (e.g., lower educational levels) were more likely to fail at this new role. At around 2 years of age, 40 percent of these children had no contact with their father. Thus, many of these young men rapidly experienced failure in this new role at a most basic level, that of having contact with their children. Accelerated entry into adult roles, without associated job or life skills and with continuance of conduct problems, can result in continued risk and failure for these young adults, as well as transmission of risk to their children.

Co-occurrence of Conduct Problems with Depressive Symptoms

In a review of clinical studies, Kovacs et al. (1988) estimated that about one-third of adolescents with major depressive disorder also qualified for a diagnosis of conduct or related disorder. Co-occurrence appeared similar for males and females. For the OYS sample, conduct problems and depressive symptoms were also found to be significantly associated (Capaldi, 1991). That such qualitatively different symptoms and behaviors develop in the same individual and exist side by side apparently presents a theoretical anomaly. Furthermore, it has spurred interest in understanding the concurrent and future outcomes for children and adolescents who experience such co-occurrence. A particular concern is risk for suicidal behavior. Conduct problems are a risk factor for suicide in both boys and girls (Cairns, Peterson, & Neckerman, 1988). Adolescent boys are at higher risk for completing suicide than girls (5 : 1; Shaffer, 1988). However, suicidal *behavior* has been found to be higher for girls with conduct disorder compared to boys (Cairns et al., 1988). Co-occurring depressive symptoms may increase risk for both sexes.

We have hypothesized (Capaldi, 1992) that antisocial youth are vulnerable to developing depressed mood because their conduct problems result in failure experiences that may be emotionally similar to the events (e.g., a traumatic event) that have been shown to trigger depression in adults and children. Capaldi (1992) found that conduct problems at 11–12 years of age predicted increased depressive symptoms by 13–14 years of

age. Evidence has been found for other explanations for the association of conduct problems and depressive symptoms, including shared genetic and environmental risks (Gjone
& Stevenson, 1997). Family contextual factors and parenting practices may contribute to
shared environmental risk (Capaldi, 1991).

For the OYS sample, we found that co-occurring conduct problems and depressive
symptoms were associated with the poorest overall levels of adjustment over either
problem alone (Capaldi 1991, 1992). The boys with co-occurring problems showed the
cluster of problems associated with conduct problems (e.g., delinquent-peer association,
a high arrest rate, parental reports of a poor relationship with the child), *plus* the cluster
of problems associated with depressive symptoms (e.g., poor relationship with friends,
self-reported poor relationship with parents), *and* the lowest levels of academic skill,
higher suicidal ideation, and some indication of earlier onset of substance use in early
adolescence. Furthermore, boys who experienced co-occurring symptoms in early
adolescence showed poorer adjustment in late adolescence in the sense of showing problems in more areas than did boys with either problem alone (Capaldi & Stoolmiller,
1999).

Conduct Problems and Violence

The topic of violence, and the degree to which one can predict which youth with conduct
problems are likely to be violent, is always of high concern to professionals in the area of
conduct-problem adolescents as well as to the general public. Findings in this area have
indicated that engagement in violent offenses appears to be part of a general pattern of
conduct-problem behavior. Capaldi and Patterson (1996) hypothesized that violent
offending at adolescence is part of a general pattern of high-rate conduct problems. Family
characteristics, parenting practices, and childhood behavior were compared for violent
adolescent arrestees and nonviolent adolescent arrestees matched for arrest frequency. The
findings generally supported the prediction that violent offenders are from similar risk
backgrounds to frequent but nonviolent offenders and had shown similar (elevated) levels
of conduct problems in earlier childhood. Furthermore, it was found that according to
self-reports of offenses, many multiple offenders with no arrests for violence were actually committing violent acts at a high rate. Thus, the bulk of violent acts committed by
adolescent offenders appear to be part of a general involvement in conduct-problem
behavior, rather than the result of a developmental pathway specific to violence. Similar
conclusions have been drawn by other researchers (e.g., Farrington, 1991).

Conduct Problems and Aggression toward a Partner

Aggression toward a partner in adulthood was commonly perceived as a behavior that
developed over time, related to longer-term relationships, particularly marriage. It was
thought that women stayed in violent relationships because of factors that made it diffi-

cult for them to leave, such as economic dependence and children in the relationship. However, in the early 1980s, it was found that relatively high rates of physical aggression toward a partner also occur among adolescent dating couples. Physical aggression toward a partner is usually defined as acts that involve some physical force, ranging from pushes and shoves to use of lethal weapons, and the context is generally defined as occurrence during a disagreement rather than during horseplay. Estimates of the prevalence of aggression toward a partner are higher in late adolescence through young adulthood, at 32–36 percent of college students, than in midadolescence, at 12–22 percent of high school students (Carlson, 1987). Psychological aggression, predominantly involving verbal aggression such as threats and insults, is significantly associated with physical aggression toward a partner for both boys and girls in late adolescence, and levels of physical and psychological aggression were as high or higher for the adolescent girl partners than for the OYS boys, including relatively high rates of observed physical aggression during a problem-solving interaction (Capaldi & Crosby, 1997).

In a series of studies we have examined developmental models of risk for aggression toward a partner, including family and peer factors, and the role of assortative partnering by antisocial behavior in predicting aggression in young couples. Capaldi and Clark (1998) tested a fully prospective model of developmental risk for aggression toward a partner, and showed that the strongest pathway of risk for boys was from unskilled parenting (poor supervision and inconsistent discipline), and the development of antisocial behavior by adolescence (figure 22.2). The association of conduct problems in childhood and adolescence and later physical aggression toward a partner in adolescence and young adulthood also has been found in recent prospective studies of young women's aggression toward a partner (Andrews et al., 2000; Magdol et al., 1997). The contributions that peer relationships may make concerning aggression toward partners are rarely considered. Capaldi et al. (2001) found that observed hostile talk about girls and women with a friend in late adolescence (which was predicted by deviant-peer association) uniquely predicted aggression toward a partner an average of 3 years later in young adulthood.

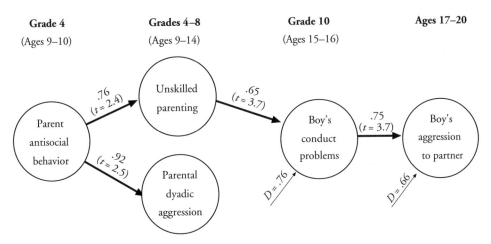

Figure 22.2 Listwise model findings for the hypothesized mediated intergenerational model.

The individual–environment interaction perspective leads to the prediction of assortative partnering by conduct problems via two processes, namely active selection and through restriction of options. Boys and girls with higher levels of conduct problems are prone to cluster into the same peer groups by midadolescence and to continue engagement in problematic behaviors. Assortative partnering by conduct problems has been found for OYS as well as other studies (Capaldi & Crosby, 1997; Krueger et al., 1998). Kim and Capaldi (2002) found that if *both* partners show higher levels of conduct problems, the couple are at heightened risk for aggression in their relationship. It would also be predicted that such assortative partnering is associated with increased risk for persistence of problematic behaviors, such as mutual engagement in drug use.

Conduct Problems and Health-Risking Sexual Behavior

A greater understanding of the etiology of health-risking sexual behavior among young people is a national research priority (APPC/NIMH, 1999). Studies of prediction of sexual-risk behavior that have been conducted have generally not examined developmental models of such behaviors. Elliott (1993) described health-compromising lifestyles as involving stable patterns of behavior associated with social environments of high risk, such as poverty and unemployment. Conduct problems are a central feature of such lifestyles and have been associated with failure both to protect and achieve personal health. We posit that a developmental model of sexual-risk behaviors should take into account both high-risk social environments, including contextual and social process factors, and the development and course of conduct problems. Accelerated life courses associated with conduct problems and with at-risk contexts are an important developmental factor in adolescent exposure to STDs.

For the OYS sample, we tested a model predicting age at first intercourse (Capaldi, Crosby, & Stoolmiller, 1996). Evidence was found supporting partial mediational effects, such that the effects of parental supervision and delinquent-peer association were mediated by the boy's characteristics and behavior, especially conduct problems. A developmental progression was found such that conduct problems were strongly associated with early onset of intercourse, but the association attenuated with age. Shown in figure 22.3 are the mean numbers of juvenile arrests for the OYS youths by age of onset for intercourse. As shown, the magnitude of the association is quite striking.

The etiology of sexual-risk behaviors was examined further for the OYS sample by a study of predictors of the three key male/female sexual behaviors associated with risk for contraction of a sexually transmitted disease, namely, frequency of intercourse, number of intercourse partners, and condom use (Capaldi et al., in press). Findings were consistent with the major hypothesis, namely, that adolescents/young men showing higher levels of conduct problems would show higher levels of risk for engaging in sexual-risk behaviors across the early lifespan (adolescence to young adulthood). Conduct problems were the strongest individual predictor of engaging in sexual-risk behaviors. Furthermore, conduct problems were significantly predictive of contraction of an STD by 22–23 years of age.

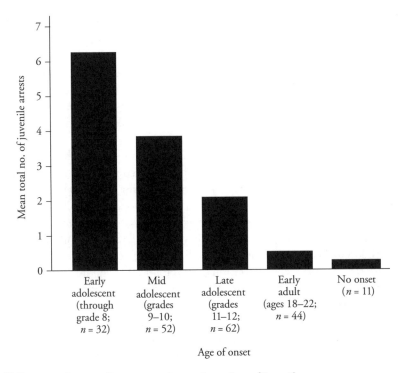

Figure 22.3   Age of onset of intercourse by total number of juvenile arrests.

Table 22.1   Correlation Matrix of Lifetime Average Sexual Behaviors and Lifetime Average Antisocial Behavior

	Frequency of intercourse	*Number of intercourse partners*	*Condom use*
Frequency of intercourse	–		
Number of intercourse partners	.33***	–	
Condom use	−.71***	−.37***	–
Conduct problems	.33***	.47***	−.48***

Gender and Ethnic Issues: Implications for Prevention and Treatment Programs

Conduct-problem behavior in girls

Understanding issues related to gender and ethnicity in the development of conduct problems is key to ensuring that conduct-disordered adolescent girls and boys from a variety of cultural backgrounds get the help and support they need to attain healthy adult functioning. Adolescent girls are less likely than boys to receive mental, social, and educational services for their conduct problems and are much more likely than boys to be incarcerated for even minor delinquent activity (Chamberlain & Reid, 1994). Despite the growth in research on conduct disorder in girls (see Keenan, Loeber, & Green, 1999 for a review), fundamental questions remain unanswered, including the nature of the developmental pattern for onset of conduct disorder in girls. The majority of girls with conduct problems appear to have an onset of these problems in adolescence (Robins, 1966).

The gender of the child, the gender of the parents, and whether there are stepparents present (Kim, Hetherington, & Reiss, 1999) should be considered in designing preventive interventions for conduct problems. Girls with behavior problems tend to have higher levels of conflict in their families compared with boys, especially conflict in the parent–child or mother–daughter dyads (Henggeler, Edwards, & Borduin, 1987). There is some evidence that parents and teachers may have different perceptions and interpretations of children's behavior problems depending on the gender of the child and gender of the reporter. However, Webster-Stratton (1996) found that children's responses to treatment were similar across gender. Interestingly, boys showed more long-term improvements when fathers were involved in the treatment (Webster-Stratton, 1996). Given that the development of conduct problems is affected increasingly by behavioral, social, and contextual variables in multiple settings outside the home, it is important that interventions for both boys and girls target multiple environments.

Ethnic issues and conduct problems

With respect to ethnicity and conduct problems, the most detailed review to date has been written by Yung and Hammond (1997). The authors would like to reiterate their point that there remains a dearth of basic developmental and clinical research on ethnic-minority children and their families regarding problem behaviors. In the United States today, one of every four Americans has ethnic-minority roots. Yet ethnic-minority children and their families continue to be treated by mental-health providers who have little training and experience in working with people from different cultural backgrounds (Vargas & Willis, 1994). Yung and Hammond (1997) describe many barriers to research, including difficulties in recruiting ethnic subjects due to location issues and high refusal rates. Work must be done to overcome these barriers so that research on the development of conduct disorders within varied cultural groups can inform intervention and treatment programs (Fisher, Storck, & Bacon, 1999; Gorman-Smith et al., 2000).

Risk and protective factors, the pattern of these influences, and children's developmental trajectories may differ between cultural groups. Thus, the rates of finishing high school in Hispanic children are much lower than for other ethnic groups. Staying in school has been found to be a protective factor against violent and delinquent behavior in Hispanic youth (Chavez, Oetting, & Swaim, 1994). Some cultural groups may be particularly vulnerable to specific risk factors (e.g., substance abuse in Native Americans and exposure to community violence for African American children; Yung & Hammond, 1997). More attention should be paid to peer-group influences within ethnic communities. Thus, differences in levels of gang membership could be a mediating factor in explaining higher levels of violent behavior. There may also be specific gender-by-ethnicity interactions (e.g., African American females have been found to engage in more violent offenses than European American females, but European American females had a greater involvement in minor status, minor property, and drug-related offences than African American females; Giordano & Cernkovitch, 1997).

Findings regarding gender and ethnic issues for conduct problems emphasize the need to intervene early, with youth in general, and to provide ethnic-minority youth with intervention approaches that are sensitive to developmental cultural contexts, including community, family, and peer-group factors (Prinz & Miller, 1991). For example, if African American girls appear to be more influenced by family processes and less susceptible to peer influences (Giordano & Cernkovitch, 1997), then interventions can focus more strongly on family relations than on peer relations.

Prevention and Treatment

To illustrate prevention approaches with parenting and peer behaviors as foci, a universal program for elementary school children designed to prevent conduct problems and conducted at the Oregon Social Learning Center (OSLC) is briefly described below. The program contains many similar components to other successful parenting interventions.

The LIFT Program – Linking the Interests of Families and Teachers

The Linking the Interests of Families and Teachers (LIFT) program is a universal preventive intervention designed for boys and girls in elementary school (Eddy, Reid, & Fetrow, 2000; Reid et al., 1999). A universal prevention targets all children in a chosen population (e.g., designated school classrooms). Following from the person–environment interaction approach, interventions affecting an entire social group (e.g., a school) provide more leverage on an individual's behaviors. Both child antisocial and child prosocial behaviors were targeted with multicomponent interventions in three settings: the home, the classroom, and the playground.

Parent training was the major theoretical focus of the intervention. The parent group-training meetings included mothers and fathers, and focused on positive reinforcement, discipline, monitoring, and problem-solving techniques that have been found to be effective with elementary school-aged children. It is important to include at least the resident father in interventions. Fathers play a major role in the well-being of their families and children, and they should not be ignored in family-focused interventions. Complementing the parent-training program was the ten-week LIFT classroom program. Activities included presentations and role-plays on specific social or problem-solving skills, small- and large-group practice time, playground time, class meetings, and presentation of daily rewards. Social and problem-solving skills conducive to positive child–peer, child–teacher, and child–parent relationships were developed.

Findings immediately following the intervention indicated significant effects for lower physical aggression toward classmates during school recess, lower parent-aversive behaviors during family problem-solving discussions, and improved social skills for the children with classmates, according to teacher ratings. Interestingly, the effects of the LIFT program were the greatest for the children who were displaying the highest rates of conduct problems (Stoolmiller, Eddy, & Reid, 2000). Findings for a three-year follow-up indicated some continuing benefits for the intervention children in lower levels of some conduct-problem behaviors, including delayed onset of association with antisocial peers, substance use, and arrests. Relative to control youth, intervention youth were 2.4 times *less* likely to be arrested.

The LIFT program is an intervention package that could be easily and inexpensively integrated into the day-to-day activities of an elementary school. In targeting an entire school class in the LIFT program, the density of reinforcement for positive behaviors for each of the individuals within the class became much higher, which provided high-rate children the opportunity to develop a new set of behaviors. In effect, each individual within the class, as well as the parents, become treatment agents.

Treatment

For youth who show repeated and severe conduct problems at adolescence resulting in multiple arrests, group programs (including group homes) or incarceration have been the traditional vehicles for both punishment and treatment. A major issue with such interventions is that they gather antisocial adolescents into groups, thus subjecting them to new delinquent-peer influences and delinquency training, which are powerfully associated with continued engagement in conduct problems at adolescence. Dishion, McCord, and Poulin (1999) provide evidence that such group interventions can actually result in iatrogenic effects, with youth showing *more* rather than fewer conduct problems afterwards. It seems that the strength of the peer influences can overwhelm the positive intervention effects.

Newer treatment programs are trying alternative approaches to aggregating antisocial youth or incarceration. Henggeler and colleagues (e.g., Henggeler & Borduin, 1990) have designed and tested a family- and home-based treatment program, termed multisystemic therapy, for serious juvenile offenders. Their intervention has been shown to improve family functioning after treatment and to reduce rearrest rates at two-year follow-up.

Sometimes, due to severe and repeated offenses, the court orders that conduct-problem youth be placed out of their homes. A highly successful program using intensive individualized residential interventions conducted at OSLC is Multidimensional Treatment Foster Care (MTFC; Chamberlain & Reid, 1998). The youth offenders are placed in a specialized foster home with parents who have been trained to manage conduct-problem youth and who receive constant support from MTFC staff. An individual treatment plan is worked out for each youth, and every aspect of their day at home and at school is involved. Each youth receives weekly skill-building, problem-solving, and aggression-management therapy from MTFC staff, and the youth's parents or guardians are coached in parenting techniques. Removing the youth from the contexts that supported conduct-problem behaviors and placing them in a specialized setting designed to reduce such behaviors can produce the leverage needed to change such serious behavior patterns. Study outcomes indicated that MTFC youth had fewer criminal referrals and returned to live with relatives more often than youth placed in more traditional care (Chamberlain & Reid, 1998). Eddy and Chamberlain (2000) found that reductions in arrest rates for the treatment group were mediated by contextual changes related to lower conduct problems; namely, increases in structured discipline and supervision, relationships with a prosocial adult mentor, and less engagement with antisocial peers.

Findings from OYS and other studies in the area confirm that conduct problems in childhood are associated with key developmental failures and have very detrimental outcomes in adolescence and young adulthood (Caspi, Elder, & Herbener, 1990; Farrington, 1991). The OYS study findings also confirmed the importance of the role of parenting practices as being implicated in the development of conduct problems in childhood. Findings from the LIFT and similar programs provide great promise that well-designed preventive interventions can make a meaningful and long-lasting improvement by reducing conduct problems. Whereas this preventive work is promising, it is difficult to change developmental patterns associated with conduct problems. The work reviewed in this chapter emphasized that the ecology of risk for conduct problems is such that children and adolescents are often embedded in social settings that provide support for such behaviors. A full range of interventions is needed if conduct problems, delinquency, and violence are to be adequately addressed.

Key Readings

Capaldi, D. M., & Clark, S. (1998). Prospective family predictors of aggression toward female partners for at-risk young men. *Developmental Psychology, 34,* 1175–1188.
This article represents the first fully prospective test with multimethod, multiagent data, including observational data of contrasting hypotheses regarding family processes that may relate to later aggression toward a partner in young men; namely, parental dyadic aggression and poor parenting, including inconsistent and coercive discipline practices. Findings indicated that the major hypothesized pathways, via unskilled parenting practices and the boys' antisocial behavior, were implicated in the intergenerational transmission of aggression.

Eddy, J. M. (2001). *Aggressive and defiant behavior: The latest assessment and treatment strategies for the conduct disorders.* Kansas City, MO: Compact Clinicals.
This volume is designed as a desk guide for clinicians working with children, adolescents, and their parents. Definitions, prevalence, and prognosis for conduct disorders are covered briefly. Diagnostic issues, characteristics, and co-occurring disorders are reviewed, along with assessment strategies. Environmentally based treatment approaches, including behavioral, cognitive, family, group, and psychodynamic approaches are presented. Two helpful appendices cover recommended resources as well as psychotropic medications for problems related to the conduct disorders, such as Attention Deficit Hyperactivity Disorder.

Keenan, K., Loeber, R., & Green, S. (1999). Conduct disorder in girls: A review of the literature. *Clinical Child and Family Psychology Review, 2,* 3–19.

Until recently, the focus of research on conduct disorder has been primarily on boys. Recent work has begun to redress that balance. This article reviews what has been learned about the precursors, developmental course, risk factors, and treatment for conduct disorder in girls, with comparisons to findings for boys. It is also helpful in identifying the gaps in our understanding of conduct disorder in girls.

Patterson, G. R., Forgatch, M. S., Yoerger, K., & Stoolmiller, M. (1998). Variables that initiate and maintain an early-onset trajectory for juvenile offending. *Development and Psychopathology, 10,* 531–547

In this article, Patterson's developmental theory regarding childhood onset of antisocial behavior, or conduct disorders, and subsequent early onset of arrest and chronic offending is explicated and tested for the Oregon Youth Study sample.

References

American Psychiatric Association (1994). *Diagnostic and statistical manual of mental disorders: DSM-IV* (4th ed.). Washington, DC: American Psychiatric Association.

Andrews, J. A., Foster, S. L., Capaldi, D. M., & Hops, H. (2000). Adolescent and family predictors of physical aggression, communication, and satisfaction in young adult couples: A prospective analysis. *Journal of Consulting and Clinical Psychology, 68,* 195–208.

APPC/NIMH Workgroup on Effectiveness of Abstinence-Only and Safer Sex Education Programs (1999). A position statement. Unpublished document.

Austen, J. (1997). *Persuasion.* Ann Arbor, MI: Tally Hall Press.

Baltes, P. B. (1983). Life-span developmental psychology: Observations on history and theory revisited. In R. M. Lerner (Ed.), *Developmental psychology: Historical and philosophical perspectives* (pp. 79–11). Hillsdale, NJ: Erlbaum.

Blumstein, A., Cohen, J., Roth, J. A., & Visher, C. A. (Eds.). (1986). *Criminal careers and career criminals* (Vol. I). Washington, DC: National Academy Press.

Bohman, M. (1996). Predispositions to criminality: Swedish adoption studies in retrospect. In G. R. Bock & J. A. Goode (Eds.), *Genetics of criminal and antisocial behavior: Ciba Foundation symposium 194* (pp. 179–197). Chichester: Wiley.

Buchanan, C. M., Maccoby, E. E., & Dornbusch, S. M. (1991). Caught between parents: Adolescents' experience in divorced homes. *Child Development, 62,* 1008–1029.

Burton, L. M., Obeidallah, D. A., & Allison, K. (1996). Ethnographic insights on social context and adolescent development among inner-city African American teens. In R. Jessor & A. Colby (Eds.), *Ethnography and human development: Context and meaning in social inquiry. The John D. And Catherine T. MacArthur Foundation series on mental health and development* (pp. 395–418). Chicago, IL: University of Chicago Press.

Cairns, R. B., Peterson, G., & Neckerman, H. J. (1988). Suicidal behavior in aggressive adolescents. *Journal of Clinical Child Psychology, 17,* 298–309.

Capaldi, D. M. (1991). Co-occurrence of conduct problems and depressive symptoms in early adolescent boys: I. Familial factors and general adjustment at 6th Grade. *Development and Psychopathology, 3,* 277–300.

Capaldi, D. M. (1992). The co-occurrence of conduct problems and depressive symptoms in early adolescent boys: II. A 2-year follow-up at Grade 8. *Development and Psychopathology, 4,* 125–144.

Capaldi, D. M., Chamberlain, P., Fetrow, R. A., & Wilson, J. (1997). Conducting ecologically valid prevention research: Recruiting and retaining a "whole village" in multimethod, multi-agent studies. *American Journal of Community Psychology, 25,* 471–492.

Capaldi, D. M., & Clark, S. (1998). Prospective family predictors of aggression toward female partners for at-risk young men. *Developmental Psychology, 34,* 1175–1188.

Capaldi, D. M., & Crosby, L. (1997). Observed and reported psychological and physical aggression in young, at-risk couples. *Social Development, 6,* 184–206.

Capaldi, D. M., Crosby, L., & Stoolmiller, M. (1996). Predicting the timing of first sexual intercourse for at-risk adolescent males. *Child Development, 67,* 344–359.

Capaldi, D. M., Dishion, T. J., Stoolmiller, M., & Yoerger, K. (2001). Aggression toward female partners by at-risk young men: The contribution of male adolescent friendships. *Developmental Psychology, 37,* 61–73.

Capaldi, D. M., & Patterson, G. R. (1991). Relation of parental transitions to boys' adjustment problems: I. A linear hypothesis; II. Mothers at risk for transitions and unskilled parenting. *Developmental Psychology, 27,* 489–504.

Capaldi, D. M., & Patterson, G. R. (1996). Can violent offenders be distinguished from frequent offenders: Prediction from childhood to adolescence. *Journal of Research in Crime and Delinquency, 33,* 206–231.

Capaldi, D. M., & Stoolmiller, M. (1999). Co-occurrence of conduct problems and depressive symptoms in early adolescent boys: III. Prediction to young-adult adjustment. *Development and Psychopathology, 11,* 59–84.

Capaldi, D. M., Stoolmiller, M., Clark, S., & Owen, L. D. (2002). Heterosexual risk behaviors in at-risk young men from early adolescence to young adulthood: Prevalence, prediction, and STD contraction. *Developmental Psychology, 38,* 394–406.

Carlson, B. E. (1987). Dating violence: A research review and comparison with spouse abuse. *Social Casework: Journal of Contemporary Social Work, 68,* 16–23.

Caspi, A., Elder, G. H., & Herbener, E. S. (1990). *Childhood personality and the prediction of life-course patterns.* New York: Cambridge University Press.

Caspi, A., Lynam, D., Moffitt, T. E., & Silva, P. A. (1993). Unraveling girls' delinquency: Biological, dispositional, and contextual contributions to adolescent misbehavior. *Developmental Psychology, 29,* 19–30.

Caspi, A., & Moffitt, T. E. (1991). Individual differences are accentuated during periods of social change: The sample case of girls at puberty. *Journal of Personality and Social Psychology, 61,* 157–168.

Chamberlain, P., & Reid, J. (1994). Differences in risk factors and adjustment for male and female delinquents in treatment foster care. *Journal of Child and Family Studies, 3,* 23–39.

Chamberlain, P., & Reid, J. (1998). Comparison of two community alternatives to incarceration for chronic juvenile offenders. *Journal of Consulting and Clinical Psychology, 6,* 624–633.

Chavez, E., Oetting, E., & Swaim, R. (1994). Dropout and delinquency: Mexican-American and Caucasian non-Hispanic youth. *Journal of Clinical Child Psychology, 23,* 47–55.

Coie, J. D., & Dodge, K. (1988). Multiple sources of data on social behavior and social status in the school: A cross-age comparison. *Child Development, 59,* 815–829.

Collins, W. A., Maccoby, E. E., Steinberg, L., Hetherington, E. M., & Bornstein, M. H. (2000). Contemporary research on parenting: The case for nature and nurture. *American Psychologist, 55,* 218–232.

Dishion, T. J., Andrews, D. W., & Crosby, L. (1995). Antisocial boys and their friends in adolescence: Relationship characteristics, quality, and interactional processes. *Child Development, 66,* 139–151.

Dishion, T. J., Andrews, D. W., Kavanagh, K., & Soberman, L. H. (1996). Preventive interventions for high-risk youth: The Adolescent Transitions Program. In R. D. Peters & R. J.

McMahon (Eds.), *Preventing childhood disorders, substance abuse, and delinquency* (pp. 184–214). Thousand Oaks, CA: Sage.

Dishion, T. J., French, D. C., & Patterson, G. R. (1995). The development and ecology of antisocial behavior. In D. Cicchetti & D. J. Cohen (Eds.), *Developmental psychopathology: Risk, disorder, and adaptation* (Vol. 2, pp. 421–471). New York: Wiley.

Dishion, T. J., McCord, J., & Poulin, F. (1999). When interventions harm: Peer groups and problem behavior. *American Psychologist, 54,* 1–10.

Dishion, T. J., Patterson, G. R., Stoolmiller, M., & Skinner, M. L. (1991). Family, school, and behavioral antecedents to early adolescent involvement with antisocial peers. *Developmental Psychology, 27,* 172–180.

Eddy, J. M. (1996). *The conduct disorders: The latest assessment and treatment strategies.* Kansas City, MO: Compact Clinicals.

Eddy, J. M., & Chamberlain, P. (2000). Family management and deviant peer association as mediators of the impact of treatment condition on youth antisocial behavior. *Journal of Consulting and Clinical Psychology, 5,* 857–863.

Eddy, J. M., Reid, J. B., & Fetrow, R. A. (2000). An elementary-school based prevention program targeting modifiable antecedents of youth delinquency and violence: Linking the Interests of Families and Teachers (LIFT). *Journal of Emotional and Behavioral Disorders, 8,* 165–176.

Elliott, D. A. (1993). *Health-enhancing and health-compromising lifestyles.* New York: Oxford University Press.

Elliott, D. S., Huizinga, D., & Ageton, S. S. (1985). *Explaining delinquency and drug use.* Beverly Hills, CA: Sage.

Elliott, D. S., & Voss, H. L. (1974). *Delinquency and dropout.* Lexington, MA: Lexington Books.

Fagot, B. I., Pears, K. C., Capaldi, D. M., Crosby, L., & Leve, C. S. (1998). Becoming an adolescent father: Precursors and parenting. *Developmental Psychology, 34,* 1209–1212.

Farrington, D. P. (1991). *Childhood aggression and adult violence: Early precursors and later life outcomes.* Hillsdale, NJ: Erlbaum.

Farrington, D. P., Gallagher, B., Morley, L., St. Ledger, R. J., & West, D. J. (1986). *Cambridge study in delinquent development: Long term follow-up.* Cambridge: Institute of Criminology, Cambridge University.

Farrington, D. P., Gallagher, B., Morley, L., St. Ledger, J. J., & West, D. J. (Eds.) (1988). *A 24-year follow-up of men from vulnerable backgrounds.* New York: Praeger.

Fisher, P. A., Storck, M., & Bacon, J. G. (1999). In the eye of the beholder: Risk and protective factors in American Indian and Caucasian adolescents. *American Journal of Orthopsychiatry, 69,* 294–304.

Forgatch, M. S., Patterson, G. R., & Skinner, M. L. (1988). A mediational model for the effect of divorce on antisocial behavior in boys. In E. M. Hetherington & J. D. Aresteh (Eds.), *Impact of divorce, single parenting, and step-parenting on children* (pp. 135–154). Hillsdale, NJ: Erlbaum.

Ge, X., Conger, R. D., Cadoret, R. J., Neiderhiser, J. M., Yates, W., Troughton, E., & Stewart, M. A. (1996). The developmental interface between nature and nurture: A mutual influence model of child antisocial behavior and parent behaviors. *Developmental Psychology, 32,* 574–589.

Giordano, P. C., & Cernkovich, S. A. (1997). Gender and antisocial behavior. In D. M. Stoff, J. Breiling, & J. D. Maser (Eds.), *Handbook of antisocial behavior* (pp. 496–510). New York: Wiley.

Gjone, H., & Stevenson, J. (1997). The association between internalizing and externalizing behavior in childhood and early adolescence: Genetic or environmental common influences. *Journal of Abnormal Child Psychology, 25,* 277–286.

Gorman-Smith, D., Tolan, P. H., Henry, D. B., & Florsheim, P. (2000). Patterns of family functioning and adolescent outcomes among urban African American and Mexican American families. *Journal of Family Psychology, 14,* 436–457.

Henggeler, S. W., & Borduin, C. M. (1990). *Family therapy and beyond: A multisystemic approach to treating the behavior problems of children and adolescents.* Pacific Grove, CA: Brooks/Cole.

Henggeler, S. W., Edwards, J., & Borduin, C. M. (1987). The family relations of female juvenile delinquents. *Journal of Abnormal Child Psychology, 15,* 199–209.

Jouriles, E. N., Bourg, W. J., & Farris, A. M. (1991). Marital adjustment and child conduct problems: A comparison of the correlation across subsamples. *Journal of Consulting and Clinical Psychology, 59,* 354–357.

Junger, M. (1994). Accidents and crime. In T. Hirschi & M. Gottfredson (Eds.), *The generality of deviance* (pp. 81–112). New Brunswick, NJ: Transaction.

Keenan, K., Loeber, R., & Green, S. (1999). Conduct disorder in girls: A review of the literature. *Clinical Child and Family Psychology Review, 2,* 3–19.

Kim, H. K., & Capaldi, D. M. (2002). Assortative partnering by antisocial behavior and depressive symptoms: Risk for aggression in romantic relationships. Manuscript.

Kim, J. E., Hetherington, E. M., & Reiss, D. (1999). Associations among family relationships, antisocial peers, and adolescents' externalizing behaviors: Gender and family type differences. *Child Development, 70,* 1209–1230.

Kovacs, M., Paulauskas, S., Gatsonis, C., & Richards, C. (1988). Depressive disorders in childhood. III. A longitudinal study of comorbidity with and risk for conduct disorders. *Journal of Affective Disorders, 15,* 205–217.

Krueger, R. F., Moffitt, T. E., Caspi, A., Bleske, A., & Silva, P. A. (1998). Assortative mating for antisocial behavior: Developmental and methodological implications. *Behavior Genetics, 28,* 173–186.

Lahey, B. B., Hartdagen, S. E., Frick, P. J., McBurnett, K., Connor, R., & Hynd, G. W. (1988). Conduct disorder: Parsing the confounded relation to parental divorce and antisocial personality. *Journal of Abnormal Psychology, 97,* 334–337.

Lipsey, M. W., & Derzon, J. H. (1998). Predictors of violent or serious delinquency in adolescence and early adulthood. In R. Loeber & D. P. Farrington (Eds.), *Serious and violent juvenile offenders: Risk factors and successful interventions* (pp. 86–105). Thousand Oaks, CA: Sage.

Magdol, L., Moffitt, T. E., Caspi, A., Newman, D. L., Fagan, J., & Silva, P. A. (1997). Gender differences in partner violence in a birth cohort of 21-year-olds: Bridging the gap between clinical and epidemiological approaches. *Journal of Consulting and Clinical Psychology, 65,* 68–78.

McCord, J. (1999). Understanding childhood and subsequent crime. *Aggressive Behavior, 25,* 241–253.

Moffitt, T. E. (1993). Adolescence-limited and life-course-persistent antisocial behavior: A developmental taxonomy. *Psychological Review, 100,* 674–701.

Newcomb, M. D. (1987). Consequences of teenage drug use: The transition from adolescence to young adulthood. *Drugs and Society, 1*(4), 25–60.

Offord, D. R., Boyle, M. C., & Racine, Y. A. (1991). The epidemiology of antisocial behavior in childhood and adolescence. In D. J. Pepler & K. H. Rubin (Eds.), *The development and treatment of childhood aggression* (pp. 31–54). Hillsdale, NJ: Erlbaum.

Pajer, K. A. (1998). What happens to "bad" girls? A review of the adult outcomes of antisocial adolescent girls. *American Journal of Psychiatry, 155,* 862–870.

Patterson, G. R. (1982). *Coercive family process.* Eugene, OR: Castalia.

Patterson, G. R., & Capaldi, D. M. (1991). Antisocial parents: Unskilled and vulnerable. In P. A.

Cowan & E. M. Hetherington (Eds.), *Advances in family research: Vol. 2. Family transitions* (pp. 195–218). Hillsdale, NJ: Erlbaum.

Patterson, G. R., Forgatch, M. S., Yoerger, K., & Stoolmiller, M. (1998). Variables that initiate and maintain an early-onset trajectory for juvenile offending. *Development and Psychopathology, 10*, 531–547.

Prinz, R. J., & Miller, G. E. (1991). Issues in understanding and treating childhood conduct problems in disadvantaged populations. *Journal of Clinical Child Psychology, 20*, 379–385.

Radke-Yarrow, M. (1998). *Children of depressed mothers.* New York: Cambridge University Press.

Raine, A. (1997). Antisocial behavior and psychophysiology: A biosocial perspective and a prefrontal dysfunction hypothesis. In D. M. Stoff, J. Breiling, & J. D. Maser (Eds.), *Handbook of antisocial behavior* (pp. 289–304). New York: Wiley.

Reid, J. B., Eddy, J. M., Fetrow, R. A., & Stoolmiller, M. (1999). Description and immediate impacts of a preventative intervention for conduct problems. *American Journal of Community Psychology, 27*, 483–517.

Robins, L. N. (1966). *Deviant children grown up.* Baltimore: Williams & Wilkins.

Robins, L. N., & Price, R. K. (1991). Adult disorders predicted by childhood conduct problems: Results from the NIMH epidemiological catchment area project. *Psychiatry, 54*, 116–132.

Rothbart, M. K., Posner, M. I., & Hershey, K. L. (1995). Temperament, attention, and developmental psychopathology. In D. Cicchetti & D. J. Cohen (Eds.), *Developmental psychopathology: Vol. 1. Theory and methods* (pp. 315–341). New York: Wiley.

Scaramella, L. V., Conger, R. D., Simons, R. L., & Whitbeck, L. B. (1998). Predicting risk for pregnancy by late adolescence: A social contextual perspective. *Developmental Psychology, 34*, 1233–1245.

Scarr, S., & McCartney, K. (1983). How people make their own environments: A theory of genotype leading to environment effects. *Child Development, 54*, 424–435.

Seligman, M. E. P., & Csikszentmihalyi, M. (2000). Positive psychology: An introduction. *American Psychologist, 55*, 5–14.

Serbin, L. A., Cooperman, J. M., Peters, P. L., Lehoux, P. M., Stack, D. M., & Schwartzman, A. E. (1998). Intergenerational transfer of psychosocial risk in women with childhood histories of aggression, withdrawal, or aggression and withdrawal. *Developmental Psychology, 34*, 1246–1262.

Shaffer, D. (1988). The epidemiology of teen suicide: An examination of risk factors. *Journal of Clinical Psychiatry, 49*, 36–41.

Stattin, H., & Magnusson, D. (1990). Pubertal maturation in female development. Hillsdale, NJ: Erlbaum.

Stoolmiller, M. (1994). Antisocial behavior, delinquent peer association and unsupervised wandering for boys: Growth and change from childhood to early adolescence. *Multivariate Behavioral Research, 29*, 263–288.

Stoolmiller, M., Eddy, J. M., & Reid, J. B. (2000). Detecting and describing preventative intervention effects in a universal school-based randomized trail targeting delinquent and violent behavior. *Journal of Consulting and Clinical Psychology, 68*, 296–306.

Tremblay, R. E., Japel, C., Perusse, D., McDuff, P., Boivin, M., Zoccolillo, M., & Montplaisir, J. (1999). The search for the age of "onset" of physical aggression: Rousseau and Bandura revisited. *Criminal Behavior and Mental Health, 9*, 8–13.

Vargas, L. A., & Willis, D. J. (1994). New directions in the treatment and assessment of ethnic minority children and adolescents. *Journal of Clinical Child Psychology, 23*, 2–4.

Walker, H. (1995). *The acting-out child: Coping with classroom disruption* (2nd ed.). Longmont, CA: Sopris West.

Webster-Stratton, C. (1996). Early-onset conduct problems: Does gender make a difference? *Journal of Consulting and Clinical Psychology, 64*, 540–551.

Wiesner, M., & Capaldi, D. M. (2001, April). The impact of childhood factors on delinquent behavior of young males: Results of a longitudinal study. Paper presented at SRCD, Minneapolis, MN.

Wilson, W. J. (1987). *The truly disadvantaged: The intercity, the underclass, and public policy.* Chicago: University of Chicago Press.

Wolfgang, M. E., Figlio, R. M., & Sellin, T. (1972). *Delinquency of a birth cohort.* Chicago: University of Chicago Press.

Yung, B. R., & Hammond, R. W. (1997). Antisocial behavior in minority groups: Epidemiological and cultural perspectives. In D. M. Stoff, J. Breiling, & J. D. Maser (Eds.), *Handbook of antisocial behavior* (pp. 474–495). New York: Wiley.

CHAPTER TWENTY-THREE

Leaving Home: The Runaway and the Forgotten Throwaway

Thomas P. Gullotta

Introduction

Each year at least half a million young people will leave their homes (Snyder & Sickmund, 1995; Whitbeck, Hoyt, & Yoder, 1999). For some young people, running away will be a short-term romantic foray into a Tom Sawyer series of adventures, ending when either boredom or an empty wallet dictates a return home. For others, it will be a desperate action to escape from family, school, or community crises with which they cannot cope. For still others, leaving home represents the only option; whether through implicit or explicit messages, these young people have learned that their families no longer want them.

A Social Historical Perspective on Running Away

Unlike Europe in the eighteenth and nineteenth centuries, with its rigid class and employment guilds, America, with its different ideas, embraced individuals who seized opportunity and followed it wherever it might lead. To illustrate, consider the exploits of a young fellow name John Levy. Born in the West Indies just before 1800, he was supposed to become a carpenter but became a sailor instead. His experiences on the high seas included robbery by pirates, abduction for war service by the British navy, and desertion from the same service. Settling into a quieter life, Levy became a pottery merchant and relocated to Boston at the advanced age of 20 (Kett, 1977). There are countless other tales, some truthful, others more fiction than fact, of young lads who – like Benjamin Franklin or Davy Crockett – defied parental authority to seize the moment. Certainly, some failed. Others, as did Franklin and Crockett, found success and acclaim.

American fiction reflects this indulgent attitude toward running away. Whether the character is Cooper's Natty Bumppo, Twain's Huckleberry Finn, or Hemingway's Nick Adams, most American writers portray leaving home as a sensible solution to seemingly unsolvable problems. The reader of the *Adventures of Huckleberry Finn,* for instance, can understand Huck's reasons for escaping from the cruelty of his drunken father when no other avenue is open to him:

> The judge and the widow went to law to get the court to take me away from him and let one of them be my guardian; but it was a new judge that had just come, and he didn't know the old man; so he said courts mustn't interfere and separate families if they could help it; said he'd druther not take a child away from its father. (Clements, 1884/1962, p. 42)

Thus, Huck's faking of his own death and running away are an acceptable way out of intolerable life circumstances.

Similarly, the reader empathizes with Hemingway's Nick Adams in his decision to escape from the game wardens who are after him for poaching. Nick's journey to the Italian front in World War I is accepted by the reader as a way in which a young man can mature into an adult. And the reader invariably agrees with Cooper's Natty Bumppo that civilization and nature do not mix. Though Natty is no longer a young man when he runs afoul of the law, he has remained so in spirit. He has always behaved honestly, truthfully, and in harmony with nature, but he gets into trouble when he kills a deer out of season with his musket (named, appropriately enough, Killdeer). His punishment by the authorities for killing the deer stands in sharp contrast to his earlier experiences, when his skills in the woods and as a scout earned him such names as Deerslayer, La Longue Carabine, Hawkeye, and Pathfinder. This experience convinces Natty that the selfish exploitation of nature by white settlers is not for him, and he becomes a voluntary outcast, following the wilderness westward.

These three brief references to American literature only serve to illustrate the hundreds of stories in print and on stage, film, and television that have contributed to our appreciation of the runaway – an appreciation of the promise of adventure the circus holds for young boys; an appreciation of the reasons why a young girl with a dog named "Toto" would leave home. In each of these stories, civilization intrudes on or smothers the natural instincts of the individual. The hero or heroine in each tale comes to face a realization that to remain with or to attempt to challenge the status quo will most assuredly result in their own personal destruction. The choice is clear: Huck paddles away in a canoe; Nick enlists in the army; Natty starts for the Great Plains; and Dorothy, with her little dog "Toto," flees from home to destinations unknown.

Major reasons for this benevolent attitude in America toward runaways can be found in the availability of land and in the value placed on individuality and ingenuity by the inhabitants of the New World. First, the sheer vastness of North America meant that success was rooted not in people's past lives but in their future intentions. With certain exceptions (women and African Americans), land was available to anyone who wanted it, and productivity was limited only by the size of the available workforce.

The influence of land on the beliefs of early Americans was remarkable. Some writers have suggested that the availability of land discouraged the rise of a noble class. Others have suggested that being thousands of miles away from "corrupted" Europe offered the promise of a society free from foreign entanglements. To Americans, these facts meant only one thing – opportunity.

Next, because individuality and ingenuity were widely believed to be the unique features separating the New World from the Old, it is understandable that the runaway was not viewed harshly. With limitless opportunities available to the resourceful, the runaway joined the thousands of other runaways (immigrants) from Europe in search of a new life (Brenner, 1970; Libertoff, 1980).

However, this tolerant attitude gradually changed. From the middle of the nineteenth century on, society increasingly viewed adolescents as consumers rather than contributors. With this redefinition of their status came increasing dependence on the family for support. Society's perception of the runaway changed as society itself changed. With the close of the frontier and the replacement of the virtue of individuality by obedience to an increasingly structured society, running away became an unacceptable response to pressure. In the next section we examine some perspectives on the forces that induce running away.

Theoretical Perspectives on the Causes of Running Away

There are several definitions of the term "runaway." The one we will use is "a youth between the ages of 10 and 17, inclusive, who has been absent from home, at least overnight, without parental or guardian permission" (Opinion Research Center, 1976, p. 3).

Remarkably, little theoretical work has been been done in recent years on runaways. This may be because this population has been lost in the wider category of "missing" youth. However, drawing on earlier work, we find that several explanations for running away have been offered.

The strain theory (Adams, 1980) proposes that deviant behavior is the result of socially induced pressure toward deviance. Psychological theories suggest runaway behavior is an expression of impulsive tendencies. The sources of strain capable of producing a deep sense of alienation can be found in the home, in school, or with friends. In particular, Brennan, Huizinga, and Elliott (1978) suggest that feelings of estrangement from family members place a youth in a state of personal "drift," creating the chance of alienation from family norms. When young people feel estranged from their families, they may turn to school or friends for support and understanding, for allegiance and commitment. If the peer group is nonconforming or the school environment is hostile or rejecting, the resulting increase in alienation may set the stage for flight from home.

The alternative-values model (Adams & Munro, 1979) is not far removed from strain theory. According to this model, runaways may be searching for new value structures and for meaning in society. As in an earlier time, leaving home reflects not only disillusionment with the status quo but hope that a new world filled with opportunity awaits those willing to take the risk. The problem for these young people "is the demands of society on individuals for systematization, conformity, and reduction of self to a piece of the system" (Adams & Munro, 1979, p. 366). For these individuals, leaving home is running away from an opposing value system that has generated conflict and hate (Adams & Looft, 1977; Adams & Munro, 1979).

In contrast to the strain and alternative-values explanations, social control theory (Adams, 1980) suggests that the runaway has failed to internalize socially acceptable behavioral norms. In social control theory this internalization insulates a youth from those situations or individuals associated with deviant behavior. If internalization has not occurred, the young person is likely to engage in criminal behavior or such deviant acts as running away. Advocates of control theory contend that weak bonds to family, school, work, or the general community, coupled with exposure to deviant behavior, increase the probability of a youth's leaving home. Thus, the early socialization of runaways produced a weak commitment to conventional norms and a low level of integration into conventional social groups and institutions (Brennan, Huizinga, & Elliott, 1978).

A last perspective for explaining the runaway's behavior is the deindividuation model (Adams & Munro, 1979), in which young people leave home to find out who they are. This need to discover one's being results from feelings of rootlessness and purposelessness.

From these perspectives an idea of the possible degree of pathology in the action of running away begins to emerge. In the strain and alternative-values models, external pressures induce young people to leave home. Because the pressures are environmental, these models do not imply that the young person is emotionally disturbed. In contrast, control theory suggests that a lack of internal restraints encourages running away. The deindividuation model, though it does not deny environmental influences, focuses primarily on the individual's feelings of helplessness and worthlessness. Thus, in the last two models, psychological dynamics are the primary cause of running away. In the next section we examine some of the research findings supporting or refuting each of these positions.

Research on Runaways

Family relationships are a crucial factor in whether a young person leaves home. Many studies report problems not only between parents and runaways, but between the parents themselves. Home life in these studies is described as tense and strife-ridden, with many households being single-parent (Brennan, Huizinga, & Eliott, 1978; English & English, 1999; Finkelhor, Hotaling, & Sedlak, 1990; Swaim & Bracken, 1997). Sexual and physical victimization is a frequent occurrence (Kaufman & Widom, 1999; Molnar et al., 1999; Rotheram-Borus et al., 1996; Simons & Whitbeck, 1991; Yoder, 1999; Yoder, Hoyt, & Whitbeck, 1998).

The early psychological literature overwhelmingly supports the idea that running away is an indicator of severe emotional problems. For example, an early study of 300 runaway boys in a state training school showed them to be friendless, immature, timid, and feeling inadequate and rejected (Jenkins, 1971). Additional evidence for this position comes from a number of other clinical studies (Edelbrock, 1980; Leventhal, 1963; O'Neal & Lee, 1959) in which running away is viewed as a psychopathological disorder manifested in the anxious, impulsive, hostile behavior of the young people these clinicians see in treatment centers. Recent publications continue to highlight the disturbed psychological profiles of these youth (Rohr, 1996).

Lately, work has focused on the increased risk for suicide confronting these young people. In particular, females are more likely to consider suicide than males, and youth who have been physically or sexually abused are at higher risk than non-abused youth (Molnar et al., 1999; Rotheram-Borus, 1993; Yoder, 1999; Yoder, Hoyt, & Whitbeck, 1998).

Still other studies have focused on the increased risk these young people face for HIV and other sexually transmitted diseases. Given that most runaway youth are education- ally ill-prepared to live independently, legitimate job opportunities are nonexistent. Rather, to earn money means panhandling, stealing, drug dealing, or exchanging sex for money. Dealing drugs more often than not results in eventually doing drugs, and IV drug use with dirty works is an invitation for HIV (Booth, Zhang, & Kwiatkowski, 1999). Similarly, unprotected sex for money is another high-risk behavior for HIV and other sexually transmitted diseases (Rotheram-Borus et al., 1996).

It would seem that there is widespread agreement about runaways and their emotional problems, but that is not so. An equally large body of work dating from the 1970s con- tradicts these findings. Essentially, this material views running away as a healthy response to the pressures of a difficult home situation or simply as an adventure. To illustrate, this literature has reported for many years that about half of the young people who run away do not run far but stay in the general vicinity of home (Nye, 1980a, 1980b; Shellow et al., 1967; Snyder & Sickmund, 1995). Most run no farther than a friend's or relative's home (Brennan, Huizinga, & Elliott, 1978; Snyder & Sickmund, 1995). Most stay away for just a brief time; many are gone only overnight (Nye, 1980a, 1980b; Snyder & Sickmund, 1995). Only a minority run away more than three times, and most run away without companions (Shellow et al., 1967; Snyder & Sickmund, 1995). Finally, running away is rarely well planned. As with Dorothy of the Wizard of Oz fame, most decisions to leave are made on the spur of the moment, when emotions are running high (Gullotta, 1979; Shellow et al., 1967).

Recent data reported by the Office of Juvenile Justice and Delinquency Prevention support these observations. About one-third of the time a family argument about house rules, friends, school, or staying out late preceded a running episode. Most runaways (94 percent) ultimately ran to a friend's or relative's house. Sixty-seven percent of caretakers knew the location of their child at least half the time, and the duration of the run was two days or less for 49 percent of the youth (Finkelhor, Hotaling, & Sedlak, 1990; Snyder & Sickmund, 1995).

What accounts for these decidedly different views of leaving home? I suspect that the answer is found in that one group has run away from home while the other has been thrown out of their homes. Unfortunately, teasing out these throwaways from those who have run away in the published literature is extremely difficult.

But first, how do we define a throwaway? A throwaway is a young person who does not willingly leave home but was forced to do so by the attitudes or actions of his or her parents or guardian (Gullotta, 1978). The throwaway comes from a family in which the parents have cut all ties to the young person. The problem is not simply "a weakening in a relationship but . . . a breakdown in the fabric of the family, a failure so severe, so emotionally tearing, that the bonds between parent and child are broken" (Gullotta, 1979, p. 113).

Several situations are capable of producing such a strong and complete rejection. One is the discovery of incest between parent and child or between children (Janus et al., 1987; Kurtz, Kurtz, & Jarvis, 1991). The abuse of drugs, criminal behavior, or promiscuity may result in the termination of the family relationship. Or the young person may be suffering from a non-responsive serious mental illness or pervasive developmental delay, like Asperger's, that makes family life torturous. In any event the breakdown of the family is complete and irreparable. In some cases it may be the end of repeated attempts, "to stop some parentally perceived undesirable behavior. In other situations, it constitutes a scapegoating or desertion of the child" (Gullotta, 1979, p. 114).

Recent studies underscore this understanding as researchers describe young people fleeing untenable circumstances (Miller, Eggertson-Tacon, & Quigg, 1990) and of living isolated, depressed, antisocial lives (Adams, Gullotta, & Clancy, 1985; Hier, Korboot, & Schweitzer, 1990). Finkelhor, Hotaling, and Sedlak (1990) report that 84 percent of these youth are over the age of 16, with nearly equal numbers of males and females. Only 19 percent come from intact homes. And in keeping with the earlier statement that family bonds were not merely strained but broken, 44 percent of their population was asked to leave home, 11 percent ran away and were refused permission to return home, and the remainder ran away and the "caretaker doesn't care" (p. 153).

Synthesis

It has been estimated that roughly 127,000 of the half-million youth who leave home each year are throwaways (Snyder & Sickmund, 1995; Whitbeck, Hoyt, & Yoder, 1999). It is my suspicion that it is among these youth that reports of high-risk sexual behavior are occurring most. It is among these youth that drug misuse is happening. It is among these youth that suicidal ideation is highest. It is among these youth that victimization past and present is most frequent. Yet, this neediest of all youth groups is lost within the wider category of runaways which in turn has disappeared into the catch-all category of "missing children."

The challenge for researchers in the coming years is to tease this group out of the runaway population. An even greater challenge exists for service providers who have yet to respond to the enormous needs of these young people. Residential facilities have not worked. Community group and foster homes have been equally ineffective. Other models of supportive care need to be developed that extend beyond minimal caretaking to truly meet the needs of these lost youth.

References

Adams, G. R. (1980). Runaway youth projects: Comments on care programs for runaways and throwaways. *Journal of Adolescence, 3,* 321–334.

Adams, G. R., Gullotta, T. P., & Clancy, M. A. (1985). Homeless adolescents: A descriptive study of similarities and differences between runaways and throwaways. *Adolescence, 79,* 715–724.

Adams, G. R., & Looft, W. R. (1977). Cultural change: Education and youth. *Adolescence, 22,* 137–149.

Adams, G. R., & Munro, G. (1979). Portrait of the North American runaway: A critical review. *Journal of Youth and Adolescence, 8,* 359–373.

Booth, R. E., Zhang, Y., & Kwiatkowski, C. F. (1999). The challenge of changing drug and sex risk behaviors of runaway and homeless adolescents. *Child Abuse & Neglect, 23,* 1295–1306.

Brennan, T., Huizinga, D., & Elliott, D. S. (1978). *The social psychology of runaways.* Lexington, MA: Lexington Books.

Brenner, R. H. (1970). *Children and youth in America* (Vol. 1). Cambridge, MA: Harvard University Press.

Clements, S. (1884/1962). *Adventures of Huckleberry Finn.* San Francisco, CA: Chandler Publishing Co.

Edelbrock, C. (1980). Running away from home: Incidence and correlates among children and youth referred for mental health services. *Journal of Family Issues, 1,* 210–228.

English, N. D., & English, L. M. (1999). A proactive approach to youth who run. *Child Abuse & Neglect, 23,* 693–698.

Finkelhor, D., Hotaling, G., & Sedlak, A. (1990*). Missing, abducted, runaway, and throwaway children in America.* US Department of Justice. Washington, DC: US Government Printing Office.

Gullotta, T. P. (1978). Runaway: Reality or myth? *Adolescence, 13,* 543–549.

Gullotta, T. P. (1979). Leaving home: Family relationships of the runaway child. *Social Casework, 60,* 111–114.

Hier, S. J., Korboot, P. J., & Schweitzer, R. D. (1990). Social adjustment and symptomatology in two types of homeless adolescents and throwaways. *Adolescence, 25,* 761–772.

Janus, M. D., McCormack, A., Burgess, A. W., & Hartman, C. (1987). *Adolescent runaways: Causes and consequences.* Lexington, MA: Lexington Books.

Jenkins, R. L. (1971). The runaway reaction. *American Journal of Psychiatry, 128,* 168–173.

Kaufman, J. G., & Widom, C. S. (1999). Childhood victimization, running away and delinquency. *Journal of Research in Crime and Delinquency, 36,* 347–370.

Kett, J. F. (1977). *Rites of passage: Adolescence in America 1790 to the present.* New York: Basic Books.

Kurtz, P. D., Kurtz, G. L., & Jarvis, S. V. (1991). Problems of maltreated runaway youth. *Adolescence, 26,* 543–556.

Leventhal, T. (1963). Control problems in runaway children. *Archives of General Psychiatry, 9,* 122–128.

Libertoff, K. (1980). The runaway child in America: A social history. *Journal of Family Issues, 1,* 151–164.

Miller, A. T., Eggertson-Tacon, C., & Quigg, B. (1990). Patterns of runaway behavior within a larger systems context: The road to empowerment. *Adolescence, 25,* 271–290.

Molnar, B. E., Shade, S. B., Kral, A. H., Booth, R. H., & Watters, J. K. (1999). Suicidal behavior and sexual/physical abuse among street youth. *Child Abuse & Neglect, 22,* 213–222.

Nye, I. F. (1980a). *Runaways: A report for parents.* Extension Bulletin # 0743. Pullman, WA: Washington State University.

Nye, I. F. (1980b). *Runaways: Some critical issues for professionals and society.* Extension Bulletin # 0744. Pullman, WA: Washington State University.

O'Neal, P., & Lee, R. (1959). Childhood patterns predictive of adult schizophrenia: 30 year follow-up. *American Journal of Psychiatry, 115,* 391–395.

Opinion Research Corporation (1976). *National statistical survey on runaway youth* (Part 1). Princeton, NJ: Opinion Research Corporation.

Rohr, M. E. (1996). Identifying adolescent runaways: The predictive utility of the personality inventory for children. *Adolescence, 31*, 605–623.

Rotheram-Borus, M. J. (1993). Suicide behavior and risk factors among runaway youths. *American Journal of Psychiatry, 150*, 103–107.

Rotheram-Borus, M. J., Mahler, K. A., Koopman, C., & Langabeer, K. (1996). Sexual abuse history and associated multiple risk behavior in adolescent runaways. *American Journal of Orthopsychiatry, 66*, 390–400.

Shellow, R., Schamp, J., Liebow, E., & Unger, E. (1967). *Suburban runaways of the 1960's.* Monographs of the Society for Research in Child Development, 32, Serial # 111.

Simons, R. L., & Whitbeck, L. B. (1991). Sexual abuse as a precursor to prostitution and victimization among adolescents and homeless women. *Journal of Family Issues, 12*, 361–379.

Snyder, H. N., & Sickmund, M. (1995). *Juvenile offenders and victims: A national report.* Washington, DC: Office of Juvenile Justice and Delinquency Prevention.

Swaim, K. F., & Bracken, B. A. (1997). Global and domain-specific self-concepts of a matched sample of adolescent runaways and nonrunaways. *Journal of Clinical Child Psychology, 26*, 397–403.

Whitbeck, L. B., Hoyt, D. R., & Yoder, K. A. (1999). A risk-amplification model of victimization and depressive symptoms among runaway and homeless adolescents. *American Journal of Community Psychology, 27*, 273–296.

Yoder, K. A. (1999). Comparing suicide attempters, suicide ideators, and nonsuicidal homeless and runaway adolescents. *Suicide and Life-Threatening Behavior, 29*, 25–36.

Yoder, K. A., Hoyt, D. R., & Whitbeck, L. B. (1998). Suicidal behavior among homeless and runaway adolescents. *Journal of Youth and Adolescence, 27*, 753–771.

CHAPTER TWENTY-FOUR

Crime, Delinquency, and Youth Gangs

Daniel J. Flannery, David L. Hussey, Laurie Biebelhausen, and Kelly L. Wester

Introduction

This chapter provides an overview of delinquent and criminal behavior among adolescents, utilizing a developmental perspective to focus on violence, mental health, and youth gangs. We identify key differences in adolescent delinquent and criminal behavior associated with gender, ethnicity, family, and community factors.

Juvenile delinquency vs. conduct disorder

Juvenile delinquency is a legal term that is defined as criminal behavior committed by minors. Delinquency is legally differentiated from status offenses, which are considered illegal only because of a child's age. The major status offenses include truancy, alcohol and drug use, running away, and incorrigibility. Historically, the juvenile justice system has been more focused on rehabilitation and treatment versus punishment; however, since the 1990s, many states have enacted tougher sentencing rules on juveniles, including the waiving or transferring of greater numbers of youthful offenders to adult courts.

It is important to differentiate delinquent behavior from the clinical diagnosis of conduct disorder. The essential feature of a conduct disorder (CD) is a repetitive and persistent pattern of behavior in which the basic rights of others or major age-appropriate societal norms or rules are violated (APA, 1994). This often includes physical aggression or the destruction of property. A young person adjudicated as delinquent may or may not meet the diagnostic criteria for conduct disorder. If an adolescent engages in delinquent/criminal behavior persistently and across settings, that person is more likely to also have a conduct disorder. Risk factors associated with poorer long-term prognosis include early age of onset, and the occurrence of more serious and frequent conduct disordered behavior.

Official data vs. self-report data

Rates of juvenile delinquency and crime have been reported using both "official" data sources like the Uniform Crime Report or National Crime Victimization Survey, and sources utilizing youth self-reports such as the Youth Risk Behavior Survey (Snyder & Sickmund, 1999). While there has been much controversy over the accuracy of self-report versus "official" data on arrest rates, evidence suggests that self-report data on occurrence of delinquent behavior are higher than official report data (Elliott, 1994). Official data may underreport rates of juvenile offending for several reasons, including: approximately half of all crimes go unreported (Snyder & Sickmund, 1999); juveniles who are "caught" are often not arrested; most adolescents report a history of engaging in delinquent or criminal activity long before they are "officially" arrested; and juveniles are usually just charged with the most serious delinquent acts. Numbers of arrests also do not equal numbers of offenders because a relatively small proportion of chronic offenders (about 6–8 percent) account for most of the arrests for juvenile criminal offending (50–70 percent) (Howell et al., 1995; Tracy, Wolfgang, & Figlio, 1990).

Incidence/prevalence

Juveniles can be exposed to violence, victimized by violence, or be perpetrators of violence, and recent research suggests a high association among these three phenomena (Singer et al., 1995; Widom, 1989). Further, exposure, victimization, and risk for perpetration are all significantly related to etiology of delinquency and criminal offending, as well as to youth gang membership and activity. Rates of incidence/prevalence are reported for youth between ages 15 and 19, unless otherwise noted.

Juvenile crime rates

Homicide. The United States is one of the most violent countries in the world, with a rate (1.66 per 100,000 population) for firearm-related deaths among children 2.7 times higher than the next closest country, Finland (.62 per 100,000) (Centers for Disease Control & Prevention, 1997; Snyder & Sickmund, 1999). Between 1985 and 1991 arrests for violent crime increased 125 percent among females (from 9,000 to 21,000 violent crime-index arrests) compared to an increase of 67 percent for males during the same period. Increases through the mid-1990s in homicide were due mostly to increases in offending among males, and the increased use of firearms in the perpetration of homicide. Guns were used in 53 percent of homicides between 1980 and 1987, but in 82 percent of all homicides committed by juveniles in 1994. For the period 1980–97, 88 percent of juvenile perpetrators of homicide were 15 years or older, 93 percent were male, and 56 percent were black. Over 90 percent of juvenile murderers kill someone of the same race. Males are much more likely to kill an acquaintance (54 percent) or a stranger (37 percent), while females are more likely to kill a family member (39 percent vs. 9

percent). Female adolescents are much more likely to use a knife (32 percent) or other violent means (e.g. strangling) to kill, than use a gun (4 percent).

Arrest rates for crime perpetrated by juveniles have decreased over the period 1997–9 (Snyder & Sickmund, 1999). For example, violent crime arrests for juveniles decreased 19 percent in 1998 compared to 1994 rates. Most of the declines have been related to: (1) reductions in violent crime in several large urban areas; (2) a decline in the use of firearms (down to 70 percent of all homicides from 82 percent); (3) a decrease in violent crime perpetrated by black males; and (4) declining rates of illicit substance use. In 1998, juveniles still accounted for 12 percent of all violent crime arrests, 6 percent of all arrests for murder, 11 percent of forcible rapes, 12 percent of aggravated assaults, and 16 percent of robberies. Female adolescents accounted for about one of every four arrests for violent crime by juveniles.

In 1997, 6 juveniles (aged under 18) were killed in the United States every day, with 50 percent of victims between the ages of 15 and 17 (Snyder & Sickmund, 1999). Compared to younger victims, youth aged 12 and over were more likely to be male victims (81 percent vs. 55 percent) and black (53 percent vs. 39 percent). In the 1980s, males accounted for 62 percent of juvenile homicide victims, a rate that increased to 71 percent in the 1990s. The ratio of juvenile homicide victims (black to white) has also varied, going from about 4:1 in the 1980s to 7:1 in 1993, before declining to 5:1 in 1997. Adolescent males are more likely to be victims of juvenile perpetrators of homicide (83 percent) than females. Victims are about equally divided by race (50 percent white, 47 percent black). Females are much more likely to be killed by another family member.

Less serious delinquent behavior. If one excludes the most serious forms of violent behavior, the prevalence of adolescent delinquent behavior is fairly common, with most adolescents reporting they have engaged in at least one form of delinquent behavior by the time they are 18. In the National Longitudinal Survey of Youth, a self-report survey of 12–16-year-olds, one in five adolescents reported they drank alcohol at least once in the last 30 days (50 percent of 14- and 15-year-olds), and one in four 14–15-year-olds said they had tried marijuana (Snyder & Sickmund, 1999). By age 12, 79 percent of 16-year-olds reported they had purposely destroyed property, 63 percent had committed assault, 60 percent had carried a handgun, 52 percent said they had belonged to a gang, 34 percent had run away from home at least once, and 34 percent had stolen something worth $50 or more (Snyder & Sickmund, 1999). One in five had been arrested by age 12, 39 percent had smoked cigarettes, and one in ten had sold drugs. According to the Center for Disease Control and Prevention's Youth Risk Behavior Surveillance System (YRBS), 37 percent of high school students reported they were in one or more fights in the previous year, with about 1 in 20 resulting in serious injury. Students in the 9th and 10th grades were more likely to get into fights than students in the 11th and 12th grades. Rates of lawbreaking for almost all behaviors were greater among adolescents who used drugs compared to non-users.

Summary. Most youth have engaged in at least one form of delinquent behavior by age 18. Delinquent acts typically committed by youth prior to age 18 include alcohol or drug use, defacing property, assault, carrying a weapon, running away, or stealing. Official crime data (i.e., arrest records) underrepresents the true incidence of delinquent behavior because not all delinquency is reported. During the past three years there has been a decline in illicit drug use, the use of firearms by juveniles, and overall reductions in violent youth crime.

Etiology

The etiology of delinquent behavior, crime, and violence is complex and multi-determined. However, it can best be understood from a developmental perspective, because the origins of adolescent violence are firmly rooted in early development and behavior (Tolan, Guerra, & Kendall, 1995). Three main findings emerge consistently in the literature on delinquency, crime and violence:

1 early onset predicts later offending;
2 there is continuity in crime (juvenile offenders are more likely to become adult offenders); and
3 chronic juvenile offenders commit a significant portion of all crimes.

Early onset

Early onset of childhood problems, specifically aggressive and disruptive behavior, is a significant and powerful risk factor for later antisocial behavior (Tremblay et al., 1992; Farrington, 1994). In fact, one of the most consistent findings throughout the research is that aggression is a relatively stable and self-perpetuating behavior that often has origins in childhood (Olweus, 1979; Huesmann & Moise, 1999). Individual differences in social behavior related to aggression can be apparent before age 2 (Kagan, 1988) in the form of temperament features and characteristics. By age 8, children's aggressive behavior across situations can be relatively stable and predictive of adult aggression (Farrington, 1990), with the early onset of violent behaviors being predictive of similar or more serious behaviors over time (Farrington, 1991; Loeber & Stouthamer-Loeber, 1987; Thornberry, Huizinga, & Loeber, 1995).

Longitudinal research by Moffitt (1993) helped to conceptualize two types of delinquency patterns, an early life-course persistent pattern, and an adolescent-limited pattern. The early life-course group of children is characterized by early onset of delinquent behavior and persistent stability across time and settings. The adolescent-limited pattern is characterized by both the onset and desistence of delinquent behaviors in adolescence. The *Diagnostic and Statistical Manual of Mental Disorders IV (DSM-IV)* makes a similar distinction in the childhood conduct disorder diagnosis by adding an early onset specifier (i.e., childhood onset prior to age 10), calling attention to the particularly poor prognosis associated with the early onset of antisocial behaviors, and increased risk in adult life for Antisocial Personality Disorder and Substance Related-Disorders (APA, 1994). Since much behavioral consolidation takes place in the elementary school years, the early onset of childhood antisocial behavior is an important risk factor for prevention and intervention efforts.

Continuity

Habitual aggressive behavior is perhaps best understood as an interaction between individual predisposing factors and environmental influences, often beginning early in development and continuing throughout adolescence and early adulthood. Boys who start their criminal careers in late childhood or early adolescence are at the greatest risk of becoming chronic offenders (Patterson, DeBarysne, & Ramsey, 1989), with the continuity of childhood antisocial and aggressive behavior often continuing through adolescence and into adulthood (Farrington et al.,1990; Huesmann & Moise, 1999). Several longitudinal studies, spanning as much as 40 years across multiple Western countries, lend support to the continuity of aggressive behavior (Farrington, 1990; McCord,1983; Moffitt, 1990).

Chronicity

While researchers disagree on exact definitions and cutoff points for defining chronic juvenile offenders, evidence supports the basic assumption that chronic criminal behavior involves three related dimensions: (1) greater frequency of offending; (2) a wider variety or number of types of crimes; and (3) more serious acts (Farrington, 1991; Loeber, 1982). Many of the chronic, high-frequency offenders are also violent offenders (Loeber & Farrington, 1998). Those children displaying more frequent and serious antisocial behavior at younger ages tend to commit high numbers of offenses, including violent or serious offenses, over the longest periods of time (Farrington et al., 1990; Loeber, 1982; Shelden & Chesney-Lind, 1993; Tracy, Wolfgang, & Figlio, 1990).

Developmental pathways

Developmentally, the incidence and prevalence of serious delinquency and violence peak in adolescence and early adulthood and are more frequent among males than females (Elliott, 1994). A primary assumption of many delinquency theories is that serious problem behaviors unfold in an ordered fashion. Developmental pathway approaches help to link patterns such as early onset, continuity, and chronicity through conceptual formulations that integrate risk factors and problem behaviors with developmental sequences. Pathway research postulates that there is a series or trajectory of escalating behaviors leading from less serious to more serious offending. In analyzing the natural histories of children's antisocial and delinquent behavior, Loeber and colleagues have proposed three overlapping pathways of development toward delinquency – overt, covert, and the authority conflict pathway (Loeber et al., 1993; Loeber & Hay, 1994). The overt pathway involves acts that tend to be directly aggressive and include physical fighting and violence. The covert pathway involves acts that are less directly aggressive and more concealed such as stealing, lying, property damage, and theft. The authority conflict pathway is the earliest pathway, and involves such behaviors as defiance, disobedience, truancy, and running away. Pathway research supplies models for determining the relative risk for antisocial behavior among subgroups of youth and helps in monitoring and evaluating interventions.

Risk factors

Risk-factor explanations for delinquency and crime involve complex person–environment interactions across individual, family, peer, school, and community levels. Individual level factors for delinquency and criminal offending include psychological and biological characteristics identifiable in children at a young age. From the individual-level perspective, risk factors for delinquency and criminal offending include premature birth (Raine, Brennan, & Mednick, 1994), male gender (Elliott, 1993), low verbal IQ (Huesmann et al., 1984), Hyperactivity-Impulsivity-and-Attention-Deficit constellations (HIA) (Farrington et al., 1990), severe aggressiveness and early conduct problems (Thornberry, Huizinga, & Loeber, 1995), exposure to violence and victimization (Flannery et al., 1998; Thornberry, 1994; Widom, 1989), and substance use (Leukefeld et al., 1998).

Research on social-cognitive deficits has identified differences in how aggressive children encode and process information, including the attribution of hostile intent and lack of social-problem-solving capacities (Huesmann et al., 1984; Lochman & Dodge, 1994). Children repeatedly exposed to violence may tend to be "hypervigilant," expect the worst, and respond aggressively to *perceived* hostility from peers or authority figures. Violence-exposed children may not have control of their reactions in situations in which they feel threatened or fearful. Consequently, they may act aggressively, without thinking, based on their misperceptions about the intentions of others.

Research on biological factors related to antisocial and aggressive behavior has examined several key factors including genetics, hormones, and neurotransmitters. Antisocial personality seems to "run" in families, regardless of gender (Plomin, Nitz, & Rowe, 1990), even without environmental transfer from parent to child. Hormone studies indicate that testosterone levels both influence and result from aggression for males (Susman & Ponirakis, 1997; Tremblay et al., 1997). Hormone levels act on sensory systems in the body, increasing or decreasing the potential for instigating a behavior. Social and physiological contexts can affect how hormones interact with behavior, such as environmental events that cause secretion of testosterone through arousal associated with stressful experiences. In a similar manner, low levels of the neurotransmitter serotonin seem to be associated with high levels of aggression, and adverse social environments may have a negative impact on serotonin function and aggression (Simon & Coccaro, 1999). As biological factors are beginning to be teased out with regard to aspects of delinquency, it is evident that more research is needed – especially on female adolescents.

Family factors

Family factors associated with the development of violent and offending behavior involve an array of characteristics and aggressive behaviors (McCord, 1979; Maguin et al., 1995). Since much of aggression is learned from interactions with others and the environment (Dodge et al., 1990; Huesmann & Eron, 1989), aggression can be taught by parents through models of behavior, reinforcement, and home conditions that frustrate or victimize the child (Patterson, DeBarysne, & Ramsey, 1989). Family risk factors include child maltreatment, parental antisocial behavior and criminality, poor family management practices, harsh or inconsistent discipline, poor parent child relations, parental rejection, and having a delinquent sibling (Eron, Huesmann, & Zelli, 1991; Maguin et al., 1995; Widom, 1989). Antisocial parents are at increased risk for rearing antisocial children and employing ineffective behavior management strategies that reward negative behavior (Patterson, DeBarysne, & Ramsey, 1989). Family stressors such as unemployment, family violence, marital discord, and divorce are also associated with delinquency (Patterson et al., 1989; McCord, 1979). Developmentally, much of learned aggression and behavior is established early on (Eron, Huesmann, & Zelli, 1991), and often nested in specific cultural and community contexts.

Peers

Negative peer influences also contribute to violent and aggressive behavior. Children who display antisocial tendencies at an early age are more likely to be rejected by their peers because of their aggressive and coercive behaviors. Antisocial behavior and peer rejection then serve as risk factors for promoting later deviant peer associations (Patterson, DeBarysne, & Ramsey, 1989). As children age, peer versus family influences take on increasing importance in contributing to delinquency and criminal behavior. Peer groups appear to be a place for consolidation of negative and aggressive behaviors for youth already headed in that direction (Loeber & Hay, 1994). Association with antisocial peers may further contribute to the escalation of antisocial behaviors including substance abuse, delinquency (Farrington & Hawkins, 1991) and school problems. Negative peer associations via gang involvement significantly increase the possibility of more serious antisocial behavior (Huff, 1996b; Thornberry, Huizinga, & Loeber, 1995).

School

Eighty percent or more of serious delinquent youth had one or more school problems including suspension, truancy, poor academic achievement, and dropout (Huizinga & Jakob-Chien, 1998). School problems are common and powerful correlates to delinquency and their relationship has been well documented (Gottfredson, 1981; Maguin & Loeber, 1996). There is substantial overlap between truancy, suspension, and serious delinquency (Huizinga & Jakob-Chien, 1998). The nature and the direction of the relationship, however, between delinquency and poor academic achievement are unclear.

Some longitudinal data have shown that poor school achievement predicts juvenile delinquency (Farrington, 1987), specifically through its association with disruptive behavior (Tremblay et al., 1992).

The school environment itself can also be a risk factor that fosters noncompliance, aggression, delinquency, and violence. Disorganized school structures with lax discipline and enforcement of rules, crowded physical space, and lack of conformity to behavior routines can increase the propensity toward aggression and violence (Flannery, 1997; Gottfredson, 1981; Guerra et al., 1995). Outside of the school environment, unsupervised after-school time is a key risk factor that has been associated with increased delinquency, substance abuse, and association with deviant peers (Flannery, Williams, & Vazsonyi, 1999).

Community factors

Neighborhood and community factors that influence delinquency development include poverty, gang involvement, availability of drugs (Maguin et al., 1995), the presence of violence or high crime (Gottfredson & Hirshi, 1990; Sampson, Raudenbush, & Earls, 1997), and low neighborhood attachment and social disorganization (Maguin et al., 1995; Sampson & Lauritsen, 1994). These factors can be addressed by large-scale, multilevel programs that can effectively mobilize and organize community structures (Hawkins & Catalano, 1992).

Summary. Aggression has been found to be a stable characteristic that is also a strong predictor of adult violence. The incidence and prevalence of juvenile delinquency has been found to peak during adolescence and early adulthood. Other risk factors of aggressive behavior include individual differences, biological and genetic factors, family influences, peer relations and perceptions, and school and community factors.

Violence Exposure and Mental Health

Exposure to violence has been linked to a number of mental health and behavioral sequelae, including increased depression (Freeman, Mokros, & Poznaski, 1993), stress (Lorion & Saltzman, 1993), fears and worries (Freeman et al., 1993), aggression (Rivera & Widom, 1990), anxiety (Singer et al., 1995), low self-esteem (Sturkie & Flanzer, 1987), posttraumatic stress (Davies & Flannery, 1998), and self-destructive behaviors (Rivara et al., 1992). These sequelae have significant effects on children's functioning at home and school, and can significantly impair a child's developmental course, adaptation, and functioning later in life.

Children and adolescents victimized by family violence are also at increased risk for perpetrating violence later in life. Thornberry (1994) showed that adolescents who had been direct victims of child maltreatment were more likely to report involvement in youth violence than non-maltreated subjects. Similarly, he showed that adolescents growing up in homes exhibiting partner violence, generalized hostility, or child maltreatment also had higher rates of self-reported violence.

Results from studies examining the relationship between violence exposure and delinquent behavior suggest that violent delinquents are more likely than nonviolent delinquents and controls to have experienced physical abuse (Rivara & Widom, 1990; Thornberry, 1994). One prospective study of young children demonstrated that the experience of physical abuse was a risk factor for the development of aggressive behaviors. Children exposed to such abuse were more likely to acquire deficient patterns of information processing compared to unexposed children (Dodge, Bates, & Petit, 1990). Several other studies also concluded that being a witness or victim of violence, including intrafamilial abuse, was associated with self-reported violence and delinquency (Flannery et al., 1998; Kaufman & Cicchetti, 1989). Adolescents victimized by violence at home are also more likely to join a gang, especially for perceived protection (Chesney-Lind & Brown, 1999). Rather than serving as a vehicle for protection, being a member of a gang increases one's chances of being a victim of violence and increases an adolescent's opportunity to engage in delinquent activity (Huff, 1996b).

There is substantial comorbidity and overlap between antisocial behavior and delinquency and drug abuse, exposure to violence and victimization, mental health problems, and school problems (Thornberry, Huizinga, & Loeber, 1995). Both delinquents and adolescent drug abusers are more likely to display low levels of educational achievement, family structure and conflict problems (Hawkins, Catalano, & Brewer, 1995), and have histories of childhood aggression that are predictive of frequent drug use and delinquency (O'Donnell, Hawkins, & Abbott, 1995). Children diagnosed with disruptive behavior disorders are at increased risk for aggressive behavior (Huesmann & Moise, 1999; Moffitt, 1990). In general, delinquents have a higher prevalence of psychological problems than nondelinquent youth (Flannery, Singer, & Wester, 2001; Huizinga & Jakob-Chien, 1998), with the most violent delinquents scoring higher on externalizing symptoms and aggressive behavior.

Summary. Exposure to violence has been found to be related to a number of mental health problems, aggressive behavior, and self-destructive behavior. Children and adolescents exposed to violence, particularly family violence, have an increased risk of becoming violent offenders themselves. Juvenile delinquents, in general, have a higher prevalence of mental health problems than nondelinquents. Violent juvenile offenders are more likely to have been exposed to violence and physical abuse than nondelinquent and control adolescents.

Gangs, Drugs, and Guns

Youth gangs

There exists little agreement on what defines or constitutes a gang (Howell, 1994; Huff, 1996a). State and local jurisdictions tend to develop their own definition and form policies based on those local criteria. However, several common criteria are typically used to define gangs:

1   there exists a formal organizational structure;
2   the group has an identified leader or leadership hierarchy;
3   the group is usually, but not always, identified with a specific territory or turf;
4   there exists recurrent interaction among the members of the group; and
5   the members of the group engage in delinquent or criminal behavior.

The last criterion, participating in delinquent or criminal behavior, is the characteristic which distinguishes gangs from other, more prosocially focused, adolescent groups.

How many kids are in gangs? Curry, Ball, and Fox's (1994) law enforcement survey for 1991 estimated that there were 4,881 gangs in the United States with 249,324 members. The 1997 National Youth Gang Survey (Office of Juvenile Justice & Delinquency Prevention, 1999) reported 31,000 gangs in 4,800 US cities, with an estimated 846,000 members under age 18. The increased numbers may be due to improvements in information gathering about gang-involved youth or real increases in gang membership and activity. One thing is certain – gangs affect more cities and jurisdictions than ever before (nearly 60 percent of all police departments in the United States reported gang problems in 1994), with dramatic increases since the 1990s in reported gang activity in rural and suburban areas. About three in four big cities report active gang activity. Just over half of suburbs now report having gangs, as do 35 percent of small cities and one in four rural communities. Gangs are no longer a uniquely urban phenomenon.

Who belongs to a gang? Gang members typically range in age from 14 to 24, with the peak age of gang membership around age 17, although in some cities the gang members are somewhat older. There is some evidence that children as young as 8 are gang-involved or gang "wannabes" (Embry et al., 1996; Huff, 1996b). According to 1995 data, 90 percent of gang members are male, mostly between ages 18 and 24 (37 percent) followed by 15–17 year-olds (34 percent) and members under 14 (16 percent). Female participation in gangs is increasing, particularly in small cities and rural areas, and some studies suggest that up to one-third of gang members are now female (Chesney-Lind & Brown, 1999); however, girls still account for a relatively small percentage of gang-involved youth (5–10 percent) (Curry, Ball, & Fox, 1994). Regarding ethnic composition, about 44 percent of gang members are Hispanic, 35 percent black, 14 percent white, and 5 percent Asian, although this varies significantly by region of the country.

Huff (1996b) identified a *developmental progression* from "hanging out" with the gang (being a gang "wannabe") to joining the gang and getting arrested. Gang members responded that they first began associating with the gang at about age 13, and joined, on average, about six months later. They were then arrested for the first time at about age 14, one year after beginning to associate with a gang and about six months after joining.

For both boys and girls, early sexual activity significantly increases the probability of engaging in delinquency (Flannery, Rowe, & Gulley, 1993) and of joining a gang (34 percent for females and 17 percent for males) (Bjerregaard & Smith, 1993). Hanging out with peers or having an older sibling who is delinquent or gang-involved also significantly increases the chances that a young person, male or female, will become delinquent or gang-involved (Rowe & Gulley, 1992).

What do gangs and gang members do? Gang-involved youth are significantly more likely to: (1) have guns or knives in school; (2) carry a concealed weapon; (3) use or sell drugs; and (4) engage in theft and property crimes. While some gang members are involved in the distribution and sale of drugs, and some gangs have evolved specifically for the purpose of drug distribution, most research consistently shows that drug trafficking is not a primary gang activity (Huff, 1996b; Klein, Maxson, & Cunningham, 1991). Most of the homicides involving gang members are over turf battles, not drug violence. Many homicides are classified as drug-related for official data if police officers merely find drugs on the victim (or large quantities of cash).

Gang membership places young people at risk for a variety of negative outcomes, including earlier onset of delinquency and victimization from violence, earlier onset of sexual intercourse, and risk for early pregnancy or the fathering of a child (Morris et al., 1996). Compared with non-gang-involved youth, adolescents in gangs were significantly more likely to be perpetrators and victims of assault, to carry a concealed weapon (79 percent vs. 22 percent), to be victims of drive-by shootings (40 percent vs. 2 percent), to be homicide victims (15 percent vs. 0 percent), and to be involved in drug use and sales. Gang members also more frequently report suicidal ideation and suicide attempts, often involving heavy substance abuse (Flannery, Huff, & Manos, 1998).

Male gang members are more likely to engage in violence and are more likely to use drugs compared to female gang members, who are more likely to commit property crimes than violence (Federal Bureau of Investigation, 1994). While academic failure appears to be a motivation for both males and females to join a gang, a lower expectation of completing school appears to be a stronger motivation for females (Chesney-Lind & Brown, 1999). Both males and females join gangs for similar reasons: having low social status, residing in disorganized neighborhoods, or being socialized on the street to join from an early age. For many youth, gang membership provides the context through which normal developmental needs are met, including a sense of group solidarity, particularly in disorganized and chaotic neighborhoods, or for youth in dysfunctional families.

Female gang involvement. There is no one "type" of female gang member. Girls in gangs can be sexual servants, individuals who are property of the male members, people who carry and conceal their male's weapons or drugs, or they may be in their own female gang, not bound to any group of males (Chesney-Lind & Brown, 1999). Female gang members tend to come from more troubled backgrounds than males (Moore, 1991), with 62 percent reporting they have been sexually abused or assaulted. In fact, girls often report joining a gang for protection from neighborhood or family violence. Female gang members report they join because they see no future for themselves, no decent career alternatives (because they dropped out of school), no marketable skills, and because they live in gendered communities where males are the breadwinners (Campbell, 1990). Recent data suggest that the future awaiting gang girls is bleak indeed; 94 percent will go on to have children and 84 percent will raise them without spouses (Chesney-Lind & Brown, 1999). One-third of them will be arrested, and the vast majority will be dependent on welfare (Campbell, 1990).

Firearms and youth violence

The use or availability of a firearm significantly increases the risk for homicide and injury in the committing of a crime by a juvenile (Berkowitz, 1994). Juvenile arrest rates for weapons violations increased 103 percent between 1985 and 1994, accounting for much of the concomitant increase in juvenile homicide rates during the same period (Fingerhut, 1993). Rates for death by firearm are six times higher for males than for females, and nine times higher for black males compared to white males. The increase in firearm deaths between 1985 and 1990 was due entirely to the increase in deaths among youth aged 10–14 (Fingerhut, Ingram, & Feldman, 1992).

Rates of juvenile crime and violence are closely tied to the use and availability of a gun, even among nonadjudicated, nonviolent youth. In a 1993 Harris poll, 60 percent of students aged 10–19 believed they could get a handgun whenever they wanted, 15 percent said they had carried a handgun in the past year and 4 percent said they had brought a gun to school in the past year (O'Donnell, Hawkins, & Abbott, 1995). Male adolescents who drop out of school are as much as three times more likely to own one or more handguns than adolescents who stay in school.

In recent surveys of male-incarcerated offenders and males in ten inner-city high schools about their use of and access to firearms (Sheley & Wright, 1993), approximately 83 percent of inmates (average age 17) and 22 percent of students said that they possessed guns, and over half of inmates said they had carried guns all or most of the time in the year or two before being incarcerated. This compared to 12 percent of high school students who reported regularly carrying guns to school; nearly one in four reported that they did so "now and then." Only 13 percent of inmates and 35 percent of high school males said they would have a lot of trouble getting a gun; nearly half of all respondents indicated that they would "borrow" one from family or friends, more than those who said they would get one "off the street" (54 percent of inmates and 37 percent of students) (Sheley & Wright, 1993). The most frequently endorsed reason for owning or carrying a gun was self-protection. These inner-city youth were convinced they were not safe in their neighborhoods and their schools.

Substance use and crime

There exists a significant relationship between substance use and delinquency, regardless of the drug type, the offense committed, or the population sampled – adolescents who use drugs are more likely to commit delinquent and violent acts than adolescents who don't (Leukefeld et al., 1998). Violent crime is particularly associated with the use of crack or involvement in the crack business. The etiology of substance use in adolescence shares many of the risk factors for delinquent and violent behavior (Snyder & Sickmund, 1995), and preventive intervention programs are beginning to include both violence and substance use as outcome behaviors targeted for reduction.

Drugs and firearms. The combination of drugs and firearms appears to contribute a great deal to both the contextual and situational determinants of violence and gang activity, and is almost exclusively responsible for trends in juvenile homicide perpetration and victimization since the 1950s (Blumstein, 1995).

Youth involved in gangs who carry weapons for self-protection and status-seeking and who may also be involved with drugs are at high risk for violence. These youth are often impulsive and frequently lack the cognitive problem-solving skills to settle disputes calmly. Fist fights turn into more lethal confrontations because guns are present. This "sequence" can be exacerbated by the socialization problems (e.g., poor parental monitoring) associated with extreme poverty, the high proportion of single-parent households, educational failures, and the pervasive sense of hopelessness about one's life and economic situation (Blumstein, 1995).

Summary. Engaging in delinquency or criminal behavior is a characteristic that distinguishes gangs from other pro-social adolescent groups. In general, gangs are no longer limited to urban areas, but have moved into suburban, small city, and rural areas due to an increase in recruitment activity.

The number of murders by adolescents, gun-related homicides by 10–17-year-old offenders, the homicide arrest rates for 14–17-year-old males, and the number of drug arrests have all significantly increased since the 1990s (Blumstein, 1995). Alcohol is present in nearly 40 percent of violent incidents, with subjects reporting that the use of alcohol prior to conflict increased the chances of the conflict being handled violently (Fagan, 1996).

Prevention and Intervention

Approaches to delinquency prevention and intervention have benefited from longitudinal studies conceptualizing the complex interplay of human development across individual and ecological factors. Due to the heterogeneous nature of violence, and its overlap with other problem behaviors, prevention and intervention strategies vary by the interaction of interventions with individual characteristics, social structures, and the contexts of development (Tolan, Guerra, and Kendall, 1995). It is difficult to separate pure prevention strategies from intervention strategies because in theory, as well as practice, they are often integrated to address multiple-need populations across different contexts.

The knowledge base regarding prevention and intervention has expanded dramatically since the 1990s and includes three commonly defined levels of prevention: primary, secondary, and tertiary. Primary prevention attempts to prevent the occurrence of the disorder within a population or group. Secondary prevention refers to early detection of a problem or disorder, often within a high-risk group, and some type of corrective remedial action. Tertiary prevention seeks to limit the negative effects or outcomes of the disorder or problem on known cases identified within a population. Paralleling the multilevel prevention model is a corresponding intervention model that also has three levels: universal, selected, and indicated. Universal interventions apply to an entire class of children based on some community-wide risk factor such as poverty. Selected interventions aid children who are part of a high-risk group or already may be displaying antisocial behaviors. Indicated interventions target known cases of delinquent or antisocial youth.

The general goal of most prevention and intervention models is to reduce risk factors and enhance protective factors across multiple life domains. Longitudinal research on risk factors and developmental pathways has helped to identify a common set of predictive factors associated with the etiology and progression of antisocial and delinquent behaviors. Cumulative research findings suggest at least two important themes: the importance of early, immediate intervention, and the need for well-coordinated multicomponent/multidimensional approaches (Henggeler, Melton, & Smith, 1992; Tolan, Guerra, and Kendall, 1995).

Early and immediate intervention is essential because at-risk children can be identified early on in their development, often prior to escalation of more serious antisocial behavior patterns (Guerra et al., 1995). Common time periods for initiating interventions are prior to school, school age, and adolescence. Ideally, comprehensive interventions implemented either before or during the early elementary school years can inhibit or postpone escalation to more serious antisocial behaviors and alter the developmental trajectories associated with the onset of antisocial behaviors (Tremblay et al., 1995). In general, comprehensive and multicomponent interventions are superior to single component interventions because they are able to address a range of delinquent behaviors by orchestrating different methodologies in an integrated and concerted fashion. This is particularly important when dealing with phenomena that are as complex and multivariate as crime and delinquency (Tolan et al., 1995).

Multidimensional levels of intervention maximize the opportunity for repetition and reinforcement across different settings by addressing the relevant levels of social structure implicated in delinquency development (Flannery & Huff, 1999). Levels of social structure include individual, peer, family, situational, and community contexts. Each of these levels may contain significant risk and protective factors that can be simultaneously influenced by integrating carefully chosen component interventions.

Evaluation and research support the efficacy of a wide variety of prevention and intervention approaches that deal with child and adolescent antisocial behavior. Some components are child focused, applying psychopharmacological interventions (Abikoff & Klein, 1992; Spencer et al., 1996) or improving interpersonal, cognitive, and social skills (Kazdin et al., 1989). Other components are parent and family focused including home visitation (Olds et al., 1988), parent management training, and family support or counseling (Yoshikawa, 1994). Effective programs may target larger social units such as a classroom or school and address both academic and social concerns (Hawkins, Doueck, & Lishner, 1988; Maguin & Loeber, 1996). The most comprehensive strategies, such as *Communities that Care* (Hawkins et al., 1992), mobilize entire communities to implement sound theory- and evidence-based approaches to address multiple interacting levels of risk and protective factors in a systematic and integrated way.

A growing body of research evidence suggests that interventions that can influence the social ecologies of at-risk children and families are the most promising (Henggeler, Melton, & Smith, 1992). Such interventions are configured to impact the naturally occurring characteristics of social structures and relationships that promote or deter violence. Family-level approaches focus on improving family transactions, particularly parenting interactions and family relationships. School-based interventions increase parental involvement, and improve school climate and the management of high-risk children (Elliott & Tolan, 1999). Programs oriented toward improving parenting in childhood and adolescence are likely to show good outcomes, particularly when pro-social behavior is reinforced across both home and school environments. Likewise, interventions that target more than one problem may have beneficial effects on other problem areas (Ellickson, Saner, & McGuigan, 1997; Leukefeld et al., 1998). These types of ecological-developmental approaches are particularly important when dealing with multiproblem youth.

The Center for the Study and Prevention of Violence (Elliott, 1997) has developed the Blueprints program for violence prevention, which identifies effective programs that meet a high standard of scientific evidence. Ten out of 400 reviewed programs have been selected and include such modalities as home visitation, school-based cognitive and skills training, family and ecological interventions, drug use prevention, and treatment foster homes. It is important to note that most of the programs that produce sustained effects involve relatively long-term and intensive interventions (Elliott & Tolan, 1999).

Summary. Many factors are associated with youth violence and criminal activity. Factors such as individual personality, genetics, biological factors, family influences and structure, peer relationships and pressure, substance use, and environmental and contextual variables are all risk factors for youth violence and criminal behavior. The overall goal of prevention and intervention programs should be to reduce risk factors and enhance protective factors across multiple life domains. Research has found that at least two important themes need to be taken into account when developing or implementing a prevention or intervention program. The first theme is that early, immediate intervention should be implemented since behavioral problems, aggression, and other risk factors can be identified at an early age. The second theme is the need for well-coordinated, multicomponent/multidimensional prevention and intervention programs given that risk factors exist across multiple levels (i.e., family, peer, individual, situational, and community).

Key Readings

Flannery, D. J., & Huff, C. R. (Eds.) (1999). *Youth violence: Prevention, intervention, and social policy.* Washington, DC: American Psychiatric Press.
This book provides useful and practical information regarding youth victims as well as perpetrators of violence and risk factors for these youths. Comprehensive information on effective intervention and prevention strategies is also presented.

Howell, J. C., Krisberg, B., Hawkins, J. D., & Wilson, J. (Eds.) (1995). *A sourcebook: Serious, violent, and chronic juvenile offenders.* Thousand Oaks, CA: Sage.
This book gives the reader a comprehensive review and discussion on implementation strategies for prevention and intervention regarding juvenile crime and delinquency. Topics include risk factors, the juvenile court system, and measurement tools.

Huff, C. R. (Ed.) (1996). *Gangs in America* (2nd ed.). Thousand Oaks, CA: Sage.
This revised and updated second edition offers an in-depth and comprehensive look at gangs. Noted contributors and scholars provide theoretical, empirical, and practical approaches to responding to the problems posed by gangs.

Loeber, R., & Farrington, D. P. (1998). *Serious and violent juvenile offenders: Risk factors and successful intervention.* London: Sage.
This book provides an in-depth look at the most current theory and research on serious and violent juvenile offenders.

Tolan, P. H., Guerra, N. G., & Kendall, P. C. (1995). A developmental-ecological perspective on antisocial behavior in children and adolescents: Toward a unified risk and intervention framework. *Journal of Consulting and Clinical Psychology, 63*(4), 579–584.
Utilizing a developmental-ecological perspective, the authors highlight six key advances for the prediction and prevention of antisocial behavior and suggest directions for future study.

References

Abikoff, H., & Klein, R. G. (1992). Attention-deficit hyperactivity and conduct disorder: Comorbidity and implications for treatment. *Journal of Consulting and Clinical Psychology, 60*, 881–892.

American Psychological Association (1994). *Diagnostic and statistical manual of mental disorders* (4th ed.). Washington, DC: American Psychological Association.

Berkowitz, L. (1994). Guns and youth. In L. D. Eron, J. H. Gentry, & S. Schlegel (Eds.), *Reason to hope: A psychosocial perspective on violence and youth* (pp. 251–279). Washington, DC: American Psychological Association.

Bjerregaard, B. & Smith, C. (1993). Gender differences in gang participation, delinquency, and substance use. *Journal of Quantitative Criminology, 9*(4), 329–355.

Blumstein, A. (1995). Violence by young people: Why the deadly nexus? *National Institute of Justice Journal, 229*, 2–9.

Campbell, A. (1990). Female participation in gangs. In C. R. Huff (Ed.), *Gangs in America* (pp. 163–182). Newbury Park, CA: Sage.

Centers for Disease Control & Prevention (1997). Rates of homicide, suicide, and firearm-related death among children – 26 industrialized countries. *Journal of the American Medical Association, 277*(9), 704–706.

Chesney-Lind, M., & Brown, M. (1999). Girls and violence: An overview. In D. Flannery & R. Huff (Eds.), *Youth violence: Prevention, intervention, and social policy* (pp. 171–199). Washington, DC: American Psychiatric Press.

Curry, G. D., Ball, R. A., & Fox, R. J. (1994). *Gang crimes and law enforcement recordkeeping* [Research in brief]. Washington, DC: US Department of Justice, National Institute of Justice, Office of Justice Programs.

Davies, H., & Flannery, D. J. (1998). PTSD in children and adolescents exposed to community violence. *Pediatric Clinics of North America, 45*(2), 341–353.

Dodge, K., Bates, J., & Petit, G. (1990). Mechanisms in the cycle of violence. *Science, 250,* 1678–1683.

Dodge, K. A., Price, J. M., Bachorowski, J., & Newman, J. P. (1990). Hostile attributional biases in severely aggressive adolescents. *Journal of Abnormal Psychology, 99*(4), 385–392.

Ellickson, P., Saner, H., & McGuigan, K. A. (1997). Profiles of violent youth: Substance use and other concurrent problems. *American Journal of Public Health, 87*(6), 985–991.

Elliott, D., & Tolan, P. (1999). Youth violence prevention, intervention, and social policy: An overview. In D. J. Flannery & C. R. Huff (Eds.), *Youth violence: Prevention, intervention, and social policy* (pp. 3–45). Washington, DC: American Psychiatric Press.

Elliott, D. S. (1993). Longitudinal research in criminology: Promise and practice. In E. Weitekamp & H. Kerner (Eds.), *Cross-national longitudinal research on human development and criminal behavior.* Dordrecht: Kluwer.

Elliott, D. S. (1994). Serious violent offenders: Onset, development, course, and termination. The American Society of Criminology 1993 presidential address. *Criminology, 32,* 1–21.

Elliott, D. S. (1997). *Blueprints for violence prevention.* Boulder, CO: Institute of Behavioral Science, Regents of the University of Colorado.

Embry, D., Flannery, D. J., Vazsonyi, A., Powell, K., & Atha, H. (1996). PeaceBuilders: A theoretically driven, school-based model for early violence prevention. *American Journal of Preventive Medicine, 12,* 91–100.

Eron, L. D., Huesmann, L. R., & Zelli, A. (1991). The role of parental variables in the learning of aggression. In D. J. Pepler & K. H. Rubin (Eds.), *The development and treatment of childhood aggression* (pp. 169–188). Hillsdale, NJ: Erlbaum.

Fagan, J. (1996). Gangs, drugs and neighborhood change. In C. R. Huff (Ed.), *Gangs in America* (2nd ed., pp. 39–74). Thousand Oaks, CA: Sage.

Farrington, D. P. (1987). Early precursors of frequent offending. In J. Q. Wilson & G. C. Loury (Eds.), *From children to citizens* (pp. 27–50). New York: Springer.

Farrington, D. P. (1990). Childhood aggression and adult violence: Early precursors and later-life outcomes. In D. J. Pepler & K. H. Rubin (Eds.), *The development of childhood aggression* (pp. 5–29). Hillsdale, NJ: Erlbaum.

Farrington, D. P. (1991). Childhood aggression and adult violence: Early precursors and later-life outcomes. In D. J. Pepler & K. H. Rubin (Eds.), *The development and treatment of childhood aggression* (pp. 5–29). Hillsdale, NJ: Erlbaum.

Farrington, D. P. (1994). Early developmental prevention of juvenile delinquency. *Criminal Behavior and Mental Health, 4,* 209–227.

Farrington, D. P., & Hawkins, J. D. (1991). Predicting participation, early onset and later persistence in officially recorded offending. *Criminal Behaviour & Mental Health, 1*(1), 1–33.

Farrington, D. P., Loeber, R., Elliott, D. S., Hawkins, J. D., Kandel, D. B., Klein, M. W., McCord, J., Rowe, D. C., & Tremblay, R. E. (1990). Advancing knowledge about the onset of delinquency and crime. In B. B. Lahey & A. E. Kazdin (Eds.), *Advances in clinical child psychology* (Vol. 13, pp. 283–342). New York: Plenum.

Federal Bureau of Investigation (1994). *Crime in the United States.* Washington, DC: US Department of Justice.

Fingerhut, L. A. (1993). *Firearm mortality among children, youth, and young adults 1–34 years of age, trends and current status.* United States, 1985–90. Advance Data from Vital Health Statistics. Washington, DC: National Center for Health Statistics.

Fingerhut, L. A., Ingram, D. D., & Feldman, J. J. (1992). Firearm and non-firearm homicide among persons 15 through 19 years of age: Differences by level of urbanization, United States, 1979 through 1989. *Journal of the American Medical Association, 267*, 3048–3053.

Flannery, D. J. (1997). *School violence: Risk, preventive intervention, and policy.* Monograph for the Institute of Urban and Minority Education, Columbia University and the ERIC Clearinghouse for Education, Urban Diversity Series No. 109.

Flannery, D. J., & Huff, C. R. (1999). Implications for prevention, intervention, and social policy with violent youth. In D. J. Flannery & C. R. Huff (Eds.), *Youth violence: Prevention, intervention, and social policy* (pp. 293–306). Washington, DC: American Psychiatric Press.

Flannery, D. J., Huff, C. R., & Manos, M. (1998). Youth gangs: A developmental perspective. In T. P. Gullotta, G. R. Adams, & R. Montemayor (Eds.), *Delinquent violent youth: Theory and interventions* (pp. 175–204). Thousand Oaks, CA: Sage.

Flannery, D. J., Rowe, D. C., & Gulley, B. L. (1993). Impact of pubertal status, timing, and age on adolescent sexual experience and delinquency. *Journal of Adolescent Research, 8*(1), 21–40.

Flannery, D. J., Singer, M., & Wester, K. (2001). Violence exposure, psychological trauma, and suicide risk in a community sample of dangerously violent adolescents. *Journal of the American Academy of Child and Adolescent Psychiatry, 40*(4), 435–442.

Flannery, D. J., Singer, M., Williams, L., & Castro, P. (1998). Adolescent violence exposure and victimization at home: Coping and psychological trauma symptoms. *International Review of Victimology 6*, 29–48.

Flannery, D. J., Williams, L. L., & Vazsonyi, A. T. (1999). Who are they with and what are they doing? Delinquent behavior, substance use, and early adolescents' after-school time. *American Journal of Orthopsychiatry 69*(2), 247–253.

Freeman, L. N., Mokros, H., & Poznaski, E. (1993). Violent events reported by normal urban school-aged children: Characteristics and depression correlates. *Journal of the American Academy of Child and Adolescent Psychiatry, 32*(2), 419–423.

Gottfredson, G. D. (1981). Schooling and delinquency. In S. W. Martin, L. B. Sechrest, & R. Rednez (Eds.), *New directions in the rehabilitation of criminal offenders* (pp. 424–469). Washington, DC: National Academy Press.

Gottfredson, M. R., & Hirschi, T. (1990). *A general theory of crime.* Stanford, CA: Stanford University Press.

Guerra, N. G., Huesmann, L. R., Tolan, P. H., Acker, R., & Eron, L. F. (1995). Stressful events and individual beliefs as correlates of economic disadvantage and aggression among urban children. *Journal of Consulting and Clinical Psychology, 63*, 518–528.

Hawkins, J. D., & Catalano, R. F. (1992). *Communities that care.* San Francisco: Jossey-Bass.

Hawkins, J. D., Catalano, R. F., & Brewer, D. D. (1995). Preventing serious, violent, and chronic offending: Effective strategies from conception to age 6. In J. C. Howell, B. Krisberg, J. D. Hawkins, & J. Wilson (Eds.), *A sourcebook: Serious, violent, and chronic juvenile offenders* (pp. 36–60). Thousand Oaks, CA: Sage.

Hawkins, J. D., Catalano, R. F., Morrison, D. M., O'Donnell, J., Abbott, R. D., & Day, L. E. (1992). The Seattle social development project: Effects of the first four years on protective factors and problem behaviors. In J. McCord & R. Tremblay (Eds.), *The prevention of antisocial behavior in children* (pp. 139–161). New York: Guilford.

Hawkins, J. D., Doueck, H. J., & Lishner, D. M. (1988). Changing teaching practices in mainstream classrooms to improve bonding and behavior in low achievers. *American Educational Research Journal, 25*, 31–50.

Henggeler, S. W., Melton, G. B., & Smith, L. A. (1992). Family preservation using multisystemic therapy: An effective alternative to incarcerating serious juvenile offenders. *Journal of Consulting and Clinical Psychology, 60*, 953–961.

Howell, J. C. (1994). Recent gang research: Program and policy implications. *Crime & Delinquency, 40,* 495–515.

Howell, J. C., Krisberg, B., Hawkins, J. D., & Wilson, J. J. (1995). *Serious, violent, and chronic juvenile offenders: A sourcebook.* Thousand Oaks, CA: Sage.

Huesmann, L. R., & Eron, L. D. (1989). Individual differences and the trait of aggression. *European Journal of Personality, 3,* 95–106.

Huesmann, L. R., Eron, L. D., Leftkowitz, M. M., & Walder, L. O. (1984). Stability of aggression over time and generations. *Developmental Psychology, 20,* 1120–1134.

Huesmann, R. L. & Moise, J. F. (1999). Stability and continuity of aggression from early childhood to young adulthood. In D. Flannery & R. Huff (Eds.), *Youth violence: Prevention, intervention, and social policy* (pp. 73–95). Washington DC: American Psychiatric Press.

Huff, C. R. (Ed.) (1996a). *Gangs in America* (2nd ed.). Thousand Oaks, CA: Sage.

Huff, C. R. (1996b). The criminal behavior of gang members and nongang at-risk youth. In C. R. Huff (Ed.), *Gangs in America* (2nd ed., pp. 75–102). Thousand Oaks, CA: Sage.

Huizinga, D., & Jakob-Chien, C. (1998). The contemporaneous co-occurrence of serious and violent juvenile offending and other problem behaviors. In R. Loeber & D. P. Farrington (Eds.), *Serious and violent juvenile offenders: Risk factors and successful intervention* (pp. 47–67). London: Sage.

Kagan, J. (1988). Temperamental contributions to social behavior. *American Psychologist, 44,* 668–674.

Kaufman, A. E., & Cicchetti, D. (1989). Effects of maltreatment on school-age children's socioemotional development: Assessments in a day camp setting. *Developmental Psychology, 25*(4), 516–524.

Kazdin, A. E., Bass, D., Siegel, T., & Thomas, C. (1989). Cognitive-behavioral therapy in the treatment of children referred for antisocial behavior. *Journal of Consulting & Clinical Psychology, 57*(4), 522–535.

Klein, M. W., Maxson, C. L., & Cunningham, L. C. (1991). "Crack," street gangs, and violence. *Criminology, 29,* 623–650.

Leukefeld, C. G., Logan, T. K., Clayton, R. R., Martin, C., Zimmerman, R., Cattarello, A., Milich, R., & Lynam, D. (1998). Adolescent drug use, delinquency, and other behaviors. In T. P. Gullotta, G. R. Adams, & R. Montemayor (Eds.), *Delinquent violent youth: Theory and interventions: Advances in adolescent development: Vol. 9* (pp. 98–128). Thousand Oaks, CA: Sage.

Lochman, J. E. & Dodge, K. A. (1994). Social-cognitive processes of severely violent, moderately aggressive, and nonaggressive boys. *Journal of Consulting and Clinical Psychology, 62*(2), 366–374.

Loeber, R. (1982). The stability of antisocial and delinquent child behavior: A review. *Child Development, 53,* 1431–1446.

Loeber, R. & Farrington, D. P. (1998). *Serious and violent juvenile offenders: Risk factors and successful intervention.* London: Sage.

Loeber R., & Hay, D. F. (1994). Developmental approaches to aggression and conduct problems. In M. Rutter & D. F. Hay (Eds.), *Development through the life cycle: A handbook for clinicians* (pp. 488–515). Oxford: Blackwell Scientific.

Loeber, R., & Stouthamer-Loeber, M. (1987). Prediction. In H. C. Quay (Ed.), *Handbook of juvenile delinquency* (pp. 325–382). New York: Wiley.

Loeber, R., Wung, P., Keenan, K., Giroux, B., Stouthamer-Loeber, M., Van Kammen, W. B., & Maughan, B. (1993). Developmental pathways in disruptive child behavior. *Development and Psychopathology, 5,* 101–133.

Lorion, R., & Saltzman, W. (1993). Children's exposure to community violence: Following a path from concern to research to action. *Psychiatry, 56,* 55–65.

Maguin, E., Hawkins, J. D., Catalano, R. F., Hill, K., Abbott, R., & Herrenkohl, T. (1995, November). Risk factors measured at three ages for violence at age 17–18. Paper presented at the meeting of the American Society of Criminology, Boston.

Maguin, E., & Loeber, R. (1996). Academic performance and delinquency. In M. Tonry (Ed.), *Crime and justice: A review of research* (Vol. 20, pp. 145–264). Chicago: University of Chicago Press.

McCord, J. (1979). Some child-rearing antecedents of criminal behavior in adult men. *Journal of Personality and Social Psychology, 37*, 1477–1486.

McCord, J. (1983). A forty year perspective on effects of child abuse and neglect. *Child Abuse & Neglect, 7*(3), 265–270.

Moffitt, T. E. (1990). Juvenile delinquency and attention deficit disorder: Boys' developmental trajectories from age 3 to age 15. *Child Development, 61*, 893–910.

Moffitt, T. E. (1993). Adolescence-limited and life-course persistent antisocial behavior: A developmental taxonomy. *Psychological Review, 100*(4), 674–701.

Moore, J. W. (1991). *Going down to the barrio: Homeboys and home girls in change.* Philadelphia: Temple University Press.

Morris, R. E., Harrison, E. A., Knox, G. W., Romanjhauser, E., Marques, D. K., & Watts, L. L. (1996). Health risk behavioral survey from 39 juvenile correctional facilities in the United States. *Journal of Adolescent Health, 117*, 334–375.

O'Donnell, J., Hawkins, J. D., & Abbott, R. D. (1995). Predicting serious delinquency and substance use among aggressive boys. *Journal of Consulting and Clinical Psychology, 63*, 529–537.

Office of Juvenile Justice & Delinquency Prevention (1999). 1997 National youth gang survey, summary (NCJ 178891). Washington, DC: Office of Juvenile Justice & Delinquency Prevention.

Olds, D. L., Henderson, C. R., Tatelbaum, R., & Chamberlin, R. (1988). Improving the life-course development of socially disadvantaged mothers: A randomized trial of nurse home visitation. *American Journal of Public Health, 78*, 1436–1445.

Olweus, D. (1979). Stability of aggressive reaction patterns in males: A review. *Psychological Bulletin, 86*, 852–875.

Patterson, G. R., DeBarysne, B. D., & Ramsey, E. (1989). A developmental perspective on antisocial behavior. *American Psychologist, 44*(2), 329–335.

Plomin, R., Nitz, K., & Rowe, D. C. (1990). Behavioral genetics and aggressive behavior in childhood. In M. Lewis & S. M. Miller (Eds.), *Handbook of developmental psychopathology* (pp. 119–133). New York: Plenum.

Raine, A., Brennan, P., & Mednick, S. A. (1994). Birth complications combined with early maternal rejection at age 1 year predispose to violent crime at age 18 years. *Archives of General Psychiatry, 51*, 984–988.

Rivara, F. P., Gurney, J. G., Ries, R. K., et al. (1992). A descriptive study of trauma, alcohol and alcoholism in young adults. *Journal of Adolescent Health, 13*, 663–667.

Rivera, B., & Widom, C. S. (1990). Childhood victimization and violent offending. *Violence & Victims, 5*(1), 19–35.

Rowe, D. C., & Gulley, B. (1992). Sibling effects on substance use and delinquency. *Criminology, 30*, 217–233.

Sampson, R., & Lauritsen, J. (1994). Violent victimization and offending: Individual-, situational-, and community-level risk factors. In A. J. Reiss & J. A. Roth (Eds.), *Understanding and preventing violence: Vol. 3: Social influences* (pp. 1–115). Washington, DC: National Academy Press.

Sampson, R. J., Raudenbush, S. W., & Earls, F. (1997). Neighborhoods and violent crime: A multilevel study of collective efficacy. *Science, 277*, 918–924.

Shelden, R. G., & Chesney-Lind, M. (1993). Gender and race differences in delinquent careers. *Juvenile and Family Court Journal, 44,* 73–90.

Sheley, J. F., & Wright, J. D. (1993). *Gun acquisition and possession in selected juvenile samples.* Washington, DC: US Department of Justice, Office of Juvenile Justice and Delinquency Prevention.

Simon, N. G., & Coccaro, E. F. (1999). Human aggression: What's animal research got to do with it? *The HFG Review, 3*(1), 13–20.

Singer, M. I., Anglin, T. M., Song, L., & Lunghofer, L. (1995). Adolescents' exposure to violence and associated symptoms of psychological trauma. *Journal of the American Medical Association, 273*(6), 477–482.

Snyder, H. N., & Sickmund, M. (1995). *Juvenile offenders and victims: A national report.* Washington, DC: US Department of Justice, Office of Juvenile Justice & Delinquency Prevention.

Snyder, H. N., & Sickmund, M. (1999). *Juvenile offenders and victims: 1999 national report.* Washington, DC: Office of Juvenile Justice and Delinquency Prevention.

Spencer, T., Biederman, J., Wilens, T., Harding, M., O'Donnell, D., & Griffin, S. (1996). Pharmacotherapy of attention-deficit hyperactivity disorder across the life cycle. *Journal of the American Academy of Child and Adolescent Psychiatry, 35,* 409–432.

Sturkie, K., & Flanzer, J. P. (1987). Depression and self-esteem in the families of maltreated adolescents. *Social Work, 32*(6), 491–496.

Susman, E. J., & Ponirakis, A. (1997). Hormones-context interactions and antisocial behavior in youth. In A. Raine, P. A. Brennan, D. P. Farrington, & S. A. Mednick (Eds.), *Biosocial bases of violence* (pp. 251–269). New York: Plenum.

Thornberry, T. P. (1994). *Violent families and youth violence.* Washington, DC: US Department of Justice, National Institute of Justice, Office of Justice Programs.

Thornberry, T. P., Huizinga, R., & Loeber, R. (1995). The prevention of serious delinquency and violence: Implications from the Program of Research on the Causes and Correlates of Delinquency. In J. C. Howell, B. Krisberg, J. D. Hawkins, & J. J. Wilson (Eds.), *A sourcebook: Serious, violent, and chronic juvenile offenders* (pp. 213–237). Thousand Oaks, CA: Sage.

Tolan, P. H., Guerra, N. G., & Kendall, P. (1995). A developmental-ecological perspective on antisocial behavior in children and adolescents: Towards a unified risk and intervention framework. *Journal of Consulting and Clinical Psychology, 63*(4), 579–584.

Tracy, P. E., Wolfgang, M. E., & Figlio, R. M. (1990). *Delinquency careers in two birth cohorts.* New York: Plenum.

Tremblay, R. E., Kurtz, L., Masse, L. C., Vitaro, F., & Phil, R. O. (1995). A bimodal preventive intervention for disruptive kindergarten boys: Its impact through adolescence. *Journal of Consulting and Clinical Psychology, 63,* 560–568.

Tremblay, R. E., Masse, B., Perron, D., Le Blanc, M., Schwartzman, A. E., & Ledingham, J. E. (1992). Early disruptive behavior, poor school achievement, delinquent behavior and delinquent personality: Longitudinal analyses. *Journal of Consulting and Clinical Psychology, 60,* 64–72.

Tremblay, R. E., Schaal, B., Boulerice, B., Arseneault, L., Soussignan, R., & Perusse, D. (1997). In A. Raine, P. A. Brennan, D. P. Farrington, & S. A. Mednick (Eds.), *Biosocial bases of violence* (pp. 271–291). New York: Plenum.

Widom, C. (1989). The cycle of violence. *Science, 244,* 160–166.

Yoshikawa, H. (1994). Prevention as cumulative protection: Effects of early family support and education on chronic delinquency and its risks. *Psychological Bulletin, 115,* 28–54.

CHAPTER TWENTY-FIVE

Eating Disorders in Adolescence

**Janet Polivy, C. Peter Herman, Jennifer S. Mills,
and Heather B. Wheeler**

Introduction

Eating disorders usually emerge during adolescence, making them especially relevant for this volume. Although the disorders may occur in adults, they are principally found in adolescents. Anorexia nervosa, for example, occurs primarily in pubertal girls, and bulimia nervosa generally appears in slightly older teenaged girls or women in their early twenties (modal age of onset is 18 years; Striegel-Moore, 1993). This raises the question, "What puts adolescents at risk for eating disorders?" The present chapter will review the literature on risk factors for eating disorders in adolescents to attempt to address this question.

We will organize our discussion of the literature according to Bronfenbrenner's (1977) ecological model for development, examining individual, family, and sociocultural factors (as well as the interactions between them) that influence the development of the disorders. In these discussions it must be remembered that, of necessity, most of the research in this area is correlational in nature, making it difficult to draw causal conclusions. We will try to separate what is known from what is merely speculative to determine what gaps in our knowledge require attention from researchers, and what we can comfortably conclude at this time.

The eating disorders actually consist of a cluster of related but distinct syndromes including anorexia nervosa (AN), bulimia nervosa (BN), eating disorders not otherwise specified (EDNOS), and possibly, binge eating disorder (BED). For the purposes of the present chapter, we will focus on the two disorders most commonly associated with adolescence (and most thoroughly studied), anorexia nervosa and bulimia nervosa. It is not entirely clear what the actual relation between these two eating disorders is, as they share some characteristics but diverge with respect to others. Where possible, we will separate the two, but much of the literature deals more generally with both of these eating disorders together; empirical studies, however, often separate them by diagnosis. Thus, much of the research literature combines diverging findings for AN and BN, making it even harder to find consistent evidence for general theoretical models of eating disorders.

The current *Diagnostic and Statistical Manual of Mental Disorders* (*DSM-IV*; American Psychiatric Association, 1994) describes anorexia nervosa (AN) as consisting of the refusal to maintain a minimally acceptable body weight for age and height (less than 85 percent of "normal"), accompanied by an intense fear of becoming fat and a disturbance in the perception of body shape and size. In addition, there is undue influence of body weight on the person's self-evaluation and/or a denial of the seriousness of the current low weight. In post-menarcheal females, absence of at least three consecutive menstrual cycles is also usually present as a result of the weight loss. In adolescents, anorexia nervosa may appear as a failure to gain weight during growth in height rather than weight loss per se.

There are two subtypes of anorexia nervosa (AN) patients. Restricting patients lose weight only by restricting their intake and/or increasing their exercising; binge eating/purging anorexics lose weight both by restriction and by purging, fasting, insulin abuse, laxative abuse, or excessive exercising following binge eating (i.e., ingestion of a very large amount of food in a short period of time) followed by purging, fasting, insulin abuse, laxative abuse, or excessive exercising. This second subtype of AN is similar in many respects to bulimia nervosa. The characteristic features of bulimia nervosa (BN) are recurrent episodes of binge eating and excessive compensatory behaviors (as in binge/purge AN), with episodes occurring at least twice a week for three months or more, excessive concern with body weight and shape, and the lack of a diagnosis of anorexia nervosa (because the patient is not sufficiently or even at all underweight) (American Psychiatric Association, 1994). In many personality and behavioral respects, bulimia nervosa patients and binge/purge anorexia nervosa patients are more alike than are restricting and binge purge anorexics. Bingeing and purging may thus be more important than weight as an indicant of which pathology is operative in an individual.

Males and females are equally affected once they have an eating disorder (Geist et al., 1999), or even show subclinical levels of pathology (Keel et al., 1998), but both community and clinical epidemiological studies (Garfinkel & Garner, 1982) indicate a sex ratio of one male case to 10–15 female cases of eating disorders. This is not true for preadolescents, however, where the sex ratio of cases is approximately equal (Field et al., 1999; Theander, 1996).

Individual Factors in the Development of Eating Disorders

There are a wide variety of individual factors that may promote the development of an eating disorder. In order to consider these somewhat systematically, we will divide them into biological factors and psychological factors. There are demographic attributes of individuals such as race and ethnicity that could be considered in this section, but these are so strongly connected to sociocultural factors that it makes more sense to treat them as such.

Biological factors

Genetic influences. The genetic contribution to eating disorders has been investigated in family studies and twin studies. Twin studies have the advantage of providing more direct genetic evidence through monozygotic (MZ) and dizygotic (DZ) comparisons. On the other hand, the twin relationship itself has been implicated as a potential risk factor for the development of an eating disorder in that it may hinder the development of personal identity (Fichter & Noegel, 1990), although there is no evidence that the prevalence of eating disorders is higher in the twin than in the non-twin population (Simonoff, 1992). In addition, twin studies often suffer from assimilation effects, whereby monozygotic twins are treated more similarly by others, which can then inflate heritability estimates. For example, if the concordance rate for MZ twins is 50 percent and the DZ concordance is 10 percent, then heritability is two times (MZ-DZ), or 80 percent, exceeding the concordance for MZ twins, which is by definition the upper limit for heritability. This problem is not unusual in twin studies in many areas, and eating disorders evince it as well.

Twin studies have yielded concordance rates for the prevalence of AN and BN of 45–75 percent for MZ twins, with most studies in the 50-percent range, while the concordance for DZ twins ranges from 0 to 31.5 percent, with most studies ranging from 1 to 7 percent (Fichter & Noegel, 1990; Treasure & Holland, 1990). The higher concordances for DZ twins come from studies that separated AN and BN, and found essentially equal levels of concordance for MZ and DZ twins on the prevalence of BN (Treasure & Holland, 1990). There thus seems to be a greater genetic component for AN than for BN. Given that BN occurs more often in older adolescent females who often have a pre-morbid history of elevated weight, bulimia may be more reflective of environmental pressures to be thin, whereas anorexia is a more direct result of a genetic predisposition (Treasure & Holland, 1995).

Despite differences in methodology and even in diagnostic criteria, results of family studies of heritability of eating disorders generally accord well with those from twin studies. Families with an eating disorder patient evinced risk levels of 4–10 percent for first-degree female relatives (males are much less likely to develop an eating disorder, and reported rates for male relatives were only .4 –1 percent) compared to rates of 0–1.1 percent for relatives of controls (e.g., Strober et al., 1990). These studies all found eating disorders to be familial, especially AN. In general, females with a first-degree relative who has an eating disorder have a two- to threefold increase in risk of developing an eating disorder. Those studies that have calculated estimates of heritability find high heritability for AN, apparently too high to be real (64 percent in Strober et al., 1990, 75–80 percent in Holland, Sicotte, & Treasure, 1988). Whatever method is used to study genetic contributors to eating disorders, the studies do agree that there are elevated rates of eating disorders in the families of patients with an eating disorder (Woodside et al., 1998), though studies of twins reared apart, which are often the most persuasive, have yet to be conducted. Moreover, AN, especially young-onset AN, seems to have a stronger genetic component than does BN.

Neurotransmitters and hormonal influences. Genetic predispositions to develop eating disorders may be expressed through physiological processes such as disturbances in neurotransmitter systems. Unfortunately, these systems are also sensitive to the effects of malnutrition, making it difficult to determine if neurotransmitter disruptions are primary or secondary to the disorder. Neurotransmitters have been studied in anorexic patients at various stages in their illness (i.e., while weight-reduced and after weight restoration) in an attempt to determine causality, though in the final analysis, even this evidence is still correlational.

Serotonin is the neurotransmitter most often studied in relation to eating disorders, possibly because of its known properties of inhibiting feeding, stimulus reactivity, and sexual activity. Anorectic patients are constrained, perfectionistic, and need order even after weight restoration, traits consistent with a disturbance of serotonergic activity (Kaye, Weltzin, & Hsu, 1993). Moreover, weight-restored anorexics still have elevated levels of brain serotonin metabolites (Kaye, Weltzin, & Hsu, 1993; O'Dwyer, Lucey, & Russell, 1996). It may be that women who develop AN have intrinsic vulnerabilities for perfectionistic, anxious, and obsessional behavior as a result of elevated serotonin levels, and these tendencies become exaggerated into pathology as a result of stress or other psychosocial stimuli (Kaye, Bastiani, & Moss, 1995).

Patients with BN also exhibit symptoms of serotonin dysregulation which may contribute to their symptoms, including binge eating (Wolfe, Metzger, & Jimerson, 1997). Kaye and his colleagues have found persistent serotonergic and related behavioral abnormalities even in recovered BN patients (Kaye et al., 1998). In addition, BN patients have reduced levels of the satiety hormone Colycystikinen following a test meal, which may explain their ability to eat such large amounts of food in a limited time, given the hormone's association with satiety (Geracioti & Liddle, 1988). This is currently an area of active research.

Andersen and Homan (1997) discuss a potential hormonal contributor to the observed sex difference in prevalence of eating disorders. Testosterone may protect against the development of eating disorders. Males with AN have lower testosterone levels than do normal males, and the decline is more gradual than that accompanying female amenorrhea. Moreover, the developmental pattern produced by testosterone production is consistent with the mesomorphic, athletic body shape culturally preferred for males; in fact, the ideal male physique is incompatible with starvation. Thirdly, the increased prevalence of eating disorders among homosexual males compared to heterosexual males may be in part a result of differences in testosterone levels, although such abnormalities have not been established. The lack of testosterone or other gonadotrophic hormones in prepubescent girls and boys may account for the equal sex ratio of anorexia nervosa cases in these children (Theander, 1996). Finally, there has been a trend toward a lower age of puberty since the 1950s for females but not so much for males. Early puberty is one factor that seems to predispose toward developing an eating disorder (Fairburn et al., 1999). Thus, the presence of testosterone may be a protective factor, while reduced levels of testosterone may contribute to the development of eating disorders.

It must be remembered, however, that the evidence for the influence of elevated serotonin and depressed testosterone on eating disorders is strictly correlational. It is thus not possible to conclude at this time that these factors are causal, and not a result of the disorder.

Psychological factors

Pubertal issues. One psychological factor with biological overtones is puberty. Pubertal changes differ in boys and girls. As Striegel-Moore (1993) points out, physical matura-tion brings boys closer to the muscular, well-developed male ideal body, but pushes girls away from the slim, preadolescent shape considered beautiful for them. The increase in body fat for pubescent girls may be particularly problematic. It is just around the time of puberty that girls develop body image dissatisfaction, feel fat, and begin to diet to lose weight, all factors that are associated with eating disorders (Polivy & Herman, 1987; Striegel-Moore, 1993), and are probably exacerbated by increased body fat. At this same time, girls must cope with heterosexual dating, which they appear to find more stressful than boys do (Striegel-Moore, 1993).

Pubertal development also coincides with increasing sex role demands. Females are expected to attempt to pursue the "superwoman ideal" of success in all spheres of life, leading to increased pressure to achieve in all dimensions – social, appearance, academic, career, and family. This superwoman ideal may be pathogenic because it requires girls to fulfill incompatible role demands, without having learned to prioritize these roles and the demands they make. This is clearly related to identity formation, which also appears to be more difficult for girls than for boys because girls are trying to negotiate an identity that incorporates conflicting goals or options (Baumeister, 1986). Archer (1989) suggests that because females try to integrate intrapersonal and interpersonal identity domains and search for goals, values, and beliefs that will please everyone else around them, they are more likely to be in a state of moratorium or identity crisis, whereas boys are able to be identity-achieved by their senior year of high school. Moreover, increasing numbers of life transitions reduce self-esteem for girls but not boys (Simmons & Blyth, 1987); the simultaneity of pubertal stresses (bodily changes, onset of dating and sexuality) appears to increase the risk for eating disorders (Levine & Smolak, 1992).

Body image. A distortion of body image such that one perceives oneself as being larger than one's actual size is a key feature of the eating disorders. For many years, research focused on perceptual theories of body image disturbance, looking for greater size esti-mation in eating disorder patients than in controls. Cash and Deagle (1997) reviewed the literature from 1974 to 1993 and concluded that attitudinal body dissatisfaction, assessed through questionnaires or self-ideal discrepancy measures, was more pronounced than was perceptual size-estimation inaccuracy. They concluded that distortions of body size estimation in eating disorder patients do not reflect a general sensory/perceptual deficit in these patients. Moreover, a unique factor in eating disorders seems to be a lack of a well-organized self-image and cohesive body image. Body image disturbances and dissatisfaction are thus seen as specific to eating disorder development (Steiger et al., 1992). Accordingly, we will focus our discussion on individual differences in body image dissatisfaction in adolescents, and their relation to eating disorders.

Negative body image or dissatisfaction is widespread in adolescent females (Koenig & Wasserman, 1995; McCarthy, 1990), who generally want to be thinner than they are, even if they are already normal weight or even thin (Raudenbush & Zellner, 1997). It is consistently found that girls have more negative body-image evaluations, are more concerned about their appearance (Muth & Cash, 1997), dislike their appearance, and feel that they have failed to meet their ideal self-concept (O'Dea & Abraham, 1999). Girls feel fatter than boys do, showing a bias toward seeing themselves as overweight, while boys tend to have accurate body perceptions (Pritchard, King, & Czajka-Narins, 1997) and are less likely to want to lose weight even when they are overweight (Steen et al., 1996). Adolescent males, on the other hand, are more likely to want to be heavier (and more muscular) (Drewnowski, Kurth, & Krahn, 1995).

Males and females may be differentially vulnerable to eating disorders not only because they have unequal levels of body image dissatisfaction, but because they use different strategies to respond to their dissatisfactions with their bodies. Girls who want to lose weight tend to skip meals, avoid sweets and fatty foods, and cut down on food intake; boys cut out sweets and snacks, but eat more healthy food (Nowak, 1998). In addition, boys who want to lose (or gain) weight are likely to use exercise to alter their body shape rather than diet (Drewnowski, Kurth, & Krahn, 1995).

This association of gender with a factor closely related to eating disorders may reflect conditions that make females predisposed toward developing an eating disorder if they are otherwise vulnerable. Negative body image may contribute to or even determine the co-occurrence of depression and eating disorders, both of which are usually related to body dissatisfaction. McCarthy (1990) suggested that this dissatisfaction, when combined with an emphasis on the importance of appearance, leads many females to attempt to obtain the thin ideal through weight-loss dieting. Dieting is generally unsuccessful as a means of long-term weight control, contributing to increased depression and lower self-esteem arising from the sense of failure and helplessness associated with unsuccessful dieting (Heatherton & Polivy, 1992). This depression may then lead to increasingly disordered eating in an attempt to reduce negative affect and regain control over appearance (McCarthy, 1990). Koenig and Wasserman (1995) tested this hypothesis in adolescents, and indeed found that problematic eating behaviors were most prevalent among those who both had a negative body image and placed a greater degree of importance on body image. As predicted, failed dieting was significantly related to depression, and in females, depression also accounted for significant variability in disordered eating. In addition, other evidence confirms that adolescent girls have more negative body images and depression (Raudenbush & Zellner, 1997; Rierdan & Koff, 1997).

Dieting. Body image dissatisfaction is often associated with another risk factor for eating disorders, dieting to lose weight. Dieting is associated with binge eating (Polivy & Herman, 1993) and with eating disorders in general (Fairburn et al., 1999; Heatherton & Polivy, 1992) in susceptible individuals (Garner et al., 1984; Polivy & Herman, 1987). As with eating disorders, dieting is most prevalent in adolescent girls, where it has been called normal or normative (Polivy & Herman, 1987; Hill & Pallin, 1998). Among girls in grades 3 to 11, 51–64.7 percent are dieting or have been dieting in the last year, and around 75 percent wish to lose weight (Schur, Sanders, & Steiner, 2000). Recent studies indicate that children as young as 8 years old want to be thin and some are already dieting (Hill & Pallin, 1998; Schur, Sanders, & Steiner, 2000). Dieting is more common in white female adolescents who use alcohol and tobacco, who have low self-esteem and negative self-worth, and whose mothers diet (Heatherton & Polivy, 1992; Hill & Palin, 1998).

The best predictor of dieting, however, appears to be the existence of a discrepancy between one's current and ideal body weight and shape (Polivy & Herman, 1987). Stice et al. (1998) found that body mass, poor body image, and perceived pressure to be thin predicted increased dieting prospectively over a nine-month period, and accounted for a significant proportion of variance in concurrent as well as subsequent dieting. Indeed, although being overweight per se seems to increase the likelihood of dieting, and being underweight is a protective factor (Stice et al., 1998), body dissatisfaction and perceived overweight (as opposed to actual weight) are more consistent correlates of dieting in adolescent females (French et al., 1997). Social and individual variables may also play a role in dieting, even when body mass index and body dissatisfaction are taken into account (Strong & Huon, 1998). For example, self-confidence, perceived parental encouragement of autonomy, and greater autonomy in terms of differentiation of self from others all seem to protect against dieting. Parental influence and pressure to diet contributed to dieting both directly, and indirectly through increasing body dissatisfaction (Strong & Huon, 1998).

Consistent with this link between dieting and autonomy, Striegel-Moore (1993) proposes that young women's pursuit of thinness and beauty via dieting is a strategy for identity affirmation; the focus on physical appearance provides a concrete way to construct an identity. Dieting can thus be seen as an adaptive response for those adolescents who are vulnerable due to an unstable sense of self, who are overly self-conscious, and/or who lack interoceptive awareness, giving them a way to cope with the challenge to their sense of self and femininity produced by adolescence (Striegel-Moore, 1993). Unfortunately, the strategy seems often to be unsuccessful, resulting in binge eating and distress, and in full-blown eating disorders when coupled with other predisposing factors.

Involvement in activities emphasizing weight/shape. Excessive exercising is related to dieting to lose weight, and is a common symptom of anorexia nervosa; eating disorder patients often have a premorbid history of strenuous exercising (Davis et al., 1997), or currently exercise compulsively (Brewerton et al., 1995). Among eating disorder patients, those who exercise an hour or more a day have greater body dissatisfaction and are less likely to binge, vomit and use laxatives, and more likely to be diagnosed with AN than with BN (Brewerton et al., 1995).

Athletes who participate seriously in sports that emphasize thinness to enhance performance or appearance (e.g., gymnastics, wrestling, figure skating, diving, and ballet) have been found to be at increased risk for eating disorders (Garner, Rosen, & Barry, 1998). Athletes and coaches frequently believe that being thinner will improve athletic performance, increasing the athlete's risk of developing disordered eating (Thompson & Sherman, 1999). Female college athletes were more weight-preoccupied the more their sport was one where leanness is emphasized (Petrie, 1996). Similarly, adolescent dancers and skaters competing at a national level had more pathological eating attitudes and higher perfectionism scores than did swimmers or nonathlete controls (Brooks-Gunn, Burrow, & Warren, 1988). Ballet dancers have long been known to develop eating disorders at many times the normal rate (Garner et al., 1987). Two to four years after initial interviewing of 11–14-year-old ballet students, 25 percent of them had developed anorexia nervosa and 14 percent had bulimic syndromes (Garner et al., 1987).

Traditionally, athletic activities emphasizing thinness did so only for females, but males have become more at risk recently, especially in sports such as wrestling, where weight level is a factor (Braun et al., 1999; Thompson & Sherman, 1999). Rowers of both sexes who have to maintain a weight criterion are at risk, with males showing even greater weight fluctuations in the off-season than do females (Sykora et al., 1993).

Reactions to eating disorder symptoms. Male and female adolescents differ in their reactions to eating disorder symptomatology. Females label their own and others' eating behavior as a binge and expect negative emotional consequences of eating, whereas males label only large amounts of food or rapid consumption of food as a binge, and do not expect affective outcomes, but gastrointestinal ones (LaPorte, 1997). Females may therefore be more likely to see their eating as pathological, and to feel upset, making them more vulnerable to other stressors.

Emotional factors

It has been suggested that maladaptive eating occurs in conjunction with body dissatisfaction and dysphoric affect, but clinical eating syndromes result only when body concerns co-occur with underlying psychopathology (Garner et al., 1984). The observed concurrence of eating disorders and depression (Strober & Katz, 1998) may be due to primary mood disturbance in anorexia nervosa and bulimia, or mood disorders secondary to an eating disorder, or a common third variable (biological or psychosocial) leading to both, such as genetic or familial transmission. In a large sample of adolescent girls, concurrent eating and mood symptoms were associated with reported body-image concerns, impulsivity, self-criticism, and lack of family cohesion (Steiger et al., 1992). Even at the subclinical level, mood and eating disturbances were associated strongly. Eating problems were linked to body image problems, but combined eating and mood disturbances were related to more severe psychological and family difficulties (Steiger et al., 1992). Early adolescent girls with more negative body images report higher levels of depressive symptoms (Rierdan & Koff, 1997), and girls as young as 8 years old who feel worse about themselves are more likely to think about dieting to improve their self-image (Hill & Pallin, 1998). Greater levels of depression are associated with more disruptive, dysregulatory eating behaviors in obese binge-purging patients (Musante, Costanzo, & Friedman, 1998). Recently, guilt and covert hostility have also been implicated in bulimia nervosa (Allen, Scannell, & Turner, 1998). Negative self-evaluation appears to be present in eating disorder patients more reliably than almost any other risk factor (Fairburn et al., 1999); however, the correlational nature of these findings makes it unclear whether dysphoric affect causes eating disorders or vice versa.

Without actually itself causing eating disorders, negative affect may make women more susceptible to external feedback and information about their weight and shape, which can then contribute to development of eating disorders. For example, Mori and Morey (1991) demonstrated that nondepressed women were unaffected by false feedback about their weight, but depressed women were more inclined to see themselves as they were (inaccurately) described. Similarly, McFarlane, Polivy, and Herman (1998) manipulated a scale so that subjects "weighed" 5 pounds more than they did in reality, and restrained eaters felt worse about themselves, felt more dysphoric, and overate in a taste-rating test; unrestrained eaters were unaffected. Restrained eaters are generally more depressed and have lower self-esteem than do unrestrained eaters (e.g., Polivy, 1996; Polivy, Heatherton, & Herman, 1988), so again, the more dysphoric individuals were more susceptible to external information about their bodies, and this information triggered behavior consistent with disordered eating.

As well as being a potential risk factor for eating disorders, emotions have long been implicated as triggers to binge eating in those with bulimia nervosa (Arnow, Kenardy, & Agras, 1995; Johnson et al., 1995; Polivy & Herman, 1993). Both negative and positive emotions have been implicated in triggering overeating, possibly through inducing a loss of self-control (Polivy & Herman, 1993). In addition, binge eating may serve an affective regulatory function for bingers; binges may reduce negative affect temporarily, or provide a distraction from or masking of the source of one's distress (Herman & Polivy, 1988; Kenardy, Arnow, & Agras, 1996; Polivy, Herman, & McFarlane, 1994). Finally, Powell and Thelen (1996) monitored affect and cognition in bulimics, who reported greater levels of negative affect and distorted cognitions both preceding and following binge episodes. Negative emotions thus seem both to trigger and result from binge eating.

Personality correlates. In addition to dysphoria, eating disorder patients exhibit a pattern of personality traits which have been shown to be consistently present premorbidly, during the disorder, and after recovery. Research on the relation of personality and eating disorders must of necessity be correlational, without evidence for causality, but the continuing presence of these traits suggests that they may constitute a predisposing risk factor for developing an eating disorder.

There has been converging evidence from clinical reports, psychometric studies, and family informants that the premorbid personality of anorexic patients is obsessional, socially inhibited, perfectionistic, compliant, and emotionally restrained (Strober & Humphrey, 1987; Wonderlich, 1995). Bulimic anorexics resemble restrictors in compliance and perfectionism, but also tend to be impulsive, emotional, and extroverted, as are BN patients (Kaye, Bastiani, & Moss, 1995). Perfectionism and negative self-evaluation seem to be the most pervasive features across AN and BN and at all stages (premorbidly, during the disorder, and post-recovery) (Fairburn et al., 1999).

Inanuma (1994) found AN patients to have obsessional premorbid personalities and preoccupation with food once self-starvation has been occurring for a few months, and a worsening of the obsessive qualities with increasing starvation. Thus, chronic starvation seems to intensify pre-existing personality characteristics such as obsessionality.

Kaye et al. (1998) report that negative affect, behavioral inhibition, obsessiveness, and perfectionism persist after recovery from AN. These characteristics might predispose individuals to try to comply with the societal preference for a thin female shape by dieting and losing weight, which may then trigger disordered eating in susceptible individuals. In sum, there are a number of personality traits linked to eating disorders. Strober and Humphrey (1987) reviewed these and proposed that genetically determined and transmitted personality factors such as obsessionality may predispose an individual to greater vulnerability to adverse familial and social experiences. We will consider such experiences next.

Family Factors in the Development of Eating Disorders

Not surprisingly, the family has been implicated in the development of eating disorders in a variety of ways. The family is a means of transmitting pathogenic cultural values to daughters, as well as making individuals vulnerable to disorders through lack of support or dysfunctional interaction and emotional response patterns. We will divide the discussion of family factors into the influence of parents, family interaction patterns, and separation–individuation issues (including the development of autonomy, of self-control, and of a separate identity).

Parental influence

The influence of one's parents can be said to begin as early as infancy. Agras, Hammer and McNicholas (1999) studied children of eating disordered mothers. Female infants sucked faster and were weaned later than offspring of noneating disordered mothers. Eating disordered mothers fed their children less regularly, were more likely to use food for nonnutritive purposes, and expressed more concern about their daughters' weight from 2 years onward than did noneating disordered mothers. By age 5, daughters of eating disordered mothers exhibited heightened negative affect. Eating disordered mothers thus appear to transmit several potential risk factors to their daughters.

Even mothers who are not themselves fully eating disordered often transmit pathogenic attitudes and values to their daughters, finding them less attractive and more in need of weight loss the more disordered they themselves are (Pike & Rodin, 1991) (although Attie & Brooks-Gunn, 1989, did not find that mothers' body image or compulsive eating contributed to their daughters' compulsive eating). Daughters are more likely to diet if their mothers do (Hill & Pallin, 1998) or encourage them to, and are more likely to use extreme weight-loss methods the more their mothers are dissatisfied with their own bodies (Benedikt, Wertheim, & Love, 1998). Perceptions of reduced maternal caring have been associated with higher levels of eating problems in both Asian-American and Caucasian females (Haudek, Rorty, & Henker, 1999).

Parental (especially maternal) comments about weight or dieting influence their children's, especially daughters', weight and shape beliefs and behaviors, as do parental modeling (Smolak, Levine, & Schermer, 1999), and pressure to diet (Strong & Huon, 1998). Twelve-year-old children report that their parents are involved in their dieting, with greater restrained eating associated with more reports of parental control of the child's eating (Edmunds & Hill, 1999).

Family interaction patterns

Early theorizing on the pathogenesis of eating disorders suggested that problems in family dynamics result in eating disorders because of their effect on autonomy and identity development. Family systems theorists (Minuchin, Rosman, & Baker, 1978) identified five patterns leading to pathology: enmeshment, overprotectiveness, rigidity, conflict avoidance, and poor conflict resolution. The few laboratory studies of family interactions show enmeshed, intrusive, hostile interactions, and negation of the child's emotional needs, although it is not clear how these potentiate or activate weight concerns in particular, rather than other forms of psychopathology (Strober & Humphrey, 1987). Recently, a longitudinal study of adolescents indicated some specificity in the risk for eating disorder symptoms on the basis of particular familial interaction patterns (Calam & Waller, 1998). Poor intrafamilial communication at age 13 predicted restricting (AN) attitudes at age 19, whereas poor role differentiation early on predicted later bulimic attitudes and behaviors.

There is ample evidence that pathological family relationships of various types are associated with the development and persistence of eating disorders (Strober & Humphrey, 1987). Bulimics and, to some extent, their parents see their families as more conflictual and disengaged and less cohesive and nurturing than do control families. Bulimics and noneating disordered individuals differ in patterns of family interaction, psychopathology and body weight. Bulimia is associated with a lack of parental affection, negative, hostile, disengaged interactions in the family, parental impulsivity, and familial alcoholism and obesity. This inadequate family environment, and the behavioral deficits it causes, may result in bulimia. Bulimia may also reflect a craving for nurturance and an attempt to control feelings of rejection and loneliness (Strober & Humphrey, 1987). Both bulimics and anorexics perceive their parents as more blaming, rejecting, and neglectful toward them than do controls, treating themselves with the same hostility and deprivation they see as coming from their parents (Humphrey, 1986).

Anorexia nervosa is related to critical comments from parents, and negative expressed emotion (le Grange et al., 1992). Levels of criticism from parents to their anorexic daughters observed early in therapy predict prognosis at 6 months, and even low levels of critical comments are associated with continuing symptoms. Similarly, high expressed emotion and low overall expressiveness in family members (Dare et al., 1994), as well as high levels of critical comments from mothers (Vanfurth et al., 1996), predict negative outcome. Levels of expressed emotion are a part of an ongoing family interaction, however, and can change. When expressed emotion decreases, patients tend to improve, while expressed emotion increased in families of patients who did not do well (le Grange et al., 1992).

Family cohesion appears to be an important variable contributing to eating disorders. Prospectively, mothers who reported that their families were less cohesive (Attie & Brooks-Gunn, 1989) had daughters with increased problematic eating attitudes two years later. Pike and Rodin (1991) also found that the mothers of eating disordered daughters complained of less satisfaction with family cohesion, and their daughters similarly wished that their families were more cohesive. In addition, in adolescent girls, disordered eating and mood symptoms are associated with a reported lack of family cohesion (Steiger et al., 1992). Moreover, Hill and Franklin (1998) report that families with a highly restrained (i.e., dieting) daughter score significantly lower on perceived family cohesion, organization and moral–religious emphasis.

Separation-individuation – autonomy, self-control and identity

Adolescent girls with eating disorders lack a normal sense of autonomy, self-control, and identity, in part because of their perceived need to live up to the high expectations of their parents and ignore their own needs, goals, values, and beliefs (Minuchin, Rosman, & Baker, 1978). They are thus disconnected from their own feelings and even bodily signals, as well as who they really are, due to their nonautonomous pursuit of parental aspirations. This perfectionistic striving appears to reflect the family system by which evaluation and rewards for goal-directed activity are, in effect, not within their own control. Rather than having internalized, self-determined, intrinsically motivated goals, anorexics or bulimics seek to please others (Minuchin, Rosman, & Baker, 1978). At the same time, they perceive their own behaviors to be controlled by impersonal, external forces (Strauss & Ryan, 1987). Indeed, Kenny and Hart (1992) found that the lack of encouragement of autonomy by parents was the main factor differentiating young women with eating disorder symptoms from non-disordered controls. Moreover, anorexia nervosa patients were observed to have parents who do not support their daughter's autonomy, negate her self-expression, and mix messages of caring and affection with enmeshment and negation of her needs (Humphrey, 1987). Parents of bulimic anorexics were also found to send mixed messages of overcontrol and support for autonomy, which was mirrored in the daughters' ambivalence, alternating between resentfully submitting and asserting themselves with their parents, who then responded with hostile control (Humphrey, 1987). Eating disordered patients also perceive their mothers (Dare et al., 1994; Rhodes & Kroger, 1992) and fathers (Calam et al., 1990) as providing "affectionless control," or lack of care and rejection combined with overcontrol and overprotectiveness. These findings are all consistent with Bruch's (1973) proposal that eating disorder patients are primarily concerned with issues of control, struggling desperately to control the one thing under their command, their bodies.

As mentioned earlier, Striegel-Moore (1993) proposed that the conflict with parents around identity and autonomy issues is more intense in adolescent girls, who score lower on measures of emotional autonomy than do boys. While increased parent–adolescent conflict is normal, girls tend to experience more conflict and related interpersonal stress within the parent–child relationship than do boys (Rudolph & Hammen, 1999). This may help to explain why eating disorders are so much more likely to occur in adolescent girls than in boys. Furthermore, although perceived family functioning seems to be independent of satisfaction with self for boys, the same is not true for girls (Wertheim et al., 1992). Therefore, the family that is conflictual, overprotective, rigid, or any of the other characteristics observed in families of anorexics or bulimics would be especially detrimental to the development of a positive, stable sense of self in females. Indeed, these attributes are antithetical to identity development in late adolescence, and, in fact, several of the self and family correlates of bulimia parallel those of identity diffusion (Auslander & Dunham, 1996).

It is not hard, then, to imagine that eating disorders are intimately linked to the effect of the family on the daughter's identity exploration and consolidation in adolescence and that this might be why such disorders are more common in adolescent females. The drive to restrain one's food intake and control one's weight may be a manifestation of a desperate search for a sense of control, autonomy, and identity, normally acquired in adolescence, but thwarted in vulnerable individuals by dysfunctional family contexts (see Bruch, 1973, for related theorizing). Moreover, these personal and familial handicaps may be exacerbated by societal pressures to achieve unattainable ideals of coping ability, identity, and appearance.

Sociocultural Factors in the Development of Eating Disorders

The Western cultural ideal that equates feminine beauty with thinness has been blamed for widespread body dissatisfaction among women (Koenig & Wasserman, 1995), and consequently for a large number of women developing eating disorders (Stice & Shaw, 1994). This sociocultural pressure to be thin is manifested through messages in the media, general sex-role expectations, and in particular racial and ethnic contexts.

Media influences

From ages 8 to 12, the amount of time children spend watching television increases from 2.5 to 4 hours a day (Harris, 1994). Adolescents also appear to pay closer attention to television than do children or, for some programs, adults (Comstock & Paik, 1991). Early adolescence is also the time when girls manifest an intense interest in fashion magazines. There is evidence that younger adolescent girls are more interested than are older girls in the magazines' messages concerning beauty and style (Levine & Smolak, 1996).

Given their heightened interest in the media, what messages are adolescent girls receiving? The magazines read by girls are ten times more likely to have articles and advertisements promoting dieting than are those read by adolescent boys (Andersen & DiDomenico, 1992). The covers of women's magazines are highly likely to contain a message regarding bodily appearance, unlike the covers of men's magazines (Malkin, Wornian, & Chrisler, 1999). In addition, a quarter of the women's magazine covers gave conflicting messages regarding weight loss and dietary habits, with the positioning of weight-related messages on the covers often implying that losing weight leads to a better life. In contrast, men's magazines focus on providing entertainment and expanding knowledge, hobbies, and activities.

Television and movies portray females in a variety of social and occupational roles, but with few exceptions, these females are thin and highly attractive (Streigel-Moore, 1993). Fouts and Burggraf (1999) analyzed 28 television situation comedies, examining the body weights of 52 central female characters (88 percent white, 10 percent black, 2 percent Asian), the verbal comments about body weight directed to them by other characters, and their comments with respect to their own body weight, shape, and dieting behaviors. Central female characters were mostly under average weight; above average weight characters were underrepresented. Thin female characters received significantly more positive verbal comments about weight and shape from male characters than did their heavier counterparts. Dieting female characters gave themselves significantly more verbal punishment for their body weight and shape than did those less involved in dieting.

The bust-to-waist ratios for actresses and models, as seen in fashion and beauty magazines, have steadily decreased over the last three decades, signifying a trend toward a slimmer, less curvaceous figure (Silverstein, Peterson, & Perdue, 1986). Playboy centerfolds and Miss Americas' weights have also decreased in this same time (Wiseman et al., 1992), while the diagnosis of eating disorders has increased markedly.

Even the toys played with by preadolescents portray cultural sex-role ideals. Brownell and Napolitano (1995) measured the ubiquitous Barbie and Ken dolls and calculated what the average healthy young women would have to change to achieve Barbie's shape, and what boys would have to do to look like Ken. A normal female would have to increase 2.4 inches in height, 5 inches in the chest, and 3.2 inches in neck length, while decreasing 6 inches in the waist to resemble Barbie; males would need to increase 2 inches in height, 11 inches in the chest, and 7.9 inches in neck circumference. Looking at American male action figures over the last 30 years, Pope et al. (1999) found that the waist, chest, and bicep circumferences of these toys have grown over time, with many contemporary figures far exceeding the muscularity of even the largest human bodybuilders. Thus, children are being presented with highly unrealistic ideals.

This raises the question, does such media exposure contribute to disordered eating attitudes and behaviors in adolescent girls? Obviously, such a causal question is difficult to answer, as most of the data are of necessity correlational. The correlations tend to support the thesis that the media images of unrealistically thin women contribute to eating disorders. As media images of women have grown slimmer, eating disorders have become increasingly prevalent in young women (Mills et al., in press). Women with higher levels of eating disorder symptomatology are also more likely to expose themselves to media images of thin women (Stice et al., 1994; Harrison & Cantor, 1997). Moreover, women exposed to thin media images in the laboratory often feel worse about themselves (Pinhas et al., 1999) (although some studies using different methodology find that such images trigger a fantasy state that makes some women feel better; Mills et al., in press). On the whole, then, media portrayals of body shapes impossible for most girls to attain appear to be at the least a contributing factor to body dissatisfaction, disordered eating behaviors, and outright eating disorders in susceptible adolescent girls.

Sex-role expectations – the superwoman myth

Midadolescence is a time when achievement concerns become intensified, and attention is directed to societal expectations such as the superwoman myth (Striegel-Moore, 1993). The "superwoman ideal" demands that women be beautiful, smart, and successful at a career, and at the same time be a nurturing partner and mother (Steiner-Adair, 1986; Streigel-Moore, 1993). Such unrealistic expectations may contribute to eating disorders; adolescent girls who had internalized this image most strongly also endorsed more disordered eating attitudes than did those who had set more realistic goals (Steiner-Adair, 1986). Steiner-Adair argues that the reason that the superwoman ideal promotes disordered eating is that it requires the adoption of conflicting attitudes and roles, which generates stress. Striegel-Moore extends this thesis, suggesting that the stress comes from the girl's inability to prioritize roles for herself, leading her to attempt to adopt whatever is currently fashionable. Focusing on appearance may seem to be the easiest way to earn approval from others.

Recent investigations of the superwoman ideal and its correlates yield a complex picture. Crago and colleagues (1996) found no evidence of increased eating disorder symptomatology in girls attending an academically competitive school, as compared to an average school, nor in those endorsing a number of roles as essential to their sense of self. Hart and Kenny (1997) examined the relation of eating disorder symptoms to three components of the superwoman ideal: valuing physical appearance, striving for success in multiple roles, and insecure parental attachment. A complex relation emerged. The hypothesized relation between symptoms and the three components of the superwoman ideal appeared, as did the connection between an emphasis on appearance and weight concern, dieting, and bulimic behaviors, but it was also the case that striving for success was positively related to social competence, at least when accompanied by secure parental attachment. It is thus possible to endorse the superwoman ideal and still be healthy, as long as other aspects of one's life and personality are solid. There may well be other socio-cultural factors that intervene, however, including race, ethnic background, and social class.

Race, ethnicity, and social class

Whereas for several decades researchers believed that eating disorders were restricted to upper- or middle-class Caucasians, it has now been demonstrated that eating disorders are a global phenomenon. They have been found worldwide and across cultures within North America, as well as within every level of socioeconomic status (Caldwell, Brownell, & Wilfley, 1997; Gard & Freeman, 1996; Striegel-Moore & Smolak, 1996), although there is still a relation between class and disordered eating attitudes, dieting, and body dissatisfaction (Ogden & Thomas, 1999). While the prevalence in nonwhite groups and nonindustrialized countries is still lower than in Caucasian and industrialized populations worldwide (Davis & Yager, 1992), in the United States, black women are as likely as Caucasian women to report body image dissatisfaction (Grant et al., 1999), fasting, vomiting, and abuse of laxatives or diuretics, and are more likely to report binge eating (Striegel-Moore et al., in press). Among the several potential explanations for the globalization of eating disorders, the most obvious is the influence of the media (Nasser, 1997), as has been discussed.

Indeed, a recent review has concluded that compared to rates for Caucasian females, eating disturbances are equally common among Hispanic females, more frequent among Native Americans, and less frequent among black and Asian American females (Crago, Shisslak, & Estes, 1996). Minority females who are younger, heavier, better educated, and more identified with white, middle-class values are at higher risk for developing eating disorders. Assimilation into the white culture can thus be a significant risk factor for non-white women, who have been found to have comparable eating attitudes to Western Caucasians after acculturation (e.g., Hispanic women, Pumariega, 1986; black women,

Abrams, Allen, & Gray, 1993; and Asian women, Davis & Katzman, 1999; Mumford, Whitehouse, & Platts, 1991).

Various explanations for the occurrence of eating disorders in immigrants or minority groups have been offered. Root (1990) proposed that the greater eating pathology found in some immigrant British Asians reflects an overcompensation to rid themselves of "deficits" that prevent them from fitting into the majority culture. DiNicola (1990) suggested that eating disorders reflect "culture change" rather than culture-specific syndromes, though this proposal has not received much support (Furukawa, 1994; Haudek, Rorty, & Henker, 1999). In fact, some researchers have found no relation at all between degree of acculturation and eating disorders (Joiner & Kashubeck, 1996; Ogden & Elder, 1998).

There are differences in the manifestation of eating disorders among nonwhite groups compared to Caucasians. For example, there is not always as much body dissatisfaction and "fear of fatness" among nonwhites with eating pathology (Lee, Ho, & Hsu, 1993). Eating problems are also related more to actual elevated weight in nonwhite groups, as opposed to perceived overweight in Caucasians (Abrams, Allen, & Gray, 1993). Black adolescent girls appear to be more likely to binge eat whereas their white peers are more likely to restrict their food intake (Striegel-Moore et al., in press), and blacks are more likely to use laxatives than are whites (Langer, Warheit, & Zimmerman, 1991).

There has been speculation that blacks are protected from developing eating disorders by having a higher ideal body size (Flynn & Fitzgibbon, 1996; Thompson, Corwin, & Sargent, 1997) and less body dissatisfaction than whites (Abood & Chandler, 1997), although some studies find no differences or attribute what is found to social class rather than race (Caldwell, Brownell, & Wilfley, 1997; Callan, Mayo, & Michel, 1993). A recent study of 6th- to 8th-grade children found that black females actually had elevated body dissatisfaction and depression (Grant et al., 1999). Nevertheless, there is evidence that blacks experience less social pressure to conform to the unrealistic thin ideal that whites struggle to attain, and that weight loss is less important for self-definition, self-esteem, and perceptions of self-control for black girls than it is for Caucasians (Striegel-Moore & Smolak, 1996). For example, black adolescent males chose heavier ideal female bodies than did white boys, and believed that others would choose as they had (Thompson, Sargent, & Kemper, 1996). In a study of white and black females' reactions to media images portraying the white beauty ideal, black respondents with high self-esteem or with high African self-consciousness reported self-evaluations that were significantly higher than the attractiveness they attributed to white standards of beauty (Makkar & Strube, 1995). Moreover, black women have less traditionally defined gender roles, may not have the pressure of the superwoman role thrust upon them, and do not have gender identities as tied to physical attractiveness as white women do. Finally, the investment in the search for understanding one's racial and ethnic identity in adolescence could itself serve as a buffer against eating disorders through the positive effect on self-esteem of providing identification with a group (Striegel-Moore & Smolak, 1996).

These equivocal findings on the effect of acculturation and ethnicity on the development of eating disorders have been addressed by theorists proposing that a "culture clash" in the parent–adolescent relationship mediates the effects of acculturation. The degree of conflict with one's parents appears to outweigh degree of acculturation in accounting for the appearance of eating disorders (Bryant-Waugh & Lask, 1991), as does perceived parental overprotection and care (Furukawa, 1994; Haudek, Rorty, & Henker, 1999), lack of family adaptability (Mildred, Paxton, & Wertheim, 1995), degree of struggle with ethnic identity issues (Abrams, Allen, & Gray, 1993; Harris & Kuba, 1996), the family's level of traditionalism (Mumford, Whitehouse, & Platts, 1991), and resentment for not being allowed to integrate into the majority white culture (Furnham & Patel, 1994). In addition, Littlewood (1995) argues that restricting one's eating allows South Asian girls in Western societies to articulate their struggle to gain personal autonomy and a separate identity in a family less open to these Western values.

Katzman and Lee (1997) take this a step further and posit a "two-world hypothesis"; eating disorders in ethnic adolescent girls reflect pressure to conform to two conflicting ideals – the values of their home countries and those of the Western society they live in, or those of their parents versus their own developing values. This is further complicated by their attempts to move from childhood to adolescence, or adolescence to adulthood.

It should be noted that when eating problems do occur in nonwhite groups, they appear to be related to the same psychosocial and health behaviors as they are in Caucasians, including low family connectedness, perfectionism, emotional distress, body dissatisfaction, and sometimes serious depression and anxiety (Davis & Katzman, 1999; French et al., 1997). As discussed above, the more a group embraces white, Western values, the greater the incidence of eating disorders. Thus, there may still be some minor differences in absolute prevalence rates and patterns of symptomatology, but it is not the case that eating disorders are exclusively a white, Western phenomenon. Some minority groups appear to enjoy a degree of protection against the disorders, possibly through identity as a group member. Others seem more susceptible, however, because of inter-generational conflicts and a struggle to define one's identity – basically through the same processes operating in Western adolescents.

Conclusion: Interactive Influences on the Development of Eating Disorders

Are we now able to answer the main question posed at the beginning of this chapter – why are adolescents, particularly adolescent girls, most likely to develop eating disorders? Despite the increase in eating disorders in males, it still seems to be primarily adolescent girls who are at risk.

Of all the risk factors reviewed here, no single one produces eating disorders. More-over, the risk-factor approach does not really allow us to make causal conclusions, as it is correlational and post hoc. This is an inherent problem in the literature because experi-mental research is impossible on such a question. But even with these caveats, what can we conclude from this literature?

Genetics does not offer us any insight into the question of why eating disorders occur in adolescent girls, but hormones may help. Early puberty in girls constitutes a risk factor. But obviously, this is not sufficient in and of itself to produce an eating disorder. All the-orizing on this issue agrees that there must be a confluence of risk factors that interact to produce an eating disorder in a particular individual. The "biopsychosocial" model has been advocated from as early as 1987, when Johnson and Connors proposed that bio-genetic predispositions, such as a genetic risk for developing an affective disorder, combine with familial factors and sociocultural pressures toward high achievement and thinness, to promote a character structure featuring affective instability and low self-esteem (Johnson & Connors, 1987). When this person then tries to achieve thinness and all its supposedly associated benefits, through prolonged caloric restriction, or dieting, the underlying affective instability is heightened, generating an enhanced susceptibility to disruptive events such as failure of any kind. These events trigger binge eating, panic about weight gain, and purging, which then cycles back into dieting.

But even a biopsychosocial theory does not fully address the question of why the problems arise in adolescents (and girls in particular), nor does it move us any closer to identifying which adolescent girls will be most at risk. Some other proposals have been offered. The psychosocial tasks of adolescence may themselves offer some insight into this issue. The "additive stress" hypothesis (Striegel-Moore, 1993) proposes that the number of life challenges encountered simultaneously determines the level of risk of developing an eating disorder. More challenges are associated with more distress, and there is some evidence that this is related to pathological eating attitudes. For example, girls who begin dating at the same time as their menarche have more pathological eating attitudes; bulimic anorexics reported more life changes prior to the onset of their disorder; and severity of life stress is related to degree of symptomatology (Levine et al., 1994).

A second, not dissimilar, hypothesis is that early maturation contributes to risk for eating disorders (Striegel-Moore, 1993). Maturing earlier than one's peers appears to cause adolescent girls a wide range of adjustment difficulties, including greater body dissatisfaction (leading to dieting). Early maturation is correlated with heightened conflict with parents, possibly because the early maturer looks older and demands more freedom. Early maturers are likely to date earlier, and may have to cope with experiences for which they are not yet ready, including sexual experiences (Striegel-Moore, 1993). Maturing early may thus be stressful for adolescents in a variety of ways, increasing their risk for developing eating disorders.

A third possible explanation for why eating disorders afflict adolescents concerns the major transitions of adolescence. Transitions are vulnerable times because of the instability resulting from the reorganization and deconstruction of personality, cognitive, and social structures (Smolak & Levine, 1996). There are several transitions young adolescents must undergo. Moving from elementary school to a larger, more complex junior high school with greater academic demands and disruptions in friendship groupings clearly involves many adjustments on the part of the child (Striegel-Moore, 1993). At this same time, they are undergoing puberty, there is an increase in sex-role demands, and evaluation and social comparison escalate markedly. The simultaneity of these demands may be overwhelming (Levine & Smolak, 1992), especially for those who do not have solid support from their families, or who have personality deficits. In fact, Levine et al. (1994) found that the combination of simultaneous puberty and dating onset, plus academic challenges, plus peer and parental valuing of thinness, discriminated normal dieting from pathological eating in middle school girls. Thus, the occurence and timing of transitions may combine with existing problems in other spheres to trigger the occurence of an eating disorder. The family's reaction to these transitions can also be a critical factor. Obviously, support and flexibility from the family can make these transitions easier, and are essential for the successful resolution of the tasks of adolescence. On the other hand, problematic interactions at home, or the "affectionless control" reported by those with eating disorders, probably make the transitional tasks more stressful and difficult.

In later adolescence, the transitions are different, but no less stressful. Upon graduating from high school, adolescents are faced with unprecedented demands for autonomy and responsibility. The conflict between independence and guilt or fear, and the stresses of the superwoman role may result in attempts to cope by controlling one's body and weight. For example, Smolak and Levine (1993) found that women with more eating disorder symptoms had greater conflictual dependence on their families than did women with only some or no eating disorder symptoms, and were "underseparated" from their families emotionally, functionally, and attitudinally compared to other women. Those with bulimic symptoms, on the other hand, while underseparated emotionally, were also "overseparated" cognitively, reporting more attitudinal independence from their parents than did controls. Thus, their beliefs, values and attitudes differ drastically from those of their parents, producing greater conflict.

The interaction of life transition challenges with predisposing individual and family factors in a context of sociocultural demands and expectations that women should be thin and attractive thus offers a potentially fruitful model for explaining why eating disorders are more likely to occur in adolescent women. Research is needed to determine the relative contributions of each factor. We still need to know what elements, or which combination, and how many are necessary and/or sufficient to produce an eating disorder in a given individual. This may help us to identify protective factors and vulnerabilities that can be supported to prevent the development of eating disorders in adolescents.

Key Readings

Heatherton, T. F., & Polivy, J. (1992). Chronic dieting and eating disorders: A spiral model. In J. Crowther, S. E. Hobfall, M. A. P. Stephens, & D. L. Tennenbaum (Eds.), *The etiology of bulimia: The individual and familial context* (pp. 133–155). Washington, DC: Hemisphere.
This chapter outlines the relation between chronic dieting and eating disorders, focusing on the authors' proposal that inevitable diet failures result in progressively worsened self-esteem and mood. Chronic dieting is thus identified and discussed as a critical individual risk factor for clinically disordered eating.

Smolak, L., & Levine, M. P. (1996). Adolescent transitions and the development of eating problems. In L. Smolak, M. Levine, & R. Striegel-Moore (Eds.), *The developmental psychopathology of eating disorders: Implications for research, prevention, and treatment* (pp. 210–231). Hillsdale, NJ: Erlbaum.
This is a developmental psychopathological discussion of eating problems and disorders, focusing on individual predispositions, triggers and developmental tasks that make both the transition into and out of adolescence particularly high-risk periods for the development of eating problems. They propose that these transitions are risky because they involve deconstructing, assessing, and reconstructing one's sense of self. Offers developmental models of dieting and eating disorders.

Striegel-Moore, R. H. (1993). Etiology of binge eating: A developmental perspective. In C. G. Fairburn & G. T. Wilson (Eds.), *Binge eating: Nature, assessment, and treatment* (pp. 144–172). New York: Guilford.

This chapter reviews developmental literature on causes of binge eating, examining questions of why eating disorders occur in adolescence, and why in females. Discusses pubertal issues, attempts at identity consolidation, and sociocultural influences contributing to development of eating disorders in adolescent girls.

Strober, M., & Humphrey, L. L. (1987). Familial contributions to the etiology and course of Anorexia Nervosa and Bulimia. *Journal of Consulting and Clinical Psychology, 55,* 654–659.

An article reviewing evidence of familial influences in anorexia and bulimia nervosa, including familial interactions, correlates, and transmission. Observational and self-report findings show that the families of eating disorder patients are enmeshed, intrusive, hostile, less supportive, and more likely to show signs of eating disorders, depressive psychopathology, and obesity. They propose that genetically determined personality factors predispose some individuals to vulnerability to adverse familial and social factors.

References

Abood, D. A., & Chandler, S. B. (1997). Race and the role of weight, weight change, and body dissatisfaction in eating disorders. *American Journal of Health Behavior, 21,* 21–25.

Abrams, K. K., Allen, L. R., & Gray, J. J. (1993). Disordered eating attitudes and behaviors, psychological adjustment, and ethnic identity: A comparison of black and white female college students. *International Journal of Eating Disorders, 14,* 49–57.

Agras, S., Hammer, L., & McNicholas, F. (1999). A prospective study of the influence of eating disordered mothers on their children. *International Journal of Eating Disorders, 25,* 253–262.

Allen, F. C. L., Scannell, E. D., & Turner, H. R. (1998). Guilt and hostility as coexisting characteristics of bulimia nervosa. *Australian Psychologist, 33,* 143–147.

American Psychiatric Association (1994). *Diagnostic and statistical manual of mental disorders* (4th ed.). Washington, DC: APA.

Andersen, A. E. (1995). Eating disorders in males. In K. D. Brownell and C. G. Fairburn (Eds.), *Eating Disorders and Obesity* (pp. 177–182). New York: Guilford.

Andersen, A. E., & DiDomenico, L. (1992). Diet vs. shape content of popular male and female magazines: A dose-response relationship to the incidence of eating disorders? *International Journal of Eating Disorders, 11,* 283–287.

Andersen, A. E., & Homan, J. E. (1997). Males with eating disorders: Challenges for treatment and research. *Psychopharmacology Bulletin, 33,* 391–397.

Archer, S. L. (1989). Gender differences in identity development: Issues of process, domain and timing. *Journal of Adolescence, 12,* 117–138.

Arnow, B., Kenardy, J., & Agras, W. S. (1995). The emotional eating scale: The development of a measure to assess coping with negative affect by eating. *International Journal of Eating Disorders, 18,* 79–90.

Attie, I., & Brooks-Gunn, J. (1989). Development of eating problems in adolescent girls: A longitudinal study. *Developmental Psychology, 25,* 70–79.

Auslander, B. A., & Dunham, R. M. (1996). Bulimia and the diffusion status of ego identity formation: Similarities of the empirical descriptors of self and parent. *Journal of Adolescence, 19,* 333–338.

Baumeister, R. F. (1986). *Identity.* New York: Oxford University Press.

Benedikt, R., Wertheim, E. H., & Love, A. (1998). Eating attitudes and weight-loss attempts in female adolescents and their mothers. *Journal of Youth and Adolescence, 27,* 43–57.

Braun, D. L., Sunday, S. R., Huang, A., & Halmi, K. A. (1999). More males seek treatment for eating disorders. *International Journal of Eating Disorders, 25,* 415–424.

Brewerton, T. D., Stellefson, E. J., Hibbs, N., Hodges, E. L., & Cochrane, C. E. (1995). Comparison of eating disorder patients with and without compulsive exercising. *International Journal of Eating Disorders, 17,* 413–416.

Bronfenbrenner, U. (1977). Toward an experimental ecology of human development. *American Psychologist, 32,* 513–531.

Brooks-Gunn, J., Burrow, C., & Warren, M. P. (1988). Attitudes toward eating and body weight in different groups of female adolescent athletes. *International Journal of Eating Disorders, 7,* 749–757.

Brownell, K. D., & Napolitano, M. A. (1995). Distorting reality for children: body size proportions of Barbie and Ken dolls. *International Journal of Eating Disorders, 18,* 295–298.

Bruch, H. (1973). *Eating disorders: Obesity, anorexia nervosa and the person within.* New York: Basic Books.

Bryant-Waugh, R., & Lask, B. (1991). Anorexia nervosa in a group of Asian children living in Britain. *British Journal of Psychiatry, 158,* 229–233.

Calam, R., & Waller, G. (1998). Are eating and psychosocial characteristics in early teenage years useful predictors of eating characteristics in early adulthood? A 7-year longitudinal study. *International Journal of Eating Disorders, 24,* 351–362.

Calam, R., Waller, G., Slade, P., & Newton, T. (1990). Eating disorders and perceived relationships with parents. *International Journal of Eating Disorders, 9,* 479–485.

Caldwell, M. B., Brownell, K. D., & Wilfley, D. E. (1997). Relationship of weight, body dissatisfaction, and self-esteem in African American and white female dieters. *International Journal of Eating Disorders, 22,* 127–130.

Callan, J. D., Mayo, K., & Michel, Y. (1993). Body size values of White and Black women. *Research in Nursing and Health, 16,* 323–333.

Cash, T. F., & Deagle, E. A. (1997). The nature and extent of body-image disturbances in anorexia nervosa and bulimia nervosa: A meta-analysis. *International Journal of Eating Disorders, 22,* 107–125.

Comstock, G., & Paik, H. (1991). *Television and the American child.* San Diego, CA: Academic Press.

Crago, M., Shisslak, C. M., & Estes, L. S. (1996). Eating disturbances among American minority groups: A review. *International Journal of Eating Disorders, 19,* 239–248.

Crago, M., Yates, A., Fleischer, C., Segerstrom, B., & Gray, N. (1996). The Superwoman ideal and other risk factors for eating disturbances in adolescent girls. *Sex Roles, 35,* 801–810.

Dare, C., le Grange, D., Eisler, I., & Rutherford, J. (1994). Redefining the psychosomatic family: Family process of 26 eating disorder families. *International Journal of Eating Disorders, 16,* 211–226.

Davis, C., Katzman, D. K., Kaptein, S., Kirsh, C., Brewer, H., Kalmbach, K., Olmsted, M. P., Woodside, D. B., & Kaplan, A. S. (1997). The prevalence of high-level exercise in the eating disorders: Etiological implications. *Comprehensive Psychiatry, 38*(6), 321–326.

Davis, C., & Katzman, M. (1999). Perfectionism as acculturation: Psychological correlates of eating problems in Chinese male and female students living in the United States. *International Journal of Eating Disorders, 25,* 65–70.

Davis, C., & Yager, J. (1992). Transcultural aspects of eating disorders: A critical literature review. *Culture, Medicine and Psychiatry, 16,* 377–394.

DiNicola, V. (1990). Anorexia multiforme: Self-starvation in historical and cultural context. Part II: Anorexia nervosa as a culture reactive syndrome. *Transcultural Psychiatric Research Review, 28*, 245–286.

Drewnowski, A., Kurth, C. L., & Krahn, D. D. (1995). Effects of body image on dieting, exercise, and anabolic steroid use in adolescent males. *International Journal of Eating Disorders, 17*, 381–386.

Edmunds, H., & Hill, A. J. (1999). Dieting and the family context of eating in young adolescent children. *International Journal of Eating Disorders, 25*, 435–440.

Fairburn, C. G., Cooper, Z., Doll, H. A., & Welch, S. L. (1999). Risk factors for anorexia nervosa – Three integrated case-control comparisons. *Archives of General Psychiatry, 56*, 468–476.

Fichter, M. M., & Noegel, R. (1990). Concordance for bulimia nervosa in twins. *International Journal of Eating Disorders, 9*, 255–263.

Field, A. E., Camargo, C. A., Taylor, C. B., Berkey, C. S., Frazier, A. L., Gillman, M. W., & Colditz, G. A. (1999). Overweight, weight concerns, and bulimic behaviors among girls and boys. *Journal of the American Academy of Child and Adolescent Psychiatry, 38*, 754–760.

Flynn, K., & Fitzgibbon, M. (1996). Body image ideals of low-income African American mothers and their preadolescent daughters. *Journal of Youth and Adolescence, 25*, 615–630.

Fouts, G., & Burggraf, K. (1999). Television situation comedies: Female body images and verbal reinforcements. *Sex Roles, 40*, 473–481.

French, S. A., Story, M., Neumark-Sztainer, D., Downes, B., Resnick, M., & Blum, R. (1997). Ethnic differences in psychosocial and health behavior correlates of dieting, purging, and binge eating in a population-based sample of adolescent females. *International Journal of Eating Disorders, 22*, 315–322.

Furnham, A., & Patel, R. (1994). The eating attitudes and behaviors of Asian and British schoolgirls: A pilot study. *International Journal of Social Psychiatry, 40*, 214–226.

Furukawa, T. (1994). Weight changes and eating attitudes of Japanese adolescents under acculturative stresses: A prospective study. *International Journal of Eating Disorders, 15*, 71–79.

Gard, M. C. E., & Freeman, C. P. (1996). The dismantling of a myth: a review of eating disorders and socioeconomic status. *International Journal of Eating Disorders, 20*, 1–12.

Garfinkel, P. E., & Garner, D. M. (1982). *Anorexia nervosa: A multidimensional perspective.* New York: Brunner/Mazel.

Garner, D. M., Garfinkel, P. E., Rockert, W., & Olmsted, M. P. (1987). A prospective study of eating disturbances in the ballet. *Psychotherapy and Psychosomatics, 48*, 170–175.

Garner, D. M., Olmsted, M. P., Polivy, J., & Garfinkel, P. (1984). Comparison between weight preoccupied women and anorexia nervosa. *Psychosomatic Medicine, 46*, 255–266.

Garner, D. M., Rosen, L. W., & Barry, D. (1998). Eating disorders among athletes - Research and recommendations. *Child and Adolescent Psychiatric Clinics of North America, 7*(4), 839.

Geist, R., Heinmaa, M., Katzman, D., & Stephens, D. (1999). A comparison of male and female adolescents referred to an eating disorder program. *Canadian Journal of Psychiatry – Revue Canadienne de Psychiatrie, 44*, 374–378.

Geracioti, T. D., & Liddle, R. A. (1988). Impaired cholecystokinin secretion in bulimia nervosa. *New England Journal of Medicine, 319*, 683–688.

Grant, K., Lyons, A., Landis, D., Cho, M., Scudiero, M., Reynolds, L., Murphy, J., & Bryant, H. (1999). Gender, body image, and depressive symptoms among low-income African American adolescents. *Journal of Social Issues, 55*, 299–315.

Harris, R. J. (1994). The impact of sexually explicit media. In J. Bryant & D. Zillman (Eds.), *Media effects: Advances in theory and research* (pp. 247–272). Hillsdale, NJ: Lawrence Erlbaum.

Harris, S., & Kuba, S. A. (1997). Ethnocultural identity and eating disorders in women of color. *Professional Psychology: Research and Practice, 28,* 341–347.

Harrison, K., & Cantor, J. (1997). The relationship between media consumption and eating disorders. *Journal of Communication, 47*(1), 40–67.

Hart, K., & Kenny, M. E. (1997). Adherence to the super woman ideal and eating disorder symptoms among college women. *Sex Roles, 36,* 461–478.

Haudek, C., Rorty, M., & Henker, B. (1999). The role of ethnicity and parental bonding in the eating and weight concerns of Asian-American and Caucasian college women. *International Journal of Eating Disorders, 25,* 425–433.

Heatherton, T. F., & Polivy, J. (1992). Chronic dieting and eating disorders: A spiral model. In J. Crowther, S. E. Hobfall, M. A. P. Stephens, & D. L. Tennenbaum (Eds.), *The etiology of bulimia: The individual and familial context* (pp. 133–155). Washington, DC: Hemisphere.

Herman, C. P., & Polivy, J. (1988). Restraint and excess in dieters and bulimics. In K. M. Pirke, D. Ploog, & W. Vandereycken (Eds.), *Psychobiology of bulimia* (pp. 33–41). Berlin: Springer-Verlag.

Hill, A. J., & Franklin, J. A. (1998). Mothers, daughters and dieting: Investigating the transmission of weight control. *British Journal of Clinical Psychology, 37,* 3–13.

Hill, A. J., & Pallin, V. (1998). Dieting awareness and low self-worth: Related issues in 8-year-old girls. *International Journal of Eating Disorders, 24,* 405–413.

Holland, A. J., Sicotte, N., & Treasure, J. L. (1988). Anorexia nervosa: Evidence for a genetic basis. *Journal of Psychosomatic Research, 32,* 561–571.

Humphrey, L. L. (1986). Structural analysis of parent–child relationships in eating disorders. *Journal of Abnormal Psychology, 95,* 395–402.

Humphrey, L. L. (1987). Comparison of bulimic–anorexic and nondistressed families using the Structural Analysis of Social Behavior. *Journal of the American Academy of Child and Adolescent Psychiatry, 26,* 248–255.

Inanuma, K. (1994). Obsessive states in anorexia nervosa. *Japanese Journal of Child and Adolescent Psychiatry, 35,* 465–476.

Johnson, C., & Connors, M. E. (1987). *The etiology and treatment of Bulimia Nervosa.* New York: Basic Books.

Johnson, W. G., Schlundt, D. G., Barclay, D. R., Carr-Nangle, R. E., & Engler, L. B. (1995). A naturalistic functional analysis of binge eating. *Behavior Therapy, 26,* 101–118.

Joiner, G. W., & Kashubeck, S. (1996). Acculturation, body image, self-esteem, and eating disorder symptomatology in adolescent Mexican American women. *Psychology of Women Quarterly, 20,* 419–435.

Katzman, M., & Lee, S. (1997). Beyond body image: The integration of feminist and transcultural theories in the understanding of self-starvation. *International Journal of Eating Disorders, 22,* 385–394.

Kaye, W. H., Bastiani, A. M., & Moss, H. (1995). Cognitive style of patients with anorexia nervosa and bulimia nervosa. *International Journal of Eating Disorders, 18,* 287–290.

Kaye, W. H., Greeno, C. G., Moss, H., Fernstrom, J., Fernstrom, M., Lilenfeld, L. R., Weltzin, T. E., & Mann, J. J. (1998). Alterations in serotonin activity and psychiatric symptoms after recovery from bulimia nervosa. *Archives of General Psychiatry, 55,* 927–935.

Kaye, W. H., Weltzin, T., & Hsu, L. G. (1993). Relationship between anorexia nervosa and obsessive and compulsive behaviors. *Psychiatric Annals, 23,* 365–373.

Keel, P. K., Klump, K. L., Leon, G. R., & Fulkerson, J. A. (1998). Disordered eating in adolescent males from a school-based sample. *International Journal of Eating Disorders, 23,* 125–132.

Kenardy, J., Arnow, B., & Agras, W. S. (1996). The aversiveness of specific emotional states associated with binge-eating in obese subjects. *Australian and New Zealand Journal of Psychiatry, 30,* 839–844.

Kenny, M. E., & Hart, K. (1992). Relationship between parental attachment and eating disorders in an inpatient and a college sample. *Journal of Counseling Psychology, 39,* 521–526.

Koenig, L. J., & Wasserman, E. L. (1995). Body image and dieting failure in college men and women – examining links between depression and eating problems. *Sex Roles, 32,* 225–249.

Langer, L. M., Warheit, G. J., & Zimmerman, R. S. (1991). Epidemiological study of problem eating behaviors and related attitudes in the general population. *Addictive Behaviors, 16,* 167–173.

LaPorte, D. J. (1997). Gender differences in perceptions and consequences of an eating binge. *Sex Roles, 36,* 479–489.

Lee, S., Ho, T. P., & Hsu, L. K. G. (1993). Fat phobic and non-fat phobic anorexia nervosa: A comparative study of 70 Chinese patients in Hong Kong. *Psychological Medicine, 23,* 999–1017.

le Grange, D., Eisler, I., Dare, C., & Hodes, M. (1992). Family criticism and self-starvation: A study of expressed emotion. *Journal of Family Therapy, 14,* 177–192.

Levine, M. P., & Smolak, L. (1992). Toward a model of the developmental psychopathology of eating disorders: The example of early adolescence. In J. H. Crowther, S. E. Hobfall, M. A. P. Stephens, & D. L. Tennenbaum (Eds.), *The etiology of bulimia: The individual and familial context* (pp. 59–80). Washington, DC: Hemisphere.

Levine, M. P., & Smolak, L. (1996). Media as a context for the development of disordered eating. In L. Smolak, M. P. Levine, & R. Striegel-Moore (Eds.), *The developmental psychopathology of eating disorders: Implications for research, prevention, and treatment* (pp. 235–257). Mahwah, NJ: Erlbaum.

Levine, M. P., Smolak, L., Moodey, A. F., Shuman, M. D., & Hessen, L. D. (1994). Normative developmental challenges and dieting and eating disturbances in middle school girls. *International Journal of Eating Disorders, 15,* 11–20.

Littlewood, R. (1995). Psychopathology and personal agency: Modernity, culture change and eating disorders in South Asian societies. *British Journal of Medical Psychology, 68,* 45–63.

Makkar, J. K., & Strube, M. J. (1995). Black women's self-perceptions of attractiveness following exposure to white versus black beauty standards: the moderating role of racial identity and self-esteem. *Journal of Applied Social Psychology, 25,* 1547–1566.

Malkin, A. R., Wornian, K., & Chrisler, J. C. (1999). Women and weight: Gendered messages on magazine covers. *Sex Roles, 40,* 647–655.

McCarthy, M. (1990). The thin ideal, depression, and eating disorders in women. *Behavioral Research and Therapy, 28,* 205–215.

McFarlane, T., Polivy, J., & Herman, C. P. (1998). The effects of false feedback about weight on restrained and unrestrained eaters. *Journal of Abnormal Psychology, 107,* 312–318.

Mildred, H., Paxton, S. J., & Wertheim, E. H. (1995). Risk factors for eating disorders in Greek- and Anglo-Australian adolescent girls. *International Journal of Eating Disorders, 17,* 91–96.

Mills, J., Polivy, J., Herman, C. P., & Tiggemann, M. (in press). Effects of media-portrayed idealized body images on restrained and unrestrained eaters. *Personality and Social Psychology Bulletin.*

Minuchin, S., Rosman, B. L., & Baker, L. (1978). *Psychosomatic families: Anorexia nervosa in context.* Cambridge, MA: Harvard University Press.

Mori, D. L., & Morey, L. (1991). The vulnerable body image of females with feelings of depression. *Journal of Research in Personality, 25,* 343–354.

Mumford, D. B., Whitehouse, A. M., & Platts, M. (1991). Sociocultural correlates of eating disorders among Asian schoolgirls in Bradford. *British Journal of Psychiatry, 158,* 222–228.

Musante, G. J., Costanzo, P. R., & Friedman, K. E. (1998). The comorbidity of depression and eating dysregulation processes in a diet-seeking obese population: A matter of gender specificity. *International Journal of Eating Disorders, 23*(1), 65–75.

Muth, J. L., & Cash, T. F. (1997). Body-image attitudes: What difference does gender make? *Journal of Applied Social Psychology, 27*, 1438–1452.

Nasser, M. (1997). *Culture and weight consciousness.* New York: Routledge.

Nowak, M. (1998). The weight-conscious adolescent: Body image, food intake, and weight-related behavior. *Journal of Adolescent Health, 23*, 389–398.

O'Dea, J. A., & Abraham, S. (1999). Association between self-concept and body weight, gender, and pubertal development among male and female adolescents. *Adolescence, 34*, 69–79.

O'Dwyer, A. M., Lucey, J. V., & Russell G. F. M. (1996). Serotonin activity in anorexia nervosa after long-term weight restoration: Response to D-fenfluramine challenge. *Psychological Medicine, 26*, 353–359.

Ogden, J., & Elder, C. (1998). The role of family status and ethnic group on body image and eating behavior. *International Journal of Eating Disorders, 23*, 309–315.

Ogden, J., & Thomas, D. (1999). The role of familial values in understanding the impact of social class on weight concern. *International Journal of Eating Disorders, 25*, 273–279.

Petrie, T. A. (1996). Differences between male and female college lean sport athletes, nonlean sport athletes, and nonathletes on behavioral and psychological indices of eating disorders. *Journal of Applied Sport Psychology, 8*(2), 218–230.

Pike, K. M., & Rodin, J. (1991). Mothers, daughters, and disordered eating. *Journal of Abnormal Psychology, 100*, 198–204.

Pinhas, L., Toner, B. B., Ali, A., Garfinkel, P. E., & Stuckless, N. (1999). The effects of the ideal of female beauty on mood and body satisfaction. *International Journal of Eating Disorders, 25*, 223–226.

Polivy, J. (1996). Psychological consequences of food restriction. *Journal of the American Dietetic Association, 96*, 589–594.

Polivy, J., Heatherton, T. F., & Herman, C. P. (1988). Self-esteem, restraint, and eating behavior. *Journal of Abnormal Psychology, 97*, 354–356.

Polivy, J., & Herman, C. P. (1987). The diagnosis and treatment of normal eating. *Journal of Consulting & Clinical Psychology, 55*, 635–644.

Polivy, J., & Herman, C. P. (1993). Etiology of binge eating: Psychological mechanisms. In C. Fairburn (Ed.), *Binge eating* (pp. 173–205). London: Guilford.

Polivy, J., Herman, C. P., & McFarlane, T. (1994). Effects of anxiety on eating: Does palatability moderate distress-induced overeating in dieters? *Journal of Abnormal Psychology, 103*, 505–510.

Pope, H. G., Olivardia, R., Gruber, A., & Borowiecki, J. (1999). Evolving ideals of male body image as seen through action toys. *International Journal of Eating Disorders, 26*, 65–72.

Powell, A. L., & Thelen, M. H. (1996). Emotions and cognitions associated with bingeing and weight control behavior in bulimia. *Journal of Psychosomatic Research, 40*, 317–328.

Pritchard, M. E., King, S. L., & Czajka-Narins, D. M. (1997). Adolescent body mass indices and self-perception. *Adolescence, 32*, 863–880.

Pumariega, A. J. (1986). Acculturation and eating attitudes in adolescent girls: A comparative and correlational study. *Journal of the American Academy of Child Psychiatry, 25*, 276–279.

Raudenbush, B., & Zellner, D. (1997). Nobody's satisfied: Effects of abnormal eating behaviors and actual and perceived weight status on body image satisfaction in males and females. *Journal of Social and Clinical Psychology, 16*, 95–110.

Rhodes, B., & Kroger, J. (1992). Parental bonding and separation–individuation difficulties among late adolescent eating disordered women. *Child Psychiatry and Human Development, 22,* 249–263.

Rierdan, J., & Koff, E. (1997). Weight, weight-related aspects of body image, and depression in early adolescent girls. *Adolescence, 32,* 615–624.

Root, M. (1990). Disordered eating in women of color. *Sex Roles, 22,* 525–536.

Rudolph, K. D., & Hammen, C. (1999). Age and gender as determinants of stress exposure, generation, and reactions in youngsters: A transactional perspective. *Child Development, 70(3),* 660–677.

Schur, E. A., Sanders, M., & Steiner, H. (2000). Body dissatisfaction and dieting in young children. *International Journal of Eating Disorders, 27,* 74–82.

Silverstein, B., Peterson, B., & Perdue, L. (1986). Some correlates of the thin standard of bodily attractiveness for women. *International Journal of Eating Disorders, 5,* 895–905.

Simmons, R. G., & Blyth, D. A. (1987). *Moving into adolescence: The impact of pubertal change and school context.* Hawthorne, NY: Aldine de Gruyter.

Simonoff, E. (1992). A comparison of twins and singletons with child psychiatric disorders: An item sheet study. *Journal of Child Psychology and Psychiatry and Allied Disciplines, 33,* 1319–1332.

Smolak, L., & Levine, M. P. (1993). Separation–individuation difficulties and the distinction between bulimia nervosa and anorexia nervosa in college women. *International Journal of Eating Disorders, 14,* 33–41.

Smolak, L., & Levine, M. P. (1996). Adolescent transitions and the development of eating problems. In L. Smolak, M. Levine, & R. Striegel-Moore (Eds.), *The developmental psychopathology of eating disorders: Implications for research, prevention, and treatment* (pp. 210–231). Hillsdale, NJ: Erlbaum.

Smolak, L., Levine, M. P., & Schermer, F. (1999). Parental input and weight concerns among elementary school children. *International Journal of Eating Disorders, 25,* 263–271.

Steen, S. N., Wadden, T. A., Foster, G. D., & Andersen, R. E. (1996). Are obese adolescent boys ignoring an important health risk? *International Journal of Eating Disorders, 20,* 281–286.

Steiger, H., Leung, F. Y. K., Puentes-Neuman, G., & Gottheil, N. (1992). Psychological profiles of adolescent girls with varying degrees of eating and mood disturbances. *International Journal of Eating Disorders, 11,* 121–131.

Steiner-Adair, C. (1986). The body politic: Normal female adolescent development and the development of eating disorders. *Journal of the American Academy of Psychoanalysis, 14,* 95–114.

Stice, E., Mazotti, L., Krebs, M., & Martin, S. (1998). Predictors of adolescent dieting behaviors: a longitudinal study. *Psychology of Addictive Behaviors, 12,* 195–205.

Stice, E., Schupak-Neuberg, E., Shaw, H. E., & Stein, R. I. (1994). Relation of media exposure to eating disorder symptomatology: An examination of mediating mechanisms. *Journal of Abnormal Psychology, 103,* 836–840.

Stice, E., & Shaw, H. E. (1994). Adverse effects of the media portrayed thin-ideal on women and linkages to bulimic symptomatology. *Journal of Social and Clinical Psychology, 13,* 288–308.

Strauss, J., & Ryan, R. (1987). Autonomy disturbances in subtypes of anorexia nervosa. *Journal of Abnormal Psychology, 96,* 254–258.

Striegel-Moore, R. H. (1993). Etiology of binge eating: A developmental perspective. In C. G. Fairburn & G. T. Wilson (Eds.), *Binge eating: Nature, assessment, and treatment* (pp. 144–172). New York: Guilford.

Striegel-Moore, R. H., & Smolak, L. (1996). The role of race in the development of eating disorders. In L. Smolak, M. P. Levine, & R. Striegel-Moore (Eds.), *The developmental psychopathology of eating disorders: Implications for research, prevention, and treatment* (pp. 259–284). Hillsdale, NJ: Erlbaum.

Striegel-Moore, R. H., Wilfley, D. E., Pike, K. M., Dohm, F., & Fairburn, C. G. (in press). Recurrent binge eating in Black American women. *Archives of Family Medicine.*

Strober, M., & Humphrey, L. L. (1987). Familial contributions to the etiology and course of Anorexia Nervosa and Bulimia. *Journal of Consulting and Clinical Psychology, 55,* 654–659.

Strober, M., & Katz, J. L. (1988). Depression in the eating disorders: A review and analysis of descriptive, family and biological findings. In D. M. Garner & P. E. Garfinkel (Eds.), *Diagnostic issues in Anorexia Nervosa and Bulimia Nervosa* (pp. 80–111). New York, Brunner/Mazel.

Strober, M., Lampert, C., Morrell, W., & Burroughs, J. (1990). A controlled family study of anorexia nervosa: Evidence of familial aggregation and lack of shared transmission with affective disorders. *International Journal of Eating Disorders, 9,* 239–253.

Strong, K. G., & Huon, G. F. (1998). An evaluation of a structural model for studies of the initiation of dieting among adolescent girls. *Journal of Psychosomatic Research, 44,* 315–326.

Sykora, C., Grilo, C. M., Wilfley, D. E., & Brownell, K. D. (1993). Eating, weight, and dieting disturbances in male and female lightweight and heavyweight rowers. *International Journal of Eating Disorders, 14,* 203–211.

Theander, S. (1996). Anorexia nervosa with an early onset: Selection, gender, outcome, and results of a long-term follow-up study. *Journal of Youth and Adolescence, 25,* 419–429.

Thompson, R. A., & Sherman, R. T. (1999). Athletes, athletic performance, and eating disorders: Healthier alternatives. *Journal of Social Issues, 55,* 317–337.

Thompson, S. H., Corwin, S. J., & Sargent, R. G. (1997). Ideal body size beliefs and weight concerns of fourth-grade children. *International Journal of Eating Disorders, 21,* 279–284.

Thompson, S. H., Sargent, R. G., & Kemper, K. A. (1996). Black and white adolescent males' perceptions of ideal body size. *Sex Roles, 34,* 391–406.

Treasure, J., & Holland, A. (1990). Genes and the aetiology of eating disorders. In P. McGuffin & R. Murray (Eds.), *The new genetics of mental illness* (pp. 198–211). Oxford: Butterworth-Heinemann.

Treasure, J., & Holland, A. (1995). Genetic factors in eating disorders. In G. I. Szmukler & C. Dare (Eds.), *Handbook of eating disorders: Theory, treatment and research* (pp. 65–81). Chichester: Wiley.

Vanfurth, E. F., Vanstrien, D. C., Martina, L. M. L., Vanson, M. J. M., Hendrickx, J. J. P., & Vanengeland, H. (1996). Expressed emotion and the prediction of outcome in adolescent eating disorders. *International Journal of Eating Disorders, 20,* 19–31.

Wertheim, E. H., Paxton, S. J., Maude, D., Szmukler, G. I., & Hiller, L. (1992). Psychosocial predictors of weight loss behaviors and binge eating in adolescent girls and boys. *International Journal of Eating Disorders, 12,* 151–160.

Wiseman, C. V., Gray, J. J., Mosimann, J. E., & Ahrens, A. H. (1992). Cultural expectations of thinness in women: An update. *International Journal of Eating Disorders 11,* 85–89.

Wolfe, B. E., Metzger, E. D., & Jimerson, D. C. (1997). Research update on serotonin function in bulimia nervosa and anorexia nervosa. *Psychopharmacology Bulletin, 33,* 345–357.

Wonderlich, S. (1995). Personality and eating disorders. In K. D. Brownell & C. G. Fairburn (Eds.), *Eating disorders and obesity: A comprehensive handbook* (pp. 171–176). New York: Guilford.

Woodside, D. B., Field, L. L., Garfinkel, P. E., & Heinmaa, M. (1998). Specificity of eating disorders diagnoses in families of probands with anorexia nervosa and bulimia nervosa. *Comprehensive Psychiatry 39,* 261–264.

CHAPTER TWENTY-SIX

Depression and Suicide during Adolescence

Alesha D. Seroczynski, Farrah M. Jacquez, and David A. Cole

Introduction

The field of psychopathology has been slow to accept the notion that children and adolescents can suffer from depression. As recently as 1992, comprehensive assessment texts for graduate training did not include information on evaluating depression in children and adolescents (e.g., Sattler, 1992), despite the fact that we have known about the existence of depression in children and adolescents for over fifty years (Spitz & Wolf, 1946). Furthermore, depressed adolescents are more likely than nondepressed teens to attempt or commit suicide, and suicide is the third leading cause of death in young people. Recent work in developmental psychopathology (Sroufe & Rutter, 1984) has advanced our understanding of depression and suicide during childhood and adolescence. The purpose of this chapter is twofold: (a) to provide an overview of depression theory and research, highlighting factors that are of particular concern during adolescence; and (b) to review factors pertaining to the incidence of suicide and parasuicidal behavior during adolescence.

Depression

Overview of depression in adolescents

Psychiatrists and psychologists have conceptualized depression in at least three different ways: as a mood, as a syndrome, and as a disorder (Angold, 1988). Depressed mood is a

The authors thank Jeremiah Wright for his diligent work on portions of this manuscript.

general feeling of negative affect, including dysphoria, sadness, and irritability. Depressive syndromes involve sets of symptoms that have been shown empirically to co-occur. Such symptoms include dysphoria, irritability, pervasive anhedonia, appetite disturbance, weight loss or gain, sleeplessness, psychomotor agitation or retardation, fatigue, feelings of guilt or worthlessness, concentration problems, and suicidal thoughts or behavior. The actual diagnosis of a depressive disorder further requires a minimum number, duration, and severity of such symptoms, as reflected in *the Diagnostic and Statistical Manual of Mental Disorders – Fourth Edition* (DSM-IV; American Psychiatric Association, 1994) and the *International Classification of Diseases* (ICD-10; World Health Organization, 1996).

Depressive disorders include bipolar disorders, dysthymic disorder (DD), and major depressive disorder (MDD). All involve impairment of social, cognitive, academic, or occupational functioning (American Psychiatric Association, 1994). Bipolar disorders involve successive episodes of mania and depression. Dysthymic disorder involves chronic episodes of depressed mood. Major Depressive Disorder is marked by one or more episodes of diagnosable depression, as described above. When depression occurs during adolescence, some symptoms of depression are especially common, including social withdrawal, academic problems, crying, avoidance of eye contact, physical complaints, and poor appetite. Irritability and aggression may also be considered part of the diagnostic picture (Pfeffer, 1996). Currently, the same diagnostic criteria are applied to adolescents as adults (American Psychiatric Association, 1994; e.g., Lobovitz & Handel, 1985). Some investigators, however, have suggested that developmental differences in the etiology, assessment, and treatment of child and adolescent depression should be more carefully examined (Cicchetti & Toth, 1998).

Recent research suggests that major depression occurs with relatively high frequency in adolescents. The point prevalence rate of depression during adolescence is between 4.0 percent and 8.3 percent (Birmaher et al., 1996), and the lifetime prevalence for MDD by adolescence is between 15 percent and 20 percent (Harrington, Rutter, & Fombonne, 1996). Unfortunately, children (like adults) with clinical depression often go untreated. As many as 70 to 80 percent of depressed teenagers do not receive treatment (Keller et al., 1991; Rhode, Lewinsohn, & Seeley, 1991).

Depression in childhood and adolescence is not necessarily brief. Longitudinal studies of children and adolescents reveal that depressive symptoms are highly stable (Cohen et al., 1995; Cole et al., 1997). The best predictor of later depression is the occurrence of a previous depressive episode. For example, 76 percent of children who first developed DD later developed MDD, and 69 percent of these children developed double depression (simultaneously occurrence of DD and MDD; Kovacs et al., 1994). The average duration of MDD in children and adolescents is seven to nine months, although 10 percent of such episodes last for more than two years (Birmaher et al., 1996).

Depression is a very debilitating disorder, associated with a wide variety of concurrent problems. Concentration problems and motivational deficits often lead to serious academic difficulties (Kovacs et al., 1984). Social withdrawal impairs interpersonal relationships (Kovacs et al., 1984). Indeed, youth who are socially withdrawn in fourth grade tend to become more withdrawn in middle school or high school (Moskowitz, Schwartzman, & Ledingham, 1985). At least one study suggests that depression in youth may be a more serious disorder that it is in adults (Radloff, 1991). Studies of adolescents reveal that depression predicts suicidality and substance abuse (Levy & Deykin, 1989), and has been associated with aggressive and delinquent behavior, especially in boys (Harrington, Rutter, & Fombonne, 1996; Young et al., 1995). Depression is also highly comorbid with anxiety (Cole, Truglio, & Peeke, 1997); children who report high levels of anxiety tend to experience greater depression in adolescence (Cohen et al., 1995).

A developmental look at depression during adolescence

In order to understand depression in adolescence, one must adopt a developmental perspective (Cicchetti & Toth, 1998). Developmental psychopathologists seek to understand the emergence of pathology in a broader developmental context. This perspective requires the simultaneous consideration of diverse disciplinary perspectives: it emphasizes individual adaptation over the course of human development, describes an integration of various developmental systems across the lifespan, and proposes a variety of possible pathways whereby pathology may develop (Cicchetti, 1993). Following is a brief overview of Cicchetti and Toth's (1998) model.

Children and adolescents confront a variety of life challenges or developmental tasks (Cicchetti & Schneider-Rosen, 1986; Sroufe, 1979; Sroufe & Rutter, 1984). The child's successful resolution of such developmental tasks influences the subsequent organization of psychological and biological resources. Successful negotiation of each task results in a healthier psychological system better prepared to meet the demands of the next developmental challenge. In contrast, the inadequate resolution of such tasks facilitates the integration of maladaptive strategies that render the individual less capable of resolving future developmental issues. Thus, early competence fosters later competence; conversely, early incompetence begets later incompetence (Cicchetti & Toth, 1998). Depression can be seen as an unsuccessful response to such developmental challenges.

Two fundamental principles of developmental psychopathology are *equifinality* and *multifinality* (Cicchetti & Rogosch, 1996). The concept of equifinality suggests that a given outcome may derive along a variety of developmental pathways. In other words, depression in different people can have different causes. In contrast, the concept of multifinality implies that any single etiological source can produce a variety of qualitatively different outcomes. In other words, a sequence of events that eventuates in depression in one person might lead to anxiety or conduct disorder or no pathology at all in another person. The practical implication is that searching for a single pathway to a specific outcome is unlikely to be fruitful.

Instead, we must consider the dynamic and transactional relations that exist between entire systems of biological, psychological, and social variables across time (Sameroff & Chandler, 1975). According to such a transactional model (Cicchetti & Toth, 1998), relatively proximal and distal processes operate upon the child. One such process is *ontogenic development*: the emergence of intrapersonal factors that affect development (e.g., the attachment relationship, the self-system, physiological regulation). A second is the *microsystem* or immediate interpersonal environment (e.g., the family, one's peer group) in which the child is imbedded. The third is the *exosystem*, those aspects of the community that have a broader or more indirect impact upon the child (e.g., father's place of employment, the local school board). The fourth process is the *macrosystem*, which entails the beliefs and values of the surrounding culture (Bronfenbrenner, 1979).

Although a complete understanding of the development of adolescent depression should involve all four levels of the ecological transactional model, the majority of research has focused on ontogenic development and the role of the microsystem. Our review of this literature is similarly constrained.

Genetic and biological factors

The genetic and biological contributors to depression are numerous and well documented (for reviews, see Depue & Iacono, 1989; Hakim-Larson & Essau, 1999; Johnson et al., 2000). Almost all such factors pertain equally to depression in adults and adolescents, and will not be reviewed here. A major exception, however, is the relation of gender to depression.

Adult women are twice as likely to suffer from depression as are adult men (Nolen-Hoeksema, 1990; Weissman & Klerman, 1977; Weissman et al., 1984). In contrast, pre-pubertal boys and girls are equally likely to experience depressive symptoms and be diagnosed with depression (Nolen-Hoeksema & Girgus, 1994). Sometime during adolescence, girls become much more likely than boys to become depressed. Although boys are less likely to report feelings of depression and although males are less apt to seek treatment for personal problems, reviews of this literature suggest that this gender difference in depression is not an artifact of differential reporting bias (Brems, 1995; Nolen-Hoeksema, 1990).

Several investigators have attempted to determine exactly when this gender difference emerges and why. In our own laboratory, we have found a prominent difference in both self- and other reports of depressive symptoms beginning in the seventh grade and continuing throughout adolescence (Cole et al., 1999). Others, however, have found that gender differences in depressive symptoms did not emerge until high school (Hankin et al., 1998; Petersen, Sarigiani, & Kennedy, 1991). In fact, Hankin and colleagues (1998) found that the incidence and lifetime prevalence of depression for boys and girls was virtually identical in adolescence until age 15, at which point the rates for girls doubled. For boys and girls, the likelihood of depression continues to climb until age 21, supporting other claims that adolescents are more often depressed than adults over age 26 (Radloff, 1991).

Several studies have attempted to explain why this gender difference emerges so clearly in early to middle adolescence. One obvious hypothesis is that hormonal changes trigger the development of depression in adolescent girls and account for this continued difference into adulthood. Although investigators have reported statistically significant hormonal effects, such effects appear to account for a very small proportion of the variance in depressive symptoms (Brems, 1995; Nolen-Hoeksema, 1990; Nolen-Hoeksema & Girgus, 1994).

One alternative explanation is the recurrence hypothesis (Hankin et al., 1998). According to the recurrence hypothesis, large numbers of males and females experience initial episodes of depression; however, previously depressed females are more likely to experience a recurrence of depression than are previously depressed males. Although this hypothesis has been supported by research with adult populations (Amenson & Lewinsohn, 1981; Lewinsohn, Zeiss, & Duncan, 1989), no such support has accrued from studies of adolescents (Hankin et al., 1998). During adolescence, the likelihood of recurrence (after an initial episode of depression) is no different for girls than for boys.

Another potential explanation centers around the interaction between biological and social factors. Petersen, Sarigiani, and Kennedy (1991) found that for both girls and boys, the synchrony of pubertal change and school change (i.e., the transition from elementary to middle school) in early adolescence significantly predicted depressed affect in late adolescence. Adolescents who experienced the onset of puberty within six months of making the middle school transition were more likely to report depressive symptoms. Girls, however, were four times more likely to experience both changes within six months of each other. For boys, the onset of puberty was substantially later than their transition into middle school. Thus, the timing of changes experienced during early adolescence may account for some of the gender differences in depression that emerge in adolescence.

In addition, when boys were faced with negative family events, they were also more likely to experience a *decrease* in negative affect, suggesting that stressful events may have a "steeling" effect on boys, but not girls (Rutter, 1981). In fact, boys may feel more confident in their ability to cope with stressful life events and the emotional distress that often results from them (Nolen-Hoeksema, 1987).

Satisfaction with one's body image is also related to adolescents' reports of depression (Grant et al., 1999; Kostanski & Gullone, 1998). Depression is significantly related to perceived body image for both boys and for girls, but the relation is stronger for adolescent girls. Kostanski and Gullone (1998) found that girls were twice as likely to report dissatisfaction with their bodies as were boys. In general, adolescent boys report higher levels of self-esteem than do girls. These findings may also help to explain the often-noted concurrence of eating disorders and depression in adolescent girls and young women (Kaye, Weltzin, & Hsu, 1993).

Cognitive factors

Cognitive models of depression in adults have garnered some support from research among adolescents. Foremost among these are Beck's cognitive model and Abramson's hopelessness model. Both are diathesis-stress models, which posit that a pattern of thinking either interacts with or is triggered by specific types of negative life events. Beck (1967, 1976) proposed that depression is predisposed by negative schemas (probably learned in childhood and probably associated with various loss experiences), which generate pessimistic views of one's self, the future, and the world. Abramson's model proposes that one's explanatory style (i.e., attributing negative events to stable and personal characteristics versus transitory or extrinsic circumstances) either potentiates or inhibits the depressive effects of negative life events.

Research provides preliminary support for such models. Depressed adolescents tend to dramatize situations, have low frustration tolerance, and make unrealistic demands on themselves and others (Marcotte, 1996). In addition, depressed adolescents tend to ascribe negative attributes to themselves and evaluate their performance as evidence of personal inadequacy and social ineptitude (Carlson & Kashani, 1988; Rutter, 1986). As a result, they are often critical of themselves and predict that they will fail, especially in achievement and interpersonal contexts. Clinically depressed adolescents also tend to think in black and white, to believe they have little control over life events, and to be pessimistic about the future (Hammond & Romney, 1995). Depressed adolescent girls also appear to ruminate excessively on their problems (Compas, Malcarne, & Fondacaro, 1988; Girgus, Nolen-Hoeksema, & Seligman, 1989). This rumination may contribute to the cognitive diathesis for depression, as preadolescent girls have been shown to adopt a ruminative and self-focused style of responding to problem vignettes (Broderick, 1998).

A recent issue of *Cognitive Therapy and Research* devoted special attention to studies on the developmental antecedents of cognitive vulnerability to depression. Several articles focused on adolescence. Rudolf, Kurlakowsky, and Conley (in press) reported that stressful life events and family disruption predicted increases in helplessness and decreases in perceived control. Garber and Flynn (in press) noted that low levels of maternal acceptance were associated with diminished self-worth in young adolescent offspring. Negative events, high levels of maternal control, and the pattern of mothers' attributions about child-related events predicted aspects of the adolescents' attributional style. In a retrospective study of late adolescents, Gibb et al. (in press) noted that individuals who showed signs of depressive cognitive errors and hopelessness were more likely than their non-risk counterparts to have histories of childhood emotional (but not physical or sexual) abuse. In a related study, Alloy et al. (in press) found that cognitive risk factors in late adolescence were related to parental attributions and feedback about negative events and to low levels of paternal acceptance and warmth.

Social influences

Depressed adolescents tend to come from distressed homes. Studies of outpatient and community youth suggest that the members of families with depressed adolescents perceive their families to be less cohesive, secure, communicative, warm, and supportive, and more tense, antagonistic, and critical, compared to members of families without depressed adolescents (Garrison et al., 1997; Lewinsohn et al., 1994; Nilzon & Palmerus, 1997; Reinherz et al., 1993; see Kaslow, Deering, & Racusin, 1994 for a review). Such family problems may be particularly salient for adolescents with longstanding depression or dysthymia (Olsson et al., 1999). Fathers are less likely to report such perceptions. Whereas mothers and adolescents tend to rate the home environment as highly conflictual, fathers of depressed adolescents do not appear to differ from controls in their reports of the family environment (Shiner & Marmorstein, 1998). This finding, however, could be related to the fact that depressed adolescents are more likely to come from divorced or father-absent homes, such that fathers may be less aware of certain family dynamics (Aseltine, 1996; Petersen, White, & Stemmler, 1991; Shiner & Marmorstein, 1998).

Reinherz et al. (1993) also identified a number of factors that appeared to put adolescents at risk for depression. One was the developmental life stage of the family. Perinatal variables such as being third born (or later), having a mother 30 years old or older, having a father 35 years old or older, and having three or more siblings were associated with depression in adolescence. These four risk factors were highly intercorrelated (.56 to .85) and represent a particular family constellation rather than four individual risk factors. Second, the onset of health problems between ages 10 and 15 was a significant antecedent of later depression for girls, but not for boys. Third, depressed females were seven times as likely than nondepressed females to have experienced the death of a parent before age 15. And fourth, early pregnancy and abortion were predictive of depression in adolescent females (although postpartum effects were not controlled).

Until recently, the majority of research has been correlational and cross-sectional in nature. Consequently, developmental and causal conclusions have been somewhat tenuous. More recent work in this area has focused on the individual contributions that adolescents, their mothers, and their fathers make towards the development and maintenance of depression in adolescence. Longitudinal studies suggest that depressed adolescents and their mothers describe their family interactions as more conflictual than do nondepressed controls (Sheeber et al., 1997, 1998; Sheeber & Sorensen, 1998). Direct observation during a laboratory task, however, revealed that neither clinically depressed adolescents nor their mothers evinced more aggressive behavior than did nondepressed controls (Sheeber & Sorensen, 1998). This raises the question as to whether real or perceived family conflict is more tightly linked to depression in adolescents.

In a large community sample, the family members' perceptions of conflict were significantly related to direct observations (Sheeber et al., 1997). Furthermore, low levels of family support and high levels of family conflict were associated with adolescent depressive symptoms in both cross-sectional and longitudinal analyses. On the other hand, the reverse was not evident. Adolescent depression did not predict deterioration in family relationships. Although the quality of family relationships appears to influence the development of depression during adolescence, the severity of the adolescents' depression does not appear to affect the quality of family relationships (Sheeber et al., 1997, 1998).

Studies also suggest that parents may inadvertently reinforce their adolescents' depressive symptoms. In response to the adolescent's exhibition of depressive behavior, mothers and fathers are more likely to emit facilitative and problem-solving behavior, as compared to parents of nondepressed adolescents. Such actions are consistent with a model of positive reinforcement (Sheeber et al., 1997, 1998). Both mothers and fathers have also been found to suppress aversive behavior in response to the adolescent's exhibition of depressive symptoms (Dadds et al., 1992; Sheeber et al., 1998). Such behavioral inhibition is consistent with a model of negative reinforcement. Adolescent depression may serve, at least temporarily, to suppress family aggression and conflict.

Divorce appears to influence adolescent depression in both direct and indirect ways (Petersen et al., 1991b; Sarigiani, 1990). Early adolescent girls with a history of emotional problems are especially vulnerable to the events surrounding divorce. Recent work suggests that divorce creates a number of secondary stressors for the adolescent. Economic hardships may be most strongly linked to adolescent depression in divorced families (Aseltine, 1996). Some of these stressors do not necessarily exist prior to the parents' divorce (Aseltine, 1996). That is, divorce appears to precipitate a number of new problems that are associated with depression in adolescents.

A few studies have examined the interplay between ontogenic development and the role of the microsystem. The interaction between depressotypic cognitions and problematic family characteristics has attracted attention. The nature of this interplay varies with the developmental level of the youth. During middle childhood, depression is most strongly associated with family conflict and nonsupport, irrespective of the presence of depressotypic cognitions such as catastrophization or overgeneralization (Leitenberg, Yost, & Carroll-Wilson, 1986; Ostrander, Weinfurt, & Nay, 1998). By early adolescence, both negative cognitive errors and an unsupportive family contribute to depression additively. Adolescents who tend to make negative cognitive errors and who come from distressed families are at greater risk for depression than are adolescents who have only one such liability. Later in adolescence, however, a multiplicative relation emerges, reflecting a cognitive-diathesis stress model of depression, much like we see operative in adults (Abramson, Metalsky, & Alloy, 1989; Beck, 1987). For older adolescents, family nonsupport appears to predict higher levels of depression only for those adolescents who report high rates of negative self-cognitions (Ostrander, Weinfurt, & Nay, 1998). The presence of one liability potentiates the depressive effect of the other.

Suicide

Overview of suicide in adolescence

The National Center for Health Statistics (NCHS) identified suicide as the third leading cause of death in adolescents (ages 15–24). Approximately 11.4 of every 100,000 adolescent deaths are attributable to suicide (NCHS, 2000). This rate is essentially twice the adolescent suicide rate in the 1970s (Bureau of the Census, 1994). These numbers become even more disturbing when one adds the fact that for every adolescent who actually commits suicide, there are somewhere between 100 to 350 suicide attempts (Berman & Jobes, 1991; Garfinkel, 1989; Jacobziner, 1965). Most suicide attempts (about seven of every eight) are so non-lethal that they do not require medical attention and may not be reported (Smith & Crawford, 1986). Consequently, any rate estimate is only an approximation. Such estimates range from 50,000 to 500,000 per year in the United States (Allen, 1987).

These numbers change dramatically when broken down by gender. Whereas *attempted* suicide is more common among girls, *completed* suicide is much more common among boys (Adcock, Nagy, & Simpson, 1991; Andrews & Lewinsohn, 1992; Bingham et al., 1994). In 1997, 627 girls committed suicide as opposed to 3559 boys (NCHS, 2000). In other words, boys were 5.7 times more likely to die by suicide than were girls. Girls, however, attempt suicide much more often than do boys. In a community sample of high school students, Cole (1989a) found that 19 percent of girls and 7 percent of boys reported having made one or more suicide attempt. The gender difference in mortality of suicide attempts is almost certainly due to the tendency of boys to use more violent and lethal methods (McIntosh, 1992).

Table 26.1   Suicide Statistics of Americans Aged 15–24, 1997

Group	Number	Rate per 100,000
Whites (both sexes)	3456	11.9
Males	2941	19.5
Females	515	3.7
Blacks (both sexes)	513	9.2
Males	447	16.0
Females	66	2.4
Hispanics (both sexes)	445	8.8
Males	398	14.4
Females	57	2.4

Source: National Center for Health Statistics (2000).

Suicide rates also vary by ethnicity (Bingham et al., 1994; Roberts, 2000). Suicide rates for white, black, and Hispanic adolescents (ages 15–24) are depicted in table 26.1. White adolescents are more likely to die by suicide than are Black or Hispanic youth. Among white adolescents, suicide is the second leading cause of death; among black and Hispanic youths, suicide is the third leading cause of death (NCHS, 2000). Although the rate of suicide has increased for all subgroups of US adolescents since the 1970s, the suicide rate for adolescent black males has increased most dramatically (Berman & Jobes, 1991). Other sources suggest that American Indian and Alaskan native adolescents have particularly high rates of suicide (Grossman, Milligan, & Deyo, 1991). The suicide rate among 15- to 24-year-old Native Americans is more than twice that for other Americans. In most ethnic groups within the United States, the incidence of suicide is greatest among the elderly; however, among Native Americans, suicide rate peaks between the ages of 20 and 24. We note, however, that there is a great deal of variation among tribes (Group for the Advancement of Psychiatry, 1996).

Over the course of adolescence, the incidence of suicide generally increases with age (Bingham et al., 1994; Brent et al., 1999). Several developmental phenomena could contribute to this change. First, older adolescents have more sophisticated cognitive skills. Not only do these abilities allow them to plan a more effective suicide attempt, but they could affect the degree to which the adolescent truly intends to die (Shaffer et al., 1996). Second, older adolescents are more likely to suffer from psychopathology (Brent et al., 1999; Groholt et al., 1998), which is a major risk factor in suicide (Shaffer et al., 1996; Rich, Young, & Fowler, 1986). Brent and his colleagues have suggested that "the relationship between psychopathology and suicide may be moderated by cognitive development, with increasing cognitive maturity making the completion of suicide more likely" (Brent et al., 1999, p. 1502).

Gay and lesbian adolescents are also an at-risk group (Nelson, 1994). According to the Secretary's Task Force on Youth Suicide, as many as 30 percent of youth suicides may be committed by homosexual adolescents (Gibson, 1989). These teenagers may be two to six times more likely to attempt suicide than are their heterosexual counterparts (Harry, 1989). The Group for the Advancement of Psychiatry's Committee on Adolescence (1996) suggests that the likelihood of suicidal behavior is particularly high upon discovery of a new sexual orientation. Gay males appear to be at particularly high risk, but this statistic may be affected by the fact that gay males tend to identify themselves as homosexual earlier (around age 15) than do females (approximately age 20 to 23; Dempsey, 1994).

Reported rates of adolescent suicide are probably underestimations. One problem is the difficulty in distinguishing suicide from other causes of death. Without the perspective of the victim, one cannot be certain whether a drug overdose, a car accident, or any other fatal accident was in reality an adolescent's suicide attempt. Accidents were the leading cause of death from 15–24-year-olds in 1997 (NCHS, 2000); how many such "accidents" might have been suicides is impossible to determine. Another problem is the reluctance to label a young person's death as a suicide. Even when friends or family members are aware of the victim's intentions, they may not call the death a suicide because of guilt, shame, or spiritual reasons (Group for the Advancement of Psychiatry, 1996). In order to spare family members from having to cope with the stigma of an adolescent suicide, some physicians may declare the cause of such deaths to be accidental. In a survey of medical examiners, Jobes and Berman (1984) found that 58 of these physicians surmised that the actual suicide rate is probably double the reported rate.

Concern about adolescent suicide is great, as well it should be. Nevertheless, the rate of adolescent suicide should be examined from a broad perspective (Bingham et al., 1994). Suicide is the third leading cause of death among adolescents. In the years since 1970, only in 1994 did it rise to be the second leading cause of death. Although 13 percent of adolescent deaths are by suicide, 42 percent are by some form of accident (most often automobile accidents), and 19 percent are by homicide (Hoyert, Kochanek, & Murphy, 1999). Clearly suicide is only one of several potentially preventable causes of adolescent death.

Methods of suicide

The various methods whereby adolescents attempt suicide differ greatly with regard to their lethality. Firearms are the most lethal method, accounting for approximately 63 percent of all adolescent suicides in the United States in 1996 (see table 26. 2). Firearms are followed by suffocation/hanging and poisoning in terms of lethality. Drug overdose is one of the least lethal methods (McIntosh, 1992), accounting for less than 5 percent of all US adolescent deaths by suicide in 1996. Indeed, drug overdose is the most common method used by adolescents who attempt but do not complete suicide (Nakamura, McLeod, & McDermott, 1994; Spirito et al., 1989). Cutting (a relatively non-lethal method of suicide) is also much more common in younger individuals (McIntosh, 1992).

Clear gender differences exist in the choice of method for attempting (not necessarily completing) suicide. Overdose is most common for female adolescents. Firearms are the most common method chosen by male adolescents. While 65 percent of male victims of suicide in 1996 used firearms, only 47 percent of female victims did (McIntosh, 2000). In recent years, however, women have begun to use firearms more frequently (McIntosh, 1992). Adolescent females attempt suicide more often than do adolescent males; however, adolescent males die by suicide more often than do adolescent females. This apparent

Table 26.2   Methods of Suicide for Americans aged 15–24, 1996

Method	Males		Females		Total	
	N	%	N	%	N	%
Firearms	2427	65.2	300	47.3	4358	100.0
Hanging (HSS)	828	22.2	145	24.6	984	22.6
Poisoning (S&L)	109	2.9	100	15.8	209	4.8
Gas poisoning	140	3.8	24	3.8	164	3.8
Jumping (heights)	60	1.6	24	3.8	84	1.9
Drowning	34	0.9	3	0.5	37	0.8
Cutting and piercing	19	0.5	1	0.2	20	0.5
Total	3724	100.0	634	100.0	4358	100.0

Notes: S&L = solid or liquid substances; HSS = hanging, strangulation, and suffocation. All percentages are computed within group.
Source: Adapted from McIntosh (2000), with permission of the author.

paradox may well be due to the fact the method most commonly used by males (i.e., firearms) is almost eight times more likely to result in death than is the method most often used by females (i.e., overdose). Furthermore, the more lethal the first attempt, the more likely there will be a suicide in the future (McIntosh, 1992).

Risk factors

A wide variety of factors appear to put adolescents at risk for suicidal behavior. Such factors can be (somewhat arbitrarily) divided into three main categories: psychological, behavioral, and familial. Most of the *psychological* risk factors relate to the prevalence of psychiatric illnesses in suicide attempters and completers. The main *behavioral* finding is the overwhelming evidence that attempted suicide is the best predictor of eventual completed suicide. Finally, *family* risk factors have most notably included family psychopathology, parental loss or separation, poor family relationships, and abusive experience.

Psychological factors

Psychiatric illness correlates with suicidal behavior. Some studies report that over 90 percent of completed suicides are committed by adolescents who could be diagnosed with a psychiatric disorder (Rich, Young, & Fowler, 1986; Shaffer, Gould, & Fisher, 1996). Suicidal behavior is most frequently associated with affective disorders, substance abuse, and conduct disorders (summarized in Berman & Jobes, 1991). Adolescents who show evidence of two such disorders are at even greater risk. Further research suggests that the suicidal behavior of mentally ill adolescents is more frequent and more lethal than that of adolescents without mental illness (Runeson & Rich, 1992; Shafii et al., 1988).

Personality disorders are also associated with suicide. Blumenthal (1990) estimated that adolescents who have been diagnosed with a personality disorder are ten times more likely to commit suicide than those who have not been so diagnosed. Particularly high rates of suicide are associated with personality disorders characterized by extreme impulsivity (e.g., borderline, histronic, and antisocial personality disorder; Stone, 1990).

The most researched mental health correlate of adolescent suicide is depression; however, this relationship is complex. Although depressed adolescents are significantly more likely to attempt and commit suicide than those who are not depressed (Shaffer, 1988; Haliburn, 2000), most depressed adolescents are not suicidal (Berman & Jobes, 1991). Some evidence suggests that hopelessness is a particularly critical component of depression when attempting to predict suicide (Beck, Kovacs, & Weissman, 1979; Morano, Cisler, & Lemerond, 1993; Donaldson, Spirito, & Farnett, 2000). Research on adult populations has found that when hopelessness is statistically controlled, the relation between depression and suicide disappears (Weissman, Beck, & Kovacs, 1979; Wetzel et al., 1980; Cole, 1988); however, research on younger populations is at odds with these findings (Asarnow, Carson, & Guthrie, 1987; Cole, 1989a). In studies of adolescents, the relation between hopelessness and suicide was not significant after accounting for depression. Depression, however, was a significant predictor. These results suggest that hopelessness may play a qualitatively different role in suicide for youth and adults. Unlike adults, most adolescents can anticipate certain major life changes that will almost certainly occur: they will eventually leave high school, and they will eventually leave home. (This is not to say that they will graduate, or that leaving home will be an amicable separation.) Nevertheless, a sense of hopelessness about the present state of affairs (e.g., "high school is miserable") may be attenuated by the expectation that certain life circumstances will eventually change ("high school will someday be over"). Such beliefs may diminish the role of hopelessness in adolescent suicide. In adulthood, one has (typically) left home, and one has indeed left school. Consequently, no future life events can be expected. This fact in-and-of-itself may potentiate the role of hopelessness during the post-adolescent years.

The *DSM-IV* (American Psychiatric Association, 1994) identifies substance abuse and dependence as factors that facilitate suicidal behavior. Furthermore, other risk factors become more predictive when combined with the lack of control and marked impulsivity that often characterize drug and alcohol abuse. In their study of psychiatric outpatients, Wannan and Fombonne (1998) found that substance abuse was almost five times greater in adolescents who were suicidal. Approximately 15 to 33 percent of suicide completers have histories of substance abuse (Hoberman & Garfinkel, 1988; Poteet, 1987). Many victims of suicide are under the influence of drugs or alcohol at the time of their death. In Hoberman and Garfinkel's (1989) study, 34 percent of the victims had used recreational drugs or alcohol within 12 hours of their death. Beck and Steer (1989) found that a diagnosis of alcohol dependence in suicide attempters at the time of hospital admission increased fivefold the risk of eventual suicide completion. Preliminary evidence suggests that the association between substance abuse and suicidal behavior may be greater in males than females (Marttunen et al., 1995). Overall, the multiplicative effect of substance abuse upon other risk factors led Brent et al. (1988) to label substance abuse the most significant stressor in the lives of suicidal adolescents.

Behavioral factors

Although depression, substance abuse, and other psychiatric illnesses are strong psychological predictors of suicidal behavior, there is no better indicator of suicide risk than a previous attempt (Lewinsohn, Rhode, & Seeley, 1994; Shafii et al., 1985; Wichstrom, 2000). Dudley and Waters (1991) found that 30 to 50 percent of completed suicides have a history of one or more previous attempt. Indeed, throughout the lifespan, past suicidal behavior is the best predictor of future suicidal behavior (Berman & Jobes, 1991).

This said, we must also note that most people who attempt suicide do not eventually die by suicide. Research suggests that fundamental differences exist between attempters and completers. The gender differences already described exemplify this distinction. The prototypical adolescent attempt is an overdose by a female, attempted after an argument, and in front of her family (Trautman, 1986). However, the most common adolescent completion, comprising almost two-thirds of all completions, is a self-inflicted gunshot by a male (Berman & Jobes, 1991). This difference highlights the need for gender to be considered when assessing suicide risk (Tomori & Zalar, 2000). Although the difference between attempters and completers should be considered carefully, the fact that a previous attempt is the best predictor of suicide is sufficient to regard any suicide attempt as a serious suicide risk factor.

Familial factors

The third major set of risk factors involves family characteristics. The most commonly cited factors include separation from parents, family history of psychiatric difficulties, family history of suicidal behavior, and childhood maltreatment (Stoelb & Chiriboga, 1998, p. 361).

Loss of or separation from a parent are reliable correlates of suicidal behavior (Cohen-Sandler, Berman, & King, 1982; Garfinkel, Froese, & Hood, 1982; Kosky, Silburn, & Zubrick, 1990). About 50 percent of suicidal adolescents come from either divorced or single-parent families (Allberg, 1990). Although statistically significant, these results should be considered carefully. After accounting for factors such as family functioning and family psychopathology, family constellation no longer contributes to suicidal behavior (Brent et al., 1988; Wannan & Fombonne, 1998). Patterns of family functioning that lead to or follow from the absence of a parent may be the more critical concern.

Family psychopathology undoubtedly correlates with adolescent suicidal behavior (Cohen-Sandler, Berman, & King, 1982; Pfeffer, 1989a; Pfeffer, Normandin, & Tatsuyuki, 1994; Garfinkel, Froese, & Hood, 1982; Roy, 1983). Depression and substance abuse are the most common psychiatric problems of parents of suicidal teens (Pfeffer, 1989b). Such parental problems are associated with high levels of stress in other family members. In 40 percent of families with a depressed parent, other family members meet a standardized criterion for therapeutic referral. For these people, living with a depressed family member produced numerous burdens (Coyne et al., 1987). In a related vein, parental suicidal behavior is also associated with adolescent suicide. Shaffer's longitudinal study suggests that at least 33 percent of suicidal adolescents have a relative who previously attempted suicide (Holden, 1986).

A history of childhood sexual or physical abuse is also a risk factor for teen suicide (Robbins, 1998; Pfeffer, 1989b). The association between abuse and suicidal behavior is stronger for adolescents than for any other age group (Pfeffer, 1989b). One researcher estimated that 16 percent of suicide attempters had been sexually abused (Coleman, 1987). Deykin, Alpert, and McNamarra (1985) studied the relation between abuse and suicidal behavior in 159 suicidal and 318 non-suicidal adolescents. Those who had attempted suicide were three to six times more likely to have been abused prior to the attempt. Abused adolescents are also often afflicted by psychiatric illnesses such as depression, substance abuse, and conduct disorder (Bayatpour, Wells, & Holoford, 1992).

For suicidal adolescents, familial relationships are often difficult and unfulfilling (Wannan & Fombonne, 1998). In his discussion of suicide and the family, Robbins (1998) noted that conflict, chaos, and a lack of cohesiveness tend to characterize these families. Such families are not well organized and the role expectations for each family member are not clearly defined (Asarnow, Carlson, & Guthrie, 1987; Hepworth, Farley, & Griffiths, 1988). The home environment is often unpredictable and unstable. Adolescents exhibiting suicidal behavior report higher levels of conflict with their parents than do other psychiatric patients (Spirito et al., 1989; Lewinsohn, Rhode, & Seeley, 1994). They generally describe their family relationships as dysfunctional because of "low levels of affection, little enjoyment of time spent with other family members, and negative views of parents" (Stillion & McDowell, 1996, p. 113).

What Is Special about Adolescence?

Many adults find it difficult to understand why a young person who has a lifetime of opportunities before them would ever consider suicide. Several aspects of adolescent development may be particularly relevant. Many of these variables concern the adolescent personal fable, an attitude about self that incorporates a sense of invincibility (e.g., "bad things won't happen to me"), uniqueness (e.g., "no one knows how I feel"), and power (e.g., "other people might have trouble, but I can handle it"). Adolescents often believe that problems afflicting others will simply not happen to them (Elkind, 1985; Lapsley, 1985). They may disregard certain natural limitations (sometimes even the permanence of death).

The adolescent personal fable has often been discussed in negative terms because of its potentially dangerous consequences, such as engaging in risky behavior (e.g., driving fast without real regard for the possibility of an accident, having unprotected sex without real concern about pregnancy or disease). The personal fable, however, may also have protective value against suicidal behavior. Cole (1989b) investigated adolescents' reports of reasons for staying alive. Adolescents who reported more reasons for staying alive were less likely to report past or recent suicidal thoughts or behaviors. More specifically, adolescents who endorsed general self-efficacy beliefs, optimistic views of the future, and life-affirming values were less likely to report suicidal thoughts or behavior. Cole speculated that adolescents who have a strong sense of their own invulnerability will likely see themselves as capable of handling life's problems, supporting the idea that aspects of the adolescent personal fable may act as a buffer against suicidal thoughts and behavior.

Adolescence is also a time when many youth establish a degree of autonomy from parents and family and take noteworthy steps in personal identity formation. Furthermore, developing stronger relationships with peers of both sexes becomes of increasing importance. Clearly, the nature and intensity of the parent–child relationship changes. Previously, the family was the primary source of support for the child; during adolescence, however, other relationships emerge that also become a source of support (Group for the Advancement of Psychiatry, 1996). During this process, some adolescents distance themselves from their parents. In such cases, young people can be left to rely completely on peers for support. Unfortunately, the identity development process is not always smooth. In our relatively age-stratified society, adolescents and their peers are apt to be undertaking these transitions simultaneously, producing a social milieu that may not be an especially dependable source of support (Robbins, 1998).

Impulsivity, fueled by a sense of invincibility and coupled with a failure to recognize one's own limitations, can lead the adolescent who feels alienated from parents, family, and peers to attempt suicide. More than half of adolescents who engage in suicidal behavior spend less than thirty minutes deliberating their actions (Hodgman & McAnarney, 1992). The report on adolescent suicide formulated by the Group for the Advancement of Psychiatry (1996) suggests that the changes that characterize adolescence leave some young people at risk. A heightened sense of self-consciousness, fluctuating levels of self-esteem, and a degree of impulsivity may set the stage: These developmental characteristics place adolescents at a heightened risk for inappropriate response to stress under the best of circumstances [*sic*]. Even a relatively minor perceived loss or rejection or disappointment in oneself can trigger self-destructive urges and behavior. When either the childrearing experiences or the cultural realities into which the adolescent is emerging compromise the psychologically healthy development or realistically constrict the options for successful adult function, adolescents are particularly at risk for suicide (Group for the Advancement of Psychiatry, 1996, p. 17).

References

Abramson, L. Y., Metalsky, G. I., & Alloy, L. B. (1989). Hopelessness depression: A theory-based subtype of depression. *Psychological Review, 96*, 358–372.

Adcock, A. G., Nagy, S., & Simpson, J. A. (1991). Selected risk factors in adolescent suicide attempts. *Adolescence, 26*, 817–828.

Allberg, W. R. (1990). Understanding adolescent suicide: Correlates in a developmental perspective. *School Counselor, 37*, 343–350.

Allen, B. (1987). Youth suicide. *Adolescence, 22*, 271–290.

Alloy, L. B., Abramson, L. Y., Tashman, N. A., Berrebbi, D. S., Hogan, M. E., Whitehouse, W. G., Crossfield, A. G., & Morocco, A. (in press). Developmental origins of cognitive vulnerability to depression: Parenting, cognitive, and inferential feedback styles of the parents of individuals at high and low cognitive risk for depression. *Cognitive Therapy and Research*.

Amenson, C. S., & Lewinsohn, P. M. (1981). An investigation into the observed sex difference in prevalence of unipolar depression. *Journal of Abnormal Psychology, 90*, 1–13.

American Psychiatric Association (1994). *Diagnostic and statistical manual of mental disorders* (4th ed.). Washington, DC: American Psychiatric Association.

Andrews, J. A., & Lewinsohn, P. M. (1992). Suicidal attempts among older adolescents; prevalence and co-occurence with psychiatric disorders. *Journal of American Academy of Child and Adolescent Psychiatry, 32*, 655–662.

Angold, A. (1988). Childhood and adolescent depression: I. Epidemiological and aetiological aspects. *British Journal of Psychiatry, 152*, 601–617.

Asarnow, J. R., Carlson, G. A., & Guthrie, D. (1987). Coping strategies, self-perceptions, hopelessness, and perceived family environments in depressed and suicidal children. *Journal of Consulting and Clinical Psychology, 55*, 361–366.

Aseltine, R. H. (1996). Pathways linking parental divorce with adolescent depression. *Journal of Health and Social Behavior, 37*, 133–148.

Bayatpour, M., Wells, R. D., & Holoford, S. (1992). Physical and sexual abuse as predictors of substance use and suicide among pregnant teenagers. *Journal of Adolescent Health, 13*, 128–132.

Beck, A. T. (1967). *Depression: Clinical, experimental, and theoretical aspects.* New York: Hoeber.

Beck, A. T. (1976). *Cognitive therapy and the emotional disorders.* Madison, NJ: International Universities Press.

Beck, A. T. (1987). Cognitive models of depression. *Journal of Cognitive Psychotherapy, 1*, 5–38.

Beck, A. T., Kovacs, M., & Weissman, A. (1979). Assessment of suicide ideation: the scale for suicide ideators. *Journal of Consulting and Clinical Psychology, 47*, 343–352.

Beck, A. T., & Steer, R. A. (1989). Clinical predictors of eventual suicide: A 5- to 10-year prospective study of suicide attempters. *Journal of Affective Disorders, 17*, 203–209.

Berman, A. L., & Jobes, D. A. (1991). Adolescent suicide: assessment and intervention. Washington DC: American Psychological Association.

Bingham, C. R., Bennion, L. D., Openshaw, D. K., & Adams, G. R. (1994). An analysis of age, gender, and racial differences in recent national trends of youth suicide. *Journal of Adolescence, 17*, 53–71.

Birmaher, B., Ryan, S. W., Williamson, D., Brent, D., Kaufman, J., Dahl, R., Perel, J., & Nelson, B. (1996). Childhood and adolescent depression: A review of the past 10 years. Part I. *Journal of the American Academy of Child and Adolescent Psychiatry, 35*, 1427–1439.

Blumenthal, S. (1990). Youth suicide: risk factors, assessment, and treatment of adolescent and young adult suicide patients. *Psychiatric Clinics of North America, 13*, 511–556.

Brems, C. (1995). Women and depression: A comprehensive analysis. In E. E. Beckham & W. R. Leber (Eds.), *Handbook of depression* (2nd ed., pp. 539–566). New York: Guilford.

Brent, D. A., Baugher, M., Bridge, J., Chen, T., & Chiappetta, L. (1999). Age and sex-related risk factors for adolescent suicide. *Journal of the American Academy of Child and Adolescent Psychiatry, 38*(12), 1497–1505.

Brent, D. A., Perper, J. A., Goldstein, C. E., Kolko, D. J., Allan, M. J., Allman, C. J., & Zelenak, J. P. (1988). Risk factors for adolescent suicide: a comparison of adolescent suicide victims with suicidal inpatients. *Archives of General Psychiatry, 45*, 581–588.

Broderick, P. C. (1998). Early adolescent gender differences in the use of ruminative and distracting coping strategies. *Journal of Early Adolescence, 18*, 173–195.

Bronfenbrenner, U. (1979). *The ecology of human development: Experiments by nature and design.* Cambridge, MA: Harvard University Press.

Bureau of the Census (1994). *Vital Statistics of the United States, 1991, 114th Ed.* Washington, DC: US National Center for Health Statistics.

Carlson, G. A., & Kashani, J. H. (1988). Phenomenology of major depression from childhood through adulthood: Analysis of three studies. *American Journal of Psychiatry, 145*, 1222–1225.

Cicchetti, D. (1993). Developmental psychopathology: Reactions, reflections, projections. *Developmental Review, 13*, 471–502.

Cicchetti, D., & Rogosch, F. (1996). Equifiniality and multifinality in developmental psychopathology. *Development and Psychopathology, 8*, 597–600.

Cicchetti, D., & Schneider-Rosen, K. (1986). An organizational approach to childhood depression. In M. Rutter, C. Izard, & P. Read (Eds.), *Depression in young people, clinical and developmental perspectives* (pp. 71–134). New York: Guilford.

Cicchetti, D., & Toth, S. L. (1998). Development of depression in children and adolescents. *American Psychologist, 53*, 221–241.

Cohen, J., Stavrakaki, C., Kruzynski, A., & Williams, V. (1995, June). Evolution of depression and anxiety from childhood to adolescence: A five-year follow-up study. Paper presented at the Biennial Meeting of the Society for Research in Child Development, Indianapolis, IN.

Cohen-Sandler, R., Berman, A. L., & King, R. A. (1982). Life stress and symptomatology: determinants of suicidal behavior in children. *Journal of the American Academy of Child Psychiatry, 21*, 178–186.

Cole, D. A. (1988). Hopelessness, social desirability, depression, and parasuicide in two college samples. *Journal of Consulting and Clinical Psychology, 56*, 131–136.

Cole, D. A. (1989a). Psychopathology of adolescent suicide: Hopelessness, coping beliefs, and depression. *Journal of Abnormal Psychology, 98*, 248–255.

Cole, D. A. (1989b). Validation of the reasons for living inventory in general and delinquent adolescent samples. *Journal of Abnormal Child Psychology, 17*, 13–27.

Cole, D. A., Peeke, L. G., Dolezal, S., Murray, N., & Canzoniero, A. (1999). A longitudinal study of negative affect and self-perceived competence in young adolescents. *Journal of Personality and Social Psychology, 77*, 851–862.

Cole, D. A., Peeke, L. A., Martin, J. M., Truglio, R., & Seroczynski, A. D. (1997). A longitudinal look at the relation between depression and anxiety in children and adolescents. *Journal of Consulting and Clinical Psychology, 106*, 586–597.

Cole, D. A., Truglio, R., & Peeke, L. (1997). Relation between symptoms of anxiety and depression in children: A multitrait–multimethod–multigroup assessment. *Journal of Consulting and Clinical Psychology, 65*, 110–119.

Coleman, L. (1987). *Suicide Clusters*. Boston: Faber & Faber.

Compas, B. E., Malcarne, V. L., & Fondacaro, K. M. (1988). Coping with stressful events in older children and young adolescents. *Journal of Consulting and Clinical Psychology, 56*, 405–411.

Coyne, J. C., Kessler, R. C., Tal, M., Turnbull, J., et al. (1987). Living with a depressed person. *Journal of Consulting and Clinical Psychology, 55*, 347–352.

Dadds, M. R., Sanders, M. R., Morrison, M., & Rebgetz, M. (1992). Childhood depression and conduct disorder: II. An analysis of family interaction patterns in the home. *Journal of Abnormal Psychology, 101*, 505–513.

Dempsey, C. L. (1994). Health and social issues of gay, lesbian, and bisexual adolescents. *Families in Society, 75*, 160–167.

Depue, R. A., & Iacono, W. G. (1989). Neurobehavioral aspects of affective disorders. *Annual Review of Psychology, 40*, 457–492.

Deykin, E. Y., Alpert, J. J., & McNamarra, J. J. (1985). A pilot study of the effect of exposure to child abuse or neglect on adolescent suicidal behavior. *American Journal of Psychiatry, 142*, 1299–1303.

Donaldson, D., Spirito, A., & Farnett, E. (2000). The role of perfectionism and depressive cognitions in understanding the hopelessness experienced by adolescent suicide attempters. *Child Psychiatry and Human Development, 31,* 99–111.

Dudley, M., & Waters, B. (1991). Adolescent suicide and suicidal behavior. *Modern Medicine of Australia, 9,* 90–95.

Elkind, D. (1985). Egocentrism redux. *Developmental Review, 5,* 218–226.

Garber, J., & Flynn, C. (in press). Predictors of depressive cognitions in young adolescents. *Cognitive Therapy and Research.*

Garfinkel, B. D. (1989, October). Depression and suicide among adolescents. Paper presented at Treatment of Adolescents with Alcohol, Drug Abuse, and Mental Health Problems Conference, Alcohol, Drug Abuse, and Mental Health Administration, Arlington, VA.

Garfinkel, B. D., Froese, A., & Hood, J. (1982). Suicide attempts in children and adolescents. *American Journal of Psychiatry, 139,* 1257–1261.

Garrison, C. Z., Waller, J. L., Cuffe, S. P., McKeown, R. E., Addy, C. L., & Jackson, K. (1997). Incidence of major depressive disorder and dysthymia in young adolescents. *Journal of the American Academy of Child and Adolescent Psychiatry, 36,* 458–465.

Gibb, B. E., Alloy, L. B., Abramson, L. Y., Rose, D. T., Whitehouse, W. G., Donovan, P., Hogan, M. E., Cronholm, J., & Tierney, S. (in press). History of childhood maltreatment, negative cognitive styles, and episodes of depression in adulthood. *Cognitive Therapy and Research.*

Gibson, P. (1989). Gay male and lesbian youth suicide. In US Department of Health and Human Services (Ed.), *Report of the Secretary's Task Force on Youth Suicide* (Vol. 3, pp. 110–142). Washington, DC: US Department of Health and Human Services.

Girgus, J. S., Nolen-Hoeksema, S., & Seligman, M. E. P. (1989, August). Why do sex differences in depression emerge in adolescence? Paper presented at the annual meeting of the American Psychological Association, New Orleans, LA.

Grant, K., Lyons, A., Landis, D., Cho, M. H., Scudiero, M., Reynolds, L., Murphy, J., & Bryant, H. (1999). Gender, body image, and depressive symptoms among low-income African American adolescents. *Journal of Social Issues, 55,* 299–316.

Groholt, B., Ekeberg, O., Wichstrom, L., & Haldorsen, T. (1998). Suicide among children and younger and older adolescents in Norway: a comparative study. *Journal of the American Academy of Child and Adolescent Psychiatry, 37,* 473–481.

Grossman, D., Milligan, C., & Deyo, R. (1991). Risk factors for suicide attempts among Navajo adolescents. *American Journal of Public Health, 81,* 870–874.

Group for the Advancement of Psychiatry, Committee on Adolescence (1996). Adolescent Suicide (Report No. 140). Washington, DC: American Psychiatric Press.

Hakim-Larson, J., & Essau, C. (1999). Protective factors and depressive disorders. In C. Essau & F. Petermann (Eds.), *Depressive disorders in children and adolescents: Epidemiology, risk factors, and treatment* (pp. 319–337). Northvale, NJ: Jason Aronson.

Haliburn, J. (2000). Reasons for adolescent suicide attempts. *Journal of the American Academy of Child and Adolescent Psychiatry, 39,* 13–14.

Hammond, W. A., & Romney, D. M. (1995). Cognitive factors contributing to adolescent depression. *Journal of Youth and Adolescence, 24,* 667–684.

Hankin, B. L., Abramson, L. Y., Moffitt, T. E., Silva, P. A., McGee, R., & Angell, K. E. (1998). Development of depression from preadolescence to young adulthood: Emerging gender differences in a 10-year longitudinal study. *Journal of Abnormal Psychology, 107,* 128–140.

Harrington, R., Rutter, M., & Fombonne, E. (1996). Developmental pathways in depression: Multiple meanings, antecedents, and end points. *Developmental Psychopathology, 8,* 601–616.

Harry, J. (1989). Sexual identity issues. In Alcohol, Drug Abuse, and Mental Health Administration, Report of the Secretary's Task Force on Youth Suicide, Volume 2. Risk factors for youth suicide (pp. 131–142). DHHS Publication No. ADM 89-1622. Washington, DC: US Government Printing Office.

Hepworth, D. H., Farley, O. W., & Griffiths, J. K. (1988). Clinical work with suicidal adolescents and their families. *Social Casework, 69*, 195–203.

Hoberman, H. M., & Garfinkel, B. D. (1988). Completed suicide in children and adolescents. *Journal of the American Academy of Child and Adolescent Psychiatry, 27*, 689–695.

Hoberman, H. M., & Garfinkel, B. D. (1989). Completed suicide in youth. In C. R. Pfeffer (Ed.), *Suicide Among Youth: Perspectives on Risk and Prevention* (pp. 21–40). Washington, DC: American Psychiatric Press.

Hodgman, C. H., & McAnarney, E. R. (1992). Adolescent depression and suicide: rising problems. *Hospital Practice, 27*, 73–96.

Holden, C. (1986). Youth suicide: new research focuses on a growing social problem. *Science, 233*, 839–841.

Hoyert, D. L., Kochanek, K. D., & Murphy, S. L. (1999). Deaths: Final data for 1997. National Vital Statistics Report, 47(19). Hyattsville, MD: National Center for Health Statistics. DHHS Publication No. (PHS) 99-1120.

Jacobziner, H. (1965). Attempted suicide in adolescence. *Journal of the American Medical Association, 10*, 22–36.

Jobes, D. A., & Berman, A. L. (1984). Response biases and the impact of psychological autopsies on medical examiners' determination of mode of death. Paper presented at the annual meeting of the American Association of Suicidology, Anchorage, AK.

Johnson, S. L., Hayes, A. M., Field, T. M., Schneiderman, N., & McCabe, P. M. (Eds.) (2000). *Stress, coping, and depression.* Mahwah, NJ: Erlbaum.

Kaslow, N. J., Deering, C. G., & Racusin, G. R. (1994). Depressed children and their families. *Clinical Psychology Review, 14*, 39–59.

Kaye, W. H., Weltzin, T. E., & Hsu, L. K. G. (1993). Serotonin and norepinephrine activity in anorexia and bulimia nervosa: Relationship to nutrition, feeding, and mood. In J. J. Mann, D. J. Kupfer, et al. (Eds.), *Biology of depressive disorders, Part B: Subtypes of depression and comorbid disorders. The depressive illness series* (Vol. 4, pp. 127–149). New York: Plenum.

Keller, M. B., Lavori, P. W., Beardslee, W. R., Wunder, J., & Ryan, N. (1991). Depression in children and adolescents: New data on "undertreatment" and a literature review on the efficacy of available treatments. *Journal of Affective Disorders, 21*, 163–171.

Kosky, R., Silburn, S., & Zubrick, S. R. (1990). Are children and adolescents who have suicidal thoughts different from those who attempt suicide? *Journal of Nervous Mental Disorders, 178*, 38–43.

Kostanski, M., & Gullone, E. (1998). Adolescent body image dissatisfaction: Relationships with self-esteem, anxiety, and depression controlling for body mass. *Journal of Child Psychiatry, 39*, 255–262.

Kovacs, M., Akiskal, H., Gatsonis, C., & Parrone, P. (1994). Childhood-onset dysthymic disorder: Clinical features and prospective naturalistic outcome. *Archives of General Psychiatry, 51*, 365–374.

Kovacs, M., Feinberg, T., Crouse-Novak, M., Paulauskas, S., & Finkelstein, R. (1984). Depressive disorders in childhood. I. A longitudinal prospective study of characteristics and recovery. *Archives of General Psychiatry, 41*, 643–649.

Lapsley, D. (1985). Elkind on egocentrism. *Developmental Review, 5*, 227–236.

Leitenberg, H., Yost, L. W., & Carroll-Wilson, M. (1986). Negative cognitive errors in children: Questionnaire development, normative data, and comparisons between children with and without self-reported symptoms of depression, low self-esteem, and evaluation anxiety. *Journal of Consulting and Clinical Psychology, 54*, 528–536.

Levy, J. C., & Deykin, E. Y. (1989). Suicidality, depression, and substance abuse in adolescence. *American Journal of Psychiatry, 146*, 1462–1467.

Lewinsohn, P. M., Rhode, P., & Seeley, J. R. (1994). Psychosocial risk factors for future adolescent suicide attempts. *Journal of Consulting and Clinical Psychology, 62*, 297–305.

Lewinsohn, P. M., Roberts, R. E., Seeley, J. R., Rhode, P., Gotlib, I. H., & Hops, H. (1994). Adolescent psychopathology, II: Psychosocial risk factors for depression. *Journal of Abnormal Psychology, 103*, 302–315.

Lewinsohn, P. M., Zeiss, A. M., & Duncan, E. M. (1989). Probability of relapse after recovery from an episode of depression. *Journal of Abnormal Psychology, 98*, 107–116.

Lobovitz, D. A., & Handel, P. (1985). Childhood depression: Prevalence using DSM-III criteria and validity of parent and child depression scales. *Journal of Pediatric Psychology, 10*, 45–54.

Marcotte, D. (1996). Irrational beliefs and depression in adolescence. *Adolescence, 31*, 935–955.

Marttunen, M. J., Henriksson, M. M., Hillevi, M. A., Heikkinen, M. E., Isometsa, E. T., & Lonnqvist, J. K. (1995). Suicide among female adolescents: characteristics and comparison with males in the age group 13 to 22 years. *Journal of the American Academy of Child and Adolescent Psychiatry, 24*, 1297–1307.

McIntosh, J. L. (1992). Methods of suicide. In R. W. Maris, A. L. Berman, J. T. Maltsberger, & R. I. Yufits (Eds.), *Assessment and Prediction of Suicide* (pp. 381–387). New York: Guilford.

McIntosh, J. L. (2000). Epidemiology of adolescent suicide in the United States. In R. W. Maris, S. S. Carnetto, J. L. McIntosh, & M. M. Silverman (Eds.), *Review of Suicidology, 2000* (pp. 3–33). New York: Guilford.

Morano, C. D., Cisler, R. A., & Lemerond, J. (1993). Risk factors for adolescent suicidal behavior: loss, insufficient familial support, and hopelessness. *Adolescence, 28*, 851–865.

Moskowitz, D. S., Schwartzman, A. E., & Ledingham, J. E. (1985). Stability and change in aggression and withdrawal in middle childhood and early adolescence. *Journal of Abnormal Psychology, 94*, 30–41.

Nakamura, J. W., McLeod, C. R., & McDermott, Jr., J. F. (1994). Temporal variation in adolescent suicide attempts. *Suicide and Life-Threatening Behavior, 24*, 343–349.

National Center for Health Statistics (NCHS) (2000). *Deaths: Final Data for 1997. Vol. 47, No. 19*. Available on-line at http://www.cdc.gov/nchs/releases/99facts/99sheets/97mortal.htm

Nelson, J. A. (1994). Comment on special issue on adolescence. *American Psychologist, 48*, 523–524.

Nilzon, K. R., & Palmerus, K. (1997). The influence of familial factors on anxiety and depression in childhood and early adolescence. *Adolescence, 32*, 935–947.

Nolen-Hoeksema, S. (1987). Sex differences in unipolar depression: Evidence and theory. *Psychology Bulletin, 101*, 259–282.

Nolen-Hoeksema, S. (1990). *Sex differences in depression*. Stanford, CA: Stanford University Press.

Nolen-Hoeksema, S., & Girgus, J. S. (1994). The emergence of gender differences in depression during adolescence. *Psychological Bulletin, 115*, 424–443.

Olsson, G. I., Nordstrom, M. L., Arinell, H., & Von Knorring, A. L. (1999). Adolescent depression: Social network and family climate – A case-control study. *Journal of Child Psychology and Psychiatry, 40*, 227–237.

Ostrander, R., Weinfurt, K. P., & Nay, R. W. (1998). The role of age, family support, and negative cognitions in the prediction of depressive symptoms. *School Psychology Review, 27*, 121–146.

Petersen, A. C., Sarigiani, P. A., & Kennedy, R. E. (1991a). Adolescent depression: Why more girls? *Journal of Youth and Adolescence, 20*, 247–271.

Petersen, A. C., White, N., & Stemmler, M. (1991b, April). Familial risk and protective factors influencing adolescent mental health. Paper presented at the biennial meeting of the Society for Research in Child Development, Seattle, WA.

Pfeffer, C. R. (1989a). Family characteristics and support systems as risk factors for youth suicide. In L. Davidson & M. Linnoila (Eds.), Report of the Secretary's Task Force on Youth Suicide, Vol. 2: Risk factors for youth suicide. DHHS Pub. No. (ADM) 89–1622; pp. 71–87. Washington, DC: US Government Printing Office.

Pfeffer, C. R. (1989b). Life stress and family risk factors for youth fatal and nonfatal suicidal behavior. In C. R. Pfeffer (Ed.), *Suicide Among Youth: Perspectives on Risk and Prevention* (pp. 143–164). Washington, DC: American Psychiatric Press.

Pfeffer, C. R. (1996). Suicidal behavior. In L. Hechtman (Ed.), *Do they grow out of it?* (pp. 121–138). Washington, DC: American Psychiatric Press.

Pfeffer, C. R., Normandin, L., & Tatsuyuki, K. (1994). Suicidal children grow up: suicidal behavior and psychiatric disorders among relatives. *Journal of the American Academy of Child and Adolescent Psychiatry, 33,* 1087–1097.

Poteet, D. J. (1987). Adolescent suicide: a review of 87 cases of completed suicide in Shelby County, TN. *American Journal of Forensic Medicine and Pathology, 8,* 12–17.

Radloff, L. S. (1991). The use of the center for epidemiologic studies depression scale in adolescents and young adults. *Journal of Youth and Adolescence, 20,* 149–168.

Reinherz, H. Z., Giaconia, R. M., Pakiz, B., Silverman, A. B., Frost, A. K., & Lefkowitz, E. S. (1993). Psychosocial risks for major depression in late adolescence: A longitudinal community study. *Journal of the American Academy of Child and Adolescent Psychiatry, 32,* 1155–1163.

Rhode, P., Lewinsohn, P. M., & Seeley, J. R. (1991). Comorbidity of unipolar depression: II. Comorbidity with other mental disorders in adolescents and adults. *Journal of Abnormal Psychology, 100,* 214–222.

Rich, C. L., Young, D., & Fowler, R. C. (1986). San Diego suicide study, I: young vs. old cases. *Archives of General Psychiatry, 43,* 577–582.

Robbins, P. R. (1998). *Adolescent suicide.* Jefferson, NC: McFarland.

Roberts, R. E. (2000). Depression and suicidal behaviors among adolescents: the role of ethnicity. In I. Cuellar & F. A. Paniagua (Eds.), *Handbook of Multicultural Mental Health* (pp. 359–388). San Diego, CA: Academic Press.

Roy, A. (1983). Family history of suicide. *Archives of General Psychiatry, 40,* 971–974.

Rudolf, K. D., Kurlakowsky, K. D., & Conley, C. S. (in press). Developmental and social-contextual origins of depressive control-related beliefs and behavior. *Cognitive Therapy and Research.*

Runeson, B. S., & Rich, C. L. (1992). Diagnostic co-morbidity of mental disorders among young suicides. *International Review of Psychiatry, 4,* 197–203.

Rutter, M. (1981). Stress, coping, and development: Some issues and some questions. *Journal of Child Psychology and Psychiatry, 22,* 323–356.

Rutter, M. (1986). Depressive feelings, cognitions, and disorders: A research postscript. In M. Rutter, C. E. Izard, & P. B. Read (Eds.), *Depression in young people: Developmental and clinical perspectives* (pp. 491–519). New York: Guilford.

Sameroff, A. J., & Chandler, M. J. (1975). Reproductive risk and the continuum of caretaking casualty. In F. D. Harowitz (Ed.), *Review of child development research* (Vol. 4, pp. 187–244). Chicago: University of Chicago Press.

Sarigiani, P. A. (1990). A longitudinal study of relationship adjustment of young adults from divorced and nondivorced families. Doctoral dissertation, Pennsylvania State University, University Park.

Sattler, J. M. (1992). *Assessment of children* (3rd ed.). San Diego: Sattler.

Shaffer, D. (1988). The epidemiology of teen suicide: An examination of risk factors. *Journal of Clinical Psychiatry, 49*(9), 36–41.

Shaffer, D., Gould, M. S., Fisher, P., et al. (1996). Psychiatric diagnosis in child and adolescent suicide. *Archives of General Psychiatry, 53,* 339–348.

Shafii, M., Carrigan, S., Whittinghill, J. R., & Derrick, A. (1985). Psychological autopsy of completed suicide in children and adolescents. *American Journal of Psychiatry, 142,* 1061–1064.

Shafii, M., Steltz-Lenarsky, J., Derrick, A. M., Beckner, C., & Whittinghill, J. R. (1988). Comorbidity in mental disorders in the post-mortem diagnosis of completed suicide in children and adolescents. *Journal of Affective Disorders, 15,* 227–233.

Sheeber, L., Hops, H., Alpert, A., Davis, B., & Andrews, J. (1997). Family support and conflict: prospective relations to adolescent depression. *Journal of Abnormal Child Psychology, 25,* 333–345.

Sheeber, L., Hops, H., Andrews, J., Alpert, T., & Davis, B. (1998). Interactional processes in families with depressed and non-depressed adolescents: reinforcement of depressive behavior. *Behavior Research and Therapy, 36,* 417–427.

Sheeber, L., & Sorensen, E. (1998). Family relationships of depressed adolescents: A multimethod assessment. *Journal of Clinical Child Psychology, 27,* 268–277.

Shiner, R. L., & Marmorstein, N. R. (1998). Family environments of adolescents with lifetime depression: associations with maternal depression history. *Journal of the American Academy of Child and Adolescent Psychiatry, 37,* 1152–1160.

Smith, K., & Crawford, S. (1986). Suicidal behavior among normal high school students. *Suicide and Life-Threatening Behavior, 16,* 313–325.

Spirito, A., Brown, L., Overholser, J., & Fritz, G. (1989). Attempted suicide in adolescence: a review and critique of the literature. *Clinical Psychology Review, 9,* 335–363.

Spitz, R. A., & Wolf, K. M. (1946). Anaclitic depression, an inquiry into the genesis of psychiatric conditions in early childhood, II. *Psychoanalytic Study of the Child, 2,* 313–342.

Sroufe, L. A. (1979). The coherence of individual development: Early care, attachment, and subsequent developmental issues. *American Psychologist, 34,* 834–841.

Sroufe, L. A., & Rutter, M. (1984). The domain of developmental psychopathology. *Child Development, 55,* 17–29.

Stillion, J. M., & McDowell, E. E. (1996). *Suicide across the life span.* Washington DC: Taylor & Francis.

Stoelb, M., & Chiriboga, J. (1998). A process model for assessing adolescent risk for suicide. *Journal of Adolescence, 21,* 359–370.

Stone, M. H. (1990). *The fate of borderline patients.* New York: Guilford.

Tomori, M., & Zalar, B. (2000). Gender differences among adolescent suicide attempters and non–attempters. *International Journal of Adolescent Medicine and Health, 12,* 177–190.

Trautman, P. (1986). Referral failure among adolescent suicide attempters. Manuscript, Columbia University, New York.

Wannan, G., & Fombonne, E. (1998). Gender differences in rates and correlates of suicidal behaviour amongst child psychiatric outpatients. *Journal of Adolescence, 21,* 371–381.

Weissman, A. M., Beck, A. T., & Kovacs, M. (1979). Drug abuse, hopelessness, and suicidal behavior. *International Journal of the Addictions, 14,* 451–464.

Weissman, M. M., & Klerman, G. L. (1977). Sex differences in the epidemiology of depression. *Archives of General Psychiatry, 34,* 98–111.

Weissman, M. M., Leaf, P. J., Holzer, C. E., Myers, J. K., & Teschler, G. L. (1984). The epidemiology of depression: An update on sex differences in rates. *Journal of Affective Disorders, 7,* 179–188.

Wetzel, R. D., Margulies, T., Davis, R., & Karum, E. (1980). Hopelessness, depression, and suicidal intent. *Journal of Clinical Psychiatry, 41*, 159–160.

Wichstrom, L. (2000). Predictors of adolescent suicide attempts: a nationally representative longitudinal study of Norwegian adolescents. *Journal of the American Academy of Child and Adolescent Psychiatry, 39*, 603–610.

World Health Organization (1996). *Multiaxial classification of child and adolescent psychiatric disorders.* New York: Cambridge University Press.

Young, S. E., Mikulich, S. K., Goodwin, M. B., Hardy, J., Martin, C. L., Zoccolillo, M. S., & Crowley, T. J. (1995). Treated delinquent boys' substance use: onset, pattern, relationship to conduct and mood disorders. *Drug and Alcohol Dependence, 37*, 149–162.

CHAPTER TWENTY-SEVEN

Sexually Transmitted Diseases among Adolescents: Risk Factors, Antecedents, and Prevention Strategies

Ralph J. DiClemente and Richard A. Crosby

Introduction

The risk of acquiring a sexually transmitted disease is one of the most significant and immediate risks to the health and well-being of adolescents. From an economic and social standpoint, these infections continue to exact a significant toll on adolescents and ultimately on society. This toll can be measured in terms of projected costs of certain infections, such as chlamydia infections (Washington, Johnson, & Sanders, 1987) and in terms of health outcomes, such as the number of ectopic pregnancies (Chow, Darling, & Greenbert, 1987) and the rate of infertility (Westrom, 1980). The real concern, however, is that in an era when a sexually transmitted infection, human immunodeficiency virus infection (HIV), can result in a fatal illness, the acquired immunodeficiency syndrome (AIDS), we have begun to measure the impact in terms of deaths of adolescents and young adults from AIDS. For this reason, the potential impact of sexually transmitted diseases is all the more significant and prevention of these infections an even higher priority.

Adolescents' Risk for STD Infection: The Scope of the Problem

Sexually transmitted diseases (STDs) recently accounted for 87 percent of all cases among the top ten most frequently reported diseases in the United States. Five of these top ten diseases were STDs (CDC, 1996). Adolescents are particularly likely to contract STDs and the long-term consequences of these infections are potentially severe. Thus, the Institute of Medicine considers STDs epidemic among adolescents and has called for development of a national STD-prevention strategy (Eng & Butler, 1997).

Table 27.1   Morbidity Associated With Selected Sexually Transmitted Diseases, including Effects for Pregnant Women

STD	Associated Morbidity
Gonorrhea and Chlamydia	Inflammation of reproductive tract tissues in both sexes Infertility and ectopic pregnancy Pelvic inflammatory disease Chronic pelvic pain Premature birth
Syphilis	Cardiovascular and nervous system disorders Congenital syphilis
Trichomoniasis	Chronic vaginal discharge Low birth weight Premature birth
Human Papillomavirus	Cancers of the vulva, cervix, anus, and penis
Herpes simplex virus types 1 and 2	Recurrent lesions and associated "flu-like" syndrome Fetal malformation and fetal brain damage Premature birth Spontaneous abortion
Hepatitis B	Chronic liver disease Cirrhosis of the liver Cancer of the liver
HIV	AIDS-related opportunistic illnesses

This chapter describes the STD epidemic among US adolescents, examines antecedents of their STD-risk behavior, and provides a review of innovative strategies designed to reduce incidence of STDs among adolescents. Throughout this chapter the term STD is inclusive of sexually transmitted infection of human immunodeficiency virus (HIV).

STDs and associated morbidity

STDs are a generic term for infections attributable to sexual transmission. They can be caused by a broad spectrum of etiologic agents, including bacteria, viruses, and parasites. The sequelae of STDs are particularly devastating to the female reproductive tract, often resulting in infertility or ectopic pregnancy. Although many common STDs can be cured with medication, viral STDs (e.g., human papillomavirus and genital herpes) remain intransigent to treatment and serve as a significant source of morbidity for adolescents as they enter adulthood. While a detailed review of each etiologic agent and its associated STD is beyond the scope of this chapter, table 27.1 provides more information about

Table 27.2   Rates* of Selected STDs among Adolescents Contrasted With Rates among the US Population, Based on Data from 1998

STD	Adolescents		US (all ages)
	(10–14 years)	*(15–19 years)*	
Chlamydia			
Male	7.9	308.4	83.1
Female	142.5	2359.4	382.2
Gonorrhea			
Male	8.5	354.6	133.7
Female	58.0	779.7	131.5
Syphilis			
Male	.1	1.9	3.0
Female	.4	4.5	2.3

* Per 100,000 population.

specific forms of morbidity associated with STDs. Collectively, the STDs displayed in the table accounted for over $16 billion of medical expenditures in 1994 (Eng & Butler, 1997).

STDs disproportionately affect adolescents

Adolescents are disproportionately affected by a wide range of STDs. In the United States, more than 15 million new cases of STDs occur annually (American Social Health Association, 1998). Each year, about one-quarter of all STDs occur among adolescents (Eng & Butler, 1997). By age 24, at least one in three sexually active young adults is estimated to have contracted an STD (Alan Guttmacher Institute, 1993). Females are much more likely than males to be diagnosed with STDs. Table 27.2 contrasts rates for specific STDs by gender between adolescents and the US population. This comparison shows that adolescents, particularly females, bear most of the STD burden. These findings are alarming because the figures do not reflect the fact that fewer adolescents than adults are sexually experienced. When sexually inexperienced adolescents are removed from the denominator, the gap between adolescents and adults becomes even greater (Berman & Hein, 1999).

Another adolescent subgroup that has experienced excess burden associated with STDs is minority adolescents. Minority adolescents, particularly African Americans, bear a disproportionate STD burden. For example, a national survey of 14–21-year-olds indicated that African Americans were more than 3.5 times as likely to report a history of STD than other adolescents, and this difference was not attributable to sexual-risk behavior or sociodemographic factors (Ellen, Aral, & Madger, 1998). Table 27.3 summarizes recent findings regarding selected STDs among predominantly minority populations of adolescents.

Table 27.3   Summary of Findings from Recent Studies Assessing the Laboratory Diagnosed Prevalence of Selected STDs among Predominantly Minority Adolescents

Study	Sample	STD	% positive
Bunnell et al., 1999	650 14–19 year old females[a], 93% were African American	chlamydia	27
		genital herpes	14
		gonorrhea	6
		trichomoniasis	3
		hepatitis B	2
		total with an STD	40
Burstein et al., 1998a	214 middle students[a] 12–17 years old, 98% were African American	males: chlamydia	2
		females: chlamydia	16
		males: gonorrhea	2
		females: gonorrhea	11
Burstein et al., 1998b	1174 12–19 year old females[a], 98% were African American	chlamydia	24
Pack et al., 2000	284 14–18 year old incarcerated males[a], 100% African American	chlamydia	14
		gonorrhea	7
Jamison et al., 1995	167 12–18 year old African American females[c]	gonorrhea	17
		chlamydia	16
		HPV[b]	17
		trichomoniasis	13
Jamison et al., 1995	287 12–18 year-old Hispanic females[c]	gonorrhea	4
		chlamydia	10
		HPV[b]	14
		trichomoniasis	3
Oh et al., 1997	315 15–18 year old females, 75% were African American	chlamydia	15
Fleming et al., 1997	2396 12–19 year olds	HSV-2[d]: African Americans	8.7
		HSV-2[d]: Hispanic	5.4
		HSV-2[d]: Caucasian	4.5

[a] Reporting current sexual activity.
[b] Human Papillomavirus.
[c] 95% of the sample reported sexual activity.
[d] Herpes Simplex Virus 2.

Adolescents and HIV. Recent evidence suggests that 50 percent of new HIV infections occur among people younger than 25 years of age and 25 percent of new HIV infections occur among persons younger than 22 years of age (Office of National AIDS Policy, 1996). Surveillance data suggests that about 17 percent of all reported AIDS cases resulted from HIV acquisition during the second decade of life, 10–19 years of age (CDC, 1999).

Table 27.4 Prevalence of HIV Infection per 1000 Adolescents for Selected Surveys, by Race/Ethnicity

Study	Sample or Site	Race/Ethnicity		
		Black	Latino	White
Burke et al., 1990	Military applicants	1.0	0.29	0.17
Kelley et al., 1990	Active-duty military[a]	5.1	4.0	1.25
St. Louis et al., 1991	Job Corps entrants	5.3	2.6	1.2
St. Louis et al., 1990	General hospital	8.3	4.9	2.7
Stricof et al., 1991	Homeless shelter	46	68	60
D'Angelo et al., 1991	Ambulatory clinics[b]	3.7	–	–
Ilegbodu et al., 1993	HIV test sites	12.9	5.2	6.2
Young et al., 1992	STD clinic	4.5	–	1.3
Lemp et al., 1994	Gay/bisexual males[c]	212	95	81
Valleroy et al., 1998	Job Corps entrants	3.8	1.2	0.7

Notes: All findings have been converted and are presented as rate of HIV-seropositive adolescents per 1000 to permit comparability with other surveys.

[a] Sample of active-duty military personnel is not exclusively comprised of adolescents.

[b] This survey does not report ethnic comparisons. More than 88% of the sample was African–American, while 12% was defined as "Other" ethnic groups. Attributable to their small proportion in the sample, comparisons with "Other" ethnic groups would not be informative.

[c] Adolescents ranged in age from 17–22.

Again, this finding is particularly alarming because adolescents, as a population, are less likely to be sexually active than their adult counterparts; yet the majority of HIV transmission among adolescents is caused by sexual contact as opposed to other methods of acquisition, e.g., injection drug use with shared needles and syringes (Rosenberg & Biggar, 1998; CDC, 1999). Table 27.4 summarizes findings from studies assessing the prevalence of HIV infection among adolescents and provides a comparison of rates by race/ethnicity.

As with other STDs, racial disparities also apply to HIV infection rates. This is observed with respect to AIDS cases among young adults; many of whom were probably infected with HIV during adolescence. Table 27.5 provides a side-by-side comparison of the percentage of AIDS cases diagnosed among young adults in 1997, by race/ethnicity, compared to the percentage of the population each race/ethnicity represented in 1997.

Increasing numbers of adolescent females are being infected with HIV. Recent surveillance data indicated that AIDS incidence rates in US cities have not abated among adolescents and young adults, with young African American females being disproportionately diagnosed with AIDS as compared to their male peers (Denning & Flemming, 1998). Recent surveillance data also indicates that 5.6 percent of the women diagnosed with AIDS were young adults (20–24 years of age), as opposed to the comparable figure of 2.5 percent among men (CDC, 1999).

Table 27.5   AIDS Cases Diagnosed among African American, Caucasian, and Hispanic Males and Females, 20 to 29 Years of Age, in 1997

Race/ethnicity	Number of diagnosed cases	% of cases	% of pop. in 1997[a]
African American	3803	44.6	14.3
Caucasian	2575	30.2	70.8
Hispanic	2021	23.7	14.9

[a] Represents percent of 34,510,593 African American, Caucasian, and Hispanic US residents in 1997, ages 20–29.

Table 27.6   Common Sexual Behaviors that Increase Adolescents' Risk for STD Infection

Behavior	Risk
Early sexual debut	If sexual activity continues, risk of STD increases because odds of encountering an infected sex partner increase. Among females, cervical ectopy is more pronounced at younger ages.
Multiple sex partners	Each new sex partner represents a new risk of STD.
A sex partner with multiple sex partners	Sex partners with a history of multiple sex partners are especially likely to transmit viral STDs such as HPV and HSV-2.
Concurrent sex partners	Overlapping sexual relationships are conducive to the spread of STDs, especially those with short incubation periods such as gonorrhea and chlamydia.
Sex unprotected by a latex condom	Correct and consistent use of latex condoms protect from most, but not all, STDs.
Frequency of sex	Risk of contracting an STD from an infected sex partner increases with each of act of sex, particularly if frequency and duration of sex compromises the integrity of genital tissue.

Antecedents of Adolescents' STD-Risk Behavior

Risk factors for STD infection

The behaviors that place adolescents at risk of STD infection, including HIV, are limited in number. Table 27.6 gives a list of these behaviors. Lack of condom use is one of the more important behaviors. Though the data is not definitive, correct and consistent condom use reduces the risk of acquiring most STDs (Stone, Timyan, & Thomas, 1999; Wald et al., 2001). Several studies have also found that number of lifetime sex partners is an important determinant of STD risk (Aral & Holmes, 1999).

Table 27.7 US High School Students Reporting Selected Sexual-Risk Behaviors, by Gender and Race/Ethnicity (%)

Race/Ethnicity	Sexually experienced	At least 4 sex partners	Condom used during last sex
African American			
male	80.3	52.8	68.4
female	65.6	25.4	58.9
Hispanic			
male	57.7	20.1	54.7
female	45.7	10.2	40.0
Caucasian			
male	43.3	11.3	62.2
female	44.0	12.1	49.2

Note: Based on a sample of 16,262 high school students surveyed in 1997 as part of the CDC YRBS.

Although the risk behaviors for STD infection have been articulated, understanding the antecedents of these behaviors has been a complex and formidable challenge confronting prevention scientists. The task is particularly difficult because empirical investigation of such a personal, and often nonpublic and nondisclosed behavior, is logistically complicated. This section of the chapter examines the antecedents of adolescents' sexual-risk behavior based on recently published, state-of-the-art empirical studies.

The context of adolescent sexual-risk behavior

Adolescents in the United States face multiple challenges; particularly challenges related to decision-making within the context of sexual behavior. Several indicators of adolescents' sexual-risk behavior have been obtained from national surveys. For example, about one-half of all school-age teens report ever having sexual intercourse and the majority of these teens remain sexually active, with one-fifth of high school seniors having sex with at least four different partners in their lifetime (CDC, 1998a). Like adults, adolescents may engage in shared sexual activities other than intercourse. A recent study of more than 2,000 urban high school students indicated that about one-half of the sample identified as virgins. Of these adolescents, 9 percent reported engaging in fellatio and 10 percent reported engaging in cunnilingus in the past year. Anal intercourse was less frequent (1 percent) for this same time period (Schuster, Bell, & Kanouse, 1996).

Despite recent trends indicating fewer adolescent males reporting sexual experience and fewer reporting four or more lifetime sex partners (CDC, 1998b), at least four of every ten sexually active adolescents reported not using a condom during last intercourse (CDC, 1998a). During the 1990s, adolescents' condom use at last intercourse was significantly lower for females than males (CDC, 1998b). Table 27.7 shows the most recent survey results from CDC, categorized by gender and race/ethnicity. Other national surveys have indicated that less than one-half of 15–19-year-old females surveyed reported current use of condoms (Piccinino & Mosher, 1998), and that about one-third of 15–19-year-old males reported not using a condom during last intercourse (Sonenstein et al., 1998). Although sizable portions of adolescents are using condoms, it is important to reiterate that the value of condoms for the prevention of some common STDs (e.g. trichomoniasis, genital herpes, and human papillomavirus) has not been definitively established (Stone, Timyan, & Thomas, 1999). Further, few studies have assessed whether or not adolescents use condoms correctly, with recent studies indicating that adolescents are unlikely to do so (Crosby & Yarber, 2001; Crosby et al., 2001a).

Adolescents' STD-Risk Behaviors Cluster With Other Health Risk Behaviors

Adolescents' STD-risk behaviors tend to cluster with other risk behavior e.g., violence, substance abuse (including tobacco and alcohol), and delinquency (Biglan et al., 1990; Boyer, 1990; Crosby, Yarber, & Kanu, 1998; Dryfoos, 1991; Jessor, Donovan, & Costa, 1991; Lowry et al., 1994). For example, a recent study of nearly 4,000 adolescents attending high schools found that use of alcohol, tobacco, or marijuana, or report of violent experiences during dates were strong predictors of reporting a greater number of lifetime sex partners among African American females. African American males were more likely to report a higher number of lifetime sex partners if they reported use of alcohol (including binge drinking), tobacco, or marijuana, or reported fighting, weapon carrying, and dating violence. Predictors of greater number of lifetime sex partners were identical for Caucasian males, with the exception of binge drinking (Valois et al., 1999).

Because adolescents' risk behaviors tend to cluster, high-risk groups of adolescents can often be easily identified. Incarcerated adolescents and those residing in drug treatment facilities are especially likely to report sexual-risk behaviors (DiClemente et al., 1991; Morris et al., 1995; Oh et al., 1994; Pack et al., 2000; St. Lawrence, Crosby, & O'Bannon, 1999; Schafer et al., 1993). Runaway youth as well as youth with emotional disorders are also likely to be at higher risk of STD infection relative to the general adolescent population (Brown et al., 1997, 1999a; DiClemente et al., 1989; Rotheram-Borus et al., 1991). Recent evidence suggests that psychologically distressed youth may be at greater risk of STD infection (DiClemente et al., 2001c).

Correlations between substance abuse (including alcohol) and adolescents' STD-risk behavior have been reported in multiple studies (e.g., Crosby, Yarber, & Kanu, 1998; Duncan, Stryker, & Duncan, 1999; Lowry et al., 1994; Santelli et al., 1998). For example, Santelli and colleagues (1998) reported data from a national survey of high school students that indicated a positive linear relationship between number of alcohol-related behaviors and number of sex partners among both females and males. Yet, whether or not substance use predisposes adolescents to risky sexual behavior has yielded mixed results (e.g., Fortenberry, 1998; Strunin, 1999). Quite possibly, adolescent risk behaviors are correlated because they share a common set of antecedents (DiClemente, Hansen, & Ponton, 1996).

Ample evidence suggests the existence of a common etiology for adolescent risk behaviors (DiClemente, Hansen, & Ponton, 1996). In fact, this hypothesis has been empirically supported in a broad range of studies investigating adolescent behavior. For example, associations have been reported between adolescents receiving less parental monitoring and their participation in antisocial activities (Patterson & Stouthamer-Loeber, 1984), high-risk sexual behaviors (Biglan et al., 1990; Small & Luster, 1994), earlier initiation of sexual activity (Romer et al., 1999), and substance use (Chilcoat & Anthony, 1996; Mulhall, Stone, & Stone, 1996; Smith et al., 1995; Steinberg, Fletcher, & Darling, 1994). Thus, lack of parental monitoring appears to be a common etiologic factor associated with multiple risk behaviors among adolescents, including STD-risk behavior (DiClemente et al., 2001a). Other common etiologies may be emotional disorders (Blum, Kelly, & Ireland, 2001; Brown et al., 1997) and lack of connectedness to family and school (Resnick et al., 1997). Below we review the evidence for associations between four different types of influences and adolescents' STD-risk behavior.

Specific antecedents of adolescents' STD-risk behavior

Family influences. STD-risk behavior of adolescents has been associated with family structure. For example, Crosby et al. (2001b) found that African American adolescent females were more likely to report sex with casual partners if they lived with a relative as opposed to one or both parents. Communities with high rates of divorce typically have higher rates of STDs among adolescents (Brewster, Billy, & Grady, 1993). The underpinnings of these findings may rest on two key factors: parental communication and parental monitoring.

Lack of communication between adolescents and at least one parent (or parent figure) about sex-related subjects (e.g., pregnancy, STDs, condom use) is an important antecedent of adolescents' STD-risk behaviors. Adolescents who engage in conversations about sex-related topics with their mothers are (1) less likely to report being sexually experienced (DiIorio, Kelly, & Hockenberry-Eaton, 1999; Jaccard, Dittus, & Gordon, 1996; Leland & Barth, 1993); (2) likely to report engaging in penile-vaginal sex less frequently (Holtzman & Rubinson, 1995; Jaccard, Dittus, & Gordon, 1996; Dutra, Miller, & Forehand, 1999); (3) more likely to report using condoms and other contraceptives (Jaccard, Dittus, & Gordon, 1996; DiClemente et al., 2001b; Dutra, Miller, & Forehand, 1999; Miller et al., 1998; Leland & Barth, 1993); and (4) likely to report fewer lifetime sex partners (Holtzman & Rubinson, 1995; Dutra, Miller, & Forehand, 1999). Open communication with their mothers about general topics has also been associated with adolescents' report of engaging in sex less frequently than those not having open conversations. Adolescents' perceived self-efficacy to use condoms has been positively associated with communication between sex partners (Lawrence, Levy, & Rubinson, 1990) and the actual implementation of these practices (Basen-Engquist & Parcel, 1992; Cobb, 1997; Rosenthal, Moore, & Flynn, 1991).

Empirical evidence has documented associations between adolescents receiving less parental monitoring and their participation in high-risk sexual behaviors (Biglan et al., 1990; Romer et al., 1999; Small & Luster, 1994). Thus, adolescents without benefit of parental monitoring may be more likely to acquire an STD. For example, DiClemente and colleagues (2001c) found that African American adolescent females reporting low parental monitoring were significantly more likely to report greater prevalence of STD/HIV-associated risk behaviors and were 1.7 times more likely to have "any" biologically-confirmed STD and 1.8 times more likely to test positive for chlamydia than their counterparts reporting higher levels of parental monitoring.

Adolescents are less likely to report early age of sexual debut if they have at least one parent who has expressed disapproval of early debut (Jaccard, Dittus, & Gordon, 1996; Miller, Forehand, & Kotchick, 1999). Data from the National Longitudinal Study of Adolescent Health indicated that adolescent females reporting their mothers did not disapprove of the respondent having sex were more likely to report infection with an STD in the subsequent year. Data from the same study indicated that adolescent females were less likely to report a subsequent STD if they perceived that even one adult cared about them (Crosby, Leichliter, & Brackbill, 2000).

Social influences. As adolescents pull away from the influence of their families, peer influences on sexual behavior become more prominent (Forehand & Weirson, 1993). Perceptions about the behaviors of their peers may be one of the most powerful influences on adolescents' sexual-risk behavior. In regard to sexual behavior, group norms frequently dictate sexual scripts; conformity to these prescribed roles is rewarded with peer approval (Fisher, Misovich, & Fisher, 1992). For example, a study of low-income African American adolescents found that condom use was four times more likely among those who perceived peer norms as supportive of condom use (DiClemente et al., 1996). Similar findings have been reported for high-risk incarcerated adolescents (DiClemente et al., 1991). Similarly, a study of low-income African American adolescent females found an inverse relationship between female adolescents' frequency of unprotected sex and the number of female peers believed to be using condoms (Crosby et al., 2000).

General perceptions of social support, as opposed to specific perceptions of peer norms regarding sexual behavior, have also been associated with adolescents' sexual-risk behavior. For example, one study showed that African American adolescents perceiving low social support were significantly more likely to engage in sex with a casual partner or a non-monogamous partner, report being coerced into unwanted sexual activity, and report recent treatment for an STD (St. Lawrence et al., 1994).

Naturally, one of the most important social influences on sexual behavior is exerted by the sex partner. This form of influence may be particularly strong when one partner has more power and control in the relationship than the other. For example, one study found that female adolescents having sex with males at least three years older were less likely to report condom use during last sex or during the past six months than their counterparts dating males closer to their own age (Miller, Clark, & Moore, 1997). Another recent study found similar associations among adolescents females reporting that their partners were two or more years older than themselves (DiClemente et al., 2002). Thus, older male partners may be resistant to protective behaviors, leaving less assertive females vulnerable to unprotected sex.

Gender-role differences contribute to unequal power in adolescent relationships. Male control of sexual decision-making has been studied as an antecedent of risky sexual behaviors for adolescent females. The finding that females have continually reported lower rates of condom use than males (CDC, 1998b) suggests that negotiating condom use may be quite difficult for adolescent females. Indeed, perceived male-partner barriers to refusing sex or negotiating condom use are strong correlates of STD-risk behavior for adolescent females (Sionean et al., 2002). A recent study reported that condom use among adolescent females was correlated with partner insistence that a condom be used but not with females' perceived control over STD-acquisition (Rosenthal et al., 1999). Consistent with this proposition, other studies have shown that more assertive women are more likely to practice safer sex (see Morokoff et al., 1997; Wingood & DiClemente, 1996 for extensive reviews). A recent study of young adult females found that high assertive communication skills, high self-control over condom use, and perceived high control over their partner's use of condoms each, independently, predicted consistent condom use by females (Wingood & DiClemente, 1998b).

Another important aspect of social influence specific to an adolescent's sex partner is length of the sexual relationship. As relationships mature, adolescents tend to use condoms less frequently (Civic, 1999; Crosby et al., 2000; Ku, Sonenstein, & Pleck, 1994). This phenomenon may occur as increased familiarity with a sex partner tends to create an illusion or sense of safety from STDs (Clark et al., 1996).

Cognitive influences. One of the most important cognitive influences on adolescents' STD-protective behavior is their perception of threat posed by STDs. Perceived threat is a psychological construct composed of perceived susceptibility and perceived severity. Thus, perceived threat of STD among adolescents occurs when they believe they can be infected with an STD and that the consequences of that infection are sufficiently severe. Greater perceived threat of HIV has been associated with adolescents' reporting a lower number of lifetime sex partners (Catania et al., 1989). Recent stabilization of previously escalating trends in adolescent risk behavior has been attributed to increased perceived threat of HIV infection (Ku et al., 1998; Piccinino & Mosher, 1998); however, empirical support for this attribution is lacking.

Although AIDS is typically perceived by adolescents as a severe disease, a great deal of variability exists regarding adolescents' perception of personal susceptibility. For example, several studies have indicated that adolescents at high risk of HIV infection do not perceive themselves as being vulnerable to HIV infection (Jemmott, Jemmott, & Fong, 1998; St. Lawrence et al., 1995, 1999a, 1999b). Adolescents are also unlikely to perceive personal susceptibility to other STDs. For example, a recent national survey indicated that more than two-thirds of sexually experienced 15–17-year-olds reported they were "not at much risk" for STDs or had "no risk for STDs" (Kaiser Foundation, 1999). However, the experience of having an STD appears to predict subsequent condom use among some adolescents (Crosby et al., 2000; Roye, 1998), indicating that perceived threat of STD may be more salient to those with a history of STD infection.

The absence or presence of perceived threat of STD infection does not necessarily translate to more or less risk behavior among adolescents. Adolescents' condom use, for example, may be motivated by perceived threat of pregnancy rather than disease (Langer, Zimmerman, & Katz, 1994; Whaley, 1999). Once an adolescent female begins using hormonal contraception, she and her partner are less likely to use barrier methods, including condoms (Roye, 1998).

A host of other factors may mediate the relationship between perceived threat and protective behaviors. The use of female-controlled contraceptive methods increases and the use of male condoms declines with the length of time the adolescent has been sexually active (Ku, Sonenstein, & Pleck, 1994). Adolescents are more likely to use condoms in a new relationship (Howard et al., 1999; Ku, Sonenenstein, & Pleck, 1992) or in a casual relationship (Biglan et al., 1990), with each of these behaviors possibly being mediated by perceived threat. Adolescents' motives for engaging in sex may mediate relationships between perceived threat of disease and condom use (Cooper, Shapiro, & Powers, 1998). For example, if the primary motive for having sex is gaining sexual pleasure, condoms may not be used because they are perceived as antithetical to this goal (Crosby et al., 2000; Jemmott et al., 1992; Norris & Ford, 1994).

Several cognitive factors appear to influence adolescents' age of sexual debut, with those debuting earlier in life being likely to report a greater number of lifetime sex partners (Durbin et al., 1993), more likely to report concurrent sex partners (Norris & Ford, 1999), and more likely to be diagnosed with repeat STD infections (Wagstaff, DeLamater, & Havens, 1999). Early debut for adolescent females has been related to sexual abuse (Nagy, DiClemente, & Adcock, 1995; Stock et al., 1997). One study found that 24 percent of females who debuted at age 13 or younger reported the experience as nonvoluntary, compared to 10 percent of those who debuted from ages 19 and 24 (Abma, Driscoll, & Moore, 1998).

Adolescent females report a greater number of lifetime sex partners if they also report a history of sexual abuse by an adult or someone older than themselves (Luster & Small, 1997). Similarly, Brown and colleagues (1997) studied a sample of emotionally disturbed adolescents and found those with a history of sexual abuse were the least likely to possess condom-use and sexual communication skills. Among young adult women (18 to 19 years of age), survivors of rape were more likely than their peers to report a greater frequency of recent sex and unprotected sex, despite being less likely than their peers to report enjoying sex (Wingood & DiClemente, 1998c).

Adolescents' ability to communicate their sexual desires and intentions to their sex partners is an important antecedent of their sexual-risk behavior. For example, Maxwell, Bastiani, and Warda (1999) found that level of sexual communication was the only variable that discriminated between condom users and non-users, of each gender, in a sample of adolescents attending STD clinics. Catania and colleagues (1989) reported that both general communication and health-protective communication among adolescents were inversely related to the reported number of sex partners; condom-specific communication was positively associated with reporting use of condoms.

Correlates of adolescents' ability to engage in sexual communication include assertive self-efficacy (DiClemente et al., 1996). Other forms of self-efficacy (e.g., condom acquisition, condom application, impulse control) are particularly important cognitive determinants of adolescents' sexual-risk behavior. Adolescents with greater self-efficacy for condom use are more likely to report they intend to use condoms (Basen-Engquist & Parcel, 1992; Jemmott, Jemmott, & Hacker, 1992; Pendergrast, DuRant, & Gaillard, 1992).

Environmental influences. Despite recent trends toward safer sexual behaviors, African American males have remained consistently likely to debut at an early age (Upchurch et al., 1998; Warren et al., 1998). For example, neighborhoods characterized by poor supervision of adolescents' behavior, inadequate community resources for adolescents, and high levels of adolescent behavior that depart from a conventional lifestyle (e.g., school dropout) have been linked to early debut (Small & Luster, 1994). Low educational achievement and pessimistic expectations about future academic success have been linked to early debut and other STD-risk factors (Harvey & Spigner, 1995; Small & Luster, 1994). Thus, apparent influences of race/ethnicity are most likely confounded by a host of environmental factors that impact STD-risk behavior (Fullilove, 1998), such as poverty and urban decay (Cohen et al., 2000).

One of the most consistent correlates of STD infection is poverty (Aral & Wasserheit, 1995). Among some impoverished adolescent populations, sex may be bartered for money and/or drugs (Lown et al., 1995; Soundheimer, 1992), leading to unprotected sex with multiple partners. Adolescents living in stressful environments are generally more likely to take sexual risks. Homeless adolescents, for example, are more likely than their same-age peers to debut early, report multiple sex partners who have a high risk of STD infection, and to report sexual abuse (Ennett et al., 1999; Eng & Butler, 1997).

Another important antecedent of adolescents' STD-risk behavior is the proximity of the sex partner to "core-group" transmitters of STDs. The concept of the core group has been used to symbolize sexual networks of individuals who have high rates of STDs. Thus, the odds of selecting a sex partner who is a core-group member constitute part of the risk environment for adolescents. Depending on the STD in question and the frequency of partner change occurring between adolescents, core groups may be quite large. For example, a recent study of syphilis transmission among adolescents and adults found sexual networks of up to 33 connected persons in a sample of less than 500 (Rothenberg et al., 2000). As the centrality (closeness of a person to the core group) of an adolescent's chosen sex partner increases, the odds of being infected by that partner also increase. Thus, adolescents living in STD epicenters are more likely to be infected with an STD due simply to the inflated odds of selecting a sex partner who is connected to a core group (Lauman & Youm, 1999). Unprotected sex with concurrent partners magnifies risk for STD infection by increasing the likelihood of being connected (directly or indirectly) to a member of a core network (Rothenberg et al., 1998; Rosenberg et al., 1999).

Environments with high STD prevalence may be a primary reason why African Americans disproportionately contract STDs. Data from a nationally representative sample of adults has shown that African Americans are more likely than Caucasians to select a high-risk sex partner, i.e., one who has an inflated risk of STD infection due to unprotected sex with multiple partners (Lauman & Youm, 1999). Thus, the higher incidence of STDs among African American adolescents may be attributable to sexual mixing patterns rather than differences in sexual behavior (Aral, 1999). Yet, low socioeconomic status is a consistent correlate of STD infection and interacts with race/ethnicity to produce higher risk of STD infection for African American, Hispanic, and other adolescent minority groups (Aral & Wasserheit, 1995). Adolescents, particularly females, often have sex with older partners, e.g., persons in their twenties. Thus, the differential prevalence of STDs in older-age racial/ethnic sexual networks may influence a similar disparity in STDs among adolescent sex partners (Ford & Norris, 1997).

Adolescents from low-income families are also likely to experience financial barriers to receiving health care. For example, the Institute of Medicine recently estimated that one-quarter of adolescents and young adults at high risk of STD infection do not have health insurance. Thus, adolescents who do not seek STD care remain likely to infect their sex partners, creating higher risk of STD infection within the sexual network.

Access to health care for suspected STD infection may also be problematic for adolescents, regardless of income. For example, communities may or may not offer readily available and confidential STD services to adolescents; transportation may also be an issue. Further, even if confidential STD care is accessible, adolescents may not perceive this to be true, perhaps fearing their sexual activity and possible diagnosis will be disclosed to parents and others (Berman & Hein, 1999). In a national survey, more than one-third of 10th-graders mistakenly believed that health departments would inform parents of an STD diagnosis and that parental consent was required for STD treatment (American Social Health Association, 1998). The social stigma of STDs and low self-efficacy for responding to an STD have also been suggested as being potential barriers to seeking care among adolescents (Fortenberry et al., 1997). Conversely, perceived social support may be an important factor in overcoming barriers to seeking STD care (Fortenberry et al., 1999).

A contextual approach

Given the diverse range of available literature on antecedents precipitating adolescents' STD-risk behavior, it is important to consider these in an integrated framework. A contextual approach, including all four influences (family, social, cognitive, and environmental) offers insights into the competing and reciprocal relationships between these influences and how they may affect sexual-risk behavior and STD acquisition. These influences reciprocally shape one another and collectively impact the balance of risk for STD infection through protective influences and risk-taking influences.

Antecedents unique to females. Both biological and psychosocial factors explain higher STD incidence among females as opposed to males. For example, the cervix of an adolescent female is a particularly vulnerable site of STD infection. This vulnerability results from cervical ectopy, a condition that is entirely normal. Similar vulnerable tissues for adolescent males do not exist. Several studies have provided evidence that use of oral contraceptives may exacerbate cervical ectopy in adolescents, leading to greater susceptibility to STDs such as chlamydia (Critchlow et al., 1995; Washington et al., 1985) and HIV (Plourde & Plummer, 1994; Wang, Reilly, & Kreiss, 1999).

Also, among adolescents engaging in penile–vaginal sex, a "biological sexism" exists in that STDs, including HIV, are typically most efficiently transmitted from male to female rather than from female to male (Bolan, Ehrhardt, & Wasserheit, 1999; Padian, Shiboski, & Jewell, 1991). For STDs that cause a discharge e.g., gonorrhea, the uninfected female partner experiences prolonged contact with the infectious discharge as this discharge (along with semen) remains in the vagina after intercourse. Alternatively, an uninfected male partner comes into contact with infectious discharge from a female only during the act of intercourse.

Behaviors unique to females also place adolescent females at higher risk of STD i_ tion than their male counterparts. Periodic douching by females is a relatively common practice, especially among African Americans (Aral, Mosher, & Cates, 1992). This practice has been related to adverse outcomes typically associated with STDs, e.g., pelvic inflammatory disease (PID) (Wolner-Hanssen et al., 1990). Sex during menstruation has been associated with increased risk of STD infection for females (Tanfer & Aral, 1996), with added risk for the male partner being minimal except with regard to HIV.

Although early diagnosis of treatable STDs is an important method of preventing subsequent morbidity, the anatomy of the female genitalia precludes casual observation of common symptoms (e.g., discharge and ulcerations). Because the male genitalia are entirely exposed, adolescent males are far more likely than their female counterparts to observe signs of STD infection. Additionally, among adolescent females who seek medical attention for an STD, the diagnosis is more difficult and less reliable than among males (Bolan, Ehrhardt, & Wasserheit, 1999).

Important psychosocial antecedents of STD risk are also unique to females. A primary limitation is that females do not have direct control over the use of a condom. Successful negotiation of condom use may be particularly problematic for adolescent females, due largely to their inexperience in sexual negotiations. This disadvantage is especially likely when the female adolescent has an older sex partner (Darroch, Landry, & Oslack, 1997; DiClemente et al., 2002; Rotheram-Borus, Jemmott, & Jemmott, 1995).

The remaining section describes efficacious approaches that have been applied to reducing male and female adolescents' incidence of STD by intervening upon the antecedents previously described; reducing factors that favor engaging in STD-risk behavior, and increasing factors that are protective from engaging in these behaviors. While there is an emerging body of intervention studies, many interventions for adolescents do not meet standards of scientific rigor (Oakley et al., 1995). Accordingly, we have included only the most rigorous studies in this section.

Preventing STD Among Adolescents: Behavioral Interventions for Adolescents at Risk for STDs

General principles of prevention

With the possible exception of hepatitis B (a vaccine-preventable STD), behavioral interventions are the most promising strategy for preventing STDs among adolescents. STD behavioral interventions have progressed from largely knowledge-based approaches to sexual communication skills-based approaches, with recent studies investigating the value of life-skills approaches, e.g., youth development programs. The primary goal of behavioral programs is to impact the antecedents associated with sexual-risk behaviors, and therefore, reduce the likelihood of exposure to STDs.

STD behavioral intervention programs for adolescents are most effective when they employ: (1) a variety of learning techniques and emphasize interactive learning; (2) a theoretical framework; (3) peer facilitators; (4) strategies to foster peer norms supportive of safer-sex behaviors; (5) gender-specific methodologies; (6) culturally specific method-ologies; and, (7) developmentally appropriate skill-based instruction (Janz et al., 1996; Kirby, 2000; Kirby & DiClemente, 1994; Wingood & DiClemente, 1996).

A diverse range of behavioral interventions designed to lower adolescents' STD inci-dence has been published. The majority of these employ strategies as outlined above. In-depth discussion of these strategies is beyond the scope of the present chapter; however, excellent reviews have been provided by Jemmott and Jemmott (2000) and Eng and Butler (1997), as well as Wingood and DiClemente (1996).

The following section describes specific examples of effective programs. Behavioral interventions have been successfully delivered to adolescents through three different venues: clinics, communities, and schools. After presenting examples pertaining to each venue, key issues relevant to intervening with adolescent populations will be discussed. A final segment will address interventions for adolescents at exceptionally high risk of STD infection, i.e., incarcerated adolescents, homeless and runaway adolescents, and HIV-positive adolescents.

Effective clinic-based STD-prevention programs

Clinic-based programs represent an ideal venue for prevention of initial STD infections and reinfection with STDs. Clinic settings offer the advantage of biomedical technology (e.g., screening for STDs) and also capture adolescents likely to be at high risk for STDs. Intervening with adolescents newly diagnosed with an STD is particularly important because a history of STD infection tends to be the most powerful predictor of adoles-cents' reinfection with an STD (Crosby, Leichliter, & Brackbill, 2000; Fortenberry et al., 1999; Richey, Macaluso, & Hook, 1999; Wagstaff, DeLamater, & Havens, 1999). For example, several studies have reported high rates of STD reinfection among adolescents, ranging from 31 percent for males to 40 percent for females, over a year's follow-up period (Fortenberry et al., 1999; Wagstaff, DeLamater, & Havens, 1999).

In a study of predominately minority adolescent females recently treated for chlamy-dia, a significant increase in condom use was reported following a single-session (20-minute) behavioral intervention delivered by a research assistant (experimental condition) as opposed to a nurse (control condition). Adolescents in the experimental condition received skills training in condom negotiation and application, as well as instruction designed to increase positive attitudes toward condoms and increased perceptions of per-ceived threat to STD. Control-group instruction consisted of individual discussion about STD and the importance of partner treatment and condom use. Despite the statistically significant intervention effect on condom use, six-month rates of reinfection with chlamy-dia in the experimental group did not differ from those in the control group; most likely because the observed increase in condom use was nonetheless inconsistent, compromis-ing the protective benefits of condom use (Orr et al., 1996). Yet, the study reported by Orr and colleagues suggests that more intensive efforts may ultimately produce clinically significant increases in condom use.

A recent study of predominantly minority male and female adolescents (12–15 years of age) attending their pediatricians' office was conducted to determine the efficacy of a tailored physician-delivered counseling session as opposed to standard-of-care treatment. Three months after the intervention, adolescents in the experimental group reported significantly fewer acts of unprotected sex during most recent intercourse (8 percent) than adolescents in the control group (43 percent). Although encouraging, this effect was not found at the nine-month follow-up period and differences in subsequent STD infection were not assessed. A portion of the intervention included efforts to facilitate improved communication about sexual issues between adolescents and their parents. The primary message expressed by pediatricians to adolescent patients was that unprotected sex is unsafe, condom-protected sex is safer, and abstinence from sexual expression with a partner is the safest behavior (Boekeloo et al., 1999).

Together, these two studies provide insight into multiple issues associated with behavioral interventions designed to lower STD incidence of adolescents. For example, each study relied on self-report of condom use as an outcome; thus the accuracy of adolescents' self-report becomes a research question. Empirical investigation of this question has shown that frequent assessments using two-week recall periods, or less frequent assessments using two-month recall periods, are most efficient for adolescents (McFarlane & St. Lawrence, 1999). Shew and colleagues (1997) found that adolescents' self-report of condom use was most valid when assessed for their last two sexual partners. Other research has indicated the utility of using computer-assisted technology and role-play to maximize the validity of adolescents' self-reported sexual behaviors (Michaud, Narring, & Ferron, 1999). Each study also highlights an inherent limitation of clinic-based intervention in that single-session programs may not be adequate to produce lasting behavior change required to avert STD infection. The latter study (Boekeloo et al., 1999) addressed a common issue of pedagogy: presentation of multiple as opposed to single prevention options to adolescents. Contrary to opinions from some public organizations, research supports the proposition that adolescents benefit from a hierarchy of prevention messages e.g., "abstinence is best, but if you must have sex use a condom" (see Jemmott, Jemmott, & Fong, 1998 in the next segment of this section for an excellent example of this research).

Effective community-based STD-prevention programs

A recent meta-analysis of community-based sexual risk-reduction interventions for adolescents showed significant effects in respect to increasing condom use, decreasing unprotected sex, and decreasing number of sexual partners, and may increase the practice of abstinence (Jemmott & Jemmott, 2000). Although the majority of the interventions reviewed were designed specifically for HIV prevention, the measured outcomes apply equally well to STD prevention. Three specific examples of community-based programs for adolescents are reviewed here.

A recent study of African American middle school students recruited for an eight-hour intervention found that both abstinence-based and safer-sex intervention can reduce sexual-risk behavior, but safer-sex interventions had greater and longer-lasting effects. Sessions were held over two consecutive Saturdays. Adolescents randomized to the safer-sex condition received messages acknowledging the value of abstinence as "best choice," but were provided with extensive material designed to enhance perceptions that condoms can be used pleasurably, and skills training designed to increase self-efficacy of condom use. Similarly, the abstinence-based condition acknowledged the value of condoms for STD protection, but provided material emphasizing positive aspects of abstinence, followed by skills training relative to negotiating abstinence and resisting social influences to have sex. Three months after the intervention, adolescents in the abstinence condition were less likely to report having sex than those in the control condition (a sequence of sessions devoted to general health); however, this effect disappeared at six and twelve-month follow-up periods. Conversely, adolescents in the safer-sex condition reported more consistent use of condoms than those in the control group at three-, six-, and twelve-month follow-up periods. At six and twelve-month follow-up periods, sexually experienced adolescents in the safer-sex condition reported significantly less sexual intercourse (using a three-month recall period) than their counterparts in the abstinence or control condition (Jemmott, Jemmott, & Fong, 1998).

St. Lawrence and colleagues (1995) provided evidence that a somewhat longer safer-sex intervention (eight sessions spread out over eight weeks, with each session lasting 1.5 to 2 hours) produced significant increases in STD-protective behavior even one year after delivery of the intervention. Adolescents were African American and ranged from 14 to 18 years of age. In addition, sexually inexperienced adolescents randomized to the safer-sex condition were less likely than control adolescents to report initiating sexual activity in the year following delivery of the intervention. Similar to the study conducted by Jemmott, Jemmott, and Fong (1998), the intervention consisted of skills training and material designed to address cognitive antecedents of sexual risk-taking, e.g., condom use self-efficacy, self-regulation, problem solving, and risk recognition.

Another intervention targeting younger African American adolescents (9–15 years of age) was conducted to determine the efficacy of delivering the intervention to naturally formed peer groups. Sessions were similar in length and number to that used by St. Lawrence and colleagues (1995), with the addition of a one-day session at a rural campsite. The intervention condition consisted of sexual communication and negotiation skills training and material promoting self-efficacy, response-efficacy (belief that STD-protective measures are beneficial), and material addressing specific barriers to adopting STD-protective behaviors. Information regarding the high prevalence of peer condom use was also provided. Compared to control adolescents, those receiving the safer-sex intervention reported significantly more condom use at the six-month, but not at the twelve-month follow-up period. Further, a dose-response effect was observed in that adolescents attending a greater number of intervention sessions were more likely to increase their condom use than those with lower attendance (Stanton et al., 1996).

Collectively, these three interventions provide evidence that interventions targeting social and cognitive antecedents of sexual-risk behavior (primarily nonuse of condoms) are effective, although benefits may decay over time. Notably underrepresented in the literature on community-based interventions for adolescents are interventions designed specifically for Hispanic populations (Jemmott & Jemmott, 2000). Also, it is noteworthy that each intervention reviewed was delivered to mixed gender audiences. Based on gender differences in antecedents of sexual behavior (see "Antecedents of Adolescents' STD-Risk Behavior," above), gender may be an important moderator of intervention effectiveness. For example, Stanton and colleagues reported that intervention-group males were more likely than intervention-group females to report increased condom use. St. Lawrence and colleagues reported that males benefited from the intervention by increasing the use of HIV-preventive behaviors (e.g., condom use); whereas females benefited from the intervention by maintaining their level of HIV-preventive behaviors (as opposed to their control-group counterparts, who decreased their HIV-preventive behaviors).

Effective school-based STD-prevention programs

Although apparently an ideal venue for intervention programs designed to prevent STD infection, US schools systems are locally controlled and thus prone to undue influence of community members objecting to sex-education programs. A recurring local-level issue is whether or not sex education (other than abstinence-only programs) leads to increased sexual activity. Kirby and colleagues (1994) reviewed numerous studies of sex-education programs in schools and concluded that education programs do not increase sexual activity among students (a finding supported by studies of intervention programs in other venues, e.g., community-based interventions). More recently, results from a review commissioned by the Joint United Nations Programme on HIV/AIDS (UNAIDS) indicated that quality sex-education programs help delay age of sexual initiation, and protect sexually active adolescents from STD infection (UNAIDS, 1997). Despite evidence-based recommendations to the contrary, the US Congress has allocated funding for *school-based abstinence-only* programs. However, scientifically rigorous studies establishing the effectiveness of these programs do not exist. Thus, examples of effective *school-based safer sex interventions* follow.

Kirby and colleagues (1991) assessed the efficacy of a 15-class period, safer-sex intervention program delivered to students in 23 health classes within 13 different California high schools. In addition to addressing social and cognitive antecedents (as previously described for community-based interventions), the program included a component designed to increase parent–adolescent communication about sexual issues. The program also provided students with practice in responding to various forms of peer or partner pressure that might lead to sex. Finally, the program was designed to supplement, rather than replace, existing health-education curricula (including sex-education materials). Compared to controls, low-risk and sexually inexperienced adolescents receiving the intervention benefited by increased use of contraceptives (including condoms) or delaying age of sexual initiation, respectively. Similar effects were not found among high-risk adolescents.

A similar, but more recent, study of nearly 4,000 9th-graders found that a school-based safer-sex intervention positively impacted a broad range of social and cognitive antecedents and increased parent–adolescent communication about sexual issues. Compared to controls, adolescents receiving the intervention reported less frequent intercourse over a three-month recall period and were more likely to report using a condom during last intercourse. Although not relevant to STD prevention, the study also found that students receiving the intervention were more likely to report use of contraceptive methods, other than condoms, during last intercourse (Coyle et al., 1999).

These studies highlight the point that sexual risk-reduction programs for adolescents may serve dual purposes: STD and pregnancy prevention. The interrelated nature of risk behaviors for STD and risk behaviors for pregnancy permit easy integration of instruction, thus serving adolescents more efficiently. More detailed discussion of the value of providing an integrated approach to STD and pregnancy prevention has been provided by Santelli et al. (1999) and Whaley et al. (1999). Further, a comprehensive discussion of principles and practices of school-based sexual risk-reduction programs has been provided by Kirby (2000).

A small percentage of US schools (less than 3 percent) have also provided condoms to students. The nature of these condom-distribution programs precludes rigorous trials of their efficacy in preventing STD infection; however, available evidence suggests these programs may increase condom use without promoting earlier age of sexual initiation (Guttmacher et al., 1997). Schools offering reproductive health-care services that include STD prevention and treatment are also few in number and are largely under-utilized by students (Crosby & St. Lawrence, 2000). This is unfortunate, because school-based clinics have the potential to lower adolescents' perceived barriers to receiving treatment and prevention services for STDs.

Effective STD-prevention programs for high-risk adolescents

A recently published study of an intervention for incarcerated males provides intriguing findings. Using a modified version of the Becoming A Responsible Teen Program (see St. Lawrence et al., 1995), St. Lawrence and colleagues (1999a) provided a six-session (one hour per session) safer-sex intervention to adolescent males in a state reformatory. Adolescents were randomized to the safer-sex intervention or an anger-management control group. Although the safer-sex intervention had a significant impact on cognitive mediators of STD-protective behaviors, adolescents in both conditions reported similar declines in sexual-risk behavior six months after their release from the facility. The authors suggested that the experience of incarceration or the relevance of the control condition to sexual behavior accounted for the null finding. Indeed, the anger-management condition included material quite similar to safer-sex programs: problem solving, resisting peer pressure, providing feedback during communication, accepting criticism, and conflict resolution.

A safer-sex intervention delivered to drug-using incarcerated males has also shown some promising results. Four group sessions were provided to adolescent males in a New York City jail; each session promoted problem-solving skills designed to reduce drug use and risky sexual behaviors. Interviews of intervention recipients and control adolescents were conducted at a follow-up interview five months after their release from jail. Compared to controls, adolescents assigned to the intervention condition reported greater increases in condom use (Magura, Kang, & Shapiro, 1994).

Homeless and runaway adolescents represent a priority group for STD prevention. Despite estimates of high rates of STD among homeless adolescents and of HIV prevalence as high as 17 percent among runaway and homeless adolescents (Lightfoot & Rotheram-Borus, 2000), few studies have been conducted to evaluate safer-sex interventions for this large population. However, a study of runaway youth in New York City demonstrated the efficacy of small-group intervention designed to increase runaway adolescents' frequency of condom use and to reduce their frequency of unprotected sex with multiple partners. The program was delivered at New York City shelter for runaways and consisted of up to 30 sessions (adolescents spending more time at the shelter received more sessions). Sessions were designed to increase knowledge about HIV/AIDS, provide coping skills and realistic expectations regarding emotional and behavioral responses to risky situations, decrease adolescents' perceived barriers to safer sex, and teach adolescents how to access health care and other important community resources. Results at three- and six-month follow-up assessments indicated that attendance to intervention sessions was positively related with reporting consistent condom use and negatively related to reporting unprotected sex with multiple partners (Rotheram-Borus et al., 1991).

Subsequent reports of success with runaway adolescents in New York City have been provided by Lightfoot and Rotheram-Borus (2000). Both sexual risk-taking and substance-abuse behaviors were reduced among a sample of more than 300 adolescents aged 11 to 17. The intervention condition focused on adolescents' social identities and roles and integration of sexual responsibility into these constructs. Skills training and social support were also built into the program. Compared to control adolescents, those in the intervention reported significantly fewer acts of unprotected sex and less substance abuse (including alcohol and marijuana). Effects were particularly strong for African American females.

Because AIDS is a particularly devastating STD, youth living with HIV (YLH) have been identified as a priority population for interventions designed to address quality of life issues and both prevent YLH from transmitting their infection to others and from being infected with other STDs and/or other strains of HIV that may exacerbate their present infection. Accordingly, Rotheram-Borus, Reid, and Rosario (1994) conducted an intervention trial for nearly 200 predominantly minority YLH (ages 13–23). Intervention content focused on social identity and social roles, as well as small-group counseling designed to help adolescents reconstruct their conceptualization of what it means to be a responsible and caring sex partner. Compared to a control group (this group received the intervention one year after the experimental group), adolescents in the experimental group reported fewer sex partners, fewer HIV-negative sex partners, less unprotected sex, and less substance abuse at a 15-month follow-up period.

Future Directions For STD Prevention

Two paradigm shifts are occurring in the field of behavioral interventions for adolescents at risk of STD infection. The first involves the convergence of prevention efforts; dictating that effective programs address overarching health concerns of adolescents rather than focusing on selected dimensions, e.g., sexual-risk behavior for STD infection. Descriptions in this chapter of adolescents' health-risk behaviors as interrelated, as well as a discussion of integrated programs and broad-based approaches, speak to the value of this paradigm shift. Youth development programs are currently being evaluated for their impact on STD-protective behavior among adolescents; and youth development programs have already been shown to lower adolescents' risk of pregnancy (Allen, Philliber, & Hoggson, 1990). Youth development programs may work because they address gaps in adolescents' development that may result from many of the family and environmental influences previously described in this chapter; whereas, most of the current approaches to promoting STD-protective behavior among adolescents have a primary focus on social and cognitive antecedents.

The second paradigm shift involves intervening with adolescents at progressively younger ages, including preadolescence. For example, a recent study by Hawkins and colleagues (1999) demonstrated that a unified youth-development program provided to students throughout their elementary school years resulted in multiple favorable outcomes as compared to students receiving the intervention only during grades five and six. The program was unified in that child-focused, developmentally appropriate training was provided to teachers, parents, and children. Outcomes were assessed when students reached 18 years of age. Favorable outcomes included less violence, less heavy drinking, and a lower likelihood of reporting sexual experience, multiple sex partners, and pregnancy (or causing a pregnancy). Other studies have supported the value of early intervention to promote STD-protective behavior of adolescents by establishing that early patterns of risk behavior tend to repeat themselves and become progressively more difficult to modify, i.e., the strongest predictor of future STD-risk behavior among adolescents was past STD-risk behavior (Sieving et al., 1997).

Other changes in current approaches to behavioral intervention are likely to include a greater emphasis on understanding relationships dynamics (Crosby et al., in press; Finer, Darroch, & Singh, 1999; Wingood & DiClemente, 1998; 2000), sexual network dynamics and STD transmission patterns in these networks (Aral et al., 1999; Rothenberg et al., 1998), and the development of interventions targeting multiple levels of causality such as family-level, environmental-level, and community-level interventions (DiClemente & Wingood, 2000). New and more innovative intervention approaches will continue to evolve, encompassing principles of adolescent development and being responsive to changes in the social and political factors that have a substantial influence on adolescents' health behavior.

Key Readings

Eng, T. R., & Butler, W. T. (Eds.) *The hidden epidemic: Confronting sexually transmitted diseases.* Washington, DC: National Academy Press.
This volume reviews the field of sexually transmitted disease prevention in the United States, with particular emphasis on adolescents. Based on recommendations from a committee assembled by the Institute of Medicine, the volume systematically outlines problems with the current national response to the STD epidemic and simultaneously describes policy-level changes that could be implemented to address these problems. The book is uniquely focused on promoting the sexual health of adolescents.

Jemmott, J. B. III, & Jemmott, L. S. (2000). HIV behavioral interventions for adolescents in community settings. In J. L. Peterson & R. J. DiClemente (Eds.), *Handbook of HIV prevention* (pp. 103–128). New York: Plenum.

This chapter provides an excellent summary of adolescents' sexual-risk behavior within the context of the Theory of Planned Behavior. It also provides an outstanding synthesis and evaluation of behavioral interventions targeting the sexual-risk behaviors of adolescents.

D'Angelo, L. J., & DiClemente, R. J. (1996). Sexually transmitted diseases including human immunodeficiency virus. In R. J. DiClemente, W. Hansen, & L. E. Ponton (Eds.), *Handbook of adolescent health risk behavior* (pp. 333–368). New York: Plenum.
This chapter provides a comprehensive view of STDs among adolescents and includes information about testing and treatment.

Crosby, R. A., & Miller, K. S. (In press). The pivotal role of the family on adolescent females' sexual health. In G. M. Wingood & R. J. DiClemente (Eds.), *Women's sexual and reproductive health: Social, psychological, and public health perspectives.* New York: Plenum/Kluwer.
This chapter provides an in-depth examination of family influences on the sexual-risk behavior of adolescent females.

References

Abma, J., Driscoll, A., & Moore, K. (1998). Young women's degree of control over first intercourse: An exploratory analysis. *Family Planning Perspectives, 30,* 12–18.

Alan Guttmacher Institute (1993). *Sex and America's teenagers.* New York: Alan Guttmacher Institute.

Allen, J. P., Philliber, S., & Hoggson, N. (1990). School-based prevention of teen-age pregnancy and school dropout: Process evaluation of the national replication of the Teen Outreach Program. *American Journal of Community Psychology, 18,* 505–524.

American Social Health Association (1998). *The National Adolescent Student Health Survey.* Oakland, CA: Third Party.

Aral, S. O. (1999). Sexual network patterns as determinants of STD rates: Paradigm shift in the behavioral epidemiology of STDs made visible. *Sexually Transmitted Diseases, 26,* 262–264.

Aral, S. O., & Holmes, K. K. (1999). Social and behavioral determinants of the epidemiology of STDs: Industrialized and developing countries. In K. K. Holmes, P. F. Sparling, P. Mardh, et al. (Eds.), *Sexually transmitted diseases* (pp. 39–76). New York: McGraw Hill.

Aral, S. O., Mosher, W. D., & Cates, W. (1992). Vaginal douching among women of reproductive age in the United States: 1988. *American Journal of Public Health, 82,* 210–214.

Aral, S. O., & Wasserheit, J. N. (1995). Interactions among HIV, other sexually transmitted diseases, socioeconomic status, and poverty in women. In A. O'Leary & L. S. Jemmott (Eds.), *Women at risk: Issues in the primary prevention of AIDS* (pp. 13–42). New York: Plenum.

Basen-Engquist, K., & Parcel, G. (1992). Attitudes, norms and self-efficacy: A model of adolescents' HIV-related sexual risk behavior. *Health Education Quarterly, 19,* 263–277.

Berman, S. M., & Hein, K. (1999). Adolescents and STDs. In K. K. Holmes, P. F. Sparling, P. Mardh, et al. (Eds.), *Sexually transmitted diseases* (pp. 129–142). New York: McGraw Hill.

Biglan, A., Metzler, C. W., Wirt, R., Ary, D., Noell, J., Ochs, L., French, C., & Hood, D. (1990). Social and behavioral factors associated with high-risk sexual behavior among adolescents. *Journal of Behavioral Medicine, 13,* 245–261.

Blum, R. W., Kelly, A., & Ireland, M. (2001). Health-risk behaviors and protective factors among adolescents with mobility impairments and learning and emotional disabilities. *Journal of Adolescent Health, 28,* 481–490.

Boekeloo, B. O., Schamus, L. A., Simmens, S. J., Cheng, T. L., O'Connor, K., & D'Angelo, L. J. (1999). A STD/HIV prevention trial among adolescents in managed care. *Pediatrics, 103*, 107–15.

Bolan, G., Ehrhardt, A. A., & Wasserheit, J. N. (1999). Gender perspectives and STDs. In K. K. Holmes, P. F. Sparling, P. Mardh, et al. (Eds.), *Sexually transmitted diseases* (pp. 117–128). New York: McGraw Hill.

Boyer, C. B. (1990). Psychosocial, behavioral, and educational factors in preventing sexually transmitted diseases. *Adolescent Medicine, 1*, 597–613.

Brewster, K. L., Billy, J. O. G., & Grady, W. R. (1993). Social context and adolescent behavior: The impact of community on the transition to sexual activity. *Social Forces, 71(3)*, 713–740.

Brown, L. K., Danofsky, M. B., Lourie, K. J., DiClemente, R. J., & Ponton, L. E. (1997). Adolescents with psychiatric disorders and the risk of HIV. *Journal of the American Academy of Child and Adolescent Psychiatry, 36*, 1609–1617.

Brown, L. K., Kessel, S. M., Lourie, K. J., Ford, H. H., & Lipsitt, L. P. (1999). Influence of sexual abuse on HIV-related attitudes and behaviors in adolescent psychiatric inpatients. *Journal of the American Academy of Child and Adolescent Psychiatry, 36*, 316–322.

Bunnell, R. E., Dahlberg, L., Rolfs, R., Ransom, R., Gershman, K., Farshy, C., Newhall, W. J., Schmid, S., Stone, K., & St. Louis, M. (1999). High prevalence and incidence of sexually transmitted diseases in urban adolescent females despite moderate risk behaviors. *Journal of Infectious Diseases, 180*, 1624–1631.

Burke, D. S., Brundage, J. D., Goldenbaum, M. S., Gardner, L. I., Peterson, M., et al. (1990). Human immunodeficiency virus infections in teenagers: Seroprevalence among applicants for U.S. Military Service. *Journal of the American Medical Association, 263*, 2074–2077.

Burstein, G. R., Gaydos, C. A., Diener-West, M., Howell, M. R., Zenilman, J. M., & Quinn, T. C. (1998a). Incident *Chlamydia trachomatis* infections among innercity adolescent females. *Journal of the American Medical Association, 280*, 521–526.

Burstein, G. R., Waterfield, G., Joffe, A., Zenilman, J. M., Quinn, T. C., & Gaydos, C. A. (1998b). Screening for gonorrhea and chlamydia by DNA amplification in adolescents attending middle school health centers. Opportunity for early intervention. *Sexually Transmitted Diseases, 25*, 395–402.

Catania, J. A., Dolcini, M. M., Coates, T. J., Kegeles, S. M., Greenblatt, R. M., & Puckett, S. (1989). Predictors of condom use and multiple partnered sex among sexually-active adolescent women: implications for AIDS-related health interventions. *Journal of Sex Research, 26*, 519–523.

Centers for Disease Control and Prevention [CDC] (1996). Ten leading nationally notifiable infectious diseases – United States, 1995. *Morbidity and Mortality Weekly Report, 45*, 883–884.

Centers for Disease Control and Prevention [CDC] (1998a). Youth risk behavioral surveillance – United States, 1997. *Morbidity and Mortality Weekly Report, 47(SS–3)*, 18–20.

Centers for Disease Control and Prevention [CDC] (1998b). Trends in sexual risk behaviors among high school students – United States, 1991–1997. *Morbidity and Mortality Weekly Report, 47*, 749–752.

Centers for Disease Control and Prevention [CDC] (1999). HIV/AIDS Surveillance Report, year-end edition (pp. 1–44). Atlanta, GA: US Department of Health and Human Services.

Chilcoat, H. D., & Anthony, J. C. (1996). Impact of parent monitoring on initiation of drug use through late childhood. *Journal of the American Academy of Child and Adolescent Psychiatry, 35*, 91–100.

Chow, W. H., Darling, J. R., & Greenbert, R. S. (1987). The epidemiology of ectopic pregnancy. *Epidemiology Review, 9*, 70–94.

Civic, D. (1999). The association between characteristics of dating relationships and condom use among heterosexual young adults. *AIDS Education & Prevention, 11*, 343–352.

Clark, L. F., Miller, K. S., Harrison, J. S., Kay, K. L., & Moore, J. (1996). The role of attraction in partner assessments and heterosexual risk for HIV. In S. Oskamp & S. C. Thompson (Eds.), *Understanding and preventing HIV risk behavior* (pp. 81–99). Thousand Oaks, CA: Sage.

Cobb, B. K. (1997). Communication types and sexual protective practices of college women. *Public Health Nursing, 14*, 293–301.

Cohen, D., Spear, S., Scribner, R., Kissinger, P., Mason, K., & Wildgen, J. (2000). "Broken Windows" and the risk of Gonorrhea. *American Journal of Public Health, 90*, 230–236.

Cooper, M. L., Shapiro, C. M., & Powers, A. M. (1998). Motivations for sex and risky sexual behavior among adolescents and young adults: a functional perspective. *Journal of Personality and Social Psychology, 75*, 1528–1558.

Coyle, K., Basen-Engquist, K., Kirby, D., Parcel, G., Banspach, S., Harrist, R., Baumler, E., & Weil, M. (1999). Short-term impact of safer choices: a multicomponent, school-based HIV, other STD, and pregnancy prevention program. *Journal of School Health, 69*, 181–188.

Critchlow, C. W., Wolner-Hanssen, P., Eschenbach, D. A., Kivat, N. B., Koutsky, L. A., Stevens, C. E., et al. (1995). Determinants of cervical ectopia and of cervicitis: age, oral contraception, specific cervical infection, smoking, and douching. *American Journal of Obstetrics and Gynecology, 173*, 534–543.

Crosby, R. A., DiClemente, R. J., Wingood, G. M., Sionean, C., Cobb, B., & Harrington, K. (2000). Correlates of unprotected vaginal sex among African American female teens: The importance of relationship dynamics. *Archives of Pediatrics and Adolescent Medicine, 154*, 893–899.

Crosby, R. A., DiClemente, R. J., Wingood, G. M., Sionean, C., Cobb, B., Harrington, K., Davies, S. L., Hook, E. W., & Oh, M. K. (2001a). Correct condom application among African American adolescent females: The relationship to perceived self-efficacy and the association to confirmed STDs. *Journal of Adolescent Health, 29*, 194–199.

Crosby, R. A., DiClemente, R. J., Wingood, G. M., Sionean, C., Cobb, B., Harrington, K., Davies, S. L., Hook, E. W., & Oh, M. K. (2001b). Correlates and STD-risk of casual sex among African American female teens. *Journal of HIV/AIDS Prevention and Education for Adolescents and Children, 4*, 55–68.

Crosby, R. A., Leichliter, J. S., & Brackbill, R. (2000). Longitudinal prediction of STDs among sexually experienced adolescents: Results from a national survey. *American Journal of Preventive Medicine, 18*, 367–372.

Crosby, R. A., & St. Lawrence, J. S. (2000). Adolescents' use of school-based health clinics for reproductive health services: Data from the National Longitudinal Study of Adolescent Health. *Journal of School Health, 70*, 22–27.

Crosby, R. A., & Yarber, W. L. (2001). Perceived versus actual knowledge about correct condom use among U.S. adolescents: Results from a national study. *Journal of Adolescent Health, 28*, 415–420.

Crosby, R. A., Yarber, W. L., & Kanu, A. (1998). The relationship of HIV/STD risk behaviors to other health behaviors among a selected sample of Indiana rural youth. *Health Education Monograph, 16*, 51–59.

D'Angelo, L. J., Getson, P. R., Luban, N. L. C., & Gayle, H. D. (1991). Human immunodeficiency virus infection in urban adolescents: Can we predict who is at risk? *Pediatrics, 88*, 982–986.

Darroch, J. E., Landry, D. J., & Oslak, S. (1999). Age differences between sexual partners in the United States. *Family Planning Perspectives, 31*, 160–167.

Denning, P. F., & Flemming, P. L. (1998). Communities at risk – Estimating the impact of the

HIV epidemic upon adolescents and young adults at the local level. Paper presented at the 126th annual meeting of the American Public Health Association.

DiClemente, R. J., Hansen, W., & Ponton, L. E. (1996). Adolescents at-risk: A generation in jeopardy. In R. J. DiClemente, W. Hansen, & L. Ponton (Eds.), *Handbook of adolescent health risk behavior* (pp. 1–4). New York: Plenum.

DiClemente, R. J., Lanier, M. M., Horan, P. F., & Lodico, M. (1991). Comparison of AIDS knowledge, attitudes, and behaviors among incarcerated adolescents and a public school sample in San Francisco. *American Journal of Public Health, 81,* 628–630.

DiClemente, R. J., Lodico, M., Grinstead, O. A., Harper, G., Rickman, R. L., Evans, P. E., & Coates, T. J. (1996). African-American adolescents residing in high-risk urban environments do use condoms: Correlates and predictors of condom use among adolescents in public housing developments. *Pediatrics, 98,* 269–278.

DiClemente, R. J., Ponton, L. E., Hartley, D., & McKenna, S. (1989). Prevalence of sexual and drug-related risk behavior among psychiatrically hospitalized adolescents. In J. Woodruff, D. Doherty, & A. J. Garrison (Eds.), *Troubled adolescents and HIV infection* (pp. 70–88). Washington, DC: Child Development Center at Georgetown University.

DiClemente, R. J., & Wingood, G. M. (2000). Expanding the scope of HIV prevention for adolescents: Beyond individual-level interventions. *Journal of Adolescent Health, 26,* 377–378.

DiClemente, R. J., Wingood, G. M., Crosby, R. A., Cobb, B. K., Harrington, K., Davies, S., Hook, E. W., & Oh, M. K. (2001a). Parental monitoring and its association with a spectrum of adolescent health risk behaviors. *Pediatrics, 107,* 1363–1368.

DiClemente, R. J., Wingood, G. M., Crosby, R. A., Cobb, B. K., Harrington, K., Davies, S. L., Hook, E. W., & Oh, M. K. (2001b). Parent–adolescent communication about sexuality-related topics and adolescents' risky sexual behaviors, communication with sex partners, and self-efficacy to discuss sexuality-related issues with sex partners. *Journal of Pediatrics, 139,* 407–412.

DiClemente, R. J., Wingood, G. M., Crosby, R. A., Sionean, S., Brown, L., Rothbaum, B., Zimand, E., Cobb, B. K., Harrington, K., & Davies, S. (2001c). A prospective study of psychological distress and sexual risk behavior among African American adolescent females. *Pediatrics, 108*(5), 1–6.

DiClemente, R. J., Wingood, G. M., Crosby, R. A., Sionean, C., Cobb, B. K., Harrington, K., Davies, S. L., Hook, E. W., & Oh, M. K. (2002). Sexual risk behaviors associated with having older sex partners: A study of African American female adolescents. *Sexually Transmitted Diseases, 29,* 20–24.

DiIorio, C., Kelley, M., & Hockenberry-Eaton, M. (1999). Communication about sexual issues: Mothers, fathers, and friends. *Journal of Adolescent Health, 24,* 181–189.

Dryfoos, J. G. (1991). Preventing high-risk behavior. *American Journal of Public Health, 81,* 157–158.

Duncan, S. C., Stryker, L. A., & Duncan, T. E. (1999). Exploring associations in developmental trends of adolescent substance use and risky sexual behavior in a high-risk population. *Journal of Behavioral Medicine, 22,* 21–34.

Durbin, M., DiClemente, R. J., Siegel, D., et al. (1993). Factors associated with multiple sexual partners among junior high school students. *Journal of Adolescent Health, 14,* 202–207.

Dutra, R., Miller, K. S., & Forehand, R. (1999). The process and content of sexual communication with adolescents in two-parent families: Associations with sexual risk-taking behavior. *AIDS and Behavior, 3,* 59–66.

Ellen, J. M., Aral, S. O., & Madger, L. S. (1998). Do differences in sexual behaviors account for the racial/ethnic differences in adolescents' self-reported history of a sexually transmitted disease? *Sexually Transmitted Diseases, 25,* 125–129.

Eng, T. R., & Butler, W. T. (1997). *The hidden epidemic: Confronting sexually transmitted diseases.* Washington, DC: National Academy Press.

Ennett, S. T., Federman, E. B., Bailey, S. L., Ringwalt, C. L., & Hubbard, M. L. (1999). HIV-risk behaviors associated with homelessness characteristics in youth. *Journal of Adolescent Health, 25,* 344–353.

Finer, L. B., Darroch, J. E., & Singh, S. (1999). Sexual partnership patterns as a behavioral risk factor for sexually transmitted diseases. *Family Planning Perspectives, 31,* 228–236.

Fisher, J. D., Misovich, S. J., & Fisher, W. A. (1992). Impact of perceived social norms on adolescents' AIDS-risk behavior and prevention. In R. J. DiClemente (Ed.), *Adolescents and AIDS: A generation in jeopardy* (pp. 117–136). Newbury Park, CA: Sage.

Fleming, D. T., McQuillan, G. M., Johnson, R. E., Nahmias, A. J., Aral, S. O., Lee, F. K., & St. Louis, M. E. (1997). Herpes simplex virus type 2 in the United States, 1976 to 1994. *New England Journal of Medicine, 337,* 1105–1111.

Ford, K., & Norris, A. (1997). Sexual networks of African-American and Hispanic youth. *Sexually Transmitted Diseases, 24,* 327–333.

Forehand, R., & Wierson, M. (1993). The role of developmental factors in planning behavioral interventions for children: Disruptive behavior as an example. *Behavior Therapy, 24,* 117–141.

Fortenberry, J. D. (1998). Alcohol, drugs, and STD/HIV risk among adolescents. *AIDS Patient Care and STDs, 12,* 783–786.

Fortenberry, J. D., Brizendine, E. J., Katz, B. P., Wools, K. K., Blythe, M. J., & Orr, D. P. (1999). Subsequent sexually transmitted infections among adolescent women with genital infection due to *Chlamydia trachomatis, Neisseria gonorrhoeae,* or *Trichomonas vaginalis. Sexually Transmitted Diseases, 26,* 26–32.

Fortenberry, J. D., Orr, D. P., Katz, B. P., Brizendine, E. J., & Blythe, J. (1997). Sex under the influence: A diary self-report study of substance abuse and sexual behavior among adolescent women. *Sexually Transmitted Diseases, 24,* 313–319.

Fullilove, R. E. (1998). Race and sexually transmitted diseases. *Sexually Transmitted Diseases, 25,* 130–131.

Guttmacher, S., Lieberman, L., Ward, D., Freudenberg, N., Radosh, A., & Des Jarlais, D. (1997). Condom availability in New York City public schools: Relationships to condom use and sexual behavior. *American Journal of Public Health, 87,* 1427–1433.

Harvey, S. M., & Spigner, C. (1995). Factors associated with sexual behavior among adolescents: A multivariate analysis. *Adolescence, 30,* 253–264.

Hawkins, J. D., Catalano, R. F., Kosterman, R., Abbott, R., & Hill, K. G. (1999). Preventing adolescent health-risk behaviors by strengthening protection during childhood. *Archives of Pediatrics & Adolescent Medicine, 153,* 226–234.

Holtzman, D., & Rubinson, R. (1995). Parent and peer communication effects on AIDS-related behavior among U.S. high school students. *Family Planning Perspectives, 27,* 235–240.

Howard, M. M., Fortenberry, J. D., Blythe, M. J., Zimet, G. D., & Orr, D. P. (1999). Patterns of sexual partnerships among adolescent females. *Journal of Adolescent Health, 24,* 300–303.

Ilegbodu, A. E., Frank, M. L., Poindexter, A. N., & Johnson, D. (1994). Characteristics of teens tested for HIV in a metropolitan area. *Journal of Adolescent Health, 15,* 479–484.

Jaccard, J., Dittus, P. J., Gordon, V. V. (1996). Maternal correlates of adolescent sexual and contraceptive behavior. *Family Planning Perspectives, 28,* 159–165 & 185.

Jamison, J. H., Kaplan, D. W., Hamman, R., Eagar, R., Beach, R., & Douglas, J. M. Jr. (1995). Spectrum of genital human papillomavirus infection in a female adolescent population. *Sexually Transmitted Diseases, 22,* 236–243.

Janz, N. K., Zimmerman, M. A., Wren, P. A., Israel, B. A., Freudenberg, N., & Carter, R. J. (1996). Evaluation of 37 AIDS prevention projects: successful approaches and barriers to program effectiveness. *Health Education Quarterly, 23*, 80–97.

Jemmott, J. B., Jemmott, L. S., Spears, H., Hewitt, N., & Cruz-Collins, M. (1992). Self-efficacy, hedonistic expectations, and condom use intentions among inner-city Black adolescent women: A social cognitive approach to AIDS risk behavior. *Journal of Adolescent Health, 13*, 512–519.

Jemmott, J. B. III, & Jemmott, L. S. (2000). HIV behavioral interventions for adolescents in community settings. In J. L. Peterson & R. J. DiClemente (Eds.), *Handbook of HIV prevention* (pp. 103–128). New York: Plenum Press.

Jemmott, J. B. III, Jemmott, L. S., & Fong, G. T. (1998). Abstinence and safer sex HIV risk-reduction interventions for African American adolescents: a randomized controlled trial. *Journal of the American Medical Association, 279*, 1529–1536.

Jemmott, J. B., Jemmott, L. S., & Hacker, C. I. (1992). Predicting intention to use condoms among African American adolescents: The theory of planned behavior as a model of HIV risk associated behavior. *Journal of Ethnicity and Disease, 2*, 371–380.

Jessor, R., Donovan, J. E., & Costa, F. M. (1991). *Beyond adolescence: Problem behavior and young adult development.* New York: Cambridge University Press.

Kaiser Foundation (1999). *What teens know and don't (but should) about sexually transmitted diseases.* Menlo Park, CA: Kaiser Family Foundation.

Kelley, P. W., Miller, R. N., Pomerantz, R., Wann, F., Brundage, J. F., et al. (1990). Human immunodeficiency virus seropositivity among members of the active duty U.S. Army 85–89. *American Journal of Public Health, 80*, 405–410.

Kirby, D. (2000). School-based interventions to prevent unprotected sex and HIV among adolescents. In J. L. Peterson & R. J. DiClemente (Eds.), *Handbook of HIV prevention* (pp. 83–102). New York: Plenum Press.

Kirby, D., & DiClemente, R. J. (1994). School-based interventions to prevent unprotected sex and HIV among adolescents. In R. J. DiClemente & J. L. Peterson (Eds.), *Preventing AIDS: Theories and methods of behavioral interventions* (pp. 117–140). New York, NY: Plenum Press.

Kirby, D., Short, L., Collins, J., Rugg, D., Kolbe, L., Howard, M., Miller, B., Sonenstein, F., & Zabin, L. S. (1994). School-based programs to reduce sexual risk behaviors: a review of effectiveness. *Public Health Reports, 109*, 339–360.

Ku, L. C., Sonenstein, F. L., Boggess, S., & Pleck, J. H. (1998). Understanding changes in teenage men's sexual activity: 1979–1995. *Family Planning Perspectives, 30*, 256–262.

Ku, L. C., Sonenstein, F. L., & Pleck, J. H. (1992). The association of AIDS education and sex education with sexual behavior and condom use among teenage men. *Family Planning Perspectives, 24*, 100–106.

Ku, L. C., Sonenstein, F. L., & Pleck, J. H. (1994). The dynamics of young men's condom use during and across relationships. *Family Planning Perspectives, 26*, 246–251.

Langer, L. M., Zimmerman, R. S., & Katz, J. A. (1994). Which is more important to high school students: preventing pregnancy or preventing AIDS? *Family Planning Perspectives, 26*, 154–159.

Lauman, E. O., & Youm, Y. (1999). Racial/ethnic group differences in the prevalence of sexually transmitted diseases in the United States: a network explanation. *Sexually Transmitted Diseases, 26*, 250–261.

Lawrence, L., Levy, S. R., & Rubinson, L. (1990). Self-efficacy and AIDS prevention for pregnant teens. *Journal of School Health, 60*, 19–24.

Leland, N. L., & Barth, R. P. (1993). Characteristics of adolescents who have attempted to avoid

HIV and who have communicated with parents about sex. *Journal of Adolescent Research, 81*(1), 58–76.

Lemp, G. F., Hirozawa, A. M., Givertz, D., Nieri, G. N., Anderson, L., et al. (1994). Seroprevalence of HIV and risk behaviors among young homosexual and bisexual men. *Journal of the American Medical Association, 272*, 449–454.

Lightfoot, M., & Rotheram-Borus, M. J. (2000). Interventions for high-risk youth. In J. L. Peterson & R. J. DiClemente (Eds.), *Handbook of HIV prevention* (pp. 129–146). New York: Plenum Press.

Lown, E. A., Winkler, K., Fullilove, R. E., & Fullilove, M. T. (1995). Tossin' and tweakin': Women's consciousness in the crack culture. In A. Aauire (Ed.), *Women and AIDS: Psychological perspectives* (pp. 90–106). Thousand Oaks, CA: Sage.

Lowry, R., Holtzman, D., Truman, B. I., Kann, L., Collins, J. L., & Kolbe, L. J. (1994). Substance use and HIV-related sexual behaviors among US high school students: Are they related? *American Journal of Public Health, 84*, 1116–1120.

Luster, T., & Small, S. A. (1997). Sexual abuse history and number of sex partners among female adolescents. *Family Planning Perspectives, 29*(5), 204–211.

Magura, S., Kang, S. Y., & Shapiro, J. L. (1994). Outcomes of intensive AIDS education for male adolescent drug users in jail. *Journal of Adolescent Health, 15*, 457–463.

Maxwell, A. E., Bastani, R., Warda, U. S. (1999). Condom use in young Blacks and Hispanics in public STD clinics. *Sexually Transmitted Diseases, 26*, 463–471.

McFarlane, M., & St. Lawrence, J. S. (1999). Adolescents' recall of sexual behavior: consistency of self-report and effect of variations in recall duration. *Journal of Adolescent Health, 25*, 199–206.

Michaud, P. A., Narring, F., & Ferron, C. (1999). Alternative methods in the investigation of adolescents' sexual life. *Journal of Adolescent Health, 25*, 84–90.

Miller, K. S., Clark, L. F., & Moore, J. S. (1997). Sexual initiation with older male partners and subsequent HIV risk behavior among female adolescents. *Family Planning Perspectives, 29*, 212–214.

Miller, K. S., Forehand, R., & Kotchick, B. A. (1999). Adolescent sexual behavior in two ethnic minority samples: The role of family variables. *Journal of Marriage and the Family, 61*, 85–98.

Miller, K. S., Forehand, R., & Kotchick, B. A. (2000). Adolescent sexual behavior in two ethnic minority samples: A multi-system perspective delineating targets for prevention. *Adolescence, 35*, 313–333.

Miller, K. S., Levin, M. L., Whitaker, D. J., & Xiaohe, X. (1998). Patterns of condom use among adolescents: The impact of mother–adolescent communication. *American Journal of Public Health, 88*, 1542–1544.

Morokoff, P. J., Quina, K., Harlow, L. L., Whitmire, L., Grimley, D. M., Gibson, P. R., & Burkholder, G. J. (1997). Sexual assertiveness scale (SAS) for women: Development and validation. *Journal of Personality and Social Psychology, 73*, 790–804.

Morris, R. E., Harrison, E. A., Knox, G. W., Tromanhauser, E., Marquis, D. K., & Watts, L. L. (1995). Health risk behavioral survey from 39 juvenile correctional facilities in the United States. *Journal of Adolescent Health, 17*, 334–344.

Mulhall, P. F., Stone, D., & Stone, B. (1996). Home alone: Is it a risk factor for middle school youth and drug use? *Journal of Drug Education, 26*, 39–48.

Nagy, S., DiClemente, R. J., & Adcock, A. G. (1995). Adverse factors associated with forced sex among southern adolescent girls. *Pediatrics, 96*, 944–946.

Norris, A. E., & Ford, K. (1994). Associations between condom experiences and beliefs, intentions, and use in a sample of urban, low-income, African-American and Hispanic youth. *AIDS Education and Prevention, 6*, 27–39.

Norris, A. E., & Ford, K. (1999). Sexual experiences and condom use of heterosexual, low-income African American and Hispanic youth practicing relative monogamy, serial monogamy, and nonmonogamy. *Sexually Transmitted Diseases, 26,* 17–25.

Oakley, A., Fullerton, D., Holland, J., Arnold, S., France-Dawson, M., Kelley, P., & McGrellis, S. (1995). Sexual health education interventions for young people: a methodological review. *British Medical Journal, 310,* 158–162.

Office of National AIDS Policy (1996). *Youth and HIV/AIDS: An American agenda.* Washington, DC: Office of National AIDS Policy.

Oh, M. K., Cloud, G. A., Wallace, L. S., Reynolds, J., Sturdevant, M., & Feinstein, R. A. (1994). Sexual behavior and sexually transmitted diseases among male adolescents in detention. *Sexually Transmitted Diseases, 21,* 127–132.

Oh, M. K., Richey, C. M., Pate, M. S., Brown, P. R., & Hook, E. W. 3rd. (1997). High prevalence of Chlamydia trachomatis infections in adolescent females not having pelvic examinations: utility of PCR-based urine screening in urban adolescent clinic setting. *Journal of Adolescent Health, 21,* 80–86.

Orr, D. P., Langefeld, C. D., Katz, B. P., & Caine, V. A. (1996). Behavioral intervention to increase condom use among high-risk female adolescents. *Journal of Pediatrics, 128,* 288–295.

Pack, R. P., DiClemente, R. J., Hook, E. W., & Oh, M. K. (2000). High prevalence of asymptomatic STDs in incarcerated minority male youth: A case for screening. *Sexually Transmitted Diseases, 27,* 175–177.

Padian, N. S., Shiboski, S. C., & Jewell, N. P. (1991). Female-to-male transmission of human immunodeficiency virus. *Journal of the American Medical Association, 266,* 1664–1667.

Patterson, G. R., & Stouthamer-Loeber, M. (1984). The correlation of family practices and delinquency. *Child Development, 55,* 1299–1307.

Pendergrast, R. A., DuRant, R. H., & Gaillard, G. L. (1992). Attitudinal and behavioral correlates of condom use in urban adolescent males. *Journal of Adolescent Health, 13*(2), 133–139.

Piccinino, L. J., & Mosher, W. D. (1998). Trends in contraceptive use in the United States: 1982–1995. *Family Planning Perspectives, 30,* 4–10.

Plourde, P. J., & Plummer, F. A. (1994). Oral contraceptives and risk of HIV: Studies among hetrerosexual women in Nairobi. In A. Nicolosi (Ed.), *HIV epidemiology: Models and methods* (pp. 107–116). New York: Raven Press.

Resnick, M. D., Bearman, P. S., Blum, R. W., Bauman, K. E., Harris, K. M., Jones, J., Tabor, J., Beuhring, T., Sieving, R. E., Shew, M., Ireland, M., Bearinger, L. H., & Udry, J. R. (1997). Protecting adolescents from harm. Findings from the National Longitudinal Study on Adolescent Health. *Journal of the American Medical Association, 278,* 823–832.

Richey, C. M., Macaluso, M., & Hook, E. W. 3rd. (1999). Determinants of reinfection with *Chlamydia trachomatis. Sexually Transmitted Diseases, 26,* 4–11.

Romer, D., Stanton, B., Galbraith, J., Feigelman, S., Black, M. M., & Li, X. (1999). Parental influence on adolescent sexual behavior in high-poverty settings. *Archives of Pediatrics & Adolescent Medicine, 153,* 1055–1062.

Rosenberg, M. D., Gurvey, J. E., Adler, N., Dunlop, M. B., & Ellen, J. M. (1999). Concurrent sex partners and risk for sexually transmitted diseases among adolescents. *Sexually Transmitted Diseases, 26,* 208–212.

Rosenberg, P. S., & Biggar, R. J. (1998). Trends in HIV incidence among young adults in the United States. *Journal of the American Medical Association, 279,* 1894–1899.

Rosenthal, D., Moore, S., & Flynn, I. (1991). Adolescent self-efficacy, self-esteem and sexual risk-taking. *Journal of Community & Applied Social Psychology, 1,* 77–88.

Rosenthal, S. L., Cohen, S. S., DeVellis, R. F., Biro, F. M., Lewis, L. M., Succop, P. A., & Stanberry, L. R. (1999). Locus of control for general health and STD acquisition among adolescent girls. *Sexually Transmitted Diseases, 26,* 472–475.

Rothenberg, R., Kimbrough, L., Lewis-Hardy, R., Heath, B., Williams, O. C., Tambe, P., Johnson, D., & Schrader, M. (2000). Social network methods for endemic foci of syphilis: A pilot project. *Sexually Transmitted Diseases, 27,* 12–18.

Rothenberg, R. B., Sterk, C., Toomey, K. E., Potterat, J. J., Johnson, D., Schrader, M., & Hatch, S. (1998). Using social network and ethnographic tools to evaluate syphilis transmission. *Sexually Transmitted Diseases, 25,* 154–160.

Rotheram-Borus, M. J., Jemmott, L. S., & Jemmott, J. B. (1995). Preventing AIDS in female adolescents. In A. O. O'Leary & L. S. Jemmott (Eds.), *Women at Risk: Issues in the Primary Prevention of AIDS* (pp. 103–130). New York: Plenum Press.

Rotheram-Borus, M. J., Koopman, C., Haignere, C., & Davies, M. (1991). Reducing HIV sexual risk behaviors among runaway adolescents. *Journal of the American Medical Association, 266,* 1237–1241.

Rotheram-Borus, M. J., Reid, H., & Rosario, M. (1994). Factors mediating changes in sexual HIV risk behaviors among gay and bisexual adolescents. *American Journal of Public Health, 84,* 1938–1946.

Roye, C. F. (1998). Condom use by Hispanic and African-American adolescent girls who use hormonal contraception. *Journal of Adolescent Health, 23,* 205–211.

Santelli, J. S., Brener, N. D., Lowry, R., Bhatt, A., & Zabin, L. S. (1998). Multiple sexual partners among U.S. adolescents and young adults. *Family Planning Perspectives, 30,* 271–275.

Santelli, J. S., DiClemente, R. J., Miller, K. S., & Kirby, D. (1999). Sexually transmitted diseases, unintended pregnancy, and adolescent health promotion. *Adolescent Medicine, 10,* 87–108.

Schafer. M. A., Hilton, J. F., Ekstrand, M., Keogh, J., Gee, L., DiGiorgio-Hagg, L., Shalwitz, J., & Schacter, J. (1993). Relationship between drug use and sexual behaviors and the occurrence of sexually transmitted diseases among high risk youth. *Sexually Transmitted Diseases, 20,* 307–313.

Schuster, M. A., Bell, R. M., & Kanouse, D. E. (1996). The sexual practices of adolescent virgins: genital sexual activities of high school students who have never had vaginal intercourse. *American Journal of Public Health, 86,* 1570–1576.

Shew, M. L., Remafedi, G. J., Bearinger, L. H., Faulkner, P. L., Taylor, B. A., Potthoff, S. J., & Resnick, M. D. (1997). The validity of self-reported condom use among adolescents. *Sexually Transmitted Diseases, 24,* 503–510.

Sieving, R., Resnick, M. D., Bearinger, L., Remafedi, G., Taylor, B. A., & Harmon, B. (1997). Cognitive and behavioral predictors of sexually transmitted disease risk behavior among sexually active adolescents. *Archives of Pediatrics & Adolescent Medicine, 151,* 243–251.

Sionean, C., DiClemente, R. J., Wingood, G. M., Crosby, R. A., Cobb, B. K., Harrington, K., Davies, S. L., Hook, E. W., & Oh, M. K. (2002). Psychosocial correlates of refusing unwanted intercourse among African American female adolescents. *Journal of Adolescent Health, 30,* 55–63.

Small, S. A., & Luster, T. (1994). Adolescent sexual activity: An ecological, risk-factor approach. *Journal of Marriage and the Family, 56,* 181–192.

Smith, C., Lizotte, A. J., Thornberry, T. P., & Krohn, M. D. (1995). Resilient youth: Identifying factors that prevent high-risk youth from engaging in delinquency and drug use. *Current Perspectives in Aging and the Life Cycle, 4,* 217–247.

Sonenstein, F. L., Ku, L., Lindberg, L. D., Turner, C. F., & Pleck, J. H. (1998). Changes in sexual behavior and condom use among teenaged males: 1988 to 1995. *American Journal of Public Health, 88,* 956–959.

Soundheimer, D. L. (1992). HIV infection and disease among homeless adolescents. In R. J. DiClemente (Ed.), *Adolescents and AIDS: A generation in jeopardy* (pp. 71–88). Newbury Park, CA: Sage.

St. Lawrence, J. S., Brasfield, T. L., Jefferson, K. W., & Allyene, A. (1994). Social support as a factor in African-American adolescents' sexual risk behavior. *Journal of Adolescent Research, 9,* 292–309.

St. Lawrence, J. S., Brasfield, T. L., Jefferson, K. W., Alleyne, E., O'Bannon, R. E. 3rd, & Shirley, A. (1995). Cognitive-behavioral intervention to reduce African American adolescents' risk for HIV infection. *Journal of Consulting & Clinical Psychology, 63,* 221–237.

St. Lawrence, J. S., Crosby, R. A., Belcher, L., Yazdani, N., & Brasfield, T. L. (1999a). Sexual risk reduction and anger management interventions for incarcerated male adolescents: a randomized controlled trial of two interventions. *Journal of Sex Education and Therapy, 24,* 9–17.

St. Lawrence, J. S., Crosby, R. A., O'Bannon III, R. O. (1999b). Adolescent risk for HIV infection: Comparison of four high risk samples. *Journal of HIV/AIDS Prevention & Education for Adolescents and Children, 3*(3), 63–86.

St. Louis, M. E., Conway, G. A., Hayman, C. R., Miller, C., Petersen, L. R., & Dondero, T. J. (1991). Human immunodeficiency virus infection in disadvantaged adolescents. Findings from the US Job Corps. *Journal of the American Medical Association, 266,* 2387–2391.

St. Louis, M. E., Rauch, K. J., Petersen, L. R., Anderson, J. E., Schable, C. A., et al. (1990). Sentinel Hospital Surveillance Group (1990). Seroprevalence rates of human immunodeficiency virus infection at sentinel hospitals in the United States. *New England Journal of Medicine, 323,* 213–218.

Stanton, B. F., Li, X., Ricardo, I., Galbraith, J., Feigelman, S., & Kaljee, L. (1996). A randomized, controlled effectiveness trial of an AIDS prevention program for low-income African-American youths. *Archives of Pediatrics & Adolescent Medicine, 150,* 363–372.

Steinberg, L., Fletcher, A., & Darling, N. (1994). Parental monitoring and peer influences on adolescent substance use. *Pediatrics, 93,* 1060–1064.

Stock, J. L., Bell, M. A., Boyer, D. K., & Connell, F. A. (1997). Adolescent pregnancy and sexual risk-taking among sexually abused girls. *Family Planning Perspectives, 29,* 200–203.

Stone, K. M., Timyan, J., & Thomas, E. L. (1999). Barrier methods for the prevention of sexually transmitted diseases. In K. K. Holmes, P. F. Sparling, P. Mardh, et al. (Eds.), *Sexually Transmitted Diseases* (pp. 1307–1322). New York, NY: McGraw Hill.

Stricof, R. L., Kennedy, J. T., Nattell, T. C., Weisfuse, I. B., & Novick, L. F. (1991). HIV seroprevalence in a facility for runaway and homeless adolescents. *American Journal of Public Health, (Suppl.) 81,* 50–53.

Strunin, L. (1999). Alcohol use and sexual behavior among "black" adolescents. *Substance Use, 34,* 1665–1687.

Tanfer, K., & Aral, S. O. (1996). Sexual intercourse during menstruation and self-reported sexually transmitted disease history among women. *Sexually Transmitted Diseases, 23,* 395–401.

United Nations Programme on HIV/AIDS [UNAIDS] (1997). Impact of HIV and sexual health education on the sexual behaviour of young people: a review update. Geneva, Switzerland.

Upchurch, D. M., Levy-Storms, L., Sucoff, C. A., & Aneshensel, C. S. (1998). Gender and ethnic differences in the timing of first sexual intercourse. *Family Planning Perspectives, 30,* 121–127.

Valleroy, L. A., MacKellar, D. A., Karon, J. M., Janssen, R. S., & Hayman, C. R. (1998). HIV infection in disadvantaged out-of-school youth: prevalence for U.S. Job Corps entrants, 1990 through 1996. *Journal of Acquired Immune Deficiency Syndromes, 19,* 67–73.

Valois, R. F., Oeltmann, J. E., Waller, J., & Hussey, J. R. (1999). Relationship between number of sexual intercourse partners and selected health risk behaviors among public high school adolescents. *Journal of Adolescent Health, 25,* 328–335.

Wagstaff, D. A., DeLamater, J. D., & Havens, K. K. (1999). Subsequent infection among adolescent African-American males attending a sexually transmitted disease clinic. *Journal of Adolescent Health, 25,* 217–226.

Wald, A., Langenberg, A. G. M., Link, K., Izu, A. E., Ashley, R., Warren, T., Tyring, S., Douglas, J. M., & Corey, L. (2001). Effect of condoms on reducing the transmission of herpes simplex virus type 2 from men to women. *Journal of the American Medical Association, 285,* 3100–3106.

Wang, C. C., Reilly, M., & Kreiss, J. K. (1999). Risk of HIV infection in oral contraceptive pill users: a meta-analysis [published erratum appears in *Journal of Acquired Immune Deficiency Syndromes, 21 (5),* 428]. *Journal of Acquired Immune Deficiency Syndromes, 21,* 51–58.

Warren, C. W., Santelli, J. S., Everett, S. A., Kann, L., Collins, J. L., Cassell, C., Morris, L., & Kolbe, L. J. (1998). Sexual behavior among U.S. high school students, 1990–1995. *Family Planning Perspectives, 30,* 170–172.

Washington, A. E., Johnson, R. E., & Sanders, L. L. (1987). *Chlamydia trachomatis* infections in the United States: what are they costing us? *Journal of the American Medical Association, 257,* 2070–2072.

Washington, A. E., et al. (1985). Oral contraceptives, *Chlamydia trachomatis* infection and pelvic inflammatory disease. *Journal of the American Medical Association, 253,* 2246–2250.

Westrom, L. (1980). Incidence, prevalence, and trends of acute pelvic inflammatory disease and its consequences in industrialized countries. *American Journal of Obstetrics & Gynecology, 238,* 882.

Whaley, A. L. (1999). Preventing the high-risk sexual behavior of adolescents: focus on HIV/AIDS transmission, unintended pregnancy, or both? *Journal of Adolescent Health, 24,* 376–382.

Wingood, G. M., & DiClemente, R. J. (1996). HIV sexual risk reduction interventions for women: a review. *American Journal of Preventive Medicine, 12,* 209–217.

Wingood, G. M., & DiClemente, R. J. (1998a). Gender-related correlates and predictors of consistent condom use among young adult African-American women: a prospective analysis. *International Journal of STD & AIDS, 9,* 139–145.

Wingood, G. M., & DiClemente, R. J. (1998b) Partner influences and gender-related factors associated with noncondom use among young adult African American women. *American Journal of Community Psychology, 26*(1), 29–51.

Wingood, G. M., & DiClemente, R. J. (1998c). Rape among African American women: sexual, psychological, and social correlates predisposing survivors to risk of STD/HIV. *Journal of Women's Health, 7,* 77–84.

Wingood, G. M., DiClemente, R. J., Oh, M. K., Crosby, R., Harrington, K., Davies, S. L., Schwebke, J. R., & Hook, E. W. (under review). Douching and STD infection among African-American adolescent females. *Journal of the American Medical Association.*

Wolner-Hanssen, P., Eschenbach, D. A., Paavonen, J., et al. (1990). Association between vaginal douching and acute pelvic inflammatory disease. *Journal of the American Medical Association, 263,* 1936–1941.

Young, R. A., Feldman, S., Bracklin, B. T., & Thompson, E. (1992). Seroprevalence of human immunodeficiency virus among adolescent attendees of Mississippi sexually transmitted disease clinics: A rural epidemic. *Southern Journal of Medicine, 85,* 460–463.

Author Index

Subject Index